Why Do You Need This New Edition?

The Seventh Edition examines the transformations in American society and the social and economic changes that affect the structure and functioning of today's families.

Some of the new topics and discussions in the Seventh Edition include:

① Updated information on racial and ethnic families, including recent controversies about immigration law, and new material on neighborhood violence and absent fathers.

② New concepts and theoretical perspectives about socialization and gender roles, as well as new material on role conflict and the second shift, gender and education, and gender roles at home.

③ A chapter on dating and mate selection incorporating current examples and updated information. Additional information on date rape, additional and updated information on same-sex relationships, and new materials on the impact of the Internet on meeting others.

④ Updated material on singlehood, cohabitation, civil unions, and other options, including postponing marriage, technology, social movements, and myths and realities about being single.

⑤ A chapter on balancing work and family life with new economic material on the recession, its impact on families, and its compounded problems (job availability, for example); as well as new information on the gender pay gap.

⑥ A chapter on families in later life showing the ways in which aging is becoming an increasingly important societal topic, and including new information on baby boomers; the recent economic crisis and its relation to aging, retirement, etc.; community support for elder care; and a new section on "Competition for Scarce Resources."

⑦ 2010 Census Update—The inclusion of data from the 2010 Census throughout brings this edition thoroughly up-to-date.

Marriages & Families
Changes, Choices, and Constraints

Seventh Edition

Census Update

Nijole V. Benokraitis
University of Baltimore

Prentice Hall

Boston Columbus Indianapolis New York San Francisco Upper Saddle River
Amsterdam Cape Town Dubai London Madrid Milan Munich Paris Montreal Toronto
Delhi Mexico City Sao Paulo Sydney Hong Kong Seoul Singapore Taipei Tokyo

Editor in Chief: Dickson Musslewhite
Publisher: Karen Hanson
Supplements Editor: Mayda Bosco
Editorial Assistant: Christine Dore
Development Editor: Maggie Barbieri
Executive Marketing Manager: Kelly May
Marketing Assistant: Janeli Bitor
Senior Production Project Manager: Pat Torelli
Manufacturing Buyer: Megan Cochran
Editorial Production and Composition Service: PreMediaGlobal
Interior Design: Carolyn Deacy
Photo Researchers: Katharine S. Cebik/Laurie Frankenthaler
Cover Designer: Kristina Mose-Libon

Credits appear on page 556, which constitutes an extension of the copyright page.

Cataloging-in-Publication Data unavailable at press time

10 9 8 7 6 5 4 3 2 1 RRD-W 15 14 13 12 11

**Prentice Hall
is an imprint of**

www.pearsonhighered.com

ISBN 10:   0-205-00673-6
ISBN 13: 978-0-205-00673-1

Brief Contents

Contents

CHAPTER 4

Racial and Ethnic Families: Strengths and Stresses 76

PART TWO

The Individual and the Developing Relationship

CHAPTER 5

Socialization and Gender Roles 104

Data Digest 105

CHAPTER 6

Romance, Love, and Loving Relationships 134

CHAPTER 7

Sexuality and Sexual Expression Throughout Life 164

PART FOUR

Parents and Children

CHAPTER 11

To Be or Not To Be a Parent: More Choices, More Constraints 290

CHAPTER 12

Raising Children: Promises and Pitfalls 318

CHAPTER 15

Separation and Divorce 414

Changes and Transitions

CHAPTER 16

Remarriages and Stepfamilies 444

Boxed Features

Applying What You've Learned

Ask Yourself

A Few Words to Students

In the past few years, I've been asking my students how many read the Preface, in this textbook or others. About one out of fifty raises her or his hand.

You're welcome to read the Preface, of course, because I write it with the student in mind. If you're like many of my students and skip the Preface, however, I wanted to say a few things to all of you before you plunge into the assigned readings.

You're going to enjoy your marriage and family course. Because the family is something *all* of us have in common, it's always been one of the liveliest classes I've taught. In fact, you'll probably remember this course as one of the most important and interesting that you've taken in college.

I hope that this textbook will be one of the reasons that your marriage and family course will be informative and memorable. Here are a few comments I've received from my own students and others outside our university:

"I'm taking four other courses this semester, but this is the only textbook that I look forward to reading each week. If writers in other subjects would be as interesting, college wouldn't be this boring."

"Frankly, I was surprised that I could apply a lot of the information to my family and relationships. I've learned a lot about dos and don'ts in marriage."

"You not only present the material in a clear way but also do it humorously."

"I like that the book has a personal touch."

"I enjoyed reading the book and have recommended it to many of my friends—to help give them a dose of reality and the facts about dating, marriage, divorce, and aging."

"I found the online tests very helpful. It was a good way to review the material in each chapter. Professor (X) used similar essay questions for exams, so I was really ready!"

"I know more about families and culture and how to deal better with relationships. This book gave me a positive outlook on family life."

"I have a better knowledge of my family. I now understand why we have some of the problems we do."

"When we were driving to Florida during spring break, I brought this book along to study for an exam. I read some of the passages to my husband to keep him awake because it was a 12-hour drive. We started discussing some issues about our marriage for the first time. It was great!"

"I talked about some of the stuff in the textbook with my teenage son when I was studying. We had some interesting conversations. Believe it or not, he read several of the chapters, and on his own!"

"The Choices boxes are VERY interesting. Moreover, I think that the Making Connections questions are extremely thought-provoking and relevant!"

Even if you shudder every time you see figures and tables, you'll enjoy this textbook. You may not agree with everything (and neither do I as I summarize the most recent research), but the material will help you think about your own family or marriage, reflect on ways to improve your current relationships, get out of bad relationships, make better decisions in the future, and understand the diversity of families in the United States and other countries.

I hope all of you enjoy your course and this textbook. The "About the Author" page provides my e-mail address if you'd like to contact me. I'm *always* happy to hear from students.

Have a good semester. And for those of you who are graduating this year, congratulations!

Dr. B (as my students call me)

Welcome to the seventh edition of *Marriages & Families: Changes, Choices, and Constraints*! There have been several notable family-related changes since the last edition. The economy began to crash in mid-2008, creating widespread unemployment, more than 1 million home foreclosures (which still continue) that increased homelessness rates, and pervasive anxiety about paying monthly bills. Practically all states slashed their school budgets, cut many social services for low-income families, and increased many parents' and children's anxiety. Older Americans on the verge of retirement had to continue working because the value of their retirement income plunged by as much as 50 percent, and many of the already retired had to take low-paying jobs to survive economically.

In 2009, President Barack Obama made universal health care a top domestic priority. One of the primary purposes of the family is to ensure the health and well-being of its members. As this book goes to press, however, it's not clear whether the new health care legislation will benefit families or the health insurance industry. By 2015, almost 15 percent of the U.S. population will be age 65 and older, putting a significant strain on the nation's health care services and federal retirement income programs such as Social Security. An important question, then, is who will pay the health costs of our aging society?

Another significant societal change since the last edition of *Marriages & Families* has been the legalization of same-sex marriage in four states after Massachusetts did so in 2004. Legalizing same-sex marriage on the state level offers family members more benefits and rights such as inheritance and medical insurance, but same-sex marriage remains a fiercely controversial issue, often dividing friends, families, and religious groups. Thus, macro-level changes, including legislation and economic fluctuations, continue to change and constrain our individual choices.

SCHOLARLY WORK, COMPREHENSIVENESS, AND READABILITY

This revision incorporates information from almost 1,100 new books, scholarly articles, and reports. Providing students with the most up-to-date material and emerging issues on family behavior enhances their "pool of knowledge" (as one of my undergraduate sociology professors used to say) and helps them make better decisions in their everyday lives.

Marriages & Families offers students a comprehensive introduction to many issues facing families in the twenty-first century. Although written from a sociological perspective, the book incorporates material from other disciplines: history, economics, social work, psychology, law, biology, medicine, and anthropology. The material also encompasses family studies, women's studies, and gay and lesbian studies, as well as both quantitative and qualitative studies. Nationally representative and longitudinal data are supplemented by insights from clinical, case, and observational studies.

Readability continues to be one of this textbook's most attractive features. A major reason why this book has been successful is that it discusses theories and recent studies in ways that students find interesting. As one of my students once said, "This is the first textbook I've had where I don't count how many more pages I have to read while I'm still on the first page."

In addition, faculty reviewers have consistently described the writing as "very clear" and "excellent." According to one reviewer, for example, "The interesting anecdotes and quotes help to maintain the student's interest while also providing examples of the subject under discussion."

CONTINUITY OF MAJOR THEMES ON THE CONTEMPORARY FAMILY

Marriages & Families continues to be distinguished from other textbooks in several important ways. It offers comprehensive coverage of the field, allowing instructors to select chapters that best suit their needs. It balances theoretical and empirical discussions with practical examples and applications.

It highlights important contemporary *changes* in society and the family. It explores the *choices* that are available to family members and the *constraints* that often limit their choices. It examines the diversity of U.S. families, using *cross-cultural* and *multicultural* material to encourage students to think about the many critical issues that confront the family of the twenty-first century.

More Changes

Changes that affect the structure and functioning of today's families inform the pages of every chapter. In addition, several chapters focus on some major transformations in American society. Chapter 4, for example, examines the growing cultural diversity of the United States, focusing on African American,

American Indian, Latino, Asian American, Middle Eastern, and interracial marriages and families. And Chapter 17 discusses the ways in which the rapid graying of America has affected adult children, grandchildren, and even great-grandchildren; family members' roles as caregivers; family relations in general; and the distribution of resources between the young and the old.

More Choices

On the individual level, family members have many more choices today than ever before. People feel freer to postpone marriage, to cohabit, or to raise children as single parents. As a result, household forms vary greatly, ranging from commuter marriages to those in which several generations live together under the same roof.

As reproductive technology becomes increasingly sophisticated, many infertile couples and even menopausal women can now have children. With the growing acceptance of civil unions, many agencies, colleges, businesses, and state governments now offer same-sex couples more health, retirement, and other benefits than ever before.

Technological advances—such as the Internet, cell phones, and texting—have decreased our privacy, but they have also brought many family members together because people can contact one another quickly and relatively inexpensively, as well as gather information about their genealogy from many sources. In addition, sometimes people find a mate through online dating services.

More Constraints

Family members' choices are more varied today than in the past, but we also face greater macro-level constraints. Our options are increasingly limited, for example, by government policies that, especially since mid-2008, have bailed out businesses for which taxpayers must pay. Some of the corporate executives of these bailed-out companies have higher salaries than ever before even though millions of workers whom the companies have laid off are struggling to keep out of poverty. In effect, then, economic changes often shape family life and not vice versa.

Political and legal institutions also have a major impact on most families through tax laws, welfare reform, and even in defining what a family is. Because laws, public policies, and religious groups affect our everyday lives, I have framed many discussions of individual choices within the larger picture of the institutional constraints that limit our choices.

Cross-Cultural and Multicultural Diversity in the United States

Contemporary American marriages and families vary greatly in structure, dynamics, and cultural heritage.

Thus, discussions of gender roles, social class, race, ethnicity, age, and sexual orientation are integrated throughout this book. To further strengthen students' understanding of the growing diversity among today's families, I have also included a series of boxes that focus on families from many cultures as well as racial and ethnic families within the United States. Both text and boxed materials should encourage students to think about the many forms families may take and the different ways in which family members interact.

WHAT'S NEW IN THE SEVENTH EDITION?

As past users know, a top priority of each new edition of this textbook is to thoroughly update national data and to provide the results of groundbreaking research that addresses the diversity of marriages and families. Because my major goal is to make each edition better than the previous one, I have revised all of the chapters to reflect the latest theory and research, and I have updated examples throughout *Marriages & Families*. Specifically, new, updated, and expanded coverage includes the following:

Chapter 1, The Changing Family

- Updates the demographic changes that characterize U.S. families, technological innovations that have changed family relationships, and the growing importance of understanding families and marriages from cross-cultural perspectives

- Offers new material on fictive kin, common law marriage, and polygamy in the United States, Europe, and some developing countries

- A **new box** ("Why Does Cousin Marriage Matter in Iraq?") shows why marrying first cousins is both encouraged and commonplace in many countries

Chapter 2, Studying the Family

- Updates family theories and studies on family self-help books, focus groups, and evaluation research

- Offers new data on the weaknesses of survey research and a heavily revised section on the ethics and politics of family research

- An updated box ("How Good Are Online Surveys?") examines the strengths and weaknesses of online research

- A **new box** ("Is My Classmate an Undercover Professor?") asks students to think about the ethical implications of participant observation

Chapter 3, The Family in Historical Perspective

- Expands the section on "The Family Since the 1960s"

- Updates the material on some common misconceptions about the modern family

- Offers a heavily revised box ("Characteristics of 'True Womanhood'") and discussion of the cult of domesticity that still affects many women's and men's attitudes and gender roles

Chapter 4, Racial and Ethnic Families: Strengths and Stresses

- Updates the material on family income and Mexican day laborers

- Offers new data on the benefits and costs of undocumented immigrants, infant deaths among U.S. minority families, residential racial/ethnic segregation, absent fathers, and the discrimination that many Middle Eastern families still face

- A revised box ("Is Bill Cosby Right about Black Families") examines the controversial question of whether low-income parents are responsible for their children's problems

Chapter 5, Socialization and Gender Roles

- Has new sections on sociobiological and symbolic interactionist theories of why gender roles differ, and new sections on gender and politics and gender and education

- Updates the analysis of the costs and benefits of traditional gender roles, peer groups, the effect of advertising, and domestic decision-making roles

- Introduces three new concepts—*gender stereotypes, gender stratification,* and *sexism*

- Uses the Global Gender Gap Index, a recent measure that gauges women's status and quality of life in 130 countries

- Has a heavily revised box on "Some Gender Inequalities in Patriarchal Societies"

Chapter 6, Romance, Love, and Loving Relationships

- Updates the material on friendship versus love, adolescents and romance, the biochemistry of love, attachment theories, and narcissism

- Expands the discussion of the role of popular culture on love

- Incorporates new studies of romantic love in other countries

Chapter 7, Sexuality and Sexual Expression throughout Life

- Updates the discussion of transgendered people, sexual scripts, and why people have sex

- Provides new data on gay men and lesbians in other countries, cross-cultural reactions to gays, the effectiveness of abstinence-only and sex education programs, virginity pledges, sex in later life, sexual infidelity, American attitudes about gay and lesbian rights, and STIs

- Has a new section on how religion affects sexual behavior

Chapter 8, Choosing Others: Dating and Mate Selection

- Provides recent data on hooking up, mail-order brides, cyberdating, the relationship between personality and dating, interracial and interethnic dating, and dating violence

- Has new discussions of friends with benefits, mate selection and wealth in the United States and other countries, interfaith dating, dowries and fraud, how mate selection methods are changing in Asia and the Middle East, and why seemingly perfect dates are often terrible partners in the long run

Chapter 9, Singlehood, Cohabitation, Civil Unions, and Other Options

- Offers a heavily revised and updated discussion of civil unions

- Updates the material on female infanticide, myths about singles, Americans' attitudes about cohabitation, single adults in later life, why people are remaining single longer, the marriage squeeze, who cohabits and why, and how cohabitation affects children

- Has new sections on economic factors and singlehood, runaway brides in China, and how wars affect being single

- Provides a **new box** ("Why Do Americans Favor or Oppose Same-Sex Marriages?") that offers both sides of the debate on this divisive issue

Chapter 10, Marriage and Communication in Committed Relationships

- Updates the discussion of why people marry, prenuptial agreements, the percentage of Americans who say they are happily married, variations of domestic roles by employment status, and marriage in midlife

- Offers recent data on who's doing most of the housework in a marriage, how intergenerational ties affect a marriage, how marriage affects women's and men's health, the empty nest syndrome, and what couples fight about

- Provides totally rewritten sections on how in-laws affect marriages, and the effect of marriage education programs on couples

- Has a heavily revised box ("Child Brides") that examines coerced marriage among girls as young as 9 years old in some countries

Chapter 11, To Be or Not to Be a Parent: More Choices, More Constraints

- Updates the discussion on the costs and effects of parenthood, U.S. fertility rates and why they've changed, infant mortality rates in the United States and other countries, the controversies about transracial adoptions and same-sex partners, and fertility drugs and other high-tech treatments for infertility

- Differentiates between *fertility, total fertility rates,* and *fertility rates*

- Offers new data on the effects of parenthood, gay adoption, international adoptions, and deciding to be child free, postpartum blues versus postpartum depression, why U.S. transracial adoption rates and U.S. abortion rates have decreased

Chapter 12, Raising Children: Promises and Pitfalls

- Updates the material on the high expectations of new mothers, first-time parents and the unexpected difficulties they encounter, parents' increased legal responsibility in raising children, myths about babies, parenting adult children who move back home, parenting in later life, lesbian and gay families, and corporal punishment of children

- Offers new data on whether mothers and fathers are better or worse parents than in the past, how and why fathers' participation in child rearing has increased, parenting variations by ethnicity and social class, overprogramming children, bed sharing, and the effect of electronic media on children

- *Role conflict*, a new concept introduced in this chapter, shows how role conflict and role strain differ in parenting, and the concept of adultification discusses why this process harms many children

- Has a new section on helicopter parents, nonresident fathers and foster care, and cyberbullying

- A **new box** ("Father Involvement in Japanese Families") examines how and why recent legislation encourages fathers' participation in child rearing

Chapter 13, Balancing Work and Family Life

Chapter 13 was heavily revised because of the recent economic downturn. Some of the changes in this chapter include

- New concepts—*work, economy, deindustrialization, globalization, offshoring, comparable worth,* and the *motherhood penalty*—discuss the significance of work and how the economy affects us on micro and macro levels, and how mothers and women are penalized in the workplace

- New material on nonstandard work hours, mass employment layoffs, and home foreclosures that affect families, corporate bailouts supported by the federal government, and bringing babies to work

- Updates discussions of flextime, telecommuting, why the rich are still getting richer whereas the middle- and working-classes are struggling to survive, why the numbers of the working poor and part-timers have increased, the effect of recent unemployment rates on families, discouraged and underemployed workers, the poverty line, the percentage of Americans living in poverty, homelessness, why employed women are often paid less than men in comparable positions, stay-at-home dads, dual-earner couples, the benefits and costs of two-income families and commuter marriages, the effect of wives who earn more than their husbands, women and minorities in the workplace, the consequences of a gender pay gap for families, sexual harassment at work, the pregnancy penalty for mothers, and elder care

- A **new box** ("Some Reasons for the Rising Inequality in America") summarizes some of the most important reasons for many Americans' recent economic problems

Chapter 14, Family Abuse, Violence, and Other Health Issues

- Introduces new concepts (*intimate partner violence*) that include unmarried partners as well as spouses and *binge eating* that the medical community has recently emphasized in eating disorders

- Updates data on child abuse, the prevalence and severity of intimate partner violence, the characteristics of abusive and violent households, familycide, internalized and heterosexist homophobia, marital rape, why women don't leave abusers, women who abuse men, sexually abused children and how abuse affects children, sibling abuse, abuse among adolescents, elder abuse, violence among same-sex couple and racial-ethnic groups, family abuse theories, substance abuse, the relationship between depression and suicide, and eating disorders

- Has new sections and data on the rise of illicit drug use among baby boomers, drunk driving, obesity, the number of Americans who have experienced intimate partner violence, and how to prevent family abuse and violence

Chapter 15, Separation and Divorce

- Introduces new concepts of *co-parenting* and *collaborative divorce* that might decrease conflict in many divorce cases

- Updates the discussion of annulments, divorce in midlife and later years, divorce rates, and why divorce rates have decreased

- Offers new data on separation without finalizing a divorce; the impact of premarital cohabitation, cultural values, social class, religious institutions, the economy, and military service on divorce; same-sex divorces; how similarity between spouses affects divorce rates; multiple parental instabilities and their effect on children; same-sex divorces; how divorce affects married people and their children; child support and visitation rights; and parental problems after divorce

- Has a **new box** ("Why Are Many Fathers Deadbeat Dads?") that examines some of the reasons why some fathers are more engaged than others with their children after a divorce

Chapter 16, Remarriages and Stepfamilies

- Has new data and discussions of remarriage characteristics, why whites have the highest remarriage rates, intergenerational financial responsibilities in stepfamilies, and women in stepfamilies as kinkeepers and gatekeepers

- Incorporates family stress theories to help explain some of the effects of stepfamilies on children

Chapter 17, Families in Later Life

- Updates life expectancy rates in the United States compared with other countries, the relationship between social class and retirement income, happiness and aging, and widowhood in later life

- Introduces several new key terms—*centenarian, old-age dependency ratio, multigenerational household,* and *living will*—to describe how our graying society is affecting younger generations

- Provides new discussions of the effect of baby boomers and their health care needs, seniors and unemployment, racial-ethnic groups and hospice care, caregiving options, and the competition for health care and other resources between the young and the old

- Has **two new boxes:** "Don't 'Sweetie,' 'Dear,' and 'Young Lady' Me!" and "Should Physician-Assisted Suicide Be Legal in Every State?"

FEATURES IN THE SEVENTH EDITION

I have maintained several popular features such as the Data Digest and the "author's files" quotations based on my students' reactions and class discussions.

Data Digest

I introduced the Data Digest in the second edition because "all those numbers" from the Census Bureau, empirical studies, and demographic trends often overwhelmed students (both mine and others). Because this has been a popular feature, I've updated the U.S. statistics and have included information about other countries. The Data Digest that introduces each chapter provides students with a thought-provoking overview of current statistics and trends and makes "all those numbers" more interesting and digestible.

The first question from my students is usually "Will this material be on the exam?" Not in my classes. I see the Data Digest as piquing student curiosity about the chapter rather than providing a lot of numbers to memorize. Some instructors tell me that their students have used this feature to develop class presentations or course papers.

Material from the Author's Files

Faculty who reviewed previous editions of *Marriages & Families,* and many students as well, liked the anecdotes and personal experiences with which I illustrate sometimes abstract theories and concepts. In this new edition, I weave more of this material into the text. Thus, I include many examples from discussions in my own classes (cited as "author's files") to enliven theoretical perspectives and abstract concepts.

PEDAGOGICAL FEATURES

The pedagogical features in *Marriages & Families*—ranging from the "Since You Asked" items to boxes in each chapter—have been designed to capture students' attention and to help them understand and recall the material. Each has been carefully crafted to ensure that it ties in clearly to the text material, enhancing its meaning and applicability.

Encouraging Students to Think More Critically

All editions of this textbook have prodded students to think about themselves and their families in the "Ask Yourself" boxes. Because of their popularity, especially in sparking lively class discussions, I've expanded two features ("Making Connections" and "Stop and Think") that were introduced in the last edition:

- **Making Connections:**   At several points in each chapter, these items ask students to link the material to their own lives by relating it to a personal experience, by integrating it with studies discussed in the chapter, or by "connecting" with classmates who might be sitting next to them in class.

⠿ MAKING CONNECTIONS

- Ask three of your friends to define *family.* Are their definitions the same as yours? Or are they different?
- According to one of my students, "I don't view my biological family as 'my family' because my parents were abusive and didn't love me." Should people be able to choose whomever they want to be as family and exclude their biological parents?

- **Stop and Think:**   These critical thinking questions are at the end of boxes throughout the textbook. The purpose of these items is to encourage reflective thought about current topics, both personally and compared with other cultures.

⠿ Stop and Think . . .

As you read articles and books about the family, ask yourself the following questions:

- Does the writer cite research or only anecdotal material as sources? If the writer cites himself or herself, are the references scholarly or only personal stories? According to one researcher, "If modern science has learned anything in the past century, it is to distrust anecdotal evidence" (Park, 2003: B20).

- Does the author describe only a few families (especially those with problems) but generalize the "findings" to all families?

- Does the writer make it sound as though life is exceedingly simple, such as following seven steps for family happiness? Family interaction and behavior are much more complex than throwing a few ingredients into the pot and stirring.

- **Since You Asked:**   Each chapter has between eight and ten questions that introduce an important idea or concept or preview a controversial issue about families and marriages. Many of these questions are similar to those that my students have raised in class or in online discussions.

Since you asked . . .
⠿ Should parents or schools be responsible for sex education?

- **Applying What You've Learned:**   This series of boxes emphasizes the connection between research findings and students' own feelings and experiences. The material, both new and revised, asks students to apply what they're reading to their own personal situations and to consider how to improve their decision making and current relationships.

Applying What You've Learned

⋮• Can I Trust This Survey?

Surveys are often used in public opinion polls and are reported on television and in newspapers. Asking a few basic questions about a survey will help you evaluate its credibility:

- *Who sponsored the survey?* A government agency, a nonprofit partisan organization, a business, or a group that's lobbying for change?

- *What is the purpose of the survey?* To provide objective information, to promote an idea or a political candidate, or to get attention through sensationalism?

- *How was the sample drawn?* Randomly? Or was it a SLOP, a "self-selection opinion poll" (see Tanur, 1994)?

- *How were the questions worded?* Were they clear, objective, loaded, or biased? If the survey questions are not provided, why not?

- *How did the researchers report their findings?* Were they objective, or did they make value judgments?

Informative and Engaging Illustration Program

Many chapters contain figures that, in bold and original artistic designs, demonstrate concepts such as the exchange theory of dating, romantic versus lasting love, and theories of mating, as well as presenting simple statistics in innovative and visually appealing ways. Many of the photographs are new. We have taken great care to select substantive photographs (rather than what I call "pretty postcards") that illustrate the material.

Outlines

Each chapter contains an opening outline. The outlines help students organize their learning by focusing on the main topics of each chapter.

OUTLINE

The Increasing Diversity of U.S. Families

Race and Ethnicity Still Matter

African American Families

American Indian Families

Latino Families

Asian American Families

Middle Eastern Families

Interracial and Interethnic Relationships and Marriages

Conclusion

Figures and Tables

Many students tend to skip over figures and tables because they're afraid of numbers, they don't trust statistics (see Chapter 2), or the material seems boring or complicated. Regardless of which textbooks I use and in *all* the courses I teach, I routinely highlight some of the figures in class. As I tell my students, a good figure or table may be more important (or at least more memorable) than the author's explanation. To encourage students to look at data, I have streamlined many figures and sometimes offer brief summaries to accompany the figures.

TABLE 2.3 | **Some Basic Principles of Ethical Family Research**

- Obtain all participants' consent to participate and their permission to quote from their responses, particularly if the research concerns sensitive issues or if participants' comments will be quoted extensively.
- Do not exploit participants or research assistants involved in the research for personal gain.
- Never harm, humiliate, abuse, or coerce participants, either physically or psychologically. This includes the withholding of medications or other services or programs that might benefit participants.
- Honor all guarantees to participants of privacy, anonymity, and confidentiality.
- Use the highest methodological standards and be as accurate as possible.
- Describe the limitations and shortcomings of the research in published reports.
- Identify the sponsors who funded the research.

Key Terms and Glossary

Important terms and concepts are boldfaced and defined in the text and listed at the end of each chapter. All key terms and their definitions are repeated in the Glossary at the end of the book.

KEY TERMS

bundling 54	familism 63	cult of domesticity 64
matrilineal 58	*compadrazgo* 63	companionate family 68
patrilineal 58	*machismo* 64	baby boomers 72

THOUGHT-PROVOKING BOX SERIES

Reflecting and reinforcing the book's primary themes, three groups of boxes focus on the changes, choices, and constraints that confront today's families. A fourth group of boxes illustrates racial-ethnic families in the United States and cross-cultural variations in other countries. The other two series of boxes help students assess their own knowledge and gain insights about family life.

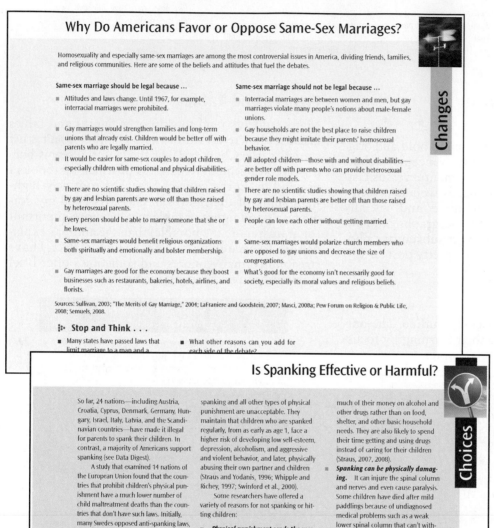

Why Do Americans Favor or Oppose Same-Sex Marriages?

Changes

Homosexuality and especially same-sex marriages are among the most controversial issues in America, dividing friends, families, and religious communities. Here are some of the beliefs and attitudes that fuel the debates.

Same-sex marriage should be legal because …

- Attitudes and laws change. Until 1967, for example, interracial marriages were prohibited.

- Gay marriages would strengthen families and long-term unions that already exist. Children would be better off with parents who are legally married.

- It would be easier for same-sex couples to adopt children, especially children with emotional and physical disabilities.

- There are no scientific studies showing that children raised by gay and lesbian parents are worse off than those raised by heterosexual parents.

- Every person should be able to marry someone that she or he loves.

- Same-sex marriages would benefit religious organizations both spiritually and emotionally and bolster membership.

- Gay marriages are good for the economy because they boost businesses such as restaurants, bakeries, hotels, airlines, and florists.

Same-sex marriage should not be legal because …

- Interracial marriages are between women and men, but gay marriages violate many people's notions about male-female unions.

- Gay households are not the best place to raise children because they might imitate their parents' homosexual behavior.

- All adopted children—those with and without disabilities—are better off with parents who can provide heterosexual gender role models.

- There are no scientific studies showing that children raised by gay and lesbian parents are better off than those raised by heterosexual parents.

- People can love each other without getting married.

- Same-sex marriages would polarize church members who are opposed to gay unions and decrease the size of congregations.

- What's good for the economy isn't necessarily good for society, especially its moral values and religious beliefs.

Sources: Sullivan, 2003; "The Merits of Gay Marriage," 2004; LaFraniere and Goodstein, 2007; Masci, 2008a; Pew Forum on Religion & Public Life, 2008; Semuels, 2008.

Stop and Think . . .

- Many states have passed laws that limit marriage to a man and a
- What other reasons can you add for each side of the debate?

Is Spanking Effective or Harmful?

Choices

So far, 24 nations—including Austria, Croatia, Cyprus, Denmark, Germany, Hungary, Israel, Italy, Latvia, and the Scandinavian countries—have made it illegal for parents to spank their children. In contrast, a majority of Americans support spanking (see Data Digest).

A study that examined 14 nations of the European Union found that the countries that prohibit children's physical punishment have a much lower number of child maltreatment deaths than the countries that don't have such laws. Initially, many Swedes opposed anti-spanking laws, predicting that the children would run wild. Instead, among youth, crime rates, drug use, and suicide rates have decreased (Straus, 2007; Gracia and Herrero, 2008). Not spanking isn't the only reason for these lower rates because there are many reasons for a person's behavior, but anti-spanking laws haven't led to the problems that many Swedes feared.

In the United States, spanking advocates say that spanking is effective, prepares children for life's hardships, and prevents misbehavior. They contend that spanking is acceptable if it is age appropriate and used selectively to teach and correct behavior rather than as an expression of rage (Trumbull and Ravenel, 1999; Larzelere, 2000; Baumrind et al., 2002).

Some pediatricians believe that a "mild" spanking (one or two spanks on the buttocks) is acceptable when all other discipline fails, but that slapping a child's face is abusive. Others argue that spanking and all other types of physical punishment are unacceptable. They maintain that children who are spanked regularly, from as early as age 1, face a higher risk of developing low self-esteem, depression, alcoholism, and aggressive and violent behavior, and later, physically abusing their own partner and children (Straus and Yodanis, 1996; Whipple and Richey, 1997; Swinford et al., 2000).

Some researchers have offered a variety of reasons for not spanking or hitting children:

- *Physical punishment sends the message that it's okay to hurt someone you love or someone who is smaller and less powerful.* A parent who spanks often says, "I'm doing this because I love you." Thus, children learn that violence and love can go hand in hand and that hitting is an appropriate way to express one's feelings (Hunt, 1991).

- *No human being feels loving toward someone who hits her or him.* A strong relationship is based on kindness. Hitting produces only temporary and superficially good behavior based on fear (Marshall, 2002).

- *Physical punishment is often due to the parent's substance abuse rather a child's misbehavior.* Parents who abuse drugs are often ineffective caregivers because intoxication impairs their decision-making abilities. Parents who abuse drugs spend

much of their money on alcohol and other drugs rather than on food, shelter, and other basic household needs. They are also likely to spend their time getting and using drugs instead of caring for their children (Straus, 2007, 2008).

- *Spanking can be physically damaging.* It can injure the spinal column and nerves and even cause paralysis. Some children have died after mild paddlings because of undiagnosed medical problems such as a weak lower spinal column that can't withstand a blow (American Academy of Pediatricians, 1998).

- *Physical punishment deprives the child of opportunities to learn effective problem solving.* Physical punishment teaches a child nothing about how to handle conflict or disagreements (Straus, 2001).

Stop and Think . . .

- When you were a child, did your parents spank you? If so, how did you feel?

- Some people maintain that spanking is synonymous with hitting. Do you agree?

- Should the United States ban spanking? Or would such laws interfere with parenting decisions?

CHANGES BOXES—some historical, some anecdotal, and some empirically based—show how marriages and families have been changing or are expected to change in the future. For example, a box in **Chapter 9, "Why Do Americans Favor or Oppose Same-Sex Marriages?"** examines some of the beliefs and attitudes that fuel continuing debates on same-sex marriage.

CHOICES BOXES illustrate the kinds of decisions families can make to improve their well-being, often highlighting options of which family members may be unaware. In **Chapter 12,** for instance, one box ("**Is Spanking Effective or Harmful?**") shows that parents have more choices than spanking to discipline their children.

CONSTRAINTS BOXES point out some of the obstacles that limit our choices. These boxes highlight the fact that although most of us are raised to believe that we can do whatever we want, we are often constrained by macro-level socioeconomic, demographic, and cultural factors. For example, a **box in Chapter 13, "Some Reasons for the Rising Income Inequality in America,"** shows that many Americans are struggling to survive economically not because they have low educational levels and lack motivation, but because of other economic factors such as corporate welfare, a surge of low-paying jobs, and offshoring.

CROSS-CULTURAL AND MULTICULTURAL FAMILIES BOXES illustrate the diversity of family structures and dynamics, both in the United States and in other countries. For example, a **box in Chapter 6, "Modern Arranged Marriages in India,"** contrasts the American open style of dating with arranged courtship and marriage in India.

APPLYING WHAT YOU'VE LEARNED BOXES ask students to think critically about research findings on a personal level. Such reflections should stimulate students to challenge common misconceptions about family life and to improve their own decision making and relationships. For example, a **box in Chapter 14, "Some Warning Signs of Intimate Partner Violence and Abuse,"** asks students to consider whether they or other family members recognize some of the signs of abuse before it actually occurs.

Some Reasons for the Rising Income Inequality in America

Constraints

Some social scientists describe the U.S. economy, especially since the late 1980s, as a U-shaped curve. That is, earnings and job growth have increased in occupations that require either high skills and educational levels (such as attorneys and doctors) or those at low skill and education levels (such as bartenders and retail sales workers)—the two vertical sides of the "U"— rather than middle-income occupations (such as librarians and accountants)—the narrow bottom of the "U." There are many interrelated reasons for the rising income inequality. For example,

- Many jobs, first in manufacturing and then in white-collar occupations, have been offshored to countries that pay low wages and offer goods and services at the lower prices that American consumers seek.
- Minimum wages have been too low to lift many families out of poverty.
- Unemployment and the number of low-wage jobs have increased.
- The top 10 percent of income groups have enjoyed gains in wages and salaries; the wages and salaries of

the remaining 90 percent have not kept up with inflation.

- As income inequality has increased, people's ability to move up the social class hierarchy has stalled, especially since the mid-1970s. For example, 60 percent of families that start at the bottom 20 percent of income groups and 52 percent of those in the top 20 percent of income groups tend to stay there.
- About 38 percent of government employees are unionized, but the number of other unionized workers has been decreasing steadily—from a high of 27 percent in 1953 to 12 percent in 2007. The decline of membership in labor unions has eroded the wages and health benefits of millions of earners, especially blue-collar workers.
- The growth of imports produced by unskilled laborers in other countries has decreased the need for similar labor in the United States.
- Between 1989 and 2007, the average CEO's pay rose 167 percent compared with 10 percent for a typical worker.

Because CEO compensation is determined by peers who serve on corporate boards rather than the market or the government, inflated CEO compensation increases the gap between the wealthy and other income groups.

Sources: Eisenbrey et al., 2007; Gordon and Dew-Becker, 2008; Autor and Dorn, 2009; Mishel et al, 2009.

Stop and Think . . .

- If the U.S. economy is a U-shaped curve, why do a large majority of Americans describe themselves as middle class?
- Some social analysts contend that many Americans are in financial trouble because, over the past decades, we've shifted from a "culture of thrift" to a "culture of debt" (Brooks, 2008: 19). Others argue that our economic crisis is due, largely, to **corporate welfare**, an array of direct subsidies, tax breaks, and other favorable treatment that the government bestows on corporations (Slivinski, 2007). With which position do you agree? Why?

Cross-Cultural and Multicultural Families

Modern Arranged Marriages in India

In India, the majority of marriages are arranged by parents or elders: "There has never been any room for romantic marriage in Indian society on the line of Western societies" (Singh, 2005: 143). Loyalty of the individual to the family is a cherished ideal. To preserve this ideal, marriages have traditionally been carefully arranged so that young men and women will avoid selecting mates that the family deems unsuitable.

There are variations in different regions and social classes, however. Educated, uppe[r] are allowed to want, but man[y] riages. One you "Love is import[ant] cient." She aske[d] research and s[ocial] parents of me[n]

and earning potential who were refined, intellectual, and good human beings. She is reportedly happily married to a man whom she had met just three times before their engagement. In other cases, children can reject undesirable candidates (Lakshmanan, 1997).

Why do arranged marriages persist in much of India? Shy people can end up with a good partner because parents and relatives seem to do a good job in choosing mates. Also, arranged marriages offer stability because the

independent couples usually live with the husband's parents. As a result, similar backgrounds and compatibility with in-laws are more important in India than in the West. The advantage is that there tends to be much family support if a marriage runs into trouble.

Stop and Think . . .

- Why are arranged marriages less fragile than marriages based on love?

Applying What You've Learned

Some Warning Signs of Intimate Partner Abuse and Violence

Numerous clues to the potential for intimate partner abuse and violence appear before the abuse actually occurs. How many of these red flags do you recognize in your or your friends' relationships?

- **Verbal abuse:** Constant criticism, ignoring what you are saying, mocking, name calling, yelling, and swearing.
- **Sexual abuse:** Forcing or demanding sexual acts that you don't want to perform.
- **Disrespect:** Interrupting, telling you what you should think and how you should feel, putting you down in front of other people, saying ugly things about your friends and family.
- **Isolation:** Trying to cut you off from family and friends, monitoring your phone calls, reading your mail or e-mail, controlling where you go, taking your car keys and cell phone.

- **Emotional withholding or neglect:** Not expressing feelings, not giving compliments, not respecting your feelings and opinions.
- **Jealousy:** Very possessive, calling constantly or visiting unexpectedly, checking the mileage on your car, not wanting you to work because "you might meet someone."
- **Unrealistic expectations:** Expecting you to be the perfect mate and meet his or her every need.
- **Blaming others for problems:** It's *always* someone else's fault if something goes wrong.
- **Rigid sex roles:** Expecting you to serve, obey, and always stay home.
- **Extreme mood swings:** Switching from sweet to abusive and violent in minutes or being very kind one day and very vicious the next.

- **Cruelty to animals and children:** Killing or punishing pets brutally. May expect children to do things that are far beyond their ability or tease them until they cry.
- **Threats of violence:** Saying things such as "I'll break your neck" and then dismissing them with "I didn't really mean it" or "Everybody talks like that."
- **Destruction of property:** Destroying furniture, punching walls or doors, throwing things, breaking dishes or other household articles.
- **Self-destructive behavior:** Abusing drugs or alcohol, threatening self-harm or suicide, getting into fights with people, causing problems at work (such as telling off the boss).

? ASK YOURSELF

If This is Love, Why Do I Feel So Bad?

If you have bad feelings about your relationship, what you're experiencing may be *control*, not love. Controllers use whatever tactics are necessary to maintain power over another person: nagging, cajoling, coaxing, flattery, charm, threats, self-pity, blame, insults, or humiliation.

In the worst cases, controllers may physically injure and even murder people who refuse to be controlled. As you read this list, check any items that seem familiar to you. Individually, the items may seem unimportant, but if you check off more than two or three, you may be dealing with a controller instead of forging your own choices in life.

☐ My partner calls me names: "dummy," "jackass," "whore," "creep," "bitch," "moron."

☐ My partner always criticizes me and makes even a compliment sound like a criticism: "This is the first good dinner you've cooked in months."

☐ Always right, my partner continually corrects things I say or do. If I'm five minutes late, I'm afraid my partner will be mad.

☐ My partner withdraws into silence, and I have to figure out what I've done wrong and apologize for it.

☐ My partner is jealous when I talk to new people.

☐ My partner often phones or unexpectedly comes by the place where I work to see if I'm "okay."

☐ My partner acts very cruelly and then says I'm too sensitive and can't take a joke.

☐ When I try to express my opinion about something, my partner either doesn't respond, walks away, or makes fun of me.

☐ I have to account for every dime I spend, but my partner keeps me in the dark about our bank accounts.

☐ My partner says that if I ever leave he or she will commit suicide and I'll be responsible.

☐ When my partner has a temper tantrum, he or she says it's my fault or the children's.

☐ My partner makes fun of my body.

☐ Whether my partner is with us or not, he or she is jealous of every minute I spend with my family or other relatives or friends.

☐ My partner grills me about what happened whenever I go out.

☐ My partner makes sexual jokes about me in front of the children or other people.

☐ My partner throws things at me or hits, shoves, or pushes me.

Source: Based on Jones and Schechter, 1992: 16–22.

ASK YOURSELF BOXES are self-assessment exercises that encourage students to think about and evaluate their knowledge about marriage and the family. They help students develop guidelines for action, either their own or on another's behalf. For example, the **"If This Is Love, Why Do I Feel So Bad?" box in Chapter 6** helps students evaluate their current situations and make the decision to leave an abusive relationship.

CENSUS UPDATE

2010 Census Update—Features fully updated data throughout the text—including all charts and graphs—to reflect the results of the 2010 Census.

A Short Introduction to the U.S. Census—A brief seven-chapter overview of the Census, including important information about the Constitutional mandate, research methods, who is affected by the Census, and how data is used. Additionally, the primer explores key contemporary topics such as race and ethnicity, the family, and poverty. The primer can be packaged at no additional cost, and is also available online in *MySearchLab*, as a part of *MyFamilyLab*.

A Short Introduction to the U.S. Census Instructor's Manual with Test Bank—Includes explanations of what has been updated, in-class activities, homework activities, discussion questions for the primer, and test questions related to the primer.

MyFamilyLab2010 Census Update gives students the opportunity to explore 2010 Census methods and data and apply Census results in a dynamic interactive online environment. It includes a series of activities using 2010 Census results , video clips explaining and exploring the Census , primary source readings relevant to the Census, and an online version of the 2010 Census Update Primer.

SUPPLEMENTS

The supplement package for this textbook is exceptional. Each component has been meticulously crafted to amplify and illuminate materials in the text.

MYFAMILYLAB (ISBN: 0205808468) MyFamilyLab is an easy-to-use online resource that allows instructors to assess student progress and adapt course material to meet the specific needs of the class. This resource enables students to diagnose their progress by completing an online self-assessment test. Based on the results of this test, each student is provided with a customized study plan, including a variety of tools to help him or her fully master the material. MyFamilyLab then reports the self-assessment results to the instructor as individual student grades as well as an aggregate report of class progress. Based on these reports, the instructor can adapt course material to suit the needs of individual students or the class as a whole.

MyFamilyLab includes several exciting new features. *Social Explorer* provides easy access to census data from 1790 to the present. You can explore the data visually through interactive data maps. *MySocLibrary* contains numerous original source readings with discussion questions and assessment exercises. *Relate/Ready: Relate* is a relationship inventory developed by a team of scholars, researchers, family life educators, and therapists from varied educational and religious backgrounds. It can be taken by individuals who might or might not be in a serious relationship or by couples who want their responses analyzed together. *Ready* is a questionnaire designed for individuals not currently in a committed relationship but who desire to be in the future. It provides information about the individual's marital readiness.

Contact your local Pearson Education representative for ordering information, or visit: www.myfamilylab.com.

INSTRUCTOR'S RESOURCE MANUAL WITH TESTS (ISBN: 020573538X)

Revised by Henry Borne of Holy Cross College in Indiana and Ann Marie Kinnell at the University of Southern Mississippi, each chapter in the manual includes the following resources: chapter learning objectives, chapter overview, lecture suggestions and classroom discussions, activities, and multimedia resources. Designed to make your lectures more effective and to save preparation time, this extensive resource gathers together the most effective activities and strategies for teaching your Marriage and Family course.

Also included in this manual is a test bank of approximately 2,000 multiple-choice, true/false, short answer, and essay questions. Additionally, each chapter of the test bank includes a ready-made ten-item quiz with an answer key for immediate use in class.

The Instructor's Resource Manual with Tests is available to adopters at www.pearsonhighered.com.

MYTEST (ISBN: 0205736149)

This computerized software allows instructors to create their own personalized exams, to edit any or all of the existing test questions, and to add new questions. Other special features of this program include random generation of test questions, creation of alternate versions of the same test, scrambling question sequence, and test preview before printing. For easy access, this software is available within the instructor section of the MyFamilyLab for *Marriages & Families, 7e* or at www.pearsonhighered.com.

POWERPOINT PRESENTATIONS (ISBN: 020573541X)

You have the option in every chapter of choosing from any of the following types of slides: Lecture, Line Art, and/or Clicker Response System. The Lecture PowerPoint slides follow the chapter outline and feature images from the textbook integrated with the text. The Line Art PowerPoint features all of the art, organized by chapter, available in a PowerPoint-ready format. The Clicker Response System allows you to obtain immediate feedback from your students regardless of class size. They are available to adopters at www.pearsonhighered.com.

ACKNOWLEDGMENTS

A number of people have contributed to this edition of *Marriages & Families: Changes, Choices, and Constraints.* First, I would like to thank my students. Their lively and passionate exchanges during class and in online discussions always help me refocus some of my research and writing. Because of their input, I always focus on the student, not faculty members, when I'm revising the textbook.

Many thanks to the excellent and very responsive staff—in reference, circulation, and interlibrary loan departments—at the University of Baltimore's Langsdale Library for their continuous support. The success of this edition, like previous ones, relied heavily on their ongoing help.

Colleagues always play a critical role in revisions. For this edition, I received valuable input from:

Kathryn Bonach, Indiana University of Pennsylvania

Xuemei Hu, Union County College

Michele Knoles, Cowley County Community College

Theresa Mariani, Bradley University

Erica Owens, West Virginia University

Jennifer F. Powell, West Virginia University

Darby Sewell, Abraham Baldwin Agricultural College

James F. Weipert, Iowa Lakes Community College

I want to express my sincere gratitude to a dedicated and extremely talented team at Pearson, including Karen Hanson, Publisher; Rochelle Diogenes, Editor in Chief, Development; Kelly May, Executive Marketing Manager; Mayda Bosco, Supplements Editor; Pat Torelli, Senior Production Project Manager; Bruce Hobart, Production Project Manager; Linda Benson, Copy Editor; Carolyn Viola-John, Development Editor; and photo researchers Kate Cebik and Laurie Frankenthaler.

I thank my family for their unfaltering patience and sense of humor throughout life's little stresses, especially my research and writing. Throughout our 43 years of marriage, Vitalius, my husband, has always been my greatest supporter, a sympathetic and intelligent sounding board, and an incredibly patient high-tech consultant. Andrius, our son, helps me maintain my sanity by keeping my computer humming. About twice a year, he updates my hardware and software and makes sure that my backup tapes are working. Gema, our daughter, manages to drag me away from the monitor and into the sunshine once in a while despite my many "But I have so much to do!" protests.

Last, but not least, I have benefited greatly from the suggestions of faculty and students who have contacted me during the past few years. I have incorporated many of their reactions in the seventh edition and look forward to future comments.

Thank you, one and all.

About the Author

Nijole V. Benokraitis, professor emerita of sociology at the University of Baltimore, taught the marriage and family course for almost 25 years. It was her favorite class, but her courses in racial and ethnic relations and gender roles ran a close second. Professor Benokraitis received a B.A. in sociology and English from Emmanuel College in Boston, an M.A. in sociology from the University of Illinois at Urbana-Champaign, and a Ph.D. in sociology from the University of Texas at Austin.

She was a strong proponent of applied sociology and required her students to enhance their knowledge through interviews, direct observation, and other hands-on learning methods. She also enlisted her students in community service activities such as tutoring and mentoring inner-city high school students, writing to government officials and other decision makers about specific social problems, and volunteering research services to nonprofit organizations.

Professor Benokraitis immigrated to the United States from Lithuania with her family after World War II as a political refugee when she was five years old. She is bilingual and bicultural and is very empathetic of students who must balance the demands of several cultural worlds.

She has authored, co-authored, edited, or co-edited ten books, including *SOC, Contemporary Ethnic Families in the United States: Characteristics, Variations, and Dynamics; Feuds about Families: Conservative, Centrist, Liberal, and Feminist Perspectives; Modern Sexism: Blatant, Subtle, and Covert Discrimination;* and *Seeing Ourselves: Classic, Contemporary, and Cross-Cultural Readings in Sociology.* Dr. Benokraitis has published numerous articles and book chapters on topics such as institutional racism, discrimination against women in government and higher education, fathers in two-earner families, displaced homemakers, and family policy.

She has received grants and fellowships from many institutions, including the National Institute of Mental Health, the Ford Foundation, the American Educational Research Association, the Administration on Aging, and the National Endowment for the Humanities. She has also served as a consultant in the areas of sex and race discrimination to women's commissions, business groups, colleges and universities, federal government programs, and the American Association of University Women's International Fellowships Program.

Dr. Benokraitis has made several appearances on radio and television shows on gender communication differences and single-sex educational institutions. She currently serves on the editorial board of *Women & Criminal Justice* and reviews manuscripts for several academic journals.

Professor Benokraitis lives in Maryland with her husband, Dr. Vitalius Benokraitis, a vice president at a technology assessment company. They have two adult children, Gema and Andrius.

The author looks forward (and always responds) to comments on the 7th edition of *Marriages & Families: Changes, Choices, and Constraints.* She can be reached at nbenokraitis@ubalt.edu.

1 The Changing Family

Two generations ago, the typical American family consisted of a father, a mother, and three or four children. In contrast, in a recent survey that asked respondents what constitutes a family, a woman in her 60s wrote the following:

My boyfriend and I have lived together with my youngest son for several years. However, our family (with whom we spend holidays and special events) also includes my ex-husband and his wife and child; my boyfriend's ex-mother-in-law and her sister; his ex-wife and her boyfriend; my oldest son who lives on his own; my mom and stepfather; and my stepbrother and his wife, their biological child, adopted child, and "Big Sister" child. Needless to say, introductions to outsiders are confusing (Cole, 1996: 12, 14).

Clearly, contemporary family arrangements are more fluid than they were in the past. Does this shift reflect changes in individual preferences, as people often assume? Or are other forces at work? As you will see in this chapter, individual choices have altered some family structures, but many of these changes reflect adaptations to larger societal transformations.

DATA DIGEST

- The **"traditional" family** (in which the husband is the breadwinner and the wife is a full-time homemaker) has declined from 60 percent of all U.S. families in 1972 to 28 percent in 2007.

- Almost 14 million American **singles ages 30 to 44 have never been married,** representing 23 percent of all people in that age group.

- Today, the **median age at first marriage** is higher than at any time since 1890: 28.4 years for men and 26.5 years for women.

- On average, **first marriages that end in divorce** last about eight years.

- The percentage of **children under age 18 living with two married parents** fell from 77 percent in 1980 to 66 percent in 2010.

- **Single-parent American households** increased from 11 percent of all households in 1970 to 32 percent in 2007.

Sources: U.S. Census Bureau, 2008, Tables 56, 580, and 1293; U.S. Census Bureau, Current Population Survey, 2008, Table MS-2; U.S. Census Bureau Press Releases, 2008. Based on Federal Interagency Forum on Child and Family Statistics, 2009.

You will also see that despite both historical and recent evidence to the contrary, we continue to cling to a number of myths about the family. Before we examine these and other issues, we need to define what we mean by *family*. First, test your knowledge about current trends in U.S. families by taking the quiz above.

WHAT IS A FAMILY?

It may seem unnecessary to define a familiar term such as *family*, but its meaning differs from one group of people to another and may change over time. The definitions also have important political and economic consequences, often determining family members' rights and obligations. Under Social Security laws, for example, only a worker's spouse, dependent parents, and children can claim benefits based on the worker's record. Many employers' health and dental benefits cover a spouse and legal children, but not adults, either heterosexual or homosexual, who are unmarried but have long-term committed relationships, or children born out of wedlock. And in most adoptions, a child is not legally a member of an adopting family until social service agencies and the courts have approved the adoption. Thus, definitions of family affect people's lives by expanding or limiting their options.

Since you asked . . .
- Does it *really* matter how we define *family*?

Some Traditional Definitions of the Family

There is no universal definition of the family because contemporary household arrangements are complex. Traditionally, *family* has been defined as a unit made up of two or more people who are related by blood, marriage, or adoption; live together; form an economic unit; and bear and raise children. The U.S. Census Bureau defines the family simply as two or more people living together who are related by birth, marriage, or adoption.

Since you asked . . .
- Are people who live together but don't have children a family?

Many social scientists have challenged such traditional definitions because they exclude a number of diverse groups that also consider themselves families. Social scientists have asked: Are child-free couples families? What about cohabiting couples? Foster parents and their charges? Elderly sisters living together? Gay and lesbian couples, with or without children? Grandparents raising grandchildren?

Some Current Definitions of the Family

For our purposes, a **family** is an intimate group of two or more people who (1) live together in a committed relationship, (2) care for one another and any children, and (3) share activities and close

In *Hannah Montana*, a popular television show, mom has died and dad is raising the kids. The show portrays a nontraditional family, but is it representative of most American families, especially single-parent households?

emotional ties. Some people may disagree with this definition because it doesn't explicitly include marriage, procreation, or child rearing, but it is more inclusive than traditional views of a wide variety of family forms.

Definitions of the family may become even more complicated—and more controversial—in the future. As reproductive technology advances, a baby might have several "parents": an egg donor, a sperm donor, a woman who carries the baby during a pregnancy, and the couple who intends to raise the child. If that's not confusing enough, the biological father may be dead for years by the time the child is actually conceived because his sperm can be frozen and stored (see Chapter 11).

Our definition of the family could also include **fictive kin,** nonrelatives who are accepted as part of the family because they have strong bonds with biological family members and provide important services and care. These ties may be stronger and more lasting than those established by blood or marriage (Dilworth-Anderson et al., 1993). James, an African American in his forties and one of my former students, still fondly recalls Mike, a boarder in his home, who is a good example of fictive kinship:

Mike was an older gentleman who lived with us from my childhood to my teenage years. He was like a grandfather to me. He taught me how to ride a bike, took me fishing, and always told me stories. He was very close to me and my family until he died. When the family gets together, we still talk about old Mike because he was just like family and we still miss him dearly (Author's files).

Fictive kin have been most common among African American and Latino communities, but a recent variation involves single mothers—many of whom are unmarried college-educated women—who turn to one another for companionship and help in child care. For example, they take turns watching one another's kids (including taking them to Saturday-morning gymnastics classes and on short summer vacations), help during crises (such as a death in the family), and call each other constantly when they need advice about anything from a child who is talking late to suggestions on presenting a paper at a professional conference (Bazelon, 2009).

Answers to "How Much Do You Know about Contemporary Family Life?"

All the answers are **false.**

1. Teenage out-of-wedlock births have decreased over the past 20 years, especially in the early 2000s (see Chapters 10 and 11).

2. Couples who are living together and plan to marry *soon* have a good chance of staying together after a marriage. In most cases, however, "shacking up" decreases the likelihood of marriage (see Chapter 9).

3. Compared with singles, married people have more and better sex and enjoy it more, both physically and emotionally (see Chapter 7).

4. College-educated women tend to postpone marriage but are more likely to marry, over a lifetime, than their non–college-educated counterparts (see Chapters 9 and 10).

5. Love is not the major or even the only reason for getting married. Other reasons include societal expectations, economic insecurity, or fear of loneliness (see Chapters 6, 10, 16, and 17).

6. Divorce rates have been dropping since the early 1980s (see Chapter 15).

7. The arrival of a first baby typically pushes mothers and fathers apart. Generally, child rearing lowers marital satisfaction for both partners (see Chapters 11, 12, and 16).

8. Social class is a more important factor than marital status in a baby's health. Low-income mothers are less likely than high-income mothers to have healthy babies, whether or not they are married (see Chapters 11–14).

9. Income levels are usually higher in stepfamilies than in single-parent families, but stepfamilies have their own set of problems, including interpersonal conflicts with new parent figures (see Chapter 16).

10. Family relationships across several generations are more common and more important now than they were in the past. People live longer and get to know their kin, aging parents and grandparents often provide financial support and child care, and many relatives maintain ties with one another after a divorce or remarriage (see Chapters 3, 4, 12, 16, and 17).

HOW ARE FAMILIES SIMILAR ACROSS SOCIETIES?

The institution of the family exists in some form in all societies. Worldwide, families are similar in fulfilling some functions, encouraging marriage, and trying to ensure that people select the "right" mate.

Family Functions

Families vary considerably in the United States and globally but must fulfill at least five important functions to ensure a society's survival (Parsons and Bales, 1955). As you read this section, think about your own family. How well does it fulfill these functions?

Since you asked . . .

:• Do we *really* need families?

REGULATION OF SEXUAL ACTIVITY Every society has **norms,** or culturally defined rules for behavior, regarding who may engage in sexual relations, with whom, and under what circumstances. In the United States, having sexual intercourse with someone under age 18 is a crime, but some societies permit marriage with girls as young as 8. One of the oldest rules that regulate sexual behavior is the **incest taboo,** cultural norms and laws that forbid sexual intercourse between close blood relatives, such as brother and sister, father and daughter, uncle and niece, or grandparent and grandchild. Sexual relations between close relatives can increase the incidence of inherited genetic diseases and abnormalities by about 3 percent (Bennett et al., 2002). Incest taboos are based primarily on social conditions, however, and probably arose to preserve the family, and do so in several ways (Ellis, 1963):

- They minimize jealousy and destructive sexual competition that might undermine a family's survival and smooth functioning. If family members who are sexual partners lose interest in each other, for example, they may avoid mating.

- Because incest taboos ensure that mating will take place outside the family, a wider circle of people can band together in cooperative efforts (such as hunting), in the face of danger, or in war.

- By controlling the mother's sexuality, incest taboos prevent doubts about the legitimacy of her offspring and the children's property rights, titles, or inheritance.

Most social scientists believe that incest taboos are universal, but there have been exceptions. The rulers of the Incan empire, Hawaii, ancient Persia, and the Ptolemaic dynasty in Egypt practiced incest, which was forbidden to commoners. Cleopatra is said to have been the issue of at least 11 generations of incest; she in turn married her younger brother. Some anthropologists speculate that wealthy Egyptian families practiced sibling marriage to prevent losing or fragmenting their land. If a sister married her brother, the property would remain in the family in the event of divorce or death (Parker, 1996).

PROCREATION AND SOCIALIZATION Procreation is an essential function of the family because it replenishes a country's population. Some married couples choose to remain child free, but most plan to raise children. Some go to great lengths to conceive children through reproductive technologies (see Chapter 11). Once a couple becomes parents, the family embarks on socialization, another critical function.

Through **socialization,** children acquire language; absorb the accumulated knowledge, attitudes, beliefs, and values of their culture; and learn the social and interpersonal skills they need if they are to function effectively in society. Some socialization is unconscious and may be unintentional, such as teaching culturally accepted stereotypical gender traits (see Chapter 5). Much socialization, however, is both conscious and deliberate, such as carefully selecting preschoolers' playmates or raising children in a specific religion.

We are socialized through **roles,** the obligations and expectations attached to a particular status or position in society. Families are important role-teaching agents because they delineate relationships between mothers and fathers, siblings, parents and children, and other relatives and nonfamily members.

Some of the rights and responsibilities associated with our roles are not always clear because family structures shift and change. If you or your parents have experienced divorce or remarriage, have some of the new role expectations been fuzzy or even contradictory? For example, children may be torn between loyalty to a biological parent and to a stepparent if the adults compete for their affection (see Chapter 16).

ECONOMIC SECURITY The family is also an important economic unit that provides financial security and stability. Families supply food, shelter, clothing, and other material resources that ensure the

The family provides the love, comfort, and emotional support that children need to develop into happy, healthy, and secure adults.

family's physical survival. Especially during the economic downturn beginning in 2008, many families have relied on their kin for loans to pay off credit debts or rent; help in caring for children while searching for a job after being laid off; and a place to live, such as with parents or grandparents, after a home foreclosure (see Chapters 13 and 17).

In traditional families, the husband is the breadwinner and the wife does the housework and cares for the children. Since the 1980s, however, many mothers have been in the labor force. The traditional family, in which Mom stays home to raise the kids, is a luxury that most families today simply can't afford. Because of high unemployment rates, depressed wages and salaries, and job insecurity, many mothers must work outside the home whether or not they want to (see Chapters 5 and 13).

EMOTIONAL SUPPORT A fourth function of the family is to give its members emotional support. American sociologist Charles Horton Cooley (1864–1929) proposed the concept of **primary groups,** those characterized by close, long-lasting, intimate, and face-to-face interaction. The family is a critical primary group because it provides the nurturance, love, and emotional sustenance that its members need to be happy, healthy, and secure. Our close friends are usually members of our primary groups, but they may come and go (especially when they move to another state). In contrast, our family is usually our steadfast and enduring emotional anchor throughout life.

Sociologists later introduced the concept of **secondary groups,** those characterized by impersonal and short-term relationships in which people work together on common tasks or activities. Members of secondary groups, such as co-workers, have few emotional ties to one another, and they typically leave the group after attaining a specific goal. While you're taking this course, for example, you, most of your classmates, and your instructor make up a secondary group. You've all come together for a quarter or a semester to study marriage and the family. Once the course is over, most of you may never see one another again.

You might discuss your course with people in other secondary groups, such as co-workers. They will probably listen politely, but they usually don't really care how you feel about a class or a professor. Primary groups such as your family and close friends, in contrast, usually sympathize, drive you to class or your job when your car breaks down, offer to do your laundry during exams, and console you if you don't get that much-deserved "A" in a course or a promotion at work.

I use a simple test to distinguish between my primary and secondary groups: I don't hesitate to call the former at 3:00 A.M. to pick me up at the airport because I know they'll be happy (or at least willing) to do so. In contrast, I'd never call someone from a secondary group, such as another faculty member with whom I have no emotional ties.

SOCIAL CLASS PLACEMENT A **social class** is a category of people who have a similar standing or rank in society based on their wealth, education, power, prestige, and other valued resources. People in the same social class tend to have similar attitudes, values, and leisure interests. We inherit a social position based on our parents' social class. Family resources affect children's ability to pursue opportunities such as higher education, but we can move up or down the social hierarchy in adulthood depending on our own motivations, hard work, connections, or even luck by being at the right place at the right time (see Chapter 12).

Social class affects many aspects of family life. There are class variations in when people marry, how many children they have, how parents socialize their children, and even how partners and spouses relate to each other. Middle-class couples are more likely than their working-class counterparts to share housework and child rearing, for example. And as you'll see in later chapters, families on the lower rungs of the socioeconomic ladder face greater risks than their middle-class counterparts of adolescent nonmarital childbearing, dropping out of high school, committing street crimes, neglecting their children, and being arrested for domestic violence (see Chapters 10, 12, and 13).

Marriage

Marriage, a socially approved mating relationship that people expect to be stable and enduring, is also universal. Countries vary in their specific norms and

Some religious groups, such as Orthodox Jews in the United States, are endogamous because they require that couples marry within their own faith.

laws dictating who can marry whom and at what age, but marriage everywhere is an important rite of passage that marks adulthood and its related responsibilities, especially providing for a family. To be legally married in the United States, we must meet specific requirements, such as a minimum age, which may differ from one state to another.

U.S. marriages are legally defined as either ceremonial or nonceremonial. A *ceremonial* marriage is one in which the couple must follow procedures specified by the state or other jurisdiction, such as buying a license, getting blood tests, and being married by an authorized official.

Since you asked . . .

- Does living together mean that someone has a common-law marriage?

Some states also recognize **common-law marriage**, a *nonceremonial* relationship that people establish. Generally, there are three requirements for a common-law marriage: (1) living together for a significant period of time (not defined in any state); (2) presenting oneself as part of a married couple (typically using the same last name, referring to the other as "my husband" or "my wife," and filing a joint tax return); and (3) intending to marry. Common-law marriages are legal in nine states and the District of Columbia. Another seven states recognize common-law marriage only under certain conditions, such as those formed before a certain date (National Conference of State Legislatures, 2009).

In both kinds of marriages, the parties must meet minimum age requirements, and they cannot engage in **bigamy**, marrying a second person while a first marriage is still legal. When common-law marriages break up, numerous legal problems can result, such as a child's inheritance rights and the father's responsibility to pay child support. Even when common-law marriage is considered legal, ceremonial marriage usually provides more advantages (such as health benefits for spouses and social approval). In addition, the rights and benefits of common-law

marriages are usually recognized only in the state that has legalized them.

Endogamy and Exogamy

All societies have rules, formal or informal, about the "right" marriage partner. **Endogamy** (sometimes called *homogamy*) requires people to marry or have sexual relations within a certain group. These groups might include those that are similar in religion (such as Muslims marrying Muslims), race or ethnicity (such as Latinos marrying Latinos), social class (such as the rich marrying the rich), or age (such as young people marrying young people). And, in many countries, marrying cousins is not only commonplace but desirable (see the box "Why Does Cousin Marriage Matter in Iraq?").

Exogamy (sometimes called *heterogamy*) requires marriage outside the group, such as not marrying one's relatives or members of the same clan or tribe. In the United States, for example, 24 states prohibit marriage between first cousins, even though violations are rarely prosecuted. Even when there are no such laws, cultural traditions and practices, as well as social pressure, usually govern our choice of sexual and marital partners. In those jurisdictions in India in which most people still follow strict caste rules, the government is encouraging exogamy by offering up to a $1,250 cash award if a male or female marries "down." This is a hefty sum when the annual income in many areas is less than half that amount (Chu, 2007).

HOW DO FAMILIES DIFFER ACROSS SOCIETIES?

Despite similarities, there are also considerable worldwide variations in family form. Some include the structure of the family and where married couples live.

Nuclear and Extended Families

Western societies tend to have a **nuclear family** that is made up of married parents and their biological or adopted children. In much of the world, however, the most common family form is the **extended family**, which consists of parents and children as well as other kin, such as uncles and aunts, nieces and nephews, cousins, and grandparents.

As the number of single-parent families increases in industrialized countries, extended families are becoming more common. By helping out with household tasks and child rearing, extended families make it easier for a single parent to work outside the home. Because the rates of unmarried people who are living together are high, nuclear families comprise only 21.5 percent of all U.S. households, down from 40 percent in 1970 (U.S. Census Bureau, 2010).

Cross-Cultural and Multicultural Families

Why Does Cousin Marriage Matter in Iraq?

According to some of my students, "It's disgusting to even think about marrying a cousin." Why, then, are such endogamous marriages prevalent in parts of the Middle East, Africa, and Asia? For example, half of all marriages in Iraq, Pakistan, and Nigeria are between first or second cousins.

This form of marriage is both legal and even preferred (instead of marrying outside of one's group) in societies in which families are organized around clans with blood relationships rather than outsiders. Each clan is a "government in miniature" that provides the services and social aid that Americans routinely receive from their national, state, and local governments.

The largest and most unified clans have the greatest amount of power and resources. These, in turn, motivate people not to trust the government, which is often corrupt, but to be attached to the proven support of kin, clan, or tribe.

Cousin marriages in Iraq (as in many other societies) create intense internal cohesiveness and loyalty that strengthen the clan. If, for example, a man or woman married into another clan, he or she would deplete the original clan's resources, especially property, and threaten the clan's unity. In addition, cousins who marry are bound tightly to their clans because their in-laws aren't strangers but aunts and uncles who know them best and

have a strong interest in supporting the marriage.

Sources: Based on Bobroff-Hajal, 2006, and Michels, 2008.

⠿• Stop and Think . . .

- What functions do endogamy and cousin marriages serve in Iraq?

- "Clan loyalty . . . strengthened by centuries of cousin marriage was always bound to undermine President Bush's fantasy of creating a truly democratic government in Iraq. Never again should the United States blithely invade a country knowing so little about its societal fabric" (Bobroff-Hajal, 2006: 9). Do you agree or disagree with this statement? Why?

Residence and Authority

Families also differ in where they live, how they trace their descent, and who has the most power. In a **patrilocal** residential pattern, newly married couples live with the husband's family. In a **matrilocal** pattern, they live with the wife's family. In a **neolocal** pattern, the newly married couple sets up its own residence.

Around the world, the most common pattern is patrilocal. In industrialized societies such as the United States, married couples are typically neolocal. Since the early 1990s, however, the tendency for young married adults to live with the parents of either the wife or husband—or sometimes with the grandparents of one of the partners—has increased. At least half of all young couples can't afford a medium-priced house, whereas others have low-income jobs, are supporting children after a divorce, or just enjoy the comforts of a parental nest (see Chapters 10 and 12).

Residence patterns often reflect who has authority in the family. In a **matriarchy**, the oldest females (usually grandmothers and mothers) control cultural, political, and economic resources and, consequently, have power over males. Some American Indian tribes were matriarchal and in some African countries, the eldest females have considerable authority and influence. For the most part, however, matriarchal societies are rare.

In China's Himalayas, the Mosuo may be a matriarchal society. For the majority of Mosuo, a family household consists of a woman, her children, and the daughters' offspring. In a practice called "walking marriage," women choose no-strings-attached lovers for a night or a lifetime. An adult male will join a lover for the evening and then return to his mother's or grandmother's house in the morning. Any children resulting from these unions belong to the female, and it is she and her relatives who raise them (Barnes, 2006).

A more widespread pattern is a **patriarchy**, in which the oldest males (grandfathers, fathers, and uncles) control cultural, political, and economic resources and, consequently, have power over females. In some patriarchal societies, like Saudi Arabia, women have few rights within the family and none outside the family, including not being able to vote, drive, work outside the home, or attend college. In other patriarchal societies, like Qatar, women can vote and run for a political office, but need permission from a husband or male relative to get a driver's license (see Chapter 5).

In **egalitarian family** structures, both partners share power and authority about equally. Many Americans think they have egalitarian families, but our families tend to be patriarchal. Employed women, especially, often complain that their husbands don't always consult them before making important decisions such as when to buy a home or new car (see Chapter 10).

Monogamy and Polygamy

In **monogamy,** one person is married exclusively to another person. When divorce and remarriage rates are high, as in the United States, people engage in **serial monogamy.** That is, they marry several people, but one at a time—they marry, divorce, remarry, redivorce, and so on.

Since you asked . . .

• Is serial monogamy a modern version of polygamy?

Polygamy, in which a man or woman has two or more spouses, is subdivided into *polygyny*—one man married to two or more women—and *polyandry*—one woman with two or more husbands. Nearly 1,000 cultures around the world allow some form of polygamy, either officially or unofficially (Epstein, 2008). There are no known cases of polyandry today, but the practice might have existed in societies in which property was difficult to accumulate. Because there was a limited amount of available land, the kinship group was more likely to survive in harsh environments if there was more than one husband to provide food (Cassidy and Lee, 1989).

The Todas, a small pastoral tribe that flourished in southern India until the late nineteenth century, illustrate polyandry. A Toda woman who married one man became the wife of his brothers—including brothers born after the marriage—and they all lived in the same household. When one of the brothers was with the wife, "he placed his cloak and staff outside the hut as a warning to the rest not to disturb him" (Queen et al., 1985: 19). Marital privileges rotated among the brothers; there was no evidence of sexual jealousy; and one of the brothers, usually the oldest, was the legal father of the first two or three children. Another brother could become the legal father of children born later.

In contrast to polyandry, polygyny is common in many societies, especially in Africa, South America, and the Mideast. In Saudi Arabia, for example, Osama bin Laden, who orchestrated the 9/11 terrorist

Law enforcement officers escort FLDS children—some of them mothers under age 18—to a temporary housing facility in San Angelo, Texas, after allegations of young girls' being sexually abused and forced into marriage.

attacks, has 4 wives and 10 children. His father had 11 wives and 54 children. No one knows the rate of polygamy worldwide, but some observers believe that polygyny may be increasing (Nakashima, 2003; Greenberg, 2006; Coll, 2008).

Western and other industrialized societies forbid polygamy, but there are pockets of isolated polygynous groups in the United States, Canada, and Europe. The Church of Jesus Christ of Latter-day Saints (Mormons) banned polygamy in 1890 and excommunicates members who follow such beliefs. Still, an estimated 300,000 families in Texas, Arizona, Utah, and Canada are headed by males of the Fundamentalist Church of Jesus Christ of Latter Day Saints (FLDS), a polygamous sect that broke off from the mainstream Mormon church more than a century ago. These dissident leaders maintain that they practice polygamy according to nineteenth-century Mormon religious beliefs. The leaders perform secret marriage ceremonies and marry girls—as young as 11—to older men (who are sometimes in their 50s and 60s) at the first sign of menstruation (Divoky, 2002; Madigan, 2003).

In 2008, state troopers raided an isolated 1,700-acre ranch near Eldorado, Texas, that housed members of the FLDS. State officials believed that the FLDS forced girls younger than 16 into sex and marriage with older men, and, in some cases, into multiple marriages—both illegal in Texas. The state won the right to remove more than 400 children from the compound to protect them from abuse, but the Texas Supreme Court ordered Child Protective Services to return the children from foster care to their parents, ruling that child welfare officials had not proven that the children were in any immediate danger.

Wives who have escaped from these plural families report forced marriage, sexual abuse, child rape, and incest. Why don't these girls refuse to marry or try to escape? They can't. Among other things, they're typically isolated from outsiders: They live in remote rural areas and their education is cut off when they're about 10 years old. Their parents support the marriages because elderly men, the patriarchs, have convinced them that "This is what the heavenly father wants" (Egan, 2005; Jones, 2009). Sexual abusers are rarely prosecuted and, even then, receive remarkable leniency. A father who was convicted of regularly molesting his five daughters spent only 13 days in jail. The presiding judge said that the abuse was really just "a little bit of breast touching" (Kelly and Cohn, 2006).

Some church elders have banished hundreds of teenage boys—some as young as 13—to reduce the competition for young wives. Gideon, 17, is one of these boys. He is one of 71 children born to his 73-year-old father, who has eight wives. Because most of the boys don't attend school past the eighth grade, they have few skills to fend for themselves after being expelled from the community (Kelly, 2005; Knickerbocker, 2006).

Some African and Middle Eastern families that immigrate to other countries continue to live in polygamous families but often run into problems. The French government, which declared polygamy illegal in 1993, estimates that there are about 20,000 polygamous families within the nation's borders. Because they are not legal residents and are not entitled to any form of social welfare such as public housing, the families end up living in crowded and impoverished conditions. Also, "tensions arise with French neighbors who tend to be flabbergasted when confronted with families consisting of a husband, two or more wives, and as many as 20 children" (Renout, 2005: 17). Whether the families immigrate to Europe or the United States, wives are reluctant to report domestic violence because they fear deportation or being branded a bad woman by family members in their native country (Bernstein, 2007; Wilkinson, 2008; Kelly, 2009).

Why is polygyny widespread in some countries? A study of marriage patterns in South Africa concluded that there is often a shortage of men (usually because of war), that poor women would rather marry a rich polygamist than a poor monogamist, that wives often pool incomes and engage in cooperative child care, and that rural wives often contact urban wives when they're looking for jobs. Thus, polygyny is functional because it meets many women's needs (Anderson, 2002).

FAMILY STRUCTURE AND SOCIAL CHANGE

Most people are born into a biological family, or *family of origin*. If a person is adopted or raised in this family, it is her or his **family of orientation.** By leaving this family to marry or cohabit, the individual becomes part of a **family of procreation,** the family a person forms by marrying and/or having or adopting children. This term is somewhat dated, however, because in several types of households—such as child-free or gay and lesbian families—procreation isn't a key function.

Each type of family is part of a larger **kinship system,** a network of people who are related by blood, marriage, or adoption. In much of the developing world, which contains most of the earth's population, the most common family form is the extended family.

For nearly a century, the nation's family structure remained remarkably stable. Between 1880 and 1970, about 85 percent of all children lived in two-parent households. Then, in the next three decades, the numbers of divorces and single-parent families skyrocketed. By 2007, almost one in four children was living in a mother-only home (see *Figure 1.1*).

Some people are concerned that the nuclear family has dwindled. Many social scientists contend, however, that viewing the nuclear family as the only normal or natural type of family ignores many other household

Since you asked . . .

- Are TV depictions of family structure realistic?

forms. One researcher, for example, identified 23 types of family structures, some of which include only friends or group-home members (Wu, 1996). Family structures have varied not only across cultures and eras but also within any particular culture or historical period (see Chapter 3).

FIGURE 1.1 Where American Children Live: Selected Years, 1880–2007

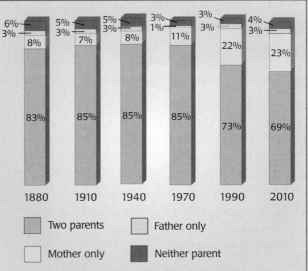

Sources: Based on Fields, 2001, Figure 7; and U.S. Census Bureau, 2008, Table 68.

As reflected in many television shows, diverse family structures are more acceptable today than ever before. At the same time, some of the most popular programs are rarely representative of real families. For example, in *Hannah Montana* and *Two and a Half Men*, a single dad is doing most of the child rearing; in *iCarly*, an older brother is taking care of his sister; and in *True Jackson VP*, the parents apparently don't exist or aren't very important in the girl's life. In reality, most American children live with both parents or only with the mother (see *Figure 1.1* on p. 11).

Clearly, there is much diversity in family arrangements both in the United States and around the world. As families change, however, we sometimes get bogged down by idealized images of what a "good" family looks like. Our unrealistic expectations can result in dissatisfaction and anger. Instead of enjoying our families as they are, we may waste a lot of time and energy searching for family relationships that exist only in fairy tales and TV sitcoms.

:•• MAKING CONNECTIONS

You may not even remember some of the television shows that came and went in the 1990s. Some, such as *Married . . . with Children, Mad about You, Home Improvement, Frasier,* and *The Bill Cosby Show,* are now syndicated. Others, such as *Life with Derek, Two and a Half Men,* and *The New Adventures of Old Christine,* offer a wide variety of family forms.

■ How many of the TV programs—in the past or now—are representative of most U.S. families? Or of your own family?

■ Do past and current shows shape our ideas about what our families should be like?

SOME MYTHS ABOUT THE FAMILY

Ask yourself the following questions:

■ Were families happier in the past than they are now?

■ Is marrying and having children the natural thing to do?

■ Are good families self-sufficient, whereas bad families rely on public assistance?

■ Is the family a bastion of love and support?

■ Should all of us strive to be as perfect as possible in our families?

If you answered "yes" to any of these questions, you—like most Americans—believe some of the myths about marriage and the family. Most of these myths are dysfunctional, but some can be functional.

Myths Can Be Dysfunctional

Myths are *dysfunctional* when they have negative (though often unintended) consequences that disrupt a family. The myth of the perfect family can make us miserable. We may feel that there is something wrong with *us* if we don't live up to some idealized image. Instead of accepting our current families, we might pressure our children to become what *we* want them to be or spend a lifetime waiting for our parents or in-laws to accept us. We may also become very critical of family members or withdraw emotionally because they don't fit into a mythical mold.

Since you asked . . .

:•• Do myths affect me and my family?

Myths can also divert our attention from widespread social problems that lead to family crises. If people blame themselves for the gap they perceive between image and reality, they may not recognize the external forces, such as social policies, that create difficulties on the individual level. For example, if we believe that only bad, sick, or maladjusted people beat their children, we will search for solutions at the individual level, such as counseling, support groups, and therapy. As you'll see in later chapters, however, and as millions of Americans have experienced since 2008, numerous family crises come from large-scale problems such as racism, greedy corporate executives in financial industries, economic downturns, and unemployment.

Myths Can Be Functional

Not all myths are harmful. Some are *functional* because they bring people together and promote social solidarity (Guest, 1988). If myths give us hope that we can have a good marriage and family life, for example, we won't give up at the first sign of problems. In this sense, myths can help us maintain emotional balance during crises.

Myths can also free us from guilt or shame. For instance, "We fell out of love" is a more face-saving explanation for getting a divorce than "I made a stupid mistake" or "I married an alcoholic."

The same myth can be both functional and dysfunctional. Belief in the decline of the family has been functional in generating social policies (such as child-support legislation) that try to keep children of divorced families from sinking into poverty. But this same myth is dysfunctional if people become unrealistically preoccupied with finding self-fulfillment and happiness.

Myths about the Past

We often hear that in the good old days there were fewer problems, people were happier, and families were stronger. Because of the widespread influence of

Like these Nebraska homesteaders, many families in the so-called good old days lived in dugouts like this one, made from sod cut from the prairie.

movies and television, many of us cherish romantic notions of life in earlier times. These highly unrealistic images of the family were presented in television shows such as *Father Knows Best* and *Leave It to Beaver* in the 1950s and early 1960s; *The Partridge Family* and *The Brady Bunch* during the 1970s; and the strong, poor, but loving rural family presented in television shows such as *The Waltons* and *Little House on the Prairie* in the 1970s and *Dr. Quinn, Medicine Woman* in the late 1990s. More recently, popular television shows such as *7th Heaven* and *Life with Derek* are probably appealing because they have resurrected images of the family in the good old days when its members solve all of their problems quickly and live happily ever after.

Many historians maintain that such golden days never existed. We idealize them only because we know so little about the past. Even in the 1800s, many families experienced out-of-wedlock births or desertion by a parent (Demos, 1986; Coontz, 1992).

Family life in the good old days was filled with deprivation, loneliness, and dangers, as the "Diary of a Pioneer Daughter" box illustrates. Families worked very hard and often were crushed by accidents, illness, and disease. Until the mid-1940s, a much shorter life expectancy meant that parental death often led to the placement of children in extended families, foster care, or orphanages. Thus, the chances of not growing up in a nuclear family were greater in the past than they are now (Walsh, 1993).

People who have the nostalgia bug aren't aware of several facts. For example, teenage pregnancy rates were higher in the 1950s than they are today, even though a higher proportion of teen mothers were married (many because of "shotgun marriages"). Until the 1970s, few people ever talked or wrote about child abuse, incest, domestic violence, marital unhappiness, sexual harassment, or gay bashing. Many families lived in silent misery and quiet desperation because these issues were largely invisible. In addition, parents spend more time with their children today than they did in the good old days (see Chapter 12).

Myths about What Is Natural

Many people have strong opinions about what is natural or unnatural in families. Remaining single is more acceptable today than it was in the past, but there is still a lingering suspicion that there's something wrong with a person who never marries (see Chapter 9). And we sometimes have misgivings about child-free marriages or other committed relationships. We often hear, for instance, that "It's only natural to want to get married and have children" or that "Gays are violating human nature." Other beliefs, also surviving from so-called simpler times, claim that family life is natural and that women are natural mothers (see Chapter 5).

The problem with such thinking is that if motherhood is natural, why do many women choose not to have children? If homosexuality is unnatural, how do we explain its existence since time immemorial? If getting married and creating a family are natural, why do millions of men abandon their children or refuse to marry their pregnant partners?

Myths about the Self-Sufficient Family

Among our most cherished values are individual achievement, self-reliance, and self-sufficiency. The numerous best-selling self-help books on topics such as parenting, successfully combining work and marriage, and having great sex also reflect our belief that we should improve ourselves, that we can pull ourselves up by our bootstraps.

We have many choices in our personal lives, but few families—past or present—have been entirely self-sufficient. Most of us need some kind of help at one time or another. Because of unemployment, home foreclosures, economic downturns, and recessions, the poverty rate has increased by 40 percent since 1970, and many of the working poor are two-parent

Diary of a Pioneer Daughter

Many scholars point out that frontier life was anything but romantic. Malaria and cholera were widespread. Because of their darkness, humidity, and warmth, as well as the gaping windows and doors, pioneers' cabins were ideal environments for mosquitoes. Women and children have been described as doing household tasks with "their hands and arms flailing the air" against hordes of attacking mosquitoes (Faragher, 1986: 90).

Historian Joanna Stratton examined the letters, diaries, and other documents of pioneer women living on the Kansas prairie between 1854 and 1890. The following selection is from the diary of a 15-year-old girl:

A man by the name of Johnson had filed on a claim just west of us and had built a sod house. He and his wife lived there 2 years, when he went to Salina to secure work. He was gone 2 or 3 months and wrote home once or twice, but his wife grew very homesick for her folks in the east and would come over to our house to visit Mother.

Mother tried to cheer her up, but she continued to worry until she got bedfast with the fever. At night she was frightened because the wolves would scratch on the door, on the sod, and on the windows, so my mother and I started to sit up nights with her. I would bring my revolver and ammunition and ax and some good-sized clubs.

The odor from the sick woman seemed to attract the wolves, and they grew bolder and bolder. I would step out, fire off the revolver, and they would settle back for a while when they would start a new attack.

Finally the woman died and mother laid her out. Father took some wide boards that we had in our loft and made a coffin for her. Mother made a pillow and trimmed it with black cloth, and we also painted the coffin black.

After that the wolves were more determined than ever to get in. One got his head in between the door casing, and as he was trying to wriggle through, mother struck him in the head with an ax and killed him. I shot one coming through the window. After that they quieted down for about half an hour, when they came back again. Their howling was awful. We fought these wolves five nights in succession. . . .

When Mr. Johnson arrived home and found his wife dead and his house badly torn down by wolves he fainted away. After the funeral he sold out and moved away (Stratton, 1981: 81).

Rebecca Bryan Boone, wife of the legendary pioneer Daniel Boone, endured months and sometimes even years of solitude when Boone hunted in the woods or went on trading trips. Besides doing household chores, she chopped wood, cultivated the fields, harvested the crops, and hunted for small game in the woods near her cabin. Although Rebecca was a strong and resourceful woman, she told a traveling preacher that she felt "frequent distress and fear in her heart" (Peavy and Smith, 1994: xi).

⸬• Stop and Think . . .

- Do historical descriptions of pioneer life differ from those that we've seen on television shows such as *The Waltons* and *Little House on the Prairie*?
- If we had time machines, would you want to be transported to the good old days of pioneers?

---

families (see Chapter 13). From time to time, these families need assistance to survive.

The middle class isn't self-sufficient, either. In the 1950s and 1960s, for example, many middle-class families were able to prosper not because of family savings or individual enterprise but as a result of federal housing loans, education payments, and publicly financed roads linking homes in the suburbs to jobs in the cities (Coontz, 1992).

Currently, all people age 65 and older, whether poor or rich, are eligible for Medicare, and the government provides numerous tax cuts for middle-income and affluent families (see Chapters 13 and 17). Even if you're in the middle class, you or other family members have probably collected unemployment payments after being laid off from a job. In addition, state-based merit scholarships are more likely to subsidize the college costs of students from rich families than those of students from poor and minority families (Fischer, 2008).

The Myth of the Family as a Loving Refuge

One sociologist has described the family as a "haven in a heartless world" (Lasch, 1977: 8). That is, one of the major functions of the family is to provide love, nurturance, and emotional support. The home can also be one of the most physically and psychologically brutal settings in society. An alarming number of children suffer from physical and sexual abuse by family members, and the violence rates between married and cohabiting partners are high (see Chapter 14).

Many parents experience stress while balancing the demands of work and family responsibilities. In addition, the U.S. unemployment rate surged from 4 percent in 2006 to almost 10 percent in mid-2009 and by April of 2011 declined only to 9.0 percent, (see Chapter 13). If nearly 1 in 10 Americans is unemployed, the anxiety underlying that unemployed person's ability to provide for his or her family is bound to negatively affect the family's dynamics and to decrease the feeling that the family is a loving refuge.

Also, family members are often unrealistic about the daily strains they encounter. For example, if people expect family interactions to always be cheery and pleasant, the level of tension may surge even when routine problems arise. And especially for families with health or economic problems, the home may be loving, but it's hardly a haven in a heartless world.

Myths about the Perfect Marriage, the Perfect Family

Here's how one woman described the clash between marital expectations and reality:

Marriage is not what I had assumed it would be. One premarital assumption after another has crashed down on my head.... Marriage is like taking an airplane to Florida for a relaxing vacation in January, and when you get off the plane you find you're in the Swiss Alps. There is cold and snow instead of swimming and sunshine. Well, after you buy winter clothes and learn how to ski and learn how to talk a new foreign language, I guess you can have just as good a vacation in the Swiss Alps as you can in Florida. But I can tell you ... it's one hell of a surprise when you get off that marital airplane and find that everything is far different from what one had assumed (Lederer and Jackson, 1968: 39).

This observation was made in 1968, but it's still very relevant today (see Chapter 10). Even if partners live together and believe that they know each other well, many may find themselves in the Swiss Alps instead of Florida after tying the knot. Numerous marriages dissolve because the partners cling to myths about conjugal life. After the perfect wedding, the perfect couple must be everything to each other: good providers, fantastic sexual partners, best friends, sympathetic confidantes, stimulating companions, and spiritual soul mates (Rubin, 1985). Are such expectations realistic?

Myths about the perfect family are just as pervasive as those about the perfect marriage. According to historian John Gillis (1996, 2004), we all have two families: one that we live *with* (the way families really are) and another that we live *by* (the way we would like families to be). Gillis maintains that people have been imagining and reimagining the family since at least the late Middle Ages because the families we are born and marry into seldom satisfy most people's need for a sense of continuity, belonging, unity, and rootedness.

MAKING CONNECTIONS

- Do media images of the family affect your perceptions? When you watch some TV shows, for example, do you feel disappointed in your own family? Or better than them?

- Do you believe any (or all) of the myths about marriage and the family that you have just read? If so, are these beliefs functional or dysfunctional in your life? How?

FAMILY VALUES: THREE PERSPECTIVES ON THE CHANGING FAMILY

We began this chapter by defining the family, examined how families are similar and different, and then considered some of the current myths about family life. Let's now look at the major theme of this chapter—how the American family is changing.

Several national surveys show that we place a high value on family. For example,

- Americans rank their family as the most important aspect of life, above health, work, money, and even religion (see *Figure 1.2*).

- Among high school seniors, 82 percent of girls and 70 percent of boys say that having a good marriage and family life is "extremely important" ("The State of Our Unions," 2007).

FIGURE 1.2 **How Important Is Family Life?**

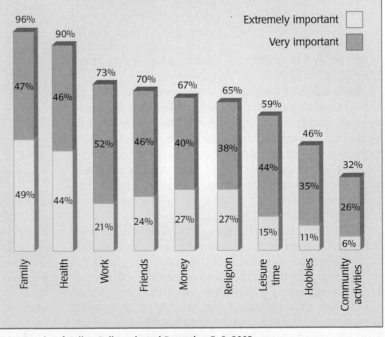

Note: Results of Gallup Poll conducted December 5–8, 2002.
Source: David W. Moore, 2003, Gallup Poll Analysis.

- Almost 77 percent of first-year college students (both women and men) say that raising a family is "very important" in their lives (*Chronicle of Higher Education*, 2008).

- Nine in 10 millennial teens (those born after 1982) say that they trust and feel close to their parents and describe themselves as happy, confident, and positive (Howe et al., 2000).

Despite such upbeat findings, many Americans worry that the family is falling apart. Some journalists and scholars refer to the "vanishing" family, "troubled" marriages, and "appalling" divorce statistics as sure signs that the family is disintegrating. Others contend that such hand-wringing is unwarranted.

Who's right? There are three schools of thought. One group contends that the family is deteriorating; a second group argues that the family is changing but not deteriorating; and a third, smaller group maintains that the family is stronger than ever (see Benokraitis, 2000, for a discussion of these perspectives).

The Family Is Deteriorating

More than 100 years ago, the *Boston Quarterly Review* issued a dire warning: "The family, in its old sense, is disappearing from our land, and not only are our institutions threatened, but the very existence of our society is endangered" (cited in Rosen, 1982: 299). In the late 1920s, E. R. Groves (1928), a well-known social scientist, warned that marriages were in a state of "extreme collapse." Some of his explanations for what he called the "marriage crisis" and high divorce rates have a surprisingly modern ring: self-indulgence, a concern for oneself rather than others, financial strain, and incompatible personalities.

Since you asked . . .

⁝⁚• Most of the families we know seem to be loving and close knit. So why do many people think that the family is in trouble?

Even some of those who were optimistic a decade ago have become more pessimistic because of recent data on family changes. Some of these data include high rates of divorce and children born out of wedlock, millions of latchkey children, an increase in the number of people deciding not to get married, unprecedented numbers of single-parent families, and a decline of parental authority in the home (see Chapters 5, 12, and 13).

Why have these changes occurred? Those who believe that the family is in trouble echo Groves, citing reasons such as individual irresponsibility, minimal commitment to the family, and just plain selfishness. Many conservative politicians and influential academics argue that the family is deteriorating because most people put their own needs above family duties. This school of thought claims that many adults are unwilling to invest their psychological and financial resources in their children or that they give up on their marriages too quickly when they encounter problems (Popenoe, 1996; Wilson, 2002).

Adherents of the family decline school of thought point out that marriage should exist for the sake of children and not just adults. Simply telling children we love them is not enough. Instead of wasting our money on a divorce industry that includes lawyers, therapists, and expert witnesses, the argument goes, we should be investing in children by maintaining a stable marriage (Whitehead, 1996).

Many of those who endorse the "family is deteriorating" perspective contend that numerous long-term trends have weakened marriage and family life. For example, fewer adults are married, more are divorced or remaining single, more are living outside of marriage or alone, and more children are born out of wedlock and live with a single parent (Popenoe, 2007).

Others maintain that if women spent more time finding husbands who are good providers, they could "devote their talents and education and energy to the rearing of their children, the nurturing of family relationships, and the building of community and neighborhood" (Gallagher, 1996: 184). The implication is that the deteriorating family could be shored up if fathers were breadwinners and mothers were homemakers.

Many of those who believe that the family is deteriorating are communitarians, people who are politically more moderate than conservatives on some family issues. For example, they accept the idea that many mothers have to work outside the home for economic reasons. Communitarians claim, however, that because many adults focus almost exclusively on personal gratification, traditional family functions such as the care and socialization of young children have become a low priority (Glenn, 1996). They contend that there has been a general increase in a sense of entitlement (what people believe they should receive from others) and a decline in a sense of duty (what people believe they should give to others).

The Family Is Changing, Not Deteriorating

Others argue that the changes we are experiencing are extensions of long-standing family patterns. For example, more women have entered the labor force since 1970, but the mother who works outside the home is not a new phenomenon. Mothers sold dairy products and woven goods during colonial times, took in boarders around the turn of the twentieth century, and held industrial jobs during World War II (see Chapter 3).

Many analysts also contend that family problems such as desertion, out-of-wedlock birth, and

Some cities and towns have refused to give unmarried partners, such as the ones pictured here, a "permit of occupancy" because they and their children are not a family. City officials say that the laws prevent overcrowding. Others argue that such laws are legislating morality by defining the family as a married, heterosexual couple and their children.

worries and harsh economic environments. And many gay and lesbian families, despite rejection by much of mainstream society, are resilient and resourceful in developing successful family relationships (Oswald, 2002; Seccombe, 2002).

Many researchers maintain that there is little empirical evidence that family change is synonymous with family decline. Instead, data support both perspectives—the belief that the family is in trouble as well as the notion that most families are resilient despite ongoing changes in gender roles, divorce rates, and alternatives to marriage such as living together (Amato, 2004).

child abuse have *always* existed. Family literature published in the 1930s, for example, included issues such as divorce, desertion, and family crises resulting from discord, delinquency, and depression (Broderick, 1988).

Similarly, there have always been single-parent families. The percentage of single-parent households has doubled in the past three decades, but that percentage tripled between 1900 and 1950. Divorce, also, is not a recent phenomenon because it became more common in the eighteenth century. Among other changes at that time, parents had less control over their adult married children because there was little land or other property to inherit and the importance of romantic love increased (Cott, 1976; Stannard, 1979).

There is no question, however, that a greater proportion of people divorce today than they did several generations ago. As a result, the decision of many singles to postpone marriage until they are older, are more mature, and have stable careers may be a sound one (see Chapters 9 and 15).

Families are changing but are also remarkably resilient, despite numerous adversities. They cope with everyday stresses and protect their most vulnerable members: the young, old, ill, or disabled. They overcome financial hardships. They handle everyday conflict and tension as children make a bumpy transition to adolescence and then to early adulthood (Conger and Conger, 2002; Patterson, 2002).

Those who hold that the family is changing, not deteriorating, point out that most poor families have stable and loving relationships despite constant

The Family Is Stronger than Ever

Do our nostalgic myths about the past misinterpret the contemporary family as weak and on the decline? Yes, according to a third school of thought. These social scientists assert that family life is much more loving today than it was in the past. Consider the treatment of women and children in colonial days: If they disobeyed strict male authority, they were often severely punished. And, in contrast to some of our sentimental notions about the good old days, only a small number of white, middle-class families enjoyed a life that was both gentle and genteel:

For every nineteenth-century middle-class family that protected its wife and child within the family circle . . . there was an Irish or a German girl scrubbing floors in that middle-class home, a Welsh boy mining coal to keep the home-baked goodies warm, a black girl doing the family laundry, a black mother and child picking cotton to be made into clothes for the family, and a Jewish or an Italian daughter in a sweatshop making "ladies" dresses or artificial flowers for the family to purchase (Coontz, 1992: 11–12).

Some social scientists argue that despite myriad problems, families are happier today than in the past because of the increase in multigenerational relationships. Many people have grandparents, feel closer to them, and often receive both emotional and economic support from these family members. The recent growth of the older segment of the population has produced four-generation families. More adults in their 60s may be stressed out because they are caring for 80- to 100-year-old parents. On the other hand, more children and grandchildren grow up knowing and enjoying their older relatives (see Chapter 17).

Some claim that families are stronger now than in the past because family members have more equitable roles at home and are more accepting of diverse family forms (such as single-parent homes, unmarried people who live together, and same-sex couples). And most Americans still believe that marriage is a lifetime commitment that should end only under extreme circumstances, such as domestic violence (Thornton and Young-DeMarco, 2001; see, also, Chapter 15).

Despite a sharp increase in the number of two-income families, mothers and fathers spend more time interacting with their children today than they did in 1965, at the height of the male-breadwinner/female-homemaker family. Single mothers have less time to spend with their families than do married mothers, but they, too, have significantly increased their time with children. Even childless and unmarried individuals are doing immense amounts of family work, with one in four American workers spending seven hours or more each week caring for an aging parent (Coontz, 2007). Thus, some maintain, most American families may be stronger and more satisfying today than in the past.

Each of the three schools of thought provides evidence for its position. Which perspective, then, can we believe? Is the family weak, or is it strong? The answer depends largely on how we define, measure, and interpret family weakness and strengths, issues we address in Chapter 2. For better or worse, the family has never been static and continues to change.

⁞• MAKING CONNECTIONS

- Which of the three perspectives on the family is closest to your own views? Why?

- Some of my students refuse to believe that many parents spend more time with their children than did earlier generations. Others agree with the studies because they believe that today's parents spend more quality time with their children. What do you think?

TRENDS IN CHANGING FAMILIES

The family is changing, but how? And why? Demographic transitions, shifts in the racial and ethnic composition of families, and economic transformations all play a role in these changes.

Demographic Changes

Two demographic changes have had especially far-reaching effects on family life. First, U.S. birthrates

have declined. Since the end of the eighteenth century, most American women have been bearing fewer children, having them closer together, and finishing child rearing at an earlier age. Second, the average age of the population has risen from 17 in the mid-1800s to nearly 37 in 2007. Both of these shifts mean that a large proportion of Americans now experiences the empty-nest syndrome—the departure of grown children from the home—at an earlier age, as well as earlier grandparenthood and prolonged widowhood. In addition, as Americans live longer, many adults must care for both children and elderly parents (see Chapters 11, 12, and 17).

We see other changes in the composition of households as well: large numbers of cohabiting couples, higher divorce rates, and more one-parent families and working mothers (see *Figure 1.3*). We'll look at these changes briefly now and examine them more closely in later chapters.

CHANGES IN FAMILY AND NONFAMILY HOUSEHOLDS
The U.S. Census Bureau divides households into two categories: family and nonfamily. A *family household* consists of two or more people living together who are related through marriage, birth, or adoption. *Nonfamily households* include people who live alone or with nonrelatives (roommates, boarders, or cohabiting couples). In 2010, 33 percent of all households were nonfamily households, a substantial increase from 19 percent in 1970 (Fields, 2004; U.S. Census Bureau, 2010).

The number of married-couple households with children under age 18 declined from 40 percent in 1970 to 22 percent in 2010 (see *Figure 1.3a*). The percentage of children under age 18 living in one-parent families more than doubled during this same period (see Data Digest). Part of the increase in one-parent families has resulted from the surge of births to unmarried women (see *Figure 1.3b*).

SINGLES AND COHABITING COUPLES
Singles make up one of the fastest-growing groups for three reasons. First, many young adults are postponing marriage. Second, and at the other end of the age continuum, because people live longer, they are more likely than in the past to outlive a partner. Third, older women who are divorced or widowed remarry at much lower rates than do older men, which increases the number of singles in their later years (see Chapters 16 and 17). Also, singles are now more likely than in the past to live alone (see *Figure 1.3c*) because they have the income to do so and enjoy their privacy (see Chapters 9 and 17).

The percentage of cohabiting couples has also climbed since 1970. This number will probably grow because there is greater societal acceptance of unmarried couples living together (see Chapters 8 and 9).

FIGURE 1.3   Some Changes in American Families since 1970

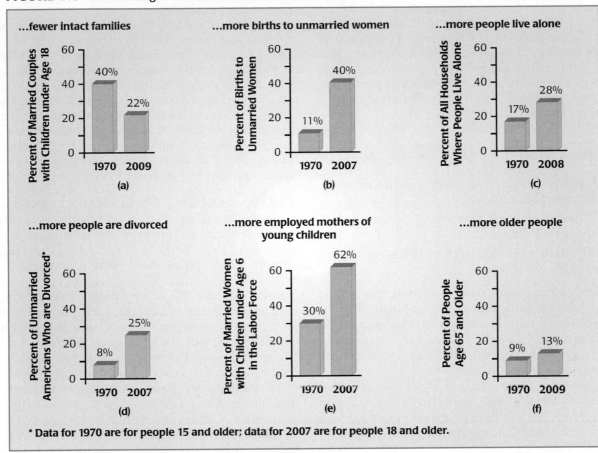

Sources: Based on data in Fields, 2004; Purcell and Whitman, 2006; Federal Interagency Forum on Child and Family Statistics, 2009; Kinsella and He, 2009; U.S. Census Bureau News, "Unmarried and Single...," 2009; U.S. Census Bureau, 2009 (1-Year Estimates), Tables 10, 55, 58, 62, 84, 578, and 580.

MARRIAGE—DIVORCE—REMARRIAGE The number of divorced people rose between 1970 and 2007 (see *Figure 1.3d*). Divorce rates have *decreased* since 2000, but almost one out of every two first marriages is expected to end in divorce. Teen marriages and marriages entered into because the woman became pregnant are especially likely to unravel (see Chapter 15).

Stepfamilies are also becoming much more common. About 12 percent of Americans are currently in their second, third, or fourth marriage. One of three Americans is now a stepparent, a stepchild, a stepsibling, or some other member of a stepfamily. We'll examine marriage, divorce, and remarriage in Chapters 10, 15, and 16.

ONE-PARENT FAMILIES As more adults remain single into their 30s and because divorce rates are high, the number of children living with one parent has increased (see Data Digest). The proportion of one-parent children living with a never-married parent rose from 4 percent in 1960 to 43 percent in 2010 (Hobbs and Stoops, 2002). And, of all one-parent households, 87 percent are mother-child families (U.S. Census Bureau, 2010). We'll look at one-parent households more closely in several later chapters.

EMPLOYED MOTHERS The high participation of mothers in the labor force since the 1980s has been one of the most striking changes in American families. The percentage of two-earner married couples with children under age 18 rose from 31 percent in 1976 to 58 percent in 2010 (U.S. Census Bureau, 2002, 2010).

In addition, six out of every ten married women with children under age 6 are in the labor force (see *Figure 1.3e*). This means that many couples are now coping with domestic and employment responsibilities while raising young children. We'll examine the characteristics and constraints of working mothers and two-earner couples in Chapter 13.

OLDER PEOPLE Americans are living longer than ever before. The 4 percent increase of people age 65 and older since 1970 may seem small (see *Figure 1.3f*), but this population rose from 19 million to 39 million between 1970 and 2008. This means that many children will enjoy having grandparents well into their own adulthood, but our aging population is also placing significant strains on family caregiving for the elderly (see Chapter 17).

Racial and Ethnic Diversity

What do you call a person who speaks three languages? Multilingual.

    What do you call a person who speaks two languages? Bilingual.

    What do you call a person who speaks one language? American.

As this joke suggests, many people stereotype (and ridicule) the United States as a single-language and a single-culture society. In reality, it's the most multicultural country in the world: Diversity is booming, ethnic groups speak many languages, and foreign-born families live in all the states.

ETHNIC FAMILIES ARE BOOMING The nation's foreign-born, 38.5 million people, account for 12.5 percent of the total U.S. population, up from 8 percent in 1990. America's multicultural umbrella includes about 150 distinct ethnic or racial groups among more than 309 million inhabitants. By 2025, only 58 percent of the U.S. population will be white—down from 86 percent in 1950 (see *Figure 1.4*). By 2050—just a few generations away—whites may make up only half of the total population because Latino and Asian populations are expected to triple in size (U.S. Census Bureau, 2009).

Because of huge immigration waves, one in five people are either foreign born or first-generation U.S. residents. Chinese, Filipinos, and Japanese people still rank as the largest Asian American groups. Since 1990, however, Southeast Asians, Indians, Koreans, Pakistanis, and Bangladeshis have registered much faster growth. Mexicans, Puerto Ricans, and Cubans are the largest groups among Latinos, but people from Central and South American countries—such as El Salvador, Guatemala, Colombia, and Honduras—have been immigrating in very high numbers.

ETHNIC FAMILIES SPEAK MANY LANGUAGES Despite the earlier joke about Americans speaking only one language, approximately 336 languages are spoken in the United States. About 20 percent—almost 56 million people—speak a language other than English at home. The largest group, 13 percent, speaks Spanish. Next are those whose primary language at home is Chinese, Vietnamese, Tagalog, French, or German (each is less than 1 percent). Other languages include Italian, Greek, Hebrew, Arabic, Russian, Navajo, Korean, Japanese, and Hindi (Shin and Bruno, 2003; U.S. Census Bureau, 2008).

In the largest cities of some states—especially those in California and Texas—the percentages of people who *don't* speak English are higher than those who *do* speak English (U.S. Census Bureau, 2008). With the advent of *globalization*—the process of integrating economic, political, and cultural systems worldwide—being bilingual or multilingual is an asset in traveling abroad or conducting business. On the other hand, as you'll see in Chapter 4, not knowing a country's native language, such as English, can block many immigrants' educational achievement and ability to find a good job.

FIGURE 1.4 Racial and Ethnic Composition of the U.S. Population, 1950–2025

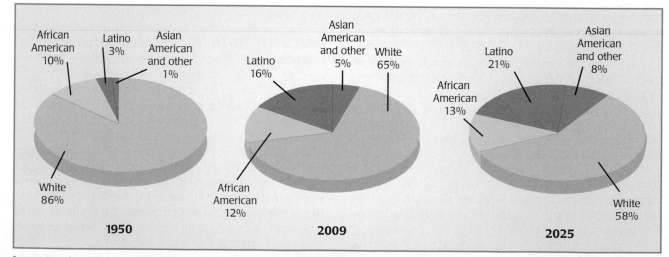

Source: Based on U.S. Census and Population Division, U.S. Census Bureau, 2009, www.socialexplorer.com/pub/reportdata/htmlresults.aspx?ReportId=R10066546.

WHERE ETHNIC FAMILIES LIVE Except for some areas of the Midwest, ethnic families live in all parts of the country but tend to cluster in certain regions (see *Figure 1.5*). Such clustering usually reflects employment opportunities and established immigrant communities that can help newcomers find housing and jobs. In some cases, however, past federal government policies have encouraged some communities to accept refugees from Southeast Asia, forced many American Indians to live on reservations, and implemented a variety of exclusionary immigration laws that limited certain Asian groups to specific geographic areas (see, for example, Kivisto and Ng, 2004).

WHY ARE FAMILIES CHANGING?

It's clear that families are changing. These changes reflect both the choices people make (such as deciding to marry later or to divorce) and the constraints that limit those choices (such as economic problems or caring for elderly parents).

To understand people's choices, social scientists often rely on a **micro-level perspective,** focusing on individuals' social interactions in specific settings. To understand the constraints that limit people's options, they use a **macro-level perspective,** focusing on large-scale patterns that characterize society as a whole. Both perspectives, and the ways in which they are interrelated, are crucial in understanding the family.

Micro-Level Influences on the Family

Consider the following scenario: Two students meet in college, fall in love, marry after graduation, find well-paying jobs, and live the good life, feasting on lobster, driving a Corvette, and the like. Then they have an unplanned child. The wife quits her job to

FIGURE 1.5 **Ethnic Diversity in the United States**
Look at where minority groups live. Do you see any patterns?

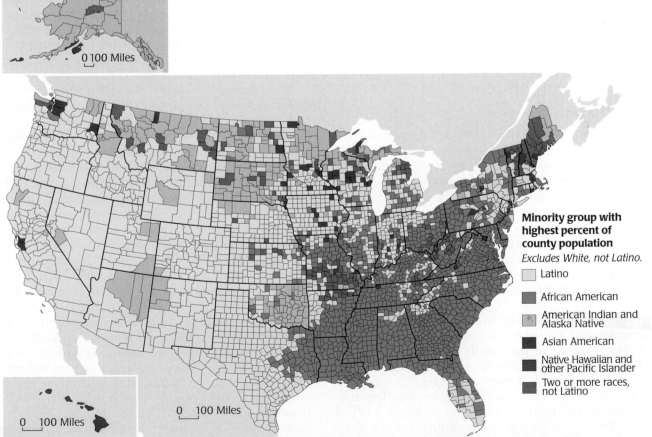

**Minority group with
highest percent of
county population**
Excludes White, not Latino.
- Latino
- African American
- American Indian and Alaska Native
- Asian American
- Native Hawaiian and other Pacific Islander
- Two or more races, not Latino

Source: Brewer and Suchen, 2001, http://www.census.gov/population/cen2000/atlas/censr01-1.pdf (accessed February 26, 2003).

take care of the baby, the husband loses his job, and the wife goes to work part time. She has difficulty balancing her multiple roles of mother, wife, and employee. The stress and arguments between the partners increase, and the marriage ends.

When I ask my students what went wrong, most of them take a micro viewpoint and criticize the couple: "They should have saved some money." "They didn't need a Corvette." "Haven't they heard about contraceptives?" and so on. Almost all of the students blame the divorce on the two people involved because they were unrealistic or immature or made bad decisions.

There's much to be said for micro-level explanations. As you'll see throughout this book, some of the biggest societal changes affecting families began with the efforts of one person who took a stand on an issue. For example, in 1986, Mary Beth Whitehead refused to give up her right to see the baby she had borne as a surrogate mother. The ensuing court battles created national debates about the ethics of new reproductive technologies. As a result, many states instituted surrogacy legislation (see Chapter 11).

On the other hand, micro explanations should be kept in perspective. Many marriage and family textbooks and pop psychology books stress the importance of individual choices but ignore macro-level variables. Micro analyses are limited because they can't explain some of the things over which families have very little control. For these broader analyses, we must turn to macro explanations.

Macro-Level Influences on the Family

The couple that got a divorce made some unwise personal choices, such as not saving their money and perhaps not using contraceptives at all or effectively. However, their relationship deteriorated, in the end, because of macro-level factors like unemployment and the unavailability of inexpensive high-quality day care services.

Constraints such as economic forces, technological innovations, popular culture, social movements, and family policies limit our choices. These are broad social issues that require macro-level explanations.

ECONOMIC FORCES The Industrial Revolution and urbanization sparked widespread changes that had major impacts on the family (see Chapter 3). By the late eighteenth century, factories replaced the local industries that employed large numbers of women and children. As families became less self-sufficient and their members increasingly worked outside the home, parents' control over their children diminished.

In the latter part of the twentieth century, many corporations moved their companies to developing countries to increase their profits. Such moves resulted in relocations and unemployment for many U.S. workers. As the U.S. economy changed, millions of low-paying service jobs replaced higher-paying manufacturing jobs. This has wrought havoc with many families' finances, contributing to the rise in the number of employed mothers. At the other end of the continuum, the higher-paying jobs require at least a college education, so people seeking them tend to postpone marriage and parenthood (see Chapters 9 and 11). The financial crisis in the United States and the rest of the world in the late 2000s resulted in high unemployment rates, reduced work hours, and financial distress, all of which disrupt family life (see Chapter 13).

TECHNOLOGICAL INNOVATIONS Advances in medical and other health-related technologies have led to a decline in infant death rates and to longer life spans. On the other hand, because the average American man or woman can now expect to live into his or her 80s and beyond, poverty after retirement is more likely. Medical services can eat up savings, and the middle-aged—sometimes called the *sandwich generation*—must cope both with the demands of raising their own children and helping their aged parents (see Chapters 12 and 17).

Since you asked . . .
- Has technology strengthened or reduced the quality of our family relationships?

Television, digital video discs (DVDs), microwave ovens, personal computers (PCs), and cell phones have also affected families. On the negative side, for example, multiple television sets in a home often dilute parental control over the programs that young children watch because many parents don't use V-chips to block specific content (Rideout, 2007). On the positive side, television can enhance children's intellectual development. For example, children ages 2 to 7 who spent a few hours a week watching educational programs such as *Sesame Street, Reading Rainbow, Mr. Wizard's World,* and *3-2-1 Contact* had higher academic test scores 3 years later than those who watched many hours of entertainment-only programs and cartoons (Wright et al., 2001).

Some people believe that electronic mail (e-mail), instant messaging (IM), text messaging, iPods, and networking sites such as Facebook are intrusive because such technologies replace close personal relationships with superficial but time-consuming online interactions. For example, people who spend more than ten hours a week on the Internet report a decrease in social activities and less time talking on the phone with friends and family (Nie and Erbring,

"But, sweety, why don't you just read my blog, like everyone else?"

© Dominique Deckmyn/www.CartoonStock.com

2000). Either because of computer problems or high usage, 65 percent of Americans spend more time with their computers than with their spouses (PR Newswire, 2007).

On the other hand, e-mail and the Internet have encouraged long-distance conversations between parents, children, and relatives that might otherwise not occur because of busy schedules. Family members who are scattered coast to coast can become more connected by exchanging photos on the Web, organizing family reunions, tracking down distant relatives, or tracing their ancestral roots. In a recent national survey, 25 percent of the parents said that the new communication technologies—including cell phones, e-mail, and the Internet—made their families feel closer than when they were growing up, and 70 percent of all couples felt that daily cell phone and e-mail contact helped them be connected throughout the day (Kennedy et al., 2008).

Also, people in their 80s and 90s say that using e-mail and the Internet makes them more "wellderly" instead of elderly: "Oh my gosh, I've never felt so young. I'm sitting around all these young people—they're on the Web and I'm on the Web. I'm talking to my granddaughter and she's off in Europe!" (White, 2008: 10B).

POPULAR CULTURE Popular culture—which includes television, the Internet, pop music, magazines, radio, advertising, sports, hobbies, fads, fashions, and movies—is one of our major sources of information *and* misinformation about our values, roles, and family life. Television is especially influential in transmitting both fact and fiction because, in a 65-year lifetime, the average American spends nine years in front of a TV set (see Chapter 5).

Compared with even five years ago, today there are many programs on black families. Asian and

Latino families are huge consumers of prime-time television, but they're almost invisible on it, except for an occasional show such as *George Lopez*. And, to my knowledge, there isn't a single family program that features Asian or Middle Eastern families. We'll examine the effects of popular culture on families in Chapter 5.

SOCIAL MOVEMENTS Over the years, a number of social movements have changed family life. These macro-level movements include the civil rights movement, the women's movement, the gay rights movement, and most recently, a marriage movement.

The *civil rights movement* of the 1960s had a great impact on most U.S. families. Because of affirmative action legislation, members of many minority groups were able to take advantage of educational and economic opportunities that improved their families' socioeconomic status. Many black and Latino students were accepted at elite colleges and universities, families received money to start small businesses, and a number of productive employees were promoted (see Chapters 4 and 13).

The *women's movements*—in the late 1800s and especially in the 1970s—transformed many women's roles and, consequently, family life. As women gained more rights in law, education, and employment, many became less financially dependent on men and started questioning traditional assumptions about gender roles.

The *gay rights movement* that began in the 1970s challenged discriminatory laws in areas such as housing, adoption, and employment. Many lesbian women and gay men (as well as sympathetic heterosexuals) believe that those challenges have resulted in only modest changes so far. There has been progress, however. Children with gay or lesbian parents, for example, are less likely to be stigmatized than they were a decade ago. Numerous companies now provide benefits to their employees' gay or lesbian partners; a number of adoption agencies assist lesbians and gays who want to become parents; numerous municipalities and states recognize civil unions; and several states have legalized same-sex marriages (see Chapters 8–12).

People who are alarmed by high divorce rates and the increase in cohabitation are joining a burgeoning *marriage movement*. Among other things, the marriage movement seeks to repeal no-fault divorce laws and wants to reduce out-of-wedlock births and state benefits for children born to unmarried low-income mothers. It also promotes abstinence among young people, lobbies for funding for programs that promote marriage, and embraces women's homemaker roles. In addition, the marriage movement encourages proponents to lobby lawmakers to pass state laws that require couples to take premarital

In 2005, tens of thousands of men converged on Washington, D.C., for the second Million Man March. The purpose of the march was to demand social and economic equality for African American and low-income families and to inspire young men, especially, to be more responsible for their children.

counseling classes and marital skills programs (see Chapter 9). As the box titled "Should Uncle Sam Be a Matchmaker?" shows, however, many people believe that the government should stay out of people's private lives.

FAMILY POLICIES Family policy refers to the measures that governments take to improve the well-being of families. Thousands of rules and regulations, both civil and criminal—at the local, state, and federal levels—affect practically every aspect of family life: laws about when and whom we can marry, how to dissolve a marriage, how to treat one another in the home, and even how to dispose of our dead. And, as you've just seen, the federal government has actively promoted marriage since 2003.

Families don't just passively accept policy changes. Instead, parents and family members have played critical roles in major social policy changes such as those dealing with the education of children with disabilities, child pornography, joint custody of children after divorce, the right of older people to die with dignity, and better nursing care facilities (see Chapters 7, 12, 15, and 17).

A CROSS-CULTURAL AND GLOBAL PERSPECTIVE ON THE FAMILY

Why does this textbook include material on subcultures within the United States (American Indians, African Americans, Asian Americans, Middle Eastern Americans, and Latinos) and cultures in other

countries? First, unless you're a full-blooded American Indian, your kin were slaves or immigrants to this country. They contributed their cultural beliefs, and their beliefs and practices shaped current family institutions. The U.S. population today is a mosaic of many cultural, religious, ethnic, racial, and socioeconomic groups. Thus, a traditional white, middle-class model is not adequate for understanding our marriages and families.

A second reason for this multicultural and cross-cultural approach is that the world today is an "international place" where "the changes facing families are not only national but are also global, encompassing social forces that transcend national and even regional or continental borders" (Karraker, 2008: 2, 5). Compared with even the late 1990s, more people are traveling outside the United States, more students from abroad attend American colleges and universities, and more exchange programs for students and scholars are offered at all educational levels.

Since you asked . . .

Why should we care about family practices and customs in other cultures?

Students value their study-abroad experiences. In a study of students at Northern Arizona University, for example, those who had participated in international study programs described their experiences as eye-opening and memorable in understanding other cultures. Consider, for example, a third-year college student who went to Italy for a year of studies:

When she sat down for dinner with her host family on her very first night, she asked for some water with her meal, a common request in the United States. Yet, the response she got from a 75-year-old Italian was not what she had expected: "Wine is for drinking, water is for washing," he said. With this, she was welcomed to the world of living and studying abroad (Van Hoof and Verbeeten, 2005: 42).

In the late twentieth century, the Internet changed our communication processes significantly, effectively shrinking the modern world and linking people across continents. As members of the global community, we should be aware of family practices and customs in other cultures.

A third reason for this text's cross-cultural emphasis is that U.S. businesses recognize the importance of understanding other societies. Since the late 1980s, more companies have been requiring their employees to take courses about other cultures before going abroad. For example, one of my students, who got a job with a *Fortune* 500 company, believed that she had an edge over some very tough competitors because of her knowledge of Portuguese and of Brazilian culture.

Fourth, understanding the customs of other countries challenges our notion that U.S. family forms are

ASK YOURSELF

Should Uncle Sam Be a Matchmaker?

In 2003, Congress passed a bill that allotted $1.5 billion over five years to promote marriage as part of welfare reform. The money was used for a variety of promarriage initiatives, including the following:

- Encouraging caseworkers to counsel pregnant women to marry the father of the child

- Reducing the rate of out-of-wedlock births

- Teaching about the value of marriage in high schools

- Providing divorce counseling for the poor

- Sponsoring programs that might produce more marriages (Brotherson and Duncan, 2004)

A very vocal marriage movement enthusiastically endorses such initiatives. According to many of its members, government programs should encourage cohabiting parents to marry and discourage married parents from divorcing (Lichter and Crowley, 2002).

Some of the movement's members justify marriage initiatives by pointing to the economic costs—from welfare to child support enforcement—that states incur because of high divorce rates and out-of-wedlock birthrates. Others, such as conservative religious groups, also endorse promarriage legislation. They maintain that the government should pass policies to support and strengthen marriage because "marriage and family are institutions ordained by God" (Wilcox, 2002).

Most recently, President Obama's administration has funded a $5 million national media campaign that extols the virtues of marriage for 18- to 30-year-olds. The campaign includes ads on Facebook and MySpace, videos on YouTube, spots on radio talk shows, ads in magazines and public transit, and a new Website, TwoOfUs.org (Jayson, 2009).

There are critics of the marriage initiatives. Some scholars point out that a husband's income is often too low to lift a family out of poverty (Ooms et al., 2004). Others charge that promoting marriage for low-income women stigmatizes them (but not high-income unmarried mothers) and compels them to stay in abusive or unhappy relationships. Many Americans also believe that a U.S. president shouldn't encourage people to marry. Such complaints might be reasonable because researchers don't know how many people are poor because they are unmarried and how many are unmarried because they are poor.

Some directors of fatherhood programs are also opposed to promarriage legislation. They believe that marriage is not a "quick fix" because many poor men have a lot of problems. As Robert Brady of the Young Fathers Program in Denver observed, "I wonder if these conservatives would be so dedicated to marriage promotion if it was their daughters they were trying to marry these guys off to" (Starr, 2001: 68).

⁙ Stop and Think . . .

- Should the government pressure low-income mothers to marry? Do you think that such strategies will reduce poverty?

- Is the government meddling in people's private affairs by using tax dollars to promote marriage? Or is it doing what's good for us?

---

the norm. According to sociologist Mark Hutter (1998: 12),

Americans have been notorious for their lack of understanding and ignorance of other cultures. This is compounded by their gullible ethnocentric belief in the superiority of all things American and not only has made them unaware of how others live and think but also has given them a distorted picture of their own life.

Hutter's perspective—and that of this book—is that understanding other people helps us understand ourselves.

Finally, families are changing around the world. Instead of clinging to stereotypes about other countries, cross-cultural knowledge and information "may result in understanding instead of conflict" (Adams, 2004: 1076).

CONCLUSION

Families are transforming, not destroying, themselves. There have been *changes* in family structures, but families of all kinds seek caring, supportive, comforting, and enduring relationships. There is nothing inherently better about one type of family form than another. Moreover, family structures don't appear by themselves. People create families that meet their needs for love and security.

The greatly expanded *choices* in family structure and function mean that the definition of family no longer reflects the interests of any one social class, gender, or ethnic group. This fluidity generates new questions. How, for example, can parents increase their family time if they experience day-to-day pressures on the job? Who will provide adequate child care when parents are employed? Is it possible to pursue personal happiness without sacrificing obligations to other family members?

Our choices often are limited by *constraints,* especially at the macro level, because of economic conditions and government policies. To deal with changes, choices, and constraints, we need as much information as possible about the family. In the next chapter, we'll see how social scientists conduct research on families, gathering data that make it possible for us to track the trends described in this and other chapters, and to make informed decisions about our choices.

SUMMARY

1. The nuclear family—composed of husband, wife, and children—is still predominant in U.S. society, but this definition of *family* has been challenged by those who believe it should include less traditional arrangements such as single parents, child-free couples, foster parents, and siblings sharing a home. Advances in reproductive technology have opened up the possibility of still more varied definitions of the family.

2. The family continues to fulfill basic functions such as bearing and socializing children, providing family members with emotional support, legitimizing and regulating sexual activity, and placing family members in society.

3. Marriages, families, and kinship systems vary in whether marriages are monogamous or polygamous, whether familial authority is vested in the man or the woman or both share power, and whether a new family resides with the family of the man or the woman or creates its own home.

4. Myths about the family include beliefs about the nature of the family in the good old days, the naturalness of marriage and family as human interpersonal and social arrangements, the self-sufficiency of the family, the family as a refuge from outside pressures, and the perfect family.

5. Social scientists generally agree that the family is changing. They disagree, however, on whether it is changing in drastic and essentially unhealthy ways, whether it is simply continuing to adapt and adjust to changing circumstances, or whether it is changing in ways that will ultimately make it stronger.

6. Many changes are occurring in U.S. families: There is more racial and ethnic diversity, family forms are more varied, and there are more single-parent families, stepfamilies, and families in which the mother works outside the home.

7. The reasons for changes in the family can be analyzed on two levels. Micro-level explanations emphasize individual behavior: the choices that people make and the personal and interpersonal factors that influence these choices. Macro-level analyses focus on large-scale patterns that characterize society as a whole and often constrain individual options. Some constraints arise from economic factors, technological advances, popular culture, social movements, and government policies that affect families.

8. Understanding the family requires an appreciation of racial, gender, ethnic, religious, and cultural diversity, both at home and around the world.

KEY TERMS

family 4
fictive kin 5
norm 6
incest taboo 6
socialization 6
role 6
primary group 7
secondary group 7
social class 7
marriage 7
common-law marriage 8

bigamy 8
endogamy 8
exogamy 8
nuclear family 8
extended family 8
patrilocal 9
matrilocal 9
neolocal 9
matriarchy 9
patriarchy 9
egalitarian family 10

monogamy 10
serial monogamy 10
polygamy 10
family of orientation 11
family of procreation 11
kinship system 11
micro-level perspective 21
macro-level perspective 21
family policy 24

MyFamilyLab provides a wealth of resources. Go to www.myfamilylab.com <http://www.myfamilylab.com/>, to enhance your comprehension of the content in this chapter. You can take practice exams, view videos relevant to the subject matter, listen to audio files, explore topics further by using Social Explorer, and use the tools contained in MySearchLab to help you write research papers.

2 Studying the Family

When my mother died, the funeral director called *twice* to confirm the information about her death before submitting it to Maryland's Division of Vital Statistics. Even though I provided the same accurate data both times, the death certificate had three errors: My mother died at age 87, *not* 88; she completed ten years of education, *not* eight; and tobacco didn't contribute to her death because no one in our family smoked.

When I see such mistakes, I wince. Here's a good example, I think, of why many people—including students—often distrust statistics. "Statistics mean never having to say you're certain," some quip. Others firmly believe the well-known quote, "There are three kinds of lies: lies, damned lies, and statistics."

Data collection isn't perfect. Even so, it's a far better source of information about families and other topics than personal opinions, experiential anecdotes, or other nonscientific ways of understanding our world. This chapter will help you evaluate the enormous amount of information we encounter on a daily basis. It will also help you understand how the researchers cited in this text collected their data. Let's begin with a discussion of why a basic understanding of family theory and research is important.

DATA DIGEST

- **The return rate for census questionnaires has decreased** over the years: 78 percent in 1970, 75 percent in 1980, 65 percent in 1990 and 2000, and 74 percent in 2010.

- During the 2000 census, **the cost per individual mailing** was $2, compared with $36 every time a census worker visited a nonrespondent's home as part of a follow-up when the questionnaire wasn't filled out.

- **People are less trusting of some types of surveys than others:** 81 percent of Americans believe scientific studies that describe the causes of disease, 63 percent trust consumer reports of products, but only 54 percent trust public opinion polls.

- DNA tests, which trace our genetic origins, have found that **at least 4 percent of Americans don't know that their father isn't a biological parent.**

- Almost **half of Americans (most of them women) purchase at least one self-help book in their lifetimes.** As a result, the sales in this genre rose from $581 million in sales in 1998 to more than $2 billion in 2008.

Sources: Edmonston, 1999; Libbon, 2000; Carpenter, 2008; Zarembo, 2009.

WHY THEORIES AND RESEARCH ARE IMPORTANT IN OUR EVERYDAY LIVES

The words *theory* and *research* are often intimidating. Many of us may distrust statistics when they're different from our beliefs. For example, many Americans believe that cohabitation decreases the chance of divorce. Most of my students are surprised when research shows that this is not the case (see Chapter 9).

Three very practical reasons show why theory and research are important: (1) What we don't know can hurt us, (2) theories and research help us understand ourselves and our families, and (3) they improve our ability to think more critically and make informed decisions in our own families.

Since you asked . . .

- Can I trust Websites on family issues?

What We Don't Know Can Hurt Us

Millions of Americans use the Internet to buy products, find jobs, and get information about family issues. When people are perplexed by problems involving divorce and stepfamilies, for example, they often seek help online.

Many Websites are maintained by people who know next to nothing about family issues but are hoping to make some money. Some of these sites charge consumers up to $5,000 to become "certified stepfamily counselors," even though there is no such certification requirement in the United States. Other sites charge people $500 for eight hours of audiotapes on how to lead marriage workshops (Siwolop, 2002). Needless to say, no one can become knowledgeable about leading such workshops after listening to only a few hours of audiotapes.

An estimated 8 million Americans (7 percent of the U.S. population) go online every day to search for health information on at least one of 17 health topics before making life-changing decisions. A majority say that what they find influences their decisions about their own treatment or that for those they care for, but only 15 percent say that they "always" check the source or the date of the health information they find online (Fox, 2006).

How accurate is the health information on the Web? Many sites contain contradictory information. In the case of depression, for example, some sites recommend St. John's wort, whereas others state that St. John's wort is ineffective. In fact, St. John's wort, if consumed with other medications such as Prozac, can sometimes be fatal (National Cancer Institute, 2004). As a result, we are likely to obtain incorrect information, and the misinformation we get could actually shorten our lives.

In other cases, we may simply be wasting our money on pills that have little effect on our health and longevity. For example, millions of Americans spend billions every year on vitamin supplements to boost or maintain their health. Several national studies that tracked people over eight years, however, concluded that vitamins C, D, and E didn't improve men's cardiovascular health and didn't offer postmenopausal women any protection from breast cancer (Chlebowskii et al., 2008; Sesso et al., 2008). Vitamins in appropriate dosages don't hurt us, but they probably don't offer the healthy benefits that many Websites selling them promise.

Theories and Research Help Us Understand Ourselves and Our Families

Theoretical perspectives and research can illuminate many aspects of our family life. For example, does spanking correct a child's misbehavior? Suppose a 2-year-old throws a temper tantrum at a family barbecue. One adult comments, "What that kid needs is a good smack on the behind." Another person immediately disagrees: "All kids go through this stage. Just ignore it." Who's right? In fact, empirical studies show that neither ignoring a problem nor inflicting physical punishment stops bad behavior (see Chapter 12).

Consider another example. Many parents believe that their children are hyperactive because they consume too much sugar and, consequently,

blame sweets for their kids' misbehavior. Consuming lots of sugar isn't healthy for any of us, but, in a controlled experiment (which we'll discuss shortly), medical researchers concluded that "sugar causes hyperactivity in children" is a myth because those who consume sugar-free and sugar-laden diets don't behave very differently (Vreeman and Carroll, 2008). Instead, there are biological or social factors that explain many children's misbehavior.

Theories and Research Help Us Make Informed Decisions

We rarely read a newspaper, newsmagazine, or Internet article without coming across statistics that affect some aspect of our lives. We listen numbly to the probabilities of dying earlier than expected because of our genetic inheritance, lifestyle, or environment. We are inundated with information on the importance of exercising, losing weight, lowering cholesterol levels, and not smoking.

Some of the information is sound, but much is biased, inaccurate, or generated by unlicensed, self-proclaimed "experts." They whip up anxieties and then sell solutions that include their own books and "consulting services." As the box "Self-Help Books: Let the Reader Beware" below shows, one of the best ways to protect yourself against quacks and con artists is to be informed.

Students in family courses that include discussions of scientific studies often feel that they and their

Self-Help Books: Let the Reader Beware

Choices

Authors of self-help books are well adjusted, free of phobias and anxieties, and bursting with self-esteem. Right? Wrong. A best-selling book on phobias, for example, lacks the author's photo because he has a phobia about having his picture taken (Quick, 1992). Husband and wife co-authors of a two-volume textbook on divorce were involved in "'the divorce from Hell'—a very public, bitter blizzard of litigation that has spawned nearly 400 legal filings," including arguments about ownership of a low-number auto tag (Ringle, 1999: C1).

Some of the most ardent leaders of the marriage movement (see Chapter 1) have been divorced at least once. And just before he died at age 94, Dr. Benjamin Spock, a family expert and author of best-selling books on childrearing for more than 50 years, agreed with his estranged sons that he had been too career driven to spend much time with his family (Maier, 1998).

Many self-help books and articles in popular magazines are bogus because they are based on personal opinion and anecdotes rather than scholarly research. As a result, many self-help materials can create five serious problems:

1. **They can threaten relationships.** Many encourage the reader to make new demands on a spouse or children. Such one-sided commands can increase conflict that the family may not be able to handle.

2. **They can make people feel inadequate.** Many popular writers tie a person's feelings of adequacy to family relationships. This ignores the satisfaction and self-confidence that people can get from work, friendships, participation in organizations, and solitary pursuits.

3. **They often reinforce gender stereotypes.** Several of the best-selling self-help parenting books insist that the best type of family is one with a breadwinner father and a stay-at-home mother and that employed mothers are selfish and neglectful (Kratchick et al., 2005).

4. **They oversimplify complex problems.** Many popular writers gloss over complicated family relationships. Reduced frequency of sexual intercourse can lead to depression, some "experts" claim. In fact, many factors may trigger depression, and sex isn't at the top of the list (see Chapters 7 and 10).

5. **They generalize limited findings.** One author interviewed 150 celebrity women (including model Cheryl Tiegs and singer Carly Simon) on their aging and then offered advice to all older women. A reviewer noted, correctly, that the experiences of such a select group of people who "have the luxury and the time to wallow in midlife crises" and to indulge in plastic surgery are not very useful for others in their 50s, 60s, and 70s who have considerably fewer options in life (Reynolds, 2007).

Stop and Think . . .

As you read articles and books about the family, ask yourself the following questions:

■ Does the writer cite research or only anecdotal material as sources? If the writer cites himself or herself, are the references scholarly or only personal stories? According to one researcher, "If modern science has learned anything in the past century, it is to distrust anecdotal evidence" (Park, 2003: B20).

■ Does the author describe only a few families (especially those with problems) but generalize the "findings" to all families?

■ Does the writer make it sound as though life is exceedingly simple, such as following seven steps for family happiness? Family interaction and behavior are much more complex than throwing a few ingredients into the pot and stirring.

instructor are on different planets. At the beginning of a semester, for example, I've heard my students grumble, "I took this course to find out how to avoid a divorce after I get married. Who cares about divorce statistics!"

In fact, by learning something about research, you will be able to make more informed decisions about finding a suitable mate and, quite possibly, avoid a divorce. In addition, knowing something about *how* social scientists study families will enhance your ability to think critically and determine what you want to do. For example, we often hear that grief counseling is essential after losing a loved one. However, four in ten Americans are better off without such counseling. Grief is normal and people work through their losses on their own, whereas counseling sometimes prolongs the feelings of depression and anxiety (Stroebe et al., 2000).

In scholarly journals, peers (other scholars) review research before it is published. In contrast, the mass media are largely immune to criticism, even when their reports are biased, simplistic, or wrong (Gans, 1979). As a result, many people who rely exclusively on the media for information often get a skewed picture of marriages, families, and other aspects of life.

This chapter will not transform you into a researcher, but it will help you ask some of the right questions when you are deluged with popular nonsense. Let's begin with the most influential theories of marriage and the family that guide social science investigations.

THEORETICAL PERSPECTIVES ON FAMILIES

Someone once observed, "I used to have six theories about parenting and no children. Now I have six children and no theories." This quip suggests that there is no relationship between theory and practice. As you saw in Chapter 1, however, theories about families are often translated into policies and laws that affect all of us.

Ideas have consequences. For example, people who theorize that the family is disintegrating might propose micro-level solutions such as cutting off public assistance to unmarried mothers. In contrast, those who theorize that the family is changing might propose macro-level remedies such as providing girls and young women with good schooling and jobs that discourage early sexual involvement and pregnancy (see Chapter 11).

As people struggle to understand family-related processes, they develop theories. A **theory** is a set of statements that explains why a particular phenomenon occurs. Theories drive research; help us analyze our findings; and, ideally, offer solutions for family problems.

> **Since you asked . . .**
>
> Why isn't there one nice, simple theory about the family?

One family sociologist compares theories to the fable of the six blind men who felt different parts of an elephant and arrived at different explanations of what elephants were like. The man who felt the side of the elephant compared it to a massive, immovable wall. The man who felt the trunk thought the elephant was like a rope that could move large objects. Similarly, different theories explain different aspects of the elephant—in this case, families (Burr, 1995).

Of the dozen or so most influential family theories, let's consider eight that are the best known: two macro-level theories (structural-functionalist and conflict), three theories that are both micro- and macro-level (feminist, ecological, and developmental), and three micro-level theories (symbolic interactionist, social exchange, and family systems) that focus on face-to-face interaction and personal dynamics (see *Figure 2.1*).

Researchers typically use more than one theoretical framework in examining any given topic because each perspective involves seeing the world differently. Because reality is complex, the "coexisting theories concentrate on a different aspect of real life" (Winton, 1995: 2). For greater clarity, let's look at each perspective separately. (Many social scientists use the terms *theories, theoretical perspectives,* and *theoretical frameworks* interchangeably.)

The Structural Functionalism Perspective

Structural-functional theory (often abbreviated to *functionalism*) examines the relationship between the family and the larger society. When functionalists study family structure, they look at how the parts work together to fulfill the functions or tasks necessary for the family's survival. For example, adult family tasks are best accomplished when spouses carry out two distinct and specialized types of roles—*instrumental* and *expressive* (Parsons and Bales, 1955).

FAMILY ROLES The husband or father, the "breadwinner," performs **instrumental roles**: providing food and shelter for the family and, at least theoretically, being hardworking, tough, and competitive. The wife or mother plays the **expressive roles** of the "homemaker": providing the emotional support and nurturing qualities that sustain the family unit and support the husband or father. These family roles characterize what social scientists call the *traditional family,* a family form that many conservative groups would like to preserve (see Chapter 1).

These and other roles that family members play are *functional.* That is, they preserve order, stability, and equilibrium. They also provide the physical shelter and emotional support that ensure a family's health and survival. Anything that interferes with these tasks is seen as *dysfunctional* because it jeopardizes the family's smooth functioning. For example,

FIGURE 2.1 Major Theoretical Perspectives on the Family

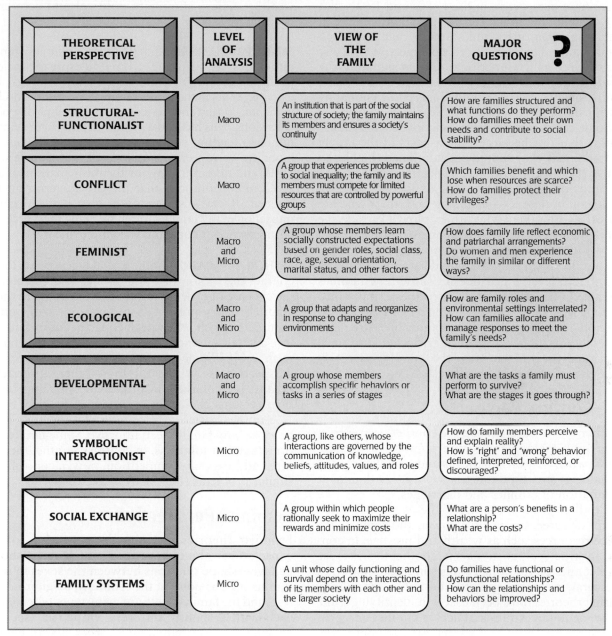

THEORETICAL PERSPECTIVE	LEVEL OF ANALYSIS	VIEW OF THE FAMILY	MAJOR QUESTIONS
STRUCTURAL-FUNCTIONALIST	Macro	An institution that is part of the social structure of society; the family maintains its members and ensures a society's continuity	How are families structured and what functions do they perform? How do families meet their own needs and contribute to social stability?
CONFLICT	Macro	A group that experiences problems due to social inequality; the family and its members must compete for limited resources that are controlled by powerful groups	Which families benefit and which lose when resources are scarce? How do families protect their privileges?
FEMINIST	Macro and Micro	A group whose members learn socially constructed expectations based on gender roles, social class, race, age, sexual orientation, marital status, and other factors	How does family life reflect economic and patriarchal arrangements? Do women and men experience the family in similar or different ways?
ECOLOGICAL	Macro and Micro	A group that adapts and reorganizes in response to changing environments	How are family roles and environmental settings interrelated? How can families allocate and manage responses to meet the family's needs?
DEVELOPMENTAL	Macro and Micro	A group whose members accomplish specific behaviors or tasks in a series of stages	What are the tasks a family must perform to survive? What are the stages it goes through?
SYMBOLIC INTERACTIONIST	Micro	A group, like others, whose interactions are governed by the communication of knowledge, beliefs, attitudes, values, and roles	How do family members perceive and explain reality? How is "right" and "wrong" behavior defined, interpreted, reinforced, or discouraged?
SOCIAL EXCHANGE	Micro	A group within which people rationally seek to maximize their rewards and minimize costs	What are a person's benefits in a relationship? What are the costs?
FAMILY SYSTEMS	Micro	A unit whose daily functioning and survival depend on the interactions of its members with each other and the larger society	Do families have functional or dysfunctional relationships? How can the relationships and behaviors be improved?

abuse of one family member by another is dysfunctional because its negative physical and emotional consequences threaten the family's continuity.

FAMILY FUNCTIONS According to many functionalists, there are two kinds of family functions. **Manifest functions** are intended and recognized; they are clearly evident. **Latent functions** are unintended and unrecognized; they are not immediately obvious. Consider weddings. The primary manifest function of the marriage ceremony is to publicize the formation of a new family unit and to legitimize sexual intercourse (see Chapter 1). Its latent functions include communicating a hands-off message to past or prospective sweethearts, outfitting the couple with household goods through wedding gifts, and redefining family boundaries to include in-laws or stepfamily members.

INSTITUTIONAL CONNECTIONS Functionalists also note that the family affects and is affected by other interrelated institutions, such as law, politics, and the economy. For example, politicians (many of whom are lawyers and businesspeople) play a major role in setting policies that determine, among other things, whether a marriage is legal, who can and cannot adopt a child, and which family members can claim Social Security payments (see Chapter 1).

CRITICAL EVALUATION Structural functionalism was a dominant perspective in the 1950s and 1960s, but later came under attack for being so conservative in its emphasis on order and stability that it ignored social change. For example, this perspective typically sees divorce as dysfunctional and as signaling the disintegration of the family rather than as indicating positive change (as when individuals end an unhappy relationship).

Some critics maintain that functionalists shouldn't assume that just because some aspects of the family are functional, they should be maintained (Ingoldsby et al., 2004). For instance, expecting males to be instrumental and females to be expressive places a burden on both sexes—including on fathers who are laid off and mothers who are employed outside the home—depending on what's going on in the economy and the particular stresses that families encounter.

Functionalism is useful in understanding families on a macro level, but it doesn't show how families interact on a daily basis. It also doesn't take into account that disagreements aren't necessarily dysfunctional but a normal part of family life. Also, feminist scholars, especially, have criticized structural functionalism for viewing the family narrowly through a white, male, middle-class lens.

The Conflict Perspective

Another macro-level theory, the conflict perspective, has a long history. It became popular in the late 1960s, when African Americans and feminists started to challenge structural functionalism as the dominant explanation of families and marriages.

Conflict theory examines the ways in which groups disagree, struggle for power, and compete for scarce resources such as wealth and prestige. In contrast to structural functionalists, conflict theorists see conflict and the resulting changes in traditional roles as natural, inevitable, and often desirable. Specifically, conflict theories have been useful in identifying some of the inequities within and across families and promoting structures and values that are less oppressive.

SOCIAL CLASS AND POWER For conflict theorists, families perpetuate social stratification. Those in high-income brackets have the greatest share of capital, including wealth, that they can pass down to the next generation. Such inheritances reduce the likelihood that all families have equal opportunities or equal power to compete for resources such as education, decent housing, and health care.

Unlike functionalists, conflict theorists see society not as cooperative and stable but as a system of widespread inequality. There is continuous tension between the haves and the have-nots. The latter are mainly children, women, minorities, and the poor. Much research based on conflict theory focuses on how those in power—typically white, middle-aged, wealthy males—dominate political and economic decision making in American society.

FAMILY PROBLEMS Conflict theorists view many family difficulties as resulting from widespread societal problems rather than individual shortcomings. For example, shifts in the U.S. economy have led to a decline in manufacturing and the loss of many well-paying blue-collar jobs. This has had a profound influence on many families, sending some into a spiral of downward mobility. We've seen unemployment rates double since 2005, and taxpayers pay for the mismanagement and greed of corporations that the U.S. government has rescued. Racial discrimination also has a negative impact on many families, often blocking their access to health services, education, and employment.

CRITICAL EVALUATION Some social scientists criticize conflict theory for stressing clashes and coercion at the expense of order and stability. According to them, conflict theory presents a negative view of human nature as selfish while neglecting the importance of love and self-sacrifice, which characterize many family relationships. Some critics also believe that the conflict perspective is less useful than other approaches because it emphasizes institutional constraints rather than personal choices in everyday family life.

Another criticism is that conflict theorists don't propose how families can improve. Some family theories focus on solutions. In contrast, conflict theories often address only competition, power, control, and similar problems (Ingoldsby et al., 2004).

Feminist Perspectives

Feminist theories examine how *gender roles*—expectations about how men and women should behave—shape relations between the sexes in institutions such as politics, the economy, religion, education, and the family. There are many types of feminism, each with a slightly different emphasis (see, for example, Lindsey, 2005, and Lorber, 2005). Despite these variations, feminist family theories generally address gender inequality, family diversity, and social change using both micro and macro approaches.

> **Since you asked . . .**
> ❖ Can men be feminists?

GENDER INEQUALITY According to Rebecca West, an English journalist and novelist who died in 1983, "I myself have never been able to find out precisely what feminism is; I only know that people call me a feminist whenever I express sentiments that differentiate me from a doormat." *Any* person—male or female, straight or gay—who believes that *both* sexes should have equal political, educational, economic, and other rights is a feminist, even if he or she refuses to identify with this label.

A core issue for feminist family scholars (both women and men) is gender inequality, both at home and in the workplace, and how gender inequality intersects with race, ethnicity, and social class. For example, the poorest older adults are most likely to be minority women, and caregivers of the old—who are predominantly women—must often leave their jobs or work only part time to accommodate caregiving (Allen and Beitin, 2007; Houser, 2007).

FAMILY DIVERSITY Feminist family scholars, more than any other group, have been instrumental in broadening our view of families. For these scholars, limiting families to the traditional nuclear definition excludes many other family forms such as long-term cohabiting couples, single parents and their children, multiethnic families, multigenerational families, same-sex families, stepfamilies, and fictive kin (see Chapter 1).

EMPHASIS ON SOCIAL CHANGE Since the early 1980s, feminist scholars have contributed to family theory and social change in several ways:

- They have pointed out that family perspectives should include families from many cultures and ethnic groups as well as interracial and interethnic families.

- They have initiated legislation to deal with family violence and have supported stiffer penalties for men who assault children and women.

- They have endorsed greater equality between husbands and wives and have pushed for legislation that provides employed women and men with parental leave rights (see Chapters 5 and 13).

- They have refocused much of the research to include fathers as involved, responsible, and nurturing family members who have a profound effect on children and the family (see Chapters 4 and 12).

CRITICAL EVALUATION Feminists have challenged discriminatory peer review processes that routinely exclude women from the old boy network. According to some critics, however, many feminists are part of an old girl network that has not always welcomed conflicting points of view from African American, Latina, Asian American, American Indian, Muslim, lesbian, and working-class women, as well as from women with disabilities, in both research and therapeutic settings (Almeida, 1994; Lynn and Todoroff, 1995; S. A. Jackson, 1998).

Another criticism is that feminist family theorists focus primarily on issues that affect women, and not men, and don't pay enough attention to other forms of oppression such as age, disability, and religion (Ingoldsby et al., 2004). In terms of ethnicity, for example, there is still considerably more contemporary feminist scholarship on white and African American families than on others, especially American Indian and Middle Eastern families (see Chapter 4).

A third criticism is that feminists, by emphasizing diversity, overlook commonalities that make families more similar than different (Baca Zinn, 2000). A related issue is whether feminist family theorists embrace only some types of diversity. For example, some feminist scholars have a tendency to view full-time homemakers as victims rather than as individuals who happily choose this role (see Chapter 10).

The Ecological Perspective

Ecological theory examines how a family influences and is influenced by its environment. Urie Bronfenbrenner (1979, 1986), a major advocate of ecological theory, proposed that four interlocking systems mold our developmental growth.

INTERLOCKING SYSTEMS These systems range from the most immediate settings, such as the family and peer group, to more remote contexts in which a child is not involved directly, such as technological changes and ideological beliefs (see *Figure 2.2*). The four systems are the following:

1. The *microsystem*, which is made up of the interconnected behaviors, roles, and relationships

FIGURE 2.2 An Ecological Model of Family Development

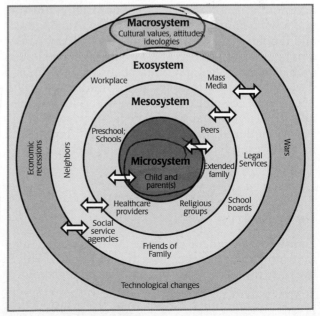

Source: Based on Bronfenbrenner, 1979.

that influence a child's daily life (such as parents' toilet-training their child).

2. The *mesosystem,* which is composed of the relationships among different settings (for example, the home, a day care center, and schools). Parents interact with teachers and religious groups; children interact with peers; health care providers interact with both children and parents.

3. The *exosystem,* which consists of settings or events that a child does not experience directly but that can affect her or his development (such as parents' employment).

4. The *macrosystem,* the wider society and culture that encompasses all the other systems.

All four of these embedded systems, or environments, can help or hinder a child's development and a family's functioning. For example, successful drug-prevention programs should be multifaceted: They must understand the teenager's specific family dynamics, address the unique needs of a particular neighborhood, and involve local organizations (such as churches, businesses, and colleges) to offer alternatives to high-risk behavior. Such alternatives include not selling alcohol to adolescents, providing education and support for parents, and involving youth in meaningful community projects (Bogenschneider, 1996).

CRITICAL EVALUATION Ecological theory is useful in explaining family dynamics and proposing programs to deal with issues such as youth violence and special needs adoptions, but critics note several limitations. Ecological theories try to explain growth as resulting from changes in the environment, but explanations of disintegration (such as aging) are notably absent. In addition, it is not always apparent exactly how and when environments produce changes in individuals and families. Finally, it's unclear how the interactions among the four systems affect nontraditional families such as stepfamilies, gay and lesbian households, and intergenerational families living under one roof. Because the ecological perspective describes primarily nuclear, heterosexual, and white families, some critics have wondered how "nontraditional" families fit in (White and Klein, 2002; Telleen et al., 2003; Schweiger and O'Brien, 2005).

The Family Development Perspective

Family development theory examines the changes that families experience over their lifespans. This is the only theoretical perspective that emerged out of a specific interest in families and still focuses exclusively on the family (rather than the relationships between unmarried couples, for example).

THE CLASSIC FAMILY LIFE CYCLE Family development theory evolved over many decades (see White and Klein, 2002, for a description of this evolution). One of the earliest variations, still popular among many practitioners, is Evelyn Duvall's (1957) model of the family life cycle.

The **family life cycle** consists of the transitions that a family makes as it moves through a series of stages and events. According to this classic model and others like it, the family life cycle begins with marriage and continues through child rearing, seeing the children leave home, retirement, and the death of one or both spouses (see *Table 2.1*).

DEVELOPMENTAL TASKS CHANGE OVER TIME As people progress through various stages and events of the family life cycle, they accomplish **developmental tasks.** That is, they learn to fulfill various role expectations and responsibilities, such as showing affection and support for family members and socializing with people outside the family.

Depending on our developmental stage, we learn to interact and handle different challenges as we grow older. For example, young children must deal with teasing, children ages 6 to 10 must cope with getting bad grades and bullying at school, older children face pressure to use drugs, and 16- to 22-year-olds report that their greatest difficulties are trouble at work and school. For adults, the greatest source of stress is family conflict. For many of the elderly, the biggest problems include a decline in physical mobility, dependence on caregivers, and paying for prescriptions and other living expenses (Ellis et al., 2001).

DEVELOPMENTAL TASKS ARE MULTIFACETED Developmental stages and tasks vary in different kinds of families, such as single-parent families, childless couples, stepfamilies, and grandparent-grandchild families. The complex situations and problems that confront families in an aging society are multigenerational. If a couple divorces, for

TABLE 2.1	The Classic Portrayal of the Family Life Cycle
Stage 1	Couple without children
Stage 2	Oldest child younger than age 30 months
Stage 3	Oldest child between ages 2-1/2 and 6
Stage 4	Oldest child between ages 6 and 13
Stage 5	Oldest child between ages 13 and 20
Stage 6	Period starting when first child leaves the family until the youngest leaves
Stage 7	Empty nest to retirement
Stage 8	Retirement to death of one or both spouses

Kinscripts: Ensuring Family Survival during Tough Times

Family life cycle patterns differ markedly in terms of needs, resources, gender roles, race and ethnicity, and social class. Studying low-income African American families, sociologists Linda Burton and Carol Stack (1993) proposed the concept of *kinscript* to explain the life courses of many multigenerational families. The kinscript arises in response to both extreme economic need and intense commitment by family members to the survival of future generations, and it requires kin-work, kin-time, and kin-scription.

Kin-work is the collective labor that families share to endure over time. It includes providing help during childbirth, intergenerational care of children or dependents, and support for other relatives. For example, a 76-year-old widower parented three preschool children after their mother started "running the streets" because he was afraid that "the service people would take the babies away" (Burton and Stack, 1993:105).

Kin-time is the shared understanding among family members of when and in what sequence kin-work should be performed. Kin-time provides for learning developmental tasks during transitions such as marriage, childbearing, and grandparenthood, and includes guidelines for assuming family leadership roles and caregiving responsibilities. A woman receiving help from her mother and other

Rebecca Anderson, 54 years old and battling lupus, became a mother again when she took in five nieces and nephews, whose three sets of parents could not care for them. Anderson's husband, Alton, who does not live with Rebecca, helps with the children occasionally, but provides no financial support.

female kin describes the complex but cooperative pattern that characterizes the care of her child:

> On the days Damen has school, my mother picks him up at night and keeps him at her home. And then when she goes to work in the morning, she takes him to my grandmother's house. And when my little sister gets out of school, she picks him up and takes him back to my mother's house. And then I go and pick him up (Jarrett, 1994: 41–42).

Kin-scription is the process by which kin-work is assigned to specific family members, usually women.

Women often find it difficult to refuse the demands of kin because they, and not men, are expected to keep families together because of the general belief that women are more nurturing than men.

⁑ Stop and Think . . .

- How does the research on kinscripts challenge the popular notion that poor families are looking for handouts rather than relying on themselves to ensure a family's survival?
- Do kinscripts describe your family? Why or why not?

instance, the ex-spouses aren't the only ones who must learn new developmental tasks in relating to their children and each other. Grandparents may also have to forge different ties with their grandchildren, an ex–son-in-law or ex–daughter-in-law, and stepgrandchildren if either of the parents remarries (see Chapters 15 and 17).

Also, the family life course may differ greatly between poor and middle-class families. As the "Kinscripts: Ensuring Family Survival during Tough Times" box shows, poor families must be especially creative and resilient to keep their members together throughout the life course.

CRITICAL EVALUATION Family development theories have generated a great deal of research, especially on

the internal dynamics of marital and family interaction. Almost all the studies are micro level, but some scholars have used the developmental approach to examine patterns of family change cross-culturally and historically (see Thornton, 2001). This perspective is especially useful for therapists and practitioners who counsel families that are experiencing problems such as constant arguments and infidelity.

Critics point out several limitations, however. First, some believe that the family life cycle stages are artificial because "the processes of life are not always so neatly and cleanly segmented" (Winton, 1995: 39). Second, despite the recent work on kinscripts and extended families, most developmental theories are limited to examining nuclear, heterosexual, and nondivorced families. For example, gay and lesbian households generally are excluded from family life course analyses (Laird, 1993).

A third criticism is that family development theory is largely descriptive rather than explanatory (Ingoldsby et al., 2004). For example, this perspective explores *how* developmental tasks change over time, but not *why* some family members are more successful than others in learning the necessary developmental skills across a life course or why even white, nuclear, middle-class families can vary quite a bit in parenting styles (see Chapter 12).

Fourth, some critics question why developmental theories often gloss over sibling relationships, which are among the most important emotional resources we have throughout life and especially after the last parent dies (McGoldrick et al., 1993). Thus, some have concluded, family development theory still "deals with a fairly small part of the elephant" (Burr, 1995: 81).

The Symbolic Interaction Perspective

Symbolic interaction theory looks at the everyday behavior of individuals. Symbolic interactionists (sometimes abbreviated as *interactionists*) examine how our ideas, beliefs, and attitudes shape our daily lives, as well as those of our families. To a symbolic interactionist, a father's batting practice with his daughter is not simply batting practice. It's a behavior that conveys messages such as "I enjoy spending time with you" or "Girls can be good baseball players."

SYMBOLS The symbolic interaction perspective looks at subjective, interpersonal meanings and how we communicate them using *symbols:* words, gestures, or pictures that stand for something. If we are to interact effectively, our symbols must have *shared meanings,* or agreed-upon definitions. Such shared meanings include wearing engagement and wedding rings, following time-honored family traditions, and celebrating important events such as birthdays and anniversaries.

SIGNIFICANT OTHERS One of the most important shared meanings is the *definition of the situation,* or the way we perceive reality and react to it. Relationships often break up, for example, because partners have different perceptions of the meanings of dating, love, communication, and sex. As one of my students observed, "We broke up because Dave wanted sex. I wanted intimacy and conversation." We typically learn our definitions of the situation through interaction with **significant others**—people in our primary groups, such as parents, friends, relatives, and teachers—who play an important role in our socialization (see Chapters 1 and 5).

FAMILY ROLES According to symbolic interaction theory, each family member plays more than one role.

The Japanese tea ceremony is an ancient ritual that involves more than just preparing and serving tea. The ceremony also requires learning the rules on proper gestures, language, clothing, utensils, and behavior.

A man, for example, may be a husband, father, grandfather, brother, son, uncle, and so on. Roles are *relational*, or complementary, because they are connected to other roles—mothers have children, brothers have sisters, and aunts have nieces and nephews. Roles also carry *reciprocal* rights and responsibilities. For instance, a mother must care of her child and expects obedience. A child has the right to be safe and fed, but is also expected to be courteous and perform assigned tasks.

Roles require different behaviors both within and outside the family, and people modify and adjust their roles as they interact with other role players. For example, you probably interact differently with Mom, Grandma, and Uncle Ned than you do with your brothers and sisters. And you probably interact still differently when you're talking to someone else's parent, a professor, or an employer.

CRITICAL EVALUATION One of the most common criticisms of symbolic interaction theory is that it ignores macro-level factors that affect family relationships. For example, families living in poverty, and especially single mothers, are likely to be stigmatized and must often raise their children in unsafe neighborhoods. Such constraints increase stress, feelings of helplessness, and family conflict—all of which can derail positive everyday interactions (Seccombe, 2007).

Some critics also contend that interactionists overlook the irrational and unconscious aspects of human behavior (LaRossa and Reitzes, 1993). That is, people don't always behave as reflectively as symbolic interactionists assume. We often act impulsively or make hurtful comments, for instance, without weighing the consequences of our actions or words.

A third criticism is that because interactionists study primarily white middle-class families—who are the most likely to cooperate in research—the findings are rarely representative of a wide range of racial, ethnic, and socioeconomic groups (Winton, 1995). As a result, according to some critics, interactionists may offer an unrealistic view of everyday family life.

The Social Exchange Perspective

The fundamental premise of **social exchange theory** is that people seek through their interactions with

> **Since you asked . . .**
>
> ::• Why don't people just leave romantic relationships or marriages when they feel unloved?

others to maximize their rewards and to minimize their costs. As a result, most people will continue in a relationship as long as there are more benefits than losses. The union often ends if another relationship offers more resources.

WHAT RESOURCES DO WE EXCHANGE? We bring to our relationships a variety of resources—some tangible, some intangible—such as energy, money, material goods, status, intelligence, control, good looks, youth, power, talent, fame, or affection. People "trade" these resources for more, better, or different assets that another person possesses. And as long as the costs are equal to or lower than the benefits, the exchanges will seem fair or balanced (see Chapters 8, 10, and 14).

From a social exchange perspective, when the costs of a marriage outweigh the rewards, the people may separate or divorce. On the other hand, many people stay in unhappy marriages or unions because the rewards seem equal to the costs: "It's better than being alone," "I don't want to hurt the kids," or "It could be worse."

ARE OUR EXCHANGES CONSCIOUS? Some of our cost-reward decisions are conscious, but many are not. Some of the research on stepfamilies shows, for example, that partners stay together even when they're unhappy because it seems easier to tolerate problems than discuss them, which may create more difficulties. As a result, family members may adapt to the existing situation rather than consciously seek a more beneficial or rewarding relationship (see Chapter 16).

CRITICAL EVALUATION Some critics have accused exchange theorists of putting too much weight on rational behavior. People don't always calculate the potential costs and rewards of every decision. For

Rod Stewart is 26 years older than his wife, Penny. Would this model have married Stewart if he were a salesclerk, for example, instead of a rock star? How do such marriages illustrate social exchange theory?

example, Linda, one of my students, spent every Saturday (the only day she wasn't working or in class) driving from Baltimore to Philadelphia to visit a grandmother who had Alzheimer's disease (see Chapter 17). Linda's mother and several nurses' aides were providing good care for the grandmother, who often didn't recognize her. Nevertheless, Linda gave up her date night because "I want to make sure Grandma is OK." In this and other cases, genuine love and concern for others can override sensible cost-benefit decisions.

Exchange theory is also limited to explaining behavior that is motivated by immediate costs or rewards. In many ethnic groups, family duties take precedence over individual rights. Traditional Asian cultures stress filial responsibility, which requires children, especially sons, to make sacrifices for the well-being of their parents and siblings (Hurh, 1998; Do, 1999). Similarly, many Middle Eastern families teach children to value family harmony rather than "me first" benefits (see Chapter 4).

The Family Systems Perspective

Family systems theory views the family as a functioning unit that solves problems, makes decisions, and achieves collective goals. The emphasis is not on individual family members but on how the members interact within the family system, how they communicate, how family patterns evolve, and how individual personalities affect family members (Rosenblatt, 1994; Day, 1995).

WHAT HOLDS FAMILIES TOGETHER? Family systems analysts are interested in the implicit or explicit rules that hold families together. A key concept is *equilibrium*. That is, a change in one part of the family or the external environment sets in motion an adjustment process to restore the family to the way it was in the past—to regain equilibrium. Thus, during stressful times such as illness, unemployment, or the death of a loved one, family members must make changes and adapt so that the family can keep on going (Broderick, 1993).

CRITICAL EVALUATION Some critics maintain that family systems theory has generated a lot of terminology but little insight into how the family really functions. Also, because the perspective originated in the study of dysfunctional families in clinical settings, some question whether the theory can be applied to healthy families. Finally, because much of research is based on case studies, the results are limited because they can't be generalized to larger groups (Holman and Burr, 1980; Nye and Berardo, 1981; Day, 1995).

Combining Theories

We've looked at eight of the major family theories separately, but researchers and clinicians often combine several of these perspectives to interpret data or choose intervention strategies. For example, a counselor might draw on social exchange, symbolic interaction, development, and systems theories to shed light on the problems in a couple's relationship.

Counselors who work with children with attention deficit hyperactivity disorders (ADHD) typically combine ecological and family systems perspectives

in conducting assessments and developing interventions (Bernier and Siegel, 1994). Instead of simply focusing on the child or the family, clinicians usually observe the child in his or her natural environment, involve the child's teacher, and educate grandparents about ADHD. Thus, both researchers and practitioners often rely on several theories to explain or respond to family-related issues.

We turn next to the ways that researchers design studies and collect information about families.

MAKING CONNECTIONS

- Return to *Table 2.1* (p. 36) for a moment. Does this model illustrate your family of orientation? What about your family of procreation? If not, how have the stages you've experienced been different?

- Why does your family behave the way it does? Which theory or theories seem to be the most useful to you in answering this question? Why?

FAMILY RESEARCH METHODS

Why are we attracted to some people and not to others? Why are young adults postponing marriage? Why have divorce rates recently declined? To answer these and other questions about the family, social scientists typically use six major research methods: surveys, clinical research, field research, secondary analysis, experiments, and evaluation research. (*Table 2.2* provides a summary of these data collection methods.)

TABLE 2.2	Six Common Data Collection Methods in Family Research	
Method	**Strengths**	**Limitations**
Surveys	Fairly inexpensive and simple to administer; interviews have high response rates; findings often can be generalized to the whole population.	Mailed questionnaires may have low response rates; respondents may be self-selected; interviews usually are expensive.
Clinical research	Helps people who are experiencing family problems; offers insights for theory development.	Usually time consuming and expensive; findings can't be generalized.
Field research	Flexible; offers deeper understanding of family behavior; can be expensive or inexpensive depending on the project's scope and location.	Difficult to quantify and to maintain observer-participant boundaries; the observer may be biased or judgmental; findings can't be generalized.
Secondary analysis	Usually accessible, convenient, and inexpensive; often longitudinal and historical.	Information may be incomplete; some documents may be inaccessible; some data cannot be collected over time.
Experiment	Attempts to demonstrate cause and effect; usually inexpensive; many available participants; can be replicated.	Volunteers and paid participants aren't representative of larger populations; artificial laboratory setting.
Evaluation research	Usually inexpensive; valuable in real-life applications.	Often political; may entail training many staff members.

Peanuts: © United Feature Syndicate, Inc.

Family researchers also rely on qualitative and quantitative approaches. In **qualitative research,** social scientists examine nonnumerical material that they then interpret. Examples of qualitative data include verbal or written narratives, letters, diaries, photographs, and other images such as Internet ads. In **quantitative research,** researchers focus on a numerical analysis of people's responses or specific characteristics. Examples include collecting or examining data on the attitudes and experiences of people who live together, family size, and age at first marriage.

Neither method is inherently better or worse than the other, but each depends on the research questions. For instance, if you wanted in-depth information on grandparents who are raising their grandchildren, you'd use qualitative methods. If, on the other hand, you wanted to find out whether the number of grandparents who are raising their children has increased over the years, you'd use quantitative methods. Or, if you were interested in both questions, you'd use both methods.

Surveys

Researchers use **surveys** to systematically collect data from respondents through questionnaires or interviews. Before the data collection begins, researchers must first decide on the population and sample.

POPULATIONS AND SAMPLES A **population** is any well-defined group of people (or things) that researchers want to know something about. Obtaining information from a population is problematic because the population (such as parents of preschool children with disabilities) may be so large that it would be too expensive and time consuming to interview every person. In other cases—such as obtaining the membership lists of religious groups or social clubs—it may be impossible even to identify the population we would like to study.

To avoid these problems, researchers typically select a **sample,** a group of people (or things) that are

> **Since you asked . . .**
>
> :: Because they've never contacted me, my family, or my friends, how can pollsters draw conclusions about our behavior or attitudes?

representative of the population they want to study. In a *probability sample,* each person (or thing) has an equal chance of being chosen because the selection is random. Researchers often get probability samples through *random-digit dialing,* which involves selecting area codes and exchanges followed by four random digits. In a procedure called *computer-assisted telephone interviewing (CATI),* the interviewer uses a computer to select random telephone numbers, reads the questions to the respondent from a computer screen, and then keys the replies into pre-coded spaces. Because the selection is random, the findings can be generalized to the population from which the sample was drawn.

In a *nonprobability sample,* researchers use other criteria, such as convenience or the availability of participants. The findings can't be generalized to *any* group because the people (or things) have not been selected randomly; that is, they have not had an equal chance of being selected for the study.

Television stations, newsmagazines, and entertainment shows often provide a toll-free number or an Internet site and encourage viewers to "vote" on an issue or a person (as is done on the popular TV contest *American Idol*). How representative are these voters of the general population? And how many enthusiasts stuff the ballot box by voting more than once? According to one observer, most

Millions of viewers choose a winner by voting for their favorite *American Idol* singer. Does the voting represent all of the show's fans? Or are such surveys a SLOP (see p. 44)?

Changes

How Good Are Online Surveys?

One of the greatest benefits of the Internet is reaching large numbers of people. Hundreds of Websites invite visitors to participate in a variety of studies that resemble scientific research, including personality tests, marketing studies, and opinion polls. How scientific are these online surveys? And can researchers draw accurate conclusions from the results?

Online surveys offer many benefits. Most important, they can ask thousands (even millions) of people lots of questions quickly and cheaply. Second, because respondents can choose when to take the survey and how much time to devote to each question, they are more likely to provide thoughtful answers. Third, researchers can ask sensitive questions ("How often do you shower?") because respondents aren't being queried face to face. In addition, marketers can use the Web's video capabilities to ask respondents what they think of a new ad campaign or image of a product (Helm, 2008).

Online surveys also have limitations. A major problem is that the numbers of respondents, though massive, haven't been chosen randomly and don't represent a population, and the results can't be generalized. Second, a related drawback is that research firms often reward participants with gifts, certificates, or cash, which means that the incentives generate self-selected groups.

Third, Internet usage varies greatly by factors such as social class and age. For example, less than half of American households that earn less than $30,000 a year use the Internet compared with almost 90 percent of those with a college degree or higher. And, of those ages 64 or older (and who comprise almost 19 percent of the adult population), only 11 percent ever use the Internet (Pew Internet & American Family Life Project, 2008; Jones and Fox, 2009). This means that the findings will be distorted because they don't include older people or those from lower socioeconomic levels.

Fourth, marketing research, especially, can be deceptive. Most reputable companies tell respondents that if they get a $10 coupon toward a future purchase, for example, the company has the right to sell any of the person's information (including credit/debit card numbers) to another company or to automatically enroll them in a membership that can cost at least $15 a month. Often, however, people who respond to these online surveys don't read the fine print that authorizes the marketers to do so (Dang, 2008).

∷• Stop and Think . . .

- Have you ever participated in an online survey? Why or why not?

- So far, there are no established federal guidelines for online surveys. Should there be such guidelines? Or should respondents be responsible for reading the fine print and making their own decisions about whether to participate?

Internet polls are "good for a few laughs" but are little more than "the latest in a long series of junk masquerading as indicators of public opinion because the participants aren't representative of everyone's opinion" (Witt, 1998: 23).

But what if a million people cast a vote? Don't such large numbers reflect how most people think? No. Because the respondents are self-selected, the pollster simply has "junk" from a very large number of people. Since the mid-1990s, the number of online surveys, including polls, has boomed. Are the results valid? The "How Good are Online Surveys?" box examines some of the benefits and costs of this data collection method.

QUESTIONNAIRES AND INTERVIEWS Researchers collect survey data using questionnaires, face-to-face or telephone interviews, or a combination of these tools. Questionnaires can be mailed, used during an interview, or self-administered to large groups of respondents. Student course evaluations are good examples of self-administered questionnaires.

The telephone is popular because it's an inexpensive way to collect data. CATI, for example, generates a probability sample and provides interviewers with a consistent set of questions.

FOCUS GROUPS Marketing companies have traditionally used *focus groups*—group interviews that target a specific topic—to gauge people's reactions to a new or "new and improved" product. Family researchers also use focus groups to explore issues—such as why teenagers use drugs—before launching a nationally representative survey. Usually, 6 to 12 members of a focus group participate in a guided discussion of a particular question or issue (Morgan, 1993; Krueger, 1994).

Focus groups can be invaluable in obtaining honest information that has not been tapped by previous studies. For example, low-income mothers are more willing to discuss child care problems with a small group of women like themselves, but would be reluctant to do so in a mailed questionnaire because they fear that child protective services will see the results and might remove children from their home (Dodson and Schmalzbauer, 2005).

Focus groups are especially useful in obtaining in-depth information on relatively new topics or understudied populations. In the case of Latino families, for instance, researchers can obtain valuable data from focus groups if they consider a number of factors—that participants from Mexico, Puerto Rico, and Central and Latin America are very diverse in

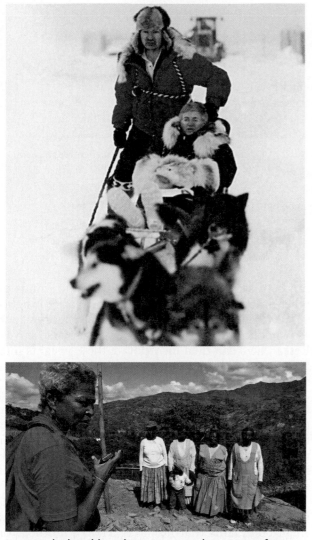

In some isolated locations, census takers must often travel to places that are inaccessible by road or without conventional postal addresses. In the 2000 census, Census Director Kenneth Prewitt was transported by dog sled to a remote village of 800 people in Unalakdeet, Alaska. Others, like an anthropologist from Washington, D.C., collect data in isolated towns in Bolivia.

their cultural experiences; that separating women and men will encourage women to open up; and that ensuring confidentiality and providing monetary incentives may be critical, especially in recruiting undocumented immigrants (Umaña-Taylor and Bámaca, 2004).

STRENGTHS Surveys are usually inexpensive, easy to administer, and have a fast turnaround rate. When assured that their answers will remain anonymous or confidential, respondents are generally willing to answer questions on sensitive topics such as income, sexual behavior, and drug use.

Face-to-face interviews have high response rates (up to 99 percent). Interviewers can also record the respondent's body language, facial expressions, and intonations, which are often useful in interpreting verbal responses. If a respondent doesn't understand a question or is reluctant to answer, the interviewer can clarify, probe, or keep the respondent from digressing. An astute interviewer can also gather information on variables such as social class by observing the respondent's home and neighborhood.

Telephone interviews provide a nearly unlimited pool of respondents because fewer than 2 percent of all households have at least one telephone (CDC Center for Disease Control). These interviews often elicit more honest responses on controversial issues than do face-to-face interviews.

LIMITATIONS One of the major limitations of surveys that use mailed questionnaires is a low response rate, often only about 10 percent (Gray, 2007). If the questions are unclear, complicated, or seen as offensive, respondents may simply throw the questionnaire away or offer opinions on subjects they know nothing about (Babbie, 2007).

Another problem is that people may skip or lie about questions that they consider inappropriate. During the 2000 census, for example, 53 percent of the people who received the long form viewed questions about income as intrusive and ignored the items; 32 percent felt the same way about questions on physical or mental disabilities (Cohn, 2000). If respondents lie or ignore questions about family characteristics, the research results will be invalid or limited because the researcher may have to scrap a key variable such as income.

There's also a problem of a survey's sponsorship. For example, the highly respected Harris poll reported, several weeks before Valentine's Day in 2005, that 37 percent of Americans said that a lobster dinner is the most romantic meal. It turned out that the poll had been sponsored by the Red Lobster restaurant chain (Moore, 2005).

A survey conducted by a team of Harvard University researchers concluded that teenagers on social networking sites (such as MySpace and Facebook) are relatively safe from online adult sexual predators because the teens themselves post naked pictures of themselves and talk about drugs, sex, and drinking. Many state attorneys, consumer groups, and parents were critical of the report because the survey was financed by interested parties such as MySpace, Facebook, Google, and Microsoft (Palfrey, 2008; Healy, 2009; Musgrove, 2009).

Unlike questionnaires and telephone surveys, face-to-face interviews can be very expensive. Because many people have become oversaturated with marketing research, they use caller ID or answering machines to avoid telephone surveys. Telephone surveys have become especially problematic because of the increased use of cell phones. Because they are charged for received calls, wireless customers may be

Applying What You've Learned

:•: Can I Trust This Survey?

Surveys are often used in public opinion polls and are reported on television and in newspapers. Asking a few basic questions about a survey will help you evaluate its credibility:

■ *Who sponsored the survey?* A government agency, a nonprofit partisan organization, a business, or a group that's lobbying for change?

■ *What is the purpose of the survey?* To provide objective information, to promote an idea or a political candidate, or to get attention through sensationalism?

■ *How was the sample drawn?* Randomly? Or was it a SLOP, a "self-selection opinion poll" (see Tanur, 1994)?

■ *How were the questions worded?* Were they clear, objective, loaded, or biased? If the survey questions are not provided, why not?

■ *How did the researchers report their findings?* Were they objective, or did they make value judgments?

---

unwilling to endure lengthy phone interviews. Also, the Federal Communications Commission requires an interviewer to enter the number when calling a cell phone, which precludes the use of random-digit dialing (Thee, 2007).

Because the survey is the research approach you will encounter most often, it's important to be an informed consumer. As the "Can I Trust This Survey?" box shows, you can't simply assume that the survey is accurate or representative of a larger population.

Clinical Research

Unlike survey research, which explores large-scale social processes and changes, **clinical research** studies individuals or small groups of people who seek help from mental health professionals and other social scientists. Many clinical researchers focus on family conflict and intervene in traumatic situations such as marital rape and incest. They also try to change negative interactions such as hostile communication patterns between partners or aspects of the family environment that might lead to eating disorders, drug use, and other problems.

Clinical research often relies on the *case study method,* a traditional approach used by social workers, psychologists, clinical sociologists, and marriage counselors. A case study provides in-depth information and detailed and vivid descriptions of family life (see LaRossa, 1984, for good examples of case studies across the life course). Clinical practitioners work with families or individuals on a one-to-one basis, but they often use several techniques such as experiments (which we'll examine shortly) and direct observation.

STRENGTHS Case studies are typically linked with long-term counseling, which can be beneficial for individuals and families. Useful intervention strategies

can be disseminated fairly quickly to thousands of other practitioners. Clinicians may also offer insights about family dynamics that can enrich theories such as symbolic interaction or family systems perspectives. Researchers can then incorporate these insights into larger or more representative studies that use surveys or other data collection methods.

LIMITATIONS Clinical research and case studies are usually time consuming and expensive. Clinicians typically see only people with severe problems or those who are willing and financially able to seek help. Therefore, the results are not representative of average families or even of troubled families.

Another problem is that clinical studies are subjective and rarely ask "Where's the evidence?" If a client complains that he has a terrible mother, for example, clinicians may try to make the patient cope better instead of meeting the mother or talking to other family members. As a result, some critics contend, subjective clinical opinions are widespread despite empirical evidence to the contrary. It is *not* true, for instance, that low self-esteem causes aggression, drug use, and low achievement. How parents treat a child in the first years of life does *not* determine a child's later intellectual and emotional success (see Chapter 12). Nor do abused children inevitably become abusive parents, causing a cycle of abuse (Tavris, 2003).

Field Research

In **field research,** researchers collect data by observing people in their natural surroundings. Field research usually is highly structured and typically involves carefully designed projects in which data are recorded and then converted into quantitative summaries. The studies examine complex communication patterns, measure the frequency of specific acts (such as the number of nods or domineering

ASK YOURSELF

Is My Classmate an Undercover Professor?

For one academic year, Cathy Small, an anthropology professor at Northern Arizona University, posed as a full-time undergraduate student and enrolled in the university where she teaches. After the university approved the project, Small paid her tuition, registered for five courses each semester, and moved into a dorm. She didn't tell her classmates that she was a professor and revealed her identity only to a few students with whom she developed close friendships.

Small found that many undergraduates valued future careers more than their coursework; that students read only the material they thought would be on an exam; that cheating was common; and that many of the dorm students spent more time socializing, drinking, and partying than preparing for classes. After returning to the classroom, Small implemented some changes because she concluded that being a student in the twenty-first century is tougher than she had imagined. Some of the changes included

assigning less reading and offering help to students with low grades.

Small's book, published under the pseudonym Rebekah Nathan (2005), received positive comments primarily from parents and college administrators who got an inside view of student life, especially the numerous pressures of a student culture that emphasizes both fun and achievement. Others, especially faculty and researchers, criticized Small's undercover research as dishonest and unethical (Hoover, 2005).

Stop and Think . . .

- Field researchers often go undercover to observe their subjects. Why, then, did some people criticize Small's participant observer role as dishonest and unethical?

- Do you think that pretending to be a student for a year is similar to being a student over a number of years? Why or why not?

---

statements), and note the duration of a particular behavior (such as length of eye contact) (Stillars, 1991). Thus, field research is much more elaborate and sophisticated than it appears to be to the general public or to an inexperienced researcher.

TWO KINDS OF OBSERVATIONS Field research includes several types of observation. In *participant observation,* researchers interact naturally with the people they are studying but do not reveal their identities as researchers (see the box "Is My Classmate an Undercover Professor?").

In *nonparticipant observation,* researchers study phenomena without being part of the situation. For example, a team of Canadian researchers followed more than 400 parents and their 2-to-5-year-old children around grocery stores, noting parents' interaction with their kids. The researchers found that good-looking children, especially boys, got more attention from their parents. The "pretty kids" were more likely than the unattractive ones to be buckled into the shopping cart instead of allowed to stand up in the cart and to be held by the hand instead of being permitted to wander away (Harrell, 2005, 2006).

In many studies, researchers combine both participant and nonparticipant observation. For example, sociologist Elijah Anderson (1999) examined households in West Philadelphia, an inner-city black community with high crime rates. Anderson teaches at the University of Pennsylvania, but he "hung out" in West Philadelphia to learn why some poor residents take

extraordinary measures to conform to mainstream values such as maintaining a strong family life, whereas others engage in crime and violence.

STRENGTHS Field research is more flexible than some other methods. For instance, the researcher can decide to interview (rather than just observe) key people after beginning to collect data. Most important, because field research rarely disrupts a natural setting, the people being studied aren't influenced by the researcher's presence. For example, sociologist Phillip Davis (1996) and some of his research assistants have observed adults' verbal aggression and corporal punishment of children in public settings such as indoor shopping malls, zoos, amusement parks, flea markets, city streets, rapid transit stations, bus depots, and toy stores.

LIMITATIONS If a researcher needs elaborate recording equipment, must travel far or often, or lives in a different society or community for a long time, field research can be expensive. Researchers who study other cultures must often learn a new language, a time-consuming task.

A field researcher may encounter barriers in collecting the desired data. Homeless and battered women's shelters, for example, are usually—and understandably—wary of researchers' intruding on their residents' privacy. Even if the researcher has access to such a group, it's often difficult to maintain objectivity while collecting and interpreting the data because the topic can evoke strong emotional reactions such as anxiety, anger against perpetrators, and sympathy for subjects.

It may also be difficult to balance the role of participant and observer. In Anderson's studies in West Philadelphia cited earlier, he became personally involved with some of his research participants. Instead of being a detached observer, Anderson hired an ex–drug dealer as a part-time research assistant, found lawyers or jobs for community members, encouraged his respondents to avoid committing crimes, and even lent them money. In these and other ways, the researcher may bias the research by succumbing to the impulse to fix a problem and to protect the people being studied from harm (Fine, 1993; Cose, 1999).

Another problem with field research is the observer's ability (or lack of it) to recognize and address her or his biases. Because observation is very personal and subjective, it can be difficult to maintain one's objectivity while collecting and interpreting the data (see Venkatesh, 2008).

Secondary Analysis

Family researchers also rely heavily on **secondary analysis,** an examination of data that have been collected by someone else. The data may be historical materials (such as court proceedings), personal documents (such as letters and diaries), public records (such as federal information on immigration or state or county archives on births, marriages, and deaths), and official statistics (such as Census Bureau publications).

The availability and usage of large-scale data sets have grown dramatically in the past two decades. The *Journal of Marriage and Family,* a major periodical in the field of family studies, reflects the growing reliance on secondary data sources. In 2003, 75 percent of the studies published in this journal used secondary data analysis, compared with only 33 percent in 1983 (Hofferth, 2005).

Many of the statistics in this textbook come from secondary analysis. The sources include the U.S. Census Bureau and other government agencies, reputable nonprofit organizations, and university research centers (see Greenstein, 2006, for a good summary of the major sources of secondary analysis in family research).

STRENGTHS Secondary analysis is usually accessible, convenient, and inexpensive. Census Bureau information on topics such as household income, the number of children in single-parent families, and immigration is readily available at college and university libraries and on the Internet.

Because secondary data often are *longitudinal* (collected at two or more points in time) rather than *cross-sectional* (collected at one point in time), they offer the added advantage of allowing the researcher to examine trends (such as age at first marriage) over time. And, increasingly, both longitudinal and cross-sectional publications provide the reader with colorful pie charts and other figures that are easy to read, understand, and incorporate into PowerPoint® presentations.

Another advantage of secondary analysis is the high quality of the data. Nationally known survey organizations have large budgets and well-trained staff who can quickly handle any data collection problems. Because the samples are representative of national populations, readers can be more confident about generalizing the findings.

LIMITATIONS Secondary analysis has several drawbacks. First, secondary data may not provide all the information needed. For example, some of the statistics on remarriages and redivorces have been collected only since the early 1990s. Therefore, it is impossible for a researcher to make comparisons over time, especially before 1990.

Second, secondary analysis of historical materials may be problematic because the documents may be fragile, housed in only a few libraries in the country, or part of private collections. Determining the accuracy and authenticity of historical materials also may be difficult.

Third, the data may not include information the researcher is looking for. If you wanted to examine some of the characteristics of couples who are separated but not divorced, for example, you'd find little national data. Consequently, you'd have to rely on studies with small and nonrepresentative samples or collect such information yourself (see Chapter 15).

Experiments

Unlike surveys, field research, and secondary analysis, an **experiment** is a controlled artificial situation that allows researchers to manipulate variables and measure their effects. A researcher tests a prediction, or *hypothesis,* stating that one specified variable causes another ("Watching a film on racial discrimination reduces prejudice."). The *independent variable* (watching a film on racial discrimination) predicts that there will be an effect on the *dependent variable* (reducing prejudice).

In the *experimental group,* the subjects are exposed to the independent variable (watching the film). In the *control* group, they are not. Before the experiment, the researcher measures the dependent variable (prejudice) in both groups using a *pretest.* After the experimental group is exposed to the independent variable (the film on racial discrimination), the researcher measures both groups again using a

Researchers often study interaction by observing people in natural settings. What are the advantages and disadvantages of experimental designs such as this one?

posttest. If the researcher finds a difference in the measures of the dependent variable, she or he assumes that the independent variable has a causal effect on the dependent variable.

Experimental family research is rare because "Children or adults cannot be assigned at random to different family types, to different partners, to different income groups" (Hofferth, 2005: 903–4). In contrast, medical researchers routinely search for cause-effect relationships between many variables, such as diet and blood pressure or stress and physical illness. Still, experimental designs are useful in studying family-related issues such as the effectiveness of anger management workshops and interaction skills between partners, and the usefulness of support groups in coping with the death of a child or divorce (see, for example, Ebling and Levenson, 2003, and Fetsch et al., 2008).

STRENGTHS A major advantage of the controlled (laboratory) experiment is its isolation of the causal variable. For example, if students who get information in sex education classes show changes in their attitude toward casual sex, a school might decide to provide such information for all of its students.

Another strength of experimental designs is their low cost. Usually, there's no need to purchase special equipment and most participants expect little or no compensation. Also, experiments often are less time consuming than data collection methods such as field research.

A third advantage is that experiments can be replicated over many years and with different participants. Such replication strengthens the researchers' confidence in the *validity,* or accuracy, and *reliability,* or consistency, of the research findings.

LIMITATIONS One disadvantage of laboratory experiments is their reliance on student volunteers or paid respondents. Students often feel obligated to participate as part of their grade, or they may fear antagonizing an instructor who's conducting a study. Students might also give the answers that they think the instructor expects. In the case of paid subjects, those who are the busiest, don't need the extra cash, move, or become ill may not participate fully or may drop out of the study.

A second and related disadvantage is that the results of experimental studies can't be generalized to a larger population because they come from small or self-selected samples. For example, college students who participate in experiments aren't necessarily representative of other college students, much less of people who aren't in college.

A third limitation is that experiments, especially those conducted in laboratories, are artificial. People *know* that they're being observed and may behave very differently than they would in a natural setting (Babbie, 2007).

Evaluation Research

In **evaluation research,** which relies on all the standard methodological techniques described in this section, researchers assess the efficiency and effectiveness of social programs in both the public and private sectors. Many government and nonprofit agencies provide services that affect the family both directly and indirectly. Work-training programs, drug rehabilitation programs, and programs to prevent or deal with teenage pregnancy are examples.

Local, state, and national governments have cut their social service budgets since the early 1980s. As a result, service delivery groups have become increasingly concerned about doing more with less. Evaluation research helps agencies determine how to achieve the best results at the lowest possible cost (Kettner et al., 1999).

Like clinical research, evaluation research is *applied.* It assesses a specific social program for a specific agency or organization, evaluating that program's achievements in terms of its original goals (Weiss, 1998). Administrators often use the final reports to improve a program or to initiate a new service such as an after-school program.

STRENGTHS Evaluation research is a valuable tool because it examines actual efforts to deal with problems that confront many families. If researchers use secondary analysis rather than collect new data, the expenses can be modest. In addition, the research findings can be valuable to program directors or agency heads because the findings highlight discrepancies between the original objectives and the way the program is actually working, allowing managers to keep a program on course (Peterson et al., 1994).

LIMITATIONS Evaluation research can be frustrating. Politics often play an important role in what is evaluated and for whom the research is done. Agency heads typically solicit the research, but they may ignore the results if the study shows that the program isn't tapping the neediest groups, the administrators are wasting money, or caseworkers are making serious mistakes.

Some evaluations are inadequate because they are poorly designed. Marriage enrichment and preparation programs have mushroomed since the early 1990s. Are they effective? The results are mixed. An evaluation of 13 such programs found that only four were useful in increasing a couple's level of communication, improving problem-solving skills, or strengthening a relationship. The other nine programs claimed success but never examined any outcomes or the outcome measures were seriously flawed (Jakubowski et al., 2004).

A systematic review of 39 evaluations of marriage and relationship programs found that even the best-designed evaluations had numerous methodological problems: The sample sizes were very small, practically all the participants were middle-class whites, there were no measures of couples' outcomes over time, the evaluators studied programs that they themselves had created, and the authors sometimes presented only positive results (Reardon-Anderson et al., 2005; see, also, Silliman and Schumm, 2000).

Conclusion

Researchers have to weigh the benefits and limitations of each research approach in designing their studies (see *Table 2.2* on p. 40). Often, they use a combination of strategies to achieve their research objectives. Despite the researcher's commitment to objectivity, ethical debates and politically charged disagreements can influence much family research.

:: MAKING CONNECTIONS

- If you get information from the Internet, how do you determine whether the material is accurate?

- In 1985, advice columnist Ann Landers asked her readers, most of whom were women, "Would you be content to be held close and treated tenderly, and forget about 'the act'?" Of the 90,000 women who deluged Landers's mailbox, 71 percent said "yes!" and 40 percent of them were under age 40 (see Angier, 1985). Landers concluded (and her conclusions are still cited by some journalists and self-help books) that American women don't care about sex, and much of the media publicized Landers's conclusion as a fact. Do you see any problems with Landers's question construction, the sample, and her conclusion?

THE ETHICS AND POLITICS OF FAMILY RESEARCH

Researchers don't work in a vacuum. Many people have very strong opinions about family issues (see Chapter 1). There is also pressure in universities to supplement shrinking budgets with outside funding sources. It's not surprising, then, that researchers sometimes encounter ethical and political dilemmas.

> **Since you asked . . .**
>
> :: If I participate in a research project, how can I be sure that any information about me will be confidential?

Researchers today operate under much stricter guidelines than they did in the past. This doesn't guarantee, however, that everyone is ethical, despite stringent ethics codes.

Ethics Codes and Scientific Misconduct

Because so much research relies on human subjects, the federal government and many professional organizations have devised ethics codes to protect research participants. Among other professional organizations, the National Council on Family Relations and the American Sociological Association publish codes of ethics to guide researchers. *Table 2.3* summarizes the key elements of these codes, regardless of the research design.

For the most part, violations of ethics codes are unintentional because they result from ignorance of statistical procedures, simple arithmetic mistakes, or inadequate supervision. Of the thousands of studies published every year, peers have typically reviewed the material and scholars have evaluated the funding requests.

www.benitaepstein.com

© Benita Epstein 1996

"I already wrote the paper. That's why it's so hard to get the right data."

TABLE 2.3	Some Basic Principles of Ethical Family Research

- Obtain all participants' consent to participate and their permission to quote from their responses, particularly if the research concerns sensitive issues or if participants' comments will be quoted extensively.
- Do not exploit participants or research assistants involved in the research for personal gain.
- Never harm, humiliate, abuse, or coerce participants, either physically or psychologically. This includes the withholding of medications or other services or programs that might benefit participants.
- Honor all guarantees to participants of privacy, anonymity, and confidentiality.
- Use the highest methodological standards and be as accurate as possible.
- Describe the limitations and shortcomings of the research in published reports.
- Identify the sponsors who funded the research.

Some data collection methods are more susceptible than others to ethical violations. Surveys, secondary analysis, and content analysis are less vulnerable than are field research and experiments because the researchers typically don't interact directly with subjects, interpret their behavior, or become personally involved with the respondents. In contrast, experiments and field research can raise ethical questions (see the box "Is My Classmate an Undercover Professor" on p. 45).

HOW OFTEN DO RESEARCHERS VIOLATE ETHICS CODES? In one of the largest and most systematic surveys to date, the researchers offered a conservative estimate of 2,325 possible instances of scientific medical misconduct nationally per year at academic institutions that received grants from the Department of Health and Human Services. The violations included faking research results, plagiarism, not presenting other people's data that contradicted researchers' own findings, not adequately protecting human subjects, cutting corners to complete a project, and changing the research design or study results to please the group that sponsored the research (Titus et al., 2008; see also, Mello et al., 2005, and DeVries et al., 2006).

Social scientists seem to be less likely than medical scientists to engage in unethical behavior. One of the reasons may be that social science research is rarely supported by corporations (such as tobacco and pharmaceutical companies) that have vested interests in getting the findings they want to promote a product (such as a drug) or medical procedure.

HOW DOES UNETHICAL RESEARCH AFFECT US? Ethical violations affect all families. For example, the National Alliance for the Mentally Ill, despite its numerous contributions, embraces claims on the prevalence of mental disorders—based on methodologically flawed studies—that contend that half of Americans suffer from a mental disorder, especially depression, at some point in their lives. In fact, scientific studies show that about 75 percent of depressive symptoms are normal and temporary (such as worrying about an upcoming exam or grieving the death of a family member or friend). If mental health organizations can convince politicians that mental illness is widespread, they can get more funding for mental health services, including normal and temporary depression. And pharmaceutical companies are eager to sell costly antidepressant drugs. As a result, many mental health organizations and pharmaceutical companies benefit by labeling even normal depression as an "overwhelming problem" (Horwitz and Wakefield, 2006: 23).

Hundreds of Harvard University Medical School students and faculty members have recently protested the ties between industry and researchers that affect both individuals and families in the work they are doing in Harvard's classrooms, laboratories, and 17 teaching hospitals and institutes. A fourth-year medical student said that he felt violated, for example, when he learned that a professor in a pharmacology class was also a paid consultant to ten drug companies. School officials dismissed such complaints because corporate support is vital to faculty research, even though Harvard University has the second-largest nonprofit international financial endowment (almost $37 billion in 2008) after the Bill and Melinda Gates Foundation (Mangan, 2009; Munson, 2009).

Political, Religious, and Community Pressures

Former Senator William Proxmire became famous (or infamous, some believe) for his "Golden Fleece" awards to social research projects that he ridiculed as a waste of taxpayers' money. Some of his examples included studies of stress and why people fall in love. The legitimacy of social science research becomes especially suspect in the eyes of political and religious groups when the studies focus on sensitive social, moral, or political issues.

One of the most controversial research topics is human sexuality. Alfred Kinsey and his colleagues carried out the first widely publicized research on sexuality in the late 1940s and early 1950s. The studies had some methodological limitations, such as using only volunteers, but many social scientists consider Kinsey's research a major springboard that launched scientific investigations of human sexuality in subsequent decades.

Many people are still suspicious of research on sex, especially when the findings contradict their personal beliefs. A bigger concern, for many scientists, is that the U.S. government may be part of the problem of providing inaccurate health information rather than solutions. Over the years, for example, a number of studies have shown that abstinence-only education programs don't work, that teens know little about sex, including about sexually transmitted diseases and contraceptives (see Chapter 7). Nonetheless, between 2002 and 2008, the Bush administration funded 2,000 "pregnancy resource centers," which are often affiliated with religious antiabortion groups. Counselors at some of these centers are still telling women with unintended pregnancies that abortion increases the risk of breast cancer and infertility and creates long-lasting psychological trauma even though such claims are false (Kaufman, 2006).

In its most extreme form, doing research on topics that politicians don't approve of may jeopardize a scholar's current or future employment. For example, a tenured professor at a large research university came close to being fired by a Republican governor who disapproved of his research on abstinence education (Bailey et al., 2002). More recently, some sociology and education faculty at Georgia State University who taught sexuality courses but listed topics such as oral sex and male prostitution as their research interests were grilled by several legislators who threatened to fire the faculty (Stombler, 2009).

::• MAKING CONNECTIONS

- Some researchers violate ethical guidelines to bring in more money for their institutions. Is this acceptable, especially if the grants provide funds that can be used to reduce class sizes, pay for much-needed computer labs, and increase library staff and student services?

- On a number of sites (such as www.pickaprof.com and www.ratemyprofessors.com), students can say anything they want about faculty. Should students identify themselves instead of submitting the evaluations anonymously? Are the comments representative of all the students in a course? Should faculty set up similar public sites and evaluate students by name?

CONCLUSION

Understanding marriage and the family is *not* an armchair activity dominated by scholars and philosophers. On the contrary, like the family itself, the study of marriage and the family reflects *changes* in the evolution of theories and *constraints* resulting from the limitations of research designs. There has been much progress in family research, and researchers have more *choices* in the methods available to them. At the same time, "there is plenty of reason for marriage and family scholars to be modest about what they know and humble about what they do not" (Miller, 1986: 110).

Research is sometimes inadequate because social scientists ignore the historical context that has shaped the contemporary family. We look at some of these historical processes in the next chapter.

SUMMARY

1. Many people are suspicious of statistics, but all kinds of data are becoming increasingly important in our daily lives. Information derived from social science research affects much of our everyday behavior, shapes family policies, and provides explanations for social change.

2. Both theory and research are essential to understanding marriages and families.

3. Some of the most influential theories of the family include two macro-level perspectives (structural functionalism and conflict theory), three micro-macro level theories (feminist, ecological, and developmental), and three micro-level theories (symbolic interactionism, social exchange, and family systems). Researchers and clinicians often use several theoretical perspectives in interpreting data or choosing intervention strategies.

4. The survey is one of the most common data collection methods in family research. Surveys rely on questionnaires, interviews, or a combination of these techniques. Both questionnaires and interviews have advantages and limitations that researchers consider in designing their studies.

5. Clinical research and case studies provide a deeper understanding of behavior because they enable researchers to study attitudes and behavior intensively and over time. Such research, however, is also time consuming and limited to small groups of people.

6. Field research offers in-depth insights on the family, but the results can be difficult to quantify and can't be generalized, and the researcher may experience difficulty in balancing observation and participation.

7. Experiments try to establish cause-effect explanations. It is impossible to prove such associations, however, because experiments are usually conducted in artificial settings that don't represent people's behavior in natural environments.

8. Secondary analysis uses data collected by other researchers (such as historical documents and official government statistics). It is usually an accessible, convenient, and inexpensive source of data, but it may not provide information about the variables that a researcher wants to examine.

9. Evaluation research, an applied research technique, often assesses the effectiveness and efficiency of social programs that offer services to families and other groups. If the results are unflattering, however, politicians and administrators may ignore the findings and never publish the reports.

10. Social scientists must adhere to professional ethical standards, both in conducting research and in reporting the results. Because political issues often affect research, however, collecting data is not as simple as it seems.

KEY TERMS

theory 32
structural-functional theory 32
instrumental role 32
expressive role 32
manifest functions 33
latent functions 33
conflict theory 34
feminist theories 34
ecological theory 35

family development theory 36
family life cycle 36
developmental tasks 36
symbolic interaction theory 38
significant others 38
social exchange theory 39
family systems theory 39
qualitative research 41
quantitative research 41

surveys 41
population 41
sample 41
clinical research 44
field research 44
secondary analysis 46
experiment 46
evaluation research 47

PEARSON
myfamilylab MyFamilyLab provides a wealth of resources. Go to www.myfamilylab.com <http://www.myfamilylab .com/>, to enhance your comprehension of the content in this chapter. You can take practice exams, view videos relevant to the subject matter, listen to audio files, explore topics further by using Social Explorer, and use the tools contained in MySearchLab to help you write research papers.

3 The Family in Historical Perspective

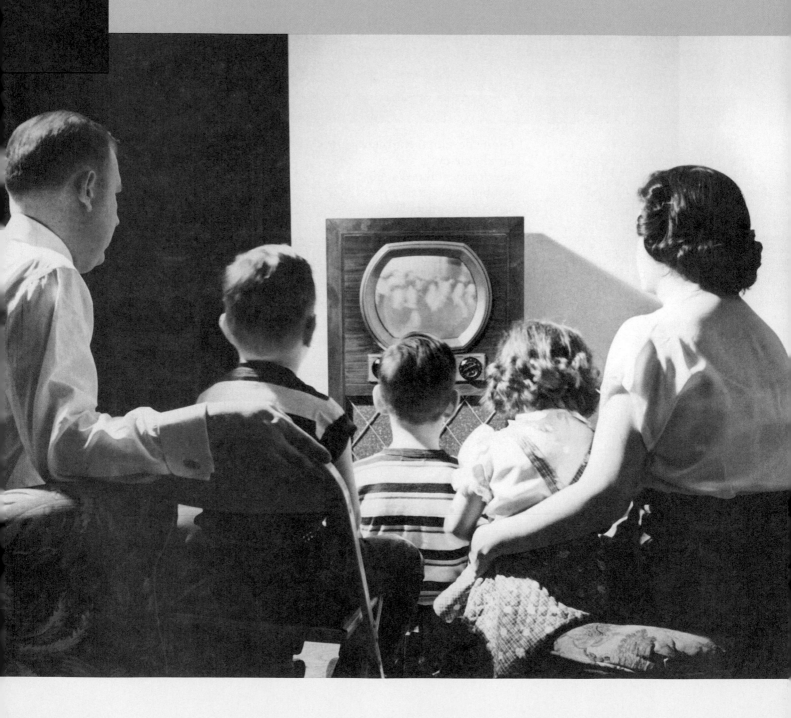

In 1890, Joel Coleman, a recent Jewish immigrant to New York City who was living in a crowded and dilapidated tenement house, wrote home:

Dear Father, I can tell You very little about my great achievements. I am not yet a wealthy man, but for sure not a beggar either. . . . Right now, during the winter, work is very slow. It happens every winter; therefore, we see to it that we have put something aside for those winter months. On the whole my life here is not bad and I cannot complain about America, except for one thing—my health was better at home, in Poland, where the air was better. Here I often get sick, but I prefer not to write about it (Wtulich, 1986: 218).

Other immigrants' letters, like Coleman's, often spoke of loneliness, low wages, hard and intermittent work, language barriers, poverty, and numerous hardships. Life was difficult and unpredictable in the "land of plenty."

When social scientists examine the past, they find that the good old days never existed for most people. Historians, especially, have raised some

DATA DIGEST

- Between **20 and 33 percent of colonial women were pregnant at the time of marriage**.

- During the **Great Depression,** one of four Americans was unemployed and farm income fell by 50 percent.

- The fathers of **nearly 183,000 children** were killed during World War II.

- Of the almost 7 million **women who were employed** during World War II, 75 percent were married.

- **African American women** made some of the greatest **employment gains** during World War II. Those working as servants fell from 72 percent to 48 percent, and the proportion employed in the war industry grew from 7 percent to almost 20 percent.

- **Divorce rates surged** from 321,000 in 1942 to 610,000 in 1946, after the end of the war. By 1950, a million veterans had been divorced.

- About 62 percent of Americans **attend a family reunion** every year.

Sources: Demos, 1970; Chafe, 1972; Hawke, 1988; Tuttle, 1993; Mergenbagen, 1996; Fetto, 2001.

53

interesting questions: Were the colonists as virtuous as they have been portrayed, especially in K–12 textbooks? Did people really pull together to help each other during the Great Depression? Were the 1950s as fabulous as many people insist they were? This chapter addresses these and similar questions.

THE COLONIAL FAMILY

Colonial families differed from modern ones in social class, religious practices, and geographic dispersion, but factors such as family roles and family structure were very similar. The diversity that characterizes modern families also existed in colonial times.

Family Structure

The nuclear family was the most prevalent family form both in England and in the first settlements in the United States. An elderly grandparent or an apprentice sometimes lived with or near his or her family, but few households were made up of extended families for long periods (Goode, 1963; Laslett, 1971). Families typically started out with six or seven children, but high infant death rates resulted in small households, with large age differences between the children.

The Puritans who migrated to New England and founded Plymouth colony in Massachusetts in 1620 were Protestants who adhered to strict moral and religious values. They believed that the community had a right to intervene in families that did not perform their duties properly. In the 1670s, for example, the Massachusetts General Court directed towns to appoint parish officers to ensure that marital relations were harmonious and that parents disciplined unruly children (Mintz and Kellogg, 1988).

Few people survived outside families during the colonial period. Most settlements were small (fewer than 100 families), and each family was considered a "little commonwealth" that performed a variety of functions. The family was a

- Self-sufficient *business*, in which all family members worked together to produce and exchange goods
- *School* that taught children to read
- *Vocational institute* that instructed children and prepared them for jobs through apprenticeships
- Miniature *church* that guided its members in daily prayers, personal meditation, and formal worship in the community
- *House of correction* to which the courts sentenced idle people and nonviolent offenders to be servants

- *Welfare institution* that gave its members medical and other care and provided a home for relatives who were orphaned, aging, sick, or homeless (Demos, 1970)

As you'll see later in this chapter, all these functions changed considerably with the onset of industrialization.

Sexual Relations

The Puritans tried to prevent premarital intercourse in several ways. One was **bundling**, a New England custom in which a fully dressed young man and woman spent the night in a bed together, separated by a wooden board.

The custom was adopted because it was difficult for the young suitor, who had to travel many miles (either by foot or horseback), to return home the same night, especially during harsh winters. Because the rest of the family shared the room, it was considered quite proper for the bundled young man and woman to continue their conversation after the fire was out (McPharlin, 1946).

Despite safeguards such as bundling, premarital sex was common because a large number of colonial

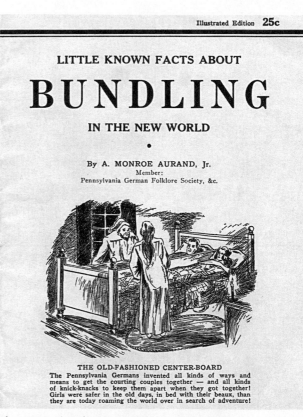

Illustrated Edition **25c**

LITTLE KNOWN FACTS ABOUT

BUNDLING

IN THE NEW WORLD

•

By A. MONROE AURAND, Jr.
Member:
Pennsylvania German Folklore Society, &c.

THE OLD-FASHIONED CENTER-BOARD
The Pennsylvania Germans invented all kinds of ways and means to get the courting couples together — and all kinds of knick-knacks to keep them apart when they got together! Girls were safer in the old days, in bed with their beaux, than they are today roaming the world over in search of adventure!

The Pennsylvania Germans invented various ways to keep courting couples apart when they were together. What do you suppose might have happened to the centerboard shown in this sketch after the young woman's parents went to bed?

women were pregnant at the time of marriage (see Data Digest). Keep in mind, however, that sexual activity was generally confined to engaged and married couples. The idea of a casual meeting that included sexual intercourse would have been utterly foreign to the Puritans.

Out-of-wedlock births were also fairly common among young women who immigrated to the southern colonies as indentured (contracted) servants. They typically came to the United States alone because they were from poor families that could not afford to migrate together. Because these very young (under age 15) women were alone and vastly outnumbered by men, they were vulnerable to sexual attacks, especially by employers (Harari and Vinovskis, 1993).

Puritans condemned adultery and illegitimacy because they threatened family stability. Sometimes local newspapers denounced a straying spouse publicly:

Catherine Treen, the wife of the subscriber, behaved in the most disgraceful manner, by leaving her own place of abode, and living in a criminal state with a certain William Collins, a plaisterer, under whose bed she was last night, discovered, endeavoring to conceal herself. Her much injured husband thinks it absolutely necessary to forewarn all persons from trusting after such flagrant proof of her prostitution (cited in Lantz, 1976: 14).

Few records, however, documented men's extramarital affairs. Although frowned upon, a husband's infidelity was considered normal. And because the courts did not enforce a father's economic obligation, it was women who paid the costs of bearing and raising out-of-wedlock children (Ryan, 1983). As you can see, the double standard (which we discuss later) is not a modern invention.

Husbands and Wives

Husbands and wives worked together to make sure that the family survived. As in modern society, colonists expected spouses to have strong relationships. Inequalities, however, were very much a part of early American family life.

PERSONAL RELATIONSHIPS In general, women were subordinate to men; the wife's chief duty was to obey her husband. New England clergymen often referred to male authority as a "government" that women must accept as "law." In the southern colonies, husbands often denounced assertive wives as "impertinent" (Ryan, 1983). A woman's social status and her power and prestige in the community came from the patriarchal head of the household, usually her husband or father, but other patriarchal heads included a brother or other male relative, such as an uncle (see Chapter 1).

At the same time, the "well-ordered" family was based on a number of mutual responsibilities. Husbands and wives were expected to show each other "a very great affection." They should be faithful to each other and were instructed to be patient and to help each other: "If the one is sick, pained, troubled, distressed, the other should manifest care, tenderness, pity, compassion, and afford all possible relief and succour" (Scott and Wishy, 1982: 86).

In the Plymouth colony, women had the right to transfer property. In 1646, for example, when a man wanted to sell his family's land, the court called in his wife to make sure that she approved of the sale. The courts also granted liquor and other business licenses to women. And they sometimes offered a woman protection from a violent husband. For example, the Plymouth court ordered a whipping for a man who kicked his wife off a stool and into a blazing fireplace (Demos, 1970; Mintz and Kellogg, 1988). Such protections were not typical in other colonies, however.

In a few cases, the local courts permitted divorce. The acceptable grounds were limited to desertion, adultery, bigamy, and impotence. Incompatibility was recognized as a problem but was not serious enough to warrant divorce. It was not until about 1765, when romantic love emerged as a basis for marriage, that "loss of affection" was mentioned as a reason for divorce (Cott and Pleck, 1979).

WORK AND THE ECONOMY Men were expected to be industrious, hardworking, and ambitious, and they were responsible for the family's economic survival. Husbands and wives often worked side by side. Men, women, and children all produced, cultivated, and processed goods for the family's consumption. When necessary, men cared for and disciplined the children while women worked in the fields.

Much of women's work was directed toward meeting the needs of others. In his 1793 *Female Guide,* a New Hampshire pastor defined women's role as "piety to God—reverence to parents—love and obedience to their husbands—tenderness and watchfulness over their children—justice and humanity to their dependents" (quoted in Cott, 1977: 22–23).

Both sexes were praised for being wealthy and industrious, but men were expected to initiate economic activity and women were expected to support them and to be frugal. In 1692, Cotton Mather, an influential minister and author, described women's economic role as being only "to spend (or save) what others get" (Cott, 1977).

In some cases, unmarried women, widows, and those who had been deserted by their husbands turned their homemaking activities into self-supporting businesses. Some used their homes as inns, restaurants, or schools and sold homemade foods. Others made a

FIGURE 3.1 Rules for Colonial Children

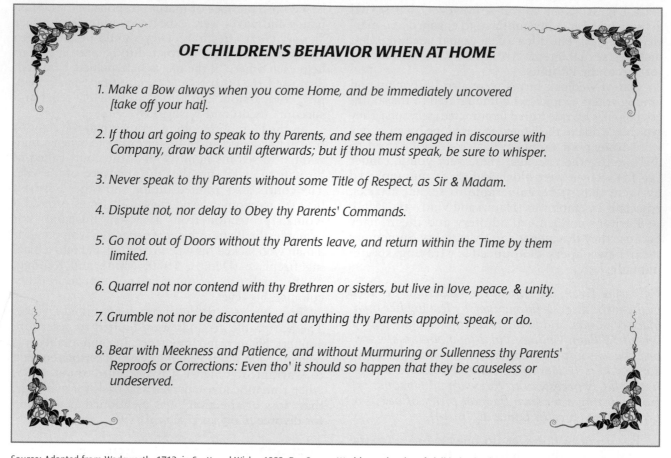

OF CHILDREN'S BEHAVIOR WHEN AT HOME

1. *Make a Bow always when you come Home, and be immediately uncovered [take off your hat].*

2. *If thou art going to speak to thy Parents, and see them engaged in discourse with Company, draw back until afterwards; but if thou must speak, be sure to whisper.*

3. *Never speak to thy Parents without some Title of Respect, as Sir & Madam.*

4. *Dispute not, nor delay to Obey thy Parents' Commands.*

5. *Go not out of Doors without thy Parents leave, and return within the Time by them limited.*

6. *Quarrel not nor contend with thy Brethren or sisters, but live in love, peace, & unity.*

7. *Grumble not nor be discontented at anything thy Parents appoint, speak, or do.*

8. *Bear with Meekness and Patience, and without Murmuring or Sullenness thy Parents' Reproofs or Corrections: Even tho' it should so happen that they be causeless or undeserved.*

Source: Adapted from Wadsworth, 1712, in Scott and Wishy, 1982. For George Washington's rules of civil behavior for adults, see Haslett (2004).

living by washing, mending, nursing, serving as midwives, or producing cure-all and beauty potions.

Some widows continued their husbands' businesses in masculine areas such as chocolate and mustard production, soap making, cutlery, coach making, rope making, publishing, printing, horseshoeing, net making, and whaling and running grocery stores, bookstores, drugstores, and hardware stores. And some of these businesswomen advertised regularly in the local newspapers (Matthaei, 1982).

In general, however, the economic roles of women, especially wives, were severely constrained. Women had little access to credit, could not sue to collect debts, were not allowed to own property, and were rarely chosen as executors of wills (Ryan, 1983).

Children's Lives

Poor sanitation, crude housing, limited hygiene, and dangerous physical environments characterized colonial America. Between 10 percent and 30 percent of all children died before their first birthday, and fewer than two out of three children lived to see their tenth birthday. Cotton Mather (1663–1728) fathered 14 children, but only one outlived his father: seven died shortly after birth, one died at age 2, and five died in their early 20s (Stannard, 1979).

Since you asked . . .

- Why did colonial women have so many children?

Children's lives were dominated by the concepts of repression, religion, and respect (Adams, 1980). Puritans believed that children were born with original sin and were inherently stubborn, willful, selfish, and corrupt. The entire community—parents, school, church, and neighbors—worked together to keep children in their place.

Compared with contemporary children, colonial children were expected to be extraordinarily well behaved, obedient, and docile (see *Figure 3.1*). Within 40 years of their arrival in Plymouth, however, many colonists worried that their families were disintegrating, that parents were becoming less responsible, and that children were becoming less respectful of authority. Ministers repeatedly warned parents that their children were frequenting taverns, keeping "vicious company," and "tending to dissoluteness (unrestrained and immoral behavior)" (Mintz and Kellogg, 1988: 17). These concerns sound pretty modern, don't they?

Wealthy southern families were more indulgent of their children than were well-to-do families in the northern colonies, but in less affluent families child labor was nearly universal. Even very young children worked hard, either in their own homes as indentured servants or as slaves. For example, several shiploads of "friendless boys and girls," who had been kidnapped in England, were sent to the Virginia colony to provide cheap and submissive labor for American planters (Queen et al., 1985).

Because girls were expected to be homemakers, they received little formal education. The New England colonies educated boys, but girls were generally barred from schooling. They were commonly admitted to public schools only during the hours and seasons when boys were occupied with other affairs or were needed in the fields. As one farmer stated, "In winter it's too far for girls to walk; in summer they ought to stay at home to help in the kitchen" (quoted in Earle, 1899: 96). Women who succeeded in getting an education were often ridiculed:

John Winthrop—the first governor of the Massachusetts Bay Colony—maintained that such intellectual exertion [as education and writing books] could rot the female mind. He attributed the madness of Ann Hopkins, wife of the Connecticut governor, to her intellectual curiosity: "If she had attended her household affairs . . . and not gone out of her way to meddle in the affairs of men whose minds are stronger, she'd have kept her wits and might have improved them usefully" (Ryan, 1983: 57).

Social Class and Regional Differences

The experiences of colonial families differed because of a number of regional and social class variations. In a study of Salem, Massachusetts, families between 1790 and 1810, sociologist Bernard Farber (1972) identified three social classes with very different socialization patterns that supported the economic structure:

- In the *merchant class,* or upper class, the patriarchs typically were shipping and commercial entrepreneurs. Family businesses were inherited, and partnerships were expanded through first-cousin marriages.

- Highly skilled occupations, apprenticeship systems, and cooperation among relatives characterized the *artisan class,* or middle class. Children were encouraged to be upwardly mobile and to find secure jobs.

- The *laboring class,* or working class, was made up mainly of migrants to the community. These

people, who had no voting privileges and little education, provided much of the unskilled labor needed by the merchant class.

Colonial families also differed from one region to another. In the northern colonies, people settled in villages; in the southern colonies, they settled on isolated plantations and farms. There was an especially rigid stratification system among wealthy families, poor whites, indentured servants, and black slaves in the southern colonies.

After reading this section, some of my students dismiss the colonial family as a relic of the past. Others believe that their families of orientation reflect some similar characteristics. Take the quiz "How Colonial Is Your Family?" to decide for yourself.

EARLY AMERICAN FAMILIES FROM NON-EUROPEAN CULTURES

European explorers and settlers who invaded North America in the sixteenth and seventeenth centuries pushed the original inhabitants, American Indians and Mexicans, out of their territories. Except for adults who arrived in the colonies as servants—and in general they chose to indenture themselves—African Americans are the only people who did not come to America voluntarily.

The experiences of these three groups were quite different. Some families and tribes fared better than others, and there was considerable diversity within each group.

American Indians

Many anthropologists believe that American Indians migrated to North America from northeastern Asia over a period of 30,000 years. By the time European settlers arrived, there were almost 18 million Indians living in North America who spoke approximately 300 languages. Tribes today speak 150 native languages, but many are vanishing quickly (Greenberg and Ruhlen, 1992; Trimble and Medicine, 1993; Ashburn, 2007; see, also, Chapter 4).

American Indians were enormously diverse racially, culturally, and linguistically. This variation was reflected in kinship and family systems as well as in interpersonal relations.

Since you asked . . .

▶ Is it true that American Indian women were dominated by their men?

FAMILY STRUCTURE Family structures and customs varied from one Indian society to another. For

Applying What You've Learned

❖ How Colonial Is Your Family?

Answer the following questions based on the family you grew up in.

Yes	No	
☐	☐	**1.** The main focus of my family was making ends meet.
☐	☐	**2.** The children in our family began to do chores as early as possible.
☐	☐	**3.** Discipline was harsh at times.
☐	☐	**4.** The needs of the family were more important than individual needs.
☐	☐	**5.** Our family was the center of our everyday lives.
☐	☐	**6.** Religion was a main theme in our family.
☐	☐	**7.** Father's rule was most important in our family.
☐	☐	**8.** We learned basic reading, writing, and arithmetic at home.
☐	☐	**9.** We had to get along with one another.
☐	☐	**10.** My parents often ignored my feelings.
☐	☐	**11.** My parents had a big say in whom I dated.
☐	☐	**12.** For my parents, romance was not as important as hard work in a potential mate.
☐	☐	**13.** My parents didn't really love each other.
☐	☐	**14.** One of my parents was subordinate to the other most of the time.
☐	☐	**15.** My parents still have strong control over my life.

Source: Based on Hammond and Bearnson, 2003: 24.

KEY TO "HOW COLONIAL IS YOUR FAMILY?"
Add up all the "yes" answers. A score of 15 represents high colonial family traits. A score of 0 signifies no traits. If you received a high score, does this surprise you? Do high scores suggest that many modern families have traces of the colonial family? Or not?

example, polygyny was common in more than 20 percent of marriages among Indians of the Great Plains and the northwest coast. In contrast, monogamy was the norm among the Hopi, Iroquois, and Huron nations. Some groups, such as the Creek, allowed polygyny, but few men took more than one wife because only the best hunters could support more than one wife and all of the children (Price, 1981; Braund, 1990).

Approximately 25 percent of North American Indian tribes were **matrilineal,** which means that children traced their family descent through their mother's line rather than through that of the father (**patrilineal**). The women owned the houses, the household furnishings, the fields and gardens, the work tools, and the livestock, and all this property was passed on to their female heirs (Mathes, 1981).

Historians say that Indian women were often better off than their white counterparts. In contrast to filmmakers' stereotypes of the docile "squaw," Indian women actually wielded considerable power and commanded respect in many bands and tribes. The box "American Indian Women: Chiefs, Physicians, Politicians, and Warriors" describes some of the roles of Indian women.

MARRIAGE AND DIVORCE American Indian women typically married between ages 12 and 15, after reaching puberty. Men married at slightly older ages, between 15 and 20, usually after they had proven their ability to hunt and to provide for a family. Some parents arranged their children's marriages; others allowed young men and women to choose their own spouses.

Family structures and customs also varied. Among the Shoshone, there were no formal marriage ceremonies; the families simply exchanged gifts. Also, there were no formal rules of residence. The newly married couple could live with the family of either the groom or the bride or establish its own independent home.

Among the Zuñi of the Southwest, marriages were arranged casually, and the groom moved into

Cross-Cultural and Multicultural Families

American Indian Women: Chiefs, Physicians, Politicians, and Warriors

European Christian missionaries and U.S. federal government agents saw Indian women as too powerful and independent and discouraged egalitarian gender roles that many American Indian tribes espoused. Nonetheless, many American Indian women and men had equal relationships. Besides being wives and mothers, they were also chiefs, physicians, politicians, and warriors.

Chiefs: In some cases, women became chiefs because of their achievements in battle. In other cases, they replaced husbands who died. Like their male counterparts, female chiefs could declare war, resolve disputes in the community, and punish offenders.

Physicians: Women could be medicine women, or shamans, the Indian equivalent of doctors. In many Indian cultures, women also played crucial roles as spiritual leaders.

Politicians: Because a number of tribes were matrilineal and matrilocal, many women had political power. Among the Lakota, for example, a man owned only his clothing, a horse for hunting, weapons, and spiritual items. Homes, furnishings, and other property belonged to women. In many tribes, women were influential decision makers.

Warriors: Among the Apache, some women warriors were as courageous as the men, and Cheyenne women distinguished themselves in war. Lakota women maintained warrior societies, and among the Cherokee, one of the fiercest warriors was a woman who also headed a women's military society.

Women could stop war parties by refusing to supply the food needed for the journey. An Iroquois woman could initiate a war party by demanding that a captive be obtained to replace a murdered member of her clan. Creek women often were responsible for raising "war fervor" against enemies (Mathes, 1981; Braund, 1990; Stockel, 1991; Jaimes and Halsey, 1992).

❖ Stop and Think . . .

- How did the roles of many white female colonists differ from those of their American Indian counterparts?

Lozen, an Apache Indian, was a brave warrior and fought alongside Geronimo in the late 1800s. She was also a midwife and a healer.

- Does this description of the varied roles American Indian women assumed reflect the images of them that you've seen in Hollywood movies or television shows?

---

the bride's household. Divorce was easy among the Zuñi and other tribes. If a wife was fed up with a demanding husband, she would simply put his belongings outside their home, and they were no longer married. The man accepted the dismissal and returned to his mother's household. If a husband wanted a divorce, he would tell his wife he was going hunting and then not return home (Stockel, 1991).

In the Great Plains, most Teton parents arranged marriages, but some unions were based on romantic love. Marriages were often lifetime associations, but divorce was easy and fairly common. A man could divorce a wife for adultery, laziness, or even excessive nagging. Both parties usually agreed to divorce, but a man could humiliate a wife by casting her off publicly at a dance or other ceremony.

CHILDREN Most Indian families were small because of high infant and child death rates. In addition, mothers nursed their children for several years, often abstaining from sexual relations until the child was weaned.

Among most American Indian nations, childhood was a happy time and parents were generally kind and loving. Mohave and Zuñi parents, for example, were indulgent; children were carefree, and discipline was rare and mild. Children were taught to be polite and gentle. Unruly children were frightened into conformity by stories of religious bogeymen rather than by physical punishment. Grandparents on both sides of the family played an active role in educating children and telling stories that reinforced the tribe's values.

PUBERTY In most Indian societies, puberty rites were more elaborate for girls than for boys. Among the Alaskan Nabesna, for example, a newly menstruating girl was secluded, forbidden to touch her body (lest sores break out) or to travel with the tribe, and had

Mother Goose & Grimm

to observe strict food taboos. In contrast, among the Mohave, the observance of a girl's puberty was a private family matter that did not include any community rituals.

Among the Teton, a boy's puberty was marked by a series of events, such as his first successful bison hunt, his first war party, his first capture of enemy horses, and other brave deeds, all of which his father commemorated with feasts and gifts to other members of the tribe.

Some tribes also emphasized the *vision quest,* a supernatural experience. After fasting and taking ritual purifying baths in a small, dome-shaped sweat lodge, a young boy left the camp and found an isolated place, often the top of a butte or other elevated spot. He then waited for a vision in which a supernatural being instructed him on his responsibilities as an adult (Spencer and Jennings, 1977).

THE IMPACT OF EUROPEAN CULTURES The French, Spanish, Portuguese, and British played a major role in destroying much of American Indian culture. Europeans exploited the abundant North American resources of gold, hardwood forests, fertile land, and fur. Missionaries, determined to convert the "savages" to Christianity, were responsible for some of the cultural destruction. Disregarding important cultural values and beliefs, missionaries tried to eliminate religious ceremonies and practices such as polygyny and matrilineal inheritance (Price, 1981).

Indian tribes coped with military slaughter, enslavement, forced labor, land confiscation, coerced mass migration, and involuntary religious conversions (Collier, 1947). By the end of the seventeenth century, staggering numbers of American Indians in the East had died from diseases for which they had no immunity, such as influenza, measles, smallpox, and typhus. The Plymouth colony was located in a deserted Indian village whose inhabitants had been devastated by epidemics carried by European settlers.

By the 1670s, only 10 percent of the original American Indian population of New England survived. At least 50 tribes became extinct as a result of disease and massacre. In the eighteenth and nineteenth centuries, the diversity of American Indian family practices was reduced even further through ongoing missionary activities, intrusive federal land policies, and intermarriage with outside groups (John, 1988).

African Americans

One colonist wrote in his journal that on August 20, 1619, at the Jamestown settlement in Virginia, "there came . . . a Dutch man-of-warre that sold us 20 negars." These first African Americans were brought over as indentured servants. After their terms of service, they were free to buy land, marry, and hire their own labor.

These rights were short lived, however. By the mid-1660s, the southern colonies had passed laws prohibiting blacks from testifying in court, owning property, making contracts, legally marrying, traveling without permission, and congregating in public places. The slave trade grew in both the northern and southern colonies over several decades.

Some early statesmen, such as President Thomas Jefferson, publicly denounced slavery but supported it privately. In 1809, for example, Jefferson maintained that "the Negro slave in America must be removed beyond the reach of mixture" for the preservation of the "dignity" and "beauty" of the white race. At the same time, Jefferson had a slave mistress, Sally Hemmings, and fathered children with her. Inconsistent to the end, he freed five of his slaves in his will but left the other 182 slaves to his heirs (Bergman, 1969).

> **Since you asked . . .**
>
> :• Did slavery destroy the black family?

FAMILY STRUCTURE Until the 1970s, sociologists and historians maintained that slavery had emasculated

A Slave Auction

Constraints

In the mid-1970s, Alex Haley, a journalist who had taught himself to read and write and had a 20-year career in the U.S. Coast Guard, was catapulted to fame when his book *Roots: The Saga of an American Family* (1976) became a best-seller and was made into one of the first miniseries on television. In the book, Haley traced six generations of his ancestors, the first of whom was abducted at age 16 from Gambia, West Africa, in 1767. The following excerpt is a powerful description of how African families were destroyed by slavery:

During the day a number of sales were made. David and Caroline were purchased together by a Natchez planter. They left us, grinning broadly, and in a most happy state of mind, caused by the fact of their not being separated. Sethe was sold to a planter of Baton Rouge, her eyes flashing with anger as she was led away.

The same man also purchased Randall. The little fellow was made to jump, and run across the floor, and perform many other feats, exhibiting his activity and condition. All the time the trade was going on, Eliza was crying aloud

and wringing her hands. She besought the man not to buy him, unless he also bought herself and Emily. She promised, in that case, to be the most faithful slave that ever lived.

The man answered that he could not afford it, and then Eliza burst into a paroxysm of grief, weeping plaintively. Freeman turned round to her, savagely, with his whip in his uplifted hand, ordering her to stop her noise, or he would flog her. Unless she ceased that minute, he would take her to the yard and give her a hundred lashes. . . . Eliza shrunk before him and tried to wipe away her tears, but it was all in vain. She wanted to be with her children, she said, the little time she had to live.

All the frowns and threats of Freeman could not wholly silence the afflicted mother. She kept on begging and beseeching them, most piteously, not to separate the three. Over and over again she told them how she loved her boy. A great many times she repeated her former promises—how very faithful and obedient she would be, how hard she would labor day

and night, to the last moment of her life, if he would only buy them all together.

But it was of no avail; the man could not afford it. The bargain was agreed upon, and Randall must go alone. Then Eliza ran to him, embraced him passionately, kissed him again and again, and told him to remember her—all the while her tears falling in the boy's face like rain.

Freeman damned her, calling her a blubbering, bawling wench, and ordered her to go to her place, and behave herself, and be somebody. . . . He would soon give her something to cry about, if she was not mighty careful, and that she might depend on.

The planter from Baton Rouge, with his new purchase, was ready to depart. "Don't cry, mama. I will be a good boy. Don't cry," said Randall, looking back, as they passed out of the door.

What has become of the lad, God knows. It was a mournful scene indeed. I would have cried myself if I had dared.

Source: Adapted from Solomon Northrup, cited in Meltzer (1964: 87–89).

---

black fathers, forced black mothers to become the matriarchs of their families, and destroyed the African American family. Historian Herbert Gutman (1983) dispelled many of these beliefs with his study of 21 urban and rural communities in the South between 1855 and 1880. Gutman found that 70 to 90 percent of African American households were made up of a husband and wife (although they couldn't marry legally) or a single parent and her or his children.

Most women were heads of households not because they had never married, but because their husbands had died or were sold to another owner. Women usually had only one or two children. Thus, according to Gutman, in the nineteenth century, black families were stable, intact, and resilient.

MARRIAGE Throughout the colonies, it was difficult for a slave to find a spouse. In northern cities, most slaves lived with their masters and were not allowed to associate with other slaves. In the southern colonies,

most slaves lived on plantations that had fewer than ten slaves. Because the plantations were far apart, it was difficult for slave men and women to find a mate of roughly the same age. In addition, overwork and high death rates due to disease meant that marriages did not last very long (Mintz and Kellogg, 1988).

To ensure that slaves would remain on the plantations and bear future slaves, many owners encouraged them to marry (even though the marriages were not recognized legally) and to have large families. Yet marriages were fragile. As the box "A Slave Auction" shows, owners often separated family members. Studies of slave families in Mississippi, Tennessee, and Louisiana show that such auctions ended 35 to 40 percent of marriages (Gutman, 1976; Matthaei, 1982).

HUSBANDS AND FATHERS Several black scholars have noted that white, male, middle-class historians and sociologists have misrepresented the slave family (McAdoo, 1986; Staples, 1988). One example is the portrayal of husbands and fathers. In contrast to popular conceptions of the African American male as powerless, adult male slaves provided important role models for boys:

Trapping wild turkeys required considerable skill; not everyone could construct a "rabbit gum" equal to the guile of the rabbits; and running down the quick, battling raccoon took pluck. For a boy growing up, the moment when his father thought him ready to join in the hunting and to learn to trap was a much-sought recognition of his own manhood (Genovese, 1981: 239–40).

These activities increased families' nutritional intake and supplemented monotonous and inadequate diets.

African male slaves also often served as surrogate fathers to many children, both blood relatives and others. Black preachers, whose eloquence and morality commanded the respect of the entire community, were also influential role models. Men made shoes, wove baskets, constructed furniture, and cultivated the tiny garden plots allotted to their families by the master (Jones, 1985).

WIVES AND MOTHERS Many historians describe African American women as survivors who resisted the slave system. Mothers raised their children, cooked, made clothes for their families, maintained the slave cabin, and toiled in the fields. Because the African American woman was often both a mammy to the plantation owner's children and a mother to her own, she experienced the exhausting *double day*—a full day of domestic chores plus a full day of work outside the home—at least a century before middle-class white women coined the term and later substituted *second shift* for *double day* (see Chapters 5 and 13).

Black women got little recognition for such grueling schedules and were often subjected to physical punishment. Pregnant slaves were sometimes forced to lie face down in a specially dug depression in the ground, which protected the fetus while the mother was beaten, and some nursing mothers were whipped until "blood and milk flew mingled from their breasts" (Jones, 1985: 20).

In the South, children as young as 2 or 3 were put to work. They fetched things or carried the train of a mistress's dress. Masters often gave slave children to their own offspring as gifts (Schwartz, 2000).

Only a few female slaves worked in the master's home, known as "the big house." Most females over age 10 worked in the fields, sunup to sundown, six days a week. As a result, mothers had to struggle to maintain a semblance of family life:

Occasionally, women were permitted to leave the fields early on Saturday to perform some chores around the slave quarters. Their homes were small

The kitchens were so hot, especially in summer, there was often a separate building to prevent fires and keep the temperature down in the main house.

cabins of one or two rooms, which they usually shared with their mate and their children, and perhaps another family secluded behind a crude partition (Ryan, 1983: 159).

Popular films such as *Gone with the Wind* often portray house slaves as doing little more than adjusting Miss Scarlett's petticoats and announcing male suitors. In reality, domestic work was as hard as fieldwork. Fetching wood and water, preparing three meals a day over a smoky fireplace, and washing and pressing clothes for an entire family was backbreaking labor.

Female servants sometimes had to sleep on the floor at the foot of the mistress's bed. They were often forced into sexual relations with the master. Injuries were common: Minor infractions met with swift and severe punishment, and servants suffered abuse ranging from jabs with pins to beatings that left them disfigured for life (Jones, 1985).

ECONOMIC SURVIVAL *Ethnic Notions,* a memorable documentary, shows that many Hollywood movies, books, and newspapers have portrayed slaves as helpless, passive, and dependent people who couldn't care for themselves. Recent evidence has challenged such stereotypes. For example, an archaeological team that excavated Virginia plantations found evidence that some enslaved Africans were entrepreneurs: They traded fish and game for children's toys, dishes, and other household items (Wheeler, 1998).

Also, many slaves hid important personal possessions and items stolen from plantation owners in underground storage areas. Thus, slaves were hardly meek or submissive. Instead, they used effective tactics such as negotiating with their masters over assigned tasks and breaking tools to slow the pace of their work (Berlin, 1998; Morgan, 1998).

AFTER EMANCIPATION After slavery was abolished in 1863, many mothers set out to find children from whom they had been separated many years earlier. Numerous slaves formalized their marriages, even though the $1 fee for the marriage license equaled about two weeks' pay for most. A legal marriage was an important status symbol, and a wedding was a festive event (Degler, 1981; Staples, 1988; King, 1996).

Some writers have claimed that the African American family, already disrupted by slavery, was further weakened by migration to cities in the North in the late 1800s (Frazier, 1939; Moynihan, 1970). However, many black migrants tried to maintain contact with their families in the South. When black men migrated alone, "a constant flow of letters containing cash and advice between North and South facilitated the gradual migration of whole clans and even villages" (Jones, 1985: 159). Others returned home frequently to join in community celebrations or to help with planting and harvesting on the family farm. Thus, many African American families remained resilient despite difficult conditions.

Mexican Americans

After 30 years of war and conflict, in 1848 the United States annexed territory in the West and Southwest that was originally part of Mexico. Despite the provisions of the Treaty of Guadalupe Hidalgo, which guaranteed security of their property, the federal government confiscated the land of most Mexican families. Land speculators defrauded countless other landowners. Most of the Mexicans and their descendants became laborers. The loss of land, an important economic base, had long-term negative effects on Mexican American families (see Chapter 4).

WORK AND GENDER Whether they were born and grew up in the United States or migrated from Mexico, Mexican laborers were essential to the prosperity of southwestern businesses. Employers purposely avoided hiring Mexicans for skilled jobs because "they are available in such [great] numbers and . . .they [would] do the most disagreeable work at the lowest wages" (Feldman, 1931: 115).

During the 1800s, men typically worked on the railroads or in mining, agriculture, ranching, or low-level urban occupations (such as dishwashing). Women worked as domestics, cooks, live-in house servants, or laundresses; in canning and packing houses; and in agriculture (Camarillo, 1979).

By the 1930s, Mexican women made up a major portion of the workers in the garment-manufacturing sweatshops in the Southwest. American labor codes stipulated a pay rate of $15 a week, but Mexican women were paid less than $5, and some earned as little as 50 cents a week. If the women protested, they lost their jobs. Illegal migrants were especially vulnerable because they were intimidated by threats of deportation (Acuna, 1988). Despite the economic exploitation they faced, many Mexican families preserved traditional family structures, family roles, and child-rearing practices.

FAMILY STRUCTURE Mexican society was characterized by **familism;** that is, family relationships took precedence over individual well-being. (You'll see in Chapter 4 that familism still characterizes much of contemporary Latino culture, including that of Mexican Americans.) The nuclear family often embraced an extended family of several generations, including cousins, in which kin provided emotional and financial support.

> **Since you asked . . .**
>
> **::•** Why were many Mexican families tightly knit?

A key factor in conserving Mexican culture was the practice of **compadrazgo,** in which parents, children, and the children's godparents maintained close relationships. The *compadres,* or co-parents, were godparents who enlarged family ties, similar to the fictive kin described in Chapter 1. Godparents were close family friends who had strong ties with their godchildren throughout life and participated in rites of passage such as baptism, confirmation, first communion, and marriage.

The godparents in the *compadrazgo* network provided both discipline and support. They expected obedience, respect, and love from their godchildren. They were also warm and affectionate and helped the children financially whenever possible. For girls, who led cloistered and protected lives, visiting their godparents' families was a major source of recreation (Williams, 1990).

FAMILY ROLES Women were the guardians of family traditions, even though many mothers worked outside the home because of economic necessity. Despite the disruptions caused by migratory work, women nurtured Mexican culture through folklore, songs, baptisms, weddings, and celebrations of birthdays and saints' days (Garcia, 1980). In the traditional family, women defined their roles primarily as homemakers and mothers, whereas the male head of the family had all the authority. Masculinity was expressed in the concept of **machismo,** which stresses male attributes such as dominance, assertiveness, pride, and sexual prowess (see Chapter 4 for recent controversies about the *machismo* concept).

This notion of male preeminence carried with it the clear implication of a double standard. Men could engage in premarital and extramarital sex, for example, but women were expected to remain virgins until marriage; to be faithful to their husbands; and to limit their social relationships, even after marriage, to family and female friends (Mirande, 1985; Moore and Pachon, 1985).

CHILDREN The handful of diaries, letters, and other writings available to us today suggests that, at least in middle- and upper-class families, children were socialized according to gender. Boys did some of the same domestic chores as their sisters, but they had much more freedom than girls did. Young girls were severely restricted in their social relationships outside the home. A girl was expected to learn how to be a good mother and wife—a virtuous example for her children and the "soul of society" (del Castillo, 1984: 81).

According to the diary of a teenage girl who lived on the outskirts of San Antonio, Texas, from 1889 to 1892, her brother was responsible for helping with tasks such as laundry and chopping wood. He was allowed to go into town on errands and to travel around the countryside on his horse. In contrast, she was not allowed to go into town with her father and brother or to attend chaperoned dances. She could not visit neighbors, and she attended only one social event in a six-month period, when her family traveled into town to visit her aunt during Christmas (del Castillo, 1984).

THE EUROPEAN INFLUENCE Although they suffered less physical and cultural destruction than American Indians did, Mexican Americans endured a great deal at the hands of European frontiersmen, land speculators, and politicians. By the mid-1800s, when most Mexican Americans were beginning to experience widespread exploitation, newly arrived European immigrant families were also harnessed under the yoke of industrialization.

⁘ MAKING CONNECTIONS

■ Look at *Figure 3.1* on p. 56 again. Some of my students think that such rules for colonial children were ridiculous. Others think that we should resurrect some of these practices because many parents are too permissive. What do you think?

■ Regardless of your cultural heritage, did your ancestors' experiences affect your family's values and behavior?

INDUSTRIALIZATION, URBANIZATION, AND EUROPEAN IMMIGRATION: 1820 TO 1930

The lives of many U.S. families changed dramatically from about 1820 to 1930 as a result of two massive immigration waves from Europe. More than 10 million immigrants—mostly English, Irish, Scandinavian, and German—arrived during the first wave, from 1830 to 1882. During the second wave, from 1882 to 1930, immigrants were predominantly Russian, Greek, Polish, Italian, Austrian, Hungarian, and Slavic.

The Industrial Revolution led to extensive mechanization, which shifted home manufacturing to large-scale factory production. As the economic structure changed, a small group of white, Anglo-Saxon, Protestant (often referred to as WASP), upper-class families prospered from the backbreaking labor of Mexicans, Asians, European immigrants, and many American-born whites. European immigrants endured some of the most severe pressures on family life.

Family Life and Social Class

Immigrants, poor single women and mothers, and low-income family members had to work outside the home to earn enough to purchase goods and services. By the late eighteenth century, the family lost its function as an economic unit in higher-income classes. The growth of new industries, businesses, and professions helped create a new middle class and a new ideology among upper- and middle-class white families about the home, work, and the ideal of womanhood later termed the *cult of domesticity* (Welter, 1966).

THE DEBUT OF THE "CULT OF DOMESTICITY" The **cult of domesticity** glorified women's domestic role. This ideology defined the world of work as male, and the world of the home as female. Women were viewed as less vigorous and forceful than men and therefore less suited to public life, including the rough world of work that exposed people to temptations, violence, danger, corruption, and selfishness.

Such attitudes encouraged separate spheres of activity: By the early 1800s, most middle- and upper-class men's work was totally separated from the household, and family life revolved around the man's struggle to make a living (and be the "bread-winner"). The good wife

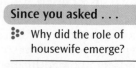

Since you asked . . .

⁘ Why did the role of housewife emerge?

turned the home into a comfortable retreat from the pressures that the man faced in the workplace and stayed home to raise and nurture their children (and be the "housewife").

Characteristics of "True Womanhood"

One author describes nineteenth-century working-class women as "without corsets, matrons with their breasts unrestrained, their armpits damp with sweat, with their hair all over the place, blouses dirty or torn, and stained skirts" (Barret-Ducrocq, 1991: 11). Expectations for upper-class women (whom middle-class women tried to emulate) were quite different because the cult of domesticity required every good and proper young woman to develop and adhere to four cardinal virtues: piety, purity, submission, and domesticity.

Piety True women were believed to be more religious and spiritual than men. Motherhood was a religious obligation, and a lack of religion in females was considered "the most revolting human characteristic." If a woman had to read, she should choose spiritually uplifting books from a list of "morally acceptable authors," preferably religious biographies.

Purity True women were pure in heart, mind, and body, and the loss of virginity before marriage was worse than death. In *The Young Lady's Friend* (1837),

Mrs. John Farrar gave practical advice about staying out of trouble: "Sit not with another in a place that is too narrow; read not out of the same book; let not your eagerness to see anything induce you to place your head close to another person's." Without sexual purity, a woman was a lower form of being, a "fallen woman," unworthy of a man's love and unfit for any company.

Submission Men were the movers and doers, whereas good women were to be passive bystanders. True women were expected to be gentle, passive, obedient, childlike, weak, dependent, and protected. Unlike men, they should work silently, unseen, and only for affection, not for money or ambition. A woman should stifle her own talents and devote herself "to sustain her husband's genius and aid him in his arduous career."

Domesticity Domesticity was a woman's most prized virtue. Woman's place was in the home, which was supposed to be a cheerful place, so that

brothers, husbands, and sons would not go elsewhere to have a good time. Women should keep busy at morally uplifting tasks, one of which was housework. For example, the repetitiveness of routine tasks (such as making beds) inculcated patience and perseverance, and proper management of the home was considered a complex art: "There is more to be learned about pouring out tea and coffee than most young ladies are willing to believe."

Sources: Welter, 1966: 151–74; Ryan, 1983.

Stop and Think . . .

- How do you think that the characteristics of true womanhood affected attitudes toward poor, employed, minority, and immigrant women?

- How did the cult of domesticity shape many women's and men's roles in terms of their choices and constraints? Do you think that any of the four virtues still reflect our attitudes toward women today?

Between 1820 and 1860, women's magazines, ministers' sermons, and physicians in popular health books defined and applauded the attributes of "true womanhood." Women were judged as "good" if they displayed four cardinal virtues (see the box "Characteristics of 'True Womanhood'").

New attitudes about the true woman became paramount in redefining the role of the wife as nurturer and caregiver rather than as workmate. Many lower socioeconomic women were not seen as true women because, like men, they worked outside the home. In these social classes, many children often dropped out of school to work and to help support their families. In addition, most spouses in these families had little time to show love and affection to their children or to each other.

As romantic love became the basis for marriage, couples had more freedom in choosing their partners based on compatibility and personal attraction. As households became more private, ties with the larger community became more fragile, and spouses turned to each other for affection and happiness much more than in the past (Skolnick, 1991).

CHILDREN AND ADOLESCENTS Fathers' control over their children began to erode. By the end of the

seventeenth century, fathers had less land to divide among their sons. This meant that they had less authority over their children's sexual behavior and choice of a marriage partner. The percentage of women who were pregnant at the time of their marriage shot up to more than 40 percent by the mid-eighteenth century, suggesting that parents had become less effective in preventing premarital intercourse (Mintz and Kellogg, 1988).

Because a marriage was less likely to involve a distribution of the family's land and property, children were less dependent on their fathers for economic support. Moreover, new opportunities for nonagricultural work, along with labor shortages in cities, prompted many children to leave home and thus escape from the authority of strict fathers.

Perhaps the biggest change was that, largely in the middle class, adults started to view and treat children as more than "miniature adults." Children began to spend more time playing than working, and adolescence became a stage of life that did not involve adult responsibilities.

People published more books for and about children. Adults began to recognize children's individuality by giving them names that were different from their father's or mother's. They also began, for the

These Pennsylvania miners and "breaker boys"—youngsters who sorted the mined coal into categories—worked as many as 14 hours a day for very low pay. Like most miners of this period, they were immigrants who performed back-breaking labor during the U.S. Industrial Revolution.

With the advent of the Industrial Revolution in the United States, young women made up a large segment of the new factory labor force, especially in textile mills. They worked six days a week, 12 or more hours a day. The wages were low, the factories were poorly lit and unventilated, and the machinery was often unsafe, resulting in injuries.

first time, to celebrate birthdays, especially those of children. There was also a decline in physical punishment, and physicians and others began to recognize the early onset of sexual feelings in children (Ariès, 1962; Degler, 1981; Demos, 1986).

Among the working classes and the poor, however, child labor was widespread, and children were a critical resource in their family's survival. In a survey of Massachusetts working-class families in 1875, for example, children under age 15 contributed nearly 20 percent of their family's income (Mintz and Kellogg, 1988).

The Impact of Immigration and Urbanization

Immigration played a key role in the Industrial Revolution in the United States. Immigrants provided a large pool of unskilled and semi-skilled labor that fueled emerging industries and gave investors huge profits.

In the first large waves of immigration in the late 1800s, paid middlemen arranged for the shipment of immigrants to waiting industries. For example, Asians were channeled into the western railroads, Italians were funneled into public works projects and used as strikebreakers, and Hungarians were directed toward the Pennsylvania coal mines. Later immigrants followed these established paths into industrial America (Bodner, 1985).

Very few immigrant families escaped dire poverty. Because men's wages were low, most married women were also in the labor force. Some worked at home making artificial flowers, threading wires through tags, or crocheting over curtain rings. Some were cleaning women or seamstresses, did laundry, or sold cakes. Others took in boarders and lodgers, especially after their children left home (Hareven, 1984; Weatherford, 1986).

Like the men, women of different ethnic groups tended to move into specific jobs. For example, Italian women were more likely than Polish or Greek women to reject domestic labor, which would take them out of the Italian community and into other people's homes. Instead, they were more likely to work as seasonal laborers for fruit- and vegetable-processing companies and to do seamstress work at home (Squier and Quadagno, 1988). By the turn of the nineteenth century, a woman's occupation was usually tied to her race and ethnicity. That is, Asian, African American, and immigrant women worked in laundering, food processing, tobacco production, and textile factories, whereas white women—especially those with some schooling—were stenographers and teachers.

Family Life and Work

By 1890, all but 9 of the 369 industries listed by the U.S. Census Bureau employed women. Many of these industries were especially eager to hire "greenhorns" and women "just off the boat" who would work for low wages. Green-horns were often under-paid or not paid at all. In

Since you asked . . .

⁘• Are employed mothers a modern phenomenon?

Cross-Cultural and Multicultural Families

Stereotypes about European Immigrants

On October 28, 1886, President Grover Cleveland dedicated the Statue of Liberty in New York Harbor, on whose pedestal are inscribed Emma Lazarus's famous welcoming words: "Give me your tired, your poor, your huddled masses yearning to breathe free." As the following examples show, however, Lazarus's poem did not reflect the reality:

> 1886: The U.S. consul in Budapest advised that Hungarian immigrants were not "a desirable acquisition" because, he claimed, they lacked ambition and would work as cheaply as the Chinese, which would interfere "with a civilized laborer's earning a 'white' laborer's wages."
>
> 1891: Congressman Henry Cabot Lodge called for restrictions on immigration because (referring especially to Jewish and Polish immigrants) the immigrants represented the "lowest and most illiterate classes," which were "alien to the body of the American people."

1910: Members of the eugenics movement contended that through intermarriage, immigration would contaminate the "old stock" of white Anglo-Saxon Americans with feeblemindedness, criminality, and pauperism. Many eugenicists, such as Robert DeCouncey Ward of Harvard, were faculty members at prestigious eastern universities.

1914: Edward A. Ross, a prominent sociologist at the University of Wisconsin and a self-proclaimed immigration watchdog, wrote: "That the Mediterranean people are morally below the races of northern Europe is as certain as any social fact."

1922: Kenneth L. Roberts, a Cornell graduate, served as a correspondent for the *Saturday Evening Post* on immigration questions. He warned that "if a few more million members of the Alpine, Mediterranean, and Semitic races are poured among us, the result must

inevitably be a hybrid race of people as worthless and futile as the good-for-nothing mongrels of Central America and Southeastern Europe."

1946: After World War II, the immigration of displaced persons revived old fears. Several influential senators argued that political immigrants should not be permitted to enter the United States because of their "alien philosophies" and "biological incompatibility with Americans' parent stocks."

Source: Carlson and Colburn, 1972: 311–50.

⁘ Stop and Think . . .

- Did your ancestors experience prejudice and discrimination? Did such experiences shape how they raised their children?

- If you're a recent immigrant, what kinds of prejudice and discrimination have you and your family encountered?

---

some cases, employers delayed wage payments for several months and then closed their shops, disappearing overnight (Manning, 1970).

By the late 1800s, Irish girls as young as 11 were leaving home to work as servants; 75 percent of all Irish teenage girls were domestic servants. Even though they were hired only for housekeeping, many had to care for children, were sexually assaulted by their male employers, and were not paid their full wages (Ryan, 1983).

Most manufacturing jobs were segregated by sex. In the tobacco industry, for example, even though cigar rolling traditionally had been a woman's task in Slavic countries, men obtained these well-paying jobs. Immigrant women were relegated to damp and smelly basements, where they stripped the tobacco, which was then rolled by men who worked "upstairs" under better conditions and for much higher wages (Ryan, 1983).

HOUSING One of the biggest problems for immigrant families was the lack of decent housing in densely

populated cities. One Philadelphia tenement house, for example, housed 30 families in 34 rooms. A Lithuanian couple and their five children lived in a tiny closet of a home that contained only slightly more air space than the law required for one adult. The buildings were jammed together so tightly that the immigrant population of one block in New York City was equal to that of an entire town. Women increased their kitchen wall space by reaching out the window and hanging utensils on the outside wall of the house next door (Weatherford, 1986).

HEALTH Epidemics and disease were rampant among immigrant families. A cholera epidemic that barely touched the rest of New York City's population killed nearly 20 percent of the residents of a crowded immigrant neighborhood. Because a third of tenement rooms had no windows or ventilation, many immigrants contracted tuberculosis, which, at the time, was incurable.

In Lawrence, Massachusetts, where 90 percent of the population consisted of immigrants, a third of the spinners in the textile mills died of respiratory diseases, such as pneumonia and tuberculosis, before they had worked there for ten years. These diseases were triggered by the lint, dust, and machine fumes of the unventilated mills. Moreover, the excruciating noise of the mills often resulted in deafness, and many workers were injured by faulty machines (Weatherford, 1986).

FAMILY CONFLICT Epidemics and dilapidated housing weren't the only problems the immigrant families faced. Most suffered many of the ills that come with poverty and isolation in a strange and often hostile new environment: crime, delinquency, a breakdown of marital and family relations, and general demoralization. Living quarters shared with relatives put additional pressures on already strained marital ties (Thomas and Znaniecki, 1927).

PREJUDICE AND DISCRIMINATION Like American Indians, Mexicans, and African Americans, most European immigrants met with enormous prejudice, discrimination, and economic exploitation. Much inequality was created and reinforced by high-ranking, highly respected, and influential people who had been educated in the most prestigious colleges and universities in the United States (see the box "Stereotypes about European Immigrants" on p. 67).

Despite the prejudice and discrimination they encountered, most immigrant families overcame enormous obstacles. Rarely complaining, they worked at low-status jobs with low wages and encouraged their children to achieve and move up the social class ladder.

THE MODERN FAMILY EMERGES

The Great Depression of the 1930s, World War II, the baby boom of the 1950s, and the increasing economic and political unrest of the decades since the 1960s have all influenced the American family—sometimes for better, sometimes for worse. Some social scientists maintain that the modern family emerged around 1830: Courtship became more open, marriages were often based on affection rather than financial considerations, and parents centered more of their attention on children. Others believe that the modern family emerged at the beginning of the twentieth century, especially with the rise of the "companionate family" (Burgess et al., 1963; Degler, 1983).

The Rise of the Companionate Family (1900–1930)

At the turn of the twentieth century, married couples, particularly in the white middle class, morphed into what sociologists Ernest Burgess and Harvey Locke (1945) called the **companionate family.** These were families that were built on mutual affection, sexual attraction, compatibility, and personal happiness between husbands and wives. Thus, unlike the past, husbands and wives weren't just economic units, but depended on each other for company and a sense of togetherness. The companionate family also included a couple's children: The affection between parents and children was more intimate and more open, and adolescents enjoyed greater freedom from parental supervision.

This new independence generated criticism, however. Many popular magazines, such as *The Atlantic Monthly, The Ladies' Home Journal,* and the *New Republic,* contained articles with concerns about "young people's rejection of genteel manners, their defiant clothing and hairstyles, their slang-filled language, and their 'lewd' pastimes . . . (such as smoking, attending petting parties, and going out on school nights). Public condemnation and moral outrage were widespread" (Mintz and Kellogg, 1988: 119). Do any of these complaints about young people sound familiar?

The Great Depression (1929–1939)

On October 29, l929, the U.S. stock market crashed and the Great Depression of the 1930s began. By 1932, massive layoffs put millions out of work. Banks failed, wiping out many families' savings. Hunger became common and long breadlines formed at charities distributing food. Still, families had a wide variety of experiences, resulting from factors such as residence, social class, gender, race, and ethnicity.

URBAN AND RURAL RESIDENCE Many people who farmed land owned by others could not pay their rent either in cash or in a share of the crops. Husbands sometimes left their families to search for jobs. Some women who could not cope with such desertion took drastic steps to end their misery. In 1938, for example, in Nebraska, a mother of 13 children committed suicide by walking into the side of a train because "she had had enough" (Fink, 1992: 172).

Even when husbands remained at home, some families lost their land and personal possessions. Parents made enormous sacrifices to feed their children. As one jobless father stated, "We do not dare to use even a little soap when it will pay for an extra egg or a few more carrots for our children" (McElvaine, 1993: 172).

> **Since you asked . . .**
>
> ⁝• Did the Great Depression have a devastating impact on *all* Americans?

To help support their families, many young men and women who had been raised on farms moved to cities seeking jobs. Young women were more likely to find jobs because there was a demand for low-paid

Some working-class children became part of the "transient army" that drifted from town to town looking for work. Most slept in lice-ridden and rat-infested housing when they could afford to pay 10 or 15 cents for a urine-stained mattress on the floor. Others slept on park benches, under shrubbery and bridges, in doorways, in packing crates, or in abandoned automobiles (Watkins, 1993).

As blue-collar employment in the male-dominated industrial sectors decreased, white-collar clerical and government jobs increased. Women took many of these jobs. The wages of white, middle-class women enabled their families, even during the Great Depression, to maintain the standard of living and consumer habits that they had enjoyed during the affluent 1920s.

Upper-middle-class families fared even better. Fairly affluent families made only minor sacrifices. Some families cut back on entertainment, did not renew country club memberships, and decreased services such as domestic help. Few reported cutbacks in their food budgets, however, and many of these families continued to take summer vacations and buy new cars (Morgan, 1939).

RACE The Great Depression was an economic disaster for many white people, but African Americans suffered even more. Unemployment was much higher among blacks than among whites. As layoffs began in 1929 and accelerated in the following years, blacks were often the first to be fired. By 1932, black unemployment had reached approximately 50 percent, twice as high as the national average. As the economic situation deteriorated, many whites successfully demanded that employers replace blacks with whites in unskilled occupations such as garbage collector, elevator operator, waiter, bellhop, and street cleaner.

In some government jobs, employers set an unofficial quota of 10 percent black, on the theory that this represented, roughly, the percentage of African Americans in the general population. In fact, the percentage of government employees who were black was only about 6 percent. Even those who were able to keep their jobs faced great hardship. A study conducted in Harlem in 1935 found that the wages of skilled black workers who could find work dropped nearly 50 percent during the Great Depression (McElvaine, 1993; Watkins, 1993).

GENDER ROLES In many families, unemployment wreaked havoc on gender roles. The authority of the husband and father was based on his occupation and his role as provider. If he lost his job, he often suffered a decline in status within the family. Understandably, men were despondent: "Sometimes the father did not go to bed but moved from chair to chair all night long" (Cavan and Ranck, cited in Griswold, 1993: 148).

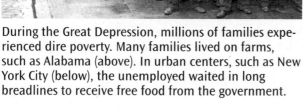

During the Great Depression, millions of families experienced dire poverty. Many families lived on farms, such as Alabama (above). In urban centers, such as New York City (below), the unemployed waited in long breadlines to receive free food from the government.

domestic help. The money they sent home from their wages of $10 or so a week helped their families buy clothes and other necessities.

SOCIAL CLASS The most devastating impact of the Great Depression was felt by working-class and poor families. More than half of all married women—especially those in poor southern states such as South Carolina, Mississippi, Louisiana, Georgia, and Alabama—were employed in low-paying domestic service or factory jobs (Cavan and Ranck, 1938; Chafe, 1972).

When working-class mothers found jobs, older children, especially girls, looked after their younger brothers and sisters and often had to drop out of school to do so (McElvaine, 1993). Boys were expected to work after school or drop out of school to supplement their family's meager income. In contrast to middle-class children, those from working-class families did not enjoy a carefree adolescence.

Men who could not provide for their families often became depressed, preoccupied and abusive; drank more; or spent much of their time searching for jobs. As fathers became physically and emotionally distant, their power in the family and their children's respect for them often decreased, and adolescents became more independent and rebellious (Griswold, 1993).

In 1932, an executive order decreed that only one spouse could work for the federal government. The widespread unemployment of men therefore put pressure on women, especially married women, to resign from some occupations. In addition, school boards fired married female teachers, and some companies dismissed married women. More than 77 percent of the school districts in the United States would not hire married women, and 50 percent had a policy of firing women who got married (Milkman, 1976; McElvaine, 1993).

When women did work, the federal government endorsed lower pay rates for women. For example, the federal Works Progress Administration (WPA) paid men $5 per day, compared with only $3 for women (Milkman, 1976).

World War II (1939–1945)

World War II triggered even greater changes in work roles and family life. Families began to experience these changes after the United States entered the war in 1941.

WORK ROLES Workers were scarce, especially in the defense and manufacturing industries, because many able-bodied men had been drafted. Initially, employers were unwilling to recruit women for traditionally male jobs. And many women, especially white middle-class women, were reluctant to violate traditional gender roles.

In 1942, however, prompted by both the Women's Bureau of the U.S. Department of Labor and organized women's groups, employers began to fill many jobs, especially those in nontraditional positions, with women. The government, supported by the mass media, was enormously successful in convincing both men and women that a woman's place was in the workplace and not the home:

In all the media, women at work were pictured and praised, and the woman who did not at least work as a volunteer for the Red Cross was made to feel guilty. . . . Even the movies joined in. The wife or sweetheart who stayed behind and went to work became as familiar a figure as the valiant soldier-lover for whom she waited (Banner, 1984: 219).

Millions of women, including mothers and even grandmothers, worked in shipyards, steel mills, and

Millions of women worked in American factories, steel mills, and shipyards during World War II. Many found it hard to give up their new-found jobs and financial independence, but most were replaced by men who returned from the war in 1945.

ammunition factories (see Data Digest). They welded, dug ditches, and operated forklifts. For the first time, black women were recruited into high-paying jobs, making some of the greatest economic gains of all women during that period.

Hundreds of thousands of domestic servants and farm workers left their jobs for much better-paying positions in the defense and other industries. In the superb documentary film, *The Life and Times of Rosie the Riveter,* black women describe the pride and exhilaration they felt at having well-paying jobs that they genuinely enjoyed.

Because of the labor shortage, this was the only time when even working-class women were praised for working outside the home. Two of the best-selling magazines during that time, the *Saturday Evening Post* and *True Story,* supported the government's propaganda efforts by portraying working-class women in very positive roles:

Stories and advertisements glorified factory work as psychologically rewarding, as emotionally exciting, and as leading to success in love. Both magazines combated class prejudice against factory work by portraying working-class men and women as diligent, patriotic, wholesome people. . . . Working-class women were resourceful, respectable, warm-hearted, and resilient (Honey, 1984: 186–87).

Daddy's Coming Home!

Soldiers returning from World War II encountered numerous problems, including unemployment and high divorce rates. Historian William M. Tuttle Jr. (1993) solicited 2,500 letters from men and women, then in their 50s and 60s, who had been children during World War II. What most of these people had in common were the difficulties they and their families experienced in adjusting to the return of their fathers from military service.

Some children feared that their fathers would not stay and therefore avoided becoming too attached. Others were bitter that their fathers had left in the first place.

One "war baby" was 18 months old when her father returned from the war. When her mother told her to hug her Daddy, she ran to a large framed photo of him and took it in her arms.

Some children, especially those who were preschoolers at the time, were frightened of the strange men who suddenly moved into their homes. One woman remembered watching "the stranger with the big white teeth" come toward her. As he did, the 4-year-old ran upstairs in terror and hid under a bed.

Some recalled feeling angry because their fathers' return disrupted their lives.

Grandparents had often pampered children whom they helped to raise. In contrast, the returning father, fresh from military experience, was often a strict disciplinarian and saw the child as a brat.

If the children had been very close to their mothers, they became resentful of their fathers for displacing them in the mother's affections. Others were disappointed when the idealized image they had constructed of Daddy did not match reality or when a father who had been described as kind, sensitive, and gentle returned from the war troubled or violent.

Readjustment was difficult for both children and fathers. Some households adjusted to the changes, but in many families the returning fathers and their children never developed a close relationship.

⁝⋅ Stop and Think . . .

- Do you think that the relationship between children and fathers helps explain the spike in divorce rates in 1946? Why or why not?

The G.I. Bill enabled many World War II veterans to go to school and improve their job opportunities. But for many vets with families, such as William Oskay Jr. and his wife and daughter, daily life required many sacrifices and hardships.

- In 1973, at the end of the Vietnam War, Congress replaced the draft with an all-volunteer military force. Based on your personal experiences or readings, do you think that the volunteer soldiers who have returned from the wars in Iraq and Afghanistan have experienced fewer family difficulties than World War II soldiers?

FAMILY LIFE Divorce rates had been increasing slowly since the turn of the century, but they reached a new high a year after the end of World War II. In 1940, one marriage in six had ended in divorce compared with one in four in 1946 (Mintz and Kellogg, 1988).

Some wives and mothers who had worked during the war enjoyed their newfound economic independence and decided to end unhappy marriages. In other cases, families disintegrated because of the strains of living with a man who returned partially or completely incapacitated. Alcoholism, which was rampant among veterans, was believed to be the major cause of the increase in divorces after the war (Tuttle, 1993).

For some people, the war postponed rather than caused divorce. Some couples, caught up in war hysteria, courted briefly and married impulsively. In many cases, both the bride and the young soldier matured during the husband's prolonged absence and had little in common when they were reunited (Mowrer, 1972).

Perhaps one of the greatest difficulties that many families faced was their children's reaction to fathers whom they barely knew or had never even seen. As the box "Daddy's Coming Home!" shows, despite widespread rejoicing over the end of the war, a father's return was unsettling for many children.

THE GOLDEN FIFTIES

After World War II, propaganda about family roles changed almost overnight because returning veterans needed jobs. Women were no longer welcome in the workplace. Ads now depicted happy housewives engrossed in using household appliances and the latest consumer products. The women portrayed in short stories and in articles in women's magazines were no longer nurses saving soldiers' lives on the battlefield, but mothers cooking, caring for their children, and pleasing their husbands. In the 1950s, middle-class people, especially, became absorbed in their families.

Gender Roles

Movies and television shows featured two stereotypical portrayals of women: innocent virgins such as Doris Day and Debbie Reynolds or sexy bombshells such as Marilyn Monroe and Jayne Mansfield. Television applauded domesticity on popular shows such as *I Love Lucy, Ozzie and Harriet, Leave It to Beaver,* and *Father Knows Best.*

Once again, and reminiscent of the cult of domesticity that arose during the 1800s, popular culture encouraged women to devote their lives to being good wives and nurturing mothers. For example, marriage manuals and child care experts such as Dr. Benjamin Spock advised women to please their husbands and to be full-time homemakers. By the mid-1950s, 60 percent of female undergraduates dropped out of college to marry (Banner, 1984).

When suburbs mushroomed during the 1950s, many critics mocked the small, detached, single-family homes as "cookie cutters" (above). Are houses practically stacked on top of each in some recently developed suburbs—such as the one south of Denver, Colorado (below)—more original and not cookie cutters?

The post–World War II period produced a generation of **baby boomers,** people born between 1946 and 1964, when birth rates surged. Family plans that had been disrupted by the war were renewed. Women continued to enter the job market, but many middle-class families, spurred by the mass media, sought a traditional family life in which the husband worked and the wife devoted herself to the home and the children.

The editor of *Mademoiselle* echoed a widespread belief that women in their teens and 20s should avoid careers and instead raise as many children as the "good Lord gave them." And many magazine and newspaper articles encouraged families to participate in "creative" activities such as outdoor barbecues and cross-country camping trips (Chafe, 1972).

Moving to the Suburbs

In the 1950s suburbs mushroomed, attracting nearly two-thirds of those who had lived in cities. The interest in moving to the suburbs reflected a number of structural and attitudinal changes in American society.

The federal government, fearful of a return to an economic depression, underwrote the construction of homes in the suburbs (Rothman, 1978). The general public obtained low-interest mortgages, and veterans were offered the added incentive of purchasing a home with a $1 down payment. There was a huge demand for housing and from 1945 to 1960, 15 million housing units were built. By 1960, 60 percent of Americans owned their own homes (Buhle et al., 2008).

Homeownership rates climbed steadily over the years, reaching 69 percent in 2004. In mid-2009, however, because of unemployment, home foreclosures, and the financial crisis, American homeownership dropped to 67 percent (Callis and Cavanaugh, 2009), and it continues to decline as this book goes to press.

Massive highway construction programs and automobile ownership enabled people to commute from the suburbs to the city. Families wanted more room and an escape from city noise, dirt, and

Since you asked . . .

- How did suburban living change family life?

Mad Men, a popular television show that began in 2007, suggests how gender roles began to change at the end of the 1950s. For example, some middle-class suburban housewives started to feel lonely and ignored as their successful husbands worked long hours. Some wives turned to alcohol and extramarital affairs to counteract their feelings of alienation.

crowding. One woman still recollects moving to the suburbs as "the ideal life": "We knew little about the outside world of poverty, culture, crime, and ethnic variety" (Coontz, 2005: 240).

The greater space offered more privacy for both children and parents: "The spacious master bedroom, generally set apart from the rooms of the children, was well-suited to a highly sexual relationship. And wives anticipated spending many evenings alone with their husbands, not with family or friends" (Rothman, 1978: 225–26).

The suburban way of life added a new dimension to the traditional role of women:

The duties of child-rearing underwent expansion. Suburban mothers volunteered for library work in the school, took part in PTA activities, and chauffeured their children from music lessons to scout meetings. Perhaps most important, the suburban wife was expected to make the home an oasis of comfort and serenity for her harried husband (Chafe, 1972: 217–18).

An Idyllic Decade?

Were the fifties as idyllic as earlier generations fondly recall? Some writers argue that many of these nostalgic memories are myths. "Contrary to popular opinion," notes historian Stephanie Coontz (1992: 29) "*Leave It to Beaver* was not a documentary." In fact, the golden fifties were riddled with many family problems, and people had fewer choices than they do today. For example,

- *Consumerism* was limited primarily to middle- and upper-class families. In 1950, a supermarket stocked an average of 3,750 items; in the 1990s, most markets carried more than 17,000 items.

- Black and other ethnic families faced *severe discrimination* in employment, education, housing, and access to recreational activities.

- *Domestic violence and child abuse,* though widespread, were invisible (see Chapter 14).

- Many young people were forced into "*shotgun*" *marriages* because of premarital pregnancy; young women—especially if they were white—were pressured to give up their babies for adoption.

- About 20 percent of mothers had *paying jobs.* Child care services are still inadequate today, but they were practically nonexistent in the 1950s.

- *Open homosexuality was taboo* because only heterosexuality was considered normal. As a result, practically all lesbians and gay men kept their sexual orientation a secret and married people of the opposite sex.

- Many people, including housewives, tried to escape from their unhappy lives through *alcohol or drugs.* The consumption of tranquilizers, largely unheard of in 1955, soared to almost 1.2 million pounds in 1959 (Coontz, 1992; Crispell, 1992; Reid, 1993).

⠿• MAKING CONNECTIONS

- Some of your grandparents or parents probably lived through the Great Depression and World War II. How did they survive these turbulent periods? If your kin were poor, how did these eras shape their attitudes and values about jobs, money, food, and other issues?

- Many Americans—and often regardless of age—view the 1950s as the good old days when, presumably, families were happy and closely knit. Do you wish that you could have been raised during the 1950s? Why or why not?

THE FAMILY SINCE THE 1960s

When I was in graduate school during the early 1970s, our family textbooks typically covered three major topics—courtship, marriage, and having children—and in that order. The authors sometimes devoted a chapter to premarital sex and one to black families, but they often described divorce, interfaith marriage, premarital pregnancy, and homosexuality as deviant or problems (see, for example, Reiss, 1971). We never read (or heard) about family violence and almost nothing about singlehood, cohabitation, stepfamilies, or one-parent families.

American families have experienced numerous changes since the 1960s and 1970s. As you saw in Chapter 1, technological innovations have transformed everyday communication, young people have greater access to and are more influenced by popular culture than ever before, social movements challenged traditional attitudes about family life, and social scientists became more interested in examining families in other societies. Since the l970s, three of the major shifts have occurred in family structure, gender roles, and economic concerns.

Family Structure

In the 1970s, families had lower birth rates and higher divorce rates compared with the 1950s and 1960s, and larger numbers of women entered colleges and graduate schools. In the 1980s, more people over age 25 postponed marriage, and many who were already married delayed having children (see Chapters 9 and 11).

Out-of-wedlock births, especially among teenage girls, declined in the late 1990s and began to climb in 2006, but the number of one-parent households increased dramatically (see Chapters 7 and 9). The number of two-income families burgeoned, along with the number of adult children who continued to live at home with their parents because of financial difficulties (see Chapter 12).

Gender Roles

In her influential book, *The Feminine Mystique* (1963), Betty Friedan (1921–2006) criticized the push toward domesticity and documented the dissatisfaction of many college-educated women who felt unfulfilled in their full-time roles as wives and mothers. Friedan's book didn't change gender roles overnight. In 1975, for example, and even though I worked full time as a college professor, I couldn't take out a credit card in my own name and needed my husband's signed permission to get a credit card even in his name. Nonetheless, *The Feminine Mystique* had an enormous impact in sparking the women's movement in the late 1960s and challenging traditional roles throughout the 1970s and 1980s.

We'll cover these topics in later chapters, but by the early 1980s, women's employment was becoming central to a family's economic advancement, and two-income families faced the stressful tasks of juggling and negotiating work and family life. On the positive side, many women believed that employment brought them more respect from society and their partners and greater decision-making power in their marriages. The percentage of stay-at-home dads is still tiny, but social acceptance of such family arrangements accelerated. Perhaps most important, men experienced less pressure to be the sole breadwinner.

Economic Concerns

The twenty-first century began with numerous problems that affected families. The stock market plunged. Many older people had to go back to work because their retirement portfolios shrank by at least 50 percent. Many young adults were laid off from promising high-tech jobs and scurried to find *any* employment that paid more than a minimum wage (see Chapters 13, 17, and 18).

Health care costs skyrocketed. After the terrorist attacks on September 11, 2001, federal and state governments funneled billions of dollars into homeland security and the war in Iraq. And, in mid-2008, the U.S. economy spiraled downward as the federal government spent a trillion taxpayer dollars to bail out numerous corporations. As a result, agencies gutted many family programs and services, especially for poor and working-class families.

CONCLUSION

If we examine the family in a historical context, we see that *change,* rather than stability, has been the norm. Moreover, families differed by region and social class even during colonial times.

We also see that the experiences and *choices* open to American Indians, African Americans, Mexican Americans, and many European immigrants were very different from those available to white middle-class Americans, all of whose lives were romanticized by many television programs during the 1950s.

Macro-level *constraints* such as wars and shifting demographic characteristics have also influenced families. Many families survived despite enormous hardships, disruptions, and dislocations. They are still coping with macro-level constraints such as an unpredictable economy as well as with micro-level variables such as greater choices in family roles. The next chapter, on racial and ethnic families, examines some of the ongoing changes, choices, and constraints.

SUMMARY

1. Historical factors have played an important role in shaping the contemporary family. The early exploitation of American Indian, African American, and Mexican families has had long-term economic effects on these families.

2. The colonial family was a self-sufficient unit that performed a wide variety of functions. Children were part of the family workforce and were expected to be docile and well behaved. Wives' work was subordinate to that of their husbands, and family practices varied in different social classes and geographic regions.

3. American Indian families were extremely diverse in function, structure, puberty rites, and child-rearing patterns. European armies, adventurers, and missionaries played major roles in destroying many tribes and much of American Indian culture.

4. Contrary to popular belief, many African American slave households had two parents, men played important roles as fathers or surrogate fathers, and most women worked as hard as the men in the fields. Instead of succumbing to subordination, many slaves were resourceful and resilient in maintaining their families. Nonetheless, all of these families experienced numerous hardships and inequalities.

5. After 1848, most Mexican American families in the newly annexed U.S. territories in the Southwest and West lost their lands to European American settlers. Despite severe economic exploitation, many families survived because of cohesive family networks and strong family bonds.

6. In the late eighteenth century, industrialization changed many aspects of the family. Marriages were based more on love and choice than on economic considerations, and parental roles became more gender segregated. In the upper and middle classes, the notion of the true woman, who devoted most of her time to looking beautiful and pleasing her husband, emerged.

7. Millions of European immigrants who worked in labor-intensive jobs at very low wages fueled the rapid advance of industrialization. Many immigrants, including women and children, endured severe social and economic discrimination, dilapidated housing conditions, and chronic health problems.

8. Working-class families, especially among African Americans, experienced the most devastating effects during the Great Depression. Middle-class families sometimes cut back on luxuries, but working-class men experienced widespread unemployment, and their wives worked in menial and low-paying jobs.

9. World War II had a mixed effect on families. For the first time, many women, especially black mothers, found jobs that paid a decent salary. However, death and divorce disrupted many families. After the war, suburbs boomed and birth rates surged. The family roles of white middle-class women expanded to include full-time nurturance of children and husbands, whereas their husbands' roles were largely limited to work. The golden fifties is a mythical portrayal of the family in that decade.

10. Since the 1960s, many Americans have experienced numerous changes in family structure, gender roles, and economic problems.

KEY TERMS

bundling 54
matrilineal 58
patrilineal 58

familism 63
compadrazgo 63
machismo 64

cult of domesticity 64
companionate family 68
baby boomers 72

PEARSON **myfamilylab** MyFamilyLab provides a wealth of resources. Go to www.myfamilylab.com <http://www.myfamilylab .com/>, to enhance your comprehension of the content in this chapter. You can take practice exams, view videos relevant to the subject matter, listen to audio files, explore topics further by using Social Explorer, and use the tools contained in MySearchLab to help you write research papers.

4 Racial and Ethnic Families
Strengths and Stresses

In 2008, the election of African American Barack Obama to the office of president of the United States affirmed many Americans' belief that the United States is a land of opportunity. Obama was born to a white American mother and a black Kenyan father, but his parents separated when he was two years old and divorced three years later. Obama then lived in a small apartment with his mother's parents in Hawaii. His grandmother worked in a bank and his grandfather was a furniture salesman. Thus, despite his modest early background and parents' divorce, Obama achieved the pinnacle of political power and recognition at age 47.

In this chapter, we focus on contemporary African American, American Indian, Latino, Asian American, and Middle Eastern families. We'll also examine marriage and dating relationships across racial and ethnic lines. Let's begin with an overview of the growing diversity of American families.

DATA DIGEST

- Canada and the United States **represent only about 5 percent of the world's population but receive more than half of the world's immigrants.**

- **Four states and the District of Columbia are "majority-minority,"** meaning that whites make up less than half of the population. Hawaii leads the nation with 75 percent minority, followed by the District of Columbia (67 percent), California (58 percent), New Mexico (58 percent), and Texas (53 percent).

- In 2000, 31 percent of African Americans and 56 percent of whites said that **race relations in the United States were generally good;** these numbers increased, respectively, to 59 percent and 65 percent in mid-2009.

- The largest numbers of **people with Middle Eastern roots who immigrated to the United States** in 2009 came from Pakistan (21,600), Iran (18.6), Egypt (8,800), Israel (5,600), and Iraq (21,100).

- In 2009, more than 7.5 million Americans said that **they identified with two or more races,** a 87 percent increase since 2000.

Sources: Martin and Zürcher, 2008; U.S. Census Bureau, 2010, Tables 6, 49; "U.S. Hispanic Population Surpasses . . .," 2008; NY Times-CBS survey, 2009.

THE INCREASING DIVERSITY OF U.S. FAMILIES

You saw in Chapter 1 that U.S. households are becoming more diverse in racial and ethnic composition. As the number and variety of immigrants increase, the ways in which we relate to one another become more complex.

To understand some of this complexity, think of a continuum. At one end of the continuum is **assimilation,** or conformity of ethnic group members to the culture of the dominant group, including intermarriage. At the other end of the continuum is **cultural pluralism,** or maintaining many aspects of one's original culture—including using one's own language and marrying within one's own ethnic group—while living peacefully with the host culture.

Still others—those in the middle of the continuum—blend into U.S. society through **acculturation,** the process of adopting the language, values, beliefs, roles, and other characteristics of a host culture (such as attaining high educational levels and securing good jobs). Like cultural pluralism, acculturation does not include intermarriage, but the newcomers merge into the host culture in most other ways.

Changes in Our Immigration Mosaic

The current proportion of foreign-born U.S. residents is small by historical standards. In 1900, about 15 percent of the total U.S. population was foreign born, compared with 12.6 percent in 2009 (U.S. Census Bureau, 2009, 1-Year Estimates).

> **Since you asked . . .**
>
> :• How has U.S. immigration changed?

There has also been a significant shift in many immigrants' country of origin. In 1900, almost 85 percent of immigrants came from Europe. In 2009, in contrast, Europeans made up only 13 percent of all new immigrants. Today, immigrants come primarily from Asia (mainly China and the Philippines) and Latin America (mainly Mexico) (see *Figure 4.1*).

UNDOCUMENTED IMMIGRANTS The United States admits more than 1 million immigrants every year—more than any other nation. Another 12 million immigrants, 59 percent of them from Mexico, are undocumented (illegal) (Passel and Cohn, 2009). Undocumented immigrants represent 31 percent of the foreign-born population (see *Figure 4.2*). Many Americans believe that undocumented immigrants are "moochers." In fact, however,

- More than 90 percent of the men work, and most pay payroll and sales taxes.

- They aren't eligible for welfare, food stamps, Medicaid, and most other public benefits.

- Fewer than 10 percent of Mexican immigrants, both documented and undocumented, have used an emergency room, compared with 20 percent of native-born whites and Mexican Americans.

- Undocumented immigrants pay on average $80,000 per capita more in taxes than they will use in government services over their lifetimes.

- About 75 percent contribute a total of $7 billion annually in Social Security taxes and roughly $1.5 billion annually in Medicare taxes, both of which they will be unable to claim or qualify for because they're not citizens (Capps and Fix, 2005; King, 2007).

FIGURE 4.1 Origins of U.S. Immigrants: 1900 and 2009

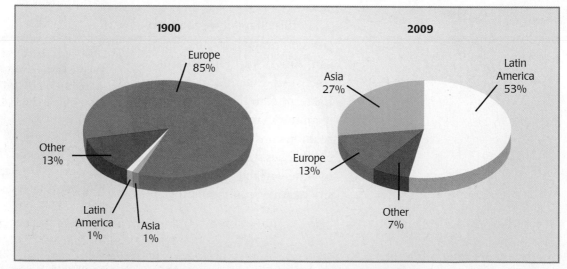

1900
- Europe 85%
- Other 13%
- Latin America 1%
- Asia 1%

2009
- Latin America 53%
- Asia 27%
- Europe 13%
- Other 7%

Note: Latin America includes the Caribbean, Central America (including Mexico), and South America.
Sources: Based on data in U.S. Department of Commerce, 1993, and U.S. Census Bureau, 2009 (1-Year Estimates), ACS09.

An additional 4 million or so are "visa overstayers"—people who arrive on a visitor's visa (from Canada, Europe, and other countries) and decide to remain in the United States. These undocumented immigrants skip over millions of others who sometimes wait years to immigrate here legally. Once foreigners are in this country, the U.S. Immigration and Naturalization Service has no way to track where they are or whether they leave when their visas expire (Lipton, 2005).

ATTITUDES ABOUT IMMIGRATION

Most Americans are ambivalent about immigration: Forty percent say that immigrants have made positive contributions in terms of food, music, and the arts, but a majority believes that immigrants have increased taxes and crime. African Americans, especially, contend that immigration has decreased job opportunities for themselves or their family (Kohut et al., 2007).

Generally, however, attitudes about legal immigration vary depending on the social context. Shortly after the 9/11 terrorist attacks, for example, 58 percent of Americans favored cutbacks in immigration compared with 39 percent in 2008 (Jones, 2008).

Illegal immigration is more controversial, but attitudes vary, as is true for legal immigration, depending on the importance of other issues. In 2006, for instance, 53 percent of Americans contended that illegal immigrants should be required to go home. In 2008—as many Americans focused on other issues such as a struggling economy, record-high gas prices, falling housing prices, and home foreclosures—illegal

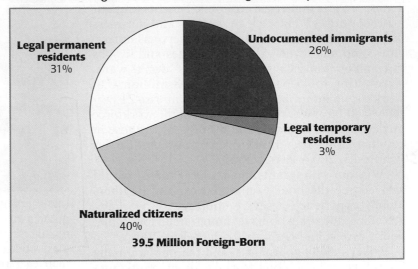

FIGURE 4.2 Legal Status of the U.S. Foreign-Born Population, 2006

- Legal permanent residents 31%
- Undocumented immigrants 26%
- Legal temporary residents 3%
- Naturalized citizens 40%

39.5 Million Foreign-Born

Source: Based on Passel, 2008.

immigration issues weren't foremost in public consciousness (Barabak, 2006; Jones, 2008).

IS IMMIGRATION HARMFUL OR BENEFICIAL? José Tenas came to the United States from Guatemala in 1987. He spent 16 days crossing through Mexico on foot and rode illegally into California in the sweltering back of a truck. Tenas washed dishes in kitchens, became a U.S. citizen, brought over his wife and children, saved his money, got a loan, and opened his own restaurant in Virginia that is now popular with local native-born residents and Latino immigrants (Williams, 2005). Tenas represents one of many illegal immigrants who have worked hard to become successful. Still, the general public and some scholars believe that all immigration, legal and illegal, has costs.

Some immigration critics allege that low-skilled workers reduce the standard of living and overload schools and welfare systems. Others note that because immigrants are younger, poorer, and less well educated than the native population, they use more government services and pay less in taxes. As a result, many Americans believe that immigrants don't share an equal burden of the expenses they incur, especially at the local level (Wood, 2009).

Immigrants themselves—both legal and illegal— also experience costs. Employment recruiters promise people good jobs and training, but immigrants at the low end of the pay scale often find themselves living in abject poverty because they don't receive the promised wages. And, as this book goes to press, many immigrants who have fought in the Iraq war have been honorably discharged but have not had their citizenship applications processed, as President Bush had promised (Bauer, 2007; Santos, 2008).

Every year, millions of immigrants become U.S. citizens. In 2008, more than 3,000 people took the oath of citizenship at Fenway Park in Boston.

Proponents argue that many immigrants, like José Tenas, provide numerous economic benefits for their host countries. They clean homes and business offices, toil as nannies and busboys, serve as nurses' aides, and pick fruit—all at low wages and in jobs that most American-born workers don't want. Accounting for 5 percent of the 148 million U.S. workers, unauthorized immigrants comprise 21 percent of all farm workers, 16 percent of the workforce in cleaning occupations, and 30 percent of those in construction and food preparation industries (Chomsky, 2007; Passel, 2008).

Without immigrants, many rural towns would shrivel (see the box "Somalis in Maine"). Others would experience a severe shortage of workers, including doctors who have immigrated from India, South Africa, and Latin America (Belsie, 2001).

Policymakers, journalists, and the public usually focus their attention on low-skilled immigrants from Mexico and other Latin American countries, but there is a large and growing number of highly skilled immigrants from Asia who attend college or are in America's high-tech workforce. In 26 states, foreign-born populations, many of them from Asia, have a higher level of educational attainment, on average, than the U.S.-born population and work in professional or managerial positions. In addition, college-educated immigrants, especially scientists and engineers, are more likely than their counterparts to hold U.S. patents and to be founders of biotech companies (Mather, 2007; Hunt and Gauthier-Loiselle, 2008).

Undocumented immigrants, most of them Latinos, comprised a quarter of the construction workers who helped rebuild New Orleans after Hurricane Katrina. Many of these workers made an average of $6.50 an hour less than legal workers and had more trouble collecting their wages (Fletcher et al., 2006).

Many scholars argue that on balance and in the long run, immigrants provide more benefits than costs. For example, they constitute an important labor force for an aging (and primarily white) America that will require many workers to support Social Security and Medicare payments for the elderly. Without large numbers of new workers, many funding programs for the elderly will be cut or decreased, requiring millions of older Americans to work well into their 70s (Bean and Stevens, 2003; Myers, 2007).

Somalis in Maine

Choices

During the 1980s, many citizens of Somalia (a country in East Africa) became refugees after fleeing famine, torture, and violence during civil wars. U.S. social service groups resettled many of the Somalis in urban centers such as Columbus, Ohio; Atlanta, Georgia; and Memphis, Tennessee. Most of the resettled parents became unhappy with their children's adaptations to American culture—dressing differently, listening to rap music, and speaking English rather than Somali at home. In addition, in neighborhoods with high crime rates, some of the adults were robbed or shot.

As a result, the Somali elders sent younger men to search for new settlements. After considerable research and discussion, the Somalis targeted

Lewiston, Maine, as a good place to live. Lewiston had a dwindling population, dilapidated housing, and few employment opportunities, but the elders believed that it was a safe town and had good schools.

Some Lewiston residents complained about the city's giving each of the 1,200 Somali families $10,000 in cash when they arrived. Others worried that the town's scarce resources were being allocated to English classes and other services at the expense of the needs of local citizens.

On the other hand, the Somalis have revitalized this dying community by shopping, paying taxes, and buying property. In addition, they opened a new restaurant, a National Basketball

Association (NBA) jersey store, and a convenience store (Jones, 2004: 69).

⁑ Stop and Think ...

- Do the goals of more recent immigrants, such as the Somalis, differ from those of earlier immigrants who came to the United States from Ireland, Poland, Italy, or other countries?

- How would you feel if about 5 to 10 percent of your town was settled by immigrants like the Somalis? Would you welcome their arrival or think that they would deplete the town's resources?

RACE AND ETHNICITY STILL MATTER

Social scientists routinely describe Latino, African American, Asian American, Middle Eastern, and American Indian families as minority groups. A **minority group** is a group of people who may be treated differently from the dominant group because of their physical or cultural characteristics, such as gender, sexual orientation, religion, or skin color. A **dominant group** is any physically or culturally distinctive group that has the most economic and political power, the greatest privileges, and the highest social status.

Minority groups may outnumber whites in a country or state (see Data Digest), but they typically have less power, privilege, and social status. Most whites, in contrast, are privileged because of their skin color.

Since you asked . . .
••• Why would many whites reject the argument that they're privileged?

Feminist educator Peggy McIntosh (1995: 76–77) describes white privilege as "an invisible package of unearned assets that I can count on cashing in each day." The box "Am I Privileged?" provides some examples of "cashing in" if you're white.

What kinds of physical and cultural characteristics differentiate minority groups from a dominant group? Two of the most important are race and ethnicity.

Race

A **racial group** is a category of people who share physical characteristics, such as skin color, that members of a society consider socially important. Both sociologists and anthropologists see race as a social label rather than a biological trait. Many biologists, similarly, view race as a social concept because there is very little genetic difference among members of different races: As few as 6 of the body's estimated 35,000 genes determine the color of a person's skin (Graves, 2001).

For social scientists, physical characteristics such as skin color and eye shape are easily observed and mark particular groups for unequal treatment: "Each of us is born with a particular collection of physical attributes, but it is society that teaches us which ones to value and which ones to reject" (Rothenberg, 2008: 3). As you'll see in this and other chapters, as long as we sort ourselves into racial categories and act on the basis of these characteristics, our life experiences will differ in terms of access to jobs and other resources and in how people treat us.

Ethnicity

An **ethnic group** (from the Greek word *ethnos*, meaning "nation") is a set of people who identify with a particular national origin or cultural heritage. Cultural heritage includes language, geographic roots, customs, traditions, and religion. Ethnic groups in

---

ASK YOURSELF

Am I Privileged?

Do we live in a color-blind society? No, according to most social scientists. White people are rarely conscious of the advantages and disadvantages associated with skin color because they enjoy a variety of everyday benefits that they take for granted. Here are a few of the 46 privileges that McIntosh (1995: 79–81) lists:

1. I can go shopping alone most of the time, fairly well assured that I will not be followed or harassed by store detectives.
2. I can turn on the television or open to the front page of the paper and see people of my race widely and positively represented.
3. I can be sure that my children will be given curricular materials that reflect their race.
4. Whether I use checks, credit cards, or cash, I can count on my skin color to send the message that I am financially reliable.
5. If a traffic cop pulls me over, I can be sure that I haven't been singled out because of my race.

6. I can be late to a meeting without having the lateness reflect on my race.
7. I can easily buy posters, postcards, greeting cards, dolls, toys, and children's magazines featuring people of my race.
8. I can do well in a difficult situation without being called a credit to my race.

Some of those who are white don't feel privileged because being white *and* wealthy *and* male brings more privileges than simply having white skin (Rothenberg, 2008). For example, low-income white females don't see any benefits in being white because their skin color doesn't seem to bring them any privileges.

••• Stop and Think . . .

■ Would you add other benefits to this list of white privileges? If so, what are they?

■ Is any discussion of white privilege now irrelevant because Obama's presidency has changed many Americans' perception of race relations?

There's much variation in skin color across and within groups. People of African descent have at least 35 different hues or shades of skin tone (Taylor, 2003). Because our skin contains different amounts of melanin (a pigment that affects skin, eye, and hair color), brown skin can vary considerably even within the same family, as pictured here.

the United States include Puerto Ricans, Chinese, blacks, and a variety of white ethnic groups such as Italians, Swedes, Hungarians, Jews, and many others.

The U.S. government acknowledges that race is a social rather than a biological concept, but it considers race and ethnicity to be two separate categories in people's self-identification. Thus, in the 2000 Census response form, the question on race included 15 separate response categories, three areas in which respondents could write in a more specific racial group, and a question on ancestry or ethnic origin. Someone who's Latino, for example, could answer questions on both ethnicity and race.

Like race, ethnicity—an individual or group's cultural or national identity—can be a basis for unequal treatment. As you saw in Chapter 3, many white European immigrants experienced discrimination because of their ethnic roots.

Racial-Ethnic Group

Sociologists often refer to a set of people who have distinctive physical and cultural characteristics as a **racial-ethnic group.** All the families we examine in this chapter are examples of racial-ethnic groups because both physical and cultural attributes are central features of their heritage. Although some people use the terms interchangeably, remember that *race* is a social concept that refers to physical characteristics, whereas *ethnicity* describes cultural characteristics. The term *racial-ethnic* incorporates both physical and cultural traits. These distinctions can become complicated because people tend to prefer some "labels" to others, and these labels change over time.

The Naming Issue

Hispanic and *Latino* are often used interchangeably for people with origins in Spanish-speaking countries,

but the labels reflect regional usage and cultural background. *Hispanic* is preferred in New York and Florida, whereas *Latino* is more popular in California and Texas. The term *Chicano* (*Chicana* for women) arose in the 1970s and is still used to refer to people of Mexican origin who were born in the United States. *Hispano* is favored to emphasize unity with Spain rather than Mexico. And a small group in southern California prefers *Mexica* to stress its indigenous Indian roots in Mexico.

Labels for blacks have also changed over time, from hurtful racial epithets to *colored, Negro,* and *Afro-American* (Kennedy, 2002). Currently, most people, including African American scholars, use *black* and *African American* interchangeably. I find the same results when I poll my black students informally. Some are vehement about using *African American* to emphasize their African ancestry; others prefer *black* (with or without a capital B).

We see similar variations in the usage of *Native American* and *American Indian.* Although these groups prefer their tribal identities (such as Cherokee, Apache, and Lumbi) to being lumped together with a single term, American Indians often dispute whether someone is full blooded or mixed blood, belongs to a tribe, or is simply a "wannabe" rather than a "real" Indian after several centuries of intermarriage (Snipp, 2002).

Racism, Prejudice, and Discrimination

RACISM Racism is a set of beliefs that one's own racial group is inherently superior to others. Using this definition, anyone can be racist if she/he believes that another group is inferior. Nationally, for example, 42 percent of whites and 36 percent of both African Americans and Latinos say that there is "widespread racism" against white Americans (Jones, 2008).

> **Since you asked . . .**
>
> ::• Can minorities be racist?

Hatred of other groups often fuels unequal treatment. Thus, racism is especially harmful when physical and cultural differences justify and preserve the social, economic, and political interests of privileged groups on a macro level (Essed and Goldberg, 2002). Within the United States, for example, because whites, as a group, have more privilege, they can affect minority families' ability to compete for high-paying jobs, to choose the neighborhoods in which they live, and to provide educational opportunities for their children. In effect, then, people can be racist on an individual level, but minorities are more likely to suffer from racism because they rarely have the power and resources to affect the dominant group on a macro level.

PREJUDICE Prejudice is an *attitude* that prejudges people, usually in a negative way, who are different from "us" in race, ethnicity, religion, or some other

Applying What You've Learned

Am I Prejudiced?

All of us, whether we realize it or not, sometimes have strong positive or negative feelings about other racial-ethnic groups. Answer the questions in this quiz as honestly as possible. After you finish, look at the key.

Usually True	Usually False	
☐	☐	**1.** Latino men have a more macho attitude toward women than do other men.
☐	☐	**2.** African Americans, both women and men, are more likely to commit crimes than are members of other racial-ethnic groups, including whites.
☐	☐	**3.** Don't trust Arab Americans. Some are decent, but most want to spread Islam and aren't loyal to the United States.
☐	☐	**4.** Asian American business owners are greedier than other business owners.
☐	☐	**5.** There are some exceptions, but most Latinos don't succeed because they're lazy.
☐	☐	**6.** The majority of Asian Americans tend to be shy and quiet.
☐	☐	**7.** Most Asian Americans are not as sociable as other groups of people.
☐	☐	**8.** Most whites are simply more capable than other groups—especially African Americans and Latinos—in doing their jobs.
☐	☐	**9.** I believe that less qualified minorities are taking away my livelihood.
☐	☐	**10.** When I was growing up, my parents said negative things about African Americans, whites, Latinos, Asian Americans, and other groups. Because of my upbringing, I feel that people outside my group are inferior.

characteristic. If an employer assumes, for example, that white workers will be more productive than those from minority groups, she or he is prejudiced. *All* of us can be prejudiced, but minorities, rather than whites, are typically the targets of discrimination. Before you read any further, take the short "Am I Prejudiced?" quiz and think about some of your feelings about racial-ethnic groups.

Generally, prejudice is less harmful than discrimination because it's in our thoughts rather than our actions. Nevertheless, prejudice may lead to discrimination.

DISCRIMINATION Discrimination is *behavior* that treats people unequally or unfairly. It encompasses all sorts of actions, ranging from social slights (such as inviting only the white kids in a child's class to a birthday party) to rejection of job applicants, and racially motivated hate crimes (see Lucas, 2008).

Discrimination also occurs *within* racial-ethnic groups. For example, immigrants from both Mexico and Central American countries, such as El Salvador, speak the same language (Spanish) and migrate to Los Angeles, California, in large numbers. El Salvadorans, however, believe that Mexican American business owners discriminate against Central and South Americans, and they pretend to be Mexican to get the low-paying jobs at these businesses (Bermudez, 2008).

Education and employment opportunities have improved since the mid-1960s, but racial-ethnic families, including African American, American Indian, Latino, Asian American, and Middle Eastern families, have to deal with prejudice and discrimination, often on a daily basis. We now turn to a closer examination of each of these five groups.

Key to "Am I Prejudiced?"

Of these ten items, the higher your score for "usually true," the more likely it is that you are prejudiced and stereotype many racial/ethnic groups. The purpose of this quiz is to get you to think about how you feel about people outside your immediate circle.

Sources: Based on material in Godfrey et al., 2000; Lin et al., 2005; and Esposito and Mogahed, 2007.

MAKING CONNECTIONS

- What do you think would be the costs and benefits of increasing or decreasing current immigration rates? Also, should the United States continue to deport illegal immigrants? Or give them temporary "guest worker" visas and a chance at citizenship?

- Provide some examples of situations in which you (or someone else) who is prejudiced might not discriminate and in which you (or someone else) who discriminates might not necessarily be prejudiced.

AFRICAN AMERICAN FAMILIES

There is no such thing as "the" African American family. Like other American families, black families vary in kinship structure, gender roles, parent-child relationships, and social class.

Family Structure

E. Franklin Frazier (1937), an African American scholar, was one of the first sociologists to point out that there are several types of black family structures: families with matriarchal patterns; traditional families similar to those of middle-class whites; and families, usually of mixed racial origins, that have been relatively isolated from the main currents of African American life. Over time, black family structures have changed, adapting to the pressures of society as a whole. When men lose their jobs, for example, some nuclear families expand to become extended families. Others welcome nonrelatives, such as fictive kin, as members of the household (see Chapter 1).

Until 1980, married-couple families among African Americans were the norm. Since then, black children have been more likely than children in other racial-ethnic groups to grow up with only one parent, usually a mother (see *Figure 4.3*). This shift reflects a number of social and economic developments: postponement of marriage, high divorce and separation rates, low remarriage rates, male unemployment, and out-of-wedlock births (topics we'll examine in later chapters).

Gender Roles

African American families are often stereotyped as matriarchal, but the egalitarian family pattern, in which both men and women share equal authority, is a more common arrangement. For example, black husbands are more likely than their white counterparts to share household chores (John and Shelton, 1997; Xu et al., 1997).

The more equal sharing of housework and child care probably reflects black husbands' willingness to pitch in because their wives are employed. Also, many

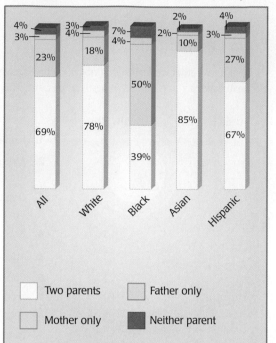

FIGURE 4.3 Where American Children Live, 2007

Legend: Two parents / Mother only / Father only / Neither parent

Note: Percentages may equal 101 due to rounding. The figures for American Indian and Alaska Native children are for 2003, the most recent available data for this group. Most of the children living with neither parent usually live with one or more grandparents.

Sources: Based on Fields, 2010, Table C3, and http://www.census.gov/population/www/socdemo/hh-fam/cps2010.html.

grew up in families in which the mother worked outside the home and black men participated in domestic labor (Penha-Lopes, 1995).

The division of domestic work is not equal, however. Black married women are still more likely than men to do most of the traditional chores, such as cooking, cleaning, and laundry, and to be overworked. Some of the instability in black marriages, as in white marriages, is a result of conflicts that occur when wives expect men to do more of the traditionally female domestic tasks (Livingston and McAdoo, 2007).

Parents and Children

Since you asked . . .

- What are some of the problems that many African American parents encounter in raising their children?

Most African American parents play important roles in their children's development. Many black fathers make a conscious effort to be involved in their children's lives because their own fathers were absent. Others are simply devoted to their kids:

[My older son and I] do everything together. I learned to roller-skate so that I could teach him

Is Bill Cosby Right about Black Families?

On several occasions, Bill Cosby has scolded low-income black parents and their kids for foolish behavior and decisions:

"It is not all right for your 15-year-old daughter to have a child," he told 2,400 fans in a high school in Milwaukee. He lambasted young men in Baltimore for knocking up "five, six girls." He tongue-lashed single mothers in Atlanta for having sex within their children's hearing "and then four days later, you bring another man into the house" (Cose, 2005: 66).

According to Cosby, many poor black parents waste what little money they have buying their kids $500 sneakers instead of "Hooked on Phonics." He also said that he was fed up with "knuck-leheads" who don't speak proper English and with women who have eight children with eight different men (American Rhetoric . . ., 2004).

Many people, regardless of ethnicity, agree with Cosby. Others think that he is picking on poor kids and their parents and that low-income youth usually make good purchasing decisions. Those who disagree with Cosby also believe that upper-middle-income blacks who benefited from the civil rights movement are too quick to criticize poor blacks who aren't achieving the same level of financial success (Chin, 2001; Dyson, 2005; Coates, 2008).

Despite criticism, especially from African Americans, Cosby repeated and elaborated on his controversial views later in a book that blamed parents for relinquishing their family responsibilities in increasing numbers, not providing proper role models, and waiting for handouts instead of taking control of their lives (see Cosby and Poussaint, 2007).

Stop and Think . . .

- Are low-income parents and their children making bad choices? Or are they adapting to problems beyond their control?
- Is Cosby right? Or is he holding poor black families to a higher standard that most other Americans don't meet?

and then go skating together. I'm the one who picks him up from school. I'm one of his Sunday school teachers, so he spends Sundays with me at church while my wife stays at home with our two-month-old son (Penha-Lopes, 1995: 187–88).

In 2004, Bill Cosby, an African American actor and author, sparked an uproar when he criticized poor black parents for raising irresponsible children (see the box "Is Bill Cosby Right about Black Families?"). The comments stirred up considerable debate that still continues.

Black, Latino, and Asian American parents are more likely than white parents to encourage their children to exercise self-control and succeed in school. This may reflect ethnic parents' concern that their children will have to work harder to overcome prejudice and discrimination (Thomas and Speight, 1999; Toth and Xu, 1999).

Because blacks, more than any other group, experience racism on an everyday basis, many parents engage in **racial socialization,** a process in which parents teach their children to overcome race-related barriers and experiences and to take pride in their ancestry. Race awareness occurs at about 2 to 3 years of age. Most African American parents talk about race with their children, but others believe that such discussions will make the child feel inferior (Phinney, 1996; Van Ausdale and Feagin, 2001; McAdoo, 2002).

The close relationship between African American parents and their children produces numerous advantages for children. In a study of the intelligence scores of black and white 5-year-olds, for example, the researchers found that the home environment was critical in fostering a child's development. Even if the family was poor, when parents provided warmth (caressing, kissing, or cuddling the child) and stimulated the child's learning (reading to the child at least three times a week), there were no differences between white and black children in intelligence scores (Brooks-Gunn et al., 1996).

Despite such positive outcomes, parents must deal with a variety of obstacles. Two of the most common are residential segregation and absent fathers.

RESIDENTIAL SEGREGATION More than 33 percent of black low-income working families and 20 percent of their Latino counterparts live in high-poverty neighborhoods, compared with only 3 percent of whites. Some housing segregation reflects individual preferences (wanting to live near those of the same race or ethnicity), but no family wants to live in high-poverty neighborhoods that don't have essential services and are overwhelmed by crime (Turner and Fortuny, 2009).

Whether in cities or suburbs, residential segregation remains the starkest for low-income African American families and perpetuates disparities in employment, education, and income. For example, residential segregation distances minority job seekers (particularly blacks) from areas of employment growth in predominantly white suburban locations because of transportation problems. Nearly half of all low-skill jobs are in white suburbs, whereas jobs in central business districts often require higher skills and educational level that low-income workers don't have (Holzer, 2001).

Residential segregation also contributes to minorities' unequal educational attainment, which reinforces their disadvantage in today's labor market. In both the poorest inner-city neighborhoods and suburbs with high concentrations of blacks and other minorities, public schools generally have low instructional quality, low test scores, and high dropout rates. Such problems are closely associated with lower employment among blacks and a wider wage gap between blacks and whites (Cashin, 2004; Turner and Fortuny, 2009).

ABSENT FATHERS Across all families, black children are the most likely to be raised by one parent, usually a mother (see *Figure 4.3* on p. 84). Some black men leave girlfriends who become pregnant because the men don't want a long-term commitment or don't have the money to support a child. Others die young, are in jail, or are involved in crime and drugs. Some out-of-wedlock fathers visit their children, play with them, and care for them while the mothers are working. The number of such fathers is increasing, but it's still low (see Chapters 9 and 12).

Female-headed households have been and can be stable over time, giving children the love and discipline they need, and female-headed families are an accepted (although not necessarily the preferred) type of family among African Americans. In addition, black adult males (such as sons, brothers, uncles, and grandfathers) often provide critical emotional and financial support to their female kin who head households (Sudarkasa, 2007).

As you'll see in later chapters, numerous studies show that fathers play a critical role in children's emotional well-being, cognitive development, academic achievement, and financial security. Thus, a father's absence can have negative outcomes on children, especially when the households are headed by teenagers or young single women who don't have or cannot depend on male family members for support.

Health and Economic Well-Being

According to one of my students, hard-working African American fathers often ignore their health:

I know many black fathers who died before reaching the age of 60. My dad was one of those men. He was a hard worker and stable provider for his family, but he died at the age of 53 due to diabetes and high blood pressure. In general, I think that black men's health often goes unnoticed (Author's files).

There's a strong relationship—across all families—among work-related stress, financial problems, and poor physical health (see Chapter 13). Minorities also

African Americans often pitch in during times of need. Morgan State University's men's basketball coach Todd Bozeman (center) adopted his nephew Okoye (right) when the boy's father, Bozeman's older brother, died in 2007 from a pulmonary embolism. Okoye's mother had died of bone cancer three years earlier. Also pictured are Bozeman's wife (front) and biological children (Klingaman, 2008).

typically receive lower-quality health care than do whites (Williams, 2007).

A primary reason for lower-quality health care is economic, and African Americans are among the poorest Americans. The percentage of black families with annual incomes of $50,000 or more increased from 21 percent in 1980 to 34 percent in 2009 (U.S. Census Bureau, 2008). Still, the median family income of African Americans is the lowest of all racial-ethnic groups (see *Figure 4.4* on p. 87).

As Congress continues to cut health services for the poor, black families—especially those headed by women—will be the ones most likely to experience health problems. Kin provide important emotional and financial support during hard times, but they may feel overburdened when economic difficulties are chronic (Lincoln et al., 2005).

More than two-thirds of African Americans (compared with less than one-third of whites) have no financial assets such as stocks and bonds. Black families inherit less wealth than do white families. This means that parents often cannot afford to give young adults money for college, large cash gifts for weddings, and down payments for their first homes (Oliver and Shapiro, 2001).

Strengths of the African American Family

Despite these and other health and economic problems, many black families have numerous strengths: strong kinship bonds, an ability to adapt family roles to outside pressures, a strong work ethic despite

FIGURE 4.4 Median Household Incomes by Race and Ethnicity, 2009

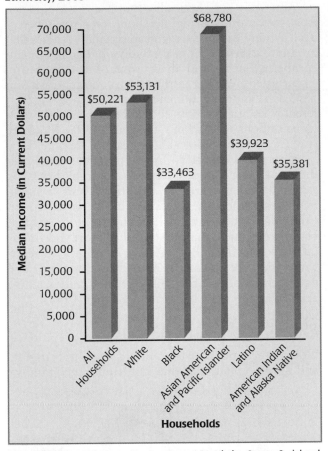

Sources: Based on U.S. Census Bureau, Current Population Survey, Social and Economic Supplements, Historical Income Tables—Households, Table H-16, 2009 (1-Year Estimates), www.census.gov (accessed March 30, 2009).

recessions and unemployment, determination to succeed in education, and an unwavering spirituality that helps them cope with adversity. Many low-income black families, especially those headed by mothers, show enormous fortitude and coping skills (Edin and Lein, 1997; McAdoo, 2002).

Numerous self-help institutions (churches, voluntary associations, neighborhood groups, and extended family networks) enhance the resilience of black families, even in the poorest communities. In the past decade, for example, many black men across the country have organized mentoring and self-help groups for adolescents and young fathers.

Despite much economic adversity, many African Americans see their families as cohesive, love their children, provide a strong religious foundation, and teach their children to be proud of their cultural heritage and to contribute to their community. Other strengths include imbuing children with self-respect, teaching them how to be happy, and stressing cooperation in the family (Hill, 2003; Peters, 2007).

AMERICAN INDIAN FAMILIES

American Indians used to be called the "vanishing Americans." Since the 1980s, however, this population has staged a surprising comeback because of higher birth rates, longer life expectancy, and better health services. American Indians and Alaska Natives make up only 1.5 percent of the U.S. population, but they are expected to comprise 2 percent of the population by 2050 (Ogunwole, 2006; "American Indian and Alaska Native . . .," 2008).

American Indian families are heterogeneous. A Comanche-Kiowa educator cautions that "lumping all Indians together is a mistake. Tribes . . . are sovereign nations and are as different from another tribe as Italians are from Swedes" (Pewewardy, 1998: 71).

Of about 150 native American Indian languages still spoken in the United States, only a handful are being passed on to the next generation and some of the last speakers, now elderly, are dying. Only 27 percent of American Indians and Alaska Natives age 5 and older speak a language other than English at home. Navajo, with about 170,000 speakers, is the most widely spoken native language in the United States, but many others are on the brink of extinction. This is a concern because, according to tribal historians and linguists, losing a language results in losing one's cultural identity (Ashburn, 2007; "American Indian and Alaska Native . . .," 2008; Clark, 2008).

Family Structure

About 62 percent of the nation's American Indian and Alaska Native children live with both parents (see *Figure 4.3* on p. 84). Compared with 40 percent of the general population, 54 percent of American

There are two remaining speakers of Kiksht, a language spoken for centuries by the Wasco tribe along Oregon's Columbia River, and neither remembers all of the words. Radine Johnson and her grandmother, who is one of the last Kiksht speakers, are working together to record and teach the language to tribal children (Clark, 2008). Pictured here, Radine is teaching Kiksht at a tribal preschool.

Indians and Alaska Natives age 30 and older live with their grandchildren and are the primary caretakers ("American Indian and Alaska Native . . .," 2008).

American Indian families have a variety of living arrangements that include large extended households, nuclear families, divorced parents, and single-parent families, on and off the reservation. Living in an extended family provides many positive resources, such as assistance with child care, money, transportation, and emotional and moral support. However, living in such households can increase stress, especially when elders in the home criticize their own children about the way they parent or because they are not making enough money (Cheshire, 2006).

In many American Indian languages, there is no distinction between blood relatives and relatives by marriage. Among some groups, aunts and uncles are considered intimate family members. Sometimes the father's brothers are called "father," uncles and aunts refer to nieces and nephews as "son" or "daughter," and a great-uncle may be referred to as "grandfather" (Sutton and Broken Nose, 1996).

Gender Roles

Research on contemporary American Indian families, husbands and wives, and gender roles is virtually nonexistent (Kawamoto and Cheshire, 2004). One exception is a study of 28 off-reservation Navajo families. Here, the researcher found that mothers spent significantly more time than did fathers in cleaning, food-related work, and child care responsibilities. Compared with fathers in other cultural groups, however, the Navajo fathers' involvement in household labor and child-related tasks was high—between 2 and 3 hours per day. The wives reported higher levels of commitment (always pitching in), cohesion (making sacrifices for others), and communication (expressing concerns and feelings). Both husbands and wives, however, felt equally competent in solving family problems and coping with everyday issues (Hossain, 2001).

Parents and Children

Children are important members of American Indian families. Parents spend considerable time and effort in making items for children to play with or use in activities and ceremonies (such as costumes for special dances, looms for weaving, and tools for gardening, hunting, and fishing). Many tribes teach spiritual values and emphasize special rituals and ceremonies (Yellowbird and Snipp, 2002).

Most adults teach children to show respect for authority figures by listening and not interrupting. As one tribal leader noted, "You have two ears and one mouth for a reason." Mothers, especially, strive to transmit their cultural heritage to their children. They emphasize the importance of listening to and observing adults to learn about their identity (Gose, 1994; Dalla and Gamble, 1997; Cheshire, 2001).

American Indian families emphasize values such as cooperation, sharing, personal integrity, generosity, harmony with nature, and spirituality—values that are quite different from the individual achievement, competitiveness, and drive toward accumulation emphasized by many in the white community. Families teach children that men and women may have different roles but that both should be respected for their contributions to the family (Stauss, 1995; MacPhee et al., 1996; Kawamoto and Cheshire, 1997).

Sometimes American Indian parents believe that they are losing control over their children's behavior, especially hanging around with friends and drinking. Some researchers see a relationship between American Indian adolescents' risk-taking behavior (such as using drugs and dropping out of school) and fragile family connections. For instance, migration off reservations has weakened the extended family, a principal mechanism for transmitting values and teaching accountability (Machamer and Gruber, 1998).

Elders and Grandparents

Elders are important to a child's care, upbringing, and development, and they contribute to a family's

In many states, American Indians hold powwows, gatherings that include dancing, singing, and celebrating the family. The purposes of powwows are to honor American Indian culture and to bring people together to express a sense of community with one another and with the universe.

cohesiveness and stability. Children are taught to respect their elders because old age is viewed as a badge of honor—a sign that one has done the right things and has pleased the creator. As a result, elders have traditionally played a central role in a family's decision making. They serve as mentors and advisors and reinforce cultural norms, values, and roles. Despite such contributions, elders are also dealing with an increasing number of issues ranging from poverty to poor health and minimal access to services in both urban and reservation areas (Kawamoto and Cheshire, 2004).

Because of the emphasis on family unity and cooperation, family members and tribal officials often offer elders assistance without their having to ask for it (Kawamoto and Cheshire, 1997). According to the Navajo, for example, the life cycle consists of three stages: "being cared for," "preparing to care for," and "assuming care of" (Bahr and Bahr, 1995). Thus, caring for one another and for elderly family members is a cultural value that is passed on to children.

As more women work outside the home, they are especially likely to turn their children over to their grandmother for care. Many American Indian college students return to work or teach on reservations or in other American Indian communities because

"they long for mothers, fathers, sisters, brothers, and perhaps most of all, their grandparents" (Garrod and Larimore, 1997: xi; Schweitzer, 1999).

Health and Economic Well-Being

Among American Indians/Alaska Natives ages 15 to 34, suicide is the second leading cause of death (behind unintentional injuries that include auto accidents) and occurs 2.2 times more than the national average for that age group ("Suicide," 2008). Alcohol-related violence is another problem (see the box "American Indians and Alcohol Use: Facts and Fictions").

> **Since you asked . . .**
>
> ::• Why is alcohol abuse a serious problem among many American Indians?

Many tribal leaders believe that one of the reasons for the high alcoholism and suicide rates, especially among youth, is the gradual erosion of American Indian culture. Children who live in urban neighborhoods have a particularly hard time maintaining their cultural identity and often feel like outsiders in both the American Indian and white cultures. In response, hundreds of programs nationwide are fighting addiction by reinforcing American

American Indians and Alcohol Use: Facts and Fictions

Alcohol consumption is a serious problem among many American Indians and Alaska Natives (AI/AN). Alcohol-related deaths among AI/ANs account for 12 percent of all deaths compared with 3 percent in the general population. Half of all deaths every year among AI/ANs in motor vehicle traffic crashes and from liver disease are due to alcohol. Alcohol use is often involved in suicides, and 62 percent of crimes among AI/ANs—compared with 42 percent for the general population—involve drinking by the offender (Perry, 2004; Naimi et al., 2008; "Congressional Hearing . . .," 2009).

Alcohol abuse is a problem in any community, but there are many stereotypes and myths about the "drunken Indian." In reality,

- A wide variation in the prevalence of drinking exists from one tribal group to another.
- About 75 percent of alcohol-related deaths are due to sporadic binge

drinking rather than chronic alcoholism.

- Serious injuries (such as car accidents) due to alcohol often result in death because many Indians live in rural, remote environments where medical care is far away or unavailable.
- Overall, 68 percent of alcohol-related deaths occur among males.
- There are considerable variations in alcohol-related deaths across regions. The highest death rates (more than 300 a year) are in the Northern Plains (the Dakotas, Iowa, Minnesota, and Nebraska), and the lowest (less than 100 a year) are in Alaska and the Southern Plains (Arkansas, Kansas, Oklahoma, and Texas) (May, 1999; Naimi et al., 2008).

According to many tribal leaders, several major beer companies have targeted American Indians with their mar-

keting strategies. The poorest reservations often accept sponsorship from brewing companies for annual tribal fairs and rodeos.

::• **Stop and Think . . .**

- AI/ANs die at higher rates than other Americans from tuberculosis (600 percent higher), alcoholism (510 percent higher), and diabetes (189 percent higher) (Indian Health Service, 2006). Why do we often hear about high AI/AN alcoholism rates but not about the high rates of diseases such as tuberculosis and diabetes?
- Alcohol commercials dominate most television sports programs. Should the commercials be banned in the Northern Plains? Or would such restrictions jeopardize free enterprise and freedom of speech?

Constraints

Mohegan Sun in southern Connecticut (left) is one of the largest casinos in the United States. It has spent some of its profits on college tuitions, a $15 million senior center, other social programs, and health insurance for tribal members. In contrast, some of the poorest tribes, such as the Navajo and Hopi, who have rejected gambling for religious reasons, often live in poverty (right).

Indian cultural practices and values (Sanchez-Way and Johnson, 2000; Sagiri, 2001).

About 56 percent of American Indians owned their own homes in 2007, but almost 26 percent live below the poverty level, compared with 12 percent of the general population. One out of every four civilian-employed American Indians works in a management or professional occupation, but on many reservations, where 36 percent of American Indians live, unemployment rates run about 50 percent and sometimes up to 90 percent. Also, 12 percent of the homes on reservations, compared with 1 percent of those for the general population, don't have safe and adequate water supplies and waste disposal facilities (Taylor and Kalt, 2005; Ogunwole, 2006; "American Indian and Alaska Native . . .," 2008).

Since passage of the Indian Gaming Regulatory Act in 1988, the number of American Indian–owned casinos has grown to more than 400 and account for 37 percent of the U.S. gambling industry. Few tribes have benefited, however, because many casinos are in remote areas that don't attract tourists. In other cases, tribal leaders who control official membership sometimes refuse to recognize tribal members to increase their own profits. Outside of gaming, the number of American Indian–owned businesses grew from fewer than 5 in 1969 to nearly 202,000 in 2002, most of them in construction, retail trade, and health care (Taylor and Kalt, 2005; *American Indian-and Alaska Native-Owned Firms . . .*, 2006; Kestin and Franceschina, 2007).

Strengths of the American Indian Family

Strengths of the American Indian family include *relational bonding,* a core behavior that is built on widely shared values such as respect, generosity, and sharing across the tribe, band, clan, and kin group. Harmony and balance involve putting community and family needs above individual achievements. Another strength is a spirituality that sustains the family's identity and place in the world (Stauss, 1995; Cross, 1998; Cheshire, 2006).

In some cases, tribal members have worked patiently over several generations to develop self-sufficient industries. In the remote village of Mekoryuk, Alaska, for example, Inuit women collaborated with an anthropologist at the University of Alaska–Fairbanks to begin a knitting cooperative that transforms the downy wool of musk oxen into warm and lightweight clothes. The knitters, ranging in age from 9 to 90, work in their homes, incorporate ancient patterns from traditional Inuit culture into their knitting, sell the products by mail order, and make enough money to stay out of poverty (Watkins, 2002).

MAKING CONNECTIONS

- Many American Indian languages are becoming extinct. Is this a normal part of a group's acculturation into a host society? Or should the languages be preserved at all costs?

- According to many tribal leaders, American Indian youth have high alcoholism and suicide rates because they often feel alienated from both their own and white cultures. Why do you think that youth from other minority groups—especially Latinos and Asian Americans, who are also straddling two cultures—have lower alcoholism and suicide rates?

LATINO FAMILIES

Latino families are diverse. Some trace their roots to the Spanish and Mexican settlers who established homes and founded cities in the Southwest before the arrival of the Pilgrims. Others are children of immigrants who arrived in large numbers around the turn of the twentieth century or Latinos who arrived more recently (see Chapter 3).

Spanish-speaking people from Mexico, Ecuador, the Dominican Republic, and Spain differ in their customs and in their experiences in U.S. society. We focus here primarily on characteristics that Latino families share, noting variations among different groups when possible.

Family Structure

About 70 percent of Latino children live in two-parent families, down from 78 percent in 1970 (see *Figure 4.3* on p. 84; see, also, Lugaila, 1998). Shifting social norms, economic changes, and immigration patterns have altered the structure of many Latino families. Couples are more likely to divorce, and there are more out-of-wedlock births. In addition, some young Latino children may be more likely to live with relatives than parents because new immigrants depend on family sponsors until they can become self-sufficient (Garcia, 2002; see, also, Chapters 11 and 15).

Gender Roles and Parenting

Gender and parenting roles vary on factors such as how long a family has lived in the United States, whether the wife or mother works outside the home, and the extent of the family's acculturation into U.S. society. Many Latino families, especially new immigrants, must grapple with new gender and parenting roles that are very different from those in their homeland.

GENDER ROLES Latino men often suffer from the stereotype of *machismo,* a concept of masculinity that emphasizes dominance, aggression, and womanizing (see Chapter 3). The mainstream press often ignores such positive elements of *machismo* as courage, honor, *respeto* (a respect for authority, tradition, and family), *dignidad* (avoiding loss of dignity in front of others), and close ties with the extended family. Men who have been raised in a culture with traditional conceptions of masculinity often feel honor and pride in being breadwinners and family protectors. When it is difficult to meet these gender role expectations, they may be at a greater risk than their acculturated counterparts for problems such as depression, substance abuse, violence, and reluctance to seek psychological assistance (Ojeda et al., 2008).

Some scholars contend that *machismo* is a ludicrous stereotype: Many Latino men participate in domestic work and child rearing instead of acting like macho tough guys who are domineering husbands and fathers. Among Dominican immigrants, for example, many husbands share some housework and consult their wives about expensive purchases (Pessar, 1995; González, 1996).

Other researchers report that even wives who work outside the home are often subordinate to men and are expected to follow traditional family roles. For example, a study of Puerto Rican families found that working mothers were primarily responsible for the care of the home and the children (Toro-Morn, 1998). Similarly, a study of Central American workers found that men in working-class households balked at sharing household responsibilities and child care even when their wives worked full time outside the home (Repak, 1995).

The female counterpart of *machismo* is *marianismo*. *Marianismo,* associated with the Virgin Mary in Catholicism, expects women to remain virgins until marriage and to be self-sacrificing and unassuming (De La Cancela, 1994; Mayo, 1997; see, also, Chapters 5 and 7).

PARENTING Most Latino parents, like other parents, are caring and affectionate and expect their children to be successful. They teach their children to be obedient, honest, and respectful. There are socioeconomic differences in parenting, however. Like their white counterparts, middle-class Latinos who have acculturated to U.S. society tend to be more permissive in raising their children (Harwood et al., 2002).

Even when they're in the labor force, most Latinas devote much of their lives to bearing and rearing children. As one Latina said, "To be valued [in our community] we have to be wives and mothers first." Parenting and marital conflicts sometimes erupt, however, because mothers are often overloaded by the demands of caring for their families and working outside the home (Segura, 1994; DeBiaggi, 2002).

Fathers don't do nearly as much parenting as do mothers. Nevertheless, they're warm and loving with their children. And compared with white fathers, Latino fathers are more likely to supervise and restrict their children's TV viewing, regulate the types of programs they watch, and require them to finish their homework before going outside to play (Toth and Xu, 2002; see, also, Chapter 12).

Familism and Extended Families

For many Latino households, familism and the strength of the extended family have traditionally provided emotional and economic support. In a national

Since you asked . . .

- Are Latinas dominated by macho men?

survey, for example, 94 percent of Latinos who were primarily Spanish speakers and 88 percent of those who were bilingual, compared with 67 percent of the general U.S. population, said that relatives are more important than friends (Pew Hispanic Center, 2004).

FAMILISM *Familism,* you recall, refers to family relationships in which sharing and cooperation take precedence over one's personal needs and desires (see Chapter 3). Many Mexican American families, for example, survive only because they have the emotional and economic support of kin who arrived in the United States earlier. In other cases, especially during economic downturns and family illness or death, familism helps families pull together and decreases the likelihood of stressed parents treating their children in more negative ways, such as being excessively punitive, verbally and physically abusive, or unpredictable (Kochhar, 2005; Behnke et al., 2008).

EXTENDED FAMILIES Extended family members (relatives, godparents, and even close friends) exchange a wide range of goods and services, including elderly and child care, temporary housing, personal advice, and emotional support. Some Mexicans practice "chain migration," in which those already in the United States find employment and housing for other kin who are leaving Mexico (López, 1999; Sarmiento, 2002).

The importance of extended families varies by place of residence and social class, but there's a complex relationship between these variables. For example, Mexican Americans in higher socioeconomic classes who live with or near their relatives are more able and likely to provide money or goods. On the other hand, those with higher income and education levels experience greater geographic mobility because of career opportunities, decreasing the likelihood of contact and financial help (Sarkisian et al., 2007).

Economic Well-Being

According to historian Kevin Starr, "The economy of the Sun Belt and California would collapse without Hispanics. They are doing the work of the entire culture," from harvesting the nation's food supply to providing much-needed workers at hotels, restaurants, and construction sites (cited in Chaddock, 2003: 1, 3).

ECONOMIC PROGRESS Similar to black families, the number of middle-class Latino families has increased. About 38 percent of households earn $50,000 a year or more (see *Figure 4.5*), up considerably from 7 percent in 1972, but there's a great deal of variation among Latino families. Almost 50 percent of Cuban families earn this much, compared with 40 percent of Puerto Rican families and those from Central South

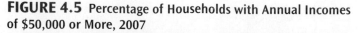

FIGURE 4.5 Percentage of Households with Annual Incomes of $50,000 or More, 2007

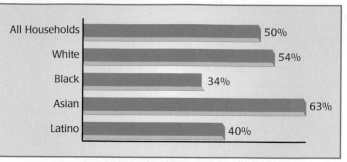

Source: Based on DeNavas-Walt et al., 2008, Table A-1.

America, and 36 percent of Mexican American families (U.S. Census Bureau, 2008).

Why are Cuban Americans generally more successful than other Latinos? Generally, economic success reflects a number of interrelated factors, especially education level, occupation, fluency in English, date of immigration, and U.S. immigration policies. The U.S. government, hoping to weaken Fidel Castro's power during the late 1950s, extended to Cuban exiles a generous welcome that included government subsidies for housing, magnanimous refugee programs that provided job training and intensive English classes, college scholarships, and other resources. No other group of immigrants, including Latinos, ever received such assistance (Suro, 1998; Acosta-Belén and Santiago, 2006; Pew Hispanic Center, 2006).

Many of the Cubans came from a middle- or upper-middle-class background. They had *human capital* (such as high educational levels and entrepreneurial skills), worked hard to develop rundown and abandoned Miami neighborhoods, and became politically active (Pérez, 1992). Many of the more recent Cuban immigrants who had much less human capital have been less successful economically (see Pew Hispanic Center, 2006).

ECONOMIC PROBLEMS Between 1995 and 2005, many newly arrived Latino workers made considerable progress, even in lower-wage jobs, in part because they were older, better educated, and more likely to be employed in a booming construction industry rather than in agriculture. As a result, the proportion of foreign-born Latino workers in the lowest 20 percent of wage jobs decreased from 42 percent in 1995 to 36 percent in 2005 (Kochhar, 2007).

The situation changed in 2007 when the most recent recession began. During a recession, the buying and selling of goods and services slows down, businesses fail, people are fired, unemployment rises, and wages and salaries are cut or stay unchanged. During economic downturns, who suffers the most?

Mexican Day Laborers in America

Angelo earned $100 for 16 hours of work at a Los Angeles construction site. Antonio stacked boxes at a Chicago warehouse for 10 hours and wasn't paid at all. Both Angelo and Antonio are *los jornaleros,* Mexican slang for "day laborers."

Day laborers are people who are paid for work on a daily or short-term basis. They often congregate on street corners before dawn and wait for employers to drive by and offer them work. When an employer drives up, the men swarm around the car or truck to be noticed and hired for the day.

Day laborers are a common sight in California and the Southwest. Increasingly, they are also working in Chicago and other cities and suburbs along the East Coast. Some researchers estimate that there are more than 118,000 of these workers across the United States, making up only a fraction of the 11 million undocumented immigrants in the country.

Day labor offers no health benefits, no job security, no overtime, and payment in cash. The employers get tax-free, cheap labor, and the workers get work.

Day laborers are overwhelmingly Mexican men who speak little English and have no more than a sixth-grade education. The 80 percent who are undocumented immigrants are especially vulnerable to unscrupulous employers, homeowners, and contractors who pay less than they promise or not at all, but day laborers don't report the abuse because they fear being deported.

In 2006, day laborers earned as much as $1,400 in a good month and as little as $350 in a typical bad month.

Groups of Latino men looking for possible work opportunities surround the car of a potential employer outside a 7-Eleven in Herndon, Virginia.

Many sent a large portion of their earnings home; others used the money to smuggle relatives across the U.S. border.

In 2008, when the economy began to crumble and many full-time Americans were laid off, day laborer jobs also dwindled. Some laborers returned to Mexico and Latin America. Those who remained experienced increased rates of hate crimes, armed assaults on their way home from a job, murders, and employers who paid less than previously or not at all.

Day laborers often handle toxic materials without proper safety equipment, perform dangerous work, and suffer injuries on the job. They possess the very traits that we celebrate—self-reliance, hard work, and raising income for their families—yet they are "widely used, abused, and despised."

Sources: Bazar and Armour, 2005; Garcia, 2006, Valenzuela et al., 2006; Semple, 2008; "False Reports . . .,"2009; Nossiter, 2009.

┇• Stop and Think ...

■ Because they work hard at jobs that most Americans don't want, why do you think that day laborers are "widely used, abused, and despised"?

■ Some activist groups are pressuring elected officials to punish the local employers who hire day laborers. Others argue that day laborers are exploited and should be protected because they provide much-needed cheap labor. What do you think? Why?

Minorities. In 2008, for example, the unemployment rates were highest for blacks (12 percent), U.S.-born Latinos (10 percent), and foreign-born Latinos (8 percent), compared with 5 percent for Asians and 6 percent for white workers (Kochhar, 2009).

Latino day laborers who seek any work they can get are among the most abused workers in America (see the box "Mexican Day Laborers in America").

However, even undocumented immigrants who have full-time jobs often experience economic exploitation. For example, a team of state inspectors in southern California who visited a dozen of the 1,600 hand carwash companies found that 20 percent of the Latino car dryers were not paid, many worked for tips only (even though this is illegal) and earned only $30 a day, and that the owners of one company saved more than $1 million by underpaying 100 Latino employees over four years. The workers knew they were being cheated but didn't complain because they feared being fired or were threatened with physical harm or deportation (Nazario and Smith, 2008).

Strengths of the Latino Family

Despite their economic vulnerability, many Latino families are resilient and adaptive. Family networks protect their members' health and emotional well-being. Many immigrants demonstrate incredible internal resources in coping with economic hardship, learning a new language, and shaping their own solutions in adjusting to a new environment (Alfaro et al., 2006; DeGarmo and Martinez, 2006).

The ability of Latino families to transmit traditional values has often offset the negative impact of prejudice and discrimination, drug use, and other risky behavior among many adolescents. As in black families, parental socialization, which emphasizes ethnic pride and identity, protects many Latino children from anger, depression, and, in some cases, violence (Quintana and Vera, 1999; Phinney et al., 2001).

ASIAN AMERICAN FAMILIES

Asian Americans encompass a wide swath of cultures and traditions. They come from at least 26 countries of East and Southeast Asia (including China, Taiwan, Korea, Japan, Vietnam, Laos, Cambodia, and the Philippines) and South Asia (including India, Pakistan, and Sri Lanka). They follow different religions, speak different languages, and use different alphabets. Asian Americans also include Native Hawaiians and other Pacific Islanders from Guam and Samoa.

Chinese are the largest Asian American group (3.5 million), followed by Filipinos (3 million) and Asian Indians (2.8 million). Combined, these three groups account for 58 percent of all Asian Americans ("Asian/Pacific American. . . ." 2009).

Regardless of their country of origin, Asian American families feel pressure to adapt to U.S. culture. Some of the changes they experience are in family structure, gender roles, and parent-child relationships.

Family Structure

Asian American family structures vary widely depending on country of origin, time of arrival, past and current immigration policies, whether the families are immigrants or refugees, and the parents' original socioeconomic status. Almost 11 percent of Asian American and Pacific Islander families have six or more members, compared with 5 percent of families nationally. Average household size varies across groups: 5.3 for Hmong and 4.0 for Laotians and Cambodians, for example, but only 2.2 for Japanese and Chinese families (McLoyd et al., 2001; 2007 American Community Survey).

Asian American families are likely to be extended rather than nuclear and might include parents, children, unmarried siblings, and grandparents. Most children grow up in two-parent homes (see *Figure 4.3* on p. 84). Female-headed homes, whether because of divorce or out-of-wedlock births, are much less common among Asian Americans than other groups.

Gender Roles

Many Asian Americans follow Confucianism, which endorses a patriarchal social structure and instructs women to obey their father, father-in-law, husband, and oldest son. The woman thus derives her status through her role as a daughter, daughter-in-law, wife, or mother. The man, in contrast, is the head of household, principal provider, decision maker, and disciplinarian (Yu, 1995; Chan, 1997).

Gender role socialization tends to be traditional in many Asian American families, but it can vary widely on the basis of social class, country of origin, and especially length of residence in the United States. For example, both Korean and Vietnamese immigrant women have almost always worked outside the home, but those in later generations have created a more gender-balanced family environment, such as men's greater participation in housework, instead of following traditional gender roles where all housework is the woman's reponsibility (Kawamoto and Viramontez Anguiano, 2006). Because Filipino culture historically has had a less patriarchal gender role structure than other groups, husbands and wives tend to have egalitarian relationships (Espiritu, 1995).

In many cases, working outside the home has not decreased the wife's homemaker role. She is still expected to cook, clean the house, and take care of the children. She bears these double roles regardless of length of residence in the United States (Ishii-Kuntz, 2004).

Tensions often arise as the husband's traditional role of breadwinner shifts. Especially in working-class families, two-paycheck couples may have multiple jobs or irregular hours. They have little time for each other, their children, or household tasks and stress builds (Fong, 2002).

Parents and Children

In many Asian American families, the strongest family ties are between parent and child rather than between spouses. Parents sacrifice their personal needs in the interests of their children. In return, they expect *filial piety*: respect and obedience toward one's parents (Chan, 1997).

FAMILY VALUES As with the Latino emphasis on familism, to Asian Americans the family is more important than the individual. The Vietnamese saying *mot giot mau dao hon ao nuoc la* ("one drop of blood is much more precious than a pond full of water") reflects the belief that family solidarity is more important than relationships with people outside the family. Even when extended kin don't live together, they may cooperate in running a family business, pool their income, and share certain domestic functions, such as meal preparation (Glenn and Yap, 2002).

Filipino ideology teaches that revealing a family problem to an "outsider"—whether a friend, teacher, or counselor—creates gossip and brings shame (*hiya*) and embarrassment to the family. Such "confessions" imply that parents are doing a bad job of raising their children. On the other hand, bottling up problems may lead to loneliness, depression, and suicidal thoughts (Wolf, 1997).

DISCIPLINE Asian American parents tend to exercise more control over their children's lives than do non–Asian American parents. They use guilt and shame rather than physical punishment to keep their children in line and to reinforce the children's strong obligations to the family. In Chinese American families, for example, *guan* ("to govern") has a positive connotation. *Guan* also means "to care for" or "to love." Therefore, "parental care, concern, and involvement are synonymous with a firm control and

governance of the child" (Chao and Tseng, 2002: 75; Fong, 2002).

Many Asian American parents are indulgent, tolerant, and permissive with infants and toddlers. As the child approaches school age, however, the parents expect greater discipline and more responsibility in grooming, dressing, and completing chores (Chan, 1997).

Most parents don't tolerate aggressive behavior and expect older children to serve as role models for their younger siblings. Parents also teach their children to conform to societal expectations because they are concerned about what other people think, both within and outside the Asian American community. Many parents not only pressure their children to excel in school but also may endure extreme hardships—even selling their house—to ensure the best college opportunities for their children (Fong, 2002). The box "How to Be a Perfect Taiwanese Kid" describes the emphasis on academic achievement.

> **Since you asked . . .**
>
> ❖ Are Asian American children really higher achievers than other American children?

The Model Minority: Fictions and Facts

Because of their educational and economic success, Asian Americans are often hailed as a "model minority." Are such labels accurate? Or misleading?

Cross-Cultural and Multicultural Families

How to Be a Perfect Taiwanese Kid

Many immigrant parents—Latino, Middle Eastern, and African—emphasize education as the route to upward mobility and success. The value of education is embodied in the Chinese proverb, "If you are planning for a year, sow rice; if you are planning for a decade, plant trees; if you are planning for a lifetime, educate people." For many Asian American parents, securing a good education for their children is a top priority (Ishii-Kuntz, 2004).

By excelling in school, the child brings honor to the family. Educational and occupational successes further enhance the family's social status

and ensure its economic well-being as well as that of the next generation (Chan, 1999). The following tongue-in-cheek observations about how to be the perfect Taiwanese kid (Ng, 1998: 42) from the parents' perspective would apply to many other Asian American families as well:

1. A perfect score on the SAT [Scholastic Aptitude Test].
2. Play the violin or piano at the level of a concert performer.
3. Apply to and be accepted by 27 colleges.
4. Have three hobbies: studying, studying, and studying.

5. Go to a prestigious Ivy League university and win a scholarship to pay for it.
6. Love classical music and detest talking on the phone.
7. Become a Westinghouse, Presidential, and eventually a Rhodes Scholar.
8. Aspire to be a brain surgeon.
9. Marry a Taiwanese American doctor and have perfect, successful children (grandkids for *ahma* and *ahba*).
10. Love to hear stories about your parents' childhood, especially the one about walking 7 miles to school without shoes.

FICTIONS ABOUT THE MODEL MINORITY Asian American families have the highest median income in the country (see *Figure 4.4* on p. 87). Such figures are misleading, however, because many Asian American households are larger than average, as you saw earlier, and include more workers. In addition, lumping all Asian Americans together as a "model minority" ignores many subgroups that are not doing well because of low educational levels and language barriers.

The most successful Asian Americans are those who speak English relatively well *and* have high educational levels. Overall, Asian Americans have higher educational levels than any other racial-ethnic group. Half have at least a college degree compared with 29 percent of the white population. There's considerable variation across groups, however. For example, 36 percent of Asian Indians have a graduate or professional degree compared with 7 percent of Vietnamese and 3 percent of Cambodians (U.S. Census Bureau, 2008; "Asian/Pacific American . . .," 2009).

Many recent Asian American immigrants with top-notch credentials from their homeland experience underemployment in the United States. For example, some Korean doctors work as hospital orderlies and nurses' assistants at the same time that they prepare for the English-language test and the medical exam in their field of specialization (Jo, 1999). The "Dangers of the Model Minority Myth" box describes some negative effects of the model minority image on Asian Americans and on American society in general.

FACTS ABOUT THE MODEL MINORITY Why have many Asian American families become successful? There are three major factors.

First, the U.S. Immigration and Naturalization Service screens immigrants, granting entry primarily to those who are the "cream of the crop." For example, nearly 66 percent of Filipino immigrants are professionals, usually nurses and other medical personnel, and more than two-thirds of all Asian Americans from India are professionals with advanced degrees beyond college. Also, foreign-born professionals are usually willing to work the long hours demanded by public hospitals and to work for lower salaries (Adler, 2003; "Asian/Pacific Americans . . .," 2009).

Second, the Buddhist and Confucian values and traditions of many Asian immigrants resemble the traditional middle-class prerequisites for success in America. All three ideologies emphasize hard work, education, achievement, self-reliance, sacrifice, steadfast purpose, and long-term goals.

Asian American and American traditions differ in at least one important way, however. Whereas American values stress individualism, competition, and independence, Buddhist and Confucian traditions emphasize interdependence, harmony, cooperation, and pooling resources. For example, many Korean immigrants have been able to secure capital to start

Asian American youths, such as Kavya Shivashankar of Olathe, Kansas, often win spelling bees and science contests. In 2009 Shivashankar won the Scripps National Spelling Bee with the correct spelling of "laodicean." (I, too, had to look it up.)

a small business through *kae* (or *kye*), a credit rotation system in which about a dozen families donate $1,000 or more to help a shopkeeper set up a new business (Yoon, 1997).

The rotating savings and credit organization is common to many ethnic groups: Ethiopians call it *ekub*, Bolivians call it *pasanaqu* (to "pass from hand to hand"), and Cambodians call it *tong-tine*. All operate on the same basic principles: Organize a group of close friends; agree on how much and how often to pay into the kitty; and determine how the money will be distributed, whether by lottery or according to need. The winner can use the funds to start a business, pay for a wedding, put a down payment on a home, or pay for college tuition (Suro, 1998).

A third reason for many Asian American families' success is fairly straightforward: They usually work harder than their non-Asian counterparts. For example, Asian American students are more likely than other racial-ethnic groups, and often white students, to finish high school, enroll in and graduate from college, and achieve graduate degrees (Carey, 2005; Pryor et al., 2007). In addition, most Asian students are active in extracurricular activities—such as school clubs, athletics, and community service—but they typically spend twice as much time on homework as other American students, and less time

Cross-Cultural and Multicultural Families

Dangers of the Model Minority Myth

Sociologist William Petersen (1966: 21) first used the phrase "model minority" when he described Japanese Americans as an unparalleled success story:

By any criterion that we choose, the Japanese Americans are better than any other group in our society, including U.S.-born whites. They have established this remarkable record, moreover, by their own almost totally unaided effort. Every attempt to hamper this progress resulted only in enhancing their determination to succeed.

Since then, many Asian American and other scholars have challenged the notion of Asian Americans as a "model minority" as being little more than a myth that results in racial stereotyping and six dangers (Do, 1999: 118–22; see, also, Chou and Feagin, 2008):

Danger 1: The model minority image distorts and ignores the differences within Asian American communities. Vietnamese Americans, for example, share many cultural characteristics and customs, but they are a diverse group in time of arrival, educational levels, English proficiency, and support received after landing on U.S. shores.

Danger 2: The model minority stereotype creates tension and antagonism within and across Asian American subgroups. If recently arrived immigrants aren't as successful as their predecessors, there must be something wrong with them. Other immigrants have done very well, after all.

Danger 3: Model minority images can lead to verbal and physical assaults. White supremacist groups, who resent many Asian Americans' educational and occupational accomplishments, often target Asian Americans with hate crimes, including murder.

Danger 4: The model minority myth camouflages ongoing racial discrimination in U.S. society by blaming the victim. If some groups—such as blacks, Latinos, and American Indians—don't succeed, it must be their own fault rather than the fault of U.S. policies or racism.

Danger 5: As with any stereotype, the model minority image denies its members' individuality. Although many Asian American students are interested in teaching, social work, dance, and theater, they are often pressured to pursue careers in law, medicine, engineering, dentistry, computer science, or the biological sciences.

Danger 6: The model minority myth deprives individuals of necessary social services and monetary support. Asian Americans typically are excluded from many civil rights policies, such as affirmative action programs, because they are labeled as achievers (Ancheta, 1998).

⠿ Stop and Think …

- Why do you think these myths about Asian Americans as a model minority are so widespread?

- How do such myths and stereotypes affect Asian Americans' relationships with classmates, co-workers, employers, and employees?

---

watching television, socializing with friends, or working after school (Saito, 2002).

Strengths of the Asian American Family

As in the case of Latino families, researchers emphasize that Asian American families vary significantly in their country of origin, time of immigration, ability to speak English, and other factors. Generally, however, the strengths of Asian American families include stable households in which parents encourage their children to remain in school and offer personal support that reduces the stress produced by discrimination and leads to better emotional health (Barringer et al., 1993; Leonard, 1997).

Traditional Asian American families are changing. Still, many young adults want to maintain the close-knit character of their family life, which emphasizes cooperation, caring, and self-sacrifice (Kibria, 1994; Zhou and Bankston, 1998).

MIDDLE EASTERN FAMILIES

The term *Middle East* refers to "one of the most diverse and complex combinations of geographic, historical, religious, linguistic, and even racial places on Earth" (Sharifzadeh, 1997: 442). The Middle East encompasses about 30 countries that include Turkey, Israel, Iran, Afghanistan, Pakistan, and a number of Arab nations (such as Algeria, Egypt, Iraq, Jordan,

Tony Shalhoub plays the neurotic but brilliant crime investigator in the popular television series, *Monk*. Shalhoub's father emigrated from Lebanon as an orphan and married a Lebanese American woman. Shalhoub, who had nine brothers and sisters, was born in Green Bay, Wisconsin, in a Lebanese American community. He has turned down numerous scripts that he believed had racist overtones.

Kuwait, Lebanon, Palestine, Saudi Arabia, Syria, and the United Arab Emirates).

Of the almost 56 million people in the United States who speak a language other than English at home, about 4 percent speak Middle Eastern languages such as Armenian, Arabic, Hebrew, Persian, or Urdu (U.S. Census Bureau, 2008). As in the case of Asian American families, Middle Eastern families make up a heterogeneous population that is a "multicultural, multiracial, and multiethnic mosaic" (Abudabbeh, 1996: 333).

Family Structure

As in other ethnic groups, Middle Eastern family structures vary. However, many share similar values and attitudes about family life.

FAMILY SIZE "Wealth and children are the ornaments of this life," says the Qur'an, the sacred book of Muslims. In traditional Middle Eastern societies, not having children is a reason for great unhappiness. A study of a working-class Arab American community in Dearborn, Michigan, found that 38 percent had five or more children (Aswad, 1994).

The number of children declines, however, among people who are U.S. born and members of higher socioeconomic classes. U.S.-born Arab American women have low fertility rates: just under two children per lifetime (which is lower than the average among all U.S. women). Many women postpone childbearing and have fewer children because they pursue college and professional degrees and have high employment rates (Kulczycki and Lobo, 2001).

NUCLEAR AND EXTENDED FAMILIES Most Middle Eastern children (84 percent) live with both parents, compared with 71 percent of all American children. Middle Eastern families frown on divorce. Iranians, for example, view divorce as a calamity (*bala*) and equate it with an "unfortunate fate" that should be avoided at all costs. Divorce rates for U.S.-born Middle Eastern families are increasing, but the percentages are much lower than the national average (almost half of all marriages). Unless a parent is a widow or a widower, single parenthood is seen as abnormal (Aswad, 1997; Hojat et al., 2000).

Nuclear families are the norm, but extended family ties are important. "The typical Lebanese," for example, "views family as an extension of him or herself" (Richardson-Bouie, 2003: 528). Households composed of parents and children maintain close contact with relatives. These relationships provide financial, social, and emotional support.

Whenever possible, Middle Eastern families try to bring relatives from their homelands to stay with them over long periods to attend U.S. colleges and universities, to work, or just to visit. According to a young Algerian woman, her 26-year-old female cousin lived with their family for six years while attending graduate school. Both women had strict curfews (Shakir, 1997).

One of my Turkish students told his classmates that his American-born parents "kicked me down to the basement" because a visiting uncle was to use his bedroom for the next year or so. The other students were appalled, but he just shrugged: "Relatives are important in Turkish families."

Marriage and Gender Roles

For most Middle Easterners, and unlike many Western families, the family is the center of everything. Shame against the family should be avoided at all costs, age and wisdom (instead of youth and beauty) are honored, and friends are treated courteously but are not seen as important as family members (Office of the Deputy Chief . . ., 2006). Many Middle Eastern families value close and reciprocal ties between husbands and wives. Marriage is often a "family affair," and gender role expectations are usually clearly delineated.

> **Since you asked . . .**
>
> :: How has acculturation changed Middle Eastern families?

MARRIAGE Marriage is endogamous (see Chapter 1), favoring unions between cousins in some groups and, in general, between people from the same national group. Marriage is a sacred ceremony and is regarded as central to the family unit.

Marriage is usually a contract between two families and is rarely based on the Western concept of romantic love. Marriages are often arranged or semi-arranged in the sense that children can turn down their parents' choices of a suitable mate.

Some of these practices are changing, and they vary from one group to another. Among Iranians, Lebanese, and Palestinians, especially those from upper- and middle-class families, young adults tend to choose their own marital partners but usually seek parental approval. Others visit their homelands to meet prospective partners that their kin (especially mothers and aunts) have singled out for marriage (Jalali, 1996).

GENDER ROLES Middle Eastern cultural attitudes mandate distinct gender role expectations. Men have been socialized to be the providers for the family and to protect their wives, children, and female kin. A "good" husband, then, supports his family and makes decisions that promote the family's well-being. In most cases, the husband is the highest authority in the family and has the final decision on family issues (Aswad, 1999; Joseph, 1999).

Women anchor the family's identity. A "good" wife takes care of the home and children, obeys her husband, and gets along with her in-laws. She doesn't challenge her husband, especially in public, and doesn't work outside the home, especially when the children are young. Men have many privileges, but women have considerable influence and status at home and in child rearing (Simon, 1996).

A wife should always act honorably and do nothing that humiliates her husband and relatives. Premarital sex and extramarital affairs are out of the question because they bring shame to the family and kin. According to some young women, such gender role expectations are comforting rather than restrictive because they protect women from assaults and competition for dates (Shakir, 1997).

Gender roles are changing, however. Many Middle Eastern women must work out of economic necessity. The women who are most likely to be employed, however, at least among Arab Americans, are those without children at home. In effect, then, patriarchal systems dictate that Middle Eastern women in some groups can be in the labor force only when they don't have traditional responsibilities such as raising children (Read, 2004).

Parents and Children

According to an Arabic saying, "To satisfy God is to satisfy parents." Satisfying parents means following the family's customs and traditions, respecting one's cultural identity, and living up to gender role expectations.

ETHNIC IDENTITY Parents and children usually have strong bonds. In a study of Arab Canadian teenagers,

for example, nine out of ten respondents said that they talk to their parents, usually the mother, about their personal lives and problems (Abu-Laban and Abu-Laban, 1999).

This trust and confidence reflects the Middle Eastern belief that parents are an important resource. Parents also teach their children to feel a lifelong responsibility to their siblings and parents and to respect their aunts, uncles, cousins, and grandparents (Ajrouch, 1999).

Parents reinforce ethnic identity by encouraging their children to associate with peers from their own culture. Many Armenian children, for example, attend language school on weekends. These adolescents not only learn their language but also associate with Armenian classmates who have similar cultural values (Phinney et al., 2001).

GENDER ROLE EXPECTATIONS Many Middle Eastern parents have a double standard in dating and curfews. Girls are guarded because husbands want a virgin bride and not "damaged goods" (see Chapter 1). Brothers have every right to scold or pressure their sisters if they act in any way that could tarnish the family name.

Boys are expected to marry within their ethnic group, but they have much more freedom to date, both inside and outside their group. According to a Lebanese mother, "We just feel the boy can take care of himself. If a boy goes out with a girl, nobody's going to point a finger at him." In contrast, a girl who dates or dresses "the wrong way" will ruin her reputation and dishonor the family's name (Simon, 1996; Ajrouch, 1999).

Girls are expected to perform traditional domestic chores and serve men. Some girls accept these roles, but others complain. According to a young Lebanese woman,

So many times I would be asked to fix my brother's bed. I was told, "He is a boy." And I would say, "He has arms and legs." Or sometimes he would be sitting, and he would say, "Go get me a glass of water." I would say, "Never! Get your own." My family would say to me, "Your head is so strong, it cannot be broken with a hammer" (Shakir, 1997: 166).

The double standards create conflict between daughters and their parents. Middle Eastern teenage girls who spend much time with their American friends, especially, balk at the restrictions on dating. These and other disagreements can strain intergenerational relationships.

Economic Well-Being and Poverty

Middle Eastern Americans tend to be better educated and wealthier than other Americans. For example, Arab Americans are nearly twice as likely as the average U.S. resident to have a college degree—41 percent compared with 24 percent. The median income for an Arab family, $52,300, is about $2,100 more than the median income of all U.S. families. As in other groups, however, there are wide variations. For example, Lebanese have higher median family incomes (almost $61,000) than Moroccans ($41,000). Because of their generally higher educational levels, the proportion of U.S. Arabs working in management jobs is higher than the U.S. average, 42 percent and 34 percent, respectively (Brittingham and de la Cruz, 2005; Office of the Deputy Chief . . ., 2006).

Not all Middle Eastern Americans are successful, of course. The proportion of U.S. Arabs living in poverty (17 percent) is higher than the general population (12 percent). Lebanese and Syrians have the lowest poverty rates, 11 percent, compared with more than 26 percent for those from Iraq and many other Middle East countries (Brittingham and de la Cruz, 2005).

Prejudice and Discrimination

All ethnic families have experienced prejudice and discrimination (see Chapter 3). For decades, many Middle Eastern Americans have encountered prejudice and discrimination in the workplace, school, and public places. Even years after the 9/11 terrorist attacks, many Middle Eastern Americans are adopting self-imposed restrictions to prevent threats of violence: They avoid flying and crossing the border into Canada, Anglicize their names (Osama Nimer, electrician, is now Samuel Nimer), trim their beards, steer clear of wearing distinctive head scarves, speak English instead of Arabic in public, display the American flag, and watch what they say (Marvasti and McKinney, 2004; Hampson, 2006).

Despite the increased diversity of the U.S. population, Middle Eastern children are often ridiculed because of their "funny names" and "strange behavior" (such as not attending proms because Islam discourages dances). Patients may distrust Middle Eastern physicians and other qualified practitioners, especially since 9/11, because they suspect that these health providers might be terrorists who would purposely endanger their health (Marvasti and McKinney, 2004).

Some Middle Easterners, many of whom are Muslims, have complained, unsuccessfully, that public schools and colleges close schools for Christian and Jewish holidays (such as Christmas and Rosh Hashanah, respectively) but not Islamic holy days such as the end of Ramadan, a month of daylong fasting and reflection (Davis, 2007). In addition, according to some scholars, denying visas to Middle Easterners since 9/11, especially to those of Arab origin, has cost the United States billions of dollars every

In 2009, AirTran removed nine Muslim Americans, including Kashif Irfan and his sons (pictured here). The airline suspected that they were terrorists after one of the women remarked, casually, to a passenger, that it's not safe to sit next to the engines in the event of an accident or explosion. One of the men was a U.S. anesthesiologist and another a U.S. attorney. Eight of the travelers were native-born Americans and the ninth was a legal and permanent U.S. resident. The Muslims said that they were targeted because some of the men wore beards and the women wore head scarves (Gardner and Hsu, 2009).

year in U.S. exports, tourism, and college student enrollments (Smith, 2007).

These and other instances of prejudice and discrimination have a negative impact on parents and their children. Nevertheless, Middle Eastern families—like African Americans, American Indians, Latinos, and Asian Americans—show enormous resilience in overcoming obstacles.

Strengths of the Middle Eastern Family

Middle Eastern Americans cope with prejudice and discrimination because they have a strong ethnic identity, close family ties, and religious beliefs that secure children to their communities. Most important, perhaps, many Middle East families have extended kin networks and relatives on whom they can count during hard times (Ajrouch, 1999; Hayani, 1999).

:: MAKING CONNECTIONS

■ If you're a member of a racial-ethnic family, what do you see as its major strengths? What about its problems?

■ What are some of the costs and benefits of maintaining one's ethnic-racial identity instead of acculturating?

INTERRACIAL AND INTERETHNIC RELATIONSHIPS AND MARRIAGES

In 1997, professional golfer Tiger Woods said he was "Cablinasian," a word he'd made up as a boy, because he was one-eighth Caucasian, one-fourth black, one-eighth American Indian, one-fourth Thai, and one-fourth Chinese. Many blacks were upset that Woods seemed to downplay his African American roots, but Woods maintained that he was embracing all parts of his multicultural heritage.

Growing Multiracial Diversity

As you saw earlier in this chapter, the 2000 Census allowed people to mark more than one race and ethnicity for the first time, which generated about 126 categories and combinations. Almost 98 percent reported only one race, but 1 in 40 was the product of two or more racial groups (see *Figure 4.6*). About 4 percent of children under age 18 were identified as multiracial, compared with 2 percent of adults. Almost a third of those reporting two or more races were Latinos. Hawaii has the largest proportion of people—21 percent—who identify themselves as belonging to two or more races, followed by Alaskans and Californians (5 percent each) (Jones and Smith, 2001; Jones, 2005).

Interracial and Interethnic Dating and Marriage

It's now fairly common for people to date someone from a different racial or ethnic group—48 percent

FIGURE 4.6 Percentage of Americans Who Identify with More than One Race

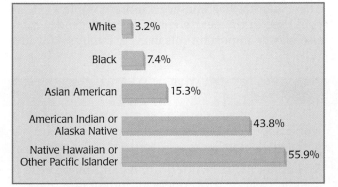

Note: Of the almost 309 million U.S. population in 2010, 2.9 percent identified themselves with two or more races. Only 0.3 percent said they were three or more races.
Source: Overview of Race and Hispanic Origin: 2010, released March 24, 2011 http://2010.census.gov/news/releases/operations/cb11-cn125.html.

of Americans overall say they have done so, including 69 percent of Latinos, 52 percent of blacks, and 45 percent of whites (Jones, 2005).

Interracial and interethnic marriages reflect *exogamy* or marrying outside of one's particular group (see Chapters 1 and 8). Laws against **miscegenation,** marriage or sexual relations between a man and a woman of different races, existed in America as early as 1661. These laws initially prohibited marriage between whites and black slaves and later were extended to include free blacks. It wasn't until 1967, in the U.S. Supreme Court's *Loving v. Virginia* decision, that antimiscegenation laws were overturned nationally. Since that time, racial-ethnic intermarriages have increased slowly—from 0.7 percent in 1970 to 5.4 percent of all married couples in 2000 (Fields and Casper, 2001). Thus, about 95 percent of all couples marry someone of the same race.

PREVALENCE OF RACIAL-ETHNIC INTERMARRIAGES When people think about racial intermarriage, they generally assume that it's between blacks and whites. This is a misconception. Of the 3 million racial-ethnic intermarriages, the out-marriage rates are lower for whites and blacks than for Latinos, Asian Americans, and American Indians (Farley, 2002). Whereas black men are more likely to marry white women than women in other racial-ethnic groups, white men are more likely to marry Latino, Asian American, and American Indian women (and in that order) than African American women (Fields and Casper, 2001).

> **Since you asked . . .**
>
> ⫶• Why have many Americans' attitudes about interracial marriage changed?

Why have racial-ethnic intermarriages increased? And why do the rates vary across and within racial-ethnic groups? There are a number of interrelated factors, both micro level and macro level. Let's begin with proximity and changing attitudes.

PROXIMITY We tend to date and marry people that we see on a regular basis. The higher the educational level, the greater the potential for intermarriage because highly educated minority members often attend the same colleges, and their workplaces and neighborhoods are more integrated than in the past (Kalmijn, 1998; Qian, 2005).

An increase in interracial marriages also reflects changing attitudes. In 1958, only 4 percent of Americans approved of marriage between blacks and whites. By 2007, 77 percent approved, but whites were more likely to disapprove (19 percent) than were blacks (10 percent) and Latinos (10 percent) (Carroll, 2007).

American model Heidi Klum has a daughter from a previous relationship with an Italian businessman. In 2005, she married musician Seal, the son of Nigerian and Brazilian parents. They are expecting their third child as this book goes to press. Do such high-profile people encourage greater acceptance of interracial marriage?

AVAILABILITY OF POTENTIAL SPOUSES People often marry outside of their racial-ethnic group because of a shortage of eligible spouses within their own group. Because the Arab American population is so small, for example, 80 percent of U.S.-born Arabs have non-Arab spouses. In contrast, intermarriage rates among Latinos and Asian Americans have decreased since 1990—for both women and men—because the influx of new immigrants has provided a larger pool of eligible mates (Kulczycki and Lobo, 2002; Qian and Lichter, 2007). Some demographers predict, however, that by 2100, more than half of all Asian Americans, Pacific Islanders, and Latinos will have intermarried (Edmonston et al., 2002).

ACCULTURATION The racial-ethnic groups that are most acculturated are the most likely to intermarry. For example, the Asian Americans who are less likely to out-marry are those who live in ethnic enclaves, do not speak fluent English, and have lived in the United States a short time (Shinagawa and Pang, 1996).

Among Japanese Americans, in contrast, intermarriage rates are high because many families have been in the country for four or five generations, have acculturated, and are generally more accepting of intermarriage than are more recent immigrants. In addition, the number of Japanese Americans is small compared with that of other Asian American groups. This decreases the opportunities for Japanese Americans to find a desirable mate within their own group (Hwang et al., 1994; Rosenfeld, 2002).

⋮⋮ MAKING CONNECTIONS

- How do you feel about interethnic and interracial dating and marriage? Do your views differ from those of your parents or grandparents?

- Are racial-ethnic intermarriages desirable because they reflect an acceptance of other groups? Or do they dilute cultural heritages?

CONCLUSION

The racial and ethnic composition of American families is *changing*. There has been an influx of immigrants from many non-European countries that is expected to continue in the future. There are also many variations both between and within racial-ethnic groups in family structure, extended kinship networks, and parenting styles. This means that families have more *choices* outside the traditional, white, middle-class family model.

These choices often are steeped in *constraints*, however. Even middle-class racial-ethnic minorities confront stereotypes and discrimination on a daily basis. Because many children are multiracial, they must live in at least two cultural and social worlds. These worlds become even more complicated, as you'll see in the next chapter, because gender roles also play an important role in every family's daily life.

SUMMARY

1. U.S. households are becoming more diverse in their racial and ethnic composition. Demographers project that if current immigration and birth rate trends continue, by 2050 only half of the U.S. population will be white.

2. Many Americans are ambivalent about the high rates of immigration to the United States. Some are grateful that immigrants provide important work at both the low-wage and professional levels. Others worry about national security and "diluting our national identity."

3. Latino, African American, Asian American, Middle Eastern, and American Indian families are minority groups. One of the most important characteristics of a minority group is its lack of economic and political power relative to the dominant group because of racism, prejudice, and discrimination.

4. Black families are heterogeneous. They vary in kinship structure, values, and social class.

5. American Indian families are complex and diverse. They speak many languages, practice different religions and customs, and maintain a variety of economic and political styles. Because of assimilation into mainstream U.S. society, a number of tribes are losing their language and customs.

6. Latino families differ in a number of ways, including when they settled in the United States, where they came from, and how they adapted to economic and political situations. In addition, family structure and dynamics vary greatly by social class and degree of acculturation.

7. Asian American families are even more diverse than American Indian and Latino families. Asian American family structures vary depending on the family's origin, when the immigrants arrived, and the socioeconomic status of the parents.

8. Middle Eastern families come from about 30 countries. They speak many languages and practice different religions, but most place a high value on nuclear and extended families, teach traditional gender roles, and reinforce their children's ethnic identity.

9. The number of multiracial Americans is increasing. Much of this population consists of children under age 18.

10. The rates of interracial and interethnic marriage have been increasing slowly since 1967. Some of the reasons for the growing number of these marriages include proximity in school and workplaces, greater public acceptance of racial-ethnic intermarriage, acculturation, and a shrinking pool of eligible marriage partners in some groups.

KEY TERMS

assimilation 78
cultural pluralism 78
acculturation 78
minority group 81
dominant group 81

racial group 81
ethnic group 81
racial-ethnic group 82
racism 82
prejudice 82

discrimination 83
racial socialization 85
miscegenation 101

PEARSON myfamilylab MyFamilyLab provides a wealth of resources. Go to www.myfamilylab.com<http://www.myfamilylab.com/>, to enhance your comprehension of the content in this chapter. You can take practice exams, view videos relevant to the subject matter, listen to audio files, explore topics further by using Social Explorer, and use the tools contained in MySearchLab to help you write research papers.

5 Socialization and Gender Roles

Norman Rockwell, "The Shiner." Printed by permission of the Norman Rockwell Family Agency. Copyright © 1953 The Norman Rockwell Family Entities.

Do you know what would have happened if there had been Three Wise Women instead of Three Wise Men? They would have asked for directions, arrived on time, helped deliver baby Jesus, cleaned the stable, made a casserole, brought practical gifts, and there would be peace on Earth. Does this joke stereotype women and men? Or do you think that it contains a kernel of truth?

You saw in Chapter 1 that socialization, a major function of the family, establishes our social identity, teaches us role taking, and shapes our behavior. In this chapter, we examine gender roles in the context of socialization: how we learn these roles and how they affect our everyday lives and family relations. Let's begin by looking at whether women and men are as different as the mass media and some self-help writers often claim. First, however, take the quiz in the "Ask Yourself" box to see how much you already know about women and men.

DATA DIGEST

- Nearly 800 million people in the world (16,3 percent of the world's population) are illiterate; **sixty-four of them are women.**

- Among 130 countries, the United States **ranks only 67 in the number of women at the highest-ranking political positions,** and well below developing countries such as Bangladesh (#13), Cuba (#14), Peru (#30), and Tanzania (#14).

- White men comprise only **28 percent of the U.S. population age 18 and older,** but they account for 78 percent of *Fortune* 500 board of directors, 84 percent of state governors, 59 percent of the U.S. Congress, 77 percent of partners in law firms, 56 percent of the U.S. Supreme Court Justices, 68 percent of college presidents, 77 percent of tenured professors, and 74 percent of high school principals.

- If the **typical stay-at-home mother in the United States were paid for her work** as a housekeeper, cook, chauffeur, and psychologist—among other roles— **she would earn at least $115,000 a year.**

- Among first-year American college students, 26 percent of the men and 16 percent of the women say that "the activities of married women are **best confined to the home and family."**

Sources: American Bar Association, 2007; King and Gomez, 2007; Planty et al., 2007, 2008; Pryor et al., 2007; World Bank, 2007; Wulfhorst, 2007; Catalyst, 2008; *Chronicle of Higher Education,* 2008; Hausmann et al., 2008; U.S. Census Bureau, 2008; Center for American Women and Politics, 2009; Central Intelligence Agency, 2009.

ASK YOURSELF

A Gender Quiz: Are Women and Men Different?

True False

☐ ☒ **1.** Women are the weaker sex.

☐ ☐ **2.** Boys are more group centered, active, and aggressive than girls.

☐ ☐ **3.** Women are more emotional than men.

☐ ☐ **4.** Women talk more than men.

☐ ☐ **5.** Women suffer more from depression.

☐ ☐ **6.** Women are more likely than men to divulge personal information.

☐ ☐ **7.** Men smile more often than women.

True False

☐ ☐ **8.** Women and men don't care whether a baby is a boy or a girl ("Just as long as it's healthy").

☐ ☐ **9.** Most women are confident about managing their financial affairs.

☐ ☐ **10.** A heart attack is more likely to be fatal for a man than for a woman.

(The answers to this quiz are on p. 112.)

GENDER MYTHS ABOUT FEMALE-MALE SIMILARITIES AND DIFFERENCES

Many Americans think that men and women are very different. Both sexes often describe men as aggressive, courageous, and ambitious. In contrast, they see women as emotional, talkative, patient, and affectionate (see *Table 5.1*).

Do these traits characterize you, your family members, and friends? Probably not. Your mom may be aggressive and ambitious and your dad emotional and talkative. Or both may be aggressive, emotional, or talkative, depending on the situation. And either or both parents may change over the years.

We tend to associate stereotypically female characteristics with weakness and stereotypically male characteristics with strength. We may criticize women for being emotional, for example, but praise men for being the "strong silent type."

Consider, also, how often we describe the same behavior differently for women and men:

- He's firm, but she's stubborn.
- He's careful about details, but she's picky.
- He's honest, but she's opinionated.
- He's raising good points, but she's "bitching."
- He's a man of the world, but she's "been around."

TABLE 5.1	The Top Ten Personality Traits Ascribed to Men and Women	
Trait	**More True of Men**	**More True of Women**
1. Aggressive	68%	20%
2. Courageous	50	27
3. Ambitious	44	33
4. Easygoing	55	48
5. Intelligent	21	36
6. Creative	15	65
7. Patient	19	72
8. Talkative	10	78
9. Affectionate	5	86
10. Emotional	3	90

Source: Newport, 2001: 34.

Is There a Difference Between Sex and Gender?

Many people use the terms *sex* and *gender* interchangeably, but they have distinct meanings. Sex is a biological designation, whereas gender is a social creation that teaches us to be masculine or feminine as we perform various roles.

SEX Sex refers to the biological characteristics with which we are born: our chromosomal, anatomical, hormonal, and other physical and physiological attributes. Such biological characteristics determine whether we have male or female genitalia, whether we will menstruate, how much body hair we will have and where it will grow, whether we're able to bear children, and so on.

Sex influences our behavior (such as shaving beards and wearing bras), but it does *not* determine how we think, feel, and act. We learn to be feminine or masculine through our gender, a more complex concept than sex.

GENDER Gender refers to learned attitudes and behaviors that characterize people of one sex or the other. Gender is based on social and cultural expectations rather than on physical traits. Thus, most people are *born* either female or male, but we *learn* to be either women or men because we associate conventional patterns of behavior with each sex.

If you've shopped for baby cards, you might have noticed that most of the cards for girls are pink, whereas those for boys are blue. The cards usually portray the baby girls as playing with their toes, sitting in a bubble bath, or gazing at a mobile hanging above their crib. The cards for boys usually depict sports-related items such as baseballs, toys such as train sets, and even laptops. What's the message in these cards? It's that female infants are passive and ornamental whereas male infants are active and involved.

GENDER IDENTITY Children develop a **gender identity,** a perception of themselves as either masculine or feminine, early in life. Many Mexican baby girls but not boys have pierced ears, for example, and hairstyles and clothing for American toddlers differ by sex. Gender identity, which typically corresponds to a person's biological sex, is learned in early childhood and usually remains relatively fixed throughout life.

Regardless of sex, gender, and gender identity, both sexes experience emotions such as anger, happiness, and sadness just as deeply. What differs is *how* women and men express their emotions because men are more likely to suffer in silence, whereas women tend to show their emotions more openly (Simon and Nath, 2004). Such differences are usually due to gender roles.

GENDER ROLES One of the functions of the family is to teach its members appropriate **gender roles,** the characteristics, attitudes, feelings, and behaviors that society expects of females and males. As a result, we

Many people view female athletes as "unfeminine," "butch," or "less powerful" than men. How accurate are such stereotypes in describing most female athletes, such as Serena Williams, pictured here?

TABLE 5.2	The Nature-Nurture Debate	
Nature	**Nurture**
Differences in male and female beliefs, attitudes, and behavior are	Differences in male and female beliefs, attitudes, and behavior are
Innate	Learned
Biological, physiological	Psychological, social, cultural
Due largely to heredity	Due largely to environment
Fairly fixed	Very changeable

learn to become male or female through interactions with family members and the larger society. In most societies, for example, men are expected to provide shelter, food, and clothing for their families, and women are expected to nurture their children and tend to the family's everyday needs (see Chapters 12 and 13).

Social scientists often describe our roles as *gendered,* the process of treating and evaluating males and females differently because of their sex:

To the extent that women and men dress, talk, or act differently because of societal expectations, their behavior is gendered. To the extent that an organization assigns some jobs to women and others to men on the basis of their assumed abilities, that organization is gendered. And to the extent that professors treat a student differently because that student is a man or a woman, their interaction is gendered (Howard and Hollander, 1997: 11).

Because gender roles are learned and not innate, we can change them. Many women now pursue college degrees and contribute to the family's finances, and many men participate in raising children and doing housework more than they did in the past.

For the most part, however, we still live in a society with fairly rigid gender roles and widespread **gender stereotypes,** expectations about how people will look, act, think, and feel based on their sex. For example, society holds that boys are *physically* aggressive (they hit and punch), whereas girls are *socially* aggressive or "mean" (they spread rumors, gossip, and intentionally exclude others).

Such views are gender stereotypes and myths, according to a recent analysis of almost 150 studies of aggression in young children and adolescents. The researchers concluded that boys—regardless of age—are almost as likely as girls to be mean and that the two types of aggression are linked. That is, if boys and girls are physically aggressive, they are also likely to be socially aggressive (and vice versa) because of similar problems such as low self-esteem, poor peer relations, and low prosocial behavior (such as sharing and cooperating) (Card et al., 2008).

Social scientists underscore the role of learning, socialization, and culture in explaining human development. Many biologists maintain that the differences in women's and men's behavior reflect innate biological characteristics, not social and cultural expectations. This difference of opinion is often called the *nature-nurture debate* (see *Table 5.2*).

THE NATURE-NURTURE DEBATE: IS ANATOMY DESTINY?

How Important is Nature?

Since you asked . . .

• Are people automatically masculine or feminine because they were born male or female?

Those who argue that nature (biology) shapes behavior point to three kinds of evidence: health differences between men and women, the effects of sex hormones, and some cases of unsuccessful sex reassignment. Let's look at each of these briefly.

HEALTH DIFFERENCES There are some documented biological differences between men and women. For example, the senses of smell and taste are more acute in women than in men, and hearing is better and lasts longer in women than in men; women have a higher risk than men of developing diabetes; and some conditions (such as migraine headaches and breast cancer) are more common in women, whereas others (such as hemophilia and skin cancer) are more common in men (McDonald, 1999; Kreeger, 2002a, 2002b).

EFFECTS OF SEX HORMONES Scientists don't know why women and men differ, but they believe that hormones provide part of the answer. All males and females share three sex **hormones,** chemical substances secreted into the bloodstream by glands of the endocrine system. These hormones are *estrogen* (dominant in females and produced by the ovaries),

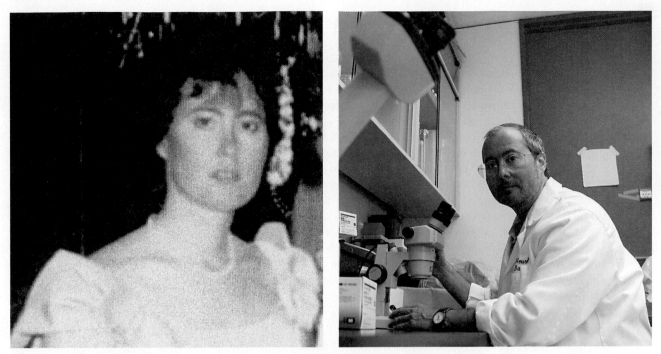

On the left: A photo of Dr. Ben Barres as a bridesmaid in 1988 before he underwent sex surgery. On the right, Dr. Barres, a neurobiologist at Stanford University's Medical Center, says that "By far, the main difference I have noticed is that people who don't know I am transgendered treat me with much more respect" than when he was a woman. "I can even complete a whole sentence without being interrupted by a man."

progesterone (present in high levels during pregnancy and also secreted by the ovaries), and *testosterone* (dominant in males and produced by the testes). All these hormones are produced in minute quantities in both sexes before puberty.

After puberty, varying levels of these hormones in males and females produce different physiological changes. For example, testosterone, the dominant male sex hormone, strengthens muscles but threatens the heart. It triggers the production of low-density lipoprotein, which clogs blood vessels. Therefore, men are at twice the risk of coronary heart disease as are (premenopausal) women. The dominant female sex hormones, especially estrogen, make blood vessels more elastic and strengthen the immune system, making females more resistant to infection (Wizemann and Pardue, 2001).

UNSUCCESSFUL SEX REASSIGNMENT Some scientists point to unsuccessful attempts at sex reassignment as another example favoring the nature-over-nurture argument. Beginning in the 1960s, John Money, a highly respected psychologist, published numerous articles and books in which he maintained that gender identity is not firm at birth but is determined as much by culture and nurture as by hormones (see, for example, Money and Ehrhardt, 1972).

Several scientists have challenged such conclusions, however. As the box "The Case of Brenda/David" on the next page shows, Money's most famous sex reassignment experiment does not support his contention that infants born as biological males can be successfully raised as females.

How Important Is Nurture?

Most social scientists maintain that culture, or nurture, shapes human behavior. They often point to three types of data to support their argument: global variations in gender roles, international differences in male violence rates, and successful sex reassignment cases.

CROSS-CULTURAL VARIATIONS IN GENDER ROLES
In a classic study, anthropologist Margaret Mead (1935) observed three tribes that lived within short distances of one another in New Guinea and found three different combinations of gender roles. Among the Arapesh, both men and women were nurturant with their children. The men were cooperative, sensitive, and rarely engaged in warfare.

The Mundugumors were just the opposite. Both men and women were competitive and aggressive. Neither parent showed much tenderness, and both often used physical punishment to discipline the children.

The Tchumbuli demonstrated the reverse of Western gender roles. The women were the economic providers. The men took care of children, sat around gossiping, and spent a lot of time decorating themselves

Choices

The Case of Brenda/David

In 1963, twin boys were being circumcised. The penis of one of the infants, David, was accidentally burned off. Encouraged by John Money, the parents agreed to reassign and raise David as "Brenda." Brenda's testicles were removed and later surgery would construct a vagina. Money reported that the twins were growing into happy, well-adjusted children, setting a precedent for sex reassignment as the standard treatment for 15,000 newborns with similarly injured genitals (Colapinto, 1997, 2001).

In the mid-1990s, a biologist and a psychiatrist followed up on Brenda's progress and concluded that the sex reassignment had not been successful. Almost from the beginning, Brenda refused to be treated like a girl. When her mother dressed her in frilly clothes as a toddler, Brenda tried to rip them off. She preferred to play with boys and stereotypical boys' toys such as machine guns. People in the community said that she "looks like a boy, talks like a boy." Brenda had no friends, and no one would play with her: "Every day I was picked on, every day

I was teased, every day I was threatened" (Diamond and Sigmundson, 1997: 300).

When she was 14, Brenda rebelled and stopped living as a girl: She refused to wear dresses, urinated standing up, refused to undergo vaginal surgery, and decided that she would either commit suicide or live as a male. When her father finally told her the true story of her birth and sex change, David recalls that "all of a sudden everything clicked. For the first time things made sense and I understood who and what I was" (Diamond and Sigmundson, 1997: 300).

Brenda had a mastectomy (breast removal surgery) at the age of 14 and underwent several operations to reconstruct a penis. Now called David, he was able to ejaculate but experienced little erotic feeling. At age 25, he married a woman several years older than he was and adopted her three children. He committed suicide in 2004 at the age of 38, an act that some researchers attributed to the physical and mental torments he suffered in childhood that "haunted him the rest of his life" (Colapinto, 2004).

Several Johns Hopkins scientists followed 14 boys who had been surgically altered as infants and raised as girls. The infants had a rare disorder, occurring once in every 400,000 births, in which the penis was small or nonexistent, despite the presence of testicles. Five of the boys were happily living as girls. The others were living as males or had reassigned themselves, taking on boys' names and dressing in masculine clothes (Reiner and Gearhart, 2004).

In contrast to Money's theories, then, some scientists maintain that David's case is evidence that gender identity and sexual orientation are largely innate. Nature, they argue, is stronger than nurture in shaping a person's sexual identity.

⁞• Stop and Think …

■ What would you do if you had to make a decision about a child's sex reassignment?

■ Because some boys who had been surgically altered are happily living as girls, should scientists conclude that gender identity and sexual orientation are biological?

---

for tribal festivities. Mead concluded that attributes long considered either masculine (such as aggression) or feminine (such as nurturance) were culturally—rather than biologically—determined.

Those of you who are familiar with Mead's work may know that some anthropologists have challenged her findings regarding sexual behavior in Samoa (for example, see Freeman, 1983, and Shankman, 1996). The New Guinea study hasn't elicited any similar controversies.

CROSS-CULTURAL VARIATIONS IN MALE VIOLENCE
If men were innately aggressive, they would be equally violent across all societies. This is not the case. The proportion of women who have ever suffered physical violence by a male partner varies considerably: 80 percent in Vietnam, 61 percent in Peru, 20 percent in the United States, and 13 percent in Japan (Chelala, 2002; Rennison, 2003; World Health Organization, 2005). Such variations presumably reflect cultural laws and practices and other environmental factors (nurture) rather than biology or genetics (nature) (Chesney-Lind and Pasko, 2004).

Male violence and aggression are more likely to occur in patriarchal rather than matriarchal societies. In a patriarchy, men hold the positions of power and authority—political, economic, legal, religious, educational, military, and domestic. In a matriarchy, in contrast, women control cultural, political, and economic resources and, consequently, have power over men.

Some patriarchal cultures, however, exercise much more control than others over women's behavior. In some Middle Eastern countries, for example, women (but not men) are killed if they dishonor the family by engaging in premarital or extramarital sex (see Chapters 7 and 14). As the box "Some Gender Inequalities in Patriarchal Societies" shows, men can engage in considerable discrimination and violence against women because cultural and religious values, customs, and laws relegate females to second-class citizenship.

This does not mean, however, that *all* men are aggressive and *all* women are nonviolent. In the United States, for example, women make up 18 percent of all those arrested for violent crimes, including homicide (Federal Bureau of Investigation, 2007).

Cross-Cultural and Multicultural Families

Some Gender Inequalities in Patriarchal Societies

Women make up half the world's population, do two-thirds of the world's work, earn one-tenth of the world's income, and own one-hundredth of the world's property. In some of the most patriarchal countries around the world, women have few legal rights, their movements are severely restricted, and violence is a common occurrence:

- **Afghanistan:** In the countryside, tribal leaders deploy religious police to enforce stringent controls on women's behavior. Many girls cannot attend school, and laws dictate that families murder their own women if they have been "dishonored" by rape during a war.

- **China:** A culture that values boys more than girls, China has used advances in sonogram technology to help prospective parents identify—and abort—female fetuses. Despite official condemnation of this practice, the gap between the number of male and female births is widening.

- **Congo:** Women need a husband's permission for most routine legal transactions, including accepting a job and opening a bank account.

- **Nigeria:** The penal code allows a man to "correct" his wife as long as the "correction" does not leave a scar or necessitate a hospital stay of 21 or more days.

- **India and Pakistan:** If a groom and his family decide that a bride's dowry is too small, she may be persecuted or burned to death. Abortion of female fetuses is still widespread in India (see Chapter 7).

- **Norway:** Women are still hired last, fired first, paid less than men, and excluded from the top jobs.

- **Qatar:** Women need a male's permission to obtain a driver's license.

- **Saudi Arabia:** A divorced woman may keep her children until they are 7 years old. After that, although she may visit them, the father's relatives raise them. Women are not allowed to vote, drive cars, or ride bicycles.

- **Syria:** A husband can legally prohibit his wife's departure from the country.

- **Turkey:** In some regions, young girls are killed by their fathers or brothers because they have shamed the family by going out with boys or marrying someone from a different sect. Among health workers, 69 percent of the women and 85 percent of the men say that wives deserve beatings if they criticize the man, lie to him, or are unfaithful.

- **Yemen:** By law, a woman must obey her husband and not leave the home without his consent.

Sources: Dauer, 2002; "Pakistani girl describes . . .," 2002; *State of the World's Mothers,* 2003; Brandon, 2005; U.S. Department of State, 2008; Forsloff, 2009; Seager, 2009; Sommers and Birch, 2009.

⁞• Stop and Think …

- "One can judge the health of a society by the way it treats its women." Do you agree or disagree? Why?

- Do you think that women would experience greater equality if more legislators and heads of state were women? Why?

SUCCESSFUL SEX ASSIGNMENT As you saw earlier, some scientists cite the Brenda/David case as evidence of the imprint of biology on gender roles and identity. Others maintain that successful sex assignments of intersexuals demonstrate the powerful effects of culture.

Intersexuals—also known as *hermaphrodites*—are people born with both male and female sex organs (internal and/or external). The incidence of ambiguous genitalia—so that the sex of the newborn is not immediately apparent—is about 1 in every 8,000 to 10,000 births (O'Mara, 1997).

Typically, parents of such infants choose a sex for the child and pursue surgical and hormonal treatments to change the ambiguous genital organs. The parents raise the child in the selected gender role: The name is male or female, the clothes are masculine or feminine, and the child is taught to behave in gender-appropriate ways. Such sex assignments, most of which are successful, suggest that socialization may be more important than biology in shaping a child's gender identity.

In addition, thousands of American transsexuals who have undergone sex surgery report living happily and not regretting the surgery (Vitello, 2006).

What Can We Conclude about the Nature-Nurture Debate?

What does all this information tell us, ultimately, about the nature-nurture debate? Several things. First, women and men exhibit some sex-related genetic differences. Boys, for example, are more likely to suffer from genetic defects, physical and mental disabilities, reading difficulties, and school and emotional problems. There is no evidence, however, that boys' (or girls') hormones *cause* physical or behavioral maladies.

Second, cross-cultural research shows much variation in the characteristics that are typically ascribed to men and to women (see *Table 5.1* on p. 106). The most patriarchal societies teach women to be obedient and submissive, whereas industrialized countries tend

Answers to "A Gender Quiz: Are Women and Men Different?"

1. **False.** Infant mortality rates vary by race and ethnicity, but the death rate for male infants is 18 percent higher than for female infants. And, on average, American women live about 5 years longer than men.

2. **True.** Boys' play is typically hierarchical, group centered, competitive, physical, and aggressive. Girls usually engage in more reciprocal, verbal, and cooperative kinds of play.

3. **False.** Both sexes are equally emotional, but men and women express their feelings differently. Men may churn more internally whereas women externalize (act out) their emotions through facial and verbal expressions.

4. **False.** In most situations, men tend to talk more and longer than women.

5. **True.** Women are two to three times more likely than men to suffer from depression. Women's societal roles affect their happiness, and unhappiness, in turn, can affect brain functions. In addition, women's brains produce less of the feel-good chemical serotonin.

6. **False.** Both sexes self-disclose by divulging personal information but are more comfortable doing so with women than with men.

7. **False.** Women smile much more than men, probably because they are expected to do "emotion work." Smiling is one way to restore harmony and reduce tension when people disagree.

8. **False.** In a recent Gallup poll, 45 percent of men compared with 32 percent of women said that if they could have only one child, they would prefer a boy.

9. **False.** About 67 percent of American women say that they have little knowledge about financial affairs or how to manage and invest their money.

10. **False.** A heart attack is more likely to be fatal for a woman than for a man. Women with heart disease are less likely than men to be diagnosed correctly or treated promptly and are less likely to receive cardiac rehabilitation.

Sources: Sugg, 2000; Misra, 2001; Vaccarino et al., 2002; Vakili et al., 2002; LaFrance et al., 2003; Wood, 2003; "Financial experience...," 2006; Mathews and MacDorman, 2007; Newport, 2007.

---

to be more tolerant of men and women who don't enact stereotypical gender roles.

Finally, nature and nurture interact to explain our behavior. Parenting, for example, has a strong effect on children's behavior despite their genetic makeup. A child with a difficult temperament—irritability, hostility, or aggressiveness—can become more sociable and learn self-control if his or her parents are continuously patient and loving (see Chapter 12). Identical twins are the same genetically, but they may differ dramatically in personality, level of aggression, and mental disorders, depending on environmental factors such as parental behavior and peer influences (Sinha, 2004; Brendgen et al., 2005).

In effect, nature and nurture interact in socialization processes and outcomes. Reviews of the research on the differences between the sexes concluded that females and males are much more alike than different on a number of characteristics, including cognitive abilities, verbal and nonverbal communication, leadership traits, and self-esteem (Hyde, 2005, 2006). Why, then, do gender roles differ?

WHY DO GENDER ROLES DIFFER?

A common misconception is that our gender roles are carved in stone by about age 4. In fact, gender roles change throughout the life course. There are many explanations for these changes, but let's consider five of the most common theories: (1) sociobiology, (2) social learning, (3) cognitive development, (4) symbolic interaction, and (5) feminist theories. (*Table 5.3* on p. 113 summarizes these theories.)

Sociobiology

Sociobiology is the study of how biology affects social behavior. Sociobiologists argue, for example, that evolution and genetic factors (nature) can explain why men are generally more aggressive than women. To ensure the propagation of their genes, males must prevail over their rivals. The competition includes aggression, violence, weapons, and plain nastiness: "In the animal world, human and nonhuman, competition is often intense. Males typically threaten, bluff, and if necessary fight one another in their efforts to obtain access to females" (Barash, 2002: B8).

Sociobiological explanations are controversial because there is hardly a single behavior that is not influenced socially. As you saw earlier, male aggression and violence vary considerably across societies. And, when cultural groups are invaded or attacked by enemies, women warriors can be as fierce as their male counterparts (see Chapter 3 on American Indian women during colonial times).

TABLE 5.3	Theoretical Explanations of Gender Roles
Perspective	**View of Gender Roles**
Sociobiology	Evolution and genetic factors (nature) determine gender roles
Social learning	Gender role socialization can be direct (rewarding or punishing behavior and role modeling) and indirect (imitation and modeling)
Cognitive development	Children learn appropriate gender attitudes and behavior as they pass through a series of developmental steps
Symbolic interaction	Gender roles are social constructions that emerge through day-to-day interaction and vary across situations because of other people's expectations
Feminism	Gender roles differ due to socialization, patriarchy, and gender scripts

Social Learning Theory

The central notion of **social learning theory** is that people learn attitudes, beliefs, and behaviors through social interaction. The learning is a result of reinforcement, imitation, and modeling (Bandura and Walters, 1963; Lynn, 1969).

Since you asked . . .

- Are mothers responsible for their daughters' obsession with beauty and appearance?

Reinforcement occurs when we receive direct or indirect rewards or punishments for particular gender role behaviors. For example, a little girl who puts on her mother's makeup may be told that she is cute, but her brother who does the same thing will be scolded ("boys don't wear makeup"). Children also learn gender roles through indirect reinforcement. For example, if a little boy's male friends are punished for crying, he will learn that "boys don't cry."

Children also learn to behave as boys or girls through *observation* and *imitation*. Even when children are not directly rewarded or punished for "behaving like boys" or "behaving like girls," they learn about gender by watching who does what in their families. A father who is rarely at home because he's always working sends the message that men are supposed to earn money. A mother who is always complaining about being overweight or old sends the message that women are supposed to be thin and young.

Because parents are emotionally important to their children, they are typically a child's most powerful *role models*. Other role models include caregivers, teachers, friends, and celebrities. According to a multiethnic study of Los Angeles adolescents, teenagers who said that their role model was someone they knew (a parent, relative, friend, or doctor outside the family) had higher self-esteem, higher grades, and lower substance use than peers whose role models were sports figures, singers, or other media characters. The researchers concluded that role model selection can have a positive or negative outcome on a teenager's psychosocial development (Yancey et al., 2002).

Social learning theories contribute to our understanding of why we behave as we do, but much of the emphasis is on early socialization rather than on what occurs throughout life. Thus, these theories don't explain why gender roles can change in adulthood or later life. Social learning theories also don't explain why reinforcement and modeling work for some children but not others, especially those in the same family, and even identical twins.

Cognitive Development Theory

In contrast to social learning theories, **cognitive development theory** argues that children acquire female or male values on their own by thinking, reasoning, and interpreting information in their environment. According to this perspective, children pass through a series of developmental stages in learning gender-appropriate attitudes and behavior.

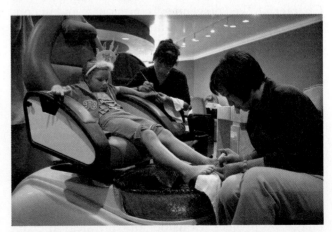

This 2-year-old is getting a manicure and pedicure at a local spa for kids. *Toddlers & Tiaras,* a TLC reality show on television, features little girls who compete in beauty pageants.

By age 3 or 4, a girl knows that she is a girl and prefers "girl things" to "boy things" simply because she likes what is familiar or similar to her. By age 5, most children anticipate disapproval from their peers for playing with opposite-sex toys, and they avoid those toys as a result. After acquiring masculine or feminine values, children tend to identify with people of the same sex as themselves (Kohlberg, 1969; Maccoby, 1990; Bussey and Bandura, 1992).

According to cognitive development theory, children use cues to evaluate the behavior of others as either gender appropriate ("good") or gender inappropriate ("bad"). They are motivated to learn the correct ways to categorize themselves and to fit into their social worlds. Such sex typing may become more rigid during adolescence, when young people want to conform to their peers' gender stereotypes, but more flexible during adulthood because peers are less influential in our behavior. Generally, however, people who have internalized sex-typed standards tend to expect stereotypical behavior from others (Hudak, 1993; Renn and Calvert, 1993).

Developmental theories offer useful insights on the relationship between maturation and learning gender roles, but they say little about individual differences among children (why one daughter is a tomboy, for example, whereas another is very feminine). (We'll examine an influential cognitive development theory in depth in Chapter 12.) Another limitation is that developmental theories exaggerate gender learning as something that children do themselves. Instead, according to symbolic interactionists, learning gender roles is shaped by our cultural context.

Symbolic Interaction Theories

For symbolic interactionists (also known simply as *interactionists*), gender roles are *socially constructed categories* that emerge in social situations (see Chapter 2). We "do gender," consciously and unconsciously, by accommodating our behavior to other people's gender role expectations. Among co-workers, for example, both sexes are more likely to interrupt women than men because men are generally viewed as more authoritative than women (West and Zimmerman, 1987; Robey et al., 1998).

In a process that sociologist Erving Goffman (1959, 1969) called *impression management,* we provide information and cues to others to present ourselves in a favorable light while downplaying or concealing our less appealing qualities. According to Goffman, all of us engage in impression management almost every day by controlling the image we project. Consider our physical appearance. Cosmetic-surgery procedures performed on American girls age 18 and younger have nearly doubled over the past decade, and nearly 14 percent of Botox injections (toxins that temporarily diminish wrinkles and frown lines) are given to

women in the 19 to 34 age group (Jeffreys, 2005; Bennett, 2009). Men color their hair, get hair transplants, and also get injections or plastic surgery to appear younger than they are.

Symbolic interaction theories have been valuable in explaining how gender and gender roles shape our everyday lives. One limitation is that interactionists credit people with more free will than they have. For both sexes, for example, impression management is more difficult for lower socioeconomic groups and the elderly because they have fewer resources to purchase goods and services to enhance the image they project (Powers, 2004). In addition, interactionists tend to downplay or ignore macro-level and structural factors that affect our gender roles. For example, when millions of Americans are fired because of a plunging economy, gender roles become unpredictable and stressful, especially if one or both partners can no longer provide for a family.

Feminist Theories

Many feminist scholars, like interactionists, view gender as a socially constructed role that is taught carefully and repeatedly. Consequently, one's *gender script*—how society says you're supposed to act based on your sex—becomes "so natural as to be seen as an integral part of oneself" (Fox and Murry, 2001: 382).

Gender scripts result, over time, in valuing men more than women. Even in Women's Studies courses, many of the female college students want to focus on male experiences and perspectives, are concerned that men in the class may feel discomfort, and sometimes even express a preference for male faculty in these courses (Sharp et al., 2008).

For most feminist theorists, the much lower number of women in powerful positions (see Data Digest) is due to **sexism,** an attitude or behavior that discriminates against one sex, usually females, based on the assumed superiority of the other sex. If people changed their individual attitudes about traditional roles, according to feminist scholars, behavior would change on a macro level. If, for example, boys were taught to cook and clean, they would be more likely to do so in adulthood. If girls were taught to be independent, they would be more likely to fend for themselves instead of relying on a man for economic support in adulthood.

Feminist perspectives have provided insightful analyses of gender roles but have been criticized for being too narrow. For example, in industrialized patriarchal societies, women in upper classes have more status and privileges than do men in lower classes and are less confined to playing traditional gender roles. Also, one might question whether gender scripts are as rigid, especially over time, as many feminists claim.

:•• MAKING CONNECTIONS

■ Drawing on your own experiences and your knowledge of people of both sexes, do you think that women and men are similar? Or different?

■ Think about how you were raised. Who played a major role in teaching you what it means to be masculine or feminine? What happened, if anything, when you broke the rules?

HOW DO WE LEARN GENDER ROLES?

We learn gender roles from a variety of sources. The most important socialization agents are parents (and other adult caregivers), peers, teachers, books, and popular culture.

Parents

Parents usually are a child's first and most influen-

Since you asked . . .

:•• Why are parents critical in shaping our gender roles?

tial socialization agents, often treating male and female infants differently from birth. They hold girls more gently and cuddle them more. Fathers, especially, are more likely to jostle and play in a rough-and-tumble manner with boys (Parke, 1996). Parents also shape their children's gender roles through differential treatment in several important ways, including talking, setting expectations, and providing opportunities for various activities.

TALKING Parents often communicate differently with boys than with girls, starting at a very early age. Even when babies are as young as 6 to 14 months, mothers often talk more to their daughters than to their sons and comfort and hug their daughters more often. This suggests that girls are supposed to interact with other people and to be more verbal. In contrast, mothers talk less often with boys and give them more room to explore their environment on their own, which teaches and reinforces a sense of independence. Thus, even babies receive gendered messages about their expected behavior months before they start to speak (Clearfield and Nelson, 2006).

Fathers tend to use more directives ("Bring that over here") and more threatening language ("If you

do that again, you'll be sorry") with their sons than with their daughters. Mothers tend to ask for compliance rather than demand it for both sons and daughters ("Could you bring that to me, please?"). These parental differences send the message that men are more authoritative than women.

By the time they start school, many boys use threatening, commanding, and dominating language ("If you do that one more time, I'll punch you"). In contrast, many girls seek agreement and cooperation ("Can I play, too?") (Shapiro, 1990).

SETTING EXPECTATIONS When parents *expect* their daughters to do better in English and their sons to excel in math and sports, they provide the support and advice that enable the children to do so. This sex-stereotypical encouragement builds up the children's confidence in their abilities and helps them master the various skills (Eccles et al., 2000).

Nationally, 10- to 17-year-old boys spend about 30 percent less time than girls doing household chores and more than twice as much time playing. In addition, boys are up to 15 percent more likely than girls of the same age to get an allowance for doing household chores (Swanbrow, 2007).

The ways that parents divide up household tasks between themselves and their children are also gender typed. Parents typically assign child care and cleaning to daughters and home maintenance work to sons. Girls are also given these duties much earlier in childhood and adolescence than are boys (Leaper, 2002). These gender-stereotyped responsibilities lay the foundation for role differences in adulthood (as you'll see shortly).

Parents are important socialization agents. This 3-year-old may be inspired to follow in his father's occupational footsteps.

Mothers sometimes start criticizing their children's—especially their daughters'—weight and physical appearance in elementary school. And throughout adolescence, fathers make more appearance-related comments to their daughters than to their sons (Schwartz et al., 1999; Smolak et al., 1999). Such gender-typed expectations may result in girls' negative body images and eating disorders (see Chapter 14).

PROVIDING OPPORTUNITIES Here's what one of my students said when we were discussing this chapter:

Some parents live their dreams through their sons by forcing them to be in sports. I disagree with this but want my [9-year-old] son to be "all boy." He's the worst player on the basketball team at school and wanted to take dance lessons, including ballet. I assured him that this was not going to happen. I'm going to enroll him in soccer and see if he does better (Author's files).

Is this mother suppressing her son's natural talent in dancing? We'll never know because she, like many parents, expects her son to perform gender roles that meet with society's approval.

During childhood and adolescence, parents provide children with activities and opportunities that our culture defines as gender appropriate. Fathers, especially, are still more likely to stress the importance of a career or occupational success for their sons than for their daughters. As a result, parents are more likely to provide opportunities for their sons than for their daughters to attend computer summer camps, more likely to explain science exhibits to their sons than to their daughters, and more likely to pressure boys to attend college (Crowley et al., 2001; Kladko, 2002).

Play and Peer Groups

Play is important in children's development because it provides pleasure; forms friendships; and builds communication, emotional, and social skills. Peer groups also play a significant role in our socialization. A **peer group** consists of people who are similar in age, social status, and interests. All of us are members of peer groups, but peers are especially influential until about our mid-20s. After that, co-workers, spouses, children, and close friends are usually more central than the peers in our everyday lives. Play and peer groups are important sources of socialization, but they can also encourage gender-stereotypical attitudes and behavior.

PLAY From an early age, play with toys is generally gender typed. In 2008, the five top-selling toys for girls were Barbie dolls, followed by Hannah Montana films and games; generic dolls; and Nintendo Wii, a video game console. The top-selling toys for boys were video games, followed by Nintendo Wii, Lego, cars, and transformers (Stead, 2008).

Girls' sections of catalogs and toy stores are swamped with cosmetics, dolls and accessories, arts and crafts kits, and housekeeping and cooking wares. In contrast, boys' sections feature sports equipment, building sets, workbenches, construction equipment, and toy guns (see the box "Are Children's Toys Becoming More Sexist?").

Barbie was the top-selling toy in the twentieth century (Towner, 2009). According to many critics, the problem with Barbie dolls is that they idealize unrealistic body characteristics such as large breasts, a tiny waist, and small hips (see *Table 5.4*). One of the results is that many girls and women try to achieve these fictional expectations through diets (that may lead to eating disorders) and cosmetic surgery (see Chapter 14).

Male action figures have grown increasingly muscular over the years. GI Joes, for example, have biceps that are twice as large as those of a typical man and larger than those of any known bodybuilder. These action figures (and comic strip heroes) put boys at risk of developing the "Barbie syndrome"—unrealistic expectations for their bodies. As a result, some researchers maintain, increasing numbers of men are becoming preoccupied with working out and taking dangerous drugs such as anabolic steroids (Field et al., 2005).

PEERS By as early as age 2, most toddlers are learning to interact with peers. One of the most widely recognized social characteristics of childhood is young children's preference for same-sex play partners. The more time boys spend with other boys, the greater the likelihood that they will learn to be rough, aggressive, competitive, and active. The more time girls spend with other girls, the more likely they are to be cooperative rather than assertive, to play quiet games, and to be less physical in their play than boys. Thus,

© Vahan Shirvanian/www.CartoonStock.com

Are Children's Toys Becoming More Sexist?

Many people say that most children's toys today are more unisex than they were during the 1980s and the 1990s. Are they right?

According to sociologists Caryl Rivers and Rosalind Barnett (2005), large toy stores have returned to "selling girls on primping and passivity" and portraying boys as active and creative. For example,

- Toys Я Us catalogs offer no pictures of girls on their sports page or of girls playing with cars and trucks. Boys, meanwhile, are seen playing basketball or with an electronic hockey game.
- Pages devoted to building sets feature boys playing with Legos, Tinker Toys, and Lincoln Logs. Girls are offered Cinderella Castle blocks and a cheap toddler block set.

- No boys are pictured on the dolls page, on which you can find a Cinderella carriage, a Barbie primp-and-polish styling head for hairdos, a Hollywood party limo, and scores of Barbies.
- The aisles of most American toy stores or toy departments have the same gender-coded sections as in the past. Hot items for girls are the big-eyed Bratz dolls (which are even more overtly sexual than Barbie) and sport navel-baring tops, hooker boots, and miniskirts.
- A growing trend is makeovers for girls ages 5 to 13 in local shopping malls, sponsored by a group known as Club Libby Lu. The club counselors create fancy hairstyles and apply sparkly makeup to the little girls, who wind

up looking like beauty pageant contestants.
- After protests from some teenage girls, Abercrombie & Fitch removed a T-shirt with "Who needs brains when you have these?" emblazoned across the wearer's chest. But the company still sells girls' T-shirts with logos such as "Available for parties," "Do I make you look fat?" and "Blondes are adored, brunettes are ignored."

⁝• Stop and Think ...

- Do you agree with the writers that toys are becoming more sex typed?
- Why do many parents endorse makeovers for little girls? What messages are they sending their daughters and sons?

the more both girls and boys play with same-sex partners, the more likely they are to participate in gender-typed play (Martin and Fabes, 2001).

Whether parents like it or not, peer influence usually increases as children get older. Especially during the early teen years, peers often reinforce desirable behavior or skills in ways that enhance a child's self-image ("Wow, you're really good in math!"). Peers also serve as positive role models because children acquire a wide array of information and knowledge by observing their peers. Even during the first days of school, children learn to imitate their peers by standing in line, raising their hands in class, and being quiet while the teacher is speaking. When children are assigned to classrooms in elementary school every fall, there's usually a quick grapevine about how to

behave ("If you don't do your homework even once, Mrs. Hill will call your parents!").

Peers also teach new skills. A child who's talented in art may help a schoolmate during an art class, and one who's good in sports may teach others how to control the soccer ball or hold a baseball bat properly. And, in many cases, peer acceptance (whether one is a jock, a computer geek, or on the yearbook staff) promotes friendship and a sense of fitting in. Thus, peer groups can be important sources of support for teens and increase their self-esteem, especially for adolescents who have poor relationships with their parents or feel insecure about their appearance or abilities (Strasburger and Wilson, 2002).

Not all peer influence is positive, however. Some cliques encourage high-risk behavior in teenagers that

TABLE 5.4	Real Women and Barbie	
	Average Woman	**Barbie**
Height	5'4"	6'
Weight	145 lbs	101 lbs
Dress size	11–14	4
Bust	36–37" *	39"
Waist	29–31"	19"
Hips	40–42"	33"

* Without breast implants
Source: Data cited in Anorexia Nervosa and Related Eating Disorders, Inc., 2006.

includes sexual activity, smoking, drinking alcohol, and using other drugs. In our society, being popular is seen as essential by many adolescents. Being disliked by one's peers may lead to feelings of isolation, loneliness, and alienation, but trying to be popular can have negative effects. Boys and girls who hang out with peers who bully, for example, tend to do more bullying themselves. If girls want to join the inner circle, they may bully even their closest friends by tormenting them with gossip and sarcastic comments (Wiseman, 2002; Espelage et al., 2003; see also, Chapter 12).

Feeling unpopular can be especially harmful for teenage girls. Among girls ages 12 to 19, those who see themselves as unpopular gain more weight every year than do those who see themselves as popular (McNeeley and Crosnoe, 2008). The reasons for the weight gain aren't clear, but it might be an emotional response to feeling rejected and a way to comfort themselves rather than engaging in athletic and other extracurricular school activities.

Such responses to feeling unpopular are unfortunate because teenage girls' and boys' self-assessments often differ from those of their peers. For example, among middle school students, about 75 percent of those who perceive themselves as unpopular are viewed as popular by their peers (McElhaney et al., 2008). Such findings suggest, as symbolic interactionists might say, that many preteens and teens experience unnecessary anguish because there's a disconnect between how they see themselves and what their peers think of them.

Teachers and Schools

Teachers and schools send a number of gender-related messages that follow boys and girls from preschool to college.

ELEMENTARY AND MIDDLE SCHOOLS In elementary and middle schools, boys usually get more time to talk in class, are called on more often, and receive more positive feedback than do girls. Teachers are more likely to give answers to girls or to do the problems for them but to expect boys to find the answers themselves. Expecting more from boys increases their problem-solving abilities, decision-making skills, and self-confidence in finding answers on their own (Sadker and Sadker, 1994).

Since you asked . . .

How do teachers help shape our gender roles?

Even when their behavior is disruptive, "problem girls" often receive less attention than do either well-behaved boys or "problem boys." Teachers tend to emphasize "motherwork" skills for girls, such as nurturance and emotional support. Both sexes are evaluated on academic criteria, work habits, and knowledge, but teachers are more likely to also eval-

uate girls on nonacademic criteria such as grooming and personal qualities such as politeness and appearance (Martin, 1998).

Michael Gurian, a self-proclaimed "teacher and therapist" maintains that nature intends girls to have and nurture children. He contends that by age 10, the development of a girl's brain causes her to be concerned about being pretty and popular, and she has a natural drive to connect with others. The author declares unequivocally that the structure of most girls' brains makes it difficult for them to grasp subjects such as calculus and physics and that women lack natural technical ability. He argues that if they put too much emphasis on achievement and careers, girls will suffer lifelong misery (Gurian and Henley, 2000; Gurian, 2002).

Scholars have dismissed such notions as "stereotypes of the first order" that will limit children's creativity and options. Girls in other countries—such as Japan, Russia, Germany, and Bulgaria—have won numerous medals in international math competitions (Begley, 2008). In the United States, however, teachers have lined up to buy Gurian's books, some principals have required their teachers to read them, and thousands of teachers have received training from Gurian's Colorado-based institute that promotes his unscientific views (Rivers, 2002; Chandler and Glod, 2008).

HIGH SCHOOL In high school, guidance counselors, who play an important role in helping students make career choices, may be particularly guilty of sex stereotyping. Even well-intentioned counselors often steer girls into vocational training, such as secretarial work or data processing, rather than college preparatory programs. And during summer vacations, teachers and counselors often help boys, but not girls, find jobs (Gerber, 2002).

In some college preparatory programs, counselors and teachers advise girls to take courses in the social sciences and humanities rather than in mathematics or the physical sciences. For example, according to Dr. Suzanne Franks, founding director of the Women in Engineering and Science Program at Kansas State University, some middle and high schools dismiss nontraditional opportunities for girls as inappropriate:

We contacted a school in Western Kansas to notify [it] of an opportunity to send some of [its] middle school girls on an industry tour we were sponsoring, where the girls could meet women engineers and scientists and see what they did for a living. We were flatly turned down, with the explanation being "I can assure you that none of our girls would be interested in such a thing" (Personal correspondence, October 9, 2002).

COLLEGE Women earn almost 58 percent of all bachelor's degrees and 60 percent of all master's degrees. Still, most women college students focus on traditional female-dominated disciplines such as literature, social work, teaching, and nursing (Planty et al., 2008).

Some people argue that women choose these lower-paying fields because they enjoy them. Others maintain that women aren't exposed to science and math courses that might pique their interest in male-dominated fields such as engineering and computer science (Margolis and Fisher, 2002).

Popular Culture and the Media

Media myths and unrealistic images assault our gender identity on a daily basis. A few examples from advertising, newspapers and magazines, television, and music videos illustrate how the media reinforce sex stereotyping from childhood to adulthood.

ADVERTISING The average young person under age 18 views more than 3,000 ads every day on television, the Internet, billboards, and in magazines (Strasburger et al., 2006). And, it's been estimated that girls ages 11 to 14 are subjected to about 500 advertisements a day, "the majority of them nipped, tucked, and airbrushed to perfection" (Bennett, 2008: 43).

Victoria's Secret—in catalogs, commercials, and ads—is not about lingerie but "the sheer sexual objectification of women." An ad for the perfume *Basic Instinct* portrays a woman with disheveled hair ("in a sexy way, of course") and a little black dress whose straps are falling off her shoulders. Her hands are tied behind her back and she has been thrown to the ground, implying rape. The perfume's name suggests that a woman's basic instinct is to play the part of a sexual victim. In other cases, images of corporate

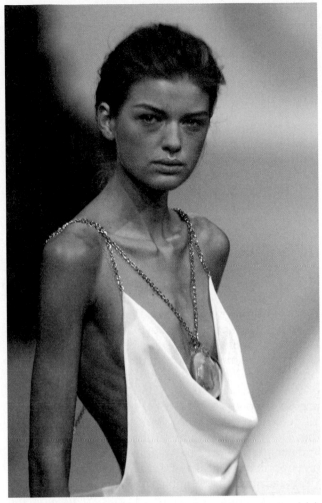

Concerned that ultrathin images of models promote girls' and young women's eating disorders, Spain and Italy now require models to have a healthy body mass index (BMI). More recently, France passed a law that makes it a crime to promote "excessive thinness" or extreme dieting (Abend and Sachs, 2008). Should the United States pass similar laws?

New Dove Firming. As tested on real curves.

ESNI0186543   NEW YORK, NEW YORK: THE NEW DOVE ADVERTISING CAMPAIGN, FEATURING "REAL" WOMEN AND NOT SUPER MODELS, HIGH ABOVE TIMES SQUARE. 2005 ©Lee Snider / The Image Works

Dove's beauty products sales surged up to 30 percent a few weeks after it began an advertising campaign featuring "normal-sized" women with "real curves." It turns out that the models' photographs were retouched (Collins, 2008). Do you think these models represent the average American woman? And why do they appear only in their underwear?

women flaunting their cleavage make it clear that femininity means sexiness, not intellectual or professional competence (Janson, 2005: 26, 27).

One result of such ads is that many women, especially white women, are unhappy with their bodies. In an analysis of 77 recent studies of media images of women, the researchers concluded that exposure to media depicting ultrathin actresses and models significantly increased women's concerns about their bodies, including how dissatisfied they felt and their likelihood of engaging in unhealthy eating behaviors, such as excessive dieting (Grabe et al., 2008).

Millions of others turn to cosmetic surgery. Women have 91 percent of all procedures, and the most common cosmetic surgery is for breast augmentation. In 2007 alone, almost 3 million women ages 19 to 34 had breast implants, whereas penis implants aren't even mentioned in the report (American Society for

Aesthetic Plastic Surgery, 2009). Many American women want to appeal to men who think big breasts are sexy. In contrast, men aren't seeking penis implants to appear more masculine or to increase their self-confidence.

NEWSPAPERS AND MAGAZINES Newspapers routinely marginalize women. A survey of 104 national and local newspapers found that in 3,500 frontpage stories, male sources outnumbered female sources almost three to one. Men were more likely to be quoted in stories about politics, business, parenting, religion, and science. Women were more likely to be cited in stories about health, home, food, fashion, travel, and ordinary people ("Newspaper content...," 2001). Thus, even though women have the greater responsibility for child rearing, men are quoted as parenting experts.

At many of the major newspapers, only a handful of the staff who write opinion pieces on the editorial pages are women—3 percent at the *Wall Street Journal,* 14 percent at the *Washington Post,* and 18 percent at the *New York Times.* The result is that women's voices and perspectives are rarely part of the national debates on important political and social issues (Jenkins, 2008).

Magazines that emphasize women's appearance (such as *Cosmopolitan, Glamour,* and *Vogue*) hold the largest share of the magazine market. About 60 percent of women read such women's magazines during the year, compared with just 7 percent who read business or financial magazines. Ad pages and dollars for most magazines have declined, but they have increased for the top women's magazines (Wellner, 2002). In effect, then, women are exposed to more beauty ads and traditional images of femininity than ever before.

ELECTRONIC MEDIA On average, seventh- to twelfth-graders spend almost 7 hours a day with electronic media—usually watching television—compared with about 2 hours each with parents and friends and less than 1 hour per day doing homework (Rideout et al., 2005). A surge of popular reality television shows, especially *Dancing with the Stars* and *American Idol,* has led to a greater diversity of racial and ethnic faces, both female and male. In other programs (such as *House, Grey's Anatomy,* the *CSI* series, and *The Closer*), the regulars include females (usually white) and black and Latino males.

For the most part, however, white men dominate prime-time television in central roles (see *Figure 5.1*). Also, girls are much less likely than boys to see women in leading roles that offer positive, strong, and competent role models, especially those that

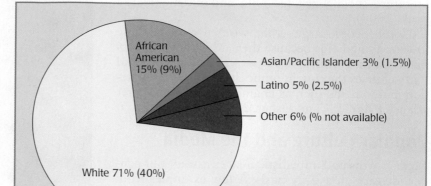

FIGURE 5.1 Racial Diversity of Prime-Time Characters on Television

Note: The numbers in parentheses indicate male actors.
Source: Based on Asian American Justice Center, 2006, Figure A.

represent their race or cultural heritage (Glaubke and Heintz-Knowles, 2004).

Are movies different? According to a study of the top-grossing G-rated animated and live-action films for children between 1990 and 2004, only 28 percent of the speaking characters were female. Most of the movies and cartoons were dominated by male characters and male stories. Minority males (whether boys or adults) were hard to find even though minority men make up almost a third of the U.S. population. Moreover, almost twice as many minority males (62 percent) as white males (38 percent) were portrayed as physically aggressive, violent, and dangerous. The study concluded that such disproportionate numbers offer young children a transparent message that being male and white is not just the norm, but preferable, and that white males are more trustworthy than their minority counterparts (Kelly and Smith, 2006). (We'll examine the impact of other electronic media, especially video games, in Chapter 12.)

⁖› MAKING CONNECTIONS

- According to the Parents Television Council (2008), of the top 20 most popular prime-time TV shows watched by children ages 2 to 17 in 2008, the worst offenders—because of violence, language, and crude sexual content—were *Family Guy, American Dad, Heroes, House,* and *The Moment of Truth.* Do you agree? What programs do *you* think are unsuitable for children?

- To decrease advertisers' influence on children, many European countries have banned TV ads on children's television programs. Should the United States do the same? Why or why not?

In 2009, the Disney studios released *The Princess and the Frog,* an animated film that features Maddy, a 19-year-old, as its first black princess. Many African American parents are delighted, but some critics are asking why the hero is a white prince.

TRADITIONAL VIEWS AND GENDER ROLES

According to one of my male students, "When a woman attempts to assume the head position in the family, it will probably lead to a loss of order and stability in the family." This remark sparked a lively class discussion, but such traditional views of gender roles are fairly common. Here are a few more examples:

Since you asked . . .

- Should the man be the boss in the family?

- The Southern Baptist Convention doctrine opposes female pastors and says wives should submit to their husbands ("Baptist missionaries . . . ," 2003).

- In disagreeing with the call of a female referee, Cedric Maxwell, a Boston Celtics radio commentator, said on the air: "Go back to the kitchen. Go in there and make me some bacon and eggs, would you?" ("Celtics broadcaster . . . ," 2007). Because the sexist remark generated considerable criticism, he apologized.

- Kansas state senator Kay O'Connor, an elected official, said that there was no reason to celebrate the passage of the Nineteenth Amendment, which allowed women to vote. She believes that mothers should stay home to rear their children and that "the man should be the head of the family" (Bullers, 2001).

Instrumental and Expressive Roles

You'll recall that functionalists developed a model of the family in which the male fulfilled an instrumental role and the female fulfilled an expressive role. Many critics view these descriptions of traditional gender roles as outmoded (see Chapter 2), but they're a reality in many American and worldwide homes. Let's take a closer look at these two types of roles.

INSTRUMENTAL ROLES Traditionally, *instrumental role players* (husbands and fathers) must be "real men." A "real man" is a procreator, a protector, and a provider. Producing children proves his virility, and having boys is especially important to carry on his family name.

The procreator must also be a protector, who is always strong and powerful in ensuring his family's physical safety. The provider works hard even if he is overwhelmed by multiple roles such as the "responsible breadwinner," "devoted husband," and "dutiful son" (Gaylin, 1992; Betcher and Pollack, 1993). If the traditional man is a "superman," the traditional woman is an only slightly more modern version of the "true woman" you met in Chapter 3 who is obedient and faithful and anticipates her husband's and children's every need.

EXPRESSIVE ROLES Traditionally, *expressive role players* (wives and mothers) provide the emotional support and nurturing qualities that sustain the family unit and support the husband/father. They should be warm, sensitive, and sympathetic. For example, the expressive role player consoles a teenage daughter when she breaks up with her boyfriend, encourages her son to try out for Little League, and is always ready to comfort a husband who has had a bad day at work.

One of women's expressive roles is that of kin-keeper, a role that is often passed down from mother to daughter. Kin-keepers are important communication links among family members. They spend much time maintaining contact with relatives, visiting friends and families, organizing family reunions, or holding gatherings during the holidays or for special events such as birthdays and anniversaries. They also often act as the family helper, problem solver, or mediator (Rosenthal, 1985).

Some Benefits and Costs of Traditional Gender Roles

Traditional gender roles have both benefits and costs (see *Table 5.5*). They may be chosen consciously or a product of habit, custom, or socialization. Remember, too, that traditional relationships vary. In some, the partners feel loving and committed; in others, they feel as though they are trapped or sleepwalking.

By permission of John L. Hart FLP and Creators Syndicate, Inc.

BENEFITS Traditional gender roles provide stability, continuity, and predictability. Because each person knows what is expected, rights and responsibilities are clear. Husbands and wives don't have to argue over who does what: If the house is clean, she is a "good wife;" if the bills are paid, he is a "good husband."

Using the exchange model (see Chapter 2), if the costs and benefits of the relationship are fairly balanced and each partner is relatively happy, traditional gender roles can work well. As long as both partners live up to their role expectations, they are safe in assuming that they will meet the other's needs financially, emotionally, and sexually.

The traditional gender role model seems to work well for conservative, Protestant, churchgoing women. At a number of Christian liberal arts colleges, for example, women aren't allowed to pursue a divinity degree, but they can take courses on how to cook, manage time, "joyfully submit to their husbands," meet their husbands' needs, and keep a marriage exciting (Sisson, 2007: 3).

Some women stay in traditional relationships because they don't have to make decisions or be responsible when things go wrong. An accommodating wife can enjoy both power and prestige through her husband's accomplishments. A good mother not only controls and dominates her children but can also be proud of guiding and enriching their lives (Harris, 1994).

When a traditional husband complained about his traditional wife's spending too much money, the wife composed and gave her husband the following "help wanted" ad:

I need someone full time who is willing to be on call 24 hours a day, seven days a week. Sick leave only when hospitalization is required. Must be able to cook, clean house, do laundry, care for children, feed and clean up after dog, do yard work, mow lawn, shovel snow, do shopping, do menu planning, take out trash, pay bills, answer phone and run errands. Must be able to pinch pennies. Also must be a friend

TABLE 5.5	Some Benefits and Costs of Traditional Gender Roles			
For Men . . .			**For Women . . .**	
Benefits	**Costs**	**Benefits**	**Costs**	
■ A positive self-image in being the provider	■ Loss of identity in the case of unemployment	■ Not having to juggle employment and domestic tasks	■ Loss of financial security if there's a separation or divorce	
■ Little marital stress in climbing a career ladder because the wife takes care of the kids and the home	■ Little time with wife or children	■ Time to focus on the husband-wife relationship	■ Is often alone because the husband is working long hours or makes numerous out-of-town trips	
■ Doesn't have to do much, if any, housework or child care	■ Wife may feel unappreciated or overburdened	■ Lots of time with children	■ Feeling useless when children leave home	
■ Has a sexual partner who isn't stressed out by having a job and caring for the family	■ Wife may feel taken for granted because she should always be available for sexual intercourse	■ Nurturing a husband and children and enjoying their accomplishments	■ Feeling like a failure if the children aren't successful, or feeling isolated and helpless if the husband is abusive	

and companion. Must be patient and cannot complain. If you are interested, please leave a message. I will contact you when I feel like talking. Speak only when you have something to say that might interest me. Otherwise, shut up and get to work.—C. L. in Utah ("Want ad proves. . .," 1997).

This ad is a good example of how men benefit from traditional marriages, especially because wives don't nag their husbands about sharing domestic chores. The wives benefit because they don't have the tension of being pulled in many directions—such as juggling jobs and housework. Such clearly designated duties can decrease both partners' stress.

COSTS Traditional gender roles have their drawbacks. Even when traditional families try to scale down their standard of living, a sole breadwinner is under a lot of economic pressure: "When mothers quit work to care for babies, fathers must shoulder unbearable stress to provide for more dependents" (Alton, 2001: 20).

The dutiful worker, husband, and father may feel overwhelmed by his responsibilities and may be unhappy with his life. A traditional man may believe that he never quite lives up to the standard of manhood. Although he has not failed completely, he may feel that he has not succeeded, either (Gaylin, 1992).

Sometimes the seemingly distant man is quiet because he is continuously worried about the family's economic well-being. Because many men derive their self-esteem from work and the breadwinner role, losing a job can send some men into severe depression, seeking solace in alcohol, frustrated rages that end in violence, and even suicide (Scelfo, 2007; Dokoupil, 2009).

In terms of costs, a traditional wife can expect little relief from never-ending tasks that may be exhausting and monotonous. And what are her options if she's miserable? Traditional values such as being nurturant, dependent, and submissive can discourage some women from leaving abusive relationships. If she's been out of the workforce for a number of years, she might be worse off after a divorce. Or a woman who has left all the money matters to her husband may find after his death that he did little estate planning and that their finances are in disarray (see Chapters 14, 15, and 17). Gender role stereotypes reflect another cost of traditional roles. The box "Should *You* Enroll in These Classes?" offers a tongue-in-cheek look at such stereotypes.

WHY DO TRADITIONAL GENDER ROLES PERSIST?
Traditional gender roles endure for several reasons. For many families, traditional gender roles are rewarding, especially when a couple works out mutually satisfying arrangements to share breadwinning and family care responsibilities. Whether the reasons are based on religious beliefs, cultural values, or socialization, traditional gender roles can provide a sense of accomplishment in meeting a family's needs.

Second, traditional gender roles are profitable for business. The unpaid work that women do at home (such as housework, child rearing, and emotional support) means that companies don't have to pay for child care services or counseling for stressed-out male employees.

If there is only one breadwinner, many men may work extra hours without additional pay to keep their jobs. Thus, companies increase their profits. If women believe that their place is in the home, they will take part-time jobs that do not provide benefits, will work for less pay, and will not complain. This

---

Applying What You've Learned

⁞• *Should* You *Enroll in These Classes?*

Humor fulfills a number of functions, including relieving tension and expressing an opinion on a controversial or sensitive topic. Consider this list of "college seminars for sexist men and women." Do the suggested courses contain a kernel of truth? Or are they stereotypes?

Seminars for Men

1. You, Too, Can Do Housework
2. Easy Laundry Techniques
3. Get a Life—Learn to Cook
4. Spelling—Even You Can Get It Right
5. How to Stay Awake after Sex
6. Garbage—Getting It to the Curb
7. How to Put the Toilet Seat Down
8. Combating Stupidity

Seminars for Women

1. You, Too, Can Change the Oil
2. Elementary Map Reading
3. Get a Life—Learn to Kill Spiders
4. Checkbook Balancing—Even You Can Get It Right
5. How to Stay Awake during Sex
6. Shopping in Less Than 16 Hours
7. How to Close the Garage Door
8. Combating the Impulse to Nag

increases the corporate world's pool of exploitable and expendable low-paid workers.

Third, traditional roles maintain male privilege and power. If women are seen as not having leadership qualities (see *Table 5.1* on p. 106), men can dominate political and legal institutions. They can shape laws and policies to maintain their vested interests without being challenged by women who are unhappy with the status quo.

GENDER ROLES IN ADULTHOOD

We've looked at some of the processes in learning gender roles. What are the effects in adulthood? **Gender stratification** refers to people's unequal access to wealth, power, status, prestige, opportunity, and other valued resources because of their gender. We'll examine gender stratification in greater depth in later chapters. Let's look briefly at gender inequality in the family, workplace, politics, education, religion, and everyday interactions.

Gender and Family Life: Who Does the Work?

Years before her death in 1977, Heloise Cruse (of "Hints from Heloise") remarked, "I think housework is the reason most women go to the office." Indeed, if they were free to do either, 58 percent of Americans—both men and women—would prefer to have a job

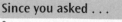

Since you asked . . .

- If you had a choice, would you rather be employed or stay at home and take care of the house and family?

outside the home rather than staying at home and taking care of the house and family (Saad, 2007). Few adults have this either-or choice, however, and employment rarely lightens women's domestic workload.

Many women's private and public roles have changed dramatically in the past few decades: Sixty-seven percent of married mothers are in the labor force, compared with 50 percent in 1970 (U.S. Census Bureau, 2008). Has women's employment changed gender roles at home? Only somewhat.

THE "SECOND SHIFT" In many cases, one of the major sources of tension is that many fathers don't participate very much in the *second shift*—the household work and child care tasks that many mothers face after coming home from work (Hochschild, 1989). Increasingly, more couples say that they share these tasks, but how equal is the division of domestic labor?

Having a husband creates an extra 7 hours of housework a week for women, but many couples say that they share domestic tasks more equally than did their parents or grandparents. Still, there continues to be a significant division of labor along traditional gender lines, such as 68 percent of wives doing the laundry (Newport, 2008; Stafford, 2008).

Men are doing more in the home, but women shoulder twice as much child care and housework as men. Women's domestic work declined from 50 hours in 1965 to about 26 hours in 2004, whereas men's increased from 12 to 16 hours. These changes are due partly to men's greater efforts and partly to a decrease in the amount that women do because of full-time employment (Bianchi et al., 2006; England, 2006; Jackson, 2006). For the most part, however, neither employed women nor full-time homemakers are doing as much housework as in the past. Instead, most of us have adapted to messier and dustier homes.

ARE GENDER ROLE CONTRIBUTIONS MORE BALANCED? Because the gap between the sexes' child care and domestic chores has narrowed, several sociologists have concluded that men have made substantial progress in lessening the burden of women's second shift (Sullivan and Coltrane, 2008).

Army Pfc. Lori Piestewa was the first female American soldier killed in combat in Iraq and the first American Indian woman killed while fighting for the U.S. military. Here, Piestewa's older daughter, age 4, attends a memorial service for her mom with her grandparents, who are raising the girls.

However, women sometimes complain that men's participation is peripheral:

I'm always amused when my husband says that he'll "help" me make our bed. I guess he "helps" because he feels making the bed is my responsibility, not his, even though we both sleep in it. When I mow the lawn, it's no big deal. But when he occasionally helps make the bed or does the dishes, he expects a litany of thank-you's and hugs (Author's files).

A heavier housework load combined with full employment means that women often experience greater stress than men. Because they have either more responsibility or a greater share of the domestic work, women often multitask, like writing checks while returning phone calls or responding to e-mail. In addition, women do more of the tedious household chores, such as scrubbing the toilet, whereas men prefer to tend to their children and do fun things with them such as going to the movies or playing video games.

WHO MAKES THE EVERYDAY HOUSEHOLD DECISIONS? Among married couples and those living together, women make more decisions—almost twice as many as men—in planning weekend activities, household finances, major purchases for the home, and TV watching (see *Figure 5.2*). Women seem to have the final say in many decisions, and 80 percent of both sexes are happy with this situation (Morin and Cohn, 2008). Note, however, that

- Less than a third of the couples share equally in decision making.
- Men (37 percent) are more likely than women (30 percent) to say that men manage the family finances.
- Older couples (ages 65 and older) are twice as likely as younger couples (ages 18–49) to share decision making equally (Morin and Cohn, 2008; St. George, 2008).

These more specific results suggest that both sexes may be exaggerating women's decision-making power, especially on important issues such as finances. In addition, older couples appear to be more egalitarian than many of their younger counterparts, which suggests that younger generations aren't as egalitarian as they think they are and that decision making becomes more balanced in long-term relationships.

FATHERS AND CHILDREN After her parents divorced, Ianna moved in with her father. When she was 5, he gave her a rod and took her out on a fishing boat for the first time. By age 11, Ianna outfished most adult men, including landing a 35-pound yellowtail. She plays with and collects dolls but says that her numerous fishing awards are "cool" (Benning, 2005). Ianna's fishing talents wouldn't have blossomed if her dad hadn't taken the time to introduce her to the sport.

Many of today's fathers are probably correct in thinking that they're doing a better parenting job than their fathers did (see Chapter 12). For example, the amount of time that employed fathers spend with their children under age 13 on workdays has increased from 2 hours to 3 hours (compared with 4 hours for mothers). Also, the percentage of employed women who say that their husbands or intimate male partners take or share greater responsibility for child care has increased from 21 percent in 1992 to 30 percent in 2008 (Galinsky et al., 2009).

Gender and the Workplace

There has been greater workplace equality, but we still have a long way to go. In the United States (as around the world), most occupations are gendered: The average male employee still doesn't have options for flexible schedules, paternity leaves, or extended absences for household matters, and women often think that they have to postpone or forgo having children if they want to pursue a career.

We'll examine family and work roles at some length in Chapter 13. Here, let's briefly consider gender discrimination and sexual harassment—two work-related gender inequities that affect women, men, their partners, and their families.

GENDER DISCRIMINATION When someone asked a top executive why there are so few high-ranking

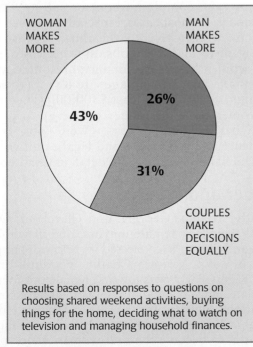

FIGURE 5.2 Who Makes the Decisions at Home?

WOMAN MAKES MORE

MAN MAKES MORE

26%

43%

31%

COUPLES MAKE DECISIONS EQUALLY

Results based on responses to questions on choosing shared weekend activities, buying things for the home, deciding what to watch on television and managing household finances.

Source: Morin and Cohn, 2008.

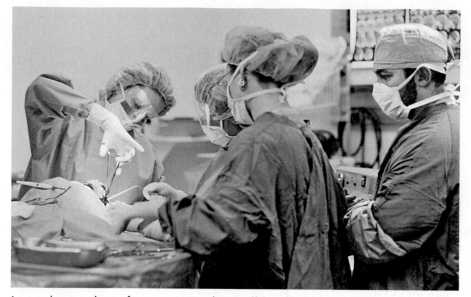

Increasing numbers of men are pursuing traditionally female occupations such as nursing, whereas more women are becoming physicians, including brain surgeons, a traditionally male-dominated occupation.

women in the advertising industry, he replied that it's because they aren't good enough. Women don't deserve to be promoted, he said, because their roles as caregivers and childbearers prevent them from working hard and succeeding in top positions (Bosman, 2005).

Such attitudes result in a *glass ceiling*, a collection of attitudinal or organizational biases in the workplace that prevent women from advancing to leadership positions. Organizational barriers reflect, in large part, stereotypes about gender roles. For example, senior-level U.S. executives—both men and women—typically describe women as better at stereotypically feminine caretaking skills such as supporting and encouraging others, and men as excelling at masculine taking-charge skills such as influencing superiors and problem solving. Because many promotions are based on taking charge rather than caretaking skills, women often suffer because they are considered too tough (a masculine trait) or too soft (a feminine trait). Thus, women often experience a double bind—that nagging sense that whatever you do, you can do no right (Sabattini et al., 2007; Foust-Cummings et al., 2008).

There's also a double standard in how co-workers and bosses interpret the same behavior. For example, whether women are supervisors or clerical workers, if they lose their temper, they are overwhelmingly seen as too emotional, incompetent, out of control, weak, and worth less pay. Their angry male counterparts, in contrast, are often viewed as authoritative and reasonable (Brescoll and Uhlmann, 2008).

SEXUAL HARASSMENT Sexual harassment is any unwelcome sexual advance, request for sexual favors, or other conduct of a sexual nature that makes a person uncomfortable and interferes with her or his work. Harassment includes touching, staring at, or making jokes about a person's body; unreciprocated requests for sexual intercourse; rape; and any other form of unwanted sex.

A landmark Supreme Court decision in 1986, *Meritor Savings Bank v. Vinson,* ruled that sexual harassment violates federal antidiscrimination laws. Sexual harassment in the workplace had a generally low profile, however, until the Senate confirmation hearings for Clarence Thomas, a candidate for the U.S. Supreme Court in October 1991. Sexual harassment suddenly received national media coverage when Anita Hill, a law professor at the University of Oklahoma, testified that in the early 1980s, Thomas had sexually harassed her while he was her supervisor and the director of the Equal Employment Opportunity Commission (EEOC). Despite the allegations, Congress approved Thomas's appointment to the U.S. Supreme Court.

National surveys show that almost half of all working women experience some form of sexual harassment in the workplace (Waldref, 2008). Very few, however, complain about or sue for sexual harassment. In most cases, especially in lower-level positions, women tolerate the abuse because they don't want to lose their jobs. In other cases, even when women have some financial resources, they know that a lawsuit will take 7 to 8 years to settle and might cost them at least $300,000. Therefore, few women have the money or energy to pursue sexual harassment lawsuits. (We'll look at the prevalence, consequences, and legal ramifications of sexual harassment in more detail in Chapter 13.)

Gender and Politics

Recently, Atlanta, Georgia, and Cleveland, Ohio, elected their first female mayors, one of whom is black, and Puerto Rico elected its first woman governor. In 1872, Victoria Chaflin Woodhull of the Equal Rights Party, was the first female presidential candidate. Since then, about 36 women have sought the nation's highest office. In 2007, Senator Hillary Rodham Clinton engaged in a "whisker-close but losing battle to become the first woman major party presidential nominee," a historic run that came close to breaking the glass ceiling of a male-dominated U.S. presidency (Halloran, 2008: 34). She lost to Senator Barack Obama.

Worldwide, the United States lags far behind many other nations, including some developing countries, in women's political empowerment (measured by the number of women serving as head of state or in decision-making government positions). Of 188 countries, the United States ranks only 71 in women's political empowerment (Inter-Parliamentary Union, 2009). According to the president of a U.S. organization working to advance women in political leadership, "It will take [women] till 2063 to reach parity [with men]" (Feldmann, 2008: 2).

Why are there so few women in political offices? One reason may be that women, socialized to be nurturers and volunteers, see themselves as supporters rather than movers and doers. As a result, they may spend many hours organizing support for a candidate rather than running for a political office themselves.

Second, women are less likely than men to receive encouragement to run for office from a political source (such as a party leader). As a result, even successful women are twice as likely as men to rate themselves "not at all qualified." In contrast, men with similar credentials are two-thirds more likely than women to consider themselves "qualified" or "very qualified" to run for office (Fox and Lawless, 2004).

Third, there is still "a lingering sexism," among both men and women, that "from the pulpit to the presidency," men are better leaders (Tucker, 2007: A9). The pervasive sexism in media coverage of political candidates was especially evident during the 2008 presidential campaigns. From the beginning, some reporters and news commentators criticized Senator Clinton's appearance ("She looked haggard") and voice ("cackling laugh"), described her as a "nagging wife," and referred to her as Hillary but never called Senators Barack Obama and John McCain by their first names or made demeaning comments about their gender, looks, or personalities (Long, 2008; Wakeman, 2008).

Gender and Education

When boys and girls enter kindergarten, they perform similarly on both reading and mathematics tests. By the third grade, however, boys, on average, outperform girls in math and science, whereas girls outperform boys in reading. These gaps increase throughout high school (Dee, 2006). Some of the reasons for these differences include parental socialization, teacher expectations, and counselors steering girls and boys into courses that focus on gender-stereotyped disciplines (such as social work for girls and engineering for boys).

In higher education, "women face more obstacles as faculty than they do as managers and directors in

Only 20 percent of our 3 million teachers are men. In elementary schools, only 9 percent are males, down from 18 percent in 1981. A major reason for the decline is low salaries, compared with other occupations, but gender stereotypes are an important factor. Especially in the lower grades, men who show nurturing skills or affection for children may be accused of being gay or a pedophile (Provasnik and Dorfman, 2005; Bonner, 2007; Scelfo, 2007).

corporate America" (West and Curtis, 2006: 4). Even when women earn doctoral degrees in male-dominated fields, they are less likely than men to be hired. For example, women have received more than 45 percent of all Ph.D.'s in biology for the past 15 years, but only 14 percent of full-time biology professors are women (Handelsman et al., 2005). Once hired, women faculty members are less likely than their male counterparts to be promoted. For nearly 25 years, one-third of all recipients of doctoral degrees have been women, but 76 percent of full professors are men (see *Table 5.6*).

Gender and Religion

Religion shapes gender and family roles in many ways. For example, the Ten Commandments teach children to honor their parents and married couples to be faithful to each other. Studies of Catholics, mainline Protestants (such as Episcopalians, Methodists, and Lutherans), and evangelical Protestants (such as Southern Baptists and Assemblies of God congregants) have found that fathers in all these faiths were more likely than fathers with no religious affiliation to spend more time with their children. The former were more likely to interact with their children (including working on projects, talking to them, and helping with reading or homework); have family dinners; and participate in youth-related activities such as sports, school functions, and religious youth groups (Wilcox, 2002; Chatters and Taylor, 2005).

Religion also shapes the division of labor in the home. In evangelical households, wives, including those who work outside the home, spend 4 to 5 more hours per week performing tasks that are traditionally defined as women's work (cooking, cleaning, and

TABLE 5.6	As Rank Increases, the Number of Women Faculty Decreases
Percentage of Full-Time Female Faculty Members, by Rank	
Professor	24
Associate Professor	38
Assistant Professor	45
Instructor	52

Note: Of the almost 632,000 full-time faculty in 2005, 49 percent were women.
Source: Based on U.S. Department of Education, 2006, Table 227.

laundry). Some female evangelicals have challenged such gendered housework, but many believe that it is divinely ordained that men provide for and protect the family and that women support men by taking on most of the household responsibilities (Bartkowski, 2001; Ellison and Bartkowski, 2002; Gallagher, 2003).

At religious colleges and universities, some female faculty members believe that their expected gender roles are constraining. Often there are few full-time faculty members at these institutions who are women. Those who are hired may feel alienated because many Christian colleges constantly remind female students that once they get married and have children, "God does not expect them to work outside the home" (Mock, 2005: B24). In effect, then, some of these women faculty wonder if they're effective in providing their female students with role models they will aspire to follow after college.

Gender and Interaction

Women and men are more similar than different in their interactions. A study that recorded conversations of college students in the United States and Mexico found that women and men spoke the same number of words daily—about 16,000. An analysis of studies published since the 1960s concluded that men are generally more talkative than women, but their talkativeness depends on the situation. During decision-making tasks, men are more talkative than women, but when talking about themselves or interacting with children, women are generally more talkative than men (Leaper and Ayres, 2007; Mehl et al., 2007).

Other studies support the findings that our cultural norms and gender role expectations shape the sexes' communication patterns. Generally, women are socialized to be more comfortable talking about their feelings, whereas men are socialized to be dominant and take charge, especially in the workplace. Because women tend to use communication to develop and maintain relationships, *talk is often an*

end in itself—a way to foster closeness and understanding. Women often ask questions that *probe for a greater understanding* of feelings and perceptions ("Do you think it was deliberate?" or "Were you glad it happened?"). Women are also much more likely than men to do *conversational "maintenance work,"* such as asking questions that encourage conversation ("Tell me what happened at the meeting") (Lakoff, 1990; Robey et al., 1998).

Compared with female speech, men's speech often reflects *conversational dominance,* such as speaking more frequently and for longer periods of time. Men also show dominance by interrupting others, reinterpreting the speaker's meaning, or rerouting the conversation. They tend to express themselves in assertive, often absolutist, ways ("That approach won't work"). Compared with women's language, men's language is typically more forceful, direct, and authoritative rather than tentative (Tannen, 1990; Mulac, 1998; see, also, Chapter 10).

Is Androgyny the Answer?

Some social scientists believe that **androgyny** may be the solution to sexist gender roles. Androgyny refers to the blending of both masculine and feminine characteristics in the same person.

According to psychologist Sandra Bem (1975), who did much of the pioneering work on androgyny, our complex society requires that people have both kinds of characteristics. Adults must be assertive, independent, and self-reliant, but they must also relate well to other people, be sensitive to their needs, and give them emotional support.

Androgyny allows people to play both instrumental and expressive roles because both men and women demonstrate humanity's "graces and furies":

Both are equally likely to be empathic, kind, altruistic, and friendly and to be mean, hostile, aggressive, petty, conformist, and prejudiced. Both sexes can be competitive or cooperative, selfish or nurturant, loving parents or indifferent ones—and reveal all of those qualities on different occasions (Tavris, 2002: B8).

Androgyny might be especially beneficial for men. Many might relax on weekends, refrain from engaging in risky sexual behavior (to demonstrate their sexual prowess), live longer, and stop worrying about being "real men." If we felt more comfortable when children display nontraditional gender traits, assertive girls and nonaggressive boys would be happier and emotionally healthier (Martin, 1990).

:• MAKING CONNECTIONS

■ Some people maintain that instrumental and expressive roles no longer exist. Others argue that both roles are alive and well. Think about your parents, your spouse or intimate partner, or your friends. Does their behavior reflect instrumental and expressive roles? What about your behavior?

■ Do you think that androgyny might take some of the pressure off men, giving them more freedom to be and do whatever they want? Or do you think that androgynous men would be dismissed as wimps and sissies?

A GLOBAL VIEW: VARIATIONS IN GENDER ROLES

Since you asked . . .

:• Are there any countries where women are better off than men?

Since each culture has its own norms and values, the degree of equality between men and women differs widely from one society to another. Such cross-cultural variations constitute some of the best evidence that gender roles are learned rather than innate.

There is no easy way to compare the status of women around the world. Still, the Global Gender Gap Index (GGGI) is a measure that sheds some light on women's status and quality of life in 130 countries, representing more than 90 percent of the world's population. The GGGI is based on key indicators in four fundamental categories: economic participation and development, educational attainment, political empowerment (women and men in the highest political positions), and health and survival (Hausmann et al., 2008).

The index is not an overall measure of a country's development or wealth, but it gauges the relative equality between men and women on an indicator. For example, Sri Lanka has been plagued with civil wars and a high poverty rate, but it has one of the smallest gender gaps in women's political rights and health. As *Figure 5.3* shows, most of the world's women live in countries that rank from "medium" to the "bottom 10 countries" on the GGGI. Let's begin with the top 10 countries—those that have the greatest equality between the sexes.

Top Ten Countries

Norway, Finland, Sweden, Iceland, New Zealand, the Philippines, Denmark, Ireland, the Netherlands, and Latvia rank highest (and in that order) on the GGGI. Being in the top ten doesn't mean that women live in paradise, however. For example, Sweden ranks at the top, but female undergraduates report sexual harassment, and women faculty members—only 11 percent of whom are tenured—complain about widespread discrimination in the awarding of postdoctoral fellowships, hiring practices, and promotion criteria (Bollag, 2002a, 2002b).

There's also wide variation among the top ten countries on several of the indicators. For example, Ireland ranks at the top in the sexes' high school graduation rates, but only 81st on the sexes' health and survival. One of the reasons for the low rank may be high rates of domestic violence against women and reported rapes (Hausmann et al., 2008; Scager, 2009).

High-Rank Countries

The countries that rank high but not at the top of the GGGI include the United States, Canada, South Africa, most of the European countries and those in East Europe, Australia, South Korea, Cuba, Argentina, Portugal, Greece, and several countries in the Middle East (Israel and Kuwait).

Again, women and men are not fully equal in these societies. Some of the high-rank countries have positive characteristics such as high female literacy rates, low maternal mortality rates, and high percentages of female university students. Yet domestic violence is widespread: Fifty-three percent of women in Portugal and 38 percent in Australia report having experienced physical abuse by a male partner (Seager, 2009).

Middle-Rank Countries

The middle-rank countries are primarily those in Central and South America, northern and southern Africa, Russia, and much of the Middle East. Especially in Islamic cultures, there is a great deal of variation in women's roles in the family, education, and politics and in employment opportunities. Each country interprets women's rights under Islam somewhat differently, and within each country social class is a determining factor in women's privileges.

In the Arab world, the overall female literacy rate is only 50 percent, but it ranges from a low of

FIGURE 5.3 The Gender Gap around the World

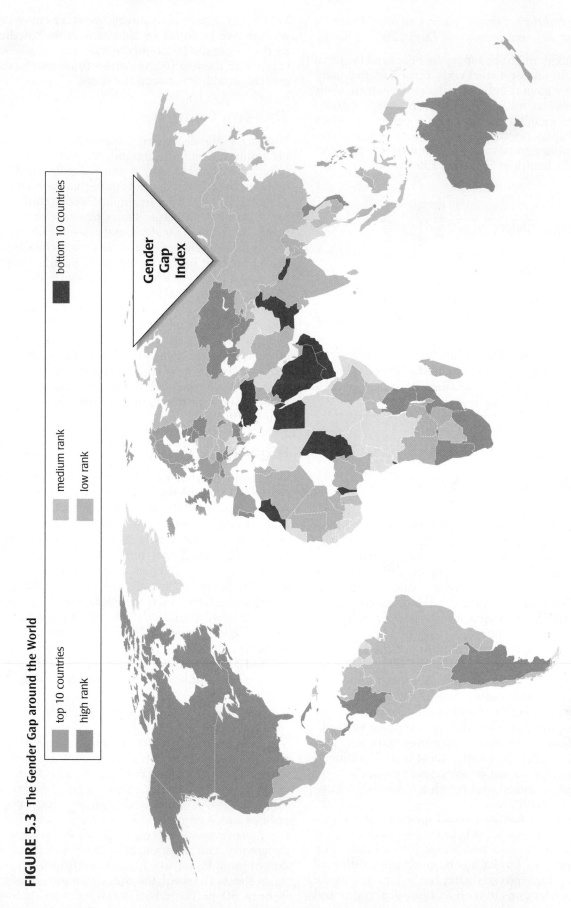

Sources: Based on Hausmann et al., 2008, Table 3a, and Seager, 2009: 17.

Women in Kenya, Africa, acquired the right to vote only in 1963 but now constitute 54 percent of the country's voting population. In both tribal villages and urban centers, women line up to vote for important issues such as the right to inherit money and property.

13 percent in Afghanistan to almost 85 percent in Jordan. In some countries (including Kuwait, Indonesia, China, Thailand, and Saudi Arabia), thriving sex industries are fed by a steady supply of young women—mostly from Bangladesh, India, the Philippines, Sri Lanka, and other poor countries where the women cannot find employment. The unsuspecting women are told that they are accepting overseas jobs as maids or domestic laborers. Instead, they are forced into prostitution. Child rape, prostitution, and pornography are widespread (UNICEF, 2006; Lampman, 2008; Central Intelligence Agency, 2009).

Low-Rank Countries

The low-rank countries include India, several Middle Eastern countries, and a number of African societies. In much of Africa, women's life expectancy is well under 55 years, with a low of 33 in Swaziland. Early death results primarily from AIDS but also reflects high death rates during childbirth because of poor nutrition, the scarcity of trained health personnel, and murder by husbands after marriage. In African countries, female literacy rates range from a low of 14 percent in Somalia to a high of 95 percent in Lesotho (Central Intelligence Agency, 2009).

In Nigeria and Somalia, females can be stoned to death for being raped by strangers; infidelity; or, in the

case of divorced women, having sexual relations without having remarried. In a recent case in Palestine, a married woman and mother of four was murdered by her male cousins to restore the family's honor because they (but not her husband or immediate family) accused her of having an affair (Prusher, 2007; "Girl is stoned . . .," 2008).

Bottom Ten Countries

The lowest-ranked countries on the GGGI are in Africa (Morocco, Benin, Egypt, and Chad), Arab countries (Yemen, Saudi Arabia, Turkey, and Bahrain), and southern Asia (Pakistan and Nepal) (see *Figure 5.3*). Women have short life expectancies for the same reasons as women in the low-ranked African societies. Their literacy rates are typically under 50 percent, women's participation in government is negligible, and rates of sex trafficking of women to other countries are high (Seager, 2009).

In Saudi Arabia, women aren't allowed to drive, vote, hold a political office, or even study the same subjects as men in college. Most jobs (in education, medicine, and banking) are segregated by sex, and women who are raped are punished by lashing, imprisonment, or both because they should not have been traveling without a male relative (Fleishman, 2007).

Some countries are struggling to improve women's status, but progress is mixed. In Afghanistan, for example, women vote, hold a quarter of the seats in parliament, and are legally allowed to work outside the home. However, because many Afghan families won't allow their daughters to be where they may be seen by unrelated men, and there are few female teachers, the ratio of boys to girls in primary school

Although they were ousted from power, the Taliban are still strong in southern Afghanistan. In a country where 87 percent of women are illiterate, and where coeducation is forbidden, gunmen have killed teachers and schoolgirls or sprayed their faces with burning acid. In other cases, they have torched schools to stop girls from learning. Pictured here are Afghan girls attending a makeshift classroom after their school was burned down.

is roughly 2 to 1 and drops to four boys for every girl in high school. In more than 80 percent of the rural districts, there are no girls in secondary schools at all, and only 10 percent of girls obtain a high school diploma. The Afghan parliament recently passed a law that forbids minority Shia women from leaving their homes without permission from a male relative and allows marital rape (Baker, 2008; Abawi, 2009; Filkens, 2009).

CONCLUSION

The past 25 years have seen the beginning of dramatic *changes* in some aspects of gender roles. More people today say that they believe in gender equality, and unprecedented numbers of women have entered colleges and the labor force.

But do most people really have more *choices*? Women have become increasingly resentful of the burden of both domestic and economic responsibilities, especially in a society that devalues them and their labor. Men, although often freed from the sole-breadwinner role, believe that their range of choices is narrowing as women compete with them at work.

Significant change in gender roles elicits *constraints* for both sexes at every level: personal, group, and institutional. Those who benefit the most from gender role inequality resist giving up their privileges and economic resources. In the next chapter, we examine how changes in gender roles affect love and intimate relationships.

SUMMARY

1. *Sex* and *gender* are not interchangeable terms. Sex refers to the biological characteristics we are born with. Gender refers to the attitudes and behavior that society expects of men and women.

2. Children develop a gender identity early in life that remains fairly fixed. Our gender roles are fairly rigid and can result in gender stereotypes and myths.

3. Scholars continue to debate how much of our behavior reflects nature (biology) or nurture (environment). Biology is important, but there is little evidence that women are naturally better parents, that men are naturally more aggressive, or that men and women are inherently different in other ways than anatomy.

4. A number of theoretical perspectives offer insights on understanding gender roles. Sociobiologists contend that biology determines women's and men's behavior. Social learning theory posits that we learn gender roles by reward and punishment, imitation, and role modeling. Cognitive development theory maintains that children learn gender identity by interacting with and interpreting the behavior of others. For symbolic interactionists, gender roles are socially constructed categories that emerge in social situations. Feminist approaches argue that gender roles differ due to socialization (especially by parents), patriarchy, and gender scripts.

5. We learn gender role expectations from many socialization agents—parents, peers, teachers, and the media. Many of these socializing influences continue to reinforce traditional male and female gender roles.

6. Traditional gender roles are based on the beliefs that women should fulfill expressive functions and that men should play instrumental roles. Traditional roles have both positive and negative consequences. On the positive side, men and women know what is expected of them. On the negative side, traditional roles often create stress and anxiety and seriously limit choices.

7. During much of our adult life, our activities are sex segregated. Typically, men and women play different roles in the home, the workplace, politics, education, and religion.

8. Men and women tend to communicate differently. These differences are often unintentional, but they reinforce our gender role interactions and expectations.

9. Some scholars contend that androgyny may be the solution to sexist gender roles, and especially beneficial for men.

10. There is wide variation among cultures in the degree of equality between women's and men's gender roles. Many societies are male dominated; others are much more progressive than the United States.

KEY TERMS

sex 107
gender 107
gender identity 107
gender roles 107
gender stereotype 108

hormones 108
sociobiology 112
social learning theory 113
cognitive development theory 113
sexism 114

peer group 116
gender stratification 124
sexual harassment 126
androgyny 128

PEARSON **myfamilylab** My Family Lab provides a wealth of resources. Go to www.myfamilylab.com <http://www.myfamilylab.com/>, to enhance your comprehension of the content in this chapter. You can take practice exams, view videos relevant to the subject matter, listen to audio files, explore topics further by using Social Explorer, and use the tools contained in MySearchLab to help you write research papers.

6 Romance, Love, and Loving Relationships

Many popular movies have been about love: first love (*Titanic*), obsessive love (*Fatal Attraction*), self-sacrificing love (*The Bridges of Madison County*), love that survives obstacles (*The Notebook*), falling in love with someone from the wrong side of the tracks (*Pretty Woman*), and aging love (*On Golden Pond*). Love means different things to different people. As the box "On Love and Loving" shows, love has been a source of inspiration, witticisms, and even political action for centuries.

In this chapter, we explore the meaning of romance and love, why we love each other, the positive and negative aspects of love, and how love changes over time. We also look at some cross-cultural variations in people's attitudes about love. Let's begin with friendship, the root of love.

DATA DIGEST

- **Love is great for business.** On a typical Valentine's Day, Americans spend more than $400 million on roses, purchase more than $600 million worth of candy, and send more than 1 billion cards (compared with 150 million on Mother's Day). In 2005, men spent an average of $218 on Valentine's Day gifts compared with women's $146.

- More than half of all American adults (52 percent) believe in love at first sight and **almost 75 percent believe that there is "one true love."**

- **Men are more likely than women to initiate romantic e-mail.** Of the people who engage in online chats, 64 percent—most of them men—say they experience "online chemistry."

- **Does love make life richer or fuller?** Yes, say 37 percent of people born between 1965 and 1980 compared with only 9 percent of those born before 1930.

- **Should women propose to men?** Yes, according to 77 percent of men but only 63 percent of women.

Sources: Carlson, 2001; Yin, 2002; Alvear, 2003; White, 2003; Armstrong, 2004; Soukup, 2005.

LOVING AND LIKING

Love—as both an emotion and a behavior—is essential for human survival.

Since you asked . . .

∷ Is it possible to love someone you don't like?

The family is usually our earliest and most important source of love and emotional support (see Chapter 1). It is in families that we learn to love ourselves and, consequently, to love others.

Self-Love

Actress Mae West once said, "I never loved another person the way I loved myself." Such a statement may seem self-centered, but it's insightful. Social philosopher Erich Fromm (1956) saw self-love, or love for oneself, as essential for our social and emotional development and as a prerequisite for loving others.

For social scientists, self-love is an important basis for self-esteem. People who like themselves are more open to criticism and less demanding of others. Those who don't like themselves may not be able to reciprocate friendship. Instead, they constantly seek relationships that will bolster their own poor self-image (Casler, 1974).

Friendship

A *friend* is someone for whom you feel affection and respect, can count on for assistance, and with whom you discuss important personal topics. A consistent finding of a number of studies on friendship is that friends have a big effect on our physical, social, and psychological health, and sometimes a bigger impact than our family relationships. For example, people ages 70 and older who have social networks—especially those including friends and not just family members—live longer; a person's chances of becoming obese increase nearly 60 percent if she or he has a friend who is obese; those with friends are generally happier than their isolated counterparts; and those with strong friendships may even be less likely than others to get colds, presumably because they experience less stress because friends offer physical assistance (such as picking up medicine and running errands) and emotional support (Giles et al., 2005; Christakis and Fowler, 2007; Parker-Pope, 2009).

Changes

On Love and Loving

Throughout the centuries many writers have commented on the varieties, purposes, pleasures, and pain of love. Here are some examples:

- **Jesus (4 B.C.–A.D. 29):** "A new commandment I give unto you, that ye love one another."

- **I Corinthians 13:4–7:** "Love is patient and kind; love is not jealous or boastful; it is not arrogant or rude. . . . Love bears all things, believes all things, hopes all things, endures all things."

- **William Shakespeare (1564–1616):** "To say the truth, reason and love keep little company together nowadays" (from *A Midsummer Night's Dream*).

- **Hindustani proverb:** "Life is no longer one's own when the heart is fixed on another."

- **Abraham Cowley (1618–1667):** "I love you, not only for what you are, but for what I am when I am with you."

- **Ninon de Lenclos (1620–1705):** "Much more genius is needed to make love than to command armies."

- **Irish saying:** "If you live in my heart, you live rent free."

- **Elizabeth Barrett Browning (1806–1861):** "How do I love thee? Let me count the ways. I love thee to the depth and breadth and height my soul can reach."

- **Henry Wadsworth Longfellow (1807–1882):** "Love gives itself; it is not bought."

- **Japanese saying:** "Who travels for love finds a thousand miles only one mile."

- **William Thackeray (1811–1863):** "It is best to love wisely, no doubt; but to love foolishly is better than not to be able to love at all."

- **Robert Browning (1812–1889):** "Take away love and our earth is a tomb."

- **Benjamin Disraeli (1804–1881):** "The magic of first love is our ignorance that it can ever end."

- **Marlene Dietrich (1901–1992):** "Grumbling is the death of love."

- **Turkish proverb:** "When two hearts are one, even the king cannot separate them."

- **Anonymous:** "Nobody is perfect until you fall in love with them."

- **Che Guevara (1928–1967):** "The true revolutionary is guided by a great feeling of love."

- **John Lennon (1940–1980):** "All you need is love."

- **Katherine Hepburn (1907–2003):** "Sometimes I wonder if men and women really suit each other. Perhaps they should live next door and just visit now and then."

- **Cher (1946–):** "The trouble with some women is that they get all excited about nothing—and then marry him."

- **Jay Leno (1950–):** "Today is Valentine's Day—or, as men like to call it, Extortion Day!"

A woman recently complained that Facebook's 5,000 limit was too low for her vast array of friends (Daum, 2009). Is someone on your Facebook page or in your Twitter circle *really* a friend? Most Americans' number of friends has shrunk from three to two since the late 1980s, and 25 percent of the population ages 18 and over report having no close friends at all. Our declining number of close social ties is due to many factors, including longer commutes and work hours and greater reliance on technologies—most notably cell phones, texting, and the Internet, that lower the probability of having face-to-face visits and interactions with people but foster a wide array of "weak ties" that many people mistake for friendship (McPherson et al., 2008).

Such research findings suggest that many of us have few, if any, friends over our lifetime, but we often hear self-help books proclaim that only friends become lovers or intimate partners. Is this true? Or do friendships and love differ?

The family is usually our earliest and most important source of love and emotional support.

Love and Friendship

Do you like people whom you don't love? Sure. Do you love people whom you don't like? No—at least not in a healthy relationship. In his classic research on "the near and dear," Keith Davis (1985) identified eight important qualities of friendship:

- **Enjoyment.** Friends enjoy being with each other most of time. They feel at ease despite occasional disagreements.

- **Acceptance.** Friends accept each other the way they are. They tolerate faults and shortcomings instead of trying to change each other.

- **Trust.** Friends trust and look out for each other. They lean on each other during difficult times.

- **Respect.** Friends respect each other's judgment. They may not agree with the choices the other person makes, but they honor his or her decisions.

- **Mutual support.** Friends help and support each other without expecting something in return.

- **Confiding.** Friends share experiences and feelings. They don't gossip about each other or backstab.

- **Understanding.** Friends are sympathetic about each other's feelings and thoughts. They can often "read" each other without saying very much.

- **Honesty.** Friends are open and honest. They feel free to be themselves and say what they think.

Love includes all these qualities and three more—sexual desire, priority over other relationships, and caring to the point of great self-sacrifice. A relationship can start off with friendship and develop into love. It's unlikely, however, that we can "really" love someone who isn't a friend. Love, like friendship, is a process that develops over time.

But just what is love? What attracts lovers to each other? And are lust and love similar?

WHAT IS LOVE?

Love is an elusive concept. We have all experienced love and feel that we know what it is. When asked what love is, however, people give a variety of answers. According to a nine-year-old boy, for example, "Love is like an avalanche where you have to run for your life." And according to a six-year-old girl, "Love is when mommy sees daddy on the toilet and she doesn't think it's gross." Before you read any further, test your general knowledge about love in the box "How Much Do You Know about Love?"

Some Characteristics of Love

During the war in Iraq, a U.S. soldier wrote his 15-month-old daughter a letter that said, in part, "You are the meaning of my life. You make my heart pound with joy and pride. No matter what happens to me or where we go, you will always know that I love you." The letter was found on the soldier's body when he died in the crash of a Black Hawk helicopter shot down by insurgents (Zoroya, 2005).

As the letter illustrates, parental love is strong and deep. Still, people often make a distinction between "loving someone" (family members, relatives, and friends) and "being in love" (a romantic relationship). Both types of love, nonetheless, are multifaceted, based on respect, and often demanding.

ASK YOURSELF

How Much Do You Know about Love?

The following statements are based on the material in this chapter.

Fact	Myth	
☐	☑	**1.** There is an ideal mate for every person; just keep looking.
☐	☐	**2.** Women are more romantic than men.
☑	☐	**3.** Love conquers all.
☑	☐	**4.** Men's and women's love needs are different.
☐	☐	**5.** Real love lasts forever.
☑	☐	**6.** Everybody falls in love sooner or later.
☐	☑	**7.** Love brings happiness and security.
☐	☑	**8.** Love endures and overcomes all problems.
☐	☐	**9.** Men are more interested in sex than in love.
☐	☑	**10.** I can change the person I love.

(The answers to these questions are on page 140.)

LOVE IS MULTIFACETED Love has many dimensions. It can be romantic, exciting, obsessive, and irrational. It can also be platonic, calming, altruistic, and sensible. Love defies a single definition because it varies in degree and intensity and in different social contexts. At the very least, and as you will see shortly, love includes caring, intimacy, and commitment.

LOVE IS BASED ON RESPECT Love may involve passionate yearning, but respect is a more important quality. If respect is missing, the relationship is not based on love. Instead, it is an unhealthy or possessive feeling or behavior that limits the lovers' social, emotional, and intellectual growth (Peele and Brodsky, 1976).

LOVE IS OFTEN DEMANDING Long-term love, especially, has nothing in common with the images of infatuation or frenzied sex that we get from movies, television, and romance novels. These misconceptions often lead to unrealistic expectations, stereotypes, and disillusionment.

In fact, real love is closer to what one author calls "stirring-the-oatmeal" love (Johnson, 1985). This type of love is neither exciting nor thrilling but is usually mundane and unromantic. It means paying bills, scrubbing toilet bowls, being up all night with a sick baby, and performing myriad other tasks that aren't very sexy.

Some partners take turns stirring the oatmeal. Others break up or get a divorce. Whether we decide to tie the knot or not, why are we attracted to some people and not others?

The Born Loser: © Newspaper Enterprise Association, Inc.

What Attracts People to Each Other?

Many people believe in "true love" and that "there's one person out there that you're meant for" (see Data Digest). Such beliefs are romantic but unfounded. Cultural norms and values, not fate, bring people together. We will never meet millions of potential lovers because they are filtered out by formal or informal rules on partner eligibility based on factors such as age, race, social class, religion, sexual orientation, health, or physical appearance (see Chapter 8).

Beginning in childhood, parents indirectly encourage or limit future romances by living in certain neighborhoods and selecting certain schools. During the preteen years, group practices and expectations shape romantic experiences. For example, even seventh-graders have rules, such as not going out with someone their friends don't like, or telling parents as little as possible for as long as possible because "Parents nose around, get into people's business, and talk to other parents" (Perlstein, 2005: 33).

Romance may cross cultural or ethnic borders, but criticism and approval teach us what is acceptable and with whom. All societies—including the United States—have rules about homogamy (dating and marrying within one's group) and exogamy (dating and marrying someone outside an acceptable group) (see Chapters 1 and 4).

Even if we "fall in lust" with someone, our sexual yearnings will not necessarily lead to falling in love if there are strong cultural taboos against it. These taboos explain, in part, why we don't always marry our sexual partners.

Do Lust and Love Differ?

Lust and love differ quite a bit. Psychologists Pamela Regan and Ellen Berscheid (1999) differentiate among sexual arousal (or lust), sexual desire, and love—especially romantic love. They describe *sexual arousal* as a physiological rather than an emotional response, one that may occur either consciously or unconsciously (see Chapter 7). *Sexual desire,* in contrast, is a psychological state in which a person wants "to obtain a sexual object that one does not now have or to engage in a sexual activity in which one is not now engaging" (p. 17).

Sexual desire may or may not lead to *romantic love,* an intense feeling that can provide ecstasy when fulfilled or deep suffering when the feeling isn't reciprocated. Once desire evaporates, disillusioned and disappointed lovers will wonder where the spark in their relationship has gone and may reminisce longingly about "the good old days."

This does not mean that sexual desire *always* culminates in sexual intercourse or that romantic love and love are synonymous. Married couples may love each other even though they rarely, or never, engage in sexual intercourse for health and other reasons. Regardless of the nature of love, healthy loving relationships reflect a balance of caring, intimacy, and commitment.

CARING, INTIMACY, AND COMMITMENT

As you'll also see later in this chapter, people fall in love for many reasons: They are physically attracted to each other, have shared interests, seek companionship, or simply want to have fun. In any type of love, however, caring about the other person is essential.

Since you asked . . .

:::• Can there be intimacy without sex?

Caring

Love includes *caring,* or wanting to help the other person by providing aid and emotional support (Cutrona, 1996). Although we often use metaphors for love such as "I'm crazy about you" or "I can't live without you," these terms of endearment may not be translated into ongoing, everyday behavior such as valuing your partner's welfare as much as your own.

Caring means responding to the other person's needs. If a person sees no evidence of warmth or support over time, there will be serious doubts that a partner *really* loves her or him.

This doesn't mean that a partner should be submissive or docile. Instead, people who care about each other bolster each other's self-esteem and offer encouragement when there are problems. When a person is sensitive to a partner's needs, the relationship will become more intimate and will flourish.

Intimacy

Definitions of intimacy vary, but all of them emphasize feelings of closeness. In his analysis of couples, for example, P. M. Brown (1995: 3) found that people experience intimacy when they

- Share a mutual emotional interest in each other
- Have some sort of history together
- Have a distinct sense of identity as a couple
- Hold a reciprocal commitment to a continued relationship
- Share hopes and dreams for a common future

Still other writers distinguish among three kinds of intimacy—*physical* (sex, hugging, and touching), *affective* (feeling close), and *verbal* (self-disclosure). They also point out that physical intimacy is usually

? Answers to "How Much Do You Know about Love?"

All ten statements are myths. Eight or more correct answers indicate that you know a myth when you hear one. Otherwise—watch out!

1. We can love many people, and we can love many times. This may be one reason why many people marry more than once.

2. Men fall in love more quickly, are more romantic, and suffer more intensely when their love is not returned.

3. Because almost one out of two marriages ends in divorce, love is not enough to overcome all problems and obstacles. Differences in race, ethnicity, religion, economic status, education, and age can often stifle romantic interest.

4. As in friendship, both men and women want trust, honesty, understanding, and respect from those they love.

5. Love can be genuine but not last forever. People today live much longer, the world is more complex, and even marital partners change as they mature and grow older.

6. Some people have deep-seated emotional scars that make them suspicious and unloving; others are too self-centered to give love.

7. Love guarantees neither happiness nor security. As you'll see shortly, love doesn't "fix" people who are generally insecure or anxious about themselves or their relationships.

8. People who love each other make sacrifices, but emotional or physical abuse should not be tolerated. Eventually, even "martyrs" become unhappy, angry, depressed, and resentful.

9. During the romantic stage, both women and men may be more interested in sex than in love. As love matures, both partners value attributes such as faithfulness and patience and making the other person feel wanted.

10. You can only change yourself. Trying to change someone usually results in anger, resentment, frustration, and unhappiness.

---

the least important of the three (see, for example, Piorkowski, 1994).

Self-disclosure refers to communication in which one person reveals his or her honest thoughts and feelings to another person with the expectation that truly open communication will follow. In intimate relationships, partners feel free to expose their weaknesses, idiosyncrasies, hopes, and insecurities without fear of ridicule or rejection (P. M. Brown, 1995).

Lovers will reveal their innermost thoughts, and marital partners feel comfortable in venting their frustrations because their spouses are considered trustworthy, respectful, and their best friends or confidantes. Self-disclosure does *not* include nagging, which decreases intimacy. If you pick at your partner, you're saying "I'm better than you. Shape up." Most people resent nagging because it implies superiority by the person who's nagging.

Intimacy includes more than the relationship between two adults. It is also a bond between children and parents, adult children and their parents, children and stepparents, children and grandparents, and so on. Much research has emphasized the role of the mother in intimate ties with children, but a father's love is just as important. If a father is close to his children, he can play a crucial role in their development of self-esteem, their emotional stability, and their willingness to avoid drugs and other risky behavior (Rohner and Veneziano, 2001).

In adult love relationships, intimacy increases as people let down their defenses, learn to relax in each other's company, and find that they can expect reciprocal support during good and bad time (Josselson, 1992). Caring and intimacy, in turn, foster commitment.

Commitment

Many of my students, especially the women, complain that their partners are afraid of "the big C"—commitment. The ultimate commitment is marriage, but as our high divorce rates show, marriage and commitment don't always go hand in hand (see Chapter 15).

Commitment is a person's intention to remain in a relationship and work through problems. Mutual

Peanuts: © United Feature Syndicate, Inc.

commitment can arise out of (1) a sense of loyalty and fidelity to one's partner; (2) a religious, legal, or moral belief in the sanctity of marriage; (3) continued optimism about future rewards—emotional, financial, sexual, or others; and (4) strong emotional attachments, dependence, and love. Many people end their relationships, even if they still love each other, if they feel that mutual commitment is not increasing (P. M. Brown, 1995; Fehr, 1999; Sprecher, 1999).

In a healthy relationship, commitment has many positive aspects, such as affection, companionship, and trust. Each partner is available to the other not just during times of stress but day in and day out. Even when we're tempted to be unfaithful if our partners don't pay as much attention to us as we'd like or if we feel overwhelmed with daily responsibilities, committed partners will persevere during rough times.

Commitment in a secure relationship is not a matter of hearts and flowers. Instead, it is behavior that demonstrates—repeatedly and in a variety of situations—that "I'm here, I will be here, I'm interested in what you do and what you think and feel, I will actively support your independent actions, I trust you, and you can trust me to be here if you need me" (Crowell and Waters, 1994: 32).

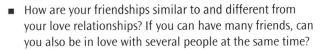

:• MAKING CONNECTIONS

- How are your friendships similar to and different from your love relationships? If you can have many friends, can you also be in love with several people at the same time?

- How many times have you been in love? Were your feelings similar in all cases? Or did they change as you grew older?

SOME THEORIES ABOUT LOVE AND LOVING

Why and how do we love? Biological explanations tend to focus on why we love. Psychological, sociological, and anthropological approaches try to explain how as well as why.

Since you asked . . .
:• Is love due to biochemical changes in the body?

The Biochemistry of Love

Biological perspectives maintain that love is grounded in evolution, biology, and chemistry. Biologists and some psychologists see romance as serving an evolutionary purpose: drawing men and women into long-term partnerships that are essential to child rearing. On open and often dangerous grasslands, for example, one parent could care for offspring while the other foraged for food.

When lovers claim that they feel "high" and as if they are being swept away, it's probably because they are. A meeting of eyes, a touch of hands, or a whiff of scent sets off a flood of chemicals that starts in the brain and races along the nerves and through the bloodstream. The results are familiar: flushed skin, sweaty palms, and heavy breathing (Ackerman, 1994).

Natural amphetamines such as dopamine, norepinephrine, and phenylethylamine (PEA) are responsible for these symptoms. PEA is especially effective; it revs up the brain, causing feelings of elation, exhilaration, and euphoria:

No wonder lovers can stay awake all night talking and caressing. No wonder they become so absentminded, so giddy, so optimistic, so gregarious, so full of life. Naturally occurring amphetamines have pooled in the emotional centers of their brains; they are high on natural "speed" (Fisher, 1992: 53).

PEA highs don't last long, though, which may explain why passionate or romantic love is short lived.

What about love that endures beyond the first few months? According to the biological perspective, as infatuation wanes and attachment grows, another group of chemicals, called *endorphins,* which are chemically similar to morphine and reside in the brain, takes over. Unlike PEA, endorphins calm the mind, eliminate pain, and reduce anxiety. This, biologists say, explains why people in long-lasting relationships report feeling comfortable and secure (Walsh, 1991; Fisher, 2004; Brizendine, 2006).

Medical researchers contend that the loss of a loved one ("a broken heart") may be linked to physical problems. According to brain images and blood tests, traumatic breakups can release stress hormones that travel to cells in one part of the brain. The resulting stress can bring on chest pain and even heart attacks (Najib et al., 2004; Wittstein et al., 2005).

There are two major problems with biological perspectives. First, they typically rely on tiny samples of volunteers (9 to 17 people, in some cases), and usually only women. Second, chemicals (such as dopamine) that apparently trigger intense romantic love are also found in gamblers, cocaine users, and even people playing computer games (Young, 2009). Thus, it's not clear how hormones "cause" love.

Sociological perspectives—and some psychological theories—claim that culture, not PEA, plays the role of Cupid. The social science theories that help us understand the components and processes of love include attachment theory, Reiss's wheel theory of love, Sternberg's triangular theory of love, Lee's research on the styles of loving, and exchange theories.

Attachment Theory

Attachment theory proposes that our primary motivation in life is to be connected with other people because this is the only true security we will ever have. British psychiatrist John Bowlby (1969, 1984) asserted that attachment is an integral part of human behavior from the cradle to the grave. Adults and children benefit by having someone look out for them—someone who cares about their welfare, provides for their basic emotional and physical needs, and is available when needed.

American psychologist Mary Ainsworth (Ainsworth et al., 1978), one of Bowlby's students, assessed infant-mother attachment in her classic "strange situation" study. In both natural and laboratory settings, Ainsworth created mild stress for an infant by having the mother temporarily leave the baby with a friendly stranger in an unfamiliar room. When the mother returned, Ainsworth observed the infant's behavior toward the mother and the mother's reactions to her baby's behavior.

Ainsworth identified three infant-mother attachment styles. She characterized about 60 percent of the infants as *secure* in their attachment, with sensitive and responsive mothers. The babies showed some distress when left with a stranger, but when the mother returned, they clung to her for just a short time and then went back to exploring and playing.

About 19 percent of the infants displayed *anxious/ambivalent* attachment styles when their mothers were inconsistent—sometimes affectionate, sometimes aloof. The infants showed distress at separation but rejected their mothers when they returned. The remaining 21 percent of the infants, most of whom had been reared by caregivers who ignored their physical and emotional needs, displayed *avoidant* behavior by ignoring the mothers after they returned.

Some of the infant attachment research has been criticized for relying almost exclusively on laboratory settings instead of natural ones and for not addressing cross-cultural differences in child-rearing practices (see Feeney and Noller, 1996). Despite such criticisms, some researchers propose that adult intimate relationships often reflect these three attachment styles.

Using a "love quiz" based on Ainsworth's three attachment styles, psychologist Cindy Hazan and her associates interviewed 108 college students and 620 adults who said they were in love (Hazan and Shaver, 1987; Shaver et al., 1988). The respondents were asked to describe themselves in their "most important romance" using three measures:

- **Secure style:** I find it easy to get close to others and am comfortable depending on them and having them depend on me. I don't often worry about being abandoned or about someone getting too close to me.

- **Avoidant style:** I am somewhat uncomfortable being close to others; I find it difficult to trust them completely and to depend on them. I am nervous when anyone gets too close and when lovers want me to be more intimate than I feel comfortable being.

- **Anxious/ambivalent style:** Others are reluctant to get as close as I would like. I often worry that my partner doesn't really love me or won't want to stay with me. I want to merge completely with another person, and this desire sometimes scares people away.

The researchers also asked the respondents whether their childhood relationships with their parents had been warm or cold and rejecting. *Secure adults* (about 56 percent of the sample), who generally described their parents as having been warm and supportive, were more trusting of their romantic partners and more confident of a partner's love. They reported intimate, trusting, and happy relationships that lasted an average of ten years.

Anxious/ambivalent adults (about 20 percent) tended to fall in love easily and wanted a commitment almost immediately. *Avoidant adults* (24 percent of the sample) had little trust for others, had the most cynical beliefs about love, and couldn't handle intimacy or commitment.

Several studies have tracked attachment styles from toddlerhood to adulthood and have found that attachment styles can change over the life course regardless of a person's early childhood experiences. If, for example, we experience disturbing events such as parental divorce, the breakup of a relationship, being dumped a few times in succession, or our own divorce, we may slip from a secure to an avoidant style. Alternatively, positive experiences, including romantic love, can change a person from an avoidant to a secure attachment style (Hollist and Miller, 2005; Simpson et al., 2007; McCarthy and Casey, 2008).

Therefore, "the view that children's experiences set attachment styles in concrete is a myth" (Fletcher, 2002: 158). Instead, critics point out, events such as divorce, disease, and financial problems are far more important in shaping a child's well-being by age 18 than any early bonding with his or her mother (Lewis, 1997; Hays, 1998; Birns, 1999).

Reiss's Wheel Theory of Love

Sociologist Ira Reiss and his associates proposed a "wheel theory" of love (see *Figure 6.1*) that generated much research for several decades. Reiss described four stages of love: rapport, self-revelation, mutual dependency, and personality need fulfillment (Reiss, 1960; Reiss and Lee, 1988).

FIGURE 6.1 The Wheel Theory of Love

Reiss compared his four stages of love to the spokes of a wheel. As the text describes, a love relationship begins with the stage of rapport and, in a lasting relationship, continues to build as the wheel turns, deepening the partners' rapport, fulfillment, and mutual dependence and increasing the honesty of their self-revelation.

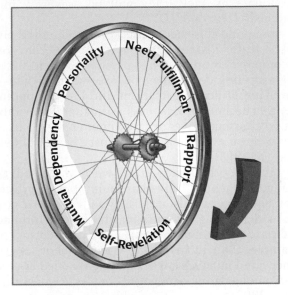

Source: Based on Reiss, 1960: 139–45.

In the first stage, partners establish *rapport* based on cultural backgrounds with similar upbringing, social class, religion, and educational level (see Chapter 1 on endogamy). Without this rapport, according to Reiss, would-be lovers do not have enough in common to establish an initial interest.

In the second stage, *self-revelation* brings the couple closer together. Because each person feels more at ease in the relationship, she or he is more likely to discuss hopes, desires, fears, and ambitions and to engage in sexual activities.

In the third stage, as the couple becomes more intimate, the partners' *mutual dependency* increases: They exchange ideas, jokes, and sexual desires. In the fourth and final stage, the couple experiences *personality need fulfillment*. The partners confide in each other, make mutual decisions, support each other's ambitions, and bolster each other's self-confidence.

Like spokes on a wheel, these stages can turn many times—that is, they can be repeated. For example, partners build some rapport, then reveal bits of themselves, then build more rapport, then begin to exchange ideas, and so on.

The spokes may keep turning to produce a deep and lasting relationship. Or, during a fleeting romance, the wheel may stop after a few turns. The romantic wheel may "unwind"—even in a single evening—if the relationship droops because of arguments, lack of self-disclosure, or conflicting interests.

Sociologist Dolores Borland (1975) modified the wheel theory, proposing that love relationships can be viewed as "clock springs," such as those in a watch. Relationships can wind up and unwind several times as love swells or ebbs. Tensions, caused by pregnancy and the birth of a child, for example, may wind the spring tightly. If the partners communicate and work toward a common goal, such tensions may solidify rather than sap the relationship. On the other hand, relationships can end abruptly if they are so tightly wound that the partners cannot grow or if one partner feels threatened by increasing or unwanted intimacy.

Others note that both the wheel theory and the clock-spring theory ignore the variations in intensity between stages of a relationship. People may love each other, but the intensity of their feelings may be high on one dimension and low on another. For example, a couple may have rapport because of similar backgrounds but may experience little personality need fulfillment because one partner is unwilling to confide in the other (Albas and Albas, 1987; Warner, 2005).

Sternberg's Triangular Theory of Love

Instead of focusing on stages of love, psychologist Robert Sternberg and his associates (1986, 1988) have proposed that love has three important components: intimacy, passion, and decision/commitment:

- *Intimacy* encompasses feelings of closeness, connectedness, and bonding.
- *Passion* leads to romance, physical attraction, and sexual consummation.
- *Decision/commitment* has a short- and a long-term dimension. In the short term, partners make a decision to love each other; in the long term, they make a commitment to maintain that love over time.

According to Sternberg, the mix of intimacy, passion, and commitment can vary from one relationship to another. Relationships thus range from *nonlove*, in which all three components are absent, to *consummate love*, in which all the elements are present.

Even when all three components are present, they may vary in intensity and over time for each partner. Sternberg envisions these three components as forming a triangle (see *Figure 6.2*). In general, the greater the mismatching of dimensions, the greater is the dissatisfaction in a relationship.

FIGURE 6.2 The Triangular Theory of Love

This theory of love suggests how people can be very close on some dimensions but very far apart on others.

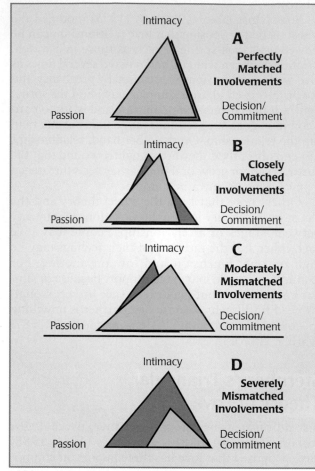

Source: Adapted from Sternberg, 1988.

Let's use Jack and Jill to illustrate this model. If Jack and Jill are "perfectly matched" (*Figure 6.2A*), they will be equally passionate, intimate, and committed, and their love will be "perfect." Even if the degree to which each of them wants intimacy and

commitment varies a little, they may still be "closely matched" (*Figure 6.2B*).

If both are about equally passionate, but Jack wants more intimacy than Jill does, and Jill is unwilling to make the long-term commitment that Jack wants, they will be "moderately mismatched" (*Figure 6.2C*). And if they want to marry (make a commitment), but Jill is neither as intimate nor as passionate as Jack, they will be "severely mismatched" (*Figure 6.2D*).

Some find this theory useful for counseling purposes. If, for instance, people recognized that love encompasses more than just passion—which is actually a fleeting component of love—there would be fewer unfulfilled expectations and less disappointment. A decline of passion is normal and inevitable if a relationship moves on to commitment, which creates a more stable union than just "being in love" (García, 1998).

Like the other perspectives we've discussed, the triangular theory of love has limitations. "Perfectly matched" exists only in Disney movies. Also, love varies depending on one's marital status. Intimacy and passion are much stronger in casual dating, for example, than in marriage. Commitment, on the other hand, is much higher among married couples than among dating or engaged couples (Lemieux and Hale, 2002).

Lee's Styles of Loving

Canadian sociologist John Lee (1973, 1974) developed one of the most widely cited and studied theories of love. According to Lee, there are six basic styles of loving: eros, mania, ludus, storge, agape, and pragma, all of which overlap and may vary in intensity (see *Table 6.1*).

EROS Eros (the root of the word *erotic*) means love of beauty. Because it is also characterized by powerful physical attraction, eros epitomizes "love at first sight." This is the kind of love, often described in romance

TABLE 6.1	Lee's Six Styles of Love	
	Meaning	**Major Characteristics**
Eros	Love of beauty	Powerful physical attraction
Mania	Obsessive love	Jealousy, possessiveness, and intense dependency
Ludus	Playful love	Carefree quality, casualness, fun-and-games approach
Storge	Companionate love	Peaceful and affectionate love based on mutual trust and respect
Agape	Altruistic love	Self-sacrificing, kind, and patient
Pragma	Practical love	Sensible, realistic

Source: Adapted from Lee, 1973, 1974.

novels, in which the lovers experience palpitations, light-headedness, and intense emotional desire.

Erotic lovers want to know everything about each other—what she or he dreamed about last night and what happened on the way to work today. They often like to wear matching T-shirts and matching colors, to order the same foods when dining out, and to be identified with each other as totally as possible (Lasswell and Lasswell, 1976).

MANIA Characterized by obsessiveness, jealousy, possessiveness, and intense dependency, **mania** may be expressed as anxiety, sleeplessness, loss of appetite, headaches, and even suicide because of real or imagined rejection by the desired person. Manic lovers are consumed by thoughts of their beloved and have an insatiable need for attention and signs of affection.

Mania is often associated with low self-esteem and a poor self-concept. As a result, manic people typically are not attractive to individuals who have a strong self-concept and high self-esteem (Lasswell and Lasswell, 1976).

LUDUS Ludus is carefree and casual love that is considered "fun and games." Ludic lovers often have several partners at one time and are not possessive or jealous, primarily because they don't want their lovers to become dependent on them. Ludic lovers have sex for fun, not emotional rapport. In their sexual encounters, they are typically self-centered and may be exploitative because they do not want commitment, which they consider "scary."

STORGE Storge (pronounced "STOR-gay") is a slow-burning, peaceful, and affectionate love that comes with the passage of time and the enjoyment of shared activities. Storgic relationships lack the ecstatic highs and lows that characterize some other styles. For many social scientists, storgic love is equivalent to **companionate love** that is characterized by feelings of togetherness, tenderness, and deep affection, as well as by sharing and supporting each other over time (Brink, 2007).

In companionate love, sex occurs later than in erotic, manic, and ludic love because the partners' goals are usually marriage, home, and children. Even if they break up, storgic lovers are likely to remain good friends. Because there is mutual trust, temporary separations are not a problem. In storgic love, affection develops over the years, as in many lasting marriages. Passion may be replaced by spirituality, respect, and contentment (Murstein, 1974).

AGAPE The classical Christian type of love, **agape** (pronounced "AH-gah-pay"), is an altruistic, self-sacrificing love that is directed toward all humankind. Agape is always kind and patient and never jealous or demanding, and it does not seek reciprocity. Lee points out, however, that he did not find an outright example of agape during his interviews.

Intense agape can border on masochism. For example, an agapic person might wait indefinitely for a lover to be released from prison, might tolerate an alcoholic or drug-addicted spouse, or might be willing to live with a partner who engages in illegal activities or infidelity (Lasswell and Lasswell, 1976).

PRAGMA Pragma is rational love based on practical considerations, such as compatibility. Indeed, it can be described as "love with a shopping list." A pragmatic person seeks compatibility on characteristics such as background, education, religious views, occupational interests, and recreational pursuits. If one person does not work out, the pragmatic person moves on, quite rationally, to search for someone else.

Pragmatic lovers look out for their partners, for example, encouraging them to ask for a promotion or finish college. They are also practical when it comes to divorce. For example, a couple might stay together until the youngest child finishes high school or until both partners find better jobs (Lasswell and Lasswell, 1976).

Researchers have developed dozens of scales to measure Lee's concepts of love (see Tzeng, 1993). Use the "What Do *You* Expect from Love?" box to reflect on some of your attitudes about love.

Exchange Theory

Social scientists often describe love as a *social exchange process* (see Chapter 2). Romantic and long-term love relationships involve social exchanges in the sense that they provide rewards and costs for each partner. If the initial interactions are reciprocal and mutually satisfying,

Erotic love is initially passionate but usually short lived. It can also develop into a companionate love that includes commitment, intimacy, and a sharing of common interests and activities with a long-term partner.

Applying What You've Learned

What Do You Expect from Love?

Use this scale to examine your own and your partner's feelings. If you've never been in love or don't have a partner now, answer in terms of what you think your responses might be in the future. There are no wrong answers to these statements; they're designed simply to increase your understanding of different types of love. For each item, mark **1** for "strongly agree," **2** for "moderately agree," **3** for "neutral," **4** for "moderately disagree," and **5** for "strongly disagree."

Eros

1. My partner and I were attracted to each other immediately after we first met.
2. Our lovemaking is very intense and satisfying.
3. My partner fits my standards of physical beauty and good looks.

Ludus

4. What my partner doesn't know about me won't hurt him/her.
5. I sometimes have to keep my partner from finding out about other partners.
6. I could get over my partner pretty easily and quickly.

Pragma

7. In choosing my partner, I believed it was best to love someone with a similar background.
8. An important factor in choosing my partner was whether or not he/she would be a good parent.
9. One consideration in choosing my partner was how he/she would affect my career.

Agape

10. I would rather suffer myself than let my partner suffer.
11. My partner can use whatever I own as she/he chooses.
12. I would endure all things for the sake of my partner.

Storge

13. I expect to always be friends with the people I date.
14. The best kind of love grows out of a long friendship.
15. Love is a deep friendship, not a mysterious, passionate emotion.

Sources: Lasswell and Lasswell, 1976, pp. 211–24; Hendrick and Hendrick, 1992a, 1992b; Levesque, 1993, pp. 219–50.

---

a relationship will continue. If, however, our needs are mismatched (see *Figure 6.2* on p. 144) or change drastically over time, our love interests may wane or shift between adolescence and later life.

LOVE DURING ADOLESCENCE Exchange theory is especially helpful in explaining why romantic love is short lived among adolescents. Adolescent love is usually intense but also self-centered. Because adolescents are still "finding themselves," they often form relationships with peers who offer many benefits and few costs ("I can call him whenever I'm lonely" or "I'm hookin' up with a knockout cheerleader this weekend").

LOVE DURING ADULTHOOD As we mature, our perceptions of rewards and costs usually change. We might decide, for example, that nurturing a relationship with someone who's patient and confident outweighs the benefits of being with someone who's "a good catch" or "a knockout" but is controlling and self-centered.

LOVE DURING LATER LIFE We also weigh the costs and benefits of love later in life. In a national survey of people ages 60 and over, 90 percent said that they wanted a romantic partner who had moral values, a pleasant personality, a good sense of humor, and intelligence ("Half of older Americans . . . ," 1998).

The survey found several distinct differences between men and women, however. Most women were interested in financial security, whereas most men wanted partners who were interested in sex. Men (67 percent) were more likely than women (48 percent) to want a partner with a terrific body. Because older women are less likely than men to be affluent, they may see the benefits of a love relationship differently than do men (see Chapters 8 and 17).

MAKING CONNECTIONS

- Return to *Figure 6.2* on p. 144 and think about your current love relationship. (If you are not currently involved with someone, reflect on a past relationship.) Are you and your partner matched in intimacy, passion, and commitment? Or is any one of these characteristics not important in your relationship?

- Think about Lee's styles of loving (*Table 6.1* on p. 144). Do you and your partner have similar or different attitudes about love? If your styles of loving differ, does this create problems, or does it make the relationship more interesting? Did your past relationships break up because your partner's style of loving was different from yours?

FUNCTIONS OF LOVE AND LOVING

Functionalist Theory

One historian argues that love is dysfunctional because it creates high divorce rates. That is, because many Americans are in love with love, their unrealistic expectations result in unhappiness and the dissolution of marriages (Coontz, 2005).

In contrast, a number of researchers and family practitioners believe that love is at the core of healthy and well-functioning relationships and families. One psychologist goes even further by maintaining that "love is as critical for your mind and body as oxygen" (McGrath, 2002). Whether or not you agree with such an assertion, love fulfills many purposes that range from ensuring human survival to providing opportunities for recreation.

> **Since you asked . . .**
>
> ❖ Is love as critical as oxygen for our survival?

Over the years, many U.S. soldiers deployed to Iraq and Afghanistan have found strength by thinking of their loved ones at home (see Platt, 2006). Here, an American soldier shows photographs of his children to young Iraqis in Beijia, a village south of Baghdad.

Love Ensures Human Survival

In a tongue-in-cheek article, one writer suggested that romantic love is a "nuisance" and "a nasty trick played upon us by nature to keep our species going," especially during the childbearing years (Chance, 1988: 23). In fact, love *does* keep our species going. Because children can be conceived without love, there is no guarantee that people who engage in sex will feel an obligation to care for their offspring and make sure they survive. Unlike sex, love implies a commitment. By promoting an interest in caring for helpless infants, love ensures the survival of the human species.

Perhaps the most dramatic example of the effects of the lack of love is suicide. People who commit suicide often feel socially isolated, rejected, unloved, or unworthy of love. According to some military leaders, for example, about 60 percent of U.S. Army suicides are due to failed relationships, especially intimate relationship problems (Schindler, 2009).

Love doesn't guarantee that we'll live to be 100, of course. Instead, researchers suggest, there is a link between loving relationships and enjoying better health.

Love Enhances Our Physical and Emotional Health

Numerous studies show a connection between our emotions and our physical and emotional well-being. Babies and children who are deprived of love may develop a wide variety of problems—depression, headaches, physiological impairments, and psychosomatic difficulties—that sometimes last a lifetime.

In contrast, infants who are loved and cuddled typically gain more weight, cry less, and smile more. By age 5, they have higher IQs and score higher on language tests (Hetherington et al., 2005).

Chronic stress, whether due to a demanding job or to an unloving home life, elevates blood pressure. Arguing or just thinking about a fight also raises blood pressure. People in unhappy marriages may be less healthy because stress can change the levels of certain hormones in the blood and weaken the immune system. As a result, people who are stressed face a higher risk of heart disease and other illnesses (Kiecolt-Glaser and Newton, 2001; Cacioppo et al., 2002; Glynn et al., 2002).

According to a highly respected heart physician, love is good medicine:

Love and intimacy are at the root of what makes us sick and what makes us well. . . . People who feel lonely are many times more likely to get cardiovascular disease than those who have a strong sense of connection and community. I'm not aware of any other factor in medicine—not diet, not smoking, not exercise, not genetics, not drugs, not surgery—that has a greater impact on our quality of life, incidence of illness, and premature death. In part, this is because people who are lonely are more likely to engage in self-destructive behavior (Ornish, 2005: 56).

In effect, positive feelings can contribute to better health. Friends, family, and loving relationships over a lifetime can help counteract the normal wear and tear of life as we age. People in their 70s who have had a lot of supportive friends, good relationships with their parents and spouses, and little criticism from their spouses and children suffer from fewer risk factors for diseases and death, including high blood pressure, high cholesterol levels, and abnormal blood sugar metabolism than those who have not enjoyed good relationships (Seeman et al., 2002).

Overall, love is critical for our emotional and physical well-being. In contrast, isolation, loneliness, hostility, anger, depression, and similar feelings often contribute to suffering, disease, and premature death.

Love Improves the Quality of Our Lives

Love fosters self-esteem. From a solid basis of loving family relationships, children acquire the confidence to face the world outside the family (Bodman and Peterson, 1995). Terminally ill patients and paraplegics often report that they can accept death or cope with their disabilities when they are surrounded by supportive, caring, and loving family members and friends (see Chapter 17).

Not having a secure base of love, on the other hand, can lead to aggression, hostility, diminished self-confidence, and emotional problems. At least half of all teenage runaways are escaping a home in which there is no love, as evidenced by violence, abuse, or incest. Battered wives become suspicious, fearful, and bitter (see Chapter 14).

Love Is Fun

Without love, life is "a burden and a bore" (Safilios-Rothschild, 1977: 9). Love can be painful, as you'll see shortly, but it is also enjoyable and often exciting. For example, it is both comforting and fun to plan to see a loved one; to travel together; to write and receive e-mail and text messages; to exchange presents; to share activities; to have someone care for you when you are sick or grumpy; and to know that you can always depend on someone for comfort, support, and advice.

One of the biggest myths in our popular culture is that love just happens. Numerous movies, especially those targeted at women (sometimes called "chick flicks"), appeal to female viewers who long for romance and a dashing guy who will sweep them off their feet and solve all their love problems. Past and current examples include *Gone With the Wind* (1939), *An Officer and a Gentleman* (1982), *How Stella Got Her Groove Back* (1998), and *Confessions of a Shopaholic* (2009). In reality, love doesn't appear out of nowhere. To get and keep love, one has to be active and take some chances.

FIGURE 6.3 Who's in Love?

This Gallup poll asked people, "Would you say you are—or are not—in love with someone right now?" Here are the responses of the 72 percent who said "yes."

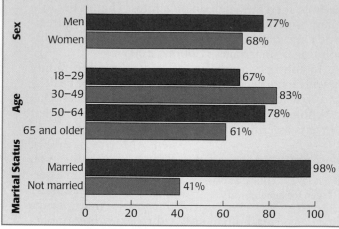

Source: Based on Saad, 2004.

EXPERIENCING LOVE

When we discuss this chapter, I ask my students "Who do you think is in love with someone right now?" Most say that it's probably women, twenty-somethings, and singles. Wrong on all counts. According to a national poll, those who say that they are in love are most likely to be men, those between the ages of 30 and 49, and people who are married (see *Figure 6.3*).

Why do so many of us assume that only young unmarried adults, especially women, are the most likely to seek and experience love? Among other reasons, we're inundated with Hollywood images of love that have nothing to do with real life. Movies rarely portray love between married couples. Instead, most movies and television shows emphasize sex rather than love, especially among young adults or unfaithful married couples (see Chapter 5).

For most people, caring, trust, respect, and honesty are central to love. There are some differences, however, in the ways that men and women conceive of love and express it. And although heterosexuals and homosexuals share many of the same feelings and behaviors, there are also some differences in their experiences of love.

Are Women or Men More Romantic?

During a recent online discussion, Emily, one of my students, wrote the following:

It's important to distinguish the truly romantic men from the "What-do-I-need-to-do-to-get-her-in-bed" romantic men. Truly romantic men do things for you that take a substantial amount of time and energy and involve some sacrifice on their part. For example, for Valentine's Day my boyfriend spent hours making me an absolutely beautiful Valentine's Day card. That meant more to me than dinner at a fancy restaurant (Author's files).

Many of the female students in class thought that Emily's boyfriend was an exception. Contrary to such popular opinion, however, many men seem to fall in love faster and are more likely than women to initiate romantic e-mail exchanges (see Data Digest).

Adolescent boys are at least as romantic as adolescent girls, but they are more reluctant to talk about their emotions to avoid ridicule by male peers, and they have lower levels of confidence navigating romantic relationships. Family instability also has a greater impact on boys' than on girls' romantic relationships: Boys from homes with parental divorces, remarriages, and cohabitations are more likely than their female counterparts to have romantic relationships and more romantic partners in grades 7 through 12. The reasons for these sex differences are unclear, but they may be due to boys' dealing with family stress through romance rather than same-sex friendships, especially if discussing family problems is more acceptable among girls than boys (Giordano et al., 2006; Cavanagh et al., 2008).

According to a national poll, 17 percent of men compared with 14 percent of women think about a past love every day. And almost one in four men (24 percent), compared with only one in ten women (11 percent), say that they have been in love five or more times since they turned 18. Men are also just as likely as women to believe that "true love lasts forever" and that there is only one person "out there" who's meant for them (Covel, 2003; Popenoe and Whitehead, 2003).

Both women and men tend to link love and sex in their romantic relationships (Hendrick and Hendrick, 2002). Women are more likely to expect some of the trappings of romantic love, however. For example, whereas 62 percent of men say that "just spending time together" would be an ideal Valentine's Day celebration, 53 percent of women would probably break up with someone who didn't give them a gift (Yin, 2002; Christenson, 2003).

Do such data suggest that women are more materialistic than men in their love relationships? Or that women are more likely than men to see gifts as tangible proof of a partner's affection? For example, one of women's biggest complaints is that the men who profess to love them are reluctant to marry. Women sometimes belittle men for being "commitment dodgers," "commitment phobics," "paranoid about commitment," and "afraid of the M word" (Crittenden, 1999; Millner and Chiles, 1999). Romance and commitment are different, however. Men can be very

romantic but not see love as necessarily leading to marriage (see Chapter 9).

Are Women or Men More Intimate?

Some years ago, advice columnist Ann Landers sparked a nationwide controversy when she reported that many of her female readers preferred being touched, hugged, cuddled, and kissed over having sexual intercourse (see Chapter 2). When women complain about a lack of intimacy, they usually mean that the man doesn't communicate his thoughts or feelings. Many men believe that such criticisms are unfair because they show intimacy through sex. Whereas many women want to feel close emotionally before being sexual, many men assume that sex is the same as emotional closeness (Piorkowski, 1994).

Since you asked . . .

:• Are men are more interested in sex than women?

Love relationships and intimacy are complex. For women, intimacy may mean talking things over. For men, as the box "Do I Love You . . . ?" shows, it may mean *doing* things (such as taking care of the family cars). According to one woman, Eddie, her husband, shows his love through "small, everyday courtesies":

Eddie cleans the bugs off my windshield so I don't have to. He removes all his favorite cassettes from the tape deck in the car and puts mine in before I go to work. . . . At home, he makes sure I have my favorite bottled water in the fridge (Ann Landers, 2001: 3D).

Men and women may show affection differently, but there are more similarities than differences in their attitudes toward love. In a study based on Lee's typology (see *Table 6.1* on p. 144), the researchers analyzed the attitudes of people ages 17 to 70. They found that *both* women and men valued passion (eros), friendship and companionship (storge), and self-sacrifice (agape). As a result, the researchers criticized the shallowness of popular books, such as Gray's *Men Are from Mars, Women Are from Venus*, that trumpet "the radical differences in men's and women's approach to partnering relationships" (Montgomery and Sorell, 1997: 60).

Same-Sex Love

Homophobia, fear and hatred of homosexuals, has decreased in the past decade or so. One result is that lesbians and gay men are more likely to openly admit that they are lovers, to have commitment ceremonies, and to get married in the states that have legalized same-sex marriage (see Chapters 7 and 9).

Heterosexual and same-sex love are very similar. Regardless of sexual orientation, most partners want

"Do I Love You? I Changed Your Oil, Didn't I?"

Are men less loving than women because they equate love with sex and rarely talk about their feelings? Not according to sociologist Francesca Cancian (1990: 171). She maintains that the fault lies not in men but in women's definitions of loving, which ignore masculine styles of showing affection:

We identify love with emotional expression and talking about feelings, aspects of love that women prefer and in which women tend to be more skilled than men. At the same time we often ignore the instrumental and physical aspects of love that men prefer, such as providing help, sharing activities, and sex.

Cancian calls excluding men's ways of showing affection the "feminization of love." Because of this bias, men rarely get credit for the kinds of loving actions that are more typical of them. According to Carol Tavris (1992: 255),

What about all the men . . . who reliably support their families, who put the wishes of other family members ahead of their own preferences, or who act in a moral and considerate way when conflicts arise? Such individuals are surely being mature and loving, even if they are not articulate or do not value "communication."

Many social scientists contend that a man who is a good provider, changes the oil in his wife's car, or fixes his child's bike is showing just as much love as a wife who tells her husband she loves him and shares her innermost thoughts and feelings with him. One might even argue that actions are more important than words in showing love.

According to Cancian, the feminization of love intensifies conflicts over intimacy. As the woman demands more verbal contact, the man feels increased pressure and withdraws. The woman may then intensify her efforts to get closer. This leads to a vicious cycle in which neither partner gets what she or he wants. As the definition of love becomes more feminized, men and women move further apart rather than closer together (Tucker, 1992). One way to break this cycle is to give both men and women credit for the things they do to show their love for each other and for their families.

⁚⁚ Stop and Think . . .

- Do you agree or disagree with Cancian that women have feminized love? Why?
- Consider your parents', your friends', and your own relationships. Do you think women and men express their love differently? If so, how do they differ?

---

to be emotionally close, expect faithfulness, and usually plan to grow old together (Clark, 1999). Breakups are generally as painful for same-sex partners as they are for heterosexual couples. A few years ago, for example, one of my best students was devastated when his partner left. The student's grades plummeted because he was unable to concentrate on his courses. He became depressed and wanted to drop out of college. Thanks to counseling and supportive friends, he finished his senior year and graduated with honors.

Barriers to Experiencing Love

A number of obstacles can block our search for love. Some are *macro level*—for example, the impersonality of mass society, demographic variables, and our culture's emphasis on individualism. Others are *micro level*—such as personality characteristics and family experiences.

Understanding some of these barriers can give us more choices and more control over our decisions and lives. Recognizing some of the macro-level hurdles, especially, can help us accept some constraints that we can't change.

MASS SOCIETY AND DEMOGRAPHIC FACTORS Our society's booming technologies—such as answering machines, texting, electronic mail, and online shopping—decrease opportunities for face-to-face interaction and tend to dehumanize interpersonal communication. In response, a love industry has mushroomed. Computerized matchmaking, Internet chat rooms, personal ads, singles bars, speed dating, and dozens of books promise singles that they can find love and counteract the isolation and impersonality of our society (see Chapter 8).

Demographic variables such as age, income, and occupation also shape our love experiences. Because older men tend to marry younger women, older women typically face a shortage of prospective partners. If women are financially independent, however, they are less likely to plunge into a relationship, including marriage, because they are unwilling to be burdened with additional housework.

Financial stress has recently battered the romantic lives of those, especially men, who used to have large incomes. For example, a 27-year-old investment banker with a Cleveland firm would fly regularly to Manhattan to see his girlfriend and take her to upscale restaurants and expensive Broadway plays.

After being laid off from his six-figure job, he moved back to Virginia to live with his mother, takes a bus to visit his girlfriend, and can no longer afford lavish dinners and activities. He says that his girlfriend is trying to be understanding, but that the situation has put stress on their relationship, and he feels less of a man for not being able to provide even for himself (Bahrampour, 2009).

THE DOUBLE STANDARD As you saw in Chapter 5, there is still a great deal of discrimination against women. The double standard is one of the most damaging forms of inequality because it can dampen the development of love. Many women feel angry and resentful of men because our society still condones men's having sex without love but labels women who do so as "sluts" and "tramps." This double standard creates a lack of mutual trust and respect. As you'll see in Chapter 7, a majority of men would like to marry virgins but label women who don't have sex in a casual relationship as "frigid" or "ice queens."

"ME-FIRST" INDIVIDUALISM Our cultural values encourage individualism and competition rather than community and cooperation. This emphasis on the individual leads to a preoccupation with self (Bellah et al., 1985; Kass, 1997).

We still hear statements such as "Look Out for Number One" and "If it feels good, do it." Measuring love solely in terms of feeling good leaves us unequipped to handle its hard, painful, or demanding aspects, such as supporting a partner during unemployment or caring for a loved one who has a long-term illness.

Some social scientists maintain that we have been steeped in narcissistic messages that preach self-improvement and self-serving behavior, often at the expense of the couple or the family (Elshtain et al., 1993; Wilson, 2002). As a result, these writers argue, there has been an emphasis in our culture, especially in the popular media, on fleeting sexual liaisons rather than on long-term commitments.

PERSONALITY AND FAMILY CHARACTERISTICS Sometimes individual personality traits or family history get in the way of love. Biochemistry may initially attract people to each other, but similar personalities, feelings, and interests strengthen a romantic relationship and keep it going. If, for example, one partner is usually pessimistic or withdrawn while the other is typically optimistic and outgoing, romantic attraction and commitment will diminish. Romantic liaisons also tend to fizzle if a person's social network of family members or close friends disapproves of the relationship *and* if he or she has not yet invested large amounts of time,

resources, or emotions (Gonzaga et al., 2007; Lehmiller and Agnew, 2007).

Many children, especially girls, whose parents have undergone hostile divorces report that they are cynical about love or afraid to fall in love. Or a child who was molested by a family member or relative may be distrustful of intimate relationships (Rodberg, 1999; see, also, Chapter 14).

Despite such difficulties, some social scientists believe that couples can overcome past problems and forge healthy adult relationships, especially if they are determined to do so, and regardless of social class and race or ethnicity (Busby et al., 2005; Hill, 2005). Still, many of our love connections go awry. Some parents may be so suffocating that even adult children may never become independent enough to pursue love or marry people who don't meet parental approval. For the most part, however, you and I—and not our parents, stepparents, grandparents, or other family members—are responsible for the kinds of relationships we enter into and pursue over time.

WHEN LOVE GOES WRONG

At the beginning of the chapter, I noted that some philosophers believe that self-love promotes love for others. However, self-love can also lead to *narcissism,* an inflated love of self that derails romantic relationships. Jealousy and other controlling forms of behavior are also hazardous to our emotional and physical well-being.

Narcissism: Playing with Love

Narcissists are people who have exaggerated feelings of power and self-importance. They believe that they are unique and smarter and more attractive than others, and they constantly seek attention. Narcissists can be enjoyable dating partners because they can be charming and flattering to get what they want. However, don't expect them to be interested in a long-term, committed relationship because they treasure material wealth over emotionally warm ties and are more interested in themselves than others (Twenge and Campbell, 2009).

To maintain their dominance in romantic relationships, many narcissists resort to game-playing (ludic) love. Narcissists see themselves as superior to their partners and seek status—a spotlight on themselves—rather than meeting their partners' needs. As a result, they may be unfaithful, break confidences, and keep their partners guessing about the extent of their commitment.

If a partner gets fed up with their "me, me, me" self-focus, narcissists aren't bothered by breaking up.

Pop/rock singer Tina Turner, born in 1939, abruptly left her husband, Ike, after an especially vicious beating. She fled in 1976 after 14 years of a marriage that became increasingly controlling and abusive. Tina reportedly had nothing more than 36 cents and a gas station credit card. Hiding from Ike, she stayed with various friends, relied on food stamps to survive, and slowly rebuilt her singing career. Here, she performs at a children's benefit in London in 2007.

Because they may have already been cheating, they can link up right way with another "trophy" romance waiting in the wings. In some cases, narcissists can be dangerous. If they feel rejected—even outside of dating relationships—they can become angry, aggressive, and even violent (Campbell et al., 2002; Twenge and Campbell, 2003).

Jealousy: Trying to Control Love

A few years ago, a 78-year-old great-grandmother killed her 85-year-old

Since you asked . . .

∴• Is intense jealousy a proof of one's love?

ex-boyfriend, shooting him in the head four times as he read a newspaper in a senior citizens' home. She was angry that their year long romance was ending and that the man had found another companion. "I did it, and I'd do it again!" she shouted to the police (Bluestein, 2005).

Regardless of age, people experience *jealousy* when they believe that a rival is competing for a lover's affection. The jealous person feels threatened and is suspicious, obsessive, angry, and resentful. Some people are even jealous when their partner spends time with family members or relatives, or in pursuing hobbies (Brehm, 1992; Hanna, 2003).

WHY ARE LOVERS JEALOUS? Love flourishes when it is based on trust and respect. In contrast, jealousy is usually an unhealthy manifestation of insecurity, low self-confidence, and possessiveness (Douglas and Atwell, 1988; Farrell, 1997). All of us have some of these traits, so why are some of us more jealous than others?

Jealous people tend to depend heavily on their partners for their own self-esteem, consider themselves inadequate as mates, and believe that they are more deeply involved in their relationship than their partner is. For example, college students who grew up in homes characterized by continual parental conflict or rejecting, overprotective parents are more likely than others to report jealousy and fears of abandonment in their love relationships (Hayashi and Strickland, 1998).

In some cases, people who are jealous have been or are still unfaithful to their partners. They distrust a partner because of their own cheating. In other cases, jealousy is triggered by rivalry. A staple of sitcom romances is that a little bit of jealousy is good for a relationship: It reminds a partner not to take the loved one for granted. In reality, jealousy is hostile and destructive.

ARE WOMEN OR MEN MORE JEALOUS? There is ongoing debate about this question. According to evolutionary psychologists, jealousy evolved a million or so years ago. Men worried about sexual infidelity because they might unknowingly end up raising someone else's child rather than passing on their own genes.

In contrast, women were more concerned about their partners' emotional rather than their sexual entanglements. If a man became emotionally attached to other women, who would bring home the food and ensure their children's survival? Thus, according to evolutionary psychologists, twice as many men as women report being more upset by imagining their partners' enjoying passionate sexual intercourse with other people than by imagining their partners' forming a deep emotional attachment (Buss et al., 1996; Buss, 2000).

Some researchers have criticized evolutionary perspectives for relying on samples of college students, whose responses are not representative of the larger population (DeSteno et al., 2002). Others contend that evolutionary studies are limited because they ask only hypothetical questions ("How would you feel *if* your partner were unfaithful?").

When one researcher asked people (other than college students) about their *actual* experiences, she found that men and women—whether heterosexual or gay—were more jealous of emotional than of sexual infidelity. Greater jealousy of a partner's emotional affairs may be due to two reasons. First, they blame themselves ("Maybe I don't satisfy her or him sexually"). Second, they see an emotional affair as more threatening because it could develop into a long-term relationship that may produce offspring

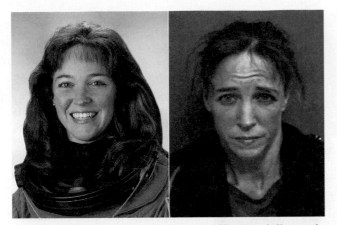

Astronaut Lisa Marie Nowak, a naval officer and divorced mother of three who juggled a career and motherhood, flew aboard space shuttle Discovery in 2006 (left). Six months later, she was arrested (right) and charged with attempting to kidnap and murder a younger woman at NASA who Nowak believed was romantically involved with another astronaut she was in love with. The incident received widespread national coverage because, among other things, Nowak wore diapers during the 900-mile drive from Houston to Orlando (where the attack occurred) so she wouldn't have to stop to go to the bathroom.

who compete for the father's affection and resources (Harris, 2003).

JEALOUSY AND STALKING Some jealous lovers become obsessed with the desired partner. They constantly daydream about him or her; make numerous phone calls; send flowers, cards, gifts, and love letters; or continuously check up on a partner's whereabouts.

Stalking—behaviors (such as telephone harassment and spying) that invade a person's privacy and cause fear—is a serious problem. California passed the first anti-stalking law in 1990. By the mid-1990s, all 50 states had adopted similar legislation. Unfortunately, these laws rarely discourage suitors (almost always men) from threatening, harassing, or even killing those who reject them.

We often hear about people who stalk celebrities—such as the man who scaled the eight-foot wall around pop star Madonna's property or the woman who broke into the home of talk show host David Letterman. However, most stalking in the United States involves average people. In 2006, for those ages 18 and older,

- Of the 3.4 million stalking cases, 74 percent of the victims were women.

- Males were as likely to be stalked by a male (41 percent) as by a female (43 percent).

- Women were significantly more likely to be stalked by a male (67 percent) than by a female (24 percent).

- Among both sexes, only about 10 percent of all victims were stalked by a stranger.

- Most of the stalkers were current or past intimate partners (30 percent) or a friend, roommate, relative, or neighbor (45 percent). (Baum et al., 2009).

Cyberstalking is threatening behavior or unwanted advances using e-mail, instant messaging, texting, and other electronic communications devices. Many chat rooms may evolve into offline stalking, including abusive or harassing phone calls, vandalism, threatening or obscene mail, trespassing, and physical assault. Cyberstalking can be as menacing as offline stalking because the perpetrators can be anywhere in the country and can post inflammatory messages on bulletin boards and in chat rooms, and electronic communications are difficult to trace (Working to Halt Online Abuse, 2008; Baum et al., 2009).

IS JEALOUSY UNIVERSAL? Although it is widespread, jealousy is *not* universal. Surveying two centuries of anthropological reports, Hupka (1991) found two types of cultures: In one, jealousy was rare (for example, the Todas of southern India); in the other, jealousy was common (for example, the Apache Indians of North America).

Toda culture discouraged possessiveness of material objects or people. It placed few restrictions on sexual gratification, and it did not make marriage a condition for respecting women. In contrast, Apache society prized virginity, paternity, and fidelity. While a man was away from home, for example, he had a close relative keep secret watch over his wife and report on her behavior when he returned.

Based on the variations he found in different cultures, Hupka concluded that jealousy is neither universal nor innate. Instead, jealousy is more common in societies in which women are regarded as property and expressing jealousy is culturally acceptable.

Other Controlling Behavior

Jealousy is not the only type of unhealthy, controlling behavior that may occur in love relationships. Threatening to withdraw love or creating guilt feelings can be deeply distressing. Inflicting severe emotional and physical abuse can also be devastating.

"IF YOU LOVED ME . . ." Controlling people want power over others. For example, one of the most common ways of pressuring people to have sex (used especially by men) is to accuse a partner of not loving them: "If you *really* loved me, you'd show it" (see Chapter 7).

People threaten to withdraw love to manipulate other kinds of behavior as well. Faculty members

Filmed in 1987, *Fatal Attraction* has become a "modern classic" in dramatizing some of the negative effects of stalking.

hear many accounts of students who choose majors they hate because they don't want to disappoint parents who insist that they become a doctor, a lawyer, an accountant, and so on. I've seen women drop out of college because their husbands or boyfriends blamed them for always studying instead of demonstrating their love by taking care of the house, preparing dinner on time, and being free on weekends. Using pressure and ultimatums, controllers force their partners or family members to give up their own interests to please the controller.

Controllers are not all alike: "A wealthy executive may use money and influence, while an attractive person may use physical allure and sex" to manipulate others (Jones and Schechter, 1992: 11). Moreover, as the box "If This Is Love, Why Do I Feel So Bad?" on p. 155 shows, controllers use a variety of strategies to dominate and control a relationship. They may also switch strategies from time to time to keep the controlled person off balance.

GUILT TRIPS People often use guilt to justify actions that have nothing to do with love. Parental psychological control involves the use of strategies such as love withdrawal and guilt to control children's behavior. *Behavioral control* is usually direct ("I have to ask my mom's permission to go out with friends"). *Psychological control* is more covert and manipulative ("My mom refuses to talk to me when she is angry with me"). Behavioral control generally has positive effects such as higher academic achievement and staying out of trouble. In contrast, some of the negative consequences of psychological control include adolescents' sacrificing their interests to preserve the parent-child relationship. Doing so may result in developing depressive symptoms such as feeling sad or having low self-esteem (Mandara and Pikes, 2008; see, also, Chapter 12 on parenting styles).

Guilt trips don't end when children become young adults. Older parents and relatives sometimes use guilt to manipulate middle-aged children. One of the most disabling guilt trips is the "affection myth," in which children are taught that love is synonymous with caregiving. Children and grandchildren may think that regardless of their own circumstances, they must care for needy elderly family members at home. As a result, younger family members sometimes endure enormous stress, even though their elderly relatives would get much better medical care at a good-quality nursing facility (see Chapter 17).

In other situations, married couples or those who are living together try to control the other through a sense of obligation: "If you are the right kind of person, you will take care of me and never leave. Can't you see how much I care about you?" (Harvey and Weber, 2002: 90). Such comments indicate emotional blackmail, not love.

EMOTIONAL AND PHYSICAL ABUSE People sometimes use love to justify severe emotional or physical neglect and abuse. A partner who is sarcastic or controlling or a parent who severely spanks or verbally humiliates a child is not expressing love for the child's own good, as they often insist. They are simply being angry and brutal. Violence is *never* a manifestation of love (see Chapter 14).

"The most insidious aspect of family violence" is that children grow up unable to distinguish between love and violence and believe "that it is acceptable to hit the people you love" (Gelles and Cornell, 1990: 20). The film *What's Love Got to Do with It?*, based on singer Tina Turner's biography, portrays Turner as enduring many years of violence because she believed that doing so proved her love and commitment to her husband, Ike.

OTHER PERVERSE REASONS FOR LOVE Some people are in love for "dubious and downright perverse

ASK YOURSELF

If This is Love, Why Do I Feel So Bad?

If you have bad feelings about your relationship, what you're experiencing may be *control,* not love. Controllers use whatever tactics are necessary to maintain power over another person: nagging, cajoling, coaxing, flattery, charm, threats, self-pity, blame, insults, or humiliation.

In the worst cases, controllers may physically injure and even murder people who refuse to be controlled. As you read this list, check any items that seem familiar to you. Individually, the items may seem unimportant, but if you check off more than two or three, you may be dealing with a controller instead of forging your own choices in life.

☐ My partner calls me names: "dummy," "jackass," "whore," "creep," "bitch," "moron."

☐ My partner always criticizes me and makes even a compliment sound like a criticism: "This is the first good dinner you've cooked in months."

☐ Always right, my partner continually corrects things I say or do. If I'm five minutes late, I'm afraid my partner will be mad.

☐ My partner withdraws into silence, and I have to figure out what I've done wrong and apologize for it.

☐ My partner is jealous when I talk to new people.

☐ My partner often phones or unexpectedly comes by the place where I work to see if I'm "okay."

☐ My partner acts very cruelly and then says I'm too sensitive and can't take a joke.

☐ When I try to express my opinion about something, my partner either doesn't respond, walks away, or makes fun of me.

☐ I have to account for every dime I spend, but my partner keeps me in the dark about our bank accounts.

☐ My partner says that if I ever leave he or she will commit suicide and I'll be responsible.

☐ When my partner has a temper tantrum, he or she says it's my fault or the children's.

☐ My partner makes fun of my body.

☐ Whether my partner is with us or not, he or she is jealous of every minute I spend with my family or other relatives or friends.

☐ My partner grills me about what happened whenever I go out.

☐ My partner makes sexual jokes about me in front of the children or other people.

☐ My partner throws things at me or hits, shoves, or pushes me.

Source: Based on Jones and Schechter, 1992: 16–22.

reasons" (Solomon, 2002: 1). In many cases, we profess love for someone because we are really afraid of being alone or coping with changes (such as meeting new people after breaking up). Or we might stay in a bad relationship because we want to avoid a partner's hostility after breaking up.

In other cases, we don't want to hurt someone's feelings by saying we don't love her or him. And if we promise to "love, honor, and obey" (although many couples have substituted "cherish" for "obey" in their marital vows), we feel an obligation to love our spouse even though our love has dwindled over the years (or we never really loved him or her to begin with). In addition, is it realistic to promise to love someone for the next 50 to 60 years—especially if her or his behavior becomes offensive or abusive?

Edward Leedskin, born in Latvia in 1887, was engaged to marry his one true love. His 16-year-old sweetheart canceled the wedding just one day before the ceremony. Heartbroken, Leedskin immigrated to the United States. Filled with obsession and undying passion, he labored for more than 28 years to build "Coral Castle," a monument dedicated to his lost love, in southern Florida. Leedskin was just 5 feet tall and weighed only 100 pounds but used blocks of coral rock, some weighing as much as 30 tons, without any human assistance or modern machinery.

Unrequited Love

In unrequited love, one does not reciprocate another's romantic feelings. Why not? First, someone who's average in appearance may fall in love with someone who's gorgeous. Because people tend to choose partners who are similar to themselves in dating and marriage (see Chapter 8), love for someone who is much better looking may go unrequited.

The rebuff is especially painful if the person senses that physical appearance is the major reason for being cast aside (Baumeister and Wotman, 1992). We often hear both women and men complain that the object of their affections "never took the time to get to know me." These accusations imply that other characteristics such as personality, intelligence, and common interests should be more important than looks.

❖ MAKING CONNECTIONS

- Are you a narcissist? If not, have you ever gone out with one? If so, how long did the relationship last? Did you enjoy the relationship in some ways?

- Have you ever dumped someone? If so, how did you cut the strings? Or, if you were the one who was dumped, how did you deal with the situation?

Second, love may be unrequited when only one of the partners wants to progress from hooking up or casual dating to a serious romance. It can be very upsetting, even traumatic, to realize that the person one is dating, and perhaps having sexual relations with, is in the relationship just for the fun of it (as with ludic lovers, including narcissists) and does not want to become more serious or exclusive.

Some people wait, sometimes for years, for someone to return their love. They assume that the situation is bound to get better (Duck, 1998). It's emotionally healthier to let go of an unrequited love and develop relationships with people who care about you.

HOW COUPLES CHANGE: ROMANTIC AND LONG-TERM LOVE

Romantic love can be both exhilarating and disappointing. In contrast, long-term love provides security and constancy. Let's begin with some of the characteristics of romantic love.

Some Characteristics of Romantic Love

Romantic love is usually a passionate and dizzying experience:

- Lovers find it impossible to work, study, or do anything but think about the beloved.

- Their moods fluctuate wildly; they are ecstatic when they hope they might be loved, despairing when they feel that they're not.

- They find it impossible to believe that they could ever love again.

- They fantasize about how their partner will declare his or her love.

- They care so desperately about the other person that nothing else matters; they are willing to sacrifice anything for love.

- Their love is "blind," and they idealize each other (Tennov, cited in Hatfield, 1983: 114).

Romantic love is intense, emotional, passionate, and sometimes melodramatic (see *Table 6.2*). It can also be self-absorbed and self-serving. As you saw earlier, for example, narcissists enhance their own self-esteem rather than express interest in their partner ("Tell me what else you like about *me*" versus "How are *you* doing?").

TABLE 6.2	How Would You Describe Passionate Love?

Over the years, Professor Sharon L. Hanna (2003: 288–89) asked her students at Southeast Community College in Lincoln, Nebraska, to describe passionate love as if they were writing "an all-consuming romantic novel." Here are some of the students' contributions. Does any of this sound familiar?

Survival

"I can't live without you."
"I'm nothing without you."
"If you ever leave me, I'll die."

Physical sensations

"Love feels zingy, and you get dingy."
"I just melt when you look at me."
Walking on air or clouds, weak knees, dizziness
Palpitating heart, shortness of breath; can't eat, sleep, or think

Perfection

"No one has ever loved like this before."
"It's perfect. You're perfect."
"Nothing will ever go wrong."

Exaggerated promises

"All I need is you."
"I'd do anything for you."
"I'll never look at another man (or woman)."

Exclusivity and possessiveness

"You're the only one for me."
"You belong to me and I belong to you."
"I'm jealous and you're jealous, and that means we're in love."
"Just the two of us. Nothing else matters."

People in cultures that have arranged marriages, as you'll see shortly, often see romantic love as frivolous, but those in Western countries tend to take it very seriously: Romantic love is considered the most legitimate reason for dating, living together, getting married, or getting a divorce ("the spark is gone"). Romantic love thrives on two beliefs—love at first sight and fate.

Since you asked . . .

- If you don't feel romantic about your partner, can you still be in love with him or her?

LOVE AT FIRST SIGHT Romantic love was less common in the United States in the 1800s than it is today for several reasons: Life expectancy was shorter, living in isolated towns and homes made it difficult to meet a variety of lovers, and most people did not live long enough to fall in love more than once. Today, with increased life spans, greater geographic mobility, and high divorce rates, we may fall in love with many people during our lifetime.

More than half of Americans believe in love at first sight, but such beliefs decrease with age and experience. People who are now in their 70s are less likely than those in their 20s to believe that love is as good as people expect (see Data Digest). People who are in a romantic relationship report being happier than those who aren't. Still, people who are older—and especially those who have been married a while—are more likely to view love as a commitment rather than as a series of thrills or highs (Dush et al., 2005; see, also, Chapter 10).

FATE Some people see fate as an important component of romantic love. Songs tell us that "you were meant for me" and "that old black magic has me in its spell." In reality, fate has little to do with romance. Romantic love is typically ignited not by fate but by factors such as a similar socioeconomic background, physical attractiveness, and a need for intimacy (Shea and Adams, 1984; Benassi, 1985).

By permission of John L. Hart FLP and Creators Syndicate, Inc.

Love in Long-Term Relationships

Many people equate romance with love, not realizing that it's only a stepping-stone. Romance draws people together and jump-starts love, but it often fizzles as the first few months (or years) of passion evaporate (Brander, 2004; Brink, 2007).

Some characteristics of romantic and long-term love overlap. Both reflect attributes such as trust, understanding, and honesty (see *Figure 6.4*). There are also some striking differences.

First, romantic love is fairly simple compared with lasting love, which is more demanding. It takes much less effort to plan a romantic evening than to be patient with a partner day after day, year after year. Thus, it's easier to fall in love than to stay in love.

Second, romantic love is often self-centered, whereas long-term love is altruistic. Romantic lovers are usually swept away by their own fantasies and obsessions, but lasting love requires putting the partner before oneself and making him or her feel cherished. Love that is not obsessive also characterizes long-term relationships (Acevedo and Aron, 2009).

Third, romance is typically short lived because love changes over time. Flaws that seemed cute during a whirlwind courtship may become unbearable a year after the wedding. For example, his dumpy furniture may have seemed quaint until she realized that he refuses to spend any money on home furnishings. And values, especially religious beliefs, become increasingly important after the birth of the first child (Trotter, 1986).

Fourth, long-term love grows and develops, whereas romantic love is typically immature. Romantic lovers often feel insecure about themselves or the relationship. As a result, one of the partners may demand constant attention, a continuous display of affection, and daily "I love you" reassurances (Dilman, 1998). Most of us appreciate tokens of love, verbal or behavioral. However, never-ending and self-absorbed commands such as "prove to me that you love me" can become tedious and annoying.

Fifth, companionate (storgic) love is more characteristic of long-term relationships compared with passion and game playing in romantic love. Those who are the happiest describe their love as companionate and committed. Committed partners, ruled by the head as much

FIGURE 6.4 Romantic Love and Long-Term Love: How Do They Differ?

If you are currently (or have been) in a relationship with someone, is (was) your relationship one of romantic love? Or long-term love?

Unique to Romantic Love	Common to Both	Unique to Long-Term Love
• Romantic Walks	• Trust	• Patience
• Obsession	• Caring	• Independence
• Longing	• Communication	• Putting Other
• Candlelit Trysts	• Honesty	before Self
• Going Out For Dinner	• Friendship	• Possibility of
• Picnics and Sunsets	• Respect	Marriage
• Playfulness	• Understanding	• Making Other
• Fantasy	• Having Fun	Feel Wanted
• Physical Attraction	Together	
• Loss of Sleep	• Passion (but More	
• Ecstasy	Intense in	
	Romantic Love)	

Source: Based on Fehr, 1993, pp. 87–120.

as the heart, are faithful to each other and plan their future together (Hecht et al., 1994).

Finally, demographic variables play a role in sustaining love. For example, an analysis of two national polls found an association between socioeconomic status and long-term relationships: "Having enough income to be out of poverty may alleviate financial problems enough to reduce stress and thereby facilitate feelings of love" (Smith, 1994: 34). So, although money may not buy love, its absence can cause couples to fall out of love.

What does long-term love look like? Here's one description:

Happy couples have similar values, attitudes, interests, and to some degree, personality traits.

They also share a philosophy of life, religion, vision, or passion that keeps them marching together in spite of minor differences. . . . They are autonomous, fair-minded, emotionally responsive individuals who trust one another and love spending time together. . . . Because they are separate selves, they also enjoy spending time apart to solidify their own individuality without feeling threatened by potential loss or abandonment (Piorkowski, 1994: 286).

For more ideas on how to achieve a satisfying, lasting relationship, see the box "Helping Love Flourish."

Helping Love Flourish

Choices

Several family practitioners (Hendrix, 1988; Osherson, 1992) have suggested some "rules" for creating a loving environment. Although these rules do not guarantee everlasting love, they are worth considering:

- Relationships do not just happen; we create them. Good relationships are the result of conscious effort and work.
- One partner should be pleased, rather than threatened, by the other partner's successes or triumphs.
- A lover is not a solution to a problem. Love may be one of life's greatest experiences, but it is not life itself.
- Love is about acceptance: Being sympathetic to another's flaws and cherishing the person's other characteristics that are special and lovable. People who feel loved, accepted, and valued are more likely to treat others in a similar manner.
- Lovers are not mind readers. Open communication is critical.
- It's not what you say but what you do that maintains love.
- Stable relationships are always changing. We must learn to deal with both our own changes as individuals and the changes we see in our mates.
- Love is poisoned by infidelity. If a loved one is deceived, it may be impossible to reestablish trust and respect.
- Blame is irresponsible. It discourages communication, makes people feel angry, and damages self-esteem.
- Love does not punish but forgives. It may be difficult to forget occasional cruel words or acts, but forgiveness is essential in continuing a healthy relationship.
- Even though partners are very close, they must respect the other person's independence and his or her right to develop personal interests and other friendships.

A GLOBAL VIEW OF LOVE

People in all known societies have intimate and loving relationships, but the meaning and expression of love vary from one culture to another. In Western societies that emphasize individualism and free choice, love may or may not result in marriage. In cultures that stress the group and the community, arrangements between families are more important than romantic love.

Romantic Love

In the United States, love hasn't always been the basis for getting married. The early colonists believed that marriage was far too important to be based on love; politics and economics, not romance, were the key factors in selecting an appropriate partner. It was only in the early twentieth century that people came to expect marriage to be based on love, sexual attraction, and personal fulfillment (Coontz, 2005; see, also, Chapter 3).

Because romantic love exists in at least 89 percent of societies, it is a nearly universal phenomenon. A number of studies in China, Hong Kong, Taiwan, and Hawaii have found that many people, especially the young, believe in passionate love (Jankowiak and Fischer 1992; Doherty et al., 1994; Cho and Cross, 1995; Goodwin and Findlay, 1997).

Romance is least important in societies in which kin ties take precedence over individual relationships. In Burma, India, and Mexico, college students said that storgic, agapic, and pragmatic love are more desirable than manic, erotic, and ludic love styles. In much of China, similarly, love is tempered by recognition that a match needs parental approval. In Saudi Arabia and some other Middle Eastern countries, public embracing between men and women is taboo, the sexes cannot mix in public, and a woman who is caught with an unrelated man can be flogged, arrested, or killed (Moore, 1998; Slackman, 2008).

Many Arab nations celebrate Valentine's Day with much fanfare. In 2002, however, Saudi Arabia officially banned Valentine's Day and prohibited stores from selling red roses and displaying tokens of affection. A year later, Iranian police ordered shops in Tehran to remove heart-and-flower decorations, images of couples embracing, and other corrupt materials that symbolized decadent Western holidays ("Valentine's a 'Worthless' Day?" 2002; "Police in Iran . . .," 2003).

As you saw in Chapter 1, the Indian government endorses mixed unions across caste lines, but not everyone supports such policies. Also, some radical groups have denounced celebrating Valentine's Day—especially popular among young, middle-class urbanites—as offensive to Indian culture and have tried to disrupt businesses that sell Valentine's Day gifts and cards (Wax, 2008; Magnier and Ramaswamy, 2009).

In Japan, which has one of the highest divorce rates in the world, expressing love and affection is uncommon, especially among men, who rarely see

Many marriages in India are still arranged (see text), but "Bollywood" films are very popular. These movies feature romantic love, passion, infatuation, and even obsession. Why do you think that the films are so popular?

their wives and children because their companies pressure them to put their job first and demonstrate their loyalty by working long hours. To increase husbands' appreciation of their wives, a man founded a Devoted Husband Organization and declared January 31 as "Beloved Wives Day," during which a husband is supposed to tell his wife that he loves her for all that she does every day for him and their family. Beloved Wives Day hasn't become a national holiday, but more men are joining the Devoted Husband Organization to show respect and affection for their wives and to avoid divorce (Kambayashi, 2008).

Arranged Love

In the United States and other Western countries, people often become engaged and then inform family and friends. Worldwide, a more typical pattern is **arranged marriage,** in which parents or relatives choose their children's partners. It is expected that the partners' love for each other will grow over time.

In many countries, arranged marriages are the norm because respect for parents' wishes, family tra-

ditions, and the kin group are more important than romantic love and the well-being of the community is valued more highly than the feelings of the individual. In fact, people in many societies find American beliefs about dating and romance at least as strange as some Americans find the concept of arranged marriages (see the box "Modern Arranged Marriages in India").

In arranged marriages in Sri Lanka, men and women who fall in love usually tell their parents about their choices. In Turkey, about 52 percent of women live in arranged marriages, but there is a trend toward love marriages among younger, better-educated, and urban women. In Canada, some second-generation Muslim Pakistani women are rebelling against arranged marriages. Others participate willingly because they can't find a suitable partner on their own or believe that their parents know best (de Munck, 1998; Zaidi and Shuraydi, 2002; Nauck and Klaus, 2005).

Love is important in all societies. It may manifest itself differently in various cultures and historical eras, but "overall, people are more similar than different" (Hendrick and Hendrick, 2003: 1065).

Cross-Cultural and Multicultural Families

Modern Arranged Marriages in India

In India, the majority of marriages are arranged by parents or elders: "There has never been any room for romantic marriage in Indian society on the line of Western societies" (Singh, 2005: 143). Loyalty of the individual to the family is a cherished ideal. To preserve this ideal, marriages have traditionally been carefully arranged so that young men and women will avoid selecting mates that the family deems unsuitable.

There are variations in different regions and social classes, however. Educated, upper-middle-class women are allowed to marry whomever they want, but many opt for arranged marriages. One young woman explained: "Love is important, but it's not sufficient." She asked her parents to research and solicit proposals from parents of men with a good education

and earning potential who were refined, intellectual, and good human beings. She is reportedly happily married to a man whom she had met just three times before their engagement. In other cases, children can reject undesirable candidates (Lakshmanan, 1997).

Why do arranged marriages persist in much of India? Shy people can end up with a good partner because parents and relatives seem to do a good job in choosing mates. Also, arranged marriages offer stability because the couple's families stand behind them: "If the relationship between the couples is about to go haywire . . . parents of both spouses make concerted efforts to resolve the crisis" (Singh, 2005: 144).

Arranged marriages persist, also, because of family ties. Even financially

independent couples usually live with the husband's parents. As a result, similar backgrounds and compatibility with in-laws are more important in India than in the West. The advantage is that there tends to be much family support if a marriage runs into trouble.

❖ Stop and Think . . .

- Why are arranged marriages less fragile than marriages based on love?

- In arranged marriages, factors such as social class and religion are more important than romantic love or physical attraction. If Americans endorsed arranged love, do you think that our divorce rates would decrease? Why or why not?

⁝⁚ MAKING CONNECTIONS

- Have you ever experienced love at first sight? If so, was the person similar to you in physical appearance or very different? How long did the love last? Why do you think that some people are more likely than others to fall in love at first sight?

- Some of my students—including those in their 30s and 40s—believe that long-term relationships are pretty boring because the romance wanes quickly. Do you agree?

CONCLUSION

When love is healthy, it *changes* how we feel about ourselves and others. Love can inspire us and motivate us to care for family members, friends, and lovers. Love also creates *choices* in the ways in which we may find happiness during dating, marriage, and old age. There are *constraints,* however, because we sometimes confuse love with jealousy or controlling behavior.

Love is essential to human growth and development, but it is often shrouded in myths and hampered by formidable barriers. For those who are willing to learn and to work at it, love is attainable and can be long lasting. Do love and sex go together? Not always. We examine this and related issues in the next chapter.

SUMMARY

1. Love is a complex phenomenon that varies in degree and intensity in different people and social contexts. Minimally necessary for a loving relationship are willingness to accommodate the other person, to accept his or her shortcomings, and to have as much concern about his or her well-being as one's own.

2. Friendship is the root of love. Friendship and love share characteristics such as trust, respect, honesty, and mutual support.

3. Caring, intimacy (including self-disclosure), and commitment form the foundations of love. These characteristics strengthen relationships and help love flourish.

4. There are many approaches to understanding love and loving: Attachment theory proposes that warm, secure, loving relationships in infancy are essential to forming loving relationships in adulthood; Reiss described four stages of love; Sternberg focused on the relationships among passion, intimacy, and decision/commitment; Lee identified six styles of loving; and exchange theorists see love as a series of mutually beneficial transactions.

5. Love serves many functions, and people fall in love for a variety of reasons. Availability of partners is one factor. Others include the desire to have children, the drive for survival of the species, quality of life, inspiration, and just plain fun.

6. Despite popular beliefs, men are usually more romantic than women and suffer more when a rela-

tionship ends. Women are more likely to express their love verbally and to work at a relationship, but they are also more pragmatic about moving on when love goes awry. There are more similarities than differences, however, between women's and men's love relationships.

7. There are many obstacles to love. Macro-level barriers include the depersonalization of mass society, demographic factors, the double standard, our society's emphasis on individualism, a negative view of gay and lesbian love, and family pressures. Micro-level obstacles include personality characteristics and childhood experiences.

8. Several kinds of negative and controlling behavior can kill love. Narcissism and jealousy are usually destructive and sometimes even dangerous. Other harmful behaviors include threatening a partner with the withdrawal of love, making the partner feel guilty, and causing physical and emotional pain.

9. Romantic love can be exhilarating, but it is often short lived and can be disappointing. In contrast to romantic love, long-term love is usually secure and constant and adapts over the life course.

10. There is a great deal of variation among cultures in how people express love. Some societies embrace love. Others view love as less important than marrying someone who meets with the approval of parents and kin.

KEY TERMS

self-disclosure 140
attachment theory 142
eros 144
mania 145

ludus 145
storge 145
companionate love 145
agape 145

pragma 145
homophobia 149
arranged marriage 161

myfamilylab My Family Lab provides a wealth of resources. Go to www.myfamilylab.com <http://www.myfamilylab.com/>, to enhance your comprehension of the content in this chapter. You can take practice exams, view videos relevant to the subject matter, listen to audio files, explore topics further by using Social Explorer, and use the tools contained in MySearchLab to help you write research papers.

7 Sexuality and Sexual Expression Throughout Life

In the movie *Annie Hall*, a therapist asks two lovers how often they have sex. The male rolls his eyes, and complains, "Hardly ever, maybe three times a week!" The female exclaims, "Constantly, three times a week!" As this anecdote illustrates, sex is more important for some people than others. Besides physical contact, sex provides an opportunity to express loyalty, passion, and affection.

Culture shapes our sexual development, attitudes, and actions. As a result, there are significant differences from one society to another in defining what is normal or abnormal. In addition, sexual behavior changes throughout life and varies over the years. Before you read any further, take the "How Much Do You Know about Sex?" quiz.

DATA DIGEST

- Nearly half of all high school students (50 percent of males and 46 percent of females) have had sexual intercourse. The **median age at first intercourse is 16.9 years for boys and 17.4 years for girls.**

- By age 20, **75 percent of Americans have had premarital sex.**

- The proportion of adults **who first had sex before the age of 15** was highest for persons with less than a high school education (27 percent) compared with persons with a high school education (19 percent) and those with more than a high school education (10 percent).

- Among those ages 15 to 44, 6 percent of men and 11 percent of women **have had sexual contact with a same-sex partner** at least once.

- A majority (54 percent) of **women and men ages 75 to 85 engage in sexual activities** (including vaginal intercourse and oral sex) two to three times each month.

- Worldwide, **33 million people are living with HIV.** In 2007, 2 million people died of AIDS. The largest number of deaths occurred in sub-Saharan Africa (1.5 million).

Sources: Mosher et al., 2005; Finer, 2007; Fryar et al., 2007; Lindau et al., 2007; Kaiser Family Foundation, 2008; UNAIDS, 2008.

ASK YOURSELF

How Much Do You Know about Sex?

1. Birth control pills offer protection against sexually transmitted infections (STIs). ☐ True ☐ False
2. Out of every ten married American men, how many would you estimate have ever had an extramarital affair?
   a. Fewer than one out of ten
   b. One out of ten (10 percent)
   c. About two out of ten (20 percent)
   d. About three out of ten (30 percent)
   e. About four out of ten (40 percent)
   f. About five out of ten (50 percent)
   g. About six out of ten (60 percent)
   h. More than six out of ten
3. If your partner is truly meant for you, sex is easy and wonderful. ☐ True ☐ False
4. Petroleum jelly, skin lotion, and baby oil are good lubricants to use with a condom or diaphragm.
   ☐ True ☐ False
5. About 10 percent of the U.S. population is exclusively homosexual. ☐ True ☐ False
6. A woman or teenage girl can get pregnant during her menstrual flow (her period). ☐ True ☐ False

7. A woman or teenage girl cannot get pregnant if the man withdraws his penis before he ejaculates.
   ☐ True ☐ False
8. Douching is an effective method of birth control.
   ☐ True ☐ False
9. A person can become infected with an STI only when a partner's symptoms are visible. ☐ True ☐ False
10. Menopause, or change of life, causes most women to lose interest in having sex. ☐ True ☐ False
11. What do you think is the length of the average man's erect penis?
    a. 2–4 inches
    b. 5–7 inches
    c. 8–9 inches
    d. 10–11 inches
    e. 12 inches or longer
12. In the United States, syphilis is one of the two most common STIs. ☐ True ☐ False

(Answers are on page 169.)

SEXUALITY AND HUMAN DEVELOPMENT

Sexuality is much more complex than just physical contact. Among other things, it is the product of our sexual identity, sexual orientation, and sexual scripts.

Sexual Identity

Our **sexual identity** is our awareness of ourselves as male or female and the ways in which we express our sexual values, attitudes, feelings, and beliefs. It involves placing ourselves in a category created by society (such as female and heterosexual) and learning, both consciously and unconsciously, how to act in that category.

Sexuality is a multidimensional concept that incorporates psychological, biological, and sociological components such as sexual desire, sexual response, and gender roles (Bernhard, 1995). *Sexual desire* is the sexual drive that makes us receptive to sexual activity. *Sexual response* encompasses the biological aspects of sexuality, which include experiencing pleasure or orgasm. *Gender roles* are the behaviors that women and men enact according to culturally prescribed expectations (see Chapter 5).

In a typical situation, a man may be aroused by a woman's cleavage because our society considers breasts sexy (sexual desire), may experience an erection (sexual response), and may then take the initiative in having sexual intercourse with a woman whom he finds attractive (gender roles). But what if the man is aroused by other men rather than by women?

Sexual Orientation

Sexual identity incorporates **sexual orientation,** a preference for sexual partners of the same sex, the opposite sex, both sexes, or neither sex:

- **Homosexuals** (from the Greek root *homo,* meaning "same") are sexually attracted to people of the same sex. Male homosexuals prefer to be called *gay;* female homosexuals are called *lesbians. Coming out* is a person's public announcement of a gay or lesbian sexual orientation.
- **Heterosexuals,** often called *straight,* are attracted to partners of the opposite sex.
- **Bisexuals,** sometimes called *bi's,* are attracted to members of both sexes.
- **Asexuals** lack any interest in or desire for sex.

Sexual orientation isn't as clear-cut as most people believe it to be. Asexuality may be a temporary condition because of the effects of medications.

Bisexuals may be attracted to people of both sexes but engage in sexual behavior primarily with women or with men. Heterosexuals might fantasize about having same-sex experiences. And homosexuals who haven't come out may have sexual intercourse only with heterosexual partners because they fear the consequences of violating cultural norms (Kinsey et al., 1948; Rieger et al., 2005).

In what one author has called being "on the down low," black men who sometimes sleep with other men see themselves as straight and don't disclose their male relationships to their female sex partners, friends, or family members (King, 2004). Black men aren't the only ones who are on the down low: White men who are married and hold high-ranking leadership jobs may frequent chat rooms and use code words such as "bimm" (bisexual married male) and "m4m" (married male for married male) (Vargas, 2004).

Heterosexuality is the predominant sexual orientation worldwide, but homosexuality exists in all societies (see the box "Homosexuality in Non-Western Cultures"). Many gays and lesbians deny or try to suppress their sexual orientation because our society is still characterized by **heterosexism,** the belief that heterosexuality is superior to and more natural than homosexuality.

According to some estimates, about 2 percent of Americans are **transgendered,** but some researchers believe that the numbers may be twice as high (Gorman, 1995; Wilson, 2005). This term encompasses several groups:

- **Transsexuals:** people who are born with one biological sex but choose to live their life as another sex—either by consistently cross-dressing or by surgically altering their sex (see Chapter 5).

- **Intersexuals:** people whose medical classification at birth is not clearly male or female (this term has replaced *hermaphrodites*).

- **Transvestites:** people who cross-dress at times but don't necessarily consider themselves a member of the opposite sex.

Transgendered people include gays, lesbians, bisexuals, and men and women who don't identify themselves with any specific sexual orientation (the acronym is GLBT). GLBTs are becoming increasingly more visible and accepted. Australia became the first country in the world to issue a passport that lists a person's sex as "indeterminate." About 125 of the *Fortune* 500 companies, up from almost zero in 2002, offer health benefits that include everything from regular hormone treatments to sex assignment surgery. So far, 13 states and the District of Columbia have passed laws that prohibit discrimination in housing, employment, and public accommodations for GLBTs (Butler, 2003; Belkin, 2008;

Meredith (right) and Lynn Bacon remain married despite Meredith's sex change in 2005. Meredith, who used to be Wally, is a popular faculty member at the University of Nebraska. Some people were shocked by the transformation, but most students, faculty, and administrators were supportive. Meredith says that since her decision for the sex change at age 59, this is "the first time I've been completely happy" (Wilson, 2005: A11).

Marimow, 2008). And, increasingly, journalists are writing supportive articles about GLBTs (see, for example, Vitello, 2006, and Rosenberg, 2007).

WHAT DETERMINES SEXUAL ORIENTATION? No one knows why we are heterosexual, gay, or bisexual. *Biological theories* maintain that sexual orientation has a strong genetic basis because, at least for males, the more genes one shares with a homosexual relative, the more likely it is that one will be homosexual.

Since you asked . . .

- Do we inherit our sexual orientation?

These studies suggest that a particular region of the X chromosome may hold a "gay gene" that results in male homosexuality (Bailey et al., 1993; Hamer et al., 1993).

Cross-Cultural and Multicultural Families

Homosexuality in Non-Western Cultures

In their classic studies, anthropologists Clelland Ford and Frank Beach (1972) examined data on 190 societies in Oceania, Eurasia, Africa, North America, and South America. They drew three conclusions about homosexuality: (1) Social attitudes toward homosexuality are widely divergent; (2) homosexuality occurs in all societies, regardless of societal reactions; and (3) males seem more likely than females to engage in homosexual activity.

Despite many attempts to repress homosexuality, especially by Western missionaries, homosexuality is common in many parts of Africa. For example, woman-to-woman marriage has been documented in more than 30 African populations, including at least nine groups in southern Africa (Carrier and Murray, 1998).

An estimated 100 million Chinese, or 7 percent of the country's population, are gay. Chinese officials disapprove of homosexuality, but Chinese psychiatrists have recently stopped classifying homosexuality as a mental disorder. Some gays and lesbians have celebrated weddings, although these marriages are not recognized legally (Hinsch, 1990; Chu, 2001; "*Reuters* highlights. . . ," 2002).

Homosexuality is better tolerated in some countries than in others. For example:

- In Egypt and many African countries, gays can be stoned, imprisoned, or killed (Wax, 2005).

- Nigeria's laws prescribe a 14-year imprisonment for homosexuals (Modo, 2005).

- In India, where homosexual acts are illegal, gay men and lesbians can be fired from their jobs, imprisoned, and serve longer sentences than most of those convicted of rapes and murders (Wax, 2008).

- In many countries in Asia and the Middle East, including Iran and Iraq, gays are not only punished legally but are murdered by either death squads or family members who reject them. In Iraq, more than 430 gay men who have come out have been murdered since 2003 ("Iranian Gays. . . , 2007; Samuels, 2008; Williams and Maher, 2009).

- In Afghanistan, homosexuality—including with young boys—has "long been a clandestine feature of life," even though it is not practiced openly (C. S. Smith, 2002: 4).

- Although gays aren't prosecuted, two-thirds of South Koreans believe that homosexuality is wrong and sinful. Because Confucian beliefs stress the continuity of families along bloodlines, homosexuality threatens a family's permanence (Prusher, 2001).

- Thailand doesn't tolerate homosexuality, but one university allows gay males (called "ladyboys") to "flout the campus dress code, which demands that men wear trousers and ties" (McNeill, 2008: A6).

- There is considerable variation in Latin America. Gay relationships are fairly open in some cities. In other cases, government and university officials define homosexuality as an illness that can and should be cured (Parker and Cáceres, 1999; Chauvin, 2002).

Some biologists theorize that brain structure may also be associated with sexual orientation because the size of the hypothalamus—an organ deep in the center of the brain that is believed to regulate the sex drive—differs between heterosexual and gay men. Other scientists have found no evidence of a biological influence on homosexuality. If there's a strong genetic predisposition, gay children would come from gay households and straight children from straight households. This isn't the case, however, because most gay men and lesbians are raised by heterosexuals (LeVay, 1993; Hamer et al., 1993; Burr, 1996; Rice et al., 1999).

Social constructionist theories hold that sexual behavior is largely the result of social pressure and that culture, not biology, plays a large role in forming our sexual identity. For example, and despite their homosexual inclinations, many straight men who have sex with other men refuse to accept the possibility that they're gay or bisexual. In effect, then, and because of societal pressure to be straight, many gay men and lesbians are living heterosexual lives (Golombek and Tasker, 1996; Patterson, 2002).

One example of social constructionist theories is the case of *hijras*. An estimated 50,000 to 5 million live in India alone and are considered members of a "third sex"—neither male nor female. Most are born male, and some are intersexuals (with ambiguous genitalia), but all dress as women and act in feminine ways. The word *hijra* is sometimes used in a derogatory way, but *hijras* often perform religious ceremonies that are supposed to bring good luck and fertility, and some have been elected to high political positions (Ilkkaracan and Jolly, 2007).

So far, no study has shown conclusively that there is a gay gene or that the environment causes sexual orientation (Brookey, 2002). At this point, researchers speculate that a combination of genetic and cultural factors influence our sexual orientation.

SEXUAL ORIENTATION AND GENDER Some researchers assert that gender is a more powerful factor than sexual orientation in shaping a person's behavior. That is, there are more similarities between straight and gay men and between straight women and lesbians than there are between lesbians and gays. For example,

- Lesbians and heterosexual women usually have monogamous relationships; gays and heterosexual men are more likely to have more than one lover at a time.

- For lesbians and heterosexual women, love and sex usually go hand in hand; many gays and heterosexual men often separate emotional intimacy from sex.

- Compared with gay and heterosexual men, lesbians and heterosexual women aren't interested in having sex with strangers (or in public places). Both groups of men, but not women, are likely to "cruise" for sexual partners.

- Heterosexual and homosexual men—not women—are the mainstay of some industries, including prostitution, pornography, topless or gay bars, escort services, and adult bookstores (Caldwell and Peplau, 1990; Goode, 1990; Fryar et al., 2007).

Such findings may seem like male bashing, but the researchers are simply pointing out that gender roles may be more important than sexual orientation in shaping our sexual scripts.

Sexual Scripts

We like to think that our sexual behavior is spontaneous, but most of us have internalized sexual scripts. A **sexual script** specifies the formal or informal norms for legitimate or unacceptable sexual activity, the eligibility of sexual partners, and the boundaries of sexual behavior. Gender, race, and ethnicity, among other factors, shape our sexual scripts in important ways.

GENDER AND SEXUAL SCRIPTS Women are more assertive in sexual encounters today than in the past, but most sexual behavior is still highly gendered. As you saw in Chapter 5, boys are typically expected to be masculine and girls are supposed to be feminine. One of the negative effects of male sexual scripts is the expectation that boys and men will be sexually aggressive and always ready for sex, and that their sexual urge is uncontrollable. Many sexually healthy men in their 20s, 30s, and 40s use impotence drugs—such as Viagra and Levitra—because they believe the myth that a "real man" is always interested in sex and always ready to be a sexual superman. Some companies even sell men's briefs that have a sling which provides a lift for a penis, making it appear larger than it is. Women, too, try to live up to unrealistic sexual scripts. For example, millions of American women undergo breast augmentation surgery—despite the chance of infection or even death—because we live in a culture in which large breasts "are part of the ideal female body" (Roan, 2005: F1; Setoodeh, 2007).

In virtually every media form, including television, music videos, magazines, video games, the Internet and advertising, girls and women are sexualized (for example, dressed in revealing clothes) and physical beauty is emphasized. Such sexualization can result in girls' and women's being dissatisfied with their bodies, low self-esteem, tolerating sexual harassment and sexual violence, and a greater likelihood of having sex at an early age (Zurbriggen et al., 2007).

RACE, ETHNICITY, AND SEXUAL SCRIPTS Race and ethnicity also shape sexual scripts. Among many Latinos, for example, "good women" are not expected to be highly sexual or to take the initiative in sexual relations. Men, on the other hand, are expected to be passionate and to use sexual conquest as proof of masculinity. Whereas 77 percent of black women say that they would have sex only if they were in love, only 43 percent of black men agree. Among whites, boys engage in sex earlier than girls and have more sexual partners (Mahay et al., 2001; Centers for Disease Control and Prevention, 2008).

Among recent and even second-generation immigrants, men's and women's sexual scripts differ. In many Middle Eastern, Latino, and Asian families, for example, parents monitor their daughters' sexual behavior but allow sons much more freedom (see Chapter 4).

The Double Standard Revisited

You'll recall that the double standard emerged during the nineteenth century (see Chapter 3). Some

Answers to "How Much Do You Know about Sex?"

Scoring the test:

Each question is worth 1 point. Score each item and add up your total number of points. A score of 11 or 12 is an "A," 9 or 10 a "B," 8 a "C," 7 a "D," and below 7 an "F."

Correct answers:

1. false, 2. c, 3. false, 4. false, 5. false, 6. true, 7. false, 8. false, 9. false, 10. false, 11. b, 12. false.

In Seattle, Washington, "sexpresso" coffee stands are booming (left). The workers, all of whom are women and paid a minimum wage, are scantily clad. The customers, almost all of them men, order drinks with names such as "Wet Dream" and "Sexual Mix." In the center is a Ralph Lauren ad for women's clothes. On the right is a 10-year-old girl who appears with adult models in swimsuit shows. How do such images reinforce women's sexual scripts? And why do many companies use women's sexuality to sell their products?

believe that the *sexual double standard*—in which sexual intercourse outside of marriage is acceptable for men but not women—has eroded. Others argue that the sexual revolution made only a small dent in the double standard.

In the late 1940s, social norms emphasized that love, sex, and marriage were deeply intertwined. By the early 1960s, the so-called sexual revolution had led to greater openness about sexuality. A growing acceptance of recreational sex replaced the emphasis on reproductive sex, and the invention of the birth control pill separated sex and childbearing for women. By the mid-1970s, the fear of pregnancy, the concepts of sin and guilt, and the value of virginity had changed, especially for teenagers. According to one writer, "The Pill did more for the equality of women than any other single factor in the twentieth century" (Potts, 2003). Is this really true?

THE SEXUAL REVOLUTION AND THE DOUBLE STANDARD Some scholars believe that the sexual revolution broke down the old sexual double standard because it permitted sexual intercourse outside of marriage for both women and men. Both sexes expressed their sexuality more freely instead of feeling compelled to follow the traditional sequence of dating, love, marriage, sex, and parenthood (Fisher, 1999).

Others contend that the sexual revolution resulted in more costs than benefits, especially for women. Women "were pressured more than ever [by men] to be sexually liberated . . . and then were accused of being uptight and puritanical if [they] didn't want sex" (Elshtain, 1988: 41). As women became free sexual agents, many men no longer felt a commitment to marry or to raise the children they had fathered (Crittenden, 1999).

About 30,000 American women undergo vaginal surgery (hymenoplasty) every year to regain their virginity. Cosmetic surgeons can repair the hymen for about $5,000. This "revirgination" is especially popular among women whose lovers want to experience

intercourse with a virgin ("Like a virgin?" 2006). Such intrusive surgery is one of the most recent examples of some women's efforts to live up to a sexual double standard.

SEXUAL ASSAULTS, SEXUAL DYSFUNCTIONS, AND THE DOUBLE STANDARD Another indicator of the persistence of the double standard is the high rate of rape and other sexual assaults on women (see Chapters 8 and 14). Much sexual violence is still dismissed as masculine misbehavior rather than as a criminal assault (McFarlane and Malecha, 2005; Taylor and Gaskin-Laniyan, 2007).

Attitudes toward sexual dysfunctions offer further evidence of the double standard. Viagra, the male impotence pill, got front-page coverage when it came on the market in 1998. Insurance companies immediately covered the costs of Viagra, about $10 per pill, but still do not pay for female contraception methods such as birth control pills, which typically cost around $30 per month. (*Appendix D* provides information on the effectiveness of common contraceptive methods.)

Nationwide, more women (43 percent) than men (31 percent) suffer from sexual difficulties such as an inability to achieve orgasm or the experiencing of pain during sexual intercourse (Laumann et al., 2001). Nevertheless, much pharmacological research focuses on erectile dysfunctions rather than on women's sexual problems.

The sexual double standard is not limited to the United States and other Western nations. Female genital mutilation/cutting, still practiced extensively in many parts of the world, reflects a double standard that allows men to mutilate women under the guise of making them more marriageable. Men have no comparable constraints. In 1979, the World Health Organization denounced the practice as indefensible on medical and humane grounds. As the "Tradition or Torture?. . . " box shows, however, millions of girls are still subjected to these procedures.

Cross-Cultural and Multicultural Families

Tradition or Torture? Female Genital Mutilation/Cutting

This 4-year-old in Kurdistan, Iraq, screams in pain during her circumcision. In another case in the same region, a 7-year-old girl prepared happily for a party that her mother promised. Instead, she was circumcised. As the operator sliced off part of the little girl's genitals, she "let out a high-pitched wail heard throughout the neighborhood" (Paley, 2008: A9).

Most of the 140 million girls and women who have undergone female genital mutilation/cutting (FGM/C) live in 28 African countries, Indonesia, and some Middle Eastern countries. FGM/C is also increasing in Europe, Australia, Canada, and the United States, primarily among immigrants. Each year, an estimated 3 million girls undergo FGM/C.

There are several types of FGM/C. The two most common, which remove all or part of the female's external genitalia, or vulva, are excision and infibulation. (*Appendix A* provides information on sexual anatomy.) In *excision,* part or all of the clitoris and the labia minora are removed. This operation often results in the growth of scar tissue that blocks the vaginal opening.

Infibulation combines removal of the clitoris and labia minora with excision of the inner layers of the labia majora. The raw edges of these inner layers are then sewn together with cat gut or acacia thorn. A sliver of wood or straw is inserted into the tiny opening that remains, allowing the slow, often painful passage of urine and menstrual flow.

When the woman marries, her husband may use his penis, razors, knives, or other instruments to penetrate the vagina during intercourse, and the opening must be further

enlarged for childbirth. In many cases, the opening is reclosed in another excision or infibulation, and the cycle begins again.

The age at which a girl undergoes FGM/C varies from one country to another. Among some groups, the girl may be only a few days old. In Egypt and many countries of central Africa, she may be anywhere from 3 to 14 years old.

The younger the girl, the less aware she is of what's going to happen to her and, therefore, the less she resists. She is usually immobilized, with her arms tied behind her back, while women (sometimes including her mother) hold her thighs apart.

The operator, typically an elderly village woman, cuts off the clitoris and then scrapes the labial flesh even though the little girl howls and writhes in pain. The procedure lasts from 15 to 20 minutes, depending on the operator's competence and the extent of the child's struggling.

In rural areas, the instruments used may include razor blades, scissors, kitchen knives, or pieces of glass. Members of the elite and professional classes in urban areas use antiseptics and anesthesia during FGM/C.

FGM/C can have a number of immediate and long-term complications:

- The girl could hemorrhage and die.
- The operator's poor eyesight or the child's resistance could cause cuts in other organs (such as the urethra or bladder).
- A rupture of the internal division between the vagina and the bladder or rectum could cause continual dribbling of urine or feces for the rest of the woman's life.
- The woman could feel severe pain during intercourse or become sterile because of infections in her reproductive organs.
- During childbirth, even if the birth canal opening is enlarged, the woman could experience perineal tears or even die because the baby cannot emerge through the mutilated vulva.

Cultures that practice FGM/C justify it on the grounds that it controls a girl's sexual desires and, therefore, preserves her morality, chastity, and fidelity. Because virginity is a prerequisite for marriage, FGM/C ensures a girl's marriageability and the family's honor. In parts of Nigeria, for instance, FGM/C allows a future mother-in-law to verify the virginity of the bride. Even disapproving mothers participate because if they refused, their daughters would be ostracized, remain

Continued

Cross-Cultural and Multicultural Families   *Continued*

unmarried, and become financially destitute.

FGM/C has been banned in some African countries, but an estimated two-thirds of the young girls in those countries have been circumcised, often against their will. Many African and Egyptian women have protested FGM/C, but the practice continues.

Sources: United Nations Children's Fund, 2005; Bauldauf, 2008; "Egyptian activists . . . ," 2008; Paley, 2008; Mullen, 2009.

Stop and Think . . .

- FGM/C is an important ritual in many countries. Should the United States and other nations interfere if they don't agree with these customs?

- Should male infants in the United States be circumcised? What if other countries denounced this practice as barbaric?

- Even though breast implants and liposuction are voluntary, are they more civilized than FGM/C in making women's bodies more acceptable to men?

WHY WE HAVE SEX

Since you asked . . .

- Why is our sexual behavior different in casual and committed relationships?

Sex, including the first experience of intercourse, doesn't "just happen." It typically progresses through a series of stages such as appro-aching, flirting, touching, or asking directly for sex. Although it may be passionate, first-time sex typically occurs after some planning and thought. Even among adolescents, most sexual behavior is not impulsive but usually involves reasoned action and considerations about the consequences (Sprecher and McKinney, 1993; Gillmore et al., 2002).

People have sex for pleasure and for procreation, but also to get rid of a headache, to celebrate a special occasion, to get a promotion, and to feel closer to God. After asking almost 2,000 college students why they have (or would have) sex, the researchers came up with 237 reasons that they grouped into four categories (see *Table 7.1*), and they found that many of the reasons were gendered. For example, men were more likely to use sex to gain status or enhance their reputation, whereas women were more likely to say that they wanted to express their love for a person. Overall, the researchers concluded that our motives for having sex are complex.

Sex the First Time

We also have different reasons for having sex the first time. The explanations range from interpersonal decisions to structural factors.

INTERPERSONAL REASONS For some people, sex is an expression of affection and a means of communication. The majority of first sexual relationships are with a romantic partner. In a national study of those ages 12 to 21, the 45 percent who had had sexual intercourse were romantically involved and progressed from activities such as holding hands and kissing to exchanging presents and touching a partner's genitals (O'Sullivan et al., 2007). Others experience physical arousal and follow their impulses or are simply curious about sex.

PEER PRESSURE At least 10 percent of girls who first have sex before age 15 describe it as unwanted. Among adolescents ages 15 to 17, 36 percent of males and 29 percent of females say that they were pressured to have sex—usually by male friends or boyfriends (Albert et al., 2003; Holt et al., 2003). A teenage boy might have sex so that he will no longer be teased and harassed about being a virgin or to quash rumors that he is gay (Pascoe, 2007).

If a boy is older, bigger, stronger, more popular, or more powerful than a girl, she may have trouble saying no, especially when drinking alcohol or using other drugs. In addition, one partner may feel obligated to have sex for fear of hurting the other's feelings or losing his or her interest (Abrahams and Ahlbrand, 2002).

PARENTAL INPUTS Parents, especially mothers, play a key role in promoting (although unintentionally) or discouraging first-time sex. Mothers are likely to delay their teenage daughters' first sexual experience if they disapprove of adolescent sex, have close relationships with their daughters, and frequently talk with the parents of their daughters' friends. Mothers have more influence on daughters than on sons, but boys who have close relationships with their mothers are also more likely to delay sexual intercourse (Davis and Friel, 2001; McNeely et al., 2002; Albert et al., 2003).

TABLE 7.1	Why People Have Sex	
Category	Reasons	Examples
Physical	Stress reduction, pleasure, physical desirability, and experience seeking	"The person had beautiful eyes" or "a desirable body," or "was a good kisser" or "too physically attractive to resist." Or "I wanted to achieve an orgasm."
Goal Attainment	Obtaining resources, social status, and revenge	"I wanted to even the score with a cheating partner" or "break up a rival's relationship" or "make money" or "be popular." Or "because of a bet."
Emotional	Love, commitment, and expression of feelings	"I wanted to communicate at a deeper level" or "lift my partner's spirits" or "say 'Thank you.'" Or just because "the person was intelligent."
Insecurity	Boosting one's self-esteem, duty, pressure, and guarding a mate from competitors	"I felt like it was my duty," "I wanted to boost my self-esteem," or "It was the only way my partner would spend time with me."

Source: Based on Meston and Buss, 2007.

STRUCTURAL FACTORS Structural factors also affect first-time sex. Teenagers are more likely to engage in sex at an early age if they experience family turbulence that includes parental conflict before or during a divorce, remarriage, and redivorce; if they live with single parents who are sexually active; in cohabiting households in which an adult does not have much authority; or in neighborhoods in which adults who are role models don't have steady jobs and bear children out of wedlock. In such situations, adolescents may disengage from their parents, looking to peers for emotional support, and thereby hasten their entry into sexual activity (Moore and Chase-Lansdale, 2001; Wu and Thompson, 2001; Upchurch et al., 2001).

Social institutions, especially religion, also affect first-time sex. As you'll see shortly, teens and young adults who say they are religious tend to postpone sexual activity even though it typically occurs before marriage.

Sex in Committed Relationships

Sex serves many functions in both short- and long-term relationships. In short-term relationships, sex can be an expression of love and affection. It can increase intimacy and a feeling of closeness that is emotional (expressing feelings), social (sharing friends), intellectual (sharing ideas), and recreational (sharing interests and hobbies). Sex can encourage self-disclosure, telling a partner about one's hopes and insecurities. It also involves an exchange of resources such as trading sex for status or attention (see Chapters 2, 6, and 10 on exchange theories).

All of these characteristics, plus several others, exist in long-term relationships. When a close bond continues over time, sexual and other physical expressions of intimacy maintain the relationship and foster interdependence because the partners rely on each other for sexual satisfaction. In addition, many people in long-term relationships have sex because they want children and plan to raise them together.

How Much Do We Know about Sex?

John Barrymore, the noted American actor, once said, "The thing that takes up the least amount of time and causes the most amount of trouble is sex." If sex causes a lot of trouble, it's probably because most people know very little about it.

How did you do on the quiz on page 166? According to some instructors, their students—like mine—usually get a C (especially if they're honest in reporting their scores). But even if you got a C, you know more about sex than most of your peers or even the average American adult (Reinisch and Beasley, 1990).

HOW INFORMED ARE ADOLESCENTS ABOUT SEX? A health educator who visits eighth graders says that although some of the children are sexually active, most don't know what sexually transmitted diseases are, how they can be prevented, when a girl can get pregnant, or how birth control works. Some teenage girls in Texas, under the mistaken belief that they got pregnant through oral sex, call their children "spit babies" (Reimer, 1999; Connolly, 2003). (*Appendix D* describes contraceptive methods.)

On the national level, a survey of 13-year-olds found that fewer than one-third were able to identify the most effective pregnancy prevention method (the pill), only two-thirds knew the most effective STI prevention method (condoms), and only 8 percent correctly identified the point in the female fertility cycle when pregnancy is most likely to occur (about 14 days before the start of menstruation). Among 14-years-olds in this study,

- 50 percent believed that it is illegal for youth under 16 to buy condoms (it's legal).

- 20 percent believed (incorrectly) that "you could tell if a person has HIV/AIDS by looking at him/her."

- 39 percent of the boys and 51 percent of the girls agreed with the statement "Most teens our age are having sex" (not true—see Data Digest) (Albert et al., 2003).

Moreover, although 75 percent of teenagers ages 15 to 17 have engaged in oral sex, 20 percent didn't know that oral sex can result in an STI (Holt et al., 2003).

HOW INFORMED ARE YOUNG ADULTS ABOUT SEX?
A number of college students also have information gaps about sex. Some believe, for example, that they cannot contract HIV if they are in monogamous relationships. In fact, being in a monogamous relationship with an infected partner can be fatal.

Nationally, young adults ages 18 to 24—especially those who are sexually active—have serious misconceptions about sex:

- 71 percent believe that birth control methods other than condoms provide safe sex.

- 60 percent don't know that STIs can cause some kinds of cancer.

- 50 percent don't know that one in four sexually active people under age 25 will get an STI during the year.

- 36 percent believe that oral sex cannot transmit STIs.

⁞• MAKING CONNECTIONS

- How would you describe your sexual scripts? Have they remained constant or changed over time? Do your sexual scripts—or those of your friends, partners, and children—reflect a sexual double standard?

- Thinking about yourself, your friends, or your children, why do people have sexual intercourse the first time? Or why have you or your friends remained virgins?

- Have you heard myths about sex from your friends, partners, or children?

- 20 percent believe that withdrawing the penis before ejaculation is a form of safe sex (Holt et al., 2003).

As this study shows, young people (and older people as well, as you'll see later in this chapter) often lack knowledge about core sexual issues and their impact on health. Why are many of us so misinformed?

WHO INFLUENCES OUR SEXUAL BEHAVIOR?

What we believe is normal sexual behavior is neither normal nor natural but is learned in a cultural context. Some societies, for example, view kissing as repulsive:

When the Thonga first saw Europeans kissing they laughed. . . . "Look at them—they eat each other's saliva and dirt." The Siriono never kiss, although they have no regulation against such behavior. The Tinguian, instead of kissing, place the lips near the partner's face and suddenly inhale (Ford and Beach, 1972: 49).

Regardless of the cultural context, people become sexual over time as they are exposed to different sources of information about sex and sexuality. The primary sources of information about anatomy, values, and sexual expression are parents, peers, siblings, religion, the media and popular culture, and sex education programs in schools.

From Parents

When reporters asked Charles Barkley, the former National Basketball Association star, how he'd handle his 12-year-old daughter's future boyfriends, he said, "I figure if I kill the first one, the word will get out." Although humorous, Barkley's statement reflects a fairly typical—but unrealistic—parental stance: "I'll make sure my kid won't have sex."

As you saw earlier, parents affect our sexual scripts by what they say (or don't say) about sex. Ideally, parents (or guardians) should be the first and best sex educators because they are experienced and have their children's interests at heart. However, as *Figure 7.1* shows, many adolescents and young adults are more likely to obtain information about sex from friends, the media, and sex education classes than from parents. Compared with other groups, black youth are the most likely to learn about sex from their parents (see *Figure 7.1*). This may reflect greater openness in discussing sex or greater concern, especially on the part of single mothers, that girls are often deceived by men who promise them marriage or a stable relationship (Hill, 2005).

A study of students ages 10 to 15 found that only 6 percent said they wanted to talk to their parents

FIGURE 7.1 How Do Young People Learn about Sex?

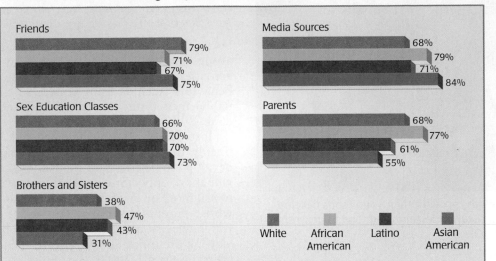

Source: Based on Holt et al., 2003, Table 30.

about sex and pregnancy. It wasn't clear whether the percentage was so low because the parents had already discussed such topics, whether the adolescents were too embarrassed to ask their parents about sex, or whether peers were the preferred sources of information (Richardson, 2004). Other reasons for not discussing sexuality range from parents not knowing (or wanting to know, sometimes) that their kids are sexually active to simply not wanting to talk about sex.

DO PARENTS KNOW THEIR CHILDREN ARE SEXUALLY ACTIVE? Only about one-third of parents of sexually active 14-year-olds know that their children have had or are having sex (Albert et al., 2003). The number of parents who are not aware that their older teens are sexually active is probably higher because 15- to 17-year-olds are almost twice as likely to talk to their friends than to their parents about birth control methods (Kaiser Family Foundation, 2004).

Teenagers may be reluctant to discuss sex with their parents because they don't want to disappoint, hurt, or shock them. Many teenagers believe that their parents see them in an unrealistically innocent light, and they don't want to tarnish this idealized image:

A 16-year-old girl: "They have so much faith and trust in me. It would just kill them if they found out I had made love before. There's a lot of pressure on me to be good since I'm the most successful of my brothers and sisters. They feel I'm a reflection of all their efforts and their ideal child" (Hass, 1979: 168).

The Hass research was published about three decades ago, but the reasons for parents' not knowing about

their children's sexual activities are similar today. For example, 83 percent of teenagers in one survey said that their peers "fool around" during coed sleepovers, even though many parents are confident that the teens obey clear rules such as no drinking, no drugs, and no sex. In another national study, 95 percent of college students who live on campus said that they participate in sexual activities they would not want their parents to know about (McCarroll, 2002; Society for Adolescent Medicine, 2004).

DO PARENTS TALK ABOUT SEX? Many parents are unsure of how to begin a conversation with their children about sex. They often feel unprepared to discuss important issues such as abstinence, contraception, and prevention of STIs. Some of this discomfort may reflect the fact that sex education programs were unavailable when they were youngsters and sexuality was deemed an inappropriate topic for discussion in the home. They are often opposed to comprehensive school-based sex education, but, compared with parents who endorse such education, they talk to their children in less depth about sex and are less likely to encourage questions, especially from children in elementary and middle school (Eastman et al., 2005; Byers et al., 2008).

Parents also worry that discussing both sex and birth control sends their children mixed messages. As one of my students said, "How does a parent provide information on birth control but also teach their children to 'just say no'?" There's no easy answer, but, as you'll see shortly, many sex educators maintain that teaching only abstinence is unrealistic because most teens engage in premarital sex.

Some parents may not want to talk about sex because they recognize that they don't practice what

Fathers who discuss sex with their young sons develop closer ties with their adolescents and tend to delay sexual intercourse.

they preach and are poor role models. They themselves may sleep around, have children out of wedlock, condone sleepovers that they suspect include sexual activity, and oversexualize 5- to 6-year-old girls by encouraging them to wear makeup and adultlike clothes (Haffner, 1999; Saltzman, 1999).

Recently, for example, some feminist scholars have been concerned about girls' Halloween costumes becoming more sexualized and targeted at younger ages than ever before. Some of the most popular costumes that parents bought for their 7- and 8-year-old daughters included sexy princess, nurse, and witch costumes, and even dressing up as prostitutes (Healy, 2008).

Nationwide, about 90 percent of parents and caregivers said that their 11- to 14-year-olds could be open with them in discussing sex, contraception, and pregnancy, but only 67 percents of these adolescents thought that their parents or caregivers would be comfortable with such discussions. Furthermore, only 41 percent of the children ages 11 to 14 said that their parents have had conversations with them about sex or birth control (Albert et al., 2003).

ARE PARENTAL DISCUSSIONS OF SEX EFFECTIVE? Many adolescents think their parents are old-fashioned. Instead of discussing the implications of sex, such as the long-term responsibilities involved in raising a child, parents often lapse into "adult-speak," telling them "Don't do it" or "Stay vertical."

According to one of my African American students, parent–child interaction is critical in discouraging early sexual activity:

When my niece was attending high school, her parents would communicate with her very frequently on issues relating to sex such as unwanted pregnancy, STI diseases including HIV and AIDS, and the roles and responsibilities of being a parent. My niece did

not have sex until she was 21 years old even though she was surrounded with teen female families and friends who were having sex (Author's files).

Such discussions—across all racial and ethnic groups—as well as parental supervision of teenagers' activities often result in postponing sex, safer sexual behaviors (such as using condoms), and fewer sexual partners (Hutchinson, 2002; Frisco, 2005; Jones et al., 2005).

Instead of having a single "big talk," parents who openly discuss sex topics more than once often develop closer ties with their adolescents and provide more opportunities for their maturing children to ask more or different questions. Also, adolescents whose parents disapprove of sex at a young age, watch television shows together, and limit television viewing are more likely to delay sexual intercourse (Bersamin et al., 2008; Martino et al., 2008).

These and similar findings show that parents can have considerable influence on their children's sexual behavior, but not all parents are knowledgeable about sex (see the box "How Much Do Parents Know about Sex?"). In fact, parental ignorance might increase their children's risky sex behavior.

From Peers and Siblings

Peers are among the most common sources of knowledge about sex, especially for white adolescents and young adults (see *Figure 7.1* on p. 175). Because peers typically are misinformed about sex, however, the instruction may be similar to the blind leading the blind. As you saw earlier, many adolescents know little about topics such as the proper use of condoms, women's fertile periods, and contraceptives.

Even though they aren't the best sources of information, peers can be helpful. Often they are more open than parents about discussing sex, offer support when a friend feels insecure about visible signs of maturing (such as the growth of breasts or facial hair), and encourage friends to seek information about birth control if parents are unwilling to talk about contraception (Gecas and Seff, 1991). College students who feel distant with their parents also cite friends as important sources of support and learning when they've regretted their sexual decision making, such as having unprotected sex or having sex with people they barely know (Allen et al., 2008).

Young people are least likely to learn about sex from their brothers and sisters (see *Figure 7.1* on page 175), but older siblings can play an important role in their younger siblings' sexuality. Older siblings may not tell their younger brothers and sisters to "just say no" to sex. But, especially if the children have close relationships and if the older kids supplement parental

Applying What You've Learned

How Much Do Parents Know about Sex?

Many parents insist that they, and not the schools, should teach their children about sex. But what if parents aren't as well informed as they think they are?

In a study of almost 1,100 parents of children ages 13 to 17 in Minnesota and Wisconsin, the researchers found that many parents didn't know as much about sex as they should (Eisenberg et al., 2004). For example,

- 55 percent said that condoms are "only somewhat effective" in preventing pregnancy. In fact, if used correctly and consistently, condoms can prevent pregnancy in 97 percent of all instances of sexual intercourse.

- 47 percent said that condoms are "somewhat effective" in preventing sexually transmitted infection. In fact, and if used correctly, condoms can prevent sexually transmitted infections in 98 percent to 100 percent of cases.

- 43 percent said that correct and consistent use of the pill is effective "most of the time" in preventing pregnancy. In fact, the pill is effective 99.9 percent of the time if used correctly.

Compared with Americans, the French have a reputation for a more open attitude about sex, and French children are bombarded even more than American children with sexual images in films, ads, songs, and on the Internet. Nonetheless, many French parents, like their American counterparts, are uncomfortable in discussing some topics, especially sexual intercourse.

To encourage parents to talk to their children about such sensitive topics, an exhibit at a science museum in Paris—aimed at 9- to 14-year-olds—uses popular children's comic strip characters and booths with headphones to illustrate and answer questions about sex and reproduction. For example, younger children get answers to questions such as "What does making love mean?" and "If a pregnant woman eats spinach, does the baby in her tummy taste it, too?" Teenagers can get answers to questions such as "I have one breast bigger than the other; is that normal?" or "What is masturbation?" Some parents have objected to the exhibit, but many support it, including a mural that details and explains the sexual act (Baum, 2008).

Stop and Think . . .

- Many parents don't have accurate information about the effectiveness of condoms and the pill. Is it just as well, then, that they don't discuss sex with their children?
- Should U.S. science museums set up exhibits, similar to the one in Paris, that teach children about sex?

information about sex, older siblings can play a beneficial role in advising their younger siblings, especially boys, to practice safer sex—for example, to use condoms (Kowal and Blinn-Pike, 2004).

From Religion

When sociologists and other social scientists study people's religious behavior, they measure *religiosity*, the way that people demonstrate their religious beliefs. The measures include how often people attend religious services, how involved they are in religious activities, and whether they think their religion actually influences their everyday decisions.

Religious parents who monitor their children's activities and have strong parent-child relationships tend to delay their children's sexual activity. However, parents with similar characteristics who are not highly religious can have the same effects, which suggests that parents with low levels of religiosity can still influence their children's sexual behavior (Manlove et al., 2008).

Except for a very small minority of evangelical college students who attend religious institutions, most college students keep religion and sex separate. Others redefine sex. For example, evangelical students who have had oral or anal sex still consider themselves virgins because they view such behaviors as not "real sex" (Freitas, 2008).

In one of the most comprehensive and methodologically rigorous national studies of American teenagers, sociologist Mark Regnerus (2007) concluded that although one might expect a powerful tie between religiosity and sexual behavior, this is rarely the case. Indeed, religion and sexuality interact in complex (and sometimes surprising) ways. For example, 80 percent of teenagers who identified as evangelical or born-again Christians said that sex should be saved for marriage, but they were more likely than their mainline Protestant, Jewish, or Catholic counterparts to lose their virginity and at an earlier age. There are several reasons for this seeming contradiction: When evangelical parents say they talk to their kids about sex, they usually mean morals, not the mechanics (such as unprotected sex); religion affects adolescents' sexual attitudes more than their actions; and it is difficult to resist temptations when steeped in the mass media's constant barrage of sexual images.

From the Media and Popular Culture

Many of us, especially young people, often obtain information about sex from the media and popular culture (see *Figure 7.1* on p. 175). Television, movies, music, magazines, romance novels, the Internet, and, sometimes, pornographic materials are powerful sources of information—or misinformation—about sex.

MAGAZINES You don't have to go to adult bookstores to find magazines that sell sex. *Playboy, Penthouse, Hustler,* and other magazines for men are sold openly at drugstores, newsstands, and many discount stores. According to some critics, magazines such as *Men's Health* and *Men's Fitness* are more about sex than about physical health (Kuczynski, 2001).

Many women's magazines also sell sex. Nearly every article and ad in *Cosmopolitan* is about sex. *Redbook* and *Mademoiselle* also have a heavy dose of articles about sex (e.g., "35 sexy new ways to touch your man"). Even magazines that target young teenage and preteen girls, such as *YM,* often have sex-related articles ("Look summer sexy") (King, 2002; see, also, Chapter 5).

MOVIES Rating systems are not strictly enforced (few moviegoers are stopped from seeing R-rated films, for example), and X-rated videos are accessible to people in most age groups. Also, film ratings have become more lenient. Since 1992, many films that were rated PG-13 ("Parents strongly cautioned") are now rated PG ("Parental guidance suggested"). This "ratings creep" has increased the likelihood that adolescents and even young children learn about sex from movies (Thompson and Yokota, 2004).

Because marital sex is rarely portrayed, movies give the impression that only sexual activities outside of marriage are common or enjoyable. Also, the emphasis on casual sex sends the message that there is no connection between sex and commitment (Brown et al., 2002).

TELEVISION Sex is a staple on most television shows, ranging from 28 percent of reality shows to 96 percent of soap operas (Kunkel et al., 2003). *How* and *how much* sex is portrayed on television has changed. Today, 70 percent of all shows contain some sexual content, up from 56 percent in 1998. Shows that depict sexual intercourse have also increased— from 7 percent in 1998 to 11 percent in 2005 (Kunkel et al., 2005).

Does sex-saturated TV content affect behavior? A national study of 12- to 17-year-olds found that the 10 percent of adolescents who watched the most sexually related content were twice as likely to engage in sexual intercourse a year later as were those who saw the least amount of sexual content (Kunkel et al., 2005). Another national study that tracked 12- to 17-year-olds for three years found that those who viewed the most sexual content on TV were more than twice as likely to become pregnant or father an out-of-wedlock baby as were teens who watched very little (12 percent vs. 5 percent) (Chandry et al., 2008).

Such studies haven't established a causal relationship because it may be that adolescents who are most interested in becoming sexually active are also most likely to watch sexually explicit TV shows. Nevertheless, nearly three out of four teens ages 15 to 17 say that viewing sex on TV influences the sexual behavior of kids their age (Collins, 2005).

THE INTERNET Among parents with children age 9 or older who use the Internet at home, almost 60 percent do not use controls to block access to Websites, and 61 percent never look in a child's e-mail inbox (Rideout, 2007). Thus, most parents are surprisingly confident that their children, including preteens and young teens, are not exposed to unwanted sexual or other information.

As access to the Internet expands, more and more young people are turning to the Web as a source of health information. The Children's Internet Protection Act of 2000 requires that schools and libraries

Television programs rarely portray the negative aspects of casual or unprotected sex, which can result in STIs or unwanted pregnancies, but television can also be a positive force in providing sexual information. One episode of *Grey's Anatomy* presented a key fact—that an HIV positive woman who gets the proper treatment has more than a 90 percent chance of having a healthy baby. The proportion of viewers who were aware of this fact quadrupled, from 15 percent before the show to 61 percent after it aired (Rideout, 2008).

use Web-browsing filters to block pornographic content or risk losing federal funds. Nationally, from 23 percent to 60 percent of the blocked sites include medically accurate information about herpes, birth control, safer sex, and gay health. The barred sites also include information about women's health and STIs maintained by medical journals and government agencies. Thus, filtering products often prevent adolescents from accessing important information from these sites (Richardson et al., 2002; Rideout et al., 2002).

From Sex Education

As you've seen, many parents do *not* teach their children about sex, and the media and popular culture deluge people with unrealistic portrayals of sexuality. Consequently, many schools and community groups have assumed responsibility for teaching children and adolescents about sex.

Since you asked . . .

Should parents or schools be responsible for sex education?

About 90 percent of parents approve of schools' providing a *comprehensive sexuality education* (CSE) that includes teaching about abstinence but also provides medically accurate information about condoms and other contraceptives. Even though only 10 percent of parents want an abstinence-only curriculum in public schools, this is what 27 states teach (Eisenberg et al., 2008; Boonstra, 2009). President Obama plans to eliminate most money for abstinence-only sex education and shift the funds to teen pregnancy prevention programs.

A major reason for this is that in 2001 the Bush administration established a federal program to fund abstinence-only curricula, which has cost more than $1 billion so far. Abstinence-only proponents argue that "Just say no" programs to delay sex until marriage work. When abstinence-only education programs evaluate their own effectiveness, the results are always positive. According to critics, however, much of the research does not meet basic requirements of scientific rigor, such as using a control group, and looks at attitudes and intentions rather than behavior (Beil, 2008; Crosse, 2008).

A number of recent and nationally representative studies show that abstinence-only programs don't work. For example,

- Many teens are already sexually active, and 88 percent of middle and high school students who pledge to remain virgins until marriage end up having premarital sex anyway (Brückner and Bearman, 2005; Fortenberry, 2005).

- Among students in grades 7 through 12, almost half of those who had reported taking a virginity pledge denied having done so a year later and most were sexually active (Rosenbaum, 2006).

- Among 15- to 19-years-olds, abstinence-only education did not reduce the likelihood of engaging in premarital intercourse; those who received a CSE program had a lower risk of pregnancy because of condom usage (Kohler et al., 2008).

- A longitudinal study that evaluated four promising abstinence-only and CSE programs in grades 3 through 8 found that kids in abstinence-only programs were no more likely to abstain from sex than those in CSE programs, had similar numbers of sexual partners, and initiated sex at the same age, and that youth in both groups got only about half of the answers correct on understanding the health consequences of contracting sexually transmitted infections (Trenholm et al., 2008).

- A review of 56 studies that evaluated abstinence-only and CSE programs found that most abstinence-only programs did not delay initiation of sex; two-thirds of the CSE programs both delayed young people's initiation of sex and increased condom and contraceptive use (Kirby, 2008).

It's also not clear why many of the abstinence-only groups oppose giving teenagers information about condoms and birth control. If teens are *really* going to abstain from sex until marriage, why should CSE curricula change their behavior? Also, as some researchers point out, promoting abstinence until marriage ignores the fact that since the 1950s, about

This teacher is talking to ninth graders about STIs and contraception. Do you think teachers should provide this information? Or should parents be responsible for educating their children about sexuality?

90 percent of Americans have engaged in premarital sex and that it's unrealistic to expect never married women in their 30s and 40s to remain virgins (Lindberg and Singh, 2008).

Which sex education programs are most effective? They are those that are comprehensive, present information on reproductive systems, emphasize abstinence but also discuss condoms and other birth control methods, begin in elementary school before adolescents engage in intercourse, and target high-risk groups such as African American youth who live in poor neighborhoods (Mueller et al., 2008; Sullivan, 2009).

Some scholars propose that teaching about sexuality is the responsibility of both parents and schools, but in different ways: "Parents should play the primary role in imparting to their children social, cultural, and religious values regarding intimate and sexual relationships, whereas health education professionals should play the primary role in providing information about sexuality and developing related social skills," and that both groups should support each other in teaching responsible sexual conduct to adolescents (Shtarkshall et al., 2007: 117–18).

MAKING CONNECTIONS

- Were there any experiences in your home life when you were growing up that influenced your sexual behavior or sexual decision making?

- What kind of sex education classes, if any, did you have in elementary, middle, and high school? Did the classes influence your behavior?

- Do you think it's realistic to expect abstinence-only and CSE parents to work together in fostering adolescents' sexual literacy and behavior? Why or why not?

SEXUAL BEHAVIORS

Many of us have fairly conventional sex lives. For example, most U.S. adults have one or no sex partners during any given year (see *Figure 7.2*). Keep in mind that sex is not just sexual intercourse; it also encompasses many other behaviors, including flirting, kissing, autoeroticism, and oral and anal sex.

Flirting

Flirting, or acting amorously, is usually one of the first steps to capture another person's attention. Whether flirting is nonverbal (such as sustained eye

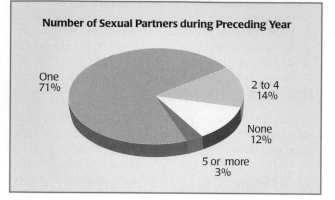

FIGURE 7.2 Sex is Largely Monogamous
This nationwide U.S. survey of sexual behavior is now more than a decade old, but the data are still considered the most authoritative available. These findings surprised many people. Why do you think this was the case?

Number of Sexual Partners during Preceding Year

One 71%
2 to 4 14%
None 12%
5 or more 3%

Source: Based on Laumann et al., 1994: 177–80; 369.

contact) or verbal (such as whispering "You're hot!" into someone's ear), it signals sexual interest.

One of the problems with flirting is that the messages may be mistaken for friendliness. Especially in the case of nonverbal cues, men are more likely than women to mistake being friendly as flirting, which sometimes results in men's sexual coercion of women (Haselton, 2003; Farris et al., 2008).

Increasingly, however, female teens (ages 13 to 19) and young adult women (ages 20 to 26) see sending nude or semi-nude pictures of themselves to men on cell phones or the Internet with whom they want to hook up or date as "only flirting," and they assume that the photos are private. Instead, at least 20 percent of the recipients have forwarded the photos to people whom the sender doesn't know (The National Campaign to Prevent. . . , 2008).

Kissing

In some parts of India, public kissing brings a $12 fine because it is considered a "highly erotic act" that couples shouldn't experience until they're married and it reflects permissive Western cultural norms about sexual behavior. A city mayor in central Mexico had to retract an edict, after numerous protests, that violators of a public-kissing ban would be punished (Sappenfield, 2007; Ellingwood, 2009).

In the United States, in contrast, public kissing is acceptable (or at least tolerated) in public spaces such as stores, restaurants, classrooms, or on the street. Thus, unlike some other societies, Americans see kissing in public as perhaps in bad taste but normal in expressing one's sexuality.

Autoeroticism

Autoeroticism refers to arousal of sexual feeling without an external stimulus. Two of the most common forms of autoeroticism are sexual fantasies and masturbation.

SEXUAL FANTASIES Most of us, but men more than women, have *sexual fantasies,* mental images of sexual activities. Sexual fantasies often mirror gender roles (see Chapter 5). Women's fantasies, for example, are typically romantic, passive, and submissive. Men are more likely to fantasize about a large number of partners and encounters that won't lead to a relationship (Battan, 1992; Geer and Manguno-Mire, 1996).

Sexual fantasies are emotionally and psychologically healthy. They can provide a safety valve for pent-up feelings or a harmless escape from boring, everyday routines: "to be covered in whipped cream and wrestle my lover, then the loser has to lick it off" or "having sex on the 50-yard line at a sold-out football game" (Patterson and Kim, 1991: 79).

Fantasies can also boost our self-image because we don't have to worry about penis or breast size, physical attractiveness, height, or weight. Because we have total control in producing and directing the fantasy, we can change or stop it whenever we want (Masters et al., 1992).

MASTURBATION When asked about what sex would be like in the future, comedian Robin Williams said: "It's going to be you—and you." **Masturbation** is sexual self-pleasuring that involves some form of direct physical stimulation. It may or may not result in orgasm, but it typically includes rubbing, stroking, fondling, squeezing, or otherwise stimulating the genitals. It can also involve self-stimulation of other body parts, such as the breasts, the inner thighs, or the anus.

Since you asked . . .

• Is masturbation abnormal?

Masturbation often begins in childhood and continues throughout life. Prepubertal children may stimulate themselves without realizing that what they are doing is sexual. For example, one girl learned when she was 8 years old that she could produce an "absolutely terrific feeling" by squeezing her thighs together (Nass et al., 1981). Thus, many children discover masturbation accidentally.

More than three times as many men as women report masturbating at least once a week. Black men (60 percent) are twice as likely as whites, Latinos, and Asians to say that they have never masturbated (Laumann et al., 1994). It's not clear whether masturbation rates among African American men are lower than among other groups because black men have traditionally viewed masturbation as an admission of inability to seduce women or whether this activity reflects only men in lower socioeconomic groups (Belcastro, 1985; Timberlake and Carpenter, 1990).

Like sexual fantasies, masturbation fulfills several needs: It can relieve sexual tension, provide a safe means of sexual experimentation (avoiding disease and unwanted pregnancy), and ultimately transfer learning about one's sexuality to two-person love-making. Masturbation can be as sexually satisfying as intercourse, and it does not hinder the development of social relationships during young adulthood or create problems in a marriage (Leitenberg et al., 1993; Kelly, 1994).

Oral and Anal Sex

In 1998, President Clinton wagged his finger at the television audience and proclaimed, "I want to say one thing to the American people. . . . I did not have sexual relations with that woman, Miss Lewinsky. . . . Never. These allegations are false." It turned out, however, that Monica Lewinsky (a White House intern) and former President Clinton routinely had oral sex.

Like many teenagers and college students, President Clinton apparently defined oral sex as not *really* sex. Some writers call this behavior "outercourse," a way of rationalizing sexual behavior because it's "almost sex" and an alternative to sexual intercourse (Harvey and Weber, 2002; Kamen, 2002).

Oral sex includes several types of stimulation. **Fellatio** (from the Latin word for "suck") is oral stimulation of a man's penis. **Cunnilingus** (from the Latin words for "vulva" and "tongue") is oral stimulation of a woman's genitals. Fellatio and cunnilingus can be performed singly or simultaneously. Simultaneous oral sex is sometimes called "69," indicating the physical positions of the partners. *Anal sex* is the manual stimulation of the rectum that involves inserting a penis, finger, dildo (penis-shaped object), or vibrator.

Over half of males (55 percent) and females (54 percent) ages 15 to 19 report having had oral sex with someone of the opposite sex; 24 percent of males and 22 percent of females in this age group have had oral sex but not vaginal intercourse. Approximately 10 percent of both males and females have engaged in anal sex with someone of the opposite sex, and about 5 percent of males have had oral or anal sex with a male. Both oral and anal sex are much more common among teens who have already had vaginal intercourse than among those who have not, suggesting that teens initiate a range of sexual activities around the same time, rather than substituting one for another (Kaiser Family Foundation, 2008; Lindberg et al., 2008). By age 44, most people have had vaginal intercourse, but 90 percent of men and 88 percent of women have experienced oral sex (see *Figure 7.3*).

Some people find oral and anal sex pleasurable or engage in it to please their partner. Others complain about the odors (although bathing solves the problem for both sexes), do not enjoy it, or find it revolting. According to a female college student, for example, oral sex is like "blowing your nose in my mouth" (Wade and Cirese, 1991: 334). Some people believe that the anus is dirty or unappealing, but anal sex can be pleasurable because the anus has a lot of sensitive nerve endings (Hock, 2007).

Oral and anal sex, like other sexual behaviors, depends on personal preference. Many people don't realize, however, that sexual diseases can be transmitted orally and anally, resulting in syphilis, gonorrhea, and herpes, as well as the papilloma virus, which can cause cervical cancer (Halpern et al., 2000; Schvaneveldt et al., 2001).

Sexual Intercourse

Most people assume that sexual intercourse refers to heterosexual, vaginal-penile penetration, but the term applies to any sort of sexual coupling, including oral and anal. *Coitus* specifically means penile-vaginal intercourse. Unless noted otherwise, we will use *sexual intercourse* to refer to coitus.

VARIATIONS BY AGE AND MARITAL STATUS Some adolescents begin to be sexually active in their early teens. On average, however, the first heterosexual intercourse takes place between the ages of 16 and 17 for both sexes (see Data Digest). The frequency of

sexual intercourse peaks between ages 25 and 34 and then declines over the years. Over time, as you'll see shortly, people develop other priorities such as providing for a family or working at least 60 hours a week to keep a job or be promoted (see Chapter 13).

Married couples and cohabitants have much higher rates of sexual intercourse than single people. For example, about 25 percent of singles, compared with only 11 percent of married people have sexual intercourse only a few times a year (Laumann et al., 1994). Such figures challenge popular perceptions of "swinging singles." Having an easily accessible partner, such as in marriage or cohabitation, seems to have the largest impact on the frequency of sexual activity.

SEX AND THE GENDER GAP Overall, women report an average of six sex partners in their lifetimes, compared with 20 for men. That is, men have more than three times as many sex partners as do women (see *Figure 7.4*). Only 34 percent of women, compared with 70 percent of men, say that they think about sex every day. And although women express satisfaction with their sex lives, only 59 percent say that they enjoy sex "a great deal," compared with 83 percent of men (Langer et al., 2004).

These differences are probably due to gender roles. Women are more likely than men to be balancing jobs and domestic responsibilities and therefore have less time to think about and enjoy sex (see Chapter 5). Also, traditional male sexual scripts focus on sex as recreational, whereas traditional female sexual scripts focus on feelings, emotions, and commitment. Our sexual scripts have become more egalitarian, but many people still follow the traditional ones. As comedian Jay Leno quipped, "According to

FIGURE 7.3 Types of Sexual Contact

Percentage of U.S. males and females ages 25 to 44 years who have had each type of sexual contact, 2002.

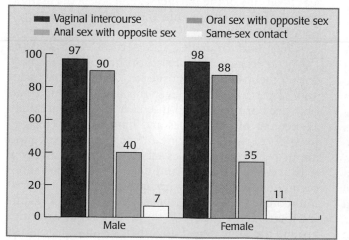

Source: Adapted from Mosher et al., 2005, Figure 4.

FIGURE 7.4 Over a Lifetime, Men Have More Sex Partners than Women

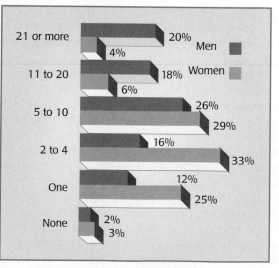

Source: Based on Langer et al., 2004, p. 4.

a new survey, 76 percent of men would rather watch a football game than have sex. My question is, why do we have to choose? Why do you think they invented halftime?"

SOME MYTHS ABOUT SEX AND SEXUAL RESPONSE

Fantasies, sounds, smells, touch, sexy pictures, dreams, hearing the person we love say "I love you," and a variety of other stimuli can arouse our sexual feelings. Our **sexual response** is our physiological reaction to sexual stimulation. Sexual response can vary greatly by age, gender, and health. Despite these variations, there are a number of myths about sex and sexual response that many people believe:

- *"Withdrawal is an effective birth control method."* In males, the first responses to sexual stimulation are swelling and erection of the penis. The penis may emit several drops of fluid that are not semen but may contain sperm cells. If this fluid is discharged while the penis is in the vagina, the woman can be impregnated. Thus, withdrawal before ejaculation can still result in a pregnancy.

- *"Erections, ejaculations, and orgasms are connected."* Penile erections, ejaculations, and orgasms do not occur simultaneously because they are affected by different neurological and vascular systems. Thus, men who argue that a penile erection must be followed by ejaculation during sexual intercourse lest they suffer dire consequences ("blue balls") are, quite simply, wrong. There is no evidence that any man has ever died of a "terminal erection." Many partners are fully satisfied by tender sexual activities that do not necessarily include orgasm.

- *"The bigger the penis, the better the sex."* One of some men's biggest concerns is that their penis isn't big enough to stimulate women during intercourse (Reinisch and Beasley, 1990). There is no association between clitoris, breast, or penis size and orgasm. Similarly, there is no evidence for the belief that compared with white men, African American men have larger penises, greater sexual capacity, or an insatiable sexual appetite (although some of my black male students would like to think so).

- *"We can always tell if a partner has had an orgasm."* Except in the movies, women's orgasms are rarely accompanied by asthmatic breathing and clutching of the bedposts. Orgasm can be explosive or mild, depending on a woman's emotional or physical state, stress, alcohol consumption, and a variety of other factors. Nearly half of women and 11 percent of men say that they have faked orgasms, mainly to please their partner or to "get done" (Langer et al., 2004).

- *"An orgasm is necessary for good sex."* Some marriage manuals promote simultaneous orgasm (both partners experiencing orgasm at the same time) as the ultimate in sexual pleasure. Many people try to fine tune the timing of their responses, but working so hard at sex becomes a chore rather than a satisfying experience. Simultaneous orgasm can be exhilarating, but so can independent orgasms. An estimated 5 to 10 percent of women never experience an orgasm yet enjoy sex throughout the life course (Lloyd, 2005).

SEXUALITY THROUGHOUT LIFE

We may love dozens of people over our lifetime, but we usually have sex with very few of them (see *Figure 7.4* on p. 182). We might also have sex with people whom we don't love. There can be many sexual relationships during the life course, and a diversity of sexual unions. There is also another option: abstinence.

Virginity and Abstinence

A *virgin* is someone who has never experienced sexual intercourse. Nearly half (48 percent) of all American high school students reported ever having had sexual intercourse, a decline from 54 percent in 1991 (Eaton et al., 2008). There are numerous factors for early sexual intercourse among adolescents (see *Table 7.2*). But why are some teens with similar characteristics more likely to abstain than others? Also, why do many adults go without sex?

WHY TEENS ABSTAIN FROM SEXUAL INTERCOURSE

There are several possible explanations for the decline of teen sexual intercourse since the early 1990s. First, some credit the abstinence movement, especially religious and medical groups that advocate chastity for either moral or health reasons. Since 1993, numerous church groups have encouraged kids to publicly sign chastity-until-marriage pledges. The government spends more than $200 million annually on abstinence-promotion programs, including virginity pledges, but do they work?

Since you asked . . .
- Should adolescents take abstinence pledges?

Several national studies have found that abstinence pledges delay intercourse, especially among young teens, but that pledgers are just as likely as nonpledgers to report premarital intercourse, and that between 82 percent and 88 percent of pledgers

TABLE 7.2	Factors Related to Early Sexual Intercourse among Adolescents

- Alcohol or other drug use
- Delinquent behavior
- Dating before age 16 or involvement in a committed relationship
- Having a low grade point average or dropping out of school
- Frequent moves that divert parental attention and decrease parental supervision; adolescents' use of sex to establish new friendships or combat loneliness
- Parental divorce during adolescence
- Poverty
- Physical or sexual abuse at home or by relatives
- Minimal parental monitoring of teens' activities and friends
- Permissive parental values toward sex, including a parent who cohabits or sleeps with overnight guests
- Lack of neighborhood monitoring of adolescents, especially teens

During a purity ball, girls as young as four promise their dads to remain virgins and fathers vow to protect their daughters' chastity until marriage. There were 4,000 such events in 2007 (Gibbs, 2008). Why aren't there purity balls or similar events for boys?

who have sexual intercourse deny having taken a pledge. When pledgers break their promise, they are less likely than nonpledgers to use contraceptives because abstinence-only programs foster negative attitudes about birth control. Also, rates of sexually transmitted disease are similar for pledgers and non-pledgers ages 18 to 24 (Brückner and Bearman, 2005; Rosenbaum, 2009; Thomas, 2009).

Second, and as you've already seen, many teenagers now substitute "outercourse," including oral and anal sex, for sexual intercourse. About 89 percent of adolescents agree that someone who has had vaginal-penile intercourse is not an abstainer, but almost half believe that a wide range of other sexual behaviors—including genital touching and oral and anal sex—aren't "really sex," and don't violate their morals or religious views about abstaining from sex until marriage (Bersamin et al., 2007; Masters et al., 2008). In effect, then, most adolescents are sexual but have changed their definition of sex to justify their behavior.

Third, family dynamics—such as child-parent connectedness and good communication—may delay sexual initiation. As you saw earlier, regardless of religiosity, parents who monitor their children's activities and have strong parent-child relationships can delay their children's first sexual intercourse.

WHY ADULTS ABSTAIN FROM SEXUAL INTERCOURSE Major reasons for adult abstinence include not having a partner, chronic illness, mental health problems, sexual dysfunctions, and a partner's infidelity. From a social exchange perspective, many partners remain in celibate relationships because companionship, love, and friendship outweigh the lack of sexual activity (Donnelly and Burgess, 2008). Unlike food, sleep, and shelter, sex is not necessary for physical survival. Sexual relationships can certainly be satisfying and rewarding, but neither virginity nor abstinence is fatal.

Sex and Adolescents

The first sexual experience can be happy and satisfying. It can also be a source of worry, disappointment, or guilt:

My first time was very unpleasant. The boy I was with rushed and fumbled around and then came so fast it was over before it started. I thought, "What's so great about this?" For weeks afterward, I was afraid I had V.D. [venereal disease] and had bad dreams about it (Masters et al., 1992: 226).

In England and Scotland—countries that are similar to the United States in many ways—almost three-quarters of 13- to 16-year-olds evaluated their early sexual experiences positively, but 19 percent of the girls and 10 percent of the boys felt pressure to have sex the first time and did not enjoy it. Also, 38 percent of the females and 20 percent of the males wished they had postponed their first sexual intercourse until they were older (Wight et al., 2008).

Many adolescents have sexual intercourse before they understand sexual anatomy and contraception or develop sexual values. By the ninth grade, 27 percent of girls and 38 percent of boys have had sexual intercourse. By the twelfth grade, 65 percent of all high school students have done so, and 23 percent have had four or more sex partners (Eaton et al., 2008). The rates are higher for black and Latino adolescents than for their white counterparts, and for boys than girls (see *Figure 7.5*).

REASONS FOR ADOLESCENT SEX "Raging hormones," the old explanation for adolescent sex, is more fiction than fact. Adolescents who mature early are likely to become sexually active at a younger age than

FIGURE 7.5 Sexually Experienced Teens, 2007

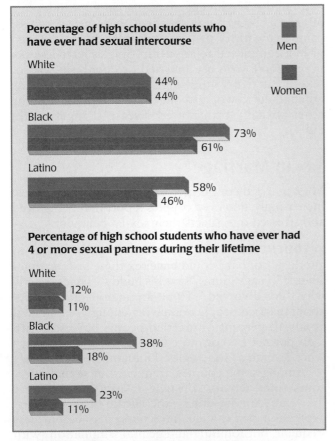

Source: Based on Eaton et al., 2008, Tables 61 and 63.

their later-maturing peers, but young people's interest in sex is affected by a variety of factors.

For young girls, sex still occurs most often in the context of close, romantic relationships. For example, 75 percent of girls ages 15 to 19 had their first sexual experience with someone with whom they were going steady (Abma et al., 2004). There are no comparable national data for men, but some studies suggest that young males are more casual about sex and may go steady to get sex (see Chapter 7).

One reason for early premarital sex, you recall, especially for boys, is *peer pressure. Parental factors* also play an important role in whether a teen engages in early premarital sex. As you saw earlier, young teens (those between ages 14 and 16) are less likely to engage in sexual intercourse and have fewer partners if their mothers, in particular, monitor their activities, maintain good communication, and have strict attitudes about adolescent sex.

Parental monitoring doesn't guarantee abstinence, however. One-third of 12-year-olds, for example, have attended a party with no adults in the house. By age 14, this percentage increased to 51 percent for boys and 42 percent for girls. In about half of the sexual encounters, an adult was at home during the party (Albert et al., 2003). Thus, teens were often having sex at home, just down the hall from a parent.

Environmental variables also influence how early sexual intercourse occurs. Teens who are more likely to engage in sexual activities are those who live in single-parent or remarried families, have more opportunities for sex (as in steady dating), associate with delinquent peers, use alcohol and other drugs, or have been sexually abused (see *Table 7.2* on p. 184).

Cultural attitudes and expectations also influence teens' sexual experiences. Young Latinos, for instance, are much more likely than Latinas to report that they've had sexual intercourse and that they've had more partners (see *Figure 7.5*). The double standard that we discussed earlier in this chapter and in Chapters 5 and 6 probably explains some of the gender differences.

Two concepts that are common in Latin American cultures promote female premarital abstinence: *verguenza* (shame), which connotes embarrassment about body parts and the notion that good girls should not know about sexuality, and *marianismo* (from the name of the Virgin Mary), which reflects values related to chastity, purity, and virtue. If young Latinas endorse these cultural values, they are likely to delay sexual activity (Liebowitz et al., 1999). As immigrants become assimilated into U.S. culture, their children often internalize peer values and behaviors that encourage early sexual intercourse (see Chapters 4 and 12).

FORCED SEXUAL INTERCOURSE Nationwide, 11 percent of female and 5 percent of male high school students say that they have had sex when they did not want to. Black and Latino students (11 percent and 9 percent, respectively) are more likely than white students (7 percent) to have been forced to have sexual intercourse. About 18 percent of those whose first sex occurred at age 14 or younger say that it was involuntary (Abma et al., 2004; Eaton et al., 2008).

For young girls, the most common factors associated with unwanted sex include the mother's having an abusive boyfriend, illicit drug use (by the parent, the victim, or a nonparental abuser), lack of parental monitoring in the home, a history of sexual abuse in the victim's family, and the victim's living apart from her parents before age 16. Adolescent boys report unwanted sexual touching (kissing, petting, fondling) and a romantic partner's threatening to withhold love (Small and Kerns, 1993; Christopher and Kisler, 2004).

Sex and Singles

Women and men are staying single longer for a variety of reasons—higher education, military service, and careers. Postponing marriage increases the likelihood of premarital sex. Divorced and widowed individuals may find a new sexual partner whom they may or may not marry (see Chapter 8). Premarital sex isn't limited to Western nations. For example, in 2005, 70 percent of Beijing residents said that they had sexual relations before marriage, compared with just 16 percent in 1989 (Beech, 2005).

WHO INITIATES SEXUAL CONTACT? Traditional sexual scripts dictate that the man should initiate sexual contact because "nice girls don't." But many young women frequent singles bars and clubs or call, e-mail, or text message men on cell phones. They also invite sexual contact in other ways, such as going to a man's apartment or dorm room. In steady dating relationships, women may touch or stroke a partner or make sensuous comments about his appearance to arouse him (O'Sullivan and Byers, 1993).

Many young women rationalize sexual intercourse in the same way that earlier generations justified petting ("It's O.K. if I love him"). The growing number of women who have casual sex when "hookin' up," however, suggests that these traditional views are changing, especially in the case of "friends with benefits" who have casual sex (see Chapter 8).

WILL YOU STILL LOVE ME TOMORROW? Maybe. Young adults, especially women, view casual sex less favorably than they did a generation ago. In 1980, for example, 50 percent of first-year college students said that "if two people really like each other, it's all right for them to have sex even if they've known each other for a short time." In 2005, 45 percent of first-year college students (58 percent of the men and 34 percent of the women) agreed with this statement (*Chronicle of Higher Education*, 2006: 19).

And will you respect me tomorrow? Not if we're having casual sex, according to some researchers. Many men still have a double standard. They often judge sexually permissive women as terrific for casual dates or as regular sexual partners but unacceptable for long-term commitments or as marriage partners (see Chapter 8).

Stereotypes and double standards are more common in some social contexts than in others. Many women consume alcohol both in private (parties, dates) and public (sporting events). In bars, many men perceive women drinkers as "loose" and "sexually easy," especially if they dress in a "provocative" manner. As one man said, appearance increases the risk of aggression: "Some girls whose boobs are hanging out, skirts up to here, no underwear on, you know something's going to happen" (Parks and Scheidt, 2000: 936). In contrast, men feel free to dress and act any way they want without being labeled as loose.

ARE SINGLES HAPPY WITH THEIR SEX LIVES? Nationally, 53 percent of young singles (under age 30) report being "very satisfied" with their sex lives, compared with 77 percent of people who are married or in a committed relationship. Singles have less sex than people who are married or cohabiting. Also, sexually active young singles are twice as likely as other adults to worry about contracting HIV or some other sexually transmitted disease (Langer et al., 2004).

Sex in Marriage

Most married couples are happy with their sex lives. Increasingly, however, couples report that being tired and stressed out affects their sexual behavior.

FREQUENCY OF SEX "I got married," says one guy to another, "so that I could have sex three or four times a week." That's funny," says his buddy. "That's exactly why I got divorced." There are many similar jokes about married people not having enough sex. In fact, about 40 percent of married people have sex with their partner two or more times a week, a rate that's twice as high as for singles (Laumann et al., 1994).

Among some couples, frequency of sexual intercourse may remain constant or even increase over the years. Among others, the nature of their sexual expression may change: Intercourse may become less frequent, but fondling and genital stimulation (with

By permission of Dave Coverly and Creators Syndicate, Inc.

or without orgasm) may increase. Overall, the frequency of marital sex typically decreases over time. As a marriage matures, concerns about earning a living, making a home, and raising a family become more pressing than the desire for lovemaking.

Consciously or not, some married women, especially mothers, avoid sex because they're angry:

Mad that he would never think to pick up diapers or milk on his way home . . . He doesn't help around the house enough or with the kids. He sees the groceries sitting on the counter. Why doesn't he take them out of the bag and put them away? (Deveny, 2003: 45, 46).

In most cases, marital sex decreases in frequency because couples are overworked, are anxious about the economy, and devote much of their time to raising kids. About 53 percent of adults say that everyday fatigue has sapped their sex lives (ConsumerReports.org, 2009).

QUALITY OF SEX The frequency of sex decreases, but the longer people are married, the more likely they are to report that they are very satisfied with their sex lives. Sex is especially satisfying if both spouses believe—in terms of exchange theory—that their rewards and costs are similar and that they have a mutually satisfying emotional relationship (Lawrance and Byers, 1995; Waite and Joyner, 2001). Such findings support the idea, discussed in Chapter 6, that sexual intercourse is more than just the sexual act—it also involves intimacy, commitment, and love.

The false notion that most married couples have unhappy sex lives has become big business. We have become so obsessed with this subject that sex manuals are constantly on best-seller lists. For example, one writer insists that having sex about once a month is synonymous with a "sexless" or "sex-starved" marriage (Weiner-Davis, 2003).

Newsmagazines and pharmaceutical companies are fanning such opinions to increase sales. Less frequent marital sex is neither unusual nor abnormal. Even young married couples report that companionship is often more important than sexual passion. As one man stated,

On my list [sex] would come fourth. Marriage, as far as I'm concerned, is friendship and companionship; that ranks first. Then there's consideration for one another, and then trust, and then fourth I'd say your physical relationship. And those three that come before hopefully enhance what you experience in your physical relationship (Greenblatt, 1983: 298).

Sex during the Middle Years

As we mature, our sexual interests, abilities, and responses change. Although a majority of adults ages 45 and older agree that a satisfying sexual relationship is important, it's not their top priority. Good health, close ties with friends and family, financial security, spiritual well-being, and a good relationship with a partner are all rated as more crucial than a fulfilling sexual connection (Jacoby, 2005). Our priorities shift, in part, because of the physiological changes that accompany aging.

MENOPAUSE Early in the twentieth century, many women died, often in childbirth, long before they experienced **menopause,** the cessation of the menstrual cycle and the loss of reproductive capacity, or "the change of life," as it was once called. *Perimenopause,* also a normal phenomenon, usually precedes menopause. Menopause typically begins in a woman's mid-40s to early 50s, but perimenopause can begin in the early 40s and last four to five years.

The symptoms of both perimenopause and menopause include hormonally induced hot flashes (a sudden experience of overall bodily heat, sometimes accompanied by sweating), irregular menstrual cycles with uncharacteristically heavy or light bleeding, mood changes, fatigue, migraine headaches, backaches, insomnia, loss or increase of appetite, diarrhea or constipation, and urinary incontinence (Northrup, 2001). Because of such changes, one of my older students defines menopause as "Everyone around you suddenly has a bad attitude."

Some (lucky) women hardly notice that they are going through menopause. Hot flashes affect about

75 percent of all women, but they usually last only a few minutes. Even when the symptoms are severe, most women do not consider menopause a crisis but a liberating time of life: Many enjoy sex more because they are no longer bothered by menstruation, the need for contraception, or the fear of pregnancy (Fisher, 1999).

IS THERE A MALE MENOPAUSE? The levels of a man's main sex hormone, testosterone, begins to drop as early as age 30. By age 50, 10 percent of all U.S. men have low levels of testosterone. Few medical researchers, however, view this biological change as "male menopause." Unlike women, men don't have menstrual periods or a well-defined period of time in which hormone production stops completely; some men at age 80 and older can continue to father children, and testosterone deficiencies can be due to alcohol abuse; depression; and lung, liver, and kidney disease (Federman and Walford, 2007; Mayo Clinic Staff, 2007).

Only a small percentage of men with low testosterone levels experiences nervousness, depression, decreased sexual performance (which often can be treated medically), inability to concentrate, irritability, and similar problems. It may be that such symptoms reflect a more general midlife crisis in which men look back over their lives and feel distress at not having achieved what they had planned as well as the accumulated effects of a lack of exercise, unhealthy diets, and normal aging (Gould et al., 2000; Federman and Walford, 2007).

Sex and Later Life

An 80-year-old husband says, "Let's go upstairs and make love." His 75-year-old wife replies, "Pick one, dear. I can't do both." This is one of my aging aunt's favorite jokes. Despite such jokes, many men and women remain sexually active into their 70s, 80s, and beyond.

SEXUAL ACTIVITY Sexual activity among older people declines but doesn't disappear, especially for those with a regular partner. One of the most recent and comprehensive studies of American adults ages 57 to 85 found that the majority have an active love life. Among 75- to 85-year-olds, for example,

- About 39 percent of the men and 17 percent of the women are sexually active.
- Nearly 25 percent have sex four or more times a month.
- More than 25 percent of the men and 33 percent of the women either gave or received oral sex in the past year (Lindau et al., 2007).

However, men and women hold sharply different opinions about sex. For example, 35 percent of women

ages 57 to 85 rated sex as "not at all important" compared with 13 percent of men. Among these women, 45 percent lacked an interest in sex, 39 percent experienced vaginal dryness that made sex uncomfortable or painful, and 34 percent didn't have orgasms (Lindau et al., 2007). Many women's lower interest in sex reflects several factors, including their or their partner's health.

HEALTH AND SEXUALITY It's not until about age 70 that frequency of sexual activity, in both men and women, begins to decline significantly. This generally results from poor health and habits. Smoking, alcoholism, heart disease, and vascular illnesses can decrease sexual desire and activity in both sexes, as can prostate problems in men.

For women, the drop in estrogen levels after menopause can decrease sexual desire and make sex painful because the walls of the vagina become thin and dry. In addition, especially for women, a mix of stress, anger, and a cooling relationship can dampen sexual desire. Some illnesses, such as diabetes, as well as some medications for high blood pressure can also decrease sexual interest for both sexes and cause impotence in older men (Lindau et al., 2007).

Despite these difficulties, older men and women engage in sex and enjoy it. A reporter asked a 90-year-old woman who married an 18-year-old man, "Aren't you afraid of what could happen on the honeymoon? Vigorous lovemaking might bring on injury or even a fatal heart attack!" She smiled and replied, "If he dies, he dies!"

Fred Thompson—a politician, actor, and attorney—married a second wife who was 24 years younger than he was. In this marriage, he fathered a second child at age 64. Why, in contrast, are most men unlikely to marry women twice their age? And how do many people feel about a woman who marries a man half her age?

MORE DOUBLE STANDARDS AND SEXUAL SCRIPTS
Gray-haired men in their 60s are considered distinguished, but their female counterparts are just old. Men are not under the same pressure as women to remain young, trim, and attractive. When comparing her own public image with that of her actor husband, the late Paul Newman, actress Joanne Woodward once remarked, "He gets prettier; I get older."

The aging process may enhance a man's desirability because he has more resources and power. In contrast, an older woman may be regarded as an asexual grandmother: "Because attractiveness is associated with feelings of well-being, a perceived decline in appearance can be particularly devastating for women" (Levy, 1994: 295–96).

As in earlier stages of life, older men's sexual scripts usually focus on intercourse and orgasm. Older women are often more interested in relational and nongenital activities such as hugging and holding hands. Such differences may explain why 40 percent of older men but only 15 percent of older women without regular sex partners rate their sex life at the bottom of the satisfaction scale (B. K. Johnson, 1996; Jacoby, 2005).

As people age, the biggest impediment to sex, especially for widows or divorcees, is a partner gap. Because our culture frowns on liaisons and marriages between older women and younger men but approves of matches between older men and younger women, single older women have a small pool of eligible sexual partners (see Chapters 6, 9, and 17).

⁝• MAKING CONNECTIONS

- Have you ever been pressured to have sex? How did you react? What advice would you give younger people who would like to resist such pressure from their friends and girlfriends or boyfriends?

- What kind of sex do you enjoy most? Least? Why? If you haven't had sexual intercourse yet, do you fantasize about it?

- How would you feel if your widowed 80-year-old parent, grandparent, or great-grandparent had an unmarried sexual partner?

SEXUAL INFIDELITY

Almost 90 percent of Americans agree that having an extramarital affair is morally wrong. Most of the remaining 10 percent don't view infidelity as a moral issue, but it's not clear why. One reason may be that people define infidelity differently. For example, some married women and men don't see extramarital sex

as cheating if a partner has no interest in sex (Weaver, 2007; Newport, 2008).

What Is Sexual Infidelity?

Some people use the terms *affair, infidelity, adultery, unfaithful,* and *extramarital sex* interchangeably. Others define infidelity more broadly as "a breach of trust, a betrayal of a relationship, a breaking of an agreement" in *any* committed relationship—married or not (Pittman, 1990: 20).

For some, extramarital sex is more damaging than other forms of infidelity, such as that between people who live together, because a married partner breaks a civil contract that's legally binding. Many are also violating a religious promise to be faithful.

EMOTIONAL INFIDELITY Emotional infidelity can be devastating to both married and unmarried couples. Almost one out of four American women believe that a sexual act is not necessary for a person to be unfaithful; lust is enough to qualify (see *Table 7.3*).

Many family therapists agree that affairs do not have to include sexual intercourse because infidelity is any betrayal of the expectation of emotional or sexual exclusivity in a committed relationship. Thus, emotional infidelity includes secrecy (meeting someone without telling your spouse or partner), emotional intimacy (confiding things you haven't told your spouse or partner), and even being mutually attracted to someone else (Glass, 2002).

ONLINE INFIDELITY You might have noticed that only 42 percent of men but 64 percent of women consider a virtual tryst (cybersex) to be cheating (see *Table 7.3*). The people involved may never meet, but some cyber affairs may eventually break up a marriage or a relationship. In almost 30 percent of cyber affairs, the relationship escalates from e-mail to telephone calls to personal contact (Greenfield, 1999).

Since you asked . . .

⁝• Isn't online sex just a harmless form of entertainment?

Some family practitioners believe that Internet romances are betrayals because they reflect emotional infidelity: People share personal information (including comments about marital dissatisfaction), become more secretive, and may spend more time with a cyber lover than with a spouse or partner (Young, 2001). Because online infidelity violates a trust, it can elicit hurt, anger, depression, a deep sense or betrayal, and insecurity.

How Common Is Sexual Infidelity?

Infidelity makes great fodder for talk shows, but extramarital sex is not a common occurrence. How many U.S. spouses are unfaithful is unclear because

TABLE 7.3 | Is This Infidelity?

Percentage of people who strongly agree that the following acts constitute infidelity in a committed relationship:

	Men	Women
Intercourse with another man or woman	88	94
Oral sex with another man or woman	85	93
Fondling another man or woman	78	88
Kissing another man or woman	51	69
Telephone sex	48	69
Cybersex	42	64
Holding hands with another man or woman	35	48
Lustfully thinking about another man or woman	17	23
Flirting with another man or woman	16	21
Looking at another man or woman	6	6

Do you see any differences between women's and men's responses? Do you agree that telephone sex and cybersex constitute infidelity?

Source: Covel, 2003: 16.

studies report slightly different results. However, several highly respected national surveys show that in any given year, about 4 percent of married people (4 percent of men and 3 percent of women) have sex outside of their marriage. Over a lifetime, about 16 percent say that they have had extramarital sex (21 percent of men and 12 percent of women). This rate has fluctuated only slightly since 1991 (Morin, 1994; Smith, 2006; Taylor et al., 2006). In committed relationships, married and unmarried, the numbers are similar—16 percent of the partners admit to having cheated, but the numbers are higher for men (21 percent) than for women (11 percent) (Langer et al., 2004).

These numbers may seem high, especially since 90 percent of Americans believe that marital infidelity is always wrong, up from 70 percent in 1970 (Newport, 2008). But year after year, my students refuse to believe that most married people are faithful because talk shows say that at least half of all married people have cheated or because of their own personal experiences. For example,

"I work as a bartender part time and hang out in bars on the weekends. I watch people leave my bar all the time and all I can think of is his poor wife waiting at home."

"I find it hard to believe that only 16 percent of married people have cheated. Most are lying."

"A lot of men, single or married, think with their penis. You'll never convince me that only about 21 percent of men have cheated on their wives." (Author's files)

Their suspicions may be correct because married women report lower rates of extramarital sex in interviews than in computer-assisted self-reports (Whisman and Snyder, 2007). Until these studies are replicated, however, the available surveys show that sexual infidelity isn't as rampant as most Americans believe.

Why Are Spouses and Partners Unfaithful?

Popular magazines routinely imply that it's the woman's fault if a man is unfaithful. The articles offer advice on how to please a husband or boyfriend, such as having cosmetic surgery, losing weight, buying sexy lingerie, preparing romantic dinners, and not nagging. Magazines very rarely advise a husband to please his wife so that *she* will not be tempted to have an affair.

The complex reasons for adultery include both macro and micro explanations. Although they overlap and are often cumulative, let's look at them separately for greater clarity.

MACRO REASONS Among the many macro explanations for extramarital sex, several are especially significant:

1. *Economic problems* place strains on families. Unemployment, underemployment (employment below a person's level of training and education), and layoffs can create pressures that may increase the incidence of sexual infidelity. Husbands and wives who must work different shifts or are separated because of military duty

Desperate Housewives, a television show that often focuses largely on extramarital sex, has been a hit since it first aired in 2004. Why?

or frequent business trips may develop intimate relationships with others.

2. *The purpose of marriage* has changed for many people. Procreation is still important, but many couples marry primarily for companionship and intimacy (see Chapter 1). When these needs are not met, outside relationships may develop.

3. *The anonymity of urban life* provides opportunities for and conceals adultery more easily than is the case in small towns, where people are more likely to know one another.

4. Because today people *live longer,* marriages can last as long as 60 years, increasing the chances for conflict, dissatisfaction, and infidelity.

5. Because there are now more women in the workplace and they have more contact with men, there is *greater opportunity for sexual infidelity.* About 37 percent of the women and men who cheated said that they did so with a co-worker (Langer et al., 2004).

6. *Gender roles* also affect infidelity. The assumption that men will be "naughty" is

built into phrases such as "boys will be boys," but the consequences for cheating woman are much harsher, such as being accused of abandoning her spouse and children and being labeled "a slut." Also, many people—both women and men—often blame the woman and not the man if he is unfaithful ("She probably let herself go") (Baird, 2008; Goodman, 2008; Stanley, 2008).

7. New *technology* has increased opportunities for cyber flirting. People can log on to their computers and engage in cyber affairs while their spouse is sleeping (Gardner, 2004).

MICRO REASONS There are also a number of micro explanations for sexual infidelity:

1. *The need for emotional or sexual satisfaction* may propel people into extramarital sex. Women who are unfaithful often feel that their husbands do not communicate with them, have no time for them except in bed, and feel emotionally deprived. In one survey, 22 percent of the women said that loneliness was their top reason for having an affair. Men, in contrast, often want more sex than they're getting (Weaver, 2007).

2. Both sexes, but twice as many men as women, have extramarital sex as well as a committed relationship, because it's *exciting.* As a 38-year-old man in a committed relationship said, "I like variety and a more wild sex life." Women, in contrast, are more likely to be unfaithful if they seek emotional attention or fall in love with someone else (Weaver, 2007).

3. Sexual infidelity is an *ego-enhancer.* As some people grow older, they may try to prove to themselves that they are still physically and socially desirable and attractive. As one unfaithful wife said, "He tells me my skin is soft. He makes me feel sexy again" (Ali and Miller, 2004: 49). Men with low self-esteem are more likely than women with low self-esteem to engage in infidelity to bolster their egos, especially those whose pregnant wives have less interest in sex over the course of a pregnancy (Whisman et al., 2007).

4. Sexual infidelity reflects a *social exchange.* Men who are involved in extramarital affairs are generally older and have much higher incomes than their female partners. Often they are the woman's boss or mentor. Aging but powerful men get sex in exchange for a younger woman's attraction to their status, power, prestige, or wealth.

5. Both sexes are unfaithful because they think that they *can get away with it.* As what one

By permission of John L. Hart FLP and Creators Syndicate, Inc.

journalist dubbed "alpha males," many politicians assume that they "can get away with stuff" because they're rich or powerful (Page, 2008: 15A). Moreover, 39 percent of men and 23 percent of women say that they would probably forgive a significant other who has had sex with someone else (Orr and Stout, 2007). Thus, at least among some unmarried couples, people know that discovery of infidelity won't necessarily end their relationship.

6. People sometimes have extramarital sex as a form of *revenge or retaliation* against a spouse for involvement in a similar activity or "for some sort of nonsexual mistreatment, real or imagined, by the spouse" (Kinsey et al., 1953: 432).

7. An extramarital relationship may provide a *way out of marriage.* Some people might deliberately initiate an affair as an excuse to dissolve an unhappy marriage (Walsh, 1991).

Often, macro and micro reasons overlap in explaining sexual infidelity. For example, people who describe themselves as religious are less likely to have extramarital affairs because Christianity, Islam, and Judaism prohibit infidelity (see, for example, Allen et al., 2005, and Whisman et al., 2007).

However, professions of being religious but low attendance rates at services are better predictors of infidelity. That is, when both spouses attend services, have a network of people who actively support faithfulness, and hear sermons on marital fidelity and the importance of marriage, they are less likely to engage in extramarital sex (Atkins and Kessel, 2008). Thus, religion (a macro-level variable) is less important than religiosity (a micro-level variable) in affecting sexual infidelity.

What Are Some of the Consequences of Sexual Infidelity?

Only 10 percent of Americans say they would definitely forgive their spouse for having an affair and 62 percent say they would get a divorce (Jones, 2008). One clinician describes the discovery of a

spouse's affair as the "emotional equivalent of having a limb amputated without an anesthetic" (McGinnis, 1981: 154). The injured spouse typically feels deceived, betrayed, and depressed. The aggrieved person may also experience doubts about his or her own desirability, adequacy, or worth.

Marriage counselors point out that most extramarital affairs devastate the entire family. They can have an especially negative impact on children, who often feel insecure and confused, particularly if the marriage collapses because of the affair. Because very young children are self-centered, they may feel that they are somehow to blame for what has happened (see Chapter 15).

Extramarital sex also has broad structural implications for society as a whole. Group solidarity is necessary for a society's survival. Because family members depend on one another for emotional support, their unity and cohesiveness can be threatened by sexual intruders.

⁘► MAKING CONNECTIONS

■ Do you think that emotional infidelity, including cybersex, is a form of sexual infidelity? Or just a harmless romantic game (the ludic love discussed in Chapter 6)?

■ Would you tell a co-worker, friend, relative, or family member that his or her partner or spouse is unfaithful? Would you want to be told?

GAY, LESBIAN, AND BISEXUAL SEX

The percentage of gays and bisexuals in the U.S. population is small, but their sexual activities have triggered a wide range of public reactions. Let's begin by looking at the extent of homosexuality in the United States.

The Extent of Homosexuality

How many GLBT people are there in the United States? No one knows for sure, but about 8 percent

FIGURE 7.6 Sexual Orientation

Percentage distribution of men and women ages 18 to 44: United States, 2002.

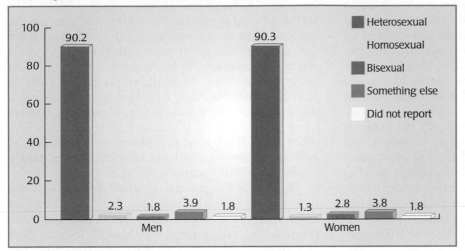

Source: Mosher et al. 2005, Figure 8.

of Americans identify themselves as homosexual or bisexual (see *Figure 7.6*). A higher number, 18 percent, who consider themselves straight have had same-sex sexual contact (Mosher et al., 2005).

Same-Sex Behavior

Except for penile-vaginal intercourse, gay couples do everything that heterosexuals do. Their sexual activities include kissing, caressing, hugging, nipple stimulation, oral and anal sex, and other nongenital touching or foreplay.

Lesbian sexual activities include cunnilingus; manual masturbation; body-to-body rubbing of breasts or clitorises; and slow, sensual body caressing. Although some lesbians report using dildos (objects to stimulate sexual arousal), the most popular activities include oral sex and nongenital acts such as kissing. Like heterosexuals, homosexuals use a variety of positions to achieve sexual satisfaction, and not all couples participate in or enjoy all sexual activities (Hock, 2007).

Societal Reactions to Homosexuality

Societies vary greatly in their responses to homosexuality (see the box "Homosexuality in Non-Western Cultures" on p. 168). African countries are among the least tolerant of homosexuality. In Canada and some of the European countries that have legalized same-sex marriages (a topic we'll discuss in Chapter 10), the general public is more accepting of GLBTs, but there's considerable variation across cities and regions (Naurath, 2007). In the United

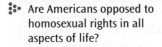

Since you asked . . .

• Are Americans opposed to homosexual rights in all aspects of life?

States, societal reactions range from homophobia to growing acceptance of gays and lesbians.

HOMOPHOBIA Homophobia, the fear and hatred of homosexuality, is less overt today than in the past but is still widespread. Some parents have blocked health curricula that discuss homosexuality in public schools. Others have demanded the right to pull their kindergarten children out of classes that use books containing pictures of same-sex parents (Simon, 2005).

Homophobia often takes the form of *gay bashing*: threats, assaults, or acts of violence directed at homosexuals. Of the more than 9,000 hate crimes reported to U.S. law enforcement agencies in 2007, 16 percent of the victims were GLBT (Federal Bureau of Investigation, 2008).

Minority GLBTs are the most likely to encounter prejudice and discrimination. Asian American lesbians feel that they face additional obstacles. They rarely appear in the mainstream or GLBT media because of the stereotype that there are no gay Asians. Coming out would bring shame on the parents because relatives, friends, and other members of Asian communities view GLBTs as abnormal. These women also experience more verbal and physical assaults because they are "triple rejects"—women, Asian, and lesbian (Foo, 2002).

Former Minnesota Vikings defensive lineman Esera Tuaolo sings "Jesus Loves Me," in Eden Prairie, Minnesota, site of a summit meeting of pastors who want Minnesota's state constitution amended to ban gay marriage. Tuaolo came out two years after retiring from pro football to say he was gay.

INCREASING ACCEPTANCE The percentage of Americans who believe that homosexuality is an acceptable way of life increased from 43 percent in 1978 to 55 percent in 2008 ("Homosexual relations," 2008). Still, many people are divided on the issue. About 55 percent of Americans oppose legalizing homosexual unions, but large numbers believe that gay men and lesbians should have equal rights in job opportunities and protection against hate crimes (see *Figure 7.7*).

Five states have legalized same-sex marriage as this book goes to press and numerous municipal jurisdictions, corporations, and smaller companies now extend health-care coverage and other benefits to the partners of their gay and lesbian employees. Many states allow gay partners to jointly adopt children on the same basis as unmarried couples. Large numbers of colleges and universities have health and other benefits for gay and lesbian couples, offer courses or programs in gay and lesbian studies, and provide funding for gay student clubs. And there are more than 3,700 gay-straight alliances (GSAS)—clubs for gay and gay-friendly kids—on high school campuses, up from just 100 in 1997 (Cloud, 2008; see, also, Chapter 11).

Commercial television has also changed in its portrayal of gays and lesbians. In an episode of the popular 1970s show *Marcus Welby, M.D.*, Dr. Welby advised a patient to suppress his homosexual tendencies to be a good husband and father. Since the mid-1990s, in contrast, a multitude of gay characters have appeared in leading and supporting roles on prime-time TV in popular programs such as *Friends, Will & Grace, ER, The Simpsons, Grey's Anatomy, Brothers and Sisters, Desperate Housewives, Greek, The Office*, and *Ugly Betty*, among others. In 2005, *Brokeback Mountain*—a film about gay cowboys—received the Golden Globes award for best motion picture of the year.

Does such programming reflect progress? Some think so, but others are offended. Ambivalence about homosexuality is especially evident in religious institutions. Some denominations have welcomed gays as members and ordained GLBT ministers and even bishops. Others find themselves polarized and divided over homosexuality. Ethnic gay men and lesbians face additional hurdles in their families and communities because of cultural, religious, and generational differences (see Chapters 8 and 9).

:• MAKING CONNECTIONS

- How would you react if your best friend told you she or he was gay? What if one of your parents did so? Your brother or sister? Your adolescent daughter or son? Or, if you're gay and have come out, how did other people react?

- How does gay bashing affect all of us and not just the victims?

SEXUALLY TRANSMITTED INFECTIONS, HIV, AND AIDS

Sexual expression is not always smooth and carefree. *Appendix B* provides information about sexual problems and dysfunctions and their treatment. Here we'll briefly examine STIs—diseases, infections, and illnesses that are conveyed almost solely through sexual intercourse.

STIs

Sexually transmitted infections (STIs) are diseases that are spread by contact, either sexual or nonsexual, with body parts or fluids that harbor specific microorganisms (generally bacterial or viral). (STI corresponds to but has recently been replacing another frequently used term, **sexually transmitted disease [STD]**.) The term *sexually transmitted* indicates that sexual contact is the most common means of spreading infections.

FIGURE 7.7 Attitudes about Gay and Lesbian Rights

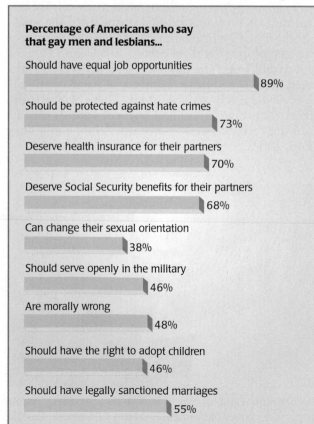

Percentage of Americans who say that gay men and lesbians...

Should have equal job opportunities — 89%

Should be protected against hate crimes — 73%

Deserve health insurance for their partners — 70%

Deserve Social Security benefits for their partners — 68%

Can change their sexual orientation — 38%

Should serve openly in the military — 46%

Are morally wrong — 48%

Should have the right to adopt children — 46%

Should have legally sanctioned marriages — 55%

Source: Based on Saad, 2008, and "Homosexual Relations," 2008.

PREVALENCE There are approximately 19 million new cases of STIs in the United States every year. STIs affect women and men of all backgrounds and economic levels, but nearly half of all STIs occur in people under age 25 (Fenton and Douglas, 2009).

There are at least 50 types of STIs (see *Appendix E* for more information about some of these diseases, their symptoms, and treatment). Today *syphilis* is the least common STI; the most common is *chlamydia*, a bacterial infection, followed by *gonorrhea* and *human papilloma virus* (HPV) (see *Figure 7.8*). Approximately 20 million Americans have HPV, which infects women's and men's genital areas and can result in genital warts and cancers in the cervix, vulva, penis, anus, and head and neck (CDC, 2008a).

One in four young women ages 14 to 19 has had at least one of the four most common STIs—HPV, chlamydia, genital herpes, and a parasite called trichomoniasis. Among those infected, 15 percent have had more than one of the diseases, and HPV is becoming the most prevalent (CDC Press Release, 2008).

EFFECTS OF STIs Most of the time, STIs cause no symptoms, particularly in women. Even when there are no symptoms, however, a person who is infected can pass the diseases on to a partner. STIs can cause

cancer, birth defects, miscarriages, and in some cases death. Untreated chlamydia can cause permanent damage to the reproductive organs, often resulting in infertility in women and sterility in men. Gonorrhea can result in infertility in men. A baby born to an infected mother may become blind.

Without early screening and treatment, 10 to 40 percent of women with gonorrhea develop *pelvic inflammatory disease* (PID). PID can result in infertility in women and life-threatening (ectopic) pregnancy when, for example, the fertilized egg implants itself in the fallopian tube rather than the uterus. The tube can rupture and, without surgical intervention, cause death. Certain types of HPV cause cervical cancer and other genital cancers. There is treatment for HPV, but no cure for herpes or genital warts.

HIV and AIDS

One of the most serious (and still fatal, in many cases) STIs is the **human immunodeficiency virus (HIV)**, the virus that causes AIDS. **Acquired immunodeficiency syndrome (AIDS)** is a degenerative condition that attacks the body's immune system and makes it unable to fight a number of diseases, including some forms of pneumonia and cancer.

PREVALENCE First reported on June 5, 1981, AIDS had taken the lives of almost 546,000 Americans by the end of 2006. An estimated 1.1 million Americans are living with AIDS. Almost 56,300 new HIV infections occur each year (CDC, 2008b). AIDS death rates have been decreasing, but some populations have become more vulnerable. As *Figure 7.9* shows, the prevalence of HIV is highest among men, African Americans, and men having sex with men (MSM).

HOW HIV SPREADS Childbirth and breast milk can pass on HIV, but the most common infections are through sexual contact and other behaviors that transmit blood and semen:

- **Anal sex.** A major reason why gay men have high rates of HIV/AIDS is that they

FIGURE 7.8 Cases of Selected STIs in the United States, 2007

These figures are conservative because many people don't realize that they're infected and don't seek medical care. The actual rates may be four to five times higher.

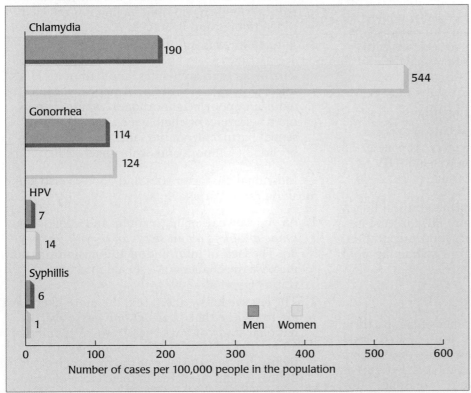

Number of cases per 100,000 people in the population

Sources: Based on Centers for Disease Control and Prevention, 2008; and Watson et al., 2008.

FIGURE 7.9 Americans Living with HIV/AIDS, 2006

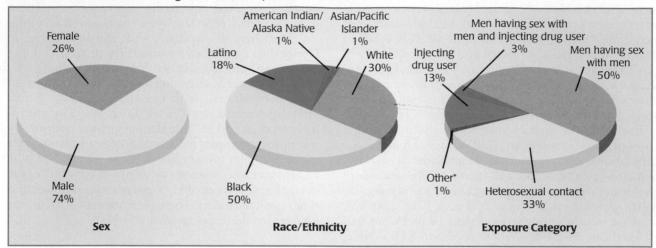

*Includes hemophilia, blood transfusion, and risk not reported or not identified.
Source: Based on CDC, 2008b.

engage in anal sex. This practice causes rectal bleeding and permits the passage of HIV from one person to another.

- **Oral sex.** A partner who has bleeding gums, cuts, or sores in the mouth or throat can transmit HIV.

- **Drug use.** Using any kind of drug, including alcohol and marijuana, can impair one's judgment and reduce the likelihood of using condoms. The rate of methamphetamine (meth) use has tripled since 2001, especially among MSM. Meth increases arousal and reduces inhibitions, prompting users to seek sex with multiple partners, some of whom may be infected with HIV (Markowitz et al., 2005).

- **Sharing needles.** Drug users often share a needle to inject drugs, infecting others.

- **Multiple partners.** A sexual liaison exposes people to a chain of past partners. Anyone in the chain who is infected can transmit HIV to numerous later partners (Bearman et al., 2004).

Some myths about HIV transmission still linger, but none of the following transmit HIV: insect bites, sweat, tears, sneezing, coughing, food preparation, toilet seats, blood donations, or a swimming pool that uses chlorine.

Why STIs Are Spreading

Why are STI rates rising? As in other situations, there are both macro-level constraints and micro-level choices. In terms of macro reasons, for example,

Since you asked . . .

:•• Why are STIs more dangerous to women than to men?

1. Some groups *aren't informed about infectious diseases.* The number

of HIV-positive people over age 50 has been rising sharply. Many are sexually active, but older women, especially, are not concerned about becoming pregnant, don't think they're at risk, and don't insist that their partners wear condoms (Kotz, 2007).

2. *Assimilation increases risky behavior.* As immigrants become more Americanized, they lose the "healthy immigrant effect," which includes avoiding drugs that increase the likelihood of risky sexual behavior and having unprotected MSM (Flores and Brotanek, 2005).

3. *Poverty spreads infections.* African Americans are six times more likely to be infected with chlamydia than are whites, and half of all HIV-infected people are African Americans. Minority women in poor neighborhoods, where there is often a scarcity of eligible men, usually select sexual partners from the same high-risk neighborhood (Adimora and Schoenbach, 2005).

Individual characteristics and choices also spike infection rates. For example,

1. As you saw earlier, both adults and adolescents *know a lot less about sex than they think they do.* The lack of information and misinformation increase the chances of a sexual infection (Eisenberg et al., 2004).

2. The less we know about sex, the more likely we are to believe that "*it won't happen to me.*" A national study of boys ages 15 to 17 found that 53 percent believed that a condom should fit tightly, leaving no space at the tip (Rock et al., 2005). A tight fit increases the chance of breakage and semen escaping during intercourse.

3. *Attitudes and behavior don't always mesh.* About 84 percent of sexually active adults ages 18 to 35 said that they take the necessary

precautions to protect themselves against sexually transmitted diseases. However, 82 percent said that they never use protection against STIs for oral sex, 64 percent never use protection for anal sex, and 47 percent never use protection for vaginal sex. Also, 93 percent said that their current partner did not have a STI, but about one-third had never discussed the issue with their partners (Lilleston, 2004).

4. *Some people lie.* About 43 percent of black men, 26 percent of Latino men, and 7 percent of white men reported being on the down low, but they didn't tell their female partners. Approximately 58 percent of MSM avoid testing because they are afraid of learning that they have HIV or worry that others will find out about the results (Sifakis et al., 2005; Wahlberg, 2005).

5. *Heterosexual women are especially vulnerable.* They are more than twice as likely as men to become infected with HIV for several reasons. First, the genital surface exposed to the virus is much larger in women than in men. Second, vaginal secretions from an HIV-infected woman are believed to be less potent than an infected man's semen, which is capable of packing high concentrations of the virus. Third, a man's exposure to the virus is limited to the duration of the sex act, but semen remains in a woman's body after intercourse. Fourth, women may not be aware that their male partners are having MSM. Finally, a majority of even college-educated women believe that they won't contract HIV or other STIs. As a result, they don't use condoms even when they have multiple sex partners (Nicolosi et al., 1994; Yarnall et al., 2003; Payne, 2008).

Since the mid-1990s, drugs have prolonged the life spans of people with AIDs, but at what cost? A 59-year-old man says that compared with his 84-year-old father, he has more and more severe illnesses that include diabetes, cardiovascular disease, kidney failure, a bleeding ulcer, severe depression, and rectal cancer. Medical researchers suspect that there is a strong connection between HIV/AIDS drugs and medical problems, but they are just beginning to study the first AIDS survivors who are now entering their fifties (Engels, 2008; Gross, 2008).

Africa has the highest rates, worldwide, of adults and children who die of AIDS. To combat the spread of HIV infection, many government officials, public health experts, and community activists have worked together to inform communities about HIV/AIDS using brochures, billboards, and door-to-door visits. Here, an HIV/AIDS educator addresses youth in Uganda.

Preventing STIs

Some sex educators advise parents to start talking about STIs when their children are in early elementary school. If preteens don't get accurate information about sex, they are less likely to use condoms, to use them correctly, or not to use dental dams during oral sex. As noted throughout this chapter, many adolescents have little information about STIs, including HIV/AIDS. Therefore, trusted adults—parents, teachers, and other community members—must become more informed themselves and then talk frankly with youth about how casual sex can lead to serious health consequences.

CONCLUSION

One of the biggest *changes* since the turn of the century is that we are better informed about our sexuality. Today we have more *choices* in our sexual expression, and most people recognize that sexuality involves more than just the sex act. Instead, sexuality has emotional, intellectual, spiritual, and cultural as well as biological components.

There are also a number of *constraints*. We are often unwilling to give young people the information they need to make thoughtful decisions about sex. Gay men and lesbians still face discrimination and harassment because of their sexual practices. And our health and lives and the lives of our children are threatened by the rising incidence of STIs and HIV infection.

These changes have significant effects on both women and men in their search for suitable marriage partners and other long-term relationships. We'll look at some of these issues in the next several chapters.

SUMMARY

1. Sex is more important for some people than for others in providing physical contact and expressing loyalty, passion, and affection.

2. Human sexuality incorporates several components, including sexual identity, sexual orientation, and gender roles. Biological theories maintain that genes and sex hormones determine sexual preference, whereas social constructionist theories emphasize social and environmental factors.

3. We like to think that our sexual behavior is spontaneous, but sexual scripts shape most of our sexual activities, attitudes, and relationships.

4. Much of our information, and misinformation, comes from peers and the media. There are variations from one state to another, but many sex education programs are funded generously only if they emphasize abstinence-only approaches.

5. Sexual activity encompasses many behaviors other than sexual intercourse, such as fantasies, masturbation, petting, and oral sex.

6. Adolescent girls are more likely to romanticize sex, whereas adolescent boys typically see sex as an end in itself. The reasons for early premarital sex

include peer pressure, environmental factors, and cultural expectations.

7. Marital sex typically decreases in frequency over the course of a marriage, but married couples enjoy a variety of other sexual activities in addition to intercourse.

8. Despite many stereotypes about sexuality and aging, people ages 70 and older continue to engage in sexual activities, including intercourse, masturbation, and sexual fantasy.

9. Gay and lesbian partners experience many of the same feelings as do heterosexuals, and face some of the same problems in their relationships. Major factors that differentiate gay and lesbian couples from heterosexual couples are society's disapproval of homosexual practices and their consequent lack of legal rights in many areas.

10. More people are informed about STIs, HIV, and AIDS, but many still engage in high-risk behaviors such as sharing drug needles, having sex with many partners, and not using condoms. The rates of new HIV infections are especially high among male-male couples, minorities, and heterosexual women.

KEY TERMS

sexual identity 166
sexual orientation 166
homosexual 166
heterosexual 166
bisexual 166
asexual 166
heterosexism 167
transgendered 167
transsexuals 167

intersexuals 167
transvestites 167
sexual script 169
autoeroticism 181
masturbation 181
fellatio 181
cunnilingus 181
sexual response 183
menopause 187

homophobia 193
sexually transmitted infections (STIs) 195
sexually transmitted diseases (STDs) 195
human immunodeficiency virus (HIV) 195
acquired immunodeficiency syndrome (AIDS) 195

 MyFamilyLab provides a wealth of resources. Go to www.myfamilylab.com<http://www.myfamilylab.com/>, to enhance your comprehension of the content in this chapter. You can take practice exams, view videos relevant to the subject matter, listen to audio files, explore topics further by using Social Explorer, and use the tools contained in MySearchLab to help you write research papers.

8 Choosing Others
Dating and Mate Selection

Someone once joked that dating is the process of spending a lot of time and money to meet people you probably won't like. Yet some of the most popular television programs are courtship competitions, such as *Age of Love, The Bachelor, The Bachelorette, Next, Rock of Love,* and *Hitched or Ditched.* Why are these shows so popular?

Singlehood has its advantages (see Chapter 9). Most of us, however, seek intimacy with a lifelong partner. Regardless of which words we use—"dating," "going out," "hooking up," "having a thing," or "seeing someone"—mate selection is a process that, many people hope, will result in finding an intimate partner or marriage mate.

As the box "Courting throughout U.S. History" shows, dating is a recent invention. It emerged in the United States in the twentieth century and became a well-established rite of passage in the 1950s. How we date has changed, but why and whom we date and why we break up have been fairly constant over time. Let's begin with the question of how often people date.

DATA DIGEST

- Among twelfth-grade students, **those who said that they never date** increased from 15 percent in 1976 to 27 percent in 2006.

- In 2009, 20 percent of all **never-married adults** were between the ages of 30 and 44.

- Among all singles age 18 and older, **55 percent are not in a committed relationship and are not looking for a romantic partner.** Among those who are seeking relationships, about half had been on no more than one date in the previous three months.

- About 66 percent of Americans **would not consider dating someone who didn't like their dog.**

- In 2006, **31 percent of American adults—63 million people—knew someone who had used a dating Website,** and 15 percent—30 million people—knew someone who had been in a long-term relationship with or married someone he or she met online.

Sources: American Kennel Club, 2006; Child Trends Data Bank, 2006; Madden and Lenhart, 2006; Rainie and Madden, 2006; U.S. Census Bureau, 2008.

Courting Throughout U.S. History

Changes

Young people in colonial America often experienced premarital sex. As a young woman wrote passionately to her lover,

O! I do really want to kiss you. How I should like to be in that old parlor with you. I hope there will be a carpet on the floor for it seems you intend to act worse than you ever did before by your letter. But I shall humbly submit to my fate and willingly, too, to speak candidly (Rothman, 1983: 401).

There were also practical considerations. In colonial New England, an engaged woman's parents conducted economic negotiations with the family of her fiancé, and most young men could not even think about courtship until they owned land. They were advised to "choose by ears, as well as eyes" and to select women who were industrious, hardworking, and sensible. Affection was expected to blossom into love after marriage.

Many colonial women were very down-to-earth about courtship. A New York woman wrote,

I am sick of all this choosing. If a man is healthy and does not drink and has a good little handful of stock and a good temper and is a good Christian, what difference can it make to a woman which man she takes? (Ryan, 1983: 40–41).

Before the Industrial Revolution, most courtships took place within the hustle and bustle of community life. Young people could meet after church services, during picnics, or at gatherings such as barn raisings and dances. Buggy rides were especially popular: There was no room in the buggy for a chaperone, and "the horse might run away or lose a shoe so that one could be stranded on a lonely country road" (McPharlin, 1946: 10).

At the turn of the twentieth century, especially among the middle classes, gentlemen "called" on women. A woman or her mother invited a suitor to visit at the woman's home, and other family members would be present. If the relationship proceeded toward engagement, the couple enjoyed some privacy in the parlor (Bailey, 1988).

With the advent of bicycles and telephones, parlor sofas and porch swings were quickly abandoned. People began to use the term *dating*, which referred to couples setting a specific date, time, and place to meet. When the automobile came into widespread use in the early 1920s, dating took a giant step forward. "The car provided more privacy and excitement than either the dance hall or the movie theater, and the result was the spread of petting" (Rothman, 1984: 295). Young people now had the mobility to meet more frequently, informally, and casually.

Until the early 1970s, dating reflected a strict and gendered code of etiquette. Men initiated dates and paid all the expenses. Women waited to be asked out and provided companionship (and sometimes sex) during a date.

Stop and Think . . .

- Did the colonists have the right idea in being practical about courtship? Or should courtship always involve love?

- Talk to your parents, grandparents, or other relatives about dating in the 1950s and 1960s. What were some of the advantages and disadvantages of the dating rituals?

HOW OFTEN DO WE DATE?

Many traditional college students (those who are living on campus and are under age 25) dismiss **dating**—the process of meeting people socially for possible mate selection—as old fashioned

Since you asked . . .

- Is dating dead? Or has it changed?

because "there's no time, no money, and no need" (Wolcott, 2004: 11). Dating may be dead on many traditional college campuses, but this is not the case elsewhere.

A majority of Americans age 18 and older either are dating or would like to (see Data Digest). Dating has declined among people under age 18, but 24 percent of high school seniors say that they date frequently (see *Figure 8.1*). How we meet people and what we call dating has changed, as you'll see shortly, but dating is as popular as ever.

WHY DO WE DATE?

The reasons for dating seem self-evident, but dating is more complex than just getting together. Sociologists describe the dating process as a **marriage market** in which participants compare the assets and liabilities of eligible partners and choose the best available mate.

Everyone has a "market value," and whom a person "trades" with depends on one's resources. Like most other choices we make, dating involves taking risks with the resources we invest. The more valuable the catch we seek, the more likely we are to devote time and money to looking attractive, accommodating the partner's personality or interests, or getting along with her or his family and friends. In contrast, one-night stands entail few risks (assuming that the partners don't contract STIs and the woman doesn't become pregnant) and little investment of resources.

Also, people might use their resources differently depending on whether the relationship is new. As one

FIGURE 8.1 How Often Do Teenagers Date?

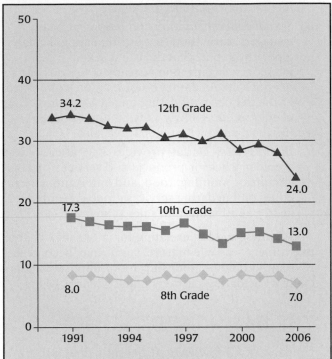

Source: Child Trends Data Bank, 2006, Figure 2.

of my students observed, people may invest more time than money in a partner if they are no longer in the trading stage in the marriage marketplace:

It's very expensive to date. When two people are in a comfortable relationship, they tend not to go out as much. The quiet nights at home are considerably less expensive than extravagant nights on the town. The longer you date someone, the less need there is to impress that person with fancy dinners and costly dates (Author's files).

Dating fulfills a number of specific functions that vary according to a person's age, social class, and gender. Dating functions can be either *manifest*—the purposes are visible, recognized, and intended—or *latent*—the purposes are unintended or not immediately recognized (see Chapter 2). Keep in mind that these functions often overlap.

Manifest Functions of Dating

Dating fulfills several important manifest functions:

- *Maturation:* Dating sends the message that an adolescent is reaching puberty. She or he becomes capable of engaging in developmental tasks such as emotional intimacy outside the family and, often, sexual expression (see Chapter 7).

  Since you asked . . .
  - Why are my parents and friends so critical of the people I date?

- *Fun and recreation:* Going out with people we like relieves boredom, stress, and loneliness. Online dating sites report that their membership spikes during stressful economic times, probably because people seek relationships to lessen their anxiety (Carpenter, 2008). And, as more people postpone marriage (see Chapter 9), dating has become an important recreational activity.

- *Companionship:* Regardless of one's age, dating can be a valuable source of companionship. It can also ease the heartbreak of being widowed. One of my students described her 72-year-old mother as being very depressed after the death of her husband, to whom she had been married for 50 years, until she "met a wonderful man and they started socializing."

- *Love and affection:* Dating provides a socially accepted way of enjoying intimacy. Both women and men say that they initiated a date because they were in love or wanted a caring and serious relationship (Clark et al., 1999). The relationship may fizzle, but dating is a way of getting closer to another person.

- *Mate selection:* In a cartoon, a woman, hand on the doorknob of her apartment, turns to her date and says: "I had a nice time, Steve. Would you like to come in, settle down, and raise a family?" Whether or not people admit it, dating is usually a search for a marital partner. Adolescents often become angry if their parents criticize their dates with remarks such as "We don't want you to marry this guy" or "She's not good

Dilbert: © Scott Adams/Distributed by United Feature Syndicate, Inc.

The Wodabe, a nomadic West African tribe, value and honor male beauty. The males perform a dance, showing off the whiteness of their teeth and eyes, at an annual competition at which women select the most beautiful man.

enough for you." The teenager's impatient rebuttal is usually "I'm not going to marry him (her). We're just going out!"

Parents are often judgmental because they know that dating can lead to marriage. In contrast, there is little need for dating in cultures in which parents arrange their children's marriages (see Chapters 5 to 7).

Latent Functions of Dating

Dating also fulfills several important latent functions:

- *Socialization:* Through dating, people learn about expected gender roles; family structures that differ from their own; and different attitudes, beliefs, and values. This kind of learning may be especially valuable for adolescents, who can test and hone their communication skills in one-on-one settings (Berk, 1993).

- *Social status:* Going out with an attractive or successful person enhances one's status and prestige. Being popular or going out with someone who's popular can also increase one's standing in a social group.

- *Fulfillment of ego needs:* Being asked out on a date or having one's invitation accepted boosts a person's self-esteem and self-image.

Self-confidence rises if the date goes well or if the partner is flattering and attentive.

- *Sexual experimentation and intimacy:* Many teenagers learn about sex during dating. Females, especially, report that their first sexual intercourse occurred in a steady or serious dating relationship. As dating becomes more committed or the frequency of dating increases, young people are more likely to want and have sex (Michael and Bickert, 2001; see, also, Chapter 7).

- *Big business:* Dating provides a significant economic market for products and services such as clothing, grooming, food, and entertainment. In 2006, online dating services alone generated nearly $650 million in sales (Quenqua, 2007).

Manifest and latent dating functions may change over time. As people mature, status may become less relevant and companionship more important, especially if the dating partners plan to marry.

THE DATING SPECTRUM

Unlike it was a few generations ago, dating today is distinct from courtship and may or may not end in marriage. Traditional dating is still common, but there are a number of newer forms of getting together, as well as some combinations of traditional and contemporary dating.

Traditional Dating

The *traditional date,* which predominated through the 1970s, is still a fairly formal way of meeting potential spouses. In traditional dating, males and females follow clear, culturally defined gender role scripts, at least among the middle classes. The girl waits to be asked out, the boy picks her up at her home, and Mom and Dad chat with the boy. The boy has specific plans for the evening (such as a dinner, concert, or party), pays for everything, and brings the girl home before curfew.

Some older television programs, such as *Happy Days* and *The Brady Bunch,* although idealized, portray this type of dating. Men pay for the date, but what exactly are they buying? A good time, perhaps. Or female companionship. But there is always "an uncomfortable undercurrent of sexual favors lurking in the background" (Stone and McKee, 2002: 70). The expectation is unstated, but members of both sexes often assume that the woman will show her gratitude in some way—usually through a goodnight kiss, petting, or intercourse.

CULTURAL VARIATIONS ON TRADITIONAL DATING
The popularity of traditional dating is particularly evident in formal events such as *coming-out parties* or debutante balls, at which young women, usually from the upper classes, are introduced to society (Kendall, 2002). Other cultural rites of passage include the *bat mitzvah* for girls and the *bar mitzvah*

The *quinceañera* has many rituals. After a traditional waltz in which the young woman dances with her father, she tosses a bouquet to the boys to determine who will win the first dance with her.

for boys in Jewish communities. These rituals mark the end of childhood and readiness for adult responsibilities and rights, including dating.

In many Latino communities, the *quinceañera* (pronounced kin-say-ah-NYAIR-ah) is a coming-of-age rite that celebrates a girl's entrance into adulthood on her fifteenth birthday. *Quince* (pronounced KEEN-say) means 15 in Spanish. The *quinceañera* is an elaborate and dignified religious and social affair sponsored by the girl's parents. It typically begins with a Catholic Mass and is followed by a reception at which 14 couples (each couple representing one year in the girl's life before the *quince*) serve as her attendants. The girl may be allowed to date boys after her *quinceañera*. There is no comparable rite of passage for Latino boys.

The *quinceañera* "can be as elaborate as the finest wedding and as expensive and as time consuming to organize" (Garcia, 2002: 73). Because the celebration reflects pride in the girl's heritage and is one of the most memorable events in her life, even working-class parents save money for years to host a typical celebration, which costs between $10,000 to $20,000 for gowns, photographers, the banquet hall, music (often a mariachi band), limos, food, and party favors.

Quinceañeras are a multi-million-dollar industry. Many large retail and bridal stores carry a large selection of gowns and accessories, and travel agencies offer *quinceañera* celebrations to numerous destinations that are often booked solid into the next year. And, perhaps as a sure sign that this event is an important ceremony, a *Quinceañera Barbie* is available in toy stores throughout the nation (Miranda, 2004).

GOING STEADY Going steady and "getting pinned" were common in the 1930s and became especially popular after World War II. A couple was pinned when a young man gave his fraternity pin to his girlfriend as a symbol of his affection and commitment. *Going steady,* which often meant that the partners were seeing only each other, usually came after a couple had a number of dates, and it sometimes preceded engagement. Typically, however, going steady was short lived because it just meant that you like one boy better than the rest (Breines, 1992; Tuttle, 1993).

A modern version of going steady is "going with" or "going together." For many middle school students, "going with" signals the transition from childhood to adolescence. The couples are not planning to get engaged, but they are also not seeing others. "Going with" sometimes starts before puberty, even though the relationships of fourth, fifth, and sixth graders usually break up after a few weeks (Merten, 1996; Albert et al., 2003). For older adolescents, such liaisons may last for months or even years.

The advantage of "going with" is having a stable relationship when many other things in life are changing and unpredictable (such as physiological changes, divorcing parents, and preparation for college or a job). The disadvantage is that such relationships discourage adolescents from meeting new people—especially when they are experiencing many developmental changes in a short period (see Chapter 2).

Contemporary Dating

In contrast to "real dates" in the traditional sense, much of contemporary dating is usually casual and includes hanging out, getting together, and "hooking up." There are also traditional-contemporary combinations that can lead to cohabitation, engagement, and marriage.

Since you asked . . .

- What are the benefits and costs of casual dating?

HANGING OUT Parents and adolescents in many American homes engage in a familiar dialogue:

Parent: Where are you going?
Teenager: Out.
Parent: What will you do?

Teenager: Just hang out.

Parent: Who will be there?

Teenager: I don't know yet.

Parent: When will you be back?

Teenager: I'm not sure.

Whether hanging out occurs on a neighborhood street corner, at a fast-food place, or in a mall, it is a time-honored adolescent pastime. A customary meeting place may be set, with people coming and going at different times. Or, once a group gets together, the members decide what they want to do and the information is quickly spread by e-mail, instant messaging, or text messages. Hanging out is possible both because many parents respect their teenagers' privacy and independence and because most 16- and 17-year-olds have access to cars.

GETTING TOGETHER *Getting together* is more intimate and structured than hanging out. A group of friends meets at someone's house or a party. Either males or females can organize the initial effort, and the group often pools its resources, especially if alcohol or other drugs are part of the activities. Because participants are not dating, there is a lot of flexibility in meeting new people.

Getting together typically involves "floating." The group may meet at someone's house for a few hours, decide to go to a party later, spend a few hours at a mall, and wind up at another party. Adolescents see getting together as normal and rational—"You get to meet a lot of people" or "We can go someplace else if the party is dead"—but it concerns many parents. Even if teenagers call home from the various locations, parents worry that the gatherings can become unpredictable or dangerous because of drug use.

Nevertheless, getting together is a popular form of dating for several reasons. Because the activities are spontaneous, there is little anxiety about preparing for a formal date or initiating or rejecting sexual advances. The experience is less threatening emotionally because the participants don't have to worry about finding a date or getting stuck with someone (for example, a blind date) for the entire evening.

It also relieves females of sexual pressure because they may help organize the get-together, share in the expenses, and come alone or with friends (rather than as part of a couple). People may pair off, participate in the group as a couple, or gradually withdraw to spend more time together, but there is less pressure to have a date as a sign of popularity.

Finally, getting together decreases parental control over the choice of friends. Parents usually don't know many of the adolescents in the group and are less likely to disapprove of friendships or compare notes with other parents.

Hooking up doesn't necessarily imply an interest in a relationship, but it often involves a casual sexual experience.

HOOKING UP *Hooking up* refers to physical encounters, no strings attached. It's a vague term that can mean anything from kissing and genital fondling to oral sex and sexual intercourse. Besides providing an opportunity for sex, hooking up is a way for people to find relationships. After an initial hook up, partners may develop a relationship in which they hang out and hook up again or, in some cases, start dating and become exclusive couples (Bogle, 2008).

At many high schools, hooking up is more common than dating. At some college campuses, 76 percent of the students have hooked up five times, on average, and 28 percent have had ten or more such encounters (England et al., 2007). It seems, then, that hooking up isn't a passing fad but is becoming the norm, especially among young people.

Hooking up commonly, but not always, takes place when both people are drinking. They might also hook up with casual friends or a former girlfriend or boyfriend. In the case of "friends with benefits" (FWB), a variation of hooking up, friends have sex with each other as a form of recreation that involves everything from kissing to sexual intercourse (Denizet-Lewis, 2004; Bisson and Levine, 2009).

Hooking up has its advantages. It's much cheaper than dating. Also, it's assumed that hooking up requires no commitment of time or emotion: "A girl and a guy get together for a physical encounter and don't necessarily expect anything further" (Wolcott, 2004: 11). In addition, hook ups remove the stigma from those who can't get dates but can experience sexual pleasure, and they make people feel sexy and desirable (Bogle, 2008).

Hooking up also has disadvantages, especially for women. Among college students, for example, men are more likely than women to initiate sex, more than twice as many men as women experience an orgasm, both sexes describe the women as "sluts" (whereas the men call the experiences "scoring"), and women who hook up generally get a bad reputation as being "easy" (England et al., 2007; England and Thomas, 2009). In effect, then, and despite the advantages of hooking up, the sexual double standard persists (see Chapter 7).

FWB sex also has costs and benefits. Such encounters provide a relatively safe and convenient environment for recreational sex because both people feel comfortable and trust each other. The disadvantages include complications such as wanting an unreciprocated romantic commitment, which can end a friendship, and creating conflict among a close circle of friends whose relationships don't include sex (Bisson and Levine, 2009).

Traditional-Contemporary Combinations

Several dating patterns incorporate both traditional customs and contemporary trends. For example, even though it's now more acceptable for members of either sex to initiate a date or to invite someone to a prom or dinner date, many gender scripts remain remarkably traditional.

PROMS AND HOMECOMING PARTIES *Proms* and *homecoming parties* are still among the most popular traditional dating events (Best, 2000). As in the past, they are formal or semiformal. Women receive corsages; men are typically responsible for transportation and other expenses; and both men and women, but especially women, invest quite a bit of time and money in preparing for these events.

Contemporary changes in the characteristics of proms include "turnabout" invitations (those extended to men by women) and dining out beforehand with a large group of couples. Couples might prolong the event by holding a group sleepover (presumably chaperoned by parents), staying out all night and returning after breakfast, or continuing the festivities into the weekend at a nearby beach or other recreational area.

DINNER DATES One of the most traditional forms of dating, the *dinner date* is still popular today, particularly among adults who are in their 30s or older. According to a national survey, 52 percent of women and 57 percent of men said that they preferred a "nice dinner" as a first date (*2006 Dating Trends Survey*, 2006).

Dinner dates, like first dates of any kind, are still highly scripted. The man typically initiates the date, opens doors, and starts sexual interaction (such as kissing the woman goodnight or making out). The women spends a good deal of time on her

Fatima Haque and her friends in Fremont, California, may have invented a new American ritual: the all-girl Muslim prom. It's a response to Muslim religious and cultural beliefs in which dating, dancing with or touching boys, or appearing without wearing a hijab (a head scarf or a veil that covers the face) is not permitted.

appearance, depends on the man to make the plans, and often responds to a sexual overture rather than making the first move. Thus, making a good impression early in the dating relationship is still largely synonymous with playing traditional gender roles. As in the past, men are much more likely than women to initiate a first date, including a dinner date, because they generally are more interested than women in sexual intimacy (Rose and Frieze, 1993; Regan, 2003).

The rise of the women's movement in the 1970s led to the custom of *going Dutch,* or splitting the costs of a date. Sharing dating expenses frees women to initiate dates and relieves them from feeling that they should "pay off" with sex.

When women ask men out, however, the rules about who picks up the check aren't clear. About half of Americans believe that the person who initiated the date should pay for it, but more than one-third think that the man should *always* pay for the date. Thus, the rules are vague: "Some men tell tales of women who ask them out and then expect them to pick up the tab" (Campbell, 2002: 4).

Perhaps the least gender-typed dating, at least on first dates, is between same-sex partners. A study of lesbians and gay men found little gender typing compared with heterosexual dating: Both partners participated more equally in orchestrating the date, maintaining the conversation, and initiating physical contact. There was also less concern about appearance (Klinkenberg and Rose, 1994). Because there are no more recent studies of same-sex dating, however, it's not clear whether these behaviors have changed.

Dating in Later Life

Dating after divorce or after being widowed can be both therapeutic and intimidating. It can enhance one's self-esteem, decrease loneliness, and involve reassessing one's strengths and weaknesses as one forges new relationships. Dating can also provide companionship while one is still grieving a spouse's death.

Dating can also be daunting. A recently divorced person may be bitter toward the opposite sex, or a parent may worry about a child's reactions to her or his dating. Widowed people may be nervous about reentering the marriage market, feel guilty about their romantic yearnings, and experience anxiety about their physical appearance or sex appeal.

However, many divorced and widowed people establish new and satisfying relationships through dating (see Chapters 15 and 17). Some seek out their teen heartthrobs online, rekindle the old flame, and marry. Not all reunions have a happy ending, of course. People change over the years, and our memories of our first love are usually highly romanticized. For example, the class Don Juan is still attentive, but now he's also bald and fat, has bad breath, and cheats on his wife. In other cases, however, sparks fly again and both partners see the same person they had loved, just older (Russo, 2002).

ꞏ• MAKING CONNECTIONS

- Many teenagers and young adults think that hooking up decreases the artificiality and pressure of dating. Some maintain, however, that such recreational sex means less romance, less excitement, less passion, and less intimacy because many women are giving out "free samples" (Mansfield, 2004). What do *you* think?

- How does one refer to a romantic partner, especially in social situations? "Significant other" can mean a parent, sibling, or close friend; "partner" or "companion" doesn't sound quite right; "lover" isn't acceptable in most social circles; "boyfriend" or "girlfriend" seems inappropriate unless you're a teenager; and "the person I'm seeing" might elicit questions about your relationship. Which term(s) do you, your family members, and friends use? Why?

MEETING OTHERS

Many people meet their dating partners through friends and family members. But there are many other avenues, including clubs, college classes, and recreational activities such as hiking, bicycling, and bowling. People have also relied on other strategies that range from personal classified ads to online dating sites.

Personal Classified Advertisements

Personal classified advertisements used to be published in the back pages of adult magazines. Now mainstream, suburban, religious, and local newspapers also carry personal ads.

People who place personal ads are usually very selective in their self-descriptions because both sexes are quite conscious of their cultural gender scripts. Because women know that men want attractive partners, they emphasize their appearance and femininity. Men, aware of women's expectations, describe their success, professional status, homeownership, education, or caring and sensitive nature. Single women rarely mention having children because men might not be willing to support offspring from a previous relationship (Dunbar, 1995; Raybeck et al., 2000). Thus, people barter the qualities that they see as most important in the marriage market.

The advantages of classified ads include anonymity, low cost, time savings, and the receipt of numerous responses. A major disadvantage is that advertisers often exaggerate their attributes. As one of my male students said, "I called her because she said she was gorgeous and intelligent. She was neither."

Mail-Order Brides

American men seeking wives can access one or more of 200 international services that publish photographs and descriptions of women, usually from economically disadvantaged regions such as the Philippines, Russia, Ukraine, and other Eastern European and South Asian countries.

Most of the men are white, college educated, and anywhere from 20 to 50 years older than the young brides they seek. Complaining that American women are too independent, too demanding, and too critical, the men typically want women with relatively little education who are raised in cultures in which a married woman is expected to be a subservient homemaker. Many U.S. brokers adorn their sites with photos of bikini-clad women and market the women as quiet, submissive, and easily controlled (Weir, 2002; Terzieff, 2006).

An estimated 4 percent of the 100,000 to 150,000 women seeking U.S. husbands find them. Because the mail-order bride business is largely unregulated, there's no way of knowing how many of these marriages are successful. Often, however, the American Prince Charming turns out to be an abuser. Some have murdered their wives; some have beaten, choked, and raped their brides; and others control their spouses by denying them any contact with their families at home or with their American neighbors (Hanes, 2004).

Beginning in 2006, the International Marriage Broker Regulation Act required U.S. men seeking a visa for a prospective bride to disclose any criminal convictions for domestic violence, sexual assault, or child abuse. Broker agencies are angry about the law, but its enforcement is weak. Most of the women stay in abusive relationships and don't report assaults because they speak little English; have no money and no friends in the United States; don't know that they can leave abusive husbands without being deported; and fear that their families will blame them, and not their husbands, for a breakup (Milbourn, 2006; Terzieff, 2006).

In other cases, the women advertising through matchmaking Websites are more interested in entering the United States than finding a good husband. It is not uncommon, for example, for an Internet bride to leave the marriage immediately after obtaining legal permanent resident status (Robinson, 2008).

Professional Matchmakers

In Shanghai, China, a 25-year-old lawyer has become wealthy by finding virgin brides for at least 50 men who are millionaires. Hundreds of women sent in applications, complete with photos and personal information, but others have denounced such matchmaking as crass and insulting: "People's beauty derives from their inner qualities, not their virginity. Those girls have sold themselves like cheap merchandise" (French, 2006: A4).

In the United States, online dating is booming, but some find the process too time consuming, are disappointed with the results, or want more privacy. As a result, professional matchmaking services are thriving.

Some matchmakers charge little for their service—$50 per introduction, plus a $50 one-time registration fee—but many fees are considerably higher. For example, one New York enterprise, Serious Matchmaking Incorporated, charges fees beginning at $20,000 for an initiation fee, plus $1,000 for a one-year membership that includes 12 dates. The services consist of an "image consultant" who suggests wardrobe changes (for both women and men) and a trip to a bridal shop so that a woman can visualize herself getting married.

Professional matchmakers, such as the one on the right, arrange dates between singles who are hoping to find a mate.

In addition, members must be willing to date imperfect people who aren't soul mates and to be less picky in choosing a mate. Many of the consultants themselves are single and haven't yet found a marriage mate. After spending thousands of dollars with a consultant, one woman said that she eventually met her man through an online dating service at a cost of $160 (Marder, 2002; Thernstrom, 2005).

How successful are matchmakers in finding mates? They may be better at getting rich than they are at marrying people off. For example, Daniel Dolan, a Harvard-trained corporate lawyer, has become a multimillionaire after setting up and franchising his "It's Just Lunch" (IJL) matchmaking service. The purpose of IJL is to set up busy professionals with meetings over lunch. The brochures and online advertising claim that "dating experts" thoughtfully pair up people based on personality, appearance, and goals (Fass, 2004).

Many participants in IJL, however, have complained about numerous problems. Nationally, for example, both women and men said that they wasted $1,200 to $1,500 for a year's membership fees because they had only one or two dates (which were disastrous); IJL never met their basic dating criteria (such as age, distance, weight, interests, health, not smoking, and not having children); members did not receive refunds when dates didn't show up; and IJL sales representatives didn't return calls involving complaints or pressured people to accept dates that they didn't want because "your criteria are unrealistic [or] inflated" ("It's Just Lunch," 2006).

Speed Dating

One of my friends recently participated in an 8-Minute Dating encounter at a local restaurant. He and 13 other guys attended an event at which they met 14 women. The participants went from one table to another, spending 8 minutes chatting with each person. At the end of an hour or two, they "graded" one other. If two people chose each other and wanted to meet, the organizer of the event e-mailed contact information to both parties.

This is an example of the fast-growing *speed dating* industry that emerged in 1999. The purpose of speed dating is to allow people to meet each other face to face, within a short period, to decide whether there is mutual interest in another date.

Since 1999, speed dating has spawned a number of companies that serve heterosexuals, gays, and a variety of ethnic and age groups. Because American Muslims are prohibited from dating at all before marriage, speed dating (known as *halal* dating) offers the opportunity for women and men to meet each other while being chaperoned. A young sheikh, or religious leader, usually leads a group discussion about the importance of marriage before the participants break up into speed dating groups (Al-Jadda, 2006).

Speed dating has several advantages. It is inexpensive (about $30 per function), takes little time, guards against stalking because the participants use only their first names, usually draws people from the same region, and avoids the awkwardness of blind dates. Some people initially feel embarrassed or uncomfortable about attending ("What if someone I know is there?"). According to the events' organizers, however, more than half of the participants meet someone with whom there is mutual interest in another date (Morris, 2003).

Speed dating also has several disadvantages. Because the participants engage in only a few minutes of conversation, they often rate potential partners on very superficial criteria such as appearance rather than more substantive traits such as values and lifestyle. Also, people who are shy may be crossed off someone's list even though they may be wonderful marriage mates over the long term (see Chapter 6).

Dating services report that numerous service members are finding romance with someone in the United States while serving in Iraq or Afghanistan. Some of these long-distance courtships have led to marriage.

Cyberdating

Millions of people are turning to the Internet to find romance and dates (see Data Digest). They can subscribe to discussion groups and chat rooms, meet hundreds of potential partners online, and discuss anything from radishes to romance. There are more than 800 online dating sites, and new ones keep popping up. Some of the largest—such as Match.com, eHarmony.com, and Matchmaker.com—have from 10 million to 50 million profiles in their databases.

Numerous dating sites—and many are free—now exist for almost every imaginable group. A few examples include Jdate.com (for Jewish singles), PlanetOut.com (for gays, lesbians, and bisexuals), TheSpark.com (for people with a weird sense of humor), OnlyFarmers.com, Catholic-Singles.com, and BlackPlanet.com. Sites such as Muslim-Match.com help hundreds of thousands of Muslims worldwide find partners with similar Islamic views and levels of religious commitment (Armario, 2005).

A major advantage of online dating is its accessibility and low cost. A fee of $20 to $25 a month provides instant access to tens of thousands of eligible singles, and subscribers can sift candidates based on height, age, income, mutual interests, and dozens of other traits. Subscribers can have up to three dates a week while corresponding with several dozen people at the same time. Another advantage is that subscribers can use code names and remain anonymous as long as they wish. Because physical appearance is in the background, verbal intimacy can lead to enduring relationships or even marriage.

People age 55 and older are the fastest-growing group of online dating service users. One reason is that the youngest baby boomers turned 60 in 2006, have high divorce rates, and are now looking for new mates. The Internet can be especially helpful to older women: Many don't have the same dating opportunities as men or find that men their age in their own community are looking for younger women. Among those age 55 and older, only 14 percent of women, compared with 22 percent of men, say that their most important reason for dating is to find a marriage mate, but members of both sexes are seeking companionship in their later years (Johnston, 2005;

During this speed dating event in New York City, dozens of singles spend five to ten minutes with each person. Event organizers send contact information by e-mail if the participants choose each other.

Wilkinson, 2005; Kantrowitz, 2006; see, also, Chapter 17).

Cyberdating also has its downside. Some complain that the dating sites have "a whole population of rebound people" who have not recovered from breakups. And some hot prospects simply disappear with no explanation after weeks of intensive e-mailing. In other cases, after rekindling romances with past sweethearts online, some people have had extramarital affairs with them or have divorced their spouses (Mahoney, 2004; Dotinga, 2005).

Another disadvantage is that electronic romances can be deceptive and superficial. As with classified personal ads, people may be dishonest or have an unrealistically high opinion of themselves. Women tend to lie about their age and weight ("Her photo must have been taken 10 years and 40 pounds ago"). Men tend to lie about their weight, height, income, and occupation. Moreover, about 20 percent of online male daters are married (Brooks, 2003; Fernandez, 2005).

Rejected suitors may start stalking or harassing their love interests. In addition, people who use the Internet to find real-life sex partners are much more likely to have engaged in risky behavior. As a result, people who seek sex using the Internet are at greater risk of contracting STIs and HIV (McFarlane et al., 2000; Booth, 2005).

Some women who believe that they've encountered lying and cheating men online are fighting back. Websites such as DontDateHimGirl.com are dedicated to outing men who are married or on the down low (see Chapter 7) or who lie about their personal characteristics (such as age, educational attainment, and weight). Some men have been outraged by such public accusations, but few have contested the charges (Alvarez, 2006).

More recently, millions of singles have turned to cellphone-based services. The programs help users find others to exchange text messages and even find, on a handset's digital map, nearby people who share their interests. Skype, an Internet phone service, lets singles connect all over the world for free. Webcams and microphones allow people to see and hear each other. Often, after one or two phone calls or video communications, people can decide if they're compatible (Semuels, 2006, 2008).

CHOOSING WHOM WE DATE: CHOICES AND CONSTRAINTS

Many Americans believe that "I can date anyone I want." This is a misconception. Most of us select dating partners and marry people who are similar to ourselves because filtering processes shape and limit our choices.

FIGURE 8.2 The Filter Theory of Mate Selection
According to filter theory, most of us narrow our pool of prospective partners by selecting people we see on a regular basis who are most similar to us on variables such as age, race, ethnicity, values, social class, sexual orientation, and physical appearance.

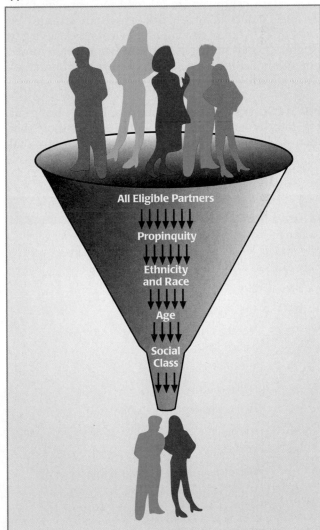

All Eligible Partners

Propinquity

Ethnicity and Race

Age

Social Class

MAKING CONNECTIONS

- How do *you* meet other eligible singles? Or are you waiting for Cupid to come to you?

- Millions of people have paid up to $350 for a two-day weekend workshop on how to snag a date (Stout, 2005). Is successful dating teachable? Or do most people land good dates through a trial-and-error process?

- Have you or your friends ever tried online dating? If so, were you happy with the results? If you've never cyber-dated, why not?

Homogamy and Filter Theory: Narrowing the Marriage Market

Theoretically, we have a vast pool of eligible dating partners. In reality, our field of potential partners is limited by our culture. According to **filter theory**, we sift eligible people according to specific criteria and thus narrow the pool of potential partners to a small number of candidates (Kerckhoff and Davis, 1962). *Figure 8.2* depicts the filter theory of mate selection.

The major filtering mechanism is homogamy. Often used interchangeably with the term *endogamy* (see Chapters 1 and 4), **homogamy** refers to dating or marrying someone with similar social characteristics, such as ethnicity and age. Some of the most important filtering variables are propinquity; physical appearance; and social characteristics such as race or ethnicity, religion, age, social class, and values and personality.

PROPINQUITY Geographic closeness, or **propinquity**, is one of the first filters that shapes whom we meet, get to know, interact with, and subsequently date and marry. Most people who are currently in serious long-term relationships or are married met through family and friends or in a work or school setting (see *Table 8.1*). And a growing number of cities have gay neighborhoods in which men and women easily meet potential partners at the grocery store, the library, or church (Sullivan, 2006).

PHYSICAL APPEARANCE Once propinquity brings us together, looks matter. A number of studies show that men and women choose partners whose physical

Men assign more importance to physical attractiveness than women do, but members of both sexes tend to choose partners whose physical appearance is similar to their own.

attractiveness is similar to their own (Berscheid et al., 1982; Feingold, 1988; McNulty et al., 2008).

Physically attractive people benefit from a "halo effect": They are *assumed* to possess other desirable social characteristics such as warmth, sexual responsiveness, kindness, poise, sociability, and good character. They are also seen as likely to have more prestige, happier marriages, greater social and professional success, and more fulfilling lives. In reality, life satisfaction is much the same for both attractive and less attractive people (Brehm et al., 2002; Olson and Marshuetz, 2005).

Throughout the world, men (regardless of their looks) are more likely than women to want an attractive mate (Buss and Schmitt, 1993). In the United States and many other Western countries, and especially for women, attractiveness is synonymous with slimness and youth.

The pressure to look good begins as early as middle school. Overweight girls ages 12 to 18 are less likely than their thinner counterparts to date. In adulthood, a woman's physical attractiveness is a key factor in being asked out on a first date. It's not surprising, then, that in 2006 almost 12 million teenage girls and women (up from 2 million in 1997) underwent cosmetic surgery to enlarge their breasts, reshape their noses and ears, and decrease fat through liposuction. In contrast, only 1 million men underwent cosmetic surgery (American Society for Aesthetic Plastic Surgery, 2009).

TABLE 8.1	Most People Find Each Other Offline
Most of the people in marriages and long-term relationships first met offline. So if your mom, classmate, best friend, or co-worker wants to fix you up with someone, go for it!	
38%	Met at work or school
34%	Met through family or friends
13%	Met at a nightclub, bar, café, or other social gathering
3%	Met through the Internet
2%	Met at church
1%	Met by chance, such as on the street
1%	Met because they lived in the same neighborhood
1%	Met at a recreational facility such as a gym
1%	Met on a blind date or through a dating service
6%	Met in a variety of other ways, such as growing up together

Source: Madden and Lenhart, 2006: 6.

Businesses are delighted by women's obsession with their looks. Says one marketing analyst, "Anything with the words 'age defying' sells" (Mayer, 1999: A1). As a result, we can be seduced into believing that we've halted or slowed the aging process by using a variety of products, and most of those products target women. Among them are age-defying toothpaste, hosiery, creams, and makeup.

Online makeover businesses are also flourishing. The services—which can cost up to $2,000—rewrite personal profiles, start initial e-mail conversations, airbrush photos, or hire professionals to take the most flattering pictures (Alsever, 2007).

Culture matters, too, in perceptions of beauty. Several Nigerian communities prize hefty women and "hail a woman's rotundity" as a sign of good health, beauty, and a family's wealth. Teenage girls spend several months in a "fattening room" eating starchy food such as yams, rice, and beans. The fattening room is a centuries-old rite of passage from girlhood to womanhood. Some younger women are starting to abandon this ancient practice because of community campaigns to lose weight for health reasons. However, many girls and women still follow the custom (Soares, 2006).

ETHNICITY AND RACE More than any other group, African American women face what one black journalist calls a "marriage crunch": "The better educated we are, the less likely we are to meet brothers who can match our credentials. The more successful we are, the less likely we are to meet brothers who can match our pocketbooks" (Chambers, 2003: 136).

Since you asked . . .

•• Why do some African Americans disapprove of interracial dating?

One in nine black men ages 20 to 34 is in prison or jail, decreasing the pool of eligible partners. Since 1976, nearly twice as many black women as black men have earned bachelor's, doctoral, and professional degrees (in fields such as medicine, law, and theology). Thus, many well-educated and successful black women find that they have priced themselves out of the market for finding a mate (Planty et al., 2008; Pew Center on the States, 2009).

Unlike the film *How Stella Got Her Groove Back*, most successful black women are unlikely to find happiness with a man who is 20 years younger than they are or one who's not intimidated by their achievements (Cose, 2003). What choices do these women have? Some are staying single; others are interdating.

About 55 percent of Americans have *interdated*—gone out with a member of another racial or ethnic group. Interdaters are more likely to be men than women and more likely to be Asian American or African American than Latino or white (Jones, 2005; Wellner, 2005).

The amount of interdating often depends on a person's social networks. Among college students, for example, those who are the most likely to develop interethnic and interracial romantic relationships have close friends who are ethnically diverse and who support interdating across ethnic or racial boundaries. As an Asian American female stated, "Currently, I'm in a relationship with a Caucasian. Three of my close friends are also in interethnic relationships" (Clark-Ibáñez and Felmlee, 2004: 300).

Interdating has increased, but some groups don't embrace the change. At some high schools in the South, black and white students date one another without their parents' knowledge, but white parents have refused to sponsor integrated proms. Instead, there's "the black-folks prom" and "the white-folks prom" (Corbett, 2009). As the box "Why I Never Dated a White Girl" shows, a number of African Americans endorse homogamy and disapprove of interracial dating.

RELIGION Religion can also affect dating and mate selection. All three of the major religions practiced in the United States—Catholicism, Protestantism,

The top row shows photographs of online daters before they used the services of makeover coaches. The bottom row shows their "after" photos.

Cross-Cultural and Multicultural Families

Why I Never Dated a White Girl

Interdating is fairly common, but still controversial. For example, 41 percent of black teens who have interdated say that their parents disapproved (Wellner, 2005).

Author Lawrence Otis Graham (1996: 36–56) explains why he's never dated a white woman and, presumably, why other black men shouldn't either:

- **Objection 1:** When black leaders or advocates marry outside their race, such decisions demonstrate less commitment to black people and our causes.

- **Objection 2:** We fear that inter-marrying blacks are making a statement to black and white America that black spouses are less desirable partners and are therefore inferior.

- **Objection 3:** Interracial marriage undermines our ability to introduce our black children to black mentors and role models who accept their racial identity with confidence and pride.

- **Objection 4:** Because it diffuses our resources, interracial marriage makes it difficult to build a black America that has wealth, prestige, and power.

- **Objection 5:** We worry that confused biracial children will turn their backs on the black race once they discover that it's easier to live as a white person.

- **Objection 6:** Today's interracial relationships are a painful reminder of a 250-year period in black Ameri-

can history when white people exploited our sexuality.

⁝• Stop and Think . . .

- Do you agree with Graham's reasons for not dating and marrying outside the African American community? Or do you think that his objections are outdated?

- Graham states why he believes that interracial dating and marriage are dysfunctional. Think back to the discussion of manifest and latent functions of dating at the beginning of the chapter. Are there ways in which interdating is functional?

and Judaism—have traditionally opposed interfaith marriages in the belief that they weaken individuals' commitment to the faith. The Roman Catholic Church encourages interfaith couples to ensure that their children will be raised as Catholics. And some Jews consider intermarriage a serious threat to Jewish identity and culture. As a result, many Jewish congregations do an "exemplary job of providing opportunities for unmarried people to get to know one another" to promote religious and ethnic endogamy (Glenn, 2002: 55).

AGE In some African and Asian countries, girls under age 13 are often married off to men who may be 30 or 40 years older. Americans are age-endogamous because they tend to date and marry within the same age group. Typically the man is a few years older than the woman. Among people who are dating, a large majority (68 percent) say that they would not marry a man who is 10 or more years younger than they are; 65 percent of men say that they would not marry a woman who is 10 or more years older than they are (*2006 Dating Trends Survey,* 2006; see, also, Chapter 10).

Men often seek younger women because they want to have families. In some cases, however, a woman may find that a much older man may be unwilling to have children, especially if he has a family from a previous marriage or is expected to share in the child-rearing responsibilities. Large age differences may also lead to generation gaps in attitudes

about lifestyle, such as music preferences, recreation, and family activities.

Successful women who have their own resources sometimes seek younger, attractive men with few assets but who can be "molded" (Moore et al., 2006). There's little evidence, however, that such unions are widespread.

SOCIAL CLASS Most people date and marry within their social class because they and their partner share similar attitudes, values, and lifestyles. Even when people from different racial and ethnic groups inter-marry, they usually belong to the same social class (Kalmijn, 1998).

Many of us face strong pressures to date people of similar (or preferably higher) social standing. Despite the popularity of films such as *Pretty Woman*, in which a powerful business mogul marries a prostitute, very few of the rich and powerful marry outside their social group (Kendall, 2002).

Parents may not have to exert much pressure on their children to date someone of their own kind because communities are typically organized by social class. Schools, churches, and recreational facilities reflect the socioeconomic status of neighborhoods. Thus, it is highly unlikely that children living in upper-class neighborhoods will ever meet children from middle-class, much less working-class, families.

Talk show host Larry King is almost the same age as the father of his seventh wife, Shawn. Why are most families and friends less likely to approve of age heterogamy in mate selection if the woman is 25 to 30 years older than the man?

One researcher has described colleges and universities as "matrimonial agencies" that are arranged hierarchically because students at Ivy League, private, state-supported, and community colleges have few chances to meet one another. Because they influence their children by encouraging them to attend college and helping them choose a school, many parents further narrow their dating choices in terms of social class (Eckland, 1968).

Social class also interacts with other variables to promote homogamy. Blue-collar and white-collar workers rarely meet each other in the workplace because they occupy different physical spaces and have different schedules. At colleges and universities, for example, staff and maintenance workers are usually housed in different buildings or floors and rarely interact. If we add religion, age, and physical appearance to the mix, homogamy reduces the number of eligible dating partners even further.

VALUES AND PERSONALITY Mate selection methods may have changed, but has there been a corresponding change in the values that shape our choices? College students' responses in three widely spaced studies—1939, 1956, and 1967—didn't change much (Hudson and Henze, 1969). Students said that they wanted partners who were dependable, emotionally stable, intelligent, sociable, good-looking, healthy, pleasant, and had a religious background and social status similar to their own.

The characteristics of the "ideal partner" had changed only somewhat by the late 1990s. As the box "What Are the Most Important Qualities in a Mate?" shows, both sexes are remarkably similar in

valuing traits such as mutual attraction, good character, emotional maturity, and a pleasant personality. Both men and women say that having a steady job and a good credit history and being financially responsible are more important than sexual compatibility in sustaining a dating relationship (Kristof, 2006; *2006 Dating Trends Survey,* 2006).

During the recent economic downturn, some middle-class men reported not dating at all after losing their jobs. As one man said, when he considers what it would cost to take a woman on a date, he thinks: "That's my electric bill." Some of these men admit that most women wouldn't mind paying for themselves on a date, but that doing so would shatter their self-worth and self-confidence as a self-supporting male (Goldstein, 2009).

Similar personalities are also important in dating and, eventually, marital satisfaction. Couples who are similar on characteristics such as self-reliance and compassion are generally happier because personality differences can spark conflict and negative reactions of anger and resentment. Also, people who are similar in personality tend to have similar emotional responses (such as amusement, anger, or sadness) that enhance a relationship (Gaunt, 2006; Gonzaga et al., 2007).

Homogamy narrows our pool of eligible partners. Increasing numbers of people, however, are expanding their marriage markets through heterogamy.

Heterogamy: Expanding the Marriage Market

As U.S. society becomes more diverse and multicultural, many people are dating and marrying across traditionally acceptable boundaries. Often used interchangeably with the term *exogamy* (see Chapter 1), **heterogamy** refers to dating or marrying someone from a social, racial, ethnic, religious, or age group that is different from one's own. Most societies, for example, prohibit dating or marriage between siblings and between children and their parents, aunts and uncles, or other relatives. In some countries, such as India, heterogamy rules forbid marriage between individuals of similarly named clans, even though the families have never met (Singh, 2005).

Worldwide, mate selection options are still limited by homogamy. Increasingly, however, many people have more choices in dating people of the same sex and across social classes, religions, and racial and ethnic boundaries.

Applying What You've Learned

⠶ What are the Most Important Qualities in a Mate?

What do you believe are the most important traits in a date or prospective mate? Are there any qualities that you would add to this list? Any that you would delete?

Order of Priority	Men Want	Women Want
1	Mutual attraction and love	Mutual attraction and love
2	Dependable character	Dependable character
3	Emotional stability, maturity	Emotional stability, maturity
4	Pleasant disposition	Pleasant disposition
5	Education, intelligence	Education, intelligence
6	Good health	Desire for children, home
7	Sociability	Ambition, industriousness
8	Good looks	Sociability
9	Desire for home, children	Good health
10	Ambition, industriousness	Similar educational background
11	Refinement, neatness	Good financial prospects
12	Similar religious background	Refinement, neatness

Source: Based on Buss et al., 2001.

SAME-SEX RELATIONSHIPS Most societies frown on same-sex dating because they define a marriage as valid only if it is between a man and a woman. Nevertheless, several countries now allow same-sex partners to marry. In the United States, five states have legalized gay marriages (Connecticut, Iowa, Massachusetts, New Hampshire, and Vermont). We'll examine same-sex marriages and civil unions in Chapter 9. For now, suffice it to say that recognizing gay relationships increases heterogamy by not limiting dating to opposite-sex partners.

SOCIAL CLASS RELATIONSHIPS As you saw earlier, most of us marry within our social class, but our dating and mate selection can move us up or down the social ladder. **Hypergamy** involves marrying up to improve one's social standing. Because the United States is still a race-conscious society, minority women, especially, can increase their social status by marrying a white man, even though he has a lower educational level than the woman (Fu, 2001; Tsai et al., 2002).

Hypogamy, in contrast, involves marrying down in social class. As women postpone marriage to pursue educational and career goals, they often find that a man with credentials similar to theirs just isn't available when they're ready to settle down (Whitehead, 2002). As a result, some women marry down.

Hypergamy used to describe most women in the past, but this is no longer the case. Increasing numbers of educated women make more money than their dating partners (and husbands) and do not have to rely on marriage for financial security or upward mobility (see Chapter 13).

About 90 percent of the most highly educated singles say that finding a partner who is intelligent is extremely or very important, compared with only 66 percent of those with a high school degree (see *Table 8.2*). Intelligence and being a college graduate aren't synonymous, of course. Many singles, however, use formal education as a proxy for intelligence. Note also that wealth is much less important than intelligence.

INTERFAITH RELATIONSHIPS Historically, religion has been an important factor in dating and mate selection in the United States and many other countries. Now, however, interfaith dating and marriages are common in the United States. For example, 37 percent of married people are in religiously mixed marriages (Pew Forum on Religion & Public Life, 2008).

TABLE 8.2	But Is He/She Smart?		
Percentage of single Americans who say that the following characteristics are "extremely important" or "very important" to them when looking for a mate.			
	High School or Less	Some College	College Graduate
Intelligent	66	86	90
Funny	65	73	75
Attractive	32	36	37
Athletic	10	12	16
Wealthy	8	4	5

Source: Adapted from Gardyn, 2002: 37.

Religiosity is important for people who have traditional values about gender roles (such as the belief that men should be breadwinners and women should be full-time homemakers). However, religious beliefs are less important for couples who have egalitarian attitudes about familiy roles and who seek partners with similar personalities (Gaunt, 2006). Race and ethnicity, in contrast, still play a major role in whom we date and marry.

INTERRACIAL AND INTERETHNIC RELATIONSHIPS

In 1987, nearly 50 percent of Americans—both black and white—disapproved of black-white dating. Today, 81 percent of white Americans and 97 percent of African Americans agree with the statement: "I think it's all right for blacks and whites to date each other" (Kohut et al., 2007).

More than half of Americans have interdated, and approval of interracial dating has surged, but racial intermarriage is still relatively uncommon because 95 percent of Americans marry people of the same race (see *Figure 8.3* on p. 218). The highest percentages of those who marry outside of their racial and ethnic groups are American Indians, Latino males, and Asian American women (see Chapter 4).

The percentage of black-white marriages is low—only 11 percent of all interracial marriages, compared with 26 percent of Latinos who marry outside of their group (U.S. Census Bureau, 2008). These rates suggest that social norms against white-black marriages are still much stronger than those against marriages among other racial and ethnic groups.

Black men are three times more likely than black women to marry a member of another racial or ethnic group. Why? Interracial dating still reflects a double standard. For example, black journalists such as Ellis Cose (1995) have criticized black women but not black men for dating interracially. Besides such double standards, other explanations might reflect the fact that black women who, as a group, are more likely than their male counterparts to obtain college and graduate degrees, would rather be single than marry down, and are less likely than black men to experience a boost in self-esteem because they believe that their white partners have a higher social status (Craig-Henderson, 2006). Mate selection theories provide further insights.

MAKING CONNECTIONS

- Think about the people that you've dated or the person you've married. Did filter theory influence your behavior? If so, which variables were the most important?

- Some people maintain that interracial dating and interracial marriage are healthy because such practices will break down some of the racial-ethnic barriers in our society. Others argue that interracial relationships will dilute one's cultural heritage. What do *you* think?

WHY WE CHOOSE EACH OTHER: THEORIES OF MATE SELECTION

Sociologists have offered various explanations of mate selection processes (see Cate and Lloyd, 1992, for a summary of several theoretical perspectives). In the 1950s and 1960s, some theories proposed that people are drawn to each other because of *complementary needs;* in other words, opposites attract (Winch, 1958). This and similar perspectives have fallen out of scientific favor because they are not supported by empirical data (Regan, 2003).

Since you asked . . .

- If opposites attract, why do people tend to date partners who are similar to themselves?

FIGURE 8.3 Interracial Marriages Have Increased in the United States

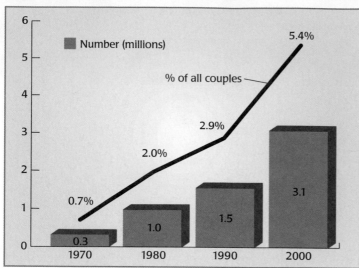

Source: Lee and Edmonston, 2005, Figure 1.

Filter theory proposes that social structure limits our opportunities to meet people who are very different from us. In this sense, the sifting process that narrows the pool of eligible candidates is largely unconscious and often beyond our control. What influences our decision to stay in a relationship or to move on? Exchange theory and equity theory maintain that satisfaction is a key factor in weighing our mate selection investments and liabilities.

Dating as Give and Take: Social Exchange Theory

According to social exchange theory, people are attracted to prospective partners who they believe will provide them with the best possible deal in a relationship (see Chapters 2 and 6). This may not sound very romantic, but social exchange theorists contend that costs and rewards form the basis of most relationships.

Social exchange theory posits that people will begin (and remain in) a relationship if the rewards are higher than the costs. *Rewards* may be intrinsic characteristics (intelligence, a sense of humor), behaviors (sex, companionship), or access to desired resources (money, power). *Costs,* the price paid, may be unpleasant or destructive behavior (insults, violence) or literal losses (money, time). The box "Am I Seeing the Wrong Person?" offers advice from practitioners for filtering out undesirable candidates as you look for a long-term relationship.

What, specifically, are some of the resources that people exchange in dating? About 62 percent of American men and 44 percent of American women have done something special for someone (saying "I love you," preparing a special meal, buying an expensive present) because they hoped it would lead to sex. People who are physically attractive trade this attribute for a

partner's higher education and income level. Among midlife adults (ages 40 to 69), men, never-married singles, and those who are sexually permissive are more willing to date people of a different race or religion or with much less money (Orr and Stout, 2007; Carmalt et al., 2008; Fitzpatrick et al., 2009). In these and similar research studies, people weigh their perceptions of rewards and costs in choosing dating partners.

Dating as a Search for Egalitarian Relationships: Equity Theory

According to **equity theory,** an extension of social exchange theory, an intimate relationship is satisfying and stable if both partners see it as equitable and mutually beneficial (Walster et al., 1973). Equity theory advances several basic propositions:

- The greater the perceived equity, the happier the relationship.
- When people find themselves in an inequitable relationship, they become distressed. The greater the inequity, the greater the distress.
- People in an inequitable relationship will attempt to eliminate their distress by restoring equity.

Equity theory reflects the American sense of fair play, the notion that one has a right to expect a reasonable balance between costs and benefits in life. If we give more than we receive, we usually become angry. If we receive more than our fair share of benefits, we may feel guilty. In each case, we experience dissatisfaction with the relationship. We try to decrease the distress and restore equity by changing our behavior, by persuading a partner to change his or her contributions, or by convincing ourselves that the inequity doesn't exist (Miell and Croghan, 1996).

Consider Mike and Michelle, who were initially happy with their dating relationship. Among other exchanges, she helped him with his calculus and he helped her write a paper for a sociology class. By the end of the semester, however, Michelle was still helping Mike with his calculus assignments but Mike was no longer available to help Michelle with her sociology papers because he had joined the swim team. According to equity theory, Mike might feel guilty and increase his help, Mike and Michelle could renegotiate their contributions, or one or both could break up the relationship.

Judgments about equity can vary depending on the stage of the relationship. As two people get acquainted, severe inequity usually ends further involvement. Once a relationship enters a stage of long-term commitment, people tolerate inequity—especially if they plan to

ASK YOURSELF

Am I Seeing the Wrong Person?

Because often "love is blind," many people overlook serious flaws and marry Mr. or Ms. Wrong. Here are some red flags that should alert you to possible problems.

- **Don Juans and other sexual predators.** Men admit using a variety of "lines" to persuade women to have sex. These Don Juans will *declare their love for you* ("I don't want to have sex with you—I want to make love to you"), *flatter you* ("You're one of the most beautiful women I've ever seen," "I've never met anyone like you before"), *make meaningless promises* ("Our relationship will grow stronger," "I swear I'll get a divorce"), *threaten you with rejection* ("Our relationship really needs to move on," "If you loved me, you would"), *put you down* if you refuse ("You're really old-fashioned"), or *challenge you* to prove that you're "normal" ("Are you frigid?" "Are you gay?").

- **Incompatibility of basic values.** Initially, it may be exciting to be with someone who's very different. In the long run, however, serious differences in values may jeopardize a relationship. If your partner likes to curl up with a mystery novel but you want to go out with friends every weekend, you may be in for trouble.

- **Rigid sex roles.** If your partner wants you to be a full-time homemaker and parent but you want a career, there may be strain.

- **Emotional baggage.** If your partner often talks about an ex-partner—comparing you with her "saintly" dead husband or his past lovers—she or he is living in the past instead of getting to know you.

- **Extreme jealousy and violent tendencies.** Stay away from someone who is possessive, jealous, or violent.

Characteristics such as a bad temper, frequent angry outbursts, constant criticism, and sudden mood swings will not decrease in the future.

- **Substance abuse.** Someone who is addicted to alcohol or other drugs is the wrong choice for a mate. Watch for slowed responses, slurred speech, glassy eyes, extreme mood swings, or failure to keep dates.

- **Excessive time spent with others.** Does your partner spend several nights a week with others while you spend time alone? If your partner is always on the phone, or if family "emergencies" often come before your needs, there will probably be similar conflicts in the future.

- **Mr. Flirt and Ms. Tease.** If your partner is flirtatious or a sexual tease, watch out. Flirting may be entertaining at first, but not over the long run.

- **Lack of communication.** Good communication is essential for a good relationship. Feelings of boredom, evidence of your partner's disinterest, or finding that you have little to talk about may signal serious communication problems that will decrease intimacy.

- **Control freaks.** Does your partner always try to change or control you or the relationship? Do you constantly feel criticized, judged, scrutinized, and corrected, especially in public? If so, stay away.

- **Blaming others for problems.** It's always someone else's fault if something goes wrong ("My boss didn't appreciate me" instead of "I was fired because I always came in late").

Sources: Powell, 1991; Collison, 1993; Kenrick et al., 1993.

---

marry—because they are optimistic about the future. In most long-term relationships, however, and especially as people face transitions (such as parenthood), perceived inequities can increase stress and dissatisfaction (Sprecher, 2001).

A GLOBAL VIEW: MATE SELECTION ACROSS CULTURES

Mate selection is an important process, but societies around the world vary considerably in how they negotiate the marriage market. A few of these variations involve differences between modern and traditional approaches, heterogamy and homogamy, and free choice versus arranged marriages.

Modern and Traditional Societies

Most countries do not have the open courtship systems that are common in Western nations. Instead, many factors—such as wealth, age, and values—promote traditional mate selection arrangements.

WEALTH In some Mediterranean, Middle Eastern, and Asian societies, the **dowry**—the money, goods, or property that a woman brings to a marriage—is an important factor for mate selection. Women with large dowries have a competitive edge in attracting the best suitors. If the bride's family fails to meet dowry expectations, their newlywed daughter may face onerous responsibilities in her new household, as well as violence and even death.

The Indian government has outlawed the dowry system, but the practice still flourishes. Many women who disapprove of dowries in principle regard them as necessary for attracting the most desirable men and as a way for young couples to obtain household goods (Srinivasan and Lee, 2004).

Whereas a dowry is a payment by the family of the bride, a **bride price** is the required payment by the groom's family. The payment varies from a few cattle to thousands of dollars. Some have criticized the bride price for treating women as property and for discouraging marriage among unemployed men. However, many defend the custom. For example, Africans argue that paying for a bride bonds families and decreases the likelihood of wife abuse. In Afghanistan, a bride price ensures a man's getting a virgin (sometimes as young as 11 years old) who will till fields, tend livestock, and bear children. In return, the bride's family delivers the girl from hunger and pays off some debts (Bearak, 2006; Calvert, 2006).

Money plays an important role in staying single or getting married. In Libya, Egypt, and other less prosperous parts of the Arab world, young men are putting off marriage because they can't provide brides with a home and a sizeable bride price, as custom demands. Across the Middle East, marriage is not only the key to adulthood and sexual activity, but also a religious obligation, which increases pressure to wed and guilt in remaining single. In Egypt, the poorest grooms and their father must save their total income for about eight years to afford a wedding. To encourage marriage in the poorest communities, the government and charities are helping finance mass weddings (Knickmeyer, 2007; Slackman, 2008).

AGE The minimum age at which people may marry varies widely from one country to another. In industrialized societies, the minimum age at marriage may be 16 or 18. In traditional societies in Africa, parents can betroth a baby girl to a friend's 4-year-old son

In some communities, charities pay for mass weddings—such as this one in Idku, Egypt—to help couples, many in their late 30s and 40s, who cannot afford to marry.

or before the girl is 10 years old or to a man who may be 20 or 30 years older than the girl (Wilson et al., 2003; Modo, 2005).

The minimum age at marriage is also low in many Middle Eastern countries. In 2002, for example, Iran passed a bill that permits girls to be married at age 13 (instead of 9) and boys at the age of 15 (instead of 14) without court permission. Female lawmakers saw the change as a major advance in protecting very young girls from early marriage ("Iranian arbitrating body . . .," 2002).

VALUES In many industrialized societies, including the United States, love is the basis for dating and marriage. In traditional societies, customs are more important than love in mate selection, including being able to support a wife and children. Other values include chastity for women, having children (rather than remaining childless), supporting aging parents, obeying in-laws, and being religious (which may mean not being able to get a separation or divorce). These and other values form the foundation of mate selection.

Heterogamy and Homogamy

Mate selection varies according to heterogamy and homogamy norms. Heterogamy, you recall, involves marrying outside one's family or kin group, whereas homogamy refers to marrying someone within one's social group, such as a person of the same race, religion, or social class.

HETEROGAMY In industrialized societies, both laws and custom prohibit people from marrying someone within her or his family. In the United States, many states don't allow marriages between first cousins (see Chapter 1). Especially if people don't have prospective marriage mates within their own social group, they marry outsiders. More than anything else, heterogamous marriages are economic decisions. For example, the number of women from mainland China who married foreigners rose from 26,000 in 1991 to 68,000 in 2006. The rates plunged in 2008, however, when the economic crisis began: "Many Chinese women married their husbands [in Germany] for their success and now [the men] are losing their jobs and cars. Many of them can't even pay their mortgages" (Ford, 2009: 5).

Heterogamy thrives in many other countries. To escape poverty, many Vietnamese women in their early 20s are marrying foreigners, mostly from Taiwan and South Korea, who are in their 40s or older. The wedding usually occurs shortly after the men spend a few days on a marriage tour to select their brides. In social exchange terms, the men—especially those from rural areas where women have moved to cities to work—find young wives who are eager to please. The women meet their obligation of saving their parents from destitution in old age, which many Vietnamese consider a child's greatest duty. The men promise to send the parents a monthly stipend. Even husbands who earn a modest living at home can help the bride's father pay off debts or open a small business. Some of the women endure ongoing abuse after the wedding, but others are happy and have no regrets (Onishi, 2007; Santana, 2008).

HOMOGAMY In many societies, mate selection is homogamous. In Afghanistan, for example, there is an old saying that "a marriage between cousins is the most righteous because the engagement was made in heaven." And across the Arab world, an average of 45 percent of married partners are related (Kershaw, 2003; Aizenman, 2005).

Homogamy has its advantages. In India—where 74 percent of the people oppose marriage across castes—homogamous mate selection ensures that people marry within their social class and can pass down their wealth to a kin group. In Turkey, homogamy ensures strong and continuing family ties (Nauck and Klaus, 2005; Benerjee et al., 2009).

Homogamy also has costs. In Cuba—and despite the government's formal policy of racial heterogeneity—racist beliefs about black inferiority and racial purity discourage people from seeking partners with lighter or darker skin colors. In Sri Lanka, classified ads for marriage partners ask respondents to indicate their caste because educated people don't want to mate with people from lower socioeconomic groups (Roschelle et al., 2005; Magnier, 2006).

Homogamy can also increase the chances of passing down diseases. In some parts of Saudi Arabia, for example, in which blood relatives range from 55 to 70 percent of married couples, such inbreeding produces several genetic disorders, including thalassemia (a potentially fatal blood disease), sickle cell anemia,

spinal muscular atrophy, diabetes, deafness, and muteness. Educated Saudis have begun to pull away from the practice, but the tradition of marrying first cousins is still deeply embedded in Saudi culture. In Afghanistan, where first-cousin marriages are common because women are prohibited from mingling with unrelated men, doctors are finding that children have a higher chance of being born with birth defects and diseases, such as brain disorders and mental retardation, that might be inherited (Kershaw, 2003; Aizenman, 2005).

Arranged and Free Choice Marriages

In arranged marriages, the family or community is more important than the individual. Arranged marriages are disappearing in some developing countries but are a mainstay in many others. As many as 90 percent of marriages in India are arranged, for example, and 71 percent of the people believe that such marriages are more successful than "love marriages" (Cullen and Masters, 2008). In Islamic societies, arranged marriages increase solidarity between families. If, for example, a newlywed couple experiences problems, family members might intervene to resolve some of the conflicts.

> **Since you asked . . .**
> ::• Do arranged marriages work better than dating in finding a mate?

Small groups of Saudi and other Middle Eastern women are challenging some strict restrictions on dating. However, many young Asians who live in the United States believe in arranged marriages because matchmakers—whether family members or friends—seem to do a good job of finding partners and women don't lose their self-respect by chasing and competing for men (Alibhai-Brown, 1993; see, also, Chapter 5).

Arranged marriages aren't paradise, however. In poor nations such as Afghanistan, parents arrange marriages between daughters and older men who are able to afford the $500 to $1,500 bride price. Thus, a 14-year-old girl may be given in marriage to a 60-year-old married man with grown children, and she is subservient to his other wives. To escape such arranged or unhappy marriages, girls and young women sometimes douse themselves with fuel and set themselves on fire. One regional hospital in Afghanistan has at least 100 such cases every year, and the numbers have been rising (Reitman, 2002).

Arranged marriages often involve marrying a first cousin as the top choice. In 2008 alone, 4,000 Pakistani girls born in Great Britain were coerced into marrying first cousins or other men during visits to Pakistan. Islam does not allow forced arranged marriages, but such cultural practices are common in societies in which men dominate and can force girls and women to marry against their will "to preserve culture and lineage" (Tohid, 2003: 7; Grose, 2008).

These men from South Korea are meeting potential brides during a marriage tour in Vietnam.

In a number of developing societies, the younger the bride, the higher the price she fetches. A father uses the bride price to ward off poverty, buy farm animals, and pay off debts. Pictured here, in Afghanistan, this 11-year-old was married off to a 40-year-old man. She had hoped to be a teacher but was forced to quit her classes when she became engaged.

In some traditional societies, men sometimes abduct women and force them into marriage (see the box "If She Says 'No,' Just Kidnap Her"). Although such practices are rare, they show that many women still have few choices regarding whom they can marry.

Open dating offers people more choices than do arranged marriages, but, as you saw, filter theory argues that people in industrialized societies, including the United States, are limited in their selection of dating and marriage mates. Arranged marriages may never take root in the United States because most people don't have strong community and family support systems after a marriage and there's a diversity of religious beliefs and values. Nonetheless, some Americans are looking into the practice because they are disillusioned with romantic love and seeking a soul mate who doesn't seem to exist (Goodale, 2008).

How Mate Selection Methods Are Changing

Some countries in Asia and the Middle East are experiencing changes in how people meet and select mates. In Baghdad, for example, many parents consider the Internet among the most harmful post-invasion developments in Iraq. A mother who discovered that her daughter was chatting with

Cross-Cultural and Multicultural Families

If She says "No," Just Kidnap Her

In some parts of Turkey, males abduct women for a number of reasons: to get a bride even though her family disapproves, to avoid dowries that the bride's family can't afford, or when both sides of the family have other mates in mind.

In some other societies, men simply kidnap women who refuse to marry them. One example is Kyrgyzstan, a country to the west of China. Even though the practice has been illegal for many years, more than half of Kyrgyzstan's married women were snatched from the street by their husbands. This custom, *ala kachuu,* translates roughly into "grab and run."

Some women don't mind *ala kachun* because it's a form of elope-

ment, but many see it as a violent act because they are taken against their will. Once a kidnapped girl or woman has been kept in the abductor's home overnight, her virginity is suspect, her reputation is disgraced, and she will find it difficult to attract a husband of her choice.

Many men in Kyrgyzstan rationalize the kidnappings. For example, snatching a woman is easier and cheaper than paying the standard bride price, which can be as much as $800, and "Men steal women to show that they are real men." And according to an old Kyrgyz saying, "Every good marriage begins in tears." That is, women are expected to adjust to the marriage.

The threat of abduction begins to haunt women in their teenage years. Some rarely leave their homes. Some women attending universities wear wedding bands or head scarves to fool men into thinking that they are already married.

Sources: Nauck and Klaus, 2005; Smith, 2005.

⁘ Stop and Think . . .

- Some women adapt to *ala kachun.* In effect, then, is this mate selection practice fairly harmless?

- Kidnapping women is illegal in Kyrgyzstan, but the law is not enforced. Does this tell us anything about patriarchal societies?

somebody online sold the computer. Arranged marriages are common, meeting members of the opposite sex is taboo unless a chaperone is present, and parents guard their daughters' virginity to ensure their marriageability. The parents' concerns seem justified because some young men who arrange dates online admit that they lie to young women, saying "I will marry you after I know you better" (Sabah, 2006).

India and China are experiencing a glut of single men and a scarcity of single women. In both countries, the preference for boys has led to the killing of millions of female infants and the deaths of many others as a result of neglect—poor nutrition, inadequate medical care, or desertion. Unmarried women have become scarce. Men in some poor rural regions of China often rely on a booming trade of kidnapped women from Vietnam and North Korea as a source of wives (Hudson and den Boer, 2004).

China has responded to the preponderance of males by implementing some Western-style mate selection methods, including newspaper and magazine ads and Internet singles services. In Beijing, on any of four days each week, hundreds of parents go to one of the city's three parks to play matchmaker, whether their children like it or not. Anxious that their mid-20s children are still unmarried because they are in fast-track jobs and don't have time to date, the parents are determined to find mates for them. They come prepared with photos and computer printouts describing the adult child and his or her desired mate. For example, "Male, 28 years old, 1.72 meters tall [about 5′ 6″;], a junior college graduate from an upper-middle-class family, seeking a shorter woman between 16 and 23 years of age, with a high school degree, a stable income, and a Beijing residence permit" (Epstein, 2005: 1A).

India has scores of sites dedicated to brokering marriages, whereas Internet dating services are much less popular. Parents post matrimonial "biodata" ads on Websites and in newspapers. The biodata include information on recreational interests, education, height and weight, complexion color, personality, monthly pay, drinking and smoking habits, and especially family history (including caste and sometimes blood type) because a marriage is a union between two families rather than between just two individuals (Abdulrahim, 2008).

Because many young couples in India who meet on a matrimonial Website marry within a few weeks, increasing numbers of parents are hiring "wedding detectives" who investigate a prospective groom's background. As India's middle and upper classes grow, so do dowries, which often invite fraud, especially by men living abroad. With an estimated 30,000 brides who are abandoned every year by suitors who disappear after collecting a dowry, detective agencies are a thriving new industry (Wax, 2008).

In Japan and South Korea, the mating game has also changed, in part because more women are acquiring a college education, finding jobs, postponing marriage, or preferring to remain single. To retain the loyalty of unmarried employees in the under-40 age bracket, several companies in Japan have engaged matrimony brokerage firms to act as matchmakers for those seeking a spouse. In South Korea, leading companies such as Samsung ask agencies to organize group blind dates as a benefit for single employees, and major banks vie for rich private customers by offering free matchmaking for their children (Thornton, 1994; Sang-Hun, 2007).

In 2005, one in five marriages in Taiwan was to a foreigner. Most were to women from China, Vietnam, and other Southeast Asian countries who met their husbands through marriage brokers. Men in rural towns, especially, have difficulty finding a wife locally who will keep house and bear children without complaint and who will care for her in-laws when they get old. Because of language barriers, abuse, and cultural differences, 40 percent of the marriages break down within five years. Other wives develop friendships

Every Sunday, parents gather at a park in Nanjing, China, to find girlfriends and boyfriends for their unmarried children. Parental matchmaking has become more aggressive because many urban Chinese youths, often in their mid- to late-20s, are busy with careers and are postponing marriage.

with brides from their own countries and adjust (Montlake, 2006).

In some parts of Spain, the Dominican Republic, Ecuador, and Colombia, women are scarce because they've left home to work in cities. To help men find mates, some enterprising farmers have organized "Cupid crusades." Women who are disenchanted with city life board a bus and spend a day with a group of bachelors: "Lonely hearts mingle over roasted lamb and a halting *pasodoble,* or two-step." An event usually lasts eight hours; the women pay $10 apiece and the men $30. Some of these encounters result in marriage (Fuchs, 2003).

HARMFUL DATING RELATIONSHIPS: POWER, CONTROL, AND VIOLENCE

A few years ago, one of my best students, Jennifer, dropped by my office to apologize for missing an exam and a week of classes. I listened quietly as she fumbled with excuses: "I was sick. . . . Well, actually, my mom was sick. . . . I've been having car problems, too." She then burst into tears and showed me a bruise around her neck. Her boyfriend had been abusing her for some time but now had tried to strangle her.

So far we've focused on the positive side of dating: how people meet and what qualities they look for in marital partners. Dating also has a dark side that includes power, control, and violence. We can recognize risk factors for sexual aggression and date rape, however, and seek solutions.

Power and Control in Dating Relationships

Sociologist Willard Waller's (1937) *principle of least interest* states that the partner who is least interested in the relationship has more power. That is, the person with more power is less dependent on the other, is less interested in maintaining the relationship, and, as a result, has more control. Conversely, the person with less power is more likely to be dependent, to try to maintain the relationship, and, as a result, to be manipulated or exploited (Lloyd, 1991; Sarch, 1993).

Men often maintain power and control during a dating relationship through direct strategies such as assertion, aggression, and discussion; women more often choose indirect strategies such as hinting, withdrawing, or attempting to manipulate a partner's emotions (Christopher and Kisler, 2004; Garbarino, 2006). The box "How Abusers Control

Dating Relationships" examines some coercive tactics in more detail.

Prevalence of Dating Violence

Control often increases as a relationship progresses from casual to more serious dating. Men are much more likely than women to use physical force and sexual aggression to get their own way or to intimidate a partner, but women can also be physically and emotionally abusive (Christopher and Kisler, 2004; Prothrow-Stith and Spivak, 2005).

Since you asked . . .

❖ Are men or women guiltier of dating violence?

DATING VIOLENCE Dating violence is widespread, especially among women ages 16 to 24 (Family Violence Prevention Fund, 2009). Consider the following statistics:

- Among 11- to 12-year olds, 41 percent who have been in a relationship know friends who have been called names, put down, or insulted via cellphone, IM, and social networking sites (such as MySpace and Facebook) (Liz Claiborne Inc., 2008).

- Among 13- to 14-year olds in relationships, 20 percent know friends and peers who have been kicked, hit, slapped, or punched by a boyfriend or girlfriend (Liz Claiborne Inc., 2008).

- Nationwide, 10 percent of high school students have been hit, slapped, or physically hurt on purpose by their boyfriend or girlfriend in the 12 months preceding the study (Eaton et al., 2008).

- One in five young women experiences rape (either completed or attempted) during college. In 80 to 90 percent of the cases, the victims and assailants know each other (Karjane et al., 2005).

- Among all adults age 18 and older, almost 22 percent of women and 3 percent of men have been raped by a current or former date, boyfriend, or girlfriend. Almost 82 percent of the male victims had been raped by another male (Tjaden and Thoennes, 2006).

- A study of university students in 32 nations found that almost a third of both sexes had physically assaulted a dating partner in the 12 months preceding the survey (Straus, 2006).

Dating violence is rarely a one-time event. Apparently, many women interpret the violence as evidence of love. According to a domestic violence counselor, "With so little real-life experience, girls tend to take jealousy and possessiveness to mean 'he loves me'" (L. Harris, 1996: 5). A Latina ninth

How Abusers Control Dating Relationships

Both men and women try to control relationships. Although the following categories describe the experiences of women who have been victims, men are also subject to abusive dating relationships.

- **Jealousy and blaming:** Blaming is often based on jealousy; almost anything the partner does is considered provocative. For example, a man may criticize his partner for not being home when he calls or for talking to another man. He may say he loves her so much that he can't stand for her to be with others, including male friends.

- **Coercion, intimidation, and threats:** Abusers may coerce compliance by threatening their partners. An abuser says things such as "I'll break your neck" or "I'll kill you" and then dismisses them with "Everybody talks like that." Abusers also threaten to commit suicide or to attack a partner's family.

- **Isolation:** Typically, abusers spend a lot of time and energy watching their victims. They accuse family and friends of "causing trouble." Abusers may deprive victims of a phone or car or even try to prevent them from holding a job. If these isolating techniques work, they break the partner's ties with other friends and increase dependence on the abuser.

- **Physical abuse:** Violent acts range from slaps and shoves to beatings, rape, and attacks with weapons. Many abusers manage to convince a partner, on each violent occasion, that "I really love you" and "This will never happen again," but it does. And in some cases the last time the abuser strikes, he or she kills.

- **Emotional and verbal abuse:** Emotional abuse is very powerful. Insults, which attack a person's feelings of independence and self-worth, are generally intended to get the partner to succumb to the abuser's

demands ("Don't wear your skirt so short—it makes you look like a hooker"). The abuser often says or implies that she had better do what the partner wants or be left without anyone.

- **Sexual abuse:** Conflicts about sex can lead to violence. Often a male abuser decides whether to have sex, which sex acts are acceptable, and whether the couple will use condoms or other contraceptive devices.

Sources. Gamache, 1990. Rosen and Stith, 1993; Shackelford et al., 2005.

Stop and Think . . .

- Have you, your friends, or relatives experienced any of these forms of abuse? How did you react?
- Do you think that we can really love someone we're afraid of?

Constraints

---

grader echoed these sentiments on why her friends tolerate abuse:

Like let's say she did something and he like, get abusive towards her. She's going to be like, well, it's because he cares about me and doesn't want me to do it again and he loves me and so he just wants me to be a good person or a good mate (Ocampo et al., 2007: 184).

The rates of violence among gay and lesbian couples are similar to those among heterosexuals, but they're highly underreported. In many cases, gays don't report dating or other violence for fear of increasing homophobia (Hoffman, 2003).

ACQUAINTANCE AND DATE RAPE Women are especially vulnerable to acquaintance and date rape. **Acquaintance rape** is rape of a person who knows or is familiar with the rapist. Acquaintance rapists may include neighbors, friends of the family, co-workers, or someone whom the victim meets at a party or get-together.

Date rape is unwanted, forced sexual intercourse in the context of a dating situation; the victim and the

perpetrator may be on a first date or in a steady relationship. Nationally, women are more likely to be raped by a date or an acquaintance than by a spouse or ex-spouse, a stranger, or a live-in partner (see *Figure 8.4*). One of the reasons date rape is so common and why it comes as a shock to the victim is that, typically, the rapist seems to be "a nice guy"—polite, clean-cut, and even a leader in the community or on campus.

Factors Contributing to Date Violence and Date Rape

There are many reasons for dating violence and date rape. Some of the most important explanations include family violence, gender roles, peer pressure and secrecy, and use of alcohol and other drugs.

FAMILY VIOLENCE A number of researchers have found an association between family violence and dating violence. Dating violence is more common among partners who had punched, shoved, or otherwise abused a sibling than among those who had not. Such violence is compounded by growing up in a family in which children see adult violence or experience

FIGURE 8.4 Rape Victims and Victim-Offender Relationships

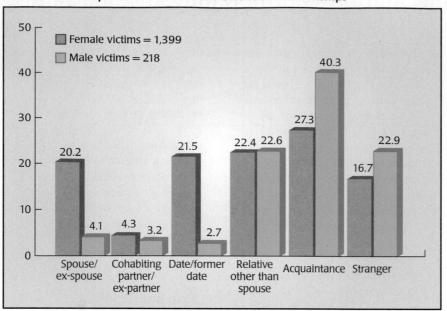

Note: Percentages by sex exceed 100 because same victims were raped by more than one person.
Source: Tjaden and Thoennes, 2006, Exhibit 13.

parent-to-child violence. Seeing that aggression produces compliance increases the likelihood of being both an assailant and a victim during dating (Noland et al., 2004; Baker and Stith, 2008; West, 2008).

GENDER ROLES Some attribute violence to *misogyny,* or hatred of women. Dating violence and date rape are ways of striking out against women (especially independent and self-confident women) who challenge men's "right" to control them.

Remember our discussion of narcissists—people who love themselves more than anyone else—in Chapter 6? Narcissistic men are especially likely to use sexual coercion during dating. They can become aggressive and even commit rape because they feel entitled to the sexual gratification that they want and expect (Bushman et al., 2003).

Generally, men who commit date rape hold traditional views of gender roles, seeing themselves as in charge and women as submissive. They initiate the date and pay the expenses, and they often claim that women lead them on by dressing suggestively. Traditional men, especially, can be sexually aggressive and not feel guilty about it because "She deserved it" or "Women enjoy rough sex." Some men who commit date rape also have stereotypical views of women's sexual behavior. They believe that women initially resist sexual advances to preserve their reputation and, because of this, prefer to be overcome sexually. In addition, some men believe that if a woman is "a tease" or "loose," she is asking for sex (Christopher, 2001; Sampson, 2002).

Women are more likely than men to blame themselves for dating violence because females are socialized to accept more responsibility than males for relationship conflict. Often, both sexes see the woman as responsible for acquaintance rape because women should know better than to visit men in their apartments or lead men on through heavy petting (Szymanski et al., 1993; Lloyd and Emery, 2000).

PEER PRESSURE AND SECRECY
Peer pressure is one of the major reasons why some people are violent and why many partners stay in abusive dating relationships. The pressure to date is fierce, and having any boyfriend is considered better than having none because teens who date are seen as more popular than those who don't (L. Harris, 1996).

Peer pressure may be even greater in college. In some cases, fraternity members and male athletes cover up incidents of sexual abuse—especially when it occurs during and after a party—instead of reporting the violence. And, on many college campuses, sorority leaders acknowledge that talking about relationship violence is not "socially acceptable" or don't know how to help members who are experiencing dating abuse (Larimer et al., 1999; Danis and Anderson, 2008: 337).

Women can also be sexually coercive. Many of the male victims report giving in to sexual arousal or verbal pressure by women. The women are more likely to have been subjected to physical force or plied with alcohol or drugs (Larimer et al., 1999; Sampson, 2002).

Secrecy protects abusers. Most teenagers remain silent about abusive relationships because they don't want their friends to put pressure on them to break up. They rarely tell their parents about the abuse because they don't feel close to them, are afraid of losing their freedom, don't want their parents to think they have poor judgment, or fear that their friends will criticize them if the parents report the abuse to the police (Ocampo et al., 2007).

Women who are members of minority racial or ethnic groups may endure dating violence for several reasons. Young Latinas and Asian/Pacific women, for instance, may be torn between duty to their values of virginity and family honor and accommodating the men they are dating. When violence occurs in a secret dating relationship, there is additional pressure to prevent parents from learning about both the

Singer/songwriter Chris Brown, 19, pleaded guilty to assaulting his girlfriend, pop singer Rihanna, 21. He is serving 5 years of probation and doing 180 days of community service. In a recent survey of 200 teenagers in Boston, 46 percent said Rihanna was responsible for the beating (Hoffman, 2009).

violence and the relationship itself. The secrecy intensifies the woman's feeling of responsibility for the violence (Yoshihama et al., 1991; Foo, 2002).

USE OF ALCOHOL AND OTHER DRUGS Although they are not the cause, alcohol and drugs play a large role in sexual assaults. In more than 75 percent of college rapes, the offender, the victim, or both had been drinking. Many college students deny any relationship between alcohol consumption and sexual aggression. Men say that they can control themselves, and women maintain that they can resist unwanted sex. However, alcohol lowers inhibitions against violence and reduces a woman's ability to resist a sexual assault. In some cases, men admit that their strategies include getting women drunk to get them into bed (Nurius et al., 1996; Sampson, 2002).

Since the mid-1990s, a growing number of college women have reported being raped after their drink was spiked with Rohypnol (also known as "roofies," "rope," and a variety of other street terms).

When it is slipped into a beverage, Rohypnol's sedating effects begin within 20 minutes of ingestion and usually last more than 12 hours. Rohypnol has been called the "date-rape drug" and the "forget me pill" because many women who have been given roofies have blacked out and been raped and had no memory of what happened. When mixed with alcohol or narcotics, Rohypnol can be fatal ("Rohypnol," 2003).

A more recent rape drug is GHB, or gamma hydroxybutyrate, a liquid or powder made of lye or drain cleaner that's mixed with GBL, gamma butyrolactone, an industrial solvent often used to strip floors. GHB is an odorless, colorless drug that knocks the victim out within 30 minutes. The coma-like effects of GHB last from three to six hours (Office of National Drug Control Policy, 2009).

Some Consequences of Dating Violence and Date Rape

Most dating violence and date rape occur in situations that seem safe and familiar. This is why these behaviors often come as a great shock to the victim, who cannot believe what is happening.

Violence and rape violate both body and spirit; they can affect every aspect of the victim's life. *Even though they are not responsible for the attack,* women often feel ashamed and blame themselves for the rape. Fear of men, of going out alone, and of being alone becomes part of their lives, as do anger, depression, and sometimes inability to relate to a caring sexual partner. *Table 8.3* lists other consequences of date violence and date rape.

Some Solutions

Because violent behavior and rape are learned behaviors, they can be unlearned. Solutions are needed on three levels: individual, organizational, and societal.

On the *individual level,* less than 5 percent of college students report completed and attempted rapes to campus authorities and/or the police. Reporting such assaults would decrease their incidence. On the *organizational level,* several federal laws require colleges to report rape and other sexual assaults. Only 37 percent of colleges comply fully with these laws. Even when assaults are reported, the perpetrators are rarely suspended or expelled. If colleges and law enforcement agencies prosecuted sexual violence, it would decrease (Karjane et al., 2005).

To make a serious dent in the incidence of dating violence and date rape, however, we must also change *societal attitudes and beliefs* about violence and about male and female dating roles. The traditional notion that it is the woman's job to maintain the tone of a relationship often leads women to blame themselves when things go wrong and to overlook, forgive, or excuse men's sexual aggression and dating violence.

TABLE 8.3	Emotional and Behavioral Problems Experienced by Victims of Date Violence or Date Rape

- General depression: Symptoms include changes in eating and sleeping patterns and unexplained aches and pains. Depressive symptoms may prevent women from attending classes, completing courses, or functioning effectively on the job.
- Feelings of powerlessness, helplessness, vulnerability, shame, and sadness.
- Loss of self-confidence and self-esteem, which may increase the likelihood of future sexual assaults.
- Changes in the victim's behavior in an intimate relationship and attitudes toward sexual relationships in general.
- Irritability toward family, friends, or co-workers.
- Generalized anger, fear, anxiety, or suicidal thoughts and attempts.
- Inability to concentrate, even on routine tasks.
- Development of dependence on alcohol or drugs.
- Unwanted pregnancy.

Sources: Benokraitis and Feagin, 1995; Larimer et al., 1999; Silverman et al., 2001; Olshen et al., 2007.

BREAKING UP

Social scientists use numerous terms for breaking up, including "uncoupling," "disengagement," and "relationship dissolution." In plain English, we dump someone or vice versa.

According to one poll, nearly half of American adults have gotten the romantic heave-ho at least twice during their lifetime, and 22 percent say that they have been dumped by significant others six to ten times (Mundell, 2002). And, a study of students at one university found that 93 percent of both sexes had been spurned by someone they passionately loved and 95 percent had rejected someone who was deeply in love with them (cited in Fisher, 2008). A classic song tells us that "breaking up is hard to do." Why, then, do so many couples break up?

Since you asked . . .
- Should we break up more often than we do?

Why We Break Up

There are numerous reasons for breaking up dating and other intimate relationships that include both micro-level and macro-level factors:

- *Individual (micro) reasons* include communication problems, different interests, emotional and physical abuse, obsessive love and controlling behavior,

stalking, mismatched love and sexual needs, self-disclosure that reveals repulsive attitudes, disillusionment, lowered affectionate behavior, infidelity, and not making a commitment (Forward, 2002; Harley, 2002; Regan, 2003).

- *Structural (macro) reasons* include moving away; economic recessions that trigger unemployment and arguments about finances; and societal reactions that disapprove of relationships between young partners, young men and older women, couples from different racial or ethnic and religious backgrounds, and same-sex partners (Martin, 1993; Regan, 2003).

How We React

Breakups are usually very painful, but people respond in different ways. Women, for example, are usually more devastated by cheating than men—who feel that betraying a friend is a greater offense than sexual infidelity. And, as you might expect, people who have fewer chips in the marriage market are more upset by dating breakups than those who have many options because they're self-confident, successful, or attractive (Feldman et al., 2000; Schmitt and Buss, 2001).

Confusion and anger are two of the most common reactions to breakups because we may not know why we were rejected. Explaining the reasons for a breakup provides a sense of closure—"a cathartic purging of feeling guilt, anger, depression, loneliness, insecurity, and confusion" (Regan, 2003: 174).

Men seem to get over breakups more quickly than women do. Shortly after a breakup, for example, 42 percent of men and 31 percent of women start dating someone else (Fetto, 2003).

Is Breaking Up Healthy?

Absolutely. Disagreements and conflict are part and parcel of any close relationship, especially before marriage. Breaking up a dating or cohabiting relationship is much less complicated than breaking up a marriage (see Chapter 15).

Some pop psychologists contend that people break up for ridiculous reasons, such as rejecting someone who texts massages during dinner, a guy who lives with his parents, or a woman who wears pumps with jeans (see Kiehl, 2007). Such reasons for breaking up may seem frivolous. On the other hand, seemingly perfect dates may be terrible partners in the long run. For example, people who are good at monitoring their behavior ("impression management," in Goffman's terms, as you saw in Chapter 5) have skills in picking up on social cues and are unlikely to say things that upset others. The downside is that because people who are good at monitoring their behavior usually mask their true feelings to avoid conflict, they don't engage in intimate communication, and, as a result, they may not be able to achieve long-term happiness in their romantic relationships. In contrast, people with fewer self-monitoring skills who don't avoid confrontation or hide their true feelings and opinions may initially seem combative, but they are ultimately more genuine, honest, loyal, and capable of making a long-term commitment (Wright et al., 2007).

One of the important functions of dating and courtship is to filter out unsuitable prospective mates. Thus, breaking up is a normal process. It can also be a great relief to end a bad relationship (see Chapter 6).

If anything, breaking up should probably occur more often than it does because most people don't circulate enough before getting married (Glenn, 2002). Ending a dating relationship provides opportunities to find a mate who may be more suitable for marriage or a long-term relationship. In addition, breaking up opens up a larger pool of eligible and interesting partners as we mature and become more self-confident before deciding to marry.

:: MAKING CONNECTIONS

- Some women stay in violent dating relationships because they have a "caretaker identity": They feel responsible for the man's behavior or want to rescue him from his problems (Few and Rosen, 2005). Have you known women who fit this description? Why do you think men are less likely to take on such caretaking roles?

- Some people believe that breaking up on e-mail or text messages is tacky. Others argue that these are quick and painless ways to end a relationship (Noguchi, 2005). What do *you* think?

CONCLUSION

We have more *choices* in mate selection today than ever before. A broad dating spectrum includes both traditional and contemporary ways to meet other people.

These choices emerge within culturally defined boundaries, or *constraints*, however. Factors that determine who selects whom for a partner come into play long before a couple marries and despite the romantic notion that "I can date anyone I want." Most people feel pressure to date and mate with people who are similar to themselves. Some partners must also deal with aggression and violence.

One response to our array of choices and constraints in mate selection is to postpone marriage. In fact, a significant *change* today is the decision of many people to stay single longer, the subject of the next chapter.

SUMMARY

1. Sociologists describe the dating process as a marriage market in which prospective spouses compare the assets and liabilities of eligible partners and choose the best available mate. In this sense, we "trade" with others, depending on what resources we have.

2. Dating fulfills both manifest and latent functions. Manifest functions of dating include recreation, companionship, fun, and mate selection. Latent functions include socialization, social status, sexual experimentation, and meeting intimacy and ego needs.

3. Forms of dating have changed over the years. Many adolescents and young adults, especially, have forsaken traditional dating for more informal methods such as "getting together" and "hooking up."

4. Adults use a variety of mate selection methods to meet a potential spouse, including personal classified ads, marriage bureaus, computerized services, and the Internet.

5. Much of our dating and mate selection behavior is shaped by homogamy—rules that define appropriate mates in terms of race, ethnicity, religion, age, social class, values, and other characteristics.

6. Our pool of eligible partners expands when we seek mates from outside our own religious, racial, or ethnic group.

7. Social exchange theory and equity theory suggest that dating partners seek a balance of costs and benefits in a relationship. The relationship is most satisfying when it is seen as egalitarian.

8. Unlike the United States and some other Western nations, most countries around the world do not have open courtship systems. Instead, marriages are often arranged by families and restricted to members of the same culture, religion, or race. The selection methods are changing in many traditional societies, however.

9. Dating is usually fun, but there are also many risks and problems. Women, especially, are often victims of sexual pressure and aggression, violence, and date rape. The reasons for such victimization include power differences between men and women, peer pressure and secrecy, and the use of alcohol and other drugs.

10. Ending a relationship may be painful, but it also provides opportunities for finding a better mate.

KEY TERMS

dating 202
marriage market 202
filter theory 212
homogamy 212
propinquity 212

heterogamy 215
hypergamy 216
hypogamy 216
equity theory 218
dowry 219

bride price 220
acquaintance rape 225
date rape 225

PEARSON
myfamilylab MyFamilyLab provides a wealth of resources. Go to www.myfamilylab.com<http://www.myfamilylab.com/>, to enhance your comprehension of the content in this chapter. You can take practice exams, view videos relevant to the subject matter, listen to audio files, explore topics further by using Social Explorer, and use the tools contained in MySearchLab to help you write research papers.

9 Singlehood, Cohabitation, Civil Unions, and Other Options

A couple who had been dating for several years went out to a Chinese restaurant for dinner. After studying the menu, the man asked the woman, "How would you like your rice: fried or cooked?" She looked him straight in the eye and replied, "Thrown."

Sound corny? Maybe not, because most people eventually marry. Until then—or if the relationship fizzles—there is more freedom than ever before to pursue other alternatives. This chapter examines four nontraditional living arrangements: singlehood, cohabitation, gay households, and communal residences. We'll look at other nonmarital households, such as single parents and widowed people, in later chapters.

Before reading further, take "A Quiz about Singles." It asks how much you know about single people and provides a preview of the chapter.

DATA DIGEST

- More than 81 percent of U.S. **high school students expect to marry** someday.

- The number of **single people** (never married, divorced, and widowed) increased from 37.5 million in 1970 to 109 million in 2008, comprising 48 percent of all Americans age 18 and older.

- The **proportion of adults who have never been married rose** from 15 percent in 1972 to 27 percent in 2010.

- The proportion of households consisting of **one person living alone** increased from 17 percent in 1970 to 27 percent in 2010.

- The number of **unmarried-couple households** has grown—from only 1 percent in 1960 to over 6 percent in 2010.

- More than 38 percent of opposite-sex, unmarried-partner households include **one or more children under age 18.**

- Almost 780,000 households are made up of **same-sex partners.**

Sources: Fields, 2004; U.S. Census Bureau, 2008; Wood et al., 2008; U.S. Census Bureau, Current Population Survey..., 2009; U.S. Census Bureau News, 2009.

ASK YOURSELF

A Quiz about Singles

True	False	
☐	☑	**1.** Men are more likely than women to live alone.
☐	☑	**2.** The age group with the largest number of people who live alone is between ages 25 and 34.
☑	☐	**3.** Living together is a good way to find out whether partners will get along in marriage.
☑	☐	**4.** Women and men who live together typically share housework and other domestic tasks.
☑	☐	**5.** The percentage of never-married people is higher for whites than for Latinos.

True	False	
☐	☑	**6.** Most singles are happier than most married people.
☑	☐	**7.** About the same percentage of people live in unmarried-couple households as in married-couple households.
☑	☐	**8.** Utah has the lowest percentage of same-sex households.
☑	☐	**9.** Rates of domestic violence are lower among gay couples than among straight couples.
☑	☐	**10.** Most elderly singles worry about growing old and dying alone.

The answers to this quiz are on p. 236.

THE SINGLE OPTION

You'll recall that many people are anxious about the state of the American family (see Chapter 1). They fear that marriage is disappearing, especially because of the increase in single people (see Data Digest). Are such concerns warranted?

Are Americans Opting Out of Marriage?

More people today than in the past are choosing not to marry, are living together, or are raising children alone. As a result, according to some social scientists, there is "a marriage problem" in the United States (Wilson, 2002).

After reading this chapter, you can decide for yourself whether we have a marriage problem. It's certainly true, however, that more people than ever believe that being single is an attractive option. This doesn't mean that singles will never marry. Instead, many young adults are simply marrying at later ages.

Many Singles Are Postponing Marriage

Many young people are pursuing a college educa-

Since you asked . . .

⁞• Is there an ideal age to get married?

tion, preparing for a job or career, and spending more time in recreational or other activities before settling down. As a result, many of us are marrying later than our parents or grandparents did.

In 1960, the median age at first marriage was 20 for women and almost 23 for men. By 2009, it had risen to almost 26 for women and more than 28 for men, the oldest ages at first marriage ever recorded by the U.S. Census Bureau (see *Figure 9.1*). (Remember that the *median* is the midpoint of cases. Thus, in 2008, half of all men were 27 or older and half of all women were almost 26 or older when they first married.)

From a historical perspective, the present tendency to delay marriage is the norm, especially for men. Men's median age at first marriage was only slightly lower in 1890 than in 2008 (26.1 and 27.4, respectively). The median for women has increased more noticeably, however, especially since 1960 (see *Figure 9.1*).

For both sexes, the younger age at first marriage in the 1950s and 1960s was a historical exception rather than the rule. As you saw in Chapter 3, World War II delayed many marriages. When the soldiers came back, there was a surge of weddings. Throughout the 1950s, the United States tried to regain normalcy by encouraging both women and men in their late teens or early 20s to marry and have babies. Young couples themselves wanted to marry and form families after men returned from the war.

In the late 1960s, feminists, especially, began to question women's traditional roles both within and outside the family. Over the past few generations, both women and men have thought more consciously and deliberately about when and whom to marry.

Is there an ideal age for first marriage? In a 1946 Gallup poll, most Americans said that the ideal age

FIGURE 9.1 Many Americans Are Marrying Later

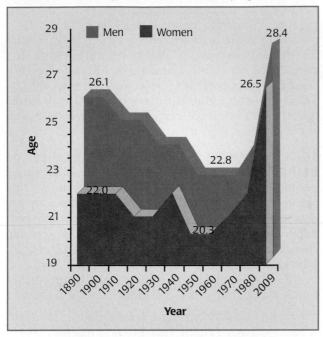

Sources: Based on data from Saluter, 1994, Table B; Saluter, 1996, Table A-33; and U.S. Census Bureau, ACS 2009 ACS09:B12007. Median Age At First Marriage: http://www.socialexplorer.com/pub/reportdata/htmlresults.aspx?ReportId=R1006 2360.

was 25 for men and 21 for women. Sixty years later, the ideal age had increased to 27 for men and 25 for women (Jones, 2006). You'll see shortly, however, that there is a growing debate, especially among some researchers and self-help writers, over whether waiting to marry is a good idea.

Being single has become much more acceptable, but many young people still feel pressure to marry. Some of my students complain that "if you're not married by the time you're 30, people think there's something wrong with you. My family and friends are constantly telling me to get married." Unmarried women, especially, often dread family get-togethers because they are asked over and over again whether they are dating "someone special." Parents drop not-so-subtle hints about having grandkids, invitations to friends' weddings pile up, and "bridesmaid dresses stare back at single women when they open their closet doors" (Hartill, 2001: 15).

The older singles are, the more often friends and relatives badger them about their marriage plans. Others complain of feeling invisible and not being invited to social or family activities with married couples unless it's to be fixed up with one of the couple's single friends (DePaulo, 2006). Despite such pressure, more people are single than ever before.

The never-married are only one cluster of a very diverse group of singles. In fact, many unmarried Americans don't identify with the word "single" because they are parents, have long-term romantic partners, or are widowed.

THE DIVERSITY OF SINGLES

There are several kinds of singles: those who are delaying marriage; the small percentage who will never marry; the currently unmarried who are divorced or widowed but may be looking for new partners; and lesbians and gay men, who are still legally barred from marrying in 44 states. In addition, people's living arrangements may vary greatly, from living alone or cohabiting during part of one's adult life to singlehood in later life.

Single Adults in General

Singlehood reflects more dimensions than simply not being married. It can be either freely chosen or unintentional, as well as either enduring or temporary (Stein, 1981):

- *Voluntary temporary singles* are open to marriage but place a lower priority on searching for mates than on other activities, such as education, career, politics, and self-development. This group also includes men and women who live with each other but aren't married.

- *Voluntary stable singles* have never married and are satisfied with that choice; are divorced or widowed but don't want to remarry; are living with someone but don't intend to marry; and those whose religion forbids marriage, such as priests and nuns. Also included are single parents—both never married and divorced— who are not seeking mates.

- *Involuntary temporary singles* would like to marry and are actively seeking a mate. This group includes people who are widowed or divorced and single parents who would like to get married.

- *Involuntary stable singles* are primarily older divorced, widowed, and never-married people who would like to marry or remarry but haven't found a suitable mate and accept their single status as permanent. This group also includes singles who suffer from some physical or psychological impairment that limits their success in the marriage market.

A person's position in these categories can change over time. For example, voluntary temporary singles may marry, divorce, and then become involuntary stable singles because they are unable to find another suitable mate. In this sense, the boundaries between being single and being married are fairly fluid for most people. For a much smaller number, singlehood is constant either because it's a choice or because some people have little to trade on the marriage market (see Chapter 8).

Some people are single longer than others. At age 62, talk show host David Letterman married his girlfriend of 23 years. At the time, their son was 5 years old.

Single Adults in Later Life

As one grows older, there is a tendency to become pickier in choosing a mate, especially because the pool of available people has decreased. And for older singles who date and want to marry or remarry, the double standard still favors men, decreasing the likelihood of their marrying older women.

AGING AND THE DOUBLE STANDARD In mate selection, aging women are typically seen as "over the hill," whereas aging men are often described as "mature" and "distinguished." Older women are also more likely than older

> **Since you asked . . .**
>
> ❖• Are most older single people lonely and unhappy?

men to remain single after divorcing or being widowed because they are caring for relatives, primarily aging parents or/and grandchildren (see Chapter 17).

There is little research on older people who have never married, probably because less than 5 percent of men and women age 65 and over fall into this category (U.S. Census Bureau, 2009). Some are isolated and others have many friends; some wish they were married, and others are glad they're single.

SOME ADVANTAGES AND DISADVANTAGES OF BEING SINGLE IN LATER LIFE Some see older single people—whether divorced, widowed, or never-married—as lonely and unhappy. Such perceptions are accurate about older singles who are living in poverty, experience poor health, don't have caregivers to help them, or have been forsaken by their family members and friends (see Chapter 17).

Marriage may be satisfying, but, on the other hand, it also limits one's freedom:

When I was a little girl and, later on, an adolescent, it never occurred to me that I would not meet the man of my dreams, get married, and live happily ever after. Now, at fifty-four, it seems unlikely, though not impossible, that this will happen. Not only do I live alone but I actually like it. I value my space, my solitude, and my independence enormously and cannot [imagine] the circumstances that would lead me to want to change it (Cassidy, 1993: 35).

Also on the positive side, never-marrieds don't have to deal with the trauma of widowhood or divorce. Many develop extensive networks of friends and relatives. They work, date, and engage in a variety of hobbies, volunteer work, and church activities and often have lasting relationships with friends and siblings.

Some singles live with others, some alone. Let's look briefly at who lives alone and why.

HOME ALONE

Because more than 90 percent of all Americans marry at least once, marriage is still the norm. Household size has been shrinking, however. In 1900, nearly half of the U.S. population lived in households of six or more people (Hobbs and Stoops, 2002). A century later, more than one in four Americans lives alone (see *Figure 9.2*). Who are the people living alone? And what explains the rise in solitary living?

 Answers to "A Quiz about Singles"

All the answers to the quiz on p. 234 are false. The answers are based on material in this and later chapters.

FIGURE 9.2 The American Household Is Shrinking

Both the decline in the average number of people per household and the rapidly rising numbers of people living alone have contributed to a smaller contemporary household.

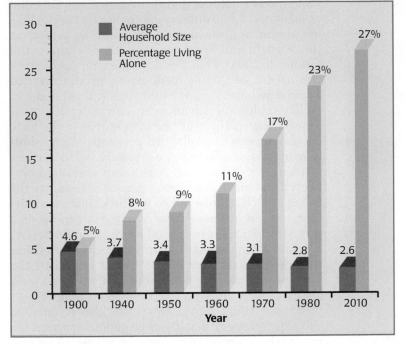

Sources: Based on Hobbs and Stoops, 2002, and U.S. Census Bureau News, 2010.

Who Is Living Alone?

Singlehood is widespread, and singles are a diverse population. Nevertheless, there are some patterns in terms of gender, age, and race and ethnicity.

GENDER AND AGE More women (15 percent) than men (13 percent) live alone. Of all age groups, older Americans are the most likely to live alone: about 27 percent in 2010, and older women are more likely than their male counterparts to live alone. There are several reasons for these gender differences. For example, on average, women live about six years longer than men, are less likely than men to remarry after a divorce or widowhood, and, if they enjoy good health and have enough income, they can care for themselves into their 80s and even their 90s (U.S. Census Bureau News, 2009; see, also, Chapter 17).

RACE AND ETHNICITY Of all people who live alone, more than 79 percent are white. Members of racial-ethnic groups are more likely to live in extended-family households because of values that emphasize caring for family members and pooling financial resources to avoid poverty (U.S. Census Bureau, 2008; see, also, Chapter 4).

Why Do People Live Alone?

Rachel, one of my graduate students, recently bought a townhouse in a nice neighborhood. Rachel is 32, has a good job as a bank manager, has no children, and hopes to marry. But, she says, "I'm not going to put off making this investment until Mr. Right comes along."

Since you asked . . .

Do people live alone because of choices or constraints?

Rachel's reasons for living alone echo those of many other singles her age. Many Americans choose to live alone because *they can afford it*. In fact, single women now buy twice as many homes as do single men. Some of the reasons include having higher educational levels and better-paying jobs, wanting a home rather than just a place to live (such as an apartment), postponing marriage, and not depending on a man to buy a house after marriage (Knox, 2006; Coleman, 2007).

A second and related reason is that *our values emphasize individualism*. Most single Americans of all ages are highly involved in their families but prefer to live alone because doing so offers more privacy and freedom than does living with parents or others.

A third reason for living alone is that Americans are *living longer and healthier lives*, making it possible for them to live independently after retirement. Even before retirement, being healthy means that people can live by themselves instead of moving in with others.

Finally, and perhaps most important, many people are living alone because they are postponing marriage or deciding not to marry. That is, they have *more options, including singlehood*. As Rachel said, she doesn't want to put her life on hold "until Mr. Right comes along."

MAKING CONNECTIONS

■ Are *you* single? Why? For example, are you single voluntarily or involuntarily?

■ Do you think there's an ideal age for marriage? If married, do you think you were too young or too old when you wed?

■ Do you or your friends live alone? Why? What are some of the benefits and costs of not living with other people?

WHY MORE PEOPLE ARE SINGLE

Many Americans say that they are single because they are not in love and are still waiting for the right person. For social scientists, being single—especially postponing marriage—reflects an interplay of macro-level factors that affect demographic variables, which, in turn, influence individual (micro-level) behavior

FIGURE 9.3 Some Reasons for Postponing Marriage

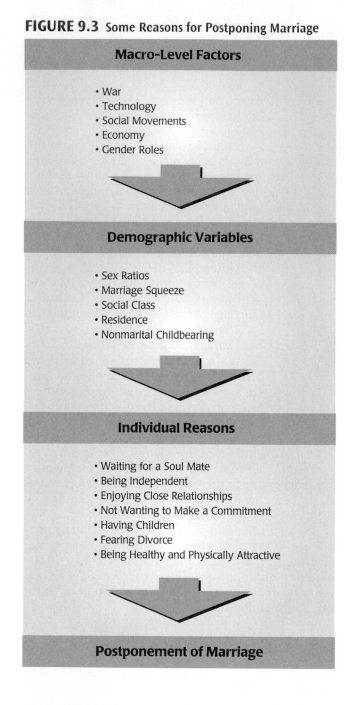

Macro-Level Factors

- War
- Technology
- Social Movements
- Economy
- Gender Roles

Demographic Variables

- Sex Ratios
- Marriage Squeeze
- Social Class
- Residence
- Nonmarital Childbearing

Individual Reasons

- Waiting for a Soul Mate
- Being Independent
- Enjoying Close Relationships
- Not Wanting to Make a Commitment
- Having Children
- Fearing Divorce
- Being Healthy and Physically Attractive

Postponement of Marriage

(see *Figure 9.3*). Let's begin with some of the macro-level factors that delay marriage.

Macro-Level Factors

A number of macro-level variables—over which we have little or no control—affect our decisions about matrimony. A few examples include war, technology, social movements, the economy, and gender roles.

WAR, TECHNOLOGY, AND SOCIAL MOVEMENTS Marriage rates tend to drop during a war. In Afghanistan, for example, decades of war killed, handicapped, or psychologically traumatized many men, leading to a shortage of potential Afghan husbands. After the U.S. invasion of Iraq in 2003, many couples—especially in Baghdad, the capital—postponed weddings because people died every day, making life unpredictable (Roug, 2005). By late 2008, 223,000 civilians and 9,000 military and police had been killed in crossfire and suicide bombings and by insurgents (Brownstein and Brownstein, 2008; O'Hanlon and Campbell, 2008). Thus, besides devastating a country's population of young men, many of the married become involuntary singles through widowhood.

Technological advances in contraceptive techniques, especially the birth control pill, have decreased rates of unplanned pregnancies and shotgun marriages. Women, especially, have greater control over childbearing, can avoid unwanted out-of-wedlock births, and aren't pressured to marry the father of a child born out of wedlock. Just as important, women in their 40s and even 50s can become pregnant by means of reproductive technologies. As a result, many women postpone marriage because they believe that they are no longer bound by the biological clock that has traditionally limited their ability to have children (see Chapters 7 and 11).

Several social movements have also resulted in delayed marriage or shaped our definitions of acceptable relationships. The women's movement opened up new educational and occupational opportunities for women, giving them career options outside marriage. The gay rights movement encouraged homosexuals to be more open about their sexual orientation and relieved the pressure to marry heterosexuals. And, most recently, there has been a surge of new books in the mass media, with titles such as *Better Single Than Sorry,* that promote singlehood (see, for example, DePaulo, 2006; Dubberley, 2007; Schefft, 2007; and Talbot, 2007).

ECONOMIC FACTORS Economic realities also play an important role in delaying or promoting marriage. Economic depressions, recessions, and unemployment tend to postpone marriage, especially for men. The well-paid, blue-collar jobs that once enabled high school graduates to support families are mostly gone. The job prospects for some college-educated men are also worsening rather than improving. In contrast, economic opportunities, as well as the belief that a person has access to those opportunities, encourage men to marry (Landale and Tolnay, 1991; see, also, Chapter 13).

Economic slumps can also reduce the marriage market for singles. When incomes plummet and people are insecure about their jobs—as Americans experienced in 2008 and 2009—unhappy married couples tend to stay together because they couldn't afford to divorce and risk the possibility of not being able to maintain separate households (Cherlin, 2009b). One result is that such involuntary marriages decrease the pool of voluntary singles.

The effects of employment on women's tendency to marry are somewhat contradictory. Being employed increases a woman's chances of meeting eligible men and may enhance her attractiveness as a potential contributor to a household's finances. On the other hand, women with high salaries may be unwilling to settle down with men who earn less than they do (Hacker, 2003; see, also, Chapter 8).

GENDER ROLES Technological and economic transitions affect gender roles. As gender roles change, so do attitudes about marriage and self-sufficiency. With the advent of washing machines, cleaning services, frozen foods, wrinkle-resistant fabrics, and 24-hour one-stop shopping, for example, men no longer need to be dependent on women's housekeeping (Coontz, 2005).

Women aren't rushing into marriage, either. Because the stigma once attached to singles living together has largely vanished, many women choose to cohabit and have babies outside marriage. In other cases, because it's difficult to juggle a career and a family, many women have chosen to advance their professional lives before marrying and starting a family.

Demographic Influences

Macro-level factors can delay marriage. Demographic shifts (such as changes in the sex ratio and the marriage squeeze), social class, and nonmarital childbearing also help explain the large number of singles.

THE SEX RATIO The **sex ratio,** expressed as a whole number, is the proportion of men to women in a country or group. A ratio of 100 means that there are equal numbers of men and women; a ratio of 110 means that there are 110 men for every 100 women (more males than females).

Worldwide, about 107 boys are born for every 100 girls. In the United States, the sex ratio is 105 at birth. In the 65 and over age group, the ratio is 75 because women tend to live longer than men (there are more females than males) (Central Intelligence Agency, 2009; see, also, Chapter 17).

In some countries, the sex ratio is highly skewed from birth. For example, the sex ratio is 114 in Armenia, 113 in Georgia, 112 in India, and 110 in China (down from 120 in the early 1990s). Because of the sex ratio imbalances, 163 million women have been deemed "missing" in the Asian region, attributed to **female infanticide,** the intentional killing of baby girls because of a preference for sons (Guilmoto, 2007; United Nations Population Fund, 2007).

According to some estimates, as many as 10 million female fetuses might have been aborted in India in the past 20 years. A law passed in India in 1994 forbids doctors from revealing the sex of a fetus to its parents because of the common practice of "sex-determined abortions." However, only a few of the wealthy districts—in which the ratios of girls to boys are at their lowest—have begun to enforce the law (Baldauf, 2006; Gentleman, 2006).

Some researchers find that sex ratios are especially skewed within different parts of a country. For example, hoping to reduce female infanticide, the Chinese government relaxed its one-child policy by allowing inhabitants in rural areas to have a second child if their first was a girl. What's happened, however, is that many couples are now aborting or killing a second or third female infant to have a son. Thus, some provinces have sex ratios of 160 for second births, contributing to an excess of 32 million males under the age of 20 in China (Zhu et al., 2009). That's roughly the size of Canada's population.

The reasons for female infanticide and, consequently, skewed sex ratios are cultural. In many Asian countries, including China and India, there is a preference for boys because they will carry on the family name, care for elderly parents, inherit property, and play a central role in family rituals. As a result, hundreds of thousands of female infants die every year because of neglect, abandonment, infanticide, and starvation. Others are aborted after ultrasound scanners reveal the sex of the child (Eberstadt, 2004; Dogra, 2006).

In adulthood, sex ratios vary due to several factors. In Africa, for example, there are more women than men because of civil wars and AIDS deaths. In Central America, there are more men than women because women often migrate to other countries—such as the United States—for jobs.

THE MARRIAGE SQUEEZE A **marriage squeeze** is a sex imbalance in the ratio of available unmarried women and men. Because of this imbalance, members of one sex can be squeezed out of the marriage market because of differences in wealth, power,

South Korea reduced its sex ratio from 112 in the late 1990s to 107 in 2009. The greater sex ratio balance has been attributed to a change in a centuries-old preference for baby boys which, in turn, decreased the number of female abortions. Among other factors, the government dismantled laws that guaranteed men their family's inheritance, educated women, and endorsed equal rights for women and men in the workplace (Sang-Hun, 2007; Central Intelligence Agency, 2009). Pictured here, girls attend the same athletic classes as boys.

TABLE 9.1	Who Has Never Married? By Age and Sex, 2009	
Age	Males (%)	Females (%)
Total, 15+	34.2	27.4
15–17 years	98.4	98.2
18–19 years	97.4	95.3
20–24 years	88.7	79.3
25–29 years	62.2	47.8
30–34 years	36.5	27.2
35–39 years	23.5	17.7
40–44 years	20.4	13.8
45–49 years	16.5	12.0
50–54 years	13.3	10.0
55–64 years	9.1	7.1
65–74 years	4.5	5.1
75+ years	3.5	3.6

Sources: Based on U.S. Census Bureau, Current Population Survey, 2008 Annual Social and Economic Supplement, 2009, Table A1, www.census.gov (accessed June 12, 2009).

status, education, age, or other factors that diminish the pool of eligible partners.

Is there a marriage squeeze in the United States? Yes. There are large numbers of never-married people, especially men, across all ages (see *Table 9.1*). If we add to the pool the 43 million people who were unmarried because of divorce, separation, or widowhood in 2008, the marriage market appears to be very large. However, homogamy narrows the pool of eligible mates. In addition, millions of women in their middle and later years experience a marriage squeeze because men their age are looking for much younger women (see Chapter 8).

Many countries are experiencing a much more severe marriage squeeze. Men in China, India, Korea, Taiwan, the Middle East, and other regions face a scarcity of young, single women because of skewed sex ratios. There are dozens of "bachelor villages" in China's poorer regions in which men can't find wives. As a result, there is a booming trade in kidnapped women who are brought to China as wives (Pomfret, 2001).

More recently, rural regions with an oversupply of bachelors have experienced wedding scams and "runaway brides." Village customs dictate that the groom's family pay the bride's family a bride price (see Chapter 8) known as *cai li*, and the bride furnishes a dowry of mostly simple household items. Because of the scarcity of women, and the shame of men's not being married by age 24 or 25, some families have saved or borrowed up to five years' worth of farming income to pay the *cai li* for brides from other provinces. A few days after the wedding, the brides and their families vanish (Fong, 2009).

SOCIAL CLASS Most low-income couples expect to marry, especially after the birth of a child, but they often retreat from marriage. A major reason is economic: They believe that they should first achieve a certain level of financial stability, save enough money to attain long-term goals (especially buying a house), and accumulate enough savings to host a "respectable" wedding. Theoretically, their living costs might be lower if they married, but many unmarried couples postpone marriage because they feel that financial worries will increase tension, arguing, and the chances of divorce (Gibson-Davis et al., 2005).

The likelihood of marriage increases with educational attainment. For example, 75 percent of unmarried people age 25 and older are high school graduates compared with 24 percent who have at least a bachelor's degree (U.S. Census Bureau Press Release, 2010). More education means more income, and more income reduces financial barriers to marriage. College-educated singles can pool their assets to pay for living expenses. They can also plan elaborate weddings and afford a down payment for a house, especially if their middle-class parents can provide generous monetary gifts.

NON-MARITAL CHILDBEARING Out-of-wedlock births are common. Still, many never-married mothers are likely to remain single because they can't find a good husband. The marriage market is especially tight for economically disadvantaged unwed mothers because prospective partners may be unwilling to make the long-term financial and emotional commitment to raise nonbiological children. Also, women who are poor are often unwilling to marry someone who has little education, is often unemployed, and has few financial resources. Because of the small pool of desirable marriage mates, many of these women cohabit rather than marry (Qian et al., 2005).

Individual Reasons

Marriage offers many benefits, but there are also incentives for being single (see *Table 9.2*). Both choices and constraints shape our attitudes and behavior about getting married or staying single. Let's begin with waiting to find an ideal partner, a soul mate.

WAITING FOR A SOUL MATE Many singles delay marriage because they are waiting to meet their "ideal mate" or "true love." In a study of never-married young singles ages 20 to 29, an overwhelming 94 percent agreed with the statement that "when you marry you want your spouse to be your soul mate, first and foremost." Another national survey of never-married single adults ages 18 to 49 found that 79 percent believed that they would eventually find and marry their "perfect mate" (Edwards, 2000; Whitehead and Popenoe, 2001).

Since you asked . . .

- Do you think that there's a soul mate out there for every person?

TABLE 9.2	Some Benefits of Marriage and Singlehood	
Benefits of Getting Married	**Benefits of Being Single**	
Companionship	Privacy, few constraints, independence	
Faithful sexual partner	Varied sexual experiences; cohabitation	
Dependability; love	Exciting, changing lifestyle	
Sharing mutual interests	Meeting new friends with different interests	
Pooling economic resources	Economic autonomy	
Social approval for settling down and producing children	Freedom from responsibility to care for spouse or children	
Becoming a part of something larger than self	A need for independence	

Sources: Based on Stein, 1981; Carter and Sokol, 1993.

Some people believe that waiting for an ideal mate is unrealistic because a marriage involves more than emotional intimacy. If a person decides that a partner is no longer a soul mate, for example, she or he will become disillusioned and bail out. Some self-help authors advise women, especially, to settle for Mr. Not-Quite-Right instead of ending up alone (see Lipka, 2008). Also, the longer one waits to marry, the smaller the pool of eligible partners, especially among the never-married (see Chapter 8).

Others contend that waiting for a soul mate isn't necessarily starry-eyed: "Perhaps more than ever before, young people have an opportunity to choose a partner on the basis of personal qualities and shared dreams, not economics or 'gender straitjackets'" (Rivers, 2001).

BEING INDEPENDENT One of the biggest benefits of singlehood is independence and autonomy because single people can do pretty much what they please. According to a 32-year-old male newscaster, "You don't have to worry about commitments to your career [affecting] your commitment to a family. I'm not ruling out marriage.... There's just no rush" (Wilson, 2001: D1). And as one of my 29-year-old female students once said, "I don't plan to marry until my feet have touched six of the seven continents."

Singles with resources, such as high education levels and high-income jobs, are especially likely to be choosy about marriage partners. If they don't find someone with the traits they seek, both sexes are saying "no thanks" to marriage rather than giving up their freedom.

ENJOYING CLOSE RELATIONSHIPS A common reason for getting married is companionship (see *Table 9.2* above). Singles who are delaying marriage rely on peers rather than a spouse for support and companionship. Especially in large cities, singles have close friends (sometimes called "urban tribes") with whom they socialize. They may meet weekly for dinner at a neighborhood restaurant, sometimes travel together, help move one another's furniture, and paint one another's apartments (Watters, 2003). As one of my unhappily married female friends recently confided, "There's nothing lonelier than being with somebody you don't want to be with."

Being unmarried is not synonymous with feeling isolated. Many singles are quite involved in family life, some live with their parents or close friends, and others spend much time with nieces, nephews, and grandchildren. Women, especially, devote much of their time and resources to supporting other family members (see Chapter 12).

MAKING A COMMITMENT There are more never-married men than women in all but the oldest age groups (see *Table 9.1* on p. 240). Why, then, do so many women complain that "there's nothing out there"?

One reason is that many men simply don't want to get married. Recently, for example, a 25-year-old complained to advice columnist "Ask Amy" that she had made it clear to her live-in boyfriend that she was ready to become engaged and to get married a year later, after both of them had finished law school.

"Why, no, I don't want to hear what the baby did."

© 1989, The New Yorker Collection, Richard Cline from cartoonbank.com. All rights reserved.

Instead, for Christmas he gave her a promise ring. She was hurt and insulted because "Where I come from, promise rings are for teenagers." It sounded as though the boyfriend was unwilling to make a commitment, but Amy chided "Anxiously Awaiting" for being immature and advised her to appreciate the boyfriend's "sweet gift" instead of pressuring him to marry (Ask Amy, 2008: 6C).

There's an old joke about single guys: "My girlfriend told me I should be more affectionate. So I got two girlfriends!" Some family practitioners believe that men are the foot draggers—especially when there's an abundance of potential girlfriends—because there's little incentive for them to marry (Pittman, 1999). For example, because of the greater acceptance of premarital sex, most men can have sex and intimate relationships without getting married. Many men also put off marriage because of stagnant wages and job losses and see marriage as a major economic responsibility that they don't want to undertake (Ooms, 2002).

In one study, 70 percent of low-income fathers-to-be under age 25 planned to marry their pregnant girlfriends but had more *social capital*—such as providing the mother with emotional support and participating in doctors' visits—than *financial capital*—such as jobs, money, and housing (Fagan et al., 2007). Because, however, and as you saw earlier, there's a strong association between higher social class and getting married, financial capital is more important than social capital and good intentions in many people's decisions to marry.

HAVING CHILDREN Couples often marry because they plan to raise a family. Nearly 70 percent of Americans, however, disagree with the statement that "the main purpose of marriage is having children" (Popenoe and Whitehead, 2003). Also, just 37 percent of Americans say it is "very important" that an unwed couple marries when the couple has a child together (Saad, 2006). Because cohabitation and out-of-wedlock parenting are widely accepted, singles of all ages feel less pressure to get married.

Though still small in number, the percentage of births to unwed women in their thirties has more than doubled—from 8 percent in 1980 to 18 percent in 2006 (Federal Interagency Forum on Child and Family Statistics, 2008). Some researchers call middle-class, professional, unmarried women who intentionally bear children "single mothers of choice" (Mattes, 1994; Hertz, 2006; see, also, Chapter 11).

Most of these women's *first* choice is to marry and *then* have children, however. As one 35-year-old mother said, "You can wait to have a partner and hope you can still have a baby. Or you can choose to let that go and have a baby on your own" (Orenstein, 2000: 149). Even if a woman finds a soul mate, he may not want to participate in child care and other domestic activities that many women now expect men to share.

FEARING DIVORCE Divorce or prolonged years of conflict between parents can have a negative effect on young adults' perceptions of marriage. Many stay single as long as possible because they worry about divorce. If children have grown up in homes where parents divorced one or more times, they are wary of repeating the same mistake. As one 21-year-old woman said, "My father left my mother when I was 6. I don't believe in divorce" (Herrmann, 2003). A 32-year-old man who works for a publishing company is in no rush to marry for similar reasons: "I would say you can never be too choosy.... Most of my friends' parents are not together anymore or on their second marriages" (Hartill, 2001: 17).

Others believe that marriage doesn't necessarily improve people's lives or relationships. According to one of my 30-something male students (with whom many of his classmates agreed),

If you have issues before marriage, you're going to have those same issues after marriage. If you marry someone else with issues, instead of one person being miserable, you have two. Many of my friends who are married aren't happy. Some are considering divorce. I feel no need to jump into a marriage (Author's files).

Many singles are postponing marriage because they see it as a lifelong commitment that they might not be able to honor. According to a 24-year-old short-order cook who lives with his girlfriend, for instance, "Marriage is a big step.... I don't want to be one of those couples that gets married and three years later gets a divorce" (Gibson-Davis et al., 2005: 1309). Thus, many singles are hesitant about matrimony not because they don't believe in marriage but because they fear divorce (see, also, Chapter 15).

BEING HEALTHY AND PHYSICALLY ATTRACTIVE Emotional and physical health and physical appeal also affect singlehood. In the marriage market, most

Singles in large cities go to many nightclubs to meet people. Despite the racial and ethnic diversity and the large pool of eligible partners, many still can't find a mate. Why not?

men are initially drawn only to good-looking women. On a scale of 10, men who are a 2 or a 3 often go after attractive women who have better options. In these mismatches, "men pursue prizes beyond their grasp, when they could be perfectly content with someone who isn't viewed as a great catch. So these men lose, not only by failing to get what they covet but also in a chance for a happy ending" (Hacker, 2003: 191). People with severe physical or emotional problems are also more likely to remain single longer or not marry at all (Wilson, 2002).

RACIAL AND ETHNIC SINGLES

Among some racial and ethnic groups, the unmarried population has increased significantly during the past few generations. Why? Many structural factors as well as attitudes and values explain some of the changes. Let's look at some of these singles more closely, beginning with African Americans.

Since you asked . . .

- Why are so many African Americans single?

African Americans

Compared with other groups, blacks are the most likely to be single, especially never married (see *Figure 9.4*). Many African Americans are postponing marriage, but an even higher proportion may never marry.

STRUCTURAL FACTORS A major reason for the high percentage of never-married black women is the shortage of marriageable African American men. This shortage reflects many structural factors. Deteriorating employment conditions, especially in urban areas, often discourage young African American men from getting married. Occupational hazards in dangerous jobs have claimed many black men's lives. Mortality rates for heart disease are almost three times higher for blue-collar workers—many of whom are black—than for managerial and professional groups, at least in part because of a lack of preventive medical care. In addition, a disproportionately large number of urban black men in their 20s and early 30s are in prison or jail (Ooms, 2002; Hill, 2005).

As a group, black men earn more than black women in every occupation (see Chapter 13). Many middle-class black men are already married, however, and most college-educated black women are reluctant to marry down. In a memorable scene in the movie *Waiting to Exhale,* the black women lament the marriage squeeze (though not in those words) and consider the merits and problems of marrying hardworking black men in lower socioeconomic levels.

FIGURE 9.4 Changes in Marital Status, by Race and Ethnicity, 1970 and 2007

The percentage of people who are married has decreased, whereas the percentage of divorced and never-married people has increased, especially among African Americans.

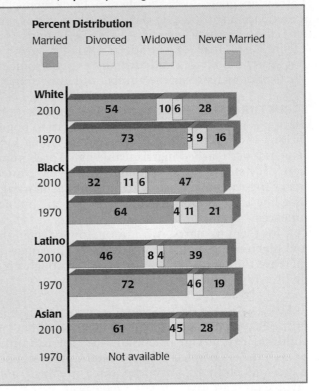

Sources: Based on Saluter, 1994: vi, and U.S. Census Bureau, 2010 Table A1.

VALUES AND ATTITUDES Homogamy generally limits the pool of eligible mates across social classes and regardless of race (see Chapter 8). Some of my black, 30-something female students have stated emphatically, "I'm making a lot of sacrifices to be in college while working full time. I don't think a man will appreciate what I've accomplished unless he's gone through the same [expletive deleted]!"

Many lower-class African American men don't see marital commitment as necessary because they can live with their girlfriends or their children's mother. Some middle-class black men may simply screen out assertive, independent, or physically unappealing women because they have a large pool of eligible romantic partners. And like many whites, blacks whose parents have divorced tend to shun marriage (Bulcroft and Bulcroft, 1993; Davis et al., 2000).

Attitudes about social mobility also affect singlehood. Many middle-class black parents emphasize educational attainment over early marriage. As a result, black women who pursue higher education may place a higher priority on academic achievement than on developing personal relationships. Others have tight social schedules because they devote most of their time to successful small businesses and to community activities (Jones, 1994; Perry et al., 2003).

Latinos

Latinas are generally less likely than black women to experience a shortage of marriageable partners, but singlehood is also increasing among Latinos (see *Figure 9.4*). There are variations among subgroups, but structural factors and attitudes explain some of the overall increases in the number of Latino singles.

STRUCTURAL FACTORS On average, the Latino population is much younger than the non-Latino population. As a result, a higher percentage of Latinos have not yet reached marriageable age. Large numbers of Mexicans who are migrating to the United States for economic reasons are postponing marriage until they can support a family. If people are undocumented (illegal) or are migrant workers, it's difficult for them to marry. In addition, low-paying jobs and high unemployment rates can delay marriage or increase the number of single people through high divorce rates (Baca Zinn and Pok, 2002).

VALUES AND ATTITUDES Familism, as you saw in previous chapters, encourages marriage and having children. In the Cuban community, for example, because of the emphasis on the importance of marriage and children, marriage rates are high and divorce rates are low. The latter have been increasing, however, as second and third generations have assimilated American values and behaviors (Pérez, 2002).

Many Puerto Rican women and men have moved away from familistic values because the relationships between families in Puerto Rico and the United States have weakened. Even though some familistic values have changed, many Puerto Rican women still have extensive kinship networks both in the United States and in Puerto Rico. As a result, single Puerto Rican mothers may remain unmarried because family members are helping them raise and financially support out-of-wedlock children (Toro-Morn, 1998; Carrasquillo, 2002).

Whether people marry also depends on family reactions. For example, familial support (encouragement and approval) increases marriage among white women but not Latinas. It may be that Latino family members are more likely than their Anglo counterparts to dampen a daughter's romance by getting too involved (Umaña-Taylor and Fine; 2003).

Asian Americans

Asian Americans and Pacific Islanders have some of the lowest singlehood rates. At ages 40 to 44, for example, only 13 percent of the men have never married, compared with 18 percent of white men, 20 percent of Latino men, and 34 percent of black men (U.S. Census Bureau, Current Population Survey . . ., 2009).

As noted in previous chapters, it's important not to lump all Asian Americans into one group because doing so obscures important differences between subgroups. There are little recent national data on these subgroups, but the available research suggests that Asian Americans share some values—such as a strong belief in the importance of marriage and family—that explain the low number of singles.

STRUCTURAL FACTORS Intermarriage decreases singlehood rates, especially among Asian American women (see Chapter 4). Marrying outside of one's own group reflects several structural factors, such as group size, sex ratios, and acculturation. For example, because Japanese Americans have been in the United States for many generations and the pool of eligible partners is small, their intermarriage rates are high (Takagi, 2002). These high rates suggest that Japanese Americans are less likely to be single because they decrease their marriage squeeze by choosing partners from a large pool.

Acculturation can also increase the number of singles. Despite the emphasis on family and marriage, many Asian Americans are experiencing higher divorce rates. Korean Americans born in the United States, for example, have a higher divorce rate than their immigrant counterparts. American-born Korean women, in particular, are more ready to accept divorce as an alternative to an unhappy marriage (Min, 2002). One of the results of acculturation, then, is a larger number of women and men who are single.

VALUES AND ATTITUDES Interracial marriages reflect a variety of individual factors. For example, college-educated Asian American women can maximize their social status by marrying the most advantaged men, regardless of race or ethnicity. Also, those who seek

Single women and men often work long hours at their jobs. Sometimes this is because they want to advance their careers, but often because they're perceived as being less burdened with home and family responsibilities and have nothing better to do.

men with the most egalitarian attitudes toward women may marry outside of their particular group (Tsai et al., 2002; Ishii-Kuntz, 2004; see, also, Chapter 8 on mail-order brides).

Cultural values can also decrease the number of singles. As you saw in Chapter 4, many Asian American households see the family as the core of society. Among Chinese Americans, for example, divorce rates are much lower than in the general population. Divorced women find it difficult to survive economically and are not readily accepted in the community (Glenn and Yap, 2002). As a result, many women avoid divorcing and becoming single again at almost all costs.

SOME MYTHS AND REALITIES ABOUT BEING SINGLE

The late comedian Rodney Dangerfield once quipped "My wife and I were happy for twenty years. Then we met!" Being married has many advantages, but some of its benefits have been exaggerated or romanticized, as the joke implies. Here are some of the most popular myths and misconceptions about singlehood:

Since you asked . . .

:•• Are there more benefits or costs in being single?

1. ***Singles are selfish and self-centered.*** In reality, married people—even those without children—are less involved than singles with their parents and siblings and less likely to visit, call, or write these and other relatives. Marriage tends to reduce community ties because married people are more immersed than singles in meeting their own needs (Gerstel and Sarkisian, 2006).

2. ***Singles are well-off financially.*** A number of single professionals and young college graduates in high-tech jobs are affluent, but more singles than marrieds live at or below the poverty level. In general, married couples are better off financially if both partners work (see Chapter 13).

3. ***Singles are usually lonely and miserable and want to marry.*** Being alone doesn't necessarily mean being lonely because many singles enjoy their solitude. Women, especially—freed from heavy marital domestic responsibilities—are happy to "spread their wings as autonomous individuals": "Not much housework, not much shopping—just for the things I like—and being able to stay out without having to let someone at home know where I am" (Kaufmann, 2008: 87). Singles who are successful and happy—whether never married, divorced, or widowed—are rarely lonely or miserable because they have other single friends who enjoy mutual recreational activities such as traveling (DePaulo, 2006).

4. ***Singles are promiscuous or don't get any sex.*** As you saw in Chapter 7, most singles are neither. Men, regardless of marital status, have more sex partners over a lifetime than do women, but married people report being happier with their sex lives than do singles and have sex more frequently. Unlike those who are married, however, singles have more sexual freedom without getting entangled emotionally or making a commitment (Kaufmann, 2008).

5. ***Singles' children are doomed to a life of poverty as well as emotional and behavioral problems.*** Single parents have their limitations, just like married parents. How children fare, however, and as you'll see in later chapters, depends largely on a parent's resources (especially income), the amount of quality parenting time, the lack of alcohol or other drug use, and a loving but authoritative relationship with their offspring.

6. ***Singles worry about growing old and dying alone.*** Because singles are more likely than married couples to be involved in family and community activities, they rarely worry about growing old and dying alone. For example, among single women age 45 and older, 81 percent said they weren't concerned about the prospect of being alone in their later years because they had friends they could depend on in times of crises (Kalata, 2006). And as you'll see in Chapter 17, older men—whether divorced, widowed, or never married—often have caregivers, especially adult daughters and female relatives, who provide companionship and help with health-related issues.

7. ***There's something wrong with people who don't marry.*** There's nothing wrong with being or staying single. Many singles simply believe that the disadvantages of marriage outweigh the benefits.

In general, many singles live happily ever after, despite the widespread stereotypes that we see in movies and on television or hear about. There are many variations, of course, but much depends on factors such as income; health; personality; and involvement with family, friends, and community service. Cohabitation is another powerful force in the lives of many single people.

:•• **MAKING CONNECTIONS**

- Why are you, your classmates, and friends single rather than married? Or married rather than single? Are there any racial/ethnic variations?

- What would you add to the discussion of the myths and realities of being single, based on your personal experiences or observations?

COHABITATION

Cohabitation is a living arrangement in which two unrelated people are not married but live together and are in a sexual relationship. The U.S. Census Bureau sometimes calls cohabitants **POSSLQs** (pronounced "possel-kews"), "persons of the opposite sex sharing living quarters" (shacking up, in plain English). Such unmarried couples also include same-sex relationships, a topic we'll cover shortly.

Cohabitation Trends and Attitudes

To the delight of some people and the dismay of others, cohabitation isn't a passing fad. Because it is based on emotional rather than legal ties, "Cohabitation is a distinct family form, neither singlehood nor marriage. We can no longer understand American families if we ignore it" (Brown, 2005: 33).

THE GROWTH IN COHABITATION The number of heterosexual unmarried couples in the United States has increased more than twelvefold—from about 0.4 million in 1960 to over 7 million in 2010 (see *Figure 9.5*). This number increases by at least another 780,000 if we include same-sex partners. Of all unmarried couples, about 1 in 7 (14 percent of all unmarried-partner households) are gay men or lesbians (U.S. Census Bureau, 2008).

Cohabitation rates have risen, but there are several reasons why these figures are probably too low. First, the Census Bureau doesn't tabulate all unmarried couples in a home but only the person who rents or owns the residence and her or his unmarried partner. Second, unmarried couples—both gay and straight—may be reluctant to disclose that they are living together. Instead, they may describe themselves as roommates or friends. Third, those who believe that they're in a common-law marriage usually don't describe or view themselves as "unmarried partners" (Gates and Ost, 2004; Manning and Smock, 2005).

As of the mid-1990s, more than 60 percent of American couples lived together before they married, compared to almost none 50 years ago. Keep in mind, however, that only 9 percent of the population is cohabiting at any time, as in 2008. In contrast, 49.7 percent of all households are married-couple families (Fields, 2004; Stanley et al., 2004; U.S. Census Bureau, 2010).

ATTITUDES ABOUT COHABITATION Acceptance of cohabitation has increased. For example, 64 percent of high school seniors approve of cohabitation before marriage, up from 40 percent in 1976. In a national survey of young adults between the ages of 20 and 29, 43 percent said that they would marry someone only if she or he agreed to live together first (Popenoe and Whitehead, 2001). And, nationally, almost half of Americans believe that partners who live together first are less likely to get divorced after they marry (Saad, 2008).

As these numbers suggest, there are also large numbers of Americans who disapprove of cohabitation, especially those who are age 65 and older. Some reject cohabitation on moral or religious grounds, but also because they believe that cohabitation has a negative effect on children (Saad, 2008). Despite such reservations, "the popular media seem to publish front page articles on cohabitation regularly" because "it makes for interesting reading" (Stanley and Rhoades, 2009: F2).

Types of Cohabitation

Many Americans see living together as a prelude to marriage, but cohabitation serves many purposes and varies at different stages of the life course. The most common types are dating cohabitation, premarital cohabitation, a trial marriage, or a substitute for a legal marriage.

DATING COHABITATION Some people drift gradually into **dating cohabitation**, which occurs when a couple who spend a great deal of time together eventually decide to move in together. Dating cohabitation is essentially an alternative to singlehood because the decision may be based on a combination of reasons, such as convenience, finances, companionship, and sexual accessibility. Such couples are unsure of the quality of their relationship, and there is no long-term commitment (Manning and Smock, 2005).

In this type of cohabitation, and especially among young adults, there is considerable **serial cohabitation**, living with one partner for a time and then with

FIGURE 9.5 Cohabiting Couples in the United States, 1960–2008

Number in Millions

Year	Value
1960	.4
1970	.5
1980	1.6
1990	2.9
2000	4.7
2010	6.4

Note: These figures are for opposite-sex unmarried partners.
Source: Based on U.S. Census Bureau, Current Population Survey, March and Annual Social and Economic Supplements, 2005 and earlier, Table UC-1, 2006, www.census.gov/population/socdemo/hh-fam/uc1.pdf (accessed September 17, 2006); and Tables UC1 and H1, 2010, www.census.gov/population/www/socdemo/hh-fam/cps2010.html.

another. Because dating cohabitation is similar to being single, partners might terminate one relationship and then move in with someone else. Even if there's an unplanned pregnancy, the man, especially, may decide to move on to another cohabiting arrangement (Wartik, 2005).

PREMARITAL COHABITATION For many people, premarital cohabitation is a step between dating and marriage. In **premarital cohabitation,** the couple is testing the relationship before making a final commitment. They may or may not be engaged but plan to marry.

TRIAL MARRIAGE In a **trial marriage,** the partners want to see what marriage might be like. This type of living together is similar to premarital cohabitation, but the partners are less certain about their relationship. Such "almost-married" cohabitation may be especially attractive to partners who doubt that they can deal successfully with problems that arise from differences in personalities, interests, finances, ethnicity, religion, or other issues.

SUBSTITUTE MARRIAGE A **substitute marriage** is a long-term commitment between two people who don't plan to marry. For many, it's an alternative to marriage, but the motives vary widely. For example, one or both partners may be separated but still legally married to someone else or may be divorced and reluctant to remarry. In some cases, one person may be highly dependent or insecure and therefore prefers any kind of relationship to being alone. In other cases, the partners believe that a legal ceremony is irrelevant to their commitment to each other and may view their non-marital cohabitation as equivalent to a common-law marriage (see Chapter 1).

Cohabitation is more complex than these four classifications suggest. Especially when children are involved, cohabitation can include two biological parents, one biological parent, or an adoptive parent. In addition, one or both partners may be never married, divorced, or remarried. These variations can create very different relationship dynamics, a topic that researchers are just beginning to explore.

Some people maintain that cohabitation is replacing marriage, but there's little evidence to support such claims. For example, 75 percent of all U.S. adolescents plan to marry in the future. By age 24, young adults are more likely to be married than living together, and by age 39, 65 percent are married compared with only 8 percent who are cohabiting (Manning et al., 2007; Saad, 2008).

Moreover, most cohabiting relationships are short lived: About half end within one year, and more than 90 percent end by the fifth year. When these relationships end, 44 percent result in marriage (Lichter et al., 2006). Whether a cohabiting relationship ends in marriage or a breakup depends, among other things, on *why* people are living together. Those with the lowest levels of commitment (dating cohabitation) are more likely to split up than those in a premarital

cohabitation, and serial cohabitation is much more likely than single-instance cohabitation to dissolve rather than end in marriage (Lichter and Qian, 2008).

Who Cohabits?

Cohabitants are a diverse group. Many of their characteristics overlap, but there are some general patterns in terms of age, gender, race and ethnicity, social class, and religion.

AGE Many people think that college-age students are the largest group of cohabitants. In fact, only 20 percent of all cohabitors are age 24 or younger. A majority, 56 percent, are between 25 and 44 (Fields, 2004; Wood et al., 2008).

Among cohabitants who are in their mid-30s to mid-40s, one or both partners may be divorced and involved romantically but not interested in remarrying. Compared with their younger counterparts, older cohabitants (those age 50 or older) report significantly higher relationship quality and stability but view their relationship as an alternative to marriage or remarriage rather than as a prelude to them. Older cohabitants are typically not having or raising children, an important reason for marriage among

People live together rather than marry for a variety of reasons. Do you think that women or men benefit more from cohabitation? Why?

younger couples (King and Scott, 2005).

The cohabitation rate for people age 65 and older has increased significantly—from less than 1 percent in 1960 to 3 percent in 2003 (Fields, 2004). Many demographers expect these numbers to climb as baby boomers age because they are healthier and live longer than previous generations.

In many cases, seniors cohabit because remarriage may mean giving up a former spouse's pension, Social Security, and medical insurance. A 72-year-old woman who lives with her 78-year-old partner, for example, has no intention of getting married because she'd lose her late husband's pension: "My income would be cut by $500 a month if I got married, and we can't afford that" (Silverman, 2003: D1).

In other cases, older couples avoid remarriage because of unpleasant divorces in the past or because their grown children fear that they will be displaced in their parents' affection—and especially their will. Moreover, widows fear a long period of caregiving for a new husband, possibly another painful loss, or want to hang on to their new sense of freedom (Greider, 2004; Levaro, 2009).

GENDER By age 30, half of all U.S. women have cohabited. When it comes to living with a man, daughters often follow their mother's lead: Young adult women whose mothers cohabited are 57 percent more likely than other women to cohabit. Also, women whose mothers have a college degree or more are significantly less likely to cohabit than are women whose mothers have less than a high school education. In this sense, attitudes about cohabitation—especially among women—may be transmitted from one generation to another (Mellott et al., 2005).

Because of the shortage of marriageable men, many low-income, cohabiting black women don't want to marry because they believe that their live-in partners will be unemployed, unfaithful, or not responsible in caring for children. Low-income white and Puerto Rican single mothers don't marry their partner, similarly, if they see the man as a poor provider or immature even though "he is the love of my life" (Jayakody and Cabrera, 2002; Edin and Kefalas, 2005).

RACE AND ETHNICITY The highest rates of cohabitation occur among American Indians/Native Alaskans and African Americans (about 17 percent for each

FIGURE 9.6 Who Is Living Together, by Race and Ethnicity

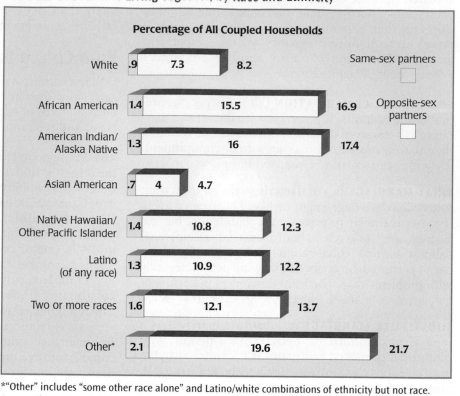

Percentage of All Coupled Households

	Same-sex partners	Opposite-sex partners	Total
White	.9	7.3	8.2
African American	1.4	15.5	16.9
American Indian/Alaska Native	1.3	16	17.4
Asian American	.7	4	4.7
Native Hawaiian/Other Pacific Islander	1.4	10.8	12.3
Latino (of any race)	1.3	10.9	12.2
Two or more races	1.6	12.1	13.7
Other*	2.1	19.6	21.7

*"Other" includes "some other race alone" and Latino/white combinations of ethnicity but not race.
Source: Simmons and O'Connell, 2003, Figure 3.

group), and the lowest rates among Asian Americans (almost 5 percent) (see *Figure 9.6*).

Latinos have relatively low cohabitation rates, but some scholars expect the numbers to rise. As the children of immigrants become more Americanized, especially those who are economically disadvantaged may retreat from marriage and enter cohabiting relationships. Even now, Latinos and blacks are more likely than whites to approve of cohabitation. In addition, many Latinos come from countries in Latin and Central America that have much higher cohabitation rates than the United States (Oropesa and Landale, 2004).

SOCIAL CLASS Race, ethnicity, and gender intersect with social class in explaining cohabitation. However, cohabitation is more common among people at lower educational and income levels. For example, 60 percent of women with no high school diploma or a general equivalency diploma (GED) cohabit, compared with 38 percent of women with a bachelor's degree or higher. Men—especially African American men—are more likely to cohabit than to marry if their earnings and educational levels are low. Men who are employed full time, especially those in professional and semiprofessional occupations, are more likely to marry their live-in partners than are unemployed men (Bumpass and Lu, 2000; Gorman, 2000; Wu and Pollard, 2000; Schoen and Cheng, 2006).

A number of studies show that dire economic circumstances reduce the odds of getting married. Cohabitors see the quality of a relationship as critical for marriage, but so are finances. Many low-income men may want to marry but believe that they can't support a family. Many black women, as you saw earlier, are unwilling to marry men with erratic employment records and low earnings. Women in low-income groups yearn for respectability and upward mobility (including home ownership and financial security). They don't marry their current boyfriend, however, if they believe that the man won't achieve economic stability (Ooms, 2002; Lichter et al., 2003; Xie et al., 2003; Carlson et al., 2004).

Across all ethnic groups, three out of four cohabitants say that they are delaying marriage because "Everything's there except money." Even a modest wedding may pose a serious obstacle to marriage for working- and middle-class young adults: "Ben, a 30-year-old railroad conductor, said he did not know how he would come up with $5,000 for a wedding, exclaiming, 'Weddings are expensive!'" (Smock et al., 2005: 688).

RELIGION Religious values also affect cohabitation rates. The most religious Americans—those who attend church weekly—are less than half as likely to cohabit as those who seldom or never attend church because they believe that premarital cohabitation is immoral and increases the odds of divorce. Thus, teenage girls who attend religious schools and religious services at least once a week are less likely to cohabit than those without such experiences (Houseknecht and Lewis, 2005).

However, about half of religious teenagers approve of cohabitation. Such acceptance suggests that because so many teens have grown up with a cohabiting parent or have experienced the divorce of their parents, wedding vows may no longer mean as much, even when youth or their parents are religious (Lyons, 2004; Cunningham and Thornton, 2005).

Some Benefits and Costs of Cohabitation

Cohabitation is usually one of the most controversial subjects in my classes. Some students believe that living together is immoral, and others argue that it's a normal part of life. As in any other relationship (including dating and marriage), cohabitation has both benefits and costs.

BENEFITS OF COHABITATION Some of the benefits of cohabitation include the following:

- Couples have the emotional security of an intimate relationship but can also maintain their independence by having their own friends and visiting family members alone (McRae, 1999).
- Partners can dissolve the relationship without legal problems, and they can leave an abusive relationship more easily (DeMaris, 2001).

- Couples who postpone marriage have a lower likelihood of divorce because being older is one of the best predictors of a stable marriage (see Chapter 15).
- Cohabitation can help people find out how much they really care about each other when they have to cope with unpleasant realities such as a partner who doesn't pay bills or has poor hygiene habits.
- Among unmarried people age 65 and older, cohabitation may increase the chances of receiving care that is usually provided by spouses (Chevan, 1996).
- Cohabitants don't have to deal with in-laws (Silverman, 2003).
- Even at lower socioeconomic levels, children can reap some economic advantages by living with two adult earners instead of a single mother. Men who experience parenthood during cohabitation are more likely than single noncohabiting fathers to become more committed to the relationship and to find employment whether the mother works or not (Cabreba et al., 2008).

COSTS OF COHABITATION Cohabitation also has costs, including the following:

- Some partners experience a loss of identity or a feeling of being trapped, especially when they are criticized for participating in activities with friends.
- Women in cohabiting relationships do more of the cooking and other household tasks than many married women do, especially when the cohabiting man is not committed to the relationship (Coley, 2002; Ciabattari, 2004).
- Compared with married couples, cohabitants have a weaker commitment to their relationship, have lower levels of happiness and satisfaction, report more alcohol problems, and are more likely to be unfaithful (Treas and Giesen, 2000; Waite, 2000).
- Spouses who cohabit demonstrate more negative behaviors after marriage (such as trying to control the partner's thoughts or feelings, verbal aggression, and anger) than spouses who don't cohabit (Cohan and Kleinbaum, 2002).
- Cohabitation dilutes intergenerational ties. Compared with their married peers, the longer people live together, the less likely they are to give or receive help from their parents, to turn to their parents in an emergency, and to be involved in extended family activities. Also, parents might sometimes avoid contact because they are unsure of their roles when their children cohabit (Eggebeen, 2005).

■ U.S. laws don't specify a cohabitant's responsibilities and rights. For example, in many states it's usually more difficult to collect child custody payments from a cohabiting parent than from one who is separated or divorced (see Chapter 11).

Often, after reading this section, students raise an important question: Should my girlfriend or boyfriend and I live together? Speaking sociologically, there's no simple answer to this question. Some of the research, however, suggests issues that you should think about before or during cohabitation (see the box "Should We Live Together?").

Even though cohabitation has some costs, many cohabitants are convinced that it leads to better marriages. Is this true? Or wishful thinking?

Does Cohabitation Lead to Better Marriages?

No, it doesn't. Generally, couples who live together before marriage have higher divorce rates than those who don't live together before marriage (Bramlett and Mosher, 2002; Phillips and Sweeney, 2005; Stanley and Rhoades, 2009).

Why is this the case? There's no single answer, but there may be a *selection effect* or a *cohabitation effect*. Most recently, some sociologists believe that an *inertia effect* also helps explain why living together has negative marital outcomes.

THE SELECTION EFFECT The selection effect suggests that people who cohabit before marriage have different characteristics than those who do not. Some cohabitants are poor marriage partners because of drug problems, inability to handle money, trouble with the law, unemployment, sexual infidelity, or mental health problems. In addition, cohabitants are less likely than noncohabitants to put effort into the relationship, less likely to compromise, tend to have poorer communication skills, and have doubts about their partner or about marriage as a lifelong commitment. It may be these characteristics that later lead to divorce (McRae, 1999; Cohan and Kleinbaum, 2002; Dush et al., 2003).

Applying What You've Learned

⁛ Should We Live Together?

Most people live together because they're unwilling to make a long-term commitment or are uncertain about whether they want to marry. Such doubts are normal and should probably arise more often than they do (see Chapter 8, especially, on breaking up).

A few social scientists are adamantly opposed to the practice of living together. According to Popenoe and Whitehead (2002), for example,

■ *You should not live together at all before marriage* because there is no evidence that cohabitation leads to better or stronger marriages. People should not live together unless they've already set a wedding date.

■ *Don't make a habit of cohabiting* because multiple experiences of living together decrease the chances of marrying and establishing a lifelong partnership.

■ *Limit cohabitation to the shortest possible period of time.* The longer you live together with a partner, the

more likely it is that you, your partner, or both will break up and never marry.

■ *Don't consider cohabitation if children are involved.* Children need parents over the long term. In addition, children are more likely to be abused by cohabitants than by biological parents.

On the other hand, people who live together give rational reasons for doing so (Olson and Olson-Sigg, 2002; Solot and Miller, 2002; Sassler, 2004):

■ *Economic advantages:* "We can save money by sharing living expenses."

■ *Companionship:* "We are able to spend more time together."

■ *Increased intimacy:* "We can share sexual and emotional intimacy without getting married."

■ *Easy breakups:* "If the relationship doesn't work out, there's no messy divorce."

■ *Compatibility:* "Living together is a good way to find out about each other's habits and character."

■ *Trial marriage:* "We're living together because we'll be getting married soon."

So where does this leave you? You might use exchange theory (see Chapters 2 and 6) in making a decision. List the costs and benefits and then decide what you want to do.

⁛ Stop and Think . . .

■ If you live with someone (or have done so in the past), why? What would you advise other people to do?

■ Look at *Appendix F* ("Premarital and Nonmarital Agreements"). Have you discussed any of these topics with someone you've lived with in the past or now?

THE COHABITATION EFFECT The cohabitation effect may also lead to marital instability. Through cohabitation, people may come to accept the temporary nature of relationships and to view cohabitation as an alternative to marriage. Cohabitants who are independent and used to having their own way, for example, may be quick to leave a marriage (DeMaris and MacDonald, 1993). Thus, cohabitation itself can increase the likelihood of divorce.

Serial cohabitation is especially harmful to marital stability because people who engage in multiple cohabitations tend to be women with low income and education levels. Generally, for those who cohabit two or more times, the odds of divorce are 141 percent higher than for women who cohabited only with the person they married. It is not clear, however, whether the divorce rates for serial cohabitors are high because of a selection effect (such as choosing partners with poor communication skills or chronic mental health problems) or a cohabitation effect (such as marriage creating new dissatisfactions that people don't want to tolerate) (Lichter and Qian, 2008; see, also, Tach and Halpern-Meekin, 2009).

THE INERTIA EFFECT Some cohabitants drift into marriage because of an inertia effect. After moving in together, a couple often makes numerous decisions that make it more difficult to break up—splitting the finances, buying furniture, getting a pet, sharing possessions, spending less time with friends, and even having a child. Instead of making a conscious decision and commitment, then, the couple may slide into marriage because of inertia ("We might as well get married because there's no reason not to") (Stanley and Smalley, 2005; Stanley and Rhoades, 2009).

Some research suggests that women who limit their cohabitation to a future husband do not experience a higher risk of divorce than women who don't cohabit before marriage. For the most part, however, there is little evidence that those who cohabit before marriage have stronger marriages than those who do not (Teachman, 2003; Popenoe and Whitehead, 2006).

How Does Cohabitation Affect Children?

Since 1960, there has been an increase of more than 900 percent in the number of cohabiting couples who live with children. In fact, nearly half of all children today will spend some time in a cohabiting family before age 16 (Bumpass and Lu, 2000).

Since you asked . . .

▶▶ Why are children of married parents better off than those of cohabiting couples?

For the most part, children who grow up with cohabiting couples—even when both are the biological

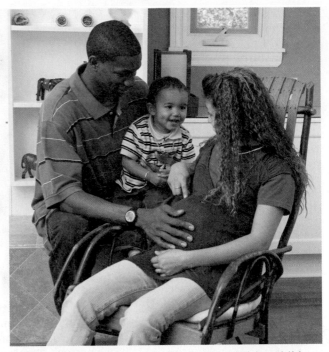

Many cohabiting couples like this one are raising children from previous relationships as well as having their own children.

parents—tend to have worse life outcomes than those who grow up with married couples. For example, children living in cohabiting households

- Experience more domestic violence because of the cohabiting men's lower investment in the relationship and because many women tolerate the assaults (Cunningham and Antill, 1995).

- Are more likely to be poor: When unmarried couples break up, men's household income drops by 10 percent, whereas women lose 33 percent; the percentage of women living in poverty increases from 20 percent to 30 percent, whereas men's poverty level remains relatively unchanged at about 20 percent (Avellar and Smock, 2005).

- Are in households in which the partners spend more on adult goods—such as alcohol and tobacco—and less on children, such as their health and education, than do married parents (DeLeire and Kalil, 2005).

- Have more academic, emotional, and behavioral problems because of poverty or because one or both adults experience more parenting problems than do married couples (Manning and Lamb, 2003; Brown, 2004; Seltzer, 2004).

Besides these difficulties, children often suffer the consequences of serial cohabitation or a parent's breakup with a partner. Nationally, children born to cohabiting versus married parents have more than five times the risk of experiencing their parents' separation. About 75 percent of children born to cohabiting parents see their parents split up before they reach age 16, compared with 33 percent of children born to married parents. The breakups increase already existing problems such as poverty for women and their children. Because cohabiting relationships are so unstable, they often aggravate personal and social difficulties for children, including behavior problems and poor academic performance (Popenoe and Whitehead, 2002; Raley and Wildsmith, 2004; Osborne et al., 2007).

Although couples say that they've found their true love, most cohabitation is short lived. Thus, many family practitioners and attorneys advise people who live together to draw up premarital and nonmarital agreements that will safeguard each person's financial assets.

Cohabitation and the Law

A few years ago, a sheriff in North Carolina fired a dispatcher because she would not marry her live-in boyfriend. North Carolina is one of seven states that have laws prohibiting cohabitation (the others are Virginia, West Virginia, Florida, Michigan, Mississippi, and North Dakota). Most of the laws are at least 200 years old and rarely enforced. In this case, however, the sheriff believed that the dispatcher's live-in arrangement was immoral and decided to enforce the law. More recently, legislators in North Dakota voted to uphold a law that can be used to prosecute unmarried couples who cohabit (Jonsson, 2006).

Even when states don't prosecute cohabitants who violate the laws, unmarried couples and their children have very little legal protection. A full 70 percent of children living with a cohabiting couple are the offspring of one of the partners, but they have few of the automatic rights and privileges enjoyed by children of married parents (Scommegna, 2002; see, also, Chapter 16).

According to many legal experts, cohabitants' best protection in financial matters is to maintain separate ownership of possessions. Cohabiting partners should not have joint bank accounts or credit cards. Shared leases should also be negotiated before the partners move in together. If partners buy real estate together, they should spell out carefully, in writing, each person's share of any profit. Cars should not be registered in a woman's name just to escape the high insurance premiums commonly charged men under 25 because, if there is an accident, the woman will be liable even if the man was driving.

Health insurance plans that cover a spouse rarely include an unmarried partner and her or his children. And if a partner dies and leaves no will, relatives—no matter how distant—can claim all of his or her possessions. If a couple has children, both partners must acknowledge biological parenthood in writing to protect the children's future claims to financial support and inheritance (Mahoney, 2002).

Discussing legal matters may not seem very romantic when people love each other. But when a cohabiting relationship ends, the legal problems can be overwhelming. Many attorneys recommend that cohabitants draw up a contract similar to a premarital document. *Appendix F* describes some of the complex issues that cohabitants are likely to encounter.

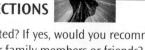

⠿ MAKING CONNECTIONS

■ Have you ever cohabited? If yes, would you recommend living together to your family members or friends? If no, why not? If you haven't lived with someone, do you plan to do so in the future?

■ A few years ago, the prestigious American Law Institute (2002) created a stir when it proposed that cohabitation be legalized. Unmarried couples would have the same rights and responsibilities as married couples regarding inheritance, child custody, debts, alimony, and health insurance, for example. Do you agree with this proposal?

GAY AND LESBIAN COUPLES

Regardless of our sexual orientation, most of us seek an intimate relationship with one special person. Because only five states have legalized same-sex marriage, most homosexuals must turn to cohabitation.

Gay and Lesbian Relationships

Gay and lesbian couples come in "different sizes, shapes, ethnicities, races, religions, resources, creeds, and quirks, and even engage in diverse sexual practices" (Stacey, 2003: 145). Of the 6 million unmarried-couple households, 780,000 are comprised of same-sex partners (U.S. Census Bureau Press Release, 2008).

Like heterosexuals, homosexual cohabitants must work out issues of communication, power, and household responsibilities. If there are children from previous marriages, gay and lesbian partners, like heterosexual parents, must deal with custody and child-rearing issues (see Chapter 12).

LOVE AND COMMITMENT Most lesbians and gay men want an enduring relationship. Gender, however, seems to shape a couple's values and practices more powerfully than does sexual orientation. Lesbian and heterosexual women, for example, are less competitive and more relationship oriented than gay or heterosexual men. In addition, both lesbian and straight women are more likely than either gay or straight men to value their relationships more than their jobs (Stacey, 2003; Roisman et al., 2008).

POWER AND DIVISION OF LABOR A majority of gay and lesbian couples report having equal power in their relationship. When power is unequal, however, and as social exchange theory predicts, the older, wealthier, and better-educated partner usually has more power. The *principle of least interest* is also pertinent (see Chapter 8). As in heterosexual couples, the person in the gay couple who is less involved in the relationship and is less dependent has more power (Patterson, 2001).

Gay life is not divided into "butch" and "femme" roles. One partner may perform many of the traditionally-female gender roles, such as cooking, whereas the other may carry out many of the traditionally-male gender roles, such as car repair. The specialization typically is based on individual characteristics, such as skills or interests, rather than on traditional husband-wife or masculine-feminine gender roles (Peplau et al., 1996; Kurdek, 2006, 2007).

PROBLEMS AND CONFLICT Like heterosexual cohabitants, gay and lesbian couples experience conflicts in four areas. In terms of *power,* all couples are equally likely to argue about finances, inequality in the relationship, and possessiveness. They are also just as likely to complain about *personal flaws* such as smoking or drinking, driving style, and personal hygiene. Couples are similar in being unhappy with some aspects of *intimacy,* especially sex and demonstrating affection. Both groups are also equally likely to criticize partners who are *physically absent,* usually because of job or education commitments. Suspicion of lingering romantic feelings may be more common among gay and lesbian cohabitants, however, because their previous lovers are likely to remain in their social network of friends, increasing the possibility of jealousy and resentment (Kurdek, 1994, 1998).

Violence is more prevalent among gay male couples than among either lesbian or heterosexual cohabitants. Compared with 8 percent of heterosexual couples, for example, 15 percent of gay cohabiting men reported being raped or physically assaulted by a male partner. About 11 percent of lesbians reported being the victim of such violence by a partner (Tjaden and Thoennes, 2000).

It's not clear why the violence rates among gay male cohabitants are so high. One explanation may be that gay men have internalized the cultural belief that aggression is an acceptable "male" way of solving conflict, even in intimate relationships. Another reason might be that gay men are more likely than lesbians to be rejected by their family and friends and to strike out against intimate partners when there are problems (see Peterman and Dixon, 2003).

RACIAL-ETHNIC VARIATIONS Gay and lesbian couples often get less social support from family members than do heterosexual couples. The greatest rejection may come from racial-ethnic families, whose traditional values about marriage and the family are often reinforced by religious beliefs because, in some faiths, homosexual behavior is considered aberrant or a sin (Hill, 2005).

In African American, Asian American, Latino, and Middle Eastern communities, family members are expected to marry and to maintain the traditional family structure (see Chapter 4). Many racial-ethnic groups also have strong extended-family systems. Thus, a gay family member may be seen as jeopardizing not only intrafamily relationships but also the extended family's continued strong association with the ethnic community (Morales, 1996; Liu and Chan, 1996; Mays et al., 1998).

Lesbian and gay couples might encounter additional problems because the partner comes from a different religion or racial-ethnic group or a lower social class. Even if both partners have come out to their family and relatives, the family might exclude a partner in subtle ways, such as inviting the heterosexual son-in-law of two years, but not the lesbian partner of 15 years, to be in a family photo (Clunis and Green, 2000).

So far, six states have legalized same-sex marriage. Do you favor or oppose gay marriage? Why?

The War over Same-Sex Unions

A majority of Americans (54 percent) support same-sex civil unions, but 56 percent oppose same-sex marriage (down from 68 percent in 1997). Opposition to both civil unions and same-sex marriage is considerably higher among those who regularly attend religious services, those who live in the South, people ages 65 and older, and those who have conservative views on family issues (Masci, 2008b; Saad, 2008). (Other terms for same-sex marriage include *gay marriage, homosexual marriage,* and *same-gender marriage.*)

Since you asked . . .

🔹 Why is same-sex marriage so controversial?

Until recently, same-sex couples were prohibited from marrying everywhere in the world, but this situation is changing in the United States and some other countries. I'm addressing gay marriage here, rather than Chapter 10, because it is still a highly contentious topic that limits many single homosexuals' choices. Let's begin with the question of why and how sexual orientation affects people's legal lives.

THE DEFENSE OF MARRIAGE ACT In 1996, President Bill Clinton signed the Defense of Marriage Act (DOMA), which bans federal benefits (such as spousal Social Security payments) unless the couple is in "a legal union between one man and one woman as husband and wife." The act also states that no U.S. state or territory has any legal duty to respect a marriage between homosexuals, even if such a marriage is valid in another state.

DOMA was a significant piece of legislation because 1,138 federal laws give only married heterosexual couples a variety of benefits, including a spouse's Social Security payments, housing and food stamps, veterans' and other military services, employment benefits, naturalization, and even privacy protection (U.S. General Accounting Office, 2004). Congress tried twice—in 2004 and 2006—to add an amendment to the U.S. Constitution to ban same-sex marriages, but failed (Vestal, 2009).

In mid-2009, President Obama extended some benefits to same-sex partners of federal workers such as allowing them to be included in the long-term-care insurance program and to use sick leave to take care of domestic partners. The order didn't include federal health and retirement benefits, which requires the passage of legislation now before Congress (Vogel, 2009). In addition, presidential orders can't overturn DOMA.

Currently, 36 states have statutes prohibiting gay marriage, including 30 states that also have constitutional bans (Vestal, 2009). This means that gays, unlike heterosexuals, don't have rights such as inheritance, child custody and visitation, adoption, and even making funeral arrangements for a partner who has died.

CIVIL UNIONS Gays have gained greater acceptance in eight states with marriage alternatives such as *civil unions* (sometimes also called *domestic partnerships* and *registered partnerships*): California, Connecticut, Hawaii, Maine, Nevada, New Jersey, Oregon, and Washington. These states give gay couples all of the legal rights enjoyed by heterosexual couples, including tax breaks, health benefits, approval of organ donations, and inheritance without a will. Some other states and local jurisdictions have implemented some of these laws, such as health benefits and adoption rights that were previously available only to married couples, and a few states and Washington, D.C., are moving toward passing bills that recognize same-sex marriages performed elsewhere (Craig, 2009; Vestal, 2009).

In about 22 countries or some of their regions, civil unions and domestic partnerships offer varying marriage benefits ranging from joint property rights to shared parenting. Partnership ceremonies are performed by a government marriage official in exactly the same manner as a heterosexual civil marriage.

Many same-sex couples argue, however, that civil union legislation isn't enough. Besides causing them to be denied federal benefits, they maintain, their inability to marry results in their being treated as second-class citizens.

SAME-SEX MARRIAGE In 2004, Massachusetts became the first state to legalize same-sex marriage. Since then, four other states have followed suit: Connecticut, Iowa, Vermont, and, most recently, New Hampshire. Worldwide, the number of countries that has legalized same-sex marriages has grown slowly. The Netherlands legalized gay marriage in 2001, followed by Belgium, Canada, Norway, Spain, Sweden, and South Africa. Twelve countries (Australia, China, Ireland, Portugal, and the United Kingdom, among others) are debating the issue.

Same-sex marriage is controversial. In the United States, those who favor same-sex marriage argue that all people should have the same legal rights regardless of sexual orientation and that marriage may increase the stability of same-sex couples and lead to better physical and mental health for gays and lesbians. Those who oppose same-sex marriage contend that such unions are immoral, weaken our traditional notions of marriage, or are contrary to religious beliefs (Sullivan, 1997; King and Bartlett, 2006). The box "Why Do Americans Favor or Oppose Same-Sex Marriages?" provides a summary of some of the major pro and con arguments in this debate.

⠿ MAKING CONNECTIONS

- Why do you think that many researchers find that straight and gay relationships are more similar than different?

- Should your state (unless it's done so already) legalize same-sex marriage? Why?

- If heterosexuals don't want to marry, should they have the same legal rights as gay couples through civil unions?

Why Do Americans Favor or Oppose Same-Sex Marriages?

Homosexuality and especially same-sex marriages are among the most controversial issues in America, dividing friends, families, and religious communities. Here are some of the beliefs and attitudes that fuel the debates.

Same-sex marriage should be legal because ...

- Attitudes and laws change. Until 1967, for example, interracial marriages were prohibited.

- Gay marriages would strengthen families and long-term unions that already exist. Children would be better off with parents who are legally married.

- It would be easier for same-sex couples to adopt children, especially children with emotional and physical disabilities.

- There are no scientific studies showing that children raised by gay and lesbian parents are worse off than those raised by heterosexual parents.

- Every person should be able to marry someone that she or he loves.

- Same-sex marriages would benefit religious organizations both spiritually and emotionally and bolster membership.

- Gay marriages are good for the economy because they boost businesses such as restaurants, bakeries, hotels, airlines, and florists.

Same-sex marriage should not be legal because ...

- Interracial marriages are between women and men, but gay marriages violate many people's notions about male-female unions.

- Gay households are not the best place to raise children because they might imitate their parents' homosexual behavior.

- All adopted children—those with and without disabilities—are better off with parents who can provide heterosexual gender role models.

- There are no scientific studies showing that children raised by gay and lesbian parents are better off than those raised by heterosexual parents.

- People can love each other without getting married.

- Same-sex marriages would polarize church members who are opposed to gay unions and decrease the size of congregations.

- What's good for the economy isn't necessarily good for society, especially its moral values and religious beliefs.

Sources: Sullivan, 2003; "The Merits of Gay Marriage," 2004; LaFraniere and Goodstein, 2007; Masci, 2008a; Pew Forum on Religion & Public Life, 2008; Semuels, 2008.

⠿ Stop and Think . . .

- Many states have passed laws that limit marriage to a man and a woman. Do you agree or not? Why?

- What other reasons can you add for each side of the debate?

Changes

COMMUNAL LIVING ARRANGEMENTS

Communes are collective households in which children and adults from different families live together. The adults may be married or unmarried. Some communes permit individual ownership of private property; others do not. There has been a great deal of historical variation in the economic, sexual, and decision-making rights in communes.

Communes in the Past

Communes are not a modern invention. They have existed since 100 B.C.E. The popularity of communal living has fluctuated in the United States, but the number of people living in communes has generally constituted only about a tenth of 1 percent of the entire population (Kantor, 1970).

Both nineteenth-century and contemporary communes have varied greatly in structure, values, and ideology. In the nineteenth century, communes wrestled with the issue of monogamy and resolved the issue in very different ways. One group, the Icarians, made marriage mandatory for all adult members. Others, such as the Shakers and Rappites, required everyone, including married couples, to live celibate lives. Still others practiced free love, permitting sexual intercourse with all members, married or not (Muncy, 1988).

Most communes have been short lived because most of the members were unwilling to give up their autonomy or private property. There was also conflict and jealousy regarding sexual relationships. As a result, many groups dwindled because of a lack of new members. For example, most of the buildings of the Shakers in Maine and other states have been turned into tourist attractions and museums or the land has been given to preservation groups (W. L. Smith, 1999; Llana, 2005).

Contemporary Communal Living

Communal living is common on college campuses. For example, fraternities, sororities, and houses that are rented and shared by five or six students fulfill many of the social and economic functions that characterize all communes, such as sharing expenses and having companionship.

A recent program, Co-Abode, matches low-income single mothers in subsidized housing. The mothers live together and split household bills, divvy up chores, care for each other's children when they want to shop, and interact daily. Children often share a room. The housing is usually in safe neighborhoods with good school districts, and an outreach program provides the mothers with referrals "for everything from dentists to lawyers and credit counselors" (Wolcott, 2003: 14).

At the other end of the age continuum, a growing number of older people—especially those who are single—are experimenting with communal living as an alternative to moving in with their children or living in a nursing home. When older people can't live alone because of physical or mental health problems, they have increasing housing options. As you'll see in Chapter 17, many elderly people live in communities that provide medical, emotional, and physical care, functions traditionally performed by the family.

CONCLUSION

There have been a number of *changes* in relationships outside, before, and after marriage. Some of our *choices* include staying single longer, cohabiting, forming same-sex households, participating in communal living arrangements, or not marrying at all. Thus, larger numbers of people are single for a greater portion of their lives.

Our choices are not without *constraints*, however. For example, many U.S. laws do not encourage or protect most of these relationships. Despite the growing numbers of unmarried people, marriage is not going out of style; it is merely occupying less of the average adult's lifetime.

Although there is less pressure to marry, most of us will do so at least once in our lives. In the next chapter, we examine the institution of marriage.

SUMMARY

1. Diverse lifestyles have always existed, but in the past 20 years the number of alternative family forms has increased, including singlehood, cohabitation, gay households, and communal living arrangements.

2. Average household size has been shrinking since the 1940s. A major reason for the decrease is the growing number of people who are postponing marriage and living alone.

3. More people are postponing marriage because there is greater acceptance of cohabitation and out-of-wedlock children.

4. Singles constitute a very diverse group. Some have been widowed, divorced, or separated; others have never been married. Some singles choose their status, whereas others are single involuntarily.

5. There are many reasons why the numbers of singles have increased since the 1970s. Some of the reasons are macro, some are demographic, and some reflect personal choices.

6. Cohabitation has boomed since the 1960s. Most cohabitation is short lived, but in some cases it is a substitute for legal marriage. Like other living arrangements, cohabitation has both benefits and costs.

7. There is no evidence that cohabitation leads to more stable or happier marriages. Cohabitants have higher divorce rates than noncohabitants, and men typically benefit more from cohabitation than women do.

8. For the most part, cohabitation is disadvantageous for children. Some of the negative effects include domestic violence, poverty, and behavioral and academic problems.

9. Legal factors often dictate living arrangements. Same-sex marriage is prohibited in all but five states. As a result, gay and lesbian partners have fewer options than do heterosexuals.

10. Communal living arrangements have changed since the turn of the twentieth century and even since the 1970s. They are less numerous and less popular today but often fulfill the economic and social needs of many people, especially low-income single mothers and elderly single adults.

KEY TERMS

sex ratio 239
female infanticide 239
marriage squeeze 239
cohabitation 246

POSSLQ 246
dating cohabitation 246
serial cohabitation 246
premarital cohabitation 247

trial marriage 247
substitute marriage 247

PEARSON
myfamilylab™ MyFamilyLab provides a wealth of resources. Go to www.myfamilylab.com<http://www.myfamilylab.com/>, to enhance your comprehension of the content in this chapter. You can take practice exams,

view videos relevant to the subject matter, listen to audio files, explore topics further by using Social Explorer, and use the tools contained in MySearch-Lab to help you write research papers.

10 Marriage and Communication in Intimate Relationships

On April 12, 1919, a young couple drove off (in a Model-T Ford) to Jeffersonville, Indiana, because the bride-to-be, 14, was under the legal age to get married in Kentucky, their home state. In 2002, the same couple—William, 104, and Claudia Lillian Ritchie, 98—celebrated their 83rd wedding anniversary. When reporters asked them the secret to their long marriage, Mr. Ritchie said that they loved each other, there was a lot of give and take, and that they didn't have very many arguments (Davis, 2002).

Most people agree that marriage has changed, but how much do you really know about it? Find out by taking "A Marriage Quiz" on the next page.

In this chapter we discuss marital expectations and rituals, consider how marriages change over the years, and examine communication processes that can strengthen or undermine intimate relationships within and outside of marriage. Let's begin by looking at why people tie the knot.

DATA DIGEST

- Among high school seniors, 82 percent of girls and 71 percent of boys say that **having a good marriage and family life is "extremely important"** to them.

- About 77 percent of men, compared with 63 percent of women, think **it's acceptable for women to propose to men.**

- In 1980, **a typical American wedding** cost $4,000. Today, it costs about $30,000.

- About 61 percent of couples **omit the word "obey" from their vows,** but 83 percent of brides take their husband's name.

- By age 35, **79 percent of U.S. adults have been married.**

- Almost 11,000 gay couples married in Massachusetts between 2004 and 2007; **two-thirds of the weddings were lesbian marriages.**

- In 2008, 88 percent of Americans said that **they were happy or "reasonably content"** in their marriages.

Sources: Armstrong, 2004; "For Richer or Poorer," 2005; Belluck, 2008; Bennetts, 2008; Chang, 2008; U.S. Census Bureau Newsroom, 2008; Fletcher, 2009; Popenoe and Whitehead, 2009.

ASK YOURSELF

A Marriage Quiz

True False

- ☐ ☐ **1.** The vast majority of today's mothers want a full-time career.

- ☐ ☐ **2.** Men and women are equally likely to say that they are happily married.

- ☐ ☐ **3.** The best single predictor of overall marital satisfaction is the quality of the couple's sex life.

- ☐ ☐ **4.** Overall, married women are physically healthier than married men.

- ☐ ☐ **5.** The keys to long-term marital success are good luck and romance.

- ☐ ☐ **6.** Marriages are much more likely to end in divorce today than 20 years ago.

- ☐ ☐ **7.** A husband is usually happier if his wife is a full-time homemaker than if she is employed outside the home.

True False

- ☐ ☐ **8.** Having children typically brings a couple closer together and increases marital happiness.

- ☐ ☐ **9.** "No matter how I behave, my partner should love me because he/she is my spouse."

- ☐ ☐ **10.** If the wife is employed full time, the husband usually shares equally in housekeeping tasks.

- ☐ ☐ **11.** Husbands usually make more lifestyle adjustments in marriage than wives do.

- ☐ ☐ **12.** "If my spouse loves me, he/she should know what I want and need to make me happy."

See p. 262 to score your answers.

WHY DO PEOPLE MARRY?

When someone announces, "I'm getting married!" we respond with "Congratulations!" rather than "How come?" In Western societies, we assume that people marry because they love each other. In fact, the principal reasons for marriage reflect moral or religious views and social norms that it's the right thing to do (see *Figure 10.1* on p. 261). We marry for a variety of other reasons, however, and some of them are negative. Let's begin with the positive reasons for getting married.

Since you asked . . .

- Because it's easier to just live with someone, why do people marry?

Some Right Reasons for Getting Married

Positive motives strengthen relationships and enhance the likelihood of marital stability. The reasons don't *guarantee* that a marriage will last, but they increase the odds of staying together, especially during rough times.

LOVE AND COMPANIONSHIP The single greatest attraction of marriage is continuous, intimate companionship with a loved one. According to 87 percent of Americans ages 18 to 30, for example, love is the major reason for taking the plunge into marriage. Even though a couple may experience conflict, the partners enjoy and look forward to each other's company (Bradbury et al., 2001; National Healthy Marriage Resource Center, 2009).

CHILDREN A traditional reason for getting married is to have children, but it's not the main one (see *Figure 10.1*). Because marriage is a social institution (unlike singlehood and cohabitation), most societies have laws and customs that protect children within marriage but not necessarily outside of it. In many industrialized countries, however, greater acceptance of out-of-wedlock children means that parenthood, rather than marriage, is often the first step into adulthood (Cherlin, 2009).

ADULT IDENTITY Developmental theory, you recall, asserts that family members progress through various stages during the life course (see Chapter 2). Finding a job and being self-sufficient marks adulthood. So does marriage because getting married says "I am an adult" to the community. A man who married at age 28 recalls,

You've made it to the next level, you've finally grown up. . . . Once I was married, it really suited me. I've found this with a lot of my married friends—you just feel more solid. You have a definite position in the world (Paul, 2002: 80).

COMMITMENT AND PERSONAL FULFILLMENT An overwhelming number of Americans (88 percent) say that marriage should be a lifelong commitment

FIGURE 10.1 Why Do People Marry?

Survey question: "Why did you decide to get married rather than just live together?"

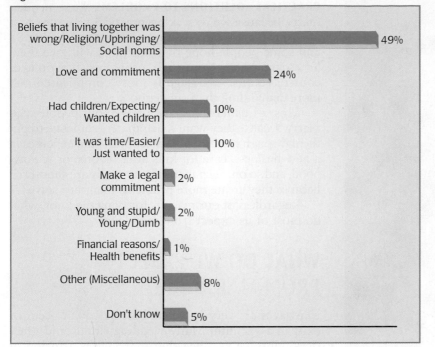

Note: These data are from a telephone survey of a randomly selected, nationally representative sample of 2,020 American adults age 18 and older who have ever married. Responses total to more than 100 percent because respondents could offer more than one answer to this open-ended question.

Source: Based on Taylor et al., 2007: 31.

Some Wrong Reasons for Getting Married

Negative motives usually derail a marriage. They may be functional in the sense that they fulfill a specific purpose, such as not feeling left out because everyone else you know is getting married. Often, however, the wrong reasons for matrimony lead to misery or divorce.

SOCIAL LEGITIMACY Getting married to legitimate an out-of-wedlock baby is one of the worst reasons for marrying (even though many religious groups would probably disagree). Often, the partners are young, one or both may not want to marry, and the couple may have only sex in common.

SOCIAL PRESSURE Sometimes parents are embarrassed that their children haven't married, and well-meaning married couples tell their single friends that marriage will bring happiness (see Chapter 8). Even if parents have been divorced, they project their own desires on their children by encouraging marriage. According to a 26-year-old media consultant, for example,

My mother was in her sixties and single. Even after her own two divorces, she was by no means turned off by the idea of marriage; in fact, she wanted more than anything to marry again. . . . Even though she didn't say it outright, she worried that I would become one of "those" women—thirty-five, lonely, careerist, with a cat and a studio apartment (Paul, 2002: 58).

ECONOMIC SECURITY When we were in graduate school, one of my friends, Beth, married a successful businessman because he was wealthy and she was struggling to pay her bills. Within a few months, Beth was staying at the library longer and longer because she dreaded going home to be with her husband. Their marriage lasted two years.

Marrying someone just for her or his money won't sustain a marriage. Among other things, a partner may be stingy and watch every penny after the wedding. One or both partners may be laid off and use up their savings very quickly. Or, even if you marry someone who's rich and then get a divorce, in most states you'll have a difficult time getting any of the money if you've been married less than ten years (see Chapter 15).

(Glenn, 2005). Commitment includes sexual fidelity, but it also encompasses other perceived responsibilities such as legitimating out-of-wedlock children to ensure their legal right to a parent's estate or health benefits.

Marriage connects people. The happiest couples report that they help each other, spend time together, and feel emotionally close. Moreover, those who believe that the quality of a marriage depends on determination and hard work are more likely to report having good marriages than couples who believe that relationships depend on fate, luck, or chance (Myers and Booth, 1999; Olson and Olson, 2000).

CONTINUITY AND PERMANENCE Much of life is unpredictable, but marriage promises stability. We expect a spouse to be a constant source of support and understanding in a shifting and changeable world.

Marriage also offers a sense of permanence and continuity by establishing one's own family. According to one of my students, "Whenever we look at our kids, my husband and I think about the wonderful things they might achieve someday. And I'm really looking forward to being a grandma."

However unintentionally, we may also marry for one or more wrong reasons.

In recent years, it's become more common for couples to have a *destination wedding,* one to which the couple, family members, friends, and/or guests travel. Some destination weddings may be close to home—such as a couple from Virginia getting married at Myrtle Beach, South Carolina—but others may involve travel to an island, such as Maldives (an island southwest of India) pictured here, Mexico, or other locations.

REBELLION OR REVENGE Young people sometimes marry to get away from their parents. They flee their families for a variety of reasons: physical, verbal, or sexual abuse; conflict between the parents or with a stepparent; or a yearning for independence. Even when the reasons for getting away from one's family are valid, rebellion is an immature reason for marriage.

In other situations, people marry on the rebound: "I'll show Jeff that other guys love me even if he dumped me." Such marriages are bound to fail because revenge doesn't solve any problems. Since the ex-partner doesn't care, an "I'll show him (or her)" attitude is irrelevant to an ex-lover.

PRACTICAL SOLUTIONS TO PROBLEMS We sometimes marry because we're seeking practical solutions to a problem. Dating can be disappointing (see Chapter 8), and some people hope that marriage will give them an escape hatch from their problems. It won't, of course, because marriage is more complicated and more demanding than singlehood.

Most of us have heard stories about people who marry because they want a helpmate—someone to put them through medical or law school, share expenses in a new business, care for kids after divorce or widowhood, and so on. Such marriages typically are short lived because they create more problems than they solve.

Regardless of our reasons for tying the knot, what do most of us expect from marriage?

WHAT DO WE EXPECT FROM MARRIAGE?

Marriages are very personal, but they don't occur or exist in a vacuum. Many wedding rituals and practices reinforce the idea that marriage is a fusion of lovers who make a lifelong commitment to each other. Some people are more guarded, however, and prepare prenuptial agreements. Let's begin by looking at the marriage rituals that presumably cement a marriage.

Marriage Rituals

Marriage is a critical rite of passage in almost every culture. In the United States, the major events that mark the beginning of a marriage are engagement, showers and bachelor or bachelorette parties, and the wedding itself.

> **Since you asked . . .**
>
> :• Why are wedding ceremonies important?

ENGAGEMENT Traditionally, an **engagement** formalizes a couple's decision to marry. According to the *Guinness Book of Records,* the longest engagement was between Octavio Guillen and Adriana Martinez of Mexico, who took 67 years to make sure they were right for each other. Most engagements are at least 65 years shorter.

Whether or not a couple follows traditional customs, an engagement serves several functions:

■ It sends a hands-off message to other interested sexual partners.

 Answer Box for "A Marriage Quiz"

All the items are false. The more "true" answers you gave, the more you believe the myths about marriage. The quiz is based on research presented in this chapter; Popenoe, 2002; and Coontz, 2006.

- It gives both partners a chance to become better acquainted with their future in-laws and to strengthen their identity as a couple.

- It provides each partner with information about a prospective spouse's potential or current medical problems (through blood tests, for example).

- It provides an opportunity for secular or religious premarital counseling, especially if the partners are of different religions or racial and ethnic backgrounds.

- It signals the intent to make the union legal if the couple has been living together or has had a child out of wedlock.

Many of India's high-income families have expensive weddings that include up to 1,000 guests and last about a week. Most weddings are less lavish, but most families follow century-long nuptial traditions. In this photo, for example, Muslims in the Kashmir region of India surround a groom as he goes to his in-laws' house to fetch his bride.

At a *bridal shower,* female friends and relatives "shower" a bride with both personal and household gifts and celebrate the beginning of a new partnership. At a *bachelor party,* the groom's friends typically lament their friend's imminent loss of freedom and have one "last fling." Some women also have *bachelorette parties* that include anything from dinner with female friends to a male strip show. Some of the bachelor and bachelorette parties are no longer a one evening local event but a weekend of fun in Las Vegas, Mexico, or resorts, especially in Florida and California.

Many men now participate in the preparations for their wedding. About 80 percent attend bridal shows, give their opinions about flowers, choose products for online bridal registries, produce original wedding invitations on their computers, and make menu choices. According to one wedding planner, "I've had grooms call me five or six times a day about small details months before their weddings" (Caplan, 2005: 67).

THE WEDDING In 2001, in an annual ceremony in Seoul's Olympic Stadium, the Reverend Sun Myung Moon, founder of the Unification Church, married 30,000 couples from more than 100 countries, including the United States. He matched the couples—all of whom were strangers—by age and education. There are no accurate statistics, but some estimate that the divorce rate for these couples is about 50 percent lower than that for U.S. couples (Burris, 2009).

Most weddings are more traditional. The wedding ceremony typically reinforces the idea that the marriage is a sacred, permanent bond. The presence of family, friends, and witnesses affirms the acceptance and legitimacy of the union. Even when the partners are very young, a wedding marks the end of childhood and the acceptance of adult responsibilities. The box "Some Cherished Wedding Rituals" illustrates the historical origins of some of our current marriage conventions.

Does a marriage last longer if the wedding ceremony is traditional rather than nontraditional (such as performing the marriage in an exotic location or in a simple civil ceremony)? There are no national data, but family practitioners emphasize that the ceremony is far less important than the marriage. If couples and their parents go into debt to pay for an elaborate wedding, both groups may experience strained relationships. Also, ignoring future in-laws before and after a marriage can alienate prospective family members who might be very supportive—emotionally and financially—when the couple runs into problems (Kiefer, 2005; Silverman, 2006).

Many brides are swept off their feet by merchandising and spend at least a year planning a perfect and often extravagant wedding ceremony (see Data Digest). Increasingly, however, attorneys are advising both women and men to invest some of their time in creating prenuptial agreements just in case the marriage fizzles after a few years.

Love and Prenuptial Agreements

Prenuptial agreements are common among the very wealthy. Most people don't create "prenups" because doing so seems unromantic and little property is

Some Cherished Wedding Rituals

Changes

Most of our time-honored customs associated with engagement and marriage, such as rings and the honeymoon, originally symbolized love and romance. Many were designed to ensure the fertility of the couple and the prosperity of their household.

Some, however, also reflected the subordinate position of the woman in the union. For example, the Anglo-Saxon word *wedd,* from which "wedding" is derived, was the payment for the bride made by the groom to her father. Thus, a wedding was literally the purchase of a woman. Here are some others:

- Before the twelfth century, the *best man* was a warrior friend who helped a man capture and kidnap a woman he desired (usually from another tribe).

- *Carrying the bride over the threshold* isn't simply a romantic gesture. Originally, it symbolized the abduction of a daughter who would not willingly leave her father's house.

- After a man captured (or bought) a bride, he disappeared with her for a while in a *honeymoon* so that her family couldn't rescue her. By the time they found the couple, the bride would already be pregnant. In America, around 1850, the honeymoon was usually a wedding trip to visit relatives. The safety and comfort of the railroad popularized more distant honeymoons.

- The *engagement ring* symbolized eternity. The medieval Italians favored a diamond ring because they believed that diamonds were created from the flames of love.

- Soldiers of ancient Sparta first staged *stag parties:* The groom feasted with his male friends on the night before the wedding. The function of this rite of passage was to say goodbye to the frivolities of bachelorhood while swearing continued allegiance to one's comrades despite being married.

- In the 1890s, the friend of a newly engaged woman in the United States held a party at which a Japanese parasol, filled with little gifts, was turned upside down over the bride-to-be's head, producing a shower of presents. The custom may have originated in Belgium, but American readers of fashion pages, learning of this event, wanted *bridal showers* of their own.

- In medieval times the wedding party's *flower girl* carried wheat to symbolize fertility. Perhaps for symmetry, the male *ring bearer* also appeared during the Middle Ages.

- In biblical times, the color blue symbolized purity. In 1499, however, Anne of Brittany set the pattern for generations to come by wearing a white wedding gown for her marriage to Louis XII of France. The *white bridal gown* came to symbolize virginity and is still worn by most first-time brides even if they aren't virgins.

- The first *wedding ring* was made of iron so that it wouldn't break. The Romans believed that a small artery or "vein of love" ran from the third finger to the heart and that wearing a ring on that finger joined the couple's hearts and destiny.

- The ancient Romans baked a special wheat or barley cake that they broke over the bride's head as a symbol of her hoped-for fertility. The English piled up small cakes as high as they could, and the bride and groom tried to kiss over the cakes without knocking the tower over; success meant a lifetime of prosperity. The cakes evolved into a *wedding cake* during the reign of England's King Charles II, whose French chefs decided to turn the cakes into an edible "palace" iced with white sugar.

- *Tying shoes to the car bumper* probably came from ancient cultures. For example, the Egyptians exchanged sandals at a wedding ceremony to symbolize a transfer of property or authority. A father gave the groom his daughter's sandal to show that she was now in his care. In an Anglo-Saxon wedding, the groom tapped the bride lightly on the head with the shoe to show his authority. Later, people began throwing shoes at the couple, and somehow this evolved into the current practice.

Sources: Based on Kern, 1992; Ackerman, 1994; Bulcroft et al., 1999.

﹕• Stop and Think. . . .

- Do you think that any of these rituals are outdated? Can you think of any new ones that have emerged in the United States?

- Have you attended a wedding ceremony, including your own, that had unusual or interesting rituals? What was their purpose?

involved at the start of most marriages, but 20 percent of couples do so ("For Richer or Poorer," 2005).

As *Appendix F* shows, prenuptial agreements cover numerous topics—from how many times partners expect to have sexual intercourse to trusts and wills. These contracts also include agreements about disposing of premarital and marital property, whether the couple will have children (and how many), the children's religious upbringing, who buys and wraps presents for relatives, and whether there will be combined or his and her savings and checking accounts.

Prenuptial agreements are controversial. Proponents contend that if there are children from a first marriage, or if one partner has considerable assets, the contract makes ending a bad marriage less complicated. Because women usually are the ones who suffer financially after a divorce, a contract gives them some legal protection (Berger, 2008; Palmer, 2008).

Applying What You've Learned

:•: Before You Say "I Do"

Some scholars contend that the best way to decrease divorce rates is to be more selective in choosing one's marital partners (Glenn, 2002). In doing so, we should spend more time planning a marriage than a wedding. Here are some questions that committed partners who are planning to wed should ask:

- What do you hope to contribute to our marriage?
- How often do you like to have time to yourself?
- Will you want to change your name after marrying?
- Which holidays will we spend with which family?
- Do you or your family have a history of any health problems, both physical and mental?

- What goals do you have in your career?
- Do you get along with co-workers?
- How much free time spent away from one another is acceptable?
- What makes you angry?
- What do you consider cheating or infidelity?
- Is religion important to you?
- Are you in debt?
- What would you do with an extra $10,000?
- Do you have to make any child support or alimony payments?
- How often do you plan to cook and clean?

- Do you want to have children? If so, how many, and who will take care of them?
- What does my family do that annoys you?
- Are there some things that you don't plan to give up in marriage?

Source: Based on Outcalt, 1998: 14–138.

:•: Stop and Think . . .

- What other questions would you add to this?
- Instead of using such self-help lists, should couples seek premarital counseling? Or are the lists sufficient?

Opponents maintain that such documents set a pessimistic tone for the marriage. Also, if the contract is executed in a state other than the one in which it was drawn up, the couple will have legal problems. Moreover, because people change over time, the contract may not reflect their future attitudes and behavior.

Regardless of how people feel about prenups, scholars and family practitioners agree that most of us don't know very much about the people we marry (see Chapter 8). The box "Before You Say 'I Do'" above suggests some questions that couples should discuss before tying the knot, including whether or not to draw up a legal premarital contract.

:•: MAKING CONNECTIONS

- If you're single, do you want to get married? If so, why? If you're married, did you marry for the right reasons, the wrong reasons, or a combination?
- Do you think that prenuptial agreements are a good idea or not? Read *Appendix F* before deciding.

TYPES OF MARRIAGES

When someone asked a happily married couple to what they owed their successful marriage of 40 years, the husband replied, "We dine out twice a week—

candlelight, violins, champagne, the works! Her night is Tuesday; mine is Friday."

As this anecdote suggests, happily married couples aren't joined at the hip. Instead, marriage reflects considerable diversity in relationships both in the United States and in other countries.

Types of Marriage in the United States

On the basis of a pioneering study of 400 upper-middle-class marriages (the partners ranged in age from 35 to 55), Cuber and Haroff (1965) identified five types of marriages. Some were happy and some were not, but all endured.

- In a **conflict-habituated** marriage, the partners fight, both verbally and physically, but do not believe that fighting is a good reason for divorce. They believe that feuding is an acceptable way to try to solve problems, and they thrive on their incompatibility. Usually the reason for the conflict is minor and the partners seldom resolve their disputes.

Since you asked . . .

:•: If a couple is fighting all the time, should they get a divorce?

- In a **devitalized** marriage, the partners were deeply in love when they married. As the years

When a marriage crosses cultural lines, the couple sometimes incorporates some of the traditions—such as the bride's wedding attire—from both cultures.

Benjamin Franklin and his wife, Deborah, presumably had a close marriage. During 18 of their 44 years of marriage, however, they lived apart because Franklin was often abroad for extended periods, including being an ambassador to France. According to some historians, Franklin enjoyed his LAT marriage (see text) because he was typically surrounded by adoring women. His wife, loyal to the end, tolerated Franklin's sexual infidelity.

go by, they spend time together—raising the children, entertaining, and meeting community responsibilities—but begin to do so out of obligation rather than love. They get along and, as a result, do not consider a divorce. One or both partners may be unhappy, but they are both resigned to staying married.

- In a **passive-congenial marriage,** the partners have a low emotional investment in the marriage and few expectations of each other. Fairly independent, they achieve satisfaction from other relationships, such as those with their children, friends, and co-workers. They often maintain separate activities and interests. Passive-congenial couples emphasize the practicality of the marriage over emotional intensity.

- In a **vital marriage,** the partners' lives are closely intertwined. They spend a great deal of time together, resolve conflicts through compromise, and often make sacrifices for each other. They consider sex important and pleasurable. When a disagreement occurs, it is over a specific issue and is quickly resolved.

- In a **total marriage,** which is similar to a vital marriage, the partners participate in each other's lives at all levels and have few areas of tension or unresolved hostility. Spouses share many facets of their lives; they may work together or have the same friends and outside interests. This type of marriage is more encompassing than a vital marriage.

Finding that approximately 80 percent of the marriages they studied fell into the first three categories, Cuber and Haroff characterized these as *utilitarian marriages* because they appeared to be based on convenience. The researchers called the last two types *intrinsic marriages* because the relationships seemed

to be inherently rewarding. In their study, vital marriages accounted for 15 percent of the population and total marriages for only 5 percent.

Several later studies found that marriages are more complex and varied (see, for example, Lavee and Olson, 1993, and Olson and Olson, 2000). The Cuber-Haroff typology and others are useful in showing that there are many types of marriages and marital relationships. None of the findings can be generalized, however, because the research is based on middle- and upper-middle-class couples or those in therapy, none of which are representative of most U.S. marriages.

Some Cross-Cultural Variations in Marriage Types

Marriage forms vary across cultures. Some couples have LAT (living apart together) relationships because of economic or personal reasons. In China, for instance, growing numbers of rural husbands are going to urban areas to look for jobs. The men work temporarily in nearby cities to increase their income while their wives take care of the farm. In these LAT marriages, "the husband works in town and the wife plows the field" (Sheng, 2005: 108).

In some Scandinavian countries, some LAT couples are married but have moved apart to save the relationship. They live in separate homes because "too many quarrels and too much irritation would have made the relationship deteriorate." Some maintain such arrangements indefinitely. For others, the LAT separation "might turn out to be the first step toward a calm divorce" (Trost and Levin, 2005: 358). In other marital forms, custom and tradition take precedence over personal options and even laws (see the box "Child Brides").

Cross-Cultural and Multicultural Families

Child Brides

When she was 11, Mwaka's father married her to a man in his 40s to repay a $16 debt. The father had borrowed the money from his neighbor to feed his wife and five children. In another case, a father gave his daughter Rachel, 12, to a 50-year-old acquaintance in exchange for a bull.

In some rural pockets throughout sub-Saharan countries—from Ghana to Kenya to Zambia—such forced marriages are fairly common. Because custom decrees that children in patriarchal tribes belong to the father, girls as young as 8 years old can be traded as marriage partners—sometimes to men in their 60s—to finance a brother's wedding, to educate sons, to buy food or cattle, or to settle debts (LaFraniere, 2005).

In Afghanistan, similarly, some farmers sell their young daughters to middle-aged or elderly men to pay off a debt. When a father appealed to a tribal council, the elders unanimously ruled that he had to give his 9-year-old daughter in marriage to the 45-year-old lender. Afghans ridicule the little girls as "loan brides," but the fathers can be killed for not repaying a loan (Yousafzai and Moreau, 2008).

Child brides are also prevalent in some Arab countries, such as Yemen, because poverty is widespread and a family needs cash (less than $350 in many cases). In addition, according to cultural beliefs, a young virginal bride can best be shaped into a dutiful wife (Hill, 2008; Worth, 2008).

For the most part, government officials have been unsuccessful in protecting the girls because many marriages are governed not by civil law but by traditional customs in which men have all decision-making authority.

❖ Stop and Think . . .

- How does forced marriage, especially for young girls, reflect and reinforce men's superior status in patriarchal societies? Who gains from such practices?

- Are child bride and loan bride customs inhumane, as some women's rights advocates claim? Or does every society have the right to establish its own rules about marriage?

MARITAL SUCCESS AND HAPPINESS

When a journalist interviewed couples celebrating their fiftieth or later wedding anniversaries, she found some common characteristics: mutual respect, common goals, supportive spouses, and a focus on communication and problem solving. Disagreements occurred, but they were toned down. As a 77-year-old woman said about her husband,

In all our 55 years, he has rarely gotten angry. If I get angry about something, we have a little argument, and he'll say something funny to me. I'll have to laugh and there goes the argument. Laughter has always been a big part of our life (Licht, 1995: 19).

Researchers usually measure marital success in terms of marital stability and marital satisfaction. *Marital stability* refers to whether a marriage is intact and whether the spouses have ever suggested divorce to each other (Noller and Fitzpatrick, 1993; Holman et al., 1994). *Marital satisfaction* refers to whether a husband or wife sees the marriage as a good one. To determine satisfaction, researchers have used concepts such as *marital conflict, contentment, commitment,* and *happiness* (Glenn, 1991; Stanley, 2007).

Measuring marital satisfaction is important for two reasons. First, longitudinal studies show that marital unhappiness is a good predictor of divorce. Second, marital unhappiness is linked to a variety of problematic outcomes, including inept parenting, psychological distress, and poor physical health—especially among wives (Amato et al., 2007).

Are Married Couples Happy?

Since 1973, the University of Chicago's National Opinion Research Center has asked nationally representative samples of Americans to rate their marital happiness. The percentage saying that their marriages are "very happy" has decreased since the 1970s (see *Figure 10.2*). Consistently, women report being less happily married than men, a gender difference we'll examine shortly.

Because happiness is a self-reported and highly subjective measure, it's impossible to know how respondents define it in marriage. Do they mean a passive-congenial marriage, for instance? Acceptance of the status quo because things could be worse? Better than being alone? Or something else?

FIGURE 10.2 Percentage of Married Americans Age 18 and Older Who said That Their Marriages Are "Very Happy," by Period

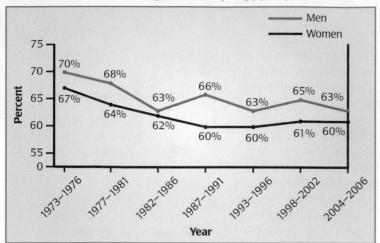

Source: Popenoe and Whitehead, 2009, Figure 4.

The measures are subjective, but many of the findings have been fairly consistent. For example, both marital stability and marital satisfaction tend to be higher for whites than for African Americans, for those with a college education or higher, for those who say that they are religious, and for those who married after age 20 instead of during their teens, but much depends on economic stress. Marital happiness decreases when couples experience poverty, job loss, and financial problems. All these events are more likely for couples at lower socioeconomic levels, of whom a disproportionate number are African American (Bradbury and Karney, 2004; Smock, 2004; Glenn, 2005; Amato et al., 2007; Brown et al., 2008; Marks et al., 2008).

Are gay marriages happier? Because these unions have been legalized in some states only recently, as you saw in Chapter 9, there are no scientific data so far. However, a journalist who interviewed gay couples who got married after Massachusetts legalized same-sex marriages in 2004 found "blissful unions,

"Is the groom male or female?"

painful divorces, and everything in between" (Belluck, 2008: 1).

Some gay couples remain committed to marriage despite their conflicts and say that the marriage had made some relatives more comfortable with the couple's intimate relationship. Some—like married heterosexuals—have disagreements over money and in-laws and whether to adopt children or have their own. They also experience widespread rejection of the legitimacy of their marriage outside of Massachusetts. Others got a divorce because they rushed into the marriage and couldn't resolve the conflicts that existed before the marriage.

Generally, higher socioeconomic status contributes to marital well-being, but it doesn't guarantee either stability or satisfaction. Individual factors are also important in shaping the quality of a marriage.

What's Important in a Successful Marriage?

Is there a recipe for an enduring and happy marriage? Researchers have been searching for an answer to this question for decades. Despite what self-help books say, there are no 5, 10, or 15 steps for living happily ever after. However, social scientists have found an association between several variables and marital success.

Since you asked . . .

➤ Why are some couples much happier than others?

COMPATIBILITY Initially, people are attracted to each other because of similar attitudes, values, and beliefs. Similar social backgrounds (such as ethnicity, religion, and education) decrease major interpersonal differences that can lead to conflict and disagreements (see Chapter 8).

After marriage, personality may become increasingly important in maintaining a relationship. Couples are happier when they have similar personalities and emotional wavelengths. Unlike dating, marriage requires regular interaction and extensive coordination in dealing with the tasks, issues, and problems of daily living (Whyte, 1990; Luo and Klohnen, 2005).

Despite popular opinion, couples who play together don't necessarily stay together. Those who participate in leisure activities together (such as watching television or going for a walk) that only one spouse likes become dissatisfied over time. Women, especially, are likely to engage in recreational activities such as golf, that only their husbands enjoy. The more time women spend in those activities, the more likely they are to end up being unhappy with their marriage (Crawford et al., 2002; Gager and Sanchez, 2003).

FLEXIBILITY Our relationships are never 100 percent compatible. One spouse may be better organized or more outgoing than the other, for example. Happily married couples, however, are more likely than their unhappy counterparts to discuss how to handle and adjust to such differences (Olson and Olson, 2000).

At the beginning of this chapter, the husband of the longest-married couple in the world said that their marriage had lasted so long because "It's a lot of give and take." Happily married people are flexible and compromise rather than trying to control their spouses or insisting on doing everything their own way. Flexible partners often accommodate the other person's needs and enjoy doing so (Schwartz, 2006).

POSITIVE ATTITUDES Spouses who like each other as people and are good friends have happier marriages. Couples whose marriages begin in romantic bliss are especially prone to divorce because it's difficult to maintain such intensity. Couples who marry after a whirlwind courtship are quickly disillusioned because they're saddled with fantasies and unrealistic expectations about married life (Pittman, 1999; Ted Huston, cited in Patz, 2000). The "How Close Is Our Relationship?" quiz may help you determine whether you and your spouse (or other partner) have positive attitudes about each other.

COMMUNICATION AND CONFLICT RESOLUTION Compared with unhappy couples, happy couples recognize and work at resolving problems and disagreements. Sometimes conflict resolution means backing off because one or both partners are hurt or angry.

Couples that have been happily married 50 years or longer say that resolving conflict is a key ingredient for marital success. For example, "When differences arise, resolve them through discussion"; "Talk out problems, work out mutual solutions, and compromise"; and "You must never be afraid to say 'sorry'" (Kurland, 2004; "Secret to Wedded Bliss," 2005).

EMOTIONAL SUPPORT According to happily married couples, emotional support is much more important than romantic love. Some of their comments about trust, cooperation, and respect are instructive:

He makes me feel smart, pretty, capable, and cherished (married 21 years).

I asked my husband why he thought our marriage was a success. He said it was because we don't compete with each other and because we respect each other's independence. I agree (married 33 years).

Whatever we had was ours, not yours or mine. We rarely borrowed money and paid all bills on time (married 60 years) (Mathias, 1992: B5; Kurland, 2004: 65).

ASK YOURSELF

How Close Is Our Relationship?

All marriages and other long-term relationships go through difficult times. When we feel valued by our partner, however, positive feelings overcome hurtful moments. This short quiz will give you an idea of whether you and your partner appreciate each other.

True False
- ☐ ☐ **1.** I look forward to spending much of my free time with my partner.
- ☐ ☐ **2.** At the end of the day, my partner is glad to see me.
- ☐ ☐ **3.** My partner is usually interested in hearing my views.
- ☐ ☐ **4.** We enjoy talking to each other.
- ☐ ☐ **5.** We have fun together.
- ☐ ☐ **6.** We are spiritually compatible.
- ☐ ☐ **7.** We share the same basic values.
- ☐ ☐ **8.** We have many of the same dreams and goals.
- ☐ ☐ **9.** Even though our activities are different, I enjoy my partner's interests.

True False
- ☐ ☐ **10.** Despite busy schedules, we make time for each other.
- ☐ ☐ **11.** My partner tells me when he or she has had a bad day.
- ☐ ☐ **12.** We make decisions together, including how to spend our money.

Sources: Based on Gottman and Silver, 1999; and Schwartz, 2006.

Scoring:

Give yourself one point for each true answer. If you score 10 or above, your marriage (or relationship) is strong. If you score below 10, your marriage (or relationship) could use some improvement.

© Mother Goose & Grim- (New) © Grimmy, Inc. King Features Syndicate

In contrast, partners in unhappy marriages try to change each other to meet their own needs. They often become frustrated and angry when their efforts fail. Instead of cooling off and thinking a problem through, the partners react while they're upset. For example, a 103-year-old man who recently celebrated his eightieth wedding anniversary advised, "When a woman is upset, keep quiet" (Mathias, 1992; B5).

Such advice is equally useful for wives. Even if hostile and sarcastic comments don't lead to verbal or physical abuse, they are unhealthy in a marriage.

HOW MARRIAGE AFFECTS HEALTH

Actress Zsa Zsa Gabor once said, "Husbands are like fires: They go out when unattended." Most American husbands must be forest fires because, according to much research, they are usually very well attended.

The Health Benefits of Marriage

Between 1972 and 2003, never-married men have become almost as healthy as their married counterparts because of better diets; regular exercise; and satisfying relationships, such as cohabitation, outside of marriage (Liu and Umberson, 2008). Overall, however, happily married people, especially men, are healthier and happier than those who are unhappily married, separated, divorced, or widowed. Married people have lower rates of heart disease, cancer, stroke, pneumonia, tuberculosis, cirrhosis of the liver, and syphilis. They attempt suicide less frequently and have fewer automobile accidents than do singles. They are also less likely to suffer from depression, anxiety, and other forms of psychological distress (Horwitz et al., 1996; Wickrama et al., 1997; Schoenborn, 2004. We'll examine the economic benefits of marriage in Chapter 13).

Since you asked . . .

⁂• Why are married people generally healthier than those who are single?

Why is there a generally positive association between marriage and physical and psychological well-being? Two major sociological explanations have focused on selection and protection effects.

THE SELECTION EFFECT Some sociologists posit that married people are healthier than their unmarried counterparts because of a "selection effect." That is, healthy and sociable people are attracted to others who are like themselves and are more desirable marriage partners because they don't depend on marriage to make them happy. In contrast, sick people tend to marry other sick people. This may be because they share similar emotional stresses and lifestyles, including poor diets and alcohol usage (Booth and Johnson, 1994; Wilson, 2002).

THE PROTECTION EFFECT Other sociologists maintain that it's not mate selection but marriage itself that makes people healthier. Receiving emotional, social, and financial support from a spouse improves one's general health and life span by reducing anxiety and preventing or lessening depression. Marriage is especially likely to have a positive effect on people who were depressed before marriage because a supportive spouse provides encouragement, economic benefits, and companionship that lowers social isolation and improves psychological well-being (Frech and Williams, 2007).

Marriage may also decrease risky activities and encourage healthy behaviors. For example, married people (especially men) are more likely than singles to quit smoking and less likely to drink heavily, to get into fights, or to drive too fast—risks that increase the likelihood of accidents and injuries (Murray, 2000; Kiecolt-Glaser and Newton, 2001).

When one partner becomes ill, the physical and emotional support that a spouse provides during recuperation after surgery or other medical treatment can help speed recovery. Such support, however, typically comes from wives rather than husbands and results in gender health differences.

Gender and Health

A number of studies show that married women are less healthy than married men. On average, women live longer than men, but, unlike husbands, many wives experience depression and other health problems.

WHY HUSBANDS ARE HEALTHY Many married men enjoy "emotional capital" because wives provide nurturing and companionship. Men routinely report that their greatest (and sometimes only) confidantes are their wives, whereas married women often talk to close friends and relatives. Thus, husbands can depend on their wives for caring and emotional support, but wives often look outside the marriage for close personal relationships (Steil, 1997; Maushart, 2002).

Wives tend to encourage behaviors that prolong life, such as regular medical checkups. Marriage also often introduces lifestyle changes that reduce some of men's bad habits such as smoking, drinking with male friends at bars, and illicit drug use, especially as part of the "singles scene" (Bachman et al., 1997).

If husbands work long hours, there's no effect on their wives' health. If wives work more than 40 hours a week, however, their husbands are significantly less healthy than other married men because they depend on their wives (even those who work long hours) to take care of their well-being, both physically and emotionally (Stolzenberg, 2001).

A review of almost 35 years of research found that a stable marriage is only one of seven factors that affect men's longevity. The other factors include alcohol use, drug abuse, smoking, exercise, coping mechanisms for stress, and depression (Cole and Dendukuri, 2003). Thus, marriage alone doesn't work miracles in extending married men's lives.

Some data suggest that marriage may be fattening to men, a negative health factor. Compared with both married women and other males, married men are more likely to be overweight or obese. The weight problems may be due to a number of variables, such as having a sedentary job, not exercising, eating high-fat meals (especially at work), or consuming alcohol (which is high in calories). Regardless of the reasons, being overweight or obese increases married men's chances of dying early due to heart disease, diabetes, or other medical problems (Schoenborn, 2004).

WHY WIVES ARE LESS HEALTHY Women typically are more attuned than men to the emotional quality of marriages. They work harder if the marriage is distressed; have many domestic responsibilities even if they work outside the home; have little time to unwind; and neglect their own health while caring for family members, including their husbands (Kiecolt-Glaser and Newton, 2001). And, as you'll see in Chapter 13, employed wives—especially those with children—are at especially high risk for depression because they often feel overwhelmed by the chronic strain of meeting the needs of their husband and children while also working full time.

African American men tend to benefit more from marriage than do African American women. Married black women report poorer physical health than unmarried black women, married or unmarried black men, and white married couples (Blackman et al., 2005).

Why is the health of African American women worse than that of single black women? So far, there's no single explanation. Black wives who are employed may experience more stress at work because of discrimination. Besides their work roles, many African American women often care for elderly relatives or the children of kin who are incarcerated or chronically ill, have more household responsibilities than their husbands, and may have to cope with an unfaithful spouse. Because of all these stresses, African American women often don't make the time to visit doctors and, generally, don't take care of themselves because they are too busy meeting the needs of their children, husband, parents, and in-laws (Shatzkin, 2005).

Marital Quality and Health

Marriage itself isn't a magic potion that makes us healthier and happier. The quality of our marriages is much more important for our health than simply getting or being married.

MARRIAGE AND LIFE SATISFACTION Many of us think that marriage will make us happier than we are. That's not the case. Generally, married people are happier than unmarried people because marriage *improves* an already happy life rather than creates one. People who are very satisfied with life and have a rich social network of family members, friends, and co-workers have little to gain from marriage. On the other hand, people who are lonely and dissatisfied with life can sometimes achieve companionship by marrying (Lucas et al., 2003).

TROUBLED MARRIAGES The quality of the marriage is critical for our emotional and physical well-being. Among other things, a spouse may increase stress levels that, over the years, can contribute to higher blood pressure, and, in turn, lead to heart disease. Emotional stress can also lead to psychological and physical problems that affect the spouses' work and family roles. A wife might medicate herself with pills and a husband might turn to alcohol to decrease the stress (Barnett et al., 2005; "Medical Memo...," 2005).

People who are unhappy in their marriages don't always end up in divorce court. Instead, they may experience marital burnout.

Marital Burnout

Marital burnout is the gradual deterioration of love and ultimate loss of an emotional attachment between partners. The process can go on for many years. In marital burnout, even if the spouses share housework and child care, one spouse may not give

Constraints

Am I Heading toward Marital Burnout?

All marriages have ups and downs. Checking off even as many as seven of the following items doesn't necessarily mean that your marriage is in trouble, but might be indicators of marital burnout. The earlier you recognize some of these symptoms, according to some family and health practitioners, the better your chances of improving your marriage.

- You've lost interest in each other.
- You feel bored with each other.
- There's a lack of communication; neither of you listens to the other.
- You seem to have little in common.
- Deep down, you want a divorce.
- There's a lack of flexibility: You can no longer compromise with each other.
- Minor irritations become major issues.
- You no longer try to deal honestly with important issues.
- You find yourself making family decisions alone.
- You have no desire for physical touching of any kind.
- Your relationships with other people are more intimate than your relationship with your spouse.

- The children have begun to act up; they have frequent problems at school, get into fights with friends, or withdraw.
- One of you controls the other through tantrums, violence, or threats of suicide or violence.
- You are both putting your own individual interests before the good of the marriage.
- You can't talk about money, politics, religion, sex, or other touchy subjects.
- You avoid each other.
- One or both of you subjects the other to public humiliation.
- You have increasing health problems, such as headaches, back pain, sleeplessness, high blood pressure, recurring colds, or emotional ups and downs.
- One or both of you is abusing alcohol or other drugs.
- Shared activities and attendance at family functions have decreased.
- One or both of you is irritable and sarcastic.

- You are staying in the relationship because it is easier than being on your own.

Sources: Based on Stinnett and DeFrain, 1985; Kayser, 1993.

⁑ Stop and Think . . .

- Have you experienced marital burnout? If so, what, if anything, did you do about it?
- Why do you think that many married couples—especially those who have been married at least 50 years—are less likely to undergo marital burnout?

---

the other emotional support. One spouse may complain that the other isn't confiding his or her innermost thoughts and feelings or doesn't want to discuss problems (R. J. Erickson, 1993; Kayser, 1993).

Marital burnout can develop so slowly and quietly that the couple is not aware of it. Sometimes one partner hides dissatisfaction for many years. At other times both partners may ignore the warning signs (see the box "Am I Heading toward Marital Burnout?"). Applying social exchange theory, when the costs in the relationship become much greater than the benefits, the couple will probably seek a divorce.

MARITAL ROLES

Marital roles are the specific ways in which married couples define their behavior and structure their time. Even if the partners have lived together before marriage, they experience changes when they marry. Who will do what housework? Who's responsible for paying the bills? Who's in charge of which child care tasks?

"His and Her Marriage"

More than 30 years ago, sociologist Jessie Bernard (1973) coined the phrase "his and her marriage." She maintained that most men and women experience marriage differently. Because men make fewer adjustments to marriage than women, Bernard wrote, "his marriage is better than hers."

NEW ROLES Whether his marriage is better than hers is debatable, but there are many gender differences in married life (Nock, 1998; Amato et al., 2007). Consider the process of identity bargaining, in which newly married partners must modify their idealized expectations and deal with the realities of living together. In **identity bargaining,** partners negotiate adjustments to their new roles as husband and wife.

In these negotiations, gender—rather than age, personality, intelligence, or employment, for example—is generally the best predictor of marital

Since you asked . . .

⁑ Why do newlyweds seem to have so many problems?

roles. According to sociologist Susan Maushart (2002), wives contribute 100 percent of the husband care—the myriad tasks of physical and emotional nurture that she calls "wifework." Wifework includes

- Performing up to three-quarters of the unpaid household labor.

- Assuming total responsibility for the husband's emotional caretaking (from organizing his underwear drawer to arranging his social life).

- Taking full responsibility for child care and drudgework (laundry, meals, shopping) so that he can enjoy leisure time (games, sports, watching television with the kids).

- Monitoring his physical well-being (providing a healthful diet, making medical appointments).

- Preparing meals tailored to his taste, appetite, and schedule.

- Maintaining his extended family relationships (buying presents, sending thank-you notes, staging and catering family gatherings).

Maushart contends that there is no reciprocal "husbandwork" in which men maintain their wives' well-being.

MORE ROLES Marriage also increases the number of roles that each partner performs, thereby raising the potential for role conflict (see Chapter 5). If both partners are employed, for example, they may feel strain in living up to extended family members' expectations to visit or spend time together. Or, in the case of one of our friends, the wife's father assumes that his new son-in-law is glad to spend Saturdays on the father-in-law's home improvement tasks. The son-in-law resents the intrusion on his weekend activities but feels that he can't refuse.

Couples also add more roles if they associate with one (or both) of the partner's friends, attend her or his religious services, or join new community organizations. Some women must take on the most demanding role of all—that of mother—if they are pregnant when they marry. A man must also cope with the multiple roles of husband and father.

Variations in Domestic Roles

Domestic work includes two major activities: housekeeping (cooking, cleaning, laundering, outdoor work, repairs) and child rearing. Domestic work varies according to factors such as age, stage of life, employment, gender, the presence of children, race and ethnicity, and social class. Let's look at a few of these variables.

GENDER The amount of housework that American women and men do has changed considerably. In 1976, women did an average of 26 hours of housework a week, compared with about 17 hours in 2005. Men did

about six hours of housework a week in 1976, compared with about 13 hours in 2005 (Swanbrow, 2008). Married people don't fully share all housework yet, but married men's participation in housework has increased appreciably since 1976 (see *Figure 10.3*). Despite men's greater contributions, wives spend the equivalent of almost two full days more on housework each week than their husbands (Lee and Waite, 2005).

EMPLOYMENT Husbands whose wives work outside the home do more household tasks, but men are less likely to pitch in if the wife earns more than her husband. A situation in which the wife earns more than her husband is still considered deviant. As a result, women may do more housework to maintain the traditional gender role expectation that women *should* do more housework than men. Otherwise, the husband is seen as economically dependent on his wife and "not really a man" (Evertsson and Nermo, 2004).

Another reason for men's lower contribution to domestic tasks may be that women's outearning their husbands is usually short lived. As you'll see in Chapter 13, many woman have higher earnings only for a few years, as when men are laid off and must settle for part-time jobs or fewer hours. In such cases, the couples' traditional division of household labor doesn't change much.

When there are huge imbalances in housework and child care, do women see the inequality as unfair? A study of 25 countries, including the United States, found that 45 percent of women believed that men do a fair share of household work even when there were dramatic differences between the sexes. Why is there such a disconnect between reality and women's perception of fairness?

The researchers concluded that much depends on the interplay among three variables: the number of hours a week women work for pay, how much they earn relative to their spouses, and, especially, women's attitudes about gender roles. When

FIGURE 10.3 Who's Doing Most of the Housework?

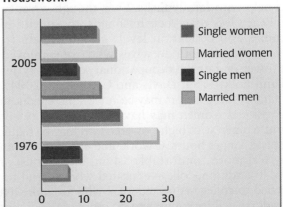

Source: University of Michigan Institute for Social Research (ISR) Panel Study of Income Dynamics, cited in Swanbrow, 2008.

housework is unequal, the women who are the most likely to be unhappy or object are those who spend many hours in the labor force, have a high income, and endorse egalitarian gender roles. On the other hand, if women have high incomes and are employed full-time but hold tradition attitudes about gender roles (for example, "A woman's job is to look after the home and family"), they are more likely to accept an imbalanced division of household labor as part of a proper woman's role, even if it leaves them alone with all of the housework (Braun et al., 2008).

THE PRESENCE OF CHILDREN Child rearing is highly rewarding, but it's also a 24-hour, 7-day job that's physically exhausting and emotionally draining. When married couples have no children, women do about 17 hours of housework a week compared to 7 for men. Among married couples with children, mothers increase their household work by almost 23 tasks per day compared with 6 tasks per day for fathers. Even when wives work full time, they are three times more likely than husbands to perform disagreeable tasks such as changing the baby's diaper and scrubbing the toilet bowl. And as the number of children increases, so does women's share of child rearing and housework. Among married couples with four or more kids, for example, mothers do an average of 28 hours of housework a week compared with only 10 hours for fathers (Huston and Holmes, 2004; Perry-Jenkins et al., 2004; Swanbrow, 2008).

Do mothers believe that men aren't doing enough? It depends on the fathers' participation. If, for example, fathers of infants perform some of the unpleasant tasks (such as changing diapers rather than just giving baths) or take on more household chores, spouses tend to see such divisions of labor as fair and experience fewer conflicts about domestic tasks (Feeney and Noller, 2002).

SOCIAL CLASS The division of household labor also varies by social class. The higher a couple's socioeconomic status, the more likely it is that the husband will help with family tasks. Even though wives typically earn less than their husbands, those with high incomes and education levels get more help from their husbands than do wives who are employed at the lower end of the occupational scale (Perry-Jenkins and Folk, 1994; Davis and Greenstein, 2004).

One or more factors may be at work here: Educated, professional women may have more authority in the home, women with high-powered jobs may be required to spend longer hours at work, and successful women may feel more comfortable asking their spouses for help. In addition, college-educated women tend to be married to college-educated men, who are more likely to endorse gender equity and do more of the domestic work than men with less education (Coltrane, 2000).

Men's contributions to housework and child care have increased since the 1970s. The longer a wife is employed, the more housework her husband often does.

Domestic Roles and Marital Quality

Men are usually happy in their marriage when there's greater equality in decision making but not housework. Women are happier when there's greater equality in decision making *and* when both spouses share more equally in housework responsibilities (Amato et al., 2003).

Mothers, especially, are least satisfied with their marriages when they have a disproportionate share of domestic and child care responsibilities, have little decision-making power, and do most of the emotional work to develop or maintain intimacy. The sense of carrying an unfair burden (rather than the actual amount of work) creates anxiety, erodes the women's emotional and psychological well-being, and increases the risk of depression (Erickson, 2005; Wilcox and Nock, 2006).

What happens when there's a gender gap in domestic roles? In time, women feel worn out and may become dissatisfied with the marriage (Piña and Bengston, 1993). In one case, the gender gap resulted in an essay that has become a classic (see the box "Why I Want a Wife").

Why I Want a Wife

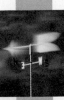

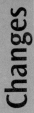

Changes

The essay excerpted here has been reprinted more than 200 times in at least ten different countries (Brady, 1990). Written by Judy Brady [then Judy Seiters] in 1972, the article satirizes the traditional view of woman as wife and mother:

I am a wife. . . . Why do I want a wife? . . . I want a wife who will work and send me to school . . . and take care of my children. I want a wife to keep track of the children's doctor and dentist appointments [and] . . . mine, too. I want a wife to make sure my children eat properly and are kept clean. . . . I want a wife who takes care of the children when they are sick, a wife who arranges to be around when the children need special care because . . . I cannot miss classes at school. . . .

I want a wife who will take care of my physical needs. I want a wife who will keep my house clean . . . pick up after me . . . keep my clothes clean, ironed, mended, replaced when need be, and who will see to it that my personal things are kept in their proper place so that I can find what I need the minute I need it. I want a wife who cooks the meals, a wife who is a good cook. I want a wife who will plan the menus, do the necessary grocery shopping, prepare the meals, serve them pleasantly, and then do the cleaning up while I do my studying. I want a wife who will care for me when I am sick and sympathize with my pain. . . .*

I want a wife who . . . makes love passionately and eagerly when I feel like it, a wife who makes sure that I am satisfied. And, of course, I want a wife who will not demand sexual attention when I am not in the mood. . . . I want a wife who assumes the complete responsibility for birth control, because I do not want more children. . . .*

When I am through with school and have a job, I want my wife to quit working and remain at home so that my wife can more fully and completely take care of a wife's duties.

My God, who wouldn't want a wife?

:• Stop and Think . . .

- Do you think that this excerpt is outdated, or does it still describe many married women's roles today?

- Write a paragraph or two that would parallel this essay on "Why I Want a Husband."

:• MAKING CONNECTIONS

- One writer, you recall, contends that wifework characterizes most marriages. Do you agree with her that there are no comparable husbandwork roles?

- Unequal housework increases men's marital satisfaction but decreases women's. How can married couples resolve this dilemma? What's worked for you, for example?

HOW MARRIAGES CHANGE THROUGHOUT THE LIFE COURSE

From a developmental perspective, people perform different roles and learn new tasks as a marriage develops its own structure and identity. Throughout the life course, we must adjust, adjust, adjust—to agreeing on specific goals, solving marital problems, and coping with unexpected crises. The adjustments begin with the first year of marriage and continue until we die.

The Early Years of Marriage

The bridal media bombard women with merchandise. Many people spend more on a wedding than a four-year degree at an average-priced state college. Because most couples don't know each other as well as they should and don't attend premarital classes, what happens after the romantic wedding ceremonies are over?

AFTER THE VOWS The first year of marriage involves basic adjustments. After the wedding, the groom takes on the new and unfamiliar role of husband. Brides, especially, often experience marriage shock. Unlike their husbands, many women must take on wifely roles such as pleasing the husband's family and friends and being the emotional guardian of the marriage (Heyn, 1997). Others experience a "wedding postpartum":

When . . . you find that your new husband blows his nose in the shower, few brides escape feeling some degree of disillusionment. You know then you're not at the champagne fountain anymore. Even though you weren't expecting perpetual bubbly from your marriage, the reality can be startling (Stark, 1998: 88).

It takes some women up to a year to feel comfortable with their new married name and the new identity of wife that it brings (Nissinen, 2000).

A second adjustment involves putting the relationship above others. While doing so, couples must also strike a balance between their relationships with their in-laws and their spouses. Parents (especially mothers) who fear losing contact with their married children sometimes create conflict by calling and visiting frequently and meddling in the couple's life (Greider, 2000; Viorst, 2003).

Beginning early in marriage, a major source of conflict is the inability to pay debts on a timely basis. Credit card debt is especially problematic because finance charges accumulate quickly, sometimes costing more that the product or service a couple buys.

SETTLING IN If both partners grew up in families whose parents were responsive to each other's emotional needs, they had good role models. Especially as newlyweds, they are more successful at weathering the effects of marital stress (Sabatelli and Bartle-Haring, 2003; Umberson et al., 2005).

Two-paycheck newlyweds—especially those who marry after a long period of independence—must make the transition from "my" money to "our" money. Adjusting to a joint bank account isn't always easy because most people aren't used to pooling their money. In addition, the couple will have to reach a consensus about paying off college loans, credit card debt, mortgage payments (if she just bought a house and he hasn't, for example), and saving for the future. And what if she's a spender and he's a saver?

Early in the marriage, assuming more debt decreases marital satisfaction. Newlyweds may be initially optimistic about their relationship and dealing with financial issues. As their credit card debt mounts, however, couples argue more about their finances, spend less time together, and think that their marriage is unfair because there are more costs than benefits (Dew, 2008).

Marriage and Children

One of the most important functions of the family is to socialize children to become responsible and contributing members of society (see Chapter 1). In some countries, teens marry at an early age and are considered adults. In Western societies, including the United States, adolescents are dependent on their parents until their late teens and even into their mid-or late 20s. This means that couples spend much of their married life raising their offspring (see Chapter 11).

YOUNG CHILDREN Socializing children takes enormous time and patience. Families with young children spend much of their time teaching them to live up to cultural expectations, and inculcating values such as doing well at school, following the rules, being kind, controlling one's temper, doing what one is asked, being responsible, and getting along with others (Acock and Demo, 1994).

In general, marital satisfaction tends to decrease after a couple has children. Most parents experience more frequent conflicts and disagreements after having children than do childless spouses. On the other hand, many couples who marry before their out-of-wedlock child is born enjoy being married. Compared with their unmarried counterparts, after the first year of marriage they report greater financial security, a stable home life, and optimism about being good parents (Timmer and Orbuch, 2001; Whiteman et al., 2007; Kamp Dush et al., 2008).

ADOLESCENTS Raising adolescents is difficult. Besides all the usual developmental tasks associated with the physical changes of puberty and emotional maturation, contemporary adolescents face more complicated lives than ever before. Both parents and children may have to cope with divorce, parental unemployment, and dangers such as violence and drugs in their schools and neighborhoods (Cotten, 1999). We'll return to the adolescent years in Chapter 12.

The potential for family stress often increases as adolescents begin to press for autonomy and independence. Conflict sometimes occurs not necessarily because of the children but as a result of a dip in the parents' happiness because of marital burnout or communication problems. Sometimes changes occur suddenly because of geographic moves. Depending on the breadwinner's (usually the father's) occupation and career stage, family members may have to adjust to a new community and form new friendships.

Marriage at Midlife

Like their younger counterparts, couples in their midlife years (between ages 45 and 65) must continually adapt to new conditions. The most common adjustments involve intergenerational ties, relationships with in-laws, the empty nest syndrome, and the boomerang generation.

INTERGENERATIONAL TIES Our family of origin, you recall, plays a significant role in shaping our values and behavior over the life course (see Chapter 1). Couples may be ambivalent about their intergenerational relationships, however. When families meet for holidays and celebrations, grandparents and other relatives may criticize the parents about how they discipline their children, especially toddlers and teenagers. Married couples may be torn between pleasing their parents or their spouses. Spouses may also experience strain about accepting financial assistance from their parents because doing so may obligate them in the future (Beaton et al., 2003).

Intergenerational ties are often positive and supportive, but irritation and ambivalence are common. A study of black and white adult children ages 22 to 49 found that parents reported more intense tension than children did, particularly regarding the children's jobs, finances, and housekeeping habits. Both parents experienced more conflict with their daughters than their sons, possibly because daughters generally have closer relationships and more contact with their parents, both of which increase opportunities for disagreements. And, both sons and daughters felt more stress with their mothers than their fathers, particularly because mothers were more likely to be critical and to offer unsolicited advice (Birditt et al., 2009).

RELATIONSHIPS WITH IN-LAWS There are numerous jokes about mothers-in-law ("Hey guys, looking for a great gift for your mother-in-law on Mother's Day? Why not send her back her daughter!"). In contrast, we rarely, if ever, hear father-in-law jokes. Why?

After a couple marries, most of the conflict is usually between female in-laws (Apter, 2009). There are many specific reasons for the friction, but there seem to be three common themes. First, women play a central role in family relationships. When a new marriage is formed and another woman enters the family circle, a mother may believe, correctly, that she is less central in her son's life and may be ambivalent about giving up the close ties with him that she enjoyed in the past. A daughter-in-law may also be guarded because she doesn't know what to expect and whether she'll be accepted. Such anxieties create a sense of insecurity on both sides (Gurner et al., 2006).

Second, American culture doesn't have clearly delineated roles for in-laws—such as showing deference to older women in the kin group or obeying a father-in-law in many Asian countries. Instead, we often hear statements such as "I'm marrying Andy, not his family." This is a misconception because in-laws, like it or not, are an important part of a couple's relationship and can account for up to 43 percent of a couple's marital satisfaction (Morr Serewicz, 2008). Even after 20 years of marriage, in-laws can intrude on a couple's marriage and create problems by treating a daughter-in-law or son-in-law with disrespect; openly criticizing how the couple raises its children; and making demands on the married couple, such as spending all holidays together (Bryant et al., 2001; Doherty, 2001). Thus, the better the relationship with in-laws, especially mothers-in-law, the better the quality of the couple's marriage.

Third, tension is compounded because of generational differences, particularly after the birth of a grandchild. Conflict arises when the newcomer and the more experienced matriarch wrestle over child care. Grandmothers feel excluded when their daughters-in-law ignore their presumably sage

First Lady Michelle Obama's mother, Marian Robinson, who has played an important role in her granddaughters' lives, represents the growing number of multigenerational families that include in-laws. When asked how she felt about relocating from Chicago to Washington, D.C., Robinson said "If somebody's going to be with these kids other than their parents, it better be me" (Toppo, 2008).

(although unsolicited) advice on proper child-rearing. The younger generation, wanting control over their parenting, often rejects the advice as old-fashioned, disapproving, and intrusive (Apter, 2009).

THE "EMPTY NEST SYNDROME" Social scientists used to characterize middle-aged parents as experiencing the *empty-nest syndrome*—depression and a lessened sense of well-being, especially among women—when children leave home. Some parents, especially mothers who have devoted their lives to bringing up children, may feel empty and useless when their kids fly from the nest.

In fact, the children's departure gives many married couples a chance to relax, enjoy each other's company, see friends, travel, and pursue their own interests. Often, both parents experience a sense of freedom and easing of responsibility that enhances their relationship (Antonucci et al., 2001).

Some sad and lonely parents might sit at home waiting for their children to call or visit, but that's not usually the case. For example, a study that tracked the marital satisfaction of more than 100 women over an 18-year period found that their marriages improved after the kids left whether the women had stayed with the same partner or remarried. Marital satisfaction increased mainly because of the quality, and not just the quantity, of time spent together after the children moved out (Gorchoff et al., 2008).

THE BOOMERANG GENERATION Children who leave the nest sometimes fly back. This recent phenomenon is known as the **boomerang generation**, young adults who move back into their parents' home after living independently for a while. In the case of a weak economy, low income, divorce, or the high cost of housing, many young adults move back into their parents' home or never leave it in the first place. Parents try to launch their children into the adult world, but, like boomerangs, some keep coming back.

Boomerang kids can have a positive or a negative impact on their parents' marital life. Co-residence has a more negative influence on remarried parents than on parents in their first marriage largely because of conflict between children and stepparents (Mitchell and Gee, 1996; we'll examine this issue in Chapter 16).

Marital satisfaction also diminishes if a child returns home several times. The multiple returns prevent some parents from enjoying the greater intimacy, privacy, and freedom to pursue new interests that they expected when their children left home. Marital satisfaction increases, however, if the children have a good relationship with their parents during co-residence. The children can provide physical and home maintenance assistance, emotional support, advice, and companionship. Thus, they can improve the overall quality of family relationships (Willis and Reid, 1999).

Marriage in Later Life

Many older couples describe their marriage as the best years of their lives. They have developed trust and intimacy over the years, enjoy each other's company, and are happier than their younger counterparts. Couples continue to make adjustments in later life, however, as evidenced by retirement and health issues.

RETIREMENT Some older couples report an upturn in marital happiness. They have few unresolved issues, settle conflicts more effectively than their younger and middle-aged counterparts, and savor the rewards of a long-term friendship.

Retirement typically brings more time to enjoy each other's company, but gender roles usually don't change very much. Husbands continue to do most of the male chores, but may take on large-scale projects such as remodeling. Men might do more shopping, but women still invest much of their time in traditionally female tasks such as food preparation, laundry, and cleaning the house (Charles and Carstensen, 2002). The biggest change in later life for both sexes is physical decline.

HEALTH AND WELL-BEING The marital quality of older couples, whether one or both are retired, depends quite a bit on the partners' health. As you saw in Chapter 7, sexual expression remains an important element in long-term marital relationships, but more so for men than for women. And, generally,

Some couples are married a lifetime; others wait a lifetime to marry. Del Martin, 87 (left), and Phyllis Lyon, 84, were the first to marry in California in June 2008 when the state allowed same-sex marriages. The law was overturned about four months later by a voter referendum. Lyon and Martin had been together more than 50 years. Martin died after the couple had been married for two months.

older spouses who feel valued are happier and live longer than unhappy older couples (Vinick, 2000; Tower et al., 2002).

A decline in health often impairs marital quality. Depression, for example, is the most common mental health illness in aging populations. The depressed spouse may have problems communicating and making decisions and may get angry quickly. The nondepressed spouse may feel confused, frustrated, and helpless (Sandberg et al., 2002). If a spouse needs long-term care, whether at home or in a nursing facility, the caregiver undergoes tremendous stress. And if a spouse is widowed, she or he may have to forge new relationships (see Chapter 17).

Power and communication issues affect marital quality throughout the life course. Most of these issues are similar whether people are married or single.

COMMUNICATION: A KEY TO SUCCESSFUL RELATIONSHIPS

People who have been married a long time usually give very similar reasons for their success: "We never yelled at each other," "We maintained a sense of humor," "We treated each other with respect," "We tried to be patient," and "We accepted what we couldn't change about each other." Effective verbal and nonverbal communication is essential to any committed relationship, not just marriage.

What Is Good Communication?

Our most intimate relationships are within the family, but being able to express thoughts and feelings and to listen are critical components of all close relationships.

Let's begin by looking at some of the major goals of effective communication in intimate relationships.

COMMUNICATION GOALS A major goal of effective communication is developing ways of interacting that are clear, nonjudgmental, and nonpunitive. A second important goal is resolving conflicts through problem solving rather than coercion or manipulation. Very little can be gained "if someone tells us how we are *supposed* to feel, how we are *supposed* to behave, or what we are *supposed* to do with our lives" (Aronson, 1995: 404).

Good communication conveys *what* we and others feel. It incorporates different approaches that are equally valid (as when people agree to disagree). Effective communication also establishes an atmosphere of trust and honesty in resolving—or at least decreasing—conflict. An important first step in successful communication is self-disclosure.

SELF-DISCLOSURE *Self-disclosure* is telling another person about oneself and one's thoughts and feelings with the expectation that truly open communication will follow (see Chapter 6). In terms of exchange theory, *reciprocal* self-disclosure increases partners' liking and trusting each other, eliminates a lot of guesswork in the relationship, and helps balance costs and benefits.

Self-disclosure is beneficial under four conditions (Derlega et al., 1993):

- *Esteem support* can reduce a person's anxiety about troubling events. If the listener is attentive, sympathetic, and uncritical, disclosure can motivate people to change significant aspects of their lives.

- A listener may be able to offer *information support* through advice and guidance. For example, people who are under stress may benefit by knowing that their problems are not necessarily due to personal deficiencies.

- Disclosure can provide *instrumental support* if the listener offers concrete help, such as shopping for food or caring for the children when the partner is sick.

- Even if a problem is not easily solved, listeners can provide *motivational support*. For example, if a husband is distressed about losing his job, his wife can encourage him to persist and assure him that "we can get through this."

When is self-disclosure harmful? If feedback is negative, disclosure may intensify a person's already low self-esteem. (Disclosure: "I'm so mad at myself for not sticking to my diet." Response: "Yeah; if you had, you'd have something to wear to the party tonight.")

Because self-disclosure is risky, many people keep secrets from their partners. In a recent national survey on married couples, for example, nearly half of the men and 41 percent of the women admitted keeping some things to themselves. It's not clear how many of the secrets were trivial or important, but 25 percent of the men said that they had kept important secrets from their wives such as debts, gambling, alcohol or drug abuse, and infidelity (Bennetts, 2008).

Many couples are reluctant to self-disclose because people gain "information power" through self-revelation that they can then use against a partner ("Well, you had an affair, so you have no right to complain about anything"). If the self-disclosure is one-sided, it sends the message that "I don't trust you enough to tell you about my flaws" (Galvin and Brommel, 2000). If a trust is violated, partners are unlikely to reveal intimate information about themselves in the future.

Do men and women differ in self-disclosure and other communication patterns? And if they differ, is the interaction innate or learned?

Sex Differences in Communication

In recent years, "communication" has become a buzzword to summarize problems in male-female relationships. We'll first consider some of the studies that suggest that men and women speak differently. Then

Dilbert: Scott Adams/Distributed by United Feature Syndicate, Inc.

Since you asked . . .

Why do women and men sometimes communicate differently?

we'll examine some of the research that shows that communication variations aren't biologically based but reflect differences in gender roles and power.

WOMEN'S SPEECH Because women tend to use communication to develop and maintain relationships, *talk is often an end in itself.* It is a way to foster closeness and understanding. A second important characteristic of women's speech is the *effort to establish equality.* Thus, women often encourage a speaker to continue by showing interest or concern ("Oh, really?" or "I feel the same way sometimes"). Or they may use affirmation, showing support for others ("You must have felt terrible" or "I think you're right").

Women often ask questions that *probe for greater understanding* of feelings and perceptions ("Do you think it was deliberate?" or "Were you glad it happened?"). Women also do *conversational maintenance work.* They may ask a number of questions that encourage conversation ("Tell me what happened at the meeting").

Another quality of women's speech is a *personal, concrete style:* Women often use details, personal disclosures, and anecdotes. By using concrete rather than vague language, women's talk clarifies issues and feelings so that people are able to understand and identify with one another. *References to emotions* ("Wasn't it depressing when . . .?") personalize the communication and makes it more intimate.

A final feature of women's speech is tentativeness. This may be expressed in a number of ways. *Verbal hedges* ("I kind of feel you may be wrong") and qualifiers ("I may not be right, but . . .") modify, soften, or weaken other words or phrases. Men often give direct commands ("Let's go"), whereas women appear to show uncertainty by hedging ("I guess it's time to go").

Women also use more *verbal fillers*—words or phrases such as "okay," "well," "you know," and "like"—to fill silences. *Verbal fluencies*—sounds such as "mmh," "ahh," and "unhuh"—serve the same purpose. Women use fillers and fluencies much more frequently when talking to men than when talking to other women (Pearson, 1985; Lakoff, 1990; Fitzpatrick and Mulac, 1995).

MEN'S SPEECH A prominent feature of men's speech is *instrumentality;* men tend to use speech to accomplish specific purposes ("Give me three reasons why I should . . ."). They often focus on problem solving: getting information, discovering facts, and suggesting courses of action or solutions. Thus, for men, speech is more often the *means to an end* rather than the end itself.

Masculine speech is also characterized by *exerting control* to establish, enhance, or defend personal status and ideas by asserting oneself and, often, challenging others ("I'll need more information to make a decision").

Men are much less likely than women to offer empathic remarks ("That must have been very difficult for you"). Men are also less likely to express sympathy or to divulge personal information.

Another feature of men's communication is *conversational dominance.* In most contexts, men tend to dominate the conversation, speaking more frequently and for longer periods. They also show dominance by interrupting others, reinterpreting the speaker's meaning, or rerouting the conversation. Men tend to express themselves in assertive, often absolutist, ways ("That approach won't work").

Compared with women's talk, men's language is typically more forceful, direct, and authoritative; tentativeness is rare. Finally, men are more apt to *communicate in abstract terms* ("What about using another paradigm?"), a reflection of their more impersonal, public style (Tannen, 1990, 1994; Roberts, 2000).

GENDER ROLES, COMMUNICATION, AND SOCIAL CONTEXT Some researchers consider the "female speech" and "male speech" dichotomy a stereotype. The notion that women and men come from two planets ignores the importance of gender roles and social context.

Gender roles shape communication. Many men don't communicate in intimate relationships because they are accustomed to being "stress absorbers" and stoics. Although the silent male is missing an opportunity for intimacy, he is protecting his loved ones from "the disappointment, frustrations, and fears that are part and parcel of his daily work life" (Nowinski, 1993: 122). Instead of focusing on disturbing feelings, many men may turn to alcohol or drugs.

Social context is also important in understanding gender communication styles. Men are more likely to use men's speech when interacting with women in general than with their wives. Husbands decrease the interaction distance between themselves and their wives by adopting a more feminine style in conversations. Women, in contrast, tend to maintain the same women's speech both with their husbands and with men in general (Fitzpatrick and Mulac, 1995).

Communication Problems

Despite our best intentions, many of us don't communicate effectively. Because communication involves *both* partners, we can't control or change our partner's interaction, but we can recognize and do something about our own communication style. Common communication problems include a variety

Nonverbal communication can be just as powerful as words in enhancing or reducing interaction. How does this couple's body language illustrate communication problems?

of issues, ranging from not listening to using the silent treatment.

NOT LISTENING Both partners may be so intent on making their point that they are simply waiting for their turn to speak rather than listening to the other person. Consider a nondiscussion with my husband that occurred while I was revising this textbook several years ago:

Me:	"I haven't had time to do any Christmas shopping yet."
My husband:	"I think you should get a new computer. What about a Mac this time?"
Me:	"And I'll probably be writing Christmas cards in February."
My husband:	"Maybe you should get a laptop."
Me:	"I'll never finish these revisions on time. What I need is a clone."
My husband:	"Will the kids be home for dinner tonight?"

This everyday exchange illustrates the common pattern of partners talking but not communicating. One of the most important components of communication is *really* listening to the other person instead of rehearsing what we plan to say when he or she pauses for a breath. Listening and responding are especially critical when partners discuss relationship problems.

NOT RESPONDING TO THE ISSUE AT HAND If partners are not listening to each other, they won't be able to address a problem. There are three common miscommunication patterns. With *cross-complaining,* partners present their own complaints without addressing the other person's point:

Wife:	"I'm tired of spending all my time on the housework. You're not doing your share."
Husband:	"If you used your time efficiently, you wouldn't be tired" (Gottman, 1982:111).

With *counterproposals,* a spouse ignores or rejects a partner's suggestions and presents his or her own ideas ("Negotiating is ridiculous because they'll never fix the windows. I want to take them to court"). With *stonewalling,* which is more common among men than women, one of the partners may "Hmmmm" or "Uh-huh," but he or she really neither hears nor responds; it's as though the partner has turned into a stone wall (Krokoff, 1987; Gottman, 1994). If a partner is addicted to alcohol or drugs, for example, she or he might refuse to talk about the problem:

Whenever someone brings up the [alcohol] issue, he proclaims that they are making a big deal about nothing, are out to get him, or are just plain wrong. No matter how obvious it is to an outsider that the addict's life may be falling apart, he stubbornly refuses to discuss it. If that does not work, he may just get up and walk out (Nowinski, 1993: 137).

BLAMING, CRITICIZING, AND NAGGING Instead of being listened to and understood, partners may feel neglected or unappreciated. They believe that their spouse or partner magnifies their faults, belittles them, accuses them unjustly, and makes them feel worthless and stupid. The criticism may escalate from specific complaints ("The bank called today and I was embarrassed that your check bounced") to more global and judgmental derision ("Don't you know anything about managing money?!").

The blamer is a faultfinder who criticizes relentlessly and generalizes: "You never do anything right," "You're just like your mother/father." In blaming and criticizing, a partner may use sophisticated communication skills to manipulate a more vulnerable partner (Gordon, 1993; Burleson and Denton, 1997). If I'm an effective blamer, for example, I can probably convince you that our budget problems are due to *your* overspending rather than *my* low salary.

SCAPEGOATING Scapegoating is another way of avoiding honest communication about a problem. By blaming others, we imply that our partners, not we, should change. We may be uncomfortable about being expressive because we grew up in cool and aloof families. Or we might be suspicious about trusting people because a good friend or intimate partner took advantage of us. Regardless of the reasons, blaming parents, teachers, relatives, siblings, friends, and past or current partners for our problems is debilitating and counterproductive (Noller, 1984).

COERCION OR CONTEMPT Partners may be punitive and force their point of view on others. If this works, coercive behavior, which is related to scapegoating, can continue. Contempt can also be devastating. The most visible signs of contempt are insults and name calling; sarcasm; hostile humor; mockery; and body language such as rolling your eyes, sneering, and curling your upper lip (Gottman, 1994).

As you saw in the "Am I Heading toward Marital Burnout?" box on p. 272, some of the red flags include efforts to control a partner through tantrums, violence, threats of violence, or threats of suicide. In addition, one partner may subject the other to public humiliation ("Will you stop interrupting me all the time?!").

THE SILENT TREATMENT People communicate even when they are silent. Silence in various contexts, and at particular points in a conversation, means different things to different people. Sometimes silence saves us from foot-in-mouth problems. Not talking to your spouse or partner, however, builds up feelings of anger and hostility. Initially, the "offender" may work very hard to make the silent partner feel loved and to talk about a problem. Eventually, however, the partner who is getting the silent treatment may get fed up, give up, or look for someone else (Rosenberg, 1993).

Power and Conflict in Relationships

Power and conflict are normal and inevitable in close relationships. Both shape communication patterns and decision making. The person who has the power to make decisions often influences many of the dynamics in marriage and other intimate relationships.

Sociologists define **power** as the ability to impose one's will on others. Whether it's a dating relationship, a family, or a nation, some individuals and groups have more power than others.

SOURCES OF POWER Power is not limited to tangible things such as money. Love, for example, is an important source of power. As you saw in Chapter 8, the *principle of least interest* explains why, in a dating relationship, the person who is less interested is more powerful than the committed partner. In marriage, similarly, if you are more committed to your marriage than your spouse is, you have less power. As a result, you may defer to your partner's wishes, do things you don't want to do, or avoid expressing negative feelings (see Olen and Blakeley, 2009).

Other nonmaterial sources of power include access to information or particular abilities or talents. For example, husbands often have more decision-making power about how to spend money on expensive items, such as houses or cars, because they are typically more knowledgeable about financial matters, investments, and negotiating contracts. In traditional households, the wife may have more

"You haven't said anything for ten years. Is everything O.K.?"

power than the husband in furnishing a home or raising children because she usually devotes more time to reading informational material; shopping; or becoming familiar with neighborhood professionals, such as pediatricians and dentists, who provide important services.

CONFLICT AND COMMUNICATION *Conflict* refers to discrete, isolated disagreements as well as chronic relationship problems. All partners and families, no matter how supportive and caring they are, experience conflict. A study of married couples found that the majority of participants reported an average of one or two "unpleasant disagreements" per month (McGonagle et al., 1993).

Comedian Phyllis Diller's quip, "Don't go to bed mad. Stay up and fight!" is actually insightful. Conflict is not in itself a bad thing. If partners recognize and actively attempt to resolve it, conflict can be a catalyst in strengthening a relationship. Before examining coping techniques, let's look at some of the issues that couples usually fight about.

WHAT DO COUPLES FIGHT ABOUT?

When asked to rate their top relationship irritants, men complain that women give them the silent treatment, bring up things the men have done in the remote past, are too critical, and stubborn in never giving in. Women complain that men forget important dates (such as birthdays and anniversaries), don't work hard enough at their jobs, noisily burp or pass gas, and stare at other women (Dixit, 2009).

Some of these irritants are more annoying than others, but what are the most serious disagreements about? Money is at the top of the list of the subjects that couples fight about. Other common issues are housework, fidelity, and children (see, also, Chapter 15 on divorce).

Money

Nationally, 51 percent of Americans don't talk about money before marriage and another 4 percent lie about their finances. It's not surprising, then, that 70 percent of newlyweds say that money issues are a serious source of disagreements as early as the first year of marriage (Ordoñez, 2007; Coplan, 2008). Some financial experts maintain, in fact, that people should find a "financial soul mate" and not a romantic one because marriage, at its core, is (or should be) a sound monetary union (Bernard, 2008).

In another national survey, 84 percent of couples said that money creates tension in their marriage and 15 percent said that they fight about money several times a month or more (Regnier and Gengler, 2006). Disagreements often arise because wives overstate debt and husbands overstate income. These dissimilar views of the family's finances increase conflict (Zagorsky, 2003).

Even when money isn't the leading source of marital conflict, the arguments about money are more pervasive, problematic, and recurrent and often go unsolved despite attempts to do so. And, compared with other conflicts (such as those over habits, relatives, child rearing, leisure activities, and communication), fights over money last longer and are more likely to lead to depressive behavior, such as withdrawal and sadness, and physical aggression, such as shouting, shoving, and slapping (Papp et al., 2009).

Arguments typically erupt over specific expenditures, but they are often based on different values, such as saving for the future or enjoying life now, entertaining lavishly or modestly, or purchasing designer rather than unknown brands. Because of different financial priorities, both married and unmarried couples sometimes lie to their partners about their spending habits (see *Figure 10.4*).

Housework

There is considerable contention over housework, including disagreements about whether it's even a problem. For example, 24 percent of husbands but 31 percent of wives say that household chores are a major source of friction (Bennetts, 2008). In another national survey, 62 percent of couples (up from 47 percent in 1990) said that sharing household tasks was very important for a successful marriage (Taylor et al., 2007). If couples can't agree on who should do what around the house, especially when both partners are employed, tension may rise and quarrels become more frequent.

Fidelity and Sex

In practically every recent national survey that I've seen, sexual infidelity is typically at the top of the list of what couples fight about, just behind money in second or third place, and always higher on the list than sex as a source of conflict. Another common pattern is that women see infidelity as a more serious problem than do men, probably because men are more likely to be unfaithful, and men are more likely than women to complain that they don't get enough sex (Taylor et al., 2007; Bennetts, 2008).

For unmarried couples, the most common violations include having sexual intercourse outside the relationship, wanting to date others, and deceiving the partner. As you saw in Chapter 7, many people, especially women, view extramarital affairs and cybersex as the most serious types of betrayal. Married and unmarried couples also argue about other violations of trust and commitment, such as lying, betraying confidences, and gossiping about each other or relatives (Jones and Burdette, 1994; Metts, 1994).

Children

Children can sometimes strengthen a relationship, but they also create strain, tension, and conflict. In addition to feeling stress because of the demands children make on them, partners may have different philosophies about issues such as discipline, the importance of teaching young

FIGURE 10.4 Is This Financial Infidelity?

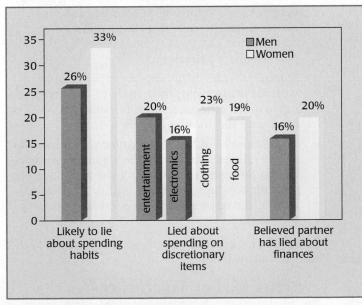

Sources: Based on Singletary, 2005; "Stats & Facts . . ." 2005.

Choices

Ground Rules for Fair Fighting

Therapists, counselors, and researchers maintain that arguing the issues is healthier than suffering in silence. Clinicians who work with unhappy couples offer the following advice for changing some of our most destructive interaction patterns (Crosby, 1991a; Rosenzweig, 1992):

1. Don't attack your partner. He or she will only become defensive and will be too busy preparing a good rebuttal to hear what you have to say.

2. Avoid ultimatums; no one likes to be backed into a corner.

3. Say what you really mean and don't apologize for it. Lies are harmful, and apologetic people are rarely taken seriously.

4. Avoid accusations and attacks; do not belittle or threaten.

5. Start with your own feelings. "I feel" is better than "You said." Focus on the problem, not on the other person.

6. State your wishes and requests clearly and directly; don't be manipulative, defensive, or sexually seductive.

7. Limit what you say to the present. Avoid long lists of complaints from the past.

8. Refuse to fight dirty:

   - No *gunnysacking,* or keeping one's complaints secret and tossing them into an imaginary gunnysack that gets heavier and heavier over time.

   - No *passive-aggressive behavior,* or expressing anger indirectly in the form of criticism, sarcasm, nagging, or nitpicking.

   - No *silent treatment;* keep the lines of communication open.

   - No *name calling.*

9. Use humor and comic relief. Laugh at yourself and the situation but not at your partner. Learning to take our-

selves less seriously and to recognize our flaws without becoming so self-critical that we wallow in shame or self-pity can shorten fights.

10. Strive for closure as soon as possible after a misunderstanding or disagreement by resolving the issue. This prevents dirty fighting and, more important, it holds the partners to their commitment to negotiate until the issue has been resolved or defused.

⫶• Stop and Think . . .

- "A good fight is an essential ingredient in building a good relationship." Do you agree? Or does keeping silent and sidestepping conflict increase affection and respect?
- Have you ever used similar rules for fair fighting in your own relationships? If so, what were the results?

---

children self-control, and the kinds of responsibilities a child should have.

As more spouses and partners collaborate in child rearing, there are more opportunities for clashes. For example, a wife may expect her husband to take on more child care tasks, but she may also resent his insistence on making decisions about the child's playmates, bedtimes, or curfews. Children are especially likely to be a source of conflict in remarriages (see Chapter 16).

How Do Couples Deal with Conflict?

Since you asked . . .

⫶• Is leaving the room the best solution to an argument?

It bears repeating that conflict is a normal part of life. What may *not* be normal or healthy is the way a family handles conflict.

COMMON CONFLICT RESOLUTION APPROACHES Intimate couples typically use four techniques to end—though not necessarily resolve—conflict: accommodation, compromise, standoff, and withdrawal (Vuchinich, 1987; Wilmot and Hocker, 2007).

- *Accommodation.* One person submits to another; the conflict ends when one person agrees with or goes along with the other.

- *Compromise.* Partners find a middle ground between their opposing positions; each must give in a little to accept a compromise. The compromise can be suggested either by a partner or by a third party.

- *Standoff.* The disputants drop the argument without resolving it; they agree to disagree and move on to other activities. No one wins or loses, and the conflict ends in a draw.

- *Withdrawal.* When a disputant withdraws, he or she refuses to continue the argument, either by clamming up or by leaving the room. Among the four coping techniques, withdrawal is the least effective because there is no resolution of the conflict.

Except for compromise, these aren't the best ways to resolve conflict.

EFFECTIVE WAYS OF HANDLING CONFLICT One of the biggest myths about interpersonal relationships is that it's okay to "say what's on your mind" and "let it all hang out." Some partners unleash "emotional napalm" to "blow off some steam" (Noller and Fitzpatrick, 1993: 178).

In some cases, couples should probably communicate less, not more, because too much talking can lead to relentless nagging, criticism, and hammering the same issues over and over. However well intentioned, constant efforts to communicate are especially futile and frustrating if partners try to change each other's personality (Dixit, 2009). For example, someone who's quiet or reserved can't suddenly become outgoing at parties to please a partner.

Displaced rage, unbridled attacks, and physical aggression aren't normal ways of handling conflict. On the other hand, denying the existence of conflict can destroy a relationship. Couples who confront their problems may be unhappy in the short term but will have a better relationship in the long run. Otherwise, the anger and bitterness will fester.

Both researchers and family practitioners have suggested effective ways of dealing with anger and strife (see the box "Ground Rules for Fair Fighting"). Such rules don't ensure a resolution. Because they are based on negotiation and compromise, however, they offer partners a better chance of developing more constructive ways of dealing with conflict.

PRODUCTIVE COMMUNICATION PATTERNS

Over time, communication problems can erode intimate relationships. It takes time to forge good communication techniques.

Psychologist John Gottman interviewed and studied more than 200 couples over a 20-year period. He found that the difference between lasting marriages and those that split up was a "magic ratio" of five to one—that is, five positive interactions between partners for every negative one:

As long as there was five times as much positive feeling and interaction between husband and wife as there is negative, the marriage was likely to be stable over time. In contrast, those couples who were heading for divorce were doing far too little on the positive side to compensate for the growing negativity between them (Gottman, 1994: 41).

Improving Your Communication Style

Yelling is one of the most damaging ways of interacting. We rarely scream at guests, employers, students, or professors. Yet we do so quite often with partners, spouses, and family members, with whom we have

"She says I'm indecisive, but I don't know."
© Anthony Kelly/www.CartoonStock.com

Since you asked . . .

- Doesn't yelling show that you love and care about a person?

our most important and longest-lasting relationships. "Hollering is just part of my personality" is no excuse for obnoxious and abusive behavior.

According to researchers and practitioners, couples can increase positive communication and decrease negative interaction patterns in the following ways:

- *Ask for information.* If your partner has a complaint ("I never get a chance to talk to you because you're always busy"), address the issue. Don't be defensive ("Well, if you were around more often, we could talk"); find out why your partner is upset.

- *Don't generalize.* Accusations such as "You always do X" increase anger and tension.

- *Stay focused on the issue.* Don't bring up past events and old grudges. If you're discussing spending habits, focus on the items that were purchased recently.

- *Be specific.* A specific complaint is easier to deal with than a general criticism. "You never talk to me" is less effective than "I wish we could have 30 minutes each evening without television or the kids."

- *Keep it honest.* Honesty not only means not lying; it also means not manipulating others. Do not resort to bullying, outwitting, blaming, dominating, or controlling. Do not become a long-suffering martyr. Truthfulness and sincerity reinforce mutual trust and respect.

■ *Make it kind.* Some people use "brutal honesty" as an excuse for cruelty. Temper honesty with positive statements about your partner.

■ *Express appreciation.* Thanking your partner for something he or she has done will enhance both the discussion and the relationship.

■ *Use nonverbal communication.* Nonverbal acts, such as hugging your partner, smiling, and holding his or her hand, can sometimes be more supportive than anything you might say.

■ *Above all, just listen.* Sharpen your emotional communication skills by being really interested in what your partner is saying rather than always focusing on yourself (Knapp and Hall, 1992; Gottman and DeClaire, 2001).

⠿ MAKING CONNECTIONS

■ Think about the conflicts you've experienced with a partner or spouse during the past year or so. What were most of the disagreements about—important or petty issues?

■ When you and your partner argue, how do you react? How does your partner respond? Do you resolve the conflict? Or does it smolder until the next eruption?

Family Therapy and Marriage and Relationship Programs

Because conflict is inevitable, family therapy and counseling have become a booming industry. Indeed, the number of couples who take premarital tests (which cost up to $500) to determine whether they should marry has increased steeply—from 100,000 couples in 1993 to 800,000 in 2004 (Barry, 2005).

In 2006, Congress approved $100 million a year for five years for marriage and relationship education (MRE) for high school classes, marriage skills training programs, and a variety of divorce reduction programs. Do therapy and MRE work? The data are mixed.

MARRIAGE EDUCATION PROGRAMS ARE EFFECTIVE

Some studies show that professional and experienced counselors can help couples identify their strengths and weaknesses and improve their relationship. For example, a review of 23 studies of programs for engaged couples concluded that the programs were generally effective. They produced immediate gains in communication processes, conflict management skills, and overall relationship

quality that lasted from six months to three years (Carroll and Doherty, 2003).

MARRIAGE EDUCATION PROGRAMS HAVE MIXED RESULTS

To determine the effectiveness of MRE programs, a team of scholars examined 13,000 research articles on marriage education, counseling, and therapy programs. Of the 39 studies that were "of the highest quality" scientifically, MRE programs had only a "moderate" effect on improving relationships and a "small" effect on improving communication (Reardon-Anderson et al., 2005).

A study of 340 high school students in Texas who took an MRE curriculum reported that the program was generally effective in helping them identify unhealthy relationship patterns, develop more realistic attitudes about relationships and marriage, and lower verbal aggression. The researchers noted, however, that among other limitations, they couldn't measure the long-term effects of the program or identify its most useful topics (Adler-Baeder et al., 2007).

A study of 49 adult couples examined three types of MRE activities: (1) a premarital workbook and exercises that the couples completed on their own, (2) six 1-hour sessions with a therapist, and (3) a six-session self-assessment process with a facilitator who was a family therapist trainee. The researchers found in a follow-up six months later, that the second program was the least effective, perhaps because it was the least structured, and that the third program was the most effective, probably because the participants could focus on the specific issues that were the most important to them (Busby et al., 2007).

MRE programs may also be useful for some adults, but they tend to attract people who may need them least. For example, a study of 7,331 couples found that the participants were people who valued marriage; were mature, kind, and considerate; wanted to improve a current relationship; and had fairly good intra- and interpersonal skills (Duncan et al., 2007). Thus, the millions of federal dollars that are being spent to improve marriage skills and reduce divorce never reach the at-risk groups that don't have the time or interest to attend MRE programs.

MARRIAGE EDUCATION PROGRAMS DON'T WORK

In one survey, people ranked marriage counseling at the bottom of the list of programs designed to improve relationships. Part of the problem is that "almost anyone can hang out a shingle as a marriage counselor" (Kantrowitz and Wingert, 1999). And, as you saw in Chapter 2, the authors of some of the best-selling self-help books include self-proclaimed therapists who have been divorced at least twice, are estranged from their children, and know less about communication than you or I do.

Many counselors have internalized cultural stereotypes about how women and men should behave based on traditional gender roles (Wright and Fish, 1997). For example, one of my students who sought premarital counseling concluded that it was "a lot of bull":

An older woman in my church told me, in so many words, to put up with whatever my fiancé would throw my way. She said that men run wild but eventually get tired or old and will settle down. She told me that good Christian women stay with their husbands even though they're miserable (Author's files).

According to one highly regarded family therapist, marital therapists do more harm than good. Many are incompetent. Others remain neutral instead of dealing with a couple's problems, or else they undermine the union ("If you're not happy, why do you stay in the marriage?") (Doherty, 2002; see, also, Cornelius and Alessi, 2007, for other criticisms of marital therapy).

Researchers also criticize MRE programs because they are expensive and there's little evidence that there are any long-term positive effects. Most important, the programs ignore broad social forces—such as unemployment and poverty—that undermine relationships and marriages by creating financial problems (Halford et al., 2002; Ooms, 2005).

CONCLUSION

Someone once said that marriages are made in heaven, but the details have to be worked out here on earth. Working out those details is an ongoing process throughout a marriage or other committed relationship. The biggest sources of conflict and *change* are disagreements over money, household work, and communication problems.

Different *choices* can have different consequences. Deciding to have a more egalitarian division of domestic work and child-rearing responsibilities, for example, can diminish some of the *constraints* that many women (and some men) encounter as they juggle multiple roles. Also, deciding to interact more honestly can result in more effective communication and greater interpersonal satisfaction.

Despite the constraints, marriage is one of the most important rites of passage for almost all of us. Another is parenthood, our focus in the next two chapters.

SUMMARY

1. Marriage, an important rite of passage into adulthood, is associated with many traditions, rituals, and rules. Many of the rituals reflect historical customs.

2. There are several types of marriage. Most endure despite conflict over issues such as parenting, communication, finances, sex, and religious attitudes.

3. What people consider to be very important in marriage hasn't changed much over the years. Both men and women consider love, sexual fidelity, and the ability to discuss feelings to be the most crucial elements of a good marriage.

4. Marriage generally increases a person's physical and mental health. Married women, however, are less likely than married men to enjoy good health.

5. Men and women often experience marriage differently. Some of these differences reflect differences in the status of men and women in society and the organization of household and child care tasks.

6. Marriage changes throughout the life course. In general, having children decreases marital satisfaction, but satisfaction increases again when adult children leave the home. Over the years, families adjust to raising young children, communicating with adolescents, and enjoying the empty-nest and retirement stages.

7. Communication is a key to successful intimate relationships. Self-disclosure is an important element of effective communication, but couples should recognize that disclosing all of their innermost thoughts might be detrimental rather than helpful.

8. Most relationships and marriages that break down do so not because of conflict but because couples don't know how to resolve conflict. Such negative coping strategies as complaining, criticizing, being defensive, and stonewalling may lead to a partner's isolation or withdrawal.

9. Conflict is unavoidable and normal. It is unrealistic to expect communication to cure all relationship problems. Nevertheless, effective communication can decrease the power struggles and hostility that can lead to breakups in marriages and other relationships.

10. Marriage and relationship education is booming. Some maintain that such programs are effective; others argue that the costs outweigh the benefits.

KEY TERMS

engagement 262
conflict-habituated marriage 265
devitalized marriage 265
passive-congenial marriage 266

vital marriage 266
total marriage 266
marital burnout 271
marital roles 272

identity bargaining 272
boomerang generation 277
power 282

11 To Be or Not To Be a Parent
More Choices, More Constraints

A successful physician in his 50s took his 80-year-old mother to a performance at the Civic Opera House in Chicago. They were making their way out the lobby doors to the physician's Mercedes when his mother turned to him and asked: "Do you have to go to the bathroom, dear?"

As this anecdote suggests, parenting never ends. We may change colleges, buy and sell houses and cars, switch careers, and marry more than once, but parenthood is a lifelong commitment. Today we are freer to decide whether to have children, but our choices are more complicated than in the past. Most people can choose when to have children and how many. Women can postpone parenthood longer than ever before, sometimes even to after menopause. We can become parents despite conception problems, and we can decide to remain child free. We cover all these possibilities in this chapter.

Parenthood is a process. *Having* children—through childbirth or adoption—is not the same as *raising* children. This chapter focuses primarily on the biological, economic, and social aspects of *becoming* a parent (or not). The next chapter examines the child-rearing roles, activities,

DATA DIGEST

- In a national study of first-year college students, 77 percent said that **having children is an "essential" or "very important" objective** in their lives.

- The **number of births** in the United States increased from 4.2 million in 1990 to more than 4.3 million in 2007.

- The percentage of **births to unmarried American women increased** from 27 percent in 1990 to 40 percent in 2007; among teenagers, **86 percent of all births are out of wedlock.**

- The number of **international adoptions decreased** from an all-time high of almost 23,000 in 2005 to about 17,500 in 2008.

- About 14 percent of **women have babies they don't want,** up from 9 percent in 1995.

- The **number of voluntarily childless women** ages 40 to 44 has doubled— from 10 percent in 1976 to 20 percent in 2006.

Sources: Chandra et al., 2005; *Chronicle of Higher Education*, 2008; Dye, 2008; U.S. Census Bureau, 2008; U.S. Department of State, 2008; Hamilton et al., 2009.

and responsibilities of being a parent. Let's begin by looking at the early stages of becoming a parent.

BECOMING A PARENT

About 72 percent of American adults have children, but almost half of all U.S. pregnancies are unintended (Chandra et al., 2005; Butler and Gilson, 2008). Whether planned or not, a couple's first pregnancy is an important milestone. Pregnancies are family affairs because both parents typically worry about the developing baby and look forward to its birth with great anticipation. The reactions of both partners to pregnancy can vary, however (Cowan and Cowan, 2000: 33–45):

- *Planners* actively discuss the issue, having jointly decided to conceive a child. They are typically jubilant about becoming pregnant. As one wife said, "When I found out that I was pregnant, I was so excited I wanted to run out in the street and tell everybody I met."

- *Acceptance-of-fate* couples are pleasantly surprised and quietly welcoming of a child, even though they had not planned the pregnancy. Often, such couples have unconsciously or intentionally made an unspoken agreement to become pregnant by using contraceptive methods only sporadically or not at all.

- *Ambivalent couples* have mixed feelings before and after conception and even well into the pregnancy. As one wife noted, "I felt confused, a mixture of up and down, stunned, in a daze." Ambivalent couples decide to have the baby because one partner feels strongly about having a child and the other complies. Or the pregnancy might be unintended, but one or both partners don't believe in abortion.

- In *yes-no couples,* one partner may not want children, even late in the pregnancy. Typically, the wife decides to go ahead with the pregnancy regardless of what her husband thinks, which sometimes causes a separation or divorce. Or, in the case of unmarried teenage couples, the father may simply stop seeing the woman after she becomes pregnant.

It's not surprising that many couples are ambivalent about parenthood because it involves both benefits and costs.

Some Benefits and Costs of Having Children

Some people weigh the pros and cons of having a baby. Many don't because it's often an emotional decision. Speaking both emotionally and practically, what are some of the benefits and costs of becoming a parent?

BENEFITS One of our thirty-something neighbors recently had their first baby. When I asked Matt how they were doing, he exclaimed, "There's nothing like it! She's the most gorgeous baby in the world!" Matt's reaction is fairly typical. For example, 96 percent of first-time parents in a national survey said that they were "in love" with their baby, and 91 percent reported being "happier than ever before" ("Bringing up baby," 1999).

Couples often believe that their lives would be incomplete without children. According to many parents, children bring love and affection; it's a pleasure to watch them grow; they bring joy, happiness, and fun; they create a sense of family; and they bring fulfillment and a sense of satisfaction (Gallup and Newport, 1990).

Unlike parents in many other countries, most Americans don't rely on their children to care for them in their old age (see Chapter 17). Instead, many say that having children brings a new dimension to their life that is more fulfilling than their jobs, their relationships with friends, or their leisure activities. Most couples place a high priority on raising happy, healthy children. Even new parents who are struggling with a colicky infant (whose abdominal distress causes frequent crying) delight in the baby's social and physical growth.

COSTS Parenthood isn't paradise. To begin with, having and raising children is expensive *Figure 11.1*

By permission of John L. Hart FLP and Creators Syndicate, Inc.

FIGURE 11.1 What a Middle-Income Married Couple Spends during the First Two Years of a Child's Life, 2007 Families earning $45,800 to $77,100 spent, on average, $10,960 per year on each child under 2. This amount does not include the costs of prenatal care or delivery.

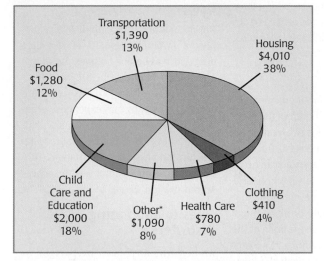

*Includes personal care items, entertainment, and reading materials.
Source: Based on Lino, 2008, Table ES1.

shows a typical year's expenses for a child 1 or 2 years old in married-couple middle-income families. Middle-income families (those earning an average of $61,000 a year) spend about 21 percent of their earnings on a child every year from the child's birth to age 17 (Lino, 2008).

Child-rearing costs are much higher, especially for low-income families, if a child is disabled or chronically ill or needs specialized care that medical or welfare benefits don't cover. And if one or both parents are laid off, they usually lose any medical benefits for themselves and their children (Lukemeyer et al., 2000).

Becoming a parent has other economic and social costs. Many women pay a "mommy tax": Their unpaid work at home doesn't count toward Social Security pensions, they often forgo educational opportunities, and they are more likely than men or childless women to live in poverty in old age or after a divorce (Crittenden, 2001).

Children also have emotional costs. Although most parents report being in love with their baby, first-time parents, especially, experience anxiety or fatigue: 56 percent say that they are stressed and worn out; 52 percent are afraid of doing something wrong; and 44 percent are unsure about what to do a lot of the time ("Bringing up baby," 1999).

As parents become more focused on the child, interpersonal relationships may deteriorate. Many mothers report feeling stressed when attempting to balance their job and household responsibilities. Others think that their husbands have become more distant emotionally—even though they're devoted

fathers—because the mothers spend most of their time caring for the infant (see Chapter 10).

Men may also feel conflicted after the birth of the first child. Many would like to be more involved, but they are still expected to be full-time breadwinners. As a result, they may work long hours, see the baby primarily on weekends, and believe that they're missing out on the parenting experience (see Chapter 13).

The Joys and Tribulations of Pregnancy

Pregnancy can be an exciting and happy time, particularly when it is planned and welcomed. For both prospective parents, it can deepen feelings of love and intimacy and draw them closer as they plan for their family's future. At the same time, pregnancy—especially the first pregnancy—can arouse anxiety about caring for the baby properly and providing for the growing child economically.

The expectant mother usually experiences numerous discomforts. In the first trimester (three-month period), she may have frequent nausea, heartburn, insomnia, shortness of breath, painful swelling of the breasts, and fatigue. She may also be constantly concerned about the health of the *fetus* (the term for the unborn child from eight weeks until birth), especially if she or the baby's father has engaged in any high-risk behaviors (see the box "Having Healthier Babies").

The second trimester can be thrilling because the mother begins to feel movements, or *quickening*, as the fetus becomes more active. *Sonograms* (diagnostic imaging produced by high-frequency sound waves) can reveal an image of the baby and its sex.

On the downside, backaches may become a problem, and fatigue sets in more quickly. In her third trimester, a woman may start losing interest in sex, which becomes awkward and difficult because of her ever-larger abdomen. She begins to retain water and may feel physically unattractive and clumsy. Once-simple, automatic tasks, like tying shoelaces or retrieving something that has fallen on the floor, may require assistance.

Vaginal births may happen quickly or be long and exhausting. Sometimes they're not possible and a woman has a *cesarean section* (surgical removal of the baby from the womb through the abdominal wall), which afterwards is more painful for the mother and entails a longer period of recovery. Both vaginal births and cesarean sections often involve bloody discharge for several weeks. Infections and fevers are also common.

Some Effects of Parenthood

You saw in Chapter 10 that marital satisfaction tends to decrease over time, a normal process. For anywhere from 70 percent to 90 percent of couples, marital bliss

Applying What You've Learned

:• Having Healthier Babies

Most babies are born healthy, but if people engage in high-risk behaviors, their baby can be born with a variety of problems. Many are due to the parents' lifestyle rather than to genetic diseases or other disorders. Here are a few examples.

Smoking

Smoking cuts off the supply of oxygen to the baby's brain; impairs the baby's growth; and is linked to spontaneous abortion, preterm (premature) birth, low birth weight, and childhood illnesses. Low birth rate is conventionally defined as less than 2,500 grams, or 5 pounds, 8 ounces.

Low birth rate (which affects 8 percent of all newborns) increases the infant's chances of sickness, retarded growth, respiratory problems, infections, low intelligence, learning problems, poor hearing and vision, and even death (Cornelius and Day, 2000; Neuman et al., 2007; Mathews and MacDorman, 2008).

Fetuses of women who smoke ten or more cigarettes per day are three times more likely to have genetic abnormalities than are fetuses of nonsmokers. By age 2, these children are more likely than those of nonsmoking mothers to show problem behaviors such as defiance, aggression, and poor social skills. In addition, children of women whose mothers and maternal grandmothers smoked during pregnancy are almost three times more likely to develop asthma by age five (de la Chica et al., 2005; Li et al., 2005; Wakschlag et al., 2006).

Alcohol

Infants experience a brain growth spurt that starts in the sixth month of the pregnancy and continues for two years after birth. However, birth defects associated with prenatal alcohol exposure can occur in the first three to eight weeks of pregnancy, before a woman even knows that she's pregnant. A single drinking binge can permanently damage the brain of the unborn child, but more than 12 percent of women drink alcohol and almost 4 percent who know they're pregnant report binge drinking (seven or more drinks per week, or five or more drinks within a few hours) (Ikonomidou et al., 2000; Denny et al., 2009).

Chronic drinking during pregnancy may lead to **fetal alcohol syndrome (FAS)**, a condition characterized by physical abnormalities such as congenital heart defects, defective joints, and often mental retardation (Baer et al., 2003). In the United States, 40,000 children are born with FAS-related disorders each year, costing the nation $6 billion in medical expenses (The FASD Center, 2009).

Drugs

During 2004 and 2005, almost 4 percent of pregnant women ages 15 to 44 used illicit drugs (such as heroin, cocaine, morphine, and opium). Mothers who use illicit drugs are likely to have infants who are addicted. The baby may experience problems such as prenatal strokes, brain damage, seizures, preterm birth, retarded fetal growth, and physical malformations (Substance Abuse and Mental Health Services Administration, 2006).

Obesity and Eating Disorders

Women who are obese, overweight, or excessively thin before becoming pregnant are at a much higher risk than normal-weight women of having infants with birth defects such as spina bifida (an abnormal opening along the spine), heart abnormalities, and other problems. Researchers suspect that obese women suffer from nutritional deficits—due to poor eating habits—that result in diabetes and health-related problems for infants. Pregnant teenagers with poor diets can hurt their baby's bone growth because the fetus is not getting enough calcium (Watkins et al., 2003; Partington et al., 2009).

---

dips within a year after the birth of their first child, whereas married couples without children become unhappier more gradually. The negative effects of parenthood tend to be greater for partners with a history of parental divorce or conflict, who cohabit before marriage, have a baby shortly after marrying, have low incomes, have high levels of negative communication before a child's birth, and experience conflict in the division of child care (Doss et al., 2009). Having a baby typically puts a sudden, drastic strain on a marriage because parenthood is steeped in romantic misconceptions: "For couples who thought that having a baby was going to bring them closer together, this is especially confusing and disappointing" (Cowan and Cowan, 2000: 18).

Do such findings imply that couples would be better off by not having children? Not at all. Some couples shouldn't have children because they neglect and abuse them, but 50 percent of Americans say that adding children to the family increases their happiness (Ali, 2008).

MOTHERS AND THEIR NEWBORNS There is a widespread myth that an instant bonding occurs between a mother and her newborn baby (see Chapter 6). In reality, it is not only mothers but also fathers, siblings, grandparents, and friends who influence children.

Since you asked . . .

:• Do mothers and fathers experience the birth of a child differently?

Historically and across cultures, many adults, not just mothers, have nurtured children. Because responsibility for the baby's care tends to fall heavily on new mothers, however, they often feel frustrated or stressed out and are more likely than fathers to experience a decline in marital satisfaction (Twenge et al., 2003).

An estimated 60 percent to 70 percent of new mothers experience *postpartum blues,* a mild mood disorder that typically occurs the first couple of weeks after childbirth (Munk-Olsen et al., 2006). The blues involve feeling moody, teary, and overwhelmed along with being happy about the baby. They are caused by chemical imbalances resulting from the sudden drop in estrogen and progesterone levels as the concentrations of these hormones in the placenta are expelled with other afterbirth tissue.

A more serious problem is *postpartum depression,* which affects up to 15 percent of mothers within the first year after giving birth and requires medical treatment (Brett et al., 2008). **Postpartum depression (PPD)** is a serious illness that can occur up to a year after childbirth. Women who experience PPD feel sad, hopeless, worthless, and have trouble caring for the baby. The causes of PPD are unknown, but they probably involve chemical imbalances as well as risk factors such as low infant birth weight, tobacco or alcohol usage, physical abuse, and emotional and financial stress before and during the pregnancy (Brett et al., 2008).

Despite physical pain, the blues, and wondering whether they'll ever get two hours of uninterrupted sleep again, most mothers are elated with their infants. Many new mothers (and sometimes fathers) can spend hours describing the baby's eating schedule, every yawn and facial expression, and even the bowel movements of "the cutest and most intelligent baby you've ever seen."

FATHERS AND THEIR NEWBORNS Our society tends to stress the importance of mothers over fathers, especially in caring for infants, but fathers are also important for infants' emotional development. Fathers are just as effective at soothing crying babies, for example, and playing with them (Diener et al., 2002).

Like mothers, many fathers worry about being a good parent. Even when they feel anxious, many men think that their task is to be calm, strong, and reassuring—a gender stereotype. Their tendency to keep their worries to themselves may increase the tension and distance between the partners. The couples who fare best are those who can listen sympathetically to each other without expecting immediate solutions (Cowan and Cowan, 2000).

Fatherhood often enhances maturity: "Being a father can change the ways that men think about themselves. Fathering often helps men to clarify their values and to set priorities" (Parke, 1996: 15).

New fathers express loving and affectionate emotions that are good for them and for their babies. Many fathers also forge stronger links with their own parents, who are often supportive grandparents (Johnson and Huston, 1998).

Jim Bob and Michelle Duggar, shown here with 17 of their 18 children, are featured on a TV reality show (*18 Kids and Counting*). The Duggars follow a lifestyle, known as Quiverfull, that views contraception as a form of abortion, believes that very large families populate "God's army," and deems that women's highest calling is to be a prolific mother and submissive wife (Joyce, 2009).

From a developmental perspective, fatherhood is an important transition in a man's life course, but some men's shift to fatherhood is problematic. They may become abusive because of increased financial responsibilities, the emotional demands of new familial roles, and the restrictions that parenthood brings (Schecter and Ganely, 1995; see also Chapter 14).

Becoming a parent seems to be an individual decision, but that's not entirely the case. Most people have a choice about conception, but having children also reflects what's going on in society and how it changes over time. Consider childbearing patterns in the last century.

HOW MANY CHILDREN DO YOU WANT?

A majority of Americans say that two children is the ideal number, and few people want more than three. This is a dramatic change from 1945, when 77 percent said that three or more children was the ideal family size (Carroll, 2007). Attitudes about family size affect **fertility,** the number of live births in a population.

Demographers describe fertility using several measures, depending on the level of specificity needed. A common measure is the **total fertility rate (TFR),** the average number of children born to a woman during her lifetime. In the early 1900s, U.S.-born white women had an average TFR of 3.5 children, compared with 2.1 children in 2007 (Kent and Mather, 2002; Hamilton et al., 2009).

A more specific measure is the **fertility rate,** the number of live children born per year per 1,000 women ages 15 to 44. Except for the baby boom blip of the 1950s, the U.S. fertility rate declined steadily

FIGURE 11.2 Fertility Rates in the United States, 1930–2007

A fertility rate is the number of live children born per year per 1,000 women ages 15 to 44.

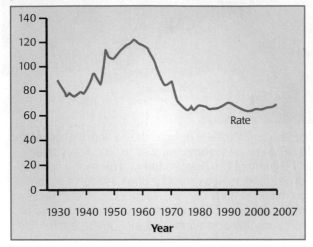

Source: Based on Hamilton et al., 2009, Figure 1.

since 1930, plateaued from the 1970s to the 1990s, and rose to almost 70 in 2007, the highest level since 1990 (see *Figure 11.2*).

Why U.S. Fertility Rates Have Changed

Except for the 1950s, why did fertility rates decrease during most of the twentieth century? And why has there recently been a slight upturn? Much of the decrease in fertility rates is due to a combination of macro-level societal factors and micro-level individual practices (see *Figure 11.3*).

MACRO-LEVEL FACTORS A major factor in fertility rates is population growth. The U.S. population increased by 22 percent between 2000 and 2007. Much of the increase was due to the arrival of immigrants, including women of childbearing age, which generated more births. In spite of the slight increase, fertility rates are still low compared with those during the 1950s and 1960s (see *Figure 11.2*).

Two related factors that have decreased fertility rates are improvements in contraceptive methods and more opportunities for women in higher education. Since the early 1960s, oral contraceptives have allowed women to space their pregnancies and delay motherhood. Because women have also had greater access to higher education, they have been able to

FIGURE 11.3 What Factors Affect Fertility?

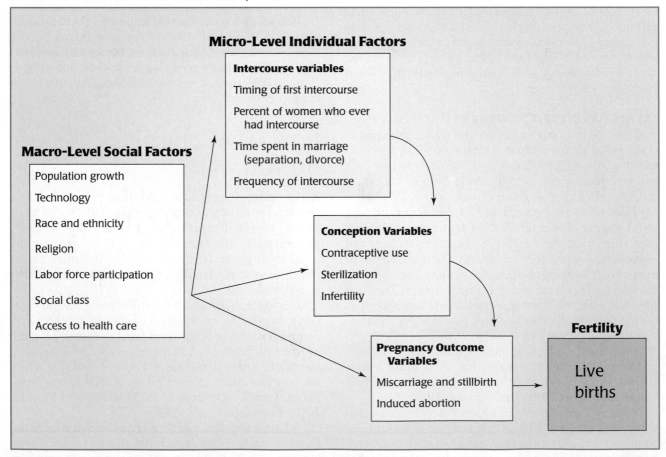

Source: Based on Chandra et al., 2005, Figure 1.

choose other roles besides the traditional ones of wife and mother (Kent and Mather, 2002).

Third, advances in medicine and hygiene have lowered infant mortality rates. Families no longer have to have six children because three or four will die before their first birthday. As a result, family size has decreased. In 1900, for example, 45 percent of all households were made up of five or more people, compared with only 10 percent of households in 2010 (U.S. Census Bureau, 2010).

A fourth reason for lower fertility rates is the economy. As the incomes of many low-skilled men under age 30 fell during the 1970s and 1980s due to factors such as technological changes and a decline in unionization, many wives sought employment to be able to continue to afford the lifestyle to which they were accustomed (see Chapter 13). As women joined the work force, many postponed having children. Postponing parenthood also means that women have fewer years in which to become pregnant (Macunovich, 2002).

Finally, demographic variables also affect fertility rates. Generally, fertility rates are higher for foreign-born women than native-born women; younger women (ages 20 to 34) than older women (ages 35 to 44); minority women, particularly Latina immigrants, than white women; women with less than a high school degree; those not in the labor force; and women living in poverty (Dye, 2008; Hamilton et al., 2009).

Many of the macro-level variables are interrelated in explaining fertility rates. For example, college-educated women tend to postpone childbearing until they have completed their education or started a career, which decreases the number of children they will have over a lifetime. Educated women also tend to be more informed about using contraceptives correctly and are better able to afford them.

MICRO-LEVEL FACTORS Macro-level factors alone don't explain fertility. We also make individual choices, such as whether we use effective **contraception** to prevent pregnancy, whether we decide to end a pregnancy through abortion, how often we have sexual intercourse, and whether we space pregnancies.

Regarding *sexual practices,* young Latinos and African Americans typically begin sexual activities earlier than their white and Asian American counterparts. They also tend to have more partners and to not use contraception. Black and Latino communities are more accepting of out-of-wedlock births and more likely to oppose abortion. All these behaviors increase the number of births during the teenage years and over a lifetime (see Chapter 7).

Relationship contexts also affect sexual practices and, consequently, fertility rates. Especially among low-income women, those who are married,

China, which has the world's largest population (almost 1.4 billion people in mid-2009), also has one of the world's lowest TFRs—1.6, compared with 2.1 for the United States, and almost 7.0 in some countries in Africa and South Central Asia. China's low TFR is due to a one-child policy, especially in urban areas, but affluent city dwellers can afford the $100,000 fine for a second child (Haub and Kent, 2008; Liu, 2008; U.S. Census Bureau, 2008).

cohabiting, and in a long-term relationship and have good communication with their partners are less likely than their counterparts to use contraceptives because they look forward to getting pregnant (Wilson and Koo, 2008).

Birth spacing, or how often women have babies, also affects fertility rates. Getting pregnant less than 18 months after giving birth and spacing children more than five years apart sometimes raises the risk of complications such as preterm births and low birth weight. In the case of close spacing, pregnancy and breast feeding use up nutrients in a woman's body. If she becomes pregnant before those nutrients are replaced, the next infant may suffer. It's not clear why, on average, intervals longer than five years may cause problems, but some researchers speculate that time could diminish a woman's reproductive capacity and lead to less viable fetuses (Conde-Agudelo et al., 2006).

About 21 percent of American women give birth a second time within 24 months of the first birth. Closer spacing of children is more common among women with lower levels of education and income, especially those living below the poverty level (Chandra et al., 2005). Thus, once again, social class affects fertility rates.

Generally, the reasons for the low fertility rates in many industrialized countries are similar to those in the United States: More women are studying longer, working, and then marrying later, which doesn't necessarily include having a baby. Men are equally likely to postpone marriage and children because success at finding and keeping a job is unpredictable.

Infant Mortality

The United States is the richest country in the world, but has a high **infant mortality rate,** the number of babies under one year of age who die per 1,000 live births in a given year. The health of infants in many countries is improving, but U.S. babies now face an increased risk of dying before reaching their first birthday. In 2006, for example, the United States had an infant mortality rate of 6.9, ranked 29th in the world, tied with developing countries such as Poland and Slovakia, and had infant mortality rates that were well above other industrialized countries such as Japan (2.8) and Sweden (2.5) (Haub and Kent; 2008; MacDorman and Mathews, 2008).

Since you asked . . .

➤ Why does the United States have a higher infant mortality rate than other industrialized nations?

Infant mortality rates are higher than the national average for black (13.6), Puerto Rican (8.3), and American Indian or Alaska Native (8.0) women. Cuban women have the lowest rate (4.4), probably because they are predominantly middle class, which means greater access to medical care (Hamilton et al., 2003; Mathews and MacDorman, 2008).

The leading causes of infant mortality are physical birth defects (due to genetic disorders and a toxic uterine environment), preterm birth, and low birth weight. Many of the reasons for these problems are unknown, but they also reflect a lack of prenatal care or inadequate access to medical care, which can result in pregnancy complications; lifestyle choices, such as smoking and using drugs; and a mother's specific medical problems, such as diabetes and hypertension (MacDorman and Mathews, 2008; Mathews et al., 2008).

➤ **MAKING CONNECTIONS**

■ If you don't have children, do you plan to have them in the future? If no, why not? If yes, at what age? And how many?

■ If you're a parent, what have been the benefits and costs of having children?

■ Suppose that you're a 17-year-old Latina. What macro- and micro-level factors are likely to affect your fertility rate? Why?

POSTPONING PARENTHOOD

"Babies vs. Career!" exclaimed a 2002 *Time* magazine cover. The cover story expressed alarm that so many women have put careers before having babies. Most of the articles discussed fertility problems and implied that voluntarily childless women (not men) are selfish and too career oriented (see Gibbs, 2002).

The numbers of first-time older mothers are rising. In the early 1970s, only 4 percent of American women having their first babies were age 30 or older. Since then, this number has increased substantially: 25 percent for women ages 30 to 34, 36 percent for women ages 35 to 39, and 70 percent for women ages 40 to 44 (Ventura, Martin, et al., 2000; Hamilton et al., 2003). Thus, despite *Time's* sensationalistic coverage, most women are postponing parenthood rather than avoiding it.

Many men, similarly, are having children later in life. The majority of children continue to be born to men ages 20 to 34. Between 1980 and 2003, however, the rate of births among men ages 40 to 44 went up 32 percent, and the rate for those ages 45 to 49 rose 21 percent. For men ages 50 to 54, the rate increased by 9 percent (Martin et al., 2005).

Why Are Many People Postponing Parenthood?

Both micro- and macro-level factors affect decisions to postpone parenthood. You'll notice as you read this section that women are usually much more likely than men to feel constrained in deciding whether and when to have children.

MICRO-LEVEL FACTORS Being single, you recall, has many attractions, including independence, the opportunity to develop a career, and more time for fun (see Chapter 9). There are similar micro-level reasons for postponing parenthood:

■ Daunting jobs and careers make it more difficult to meet prospective mates (see Chapter 8).

■ Many single women don't want to conceive or adopt a child on their own. According to a 43-year-old woman whose mother raised her and her siblings, "The hardest thing you can be is a single, working mom" (Peterson, 2002: 2D).

■ Many couples don't want nannies or child care centers to raise their children. They delay having children until they feel that one of them (usually the wife) can be a stay-at-home parent.

■ Both women and men want to build equity in homes, put some money aside, and save for retirement before having children (Poniewozik, 2002).

■ Women who enjoy their jobs and need the money to boost their family's income are often reluctant to struggle with balancing child rearing and paid work (see Chapter 13).

MACRO-LEVEL FACTORS On the macro level, economic and reproductive factors seem to play the biggest role in postponing parenthood:

■ In periods of economic recession and high unemployment, many young men don't have the resources to start a family.

- Young married couples living with their parents may postpone childbearing because they don't want to make already crowded living conditions even worse.

- Disturbed by the current high divorce rate, some young couples delay parenthood until they feel confident that the marriage will work.

- Advances in reproductive technology, as you'll see shortly, have reduced many women's concerns about their biological clock and finding a mate.

- Women and men are delaying childbearing because the United States—especially compared with many European countries—has abysmal family leave policies, no national child care programs, and rigid work schedules, as we'll see in Chapter 13.

One of the principal reasons for many women's delaying having children is that the best years for childbearing coincide with the best years for establishing a career. A woman who starts having babies at age 25, for example, will have a difficult time competing in the labor market with younger men and with women 10 years later. According to a fashion designer, 33, who dropped her X-Girl clothing line after having a baby when she was 26, "How can you come back at 36 or 37 and say, 'I'm here, guys—snap, snap, let me start another line of hip-hop clothing'?" (Poniewozik, 2002: 58).

Some Characteristics of Older Parents

"My parents had me in their mid-forties. They were always too tired to attend many of the school functions or to take me to baseball games."

"My mother had me when she was 45 and that was in 1973. I'm living proof that older moms are good parents."

As these comments by two of my students show, many of us have strong opinions about the age at which people should have kids. Like most other options in life, being an older parent has both advantages and disadvantages.

ADVANTAGES Women who give birth for the first time between ages 22 and 34 have healthier babies than those who have babies during their teenage years or after age 40. The latter may experience more problems in conceiving a child. However, mothers in their teens are more likely than their older counterparts to have babies with birth defects and to experience infant deaths: They often have poor nutrition, don't obtain adequate prenatal care, or engage in unhealthy lifestyles that include smoking and using alcohol and other drugs (Mirowsky, 2005).

Compared with younger mothers, older mothers are more likely to be married and highly educated. They also tend to work in professional occupations and to have high family incomes (Dye, 2008). Higher incomes decrease stress because the family has more resources to raise a child.

Older mothers tend to feel more self-assured, more ready for responsibility, and better prepared for parenthood than do younger women. Younger mothers sometimes feel trapped by having a baby because they still want to party, go out with friends, and have a good time (Maynard, 1997).

Men who postpone parenthood usually enjoy more advantages and have fewer constraints than older women. Most men do not face sex discrimination in the workplace, earn higher salaries, and have better health benefits. Thus, they are less likely to worry about not having the resources to raise children later in life. According to one of my students, for example, having an older dad "made life wonderful for me":

I am the youngest of four. I was only 7 years old when my dad retired. He spent a lot of time with me. He invested well and made financial decisions that were beneficial for the entire family. I think his age played a big part in having the means to make his family comfortable and raising his children without any financial burdens (Author's files).

Since you asked . . .

•• Are there any advantages to having children after age 40?

With fewer economic concerns, men remarry more often and sometimes, after a divorce, support children from two families (see Chapter 16). Also, because their careers are better established, older fathers may have more flexibility to spend their non-work hours and weekends with their families. They are often more relaxed—especially if they are financially secure and don't have to work as aggressively at a career—and have more time to forge strong emotional bonds with their offspring (Carnoy and Carnoy, 1997).

DISADVANTAGES The vast majority of children born to men of all ages are healthy, but scientists are finding that older fathers may be increasing babies' health risks, including problems such as skeletal deformities, autism, and schizophrenia (Stroh, 2006). Sperm age better than eggs, but such research suggests that biological clocks may be ticking for men and not just women.

Older parents may be more patient, mature, and financially secure, but there are drawbacks to delaying parenthood. Pregnant women in their 40s are at greater risk of having a baby with Down syndrome than are women in their 30s. Beyond health risks, there are some practical liabilities in becoming a father at a later age:

Many older parents who have postponed parenthood until they have established their careers have the resources to provide their children with educational and other opportunities. A disadvantage is that they may not live long enough to see their grandchildren.

At 52, you'd be coming out of the "terrible twos" and hosting play groups for toddlers. As you turned 55, your child would start kindergarten and you'd qualify for dual memberships in the PTA and the American Association of Retired Persons (AARP). At 60, you and your spouse would be coaching soccer.... By the time you hit 70, you'd be buried under college tuition bills. And if your child delayed marriage and family like you did, you might be paying for a wedding when you were 80 and babysitting for your grandchildren at 90 (Wright, 1997: E5).

A 16-year-old daughter of an almost 60-year-old mother believes that the "huge generation gap" has led to greater conflict because of their different attitudes and values ("How late is too late?" 2001). Moreover, some women who have waited to have children find that it is too late to have as many as they wanted.

Older mothers, especially those who have risen to powerful but demanding executive positions, may feel especially guilty about splitting their time between their family and their employer and thus cheating both (see Chapter 13). At one point or another, many midlife parents are mistaken for grandma or grandpa. Some laugh it off, but others bristle at such errors (Crandell, 2005). Finally, postponing parenthood may mean that parents will never get to see their grandchildren.

You see, then, that there are many reasons for postponing childbearing—especially for women who seek more options in education and jobs. However, millions of Americans have fewer choices because they are infertile.

INFERTILITY

Infertility is the inability to conceive a baby. It is a condition that often goes undiagnosed until a couple has had at least 1 year of unprotected intercourse or until a woman has had multiple miscarriages.

Infertility affects about 15 percent of all couples of reproductive age. Infertility rates have been fairly stable since the mid-1960s, but the likelihood of infertility increases as people delay childbearing. For example, the rate of infertility for couples between ages 30 and 34 is more than 50 percent greater than for those between ages 25 and 29 (Mosher and Pratt, 1991; Chandra et al., 2005).

Since you asked . . .

:• What causes infertility?

There are many reasons for infertility, and the reactions to it are typically distressing. First, let's look at some of the reasons for infertility.

Reasons for Infertility

Infertility is due about equally to problems in males and females; each sex independently accounts for about 40 percent of cases. Approximately 20 percent of infertile couples are diagnosed as having *idiopathic infertility.* In plain language, doctors simply don't know what's wrong.

Until recently, most infertility research focused almost exclusively on women because scientists believed that the main reason for infertility was female aging. Although it's true that women's reproductive organs age faster than other parts of their body, people of either sex can be infertile.

FEMALE INFERTILITY The two major causes of female infertility are failure to ovulate and blockage of the fallopian tubes. A woman's failure to *ovulate,* or to produce a viable egg each month, may have a number of causes, among them poor nutrition, chronic illness, and drug abuse. Very occasionally, lack of ovulation may be attributed to psychological stress (Masters et al., 1992).

The *fallopian tubes* carry the egg—whether or not it has been fertilized—from the ovaries to the uterus. The fallopian tubes can be blocked by scarring caused by **pelvic inflammatory disease (PID),** an infection of the uterus that spreads to the tubes, the ovaries, and surrounding tissues. PID, in turn, is often caused by sexually transmitted diseases such as chlamydia.

Chlamydia, a sexually transmitted bacterial infection, is often called "the silent epidemic" because it exhibits no symptoms in 75 percent of women and 33 percent of men. Chlamydia is a rapidly rising cause of PID but, once diagnosed, is easily cured with antibiotics (see Chapter 7 and *Appendix E* for more information about sexually transmitted infections).

Another important reason for women's infertility is **endometriosis,** a condition in which the tissue that forms in the endometrium (the lining of the uterus) spreads outside the womb and attaches itself to other pelvic organs, such as the ovaries or the fallopian tubes. The cause of endometriosis is unknown, but some researchers believe that women with endometriosis have certain malfunctioning genes that prevent an embryo from attaching to the uterine wall (Kao et al., 2003). Endometriosis can lead to PID, uterine tumors, and blockage of the opening to the uterus.

Excessive exercise or rapid weight loss can decrease the production of reproductive hormones. Regular use of vaginal douches and deodorants that contain certain chemicals may also kill sperm or inhibit their ability to fertilize an egg (Fogel and Woods, 1995; DeLisle, 1997).

MALE INFERTILITY Male infertility often results from sluggish sperm or a low sperm count. Chemical pollutants might play a significant role in male infertility because men have been more likely than women to work in environments in which they come into contact with toxic chemicals or are exposed to other hazardous conditions (Kenen, 1993).

Other possible causes of low sperm counts include injury to the testicles or scrotum; infections such as mumps in adulthood; testicular varicose veins that

Many couples, especially the women, are heartbroken by infertility. Why do you think that women are generally unhappier than men by the couple's inability to conceive a baby? Or do you think that men are simply more likely to hide their feelings?

impede sperm development; undescended testes (the testes normally descend from the abdominal cavity into the scrotum in about the eighth month of prenatal development); endocrine disorders; and excessive consumption of alcohol, marijuana, narcotic drugs, or even some prescription medications. The sperm of chronic smokers (men who have smoked four or more cigarettes a day for at least two years) are on average 75 percent less fertile than those of nonsmokers (Nagourney, 2005).

Several studies report that long-distance bicycle riding or tight-fitting underwear can lower sperm counts. Spending many hours each week on a bike saddle with a high nose can create enough pressure on the perineum (the area between the anus and the pubic bone) to damage the artery—sometimes permanently—that supplies blood to the penis (Guess et al., 2006).

Prolonged and frequent use of saunas, hot tubs, and steam baths may also have a negative effect because sperm production is sensitive to temperature. In the case of obese men, excess fat in the genital area could raise the temperature of the testicles, reducing the quality and quantity of sperm (Bhattacharya, 2003).

Sperm quality and the speed at which sperm travel toward an egg also decline in men older than age 50 (Marcus, 2003). Thus, men's fertility usually decreases as they age.

Reactions to Infertility

People respond to infertility differently, but couples are usually devastated. In most societies, including the United States, two cultural norms about procreation dominate. One is that all married couples *should* reproduce; the other is that all married couples *should want to* reproduce (Veevers, 1980).

For many women, then, infertility becomes "an acute and unanticipated life crisis" that involves stigma, psychological distress, grief, guilt, and a sense of violation. As one woman said, "It's a slap in the face. I feel like I'm isolated in a prison…no one understands how horrible this is" (Whiteford and Gonzalez, 1995: 29; see, also, McQuillan et al., 2003).

Though well intentioned, potential grandparents' expectations exert pressure to carry on the family line ("Do you think that I will have a grandchild before I die?"). The fact that generational continuity will come to an end may reinforce a woman's feelings of being a failure when she doesn't conceive:

My husband is Italian and for the ten years that we've been married, I have known that his having a son has been important to him, and my not being able to deliver has been a real difficult thing for me to deal with…. My mother-in-law has been pushing for a grandchild since the day we got married (Whiteford and Gonzalez, 1995: 34).

Many women, concerned that people will see them in a new and damaging light, engage in "information management" (Goffman, 1963). For example, they may avoid the topic whenever possible, or they may attribute the problem to a disease such as diabetes or kidney trouble, taking the focus off specific reproductive disorders. Because male infertility may be viewed as a defect in masculinity, women often accept responsibility for infertility themselves:

When I tell them we can't have children, I generally try to leave the impression that it's me. I may mutter "tubes you know" or "faulty plumbing" (Miall, 1986: 36).

Marital satisfaction can decrease if women blame themselves or bury their feelings instead of seeking their partner's emotional support. Coping with infertility is especially difficult if men distance themselves by making light of the situation or acting as if nothing is wrong (Peterson et al., 2006).

For many couples, infertility is socially isolating: "It often becomes difficult to socialize with family and friends whose conversation gravitates to the joys (or miseries) of parenthood." They may also avoid events ranging from family holidays that include infants and children to baby showers for pregnant co-workers (Shapiro, 2005: F15-F16).

Infertile couples sometimes enjoy vicarious parenthood through contact with children of relatives and friends. Others become increasingly involved in work-related activities and even begin to regard their childlessness as an advantage.

Some couples accept infertility as a fact of life and remain childless. A much larger group tries to adopt.

ADOPTION: THE TRADITIONAL SOLUTION TO INFERTILITY

At one time, 80 percent of U.S. babies born out of wedlock were given up for **adoption,** taking a child into one's family through legal means and raising her or him as one's own. This rate has dropped to about 2 or 3 percent because today most unwed mothers keep their babies.

Of the 1.5 million adopted children in the United States, 44 percent live with two adoptive parents, 20 percent live with one adoptive parent, and the remaining children have been adopted by a stepparent. Adoption touches many other lives, however. For example, 65 percent of Americans have experience with adoption through their family or friends, and three in ten Americans say that they have considered adopting a child (Dave Thomas Foundation for Adoption, 2007; Kreider, 2008).

A *foster child* is one who is placed by a government agency or a court in the care of someone other than his or her biological parents. Of the 510,000 foster children nationwide, at least 114,000 are eligible for adoption because their biological parents are dead or missing, have been found unfit, or have legally surrendered their rights to their children. Many of these children are hard to place, however, because they are sick, physically handicapped, biracial, nonwhite, emotionally disturbed, HIV-positive, or "too old" (Dave Thomas Foundation for Adoption, 2007; Child Welfare Information Gateway, 2009).

Whether we arrive by birth or adoption, none of us chooses our family. Adoptive families, however, often experience outside intrusions that biological parents don't (Melosh, 2002). We'll consider the benefits and costs of adoption, but let's first look at several types of adoption, beginning with transracial adoption.

Transracial Adoption

The federal Multiethnic Placement Act (MEPA) of 1994 forbids public child welfare agencies from delaying or denying a child's foster care or adoption on the basis of race, color, or national origin. In other words, MEPA supports transracial adoption and prohibits matching children and prospective parents solely on the basis of race or ethnicity, but this policy has been controversial.

Since you asked . . .
- Why are transracial adoptions controversial?

ARE TRANSRACIAL ADOPTIONS A GOOD IDEA?

Advocates maintain that many African American and

MAKING CONNECTIONS

- What are some of the advantages and disadvantages of having children during one's 20s rather than one's 40s?

- Are people's reasons for postponing parenthood valid? Or are they being selfish and self-centered in delaying childbearing?

- Suppose you hear that a couple has problems conceiving a baby. Is your first reaction "What's wrong with her?" or "What's wrong with him?" Why?

biracial children, especially those with emotional or physical disabilities, would remain in foster homes until age 18 if white parents did not adopt them. Moreover, foster homes are costly and don't provide the permanence and stability that adoption offers (Altstein, 2006; Hansen and Pollack, 2007).

Some critics contend that promoting foster care instead of transracial adoptions is self-serving because it protects social service jobs: "The more kids in foster care, the more money states get from the federal government for their overall programs, since 50 percent of foster care funds go to administrative costs, including social worker salaries" (Spake, 1998: 31).

When white adoptive families encourage their transracial children to participate in multicultural and multiracial activities, children in transracial adoptions do well. If anything, some black adoptees have complained that their white parents tried too hard to educate them about their heritage, turning dinner-table conversations into lectures on African American history (Simon, 1993; Simon and Alstein, 2000).

Transracial adopted children can benefit from learning about their birth culture, but doing so is not a prerequisite for healthy psychological development. For example, strong family ties and good peer relationships are more important to the children's well-being than identifying with their birth culture or racial heritage (Baden, 2001).

ARE TRANSRACIAL ADOPTIONS A BAD IDEA? The

National Association of Black Social Workers and the Child Welfare League, among others, oppose transracial adoptions. A leading objection to transracial adoptions is that the children "are alienated from their culture of origin" and "dislodged from the ethnic community" (Kissman and Allen, 1993: 93). Many African American (and some white) social workers contend that every child has the right to a permanent home with a family of the same race and that a white parent, "no matter how skilled or loving, could do irreparable harm to the self-esteem of a black child" (Furgatch, 1995: 19).

Some child advocates also question the wisdom of placing African American children with white parents who may not provide the children with the strategies they need to deal with everyday episodes of racism, prejudice, and discrimination (Herring, 2007; Evan B. Donaldson Adoption Institute, 2008). Even when white parents adopt African American or biracial children as infants, in adulthood some of the adoptees report struggling with problems such as rejection by extended family members, being stigmatized by black peers for being raised by white people, and not fully fitting in with either black or white friends (Samuels, 2009).

Open and Closed Adoption

Another controversial issue is **open adoption,** the practice of sharing information and maintaining contact between biological and adoptive parents

Opponents of transracial adoption maintain that white parents can't teach their African American children how to cope with being "different," to a develop a positive racial/ethnic identity, and to deal with discrimination. Do you agree?

throughout the child's life. In a **closed adoption,** in contrast, the records of the adoption are kept sealed, the birth parent is not involved in the adoptee's life, and the child has no contact with the biological parents or little, if any, information about them.

In a third option, **semi-open adoption,** sometimes called *mediated adoption,* there is communication between the adoptee and the adoptive and biological parents, but it takes place through a third party (such as a caseworker or attorney) rather than directly. *Table 11.1* provides some of the pros and cons of each of these adoption methods.

By late 2006, 23 states were providing open access to adoption records. Some birth mothers believe that such laws violate their right to privacy, especially when the birth resulted from a rape or violent relationship. Being contacted by a biological child can renew past traumas that the mothers have struggled to get over. Adopted children argue, however, that they have a right to information about their biological parents. The children maintain that even if a biological parent doesn't want to be contacted, they want to meet the parents as well as find out about health problems that have shown up in their own children and that may reflect genetic factors (Collins, 2005; National Adoption Information Clearinghouse, 2006).

Adoption by Same-Sex Partners

A few years ago, the American Academy of Pediatrics announced its support for lesbians and gay men to adopt children as well as their partners' children because "A growing body of scientific literature demonstrates that children who grow up with 1 or 2 gay and/or lesbian parents fare as well in emotional, cognitive, social, and sexual functioning as do children

TABLE 11.1	The Pros and Cons of Adoption Types		
	Closed Adoptions	**Semi-Open Adoptions**	**Open Adoptions**
Pros	■ *Birth parents* have a sense of closure and can move on with their lives.	■ *Birth parents* can maintain privacy while providing some information.	■ *Birth parents* can develop a relationship with the child as she or he grows.
	■ *Adoptive parents* are safe from the interference or co-parenting by birth parents.	■ *Adoptive parents* have a greater sense of control than in open adoptions.	■ *Adoptive parents* have a better understanding of the child's history.
	■ *Adopted children* are safe from unstable or emotionally disturbed birth parents.	■ *Adopted children* don't fantasize about birth parents.	■ *Adopted children* are less likely to feel abandoned (they can know why they were placed for adoption) and can increase their circle of supportive adults.
Cons	■ *Birth parents* may experience more distress because they lack information about their child's well-being.	■ *Birth parents* may experience more distress about the decision because they are in contact with the adoptive family.	■ *Birth parents* may be disappointed if the adoptive family fails to meet all their expectations.
	■ *Adoptive parents* don't have access to much medical information about the birth family.	■ *Adoptive parents* may have to deal with troubling communications (letters, e-mail) between birth parents and an adopted child.	■ *Adoptive parents* may have difficulties dealing with emotionally disturbed birth parents.
	■ *Adopted children* may experience identity confusion because their physical traits differ from those of their adoptive parents.	■ *Adopted children* may want more information than third parties are willing to divulge.	■ *Adopted children* may feel rejected if contact with birth parents ceases or they may play their birth and adoptive families against each other.

Sources: Based on Grotevant, 2001; National Adoption Information Clearinghouse, 2002.

whose parents are heterosexual" (Perrin, 2002: 341). About 46 percent of Americans favor adoption by gays and lesbians, up from 38 percent in 1999 (The Pew Research Center for the People & the Press, 2008).

Despite growing approval, U.S. adoption laws vary from state to state regarding *joint adoption,* when two unmarried parents adopt a child together at the same time. In Utah, only heterosexual married couples can adopt. Only five states have legalized same-sex marriage (see Chapter 10). Some contend that the 45 states that forbid same-sex marriage or those that don't allow joint adoption do so to prohibit adoptions by gay and lesbian couples. For example, some critics believe that a new Arkansas law that bans all unmarried adults from adopting children was specifically targeted at gays and lesbians (Rubin, 2008; "The best interests of the child," 2009).

About 65,000 children (4 percent of all adopted children) live with a lesbian or gay adoptive parent. This saves taxpayers as much as $130 million a year in costs for keeping children in foster and institutional care and recruiting adoptive parents (Dave Thomas Foundation for Adoption, 2007; Gates et al., 2007).

Compared with heterosexual women, lesbian partners considering adoption report equal support from friends but considerably less from family members. Nevertheless, about 40 percent of adoption agencies have placed children with gay or lesbian parents because of the belief that loving and responsible families are more important than the parents' sexual orientation ("Expanding resources for children...," 2005; Goldberg and Smith, 2008).

International Adoption

Because the waiting period for adopting a child from overseas is only one or two years, compared with seven to ten years for adopting a child in the United States, many Americans have turned to international adoptions (also called intercountry adoptions). In the past decade, about 216,000 children have been adopted from at least 20 countries (U.S. Department of State, 2008).

FIGURE 11.4 Adoptions to the United States, 1998–2008

In 2008, 57 percent of the adopted children came, in order of rank, from Guatemala, China, and Russia.

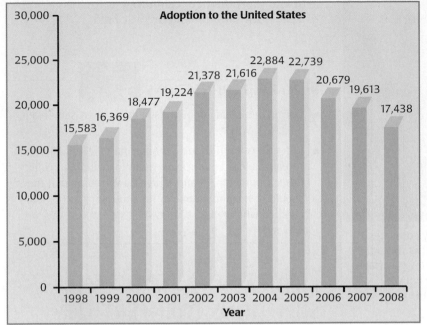

Source: U.S. Department of State, 2008.

International adoptions increased steadily from 1998 to 2004 but then started dropping (see *Figure 11.4*). The decrease is due not to American parents' loss of interest, but to some host countries' curtailing international adoptions for cultural, political, and economic reasons. For example,

- In China, as prosperity increased, the number of abandoned children decreased. Girls still make up 95 percent of children at orphanages, but many parents are now more accepting of having daughters and not just sons. Perhaps because of both of these reasons, China has tightened eligibility rules to bar intercountry adoption applicants who are single, gay, obese, older than age 50, low-income, or on antidepressants (Koch, 2007; Wingert, 2008; Webley, 2009).

- Russia, Ukraine, and South Korea—all facing declining birth rates—are encouraging domestic adoption (Wingert, 2008).

- Russia, which has at least 260,000 orphans available for adoption, has sharply limited adoptions to the United States because of 14 instances of parental abuse that resulted in a child's death, and a growing anti-American political sentiment (Weir, 2007).

- In South Korea, government officials hope to eliminate all international adoptions by 2012.

Besides encouraging domestic adoptions to have a larger force of young workers who will support the elderly (see Chapter 17), government officials "consider it shameful to send babies overseas for adoption" (Onishi, 2008: 6).

- Guatemala, where adoption processes averaged only six months, has tightened laws because of complaints that international adoptions have led to children's kidnappings; mothers having babies for compensation; and some lawyers' engaging in illegal, profitable adoption practices (Llana, 2007).

Some Rewards and Costs of Adoption

People who are thinking about adoption should do much more research than rely on a few pages of a textbook. As in the case of having a biological child, there are rewards and costs in adopting a child.

SOME REWARDS OF ADOPTION The most obvious benefit is that adoptive parents and abandoned children find people to love. Most single parents are women, who tend to adopt girls or older, minority, or mentally disabled children. Without adoption, many of these children would grow up in foster homes rather than in a stable environment.

Compared with children raised in foster homes or by never-married mothers, adopted children are economically advantaged; more likely to complete high school and hold a skilled job; and less likely to use drugs, commit crimes, or be homeless as adults (Bachrach et al., 1990; Spake, 1998). In fact, some of the most notable people in the United States and elsewhere have been adopted. They include

- Playwrights and authors (James Michener, Edgar Allen Poe, and Leo Tolstoy)

- Actors (Shari Belafonte-Harper, Ted Danson, Melissa Gilbert, and Ginger Rogers)

- Past U.S. presidents and first ladies (Gerald Ford, Herbert Hoover, and Nancy Reagan)

- Civil rights leaders and politicians (Jesse Jackson and Newt Gingrich)

- Entrepreneurs (Steve Jobs, co-founder of Apple Computer; Tom Monaghan, founder of Domino's Pizza; and Dave Thomas, founder of Wendy's)

Babies and children are orphaned in many countries. About 6,000 of these orphans are in Romania. Because there are few facilities, a number of children may have to share a crib, such as those pictured here. Even teenagers may be crowded into cribs because there are no available beds.

Most biological and adoptive parents are quite similar. Both use positive rather than negative discipline (such as praising rather than spanking), emphasize desirable behavior (such as doing well in school), and expect their children to complete college. Thus, adoptive parents function at least as well as their biological counterparts (Borders et al., 1998).

SOME COSTS OF ADOPTIONS Adoption also has disadvantages. Adoptive parents sometimes worry that a teenage girl who has not had prenatal care or used drugs could deliver a baby who may later have health problems. Adoptive parents must also sort out their feelings about having their own child versus adopting someone else's. And, about 3 percent to 8 percent of adoptions are dissolved because the adoptive parents can't cope with the child's severe behavior problems (Daly, 1999; Festinger, 2002).

Should adoptive parents be allowed to change their minds after the adoption has been finalized? In a national survey, 23 percent of Americans said "yes," 59 percent said "no," and 18 percent weren't sure (Hollingsworth, 2003). Some argue that adoptive parents make a commitment and should deal with the problems instead of returning a child. Others contend that keeping a child whom parents don't love might create even more problems for both the parents and the child.

Whereas some people adopt children, others turn to reproductive technologies. In fact, the number of infants born each year in the United States through artificial reproductive technology is higher than that of U.S.-born infants who are adopted.

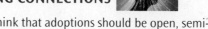

∴• MAKING CONNECTIONS

- Do you think that adoptions should be open, semi-open, or closed? Why?

- Recently, celebrities such as Angelina Jolie and Madonna received a lot of publicity by adopting children, respectively, from Vietnam and Africa. Do you think that they should have adopted one of the thousands of U.S.-born children who are languishing in foster homes? Why or why not?

MEDICAL AND HIGH-TECH SOLUTIONS TO INFERTILITY

New genetic technologies have generated some difficult medical, legal, and ethical questions. Before considering these issues, let's look at the most common medical and high-tech treatments for infertility.

Medical Treatments for Infertility

Medical treatments include *artificial insemination* and *fertility drugs*. Artificial insemination is the most common treatment for men with low sperm counts. Fertility drugs improve the chance of conception in infertile women.

ARTIFICIAL INSEMINATION Artificial insemination, sometimes called *donor insemination (DI)*, is a medical procedure in which semen is introduced artificially into the vagina or uterus at about the time of ovulation. The semen, taken from the woman's husband or from a donor, may be fresh or it may have been frozen. Artificial insemination was first performed in the 1970s and was followed by a normal pregnancy and birth. The success rate is close to 20 percent (King, 2002).

Prospective parents can browse a catalog and choose a sperm donor by eye and hair color, nationality, blood type, height, and profession. (There is an extra charge for the sperm of Ph.D.s, M.D.s, and attorneys.) According to one man in Southern California who donated sperm to help cover living expenses while in medical school, "I could fill a banquet hall with 'my' children" (Romano, 2006: A2). Because donors are typically anonymous, half siblings might

Motherhood After Menopause

Choices

The National Center for Health Statistics defines women's childbearing years as between ages 15 and 44. A woman's ovaries cease egg production after menopause, but her other reproductive organs remain viable. In later life, women can become pregnant using a younger woman's donated eggs that are fertilized with sperm from the older woman's husband or from another donor.

Since 1994, there have been 12 documented cases of women over 60 having babies, including a 62-year-old woman in California who had 11 other children. In 2007, a 67-year-old woman from Spain (pictured at right) gave birth to twin boys. A recipient of donor eggs and sperm at a Los Angeles fertility clinic, she lied to doctors about her age because the cutoff was 55. She was diagnosed with cancer shortly after giving birth, and died in 2009. It's unclear who will care for the children (Pool and Bousada, 2007; Daum, 2009).

The world's oldest mom may be a woman in India who was believed to be 70 (her exact age is unknown) when she birth to boy-and-girl twins in 2008. She already had two adult daughters and five grandchildren, but she and her husband hoped to have a son. Her 77-year-old husband—who said he was proud and happy to finally have a son who would be an heir and work the land—had spent his life savings, mortgaged his land, sold his buffaloes, and taken out a loan to pay for the in-vitro fertilization treatments (Daum, 2009).

Several countries, including France and Italy, have passed laws barring postmenopausal women from artificial impregnation because they view such practices as immoral and dangerous to women's health.

⠿ Stop and Think . . .

- Should there be strict age limits for in-vitro fertilization treatments? Why or why not?
- If we bar women in their 50s from getting pregnant, should we also require vasectomies of men who father children in their 50s, 60s, and later?

---

meet and mate, not knowing that they have the same biological father and may share the same health problems (Streisand, 2006).

FERTILITY DRUGS If a woman is having difficulty becoming pregnant, her physician often uses **fertility drugs,** medications that stimulate the ovaries to produce eggs. In 1997, a couple from Carlisle, Iowa, became the parents of the first septuplets ever born alive. The mother had been taking a fertility drug. For religious reasons, the couple refused to undergo a process known as *selective reduction:* aborting some of the fetuses to give the others a better chance to develop fully.

Fertility drugs have a high success rate: 50 to 70 percent. A primary concern, however, is that multiple births increase the chances of babies being born preterm and having a low birth weight. The babies that survive may end up with major health problems and lifelong learning disabilities, including cerebral palsy, developmental delays, and birth defects (Jones, 2007).

High-Tech Treatments for Infertility

Infertile couples have more options than ever before through **assisted reproductive technology (ART),** a general term that includes all treatments or procedures that involve the handling of human eggs and sperm to establish a pregnancy. ART accounts for more than 1 percent of all U.S. births every year (Sunderman et al., 2009).

About 12 percent of U.S. women have received some type of infertility treatment since the introduction of ART in 1981. Success rates are modest—about 30 percent overall—and decline significantly with multiple births and after age 40. Still, the number of live-birth deliveries using ART has increased steadily from about 14,500 in 1996 to about 41,400 in 2006 (Centers for Disease Control and Prevention, American Society for Reproductive Medicine, 2008). The most common ART technique is in vitro fertilization.

IN VITRO FERTILIZATION In vitro fertilization (IVF) involves surgically removing eggs from a woman's ovaries, fertilizing them in a petri dish (a specially shaped glass container) with sperm from her husband or another donor, and then transferring the embryos into the woman's uterus. (An *embryo* is the developing organism up to the eighth week of pregnancy.) IVF is an outpatient procedure conducted at nearly 400 clinics in the United States alone. More than 2 million children worldwide owe their birth to this procedure (Evans, 2009).

IVF is a miracle for many couples, but it has drawbacks. Because more than one egg is usually implanted to increase the chances of success, nearly half of all women using IVF have multiple births. Multiple-birth babies are ten times more likely than single babies to be born preterm, with a low birth weight, and/or with poorly developed organs. As with fertility drugs, a low birth weight subjects infants to medical risks ranging from lung disease and brain damage to infant death (Mitchell, 2002; Wood et al., 2003).

IVF is expensive (costing up to $25,000 per attempt), time consuming, painful, and can be emotionally exhausting. Despite the difficulties and expense, egg donation is a growing industry that allows even women who have gone through menopause to become pregnant (see the box "Motherhood after Menopause").

SURROGACY In surrogacy, a woman who is capable of carrying a pregnancy to term serves as a substitute for a woman who cannot bear children. Usually, the surrogate is artificially inseminated with the sperm of the infertile woman's husband, and if she conceives, she carries the child to term. In some cases, the infertile couple's egg and sperm are brought together in vitro and the resulting embryo is implanted in a surrogate, who carries the child for them.

A growing number of childless people, including Americans, have made India a top destination for surrogacy. In the United States, surrogate mothers are typically paid $20,000 to $25,000, and agencies collect another $50,000. In India, the total costs come to about $25,000 (Ali and Kelley, 2008; Gentleman, 2008; Zarembo and Yoshino, 2009).

Why are women surrogates? A major reason is money, especially in India. For example, Mehli, 32, and a mother of three children, delivered a healthy baby and handed the newborn over to an American couple:

She'll be paid about $5,000, a bonanza that would take her more than six years to earn on her salary as a schoolteacher. "I might renovate or add to the house, or spend it on my kids' education or my daughter's wedding," Mehli said (Chu, 2006: A1).

Some criticize surrogacy as "reproductive tourism" that exploits poor women by "renting their wombs, cheap" and risks their lives because of the possible complications of pregnancy and childbirth. Others argue that surrogacy improves the family's standard of living (the average income is about $500 a year) and that the doctors provide high-quality care. There are also cultural reasons for being a surrogate: Indian society views producing offspring as an almost sacred obligation, Hindu teachings promise rewards in the next life for good deeds performed on earth, and the mothers empathize with childless parents (Chu, 2006: A1).

PRENATAL TESTING Preimplantation genetic diagnosis (PGD) is a recent ART procedure that enables physicians to identify genetic diseases, such as cystic fibrosis or Down syndrome, in the embryo before implantation. PGD allows a couple to choose only healthy embryos for transfer into a woman's uterus.

Some critics fear that PGD will increase abortion rates because of imperfect embryos and open the door to a "new eugenics" as parents customize their babies for anything "from tissue type to eye color, broad shoulders, to extreme intelligence" (Healy, 2003: F1). On the other hand, many researchers believe that PGD will eventually produce embryos that are free of fatal diseases (Jones, 2003).

Genetic Engineering: Its Benefits and Costs

Genetic research and biotechnology have been a blessing for many couples, but some people wonder whether scientists are going too far (see the box "So What's Next? Pregnant Men?"). Some worry that genetic manipulation, because it meddles with nature, is unethical and detrimental to society. Others maintain that the benefits outweigh the costs.

Since you asked . . .

• Whom does genetic engineering benefit the most?

So What's Next? Pregnant Men?

Changes

In the movie *Junior,* a scientist loses funding for his research and implants a fertilized egg in his own body to test a wonder drug that ensures healthy pregnancies.

In real life, there are some problems with this scenario. Men don't produce the appropriate hormones, don't have ovaries or produce eggs, and don't have wombs.

However, hormones can be injected, and perhaps wombs aren't necessary. Abdominal pregnancies—those occurring outside the womb—are rare, but they happen about once in every 10,000 pregnancies.

An abdominal pregnancy may occur when the placenta, which is produced partly by the fetus, attaches to something other than the womb. In August 1979, for example, Dr. George Poretta attempted to perform an appendectomy on a Michigan woman who was suffering from stomach cramps. "I opened her up expecting to find an appendix," Poretta said, "and there was this tiny foot." The baby, a boy, weighed 3 pounds 5 ounces (Teresi, 1994: 55).

Both male and female abdomens offer a similar environment for impregnation, including a membrane, called the *omentum,* that encloses abdominal organs in which, theoretically, a fertilized egg could become implanted. Thus, fertilizing an egg in vitro and inserting the developing embryo through a small incision in the abdominal cavity of a man could produce a pregnancy (Peritz, 2003).

Scientists have recently turned stem cells (the building blocks of the human body) from both female and male mice into eggs (Hübner et al., 2003). This research suggests that even men might have the biological capacity to produce eggs.

⁞• Stop and Think . . .

■ Should we continue to develop technology that will allow men to become pregnant and deliver babies? Or is such research a sci-fi nightmare?

■ One of the advantages of creating human eggs is that there would be no need for donors. What are some possible disadvantages of creating human eggs?

THE BENEFITS OF GENETIC ENGINEERING Genetic engineering has been valuable in detecting prenatal genetic disorders and abnormalities. Two diagnostic procedures that have become fairly common are amniocentesis and chorionic villus sampling. In **amniocentesis,** which is performed in the twentieth week of pregnancy, a needle is inserted through the abdomen into the amniotic sac, and the fluid withdrawn is analyzed for abnormalities such as Down syndrome and spina bifida.

The same information can be produced at ten weeks by **chorionic villus sampling (CVS).** A catheter inserted through the vagina removes some of the *villi* (fingerlike protrusions) from the *chorion* (the outer membrane that surrounds the amniotic sac). The chief advantage of detecting abnormalities at these stages is that parents can decide on an abortion early in the pregnancy. Both amniocentesis and CVS have risks, though low (about 1 to 2 percent of all cases), of spontaneous abortions and possible deformities (Boodman, 1992).

Besides detecting prenatal abnormalities, genetic engineering produces children who are usually as healthy as children born naturally. In addition, because some women experience infertility due to cancer treatments, they can freeze their eggs before chemotherapy and doctors can later reimplant those eggs to produce healthy babies (Hobson, 2004; Shevell et al., 2005).

THE COSTS OF GENETIC ENGINEERING ART techniques increase the risk of birth defects, especially in the case of twins or multiple births (Reefhuis et al., 2009). Medical treatments for infertility are usually limited to affluent couples because the procedures are expensive and rarely covered by insurance programs. For example, repeated IVF attempts can easily cost more than $100,000 (Saul, 2009). Because only the rich can afford genetic engineering, the technology doesn't benefit all social classes.

There is also concern about issues such as parents' and scientists' right to manufacture babies, creating designer babies by choosing genes for a child's hair color and height; parents' right to reject imperfect fetuses; and the rights of both parents and embryos. Suppose that both parents of a fertilized egg that has been frozen die. Who's responsible for the frozen embryo? Should it be destroyed because the parents are dead? Should it be given to relatives? Put up for adoption? Turned over to doctors for medical research?

Since the recent birth of octuplets, many fertility experts have renewed their criticism of physicians for not limiting the number of embryos implanted during IVF to two because triplets, quadruplets, and quintuplets are 12 times more likely than other babies to die within a year. Many suffer from lifelong respiratory and digestive problems. They're also prone to a range of neurological disorders, including blindness, cerebral palsy, and mental retardation (Rochman, 2009).

Some parents conceive children to use the tissue from the umbilical cord to provide life-saving cells for a sick sibling. They might certainly love the new

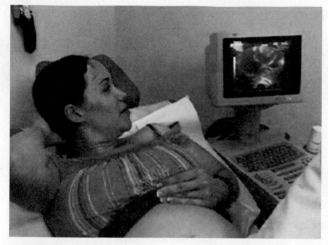

In 2009, Nadya Suleman, after using IVF, gave birth to six boys and two girls. Suleman is single, unemployed, lives with her parents, receives public assistance, and already has six children, three of whom are disabled. All of children are under the age of 8 and products of IVF.

baby as much as the other children. The question is whether it's ethical to bear babies primarily so that their tissue can be used to help other children in the family.

Finally, how many parents can a baby have? If lesbian moms split up, for example, who has parental rights: the sperm donor, the egg donor, the mother who bears the child, or all three? And who are the parents of a child who has a sperm donor, an egg donor, a surrogate mother, and a stepparent who adopts the child?

We've seen that millions of Americans invest considerable resources to have a baby, but others avoid having children. The number of non-marital births has surged since 1990 (see Data Digest), but they'd be much higher if women didn't have access to abortion. Some people see abortion as sinful; others believe that it's a responsible way to avoid parenthood, both inside and outside marriage.

⁙ MAKING CONNECTIONS

- In several European countries—including Britain, Sweden, Norway, and the Netherlands—it's illegal to sell anonymous donor sperm. Should the United States pass similar laws, even if doing so might reduce the number of donors?

- PGD allows people to select the sex of their offspring. Should all prospective parents have such a choice?

- In Europe, laws limit the number of embryos—usually to two—that can be used in a single ART procedure. Should the United States pass similar laws? Or would doing so be intrusive?

ABORTION

Abortion is the expulsion of an embryo or fetus from the uterus. It can occur naturally—as in *spontaneous abortion/* or *miscarriage*—or it can be induced medically.

Practiced by people in all societies and for centuries, abortion was not forbidden by the Catholic Church until 1869. The United States outlawed abortion in the 1800s when the practice became widespread among white, married, Protestant, American-born women in the middle and upper classes. Upper-middle-class white men became concerned that the country would be overpopulated by members of "inferior" new ethnic groups with higher fertility rates (Mohr, 1981).

Incidence of Abortion

Half of all pregnancies in the United States are unintended: Some are unwanted at the time of conception; others are mistimed because they occur sooner than the woman or couple wanted. About 40 percent of the unintended pregnancies and 22 percent of all pregnancies end in abortion. Ultimately, 33 percent of U.S. women will have had an abortion by age 45 (Jones et al., 2008b).

The number of abortions in the United States declined from 1.6 million in 1990 (the all-time high) to 1.2 million in 2005, when 2 percent of all American women had an abortion (Jones et al., 2008b). The *abortion rate,* or the number of abortions per 1,000 women ages 15 to 44, increased during the 1970s but has steadily decreased since 1980 (see *Figure 11.5*).

Who Has Abortions and Why?

The decision to have an abortion depends on structural factors, such as access to medical services, as well as individual experiences, such as a pregnancy resulting from a rape. There are some general demographic trends, however.

SOME DEMOGRAPHIC CHARACTERISTICS Abortion is most common among women who are young (in their 20s), African American or white, and never married (see *Figure 11.6*). Proportionately, 37 percent of abortions are obtained by black women; 34 percent by white women; 22 percent by Latinas; and 7 percent by women who are Asians, Pacific Islanders, American Indians, and those of mixed races. Of all women who get abortions, 60 percent have one or more children (Cohen, 2008; Guttmacher Institute, 2008).

About 43 percent of the women who have abortions are Protestant; 27 percent are Catholic; 8 percent belong to other religious groups or subgroups, including born-again Christians; and 22 percent

FIGURE 11.5 U.S. Abortion Rates Have Decreased

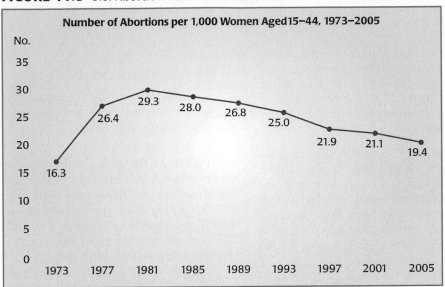

Source: Based on Guttmacher Institute, 2008.

identify themselves as having no religious affiliation (Guttmacher Institute, 2008). The last statistic is probably inflated because only 16 percent of all Americans say that they have no religious affiliation (Pew Forum on Religion & Public Life, 2008). It could be that many women who have abortions are reluctant to claim a religious affiliation because they feel guilty or ashamed. Or, as in the case of Catholics, who are forbidden to get abortions, they may not want service providers or researchers to know that they are violating religious beliefs.

SOME REASONS FOR ABORTION Some of the most frequently cited reasons for getting an abortion include the following: (1) not being ready for motherhood (usually because of age or educational goals), (2) having to leave a job because of the inability to pay for child care services, (3) not wanting to be a single mother, (4) deciding not to have more children, (5) responsibility for raising other children, and (6) not wanting others (especially parents) to know that they've had sex or are pregnant. Fewer than 1 percent of women say that the most important reason for an abortion was pressure from parents, husbands, or partners (Finer et al., 2005).

Since 1987, the major reason for abortion (74 percent of all cases) has been a financial inability to support the baby. The majority (61 percent) of American

FIGURE 11.6 Who Gets Abortions?

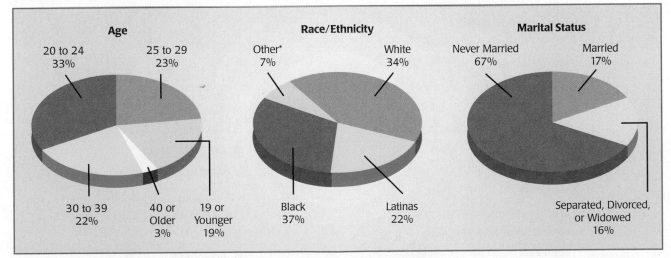

*Other refers to Asian/Pacific Islanders, American Indians, and Alaska Natives.
Source: Based on Guttmacher Institute, 2005, 2008.

women who have abortions are already mothers, and about 57 percent of women who have abortions live well below the poverty level (Boonstra et al., 2006; Jones et al., 2008b).

Many low-income women believe that having an unwanted baby would plunge them deeper into poverty and create even more parenting problems. For example, here's how a 25-year-old mother of two children, separated from her husband, explained her decision for an abortion:

Neither one of us is really economically prepared. For myself, I've been out of work for almost two years now. I just started, you know, receiving benefits from DSS [Department of Social Services] and stuff. And with my youngest child being three years old, and me . . . constantly applying for jobs for a while now . . . And with the father . . . let's just say I don't think he needs another one (Finer et al., 2005: 114).

In effect, many women seek an abortion not because they're selfish, but because they feel a responsibility to care for the children they already have. About 66 percent of women who get abortions are living at or below the poverty line and already feel stretched—financially, emotionally, and physically—and want to be good mothers to the children they have. Many, moreover, have considered adoption but regarded giving up a child too emotionally distressing (Jones et al., 2008a).

Is Abortion Safe?

Antiabortion groups contend that abortion endangers a woman's physical and emotional health. Are such claims accurate?

PHYSICAL HEALTH On the physical level, a legal abortion in the first trimester (up to 12 weeks) is safer than driving a car, using oral contraceptives, undergoing sterilization, or continuing a pregnancy (see *Table 11.2*). Abortions performed in the first trimester pose virtually no long-term risk of problems such as infertility, miscarriage, birth defects, or preterm or low birth weight. There is also no evidence, despite the claims of abortion opponents, that having an abortion increases the risk of breast cancer, causes infertility, and leads to postabortion stress disorders or suicide (Boonstra et al., 2006; Guttmacher Institute, 2008).

Since you asked . . .

- How dangerous is abortion?

TABLE 11.2	Abortion Risks in Perspective
Activity	**Chance of Dying**
Motorcycling	1 in 1,000
Illegal abortion	1 in 3,000
Driving a car	1 in 6,000
Power boating	1 in 6,000
Legal abortion after 20 weeks	1 in 11,000
Continuing a pregnancy	1 in 14,300
Oral contraceptive use (smoker)	1 in 16,000
Playing football	1 in 25,000
Sexual intercourse (risk of pelvic infection)	1 in 50,000
Legal abortion (13 to 15 weeks)	1 in 60,000
Oral contraceptive use (nonsmoker)	1 in 63,000
Tubal ligation	1 in 67,000
Using an intrauterine device	1 in 100,000
Vasectomy	1 in 300,000
Tampons (risk of toxic shock syndrome)	1 in 350,000
Legal abortion (9 to 10 weeks)	1 in 500,000
Legal abortion before 9 weeks	**1 in 1 million**

Sources: Finer and Henshaw, 2003; Guttmacher Institute, 2005.

EMOTIONAL HEALTH What about emotional health? A team of psychologists who evaluated 73 empirical studies in peer-reviewed journals published between 1990 and 2007 concluded that among adult women who had an unplanned pregnancy, the risk of mental health problems after an abortion was no greater than experiencing the normal postpartum blues (Major et al., 2008).

When women experience sadness, grief, and depression after an abortion, according to the researchers, such feelings are usually due to co-occurring factors including poverty (because low-income mothers worry about providing for a baby), a history of emotional problems and drug or alcohol abuse, or keeping the abortion secret from family and friends who stigmatize abortions. These findings were consistent with previous national studies conducted in the early 1990s (Major et al., 2008).

Why Have Abortion Rates Decreased?

More women are having unwanted babies (see Data Digest). Why, then, have abortion rates decreased? There are several reasons, ranging from personal attitudes to structural factors such as politics and laws.

ATTITUDES ABOUT ABORTION Abortion has been legal since the U.S. Supreme Court's *Roe* v. *Wade* ruling in 1973, but it is a fiercely divisive issue. Antiabortion activists insist that the embryo or fetus is not just a mass of cells but a human being from the time of conception, and that, therefore, it has a right to live. On the other hand, many abortion rights advocates believe that the organism at the moment of conception lacks a brain and other specifically and uniquely human attributes, such as consciousness and reasoning. Abortion rights proponents also believe that a pregnant woman, not the government or religious groups, should decide what will happen to her body.

More Americans describe themselves as pro-life (51 percent) than pro-choice (42 percent) on abortion for the first time since Gallup began asking the question in 1995. Despite their ideological stance, however, a majority of Americans (53 percent) say that abortion should be legal under some circumstances, such as when the mother's life is threatened or when the pregnancy is the result of rape or incest; 22 percent say that abortion should be legal under all circumstances, and 23 percent say it should be illegal under all circumstances (Saad, 2009).

Religious beliefs and practices are a key factor in people's attitudes about abortion: 61 percent of those who attend religious services at least once a week

Abortion opponents and abortion-rights activists are equally passionate in their beliefs. Both sides of this highly controversial issue often stage public protests, especially in Washington, D.C., to influence policy makers.

believe that abortion should be illegal in all or most cases. However, being religious also reflects social class. For example, as income and educational attainment rise, the importance of religion decreases, and the acceptance of abortion increases (Pew Forum on Religion & Public Life, 2008; "Abortion views by religious affiliation," 2009). Thus, social class is an important variable in many Americans' views of abortion.

CONTRACEPTIVES As much as 43 percent of the decrease in abortions since 1994 can be attributed to the use of emergency contraception (EC) (Guttmacher Institute, 2005). Sometimes called "morning-after" birth control, oral contraceptive pills taken within 72 hours after sexual intercourse prevent implantation of the fertilized ovum in the uterine wall. Anyone age 17 and older can buy EC pills without a prescription from a certified pharmacist, and as many as 89 percent of unintended pregnancies in the United States each year could be prevented with morning-after pills (Levey, 2009).

Morning-after pills are controversial, however. Opponents claim that they are *abortifacients,* substances that cause termination of pregnancy. Proponents maintain that they are contraceptives because they prevent pregnancy and abortion.

Despite the controversy, millions of teens can't access EC quickly. In a study of California, for example, the researchers found that only 36 percent of the phone calls to pharmacies were successful in accessing EC. In the other cases, calls to pharmacies in rural areas or by Spanish speakers, especially, were often fruitless because of language barriers, the pharmacists' unavailability, or the pharmacists' reluctance to suggest or sell EC because of their religious beliefs (Sampson et al., 2008). If EC were readily available, abortion rates would probably decrease even more.

ABORTION SERVICES Abortion rates have also decreased because there are fewer abortion providers. One study found that 42 percent of certified nurse-midwives and 24 percent of physician assistants want training in abortion. Because of domestic terrorism by antiabortion activists, however, few doctors perform abortions. For example, the number of abortion providers has declined by 11 percent since 1996; 87 percent of U.S. counties and 31 percent of metropolitan areas have no abortion facilities. If a woman doesn't have the resources to travel to another state, she has little choice except to bear an unwanted or unplanned baby (Hwang et al., 2005; Boonstra et al., 2006; Jones et al., 2008b).

Abortion foes have been vocal and sometimes violent in closing down abortion clinics. In mid-2009, an antiabortion activist shot and killed Dr. George Tiller in Wichita, Kansas, who provided abortions, including those late in a pregnancy. At the time, Dr. Tiller was attending church services. One of the regular protesters outside the doctor's clinic said that killing any abortion doctor is justifiable because it saves the lives of the unborn. After the murder, the family closed the clinic (Slevin, 2009).

The Bush administration funded at least 4,000 *crisis pregnancy centers* (CPCs). CPC staff—usually volunteers with no professional training—try to discourage girls and women from having abortions by "playing gruesome videos depicting bloody fetuses, withholding pregnancy test results, and even pressuring them to sign adoption papers" (Kashef, 2003: 18; see, also, Gibbs, 2007).

The Obama administration might limit or stop federal funds for CPCs, but at least eight states still use taxpayer money to subsidize CPCs that encourage women with unplanned pregnancies to have their babies, provide no information about contraception, and never discuss abortion. Most of the CPCs advertise themselves as "women's centers" and "clinics." When women arrive expecting a full range of services, the "staff" tells the women that having an abortion increases the risk of breast cancer, causes sterility, and leads to suicide and postabortion stress disorders—all of which are false (National Abortion Federation, 2006; United States House of Representatives, 2006).

A growing number of drugstores around the country don't sell condoms, won't fill prescriptions for birth control pills, or don't carry EC pills (Stein, 2008). All of these and similar policies and practices have contributed to the decrease in the number of abortions.

LAWS AND POLICIES The United States has some of the most restrictive abortion policies around the world, especially among industrialized countries (Kissling and Michelman, 2008). For example,

- 46 states allow individual health care providers to refuse to participate in an abortion and 43 states allow hospitals and clinics to refuse to perform an abortion

- 32 states and the District of Columbia prohibit the use of state funds for most abortions

- 24 states require women to receive counseling, usually 24 hours before an abortion can be performed; this means that many women must make two separate trips to clinics that are sometimes hundreds of miles away from their home

- 20 states allow the sale of "Choose Life" license plates; most of the proceeds go to antiabortion groups, are used to pay for advertisements opposing abortion, and fund CPCs

- 18 states require two physicians, not just one, to be involved in an abortion

- 17 states require that women be given "counseling" before an abortion that includes misinformation about the purported link between abortion and breast cancer, the ability of a fetus to feel pain, and the long-term negative mental consequences to women after an abortion (Guttmacher Institute; 2009a, 2009b; Joyce et al., 2009)

MAKING CONNECTIONS

- Are you for or against abortion? What are the reasons for your position?

- Many Americans assume that *Roe* v. *Wade* will continue to provide women with choices about abortion. How would you feel if the U.S. Supreme Court overturned this law?

- Are parents irresponsible if they don't abort a child who they know will be severely disabled, who will always depend on others for care, or who will probably die at an early age? Or do all fetuses have the right to be born?

CHILD FREE BY CHOICE

American author Edgar Watson Howe once said that families with babies and families without babies feel sorry for each other. Thus, the desire to have children is not universal. For example,

■ The percentage of women ages 40 to 44 who have not had children has increased since 1976 (see Data Digest).

■ 23 percent of first-year college students don't think that raising a family is essential or very important (see Data Digest).

■ 41 percent of Americans say that having children is very important to a good marriage, down from 65 percent in 1990 (Taylor et al., 2007).

■ Americans spend several billion dollars more a year on dog and cat food than they do on baby food (Bauer, 2007).

Couples without children prefer to call themselves *child free* rather than *childless* because they don't have children voluntarily rather than because one or both are infertile. *Childless* implies a lack or a loss, whereas *child free* connotes freedom from the time, money, energy, and responsibility that parenting requires (Paul, 2001).

<table>
<tr><td>**Since you asked . . .**</td></tr>
<tr><td>• Do child-free couples lead empty lives?</td></tr>
</table>

People have many reasons for being child free. Some decide not to have children because their family has a history of genetic diseases such as breast and other cancers, early Alzheimer's, and muscular dystrophy. One young married women decided "not to roll the biological dice" after testing showed that she had a 67 percent chance of passing on leukemia, the cause of her sister's death at age 8 (Handler, 2009:11).

Nationally, African American and white women ages 25 and older—especially those with a college education and job experience—have more positive attitudes than men about being child free. This gender gap doesn't mean that women dislike children or devalue parenthood. Instead, they are more aware of the challenges of balancing employment and parenthood, particularly because women still have more responsibility for housework and child care (Koropeckyj-Cox and Pendell, 2007; see, also, Abma and Martinez, 2006).

Some couples remain child free because of inertia or indecision. When couples disagree about having a child, for instance, the partner who wants a child postpones further discussion, sometimes indefinitely (Thomson, 1997).

Others marry later in life and decide not to have children. As one husband said, "I didn't want to be 65 with a teenager in the house" (Fost, 1996: 16). Some are teachers or other professionals who work with children but like to "come home to peace and quiet and a relaxing night with my husband" (May, 1995: 205). Others believe that marriage should come before parenthood:

A thirty-five-year-old divorced Black attorney who had grown up in a "secure two-parent family" wanted to have children as a part of a committed relationship with "two on-site, full-time loving parents." She had two abortions because the men involved "weren't ready for the responsibility of fatherhood," and she did not want to be a single mother (May, 1995: 193).

Some couples believe that it's irresponsible to bring more children into an already crowded world or don't think they're suited for parenthood because they'd be impatient with offspring. Others don't want to structure their lives around children's activities and school vacations and to worry about how a child will turn out, especially when they can experience parenthood vicariously through nieces, nephews, and friends' children (see Bulcroft and Teachman, 2004, for a discussion of theories of childlessness).

Several social scientists see "a social retreat from children" because the meaning and purpose of marriage has changed: "Legally, socially, and culturally, marriage is now defined primarily as a couple relationship dedicated to the fulfillment of each individual's innermost needs and drives." This emphasis on companionship has resulted in a "devaluation of child rearing," which requires sacrifice, stability, dependability, and maturity—values that "seem stale and musty by comparison to the 'child-free' values" that seem to dominate American society (Whitehead and Popenoe, 2008: 7, 35–36).

Whether there's a social retreat from having children is debatable because there are millions of families with three or more children, a growth of the ART industry, and heated arguments about which parent gets custody of the children after a breakup or divorce. However, numerous journalists have noted that many Americans now dress their pets better than themselves, spend more per year on veterinary than pediatrician bills, treat their pets more lovingly than their children, and often have pets (their "babies") instead of children (see, for example, Brady and Palmeri, 2007; Lynch, 2007; and Piore, 2007).

Today the general public is much more accepting of child-free couples than in the past, but they are still often seen as self-indulgent, selfish, self-absorbed, workaholics, less well-adjusted emotionally, and less sensitive and loving than couples with children. In fact, people who don't marry are lonelier later in life than those who don't have children (Zhang and Hayward, 2001).

Why do these stereotypes about child-free couples exist? Perhaps couples with children resent child-free couples because the latter have (or seem to have) more freedom, time, money, and fun. As you will see in the next chapter, raising children is a difficult task, and parents often feel unappreciated. Thus, a child-free life can sometimes be very attractive.

CONCLUSION

Attitudes about becoming a parent have *changed* greatly, especially during the last generation. There are more *choices* today than in the past, including postponing parenthood, becoming pregnant despite infertility, and having children outside of marriage.

These choices are bounded by *constraints*, however, and many expectations about parenthood are contradictory. We encourage young adults to postpone parenthood, yet we are still somewhat suspicious of people who decide to remain child free. We are developing reproductive technologies that help infertile couples become pregnant yet do little to eliminate hazardous work environments that increase people's chances of becoming infertile and of giving birth to infants with lifelong physical and mental disabilities.

In addition, the high costs of reproductive technologies limit their availability to couples at the lower end of the socioeconomic scale. Despite such contradictions, however, most people look forward to raising children, our focus in the next chapter.

SUMMARY

1. Parenthood is an important rite of passage. Unlike other major turning points in our lives, becoming a parent is a lifelong commitment.

2. There are both benefits and costs in having children. The benefits include emotional fulfillment and personal satisfaction. The costs include a decline in marital satisfaction and high expenses.

3. U.S. fertility rates have fluctuated in the past 70 years, but they are still relatively low. Fertility patterns have changed because of macro- and micro-level factors.

4. U.S. infant mortality rates are higher than even those of some developing countries, and African American babies continue to have the highest death rates.

5. Postponing parenthood is now common. Remaining childless as long as possible has many benefits, including independence and the opportunity to build a career. There are also costs, such as finding it difficult or impossible to have biological children later in life.

6. Approximately 15 percent of all couples are involuntarily childless. The reasons for infertility include physical and physiological difficulties, environmental hazards, and unhealthy lifestyles.

7. Couples have a variety of options if they are infertile, including adoption; artificial insemination; and a number of high-tech procedures, such as in vitro fertilization and surrogacy.

8. Some ongoing issues in the area of adoption include transracial adoption, open adoption, and adoption by same-sex couples.

9. Improved contraceptive techniques and the availability of abortion have resulted in fewer unwanted births. The incidence of abortion has declined since 1990, but abortion continues to be a hotly debated issue in the United States.

10. Couples who decide not to have children are still a minority, but remaining child free is becoming more acceptable.

KEY TERMS

fetal alcohol syndrome (FAS) 294
postpartum depression (PPD) 295
fertility 295
total fertility rate (TFR) 295
fertility rate 295
contraception 297
infant mortality rate 298
infertility 300
pelvic inflammatory
   disease (PID) 301

chlamydia 301
endometriosis 301
adoption 302
open adoption 303
closed adoption 303
semi-open adoption 303
artificial insemination 306
fertility drugs 307
assisted reproductive
   technology (ART) 307

in vitro fertilization (IVF) 308
surrogacy 308
preimplantation genetic
   diagnosis (PGD) 308
amniocentesis 309
chorionic villus
   sampling (CVS) 309
abortion 310

mYfamilylab MyFamilyLab provides a wealth of resources. Go to www.myfamilylab.com<http://www.myfamilylab .com/>, to enhance your comprehension of the content in this chapter. You can take practice exams, view videos relevant to the subject matter, listen to audio files, explore topics further by using Social Explorer, and use the tools contained in MySearchLab to help you write research papers.

12 Raising Children
Promises and Pitfalls

According to some elementary school children, the difference between moms and dads is that

"Moms work at work and work at home, and dads just go to work at work."

"Dads are taller and stronger, but moms have all the real power 'cause that's who you got to ask if you want to sleep over at your friend's house."

The kids' comments, which have been floating around on the Internet, are fairly accurate in describing parenting roles in the average American home. A Swahili proverb says that a child is both a precious stone and a heavy burden. Child rearing is both exhilarating and exhausting, a task that takes patience, sacrifice, and continuous adjustment. There are many rewards, but no guarantees.

In this chapter, we examine some of the central issues of child rearing, some of the most influential theories in child development, parenting styles in a variety of families and social classes, parents' impact on their children's development, and child care. Let's begin by looking at contemporary parenting roles.

DATA DIGEST

- Congress recognized Mother's Day as a **national holiday** in 1914. Father's Day became an official holiday in 1972.

- Of the more than 74 million American children under age 18, **66 percent live with married parents,** 27 percent live with one parent, almost 4 percent live with no parent present, and 3.6 percent live with two unmarried parents.

- About 52 percent of U.S. adults approve of spanking (down from 94 percent in 1968), but **94 percent of all American parents spank their preschool children.**

- Among 12- to 19-year-old American teenagers who were asked to name **the most influential people in their lives,** 86 percent said mom, and 73 percent rated dad in their top three.

- Teens are up to 50 percent less likely to use drugs (such as alcohol and marijuana) **if they learn about the risks of drugs from their parents** rather than friends, school programs, and the media.

- Among 25 of the richest nations of the industrialized world, **the United States ranks only 25th on six dimensions of children's well-being** that include health, safety, education, and family relationships.

Sources: Wulfhorst, 2006; UNICEF, 2010; Straus, 2008; U.S. Census Bureau News, 2008; Partnership for a Drug-Free America, 2009; TRU, 2009.

CONTEMPORARY PARENTING ROLES

Becoming a parent is a major life change. Most prospective parents are emotionally and financially invested in planning for their child's arrival. Months before the baby is born, they begin to alter their lifestyles. The pregnant mother may forgo Big Macs and increase her intake of calcium-rich dairy and fresh vegetables and eliminate cigarettes, alcohol, and other drugs, behaviors that often continue after childbirth. Most prospective parents shop for baby clothes and nursery furniture, and child-rearing manuals pile up on their nightstands.

Since you asked . . .

❖ Does parenting come naturally?

A Parent Is Born

Infants waste no time in teaching adults to meet their needs. Babies are not merely passive recipients but active participants in their own development:

The infant modulates, regulates, and refines the caretaker's activities. . . . By fretting, sounds of impatience or satisfaction, by facial expressions of pleasure, contentment, or alertness he . . . "tells" the parents when he wants to eat, when he will sleep, when he wants to be played with, picked up, or have his position changed. . . . The caretakers, then, adapt to him . . . (Rheingold, 1969: 785–86).

Rather than simply performing parental roles, people *internalize* them: "We absorb the roles we play to such a degree that our sense of who we are (our identities) and our sense of right and wrong (our consciences) are very much a product of our role-playing activities" (LaRossa, 1986: 14).

Internalizing the parental role changes both partners. As they make the transition to parenthood, they help each other learn the role of parent, deal with the ambiguity of what constitutes a good parent, and usually share in the care of their child.

Parenting does *not* come naturally. It is neither instinctive nor innate. Especially with our first child, most of us muddle through by trial and error. Many people are so anxious about being perfect parents that they often turn to experts for advice. Much of the advice can be valuable, especially on topics such as the physical care of the baby. But, as you'll see later in this chapter, some of the self-proclaimed experts, especially, promote myths that have become widely accepted.

Some Rewards and Difficulties of Parenting

Just as there are benefits and costs of having children, there are also benefits and costs of raising them:

"Mommy's not complaining, honey. Don't call your lawyer!"

"Parenting varies, being enormously satisfying and seemingly easy at times as well as confounding, difficult, and burdensome at other times" (Arendell, 1997: 22). Employed mothers and fathers, especially, are experiencing a time crunch because their parenting roles have expanded (Schor, 2002).

Sociologists often use *role theory* to explain the interactions among family members. A *role*, you recall, is a set of expected behavior patterns, obligations, and privileges (see Chapter 1). Theoretically, every role has culturally defined rights and responsibilities. In practice, however, most parents experience role conflict and role strain as norms or role expectations change.

ROLE CONFLICT AND ROLE STRAIN Playing many roles often leads to **role conflict**, the frustrations and uncertainties a person experiences when the expectations of two or more roles are incompatible. Parents routinely undergo role conflict when job and child-rearing responsibilities collide, and they are not able to attend school activities or parent-teacher meetings because of job obligations.

Role strain involves conflicts that someone feels *within* a role. Almost all people experience role strain because many inconsistencies are built into our roles. A parent may experience role strain, for example, when she or he must attend to the needs of both a younger and older child who have different schedules and interests or when parents want to be both friends and authority figures to their children. Four factors contribute to parents' role strain: unrealistic role expectations, decreased authority, increased responsibility, and high parenting standards.

UNREALISTIC ROLE EXPECTATIONS Many parents experience problems because of society's unrealistic expectations. Just as students accept the fact that some professors are better than others, most of us accept occasional mistakes from lawyers, social workers, and other professionals. Parents, however, expect and are expected to succeed with every child and may feel guilty if they "fail": "In fact, the way children turn out seems to be the only measure our culture offers for assessing whether men and women are 'good' parents" (Simon, 2008: 44).

DECREASED AUTHORITY Many parents experience role strain because they believe that they have less authority in raising kids than parents generally had in the past. For example, parents have fought state laws to educate their children at home or to take terminally ill children off life-support systems when there is no possibility of recovery. Parents must also compete with television and other media in teaching their children values, a topic we'll address later (Elkind, 2002).

INCREASED RESPONSIBILITY Parental authority has decreased, but responsibility has increased. If parents raised several children and one ran away from home, relatives and friends would probably think that these good parents had one "bad apple." In contrast, many professionals (such as psychiatrists and social workers) often automatically assume that children do not run away from good homes and might conclude that something was wrong with the parents. Such judgments increase parents' feelings of anxiety and role strain.

A growing number of states are passing laws increasing parental liability for teenage drinking in their homes, whether or not the parent is aware that there is underage drinking. If the intoxication contributes to driving accidents, especially those that result in car crash deaths, the parents can be sued in civil court for millions of dollars (Schwartz, 2007). Thus, parents—rather than their children—are held accountable for a child's misbehavior, whether it's a minor offense such as graffiti or a serious offense that involves a death.

HIGH PARENTING STANDARDS Parents have no preparation for their difficult role, yet they must live up to high standards. We receive more training to get a driver's license than we do to become parents. In contrast to previous generations, parents are now expected to be informed about the latest medical technologies, to watch their children closely for early signs of physical or mental abnormalities, and to consult with specialists immediately if they detect learning

problems. Moreover, many mothers and fathers experience contradictions in their child-rearing responsibilities.

Motherhood: Ideal versus Realistic Roles

New mothers, especially, often face enormous pressures, role conflict, and role strain. The myth that mothering comes naturally creates three problems. First, it assumes that a good mother will be perfect if she simply follows her instincts. Second, it implies that there's something wrong with a mother who doesn't devote 100 percent of her time to child rearing. Third, it discourages the involvement of other adults, especially fathers.

More than 69 percent of children under age 18 live with two employed parents. Nevertheless, mothers continue to do most of the child rearing and housework. Both employed and stay-at-home mothers spend more time caring for their children than their own mothers did (Bianchi et al., 2006; U.S. Census Bureau, 2008).

About 70 percent of Americans say that mothers today have a more difficult parenting job than did mothers 20 or 30 years ago, and 60 percent believe this about fathers. Despite the general consensus that mothering is more difficult than in the past, Americans are more critical of mothers than fathers (see *Figure 12.1*). Some of the harshest critics are older women: 65 percent of those ages 50 to 64, compared with 54 percent of women under age 50, say that mothers of children under 18 are now doing a worse job as parents than their own mothers did (Kohut and Parker, 2007).

Why is it that both employed and stay-at-home mothers spend more time caring for their children

FIGURE 12.1 Are Mothers and Fathers Better or Worse Parents Than in the Past?

Question: "All in all, do you think mothers/fathers of children under 18 are now doing a better job as parents than their own mothers/fathers did 20 or 30 years ago, a worse job, or about the same job?"

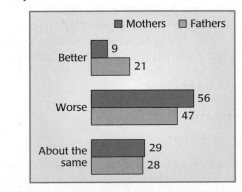

Source: Based on Kohut and Parker, 2007, 2.

than their own mothers did, but many Americans are more critical of mothers than fathers? And especially compared to mothers 20 or 30 years ago? One reason is that fathers have increased the number of hours they spend in parenting and get overwhelming credit for doing so. Another reason is that mothers, who still have the major responsibility for raising kids, have a difficult time grappling with external societal influences—such as drugs and alcohol and the impact of the electronic media—that were less prevalent or practically nonexistent 20 or 30 years ago (Kohut and Parker, 2007).

Others contend that the mass media, especially, have generated a "new momism": a highly romanticized yet demanding view of motherhood with cultural standards and ideals that are impossible to meet. For example, many newspaper articles insist that "women are the best caretakers of children, and that to be a remotely decent mother, a woman has to devote her entire physical, psychological, emotional, and intellectual being, 24/7, to her children" (Douglas and Michaels, 2004: 4).

In recent years, magazine covers have featured celebrity moms (such as Angelina Jolie and Halle Berry) who have chic maternity clothes, perfect hairdos and makeup, expensive baby products, and, of course, nannies: "When the beautiful people embrace parenting, it becomes sexy." Despite this "gloss" on motherhood, the reality is very different for the typical mother: "Real mothers are still worn out by broken sleep, worries about how to split their time between paying work and child-rearing, and what to do about child care" (Fisher, 2005). Thus, many mothers compare themselves with celebrity moms and feel inadequate and unattractive as a result.

Even when women don't compare themselves to celebrities, traditional gender roles—that many Americans still espouse, as you saw in Chapter 5—idealize the mother role and expect fathers to step aside in child rearing. Such "maternal gatekeeping" decreases a father's involvement in his children's lives. If, for example, mothers believe that men aren't capable parents, they may limit the father's accessibility to children by not encouraging him to interact with the children or to respond to phone calls from the child's teacher or doctor (McBride et al., 2005).

Generally, the greater the father's participation in raising children, the greater is the mother's satisfaction with her own parenting and the marriage (see Chapters 5 and 10). But how much do fathers contribute to child rearing?

Fatherhood: Ideal versus Realistic Roles

Fathers, like mothers, experience role conflict and role strain. They may have little opportunity to learn parenting skills, especially during the first year of a baby's life:

Fred Taylor, a successful running back for the Jacksonville Jaguars, a National Football League team in Florida, said that, in his younger days, he used to think that "his career could not be complete without at least one Pro Bowl appearance," but that was before he had four children and has enjoyed fathering them (Crouse, 2007: 1). Pictured here, Taylor is coloring with two of his children.

An old joke for musicians goes like this: A young man asks an older musician, "How do I get to Carnegie Hall?" The older man answers, "Practice, my son, practice." You can say the same for fatherhood. It takes practice to know how to handle a crying baby in the middle of the night and to diaper a squiggly baby on a changing table.... But first-time fathers who work outside of the home ... [are expected] to know how to be dads instantaneously, and this unrealistic expectation causes problems (Marzollo, 1993: 10).

Sociologist Kathleen Gerson (1997) suggests that there are three basic types of fathers:

- *Breadwinner fathers* see themselves as primary earners, even if their wives work outside the home. They view fatherhood mainly in economic terms and prefer a wife who takes responsibility for domestic tasks and child care.

- *Autonomous fathers* seek freedom from family commitments and distance themselves—usually after a marital breakup—from both their former spouse and their children (examples include deadbeat dads, who don't provide economic or emotional support for their children after a marital breakup.)

- *Involved fathers* believe that good fathering includes extensive participation in the daily tasks of child rearing and nurturing. These fathers don't necessarily share equally in their children's care, but they try to forge satisfying relationships with their wives and children.

Many involved fathers find that becoming a dad isn't as easy as they had expected. For example, a

31-year-old producer in the Public Broadcasting System says that he experienced "male postpartum depression" shortly after their son was born: "My life was gone. Movies, sleeping, long showers—all gone. We became slaves to this tiny new thing living in our home, and there was no going back." When work colleagues asked excitedly about fatherhood, all he could mutter was "Actually, it's very, very hard" and was close to tears. Helping care for the infant was exhausting, and "I was mourning the loss of my life as I knew it" (Schwartzberg, 2009: 17).

Such negative emotional reactions are normal—regardless of how much fathers love their infants and children—but we rarely hear about them. Instead, like women, men often hold a romanticized view of parenthood sparked by media images of fathers holding a peaceful and happy baby instead of the reality of coping with a whining and demanding infant who rarely sleeps through the night and requires constant care.

Mothers spend more time with children than fathers, but fathers' participation has increased. Fathers under age 29 spend an average of 4.3 hours per workday with their children, up from 2.4 hours in 1977. Fathers age 29 to 42 spend 3.1 hours per workday, up from 1.9 hours in 1977 (Galinsky et al., 2009).

Many fathers want to be close to their children, but with long commutes and demanding employers, they may have little time to do so. Despite recent media attention about the need for family-friendly work policies, many men have few choices on work hours and locations, especially since the severe recession that began in 2008. In most jobs, employees must be in the workplace at specified times, which limits the time men can spend with their children (Cowan et al., 2009).

If both partners believe that the mother is innately more nurturing, the father may back off while the mother deepens her emotional connection with the children. As fathers step back, the idea that mothers have a natural connection is perpetuated, mothers take on more child-related tasks, and fathers may be left out. In contrast, fathers who believe that men are capable of nurturing their children have more egalitarian views of gender roles: They value women's economic contributions and are more attuned to what their wives and children need (Cowdery and Knudson-Martin, 2005; Matta and Knudson-Martin, 2006).

The quality of the partners' relationship also affects parenting. When the relationship between parents is strong, fathers are more likely to be involved in caring for their children, behavior that benefits children, mothers, and fathers themselves (Cowan et al., 2009).

Parents are the primary socialization agents (see Chapters 1 and 5). How do they influence their children's development over time? Theorists have offered various answers to this question.

:•• MAKING CONNECTIONS

- Who did most of the child rearing when you were growing up? Was your mom or your dad more influential during your childhood? If you have children now, who does most of the parenting?

- A mother in London, England, wrote an essay for the *Daily Mail* newspaper entitled "Sorry, But My Children Bore Me to Death!" She said, among other things, that motherhood is tedious because she hates changing diapers, reading bedtime stories, and driving her children to numerous activities every day (Soriano, 2006). Should this mom never have had children? Or should parents be more open and honest about some of the negative aspects of having and raising children?

SOME THEORIES OF CHILD DEVELOPMENT

Social scientists have proposed a number of theories to explain child development. Three perspectives have been especially influential. George Herbert Mead (1934, 1938, 1964) focused on social interaction as the core of the developing human being. Jean Piaget (1932, 1954, 1960) was interested in the child's cognitive development: the ability to think, reason, analyze, and apply information (see Chapter 5). Erik Erikson (1963) combined elements of psychological and sociological perspectives to create a theory that encompasses adulthood as well as childhood. Refer to *Table 12.1* as we look briefly at these major theories.

> **Since you asked . . .**
>
> :•• What helps a child develop into a mature and productive adult?

Mead's Theory of the Social Self

George Herbert Mead (1863–1931), a symbolic interactionist, saw the *self* as the basis of humanity that develops not out of biological urges but from social interaction. For Mead, the newborn infant is a *tabula rasa* (the Latin phrase for a "blank slate"), with no inborn predisposition to behave in any particular way. It is only as the infant interacts with other people, Mead said, that she or he begins to develop the necessary attitudes, beliefs, and behaviors to fit into society.

The child learns first by imitating the words and behavior of significant others, the people who are important in one's life, such as parents or other primary caregivers and siblings. As the child matures, he or she understands the role of the **generalized other,** people who do not have close ties to a child but

| **TABLE 12.1** | Some Theories of Development and Socialization |

Theory of the Social Self (George Herbert Mead)	Cognitive Development Theory (Jean Piaget)	Psychosocial Theory of Human Development (Erik Erikson)
Stage 1: Imitation (roughly birth to 2) The infant does not distinguish between self and others. She or he learns behavior by mimicking significant others (primarily parents, but also siblings, teachers, and peers). **Stage 2: Play (roughly 2 to 6)** As children begin to use language and continue to interact with significant others, they distinguish between "self" and "other." The child learns social norms, especially that she or he is expected to behave in certain ways. The child also begins to understand other roles in "let's pretend" and other kinds of play. **Stage 3: Games (roughly 6 and older)** As children grow older and interact with a wider range of people, they learn to respond to and fulfill social roles. They learn to play multiple roles and to participate in organized activities (the "generalized other").	**Sensorimotor stage (birth to 2)** The child develops a physical understanding of her or his environment through touching, seeing, hearing, and moving around. The child learns the concept of object permanence (e.g., a toy exists even when it is out of sight). **Preoperational stage (2 to 7)** Children learn to use symbols. For example, they learn to represent a car with a block, moving the block around. They learn to use language to express increasingly complex ideas. However, they still have difficulty seeing things from another person's viewpoint. **Concrete operational stage (8 to 12)** Children learn to discern cause and effect: They can anticipate possible consequences of an action without having to try it out. They begin to understand the views of others. They also understand that quantities remain the same even when their shape or form changes (e.g., a fixed amount of liquid poured into a tall, thin glass and into a short, wide one is the same, even though it looks different in differently shaped containers). **Formal operational stage (13 and older)** Children can reason using abstract concepts. They can understand future consequences and evaluate the probable outcomes of several alternatives. They can evaluate their own thoughts and consider major philosophical issues, such as why pain and suffering exist.	**I. Trust vs. mistrust (birth to 1)** *Task:* To develop basic trust in oneself and others. *Risk:* A sense of abandonment may lead to mistrust and lack of self confidence. **II. Autonomy vs. shame, doubt (2 to 3)** *Task:* To learn self-control and independence. *Risk:* Parental shaming to control the child may lead to self-doubt. **III. Initiative vs. guilt (4 to 5)** *Task:* To learn new tasks and pursue goals aggressively. *Risk:* Feeling guilty for having attempted forbidden activities or been too aggressive. **IV. Industry vs. inferiority (6 to 12)** *Task:* To develop an interest in productive work rather than just play. *Risk:* Failure or fear of failure may result in feelings of inferiority. **V. Identity vs. identity confusion (13 to 19)** *Task:* To achieve a sense of individuality and of having a place in society. *Risk:* Making important decisions may lead to confusion over who and what one wants to become. **VI. Intimacy vs. isolation (20 to 30)** *Task:* To achieve close ties with others and fulfill commitments. *Risk:* Inability to take chances by sharing intimacy may result in avoiding others or in isolation. **VII. Generativity vs. self-absorption (31 to 64)** *Task:* To establish and guide the next generation—especially one's children—to create ideas and products. *Risk:* Inability to bear children or create ideas or products may lead to stagnation. **VIII. Integrity vs. despair (65 and older)** *Task:* To feel a sense of satisfaction and dignity in what one has achieved. *Risk:* Disappointments and unrealized goals may lead to feelings of alienation or despair.

who influence the child's internalization of society's norms and values (e.g., "Let's pretend that you're the daddy and I'm the mommy"). When the child has learned the significance of roles, according to Mead, she or he has learned to respond to the expectations of society (see Chapter 5).

Piaget's Cognitive Development Theory

Jean Piaget (1896–1980) was interested in the growing child's efforts to understand his or her world, to learn how to adapt to that world, and to develop an independent identity. In his four major developmental stages, Piaget traced the acquisition of abilities such as differentiating oneself from the external world; learning to use language and symbols; understanding the perspective of another person; and learning to think and reason in abstract terms about the past, the present, and the future.

Piaget believed that children play an active role in learning, processing information, and seeking knowledge. He emphasized that although some children learn faster than others, they must pass through the same four stages, at similar ages, and in the same order. Once children have mastered the tasks of one stage, they move on to the next, which is more difficult.

Erikson's Psychosocial Theory of Development

Erik Erikson (1902–1994) is one of the few theorists whose explanation of human development encompassed the entire lifespan rather than just childhood

This 4-year-old girl seems as engrossed in filling her dump truck as she might be in dressing a doll. If parents and other caretakers don't steer children toward sex-stereotypical activities, both girls and boys can enjoy a variety of games and toys as they're growing up.

and adolescence. In each of Erikson's eight stages, the developing person faces a specific challenge, or crisis, that presents both tasks and risks.

The outcome of each crisis determines whether the individual will move on successfully to the next stage. For example, a person may leave the first stage having learned to trust other people, such as parents or caregivers, or else unable to count on anyone. For Erikson, resolving each of these crises is the responsibility of the individual, but successful development also reflects the person's social relationships with family members, peers, and others.

The important point in all three of these theories is that children grow and mature by learning to deal with new expectations and changes. A child who feels loved and secure has a good chance of developing into a reasonably happy and productive member of society, one of the family's major socialization functions (see Chapter 1).

These and other theories give us some insight into children's development but say little about children's development across different types of families. How, for instance, do race, ethnicity, and social class affect parenting and children's development?

PARENTING VARIATIONS BY ETHNICITY AND SOCIAL CLASS

Positive parenting has a direct influence on children that results in fewer behavioral problems. However, there's no recipe for good parenting because much depends on variables such as whether there are one or two adults in the home, whether the parents are married or cohabiting, the number of children that demand parental time, and the degree and quality of parent-child interaction (see Dye and Johnson, 2007). Ethnicity and social class intersect in shaping our family life.

Parenting across Racial-Ethnic Families

We looked at socialization practices across a number of racial-ethnic families in Chapter 4. Some specific child-rearing tasks include spending time with children and monitoring their activities.

SPENDING TIME WITH CHILDREN An important variable in a child's well-being is the type and amount of interaction that occurs between the child and his or her parents. Interaction includes reading to children and taking them on outings.

Reading is an important activity, not only because it stimulates a child's cognitive and intellectual abilities but also because it's a way for parents to spend time with their youngsters. Also, reading prepares children for kindergarten because it sharpens their reading skills. In 2005, only 26 percent of Latino children ages 3 to 5—compared with at least 44 percent of white, black, and Asian children—had skills such as recognizing the alphabet, counting to 20 or higher, and reading or pretending to read storybooks (U.S. Census Bureau, 2011).

Latino parents are less likely to read to their young children than are African American, Asian American, and white parents (see *Table 12.2*). However, Latino parents (60 percent) are almost as likely as white parents (61 percent) and more likely than black parents (57 percent) and Asian parents (49 percent) to expect their children to graduate from college ("A child's day. . . ." 2009). Thus, many Latino parents have high educational expectations for their offspring, but they don't always have the time, language skills, or energy to engage in the daily reading activities, even when their children are very young, that prepare them for achieving a college degree.

Another way to spend time with children is to take them on outings such as to a park, playground, or zoo or to visit friends or relatives. Such trips provide opportunities for parents to talk to their children and get to know more about them. About 41 percent of white children younger than age 12 have 15 or more outings with their parents per month compared with about 26 percent of children in African American, Asian, and Latino families ("A child's day . . .," 2009).

There may be several explanations for these racial and ethnic variations in parental reading and outings. One is marital status. African American children are the most likely to live with only one parent, usually the mother (see *Figure 4.3* on p. 84). Many single parents who work have less time and energy to interact with their children. In multigenerational homes—which tend to be black, Asian, and Latino—mothers may be caring for older family members and also depend on their children, sometimes as young as age 8, for caregiving (see Chapter 17). As a result, these parents may be less aware of their children's needs and devote less time to activities such as reading and outings (Jambunathan et al., 2000). More-over, recent immigrants who don't speak English well may be uncomfortable with or unaware of recreational opportunities outside the home that are free to the public.

MONITORING CHILDREN'S ACTIVITIES African American and Latino fathers typically supervise their children's activities more closely than do white fathers. Recent Asian immigrants are also more likely to monitor their children than are U.S.-born parents. As children acculturate, parental supervision and control decrease because many adolescents conform to the values of their peer group rather than those of their family (Willie and Reddick, 2003; Coltrane et al., 2004; see, also, Chapter 4).

In monitoring television viewing, a major source of recreation for children, parents often impose three rules: the types of programs, times of day, and number of hours the child may watch. About 70 percent of white, black, Asian American, and Latino parents report setting such rules for children ages 6 to 11. These rules vary by social class, however. As a parent's educational level increases, so do restrictions on television viewing. For example, 63 percent of parents who haven't graduated from high school, compared with 74 percent of parents with a college degree, restrict television watching for children ages 6 to 11 (Dye and Johnson, 2007).

Parenting and Social Class

Many racial and ethnic parenting approaches reflect social class variations. That is, middle-class parents, regardless of race and ethnicity, are more similar to one another than to low-income and high-income parents in their child-rearing practices.

Social scientists typically measure social class using **socioeconomic status (SES)**, an overall rank of an individual's position in society based on income, education, and occupation. Sociologists have delineated as many as nine social classes in the United States (see the classic study by Warner and Lunt, 1941). For our purposes, low-SES families are those

TABLE 12.2	How Often Do Parents Read to Their Kids?	
Percentage of Children Never Read to Last Week		
Race or Ethnicity of Child	**Children 1 or 2 Years**	**Children 3 to 5 Years**
White	4	5
Black	11	8
Asian and Pacific Islander	13	10
Latino	18	14

Source: Based on data in "A child's day . . .," 2009, Tables D9 and D21.

Many schools, such as the Amistad Academy in Connecticut, are encouraging minority dads, grandfathers, and uncles to visit schools and become more involved in their children's education.

living just above or below the poverty line which, in 2008, was $21,834 for a family of four (two adults and two children) (DeNavas-Walt et al., 2009). Middle-SES families are those in blue-collar and white-collar occupations, and high-SES families are professionals and higher.

Since you asked . . .

How does social class affect parenting?

LOW-SES FAMILIES Most low-SES parents, especially recent immigrants, must grapple with numerous obstacles. Macro-level stressors such as poverty, unemployment, and racism often create interpersonal conflict. Besides living in high-crime neighborhoods, children have little physical space at home and usually attend schools that are overcrowded and underfunded (Fuligni and Yoshikawa, 2003; Votruba-Drzal, 2003).

Compared with middle-SES parents, low-SES parents typically give their infants fewer opportunities for daily stimulation and fewer appropriate play materials. Many school-related activities are free, but parents may lack the time, energy, health, and economic resources to encourage children to participate in extracurricular activities (Bornstein, 2002; Goodman et al., 2008).

Depression is higher among economically disadvantaged mothers than higher income mothers because of the stresses of poverty and unhappy relationships. Because depressed mothers are more likely to use harsh discipline strategies or no strategies at all, their children are more likely to act out and get into trouble at school and in the community as early as the third grade (Moore et al., 2006).

The most vulnerable low-SES families are those formed by adolescents. Often, teenage parents lack the skills to maintain a relationship, don't have a strong parenting alliance in raising children (especially if they are no longer romantically involved), and few resources to ensure their children's healthy development. Such problems may appear or worsen when young fathers experience employment problems because of low educational levels or one or both partners have additional out-of-wedlock children (Futris and Schoppe-Sullivan, 2007).

Especially in disadvantaged single-mother families, children are likely to undergo *adultification,* a developmental process in which, although prematurely and often inappropriately, a child assumes extensive adult roles and responsibilities within the family. Preteen children may have to raise younger siblings and be social service advocates when a parent is chronically ill, has mental health problems, or abuses drugs. Children who have demanding family responsibilities learn to take charge of situations, feel needed, develop self-confidence, and have a high level of independence. Despite such assets, adultification often leads to dropping out of school, poor academic performance, feeling anxious or depressed, and even forgoing marriage. Listen, for example, to a 68-year-old African American man:

I've been taking care of my family members since I was five and my mother told me that's what I should do. I go from one house to the other, taking care of newborn babies and sick relatives. I go where I am needed. . . . There was never any time to marry (Burton, 2007: 342).

MIDDLE-SES FAMILIES Middle-SES parents have more resources (money, time, education) to enhance their children's emotional, social, and cognitive development. Many middle-class men believe that they show their commitment to parenthood by staying in their jobs—even jobs they hate—to provide for their families. These fathers provide the means for children to pursue educational or cultural opportunities at summer camps or through music lessons and sports. Such activities often avoid the possible harmful influences of undesirable friends. Economically disadvantaged parents aren't able to provide such advantages (Ambert, 1997).

Middle-SES mothers talk to their infants more, and in more sophisticated ways, than do low-SES mothers. Such conversing facilitates children's self-expression. Middle-SES parents are also more likely than lower-SES parents to seek professional advice about a child's physical, cognitive, and emotional development (Bornstein, 2002).

HIGH-SES FAMILIES The more money parents have, the more they can spend on education, health care, reading materials, and other expenses that enhance

OK, SO MAYBE WE'VE ALL OVERSCHEDULED OUR KIDS A LITTLE...

Speed Bump © 2006 Dave Coverly. All Rights Reserved. Used with permission of Dave Coverly and Cartoonist Group.

their children's life chances. From birth to age 17, a high-income family ($115,000 a year) spends $300,000 on a child, compared with $204,000 for a middle-income family ($61,000 a year) and $148,000 for a low-income family ($29,000 a year) (Lino, 2008). Thus, a child from a high-income family enjoys considerably more material resources from birth until late adolescence than does a child in a middle- or low-income family.

Parents in higher-SES families read to their children more often, provide more outings, and are more likely to limit television viewing. Their children are involved in more extracurricular activities that broaden their self-confidence, knowledge base, and physical and intellectual abilities. For example, 5 percent of children ages 6 to 17 in low-SES homes, compared with 13 percent of children in high-SES households, participate in at least three types of extracurricular activities that include clubs *and* sports *and* lessons in subjects such as music, dance, languages, or computers (Dye and Johnson, 2007).

Children's activities are expensive. Many require special clothing and equipment, paying for hotel and restaurant bills during tournaments outside local areas, assorted costs such as car maintenance and gas, and flexibility in work schedules so children can be transported to events. Such expenses are negligible for high-income families, affordable for many middle-class parents, but daunting for low-income families (Lareau, 2003).

Most of us associate child rearing with raising children and adolescents. In fact, parenting continues until both parents die. People live much longer now than in the past, thereby creating multigenerational families, and parenting often spans a parent's entire life course.

PARENTING CHANGES OVER THE LIFE COURSE

Raising children from infancy to adulthood requires a variety of adjustments over time. Because constructive or harmful parenting practices are often passed down to the next generation, understanding the changes that take place over the life course can improve family relationships (Chen and Kaplan, 2001).

Parenting Infants and Babies

Expecting a baby is very different from *having* a baby. During the first year, infants require "continuous coverage" because "they need to be talked to, listened to, cuddled, fed, cleaned, carried, rocked, burped, soothed, put to sleep, taken to the doctor, and so on" (LaRossa, 1986: 88).

Infancy, the period of life between birth and about 18 months, encompasses only a small fraction of the average person's lifespan but is a period of both extreme helplessness and enormous physical and cognitive growth. Because parents are on call 24 hours a day, stress and fatigue quickly set in.

THE DEMANDS OF INFANTS Infants communicate hunger or discomfort by crying and fussing. Both parents experience frustration when they can't soothe a crying infant. Mothers, especially, may feel inadequate and experience strain and a decline in marital satisfaction (Crnic and Low, 2002).

Parents should recognize that crying is the most powerful way for a baby to get attention. Babies cry during the first few months for a variety of reasons. They may be unable to digest cow's milk if they are bottle-fed; if they are breast-fed, they may want to suckle even if they are not hungry; they may be in pain due to ear or urinary tract infections; they may be uncomfortable because of an allergy or other condition; they may be wet or soiled; or they may simply want some company (Kitzinger, 1989).

Sometimes parents bring colicky babies to bed with them because bed sharing quiets the infant, provides family companionship, and is convenient for breast-feeding mothers. Bed sharing is common throughout much of the world and among recent Asian immigrants in America, but it's a relatively recent trend in the United States, especially among African Americans (Willinger et al., 2003).

Should parents sleep with their infants and babies? The La Leche League, which promotes breastfeeding, endorses sleeping with a baby because the practice is safe and promotes parent-infant bonding. In contrast, the American Academy of Pediatrics discourages bed sharing with infants because it can lead to accidental deaths if the infant falls out of bed or becomes wedged between a wall or a mattress or under a pillow, or when a parent rolls on top of the baby. From 1984 to 2004, for example, infant suffocation and strangulation deaths nationally rose from 2.8 to 12.5 per 100,000 live births (Shapiro-Mendoza et al., 2009).

Another problem is that children who sleep with parents at an early age often continue to do so until they're even 11 years old because they have nightmares, are afraid of severe weather, or just want more attention. Some parents, especially mothers, encourage toddlers and older children to co-sleep because they want to avoid sexual intercourse with their partners. In most cases, however, such co-sleeping disrupts partners' sexual intimacy and the parents' ability to get a good night's rest. Some parents, in fact, are paying "sleep consultants" up to $400 an hour to learn how to dislodge their children from their beds (Green, 2007: D1).

FATIGUE, STRESS, AND CO-PARENTING Because newborns are demanding, parents have less time for each other. Mothers, in particular, are often exhausted by child care. Those who are employed are often tired and may temporarily lose interest in sex. Many wives accommodate their husbands' sexual overtures, but they may experience a temporary loss of desire. Part of the disinterest may be due to fatigue or to hearing the baby crying in the next room (Walzer, 1998).

During the first months of a baby's life, every new parent suffers from self-doubt. Fathers may be especially susceptible to a lack of self-confidence in the day-to-day care of an infant if there is maternal gatekeeping. For example, the more that a mother criticizes and nags rather than encourages the father's efforts, the more likely he is to withdraw from caring for the baby (Schoppe-Sullivan et al., 2008).

Other parental characteristics also often affect infant care and stress levels. Mothers who are more withdrawn, anxious, or depressed generally experience greater stress during their children's infancy. They are often insecure about their parenting skills and need support from their partner, such as positive statements and discussions about the difficulties of parenting (Mulsow et al., 2002).

Some of the parenting insecurity comes from self-proclaimed "experts" who give advice based on personal opinions or limited experience or who reinforce misconceptions. Parents can protect themselves by recognizing some common myths about babies.

SOME MYTHS ABOUT BABIES Some of the ideas parents have about child development, especially from self-help books and talk shows, reflect common

Millions of parents spend hundreds of dollars on educational toys, as for this 11-month-old child, to increase their intelligence. Do these toys work? Or are parents wasting their money?

misperceptions about the baby's early years. Here are some of the most widespread myths about babies:

1. *Myth 1: You can tell in infancy how bright a child is likely to be later on.* A baby's early achievements—such as reaching, sitting, crawling, or talking—are rarely good indicators of intelligence. For example, early agility in building with blocks or imitating words has almost no relationship to later performance in school (Segal, 1989).

2. *Myth 2: The more stimulation a baby gets, the better.* Babies can be overstimulated, agitated, or even frightened into withdrawal by constant assaults on their senses by an intrusive rattle, toy, or talking face. Millions of parents buy enrichment products such as flash cards and educational software for children as young as 6 months ("Your baby will learn the numbers 1–20!" according to some ads). Others play classical music all day or cassette tapes in the baby's crib that are supposed to teach the baby French or German.

   Classical music and language tapes are a waste of money because there's no evidence that they increase a baby's intelligence. In fact, some researchers have found that baby DVDs may be doing more harm than good because infants 8 to 16 months old who watch these DVDs learn fewer words than those whose parents talk to them, tell them stories, and expose them to a rich vocabulary (Zimmerman et al., 2007).

3. *Myth 3: Parents who pick up crying babies will spoil them.* It's impossible to spoil a child who is younger than 1 year old. Crying is the only way a baby can tell parents that he or she is hungry, uncomfortable, or sick. Parents should pick up their baby as much as they want

and not worry about discipline at such a young age (Bornstein, 2002).

4.   *Myth 4: Special talents surface early or not at all.* Many gifted children do not recognize or develop their skills until adolescence or even later. For example, jazz musician Louis Armstrong was a neglected and abandoned child. It was only years later, when he was living in the New Orleans Colored Waifs Home for Boys, that he was taught to play a trumpet, and his talent was ignited.

5.   *Myth 5: Parental conflicts don't affect babies.* Babies as young as 1 year old understand the facial expressions and voice tones of people around them and react accordingly. Thus, parental yelling or arguing affects a baby (Mumme and Fernald, 2003).

These and other myths create unnecessary anxiety and guilt for many parents because they set up false expectations or unrealistic goals.

Parenting Children

The quality of relationships with adults and other caregivers has a profound impact on a child's development. Some wonder, however, whether American parents have become too involved in their children's lives.

DAILY INTERACTION The benefits of warm and responsive parental interaction during the first two years of a child's life become evident as early as age 4. For example, children who have had a close and positive relationship with their parents are better able to control their behavior by showing patience, deliberation, and self-control (Kochanska et al., 2008).

The majority of children younger than 11 years old interact with their parents quite a bit. About 75 percent have dinner with one or both parents every day, and 67 percent receive parental praise three or more times a day ("Good for you" or "Way to go") ("A child's day . . .," 2009). And, as you saw earlier, father's child-rearing involvement has increased.

PARENTS' AND CHILDREN'S INPUTS Parents who encourage their 3-year-old children's curiosity (such as exploring their environment) and speaking improve the children's cognitive abilities. And children age 13 and younger who spend time in family activities and have regular bedtime schedules have fewer behavior problems than other children (Huttenlocher et al., 2002; Raine et al., 2002).

Parents shape a child's environment, but each baby arrives in the world with its own genes, physical appearance, temperament, and personality. Even children in the same family can differ greatly. Some children are easier to satisfy and soothe and have a

These preschoolers seem very attentive to their teacher's instructions on how to use a computer. If they're loved and supported by their parents and families, children are more likely to meet this and other challenges successfully.

happy demeanor. Others are more cautious and shy. Still others are difficult to please and seem constantly dissatisfied (Ambert, 2001).

There can be considerable differences even between identical twins in personality and behavior. One of my colleagues tells the story of his twin girls, who received exactly the same dolls when they were 3 years old. When the parents asked the girls what they would name the dolls, one twin chattered that the doll's name was Lori, that she loved Lori, and she would take good care of her. The second twin muttered, "Her name is Stupid," and flung the doll into a corner. By adolescence, identical twins can be very different emotionally even though they are the same age, gender, ethnicity, and social class; live in the same community; attend the same school; and share the same genetically based traits (Crosnoe and Elder, 2002; Lytton and Gallagher, 2002).

Despite children's different temperaments, parents have similarly high expectations of them. Do many parents, however, over-medicalize and overprogram their offspring?

IS CHILDHOOD TOO MEDICALIZED? In 1952, the American Psychiatric Association published the first edition of the *Diagnostic and Statistical Manual of Mental Disorders,* which describes all mental health disorders for children and adults. The number of disorders increased from 106 in 1952 to 283 in 2000, and is expected to rise for the edition to be published in 2012, especially for childhood disorders. Parent groups want the newest manual to increase the number of childhood disorders to help raise money for research and to obtain insurance coverage for expensive treatments. Others believe that the manual is little more than an excellent doorstop because it medicalizes childhood behavior that, in the past, was deemed normal or simply disobedient (Carey, 2008).

Many researchers are concerned that physicians and parents are increasingly overmedicating children. A study of 200,000 children ages 2 to 4 found that almost 2 percent were receiving stimulants (such as Ritalin), antidepressants (such as Prozac), or tranquilizers. About 4 percent of children ages 5 to 14 took Ritalin. By age 20, children might be taking a range of potent drugs that have been tested only on adults (Zito et al., 2003).

Antipsychotic drugs such as Zyprexa and Risperdal are given as quick fixes to kids who "act out." Clonidine, a blood pressure medication, is now being given to children with attention deficit hyperactivity disorder (ADHD) and even to babies who don't sleep through the night. Since 1997, spending on prescription drugs for children has risen faster than spending for any other group, including seniors. Many of the drugs have had adverse side effects, including an increase in suicidal thoughts, reduced bowel control, heart problems, and even death. Some researchers contend that the medications are unnecessary because many unruly preschoolers may be misbehaving because of stressors such as divorce, neglect, or harsh parenting styles rather than ADHD (Diller, 1998; Cordes, 2003).

In 2002, psychiatrists prescribed antipsychotic drugs to children and adolescents at five times the rate they did in 1993. A third of the children—primarily white boys—were diagnosed as having "behavior disorders" and received new drugs that were usually given only to adults. Because the drugs are largely untested, no one knows how the drugs will affect children in the long run (Olfson et al., 2006).

ARE CHILDREN OVER-PROGRAMMED? Psychologist David Elkind (2007) has criticized children's hurried lives and scolded parents for pushing children to grow up too fast. Over the past two decades, he maintains, children have lost 12 hours of free time a week,

Since you asked . . .

- Are children's lives too rushed?

including unstructured play at home and outside. Organized and more sedentary activities have supplanted free play, Elkind says, and are less likely to enrich children's imagination, curiosity, creativity, and interaction with peers.

Others argue that the lack of free play has been greatly exaggerated. Structured activities increase children's self-confidence and provide valuable interpersonal interactions. Only about 6 percent of American adolescents spend more than 20 hours a week in highly organized activities. In addition, some social scientists contend, organized activities are exciting and enjoyable; offer new skills (such as learning a sport); provide opportunities to interact with both peers and adults; and decrease the likelihood of engaging in unhealthy behaviors such as smoking, drinking, and using drugs (Mahoney et al., 2006).

Parenting Teenagers

Adolescence is a time of tremendous change. Teenagers are establishing their own identity and testing their autonomy as they mature and break away from parental supervision, a healthy process in human development (see Erikson's stages in *Table 12.1* on p. 324).

CHANGES IN PARENT-CHILD RELATIONSHIPS A good parent-child relationship may shift suddenly during adolescence. As children enter the seventh and eighth grades, there may be conflict over issues such as relationships, money, and spending time with friends.

Since you asked . . .

- Why is parenting teenagers sometimes so difficult?

As teenagers become more independent and more likely to confide in friends, parents may feel rejected and suspicious. The most difficult part of parenting adolescents, according to some mothers, is dealing with their changing moods and behavior: "She used to chatter incessantly on car rides; now . . . 'What's new in school today?' you ask. 'Nothing,' she

© Zits Partnerships. King Features Syndicate.

answers" (Patner, 1990: C5). One mother dragged her 13-year-old son to a local hospital for a battery of tests: She was convinced that he had a hearing problem because he never seemed to respond to what she was saying (Shatzkin, 2004).

For many years, people attributed such dramatic changes to "raging sex hormones." Some scientists now think that there may be a link between a teen's baffling behavior and the fact that his or her brain may be changing far more than was thought previously. For example, neural systems that respond to thrills, novelty, and rewards develop well before those that rein in questionable actions: "The teenage brain, in essence, is a turbocharged car with a set of brakes still under construction." In effect, then, the adolescent brain "is primed to seek rewards and take risks," especially when adolescents are with friends. This may explain, in part, why adolescents have more accidents when there are other passengers in the car (Monastersky, 2007: A16, A17).

Adolescent brains aren't developed enough to regulate the teen's behavior, but busy parents provide less supervision and teenagers stay up later because of increasing homework loads and Internet distractions. One of the results is that teens have a harder time getting up at dawn to get to high schools that begin early, are cranky, and may make bad decisions because they're tired (Strauch, 2003).

Regardless of the sources of change, normal adolescent development can strain a marriage. In most cases, the husband and wife are experiencing stresses in their relationship, at work, and with extended family members. Parenting teenagers adds to marital role strain but doesn't necessarily cause it. Instead, "the seeds of parents' individual and marital problems are sown long before their first baby arrives" and continue through the child's adolescence (Cowan and Cowan, 2000: ix; see, also, Grych, 2002; Schoppe-Sullivan et al., 2004).

Because of the seemingly overnight changes in many adolescents' behavior, language, clothes, and music, parents sometimes view their children as aliens from another planet (Danesi, 2003). Teenagers often do things that are silly or dangerous, but are parents too anxious about raising adolescents?

HELICOPTER AND PROBLEM PARENTS Most high school counselors applaud parental involvement but also dread "helicopter parents" who hover over their kids, micromanaging every aspect of their lives. Examples include verbally attacking teachers over their adolescents' low grades, demanding that their child be moved to another class before the school year has even begun, and showing up in the guidance counselor's office with college applications that they have filled out for their children (Krache, 2008).

Helicopter parenting diminishes teens' ability to develop their decision-making skills and to become responsible in problem solving. However, there may be a more serious and widespread problem that a recent report described as "problem parents"—those

Some teenagers are happy that car chips help parents locate them in an emergency. Others complain that such technology gives parents too much control. So, what should parents do?

who by their actions or inactions—increase their teenage children's risk of engaging in unhealthy behavior (see *Table 12.3*). The report concludes that "Problem parents are a big part of why so many teens smoke, drink, get drunk and abuse illegal and prescription drugs" (National Center on Addiction and Substance Abuse, 2008: iii).

Simply telling teens to do or not to do something is much less effective than being a good role model. And instead of giving teens undeserved praise or hovering, parents can boost their child's psychological and emotional well-being by teaching them good social skills: exhibiting positive behaviors (such as being considerate to others), practicing self-control, taking the initiative in developing social relationships, and using constructive strategies (such as discussion) to resolve conflict (Zaff et al., 2002).

MOST TEENAGERS FARE WELL Almost 90 percent of parents say that, compared to the time when they were growing up, it is harder to monitor their 12- to 17-year-olds (National Center on Addiction and Substance Abuse, 2008). One of the reasons is that employed parents, especially, often experience **role overload,** a feeling of being overwhelmed by multiple commitments. Nearly half of American parents say that they don't spend enough time with their children, but 75 percent of children ages 8 to 17 believe that working parents have a positive effect on the quality of their home life. Fathers of adolescents, especially, worry that the amount of time they spend at work is robbing them of the last opportunity to spend quality time with their children before the

youngsters go off to college or jobs (Milkie et al., 2004; Conlin, 2007).

Most adolescents manage to reach adulthood without major problems. In fact, between ages 18 and 25, the average young adult (especially a young woman) shows significantly lower levels of depressive symptoms, higher levels of self-esteem, and a greater sense of psychological well-being than before age 18. These improvements are highest among families with well-educated parents and among young adults who suffer only short periods of unemployment. Over time, however, people in their mid-20s are happier than they were at age 18 because they have married or formed new friendships (Galambos et al., 2006).

Teenagers who fare best have interrelated traits that some psychologists have labeled "the 5 Cs": competence, confidence, connection, character, and caring (Steinberg and Lerner, 2004). Most parents assume that they can nurture such traits until adolescents are at least 18 years old. Thus, parents often feel anxious, hurt, and confused when—and seemingly overnight—their 13- and 14-year-olds start spending more time with their peers and seem to care more about their friends' than their parents' opinions. As teens withdraw from the family, their parents try to keep in touch with them. Others take more drastic measures (see the box "Should Parents Track Their Teens?").

Many parents enjoy their teenagers but look forward to the end of child rearing. Often, however, children bounce back to the parental nest in young adulthood and later. According to one joke, "I childproofed my house, but they still get in."

Parenting in the Crowded Empty Nest

American poet Robert Frost wrote: "Home is the place where, when you have to go there, they have to take you in." Almost 19 million young adults ages 18 to 34 who live with their parents apparently agree (U.S. Census Bureau, Current Population Survey . . ., 2009).

RECENT TRENDS During the 1960s and 1970s, sociologists almost always included the "empty nest" in describing the family life cycle (see Chapter 2). This is the stage in which parents, typically in their 50s, find they are alone at home after their children have married, gone to college, or found jobs and moved out.

The pendulum has swung back, however. Today young adults are living at home longer than was generally true in the past. The terms *boomerang children* and *boomerang generation* used to refer to young adults moving back in with

Since you asked . . .

• Are empty nests becoming open nests?

TABLE 12.3	Are Parents Promoting Their Teens' Substance Abuse?

According to the National Center on Addiction and Substance Abuse (2008), many parents don't monitor their 12- to 17-year–olds' behavior, which increases the likelihood of substance abuse. For example,

■ 86 percent of parents say that their children are always at home by 10:00 p.m. on school nights (Monday through Thursday), but 46 percent of teens report hanging out with their friends and not being at home by 10:00 p.m. on those nights.

■ 76 percent of parents believe it is realistic to expect their teens not to smoke cigarettes; fewer than 66 percent feel the same way about their children's using marijuana (which is now more common than smoking cigarettes).

■ 50 percent of the prescription drugs that teenagers use to get high come from their parents' medicine cabinets.

■ 25 percent of teens know a parent of a classmate or friend who uses marijuana; 10 percent say that the parent smokes marijuana with people the teen's age.

Should Parents Track Their Teens?

Constraints

Car accidents are the chief cause of death and disability among teenagers, with teens being killed at four times the rate of adults. There are many contributing factors, such as inexperience behind the wheel, being distracted by cell phones and text messages, and overconfidence in their skills, but two of the most common variables are speed and intoxication or driving with someone who's drunk (Lyon, 2009).

Increasingly, then, parents are using high-tech methods to track everything from where their children are driving to what they buy and whether they show up for classes. One gadget is a cell phone that transmits location data. Another device is a debit-like card used at school lunch counters. The car chip and the global positioning system (GPS), installed in a vehicle, monitor speed, distance, and driving habits.

Parents contend that such high-tech devices increase their teens' safety, especially because kids will act more responsibly if they know they're being watched. Some teenagers don't mind the monitoring because it cuts down on the need to constantly check in. According to one 17-year-old, for example, his mom simply presses a "locate" button on a cell phone to see where he is (Harmon, 2003).

Many teens, however, complain that they feel like prisoners. "It's annoying," grumbles a 15-year-old who has been caught in a few places where he wasn't supposed to be: "It gives parents too much control." Some college students have simply left their GPS-enabled cell phones under their dorm room beds when they went off with friends ("High-tech gadgets . . .," 2005: B5).

⠿ Stop and Think . . .

- Do tracking devices keep teens safer? Or do they intrude on adolescents' privacy?
- Parents are accountable, even legally, for their teens' behavior. So should parents keep tabs on their children? Or should teens be allowed to learn from their mistakes, as their parents did?

---

their parents, but many people in their 30s, 40s, and older—often with a spouse and children in tow—are moving back home (Koss-Feder, 2009; see, also, Chapter 10).

Most young adults leave the parental nest by age 23, but the proportion of those ages 25 to 34 who are living with parents increased from 9 percent in 1960 to over 27 percent in 2008 (Fields and Casper, 2001; U.S. Census Bureau, Current Population Survey . . ., 2010). Among young adults ages 18 to 34, men are more likely than women to live with their parents (see *Figure 12.2*).

Some journalists have called boomerang children "adultolescents" because they're still "mooching off their parents" instead of living on their own, but this stage of life isn't solely an American phenomenon. The English call such young adults *kippers* ("kids in parents' pockets eroding retirement savings"). In Germany, they are *nesthockers* (literally translated as "nest squatters"), in Italy *bamboccione* (grown babies who are still attached to mama's apron strings), and in Japan *freeter* (young adults who job hop and live at home) (van Dyk, 2005; Alini, 2007).

WHY ARE ADULT CHILDREN MOVING BACK TO THE NEST? Individual and macro factors intersect in explaining the delay in many Americans' transition to adulthood, especially living independently. Among white middle classes, men, in particular, are not moving out or are returning home because they are delaying marriage and don't feel a need to establish their own homes. Others enjoy the comforts

FIGURE 12.2 Who Lives at Home?

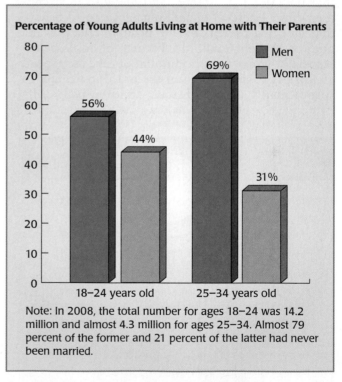

Percentage of Young Adults Living at Home with Their Parents

Note: In 2008, the total number for ages 18–24 was 14.2 million and almost 4.3 million for ages 25–34. Almost 79 percent of the former and 21 percent of the latter had never been married.

Source: Based on U.S. Census Bureau, Current Population Survey . . ., 2011, table A2.

of the parental nest: "Some parents find they have an adult on their hands who still wants Mom to cook his meals and do his laundry" (Large, 2002: 4N).

One of my male students, in his late 20s, may be representative of other men his age who enjoy living at home: "My mom loves my living with her. She enjoys cooking, cleaning my room, and just having me around. I don't pitch in for any of the expenses, but we get along great because she doesn't hassle me about my comings and goings. I have lots of freedom without worrying about bills."

Some women also move back with doting parents who support them financially. A 29-year-old elementary schoolteacher moved into her parents' home in a retirement community in Cape Cod, Massachusetts, because her $1,400-a-month apartment in Boston didn't have air-conditioning, a dishwasher, or a washing machine. She now enjoys golf and tennis privileges, yoga classes, a fancy clubhouse, and her parents' Jacuzzi bathtub—all at the parents' expense. A 32-year-old employed woman moved home with her parents because, among other things, her parents paid almost all of her credit-card expenses. And when the daughter complained about being disturbed while she slept, dad ground his coffee beans at night instead of at 5 a.m., and mom stopped doing laundry, including the daughter's, early in the morning or late at night when the daughter was sleeping (Rich, 2005; White, 2005).

Macro-level factors also encourage a large number of young adults to stay home or move back. Student loans, low wages, divorce, credit card debt, and jumping from job to job until they find work they enjoy have made it harder for young middle-class adults to maintain the lifestyles that their parents created. And the transition to adulthood gets tougher the lower you go on the economic and educational ladder. Until the late 1980s, it was possible for a high school graduate to achieve a middle-class standard of living. That's no longer the case. Instead, young adults now need a college degree to be where blue-collar people the same age were 20 or 30 years ago (see Chapter 13).

According to some sociologists, economic factors aren't the primary reason for living at home because even affluent young adults aren't living on their own. Instead, the researchers propose, many middle-class families are child centered, which means supporting their young adults while they seek post-college degrees or find jobs they like rather than those that provide a living. Perhaps most important, the stigma traditionally linked to young adults' living at home has faded because the practice is widespread enough "to be considered socially acceptable rather than an indicator of the youth's personal failure" (Danziger, 2008: F8).

Do most of these young adults save money to be able to move out of their parents' homes? Rarely. Without the responsibility of paying bills, many boomerangers have more money than they're used to and spend it instead of saving: "Most of their needs are taken care of by Mom and Dad. Many twenty-somethings are living at home, but if you look, you'll see flat-screen TVs in their bedrooms and brand-new cars in the driveway" (Grossman, 2005: 51–52).

RELATIONSHIPS BETWEEN PARENTS AND BOOMERANG CHILDREN How do adult children and parents get along when they're living under the same roof? Some parents report that they are tolerant of but unhappy with the return of their children. There is often conflict about clothes, helping out, use of the family car, and the adult child's lifestyle. The average parent spends about 20 percent of her or his retirement income to support a young adult. Parents whose adult children suffer from mental, physical, or stress-related problems, are unemployed, or unwilling to help with household expenses experience greater stress than do parents whose boomerang children don't have these difficulties (Paul, 2003; Ramachandran, 2005).

Some college-educated fathers, especially, are angry about children who move back home instead of living on their own. This may result, in part, from the fathers' higher expectations for their children's success. Others, however, are quite willing to support adult children who have a low-paying job they "love," such as photography, instead of higher-paying jobs (with health benefits) that aren't as interesting (Shellenbarger, 2008: D1)

Other research shows that co-residence brings mutual assistance. For example, adult children and

© Mike Baldwin / Cornered

"Empty-nesters. They're hoping to sell before the flock tries to move back in."

www.CartoonStock.com

their parents often benefit by sharing some household expenses and child care, especially if they respect each other's privacy and carve out spaces—such as computer rooms—that are their own (Koss-Feder, 2009).

On an anecdotal level, some of my students believe that there are many mutual payoffs to living at home. For example, "After my dad died, my mom wanted me to live at home because she was always a stay-at-home mom and was very lonely"; "My dad still treats me like a 10-year-old, but I take care of him and he helps me pay my tuition and looks after my kids when I'm in class or at work"; and "I'm not happy about my parents' telling me that they disapprove of some of my friends, but they also cheer me up when I feel down."

Parenting in Later Life

You'll see in later chapters that the majority of parents provide some form of help to at least one of their adult children, including giving advice, assisting with child care, and helping out financially. Single mothers are especially likely to move back with their older parents or grandparents if they are unemployed or can't afford housing, child care, or health care because their wages or salaries have not kept up with inflation (Palmer, 2008).

If adult children help pay for some of the household expenses, take over physically demanding chores such as mowing the lawn, and care for their aging parents who get sick or need assistance (e.g., driving to see a doctor), child-parent relationships generally improve. There are also strains, however, because adult children, their parents, or grandparents may strongly disagree about child rearing, and the young children must follow the elders' rules such as not jumping on furniture or doing their chores that might differ from their parents' rules (Fingerman et al., 2007; Koss-Feder, 2009).

Because of the wars in Iraq and Afghanistan, many older American parents have been thrust into caregiving roles that they didn't expect with more soldiers than ever surviving their war injuries. An estimated 10,000 recent veterans of these wars now depend on their parents—who are often in their 50s and 60s—for care because they are single or because their spouses can't or won't care for them:

Across the nation, parents end up scrubbing burn wounds, suctioning tracheotomy tubes, and bathing their adult children. They assist with physical and occupational therapy. They fight for benefits. They deal with mental health crises and help children who have brain injuries to relearn skills. They drive back and forth to Veterans Affairs (VA) hospitals for outpatient appointments. In short, they put their own lives on hold (Yeoman, 2008: 62–63).

You see, then, that whether people are married, unmarried, or single, they parent their children throughout their life course. What about same-sex parents? Are their child-rearing practices similar to or different from those of heterosexual parents?

∷∙ MAKING CONNECTIONS

- Think about how your parents raised you or how you're raising your children. Do you think that mothers are too critical of fathers' parenting? Or are fathers too sensitive about mothers' comments?

- Do you think that parents should welcome their adult children (including grandchildren) with open arms? Or should they enjoy their empty nest and expect their adult children to move out and cope on their own?

PARENTING IN LESBIAN AND GAY FAMILIES

Nationally, 33 percent of lesbian couples and 22 percent of gay male couples are raising children younger than 18 years old. The actual figures are probably higher, but no one knows for sure because the census does not ask any questions about sexual orientation or sexual behavior (Simmons and O'Connell, 2003; Gates and Ost, 2004).

> **Since you asked . . .**
>
> ∷∙ Does parenting differ in heterosexual and same-sex partner families?

More than one in three lesbians has given birth (you might want to refer to the discussion of artificial insemination in Chapter 11); one in six gay men has fathered or adopted a child. Gay and lesbian parents are raising 4 percent of all adopted and 3 percent of all foster children in the United States (Gates et al., 2007). Thus, large numbers of lesbians and gay men, both single and partnered, are involved in child rearing.

In most respects, lesbian and gay families are like heterosexual families: Parents must make a living and juggle work and domestic responsibilities, family members may disagree about the use of space or money, and both children and parents must develop problem-solving skills. Gay and lesbian parents face the added burden of raising children who often experience discrimination because of their parents' sexual orientation (Goldberg and Sayer, 2006; see, also, Chapters 7 and 8).

Children with Lesbian and Gay Parents

In many cases, children think that having same-sex parents is "no big deal." According to one 8-year-old, for example, "I just say I have two moms—'Mom' and

Lesbian mothers who work outside the home often have to struggle, just as heterosexual parents do, to be able to spend quality time with their children.

'Mamma Sheri.' They're no different from other parents except that they're two girls" (Gilgoff, 2004: 42). In other cases, especially during adolescence, children may try to hide the information from their friends to avoid teasing and rejection (McGuire, 1996).

Despite the particular difficulties that children in gay families face, their peer and other social relationships are similar to those of children raised in heterosexual families. A number of studies of adolescents growing up with same-sex parents have concluded that what matters is not the gender of parents but the quality of their relationships with their children. Adolescents whose parents have close and satisfying relationships are likely to do better in school and have few behavioral problems regardless of a parent's sexual orientation (Stacey and Biblarz, 2001; Wainright et al., 2004).

Do lesbian and gay parents worry about their children's' being raised in households in which a mother or father figure is absent? As in the case of heterosexual single parents, there's considerable variation in parental perceptions of providing children with female or male adult role models. For example, a study of lesbians who were planning to be mothers found that some wanted men—especially brothers, their own fathers, nephews, and close straight male friends—to be involved because they believed that children benefit from having more adults in their lives who care about them and who expose the children to different attitudes and activities. Others, like single heterosexual mothers, believed that they could do a good parenting job whether or not there was a male role model for their sons (Goldberg and Allen, 2007).

Parents with Gay and Lesbian Children

About one-third of youth ages 15 to 19 who are lesbian, gay, or bisexual do not tell their parents (D'Augelli et al., 2005). When children do come out,

many heterosexual parents have initially negative reactions because they think that their children could be heterosexual if they wanted to be. Some Asian parents, for example, view homosexuality as a chosen lifestyle, "an undesirable indulgence of individual freedom in the United States" (Leonard, 1997: 148). A child who once was familiar now appears to be a stranger. Parents may also be concerned about being stigmatized themselves.

Negative feelings are frequently followed by strong feelings of guilt and failure in their parenting roles. A common question is "Where did we fail?" Some parents may break off contact with their children, try to convince them to change their sexual orientation, or ignore the issue. Over time, others accept the child's homosexuality (Barret and Robinson, 1990; Savin-Williams and Dubé, 1998).

Regardless of their sexual orientation, mothers and fathers who are consistently involved in their children's lives in a constructive way help them grow up with a strong sense of self, a feeling of security, and a host of other positive characteristics. Parents, and regardless of sexual orientation, must also develop effective parenting styles and forms of discipline. What works and what doesn't?

PARENTING STYLES AND DISCIPLINE

Someone once said that children may not remember exactly what you did or what you said, but they will always remember how you made them feel. How do parenting styles and discipline affect children and how they feel about themselves? Parents differ greatly in their child-rearing approaches. Let's look at some general parenting styles and then more specific beliefs about discipline.

Parenting Styles

Many adolescents think that their parents have little or no effect on them, but parenting styles make a big difference in how a child turns out. A **parenting style** is a general approach to interacting with and disciplining children. Psychologist Diana Baumrind (1968, 1989, 1991) has identified four parenting styles: authoritarian, permissive, authoritative, and uninvolved.

These four styles vary on two dimensions: support and control (see *Table 12.4*). *Support,* sometimes called responsiveness, refers to the amount of affection, acceptance, warmth, and caring that a parent provides to a child. *Control,* which Baumrind also described as demandingness, is the degree of

> **Since you asked . . .**
>
> Is spanking effective in disciplining children?

TABLE 12.4	Four Common Parenting Styles		
	Parental support is . . .	Parental control is . . .	Example
Authoritarian	Low	High	"You can't have the car on Saturday because I said so."
Permissive	High	Low	"Sure; borrow the car whenever you want."
Authoritative	High	High	"You can borrow the car after you've picked your sister up from soccer practice."
Uninvolved	Low	Low	"I don't care what you do; don't bother me."

flexibility a parent shows in guiding a child's behavior. Control can range from offering suggestions to physical abuse.

AUTHORITARIAN PARENTING Parents who use an **authoritarian style** are often very demanding, rigid, and punitive. They expect absolute obedience from their children and often use forceful measures to control their behavior. Verbal give-and-take is rare because the child is expected to accept parental authority without question ("You'll do it because I said so").

Authoritarian parents typically show their children little warmth and support. The parents may be experiencing stress due to low income, parental conflict, or substance abuse. In addition, psychological factors such as depression increase the likelihood of punitive parenting styles. Children from these homes are often irritable, belligerent, and hyperactive (Bluestone and Tamis-LeMonda, 1999; Gaertner et al., 2007; Meteyer and Perry-Jenkins, 2009).

Another study suggests that authoritarian parenting styles can lead to children becoming overweight: Strict mothers who commanded their children to "Clean your plate or else!" were five times more likely than more flexible parents to have children who were overweight by the time the children entered the first grade (Rhee et al., 2006).

PERMISSIVE PARENTING In the **permissive style**, parents are usually warm and responsive but undemanding. They place few requirements on their children for orderly behavior or household tasks. According to one observer, permissive kids (and their parents) are "downright annoying": "I never expected prissy public behavior at a clothing store for toddlers, but an astounding number of preschool-age children were pulling clothes off hangers and onto the floor while their mothers smiled absently at them" (Klein, 2006: B11).

Instead of setting boundaries, permissive parents are indulgent. They don't bully or tyrannize their children, but adolescents raised in lenient households are often less mature, more irresponsible, and less able to

assume leadership positions in adulthood. They are also more likely to be rebellious and impulsive and to have behavior problems such as fighting and losing their temper (Wolfradt et al., 2003; Aunola and Nurmi, 2005).

AUTHORITATIVE PARENTING Parents who use the **authoritative style** are demanding. They impose rules and standards of behavior, but they are also responsive and supportive. These parents encourage autonomy and self-reliance and tend to use positive reinforcement rather than harsh punishment.

Unlike authoritarian parents, authoritative parents encourage verbal give-and-take and believe that the child has rights. They expect obedience, but are open to discussing and changing rules in particular situations when the need arises.

One of the most consistent research findings is that authoritative parenting styles produce children who are self-reliant, achievement oriented, and more successful in school. Authoritative fathers, especially, help adolescents resist peer pressure to use drugs (Eisenberg et al., 2005; Hillaker et al., 2008).

UNINVOLVED PARENTING In the **uninvolved style**, parents are neither supportive nor demanding because they're indifferent. They spend little time interacting with their children and know little about their whereabouts or interests.

Uninvolved parents can also be rejecting: They typically ignore a child as long as she or he doesn't interfere with the parents' activities. The most extreme examples include neglectful parents who lock their children in their bedrooms or strap them down for hours while visiting friends or going to parties (Meyer and Oberman, 2001).

Children from these homes are often immature, withdrawn, or underachieving, and may have a variety of psychological and behavioral problems, such as drug use and bullying. Because these children are used to doing what they want, they may become rebellious when confronted with demanding teachers or other authority figures (Pellerin, 2005).

Which Parenting Style Is the Most Effective?

There are some exceptions, but a number of studies show that healthy child development is most likely in authoritative families, in which the parents are consistent in combining warmth, monitoring, and discipline. Compared with adolescents whose parents are permissive, authoritarian, or uninvolved, children from authoritative households have better psychosocial development, higher school grades, greater self-reliance, and lower levels of delinquent behavior and are less likely to be swayed by harmful peer pressure (to use drugs and alcohol, for example) (Gray and Steinberg, 1999; Barnes et al., 2000; National Center on Addiction and Substance Abuse, 2008).

Authoritarian, permissive, and authoritative parenting styles often overlap. Immigrant Chinese mothers, for example, use a combination of parenting roles. They might seem authoritarian because they have high expectations about academic success, but they are also warm, nurturing, and supportive (Cheah et al., 2009).

Parenting styles also reflect cultural values. Among many recent Latino and Asian immigrants, for example, authoritarian parenting produces positive outcomes, such as better grades. This parenting style is also more effective in safeguarding children who are growing up in communities with high levels of crime and drug peddling (Brody et al., 2002; Pong et al., 2005).

Most American studies emphasize the participation of both parents in raising well-adjusted and emotionally healthy children. In other cultures, similarly, there is an increased interest in fathers playing a more active role in child rearing (see the box "Father Involvement in Japanese Families").

Discipline

A few years ago, a California legislator announced that she was planning to introduce a bill that would make spanking 3-year-old or younger children in California a misdemeanor. She abandoned the bill after newspapers around the country published numerous editorials opposing her proposal as unenforceable, that spanking little children is sometimes necessary, and that the government shouldn't interfere in parental discipline (McKinley, 2007; Vogel, 2007).

Children must learn discipline because self-control is *not* innate. Many parents believe that both verbal and corporal punishments are legitimate forms of discipline.

VERBAL PUNISHMENT A national study found that most parents, in all socioeconomic groups, used verbal and psychological aggression to control or change their children's behavior (Straus and Field, 2003):

- 50 percent yelled, screamed, and shouted at their infants and 1-year-old children, and 90 percent did the same with children ages 4 to 17.

Cross-Cultural and Multicultural Families

Father Involvement in Japanese Families

Some studies claim that if only active father-child interaction is counted (such as helping children with homework), the typical Japanese father spends only between 17 to 30 minutes with his children every day. In contrast, Japanese mothers spend almost seven hours with their children every weekday, one of the highest rates among industrialized and some developing countries.

In Japan, child rearing has for some time been the primary responsibility of stay-at-home mothers. Indeed, some view Japanese families as fatherless because the provider role dominates a father's life. These fathers are often called "7-11 husbands" because the father leaves at 7:00 a.m. and returns home at 11:00 p.m.

Many Japanese fathers would like to be more involved in child rearing,

but they face structural, cultural, and social barriers. A major obstacle is a corporate culture that requires long working hours, socializing with colleagues after work, and accepting job transfers requiring the father to leave his wife and children behind. Strong societal gender stereotypes encourage the husband to be the breadwinner and the wife to be the homemaker.

To encourage greater father involvement in child rearing, in 1995 the Japanese government passed a Child Care and Family Care Leave Act that guarantees up to one year of parental leave after the arrival of a child, with a subsidy equivalent to about 50 percent of the employee's regular wages. Fewer than 1 percent of fathers have taken this leave or plan to do so, however, because they

believe that doing so would cause too much trouble for their co-workers, other men at the office aren't taking the leave, employers aren't supportive, and the men fear losing their jobs.

Sources: Retherford and Ogawa, 2006; Christiansen, 2009; Porter and Sano, 2009.

Stop and Think . . .

- Despite men's limited parenting, Japanese children say that they respect their fathers and appreciate their hard-working provider roles. Why, then, are many families described as fatherless?

- Do you think that Japanese fathers would take paternity leave if they received 100 percent of their regular wages or salaries?

- 33 percent swore at their children, and 17 percent admitted calling them names (such as "dumb" or "lazy").

- 20 percent threatened, at least once, to kick the child out of the house.

These percentages are probably low because many parents don't want to admit to researchers that they abuse their children verbally. Also, because the incidents are so common and normal, parents don't remember all of them.

CORPORAL PUNISHMENT In 2007, about 94 percent of American parents have hit their preschool children to correct misbehavior, which is about the same percentage as in 1975, and the hitting continues on average for 12 years. About 35 percent discipline their infants by slapping a hand or leg; pinching; shaking; hitting the buttocks with a hand, belt, or paddle; or slapping the infant's face. More than half of parents have hit their children at age 12, a third at age 14, and 13 percent at age 17. Parents who hit teenagers do so an average of about six times a year (Straus and Stewart, 1999; Straus, 2008).

As with verbal punishment, corporal punishment rates are probably higher across all age groups. However, parents don't want to admit, especially regarding very young children, that they are more likely to spank their toddlers than to use other disciplinary methods such as time-outs (see Barkin et al., 2007).

Physical punishment tends to be more common among low-income parents; in the South; for boys (particularly firstborns); and by unmarried mothers, especially those under age 33, probably because they have less time and fewer money resources to engage their children in activities that relieve boredom. Also, mothers who move in with their romantic partners are more likely to spank their children than those who live only with their children. The residential change may reflect new strains for mothers that increase the likelihood of corporal punishment when children misbehave (Walsh, 2002; Guzzo and Lee, 2008).

DOES CORPORAL PUNISHMENT WORK? Spanking vents a parent's anger and frustration, but does physical punishment change a child's behavior? Spanking stops bad behavior, but only temporarily, because young children—especially preschoolers—need a "huge number of repetitions" about behaving properly (Straus, 2008: F15). Thus, physical punishment can be as ineffective as time-outs and trying to reason with a very young child, but it often has more serious long-term negative effects.

Most research shows that corporal punishment increases the child's aggression and misbehavior. In a study of preschool-age children, for example, children whose mothers threatened, insulted, spanked, or yelled at them were more likely to be disobedient and disruptive when they entered school. An analysis of 88 studies conducted over 62 years concluded that

spanking children can make them temporarily more compliant but increases the risk that they will become aggressive, antisocial, and chronically defiant (Spieker et al., 1999; Gershoff, 2002).

Recent research on adolescents and adults supports such findings. For example, adolescents in authoritarian homes (in which parents rely on spanking as a form of discipline) are more likely than children raised in authoritative homes to experience depressive symptoms such as sadness and anxiety, as well as mood swings and feeling worthless. They are also more likely than their non-spanked counterparts to hit their parents and other children and to physically abuse their dating and marital partners and their own children later in life (Christie-Mizell et al., 2008; Straus, 2008).

Many researchers and pediatricians maintain that physical punishment is a futile disciplinary method (see the box "Is Spanking Effective or Harmful?"). Increasingly, child-rearing experts recommend nonphysical forms of punishment, such as removing temptations to misbehave, making rules simple, being consistent, setting a good example, praising good behavior, and disciplining with love and patience instead of anger. These anti-spanking proponents maintain that nonphysical discipline has better long-term effects than does physical punishment, but many Americans disagree.

WHAT'S A PARENT TO DO? According to many family practitioners, it's important not to discipline too early. Children younger than 6 years old are curious and eager to learn (see *Table 12.1* on p. 324). Parents can often avoid problems by guiding their children's exploration and interest in new activities instead of yelling "Stop it!" or "I told you not to touch that!"

Effective discipline involves more than rewards and punishments. Children need three types of inner resources if they are to become responsible adults: positive feelings about themselves and others, an understanding of right and wrong, and alternatives for solving problems. The box "Some Building Blocks of Effective Discipline" lists ten building blocks that parents can use to establish these inner resources in their children.

⁞• MAKING CONNECTIONS

- According to one of my students, "Spank while they're little so the law doesn't later." Do you agree or disagree with his philosophy? Or do you think that Congress should pass a law that bans spanking?

- The California legislator who wanted to ban spanking and other physical punishment of children backed off. Many people—including Republican legislators and editors of major newspapers—claimed that the law couldn't be enforced and would interfere with parental rights to discipline their children. Should we also get rid of child/partner/spouse abuse laws because they, too, interfere with private family matters and are difficult to enforce?

Is Spanking Effective or Harmful?

So far, 24 nations—including Austria, Croatia, Cyprus, Denmark, Germany, Hungary, Israel, Italy, Latvia, and the Scandinavian countries—have made it illegal for parents to spank their children. In contrast, a majority of Americans support spanking (see Data Digest).

A study that examined 14 nations of the European Union found that the countries that prohibit children's physical punishment have a much lower number of child maltreatment deaths than the countries that don't have such laws. Initially, many Swedes opposed anti-spanking laws, predicting that the children would run wild. Instead, among youth, crime rates, drug use, and suicide rates have decreased (Straus, 2007; Gracia and Herrero, 2008). Not spanking isn't the only reason for these lower rates because there are many reasons for a person's behavior, but anti-spanking laws haven't led to the problems that many Swedes feared.

In the United States, spanking advocates say that spanking is effective, prepares children for life's hardships, and prevents misbehavior. They contend that spanking is acceptable if it is age appropriate and used selectively to teach and correct behavior rather than as an expression of rage (Trumbull and Ravenel, 1999; Larzelere, 2000; Baumrind et al., 2002).

Some pediatricians believe that a "mild" spanking (one or two spanks on the buttocks) is acceptable when all other discipline fails, but that slapping a child's face is abusive. Others argue that spanking and all other types of physical punishment are unacceptable. They maintain that children who are spanked regularly, from as early as age 1, face a higher risk of developing low self-esteem, depression, alcoholism, and aggressive and violent behavior, and later, physically abusing their own partner and children (Straus and Yodanis, 1996; Whipple and Richey, 1997; Swinford et al., 2000).

Some researchers have offered a variety of reasons for not spanking or hitting children:

- **Physical punishment sends the message that it's okay to hurt someone you love or someone who is smaller and less powerful.** A parent who spanks often says, "I'm doing this because I love you." Thus, children learn that violence and love can go hand in hand and that hitting is an appropriate way to express one's feelings (Hunt, 1991).
- **No human being feels loving toward someone who hits her or him.** A strong relationship is based on kindness. Hitting produces only temporary and superficially good behavior based on fear (Marshall, 2002).
- **Physical punishment is often due to the parent's substance abuse rather a child's misbehavior.** Parents who abuse drugs are often ineffective caregivers because intoxication impairs their decision-making abilities. Parents who abuse drugs spend much of their money on alcohol and other drugs rather than on food, shelter, and other basic household needs. They are also likely to spend their time getting and using drugs instead of caring for their children (Straus, 2007, 2008).
- **Spanking can be physically damaging.** It can injure the spinal column and nerves and even cause paralysis. Some children have died after mild paddlings because of undiagnosed medical problems such as a weak lower spinal column that can't withstand a blow (American Academy of Pediatricians, 1998).
- **Physical punishment deprives the child of opportunities to learn effective problem solving.** Physical punishment teaches a child nothing about how to handle conflict or disagreements (Straus, 2001).

Stop and Think . . .

- When you were a child, did your parents spank you? If so, how did you feel?
- Some people maintain that spanking is synonymous with hitting. Do you agree?
- Should the United States ban spanking? Or would such laws interfere with parenting decisions?

CHILD CARE ARRANGEMENTS

The Reverend Jesse Jackson reportedly said, "Your children need your presence more than your presents." Many employed parents, especially fathers, spend little time with their children. Latchkey kids must fend for themselves after school until a parent comes home from work. In many other families, employed parents must rely on child care outside the family.

Absentee Fathers

Some people believe that one of the most serious problems facing contemporary families is that the United States is becoming an increasingly fatherless society: "Never before have so many children grown up without knowing what it means to have a father" (Blankenhorn, 1995: 1).

President Obama seems to agree. He was raised primarily by his grandparents after his father abandoned the family. On Father's Day in 2009, President Obama urged fathers to stay in their children's lives:

When fathers are absent, when they abandon their responsibility to their children, we know the damage that does to our families. I say this as someone who grew up without a father in my life. That's something that leaves a hole in a

Applying What You've Learned

Some Building Blocks of Effective Discipline

As you read these guidelines, think about what worked for you when you were growing up. If you're a parent, which of this advice do you think is most effective? And what would you add to this list?

- **Show your love.** You can express your love not only through a warm facial expression, a kind tone, and a hug but also by doing things with your children, such as working on a project together, letting them help with grocery shopping, and reading their favorite books. When children feel loved, they want to please their parents and are less likely to engage in undesirable behaviors.

- **Be consistent.** Predictable parents are just as important as routines and schedules. A child who is allowed to do something one day and not the next can become confused and start testing the rules.

- **Communicate clearly.** Ask children about their interests and feelings. Whenever possible, encourage them. Constant nagging, reminding, criticizing, threatening, lecturing, questioning, and demanding make a child feel dumb or inadequate.

- **Understand problem behavior.** Observe a problem behavior and look for a pattern that may explain why; for example, a child becomes unusually cranky when tired or hungry. Children may also have behavioral problems because their parents are experiencing a stressful event, such as losing a job or divorce.

- **Be positive and patient.** Sometimes children act up because they want attention. Patience and approval of good conduct encourage children to repeat the positive behavior.

- **Set up a safe environment.** Children are doers and explorers. Removing hazards shortens the list of "no's," and changing play locations relieves boredom and prevents destructive behavior.

- **Make realistic rules.** Set few rules, state them simply, and supervise closely. Don't expect more than your child can handle; for instance, don't expect a toddler to sit quietly during long religious services.

- **Defuse explosions.** Try to avert temper tantrums and highly charged confrontations (for example, distract feuding preschoolers by involving them in other activities).

- **Teach good problem-solving skills.** Children younger than 4 years old need very specific guidance in solving a problem and positive reinforcement for following suggestions.

- **Give children reasonable choices.** Don't force them to do things that even you wouldn't want to do (such as eating a vegetable they hate). Removing children from the play area when they misbehave, and giving them a choice of other activities, is often more effective than scolding or punishing.

Sources: Goddard, 1994; Rosemond, 2000.

---

child's heart that governments can't fill (Cooper, 2009: 10).

In 2010, over 17 million American children younger than age18 (23 percent of all children, and 48 percent of black children) were living only with mothers (U.S. Census Bureau, Current Population Survey, 2009). Father absence is due to many factors including the desertion of unwed mothers, incarceration, physical or mental disabilities, drug abuse, divorce, and not paying child support. Regardless of the reason, absentee fathers usually have a negative impact on their children from birth to young adulthood, particularly in increasing the likelihood of economic and social deprivation.

ECONOMIC DEPRIVATION Nearly 29 percent of families headed by single mothers live below the poverty line compared with 6 percent of two-parent families (DeNavas-Walt et al., 2009). Many single-mother families were poor even before the father left, but his departure reduces a child's economic resources even further. Economic problems, in turn, affect a mother's ability to move into a neighborhood that has good schools, pay for child care, and provide access to enriching after-school and summer programs.

SOCIAL DEPRIVATION Most single mothers—whether unmarried, separated, or divorced—experience parenting difficulties, especially if they're poor and/or must juggle demanding employment and domestic responsibilities. Compared with children raised in single-mother households, however, those raised in single-father homes are less well behaved at school, are less successful at getting along with others, and put forth less effort in class (Downey et al., 1998; Carlson, 2006).

Single mothers sometimes get financial and other support from "social fathers," male relatives and mothers' boyfriends who are like fathers to the children. Male relatives, especially, can enhance children's cognitive abilities by giving them books, reading to them, and spending time with them (Jayakody and Kalil, 2002). If social fathers leave or move away, however, the children lose access to such resources.

Latchkey Kids

Demographers sometimes refer to families in which both parents are employed full time as **DEWKs,** or dual-employed with kids. As the proportion of DEWK families has increased, so has the number of latchkey children.

There's nothing new about children being on their own at home. The phrase *latchkey children* originated in the early 1800s, when youngsters who were responsible for their own care wore the key to their home tied to a string around their necks. Today **latchkey kids** are children who return home after school and let themselves in to an empty house or apartment, where they are alone and unsupervised until their parents or another adult comes home.

Millions of latchkey kids return from school to an empty house, where they are alone two to four hours until an adult or other caretaker arrives. Most schools don't provide after-school care. In other cases, parents—especially single mothers—can't afford expensive after-school programs.

The number of latchkey kids has doubled since the 1970s. Almost 6 million children ages 5 to 14 (15 percent of children in this age group) care for themselves on a regular basis before or after school. On average, children spend six hours per week in self-care, typically until a parent returns from work (Overturf Johnson, 2005).

As you might expect, the older children are, the more likely they are to be latchkey kids. For example, 1 percent of children in self-care are 5 or 6 years old, compared with 39 percent of 14-year-olds. Employment rather than family structure influences self-care. That is, in both married-couple and single-mother homes, about 20 percent of elementary school children spend some time in self-care if the parents are employed (Overturf Johnson, 2005).

Most children enjoy being home alone, savoring the independence. They watch television, play, read, and do homework and some chores. Others are nervous about being by themselves, don't structure their time, don't do their homework, or invite friends over, against house rules. Some researchers believe that most 6- to 9-year-olds are not ready to care for themselves regularly, and certainly less able than older children to deal with household emergencies (Belle, 1999; Vandivere et al., 2003).

Who's Minding the Kids?

Few issues make working parents as anxious as choosing child care. Parents experience stress because they worry about their children's safety and the possibility of engaging in risky behavior when unsupervised (Barnett and Gareis, 2006). The greatest concern is for children younger than age 12 because they are least able to fend for themselves.

> **Since you asked . . .**
> • How do child care centers affect young children?

CHILD CARE PATTERNS AND CHARACTERISTICS

When mothers are employed, the majority of children younger than age 5 receive care from nonrelatives, especially at child care centers and in providers' homes, but fathers are an important source of care for young children (see *Figure 12.3*). They are more likely to provide care if they work evening and weekend shifts or if they are unemployed. Fathers in low-income families are also more likely to take care of their children than are fathers in middle-class families because child care costs constitute a large proportion of a poor family's budget—35 percent compared with 6 percent for middle-class families. The arrangements vary, however, depending on the availability of care, its costs, the hours of child care programs, and race and ethnicity (Capizzano et al., 2006).

Nationally, black parents are more likely than white and Latino parents to use child care centers, whereas Latino parents are more likely to depend on

FIGURE 12.3 Who's Watching the Kids?

Primary child care arrangements for children younger than 5 years old with employed mothers.

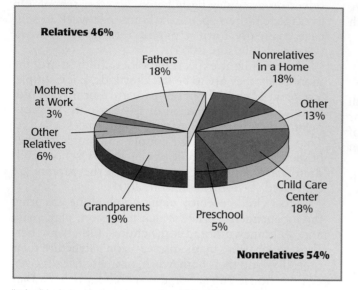

"Other" includes kindergartens and multiple child care arrangements.
Source: Based on Overturf Johnson, 2005, Table 3.

relatives. Latino parents are probably less likely to use child care centers because many are recent immigrants who do not speak English and aren't aware of child care facilities; little care is available nearby; they cannot afford the costs; or, in the case of undocumented immigrants, they aren't eligible for state programs that subsidize child care (Capps et al., 2005).

Higher-income families are more likely to use child care arrangements, including child care centers, than are lower-income families. Nationally, the average cost of a child care center for children younger than age 5 is about $10,000 a year (Urban Institute, 2008). The costs are higher for infants and for young children living in metropolitan areas. According to one of my students, for example, "I pay almost $9,000 a year for my 10-month-old son, and it isn't easy to also pay for my tuition and books." In 33 states and the District of Columbia, the annual cost of a child care center for a preschooler is more than the annual tuition at a community college or a four-year public university (Children's Defense Fund, 2008).

EFFECTS OF CHILD CARE ON CHILDREN AND PARENTS Day care is a controversial issue. Those with conservative perspectives, especially, are critical of employed mothers who place their children in child care. They maintain that working mothers are responsible for juvenile delinquency, children's poor performance in school, childhood obesity, and a host of other maladies, including playground accidents (Eberstadt, 2004).

Such accusations increase mothers' feelings of guilt, but are they valid? No. For example, children are considerably more likely to be abused by relatives than by day care workers; preschool children are almost twice as likely to be injured on playground equipment at home as in other locations (including child care centers); and the death rate among children receiving care in private homes is 16 times greater than the rate for children, especially infants, in child care centers (U.S. Consumer Product Safety Commission, 2001; Wrigley and Dreby, 2006).

A number of studies report that a well-run child care center has positive effects on children's social and cognitive development. In high-quality day care, even children from low-income families outscore more advantaged children on IQ tests by the time they enter kindergarten. The higher the quality of child care in the first three years of life—among children from both poor and middle-income families—the greater the child's language abilities and school readiness skills such as counting and knowing the alphabet (NICHD, 2003; Loeb et al., 2005).

A longitudinal study that followed preschoolers over four years concluded that the children who were cared for exclusively by homemakers did not develop differently than those who were also cared for by others. Even when children attended higher-quality centers, parent and family characteristics were two or three times more strongly linked to child development. For example, children did better when parents were more educated; when families' incomes were higher; when mothers had few or no symptoms of depression; when mothers were attentive and responsive and interacted frequently with the children; and when families had well-organized routines, books, and play materials and took part in learning activities, such as going to the library or attending a cultural festival (NICHD, 2006; see, also, Nomaguchi, 2006).

The day care centers with the best results are small and have high staff-to-child ratios (see the box "How

A high-quality child care center can enhance a child's language, social, and pre-academic skills, but parent and family characteristics are linked more strongly to child development.

? ↑

ASK YOURSELF

How Can I Evaluate the Quality of Child Care?

Following are some questions that will help you evaluate the child care programs or providers you visit. Be sure, also, to talk to parents who are using or have used the facility or a private home.

1. ***What is the staff-to-child ratio?*** The best programs have enough staff members to give children plenty of attention. Suggested staff-to-child ratios are 1 to 3 for infants, 1 to 10 for 5- and 6-year-olds, and 1 to 12 for children older than 6.

2. ***What is the staff turnover rate?*** If half the staff members leave every year, it probably means that they are paid extremely low wages or believe that the program is not run well.

3. ***How do the staff and children look?*** If the children seem unhappy, have runny noses, and seem passive, and if the staff members seem distant or lackadaisical, look elsewhere.

4. ***How well equipped is the facility?*** There should be interesting indoor activities that give children a choice

of projects, as well as ample playground space with swings, jungle gyms, and other exercise equipment. If there is no adjacent outdoor area, do the children go regularly to a park or playground? Is the facility clean and organized? Does it have a wide range of toys, books, materials, and activities?

5. ***What are the safety regulations and hygienic practices?*** Are children always accounted for when they arrive and leave? Are staff trained in first aid? What are the policies about children who take medications (for allergies, for example)?

6. ***Is the director of the center willing to have you talk to other parents who use the center?*** Better yet, does the center have video cameras so you can log on from work or home? The MyFamilyLab online provides Internet sites for a wealth of information about child care facilities.

Can I Evaluate the Quality of Child Care?"). Good child care providers often quit, however, because they earn among the lowest wages: about $21,000 a year, less than pet groomers who earn almost $22,000 a year, and rarely receive health insurance or retirement benefits. Consequently, 30 percent of day care workers leave their jobs within a year (Gable et al., 2007; Bureau of Labor Statistics, 2009).

Because of continuous state budget cuts, many low-income families aren't eligible for child care programs, must endure long waiting lists, and are subject to high co-payments that they can't afford. Even though it's the richest country in the world, the United States lags far behind other industrialized countries—such as Japan, France, Germany, and Sweden—where the government runs preschool and child care centers or pays up to 90 percent of child care costs (Forry and Walker, 2006; see, also, Chapter 13).

CURRENT SOCIAL ISSUES AND CHILDREN'S WELL-BEING

Government officials often proclaim that children are our most precious resources, tomorrow's leaders, and so on. Do public policies and parenting behavior contradict such noble sentiments? Let's look at the effects of electronic media on children, some of the risks that children face, and foster care.

The Impact of Electronic Media

The typical American child is saturated with electronic media (see Chapters 5 and 7). The American Academy of Pediatrics (2001) recommends that children younger than age 2 be kept away from all screen media to encourage creative play and interaction with parents.

Since you asked . . .

What limits, if any, should parents put on their children's use of electronic media?

Still, 68 percent of children younger than 2 view two to three hours of television daily—years before they even ask for TV. Some educators have criticized even the highly respected *Sesame Street* as "downright irresponsible" for recently producing a new DVD series targeted at children ages 6 months to 2 years. Electronic media for preschoolers can be educational, but parents often use them as nannies: "My two-year-old daughter will play a game for an hour or more at a time. I'm sure she's learning something" (Oldenburg, 2006: C1; see, also, Garrison and Christakis, 2005).

Because few television programs have educational content, some scholars believe that parents have an overly positive view of the impact of television on young children. Especially in homes in which the television is always on, even if no one is watching, parents of children younger than age 6 spend less time reading to children and these children have lower reading skills than those who have limited access to television, DVDs, videos, and other electronic media (Vandewater et al., 2005; Rideout and Hamel, 2006).

As you saw in Chapter 5, on average, seventh- to twelfth-graders spend almost seven hours a day with media compared with about two hours each with parents and friends, and less than one hour per day doing homework. Because of simultaneous activities (such as hanging out with parents and watching TV), children are actually exposed to about 8.5 hours of media content a day, more than the equivalent of a full-time job (Rideout et al., 2005).

How healthy is the ever-expanding presence of electronic media in children's everyday environment? Much depends on factors such as age, content, parental monitoring, and the frequency of an activity (see Bremer, 2005, for a review of some of this literature).

Generally, children and adolescents who watch television more than two hours a day do poorly in school because TV viewing displaces reading and homework. The presence of a bedroom television set, especially, increases viewing, which, in turn, decreases academic success. As early as the third grade, children with their own TV sets score lower in math and reading than do those without their own sets. However, computer access, especially when children use the Internet for homework, improves both reading and math scores (Borzekowski and Robinson, 2005; Hancox et al., 2005; Zimmerman and Christakis, 2005).

Other electronic media may also be harmful to adolescent development. For example, about 23 percent of children ages 10 to 14, especially African American boys, have watched at least one of 40 R-rated movies (such as *Blade, Hollow Man,* and *Scary Movie*) that have extreme examples of graphic violence (Worth et al., 2008).

More than 90 percent of American adolescents have Internet access, and about half use social networking sites such as MySpace or Facebook. Their profiles often include coarse language and photos of themselves and their friends drinking and having sex. Such profiles can make adolescents targets for online predators and decrease the teens' chances of getting into college or getting a job because university administrators and employment recruiters often access the sites. Moreover, the profiles make risky and appropriate language and behavior seem normal to younger teens (Moreno et al., 2009).

Some social scientists also wonder if video and online games can become addictive. About 92 percent of children younger than age 18 play these games regularly, but almost 9 percent of 18-year-olds might be "pathologically addicted" because, among other behavioral problems, they disobey parental limits; lose interest in sports and hobbies; choose gaming over time with family and friends; continue to play despite plummeting grades, loss of a college scholarship, or a breakup with a romantic partner;

Advergaming, which combines online games with advertising, is growing rapidly. These sites attract millions of young children and provide marketers with an inexpensive way to sell products that keep children at the computer rather than at physical activities, thereby leading to an increase in obesity.

and lose sleep, don't shower, and lose weight because they skip many meals (Martin and Oppenheimer, 2007; Wagner, 2008).

Electronic media also provide many benefits. Nationally, 25 percent of parents say that the Internet and cell phones have strengthened their family ties because of easy access to one another throughout the day and the sharing of Web experiences. Only 11 percent believe that the electronic media have weakened their family bonds, and the rest say that such technologies haven't made their family any more or less close than in the past (Kennedy et al., 2008).

Some researchers note that nearly 65 percent of teens are expressing their creativity and sharpening their writing skills by sharing artwork, photos, or videos; designing Web pages for themselves or organizations they support; and developing online blogs that include anything from descriptions and photos of their personal experiences to comments on topics such as music, movies, and politics (Donahue et al., 2008; "Teens, video games and civics," 2008). Thus, according to some researchers, the benefits of electronic media—especially the Internet—outweigh the costs.

Children at Risk

Life is improving for many American children. Compared with similar data from 2000, they are smoking and drinking alcohol less, graduating from high school in larger numbers, are less likely to die of firearm or motor vehicle injuries, and are less likely to be exposed to secondhand smoke at home (Federal Interagency Forum, 2009). So far, at least 13 states have passed laws against *cyber-bullying* (threats or humiliation spread on the Web, by cell phones, or other digital devices), and a larger number of school

In Beijing, the Chinese government defines youth (but not adult) Internet addiction as using the Web for six consecutive hours a day for three straight months. Internet addiction patients are required to stay at a treatment center for three months, isolated from the outside world, and without access to cell phones, computers, and other electronic media. The cost can total nearly $3,000—almost three months' salary for the average Chinese couple. Pictured here, young patients at an Internet addiction center follow a strict military routine (Jiang, 2009). There are no data, so far, on whether the patients change after "rehabilitation."

districts are becoming concerned about stopping bullying (Sampson, 2009; Surdin, 2009).

There's also some bad news. For example,

- On average, children ages 2 to 17 watch more than 18,000 food ads on television annually; 72 percent of the ads are for candy and snack foods, sugary cereal, and fast food (Gantz et al., 2007).

- The percentage of obese and overweight children ages 10 to 17 is at or above 30 percent in 30 states—a new record high (Trust for America's Health, 2009).

- More than 66 percent of children live in counties in which one or more air pollutants are above the allowable levels (Federal Interagency Forum, 2009).

- From 1960 to 2007, of the total federal budget, spending on children rose from just 1.9 percent to 2.6 percent, but nearly quadrupled—from 2 percent to almost 8 percent—for non-child portions of Social Security (a public retirement pension system for older people) and Medicare (a health insurance program for people age 65 and older) (Carasso et al., 2008).

- Among all industrialized countries, the United States has the highest child poverty rates (Children's Defense Fund, 2008).

If children are our most precious resource, we are squandering our assets (see the box "A Day in the Life of America's Children" on p. 348). Compared with other industrialized countries, and even some developing countries such as China, the United States is least effective in protecting its children against gun violence and has the highest child poverty rates. It is also the *only* industrialized nation in the world that does not provide guaranteed prenatal care for every pregnant woman (Children's Defense Fund, 2008).

Foster Care

The growth of poverty, child abuse, and parental neglect has increased children's out-of-home placements, including care by relatives, residential treatment facilities, group homes (which house a number of children), and shelters for runaways. The most common out-of-home placement is the **foster home,** in which parents raise children who are not their own.

In 2006, an estimated 510,000 children were in foster care at some point during the year. Of the 289,000 who exited foster care that year, 53 percent were reunited with a parent or primary caregiver; 17 percent were adopted; 16 percent went to live with a relative or guardian; and the remainder aged out of foster care at age 18, ran away, or died (Child Welfare Information Gateway, 2009).

One of most promising recent programs is releasing a child from foster care to the custody of a nonresident father, a biological father who did not live in the home from which the child was removed. Some of these fathers didn't even know that they had a child until they were contacted by the child welfare agency. In a study of four states (Arizona, Massachusetts, Minnesota, and Tennessee), 46 percent of the 1,071 fathers who had been contacted became actively involved in getting custody of a child. After reunification, the fathers had substantially lower rates of maltreatment allegations than did the mothers (Malm et al., 2008).

PROBLEMS OF FOSTER HOMES In theory, foster homes are supposed to provide short-term care until children can be adopted or returned to their biological parents. In reality, many children go through multiple placements and remain in foster care until late adolescence.

Approximately 25 to 30 percent of the children who are returned to their biological parents are soon back in foster care. Children who are older or have behavioral or emotional problems are most likely to bounce from home to home. If this happens, the foster care system may worsen children's already significant physical and mental health problems. Also, many experience fear, anger, and a sense of loss: They don't know what will happen in the future and miss seeing their family and relatives (Whiting and Lee, 2003).

Choices

A Day in the Life of America's Children

The Children's Defense Fund (2008) reports a grim existence for many American children. Every day, for example,

2	mothers die in childbirth
4	children are killed by abuse or neglect
5	children or teens commit suicide
8	children or teens are killed by firearms
78	babies die before their first birthday
201	children are arrested for a violent crime
404	children are arrested for a drug crime
1,154	babies are born to unmarried teen mothers
1,240	public school students are corporally punished
2,367	high school students drop out
2,583	babies are born into poverty
18,493	public school students are suspended

⠂• Stop and Think . . .

■ The United States ranks first in the world in defense and health expenditures, gross national product, and the number of billionaires. Why, then, are we first among 16 industrialized nations in the proportion of children living in poverty?

■ Do you think that many of our children's problems are due to macro-level variables (such as the economy and political system)? To micro-level parental variables (such as being irresponsible or uninvolved in their children's child rearing)? Or to other factors?

Foster children are especially disadvantaged in attaining a higher education. About 150,000 are qualified, but only 30,000 attend college. Of those in college, only 5 percent finish. The high dropout rate is due to a number of interrelated factors. For example, the youth don't have adults, especially parents or foster parents, who encourage them to succeed; they often lack the skills to function on their own (such as living independently) because they may have lived in as may as ten foster homes and have attended as many schools; and they may suffer from depression or anxiety because of the traumatic feelings of abandonment and living apart from their families (Wolanin, 2005).

BENEFITS OF FOSTER HOMES The obvious benefit of foster homes is that many children experience physical and emotional safety: "We had some parents that we could trust [and] they cared about me" or "You don't get beat, they teach you the right way to do stuff, they teach you not to lie, stuff like that" (Whiting and Lee, 2003: 292).

Many foster parents make sure that the kids get the medical and mental health services they need. Instead of being in a group home with many other kids who have severe behavioral problems, a child in a foster home usually lives with emotionally healthy adults (Wiltenburg, 2002).

For many, being a foster parent is a labor of love. For example, a woman, now 73, has raised nine children, adopted 11 others, and been a foster parent to 300. She lives in a modest one-story home in a black working-class neighborhood of Fort Lauderdale, Florida. She recalls, "The foster people would say: 'Mrs. Walker, they have got to move on, don't fall in love with the kids.' But I fell in love with all of them." Her oldest son, who owns a plastering business, and some of her other children help pay the bills, but the state assists by granting a monthly allowance—$297 per month per foster child (Goddard, 2008: 20).

CONCLUSION

As this chapter shows, there have been numerous *changes* in child-rearing practices in the past decade or so. Many fathers helping raise their children, but there are more at-risk children and a widespread need for high-quality day care.

Parents face many micro- and macro-level *constraints*. The most severe problems are generated by political and economic conditions. Even though the United States is one of the wealthiest countries in the world, the number of American children who live in poverty and who are deprived of basic health care and other services has increased since 1980.

Social class, race, ethnicity, and other factors shape parental *choices*. Gay and lesbian, minority, and working-class parents, for example, have to struggle to raise happy, healthy children. In the next chapter, we address the economic constraints and choices that many families confront.

SUMMARY

1. Infants play an active role in their own development. Parenting isn't innate, but a long-term, time-consuming task that must be learned through trial and error.

2. Among the major theories of child development and socialization are Mead's theory of the social self, Piaget's theory of cognitive development, and Erikson's psychosocial theory of development over the life course.

3. Many parents experience problems in raising children because they have unrealistic expectations and believe many common myths about child rearing.

4. Social scientists have identified four general parenting styles: authoritarian, permissive, authoritative, and uninvolved. These styles often vary across racial and ethnic groups and social classes.

5. Most parents maintain that physical punishment is necessary, but many scientists argue that there are more effective disciplinary methods than spanking, slapping, or verbal putdowns.

6. Parenting stretches across the life course. Largely for economic reasons, adult children are staying in their parents' home longer and often returning after living independently, sometimes with their own children.

7. In general, gay and lesbian parenting is similar to heterosexual parenting. For example, all parents must make a living and develop effective problem-solving strategies.

8. Parents are usually the most important people in their children's lives. Parenting can be stressful, however, if the father is not involved in a constructive way; if very young children are latchkey kids; and if child care is expensive, of low quality, or otherwise inaccessible.

9. Contemporary issues about children's well-being include the positive and negative impacts of electronic media, bullying and cyber-bullying, and high child poverty rates.

10. One response to at-risk families is to place children in foster homes. Many foster homes are beneficial, but some create more problems than they solve.

KEY TERMS

role conflict 320	parenting style 337	DEWK 343
role strain 320	authoritarian style 338	latchkey kids 343
generalized other 323	permissive style 338	foster home 347
socioeconomic status (SES) 326	authoritative style 338	
role overload 333	uninvolved style 338	

PEARSON
myfamilylab MyFamilyLab provides a wealth of resources. Go to www.myfamilylab.com<http://www.myfamilylab .com/>, to enhance your comprehension of the content in this chapter. You can take practice exams, view videos relevant to the subject matter, listen to audio files, explore topics further by using Social Explorer, and use the tools contained in MySearch-Lab to help you write research papers.

13 Balancing Work and Family Life

Mark Cooper was the security manager for a *Fortune* 500 company in Tempe, Arizona, overseeing a budget of $1.2 million and earning almost $70,000 a year. When the economy began to crash in mid-2008, he lost his job and now makes $12 an hour cleaning an office building for a friend's janitorial services company. His wife was initially embarrassed by his downward mobility, but now she says that she is proud of her husband for doing whatever it takes, including mopping floors and cleaning urinals, to keep their family afloat. Cooper is grateful for the job but says that he fights despair, discouragement, and depression every day (Luo, 2009).

This example illustrates the close linkage between an individual's personal life and the **economy**, the social institution that determines how a society produces, distributes, and consumes goods and services. You'll see in this chapter that economic issues are critical to a family's well-being and that social policies often hurt rather than help families. Let's begin with a brief look at why work is so important in our lives.

DATA DIGEST

- In 2009, **the median income for all U.S. households was $50,221:** $68,780 for Asian Americans, $53,131 for whites, $39,923 for Latinos, and $33,463 for African Americans.

- In 2008, and before the economic crisis peaked, **79 percent of U.S. adults said that they were worse off than five years ago;** 65 percent felt this way in 1986.

- In 2007, **60 percent of mothers of children younger than age 3 were employed,** down from 62 percent in 1998 but up from 34 percent in 1975.

- In early 2009, **59 percent of Americans opposed the government's giving financial aid to automakers, banks, and financial companies in danger of failing;** 33 percent thought the same way about helping homeowners who were in danger of losing their homes to foreclosures.

- **The United States is the only one of 22 industrialized countries that doesn't provide paid sick leave** for a worker undergoing a 50-day cancer treatment.

- Among 21 of the world's richest nations, **the government requires employers to pay full-time workers an annual leave** of 30 days in France, 22 to 25 days in eight countries, 20 days in nine countries, 10 days in two countries, and none in one country—the United States.

Sources: Ray and Schmitt, 2007; Taylor et al., 2008; U.S. Department of Labor, 2008; DeNavas-Walt et al., 2009; Heymann et al., 2009; Newport, 2009; U.S. Census Bureau, 2009 (1-Year Estimates).

THE SIGNIFICANCE OF WORK

Work is physical or mental activity that accomplishes or produces something, either goods or services. For most of us, money is a major motivator for working, but work provides other benefits as well. Generally, employment leads to better health and a sense of accomplishment and usefulness and is a major source of social identity. In addition, work provides a sense of stability and order and a daily rhythm over the life course that we don't get from many other activities (Mirowsky and Ross, 2007). Thus, work is socially as well as economically significant.

During the recent economic downturn, most Americans have been especially concerned about surviving financially. When a national poll asked Americans what they wanted President Obama to speak about in his first address to Congress in February 2009, 74 percent said economic problems such as jobs, job creation, and unemployment. A year earlier, only 47 percent were concerned about their financial well-being ("Dents in the dream," 2008; Saad, 2009).

Many people, like Mark Cooper, were demoralized because their income had plummeted, but Cooper's family is more fortunate than millions of others who can no longer pay their mortgages, struggle to pay monthly bills, and are jobless or homeless. What's especially striking is how much the economy and work have changed family lives since the last edition of this textbook.

WORK IN THE CONTEMPORARY UNITED STATES

After 30 years at a factory in Ohio that made truck parts, Jeffrey Evans was earning more than $60,000 a year. When the plant shut down in 2008, Evans could find only sporadic construction work. He restarted at the bottom as a union pipe-fitting apprentice and makes about $20,000 a year. "I lost everything I worked for all my life," he says (Eckholm, 2008: 14).

Deindustrialization, Globalization, and Offshoring

Evans isn't alone in feeling that he's losing everything that he's worked for all his life. There are many reasons for millions of Americans' recent downward slide; even those who live modestly are losing economic ground because of macro-level variables such as deindustrialization, globalization, and offshoring.

DEINDUSTRIALIZATION Evans, like many others, is a casualty of **deindustrialization,** a process of social and economic change resulting from the reduction of industrial activity, especially manufacturing.

This worker, 49, moved in with his mother, 73, after losing his job at an automotive factory. He, like millions of other Americans, is a casualty of deindustrialization and globalization.

Between 2000 and 2006 alone, 20 percent of U.S. manufacturing jobs disappeared (Helper, 2008). One of the reasons for this decline is that many companies upgraded their production methods and relied more on robots or computerization than on human labor.

Beginning in the early 1960s, employers easily replaced workers with the lowest skill levels, usually those on assembly lines, with automation (Lee and Mather, 2008). Unlike humans, a robot doesn't need health care benefits or pensions; works several shifts; doesn't complain about the boredom of performing the same task (such as spray painting a car or loading equipment); and can be programmed to perform several tasks, including welding and inspecting machine parts.

GLOBALIZATION Deindustrialization accelerated as a result of **globalization,** the growth and spread of investment, trade, production, communication, and new technology around the world. One example of globalization is a motor vehicle that is assembled in the United States with practically all of its parts manufactured and produced in Germany, Japan, South Korea, or developing countries.

OFFSHORING Whether political and economic analysts support or oppose globalization, most agree that technological changes have hastened deindustrialization because of **offshoring,** the sending of work or jobs to another country to cut a company's costs at home. Sometimes called *international outsourcing* or *offshore outsourcing,* the transfer of manufacturing jobs overseas has been going on since at least the 1970s.

Most of the offshored jobs go to India and China, but many have also moved to Canada, Hungary, the

Philippines, Poland, Russia, Egypt, Venezuela, Vietnam, and South Africa. Initially, most of the offshored jobs were blue-collar manufacturing jobs. Increasingly, however, U.S. firms have offshored high-level, well-paid information technology (IT) jobs, including jobs in accounting, computer science, and engineering. A typical accountant in India, for example, earns about $5,000 a year compared with one in the United States who earns about $63,000 a year. These large wage differentials make it very attractive for companies to lower costs by replacing U.S. employees with lower-cost overseas workers (Hira, 2008).

Some economists maintain that offshoring has few negative effects on American workers because the jobs that are lost are those with the lowest skill levels, offshoring saves taxpayers money, and American consumers benefit by buying produces and services at low prices (Liu and Trefler, 2008). Others contend that there's something wrong with a government that uses taxpayers' money to create jobs offshore—especially when experienced programmers and analysts are being forced out of the field—and that offshoring increases risks of identity theft and privacy violations (Bivens, 2006; Whoriskey, 2008).

Social Class, Wealth, and Income

Conventional wisdom says that money can't buy happiness, but as the late American entertainer Sophie Tucker once observed, "I've been rich and I've been poor—and believe me, rich is better."

Americans are more productive than ever, but who gets the largest returns from their labor? Much depends on one's *social class,* a group of people who have a similar standing or rank based on wealth, education, power, prestige, and other valued resources (see Chapter 1). **Wealth** is the money and economic assets that a person or family owns. It includes property (such as real estate), stocks and bonds, retirement and savings accounts, personal possessions (such as cars and jewelry), and income. **Income** is the amount of money a person receives, usually through wages or salaries, but it can also include rents, interest on savings accounts, dividends on stocks, or the proceeds from a business.

It is difficult to quantify social class, but income provides an idea of how many households are in upper, middle, and lower levels (see *Figure 13.1*). The methods used to measure social class vary, but most researchers agree on two points. One is that income inequality among the classes is greater in the United States than in any other Western industrialized nation. The other is that, generally, the rich are getting richer, the middle class is struggling, and the poor have gotten poorer.

THE RICH ARE GETTING RICHER U.S. wealth and income inequality is staggering. From 1979 to 2006, the richest 1 percent of U.S. households more than

FIGURE 13.1 Is the Number of Middle Class Families Shrinking?

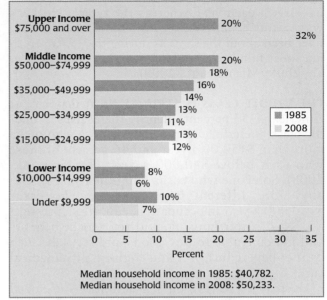

Median household income in 1985: $40,782.
Median household income in 2008: $50,233.

Source: Based on DeNavas-Walt et al., 2009, Table A-1.

doubled their share of the country's total income, rising from about 10 percent to nearly 23 percent and they now own 34 percent of all wealth; the bottom 40 percent has only 0.2 percent of all wealth and 10 percent of all income. More employed Americans own stocks because of retirement plans, such as a 401(K), but overall, fewer than half own any stock at all. The richest 20 percent own 90 percent of all stock wealth (Wolff, 2007; Mishel et al., 2009).

In 2008, there were 1,125 billionaires worldwide: 40 percent were Americans and owned 28 percent of the global income. Of the 469 richest Americans, 77 were new billionaires. Thus, even multimillionaires are now far behind the super rich. Because the median U.S. household income in 2008 was $50,303, it's difficult for most of us to imagine having an annual income of a million, much less a billion dollars ("Billionaires 2008," 2008; DeNavas-Walt et al., 2009).

When the stock market declined during 2000 and 2001, wealthy families didn't notice much difference. When the stock market started plunging in 2008, some of the rich complained about having to cut back on plastic surgery, jets, maids, tipping, and jewels. For example, when the CEO of General Motors was asked, in late 2008, if he'd take a cut in his $2.2 million salary as the company was laying off thousands of automotive workers, he said, "I do have a son in college I have to pay for somehow" (Gilson, 2009: 26).

In 2007, CEOs in the United States averaged almost $11 million a year, 344 times the take-home pay of the typical American worker. Thirty years ago, CEOs averaged "only" 30 to 40 times the typical worker's paycheck. The top 50 investment fund managers earn about $588 million each per year, more than 19,000 times as much as the average worker earns. The wealth and income of the wealthy have risen each year, whereas the typical worker's wages and benefits, after adjusting for inflation, have been about the same as during the 1970s, eroding most families' standard of living (Anderson et al., 2008; Mishel et al., 2009).

THE MIDDLE CLASS IS STRUGGLING A majority of Americans (53 percent) identify themselves as middle class, including 33 percent of those who make more than $150,00 a year and 46 percent of those who earn below $40,000 a year (Taylor et al., 2008). Someone who earns $40,000 a year is usually quite different from someone who earns $150,000 a year in occupation, education, prestige, access to better housing, and retirement benefits and in being able to buy goods and services (such as a college education and high-quality medical care).

Instead of relying on self-definitions of social class, the Pew Research Center has defined middle class as households in which the annual income fell within 75 percent and 150 percent of the median annual income—$45,000 to $90,000 in 2006. Using this measure, the researchers concluded that the middle class has been experiencing a "squeeze" (Taylor et al., 2008). For example,

- Since 1999, real median annual household income ("real" referring to income adjusted for inflation) has shown a downturn.

- Since 1983, the middle class has made income gains, but it has fallen further behind upper-income families than ever before.

- As expenses have risen, middle-income Americans have gotten deeper into debt.

In mid-2008, the stock market and housing values started to collapse simultaneously. The declines hit middle- and lower-income families the hardest because half of the assets of these groups were tied to their homes compared with 20 percent of the assets of wealthy families. By mid-2009, as house values continued to fall, 22 percent of homeowners held mortgages that were higher than the market value of their homes (Bucks et al., 2009; Trumbull, 2009).

In late 2007, 77 percent of households had mortgage, credit card, or other debt, with a median amount of $67,000. About 27 percent of middle-income household were in debt compared with less than 2 percent of those at the top 1 percent of households (Bucks et al., 2009; Mishel et al., 2009).

Many personal finance advisors blame Americans for being spendthrifts rather than savers (see, for example, Orman, 2008). Such criticism, although warranted in some cases, overlooks demographic and other structural variables that affect families' financial lives. For example, most middle class families—especially among African Americans and Latinos—depend on wages and salaries rather than wealth that has been inherited, accumulated over time, and passed on to the next generation. And, when there's a severe economic downturn, middle class people may need to withdraw funds from their retirement

FIGURE 13.2 Who's Worried about Paying Their Bills, by Education and Annual Income, 2008
Percentage of American adults who said that they worried about keeping up with monthly payments

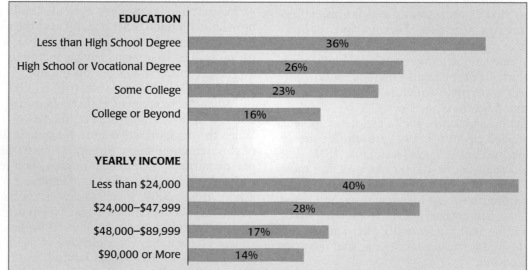

Source: Based on Gallup data in Mendes and Pelham, 2009: 2.

accounts to pay for everyday expenses. The withdrawals deplete savings, decrease retirement security, and carry tax and other penalties that may be as high as one-third of the money withdrawn (Block and Petrecca, 2009).

THE WORKING CLASS IS BARELY SURVIVING
Whereas many middle class households are managing to stay afloat, numerous working-class families are clinging to a sinking ship. Between February and December, 2008, the number of Americans who were worried about keeping up with their monthly payments rose from 21 percent to 30 percent. Latinos (30 percent) were more concerned than blacks (29 percent) and whites (22 percent) (Mendes and Pelham, 2009). As *Figure 13.2* shows, those with the lowest incomes

and educational levels—many of whom can be described as working class—were the most anxious. This isn't surprising, but note that 28 percent of those with a yearly income between $24,000 and almost $48,000 worried about keeping up with monthly bills.

A slowing economy affects all families, but why are working class households, especially, struggling more than their parents and grandparents? And why is income inequality rising in the United States, especially between the top 10 percent of workers and everybody else? The box "Some Reasons for the Rising Income Inequality in America" summarizes some of the most common explanations.

We've examined some macroeconomic changes that affect American families. How do families cope with these changes on a daily basis?

Some Reasons for the Rising Income Inequality in America

Some social scientists describe the U.S. economy, especially since the late 1980s, as a U-shaped curve. That is, earnings and job growth have increased in occupations that require either high skills and educational levels (such as attorneys and doctors) or those at low skill and education levels (such as bartenders and retail sales workers)—the two vertical sides of the "U"—rather than middle-income occupations (such as librarians and accountants)—the narrow bottom of the "U." There are many interrelated reasons for the rising income inequality. For example,

- Many jobs, first in manufacturing and then in white-collar occupations, have been offshored to countries that pay low wages and offer goods and services at the lower prices that American consumers seek.
- Minimum wages have been too low to lift many families out of poverty.
- Unemployment and the number of low-wage jobs have increased.
- The top 10 percent of income groups have enjoyed gains in wages and salaries; the wages and salaries of

the remaining 90 percent have not kept up with inflation.

- As income inequality has increased, people's ability to move up the social class hierarchy has stalled, especially since the mid-1970s. For example, 60 percent of families that start at the bottom 20 percent of income groups and 52 percent of those in the top 20 percent of income groups tend to stay there.
- About 38 percent of government employees are unionized, but the number of other unionized workers has been decreasing steadily—from a high of 27 percent in 1953 to 12 percent in 2007. The decline of membership in labor unions has eroded the wages and health benefits of millions of earners, especially blue-collar workers.
- The growth of imports produced by unskilled laborers in other countries has decreased the need for similar labor in the United States.
- Between 1989 and 2007, the average CEO's pay rose 167 percent compared with 10 percent for a typical worker.

Because CEO compensation is determined by peers who serve on corporate boards rather than the market or the government, inflated CEO compensation increases the gap between the wealthy and other income groups.

Sources: Eisenbrey et al., 2007; Gordon and Dew-Becker, 2008; Autor and Dorn, 2009; Mishel et al, 2009.

⁞• Stop and Think . . .

- If the U.S. economy is a U-shaped curve, why do a large majority of Americans describe themselves as middle class?
- Some social analysts contend that many Americans are in financial trouble because, over the past decades, we've shifted from a "culture of thrift" to a "culture of debt" (Brooks, 2008: 19). Others argue that our economic crisis is due, largely, to **corporate welfare**, an array of direct subsidies, tax breaks, and other favorable treatment that the government bestows on corporations (Slivinski, 2007). With which position do you agree? Why?

Constraints

ROAD CLOSED

HOW THE ECONOMY AFFECTS FAMILIES

Across the country, many families are struggling to survive. They have adopted a variety of techniques, including taking low-paying jobs and working nonstandard hours and part time. If these strategies fail, they find themselves among the unemployed, which, in turn, may lead to poverty and homelessness.

Low-Wage Jobs and Nonstandard Work Hours

One writer described the United States as "a nation of hamburger flippers" because of the explosion of low-wage jobs in recent decades (Levine, 1994: E1). Others work nonstandard hours to meet employers' increasing demands to provide services late into the night, around the clock, and on weekends.

LOW-WAGE JOBS The federal minimum wage, which rose from $6.55 to $7.25 an hour in 2009, increased the wages of less than 4 percent of the workforce. When adjusted for inflation, the new federal minimum was about 18 percent lower than the minimum wage between 1961 and 1981, and lower than the minimum wage required by 13 states and the District of Columbia. A person who works full-time at the minimum wage earns $14,500 a year, which is slightly below the 2009 federal poverty level of $14,570 for a family of two (Filion, 2009; Orr, 2009).

According to the Labor Department, five of the ten occupations expected to add the most jobs through 2016 are low paying, up to a maximum of about $22,000 a year. They include retail sales and home health aide jobs. Another three of the ten low-paying jobs, from about $22,000 to $31,000, include customer-service representatives, general office clerks, and nurses' aides ("Where the jobs are," 2009).

Almost 26 percent of all workers now fall into the category of the **working poor,** people who spend at least 27 weeks a year in the labor force (working or looking for work) but whose family or personal incomes fall below the official poverty level ("A profile of the working poor . . .," 2009).

Although many people think that the working poor are simply looking for government handouts, this is not the case. In fact, among almost half of low-income families, 72 percent of the adults are employed, and one parent works full time and year-round (Roberts and Povich, 2008).

Almost half of these full-time workers have no health insurance, some because small-business owners can't afford both wages and health benefits. When employers decrease health coverage to maintain

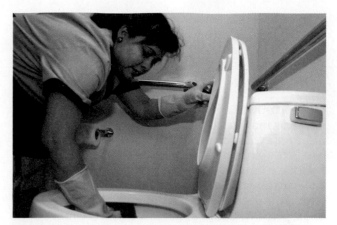

Housekeepers (who on average earn less than $19,000 a year full time) at many of the nation's fanciest hotels are experiencing more arm, shoulder, and lower-back injuries. They now typically lift king-size mattresses (which weigh 115 pounds) up to 200 times a day, must bend to scrub dozens of large tubs and Jacuzzis every day, and have greater workloads because each room requires more tasks, such as changing more pillowcases, cleaning hair dryers, and washing coffeepots.

higher profit margins, many workers simply can't afford the cost of the insurance offered by employers or private companies ("Employee compensation," 2006; Golden et al., 2006).

Low-wage earners suffer other work-related problems. A recent Government Accountability Office (GAO) study found that millions of low-income workers are subject to "wage theft" because the Labor Department's Wage and Hour Division doesn't enforce minimum wage, overtime, and child labor laws and mishandles nine out of ten complaints. In one case, the division failed to investigate a complaint that underage children were working during school hours at a California meatpacking plant with dangerous machinery. In another case, a restaurant in Indiana owed 438 employees $230,000 because the managers didn't pay for overtime or stole tips (Kutz and Meyer, 2009).

NONSTANDARD WORK HOURS In many countries, workers are needed almost around the clock because business is being conducted somewhere almost every hour of the day, including weekends. In the United States, two in five people work weekends, evenings, or nights (Dohm and Shniper, 2007).

Since you asked . . .

❖ How do parents' nonstandard work hours affect children?

These nonstandard work hours (often called *shift work*) are most common among men, African Americans, people in service occupations (such as restaurants), and those who work in hospitality industries, especially in hotels and motels (see *Figure 13.3*). People

FIGURE 13.3 Who Works Nonstandard Hours?

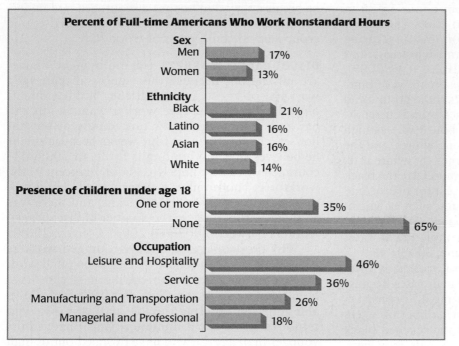

Percent of Full-time Americans Who Work Nonstandard Hours

Sex
Men — 17%
Women — 13%

Ethnicity
Black — 21%
Latino — 16%
Asian — 16%
White — 14%

Presence of children under age 18
One or more — 35%
None — 65%

Occupation
Leisure and Hospitality — 46%
Service — 36%
Manufacturing and Transportation — 26%
Managerial and Professional — 18%

Source: Based on McMenamin, 2007.

variables such as social class, the children's ages, how well the parents get along, and the quality of care provided by adults other than parents. For example, parents with nonstandard work hours experience more problems than those with daytime schedules when the children are younger than age 14, when stress increases marital conflict, and when the jobs are low paying. Shift-work parents of adolescents are generally just as likely as those with day schedules to spend as much time with their children and to know about their activities, probably because adolescents become more independent and parents have learned to cope with the challenges of shift work (Davis et al., 2006; Joshi and Bogen, 2007; Perry-Jenkins et al., 2007; Davis et al., 2008).

who work late at night, during the early morning hours, and on weekends tend to have low education levels (McMenamin, 2007). In effect, then, many who work nonstandard hours do so because they have few other choices for making a living.

Most reasons for shift work reflect the nature of the job. For example, police, firefighters, nurses, truck drivers, and hotel workers are needed around the clock. Others work nonstandard hours because of personal preference (12 percent); because child care by a spouse, partner, or relative is available only during those hours (16 percent); because the worker couldn't get a better job (8 percent); or because the job offered better pay (7 percent) (McMenamin, 2007).

The demand for nonstandard work hours is expected to increase in the future. The 30 occupations with the largest job growth until 2016 include those outside daytime schedules, such as cashiers, truck drivers, registered nurses, nursing aides and orderlies, security guards, janitors, and people who clean office buildings and hotels (Saenz, 2008).

How does shift work affect families? Atypical work schedules can create problems because one or both parents spend less time with their children (especially on weekends and evenings), provide less supervision and help with homework, and are less likely to attend school activities. Some of the negative effects include children's developing fewer language skills, doing poorly in school (and being suspended), and being more depressed (Presser et al., 2008).

Not all of the consequences of nonstandard work schedules are negative because much depends on

Part-Time Work

The average number of hours (33) that Americans worked in 2009 was the lowest level since 1964. Of the almost 28 million part timers (those who work less than 35 hours a week), 68 percent were voluntary because they didn't want to work more hours, but 32 percent were involuntary because they couldn't find suitable full-time employment or employers had reduced their hours because of a slowdown in business (Bureau of Labor Statistics, 2009; Eisenbrey, 2009).

The percentage of part-time employees, voluntary or not, is likely to increase because employers can save on health care costs or other benefits. According to an internal memo sent to Wal-Mart's board of directors, for example, the vice president for health benefits recommended reining in costs by hiring more part-time workers and not hiring unhealthy people (Greenhouse and Barbaro, 2005).

Unemployment

The U.S. unemployment rate surged from less than 5 percent in 2007 to more than 10 percent in mid-2009. According to economist Heidi Shierholz (2009), the entire growth in jobs since 2001 has been wiped out, unemployed workers have been jobless for longer periods, and a quick recovery is unlikely because the economy has fewer jobs that it did in 2001.

The job losses have been so severe that the Bureau of Labor Statistics is now reporting *mass layoffs* that occur when at least 50 claims for unemployment insurance are filed by former employees of a single establishment during a five-week period. By this standard, mass layoffs increased from about 1,480 in early 2008 to almost 2,800 in mid-2009. The largest mass layoffs were in construction, manufacturing (especially the auto industry), and wholesale and retail trade (Bureau of Labor Statistics News, 2009).

Unemployment causes widespread economic hardship for all families, but it hits some groups and sectors harder than others. Historically and currently, unemployment rates have been about twice as high among African Americans as among whites, and the Latino rate tends to about 1.5 times the white rate. Some economists predict that by mid-2010, the black unemployment rate will be 16 percent for blacks (and as high as 25 percent in some states, such as Michigan), 13 percent for Latinos, and 9 percent for whites, all higher than the current unemployment rates (Austin, 2009; see, also, Cawthorne, 2009).

African Americans and Latinos, especially men, bear disproportionate unemployment rates because they have worked in manufacturing and construction—which have had the highest number of recent layoffs. Now, however, layoffs have reached black professionals, managers, and government workers, including many who overcame discrimination and limited economic and educational opportunities to get quality jobs. State governments, typically a reliable source of employment for educated African Americans, have been laying off thousands of teachers and administrators. And, with the loss of thousands of jobs in the auto and real estate industries, many mid-level black managers find themselves unemployed (White and Lifsher, 2009).

> **Since you asked . . .**
>
> ❖ How accurate are official unemployment statistics?

In good times and in bad, African American men have the highest unemployment rates. In tough times, as during 2008–2009, their jobless rates rise higher and faster. And, compared with their white counterparts, black workers will be unemployed long after their unemployment insurance benefits end. Pictured here, laid-off workers examine listings at a job fair.

Unemployment figures are lower than they might be because they don't count discouraged and underemployed workers. Families in all racial-ethnic groups include both types of workers.

DISCOURAGED WORKERS Unemployment figures are misleading because they ignore **discouraged workers,** or those some call the "hidden unemployed." The discouraged worker wants a job and has looked for work in the preceding year but has not searched in the past four weeks because she or he believes that job hunting is futile. In 2009, discouraged workers comprised about 1 percent of the workforce. This number may seem small, but it represents at least 725,000 Americans, and there was a 70 percent increase in the number of discouraged workers between 2008 and 2009 (Cohany, 2009).

Why do people give up? Discouraged workers include retirees who believe that they can't find work because of age discrimination, mothers who have been taking care of their kids but can't find a suitable job after entering the job market, those who refuse to work for a minimum wage, and adults younger than age 25 who have dropped out of high school and don't have the necessary schooling or job experience that many employers seek (Davey and Leonhardt, 2003; Cohany, 2009).

Most discouraged workers who stop looking for jobs survive financially because they rely on the earnings of their spouses, rent out rooms in their homes, get groceries from local charitable institutions, sell off their property and receive some public assistance, and perform odd jobs such as mowing lawns and baby-sitting. Others, particularly males, may turn to illegal ways of making a living that include selling drugs (Hagan, 2008).

UNDEREMPLOYED WORKERS Unemployment rates are also misleading because they ignore **underemployed workers,** people who have part-time jobs but want full-time work or whose jobs are below their experience, skill, and education levels. The federal government doesn't track underemployment (see Haugen, 2009), but some analysts estimate that about 20 percent of Americans are underemployed, and the numbers will probably rise (Ehrenreich, 2009).

Women, particularly those with young children, are more likely than men to experience underemployment because of problems in finding and affording good child care services. Another large group of underemployed workers are professionals (engineers, physicists, and chemists)—especially men in their 50s—who are laid off when corporations want to increase their profits. Companies can hire two young college graduates for the price of one senior-level employee, and they often do so.

SOME EFFECTS OF UNEMPLOYMENT Regardless of social class, unemployment is typically overwhelming.

It can trigger a vicious "chain of adversity" that includes financial strain, depression, loss of self-confidence, decreased emotional functioning, and poorer physical health because people lose health coverage (Price et al., 2002).

Especially since 2008, many families—including those in the working and middle classes—have experienced everything from anxiety to drastic changes in lifestyles because of unemployment. For example,

- Low-wage earners are about one-third as likely as those earning more to collect unemployment benefits because they are unable to prove that their employers fired them because of layoffs. Employers can block insurance payments when they claim that workers were laid off because of poor performance or that they quit (Hagenbaugh, 2009; Whoriskey, 2009).

- Rising job losses have increased consumers' bankruptcy filings, which, in turn, ruin a person's credit rating and ability to borrow money in the future to buy a house or get an auto loan (Dugas, 2009).

- Middle class families—who could previously afford attorney services—are now turning to publicly funded legal aid groups for the poor to deal with problems such as divorce, custody, driving offenses, debt, and home foreclosures (Williams, 2009).

- Middle class families that collect up to $1,800 in monthly unemployment benefits often don't qualify for federal or state food stamps (Hennessy-Fiske, 2009).

- Millions of Americans have stopped taking prescription drugs for heart disease, diabetes, and high cholesterol because they need the money for groceries and housing. Others take their pills every other day, split them, drop the medical insurance they have, or skip doctors' appointments, all of which can cause major medical problems (Saul, 2009; Szabo and Appleby, 2009).

Moreover, the downward shift in the economy has had a "trickle-down" negative effect that has altered millions of Americans' lives. For example, when people in the banking and mortgage industries lost their jobs, so did secretaries and other office staff, attorneys, and people who clean offices. And, when unemployment increases, men are less likely to marry because they believe that they can't support a wife and family. Forming fewer new households means less demand for housing, a new car, or furniture and less work for electricians, carpenters, and real estate agents (Lopez, 2009; Shin, 2009). The most severe consequence of unemployment is poverty.

Poverty

In one national survey, 21 percent of respondents with annual household incomes of less than $20,000 described themselves as "haves," whereas 6 percent of those making more than $75,000 a year saw themselves as "have-nots" (Parmelee, 2002). How is it that the latter describe themselves as poor whereas people with an income of less than $20,000 a year do not? (Before reading any further, take the quiz "How Much Do You Know about Poverty?" on p. 360.)

There are two ways to define poverty: absolute and relative. **Absolute poverty** is not having enough money to afford the most basic necessities of life, such as food, clothing, and shelter ("what I need"). **Relative poverty** is not having enough money to maintain an average standard of living ("what I want"). People who experience relative poverty may feel poor compared with a majority of others in society, but they have the basic necessities to survive.

THE POVERTY LINE The **poverty line** is the minimum level of income that the government considers necessary for basic subsistence. To determine the poverty line, the Department of Agriculture (DOA) estimates the annual cost of food that meets minimum nutritional guidelines and then multiplies this figure by three to cover the minimum costs of clothing, housing, and other necessities. Anyone whose income is below this line is considered officially poor and is eligible for government assistance (such as food stamps and health care).

Since you asked . . .

- Is the poverty line too high or too low?

The poverty line, which in 2008 was $21,834 for a family of four (two adults and two children), is adjusted every year to reflect cost of living increases. If a family makes a dollar more than the poverty line figure, it is not officially categorized as poor and cannot receive any public assistance. Many people earn considerably less than the poverty threshold. In 2008, for example, 43 percent of poor families—a group that the Census Bureau refers to as "severely poor"—earned less than half of the poverty threshold (DeNavas-Walt et al., 2009).

Some believe that the official definition of poverty is inflated. They argue, for example, that poverty levels—which were developed in the mid-1960s—do not include the value of noncash benefits such as food stamps, tax credits, medical services (such as Medicare and Medicaid), and public housing subsidies that some Americans now receive (Eberstadt, 2009).

Others claim that the poverty line is unrealistically low because it ignores many current needs of poor people. For example, single mothers require affordable child care so that they can work and pay for transportation costs to child care centers and jobs. These critics also contend that a poor person who lives in a metropolitan area or in a state such as California or Massachusetts needs more money to survive—often three to four times more than someone who lives in the rural South—primarily because

ASK YOURSELF

How Much Do You Know about Poverty?

True False

☐ ☐ **1.** The number of Americans living in poverty has decreased since 2000.

☐ ☐ **2.** Most Americans could get out of poverty if they worked.

☐ ☐ **3.** Most poor people in the United States are white.

☐ ☐ **4.** According to the federal government, a family of four is poor if it earns less than $25,000 a year.

☐ ☐ **5.** The majority of poor children in the United States are African American.

True False

☐ ☐ **6.** The U.S. child poverty rate is higher than in most of the world's industrialized countries.

☐ ☐ **7.** Single fathers are as likely as single mothers to be poor.

☐ ☐ **8.** The poverty rate of people age 65 and older is lower than that of any other age group.

☐ ☐ **9.** Most poor people live in inner cities.

☐ ☐ **10.** Single men and veterans have been the fastest-growing groups of homeless people.

The answers to this quiz are below.

---

of higher housing costs. According to New York City's mayor, for example, the city's poverty rate is actually 23 percent rather than 19 percent (the federal government's figure), and the poverty line for a family of four should be $26,138 because of the high cost of housing (Swarns, 2008). Others add that families typically spend only one-seventh of their income on food but pay substantially more (than when the poverty line formula was established in 1964) for energy and money on transportation and that the poverty line doesn't take into account severe economic downturns and job losses (Blank, 2008).

Poverty isn't random. Instead, children, women, and racial-ethnic minorities are disproportionately poor.

CHILDREN AND OLDER ADULTS In 2008, the U.S. poverty rate was over 13 percent (39.8 million Americans), but children are almost twice as likely as older adults to be poor (see *Figure 13.4*). Children make up only 25 percent of the U.S. population but 36 percent of the poor. Among older Americans, people 65 and older and make up 13 percent of the total population but about 10 percent of the poor (DeNavas-Walt et al., 2009).

Most children living in poverty—4.4 million—are white. However, 11 percent of white children are poor, compared with 35 percent of black children, 31 percent of Latino children, and 15 percent of Asian and Pacific Islander children (DeNavas-Walt et al., 2009).

Answers to "How Much Do You Know about Poverty?"

1. False. The number of Americans living in poverty has increased since 2000 (DeNavas-Walt et al., 2009).

2. False. Most Americans living in poverty are too young, too old, or incapable of working due to physical or mental illness or disability. Also, among poor families, at least one parent usually works full time (Stanczyk, 2009).

3. True. Most poor people are white, but most white people aren't poor (see text).

4. False. The federal government's poverty threshold is much lower (see text).

5. False. White children comprise the largest group of children living in poverty, even though black and Latino children are disproportionately likely to be poor (see text).

6. True. The U.S. child poverty rate is higher than that of all industrialized countries except the United Kingdom. Even some developing countries—such as the Czech Republic, Hungary, and Poland—have much lower child poverty rates than the United States (UNICEF, 2005; Moore et al., 2009).

7. False. Female-headed households are twice as likely to be poor as male-headed households (see text).

8. True. The poverty rate for Americans age 65 and older has been among the lowest nationally because of government programs such as Social Security, Medicare, and Medicaid (see Chapter 17).

9. False. About 43 percent of the poor live in inner cities, but the rest live in urban areas outside of inner cities, the suburbs, small towns, and rural communities (DeNavas-Walt et al., 2009).

10. False. The fastest-growing group of homeless people are families with children (see text).

FIGURE 13.4 U.S. Poverty Rates by Age, 1959–2008

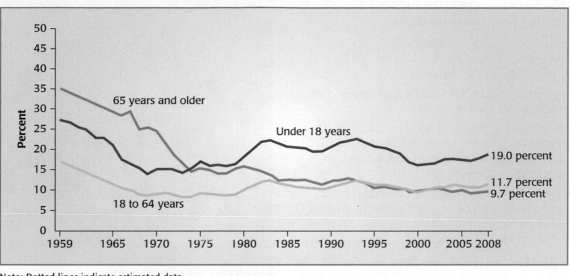

Note: Dotted lines indicate estimated data.
Source: DeNavas-Walt et al., 2009, Figure 4.

WOMEN Of all people 18 and older who are poor, 57 percent are women (DeNavas-Walt et al., 2009). Researcher Diana Pearce (1978) coined the term **feminization of poverty** to describe the likelihood that female heads of households will be poor. Because of increases in divorce and unmarried childbearing, single-mother families are at least five times more likely to be poor than are married-couple families, and they are disproportionately represented among the long-term poor, especially when unmarried and divorced fathers don't support their children (Grall, 2005). Besides marital status, other major reasons for the feminization of poverty are low-paying jobs and wage discrimination, topics we'll discuss shortly.

RACIAL-ETHNIC MINORITIES Less than half of the poor people in the United States are white (43 percent), but most white people aren't poor. As *Figure 13.5* shows, a larger proportion of people in other racial-ethnic groups are poor, and African Americans, American Indians, and Latinos are twice as likely as whites and Asian Americans to be poor.

During economic recessions, African Americans, American Indians, and Latinos are particularly vulnerable to layoffs mainly because of their lower educational levels. And, as you saw earlier, because many racial-ethnic minorities have a smaller cushion of wealth, on average, than whites do, extended unemployment takes a bigger toll.

WHY ARE PEOPLE POOR? About 69 percent of Americans say that money and wealth in this country should be more evenly distributed, but an equal percentage also believes that it's possible to start out poor and get rich through hard work (University of Connecticut . . ., 2007). Why people are poor involves

two general explanations: One blames the poor themselves, and the other emphasizes societal factors.

Proponents of an influential *culture of poverty* view contend that the poor are "deficient": They share certain values, beliefs, and attitudes about life that differ from those who are not poor, are more permissive in raising their children, and are more likely to seek immediate gratification instead of planning for the future (Lewis, 1966; Banfield, 1974). The assertion that these values are transmitted from generation to generation implies that the poor create their own problems through a self-perpetuating cycle of poverty ("like father, like son").

In contrast to blaming the poor, most sociologists maintain that a society's organization creates and

FIGURE 13.5 Percentage of Americans Living in Poverty, by Race and Ethnicity, 2007

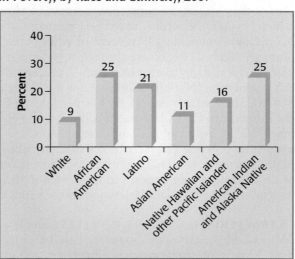

Source: Based on Bishaw and Semega, 2008, Table 9.

sustains poverty. In a classic article on poverty, sociologist Herbert Gans (1971) maintained that poverty and inequality have many functions:

- The poor ensure that society's dirty yet necessary work gets done (such as dishwashing and cleaning bedpans in hospitals).

- The poor subsidize the middle and upper classes by working for low wages.

- The poor buy goods and services that would otherwise be rejected (such as day-old bread; used cars; and the services of old, retired, or incompetent professionals).

- The poor absorb the costs of societal change and community growth (such as being pushed out of their homes by urban renewal and construction of expressways, parks, and stadiums).

Thus, according to Gans, poverty persists in the United States because many people benefit from its consequences.

Which perspective is more accurate—blaming the poor or blaming society? Some people are poor because they focus on the present, don't want to work, or don't have the skills that employers require. However, researchers find little support for the argument that poverty is transmitted from generation to generation. Instead, almost eight out of ten Americans receive public assistance for only two years. Most people are poor because of economic conditions (especially low wages), job loss, physical or mental disabilities, or an inability to afford health insurance which, in turn, can result in acute health problems that interfere with employment. And, as more companies relocate to the suburbs, poor minorities—especially those concentrated in inner cities—are unlikely to hear about employment possibilities or to have the transportation to get to even low-skill jobs (Nichols, 2006; Bernstein et al., 2007; Stanczyk, 2009).

Homelessness

One of the most devastating consequences of poverty is homelessness. According to the best estimates, about 3.5 million Americans (39 percent of whom are children) are likely to experience homelessness in a given year. This translates to approximately 1 percent of the U.S. population (National Coalition for the Homeless, 2008a). These estimates are very low because the Census Bureau can't calculate the "uncounted homeless" who live in automobiles and campgrounds, have makeshift housing (such as boxes in a city alley or under a bridge), stay with relatives for short periods, or crowd into a single motel room—often sharing it with another family—until everyone's money runs out.

CHARACTERISTICS OF THE HOMELESS Single men comprise 51 percent of the homeless, families with children 30 percent, single women 17 percent, and unaccompanied youth 2 percent. Among families, the

Family poverty rates in America's midsize counties, small towns, and rural areas have increased by about 3 percent since 1999 (Mather, 2008). As poverty grows, so do the lines at local soup kitchens and food pantries.

homeless population is estimated to be 55 percent African American, 21 percent white, 10 percent Latino, 5 percent American Indian, and 2 percent Asian. In cities, 26 percent of homeless people are considered mentally ill, 19 percent are employed, 15 percent are domestic violence victims, 13 percent are physically disabled, and 13 percent are veterans (U.S. Conference of Mayors, 2008; U.S. Department of Housing and Urban Development, 2008).

WHY FAMILIES ARE HOMELESS Homelessness is due to a combination of factors, some of which are beyond people's control. Poverty, lack of education or marketable skills, low-paying jobs, domestic violence, substance abuse, the inability of relatives and friends to help during crises, and a decline in public assistance are among the most common reasons for homelessness. Young mothers with young children are especially likely to become homeless. The homeless also include teenage runaways escaping from family violence or incest (Burt et al., 2004; National Coalition for the Homeless, 2008b; U.S. Conference of Mayors, 2008).

Two of the biggest reasons for homelessness are the lack of affordable housing, and most recently, a surge in unemployment. In terms of housing, a household must earn about $38,000 a year to afford the average two-bedroom apartment, which costs $928 a month, excluding utilities. This means that one member of the family must have a job that pays $17.84 an hour. In states with higher housing costs, such as Massachusetts, one person must earn $25 an hour—about three times the minimum wage—to rent a livable two-bedroom apartment (Wardrip et al., 2009).

In mid-2009, 1 in 84 Americans lost a home to foreclosures, an increase of 15 percent since mid-2008. When the housing market began to decline, many people couldn't sell their homes at the prices they paid for them. Others lost their jobs and couldn't keep up with the monthly mortgage payments (Armour, 2009).

Because of the housing crisis, some analysts began to differentiate between the *chronic homeless*—the longtime street residents who often suffer from mental illness, drug abuse, or alcoholism—and the *economic homeless*, the working and middles class people who were the newly displaced from homes by layoffs, foreclosure, or other financial problems caused by the 2008 economic recession. Homelessness is common in urban areas, but family homeless rates jumped by 56 percent in suburbs and rural areas (U.S. Department of Housing and Urban Development, 2008; Bazar, 2009).

We've seen that many families are struggling rather than striving. The situation would be much worse for many families if women weren't employed.

:• MAKING CONNECTIONS

■ What role do personal decisions play in financial problems? For example, should schools teach topics such as budgeting, avoiding credit card fees, getting a mortgage, and saving money?

■ What do you think can be done to reduce the numbers of homeless families? Or is it impossible to do anything at all?

WOMEN'S PARTICIPATION IN THE LABOR FORCE

Many young adults expect to work and raise children simultaneously. In a national study, for example, 75 percent of first-year college students said that being very well off financially was "very important" or "essential"; 76 percent felt the same way about raising a family. However, 26 percent of the men and 16 percent of the women said, "the activities of married women are best confined to the home and family" ("Attitudes and characteristics . . .," 2006: 18). Unless they have very high-paying jobs and expect equally high job security in the future, it's not clear how one-earner families can expect to be well off financially.

Changes in Women's Employment

The high proportions of high school and college women who say that they expect to marry, have children, and work are right on target, because many will have to work to support themselves and their families. In fact, the widespread employment of mothers is often cited as one of the most dramatic changes in family roles that occurred during the twentieth century. Except for a brief period after the end of World War II, the percentage of working women has increased steadily since the late nineteenth century (see *Table 13.1*).

Moreover, the days when mothers stay home to raise children are disappearing. There has been a dramatic increase in the numbers of employed mothers with young children (see Data Digest). In 2007, 64 percent of mothers with children younger than age 6 were in the workforce, compared with 39 percent in 1975 (U.S. Department of Labor, 2008).

More than half of all American mothers with a child younger than 1 year work, they work longer during a pregnancy, and they return to work more quickly. For example, 58 percent of women return to work within three months of childbirth, compared with 17 percent between 1961 and 1965 (Johnson, 2008). Historically, African American mothers were more likely than any other group to be employed and to work during pregnancy and after giving birth, but such gaps between black and white women have closed (see *Figure 13.6*).

Why Do More Women Work?

Why has men's participation in the labor force decreased whereas women's has increased? The decline in men's employment is due, largely, to social and economic factors. Social Security provides full benefits for retirees (most of whom were men) at age 66 and many had well-paying private pensions. Among men ages 25 to 54, in the 1980s employment rates fell for those without a college degree, especially in white-collar jobs. Many men's employment rates also dropped, as you saw earlier, because of deindustrialization and offshoring (Lee and Mather, 2008).

Factors affecting the rise in women's employment are more complex. Economic variables include an expansion of white-collar jobs and their greater availability to women, and better wages that provide an incentive for women to work.

Since you asked . . .

:• Do women's and men's reasons for being in the labor force differ?

TABLE 13.1	Women and Men in the Labor Force, 1890–2008		
	Percentage of All Men and Women in the Labor Force		Women as Percentage of All Workers
Year	Men	Women	
1890	84	18	17
1900	86	20	18
1920	85	23	20
1940	83	28	25
1945	88	36	29
1947	87	32	27
1950	87	34	29
1970	80	43	37
1990	76	58	45
2008	73	59	43

Source: Bureau of Labor Statistics, 2009.

Politically, legislation (such as the Equal Pay Act of 1963 and the Civil Rights Act of 1964 and its amendments) has made it more costly for employers to discriminate against women. And, as you saw in Chapters 5 and 7, the birth control pill gave women more control over childbearing; the women's movement during the 1960s and 1970s challenged traditional attitudes about women's place being in the home; and educational opportunities delayed marriage, childbearing, and child-rearing responsibilities.

Generally, the two principal reasons why women work outside the home are the same as men's—personal satisfaction and supporting themselves and their dependents. The opportunity to succeed and to be rewarded for competence enhances self-esteem, which, in turn, increases overall well-being. This is especially true for people who enjoy their work or are employed in stimulating, satisfying jobs (Mirowsky and Ross, 2007).

Most women can't afford to stay home because they are single parents, can't take unpaid maternity leaves for financial reasons, or are married to men with low-paying jobs. In addition, the purchasing power of families has declined considerably. After adjusting for inflation, the median income for men younger than age 44 is lower than it was in 1970 (Bucks et al., 2009). It's not surprising, then, that almost seven out of ten mothers with young children are in the labor force. Wanting a creative outlet motivates some women to work, but in most cases women are employed because of economic necessity. The box "Variations in the Working Mother Role" examines motherhood and employment more closely.

Are More Women Leaving the Workplace?

When women's labor force participation plateaued in the early 2000s, cover stories in the *New York Times* proclaimed that many women, especially college-educated women, were "opting out" of the workplace (see, for example, Gardner, 2002, and Belkin, 2003). The implication was that women are returning to traditional roles and choosing motherhood over careers because employment is too difficult for these mothers to handle.

FIGURE 13.6 Percentage of Employed Mothers with Infants

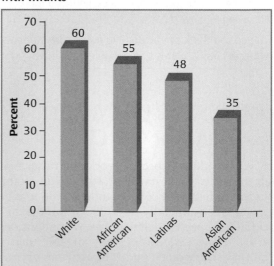

Source: Based on Dye, 2005, Table 4.

Variations in the Working Mother Role

Employed mothers reflect a variety of motivations. Here are four general categories (Moen, 1992: 42–44):

- *Captives* would prefer to be full-time homemakers. These mothers may be single parents who are sole breadwinners, wives of blue-collar workers whose incomes are insufficient to support the family, or middle class wives who find two salaries necessary to maintain a desired standard of living. Captives find their multiple responsibilities overwhelming and remain in the labor force reluctantly.

- *Conflicted* mothers feel that their employment is harmful to their children. They are likely to leave the workforce while their children are young, and many quit their jobs when they can afford to do so. Conflicted mothers include many Latinas whose husbands support their wife's employment as long as she fulfills all housework and child care duties despite her outside job. Many of these women quit their jobs as soon as the husband secures better-paying work (Segura, 1994).

- *Copers* are women with young children who choose jobs with enough flexibility to accommodate family needs. As a result, they often settle for minimally demanding jobs that offer lower wages and fewer benefits, and in the long run they forgo promotions, seniority advantages, and pay increases.

- *Committed* mothers have both high occupational aspirations and a strong commitment to marriage and family life. As the section on dual-earner families shows, however, mothers who can afford good child care and are free to pursue careers are still a minority.

⋮⋮ Stop and Think . . .

- Which group of mothers, if any, has freely chosen to work outside the home?

- Do these categories also describe employed fathers?

Changes

Women's workforce participation, as a percentage of all workers, did start to decline in 2000, but not for all women and not because they couldn't compete with men. During the economic downturns in 2001 and 2008, job losses forced many women out of the workplace (Warner, 2008). Others left the workforce, as we'll discuss later in this chapter, because family-unfriendly policies pushed them out.

Considerable research shows that education encourages women's employment. Even when there are infants at home, employment rates are appreciably higher for women with graduate or professional degrees (70 percent) and college degrees (60 percent) than for women or who are high school graduates (52 percent) or did not finish high school (36 percent) (Conlin et al., 2002; Dye, 2005).

Women who have invested more time in their education return to work more rapidly because they have a greater commitment to their careers, can command higher salaries, and have more work experience than do women with fewer years of schooling. In addition, they have the resources to purchase child care services, especially if their husbands are also employed. Others—particularly women in male-dominated professions such as engineering—are wary of taking leaves for maternity or child rearing because they believe that doing so would harm their careers (Cho, 2008; Cotter et al., 2008; Percheski, 2008).

Many women hit a **glass ceiling,** a collection of attitudinal and organizational biases in the workplace that prevent women from advancing to leadership positions. One solution is to own one's businesses.

Between 1997 and 2002, the number of women-owned businesses, many of them one-person enterprises (most in health care and retail trade), grew by 20 percent, twice the national average for all businesses. Minority women own about a quarter of these firms. In 2007, 38 percent of all self-employed people were women, compared with 27 percent in 1976 (Nance-Nash, 2005; U.S. Department of Labor, 2008).

Being employed mothers or stay-at-home moms aren't the only options. Several other possibilities reflect a couple's economic resources and personal choices.

⋮⋮ MAKING CONNECTIONS

- In a national survey, 48 percent of Americans said that mothers with preschoolers shouldn't work outside the home (Gerson, 2003). Do you agree?

- Is a woman with a college degree "wasting" her education by being a full-time homemaker?

ECONOMIC ROLES WITHIN MARRIAGE

In Chapter 5, we examined the traditional male breadwinner–female homemaker roles. There are currently two variations on the traditional division of labor within marriage: the two-person single career and the stay-at-home dad.

Dilbert: © Scott Adams/Distributed by United Features Syndicate, Inc.

The Two-Person Single Career

In the **two-person single career,** one spouse, typically the wife, participates in the partner's career behind the scenes, without pay or direct recognition. The wives of many college professors, for example, support their husband's career by entertaining faculty and students, doing library research, helping write and edit journal articles or books, and grading exams.

College presidents and their spouses often have a two-person single career. In most cases, the president is male, but female presidents are becoming more common. Whether the president is a man or a woman, the spouse spends considerable time in activities such as entertaining; organizing fund-raising events; attending campus events; meeting with faculty, students, and staff members; and often also running a household and raising their children. The spouses are expected to be available and cordial and to never say or do anything that might embarrass the president or the institution (Oden, 2008; Wilson, 2008).

The best public example of the two-person single career is that of the first lady, who often enjoys considerable power and influence behind the scenes. Nancy Reagan influenced her husband's staffing decisions, Barbara Bush criticized her husband's opponents, Hillary Rodham Clinton promoted her husband's domestic policies and defended him during his sex scandals, and Laura Bush endorsed improvements in teaching (Allgor, 2002). Michelle Obama, similarly, spends much of her time addressing groups and traveling abroad with her husband in support of the administration's domestic and foreign policies.

The military imposes numerous demands on family life that often require a two-person single career. Whether they live on military installations or in their own homes, the wives of soldiers—especially officers—on active duty must often sacrifice their own interests to support their husband's role. Families stationed overseas must cope with missing their friends and being separated from extended family (Segal and Harris, 1993; McFadyen et al., 2005).

Stay-at-Home Dads

In the movie *Daddy Day Care,* Eddie Murphy is an unemployed father who starts a "guy-run" day care center with a buddy. Stay-at-home dads (or *househusbands,* as they were called in the 1990s) are the rare men who stay home to care for the family and do the housework while their wives are the wage earners.

Since you asked . . .

❖ Are stay-at-home dads reversing gender roles?

An estimated 158,000 stay-at-home dads care for their children while their wives work outside the home. They make up about 3 percent of all stay-at-home parents during a given year, but the number is much lower during a strong economy (U.S. Census Bureau News, 2010).

REASONS Being a stay-at-home dad is usually a temporary role. Some men take on the role by default; they are unemployed or are not working because of poor health or disability. Others are retired, have remarried much younger women who are employed, or want a second chance to watch a child grow up in a second (or even third) marriage (Gutner, 2001).

Sometimes male graduate students who are supported by their wives take on a modified housekeeping role, doing household chores between classes and studying at the library. And, especially at well-financed private colleges and universities, some male faculty take advantage of generous one-year family leaves to care for their children while the mother works (Latessa, 2005).

In the past, many of these stay-at-home dads had wives who earned more than they did and had greater job security, better health care benefits, and in some cases, high-powered jobs. A number of these men took early retirement from high-level executive positions, were wealthy, and often hired a nanny to assist with child care (Morris, 2002).

More recently, most stay-at-home dads have been laid off—especially from real estate, financial services, and construction jobs—and can't find comparable work. Some take unpaid paternity leaves for up to a year when their much higher-paid wives return to work (Braiker, 2007; Gibbs, 2009).

BENEFITS AND COSTS Being a full-time dad is a mixed blessing. Some fathers find child rearing a joy because they are more intimately involved with their kids: "I know my son's and daughter's friends. I know everything they like and dislike. I have the chance to be there to answer questions" (Barovick, 2002: B10). Parents don't have to worry about the quality of day care or after-school programs.

On the other hand, some stay-at-home dads are concerned about losing their business skills and their professional place in line, and they feel unappreciated by their working wives, who may complain that the house is a mess. Even when stay-at-home dads say that it's one of the most rewarding experiences they've had, they often feel stigmatized and emasculated by unemployment because much of their identity comes from being a good provider. Says a father who lost his job at a large investment bank and is now a stay-at-home dad, "I just can't shake the feeling that I'm out of step with the world. . . . Losing my job is not necessarily the worst thing I've endured, but I wouldn't wish it on anyone" (Blomfield, 2009: 22).

In most families, parents don't have the choice of staying home with their children. Instead, both partners work either part time or full time, and sometimes both.

TWO-INCOME FAMILIES

Consider the following results when researchers asked U.S. employees to respond to the statement "It is better for all involved if the man earns the money and the woman takes care of the home:"

- In 1977, 74 percent of the men and 52 percent of the women agreed.
- In 2008, 42 percent of the men and 39 percent of the women agreed (Galinsky et al., 2009: 9).

These responses indicate that large numbers of both sexes still endorse traditional gender roles, but men's and women's attitudes about appropriate work and family roles have changed considerably over three decades and are now very similar.

Attitudes change more quickly than behavior, but they help explain why two-income families are becoming increasingly diverse. There are dual-earner and dual-career couples, trailing spouses, commuter marriages, and marriages in which wives earn more than their husbands.

Dual-Earner versus Dual-Career Families

In the past 50 years, the proportion of married women in the labor force has almost tripled. When wives work full time, the median family income can be twice as high as when they stay home (see *Figure 13.7* on the next page). The higher income characterizes both dual-earner and dual-career families.

HOW THEY DIFFER In **dual-earner couples,** also called *dual-income, two-income, two-earner,* or *dual-worker* couples, both partners work outside the home. These couples make up about 47 percent of all married couples (U.S. Census Bureau, 2010).

Despite their two incomes, dual-earner families are seldom affluent. Only a small fraction have much **discretionary income,** money remaining after the costs of basic necessities such as food, rent, utilities, and transportation have been paid. Many dual-earner families are composed of middle-aged people who are paying for their children's college education, saving for their own retirement, and sometimes helping low-income aging parents (Warren and Tyagi, 2003; see, also, Chapter 17).

In **dual-career couples,** both partners work in professional or managerial positions that require extensive training, a long-term commitment, and ongoing professional growth. The better educated the couple, the more hours they work.

There are no national data on dual-career couples, but one survey found that among more than 9,000 full-time faculty at 13 U.S. research universities, 36 percent were dual-career academic couples (Schiebinger et al., 2008). Academics tend to marry other academics because they often meet in graduate school, share similar interests, and have similar educational levels (usually a master's or Ph.D. degree), but it's not clear whether this is also true for people in other professions such as law, medicine, and high-level management.

GENDER ROLES AND PARENTING As the employee survey referred to earlier showed, many women and men endorse egalitarian gender roles regarding family and work responsibilities. Considerable research shows, however, that behavior has not caught up with attitudes because parenting is still gendered among many dual-earner and dual-career couples.

A national study of dual-earner married parents found that even though many couples said that they believed in egalitarian roles, only 9 percent of the couples made similar domestic and employment contributions. In the other cases, the mothers had more responsibility for domestic tasks, especially child care (Hall and MacDermid, 2009). When there are conflicts between work and family responsibilities, mothers are more likely than fathers to restrict their work efforts by refusing to travel or work extra hours, turning down promotions and interesting assignments, and rearranging their work schedules (Maume, 2006).

Many two-income parents work more than 46 hours per week and place a priority on spending

FIGURE 13.7 Median Family Income When Women Work Full-Time, Year-Round, 1949–2008

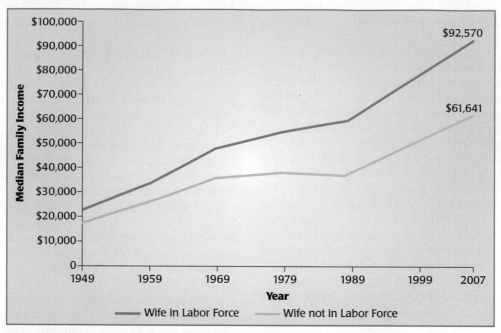

Source: U.S. Census Bureau, 2002 and 2008. "Historical Income Tables—Families," Tables F-13 and F-14, www.census.gov (accessed September 11, 2003, and August 6, 2009).

quality time with their families, but how parents define quality time is gendered. A study of 110 dual-career married couples found that mothers spent more time on planning structured activities (such as family vacations) and child-centered activities (such as having heart-to-heart talks with their children). Fathers were more likely to define quality time as any time families spent together. For example, according to a professor of computer science and father of five: "Quality time means nothing to me. . . . When you spend time with your kids, you spend time with your kids. I don't worry about what kinds of time. . . . We're always around" (Snyder, 2007: 334).

Especially in professional and managerial jobs, the norm is a 60-hour week (overwork) for both partners. The long work hours intensify gender inequality by reinforcing "separate spheres" at home and the workplace. That is, when the husband works long hours, his wife is more likely to quit because of child care responsibilities, but wives' long work hours don't affect men's employment status. Even though most women are very committed to their jobs, overwork limits their career choices and progress because cultural expectations and gender ideologies still endorse breadwinning men and homemaking women (Cha, 2009).

SOME BENEFITS AND COSTS OF TWO-INCOME FAMILIES Having two wage earners raises the family's standard of living. And if a husband's income is low or he is laid off, his wife's financial support relieves some of the pressure on him to be a provider. Two-income parents believe that they provide responsible adult role

models for their children and that their offspring are more independent and less "needy" than they would be if only one parent worked (Barnett and Rivers, 1996). Also, as you saw at the beginning of this chapter, work provides many benefits beyond income.

The most common problem for dual-earner couples is role overload, especially when their children are young. Role overload can lead to increased health risks; decreased productivity; increased tardiness, absenteeism, and turnover; and low morale at work (see Chapter 12). To achieve their goals, both partners in dual-career couples often feel driven to overwork. Having a strong professional identity along with a commitment to family life requires ongoing coping and effective conflict resolution skills that couples may not have. Overwork can also derail women's career choices and plans (Bird and Schnurman-Crook,

Mike Smith EDT (New) © King Features Syndicate.

Applying What You've Learned

∷ Juggling Competing Demands in Dual-Earner Families

As you read these suggestions for balancing work and family life, think about other strategies that have worked for you, your parents, or your friends.

■ **Emphasize the positive.** Concentrate on the benefits you get from having a job: personal fulfillment, a higher standard of living, and providing more cultural and educational opportunities for your children.

■ **Set priorities.** Because conflicts between the demands of family and job are inevitable, establish principles for resolving clashes. For example, parents might take turns staying home with sick children.

■ **Be ready to compromise.** Striving for perfection in family and job responsibilities is unrealistic. Instead, aim for the best possible balance among your various activities, making compromises when

necessary. For example, homes don't have to be immaculate.

■ **Separate family and work roles.** Many mothers, especially, feel guilty while at work because they are not with their children. And when they are at home, they feel guilty about not working on office assignments. If you must work at home, set time limits for the work and enjoy the rest of the time with your family.

■ **Organize domestic duties.** Resolve domestic overload by dividing family work more equitably between adults and children. Many families find it useful to prepare a weekly or monthly job chart in which everyone's assignments are clearly written down. It's also useful to rotate assignments so that everyone gets to do both the "better" and the "worse" jobs.

■ **Cultivate a sharing attitude.** Sit down with your partner periodically and discuss what you can do to help each other in your roles at home and at work. Most of us are happier when our spouses and partners provide a sounding board or offer encouragement.

■ **Maintain a balance between responsibilities and recreation.** If you are both working to improve your standard of living, use some of your extra income to enjoy life. Otherwise, you'll have little energy left for activities that will make life more enjoyable.

Sources: Based on Beck, 1988, and Crosby, 1991b.

2005; Cha, 2009). The box "Juggling Competing Demands in Dual-Earner Families" offers some suggestions for coping with some of the difficulties that many two-income couples encounter.

Trailing Spouses

A **trailing spouse** is the partner who gives up his or her work and searches for another position in the location where the spouse has taken a job. Some companies help a trailing spouse search for employment, but most don't.

WHO'S THE TRAILING SPOUSE? Male trailing spouses—only 10 to 15 percent of all trailing spouses—fall into five categories: (1) men who can't find suitable employment in their present location; (2) those with "portable" professions, such as photographers, computer programmers, and engineers; (3) men who take pride in and accommodate their wives' relocation because of job offers; (4) blue-collar workers, such as construction workers, who are used to changing jobs; and (5) laid-off managers and executives whose

wives are climbing the corporate ladder (Cohen, 1994; "The big picture," 2000).

In most cases, the wife is the trailing spouse because of traditional gender roles in which wives are expected to accommodate husbands' work roles (see Chapter 5). According to a faculty member, for example, about 90 percent of her male Ph.D. students apply for almost every job that "remotely matches their qualifications," even if it would require moving to a different location, compared with only 50 percent of their female counterparts, "usually because the men in their lives don't want to move" (Williams, 2001: B20).

WHAT ARE THE BENEFITS AND COSTS FOR TRAILING SPOUSES? The most obvious benefit of being a trailing spouse is that the main provider can increase his or her income and job opportunities. Especially when women hit glass ceilings, their only option for a better job may require relocation.

There are also many drawbacks. Many female instructors who are adjunct faculty members are trailing spouses. They often move with their spouses, hoping to find a full-time teaching position at the new location. Instead, often they must piece together a string of part-time teaching jobs. Says one: "After nearly two years of driving 65 miles each way to teach for less than $10,000 a semester, the truth was apparent: My car was going the distance, but my career and my spirits were in neutral" (Carroll, 2003: C4).

Another part-time instructor describes being a trailing spouse as an "esteem-crushing nightmare." The pay is low, health insurance is nonexistent, there is zero opportunity for advancement, and the wife becomes the full-time partner's caretaker, handling everything from grocery shopping to home repairs (Taz, 2005: C1).

Because of such difficulties, many couples don't or won't relocate. Instead, they try to pursue their independent careers in commuter marriages.

Commuter Marriages

In a **commuter marriage,** married partners live and work in different geographic areas and get together at various intervals, such as over weekends. Precise recent figures on commuter marriages are difficult to find, but according to some estimates, in 2006 3.6 million married couples were living apart for reasons other than marital discord. This represents almost 3 percent of all U.S. marriages, up from 2 percent in 2000. The numbers have probably increased since 2006 because many couples are accepting jobs that require living apart, sometimes in another country, because of the global economy (Center for the Study of Long Distance Relationships, 2007; Kridel, 2009).

WHY DO THEY DO IT? There are several reasons for commuter marriages. For one, if one partner (usually the wife) sees that relocation will have negative effects on her or his employment prospects, she or he may decide not to move. Second, if both partners have well-established careers in different cities, neither may be willing to make major job sacrifices after marriage. Third, a commuter marriage may avoid the stress of uprooting teenage children or elderly parents. Fourth and most important, when jobs are scarce, financial security is an important factor in launching a commuter marriage.

BENEFITS AND COSTS OF COMMUTER MARRIAGES The major benefit of a commuter marriage is the paycheck, especially when higher-paying jobs are scarce. According to a partner at a large investment firm, "Eighteen months ago anyone searching for a new job would ask to be placed in their current location. Now they come in and say 'I am prepared to move,' even, if necessary, without the family" (Conlin, 2009: 1).

Long-distance couples believe that they can devote more attention to their work during the week and that they learn to appreciate and make the most

Many parents in commuter marriages stay in touch with their children via Skype—software that enables users to transmit their voices and images through the Internet. Here, a college professor who teaches in New Orleans, reads to his children who live in Chicago with his wife.

of the time they have together. Each person is more independent and can take advantage of time alone to pursue hobbies or recreational interests that the other partner might not enjoy. As one commuter husband noted, "She can watch all the foreign movies she wants and eat sushi for lunch and dinner" (Justice, 1999: 12).

Commuter marriages also have disadvantages, including time and extra costs. Frequent airplane flights and maintaining two residences can be expensive: "Two mortgages, property tax bills, electric bills, heating fuel bills, phone bills, garbage bills, grocery lists, driveways to plow, yards to maintain, and two houses to clean" (Smith, 2009: F15).

The commuting partner may feel isolated from community and social relationships, a situation that can lead to extramarital relationships on the part of either partner, or a divorce if there has been previous marital conflict. The stay-at-home parent may resent the weekend parent, who shoulders little of the parenting responsibility. In other cases, the stay-at-home parent, who is usually the wife, sometimes doesn't look forward to the commuter's weekend visits because it means preparing more elaborate dinners and being stricter with the children (Cullen, 2007; Conlin, 2009).

Whether or not a two-income marriage involves long-distance commuting, women continue to earn less than men. There is also an increasing number of families in which the wife earns more than her husband.

When Wives Earn More

In 2008, almost 26 percent of women earned more than their husbands, up from 18 percent in 1987. These women typically work full time year-round as professionals or managers, and many have at least a college degree (U.S. Department of Labor, 2008; Galinsky et al., 2009). In other cases, as profits in farming and ranching communities decreased, wives who worked as county treasurers, as tax assessors, or in other public offices also began to earn more than their husbands (Belsie, 2003).

In many cases, a woman's higher income is short term, because her husband has been laid off, is on a short-term disability leave, or is pursuing a college or graduate degree. Wives are less likely to outearn their husbands, even if they have a college degree, when (1) their labor force participation is interrupted by having and raising children or (2) they work fewer hours per week than their husbands because they are caring for aging or disabled parents or other relatives (Winslow-Bowie, 2006). Once again, then, gender roles have an impact on women's income.

According to exchange and resource theories, the partner with the higher income typically has more power in a relationship (see Chapters 2 and 10). However, much of the literature shows that there is usually little impact on marital power when wives outearn their husbands. Many couples ignore the income differences or minimize them by having joint bank accounts and contributing equally to household expenses. They often stick to traditional roles in public, however: The husband picks up the tab at restaurants and pays for the groceries, for example. If the wife doesn't want to threaten her husband's self-esteem as the primary breadwinner, she may do more of the housework (Greenstein, 2000; see, also, Chapter 10).

High-earning wives typically enjoy a more equitable division of labor in the home than do their lower-income counterparts, but they often still bear the larger burden of housework and child care (the "second shift" discussed in Chapters 5 and 10). They may see this arrangement as fair because they tend to judge their success as wives and mothers by how much they do around the house rather than by how much they earn. Others are afraid of exercising their decision-making power because doing so might threaten their husbands' masculinity and, consequently, the relationship. Thus, gender roles, rather than the woman's income, often reinforce the husband's marital power (Tichenor, 2005).

⁞• MAKING CONNECTIONS

- If you, your friends, or your parents are two-income couples, do you and they experience more benefits or more stresses than single-income couples?

- If women earn more than their husbands, should husbands do more of the housework and child care than their wives? What about cohabiting couples?

INEQUALITY IN THE WORKPLACE

Considerable inequality exists in the workplace. Scholars continue to debate whether the inequality is due to individual characteristics (such as a low educational level and previous choices), or macro variables (such as social class and changes in the economy). There are few disputes, however, about data that show striking income differences among most women, minority men, and white male employees; a gender pay gap; and that women are considerably more likely than men to experience sexual harassment in the workplace. Let's begin by looking at the income differences between women and men and across racial/ethnic groups.

Women and Minorities in the Workplace

Large earning disparities exist across minority groups, but the differences are especially striking by sex. As you examine *Figure 13.8,* note two general characteristics. First, earnings increase—across all racial/ethnic groups and for both sexes—as people go up the occupational ladder. For example, managers and professionals make considerably more than car mechanics and truck drivers. But, across all occupations, men have higher earnings than their female counterparts of the same racial/ethnic group. At the bottom of the occupational ladder are African American women and Latinas, with the latter faring worse than any of the other groups. Thus, sex *and* race/ethnicity intersect in the workplace, producing earning disparities between workers.

At the top occupation levels—managerial and professional—Asian American men have the highest earnings because of their high educational levels, including well-paying jobs in science and medicine. In the low-skill job market, Latino men are less likely than their counterparts to have a high school degree, prior job experience, and training or certification in specific skills. Also, many of these workers with the necessary skills lack the networks or access to job information (Acs and Loprest, 2009).

The Gender Pay Gap

In mid-2009, women who worked full time year-round had a median income of $48,802, compared with $64,167 for men. This means that women earned 76 cents for every dollar men earned. (On average, a woman with a college degree earns only slightly more per year than a man with an associate degree—$55,222 and $51,894, respectively).

Since you asked . . .

⁞• Why do women earn less than men, even when their jobs are almost identical?

FIGURE 13.8 Median Weekly Earnings of Full-Time Workers by Occupation, Sex, and Ethnicity

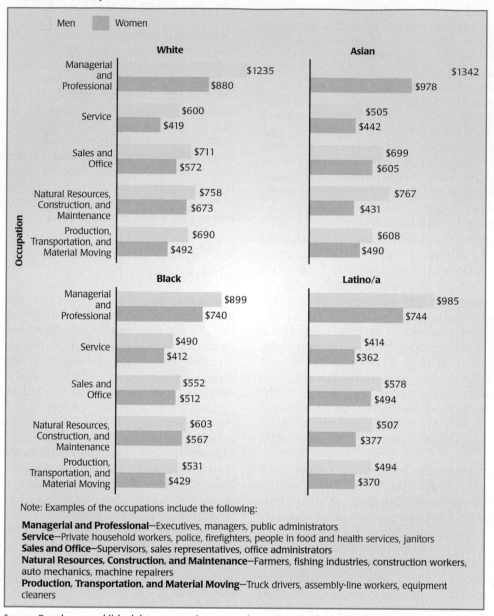

Note: Examples of the occupations include the following:

Managerial and Professional—Executives, managers, public administrators
Service—Private household workers, police, firefighters, people in food and health services, janitors
Sales and Office—Supervisors, sales representatives, office administrators
Natural Resources, Construction, and Maintenance—Farmers, fishing industries, construction workers, auto mechanics, machine repairers
Production, Transportation, and Material Moving—Truck drivers, assembly-line workers, equipment cleaners

Source: Based on unpublished data; personal correspondence; Bureau of Labor Statistics, U.S. Department of Labor, Division of Labor Force Studies, Current Population Survey, Table A-2, 2008.

Stated differently, *the average woman must work almost four extra months every year to make the same wages as a man* (Joyce, 2006; U.S. Census Bureau, 2008; Bureau of Labor Statistics News, 2009). This income difference is the **gender pay gap** (sometimes called the *wage gap, pay gap,* or the *gender wage gap*).

WHAT ARE THE CONSEQUENCES OF A GENDER PAY GAP? Over a lifetime, the average woman who works full time and year-round over four decades loses a significant amount of money because of the gender pay gap: $700,000 for high school graduates; $1.2 million for college graduates; and more than $2 million for women with a professional degree in business, medicine, or law (Murphy and Graff, 2005; Soguel, 2009).

The gender pay gap is even more costly than these figures suggest. Because raises are typically based on a percentage of one's annual income, the lower the wages, the lower the raises and possible savings. Lower wages and salaries also reduce women's purchasing power and quality of life. (Imagine, for example, what you could do with an extra $6,000 a year if you're a female college graduate.) In addition, lower wages result in lower monthly payments after retirement from Social Security and private pensions (Horn, 2006; see, also, Chapter 17).

WHY IS THERE A GENDER PAY GAP? A common explanation for the gender pay gap is that women choose fields with lower earnings (such as health care and teaching in elementary and middle schools), whereas men tend to dominate the higher-paying fields (such as engineering, mathematics, and the physical sciences). This doesn't explain, however, why women have lower earnings than men in both the highest- and lowest-paying occupations, and why the wage gaps are greater in high-income jobs (see *Figure 13.9*).

A second common explanation for the gender pay gap is that women don't take promotions that require greater job responsibility. Data show, however, that women and men younger than age 29 are equally interested in jobs with greater responsibility, and there are few differences between mothers and women without children in this age group (Galinsky et al., 2009).

Some scholars maintain that women—especially those in professional, managerial, and executive positions—are being pushed out of the workplace or are getting stuck under glass ceilings. Even in federal agencies, men with much less experience and lower educational levels are routinely promoted over more accomplished women (Stone, 2007; Waldref, 2007).

According to many women on Wall Street, even before the 2009 bailout of major companies such as Citigroup, Bank of America, and American International Group (AIG), most of the major corporations were laying off women, and none of the seven leading Wall Street banks has a single female

officer in the top executive positions such as CEO and CFO (chief financial officer). With the layoffs, according to a female director in a health care company, who was fired in late 2008, "you have taken out a whole generation of future female managing directors" (Raghavan, 2009: 78).

A third common explanation for the gender pay gap is that mothers are more likely than fathers (or other women with no children) to work part time, take leaves, or take a break from the workforce to raise children—factors that reduce wages and salaries (Dey and Hill, 2007). Some argue, however, that because only women can have babies and men's child-rearing participation is still modest, many women's earnings suffer from a **motherhood penalty** (also called a *motherhood wage penalty* and *mommy penalty*), a gender pay gap attributed to being a mother, rather than just a woman.

Employed mothers in the United States earn about 5 percent less, on average, than nonmothers with the same credentials, educational levels, work experience, and similar variables. For those younger than age 35, the pay gap between mothers and childless women is larger than the pay gap between men and women. Many employers believe that mothers are less committed than nonmothers to the workplace, less dependable, and less competent. In contrast, fathers are more advantaged than childless men because employers see them as more dedicated to the job and needing a higher starting salary. In effect, then, parenthood penalizes employed mothers and provides strong evidence of discrimination (see Correll et al., 2007, and Glauber, 2007, for these findings and literature reviews).

FIGURE 13.9 | Women Earn Less Than Men Whether They're Chief Executives or Cooks
These were five of the highest and lowest-paid occupations of full-time, year-round workers in the United States in 2007. How might you explain why the earnings differ by sex, especially in the highest-paid jobs?

Men Make More Than Women in Some of the Highest-Paid Jobs			. . . And Some of the Lowest-Paid Jobs		
Occupation	Median weekly earnings (men)	Median weekly earnings (women)	Occupation	Median weekly earnings (men)	Median weekly earnings (women)
Chief executives	$1,918	$1,536	Bartenders	$551	$404
Pharmacists	$1,887	$1,603	Personal and home care aides	$434	$373
Physicians and surgeons	$1,796	$1,062	Telemarketers	$422	$391
Lawyers	$1,793	$1,381	Waiters and waitresses	$415	$360
Computer and information systems managers	$1,598	$1,363	Cooks	$377	$341

Note: Some of the differences between men's and women's median weekly earnings may seem small, but multiply each figure by 52 weeks. Thus, in annual earnings, male physicians and surgeons average more than $90,000 a year compared with only about $55,000 for females.
Source: Based on material in U.S. Bureau of Labor Statistics, 2008, Table 39.

Overall, the gender pay gap can be partially explained by differences in education, experience, and time in the workforce, but about 41 percent of the wage gap is the result of sex discrimination in hiring, promotion and pay, bias against mothers, and occupational segregation. That is, a wage gap remains even when women and men have the same education, occupation, number of years in a job, seniority, marital status, and number of children and are similar on numerous other factors (Boraas and Rodgers, 2003; Blau and Kahn, 2006).

COMPARABLE WORTH: A SOLUTION TO THE GENDER PAY GAP? Some women have tried to remedy the gender pay gap by filing individual or *class action suits,* legal proceedings that are brought by one or more people but represent the interests of a larger group. In 2009, Dell, a computer company, agreed to pay $9.1 million to settle a class action lawsuit filed by a former employee on behalf of female Dell employees worldwide. The plaintiff alleged that Dell had systematically engaged in gender discrimination in salaries, career opportunities, and promotions. A year earlier, Dell was recognized as one of the top companies that practiced diversity and was honored by *Working Mother* magazine as one of the 100 best companies for women to work for (Shah, 2009).

Such lawsuits are costly and could be unnecessary. According to the concept of **comparable worth,** men and women should receive equal pay for doing work that involves similar skills, effort, responsibility, and work conditions. If employers instituted comparable worth policies, the benefits would far outweigh the costs. In 1982, for example, the state of Minnesota implemented comparable worth for its public sector employees, phasing in the program over a number of years. By 2002, women who worked for the state earned about 97 cents for every dollar men made, and overall personnel costs were less than 3 percent of the total state budget. Comparable worth not only cuts women's poverty rate in half but also gives women more purchasing power, which strengthens the economy (Murphy and Graff, 2005; Horn, 2006).

Employment inequality hurts all families. Many women and some men must also endure work-related abuses such as sexual harassment.

Sexual Harassment

Before reading any further, take the "Do You Recognize Sexual Harassment?" quiz to see how attuned you are to this issue.

Sexual harassment became an illegal form of sex discrimination under Title VII of the Civil Rights Act

---

ASK YOURSELF

Do You Recognize Sexual Harassment?

Is it sexual harassment if:

Yes **No**

☐ ☐ **1.** An employee uses e-mail to send sexual jokes to co-workers?

☐ ☐ **2.** An employee continues to ask a co-worker to go out on dates despite repeated refusals?

☐ ☐ **3.** Employees tell bawdy jokes to co-workers who enjoy them in non-workplace settings?

☐ ☐ **4.** Flirting occurs between mutually consenting individuals who are equal in power or authority?

☐ ☐ **5.** Male and female co-workers repeatedly talk about their sexual affairs and relationships at the office?

☐ ☐ **6.** A cashier in a restaurant greets each customer by calling him or her "honey" or "dearie"?

Yes **No**

☐ ☐ **7.** A male supervisor tells a female employee, "You look very nice today"?

☐ ☐ **8.** Employees put up pornographic material on company bulletin boards or in lockers?

☐ ☐ **9.** Employees or supervisors make frequent comments to co-workers about sexually explicit material in the media (films, television, magazines)?

☐ ☐ **10.** At the end of a staff meeting, a male manager says to two female secretaries, "Why don't you girls clean up this room?"

The answers to these questions are on p. 376.

of 1964 and again in the 1980 Equal Employment Opportunity Commission (EEOC) guidelines. According to the EEOC, the fastest-growing area of employment discrimination complaints is sexual harassment, with almost 240,000 complaints filed with the EEOC between 1992 and 2008; 85 percent of them were filed by female employees (U.S. Equal Employment Opportunity Commission, 2009a).

Sexual harassment includes the following:

- *Verbal behavior* (such as pressures for dates or demands for sexual favors in return for hiring, promotion, or tenure, as well as the threat of rape)

- *Nonverbal behavior* (such as indecent gestures and displaying posters, photos, or drawings of a sexual nature)

- *Physical contact* (such as pinching, touching, and rape)

Sexual harassment in the workplace is a display of power that is usually perpetrated by a boss and directed at a subordinate of the same or opposite sex. Because men dominate in positions of power, it is far more likely that a harasser will be a man than a woman. The superior-subordinate relationship of perpetrator and victim also accounts for the fact that women often fail to report incidents of harassment. The women believe that nothing will be done and that they risk losing their jobs if they complain. Teenage girls often tolerate unwanted comments and touching by co-workers and supervisors because they initially mistake them for innocent romantic overtures or don't know how to stop the abusive behavior (Joyce, 2004).

Sexual harassment cuts across many types of jobs. Dov Charney, the founder and CEO of the clothing manufacturer American Apparel Inc. holds meetings in his underwear and regularly refers to women as sluts and whores and uses other demeaning epithets. He is facing sexual harassment charges, but his lawyer defends Charney's behavior as "creative expression" (Bronstad, 2008).

Sexual harassment is especially common in male-dominated occupations in which female newcomers are unwelcome. For example, among firefighters, 97 percent of whom are men, many women have complained about offensive behavior such as finding feces in the women's shower stalls, unwanted touching, being referred to as "bitches," and attempted rape (Banks, 2006).

Some people claim that there is a fine line between sexual harassment and flirting or simply giving a compliment. Wrong. If someone says, "Stop it," and the perpetrator doesn't stop, it's sexual harassment. Most people know—both instinctively and because of the other person's reaction—when sexual attentions are unwelcome.

Sexual harassment can be very costly, both emotionally and financially, to its victims. What many

In 2004, a Burger King in St. Louis, Missouri, settled a sexual harassment lawsuit for $400,000. The money was paid to seven high school female employees whose boss had subjected them to groping, vulgar sexual comments, and demands for sex.

people don't realize is that sexual harassment constitutes wage discrimination because repeated harassment can cause employees (usually women) to leave or lose their jobs and, consequently, forfeit potential raises and promotions. Victims of sexual harassment may also experience emotional and behavioral problems that affect their families, including depression; changes in attitude toward sexual relationships or in sexual behaviors; irritability toward family members, friends, or co-workers; and alcohol and drug abuse (WAGE, 2006; see, also, Chapter 5).

Sexual harassment is also expensive for employers and companies. In 2004 alone, for example, several large corporations paid women almost $3 million to settle sexual harassment lawsuits. The California Supreme Court ruled that even consensual sleeping with the boss, male or female, is sexual harassment because it may result

⠿ MAKING CONNECTIONS

- Are women and men too accepting of gender pay gaps? If you're a male, how would you feel if your mother, daughter, wife, or partner was earning 33 percent less than a man in a comparable position?

- Have you, your friends, or members of your family ever observed or experienced sexual harassment? If so, what did you or they do about it?

Answers to "Do You Recognize Sexual Harassment?"

1. Yes, if repeated instances create an offensive and hostile work environment.
2. Yes.
3. No.
4. No.
5. No, if no one else is around and the talk is consensual. It could be sexual harassment if a passerby finds such talk offensive.

6. No, if the comments are directed at both sexes and aren't intentionally derogatory or degrading.
7. No.
8. Yes, this creates a hostile work environment.
9. Yes.
10. No, but it's a sexist comment.

---

in favoritism (such as promotions and pay increases) that treats the employee as "sexual playthings" and penalizes women (and men) who refuse to sleep with the boss (Dolan, 2005; Murphy and Graff, 2005).

FAMILIES AND WORK POLICIES

How family friendly are workplace policies? Some companies allow flexible work schedules and telecommuting. For the most part, however, pregnancy discrimination is common, our family leave policies are among the worst worldwide, and there is minimal support for employed parents who must care for children and aging parents. Let's begin with some of the recent changes that include bringing babies to work, flextime, and telecommuting.

Bringing Babies to Work, Flextime, and Telecommuting

By mid-2009, 126 "baby-friendly" U.S. companies let a new parent bring a baby to work every day, usually until the child was old enough to crawl. The practice is growing, especially among smaller businesses (Parenting in the Workplace Institute, 2009).

Since you asked . . .

- Should businesses allow parents to bring their babies to work?

Employers who allow babies in the workplace don't want to pay for maternity leave or day care, and they say that it's a good way to retain valued workers who, in turn, deepen their loyalty to the company. However, many co-workers don't want to put up with a baby gurgling—or worse—in the next cubicle, are distracted, less productive, and complain that employers are coddling parents (Armour, 2008; Farnsworth, 2008).

A more common accommodation for employed parents is **flextime,** a practice that allows workers to change their daily arrival and departure times. In 2007, nearly 26 percent of working women with children younger than age 18 worked flexible schedules, up from 14 percent in 1991 (Palmer, 2007).

This woman is one of the many parents, particularly mothers, who take advantage of company policies that let employees care for babies in the workplace.

Some employers endorse flextime because it decreases tardiness resulting from remaining home to see children off to school or leaving early to be there when the kids come home. Also, employees who work later shifts can accommodate more clients and customers, especially those in earlier time zones. Office workers often have the option of flextime, but county and state officials require some workers, such as public safety and school employees, to work regular hours because the public expects their services during regular office hours or because it would cost more to heat and air condition offices throughout the evening (Carson, 2008).

Telecommuting, working from home through electronic linkups to the central office, is one of the most recent flexible work styles that allow parents to combine work and child rearing. Some policy analysts encourage employers to expand telecommuting because doing so would cut a company's energy costs, reduce pollution because fewer people would be driving to work, decrease the pool of workers who experience transportation problems (especially in urban and rural areas), enhance productivity by reducing the number of trips to work, and slow offshoring jobs to other countries because more people work evenings, nights, and on weekends (Cox, 2009).

Sales representative, such as this mother, can often work from home, which enables them to interact with their children more frequently.

In 2008, however, only 30 percent of Americans telecommuted at least two days a week, up from 9 percent in 1995, but down from 32 percent in 2006, and the vast majority were in higher-income jobs that paid $75,000 or more a year. Thus, although nearly two-thirds of all jobs can be done working from home, the number of telecommuters has declined. One of the reasons for the decline may be that just 12 percent of workers believe that their companies encourage telecommuting one or more days a week (Gariety and Shaffer, 2007; Saad, 2008). There's no way of knowing whether employees' beliefs are correct, but, as the box "Working at Home: Still Not a Paradise" shows, telecommuting has both benefits and costs.

The Pregnancy Penalty

The federal Pregnancy Discrimination Act of 1978 makes it illegal for employers with more than 15 workers to fire, demote, or penalize a pregnant employee. Some state laws extend this protection to companies with as few as four employees. Despite such laws, the EEOC reports that charges of pregnancy discrimination have risen at least 33 percent in recent years. In 2008 alone, nearly 6,300 women filed complaints that they had been fired or demoted or had some of their responsibilities taken away from them when their employers learned that they were pregnant (U.S. Equal Employment Opportunity Commission, 2008b). This is just the tip of the

Working at Home: Still Not a Paradise

On the *positive side,* many telecommuters spend less money on clothes, have a more flexible work schedule, and have reduced the cost of child care. Some report that working at home brings the family closer together: A parent is available when a child returns after school, and family members sometimes get involved in business tasks.

Some companies permit telecommuting to retain talented employees who prefer to work from home. Telecommuting can also boost productivity because it improves morale (for example, people have more control over their time and schedule). Workers also waste less time (such as chatting with co-workers at the water cooler) and are less tired because they don't commute to and from a central office.

On the *negative side,* some telecommuters feel isolated, miss their co-workers,

and believe that nothing can replace face-to-face interaction. Others worry that telecommuting might make them less visible to managers who award promotions and raises, and, consequently, they work extra hours on nights or weekends because they have less "face time" (interaction between two or more people at the same time and physical location).

Telecommuting can also decrease the quality of family time. Some parents resent interruptions or distractions while they're working, worry that they can't leave job stress at the office, or find that it's hard to separate their family and business lives.

Noise from children, pets, and appliances may also decrease productivity and create tension at home. Some people are also concerned that the costs of telecommuting may be screened more carefully

by the Internal Revenue Service and increase the risk of audits.

Source: Heubeck, 2005; Gariety and Shaffer, 2007; Saad, 2008.

Stop and Think . . .

- Have you or your friends ever telecommuted? If so, what were the advantages and disadvantages?

- When employers started laying people off in 2008 and 2009, some telecommuters—including those with incomes above $70,000 a year—worried that they would be cut because they didn't have much face time at the company (see Shin, 2009). Do you think that such concerns are justified? Or are higher-paid telecommuters safe from layoffs?

Changes

iceberg because only a fraction of women who encounter pregnancy discrimination ever take action: Many aren't aware of their rights and others don't have the resources to pursue lengthy lawsuits.

Family and Medical Leave Policies

The Family and Medical Leave Act (FMLA) of 1993 allows eligible employees to take up to 12 weeks of *unpaid* annual leave, with continuation of health benefits, after the birth or adoption of a child, to care for a seriously sick family member, or to recover from their own illnesses. The box "A Tour of the Family and Medical Leave Act" provides a closer look at these rights.

BENEFITS OF THE FMLA The most obvious benefit of family leave policies is that many employees should no longer lose their jobs because of sickness, childbirth, or parental leave. Also, most employees are guaranteed the same job or an equivalent job when they return. The FMLA defines an "equivalent" position as one with the same pay, benefits, working conditions, and "substantially similar" duties and responsibilities. Most important, because the FMLA is the law, employees don't have to depend on the supervisor's good will for leave.

Many parents, especially mothers, stitch together paid leave (such as sick days and vacations) to cover childbirth and caring for an infant for a few weeks or longer. The percentage of women who had some paid leave increased from 37 percent in 1981 to 42 percent in 2000. Most companies, especially those with 1,000 or more employees, fund this pay through a general temporary disability insurance (TDI) plan that provides partial wage replacement for maternity-related

Choices

A Tour of the Family and Medical Leave Act

Workers who know their rights under the Family and Medical Leave Act (FMLA) are more likely to take advantage of its benefits.

Who is covered? Any employee is eligible for 12 weeks of leave if she or he has worked at least 1,250 hours during a 12-month period—roughly the equivalent of 25 hours a week—at a company or work site that employs at least 50 people.

The highest-paid 10 percent of employees must be granted a leave like all other employees. However, members of this group are not guaranteed a job on return if their absence causes "substantial and grievous economic injury" to their employer.

What are the purposes of leave? An employee may take family or medical leave for the birth or adoption of a child and to care for a newborn; to care for a spouse, child, or parent with a serious illness; or to recuperate from a serious illness that prevents the employee from working.

Who pays for the leave? The employee pays for the leave. A company may require or allow employees to apply paid vacation and sick leave to the 12 weeks of family leave, but it does not have to pay workers who take leave.

When should the employer be notified? In foreseeable cases, such as a birth, adoption, or planned medical treatment, 30 days' verbal or written notice is required. When that's impossible (for example, if a baby is born earlier than expected), the employer must be notified as soon as possible, generally within one or two business days. Employers can ask for medical proof that a leave is needed.

Must the leave be taken all at once? No. For example, the leave can be used to shorten the workweek when an employee wants to cut back after the birth of a child. Medical leave can also be taken piecemeal (to accommodate weekly appointments for chemotherapy treatments, for instance).

What if you believe that your rights have been violated? Any local or regional office of the U.S. Department of Labor's Wage and Hour Division, Employment Standards Administration, will accept complaints, which must be filed within two years of the alleged violation. Private lawsuits must also be filed within two years of the violation.

According to a recent Supreme Court ruling (*Nevada Department of Human Resources v. Hibbs*), state employees can now sue agencies that violate the FMLA.

⠿• Stop and Think . . .

- In contrast to the United States, 19 other industrialized countries have provided 12 to 72 weeks of paid parental leave since 1989 (Shierholz and Garr, 2008). Should we do the same, even if it means increasing everyone's taxes?

- Many U.S. employers now cover some paid maternity (but not paternity) leave under disability insurance. Why is pregnancy a "disability"? And why are men excluded from such "disability insurance"?

leaves, but only for mothers (Bond et al., 2005; Overturf Johnson and Downs, 2005).

LIMITATIONS OF THE FMLA The biggest problem is that the 60 percent of U.S. employees who work in companies with fewer than 50 employees are not covered by the FMLA (Shierholz and Garr, 2008). Small companies are much less likely than larger ones to provide employee benefits such as health insurance, paid sick leave, and disability insurance. Thus, the FMLA ignores millions of employees who already have limited benefits. In addition, the many workers in part-time, temporary positions (most of whom are women) are excluded from family leave policies.

A second problem is that 30 percent of employers with 50 or more employers offer fewer than 12 weeks of unpaid family leave, a violation of the FMLA. It's not clear whether the employers are simply unaware of the law or violate it deliberately. In fact, 90 percent of businesses that follow the FMLA report that they incur no additional costs by providing unpaid leave or actually increase their profits through higher employee morale and productivity (Smith et al., 2001; Bond et al., 2005).

A third problem is that the FMLA is of little help to many parents because it involves unpaid time off and covers only major illnesses, which typically necessitate a hospital stay. In most cases, children don't need hospitalization but instead have frequent routine illnesses. Many working parents can't afford to take any unpaid leave because of the cost or the risk of being laid off (Phillips, 2004).

Finally, employees and employers may disagree about what constitutes "equivalent" jobs or "substantially similar" responsibilities. For example, does a person have an equivalent job if it involves driving an extra 30 minutes to work to an unfamiliar office at a less desirable location?

COMPARISON WITH OTHER COUNTRIES Women who return to work quickly after childbirth are more likely than those who stay home longer to suffer from depression, poorer health, and lower productivity (Chatterji and Markowitz, 2008). Nonetheless, the United States is the only one of the 19 industrialized countries that does not guarantee paid leave at all. Out of 173 countries, 169 offer some form of paid maternity leave, and 98 countries offer at least 14 weeks of paid leave. Those that don't are three developing nations—Liberia, Papua New Guinea, Swaziland—and the United States. Also, 66 countries ensure that fathers either receive paid paternity leave or have a right to parental leave, and 31 of these countries offer 14 or more weeks of paid leave. The United States, in contrast, does not guarantee fathers any paid leave (Heymann et al., 2007).

Sweden has one of the most generous parental leave policies in the world—15 months of paid leave. The Netherlands and Spain offer 16 weeks of maternity leave at full pay, Denmark provides 18 weeks at 90 percent of the worker's salary, and Ireland offers 14 weeks at 70 percent of the worker's salary. Some countries—such as Belgium, Greece, France, and Finland—give up to 4 weeks of paid paternity leave (Moss and Wall, 2007).

Care for Dependents

One of the most serious problems facing families today is inadequate day care for young children. And, increasingly, families are confronting the need to provide services for elderly parents. What, if anything, are businesses and government doing to help families care for their dependents?

CHILD CARE As you saw in Chapter 12, high costs, poor quality, and long waiting lists are just some of the obstacles that confront working parents who seek safe and reliable care for their children. Unlike almost all other industrialized countries, we have no national child care program. Some companies that tout child care assistance actually do little more than provide a list of child care providers in the area. Only 7 percent of employers with 50 or more workers provide child care at or near the workplace (Bond et al., 2005). Because most companies charge their employees for day care services, many low-wage workers are unable to pay even the reduced costs that companies offer.

ELDER CARE The FMLA does not include elder care. Most businesses rarely provide or subsidize elder care leave, but about 79 percent of all companies say that they offer employees time off to care for elderly parents without jeopardizing their jobs (Bond et al., 2005). It's not clear, however, how much of that "time off" includes paid leave. Probably very little, because family members—especially women—provide most elder care and often have to quit their jobs to do so (see Chapter 17).

Many modern-day parents struggle to combine employment and family life. Work offers economic and psychological benefits, but many women (and sometimes men) have little choice in deciding whether they want to be employed or spend more time raising their children. Such constraints are widespread, some scholars contend, because family policies have been crafted by political and capitalist elites who are interested in wreaking more profits for themselves at the expense of the average working and middle class family (see Gilbert, 2008).

You'll recall that there was considerable concern by policymakers and employers when women's labor force participation declined slightly after 2000. There hasn't been a parallel concern in passing family-friendly legislation that improves the quality of life for employed parents and their children, including paid leave for fathers and increasing women's earnings.

CONCLUSION

Because many families are struggling financially, they have very few *choices* in the workplace, such as working part time or full time. Macro-level economic *changes*, especially during the past few years, have created numerous *constraints* that impact families. Incomes have not kept up with inflation and unemployment rates have increased, so more parents have to work. Doing so results in outsourcing young children's care, often to strangers, and spending less time supervising and interacting with adolescents.

Many parents, especially single mothers, can't afford the cost of child care. But without child care, they can't get the training for jobs that will pull them out of poverty. Many of the same economic forces also have an impact on family violence, a topic we examine in the next chapter.

SUMMARY

1. Work is important, but many families have lost economic ground because of macro-level variables such as deindustrialization, globalization, and offshoring.

2. Social class and economic changes play a major role in what happens to families. Affluent families are getting richer, an increasing number of middle class families have lower incomes, and the number of poor families is growing.

3. The economy affects families in many ways. Some must accept low-wage jobs or work nonstandard hours or only part time. Official unemployment rates aren't accurate because they don't count the millions of discouraged and underemployed workers.

4. Unemployment often leads to poverty. Many scholars contend that the poverty line is unrealistic, but they agree that children, women, and many racial-ethnic families are disproportionately poor. There are several explanations for poverty and homelessness, both of which have increased.

5. Women's participation in the labor force has increased since the 1950s but has recently leveled off. Still, many women now work longer before childbirth and return to work more quickly than in the past.

6. Economic recessions and stagnant incomes have resulted in more dual-earner families. There is a great deal of variation in these families, however, in terms of social class, gender roles and parenting, and willingness to relocate or to have a commuter marriage.

7. There is considerable inequality and discrimination in the workplace based on sex, race, and ethnicity. Some of the problems that women are especially likely to encounter are gender pay gaps, a motherhood penalty, and sexual harassment.

8. One solution for the gender pay gap is comparable worth, but few states have enacted such policies.

9. Some of the recent changes in the workplace include bringing babies to work, flextime, and telecommuting. When available, these options have both benefits and costs.

10. The Family and Medical Leave Act is supposed to protect an employee's job during illness and maternity and paternity leave, but many employers still provide only limited coverage. The United States lags behind other countries—industrialized and developing—in offering paid leaves for workers to care for their children and other family dependents.

KEY TERMS

economy 351
work 352
deindustrialization 352
globalization 352
offshoring 352
wealth 353
income 353
corporate welfare 355
working poor 356
discouraged worker 358
underemployed worker 358

absolute poverty 359
relative poverty 359
poverty line 359
feminization of poverty 361
glass ceiling 365
two-person single career 366
dual-earner couple 367
discretionary income 368
dual-career couple 368
trailing spouse 369
commuter marriage 370

gender pay gap 372
motherhood penalty 373
comparable worth 374
flextime 376
telecommuting 376

PEARSON myfamilylab MyFamilyLab provides a wealth of resources. Go to www.myfamilylab.com<http://www.myfamilylab.com/>, to enhance your comprehension of the content in this chapter. You can take practice exams, view videos relevant to the subject matter, listen to audio files, explore topics further by using Social Explorer, and use the tools contained in MySearchLab to help you write research papers.

14 Family Abuse, Violence, and Other Health Issues

Families can be warm, loving, and nurturing, but they can also be vicious and terrifying. A few years ago, for example, almost 3-year-old Andrew died after his father, a computer systems engineer, took the unresponsive child to an emergency room. The toddler's ravaged body was covered with wounds, bruises, and lacerations, some of which were recent and others that had been sustained over a period of time. Andrew weighted 13 pounds, roughly what a normal 3-month-old weighs. The boy's starvation was so advanced, his brain and heart had begun to shrink, and his muscles had atrophied so much that he couldn't walk. According to the police, Andrew's room was splattered with his blood on the ceiling, the walls, and his basinet. Andrew's mother, a full-time housewife with five other children, said that Andrew's injuries were caused by his scratching himself and falling down the stairs (Barnhardt and Scharper, 2007; Madigan, 2009).

Over a lifetime, we are much more likely to be assaulted or killed by a family member than by a stranger: "That violence and love can coexist in a household is perhaps the most insidious aspect of family violence, because we grow up learning that it is acceptable to hit the people we love" (Gelles, 1997: 12).

DATA DIGEST

- Between 1994 and 2007, the rate of **reported child abuse or neglect decreased** from 15.2 to 10.6 per 1,000 children.

- Of all **intimate partner homicides,** 75 percent of the victims are women.

- Nearly **22 percent of women who are physically assaulted by an intimate partner are injured,** compared with 4 percent of men.

- Almost **30 percent of U.S. children live in partner-violent families.**

- The **cost of child maltreatment** is almost $104 billion a year. The costs are both direct (such as hospitalization and law enforcement) and indirect (such as juvenile delinquency and adult criminality).

- Each year, spouses, adult children, or close acquaintances **injure about 192,000 people age 60 or older and kill about 500.**

Sources: McDonald et al., 2006; Teaster et al., 2006; Catalano, 2007; Fox and Zawitz, 2007; Wang and Holton, 2007; U.S. Department of Health and Human Services, 2006, 2009.

This chapter examines the different forms of domestic abuse and violence, describes their prevalence, and discusses why people who say that they love each other can be so cruel. We then turn to other family health issues, such as drug abuse, depression, suicide, and eating disorders. We'll end the chapter with a look at some prevention and intervention strategies.

INTIMATE PARTNER ABUSE AND VIOLENCE

Intimate partner violence (IPV) occurs between two people in a close relationship. The term *intimate partner* refers to current and former spouses, couples who live together, and current or former boyfriends or girlfriends. Chapter 8 examined dating violence; this chapter focuses primarily on other IPV couples.

Some social scientists use the terms *intimate partner violence* and *domestic violence* interchangeably, whereas others use the term *intimate partner* to explicitly include people who are not married (for example, divorced or single men and women and gays and lesbians). I'll use *domestic violence* more frequently later in the chapter when we look at abuse that also includes children, siblings, and older family members.

IPV is pervasive in U.S. society. In a recent national study conducted by the Centers for Disease Control and Prevention (CDC), 27 percent of women and 16 percent of men said that they had been victims of IPV at some time in their lives (Black and Breiding, 2008). These numbers are probably conservative because many people are too ashamed to report the victimization, believe that no one can help, or fear reprisal.

Types of Intimate Partner Violence

Intimate partner violence exists along a continuum from a single episode to ongoing battering. IPV includes three types of behavior:

- **Physical abuse** occurs when a person hurts or tries to hurt a partner using physical force. Examples include throwing objects, pushing, grabbing, slapping, kicking, biting, hitting, beating, and choking.
- **Sexual abuse** is forcing a partner to take part in a sex act when she or he doesn't consent. The most common examples include coercing a person to have sexual intercourse (the legal term is *rape*) or taking part in unwanted sexual activity (such as anal or oral sex).

- **Emotional abuse** is threatening a partner or his or her loved ones or possessions or harming a partner's sense of self-worth. Examples of emotional abuse include stalking, name calling, intimidation, and not letting a partner see friends and family. Such psychological and verbal abuse are equally harmful because scorn, criticism, ridicule, or neglect by loved ones can be emotionally crippling.

The CDC (2006) includes *threats* of physical or sexual abuse as another type of IPV. These are behaviors that involve words, gestures, weapons, or other means to communicate the intent to cause harm.

Often, IPV starts with emotional abuse that can escalate to physical or sexual assault. Also, several types of IPV occur together, such as when a partner berates someone verbally while pummeling her or him.

The Prevalence and Severity of Intimate Partner Violence

Women's victimization by intimate partners decreased between 1993 and 2005, but the numbers are still high and considerably higher than those for men (see *Figure 14.1*). During this period, women were five times more likely than men to experience violence by an intimate partner. In fact, almost 75 percent of all attacks by intimate partners are against women (Durose et al., 2005).

Each year, IPV results in an estimated 1,200 deaths and 2 million injuries among women compared with 330 deaths and nearly 600,000 injuries among men (Catalano, 2007; Black and Breiding,

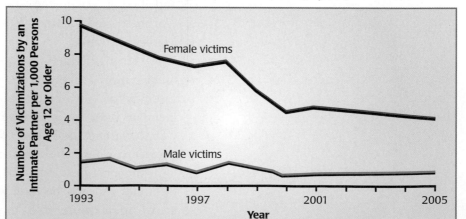

FIGURE 14.1 Violence Rates by an Intimate Partner, by Sex, 1993–2005

Source: Based on Rennison, 2003; Catalano, 2007.

2008). When victims survive an assault, women are much more likely than men to report serious psychological distress (such as depression, nervousness, and feelings of hopelessness and worthlessness) and to attempt suicide. Women's poorer mental health functioning is due to their greater likelihood of experiencing repeated abuse as well as both physical and sexual violence (Edwards et al., 2009).

Women are also more likely than men to experience serious physical injuries because they are usually smaller than their partners and more likely to use their fists rather than weapons. Female intimate partners are more likely to be murdered with a firearm than all other means combined (Violence Policy Center, 2008).

IPV is a leading cause of death for women ages 15 to 44. Pregnant women are especially vulnerable. Homicide ranks second, after auto accidents, as a major cause of death for women during pregnancy or within one year after giving birth. Sexual and physical violence usually go hand in hand during pregnancy (Chang et al., 2005; Tessier, 2008).

Most intimate partner homicides have involved spouses, but in recent years the number of deaths by spouses and girlfriends and boyfriends have been similar (see *Figure 14.2*). The reason for the drop in marital homicides is unclear, but it might reflect a number of interrelated factors such as an improved economy between 1980 and 2000; an increase in women's financial power as larger numbers entered the workforce; and postponing marriage and parenthood, both of which decrease the likelihood of violence because the partners are older, more mature, and have more skills in resolving conflict (see Chapters 10, 12, and 13). We won't know for several years whether the recent economic downturn affected intimate partner homicide rates.

We'll examine why women's victimization rates are much higher than men's shortly. First, however, let's look at some of the characteristics of IPV.

Some Characteristics of Abusive and Violent Households

Who batters? There is no "typical" batterer, but some characteristics are common to abusers (see *Table 14.1*). Some reflect macro-level influences, such as unemployment and poverty. Others are due to micro-level factors such as drug abuse. The more risk factors, the more likely the abusive and violent behavior.

In general, both male and female abusers tend to be young, poor, unemployed, cohabiting or separated and to abuse alcohol and other drugs, and they may have seen a parent, usually a father, or other male in an intimate relationship use violence to resolve conflict. Typically, however, abusive relationships reflect a combination of these and other related factors. They also vary across groups in terms of gender, age, race and ethnicity, and social class.

> **Since you asked . . .**
>
> :•• Is there *one* major reason for intimate partner violence?

GENDER Women are much more likely than men to experience IPV over a lifetime, regardless of age, race or ethnicity, annual household income, and education level (see *Table 14.2*). Men are also more likely to use a deadly weapon. In 2005, according to the most recent available data, 16 percent of women compared with 28 percent of men in IPV used a weapon, and men were almost four times more likely than women to use a firearm (Catalano, 2007).

Also, and unlike women, men are likely to commit **familycide**, murdering one's spouse, ex-spouse, children, or other relatives before attempting or committing suicide. The men who slaughter their families are sometimes called *family annihilators*. Such crimes are rare but represent up to 2 percent of all homicides a year and devastate the surviving family members, relatives, and the community (Callahan, 2009).

Family annihilators are usually white; male; middle-aged; a family breadwinner who is on the verge of a catastrophic economic loss or has been laid off; has never shown

FIGURE 14.2 Homicides of Intimates, by Relationship of Victim to Offender, 1976–2005

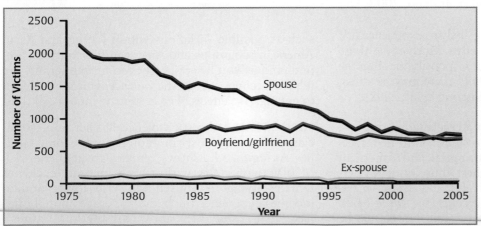

Source: Fox and Zawitz, 2007, p. 56.

TABLE 14.1	Risk Factors Associated with Intimate Partner Violence

- The woman's education or income level is higher than the man's.
- The couple is cohabiting or separated rather than married, divorced, or widowed.
- The partners' race and/or ethnicity differ.
- The man is sadistic, aggressive, or obsessively jealous.
- Either or both partners were violent during their teenage years.
- One or both partners grew up seeing a parent or intimate partner hit the other.
- The man is unemployed and the woman is employed.
- The family's income is below the poverty line.
- The man is younger than age 35.
- Either or both partners abuse alcohol and other drugs.
- The man has assaulted someone outside the family or committed some other violent crime.
- The family is socially isolated from neighbors, relatives, and the community.

Sources: MacMillan and Gartner, 1999; Tjaden and Thoennes, 2000; Rennison, 2001; Thompson et al., 2006; Catalano, 2007; Herrenkohl et al., 2007; Black and Breiding, 2008; Edwards et al., 2009.

TABLE 14.2	Percentage of Americans Age 18 and Older Who Have Ever Experienced Intimate Partner Violence	
	Women	**Men**
Total	26	12
Age		
18–24	24	18
25–34	30	21
35–44	30	18
45–54	31	16
55–64	27	13
65 and older	13	6
Race/Ethnicity		
White	27	16
Latino	21	16
Black	29	23
American Indian/Alaska Native	39	19
Asian	10	8
Multiracial	43	26
Annual Household Income		
Less than $15,000	36	21
$15,000–$24,999	29	20
$25,000–$34,999	31	16
$35,000–$49,999	27	16
$50,000 or higher	24	14
Education		
Did not graduate from high school	28	16
High school graduate	25	16
Some college	32	19
College graduate	23	14

Source: Based on Black and Breiding, 2008, Table 1.

any signs of depression, anxiety, or hostility; behaves normally; and has been plotting the murders of his wife and children sometimes for many months (Callahan, 2009). In 2008, for example, a former bank executive in Iowa, who had been accused of embezzlement, beat his wife and four children to death with baseball bats and then crashed his car ("Mother, 4 kids . . .," 2008).

AGE In general, younger rather than older people are more likely to be the victims and perpetrators of IPV, and the victimization tends to decline over time. In 2005, for example, males and females ages 20 to 24 had the highest incidence of IPV and those age 65 and older the lowest. In the same year, almost half of all victims and offenders of intimate partner homicide were between ages 18 and 34 (Catalano, 2007; Fox and Zawitz, 2007).

Teen mothers are especially likely to experience IPV for several years after a child's birth. Much of the abuse probably results from financial responsibilities that the couple can't manage. As a result, there may be stress, conflict, and violence (Harrykissoon et al., 2002).

RACE AND ETHNICITY Across all racial-ethnic groups, women are much more likely than men to be targets of IPV over a lifetime. Multiracial and American Indian women report the highest abuse rates (43 percent and 39 percent, respectively), and Asian American women the lowest (10 percent) (see *Table 14.2*).

Such national data are useful, but they should be interpreted cautiously for several reasons. First, there are still almost no data on IPV *within* ethnic-racial groups,

such as possible variations within Latino and Asian American subgroups and American Indian tribes. Second, and as you'll see shortly, recent immigrants are reluctant to report domestic violence. Third, it's difficult to untangle the effects of race, ethnicity, and social class.

SOCIAL CLASS Domestic violence cuts across all social classes, but it is most common in low-income families. As *Figure 14.3* shows, females are at greater risk of IPV than males within each income level, but females living in households with lower annual incomes experience the highest average annual rates (see, also, *Table 14.2* above for lifetime figures). Women living in households with annual incomes less than $7,500 a year are nearly seven times more

FIGURE 14.3 Average Annual Nonfatal Intimate Partner Victimization Rate, by Income and Gender, 2001–2005

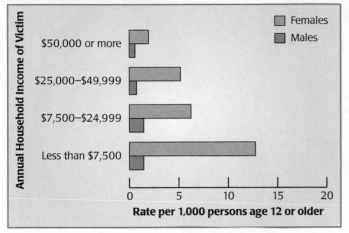

Source: Catalano, 2007, p. 16.

likely to be victimized by an intimate partner than are women living in households with an annual income of at least $75,000 (Macomber, 2006).

Social class itself doesn't cause IPV because, over a lifetime, perpetrators and victims include those from all income and education levels (Catalano, 2007; see, also, *Table 14.2* on p. 386). However, socioeconomically disadvantaged women and men are more likely than others to be living in adverse conditions that increase the likelihood of at-risk behavior. The most likely IPV perpetrators and victims are those who marry or cohabit at a young age, started to have sexual intercourse at a young age, had many sex partners, were aggressive in childhood, abuse alcohol and other drugs, are unemployed, live in poverty, and have unintended pregnancies or more children than they can afford to raise (Frias and Angel, 2005; Hill, 2005; O'Donnell, 2009).

Besides familycide, there are many other instances of IPV in middle-class families. A few years ago, for example, the police arrested a police lieutenant who had pressed his service revolver to the back of his wife's head, threatening to kill her. He was upset because his wife had come home with a regular cake instead of an ice cream cake for his 47th birthday. The lieutenant had previously supervised a domestic violence unit in his precinct on Staten Island, New York ("Officer accused . . . ," 2005).

When men have fewer economic resources than their wives, they may engage not in physical abuse but in emotional abuse (such as put-downs, threats of physical violence, and limiting the woman's movements). Especially when men have traditional views about gender roles and equate masculinity with being the primary breadwinner, they are more likely to use physical violence to compensate for their lack of income. In both types of situations, the men try to restore their control and dominance over their part-

ner through emotional or physical abuse (Kaukinen, 2004; Atkinson et al., 2005).

People in higher socioeconomic families also abuse their partners and spouses. The late host of *Dominick Dunne's Power, Privilege, and Justice,* a popular television crime series, seemed to relish exposing the greed and domestic violence among the rich and privileged. In 2007, a woman's shelter in Naples, Florida, added a new program, Women of Means, that specifically targets educated, professional and/or affluent victims of IPV. The program offers upscale services such as spas and beauty salons, and an array of attorneys, physicians, psychiatrists, dentists, and other professionals (Green, 2007). Whether wealthy women should get special treatment might be controversial, but the program shows that IPV isn't limited only to low-income groups.

Marital Rape

Marital rape (sometimes called *spousal rape* or *wife rape*) is an abusive act in which a man forces his wife to have unwanted sexual intercourse. Marital rape has been a crime in all states since 1993 and is the most common type of rape in the United States, but some states define this assault as a lesser offense than stranger rape (Polisi, 2009).

An estimated 25 percent of women nationwide have been raped by their spouses, but very few report the crime. A traditional wife, believing that she has no choice but to perform her "wifely duty," may accept the situation as normal, especially if her husband does not use a weapon or threaten her with physical harm (Michael et al., 1994; Polisi, 2009).

When women report the crime, offenders are rarely prosecuted. A wife may have difficulty proving that a rape occurred if she shows no visible signs of having been forced, such as bruises or broken bones. Some husbands use physical force, but many rely on other forms of coercion such as threatening to leave or to cheat on a wife (Hines and Malley-Morrison, 2005).

The Cycle of Domestic Violence

Since 1978, state governors have granted clemency to several hundred women who were convicted of killing their abusers. The women were pardoned based on the defense of **battered-woman syndrome,** a condition that describes a woman who has experienced many years of physical abuse and feels incapable of leaving her partner. In a desperate effort to defend themselves, such women sometimes kill the abuser.

The battered-woman syndrome is controversial because, some argue, abused women have the option of leaving the abusers instead of killing them. Others maintain that a "cycle theory of battering incidents" supports the battered-woman syndrome defense.

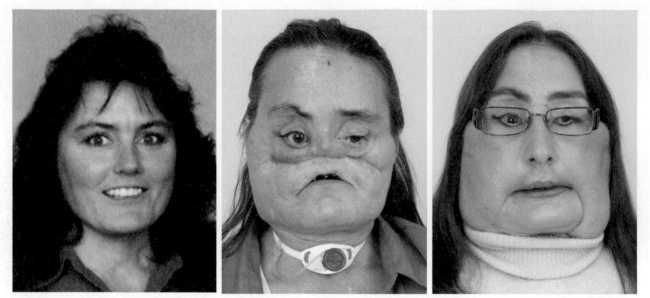

In 2004, Connie Culp's husband blasted her with a shotgun that left a hole where the middle of her face had been. He then turned the gun on himself, survived, and was sent to prison for seven years. In 2009, and after 30 operations, Culp became the fourth woman in the world to undergo a successful face transplant. The photos, from left to right, show her before the attempted murder, and before and after the face transplant.

According to this well-known theory, a tension-building phase leads to an acute battering incident. This is followed by a period of calm until the cycle starts again (Walker, 1978, 2000).

PHASE ONE: THE TENSION-BUILDING PHASE In the first phase of the cycle, when "minor" battering incidents occur, the woman tries to reduce her partner's anger by catering to him or staying out of his way. At the same time, the battered woman often believes that her partner's abuse is justified: "When he throws the dinner she prepared for him across the kitchen floor, she reasons that maybe she did overcook it, accidentally. As she cleans up his mess, she may think that he was a bit extreme in his reaction, but she is usually so grateful that it was a relatively minor incident that she resolves not to be angry with him" (Walker, 1978: 147). Although the victim hopes that the situation will change, the tension typically escalates, the man becomes more brutal, and the woman is less able to defend herself.

PHASE TWO: THE ACUTE BATTERING INCIDENT Abusers often have a Dr. Jekyll and Mr. Hyde personality in which the rational and gentle Dr. Jekyll changes, unpredictably, into an unreasonable and brutal Mr. Hyde. In this second phase, Mr. Hyde emerges, exploding in rage and beating or otherwise abusing his partner. Thus, the woman's feelings fluctuate:

I have two responses to Stu because I am responding to two different people, or two different parts of one person. There's the Stu who is very thoughtful and gentle and kind, and then there's the brutal and hostile Stu (Strasser, 2004: 210).

Some women who have lived with abuse for a long time actually anticipate this phase and trigger the violent incident to get it over with. They often deny the severity of their injuries and refuse to seek medical treatment. One woman who wanted to go to a family party with her husband and sensed that an acute battering incident was about to occur deliberately provoked it during the week so that by the weekend her husband would be pleasant for the party (Walker, 1978).

PHASE THREE: CALM (THE "HONEYMOON PHASE") Mr. Hyde becomes the kindly Dr. Jekyll in the third phase, begging the woman's forgiveness and promising that he will never beat her again: "He manages to convince all concerned that this time he means it; he will give up drinking, seeing other women, visiting his mother, or whatever else affects his internal anxiety state. His sincerity is believable" (Walker, 1978: 152).

If the victim has been hospitalized because of her physical injuries, the man often deluges her with flowers, candy, cards, and gifts. He may also get his mother, father, sisters, brothers, and other relatives to plead his case to her. They build up her guilt by telling her that he would be devastated if she left him and that a father should not be separated from his children. Because most battered women hold traditional values about love and marriage, the wife convinces herself that *this* time he'll *really* change.

Because he is now loving and kind, the battered woman believes that the "good man," the one she loves, will honor his tearful promises to change. After a while, the calm and loving behavior gives way to battering incidents, and the cycle starts all over again, often including marital rape.

Former basketball star Dennis Rodman has been arrested several times for intimate partner violence, once against his wife, and later against a girlfriend.

Why Do Women Stay?

Walker theorized that the cycle of violence often results in *learned help-lessness:* The woman becomes depressed, loses her self-esteem, and feels incapable of seeking help or escaping the abusive relationship. It's not clear whether these characteristics reflect personality traits that battered women possessed before they met the abusers, whether they are the result of the abuse, or a combination of both (Rathus and O'Leary, 1997).

> **Since you asked . . .**
>
> ⠿• Why do many battered women stay with their partners?

Still, the obvious question is "Why do these women stay?" Despite the common tendency to think of abused women as passive punching bags, many do resist or try to change the situation. Some of the strategies include hitting back; contacting local domestic violence shelters; calling the police; obtaining restraining/protection orders; disclosing their abusive experiences to family members, friends, neighbors, and/or co-workers; and terminating the relationship (Hamby and Bible, 2009).

Some women, like one of my students, find the courage to leave only when they suddenly realize that the abusive relationship has a spillover effect that harms their children:

John never laid a finger on our daughter but struck me in front of her. . . . I cringe to remember but at the time I chose to believe that what Sheri saw wasn't affecting her. One afternoon when I heard Sheri banging and yelling, I rushed to her room. . . . Sheri was hitting her doll and screaming four-letter words she often heard her father yell at me. She was just starting to talk, and that was what she was learning. That moment changed our lives forever. . . . I left John that night and never went back (Author's files).

This woman left her husband because she had some resources—a good job at the Motor Vehicle Administration, a college degree, her own checking and savings accounts, and supportive family members who provided her and Sheri with temporary housing and emotional encouragement. Most abuse victims aren't that fortunate.

There is no single reason why some women don't leave violent relationships. Instead, there are multiple and overlapping explanations.

NEGATIVE SELF-CONCEPT AND LOW SELF-ESTEEM Most batterers convince their partners that they are worthless, stupid, and disgusting: "Behind a closed door, a man calls a woman a 'slut' and a 'whore.' He tells her that she is too fat, too sexy or too frumpy, that she is 'a poor excuse for a mother,' a worthless piece of dirt" (Goode et al., 1994: 24). And, according to a 33-year-old mother of two children: "He rarely says a kind word to me. The food is too cold or . . . too hot. The kids are too noisy. . . . I am too fat or too skinny. No matter what I do, he says it isn't any good. He tells me I am lucky he married me 'cause no one else would have me" (Gelles and Straus, 1988: 68).

Such tyranny is effective because in many cultures, including ours, many women's self-worth still hinges on having a man. Sometimes women are willing to pay any price to hold on to the relationship because they believe that no one else could love them.

BELIEF THAT THE ABUSER WILL CHANGE When I asked a woman I knew, her cheek still raw from her husband's beating, why she didn't leave, she said, "I'm still in love with him, and I know he's going to change as soon as he gets past these things that are troubling him."

Our society has long nurtured the myth that women are responsible for changing men into kind and loving beings. Consider the message in the popular Walt Disney film *Beauty and the Beast.* The woman is taken captive and isolated from her friends and family. The Beast turns into a prince only after Beauty stays with him and says that she loves him despite his cruelty and threats and his breaking furniture and acting like a beast.

Many women stay in violent relationships because they are seduced by the Cinderella fantasy. The woman believes that, sooner or later, the abuser will change and she and Prince Charming will live happily ever after. As a result, millions of women stay in an abusive relationship because they hope to "rehabilitate" the man rather than break up the family (Sontag, 2002).

A college professor remained married to a batterer for 12 years because she believed that her husband would eventually change back to being a good man: "Before we married, my husband seemed to be the perfect man—kind, gentle, romantic, admiring of me and my academic successes." She clung to this illusion for over a decade even though the battering began three weeks after they married, when she learned that she was pregnant (Bates, 2005: C1).

ECONOMIC HARDSHIP AND HOMELESSNESS Because many abused women do not work outside the home or have few marketable skills, they see no way to survive economically if they leave the abuser. For example, an award-winning high school coach in Baltimore stabbed his wife 10 times with a screwdriver, leaving her partially paralyzed. The wife pleaded with the judge *not* to send the husband to jail. Ironically, she wanted him to keep working so his health insurance could pay for treating her injuries; she had worked part time and had no medical benefits (Shatzkin, 1996).

Many batterers keep their wives in economic chains. Nothing is in the woman's name—not checking or savings accounts, automobiles, or homes. Because most abusers isolate their victims from friends and relatives, the women have no one to turn to. Moreover, those who might give battered women a place to stay are afraid that they might endanger their own family. Without resources, some abused women who do leave become homeless (Browne, 1993; Choice and Lamke, 1997).

Women often have nowhere to go. Hundreds are turned away from shelters for battered women every day because of overcrowding and underfunding. In Missouri, for example, almost 4,300 women were turned away from shelters in 2004 alone because there was not enough space (Gonnerman, 2005).

NEED FOR CHILD SUPPORT Leaving a man or filing charges against him may push a woman and her children into poverty. Many women believe that even an abusive partner is better than none. As one of my students, a former abused wife who eventually left her husband, once said in class, "This man brings in most of the family's income. Without him, you can't pay the rent, buy the groceries, or pay the electric bills. If he goes to jail, he'll probably lose his job. And then what will you and the kids do?"

Since 2001, Latinas and other women in New York City have participated in the Annual Brides March against Domestic Violence. The signs tell women "You're worth a lot" and "Don't accept the mistreatment."

SHAME OR GUILT Strong cultural factors may also keep a woman from leaving an abuser. In some Asian American communities, especially, there is strong pressure not to bring shame or disgrace on the family by exposing problems such as domestic violence. Women in rural areas are especially isolated: There are no shelters, their jobs usually pay a minimum wage, and the women are afraid that disclosing abuse to co-workers or supervisors will bring gossip and shame on the family (Swanberg and Logan, 2003).

BLAMING THEMSELVES Battered women often believe that somehow they have brought the violence on themselves. Men who batter may be well-respected professional athletes, community leaders, or attorneys. The women start thinking that because the men have a good reputation, it must be their fault when the men are abusive at home (Parameswaran, 2003).

This is particularly likely if women have seen their mothers or grandmothers suffer similar treatment: "One woman whose bruises from her husband's beatings were clearly visible was told by her grandmother, 'You have to stop provoking him. You have two children, and the bottom line is you have nowhere to go. If he tells you to shut up, shut up!'" (Goode et al., 1994: 27).

Thus, an abusive tradition is passed on. Women believe that they are responsible for preventing male violence, and if they don't succeed, they must accept the consequences. Moreover, because some priests, ministers, and rabbis remind a woman that she is married "for better or for worse," religious women may feel guilty and sinful for wanting to leave (Jones, 1993; Hines and Malley-Morrison, 2005).

FEAR Fear is a *major* reason for staying in an abusive relationship. Some men threaten to kill the woman, her relatives, and even the children if the woman tries to escape. Several directors of battered women's shelters have told me that it is not unusual for husbands to track down their families from as far away as 1,000 miles and threaten violence to get them to return.

Even when judges issue protective orders, as you'll see later in this chapter, the orders are temporary and the offenders can still assault their partners at home (even when the locks have been changed), workplaces, and public places such as parking lots. Because the man has been abusive before, threats of retaliation are real and many victims live in constant fear.

THE HOME BECOMES A PRISON Both emotional and physical abuse trap the battered woman in her home. With little chance of escaping, the victim becomes a prisoner. The man is the ultimate authority, and she is punished if she disagrees with him. She must follow his "house rules" about not leaving the house or even making phone calls without his permission. In some cases, he takes the phone with him when he leaves for work. She has no control over her body, is isolated from her friends and relatives, and is watched constantly (Avni, 1991; Gonnerman, 2005).

All these factors help explain why many women stay in abusive relationships: "Staying may mean abuse and violence, but leaving may mean death. A bureaucracy may promise safety, but cannot ensure it. For many battered women, this is a risk they cannot take" (Englander, 1997: 149–50).

Also, as some social scientists point out, leaving an abusive partner isn't as clear cut as deciding to quit smoking, for example, because it's often a long *process* that involves numerous changes, such as thinking about leaving, preparing to leave (such as trying to establish secret savings and checking accounts), taking action (such as speaking to a counselor), and trying to improve the relationship. In all of these stages, women may be ambivalent about leaving and preserving a father-child relationship that's not abusive, as well as having few available resources for themselves and their children (Khaw and Hardesty, 2009).

Domestic violence takes different forms, but the goal is always the same: control of the partner through fear and intimidation. The box "Some Warning Signs of Intimate Partner Abuse and Violence" provides clues to potential problems.

Women Who Abuse Men

In 2003, a jury in Houston, Texas, sentenced a 45-year-old dentist to 20 years in prison for killing her husband, an orthodontist. The wife ran over her husband several times with her Mercedes-Benz after finding him with his mistress, a former receptionist. The case received prominent national attention because the incident involved an upper-middle-class couple and the offender was a woman.

Sociologist Michael Johnson (2005, 2008) argues that there are at least two types of IPV. In *intimate terrorism*, the primary perpetrator is a male who uses multiple and escalating control to dominate his partner. In *situational couple violence*, both the woman and the man are perpetrators. They are not necessarily seeking control, but the violence is a product of conflict that turns into disagreements that escalate to arguments, to verbal abuse, and ultimately to

---

Applying What You've Learned

⁘ Some Warning Signs of Intimate Partner Abuse and Violence

Numerous clues to the potential for intimate partner abuse and violence appear before the abuse actually occurs. How many of these red flags do you recognize in your or your friends' relationships?

- **Verbal abuse:** Constant criticism, ignoring what you are saying, mocking, name calling, yelling, and swearing.

- **Sexual abuse:** Forcing or demanding sexual acts that you don't want to perform.

- **Disrespect:** Interrupting, telling you what you should think and how you should feel, putting you down in front of other people, saying ugly things about your friends and family.

- **Isolation:** Trying to cut you off from family and friends, monitoring your phone calls, reading your mail or e-mail, controlling where you go, taking your car keys and cell phone.

- **Emotional withholding or neglect:** Not expressing feelings, not giving compliments, not respecting your feelings and opinions.

- **Jealousy:** Very possessive, calling constantly or visiting unexpectedly, checking the mileage on your car, not wanting you to work because "you might meet someone."

- **Unrealistic expectations:** Expecting you to be the perfect mate and meet his or her every need.

- **Blaming others for problems:** It's *always* someone else's fault if something goes wrong.

- **Rigid sex roles:** Expecting you to serve, obey, and always stay home.

- **Extreme mood swings:** Switching from sweet to abusive and violent in minutes or being very kind one day and very vicious the next.

- **Cruelty to animals and children:** Killing or punishing pets brutally. May expect children to do things that are far beyond their ability or tease them until they cry.

- **Threats of violence:** Saying things such as "I'll break your neck" and then dismissing them with "I didn't really mean it" or "Everybody talks like that."

- **Destruction of property:** Destroying furniture, punching walls or doors, throwing things, breaking dishes or other household articles.

- **Self-destructive behavior:** Abusing drugs or alcohol, threatening self-harm or suicide, getting into fights with people, causing problems at work (such as telling off the boss).

physical violence. In situational couple violence, the male victims may be reluctant to report the assaults because they are embarrassed (Felson and Paré, 2005).

Some maintain that focusing on male victims diminishes women's abuse: Women are 10 times more likely than men to be injured in domestic violence cases. Especially among married couples, assaults by husbands on wives are more frequent than assaults by wives on husbands (Gelles, 1997; Felson and Cares, 2005). In addition, battered men are less likely than battered women to be trapped in a relationship because they have more economic resources. It's also easier for men to walk out of an abusive situation because, typically, women take responsibility for the children.

Women aren't always the only victims when IPV is mutual. Over a lifetime, men experience abuse and violence, but at much lower levels than women (see *Table 14.2* on p. 386 and the related discussion). Reciprocal abuse and violence are also more likely when both partners are young, have a history of antisocial behavior and substance abuse, suffer from depression, and face chronic stress because of limited resources. Such characteristics increase the likelihood of verbal conflict escalating into physical abuse (Kim et al., 2008).

Intimate partner violence has negative consequences for both sexes, but men are more likely than women to be controlling across more situations and over a longer period of time (Stark, 2007; Anderson, 2008). Whether IPV is largely one-sided or mutual, it often spills over into violence against children.

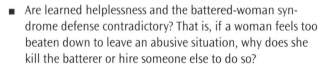

ꞏꞏ MAKING CONNECTIONS

- Are learned helplessness and the battered-woman syndrome defense contradictory? That is, if a woman feels too beaten down to leave an abusive situation, why does she kill the batterer or hire someone else to do so?

- Look, again, at the "Applying What You've Learned" box on p. 391. Do any of these characteristics reflect your current relationship with an intimate partner? If so, what, if anything, are you going to do about it?

CHILD MALTREATMENT

In 2001, Andrea Yates, a suburban homemaker in Houston, Texas, filled the bathtub and drowned each of her five children, who ranged in age from 6 months to 7 years: "It took a bit of work for her to chase down the last of the children; toward the end, she had a scuffle in the family room, sliding round on wet tile" (Roche, 2002: 44).

In 2001, Andrea Yates, a former high school valedictorian, nurse, and then full-time homemaker admitted killing her five children. In her retrial in 2006, pictured here, the jury found her guilty by reason of insanity, which means that she won't be executed under Texas law.

Abuse of and/or killing one's children is not a recent phenomenon. Among the Puritans, women were instructed to protect children "if a man is dangerously cruel with his children in that he would harm either body or spirit" (Andelin, 1974: 52). And men were not the only offenders: In 1638, Dorothy Talbie "was hanged at Boston for murdering her own daughter, a child of 3 years old" (Demos, 1986: 79).

In 1946, after observing unexplained fractures in children he had seen over the years, pediatric radiologist John Caffey suggested that the children had been abused. And in what may have been the first formal paper on the subject, in 1962 physician C. Henry Kempe and his colleagues published an article on the battered-child syndrome in the *Journal of the American Medical Association*. Nevertheless, "child abuse" became a household term only in the 1980s.

What Is Child Maltreatment?

Child maltreatment includes a broad range of behaviors that place a child at serious risk or result in serious harm, including physical abuse, sexual abuse, neglect, and emotional abuse. This term involves either acts or failure to act responsibly by a biological parent, stepparent, foster parent, adoptive parent, caregiver, or other person who is supposed to care for a child. (I sometimes use the older term **child abuse** interchangeably with *child maltreatment*.)

Since you asked . . .

ꞏꞏ Is physical abuse more harmful than emotional abuse?

PHYSICAL ABUSE *Physical abuse*, one type of maltreatment that causes bodily injury to a child,

Here, Oprah Winfrey, one of the world's richest and most influential women, launches *O: The Oprah Magazine,* one of her many successful enterprises. When she was nine years old, Winfrey's 19-year-old cousin started to molest her sexually. At age 14, she gave birth to a premature baby who died shortly after birth. Winfrey says that she was too confused and afraid to report the abuse.

includes beating with the hands or an object, scalding, and severe physical punishments. The most severe cases may result in a child's death.

SEXUAL ABUSE *Sexual abuse* is a type of maltreatment that involves the child in sexual activity to provide sexual gratification or financial benefit to the perpetrator. Sexual abuse includes making a child watch sexual acts, fondling a child's genitals, engaging the child in prostitution, committing statutory rape (having sexual intercourse with a minor), forcing a child to engage in sexual acts for photographic or filmed pornography, and engaging in incest. This category also includes sexual assault on a child by a relative or stranger.

NEGLECT *Neglect* is failure by a parent or other caregiver to provide a child with life's basic necessities. In *medical neglect,* the caregiver doesn't give the appropriate health care that will ensure the child's healthy development.

In *stimulation neglect,* parents don't cuddle and talk to their babies, don't take their children to the park (or other recreational spots), and don't play with or engage in activities that nourish the child's cognitive development (Cantwell, 1997).

Language neglect discourages the development of the child's communication skills, such as ignoring an infant's babbling, not reading to a child, and commanding young children ("Put this here" or "Don't do that") instead of conversing with the child and eliciting a response ("Where do you think we should hang this picture?") (Oates and Kempe, 1997). Neglectful caretakers are usually the child's parents but may also include people in residential centers for children or foster-care homes.

EMOTIONAL ABUSE *Emotional abuse,* sometimes referred to as *psychological maltreatment,* conveys to children that they are inferior, worthless, unloved, or unwanted. Verbal abusers devalue and reject their children with constant criticism, put-downs, and sarcasm (Briere, 1992; Brassard and Hardy, 1997).

More specifically, emotional maltreatment includes *spurning* (rejecting the child verbally and nonverbally), *terrorizing* (threatening to hurt, kill, or abandon the child), *isolating* (denying the child opportunities to interact with peers or adults inside or outside the home), and *exploiting* or *corrupting* (being a poor role model and permitting or encouraging a child's antisocial behavior) (Hart et al., 2003).

There are other forms of emotional abuse by parents, such as by those who focus on their own problems and ignore those of their children, who use guilt and other manipulations to control children's lives, who subject children to unpredictable mood swings because of alcoholism and other drug abuse, and who frequently demand that children assume adult caretaking responsibilities (see, also, the discussion of adultification in Chapter 12).

Prevalence and Characteristics of Child Maltreatment

Child maltreatment rates have decreased (see Data Digest), but there were still 794,000 confirmed cases in 2007. Because only a fraction of the total number of child victimizations are reported, it can be assumed that millions of American children experience abuse and neglect on a daily basis (U.S. Department of Health and Human Services, 2009a).

VICTIMS Although a child is often a victim of more than one type of maltreatment, the most common form of abuse is neglect (see *Figure 14.4*). From birth to age 18, girls (52 percent) are slightly more likely than boys (48 percent) to be neglected. Children younger than 1 year account for 12 percent of all

FIGURE 14.4 Types of Child Maltreatment: 2007

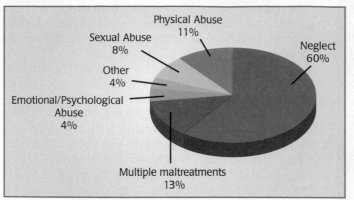

Note: "Neglect" includes medical neglect (about 1 percent of these cases). "Other" includes categories that some states report, such as babies who are born drug addicted.
Source: Based on U.S. Department of Health and Human Services, 2009a, Figure 3-4.

victims, and victimization rates decrease as children grow older (U.S. Department of Health and Human Services, 2009a).

Victimization rates by race and ethnicity range from almost 3 per 1,000 children for Asian Americans to 17 per 1,000 for African Americans (see *Figure 14.5*). Overall, however, 46 percent of all victims are white, 22 percent are black, 21 percent are Latino, and 11 percent are multiracial or from other ethnic groups (U.S. Department of Health and Human Services, 2009a). That is, child maltreatment percentages are highest among whites, but a disproportionate share of reported cases involves minority groups.

These differences among various groups are large, but there is some evidence that abuse in white, middle-class families is often underreported. According to a study of children younger than 3, for example, doctors were twice as likely to miss evidence of abuse in children from white, two-parent families as in children from minority, single-parent families. The

FIGURE 14.5 Child Victimization Rates by Race/Ethnicity: 2007

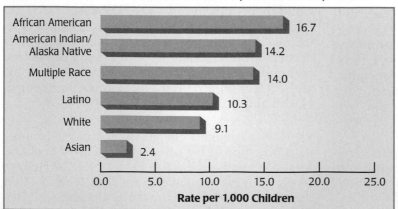

Source: Based on U.S. Department of Health and Human Services, 2009a, p. 25.

researchers attributed the misdiagnoses to physicians' lack of training (such as not recognizing head traumas) and especially to discomfort about casting suspicion on parents who seem to be solid citizens (Jenny et al., 1999).

PERPETRATORS About 80 percent of people who abuse children are parents, and more than half of them are mothers. An additional 8 percent of perpetrators are relatives or the parents' intimate partners, usually boyfriends. These figures are incomplete because about half the states don't have data on the relationship between the abused child and the offender (U.S. Department of Health and Human Services, 2009a).

FATALITIES Homicide is the leading cause of death among infants and the rates have doubled since 1970. Of the 1,760 children who died of abuse in 2007, 42 percent were younger than 1 year, and 76 percent were younger than 4 years (U.S. Department of Health and Human Services, 2009a). In effect, about five children die every day because of maltreatment.

Most mothers who kill their infants are unmarried teenagers and are usually black. Most have dropped out of high school, already have one or more children, and may have a history of mental illness ("Infant homicide," 2007).

About 70 percent of child deaths are caused by one or both of the child's parents, but half of all offenses involve just mothers or mothers and others, usually fathers and boyfriends (see *Figure 14.6*). The first two months of an infant's life are usually the most deadly. A young mother may know little about parenting and be unable to cope with the constant crying of a normal infant. As one of my students said, "My daughter had colic and she cried all night long for three months. I thought I'd go crazy."

Many researchers maintain that official child victimization statistics are far too low. For example, studies in Colorado and North Carolina have estimated that as many as 50 percent to 60 percent of child deaths resulting from abuse or neglect are not reported as caused by maltreatment. The underreporting is due to a variety of factors, including inadequate training of people who investigate deaths, incorrect information on death certificates, and parents' ability to conceal their children's deaths due to maltreatment (Child Welfare Information Gateway, 2008).

Sexual Abuse and Incest

Sexual abuse that strangers commit against children gets a great deal of media publicity, but 90 percent of all

FIGURE 14.6 Who Kills Children?

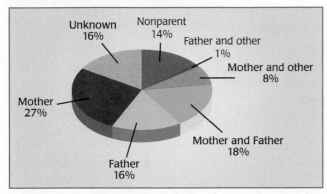

Note: Among nonparents, the largest number of perpetrators were relatives (4 percent), adults who were not the child's parents (4 percent), and a parent's girlfriend or boyfriend (3 percent).

Source: Based on U.S. Department of Health and Human Services, 2009a: Table 4-5.

these offenses are perpetrated by family members, friends of the family, and other persons children know (Gilgun, 2008). An estimated 21 percent of adolescents who run away from home do so to escape sexual abuse (Finkelhor and Ormrod, 2000).

A national study of sexually assaulted children found that 4 percent were younger than age 5, 3 percent were ages 6 to 8, 11 percent were 9 to 11, and 27 percent were 12 to 14. Among the offenders, 95 percent were men. Across all cases, 10 percent were family members (usually fathers and brothers), and 64 percent were a family friend or a child's friend or caretaker (Finkelhor et al., 2008).

Some of my former students, who are now social workers in isolated rural areas, say that incest is "much more common than people think." The abuse is difficult to prove, however, because the children are afraid to talk to anyone about the experience. One of the results of underreporting is that many people refuse to believe that incest is a serious problem (see the box "Myths and Facts about Incest" on the next page).

Incest offenders are typically fathers, stepfathers, grandfathers, and brothers. Their personality traits vary, but the perpetrators share some common characteristics: "They tend to be highly entitled, self-centered, and manipulative men who use children to meet their own emotional needs. They are often controlling and view their daughters (or sons) as owned objects" (Bancroft, 2002: 245–46).

Typically, a man who abuses his child or children starts doing so when the child is between 8 and 12 years old, although in some cases the child is still in diapers. The father may select only one child (usually the oldest daughter) as his victim, but it is common for several daughters to be victimized, either sequentially or simultaneously over the years. Incest offenders convince their daughters that the

attacks are expressions of affection ("This is how daddies show their love"). Others intimidate their victims with promises of physical retaliation against the victim and other family members. They threaten that they will be arrested or the family will break up if the incest is reported. Children remain silent out of fear and guilt because they believe that they are somehow responsible for the abuse (Allan, 2002).

Why Do Adults Abuse Children?

People tend to consider child abusers to be mentally ill, but fewer than 10 percent are thought to be so (Goldman and Salus, 2003). Some of the many reasons for child maltreatment are substance abuse, stress, poverty, partner abuse, and divorce.

SUBSTANCE ABUSE A number of studies have linked child abuse with the parents' substance abuse. Children whose parents abuse alcohol and other drugs are three times more likely to be abused and almost five times more likely to be neglected. Substance-abusing parents usually have poor parenting skills: They typically don't give their children emotional support or monitor them. As a result, the children haven't learned social control, lack social skills, and often begin using alcohol themselves at an early age (U.S. Department of Health and Human Services, 2009b).

STRESS Stress increases the likelihood of child maltreatment. As you saw earlier, intimate partner conflict, unmarried teenage parenthood, and a colicky infant aggravate stress and decrease coping skills. A study of Texas military personnel found that deployment-related anxiety explained much of the surge in child maltreatment rates after the war in Iraq began because many parents experienced difficulties, especially before the soldiers departed and after they returned (Rentz et al., 2007).

The stress of economic problems is especially likely to exacerbate child abuse. Social workers, child welfare agencies, and medical staff say that child abuse cases rose considerably in late 2008 when parents began to lose their jobs and homes (St. George and Dvorak, 2008).

POVERTY Poverty is the single best predictor of child abuse and neglect. Most poor parents aren't abusers, but children from poor families are 22 times more likely than children from families with higher incomes to be abused or neglected. Poverty and child maltreatment often co-occur when parents experience problems such as substance abuse

Myths and Facts about Incest

Constraints

Forcing, coercing, or cajoling a child into an incestuous relationship is one of the most devastating things an adult can do to a child. Even when family members are aware of incestuous behavior in the family, most neither report it nor try to stop it. Why? Because they believe in myths such as the following:

■ **Myth:** Children lie about incest.
■ **Fact:** Children rarely lie about incest. Most are too young to know the significance of the sexually exploitative acts they describe.
■ **Myth:** Children fantasize about incest. Every daughter fantasizes a romantic relationship with her father; every son imagines a romantic relationship with his mother.
■ **Fact:** A child wants and needs love and caring from a parent, not sexual intimacy.
■ **Myth:** If a child is not coerced, it is not incest.
■ **Fact:** Regardless of whether a child has been verbally seduced or violently raped, incest is a crime.
■ **Myth:** If a child experiences pleasurable feelings during the

encounter, the incest isn't harmful.
■ **Fact:** A child's physiological excitement is an automatic response to sexual manipulation and is one of the most damaging effects of incest. It can cause confusion and feelings of guilt or complicity.
■ **Myth:** The younger the victim, the less traumatic is the incest.
■ **Fact:** Incest is traumatic at *any* age. People who recall incestuous experiences vividly describe feelings of pain and humiliation.
■ **Myth:** Incest happens only in poor, disorganized, or unstable families.
■ **Fact:** Incest is more likely to be discovered in poor, disorganized, or unstable families because these families often come to the attention of social service agencies. Incest also occurs in many seemingly "normal" middle-class families.
■ **Myth:** Fathers turn to their daughters for warmth and nurturance that have been denied them by their wives.
■ **Fact:** The majority of men who are guilty of incest have received plenty

of nurturance from their mothers, wives, and other women.
■ **Myth:** Incest is usually punished by incarceration.
■ **Fact:** Perpetrators are rarely charged or imprisoned, largely because a child's testimony is seldom accepted as evidence of incest. In addition, solid physical evidence is rarely available because the event is not reported and investigated quickly enough.
■ **Myth:** A child can be seductive and thus is often responsible for the adult's sexual arousal.
■ **Fact:** Children are *never* responsible for adults' sexual arousal or physical assaults.

Sources: Faller, 1990; Adams et al., 1994; Allan, 2002; Wilson, 2006.

and domestic violence (Children's Defense Fund, 2005).

PARTNER ABUSE Child maltreatment is also more common in homes in which the woman is abused. The greater the amount of violence toward a partner, the greater is the probability of child abuse, especially by the male. Noting that 70 percent of wife beaters also physically abuse their children, Kurz (1993) posits that family violence, including child maltreatment, is a direct outcome of men's attempts to maintain control over the powerless members of the family—women and children.

DIVORCE The period just before and after divorce may make child maltreatment more likely because parental conflict and family tension are high. For example, the custodial parent may be changing residences, working longer hours, and experiencing more turmoil. Parents who are already stressed may react abusively to infants who, affected by the parents' emotional state, become more irritable and harder to soothe (see Chapter 15).

In 2006, when a woman in Maryland sought a protective order from her estranged husband, she told the judge that the husband had threatened to kill the children to punish her "by leaving her alone in the world." After a bitter divorce, the father got unsupervised visitation rights with the children. Two years later, he drowned the children—ages 2, 4, and 6—in a bathtub (Fuller and Gencer, 2008: A1). There are no national data on how many children are abused because of parental revenge during and after a divorce, but they are often the victims of parental anger.

A COMBINATION OF FACTORS Generally, child maltreatment reflects a combination of variables. For example, infant maltreatment rates are seven times higher than the average for the general population when families have a number of risk factors, including poverty, the infant's low birth weight (which requires more caretaking), more than two siblings, and an unmarried mother (Wu et al., 2004).

Interviews with 40 mothers jailed for killing their children found, similarly, that the women cited many

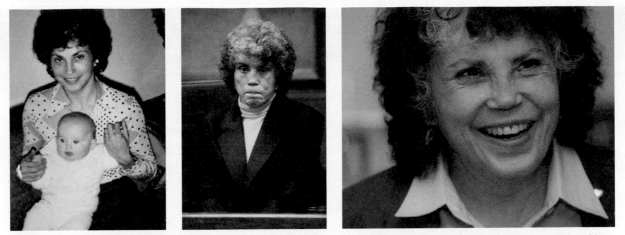

Hedda Nussbaum was the live-in lover of criminal attorney Joel Steinberg when he "adopted" infant Lisa (left). Six years later, battered beyond recognition by her "lover" (center), Hedda witnessed his arraignment for the murder of Lisa, whom he had begun to abuse as well. Doctors, teachers, and neighbors had noticed Lisa's bruises but did nothing. Late in 1987, Steinberg hit Lisa and left her lying on the floor, comatose. Lisa died three days later. Steinberg was convicted and jailed. Nussbaum, judged incapable of either harming or helping Lisa, began slowly to rebuild her life. She now spends much of her time giving lectures about helping battered women (right).

intertwined factors that accumulated over the years. The most common included growing up in a neglectful or violent home, not having mothers who were good child-rearing models, experiencing abuse from a partner, poverty, early pregnancy, and substance abuse (Oberman and Meyer, 2008).

Even if parents insist that they love their children, love isn't enough. Whether the reasons are micro level, macro level, or a combination, child abuse has a very negative impact on children's lives.

How Abuse Affects Children

Whether abuse is physical, emotional, or sexual, children often suffer from a variety of physiological, social, and emotional problems, including headaches, bedwetting, chronic constipation, difficulty communicating, learning disabilities, poor performance in school, and a variety of mental disorders. Children from violent families are often more aggressive than children from nonviolent families. Being abused or neglected as a child increases the likelihood of arrest as a juvenile by 59 percent, as an adult by 28 percent, and for a violent crime by 30 percent (Widom and Maxfield, 2001; Currie and Tekin, 2006; Carrell and Hoekstra, 2009).

Adolescents who experience maltreatment are more likely than their nonabused counterparts to engage in early sexual activity, have unintended pregnancies, suffer emotional and eating disorders, abuse alcohol and other drugs, and engage in delinquent behavior. In adulthood, abused children are twice as likely to be unemployed and in welfare programs. They are also more likely to be violent with their intimate partners (Ehrensaft et al., 2003; Zielinski, 2005; Conway and Hutson, 2008).

Childhood experiences of abuse and neglect are linked with serious life-long problems. For example, the victims are at least five times more likely to experience depression and 12 times more likely to attempt suicide. Physically abused adolescents are 12 times more likely to have alcohol and drug problems, and sexually abused adolescents are 21 times more likely to become substance abusers. As many as two-thirds of people in drug treatment programs report that they were abused as children (Putnam, 2006).

Incestuous relationships in childhood often lead to mistrust, fear of intimacy, and sexual dysfunctions in adulthood. *Table 14.3* summarizes some of the physical and behavioral signs that a child is being abused and needs protection.

❖ MAKING CONNECTIONS

- Some people believe that emotional maltreatment—of both children and adults—is less harmful than physical abuse. Do you agree?
- When child neglect occurs in lower socioeconomic families or during economic downturns, who is to blame?

HIDDEN VICTIMS: SIBLINGS AND ADOLESCENTS

Violence between siblings and abuse of adolescents are less visible, primarily because the authorities are rarely notified. Such abuse, however, can be just as devastating as the other forms of domestic abuse we've examined.

TABLE 14.3	Signs of Child Abuse	
	Physical Signs	**Behavioral Signs**
Physical Abuse	■ Unexplained bruises (in various stages of healing), welts, human bite marks, bald spots	■ Acts self-destructively
	■ Unexplained burns, especially cigarette burns or immersion burns	■ Withdrawn and aggressive, displays behavioral extremes
	■ Unexplained fractures, lacerations, or abrasions	■ Arrives at school early or stays late, as if afraid to be at home
		■ Is uncomfortable with physical contact
		■ Displays chronic runaway behavior (adolescents)
		■ Complains of soreness or moves uncomfortably
		■ Wears inappropriate clothing to cover bruises
Physical Neglect	■ Abandonment	■ Fatigue, listlessness, falling asleep
	■ Unattended medical needs	■ Steals food, begs from classmates
	■ Lack of parental supervision	■ Reports that no caretaker is at home
	■ Consistent hunger, inappropriate dress, poor hygiene	■ Frequently absent or tardy
	■ Lice, distended stomach, emaciation	■ School dropout (adolescents)
Sexual Abuse	■ Torn, stained, or bloody underclothing	■ Withdraws or is chronically depressed
	■ Pain or itching in genital area	■ Is excessively seductive
	■ Difficulty walking or sitting	■ Role reversal; overly concerned about siblings
	■ Bruises or bleeding from external genitalia	■ Displays lack of self-esteem
	■ Sexually transmitted disease	■ Experiences drastic weight gain or loss
	■ Frequent urinary or yeast infections	■ Displays hysteria or lack of emotional control
		■ Has sudden school difficulties
		■ Exhibits sex play or premature understanding of sex
		■ Threatened by closeness, problems with peers
		■ Is promiscuous
		■ Attempts suicide (especially adolescents)
Emotional Maltreatment	■ Speech disorders	■ Exhibits habit disorders (sucking, rocking)
	■ Delayed physical development	■ Antisocial; is responsible for destructive acts
	■ Substance abuse	■ Displays neurotic traits (sleep disorders, inhibition of play)
	■ Ulcers, asthma, severe allergies	■ Swings between passive and aggressive behaviors
		■ Exhibits delinquent behavior (especially adolescents)
		■ Exhibits developmental delay

Source: Based on American Humane Association, 2001.

Sibling Abuse

Sibling conflict is so common that many parents dismiss it as normal. But physical, emotional, and sexual abuse among siblings can leave lasting emotional scars.

PHYSICAL AND EMOTIONAL ABUSE Almost all young children hit a sibling occasionally, but habitual attacks are more problematic. A national study found that almost 30 percent of children ages 2 to 17 had been physically assaulted by a sister or brother at least once during the preceding year. Among those ages 6 to 12, 72 percent had been physically assaulted. In 24 percent of all cases, the assaults were serious enough to call the police (Finkelhor et al., 2005; Snyder and McCurley, 2008).

Since you asked . . .

:•• Is hitting and teasing brothers and sisters a normal part of growing up?

Although most sibling conflict does not involve weapons, it can be traumatic. Wiehe and Herring (1991) describe some of the most common forms of sibling abuse:

- **Name calling and ridicule:** Name calling and ridicule are the most common forms of emotional abuse among siblings. Victims remember being belittled about their height, weight, looks, intelligence, or athletic ability. One woman is still bitter because her brothers called her "fatso" and "roly-poly" during most of her childhood. Another woman said, "My sister would get her friends to sing songs about how ugly I was" (p. 29).

- **Degradation:** Degrading people, or depriving them of a sense of dignity and value, can take many forms: "The worst kind of emotional abuse I experienced was if I walked into a room, my brother would pretend he was throwing up at the sight of me. As I got older, he most often would pretend I wasn't there and would speak as if I didn't exist, even in front of my father and my mother" (p. 35).

- **Intimidation:** Siblings often use fear to control or terrorize their brothers or sisters. A woman in her 40s said that her siblings would take her sister and her into the field to pick berries. "When we would hear dogs barking, they would tell us they were wild dogs, and then they'd run away and make us find our own way home. We were only five or six, and we didn't know our way home" (p. 37).

- **Torturing or killing a pet:** The emotional impact on a child who loves an animal that a sibling tortures or kills can last for many years: "My second-oldest brother shot my little dog that I loved dearly. It loved me—only me. I cried

Habitual sibling disputes often have long-term negative effects. Sibling relationships that are largely conflictual early in life are likely to remain so.

by its grave for several days. Twenty years passed before I could care for another dog" (p. 39).

- **Destroying personal possessions:** Childhood treasures, such as favorite toys, can become instruments of emotional abuse: "My brother would cut out the eyes, ears, mouth, and fingers of my dolls and hand them to me" (p. 38).

Many children report that their parents rarely take physical or emotional abuse by siblings seriously: "'You must have done something to deserve it,' parents might say. My parents seemed to think it was cute when my brother ridiculed me. Everything was always a joke to them. They laughed at me. Usually their reply was for me to quit complaining—'You'll get over it'" (Wiehe and Herring, 1991: 22, 73).

However unintentionally, parents often encourage sibling violence by yelling at their kids instead of teaching them how to resolve disagreements. Parents might also escalate the violence by treating children differently or showing favoritism. They might describe one child as "the smart one" or "the lazy one." Such labeling discourages siblings' respect for one another and creates resentment. The preferred child might target a less-preferred sibling for maltreatment, especially when the parents aren't present (Updegraff et al., 2005).

A favored child might become abusive toward siblings because of his or her power and status in the family. A child's perception that she or he is less loved damages not only sibling relationships but also the child's self-image (Caffaro and Conn-Caffaro, 1998).

Sibling aggression is more dangerous than many parents think. About 10 percent of all murders in families are **siblicides,** killing of a brother or sister, and they account for more than 2 percent of all murders nationwide. The average age of siblicide victims is 33—during early and middle adulthood rather than during adolescence, as one might expect. Men are much more likely than women to be either offenders (88 percent) or victims (84 percent). The most common reason for siblicide is an argument between the perpetrator and the victim (Dawson and Langan, 1994; Fox and Zawitz, 2007).

By not discouraging sibling violence, parents send the message that it's okay to resolve conflict through fighting. Children raised in such violent environments learn that aggression is acceptable not only between brothers and sisters but also later with their own spouses and children. Such perceptions increase the likelihood of bullying at school and aggression with friends and in dating relationships (Gelles, 1997; Simonelli et al., 2002).

One of the primary functions of the family is to teach its members to be productive citizens in society (see Chapter 1). Ignoring or intervening briefly in sibling violence doesn't teach children the skills they need for regulating their behavior throughout life. Peers, teachers, employers, and co-workers rarely tolerate impulsive and negative behavior because a group's stability and productivity require problem solving, anger management, negotiation, cooperation, and compromise (Smith and Ross; 2007; Kennedy and Kramer, 2008).

SEXUAL ABUSE Sexual abuse by a sibling is rarely an isolated incident. In most instances, the episodes continue over time. They are often accompanied by physical and emotional abuse and may escalate. According to one woman,

I can't remember exactly how the sexual abuse started but when I was smaller there was a lot of experimenting. My brother would do things to me like put his finger in my vagina. Then, as I got older, he would perform oral sex on me (Wiehe, 1997: 72).

The perpetrators often threaten victims with violence: "I was about twelve years old. My brother told me if I didn't take my clothes off, he would take his baseball bat and hit me in the head and I would die. I knew he would do it because he had already put me in the hospital. Then he raped me" (Wiehe and Herring, 1991: 55). Most children say nothing to their parents about sexual abuse, either because they are afraid of reprisal or because they think their parents won't believe them.

In most cases of sibling incest, older brothers molest younger sisters. Male and female roles in families in which sibling incest occurs are often shaped by rigid gender stereotypes. Girls generally perceive themselves as less powerful than their brothers. As a result of such gender-based power differences, an older brother and a younger sister are most at risk for sibling incest. As one woman explained,

My brother was the hero of the family. He was the firstborn, and there was a great deal of importance placed on his being a male. My father tended to talk to him about the family business and ignore us

girls. My mother would hang on every word my brother said. . . . If he ever messed up or did something wrong, my parents would soon forgive and forget. When I finally confronted them as a teenager about Shawn molesting me, at first they didn't believe me. Later, they suggested that I just get over it (Caffaro and Conn-Caffaro, 1998: 53).

Adolescent Abuse

The risks of family violence and child homicide decrease as children grow older, but a staggering number of parents (or their intimate partners) abuse teenagers. As in early childhood, victimization during adolescence is the root of many problems later in life.

PREVALENCE OF ADOLESCENT ABUSE Many parents are physically and verbally abusive toward their children throughout the teen years. When adolescents fail to live up to their parents' expectations, the parents sometimes use physical force—including spanking, hitting, and beating—to assert control (see Chapter 12).

Of all child victims, an astounding 27 percent are between ages 12 and 17. Within this age group, almost 22 percent have been sexually assaulted by a family member, including adult relatives (U.S. Department of Health and Human Services, 2009a).

SOME CONSEQUENCES OF ADOLESCENT ABUSE Some teenagers strike back physically and verbally. Others rebel, run away from home, withdraw, use alcohol and other drugs, become involved in juvenile prostitution and pornography, or even commit suicide (Estes and Weiner, 2002).

A number of studies have found that compared with non-victims, abused adolescents are twice as likely to be victims of other violent crimes, perpetrators of domestic violence, and substance abusers as adults. They are also almost three times more likely to commit serious property and violent crimes. Compared with 17 percent of non-victim boys, 48 percent of boys who have been sexually assaulted engage in delinquent acts. About 20 percent of sexually assaulted girls engage in delinquency, compared with 5 percent of their non-victim counterparts (Menard, 2002; Kilpatrick et al., 2003; Wasserman et al., 2003; Herrenkohl et al., 2007).

Another aspect of family violence that receives little attention is mistreatment of the elderly. Although elder abuse is less common than other forms of domestic violence, it is a serious problem.

ELDER ABUSE AND NEGLECT

Baby boomers, now in their late 40s to early 60s, are often referred to as the **sandwich generation** because they must care not only for their own children but

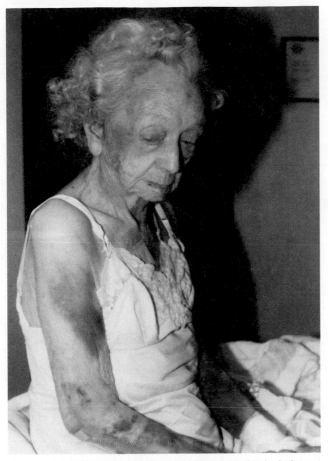

This 84-year-old woman suffered continuous physical abuse by a caregiver in the older woman's home. When arrested, the caregiver claimed that the woman had fallen out of bed.

also for their aging parents (see Chapter 1). Most people in the sandwich generation are remarkably adept at meeting the needs of both the young and the old. Others may abuse their children, their elderly parents and relatives, or both.

What Is Elder Abuse?

Elder abuse, sometimes also called *elder mistreatment,* includes the following:

- Physical abuse (such as hitting or slapping)
- Negligence (such as inadequate care)
- Financial exploitation (such as borrowing money and not repaying it)
- Psychological abuse (such as swearing at or blaming the elderly for one's own problems)
- Deprivation of basic necessities such as food and heat
- Isolation from friends and family
- Not administering needed medications

Police officers who are guest lecturers in my classes describe some horrific cases of elder abuse or

neglect. Some elderly people die of starvation, and their bodies aren't discovered for a year or more. A 71-year-old woman was left in bed for so long that her bedsores became infested with maggots.

Family members and acquaintances mistreat an estimated 5 percent of the elderly every year. Some researchers call elder abuse the "hidden iceberg" because about 93 percent of cases are not reported to police or other protective agencies (National Center on Elder Abuse, 2005). A congressman from Illinois recently complained, legitimately, that elder abuse is "under-researched, under-funded, and under-prosecuted" (cited in Edwards, 2007: 19). It remains to be seen if the data collection will improve if millions of baby boomers become victims of elder abuse.

Who Are the Victims?

Most elder abuse is hidden, but researchers estimate that 1 to 2 million Americans age 65 or older have been injured, exploited, or otherwise mistreated by a family member or caretaker. The maltreatment rates —which often involve more than one type of mistreatment—include physical abuse, 62 percent; abandonment, 56 percent; emotional or psychological abuse, 54 percent; financial abuse, 45 percent; and neglect, 41 percent (Tatara, 1998; National Center on Elder Abuse, 2005).

About 77 percent of elder abuse victims are white. Despite the revered role of grandparents among most minorities, elder maltreatment rates are also high among African Americans, Latinos, American Indians, and Asian Americans. A major difference is that whites are more likely to engage in physical abuse. Minority family members are more likely to be guilty of neglect, emotional abuse, and financial exploitation (such as keeping much of the income from the elderly person's Social Security checks) (Malley-Morrison and Hines; 2004; Teaster et al., 2006).

About 66 percent of elder abuse victims are women and 43 percent of both sexes are age 80 or older. Older women are probably more likely than older men to be abused because they tend to live longer than men. Thus, women are more dependent on caretakers because they have few economic resources, experience poor health, and may command less authority and power with family members (Teaster et al., 2006; see, also, Chapters 5 and 17).

Who Are the Abusers?

Rosa is a 79-year-old widow who lives with Michael, her 52-year-old son. Michael moved in with his mother after a divorce in which he lost custody of his two children and ownership of his home. Within a few

Since you asked . . .

- Is elder abuse more common in nursing homes than elsewhere?

months of Michael's move, he assumed responsibility for Rosa's Social Security checks and meager pension. He did not allow her to see visitors and locked her in her room when he left the house. Neighbors who never saw Rosa became suspicious and called the police (Teaster et al., 2006).

Adult children like Michael are the largest group of abusers (53 percent), followed by the victim's spouse (19 percent). In fact, 90 percent of the abusers are family members (see *Figure 14.7*).

Why Do They Do It?

Why do family members mistreat the elderly? A number of micro and macro risk factors increase the likelihood of elder abuse and neglect.

LIVING ARRANGEMENTS A shared living situation is a major risk factor for elder mistreatment. Sharing a residence increases opportunities for contact, tensions that can't be decreased simply by leaving, and conflicts that arise in everyday situations (Bonnie and Wallace, 2003).

SOCIAL ISOLATION Elder abuse is more likely when family members don't have a strong social network of kin, friends, and neighbors. Care providers who don't have supportive networks to provide occasional relief from their caretaking activities experience strain and may become violent toward their elderly parents or relatives (Kilburn, 1996).

ALCOHOL ABUSE Alcohol use and abuse are common among offenders. Daily alcohol consumption is more than twice as likely among those who abuse elders as among those who do not (Reay and Browne, 2001; Bonnie and Wallace, 2003).

IMPAIRMENT OF THE CAREGIVER OR THE CARE RECIPIENT A 70-year-old "child" who cares for a 90-year-old parent—a situation that is not uncommon today—may be frail, ill, or mentally disabled and thus unaware that he or she is being abusive or neglectful. Some elderly people suffer from dementia (deteriorated mental condition) after a stroke or the onset of Alzheimer's disease. They may pinch, shove, bite, kick, or strike their caregivers. Children or spouses, especially when they know little about debilitating diseases, are likely to hit back during such assaults (Pillemer and Suitor, 1991; see, also, Chapter 17).

DEPENDENCY OF THE OLDER PERSON ON CAREGIVER Elderly people who live with their children because they are too poor to live on their own may also suffer from incontinence, serious illness, or mental disabilities. They become physically as well as economically dependent on their caretakers. If the elderly are demanding, the caregivers may feel angry or resentful.

The dependency between the abuser and the victim is often mutual. Spouses, for example, may depend on each other for companionship. In the case of adult children and parents, although the abuser may need the older person for money or housing, the older parent needs the abuser for help with chores or to alleviate loneliness. If the adult child is still dependent on an elderly parent for housing or finances, she or he may mistreat the parent to compensate for the lack or loss of power (Payne, 2000).

MEDICAL COSTS AND FINANCIAL STRESS Having to pay medical costs for an elderly relative may trigger abuse. Unlike low-income people, middle-class families are not eligible for admission to public institutions, yet few can afford the in-home nursing care, high-quality nursing homes, and other services that upper-class families can afford. As a result, cramped quarters and high expenses increase the caretakers' stress. In addition, adult children and relatives may also divert money for their own purposes, especially if they are experiencing hard times and are jobless.

PERSONALITY Sometimes personality characteristics of older people increase their risk of abuse. Chronic verbal aggression and hostility can spark physical and verbal maltreatment by a caretaking spouse (Comijs et al., 1998).

In many cases, however, the violence begins early in a marriage and continues for decades. Some practitioners refer to this phenomenon as "domestic violence grown old." For example, women who grew up during the 1920s and 1930s were taught that "you married for life and you stuck things out," regardless of the husband's personality or aggression (France, 2006: 82).

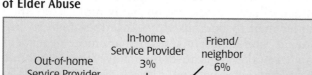

FIGURE 14.7 Relationship of Perpetrators and Victims of Elder Abuse

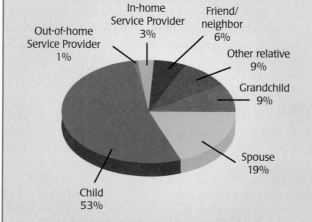

Source: Based on Tatara, 1998: Figure 4–9.

:• MAKING CONNECTIONS

- Think about your or your friends' relationships with their brothers and sisters. Are the relationships abusive? Do the parents take sibling mistreatment seriously?

- There's an old saying: "Be nice to your children because they may be taking care of you some day." Does this saying illustrate the cycle of violence?

VIOLENCE AMONG SAME-SEX COUPLES AND RACIAL-ETHNIC GROUPS

Compared with other families, there has been considerably less research on domestic violence in same-sex and racial-ethnic households. Still, neither sexual orientation nor national origin deters abuse and neglect.

Same-Sex Couples

Since you asked . . .

:• Is abuse less common among same-sex couples?

The prevalence of battering in lesbian and gay couples is about the same as it is for heterosexual couples, occurring in approximately 25 percent to 33 percent of all couples. About 10 percent of men and 2 percent of women are violent with their same-sex partners (Rennison, 2001).

A study of 288 gay and lesbian batterers reported that all the men and women had been psychologically abused as children. About 93 percent of the men and 88 percent of the women said that they had experienced physical abuse during childhood (Farley, 1996).

A study of lesbian couples found that IPV was due to two related stressors—internalized homophobia and heterosexist discrimination. *Internalized homophobia* refers to having negative feelings about being lesbian or gay because of society's rejection of homosexuality. A major reason for internalized homophobia is *heterosexist discrimination,* or being treated unfairly because of one's homosexual orientation. Examples include excluding gays and lesbians from family events, firing them from jobs, vandalizing their homes or property, and attacking them verbally or physically. The study concluded that both internalized homophobia and heterosexist discrimination increase the likelihood of lifetime IPV because lesbians and gay men "may be more likely to remain in abusive relationships because they may harbor beliefs that they deserve the abuse" (Balsam and Szymanski, 2005: 266).

In domestic violence cases, law enforcement officers generally are trained to untangle the history of the IPV incident and to arrest the aggressor rather than both people. A nationally representative sample found that most Americans believe that IPV among same-sex couples is illegal and should be taken seriously and that the police should be called. Same-sex couples are often reluctant to report IPV, however, because they fear that the police won't take the abuse seriously or will arrest both partners because they won't take the time to differentiate the victim from the assailant (Sorenson and Thomas, 2009).

Racial-Ethnic Groups

You saw earlier that across all racial and ethnic groups, women have higher IPV victimization rates than men, but women, also, are assailants (see *Table 14.2* on p. 386 and the related discussion). IPV and domestic violence may be experienced differently across racial and ethnic groups because of variations in socioeconomic status, culture, national origin, external stressors (such as discrimination), and other factors. Among Latinos, for example, there is a greater likelihood of IPV among both women and men when the cohabitors and married couples live in high-crime neighborhoods and if one or both partners abuse alcohol (Cunradi, 2009).

There are also variations among Asian American couples that reflect, among other variables, gender roles and employment status. For example, a study of married couples found that some men are more likely to be abusive when the wives violate traditional gender roles by challenging the husband's dominance in family decision making in areas such as household chores, child rearing, and finance. Because many Asian American women are employed, the association between marital violence and male dominance in a household becomes more complicated. When wives earn as much or more than their husbands and, consequently, want to have more household decision-making power, some husbands—especially those who are older—may become abusive to reassert their control (Chung et al., 2008).

Immigrant women generally experience more domestic violence than their American-born counterparts do. For example, a study in New York City found that among victims of intimate partner homicides, 51 percent were foreign born whereas 45 percent were born in the United States. In another study, 48 percent of Latinas reported that their partner's violence increased after they immigrated to the United States (cited in Family Violence Prevention Fund, 2006).

Recent immigrants rarely report IPV. Women, especially those who don't speak English well, may not report marital violence because they fear being deported or ostracized by their community. Many tolerate violence because they don't know about or

Parental conflict evokes fear and insecurity during childhood, but why does continuous exposure increase the likelihood of being either an offender or a victim of intimate partner violence or family abuse in adulthood?

don't trust social service organizations that could provide help (Foo, 2002; Raj and Silverman, 2002). Latinas may also be silent about marital rape because of cultural values that require them to remain loyal and to protect the man's honor and reputation, especially as a sign of the wife's "warmth and goodness" (Vandello and Cohen, 2003: 997).

Overall, Asian American parents have lower rates (2 percent) of severe child maltreatment (such as beating, choking, and scalding) than do whites (6 percent), African Americans (12 percent), and Latinos (16 percent). The lower rates may be due to Asian American parents' reluctance to report stigmatized behaviors such as parental aggression. However, severe assault rates vary across subgroups depending on other factors. For example, perceived societal discrimination (such as being treated with less respect) and family cultural conflict (such as arguments with family members because of different cultural values) increase the risk of severe child maltreatment (Lau et al., 2006; see, also, Pelczarski and Kemp, 2006).

EXPLAINING FAMILY ABUSE AND VIOLENCE

Why are families abusive? There many competing explanations based on medical, political, psychological, and criminological models. Let's examine, briefly, five influential perspectives—patriarchy or male dominance theory, social learning theory, resource theory,

Since you asked . . .

∷• What is the best explanation for intimate partner and family abuse?

exchange theory, and ecological systems theory. (You might want to refer to *Figure 2.1* on page 33 to refresh your memory of some of these perspectives.)

Patriarchy or Male Dominance Theory

Patriarchy or *male dominance theory* maintains that men's authority creates and condones domestic violence. Aggression against women and children, particularly female children, is common in societies in which men have power, status, and privilege. In such "intimate terrorism," men control a partner or child (Johnson, 2005).

This perspective maintains that as long as cultural values encourage men to be controlling, dominant, competitive, and aggressive rather than nurturing, caring, and concerned for the welfare of others, men will continue to express their anger and frustration through violent and abusive behavior (see, for example, Birns et al., 1994).

Social Learning Theory

According to *social learning theory*, we learn by observing the behavior of others. Some people try to avoid the behavior that they've experienced in the past, but continuous exposure to abuse and violence during childhood increases the likelihood that a person will be both an assailant and a victim as an adult (Busby et al., 2008).

No one really knows whether or how much family violence is transmitted intergenerationally through modeling or imitation (see National Research Council, 1998, for a review of some of this literature). Modeling probably plays an important role in learning abusive behavior, but many children who grow up in violent households don't themselves become abusive.

Resource Theory

According to *resource theory*, men usually command greater financial, educational, and social resources than women do, so they have more power. Men with the fewest resources are the most likely to resort to abuse. For example, a man who has little education, holds a job low in prestige and income, and has poor communication skills may use violence to maintain his dominant position in a relationship or the family. Many women cannot assert themselves simply because they have even fewer resources than their partners (Babcock et al., 1993; Atkinson et al., 2005).

A decline of resources and the resulting stress can also provoke violence. If a man's contribution to earnings decreases relative to the wife's or the man experiences spells of unemployment, the woman is more likely to experience abuse. The situation can be aggravated by living in a disadvantaged neighborhood, having a large number of children, and the wife's refusal to work more hours outside the home (Fox et al., 2002).

Exchange Theory

According to *exchange theory,* both assailants and victims tolerate or engage in violent behavior because they believe that the benefits outweigh the costs. You'll recall that many battered women stay in an abusive relationship for financial reasons. The rewards for perpetrators include release of anger and frustration and accumulation of power and control. They often spend little time in jail, and the women they abuse often take them back (Sherman, 1992).

Violence also has costs. First, it's possible that the victim will hit back. Second, a violent assault could lead to arrest or imprisonment and a loss of status among family and friends. Finally, the abuser may break up the family (Gelles and Cornell, 1990). However, if a patriarchal society condones male control of women and children, the costs will be minimal.

Ecological Systems Theory

Ecological system theory explains domestic violence by analyzing the relationships between individuals and larger systems such as the economy, education, state agencies, and the community. For example, elder abuse is highest when there is a combination of micro and macro variables: Caretakers abuse drugs or have limited resources and experience stress, older people develop physical or mental disabilities, caregivers and the elderly are physically and socially isolated from a larger community, and there are few social service agencies that provide high-quality care.

Moreover, cultural values—including television programs and movies—that demean, debase, and devalue women and children promote and reinforce abusive behavior. For example, even if hip-hop music, especially "gangsta rap," doesn't actually cause physical abuse against women, the lyrics are "often chillingly supportive of rape and violence" (Hill, 2005: 185; see, also, Chapter 5).

Using Several Theories

Researchers rarely rely on only one theory of intimate partner or domestic abuse because the reasons for human behavior, including violence, are complex. For example, resource theory suggests that men who have few assets in fulfilling a provider role are more likely to be violent toward their wives than are men with high incomes. However, men who have average incomes but lower educational and income levels than their employed wives may also resort to violence. Patriarchy or male dominance theory suggests

that these men have less egalitarian views about decision making or that they react violently when their wives pressure them to share more of the housework (Anderson, 1997). If we also consider personality variables and social exchange factors, explaining family violence becomes even more complex.

OTHER FAMILY HEALTH ISSUES

Physical abuse and violence can destroy a family, but other health-related problems can also become crises. For example, many families must cope with long-term problems such as substance abuse, depression and suicide, and eating disorders.

Substance Abuse

Eddie, a 22-year-old father of two young children, was rushed to the hospital. He died ten days later, the result of having overdosed on a mix of pharmaceutical pills. Although his parents were shocked, his mother later said that "Eddie was not the first kid to die in this neighborhood from prescription drugs" (Leinwand, 2006). Use of some drugs—whether legal or illegal—can result in **substance abuse,** an overindulgence in and dependence on a drug or other chemical that are detrimental to an individual's physical and mental health or to the welfare of others.

ILLEGAL DRUGS An estimated 8 percent of Americans (almost 20 million people) age 12 and older use illegal drugs (Substance Abuse and Mental Health Services Administration, 2008). Among racial-ethnic groups, those who are multiracial have the highest usage rates and Asian Americans the lowest (see *Figure 14.8*). Asian Americans' lower rates may result from their cultural emphasis on doing what's good for the family rather than seeking individual gratification. It's not clear why the rates are the highest for multiracial persons, but some of the reasons may reflect identity problems (see Chapter 4).

Between 2002 and 2007, illegal drug use among youth between the ages of 12 and 17 dropped from 12 percent to 10 percent, but one-third used prescription drugs illegally. About 5 million teenagers have taken prescription painkillers such as Vicodin or OxyContin or stimulants such as Ritalin or Adderall to get high. Some teens organize "pharm parties" ("pharm" being short for pharmaceuticals) at which they down fistfuls of prescription drugs that they can easily get from their parents' medicine cabinets (Office of National Drug Control Policy, 2006; Partnership for a Drug-Free America, 2008).

Medical researchers are especially concerned about the popularity among teenagers of prescription-type

Since you asked . . .

- What's a "pharm party"?

FIGURE 14.8 Illicit Drug Use by Race/Ethnicity, 2007

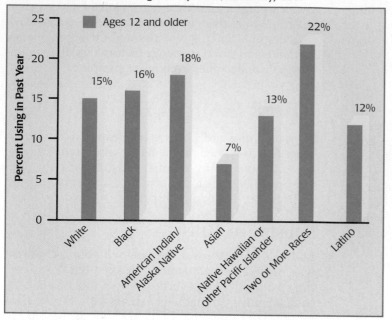

Source: Based on Substance Abuse and Mental Health Services Administration, 2008, Table G.11.

drugs, such as tranquilizers and sedatives. Like other illicit drugs, prescription-type drugs often filter down to middle school students. The problem isn't just that children can become addicted to prescription drugs. These medicines can also send kids to the emergency room: They can lead to difficulty in breathing, a drop or rapid increase in heart rate, or impaired responses when driving (Banta, 2005; Johnston et al., 2006).

Whereas illicit drug use among youth has declined, it has risen among baby boomers because many continue to use illegal drugs such as marijuana as well as tranquilizers and stimulants (which have not been prescribed). For example, among persons ages 50 to 59, the rate of illicit drug use increased from 2.7 percent in 2002 to 5 percent in 2007 (almost 3 million people), and it is expected to double by 2020. Because of their decreased metabolism and reduced body water content, older people who use illicit drugs experience a broad range of health problems that include lower cognitive and motor functions, which, consequently, increase the number of accidents, falls, injuries, and other impairments (Han et al., 2009). Such problems will put further strains on the nation's health care system, including Medicare and Medicaid (see Chapter 17).

Marijuana is the most popular illegal drug (used by 6 percent of the U.S. population, about 15 million people). Short-term effects of marijuana use include problems with memory and learning, distorted perception, difficulty in thinking and problem solving, loss of coordination, increased heart rate, and anxiety (Substance Abuse and Mental Health Services Administration, 2008).

Many users maintain that marijuana is less harmful than tobacco or alcohol, but some researchers describe it as a "gateway" drug that leads to using harder drugs. According to a study of fraternal and identical twins, for example, the twin who used marijuana before age 17 was five times more likely than his or her sibling who did not to later use cocaine, heroin, hallucinogens, sedatives, or alcohol (Lynskey et al., 2003).

In addition, some researchers are finding a co-occurrence of substance-related behaviors. Among youth ages 12 to 17, of those who use marijuana, 81 percent also drink alcohol regularly, and 45 percent sell marijuana or harder drugs such as heroin, cocaine, or LSD (McCurley and Snyder, 2008).

ALCOHOL According to the Substance Abuse and Mental Health Services Administration (SAMHSA), slightly more than half of Americans (51 percent) drank alcohol in 2007. SAMSHA defines two types of alcohol consumption as problematic:

- *binge drinking,* having five or more drinks on the same occasion at least 1 day in the past 30 days
- *heavy drinking,* binge drinking on at least 5 days in the past 30 days (Substance Abuse and Mental Health Services Administration, 2008: 3).

Thus, you're a heavy drinker if you've consumed five or more drinks on the same occasion on five or more days within a month.

In 2007, among those ages 12 to 20 (who were under the legal drinking age of 21), 19 percent were binge drinkers and 6 percent were heavy drinkers. Driving under the influence of alcohol is highest at ages 21 to 29 and then decreases, but a large number of drunken drivers are ages 16 to 20 (see *Figure 14.9*).

Even if drunk drivers don't injure or kill themselves, their family members, or others, alcohol abuse has many harmful effects. For example, 47 percent of those who begin drinking before age 14 become dependent on alcohol at some point later in their lives (Dawson et al., 2008). And, as you saw earlier in this chapter, substance abuse is often associated with intimate partner and marital violence, and children who experience domestic violence—including physical and sexual abuse—are more likely than their non-abused counterparts to use drugs and alcohol in adolescence and adulthood.

Alcohol can cause greater damage to the brain development of people younger than 25 than to any other age group. The prefrontal region of the brain

Recently, Michael Phelps, an Olympic gold medalist in swimming, was photographed smoking marijuana. Phelps, 24, issued an apology for engaging in "inappropriate" and "youthful behavior." Kellogg's Corporation withdrew his $500,000 contract, but others (Speedo, Omega, Subway, and Mazda China, for example) continued their lucrative contracts. Do such endorsements by major companies show an acceptance of using marijuana? And until what age is illicit drug use simply a "youthful mistake" rather than a crime?

plays an important role in forming the adult personality and in controlling, planning, and monitoring behaviors. Because this part of the brain develops from childhood until early adulthood, adolescents need to drink only half as much as adults to suffer the same negative effects, such as learning and memory impairments ("Underage drinkers . . .," 2002).

Adolescent drug use also leads to health problems in adulthood. Twenty years later, for example, people who used drugs as teens report more health prob-

lems, including a higher incidence of respiratory problems such as colds and sinus infections; cognitive problems such as difficulty in concentrating, remembering, and learning; and headaches, dizziness, and vision problems. Besides other problems, alcoholics are five to ten times more likely than the general population to experience depression and to commit suicide (Brook et al., 2002; Preuss et al., 2003).

Depression and Suicide

Two other serious problems that many families must deal with are depression and suicide. Both have negative impacts that affect kin and friends throughout the life course.

DEPRESSION Depression is a mental disorder characterized by pervasive sadness and other negative emotions that interfere with the ability to work, study, sleep, eat, and enjoy experiences that were formerly pleasurable (see *Table 14.4* on p. 408).

Over a lifetime, 14 percent of adolescents and 15 percent of adults (ages 18 and older) have experienced at least one major depressive episode (one that lasts at least two weeks), but fewer than half ever seek treatment. In all age groups, twice as many women as men suffer a major depressive episode every year. Although substance abuse doesn't cause depression, those who abuse alcohol and use illicit drugs are twice as likely to experience a major depressive episode as are nonusers (Bostic and Miller, 2005; Substance Abuse and Mental Health Services Administration, 2005).

SUICIDE Depression may lead to *suicide*, taking one's life. Here are some general facts about suicide:

- It is the eleventh leading cause of death among Americans.
- More than 33,000 Americans kill themselves each year, which is the equivalent of 91 suicides per day.
- Males take their own lives at nearly four times the rate of females and represent 79 percent of all U.S. suicides.
- During their lifetime, women attempt suicide about two to three times as often as men.
- Suicide rates for males are highest among those age 75 and older, and highest for females ages 45 to 54.
- Suicide is the second leading cause of death among 25- to 34-year olds and the third leading cause of death among 15- to 24-year olds.
- Among American Indians and Alaska Natives ages 15 to 34, suicide is the second leading cause of death ("Suicide," 2009; "Understanding suicide," 2009).

FIGURE 14.9 Driving Under the Influence of Alcohol, by Age: 2007

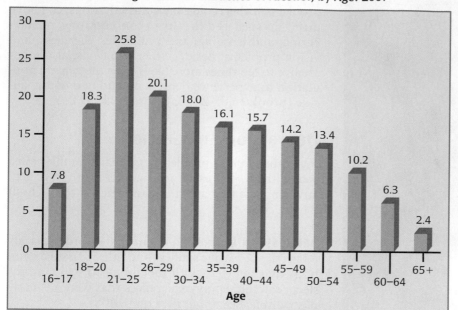

Source: Substance Abuse and Mental Health Services Administration, 2008, Figure 3.5.

Eating Disorders

Several recent studies have found an association between negative body image obsession and suicide because a negative body image often leads to self-loathing, social isolation, and depression. Teens who see themselves as either very fat or very skinny (regardless of how much they weigh) are twice as likely to think about or attempt suicide as their normal-weight counterparts. People who have a distorted body image and think obsessively about their appearance are 45 times more likely to commit suicide than people in the general population (Eaton et al., 2005; Dyl et al., 2006; Phillips and Menard, 2006).

Most people with a negative body image don't take their lives, but our self-perceptions about our weight—whether real or imagined—affect us, our families, and our quality of life. Let's begin with overweight and obesity and then examine three related eating disorders—binge eating, anorexia, and bulimia.

OVERWEIGHT AND OBESITY Overweight and obesity refer to ranges of weight that are greater than what is generally considered normal and are measured by the "body mass index" (BMI), which indicates the amount of body fat ("Defining overweight and obesity," 2009). Since the 1980s, the percentage

The causes of suicide are unknown, but taking one's life is associated with risk factors such as a history of depression or other mental illness, substance abuse, physical illness, feeling alone, living with drug users, easy access to guns and poisons, and bullying and other peer victimization among youth (Miller et al., 2007; Paulozzi et al., 2007; Srabstein et al., 2008; Kaminski and Fang, 2009; "Understanding suicide," 2009).

Most people, including teenagers, experience ups and downs throughout life. When the downs become frequent, however, parents, friends, teachers, and relatives should seriously consider the possibility that an adolescent or adult is planning suicide and should intervene when there are symptoms of suicidal behavior (see *Table 14.5*).

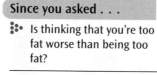

Since you asked . . .

Is thinking that you're too fat worse than being too fat?

TABLE 14.4	Some Symptoms of Depression
1. Persistent sadness, anxiety, or an "empty" feeling
2. Feelings of worthlessness, guilt, helplessness, hopelessness
3. Loss of interest or pleasure in usual hobbies and activities, including sex
4. Difficulty concentrating, remembering, making decisions
5. Fatigue and loss of energy
6. Restlessness, irritability
7. Changes in appetite and weight (weight loss or gain)
8. Disturbed sleep (insomnia or sleeping much of the time)
9. Suicidal thoughts or attempts
10. Persistent physical problems such as headaches, pain, and digestive disorders that don't respond to treatment

TABLE 14.5	Some Common Warning Signs of Suicide

- Withdrawal from family or friends
- Verbal expression of suicidal thoughts or threats, even as a joke
- Major personality changes
- Changes in sleeping or eating habits
- Drug or alcohol abuse
- Difficulty concentrating
- Violent or rebellious outbursts
- Running away
- Recent suicide of a relative or friend
- Rejection by a boyfriend or girlfriend
- Unexplained, sudden drop in quality of schoolwork or athletic interests
- Giving or throwing away prized possessions
- Sudden lack of interest in friends or usual activities
- Extreme and sudden neglect of appearance
- Eating disorders (losing or gaining weight)

Children who are overweight are likely to be overweight or obese in adulthood and experience serious health problems.

of Americans who are overweight and obese has increased. Among children ages 6 to 17, the percentage overweight increased from only 6 percent from 1976 to 1980 to 15 percent in 2006 (Federal Interagency Forum on Child and Family Statistics, 2009). Many adults are overweight, but more than one in four were obese in 2008, a rate that has more than doubled since the late 1970s (Pan et al., 2009).

Obesity is a concern because it has negative health outcomes—including heart disease, strokes, debilitating diseases such as diabetes, and early death—that affect all family members. There are many reasons for obesity, including genetics, metabolism (the way the body uses calories), and drugs, but the major reason is consuming more calories than our bodies use (i.e., overeating). Weight gain is also associated with social class. For example, families in low-income communities, many of whom are minorities, have little access to affordable healthful food choices because there are fewer chain markets, safe locations for physical activity, and inexpensive facilities that offer exercise and recreational sports ("Causes and consequences," 2009; Pan et al., 2009).

BINGE EATING Often, obesity is due to **binge eating**, consuming an unusually large amount of food and feeling that the eating is out of control. Binge eating is the most common eating disorder in the United States and affects about 4 percent of women and 2 percent of men. Most binge eaters are between the ages of 46 and 55 (Hudson et al., 2007; "Binge eating disorder," 2008).

People with binge eating disorders report more health problems, stress, muscle and joint pain, headaches, menstrual problems, trouble sleeping, and suicidal thought that do people without this eating disorder. No one knows for sure what causes binge eating disorders. Many binge eaters report problems in handling some emotions and stress, abuse alcohol, and feel depressed and isolated. On the other hand, binge eating may trigger many of these problems. Some early-stage research suggests that genes may be involved in binge eating disorders because they often occur within families ("Binge eating disorder," 2008).

Researchers in other Western countries have found that many adolescents experience low self-esteem because they have an exaggerated image of themselves as obese. A national study of adolescents in Germany found that almost 55 percent of the girls and 36 percent of the boys thought that were too fat although only 18 percent of both sexes were actually overweight. Such findings were similar for studies in England and Australia (Kurth and Ellert, 2008) and may lead to two other eating disorders—anorexia nervosa and bulimia.

ANOREXIA NERVOSA AND BULIMIA Anorexia nervosa (usually abbreviated as *anorexia*), is a dangerous eating disorder that is characterized by a fear of obesity, the conviction that one is fat, significant weight loss, and refusal to maintain weight within normal age and height limits. **Bulimia** is a cyclical pattern of eating binges followed by self-induced vomiting, fasting, excessive exercise, or use of diuretics or laxatives.

Although study results vary, at some point in their lives an estimated 4 percent of American women suffer from anorexia and another 7 percent from bulimia. Of all people affected by these disorders, 10 percent are male. Eating disorders can affect people of all ages, but 86 percent report the onset of anorexia or bulimia before age 20 (Berkman et al., 2006; National Mental Health Association, 2006).

Anorexia may cause slowing of the heartbeat, loss of normal blood pressure, cardiac arrest, dehydration, skin abnormalities, hypothermia, lethargy, potassium deficiency, and kidney malfunction. With treatment, about half of anorexics get better, about 40 percent remain chronically ill, and 10 percent die of causes related to the disease (Fichter et al., 2006).

Bulimia's binge-purge cycle can cause fatigue, seizures, muscle cramps, an irregular heartbeat, and decreased bone density, which can lead to osteoporosis. Repeated vomiting can damage the esophagus and stomach, cause the salivary glands to swell, make the gums recede, and erode tooth enamel.

Although most anorexics and bulimics are young middle-class white women, some researchers are finding that the number of Latinas and African American women with eating disorders is increasing, especially those who binge eat. A study of college students found that 5 percent of the Asian American women were bulimic, but the numbers may be increasing because more minority women are seeking treatment instead of being secretive about their condition (Tsai and Gray, 2000; Striegel-Moore et al., 2003; Brodey, 2005).

As with most mental illnesses, eating disorders are due to a combination of cultural, psychological, and biological factors. Some parents of 3-year-olds say that their daughters eat enough (even when the girls are thin), but they encourage their sons to eat more to become big and strong even though 18 percent of the boys are overweight (Holm-Denoma et al., 2005).

Other cultural and psychological factors include a history of sexual abuse, low self-esteem, and cultural norms of attractiveness. A study of girls ages 5 to 8 found that those who play with Barbie dolls rather than with Emme, a doll with a more proportional body shape, had lower body esteem and a greater desire for a thinner body, laying the foundation for the development of eating disorders (Dittmar et al., 2006).

Educator Jean Kilbourne, who has done pioneering work on the negative effects of advertising on women's body image, notes that women are conditioned to be terrified of fat: "Prejudice against fat people, especially against fat women, is one of the few remaining prejudices that are socially acceptable" (Kilbourne, 1994: 402). Consequently, the most common explanation of anorexia and bulimia is that women are trying to live up to a cultural ideal that equates thinness with beauty and success:

If I'm thin, I'll be popular. If I'm thin, I'll turn people on. If I'm thin, I'll have great sex. If I'm thin, I'll be rich. If I'm thin, I'll be admired. If I'm thin, I'll be sexually free. If I'm thin, I'll be tall. If I'm thin, I'll have power. If I'm thin, I'll be loved. If I'm thin, I'll be envied (Munter, 1984: 230).

Researchers are now finding that about half of the risk for developing anorexia could be attributed to an individual's combination of genes and brain chemistry. If there is a genetic predisposition for anorexia, for example, the brain can reduce or overproduce chemicals, especially serotonin. Some scientists theorize that by eating less, anorexics reduce the serotonin activity in their brains, creating a sense of calm, even as they are about to die of malnutrition (Frank et al., 2005; Bulik et al., 2006). However, because eating disorders typically co-occur with other problems such as depression and sexual abuse, the relationship between genes and eating disorders is still tentative.

⁚•▸ MAKING CONNECTIONS

- Should a parent who suspects his or her child of substance abuse use a home drug-testing kit? Or would this create rebellion and more problems in the parent-child relationship?
- Are you overweight or obese? Do you ever binge eat? If so, why?

COMBATING FAMILY ABUSE AND VIOLENCE

When National Football League player Michael Vick was arrested for staging dogfight events, the case got national publicity, and the public was outraged by his cruelty to animals. A law professor asked why there isn't similar outrage about athletes who abuse their partners: "The public reaction to the Michael Vick case is another reminder of how much more seriously we seem to take animal abuse than domestic violence. Penalties for animal abuse are still greater than penalties for domestic violence in some states" (Goodmark, 2007: 11A). If family violence was always in the headlines, prevention and intervention strategies might follow.

Since you asked . . .

⁚•▸ Is it *really* possible to reduce intimate partner violence and child abuse?

Raising Awareness about Family Abuse and Violence

A recent study concluded, "Domestic violence thrives on a social climate of secrecy, tolerance, and passivity" (Gracia and Herrero, 2006: 767). A greater public sense of responsibility and accountability and involvement in helping victims would increase the exposure and social control of partner violence against women.

Public education efforts to raise awareness about domestic violence have typically been aimed at women. If such efforts leave men—especially young men—out of the conversation, there'll be little change. How do you stop a 30-year-old man from beating his wife? "Talk to him when he's 12," writes a journalism professor, and as often as possible, about not abusing girls (Voss, 2003).

Preventing Family Abuse and Violence

Numerous organizations offer programs to prevent domestic violence and other family crises. Many schools and communities have implemented "keeping kids clean" programs that teach youth how to avoid risky behaviors and instruct parents in how to talk to their children more effectively about the dangers of drugs (Atkin, 2002).

Preschool programs can also reduce the likelihood of child abuse. For children of low-income parents who are involved in their children's preschool programs, the rate of maltreatment is 52 percent lower than the rate for children whose parents don't participate in such programs (Reynolds and Robertson, 2003).

The Watchful Shepherd (www.watchful.org), a nonprofit organization founded in Pennsylvania, protects at-risk children with electronic devices that children can use to contact hospital emergency personnel when they feel threatened or fear abuse. An unexpected outcome is use of the device by parents who fear that they are losing control and might hurt their child unless someone intervenes.

Caseworkers usually have the right to obtain warrants to search the homes of suspected child abusers. Many don't do so, however, because of high caseloads and our cultural norms about not "intruding" on parents.

Intervening in Family Abuse and Violence

Thousands of U.S. programs and laws are designed to intervene in family crises. Some are ineffective because the staff is overworked, the agency is underfunded, or the police and judges don't enforce domestic violence laws. These programs and interventions have had some successes, however. For example,

- Abused women who obtain permanent (rather than temporary) court orders of protection are 80 percent less likely to be assaulted again.

- Counseling generally has little effect on a batterer's attitudes or behavior. Arrests, restraining orders, and intensive monitoring by police are far more effective.

- Kaiser Permanente, a national health maintenance organization, has launched a successful program that screens and treats domestic violence victims in emergency rooms and reports the abuse to police.

- Teen substance abuse programs that involve the entire family have a higher success rate than those that treat only the adolescent.

- Women who are treated for substance abuse during pregnancy are much more likely to have healthy babies than those who don't have prenatal care.

- Nurses and trained volunteers who visit low-income adolescent mothers and reinforce their parenting skills reduce the mothers' isolation and decrease child abuse by as much as 40 percent (Centers for Disease Control and Prevention, 2003; Jackson et al., 2003; Vesely, 2005; Middlemiss and McGuigan, 2005; Paris and Dubus, 2005).

The U.S Department of Justice and nonprofit organizations have published a number of reports that describe the most promising policies and practices that integrate the efforts of domestic violence providers, child welfare agencies, law enforcement officers, and the judicial system (see, for example, Lowry and Trujillo, 2008, and Klein, 2009). If some of these programs were implemented, domestic violence and child maltreatment could be reduced.

CONCLUSION

Millions of U.S. families are experiencing negative *changes,* such as domestic violence, elder abuse and neglect, and high drug use among middle school children and teenagers. This does not mean that the situation is hopeless. As people become more informed about these and other problems, they have more *choices* in accessing supportive community resources and legal intervention agencies.

These choices are sometimes eclipsed by a number of *constraints.* Laws are not always enforced, our society still tolerates much male violence, and social service agencies are too understaffed and underfunded to deal with many health-related problems. Besides violence and health issues, many families must also deal with separation and divorce, the topic of the next chapter.

SUMMARY

1. People are more likely to be killed or assaulted by family members than by outsiders.

2. Although both men and women can be violent, abuse of women in intimate relationships results in much more serious physical and emotional damage than does abuse of men.

3. Women and children who are battered often suffer from low self-esteem and learned helplessness.

4. Women don't leave abusive relationships for a number of reasons: poor self-concept, a belief that the man they love will reform, economic hardship, the need for child support, doubt that they can get along alone, fear, shame and guilt, and being imprisoned in their homes.

5. There are four major categories of child maltreatment: physical abuse, sexual abuse, neglect, and emotional maltreatment.

6. Child maltreatment results in a variety of physiological, social, and emotional problems. Many of

these problems are long term and continue into adulthood.

7. The incidence of physical and sexual abuse among siblings and elderly abuse is greatly underreported.

8. The most influential theories of domestic violence and female victimization include patriarchy or male dominance theory, social learning theory, resource theory, exchange theory, and ecological systems theory.

9. Besides violence, families must grapple with other health-related issues such as substance abuse. Parental drug use, depression, suicide, and eating disorders also affect many families.

10. To decrease domestic violence and other family crises, we must do a better job of informing people about the problems, provide successful prevention programs, and implement better intervention strategies.

KEY TERMS

intimate partner violence (IPV) 384
physical abuse 384
sexual abuse 384
emotional abuse 384
familycide 385
marital rape 387

battered-woman syndrome 387
child maltreatment 392
child abuse 392
siblicide 399
sandwich generation 400
elder abuse 401

substance abuse 405
depression 407
binge eating 409
anorexia nervosa 409
bulimia 409

 MyFamilyLab provides a wealth of resources. Go to www.myfamilylab.com<http://www.myfamilylab.com/>, to enhance your comprehension of the content in this chapter. You can take practice exams, view videos relevant to the subject matter, listen to audio files, explore topics further by using Social Explorer, and use the tools contained in MySearchLab to help you write research papers.

15 Separation and Divorce

W

When I was in college during the mid-1960s, divorce was rare. In hushed tones, adults described the few children whose parents were divorced as "poor dears" and their parents as "disgraceful." Today, most people view divorce as a normal event that may occur in a person's lifetime. Statistically, two out of every five students reading this chapter probably come from divorced homes. Thus, both divorce rates and our reactions have changed dramatically within just one generation.

As you'll see in this chapter, divorce is a process rather than a single event, marriages fail for a number of micro- and macrolevel reasons, and divorce has both costs and benefits for adults and children. Let's begin by looking at separation, which usually precedes divorce.

DATA DIGEST

- In 2008, 70 percent of Americans ages 18 and older said that **divorce is morally acceptable,** up from 59 percent in 2001.

- On average, **first marriages that end in divorce last about eight years.**

- In 2009, **almost 55 percent of American married women had been married for at least 15 years;** 6 percent had been married for at least 50 years.

- In 2009, **among men who had ever been divorced** by age 70, 28 percent were African American, 25 percent were Latino, 20 percent were white, 11 percent were Asian, and 16 percent were multiracial or of another racial-ethnic origin.

- After a divorce, **83 percent of the custodial parents are mothers.** This proportion has been constant since 1994.

- Of the **13.7 million custodial parents in 2007,** 54 percent had a legal child support agreement.

- In the United States, **divorced households use 46 percent more electricity and 56 percent more water** per person than those in married households.

Sources: Grall, 2007; U.S. Census Bureau News, 2007; Yu and Liu, 2007; Saad, 2008.

SEPARATION: PROCESS AND OUTCOME

Separation can mean several things. It may be a temporary time-out from a highly stressful marriage during which the partners deliberate about continuing the marriage. One person may move out of the home in a trial separation, allowing the partners to see what living apart is like.

Separation can also be a permanent arrangement if the couple's religious beliefs don't allow divorce. Or a couple may seek a legal separation—that is, a temporary period of living apart, which is required by most states before the couple can be granted a divorce.

The Phases of Separation

Separation is usually a long and painful process that encompasses four phases: preseparation, early separation, midseparation, and late separation (Ahrons and Rodgers, 1987). Whether or not the partners go through all four stages, they often agonize for months or even years before making a final break.

PRESEPARATION During the *preseparation* phase, the partners may fantasize about what it would be like to live alone, escape from family responsibilities, or form new sexual liaisons. The fantasies rarely become reality, but they can make separation or divorce seem appealing.

In the later stages of the preseparation phase, the couple splits up after a period of gradual emotional alienation. Even though the financials costs of ending a marriage (especially one with children) are important considerations for separating couples, they are often less important than emotional and psychological factors such as staying in an unhappy marriage (Hewitt, 2009).

Even when people are considering separation (or have already made the decision), they often maintain a public pretense that nothing is wrong. The couple may attend family and social functions together, continuing rituals such as holding hands right up until the actual separation.

EARLY SEPARATION During the *early separation* phase, besides feeling ambivalent about leaving a marriage, the newly separated couples are plagued by many questions, both serious and trivial: What should the partners tell their family and friends? Should the children's teachers be notified? Who gets the new car? What about the vacuum cleaner, blender, and microwave?

Couples must also confront economic issues such as paying bills, buying the children's clothes, and splitting old and new expenses. The woman's economic survival may be a particularly difficult question. Even

when she is employed outside the home, a wife typically earns much less than her husband (see Chapter 13). As a result, she faces a lower standard of living, especially if the children live with her. Some people get support from family and friends, but most must cope on their own.

MIDSEPARATION In the *midseparation* phase, the harsh realities of everyday living set in. The pressures of maintaining two households and meeting the children's emotional and physical needs mount, and stress intensifies. The partners may feel overwhelmed, especially if there are additional stressors such as illness, unexpected expenses, a dependent elderly parent, or difficulties at work or in seeking a college or graduate degree.

Because of these problems, and especially when couples have been married at least ten years, they may experience "pseudo-reconciliation." That is, the earlier preseparation expectations or fantasies may be followed by a sense of loss when partners don't see their children as much; by guilt over abandoning the family; and by disapproval from parents, relatives, or friends. As a result, partners may move back in together.

This second reunion rarely lasts. Soon the underlying problems that led to the separation in the first

During a separation, the spouses must perform housework and other tasks they might not have done during the marriage.

place surface again, conflicts reemerge, and the couple may separate again (Everett and Everett, 1994).

LATE SEPARATION In the *late separation* phase, the partners must learn how to survive as singles again, such as now doing all the housework and home maintenance. Both spouses must also deal with mutual friends who have a hard time accepting the separation. Some friends may avoid both partners because the separation threatens their perceptions of their own marriages. Others may take sides, which forces a separating couple to develop new individual friendships.

Perhaps most important, partners must help their children deal with anxiety, anger, confusion, and sadness. We'll return to this topic later in the chapter.

On the positive side, separating couples often experience growth (Nelson, 1994): They may further their education, form new friendships, and enjoy a greater sense of independence and self-control.

Some Outcomes of Marital Separation

Not all separations end in divorce. Sometimes people reconcile and try to give their marriage a second chance:

After 25 years of marriage, my dad just moved out one day and lived in another state for almost three years. Then one day they reconciled and that was that. They never talk about it but my mom once commented that having dad around was better than being alone, the utilitarian marriage we discussed in class a couple of weeks ago. I'm assuming they'll stay together because my parents recently celebrated their 31st wedding anniversary (Author's files).

SEPARATION AND RECONCILIATION Data on reconciliation are practically nonexistent. According to one study, approximately 10 percent of all married U.S. couples who have separated have gotten back together, and black women were almost twice as likely as white women to do so (Wineberg and McCarthy, 1993).

A national study of black women who had reconciled found that the decision to get back together varied by age. Women separating after age 23 were substantially more likely to reconcile than were younger women. The researcher attributed this difference to three factors: Older women are more mature and more willing to make sacrifices in reuniting; they've invested more in the marriage than younger women have, especially if there are children; and they may believe that marriage should be a lifelong commitment (Wineberg, 1996).

SEPARATION WITHOUT DIVORCE Some people separate and even do the necessary paperwork, but about 6 percent never make the divorce official. If spouses, especially wives, don't have the money to get a divorce, the separation might last many years. Long-term separations are most likely among those who don't have a high school degree, have a low income, are not employed, and/or have one or more out-of-wedlock children (Bramlett and Mosher, 2002).

There are no recent national data, to my knowledge, on how many couples separate and don't get a divorce, but some estimates suggest that the rate may be much higher than 6 percent. In California, for example, 80 percent of divorcing people handle their own divorces to avoid the high lawyer fees. Of those handling their own divorce, about a third don't finalize their divorces because they don't realize that after serving the divorce petitions on their spouses and getting their signature, they must then receive a decision from a judge. Instead, many people file the papers in court and assume they're divorced. In effect, then, they're separated but not legally divorced (Garrison, 2007). In most cases, however, separations end in divorce.

SEPARATION AND DIVORCE Divorce, the legal and formal dissolution of a marriage, is not a new phenomenon. The Code of Hammurabi, written almost 4,000 years ago in ancient Mesopotamia, permitted termination of a marriage. (What was once Mesopotamia is currently composed of Iraq and parts of Syria and Turkey.) Among the nobility, especially, divorce was as easy for women as for men (Esler, 1994).

Many centuries later, in 1830, some researchers were alarmed that divorce rates had been increasing and that marriage was no longer "a permanent and lifelong state" (Thwing and Thwing, cited in Reiss,

"It's National We're History Month."

1971: 317). By the early twentieth century, a number of men ended their marriages by deserting rather than seeking a legal divorce.

TRENDS IN DIVORCE

Comedienne Roseanne Barr, married three times, has some advice for brides: "Take this marriage thing seriously—it has to last all the way to the divorce" (Scott, 2009: 2). CNN talk show host Larry King has been to the altar six times. Actor and singer Billy Bob Thornton has had five marriages, and model Christie Brinkley has divorced her fourth husband. Are such celebrities typical of the average American? Not at all.

Are U.S. Divorce Rates Alarming?

Talk show hosts and many journalists often proclaim that one in two U.S. marriages end in divorce. Such statements are misleading because they imply that in a given year, the people who marry are the same ones who get a divorce. For example, if there were 2 million marriages in the United States in 2007, the phrase "half of all marriages end in divorce" suggests that 1 million of those marriages ended in divorce. Such interpretations are incorrect because practically all of the 856,000 divorces that occurred in 2007 (National Center for Health Statistics, 2009) refer to marriages that took place in the past, perhaps even 50 years ago.

The most common (although not perfect) measure of the divorce rate is the number of divorces in a given year per 1,000 population. In the United States, the divorce rate decreased from 4.0 in 2000 to 3.5 in 2008 (National Center for Health Statistics, 2009; Tejada-Vera and Sutton, 2009). Over a lifetime, between 43 percent and 46 percent of American marriages end in divorce (Schoen and Canudas-Romo, 2006).

Whether such divorce rates are alarming depends on one's perspective. In an ideal world, *all* couples would have a happy marriage until one of the spouses died. On the other hand, a divorce is less likely today than it was 30 years ago.

Divorce Rates Have Decreased

The U.S. divorce rate rose steadily throughout the twentieth century (see *Figure 15.1*). The small peak in the early 1950s, after the end of World War II, has been attributed to divorces among

Since you asked . . .

- Why are U.S. divorce rates lower today than they were in 1980?

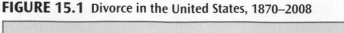

FIGURE 15.1 **Divorce in the United States, 1870–2008**

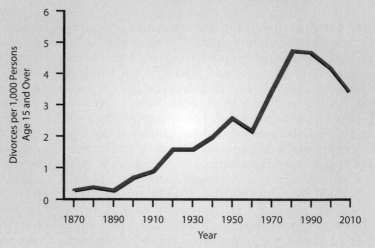

Sources: Based on Plateris, 1973; U.S. Census Bureau, 2009; and Tejada-Vera and Sutton, 2009, Table A.

people who had married impulsively before soldiers left for war. When the men returned, the couples often found that they had nothing in common. War-related family stress also increased divorce rates (see Chapter 3).

In the mid-1960s, divorce rates began to climb. They reached a plateau and remained there for a while, but started dropping in 1995. In effect, divorce rates are *lower* today than they were between 1975 and 1990.

It's not clear why this is the case. Perhaps more people are seeking premarital counseling or working harder to save their marriages. On the other hand, the lower divorce rates may reflect the growing number of couples who cohabit and/or postpone marriage. That is, many cohabiting couples in trial marriages break up instead of getting married and then divorcing. In a sense, then, remaining single longer and living with someone have decreased both marriage and divorce rates (Yin, 2007; see, also, Chapter 9).

Most people want to marry and vow to stay married. Nonetheless, many marriages end in divorce before the tenth wedding anniversary (see Data Digest), and is usually a painful experience in many people's lives regardless of when it occurs.

THE PROCESS OF DIVORCE

Like separations, few divorces are spontaneous, spur-of-the-moment acts. Instead, the divorce process is usually spread over a long period during which couples gradually

Since you asked . . .

- Can people who are divorced remain friends?

redefine their relationship and their expectations of each other. In navigating this transition, many people go through a number of stages. One widely cited process is Bohannon's (1971) six "stations" of divorce: emotional, legal, economic, coparental, community, and psychic.

Emotional Divorce

The *emotional divorce* begins before any legal steps are taken. One or both partners may feel disillusioned, unhappy, or rejected. The person who eventually initiates the divorce may feel that the marriage was never "right" to begin with, that the partners were mismatched, or that they were living a lie:

I came to realize that there had been a very long time when we really had no life together. We just sort of shared a house, and sort of took care of the kids together. But mostly I did that with the kids and he went and did his thing, and we were sort of this phony family for friends and neighbors and the relatives (Hopper, 2001: 436).

Spouses may be aloof or polite, despite their anger, or they may become overtly hostile, making sarcastic remarks or hurling accusations at each other.

The emotional divorce often progresses through a beginning phase to an end phase (Kersten, 1990). In the *beginning phase,* spouses feel disappointment in each other but hope that the marriage will improve.

During the *middle phase,* their feelings of hurt and anger increase as efforts to correct the situation seem unsuccessful. The partner who is less happy begins evaluating the rewards and costs of leaving the marriage.

In the *end phase,* one of the partners stops caring and detaches emotionally from the other. Apathy and indifference replace loving, intimate feelings. Even when the partners don't hate each other, it may be too late to rekindle the marriage.

Many couples delay the divorce as long as possible. For example, a national study of people ages 40 and older found that 17 percent had postponed getting a divorce for at least five years, primarily because they were concerned about hurting their children (Montenegro, 2004). Some couples turn to counseling, as you'll see later in this chapter, but most seek legal advice to end the marriage.

Legal Divorce

The *legal divorce* is the formal dissolution of a marriage. During this stage, couples reach agreements on issues such as child custody and the division of property and other economic assets. In part because divorce is an adversarial procedure during which each partner's attorney tries to maintain the upper hand, the process is rarely trouble free. For example,

the partner who does not want the divorce may try to forestall the inevitable end of the marriage or get revenge by making demands that the other spouse will find hard to accept, such as getting custody of the family dog.

Some issues may include **alimony** (sometimes called *spousal maintenance*), monetary payments by one ex-spouse to the other after a divorce. Other conflicts involve **child support**—monetary payments by the noncustodial parent to the custodial parent to help pay for child-rearing expenses. Because spouses often disagree on what is fair and equitable, they may use money to manipulate each other into making more concessions ("I'm willing to pay child support if you agree to sell the house and split the proceeds").

Even after a divorce is legal, couples may experience ambivalence: "Did I really do the right thing?" or "Should I have been satisfied with what I had?" Such doubts are normal, but some family clinicians caution divorcing parents not to reveal their ambivalence to their children, who may become confused or anxious, or deny the reality of divorce and fantasize about reconciliation (Everett and Everett, 1994).

Economic Divorce

During the *economic divorce,* the couple may argue about who should pay past debts, property taxes, and new expenses, such as braces, for the children. Thus, conflict over financial issues may continue long after the legal questions have been settled. In addition, the partners may try to change the child support agreement or not make the required payments.

Most financial planners now advise couples who are considering divorce to think about their retirement funds because they are often among the largest assets to be divided. They also urge prospective divorcees to go to court and renegotiate payments, especially for child support, when there are downturns in the economy. In doing so, couples may be involved in an economic divorce for several decades if their children are very young at the time of the divorce.

Coparental Divorce

The *coparental divorce* involves agreements about legal responsibility for financial support of the children, their day-to-day care, and the rights of the custodial and noncustodial parents in spending time with them. As you'll see shortly, conflict during this period may be short lived or long term, depending on how well the parents get along.

Community Divorce

Partners also go through a *community divorce,* during which they inform friends, family, teachers, and others that they are no longer married. Some people send e-mail messages to announce the divorce.

Sometimes people have divorce ceremonies, like this party, to celebrate the end of an unhappy marriage. Do you think that such ceremonies are tasteless or help people get closure on a divorce?

Others send formal printed cards, which sometimes look almost exactly like their wedding invitations did (Segrè, 2007). During this stage, relationships between grandparents and grandchildren often continue, but in-laws may sever ties. The partners may also replace old friendships with new ones, and they typically start dating again (see Chapter 16).

Psychic Divorce

In this final stage, the couple goes through a *psychic divorce* in which the partners separate from each other emotionally and establish separate lives. One or both spouses may undergo a process of mourning. Some people never complete this stage because they can't let go of their pain, anger, and resentment toward an ex-spouse, even after they remarry.

Not all couples go through all six of Bohannon's stations. Also, some couples may experience some stages, such as emotional and economic divorce, simultaneously. The important point is that divorce

Choices

How Divorced Parents Relate Can Make All the Difference to Children

Because divorcing spouses are often angry, hurt, or bitter, many divorces are hostile and painful. As the following five styles of relating to each other suggest, the more civility ex-spouses can maintain in their postdivorce relationship, the more productive their relationships will be, both with each other and with their children (Ahrons and Rodgers, 1987; Gold, 1992).

Perfect Pals

A very small group of divorced spouses share decision making and child rearing much as they did in marriage, and many feel that they are better parents after the divorce. These former spouses may even spend holidays together and maintain relationships with each other's extended families.

Cooperative Colleagues

Most divorced spouses do not consider themselves good friends, but some are able to cooperate. Working together takes effort, but they believe that it is their duty to make mutually responsible decisions about their children.

Cooperative parents want to minimize the trauma of divorce for their children and try to protect them from conflict. Such parents are willing to negotiate and compromise on some of their differences. They may also consult counselors and mediators to resolve impasses before going to court.

Angry Associates

These ex-spouses harbor bitter resentments about events in their past marriage as well as the divorce process. Some have long and heated battles over custody, visitation rights, and financial matters, for example. These battles may continue for many years after the divorce.

Fiery Foes

Some ex-spouses are completely unable to co-parent. Such partners are incapable of remembering any good times in the marriage, and each emphasizes the wrongs done by the other. Children are caught in the middle of the bitter conflict and are expected to side with one parent

and regard the other as the enemy. As in the case of "angry associates," legal battles sometimes continue for years after the divorce.

Dissolved Duos

Unlike the battling "fiery foes," the ex-spouses break with each other entirely. Noncustodial parents may leave the area where the family has been living. In some cases, one parent, usually the man, actually disappears, leaving the other parent with the entire burden of caring for the family. The children have only memories and fantasies of the vanished parent.

⁑ Stop and Think . . .

- Think about yourself, your parents, or your friends. Do any of these five styles characterize your or their divorces?
- Why, in most cases, are few parents "perfect pals" and "cooperative colleagues"? If parents say that they really care about their children, why do so many use children as pawns in divorce struggles?

is a *process* that involves many people, not just the divorcing couple, and may take time to complete. Moreover, because people differ, divorcing couples may respond to each other in varying ways, as the box "How Divorced Parents Relate Can Make All the Difference to Children" illustrates.

⁝• MAKING CONNECTIONS

■ Based on your own or your friends' experiences, how well do Bohannon's six stations describe divorce? Would you add other stages, for example? Or feel that some are considerably more important than others?

■ According to one divorce attorney, even happily married couples should prepare for a divorce, especially financially. One example includes making regular deposits into a private account that a spouse won't notice (Fogle, 2006). Is such advice cynical? Or practical and realistic?

WHY DO PEOPLE DIVORCE?

Divorce rates vary in the United States and elsewhere because they occur for three interrelated reasons: macro or societal, demographic, and micro or interpersonal. As *Figure 15.2* shows, macro variables influence demographic variables, which, in turn, may lead to interpersonal problems that end a marriage.

Macro-Level Reasons for Divorce

There are many macro-level reasons for divorce. As societal structures—such as religious institutions and the economy—change, they can contribute to an increase in divorce rates. Let's begin with the effect of changes in divorce laws.

DIVORCE LAWS All states have **no-fault divorce** laws so that neither partner needs to establish guilt or wrongdoing on the part of the other. Before no-fault divorce laws, the partner who initiated the divorce had to prove that the other was to blame for the collapse of the marriage because of adultery, desertion, or physical and mental cruelty. Couples can now simply give "irreconcilable differences" or "incompatibility" as a valid reason for divorce.

It's not clear whether and how much no-fault divorce laws contribute to divorce rates, but the increasing number of people entering the legal profession and the growth of free legal clinics have made divorce more accessible and inexpensive. Because divorce cases account for a large portion of all civil lawsuits, they provide millions of jobs for lawyers, judges, and other employees of the legal system. In child-custody or marital property disputes, especially, attorneys may hire accountants, marriage

FIGURE 15.2 Some Causes of Divorce

Macro-Level Reasons

- Divorce Laws
- Religious Institutions
- The Economy and Women's Employment
- Military Service
- Cultural Values and Social Integration
- Social Integration
- Technology

Demographic Variables

- Parental Divorce
- Age at Marriage
- Premarital Pregnancy and Childbearing
- Premarital Cohabitation
- Presence of Children
- Gender
- Race and Ethnicity
- Social Class
- Religion
- Similarity Between Spouses
- Marital Duration

Interpersonal Problems

- Extramarital Affairs
- Violence
- Substance Abuse
- Conflict over Money
- Disagreements about Raising Children
- Lack of Communication
- Irritating Personality Characteristics (Critical, Nagging, Moody)
- Annoying Habits (Smoking, Belching, etc.)
- Not Being at Home Enough
- Growing Apart

DIVORCE

counselors, psychologists, medical personnel, clergy, social workers, and mediators. Not everyone who wants a divorce can afford all these services, but their very availability sends the message that divorce is acceptable.

RELIGIOUS INSTITUTIONS No religion or religious group encourages divorce, but religious institutions affect divorce rates. American religions endorse marriage but also allow divorce, welcome divorced people into a congregation, and accept or even encourage remarriage (Cherlin, 2009a). The Catholic Church forbids divorce, but people can obtain an **annulment**, a ruling that a marriage is invalid for a variety of reasons, including adultery, pressure to marry, failure to consummate a marriage through vaginal intercourse, or a refusal to have children. Annulments have become so common that they are the "de facto religious divorces for American Catholics" (Cherlin, 2009a: 111). In these and other ways, religious institutions—however unintentionally—support if not increase divorce.

THE ECONOMY During the late nineteenth and early twentieth centuries, as the United States shifted from a preindustrial to an industrial society, extended families became less important, and the companionate marriage emerged. This type of marriage was based on the importance of emotional ties between husband and wife (friendship, romantic love, and a happy sex life) and one in which the husband was still the head of the household and the breadwinner (see Chapter 3).

What happens when men can't fulfill the male-breadwinner ideal? One might expect that hard economic times result in more marriage breakdown because financial insecurity increases marital conflict. Marital disagreements may increase, but as unemployment rises or men's work hours are reduced, divorce usually declines. Some sociologists expect that the severe 2008–2009 recession will decrease divorce rates temporarily because many unhappy couples will not have the income they need to separate and manage alone: "Fewer unhappy couples will risk starting separate households [and] . . . the housing market meltdown will make it more difficult for them to finance their separations by selling their homes" (Cherlin, 2009b: 25). In addition, whether or not there's an economic crisis, many unhappily married couples in lower socioeconomic levels stay together if they are unable to afford the costs of a divorce or of suing for child custody or child support.

The economy also affects the quality of marriage. As more couples must work nonstandard and long hours, they experience more stress and tension and spend less time together. Fatigue, demanding child-rearing responsibilities, and job instability (such as moving from job to job or finding only part-time work) can increase the likelihood of divorce (Ahituv and Lerman, 2004; see, also, Chapter 13).

MILITARY SERVICE Military service can be a source of upward mobility when recruits learn new skills, earn promotions to higher ranks and higher pay,

To combat the high divorce rates among active-duty soldiers and officers, the military offers numerous weekend retreats and marriage education classes. Pictured here, a family enjoys Christmas presents, an activity sponsored by the Army National Guard in Eugene, Oregon. The organization offers families many other services, including marital counseling.

and take advantage of education benefits to earn associate, bachelor, and graduate degrees. Having greater access to equal pay, equal benefits, and equal opportunities for promotions to higher ranks reduces marital stress associated with racial discrimination and, thus, increases marital quality and decreases the risk of divorce (Lundquist, 2006; Teachman and Tedrow, 2008).

Despite such benefits, military service—especially during the wars in Iraq and Afghanistan—is believed to have increased divorce rates because extended duty and deployment have been difficult on soldiers and their families. About one in every five married enlisted service members has filed for divorce since the beginning of the war in Iraq in 2003, a 44 percent increase over 2001. The rate of divorce among male enlistees (but not officers) has gradually increased, but the rate among female soldiers has surged. By mid-2007, female soldiers in the U.S. Army were filing for divorce at a rate three times higher than that of their male counterparts. Civilian husbands often don't understand why their military wives have to work long hours—sometimes for months at a time and often on a moment's notice. Female soldiers married to servicemen often complain that their spouses are jealous of both the women's opportunites for infidelity and their higher ranks (LaPlante, 2007). Such stresses can lead to disagreements and marital instability.

CULTURAL VALUES Americans' acceptance of divorce has grown (see Data Digest). In 2008, a large majority of Americans said that divorce is more acceptable than gambling (63 percent), having a baby outside of marriage (55 percent), or abortion (40 percent) (Saad, 2008). In another recent national survey,

67 percent of Americans said that children are better off if their unhappy parents get a divorce rather than remain married (Taylor et al., 2007).

The acceptance of divorce results from many factors. Some social scientists maintain that Americans are increasingly emphasizing individual happiness over family commitments. As more people pursue individual self-fulfillment, they seek a divorce, ignoring the needs of their spouses and children (Popenoe and Whitehead, 2009).

Since the 1970s and 1980s, many therapists and attorneys not only sent the message that "divorce is okay" but flooded the market with self-help books on how to get a divorce, how to cope with loneliness and guilt after a divorce, how to deal with child-custody disputes, as well as other divorce-related issues (see Chapter 2). And television programs such as *Divorce Court* reinforce the idea that divorce is a normal and everyday occurrence.

SOCIAL INTEGRATION Changes in cultural values and rising individualism, some sociologists maintain, have decreased **social integration**—the social bonds that people have with others and with the community at large. Less social integration increases divorce rates.

Compared with data from 2000, spouses are now less likely to interact and to spend time together and more likely to pursue interests and activities on their own rather than together. In addition, married people may value their privacy and prefer solitary activities—such as watching television or surfing the Internet—rather than socializing with friends and joining clubs (Amato et al., 2007).

There's nothing wrong with such behavior, but it decreases social integration because friends can provide emotional support, advice, and encouragement to married couples who are experiencing problems. In addition, belonging to the same organizations, such as religious congregations, can increase marital interaction and reinforce norms of marital commitment (Amato et al., 2007).

TECHNOLOGY Technological advances such as the Internet have made divorce more accessible. Many people now go online to file for divorce to save money and time and avoid the emotional clashes that can play out in lawyers' offices. Some online do-it-yourself divorces cost as little as $50 for all the necessary court forms and documents.

Some critics contend that the online services invite impulsiveness. People who have used the services, however, say that the decision to seek a divorce is always agonizing but the online accessibility saves money on legal fees. According to one proponent of online services, "You're not going to get divorced because it's on special offer" (O'Donnell et al., 1999: 8).

Although there are no national data, some researchers suspect that online dating that results in marriage may be especially likely to end in divorce. Many online daters are likely to act impulsively because they want to marry. They often don't know each other well, rush into marriage, and then discover that they have little in common or that one of the partners lied about his or her background (Gamerman, 2006; see, also, Chapter 8).

Demographic Variables and Divorce

Many demographic variables also help explain why some couples are prone to divorce. Let's begin with having divorced parents.

PARENTAL DIVORCE If the parents of one or both partners in a marriage were divorced while their children were young, the children themselves are more likely to divorce after they marry. Because children of divorced parents are less able to afford college (which tends to delay marriage), they are more likely to marry early. And the younger partners are when they marry, the more likely they are to divorce (Glenn, 2005; Wolfinger, 2005).

Some researchers believe that children of divorced parents have high divorce rates because they are less willing than those whose parents have not divorced to tolerate unhappy marriages. Others argue that many children of divorced parents have trouble making the kind of commitment that is necessary for marital success (Glenn, 2005). It's not clear, however, whether the inability to make the commitment is due to parental role models, a general suspicion that happy marriages are impossible, a higher likelihood of cohabiting (which increases divorce rates), or social class.

AGE AT MARRIAGE A number of studies have found that early age at marriage—especially younger than age 18—increases the chances of divorce. In fact, early marriage may be one of the strongest predictors of divorce. After 10 years of marriage, for example, 48 percent of first marriages of women younger than age 18 dissolved compared with 24 percent of first marriages of women who were at least age 25 at the time of the marriage (Kurdek, 1993; Bramlett and Mosher, 2002).

Those who delay marriage until their 20s are probably more mature and better able to handle the challenges of married life than are those who marry in their teens. Moreover, teen marriages are often hastened by a premarital pregnancy, another high risk factor that increases the likelihood of divorce.

PREMARITAL PREGNANCY AND CHILDBEARING Women who conceive or give birth to a child before marriage have higher divorce rates than women who conceive or have a child after marriage. Divorce is especially likely among adolescent parents, who generally lack the education or income to maintain a stable family life (Garfinkel et al., 1994; Teachman, 2002).

PREMARITAL COHABITATION Couples who live together before marriage have a higher chance of divorce if they marry, but the risk of divorce is highest among those who engage in serial cohabitation by living with different partners over time. Living together may be a way to get to know each other better, but cohabitors tend to have more lenient attitudes about divorce and to have a weaker commitment to marriage (Lichter and Qian, 2008; Popenoe and Whitehead, 2009; see, also, Chapter 9).

PRESENCE OF CHILDREN The presence of preschool children, especially firstborn children, seems to increase marital stability. This may reflect the fact that some couples stay together for the sake of the children. In addition, the presence of young children may make the divorce process more costly, both emotionally and financially (Previti and Amato, 2003; Rigt-Poortman and Seltzer, 2007).

When children are older, especially in their teens, couples may have fewer incentives to stay together. In some cases, problems with adolescent children worsen already strained marital relationships, and the marriage may fall apart (Waite and Lillard, 1991; Montenegro, 2004; see, also, Chapters 12 and 16).

GENDER Women are twice as likely as men to initiate a divorce (Amato et al., 2007). A national study of Americans between the ages of 40 and 79 found, similarly, that wives were more likely than husbands to seek a divorce, and that 26 percent of the men were shocked because they thought the marriage was happy. The women, however, said that after years of nagging, waiting for their husbands to be more responsive to relationship problems, and silently suffering, they gave up (Montenegro, 2004).

Across all age groups, women in unhappy marriages are more likely to get a divorce if they can support themselves. However, holding assets such as savings and stock jointly decreases many wives' likelihood of seeking a divorce, even in an unsatisfactory relationship. Having more financial assets and economic security enhance many wives' marital satisfaction. Even if spouses are unhappy, women in these marriages are more reluctant than men to leave because they expect that they will have a lower standard of living after a divorce. In terms of exchange theory, ironically, joint assets "can actually restrict the choices of women vis-à-vis divorce" (Dew, 2009: 29).

RACE AND ETHNICITY Divorce rates vary by race and ethnicity. In 2007, 12 percent of blacks in the United States were divorced compared with 11 percent of whites, 8 percent of Latinos, and 4 percent of Asians (U.S. Census Bureau, 2008). Across all racial and ethnic groups, African American women have the lowest marriage rates but higher divorce rates than Latinas and Asian American women (see *Figure 15.3*).

FIGURE 15.3 Marriage and Divorce among Racial-Ethnic Groups
Percentage of women age 15 and older who have ever been married and divorced, 2004.

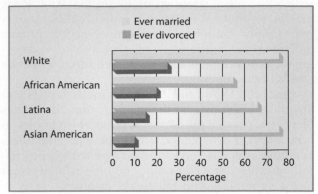

Source: Based on data in U.S. Census Bureau, Survey of Income and Program Participation (SIPP), 2004 Panel, Wave 2 Topical Module, 2007, Table 4, http://www.census.gov/population/www/socdemo/marr-div/2004detailed_tables.html (accessed August 25, 2009).

One of the most consistent research findings is that, in terms of population size and marriage rates, blacks are more likely to divorce than are people in any other racial-ethnic group. These differences persist at all income, age, educational, and occupational levels (Rank, 1987; White, 1991; Saluter, 1994). The box "Why Are African American Divorce Rates So High?" on p. 425 examines some of the reasons for these findings.

SOCIAL CLASS Low educational attainment, high unemployment rates, and poverty increase the likelihood of separation and divorce. A number of researchers have noted a "divorce divide" between people with a bachelor's degree or higher and those with a high school education or less (see Carroll, 2006). For example (and consistent with previous studies), a recent study of Americans age 18 and older found that 25 percent of college graduates have ever been divorced compared with 35 percent of those with a high school degree or less (Taylor et al., 2007).

Do people with college degrees have lower divorce rates because they're smarter? No. Rather, going to college postpones marriage, with the result that college graduates are often more mature, experienced, and capable of dealing with personal crises when they marry. They have higher incomes and better health care, which reduce stress from financial problems. Also, some of the characteristics required for completing college (such as persistence, dependability, and responsibility) also increase the likelihood of having a stable marriage (Kreider and Fields, 2002; Glenn, 2005).

Since you asked . . .

- Why do college graduates have lower divorce rates than those with less education?

Cross-Cultural and Multicultural Families

Why Are African American Divorce Rates So High?

Race and ethnicity don't "cause" divorce. Other macro, demographic, and micro/interpersonal factors are at work. This combination of factors, all of which increase the likelihood of divorce and are more prevalent among African American married couples, includes the following:

- Higher rates of teenage premarital pregnancy
- Young age at marriage
- Presence of children from previous relationships
- Serial cohabitation
- Poverty, financial strain, and male unemployment
- A major illness of a spouse when neither the wife nor husband has health insurance

Some researchers also suggest that divorce may be more acceptable among African Americans than other groups. Divorce may be less stressful because the community offers divorcing partners social support. During painful life events such as divorce, black families and churches provide love, services, money, and other resources.

Low Asian American divorce rates also reflect a combination of variables. Recent immigrants, for example, are likely to endorse traditional values that encourage staying married, even if there is domestic violence. Moreover, birth rates for unmarried Asian American women are low, another factor that decreases the risk of divorce.

Sources: Hill, 2003; Willie and Reddick, 2003; Costigan et al., 2004; Montenegro, 2004; Amato et al. 2007.

⁚• Stop and Think . . .

- Some of my African American students contend that discussions of high black divorce rates are racist ("You white folks are always emphasizing the negative"). Do you agree? And do such criticisms indicate that many Americans, including blacks, still see divorce as deviant rather than as normal?

- A national study concluded that risk factors such as age at marriage, education, and premarital child-rearing explain little of the overall difference between white and black divorce rates because there are many unknown variables (Sweeney and Phillips, 2004). What might be some of the unknown variables that researchers haven't taken into account?

Education is closely related to income, another predictor of the likelihood of divorce. In 2007, for example, 28 percent of Americans with annual incomes between $50,000 and $99,000 were ever divorced compared with 41 percent of those with annual incomes less than $30,000 (Taylor et al., 2007). We often hear that money can't buy happiness, but it can apparently reduce divorce rates. Financial problems can derail a marriage because they increase the likelihood of stress, arguments, and marital dissatisfaction.

RELIGION Decades ago, religion was an important factor in who married whom. For example, "a Catholic college graduate was more likely to marry a Catholic high school graduate than to marry a college-educated Protestant" (Cherlin, 2009a: 178-9). Currently, schooling and income are more important factors in sorting through the marriage market in finding a spouse (see Chapter 8).

According to some studies, about 21 percent of spouses have different religious affiliations, but this percentage doesn't include married couples in which one of the partners doesn't have any religious affiliation. The married couples who say that they are religious, compared with those who say that they are not religious, report more marital happiness and more commitment to their marriages, and they tend to have lower divorce rates (Amato et al., 2007).

However, such findings vary depending on the spouses' participation in religious services. If marital couples attend religious services together on a weekly or monthly basis, they are more likely to fight less and to interact more frequently because shared worshipping increases the likelihood of meeting other people who reinforce similar beliefs and experiencing social integration in a local community. On the other hand, not participating in religious services with a deeply religious spouse can increase the risk of divorce because of possible conflicts about attending religious services (Amato et al., 2007). Thus, strong religious beliefs and behavior can either strengthen or weaken a marriage.

SIMILARITY BETWEEN SPOUSES When spouses are similar to each other on demographic characteristics such as age, religion, race, ethnicity, and education, they are less likely to divorce. Those who differ on these and other characteristics face increased stresses and complications in their marriages because they may have different values and enjoy less support from family and friends (see Chapter 8).

Interracial marriages are also more likely to end in divorce. Interracial marriages among Asian Americans are the most stable, probably because of similar cultural values. Across all interracial marriages, African American men who marry white women have the highest risk of divorce, probably because they are more likely to experience greater racism and distrust than those of other racial-ethnic groups who intermarry (Clarkwest, 2007; Bratter and King, 2008; Zhang and Van Hook, 2009; see, also, Chapter 4 on interracial relationships and marriage). However, it's not clear whether many interracial marriages are more fragile because the partners are shunned by family and friends who disapprove of interracial marriages, because the romance of marrying someone who's very different wears off and the couples realize they have little in common, because prejudice from outsiders increases marital stress, or because of a combination of these and other factors.

Micro-Level/Interpersonal Reasons for Divorce

Macro-level and demographic variables affect interpersonal reasons for divorce. Because we live longer than people did in the past, a married couple may spend a significantly longer period of time together. Thus, there is a greater chance that, over the years, the partners may grate on each other's nerves. Or macro-level factors such as unemployment can create strain and aggravate existing annoyances.

Still, there are many micro-level reasons for divorce. Most overlap, as when a lack of commitment leads to infidelity, verbal or physical abuse, or poor communication. Financial difficulties create conflict for both spouses, but more women than men have been unhappy in their marriages (see *Figure 15.4*). These differences help explain why women are more likely than men to initiate a divorce.

People grow apart for many reasons, but some problems are especially likely to break up a marriage. Four common stressors are unrealistic expectations, conflict and abuse, infidelity, and communication problems.

UNREALISTIC EXPECTATIONS People now have fewer children and more time to focus on their relationship as a couple, both while the children are living at home and after they move out. One of the results is a greater chance that one of the spouses will become disillusioned. Also, couples may compare themselves to unrealistic images in films and on television and conclude that their marriage isn't as idyllic as it should be (see Chapters 1, 5, and 10).

CONFLICT AND ABUSE Arguments and conflict are major reasons for divorce for both sexes (see

FIGURE 15.4 Why People Get a Divorce, by Gender

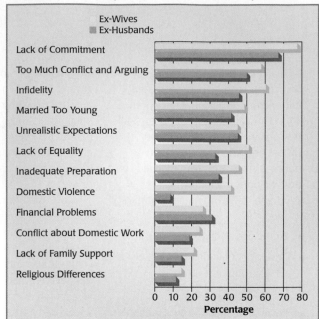

Source: Glenn, 2005: Figure 19.

Figure 15.4). The seeds of dissatisfaction are often sown years before marriage. A strong predictor of divorce is negative interaction before the couple marries. Unless people change their interaction patterns (and they usually don't), marital distress grows, increasing the likelihood of divorce (Clements et al., 2004).

Sometimes the conflict escalates into abuse, especially for wives. For example, 42 percent of women but only 9 percent of men said that domestic violence was a major reason for divorce. Among those age 40 and older, 23 percent of women, compared with only 8 percent of men, said that verbal, physical, or emotional abuse was "the most significant reason for the divorce" (Montenegro, 2004; Glenn, 2005).

INFIDELITY Cheating is another major reason for divorce, especially for women (see *Figure 15.4*). Many men claim that they're unfaithful because they're unhappy with their sex life, but there's little evidence to support such complaints. Nationally, for example, only 2 percent of men and women say that sexual incompatibility or poor sexual performance was the most important reason for a divorce (Montenegro, 2004; see, also, Chapter 7 for a discussion of the prevalence, reasons, and consequences of emotional and sexual infidelity in marriage and nonmarital relationships).

COMMUNICATION Communication problems derail many marriages (see Chapters 5 and 10). Some researchers can predict whether a newlywed couple will still be married four to six years later by observing

Hagar © 2005. King Features Syndicate.

not *what* they say but *how* they say it. Couples who stay together listen to each other respectfully even when they disagree, don't start discussions with accusatory statements ("You're lazy and never do anything around the house"), and have more positive than negative interactions . Lasting relationships may not be blissful, but the communication isn't venomous (Gottman, 1994).

There are other important reasons for divorce. Many couples stay in a marriage for the sake of the children, but continuous disagreements about how to raise and discipline children can increase marital dissatisfaction and trigger a divorce. Money is another common source of conflict in marital breakups. Wives grow disillusioned if their husbands can't find or hold a job. Unemployed or low-paid men, who already feel inadequate, complain that their wives' nagging about bills makes them feel even worse (Hetherington and Kelly, 2002; Stanley et al., 2002; Montenegro, 2004).

It bears repeating that interpersonal difficulties are often closely related to demographic and macrolevel factors. For example, many divorced black men report that financial strain created or aggravated existing communication problems. As one divorced father said, "I worked too much and spent little time at home. . . . It is ironic that my efforts to provide for my family made me vulnerable to charges of being distant and uncaring" (Lawson and Thompson, 1999: 65).

Same-Sex Divorce

In the United States, what's harder to get than a same-sex marriage? A same-sex divorce. In 2004, Massachusetts became the first state to legalize same-sex marriage, and four other states followed (see Chapter 9).

Maggie and Linda, who lived in Rhode Island, drove to Massachusetts to wed. After two years of marriage, the 10-year relationship collapsed, and Linda decided to get a divorce. She and Maggie couldn't get a regular divorce because the federal law defines marriage as being between a man and a woman. They couldn't get a divorce in Rhode Island because the state, similarly, views same-sex marriage as illegal. And they couldn't get a divorce

in Massachusetts because only residents who have lived there a year can file for a divorce (Horton, 2008). As Maggie and Linda, other married same-sex couples, and heterosexual have found, getting divorced can be much more difficult than getting married.

We know little about same-sex divorce in the United States because laws allowing same-sex marriage are recent. However, a study of same-sex divorce in Norway and Sweden, countries that have recognized same-sex marriages for some time, found several patterns. Like the United States, couples who are young when they marry are more likely to divorce. The researchers also found that lesbians were more than twice as likely to divorce as gay men (but the reasons are unclear). In addition, the divorce rates of same-sex couples were higher than those of opposite-sex couples probably because, even in Norway and Sweden, same-sex couples get less support from the community and less encouragement than heterosexual couples to make the marriage work from family and friends (Andersson et al., 2006).

MAKING CONNECTIONS

- Look again at the reasons people give for divorce in *Figure 15.4* on p. 426. Which reasons do you think justify getting a divorce? Which problems do you think are minor and couples should try to work them out instead of getting a divorce?

- Think about the people you know who have experienced a divorce. Were the reasons macro, demographic, micro/interpersonal, or a combination?

HOW DIVORCE AFFECTS ADULTS

In the film *The First Wives Club*, three middle-aged women get revenge on their ex-husbands for dumping them for younger girlfriends. Among other stereotypes, the husbands are portrayed as cads, the wives are presented as innocent victims, and getting even is fun.

In real life, divorce is usually an agonizing process for both sexes because nearly all people enter a marriage with the expectation that it will be a lifelong and mutually satisfying relationship. Divorce has significant effects in at least three areas of the ex-spouses' lives: physical, emotional, and psychological well-being; economic and financial changes; and child-custody and child-support arrangements.

Physical, Emotional, and Psychological Effects

Divorced people are worse off than married people in many ways. They report greater social isolation, more economic hardship, more stress, less social support, and less satisfying sex lives (Waite et al., 2002; Amato et al., 2007; see, also, Chapter 7 on sexual behavior).

PHYSICAL WELL-BEING Generally, divorce decreases physical well-being. A study that examined national data from 1972 to 2003 found that the self-rated health of the divorced worsened over the 31 years compared with that of married people, and more so for women than men. The health of the never-married—across all race groups and for both sexes—improved so much that their physical well-being was similar to that of married men, who typically are the healthiest due, largely, to economic resources, their wives' encouraging exercise, a healthful diet, and the avoidance of risk-taking behavior (see Chapter 10). The researchers concluded, however, that encouraging marriage for everyone to promote health may be misguided because "getting married increases one's risk for eventual marital dissolution, and marital dissolution seems to be worse for self-rated health now than at any point in the past three decades" (Liu and Umberson, 2008: 252).

Other recent studies have found, similarly, that there's a negative association between divorce and health. Among people older than age 50, for example, the divorced suffer a greater decline in physical health than do married people. Those who spent more years divorced reported about 20 percent more chronic health problems such as heart disease, diabetes, and cancer, as well as mobility problems such as difficulty climbing stairs and even walking one block. Thus, "*Being* married may protect or even improve health, *getting* divorced or becoming widowed may damage health, and *being* divorced or widowed may damage health" (Hughes and Waite, 2009: 356, emphasis in original; see, also, Zhang and Hayward, 2006).

EMOTIONAL AND PSYCHOLOGICAL WELL-BEING The psychic divorce described on p. 420 may continue for many years. Even when both partners know that their marriage can't be salvaged, they are often ambivalent about getting a divorce. They may fluctuate between a sense of loss and a feeling of freedom; they may have periods of depression punctuated with spurts of happiness. The box "Do You Know Someone with Divorce Hangover?" on p. 429 examines some of the adjustments that newly divorced people face.

Initially, divorced people of both sexes experience emotional upsets, but they tend to react differently: Women report more depression whereas men report more alcohol abuse and smoking. Such reactions reflect cultural norms about gender roles. That is, in our society women typically express stress by turning inward, whereas men are more likely to engage in high-risk behaviors. A person's emotional health usually improves, however, when he or she forms a new relationship, especially by cohabiting or remarrying (Johnson and Wu, 2002; Simon, 2002; Martin et al., 2005).

The degree of emotional and psychological distress involves other important factors. When people leave a very unhappy marriage characterized by a long period of conflict, hostility, and violence, they experience much less depression and stress than those who were simply dissatisfied. Psychological well-being problems are greatest for parents with young children at home at the time of the divorce. For women without young children, divorce appears to have few negative psychological consequences (Kalmijn and Monden, 2006; Williams and Dunne-Bryant, 2006; Amato and Hohmann-Marriott, 2007).

THE CHICKEN AND EGG QUESTION In the studies just cited and others, social scientists never imply or conclude that divorce causes physical, emotional, and psychological problems or other maladies. Rather, they note an association between divorce and poorer health. On the other hand, poor health, especially poor mental health, can decrease marital satisfaction, increasing the likelihood of a separation or divorce (Hughes and Waite, 2009).

Thus, it's not clear whether divorce lowers people's well-being or whether preexisting problems (such as depression and alcohol abuse) contribute to the likelihood of getting a divorce. Some people are prone to psychological or interpersonal problems before divorce but exhibit additional problems afterward. For example, an aggressive husband may become physically abusive with new partners after a divorce. In other cases, long-standing problems such as infidelity and substance abuse play a major role in dissolving a marriage (Amato, 2002; Lucas, 2005).

Social scientists agree, however, that a combination of factors affects well-being. A study of divorced women in Iowa found that the act of getting a divorce produced no immediate effects on physical health but had some negative effects on mental health. Ten years later, those effects on mental health led to poorer physical health. Over time, distress over financial difficulties,

⁝• Do You Know Someone with Divorce Hangover?

After a divorce, ex-spouses must accomplish three tasks: letting go; developing new social ties; and, when children are involved, redefining parental roles. Often, however, one or both ex-spouses suffer from "divorce hangover" (Walther, 1991; Everett and Everett, 1994).

In each of the following statements, fill in the blanks with the name of someone you know who has just gone through a divorce. If you agree that many of these statements describe a friend or acquaintance, you know someone with divorce hangover. Confronting these symptoms can help a person recognize and begin to overcome divorce-related stress.

Sarcasm When someone mentions the ex-spouse, _____ is sarcastic or takes potshots at the former partner. The sarcasm may be focused on the marriage in particular or unsupported generalizations: "All men leave the minute their wives turn 40" or "All women are just after their husband's money."

Using the children _____ tries to convince the children that the divorce was entirely the other person's fault and may grill the children for information about the other parent.

Lashing out _____ may try to assert control by making unreasonable demands (for example, refusing joint custody) or blowing up at a friend because the ex-spouse was invited to a party.

Paralysis _____ can't seem to get back on track by going back to school, getting a new job, becoming involved in new relationships, or finding new friends. Sometimes it's even hard for _____ to get up in the morning and go to work, clean the house, or return phone calls.

Holding on The ex-spouse's photograph still sits on _____'s piano, and his/her clothing or other possessions remain in view, keeping the ex-spouse's presence alive in _____'s daily life.

Throwing out everything _____ may throw away things of value—even jewelry, art, or priceless collections—that are reminders of the ex-spouse.

Blaming and finding fault Everything that went wrong in the marriage or the divorce was someone else's fault, _____ maintains: the ex-spouse, family, friends, kids, boss, and so on.

Excessive guilt _____ feels guilty about the divorce, regardless of which partner left the other. _____ buys the children whatever they want and gives in to the children's or ex-spouse's demands, however unreasonable they may be.

Dependency To fill the void left by the ex-spouse, _____ leans heavily on other people, particularly new romantic involvements.

---

parenting problems, lapses in health care coverage, and other stressful life events affected the women's physical well-being (Lorenz et al., 2006).

Economic and Financial Changes

Generally, marriage builds wealth while divorce depletes it. A national study of people ages 41 to 49 found that, on average, a couple's wealth increases about 16 percent for each year of marriage. In contrast, divorced couples lose about 77 percent of their shared wealth within five years of the divorce (Zagorsky, 2005).

Married couples accumulate more wealth than single people for a variety of reasons: They maintain one household, save more money, invest more of their income, and may work harder and seek promotions to pay for their children's education. Divorce reverses all these benefits. Ex-spouses often have two mortgages or rents and two sets of household expenses, and they rarely pool their assets to pay for their children's educational costs. Gender can also have a dra-

matic impact on a divorced person's economic status. As one accountant noted, "The man usually walks out with the most valuable asset, earning ability, while the woman walks out with the biggest cash drain, the kids and house" (Gutner, 2000: 106).

ALIMONY Payment of alimony is less common than in the past, but still exists. In some states, even if the wife is employed and the couple is childless, the higher earner, who is usually the man, may pay up to a third of his salary to his ex-wife for several years if they've been married longer than 10 years or if she is deemed physically or emotionally unhealthy.

GENDER According to some observers, no-fault divorce has done more harm than good to many women. Because both partners are treated as equals, each, theoretically at least, receives half of the family assets, and the ex-wife is expected to support herself regardless of whether she has any job experience or work-related skills. Even though the couple's combined wealth decreases, the economic well-being of mothers declines by 36 percent and the financial status of fathers improves by 28 percent after a divorce. Whether or not a couple has children, the woman must often fight for a portion of her ex-husband's retirement income, which he earned during the marriage (Bianchi et al., 1999; Tergesen, 2001).

A recent national study that examined the financial status of white divorced mothers with children living at home found that nearly 25 percent were living in poverty. About 5 percent of the women improved their situation by marrying successful men, finding high-paying jobs, or both. Most, however, had financial difficulties, even after moving in with parents or siblings, because they lacked marketable skills for well-paying jobs and received little, if any, alimony or child support or public assistance (Ananat and Michaels, 2008).

AGE A person's, particularly a woman's, age can also affect income after a divorce. In 1979, homemaker Terry Hekker published a best-selling book that attacked career women and trumpeted the joy of women who devote their lives to being full-time wives and mothers. Twenty years later, her husband presented her with divorce papers on their fortieth anniversary and left her for a younger woman. Hekker, who had raised five children, was devastated. Although she had no income and no marketable skills, the judge suggested that—at age

In 1997, Lorna Wendt, the wife of a wealthy General Electric corporate executive, rejected a $10 million settlement after her husband of 32 years sought a divorce. Ms. Wendt went to court, arguing that she was worth more as a full-time homemaker because she had raised their children single-handedly, entertained her husband's business associates, and made numerous business-related trips to 40 countries in support of her husband's career. The judge awarded her half the marital estate—worth about $100 million.

67—she get job training. Hekker ended up selling her engagement ring to pay for roof repairs, got a job at a salary of $8,000 a year, and started living on food stamps. Her ex-husband, meanwhile, was vacationing in Mexico with his new lover. Recently, Hekker (2009) published her second book, *Disregard the First Book,* in which she tells all women to learn to support themselves.

Hekker is fairly representative of many older divorced women. The proportion of women ages 55 to 59 who were currently divorced jumped from less than 5 percent in 1970 to over 16 percent in 2010 (U.S. Census Bureau, 2010). Because older women are less likely than older men to remarry, many live at or near the poverty level, a topic we'll discuss in Chapter 17.

Compared with young men about the same age, many younger women's incomes plunge because in 84 percent of all divorce cases, the children live with the mother (Grall, 2007). Even if both parents have child custody rights, child support payments rarely meet the mother's and children's living expenses. Let's look at child custody first and then examine child-support issues.

Child Custody

Children often are caught in the middle of custody battles:

> **Mark, age eight:** *"I don't think either one of them should get me. All they ever do is fight and yell at each other. I'd rather live with my grandma."*
>
> **Mary, age ten:** *"I hate going to my dad's because every time I come back I get the third degree from Mom about what we did and who was there and whether Dad did anything wrong or anything that made us mad. I feel like a snitch."*
>
> **Robin, age seven:** *"Mom wants me to live with her and Dad wants me to live with him. But I want to live with both of them. Why do I have to choose? I just want us to be happy again"* (Everett and Everett, 1994: 84–85).

Custody is a court-mandated ruling as to which divorced parent will have the primary responsibility for the welfare and upbringing of the children. Children live with a custodial parent, whereas they see the noncustodial parent according to specific visitation schedules worked out in the custody agreement. Because approximately 90 percent of all divorces are not contested, most child-custody cases are settled out of court (Clarke, 1995).

In some cases, fathers get child custody by default: The biological mother doesn't want to raise the children, child protective agencies seek the father's involvement, or a child wants to live with the father.

Even when they don't expect or want custody, some fathers, including those living in impoverished communities, often enjoy raising their children: "It's the best part of who I am," according to one father. However, they must often rely on kin for child-rearing support because of inflexible work schedules and low wages (Hamer and Marchioro, 2002: 126).

TYPES OF CUSTODY There are three types of custody: sole, split, and joint. In **sole custody** (about 81 percent of cases), one parent has sole responsibility for raising the child; the other parent has specific visitation rights. Parents may negotiate informally over issues such as schedules or holidays; but if they disagree, the legal custodian has the right to make the final decisions.

In **split custody** (about 2 percent of cases), the children are divided between the parents either by sex (the mother gets the daughters and the father gets the sons) or by choice (the children are allowed to choose the parent with whom they want to live).

In **joint custody,** sometimes called *dual residence custody* (about 16 percent of cases), the children divide their time between their parents, who share in decisions about their upbringing. In another 1 percent of cases, custody is awarded to someone other than the husband or wife, such as a relative (Clarke, 1995). There are two types of joint custody. In *joint legal custody,* both parents share decision making on issues such as the child's education, health care, and religious training. In *joint physical custody,* the court specifies how much time children will spend in each parent's home.

Many fathers are pushing for **co-custody,** in which parents share physical and legal custody of their children equally. Men's rights groups contend that mother-only custody is not in the best interests of the child and often leads to a father's alienation and absence (Kruk, 2008).

Women who resist co-custody legislation argue that noncustodial fathers show little evidence of taking their parenting roles seriously. Many are "Disneyland dads" who are more likely to engage in leisure activities with their children (video games, movies, sports) than to participate in school events or to supervise homework (Stewart, 2003).

SOME PROS AND CONS OF CO-CUSTODY Co-custody is a heated issue because fathers' rights groups and many women are on opposite sides of the issue. The issue is complex because the divorced parents may live far apart or are constantly fighting.

Proponents of co-custody advance several arguments:

Since you asked . . .
• Should divorced parents share custody of the children?

- Many men say that they want to care for their children and have formed organizations such as

Fathers 4 Justice, a social movement that began in Great Britain, has become popular in the United States. The fathers, both unmarried and divorced, demand better access to their children.

Fathers United for Equal Justice to lobby for co-custody laws in every state.

- Much research shows that a father's positive involvement—whether married, unmarried, or divorced—is essential to children's development.

- Co-custody eases the economic burdens of parenting, particularly for mothers.

- Because, on average, divorced fathers have higher incomes than divorced mothers, they can provide more resources for the children.

- Fathers are more likely to honor court-mandated child-support and alimony payments if they have equal child-rearing rights (Hetherington and Stanley-Hagan, 1997; Sayer, 2006).

Opponents contend that co-custody does more harm than good:

- Constantly shuttling children between two homes can create instability and confusion as well as disrupt school attendance and academic performance.

- Children may have to deal with more parental conflict because parents who argued frequently during marriage continue to do so after a divorce (about child-rearing practices, discipline, or religious upbringing, for example).

- Co-custody usually decreases child support payments to mothers, who earn less than fathers do.

- Co-custody gives men more rights than responsibilities: They have more legal control and decision-making power, whereas mothers provide most of the children's emotional and routine physical care.

■ Co-custody makes it possible for men who abused their wives or children before the divorce to continue doing so (Comerford, 2005; Kernic et al., 2005; Tessier, 2007).

One solution to such disputes might be **co-parenting,** which refers to divorced parents' being involved in making decisions about the child's education, health care, religious training, and social activities. Co-parenting doesn't mean that divorced parents must interact face to face, but it does involve some degree of communication between parents about child rearing (Markham et al., 2007).

Co-parenting plans (also called "parenting plans" or "parenting partners") are gaining popularity because they seem to benefit the children. Children adjust better to divorce when both parents continue to be active in their lives and when parents can avoid putting the children in the middle of personal feelings and conflict. Co-parenting is not a legal type of custody defined by legal statutes, but more states are requiring parents to file a co-parenting plan as part of the divorce process (Segal et al., 2009).

Generally, child custody is a contentious issue. Child support is even more combative and can have negative outcomes over the child's life course.

Child Support

When couples separate or divorce, child support is usually a critical issue. Let's begin by looking at who pays and who gets child support.

WHO PAYS AND GETS CHILD SUPPORT? Because mothers get sole custody in 84 percent of the cases (Grall, 2007), most court-ordered child support is required of fathers. Nearly half of all men neither see nor support their children after a divorce. In fact, two-thirds of noncustodial fathers spend more on car payments than they do for child support. Others ignore their children entirely, including not sending them birthday presents (Garfinkel et al., 1994; Sorensen and Zibman, 2000).

The number of noncustodial fathers who saw their 6- to 12-year-old children did rise from 18 percent in 1976 to 31 percent in 2002.

Weekly contact was most likely when the children were born within the marriage and the fathers paid child support (Amato et al., 2009).

There may be a number of reasons for the rise of noncustodial fathers' contact with their children. For example, black religious leaders have encouraged fathers to do so, the mass media has publicized the result of scholarly studies which show that maintaining father-child ties benefits both fathers and children, and fathers' rights groups have pushed fathers to see their children regularly because doing so may strengthen their goal of getting joint custody or having the mother agree to co-custody.

In 2006, almost 14 million single parents had custody of 21 million children while the other parent lived somewhere else (nonresident parent). Of all these custodial parents, a majority (57 percent) had some type of legal court agreement for child support. The top reasons for not seeking a legal award were having informal agreements, each parent providing what she or he could for support, and believing that the noncustodial parent could not afford to pay anything (Grall, 2007).

As *Figure 15.5* shows, a parent is most likely to receive the full amount of court-ordered child-support payments if she or he has at least a college degree, has divorced (rather than breaking up outside of marriage), the noncustodial parent has regular contact with the children, is age 40 or older, and works full-time year-round. The custodial parents who are the least likely to receive child support are never married black mothers who are younger than age 30, do not have a high school diploma, and depend on public assistance (Grall, 2007). Thus, those with greater

FIGURE 15.5 Custodial Parents Who Received Full Child-Support Payments Ordered by the Court: 2005

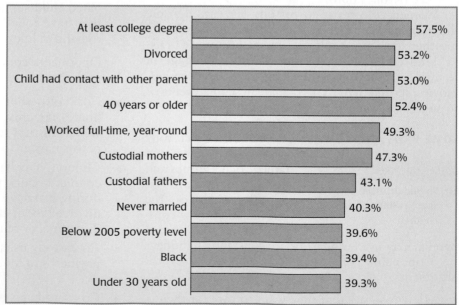

At least college degree	57.5%
Divorced	53.2%
Child had contact with other parent	53.0%
40 years or older	52.4%
Worked full-time, year-round	49.3%
Custodial mothers	47.3%
Custodial fathers	43.1%
Never married	40.3%
Below 2005 poverty level	39.6%
Black	39.4%
Under 30 years old	39.3%

Source: Grall, 2007, Figure 1.

resources, such as a college degree, are able to collect more financial support. They may have ex-husbands (and occasionally ex-wives) who can provide more support or are more aggressive about getting court-ordered awards.

Approximately 77 percent of custodial parents receive less child support than they're supposed to, and 23 percent receive none. Even when parents (most of whom as mothers) receive the full amount awarded by the court, the average amount is less than $6,000 a year and about one-third that amount if the father has a high school diploma or less and hasn't been employed for several years. Even then, fewer than 40 percent of mothers receive the full amount (Grall, 2007; Martinson and Nightingale, 2008). Thus, once again, not having resources diminishes the likelihood of getting more resources.

Some noncustodial parents provide noncash support. About 61 percent of custodial parents, typically mothers, receive birthday, holiday, or other gifts (58 percent); clothes or diapers for the children (39 percent); food and groceries (29 percent); medical assistance other than health insurance (19 percent); or partial or full payments for child care or summer camp (11 percent) (Grall, 2007). Many of the occasional contributions, such as birthday presents, have a minimal impact on improving a child's overall financial well-being.

CHILD SUPPORT AND VISITATION In 2006, 85 percent of mothers who received child support also had visitation arrangements with the child's father (Grall, 2007). Child support usually increases when it involves co-parenting, but that's not always the case (see the box "Why Are Many Fathers Deadbeat Dads?"

Many middle-class parents, especially fathers, avoid child support payments because they don't agree with the visitation rights or believe that their ex-spouse is squeezing them for money. Others rarely see their children because they work longer hours to meet their child-support obligations (Huang, 2009).

Among lower-income fathers, many are "dead broke" rather than "deadbeat dads." With low earnings, it's difficult for fathers to meet court-ordered child-support payments that might consume up to half of their wages (Martinson and Nightingale, 2008). Instead, they break off all contact with their children.

Why Are Many Fathers Deadbeat Dads?

Most noncustodial fathers say they love their kids but may evade child support orders. These nonpaying fathers generally fall into one or more of the following categories (Nuta, 1986):

- The *irresponsible parent,* representing the greatest number of child-support dodgers, simply doesn't take his parental duties seriously. He may expect others to take care of his family ("Welfare will pay" or "Her family has more money than I do"), or he thinks that taking care of himself is more important than providing for his children. The irresponsible parent often includes noncustodial fathers with psychological and drug abuse problems who do not seek employment or cannot keep a job (Dion et al., 1997).
- The *overextended parent* is overburdened with financial obligations ("I can't afford it"). Anxious to get out of

a marriage as soon as possible, he may agree to pay more support than he can afford. He may remarry and, unable to support two families, fail to provide for the children of his first marriage (Manning et al., 2003). Or he may become ill and unemployed and thus unable to make the child-support payments.

- The *parent in pain* may feel shut out of the family and distance himself physically or emotionally from his children. He may even rationalize his distancing ("She turned the kids against me"). Other fathers are angry if they believe that their visitation rights are unfair.
- The *vengeful parent* uses child support as a form of control. He may use nonpayment to change a visitation agreement or to punish his wife for initiating the divorce ("She's getting what she deserves").

Stop and Think . . .

- Do you think that any or all of these fathers have legitimate reasons for not paying child support?
- A few years ago, several businesses in Cincinnati, Ohio, posted photos of the county's "Most Wanted Deadbeat Parents" on pizza boxes. Fathers' rights groups protested, claiming that many of the fathers are unable to pay child support, and that publicly humiliating them makes them angrier, and embarrasses their children (Leving and Sacks, 2007). Do you agree or disagree? Why?
- Do you think that noncustodial mothers should be included in the classification of "deadbeat parents"?

Choices

ENFORCEMENT OF CHILD SUPPORT Since the 1980s, federal legislators have passed a number of laws to enforce court-ordered child-support awards. In 1984, Congress passed the Child Support Enforcement Amendments, which require states to deduct payments from delinquent parents' paychecks and tax returns. The Family Support Act of 1988 mandates periodic reviews of award levels to keep them consistent with the rate of inflation. In 1998, the federal government passed the Deadbeat Parents Act, which makes it a felony to cross a state line to evade child-support obligations. And, since 2006, the State Department has denied passports to noncustodial parents who owe more than $2,500 in child support ("No passports . . .," 2007).

Enforced court-ordered child-support payments often are the only monetary contributions that many fathers make. Also, there is some evidence that strengthening child-support enforcement discourages men from having children with women to whom they are not married or living with women who cannot share the financial costs of raising children (Paasch and Teachman, 1991; Aizer and McLanahan, 2005).

Despite the laws, court-ordered child support has several problems. First, states vary a great deal in the extent to which they enforce child-support laws. A second problem is that 30 percent of all parents, most of them fathers, who live in a different state than their ex-spouse can evade legal action because of local policies or practices. According to a journalism professor in North Carolina, for example, it's been very difficult to collect any child support from her ex-husband despite the Deadbeat Parents Act:

The county I filed with notifies nonpaying parents of legal action against them by putting a letter clearly marked from the child support enforcement office into the U.S. Postal Service. The nonpayer can stall proceedings by simply not signing the letter's return-receipt card (Elmore, 2005).

Do Visitation and Child Support Improve Children's Lives?

Of course, you might be thinking. The answer isn't this clear-cut, however, because visitation and child-support benefits depend on a number of variables, such as how much a parent pays and the family's social class.

Researchers who argue that child-support enforcement is "an investment that works" point to numerous advantages. For example, especially for poor mothers who are employed, child support is the second largest source of income for their families. In low-income families, getting child support may mean staying out of poverty. Low-income fathers are also more motivated to find a job and to stay employed longer. Among all families, fathers who make regular child-support payments are more involved with their children and the payments may reduce further conflict between the parents (Turetsky, 2006).

Others are more skeptical. They note, for example, that most low-income, never-married fathers—especially those who have been in prison or have few marketable skills—can't support themselves, much less their children. As a result, they may avoid their children altogether. Other fathers, regardless of social class, just don't want to be involved with their children, even when they make some of the court-ordered child support payments (Malm et al., 2006; Sayer, 2006).

Some studies have found that among low-income households, child-support enforcement rarely improves children's well-being and makes nonresident fathers' financial situation worse. This arises because the government uses fathers' payments to recoup the costs of public assistance to mothers and children. In 2007, for example, close to half the states passed along none of the collected child support to families on welfare (Eckholm, 2007; Stirling and Aldrich, 2008).

::• MAKING CONNECTIONS

- Judges have vast discretion in divorce proceedings, which vary from state to state and from case to case. The American Law Institute has proposed, instead, that a court should grant child custody to parents in proportion to the amount of time they spent caring for a child before the divorce. Do you agree with this proposal?

- As you saw, many low-income mothers and children get none of the father's child-support payments because the money helps the government compensate for public assistance costs. Are such policies fair for taxpayers? Or counterproductive because low-income noncustodial fathers have less incentive to pay child support?

HOW DIVORCE AFFECTS CHILDREN

When people marry, they expect a long and happy relationship and to raise their children to grow up as competent, well-adjusted, and equally happy adults. Instead, nearly 1 million American children undergo a parental breakup every year, and 40 percent experience a parental divorce before reaching adulthood (Amato, 2007).

Since you asked . . .
::• Can children benefit from their parents' divorce?

As you've seen throughout this chapter, divorce is almost always a painful and stressful process for adults, but some children are more resilient and adaptive than others. Before looking at some of the reasons for these variations, let's begin with the question of whether divorcing and divorced parents should treat their children like peers.

In a Divorce, Should Your Child Be Your Peer?

A 23-year-old daughter once complained to "Dear Ann," the advice columnist, that her divorced mother treated her less like a daughter and more like a girlfriend: "She has told me some hair-raising stories about her sexual escapades, and now she keeps pressing me for details about my sex life. . . . I don't want to hear all the personal stuff she tells me" (Dear Ann, 2001: C7).

As this example illustrates, divorced parents sometimes make the mistake of treating their children like peers. Particularly if the children are bright and verbal, a parent may see them as being more mature than they really are. Mothers often share their feelings about a wide range of personal issues: They may express bitterness toward their ex-husband, anger at men in general, or frustration over financial concerns or social isolation.

In response, the child may console the parent and appear concerned and caring but may also feel anger, resentment, sadness, or guilt. According to one 15-year-old girl,

Don't look to kids for emotional support. I was going through so much of my own emotional hell that my mom leaning on me was the last thing that I wanted, and it made me very, very resentful of her. My mom tried to use me as her confidant for all the bad stuff my dad did to her, but she refused to see that he was still my dad, and I still loved him (S. Evans, 2000: C4).

Many adults say that as children they often felt the need to protect their divorcing parents, especially their mother, emotionally. Instead of talking to their parents, who were preoccupied with nursing their own wounds, the children often turned to siblings or friends or tried to deal with their problems alone (Marquardt, 2005).

Some researchers maintain that the mother-child "lean on me" relationship sometimes works well. For example, a study of some first-year college students concluded that mothers' depending on their children for emotional support during and after a divorce contributed to a sense of closeness. Another study found that divorced parents' confiding in their adolescents had no negative effects if the parent was emotionally strong and didn't expect a child to become the parent's or siblings' caretaker (Buchanan et al., 1996; Arditti, 1999). Even then, however, parents might unintentionally "parentify" a child (often a girl). As

The Squid and the Whale is one of the few films that examines the difficulties that divorce creates for both children and their parents.

a result, an adolescent has difficulty in focusing on her (or his) own individual growth:

Often the only time Mom talked to Dad, and vice-versa, was through messages sent through me. Even my brother and sister used me as a courier in getting the things they wanted. . . . I would feel an overwhelming sense of loneliness and desperation in my struggles to keep the peace and save the family. . . . I believe I went far away to college unconsciously, but once I was here, I suffered from guilt in abandoning my family duties. . . . Now after three years I still feel anger and sadness and loneliness when I see that it is once again my duty to restore the harmony in the family (Brown and Amatea, 2000: 180).

Parentifying children can turn them into miniature adults who aren't emotionally ready to cope with adult burdens because they're also dealing with the normal developmental problems of growing up (see, also, the discussion of *adultification* in Chapter 12).

Parental divorce, despite some benefits, usually results in a wide range of negative consequences for children. You'll notice, as you read the next two sections, that some of the factors that hurt children before, during, and after a divorce are similar to those that can alleviate some of their pain.

What Hurts Children Before, During, and After Divorce?

A large number of studies have shown that compared with their counterparts in married families, children from divorced families experience a variety of difficulties, including lower academic achievement, behavioral problems, a lower self-concept, and some long-term health problems (Thornberry et al., 1999;

Furstenberg and Kiernan, 2001; see also, Amato, 2002, for a summary of some of this research).

Some negative effects of divorce are short term, but others last longer. Why do some children adjust to their parents' divorce better than others? Let's begin by looking at predivorce difficulties.

PARENTAL PROBLEMS BEFORE A DIVORCE Typically, divorce crystallizes rather than creates long-standing family problems. That is, partners who divorce are more likely to have poor parenting skills and high levels of marital conflict or to suffer from persistent economic stress well before a separation or divorce occurs (Furstenberg and Teitler, 1994; Doyle and Markiewicz, 2005).

Parents in these predivorce families are less involved in their children's education, have lower expectations of their children, have few discussions about school-related issues, and rarely attend school events. Besides poor academic progress, the children exhibit behavior problems and low self-concepts at least three years before the divorce (Sun, 2001).

Children can experience short-term negative outcomes even if their parents initiate divorce proceeding but then change their minds. For example, a study of students in grades 1 through 12 in a Florida school district found that when parents filed for divorce, the children underwent several years of lower test scores in school and more disciplinary problems even if the parents changed their minds (Hoekstra, 2006). Thus, parental problems that cause parents to contemplate getting divorced can have a negative effect on children's academic performance and behavior even if the parents decide to stay married.

TIMING OF DIVORCE Does it matter how old children are when parents get a divorce? A change in a parent's marital status—whether it's a divorce or a remarriage—creates parental stress that usually passes down to children. Parents' experiencing depression, juggling new parenting and financial responsibilities, and rearranging their lives can disrupt children's sense of security and create ambiguity about household rules and parental expectations (Osborne and McLanahan, 2007).

Divorces that occur in early childhood, especially before age 5, create early instability that can alter children's development and later social relationships with parents and peers. Boys who experience parental divorce in early childhood are more likely than girls to misbehave and become more aggressive (Cavanagh and Huston, 2008). The reasons for such differences are unclear, but they may be related to the sons' resentment of losing an important male role model (see Chapter 5 on gender role socialization).

One might expect that young children under age 5 are more adaptable to family instability because, from a developmental perspective, they're more flexible and more focused on their own needs rather than their parents'. They may be at greater risk of developmental problems than older children, however, because they often undergo more multiple transitions after their parents' divorce (such as moving to a poorer neighborhood and changing schools several times or adjusting to a stepparent or a parent's multiple romantic partners).

ONGOING PARENTAL CONFLICT AND HOSTILITY Often it is not the divorce itself but parental attitudes during and after the divorce that affect children's behavior and perceptions about family life. The end of a highly conflicted marriage typically improves children's well-being. Freed from anxiety, stress, and depression, their mental health improves and their antisocial behavior decreases. In fact, children with parents in high-conflict marriages fare worse as adults than those from families in which the high conflict ends in divorce. The latter are less likely to feel caught in the middle when their parents argue, don't feel as much pressure to take sides, and experience less stress when feuding parents finally break up (Amato and Afifi, 2006).

On the other hand, divorces that dissolve low-conflict marriages may have negative effects on children. The children experience the divorce as unexpected, unwelcome, and a source of turmoil and instability in their lives. Because nearly two-thirds of divorces end low-conflict marriages, some scholars question whether these marriages should be dissolved (Amato, 2003; Strohschein, 2005; Glenn and Sylvester, 2006).

Overall, within two to three years of a divorce, most adults and children adapt to their new lives reasonably well *if* they do not experience continued or new stresses. Still, the "echoes of divorce" can linger for many years. For example, youths from divorced families are more likely than their counterparts to select partners—often also from divorced families—who are impulsive or socially irresponsible and have a history of antisocial behaviors such as alcohol and drug abuse, trouble with the law, problems in school and work, and an unstable job history (Hetherington, 2003).

QUALITY OF PARENTING Children do not develop difficulties simply because their parents get a divorce. As one of my students remarked in class, "It wasn't my parents' divorce that left the most painful scars. It was their inability to be effective parents afterward."

Children's adjustment to divorce depends, to a great extent, on the quality of parenting they experience after the marriage ends. Because, as you saw earlier, many children lose touch with their noncustodial fathers, a sense of loss can continue into adulthood.

If noncustodial fathers don't take their parenting role seriously, mere contact or even sharing some good times contributes little to children's overall development. However, if these fathers play an authoritative role (such as listening to their children's problems, giving advice, and working together on projects), noncustodial fathers and children report a close relationship (Amato and Gilbreth, 1999).

Twenty years after their parents' divorce, 62 percent of children say that their relationship with their noncustodial father had improved or remained stable over time. Thus, it's not custody itself that affects the quality of the relationship but a combination of pre- and post-divorce factors, especially continued conflict between the parents, a father's low involvement with his children in the early years of a divorce, and a father's quick remarriage (Kelly and Emery, 2003; Ahrons, 2004).

According to many studies (see text), it's not the divorce itself but parental conflict during and after a divorce that is the most damaging to children.

ECONOMIC HARDSHIP A divorce may reduce domestic conflict, but the financial problems usually increase, especially for mothers. The mother's income usually drops by about a third after the divorce. Men's income typically increases, with estimates ranging from 8 percent to 41 percent. Men's income increases for a number of reasons: not having physical custody of the children, not complying with child-support orders, having higher-paying jobs than their ex-wives do, and often taking some of the family's wealth—such as stocks and bonds—with them after the divorce (Sun and Li, 2002; Barber and Demo, 2006; Sayer, 2006).

In the first two years following divorce, family income falls 30 percent for white children and 53 percent for African American children (comparable and recent data for other racial-ethnic groups are not available, to my knowledge). A major reason for this difference is that white mothers receive 10 times as much child support as do black women. The long-term economic costs of divorce are especially pronounced for black women because they are less likely to remarry and more likely to divorce after a remarriage (Page and Stevens, 2005; see, also, Chapter 16).

Most children enjoy fewer parental economic resources after a divorce, but parents' social resources also decline because one or both parents may have less time to talk to their children about course selections, school activities, and friends. Fewer resources often have long-term negative socioeconomic consequences in adulthood, including lower educational, economic, and occupational achievements (Biblarz and Gottainer, 2000).

The chances of experiencing negative socioeconomic outcomes double if, by age 18, adolescents undergo multiple parental transitions such as many romantic relationships, cohabiting, remarrying, or getting a divorce after a remarriage (Sun and Li, 2008). In effect, then, greater stability after their parents' divorce increases adolescents' well-being in adulthood.

CUMULATIVE EFFECTS OF DIVORCE Divorce usually decreases both children's and parents' well-being both initially and over the life course. If divorce interferes with children's schooling, for example, this disadvantage cumulates through life, affecting children's occupational status, income, and economic well-being. Children with low levels of educational attainment and high levels of economic hardship are at higher risk for mental health problems and more likely to experience unhappy or unstable interpersonal relationships in adulthood (Chase-Lansdale et al., 1995; Ross and Mirowsky, 1999).

Divorce increases the probability that a woman will experience economic pressures and depression. This strain and emotional distress tend to reduce the quality of parenting, which, in turn, increase a child's risk of emotional and behavioral problems and poor developmental outcomes. In addition, children may have to live with a parent with whom they don't get along and lose access to a parent with whom they've had a good relationship (South et al., 1998; Videon, 2002).

A divorce can also have negative consequences for subsequent generations through a process that some scholars call the **intergenerational transmission of divorce.** When grandparents divorce, for example, the second generation experiences lower educational attainment and problematic relationships: "These outcomes in turn become the causes of similar problems in the third generation" (Amato and Cheadle, 2005: 204).

Despite all these stressors, 80 percent of children from divorced homes navigate through troubled waters and "eventually are able to adapt to their new life and become reasonably well adjusted" (Hetherington and Kelly, 2002: 228). Among other things, children fare well if protective factors are at work during and after the divorce.

Noncustodial fathers who co-parent can maintain close relationships with their children by seeing them as often as possible, setting rules, discussing problems, and providing guidance.

What Helps Children Before, During, and After Divorce?

The biggest benefit of divorce is that it decreases the amount of stress that children undergo in a high-conflict, quarrelsome home in which adults yell, scream, throw things, or poison the atmosphere with emotional or physical abuse. The children who experience the least negative effects are those who receive support from friends, neighbors, and schools, especially when their parents are self-absorbed or depressed. Even if a nonresident parent isn't around, the most effective custodial parents provide many protective factors such as warmth, responsiveness, monitoring, involvement in the children's activities, and keeping the children out of parental battles (Rodgers and Rose, 2002; Leon, 2003).

According to researchers and family clinicians, parents can lessen some of a divorce's negative effects in many ways:

- They can reassure the children that both parents will continue to love and care for them, emphasizing that they will remain actively involved with them and that the children should always feel free to love both parents.

- They should talk about their feelings because doing so sets the stage for open communication between parents and children. Parents can discuss their unhappiness and even their anger, but they should not blame the other parent because this will force the children to take sides.

- They should emphasize that the children are not responsible for problems between their parents, pointing out that each adult is divorcing the other partner but not the children.

- They should reassure the children that they will continue to see their cousins, grandparents, and other relatives on both sides of the family.

- They should maintain an ongoing relationship with the children if they are not emotionally or physically abusive. When noncustodial parents maintain stable and frequent visitation, they give more advice to their children, and their adolescents are more satisfied and less likely to experience depression.

- They should encourage their children to talk about their feelings and experiences freely and openly with significant people in their lives such as parents, grandparents, teachers, coaches, and clergy (Barber, 1994; Harvey and Fine, 2004).

Research has consistently shown that the difficulties that children and adults who go through a divorce experience can be reduced if co-parents are civil and cooperative and work together to improve their children's well-being. Even 20 years after the divorce, according to one study, when the children are grown and have children of their own, what they want most is for their parents to just get along: "There were those special family occasions, such as graduations, weddings, and grandchildren's birthdays, that most of the grown children wanted to share with *both* of their parents" (Ahrons, 2006: 59, emphasis added).

MAKING CONNECTIONS

- Should divorced parents treat their offspring as peers rather than as children? Why or why not?

- If your parents got a divorce when you were very young, do you think it had an effect on your childhood, adolescence, or adulthood? If your parents didn't separate or divorce, do you think that they were happy? Or stayed together for the sake of the children?

SOME POSITIVE OUTCOMES OF SEPARATION AND DIVORCE

Much of this chapter has looked at the harmful effects of divorce on adults and children. In response to such negative outcomes, some groups are proposing that no-fault divorce be eliminated and that divorce laws be made tougher (see the box "Should It Be Harder (or Impossible) to Get a Divorce?" on p. 439).

Does divorce have any positive effects? In a highly publicized book, *The Unexpected Legacy of Divorce*, Wallerstein and her colleagues (2000) advised parents to stay in unhappy marriages to avoid hurting their children. However, that well-intentioned advice

Since you asked . . .

⋮• Should more unhappy
couples get a divorce?

was based on a clinical study of a small group of highly dysfunctional divorced families. In contrast, most divorced couples and their children adjust and function well over time.

Benefits for Children

The major positive outcome of divorce is that it provides options for people in miserable marriages. If a divorce eliminates an unhappy, frustrating, and stressful situation, it may improve the mental and emotional health of both ex-spouses and their children. Generally, children and young adults experience positive outcomes after their parents' divorce, but only under certain conditions: if both adults take co-parenting seriously, if the parents are always civil with each other, if the ex-spouses maintain good communication with their children and each other, if the children are comfortable staying in both parents' homes or can spend a lot of time with their nonresident parent, if a parent's

relocation doesn't disrupt the children's everyday life, and if the parents (especially fathers, who usually have more income than mothers) support their children financially throughout high school and while they are in college (Fabricius, 2003; Warshak, 2003).

After a divorce, child-mother relationships usually remain the same whereas those with noncustodial fathers decline. Continued engagement can be beneficial for both sides. For example, noncustodial fathers' and their children's ties improve when adolescents and young adults—especially those with few educational or occupational resources—feel that they can count on their fathers for advice or financial support regarding issues such as an unwanted pregnancy, cohabitation, or marriage at a young age (Scott et al., 2007).

In addition, and as you saw earlier, parental separation is better for children in the long run than growing up in an intact family where there is continuous conflict. Divorce can also offer parents and children opportunities for personal growth, more gratifying relationships, and a more harmonious family life (Hetherington and Kelly, 2002).

Should It Be Harder (or Impossible) to Get a Divorce?

According to a national study, almost 59 percent of Americans said that "Society would be better off if divorces were harder to get." On the other hand, in a national study of people age 40 and older, 64 percent of men and 76 percent of women said that they had made "absolutely the right decision" to divorce (Montenegro, 2004; Glenn, 2005).

Some people claim that the switch to no-fault divorce has led to an increase in the divorce rate in the United States and other countries. Others point out that divorce rates started increasing years before no-fault legislation was passed in the 1970s. In effect, no-fault laws simply ratified, symbolically, changes in societal values about marriage and divorce that had already occurred (Nakonezny et al., 1995; Glenn, 1997; Rodgers et al., 1997).

Marriage Savers, a ministry that wants to cut divorce rates and raise marriage rates, proposes cutting the American divorce rate in half by changing some divorce laws. Except for physically

abusive parents, couples with children under age 18 wouldn't be granted a divorce unless both parents fully agreed. Such "mutual-consent" divorce laws would not only cut the divorce rate in half, but would preserve the marriages in which one spouse doesn't want a divorce (McManus, 2008).

So, should we maintain current no-fault divorce? Or make divorce harder, even impossible, to get? Here are a few arguments from both sides:

Make Getting a Divorce More Difficult

- It's too easy to get a divorce.
- Couples break up over little things because divorce is "no big deal."
- No-fault divorces disregard the interests of children.
- Ending no-fault divorce would give more rights to the partner who doesn't want a divorce.

Leave Current Divorce Laws Alone

- Getting a divorce is already complicated, expensive, and stressful; don't make the situation worse.
- Many couples stay in destructive relationships for decades for the sake of the children.
- Children fare worse in high-conflict two-parent families than in loving single-parent families.
- Ending no-fault divorce could keep children in high-conflict homes longer and make divorce even more adversarial.

⋮• Stop and Think . . .

- Would you support a federal "mutual-consent" divorce law?
- Should we make it harder to get a divorce? Harder to get married? Both? Or should we leave things the way they are?

Constraints

ROAD CLOSED

Benefits for Adults

How do divorced people fare, emotionally and socially? During the first year, about 70 percent express doubts or ambivalence about the breakup and continue to be angry. By two years after the divorce, the problems diminish. After 10 years, most divorced people have built a satisfying new life. Many women, especially, report being more competent, better adjusted, and more fulfilled. Those who return to school or work often meet and marry men from higher socioeconomic backgrounds and say that their later marriages are more successful than their first ones (Hetherington, 2003).

Both sexes cite gains after a divorce, but women are more likely to do so than men. Women are especially likely to say that they enjoy their new-found freedom, developing their own self-identity, and not having to answer to a domineering husband (Montenegro, 2004). According to one woman, "Divorce is a happy word: I've found things that I truly love to do instead of doing things that my husband or my family thought I should do. I have hobbies and interests; I have great joy in the ways I spend my time" (Orenstein, 2000: 233).

Divorced men also report benefits such as spending more money on themselves or their hobbies, being better off financially (especially if they don't support their ex-wives or children), having more leisure time, and dating numerous people (Montenegro, 2004). As one African American author advises black men, "While the break-up may mean broken dreams, it doesn't have to mean broken homes. It may present fresh opportunities for men to reassess their lives and learn from their mistakes. And, perhaps, they won't stumble over the same rocks" (Hutchinson, 1994: 113).

These empirical studies echo many of my students' experiences. For example,

Sometimes a marriage just doesn't work out. I know because I stayed in an unhappy marriage for eleven years for the children's sake, hoping that things would work out. I gave 150 percent, but still nothing changed. To this day, nothing has changed between my ex-husband and me but he sees the kids every day and all of us are happier and healthier individuals (Author's files).

COUNSELING, MARITAL THERAPY, DIVORCE MEDIATION, AND COLLABORATIVE DIVORCE

Counseling, marital therapy, and mediation can help some families get through divorce or even avoid it. These and other strategies and interventions aren't always successful, however. Collaborative divorce is an emerging strategy for decreasing some of the emotional and financial costs of divorce.

Counseling and Marital Therapy

According to the most recent estimates, every year more than 3 percent of the nation's 57.3 million married couples see a marriage or family therapist or a mental health professional for marital problems. The average cost is at least $100 for a one-hour session, but fees vary across regions, states, and urban-rural areas (Jayson, 2005).

How effective are counseling and marital therapy? No one knows for sure because there have been no scientific national studies that have measured the results. Some argue that counseling and marital therapy are better than nothing, especially if couples seek help within a few years of experiencing problems. Others contend that some counseling and therapy can do more harm than good (Doherty, 1999; Shadish and Baldwin, 2005).

> **Since you asked . . .**
> :•• Do counseling and marital therapy prevent divorce?

ADVANTAGES Counseling can be useful, especially if therapists serve as impartial observers rather than favoring one side or the other (as attorneys do). Counselors can help couples and families decrease some difficulties, such as parenting problems. Thus, therapists can help married and divorcing parents

Many divorced parents, especially noncustodial fathers, stay in touch with their children using webcam.

build stronger relationships with each other and their children.

Family practitioners assist divorcing couples and families in a number of ways: They individualize treatment programs, help parents learn to co-parent, help children cope with fears such as losing the non-residential parent permanently, provide information on remarriage and its potential impact on the children and ex-spouse, and organize a variety of support networks (Leite and McKenry, 1996).

DISADVANTAGES Two years after ending counseling, 25 percent of couples are worse off than they were when they started. After four years of counseling or therapy, up to 38 percent are divorced (Gilbert, 2005).

Why does much counseling and therapy fail? Many therapists are poorly trained and inexperienced and may feel overwhelmed by a couple's or family's problems. And, despite similar training, in every occupation some people are more skilled than others at what they do (Doherty, 2002).

Some critics contend that many professional marriage counselors and therapists, instead of being neutral, promote marriage as a superior family form (compared with cohabitation or single-parent households, for example). Thus, they foster a lifelong commitment to marriage and do everything they can to discourage divorce. Such "faith-based values" may be beneficial for some traditional couples, but not for those in which one of the major sources of conflict may be domination of the wife by a controlling husband who expects her to sacrifice her needs to satisfy his or the children's (Leslie and Morton, 2004).

Also, not all marriages are salvageable. As you saw in Chapters 8 and 10, some of us choose the wrong partner and for the wrong reasons. In such cases, a separation or divorce may be a more effective strategy for resolving conflict than counseling and therapy.

Increasingly, many jurisdictions are ordering divorcing parents to attend educational seminars with professional counselors before going to court. The purpose of the sessions is not to convince parents to stay together but to teach them about their children's emotional and developmental needs during and after the divorce. In other cases, counseling is a preliminary step before meeting with a mediator.

Divorce Mediation

In **divorce mediation,** a trained arbitrator helps the couple come to an agreement. Issues that may be resolved in this way include custody arrangements, child support and future college expenses, and the division of marital property (such as a house, furniture, stocks, savings and retirement accounts, pension plans, cars, debts, and medical expenses). Most mediators are attorneys or mental health professionals, but accountants and others may also be trained as mediators.

ADVANTAGES Mediation will not eliminate the hurt caused by separation and divorce, but it has several advantages (see Hahn and Kleist, 2000, for a review of the conditions under which mediation is most effective). First, mediation increases communication between spouses and decreases angry confrontations that don't resolve anything.

Second, mediation generally reduces the time needed to negotiate a divorce settlement. A mediation settlement typically takes a few months; a divorce obtained through a court proceeding may take two to three years.

Third, mediated agreements generally make it easier to accommodate changes as the children grow older. For example, as a child's activities and schedule change from a Saturday morning ballet lesson at age 8 to Wednesday night driving lessons at age 15, the parents can negotiate schedules without resorting to costly and time-consuming requests for changes in court-ordered arrangements.

Finally, mediation prevents children from being pawns or trophies in a divorce contest. The mediator's approach is "Which arrangements are best for you, your spouse, and your children?" There is no room for the adversarial stance, "Which of you will win the children?"

DISADVANTAGES Mediation doesn't work for everyone. If one partner is savvier about finances than the other, for example, the less informed spouse may be at a disadvantage. In addition, an aggressive or more powerful spouse (who is usually the husband) can be intimidating.

Another problem is that mediators may be unschooled in issues pertaining to children. Because the parent, not the child, is the client, mediation may not always be in the child's best interests (Wallerstein, 2003).

Collaborative Divorce

Collaborative divorce is a method of trying to resolve disputes before finalizing a divorce in court. The process differs from mediation in that lawyers for each side are present and communication occurs among all parties—attorneys, clients, divorce coaches, a child specialist, and financial planner. The lawyers typically know each other well and have a good working relationship. Over a series of sessions, the "support team will help the couple reach a peaceful dissolution of their financial and familial relationship" (Harris, 2007: A1, A12).

ADVANTAGES Collaborative divorce offers several benefits. First, couples have more control over the outcome because they can voice their opinions, compromise, and settle issues instead of having a judge make the final decisions. Doing so can reduce much of postdivorce anger, bitterness, and resentment. Second, the process is usually less expensive and takes less time than litigation because it does not involve a multitude of steps, fees, and court costs. Third, collaborative divorce spares children the stress of watching parents fight and grieve over the breakup. Finally, because there is a full and candid exchange of information between the parties, the partner with more economic resources is less likely to hide assets or to dominate the less powerful partner (Davis, 2009).

DISADVANTAGES Collaborative divorce won't work for couples with a history of domestic violence, drug or alcohol addiction, serious untreated mental illness, or an intention to hurt the other party emotionally or financially. A second disadvantage is that collaborative divorce is available in only about six states so far and not all attorneys in those states have been trained in collaborative law. A third limitation, especially according to lawyers, is that attorneys should be fighting zealously for their clients' interest instead of reaching out-of-court agreements. Proponents of collaborative divorce, however, accuse the opponents

of being more concerned about their lucrative fees than their client's well-being (Harris, 2007).

CONCLUSION

Greater acceptance of divorce in the late twentieth and early twenty-first centuries has created *change* in family structures. Indeed, separation and divorce seem to have become "an intrinsic feature of modern family life rather than a temporary aberration" (Martin and Bumpass, 1989: 49). As this chapter shows, a large segment of the adult population flows in and out of marriage during the life course.

This means that people have more *choices* in leaving an unhappy marriage. Often, however, parents don't realize that their choices may create more *constraints* for their children, who often feel at fault, guilty, and torn between warring parents.

If parents handled divorces in more rational and civilized ways, many children would be spared the emotional pain and economic deprivation that they now suffer. Some of the pain that both parents and children experience may become even greater after parents remarry, the topic of the next chapter.

SUMMARY

1. A separation is a temporary or permanent arrangement that precedes a divorce. In most cases, separation is a lengthy process that involves four phases: preseparation, early separation, midseparation, and late separation.

2. Marital separation leads to one of three outcomes: divorce, long-term separation, or reconciliation. The outcomes of marital separation often vary by race, ethnicity, and social class.

3. Divorce rates increased rapidly in the 1970s, reached a plateau in the 1980s, and have decreased since the mid-1990s. Whereas in the past many marriages ended because of death or desertion, during the twentieth century divorce became the most common reason for marital dissolution.

4. Nearly twice as many women as men file for divorce. Some women want to legalize a husband's emotional or physical absence. Others are more independent economically and thus less inclined to tolerate their husbands' extramarital affairs or other unacceptable behaviors.

5. Divorce is often a long and drawn-out process. In most divorces, people go through one or more of six stages: the emotional divorce, the legal divorce, the economic divorce, the co-parental divorce, the community divorce, and the psychic divorce.

6. The many reasons for divorce include macro-level factors such as changing gender roles, demographic variables such as marriage at a young age, and micro/interpersonal factors such as unrealistic expectations and infidelity.

7. Divorce has psychological, economic, and legal consequences. Because child support awards typically are low, many women and children plunge into poverty after a divorce.

8. There are three major types of child custody: sole, split, and joint. Most mothers receive sole custody, but joint custody and co-parenting are becoming more common.

9. Divorce is harmful to most children. Many of the problems that lead to marital disruption begin many years before the legal breakup.

10. Counseling and divorce mediation are alternatives to the traditional adversarial approach that is typical of legal processes. Mediated divorces tend to be less bitter and less expensive and offer each partner more input in child-custody decisions. Collaborative divorce is a recent strategy that can reduce the likelihood of expensive court battles.

KEY TERMS

separation   416
divorce   417
alimony   419
child support   419
no-fault divorce   421
annulment   422

social integration   423
custody   430
sole custody   431
split custody   431
joint custody   431
co-custody   431

co-parenting   432
intergenerational transmission
   of divorce   437
divorce mediation   441
collaborative divorce   441

PEARSON myfamilylab MyFamilyLab provides a wealth of resources. Go to www.myfamilylab.com<http://www.myfamilylab.com/>, to enhance your comprehension of the content in this chapter. You can take practice exams, view videos relevant to the subject matter, listen to audio files, explore topics further by using Social Explorer, and use the tools contained in MySearchLab to help you write research papers.

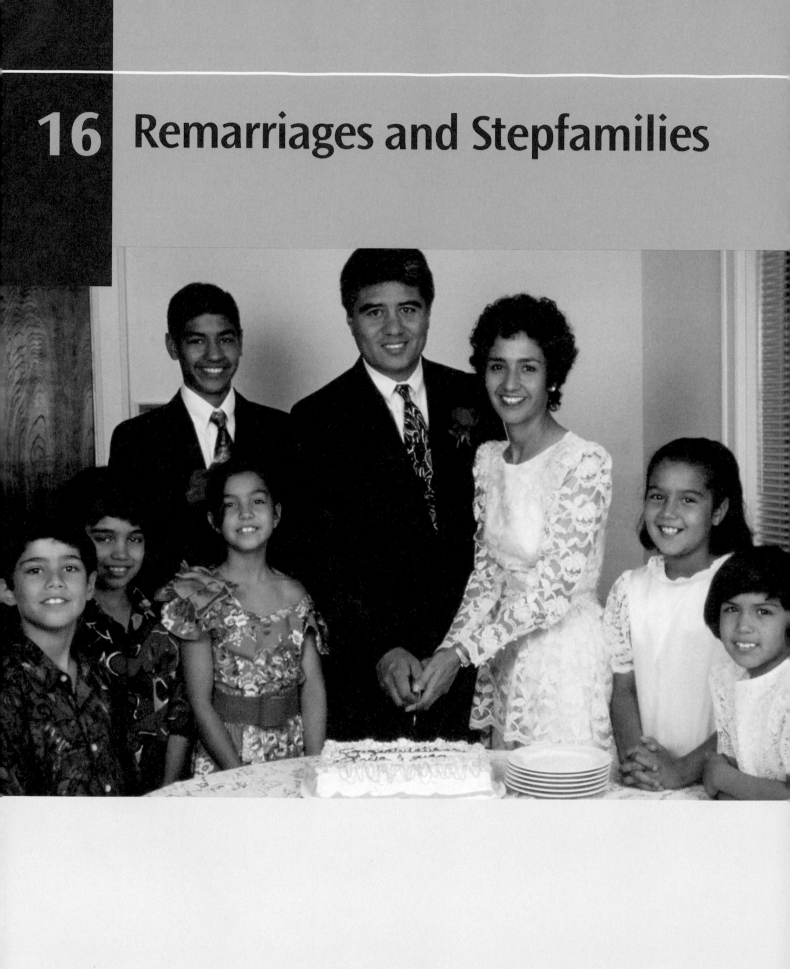

Even with high divorce rates, most people aren't disillusioned about marriage. Many remarry, some more than once, and the resulting family relationships can be intricate. Listen to a divorced mother who married a widower describe her multifaceted family relationships shortly before the marriage of her stepdaughter:

Ed will be my stepson-in-law, but there's no simple way to state the relationships between his daughter, Amy, and me. . . . Amy becomes my husband's step-granddaughter, his daughter's stepdaughter, his granddaughters' stepsister or his son-in-law's daughter. To me, the linguistic link is truly unwieldy: my husband's step-granddaughter, my stepdaughter's stepdaughter, my step-grandchildren's stepsister! (Borst, 1996, p. 16).

These family structures reflect more than just complex kinship terms because they vary in the closeness of the members' ties and everyday dynamics. Because not all remarried couples have children from current or previous marriages, we'll sometimes look at remarriage and stepfamilies separately, but the two family forms often overlap.

DATA DIGEST

- The **median time between a divorce and a second marriage is about 3.8 years.**

- **One out of three Americans** is a stepparent, a stepchild, a stepsibling, or some other member of a stepfamily.

- In 2009, 12 percent of men and 12 percent of women **had been married twice,** and 3 percent each **had been married three or more times.**

- In 2010, **5.7 percent (4.2 million) of all American children lived with a biological parent and a stepparent,** usually with a biological mother and a stepfather (3.2 million).

- About 5 percent of all **remarried couples have three sets of children:** yours, mine, and ours.

Sources: Kreider, 2005, 2008; U.S. Census Bureau News, 2007; U.S. Census Bureau Newsroom, 2008.

445

This chapter examines the prevalence and characteristics of remarriages and stepfamilies, their varied forms and relationships, and some characteristics of successful and unhappy remarriages and stepfamilies. Let's begin with dating and cohabitation, two activities that often lead to remarriage or the forming of a stepfamily.

BEING SINGLE AGAIN: DATING AND COHABITATION

Most couples form stepfamilies through remarriage, usually after a divorce, but sometimes after widowhood. Single people often become involved in *courtship* by seeking and selecting a mate (see Chapter 8). Like those who marry for the first time, they rely on two courtship avenues—dating and cohabitation—to meet and choose another mate, but they often find that these processes are now more complicated.

Dating after Divorce

Many people start dating again even before a divorce is legally final. To relieve

> **Since you asked . . .**
>
> :•• Why is it difficult for some people to start dating again after a divorce or widowhood?

some of the pain of divorce, many people rush into another relationship: "It's not unusual to see women and men frantically dating in the first year after their separation, trying to fill the void with an intense new love or even with just another warm body" (Ahrons, 1994: 65).

If people are young and have not been married very long, reentering the dating scene is fairly easy. Dating may be more awkward for those who have been married a long time because they don't know what to expect. For example, one of my friends, a woman who divorced after 16 years of marriage, wanted to pursue new relationships but was anxious about dating: "Am I supposed to pay for myself when we go to dinner? Should I just meet him at the restaurant, or do men still pick women up? What if he wants to jump into bed after the first date?"

As people age, they may become more concerned about their physical appearance. Feeling nervous about intimacy is a big reason for staying on the dating sidelines A 53-year-old recently divorced man declared, "Even I don't like looking at me naked anymore!" (Mahoney, 2003).

Those who have not dated for many years are usually apprehensive because they have less self-confidence, especially if the ex-spouse was the one who initiated the divorce. Some may avoid dating altogether, whereas parents who date frequently may feel guilty about being less available to their children.

Dating and cohabitation after a divorce or widowhood, including among midlife people, provide couples with companionship.

Courtship is usually brief because half of all women and men who remarry after a divorce from their first marriages do so within about three to four years (U.S. Census Bureau Newsroom, 2009). In other cases, cohabitation replaces dating, both in the short run and long term.

Cohabitation: An Alternative to Dating after a Divorce

Many divorced people, and some of those who are widowed after age 50 or so, prepare for remarriage by living together. More cautious about entering another marriage, they consider cohabitation a way of testing a relationship, especially if young children are present. Cohabitants who break up often increase the children's stress because they experience several transitions, such as the divorce, a parent's cohabitation, and the parent's exiting one cohabiting relationship and possibly entering another one (see Chapter 15). However, many cohabiting couples believe that children undergo less turmoil because the adults can avoid another divorce.

Half of all remarriages begin with cohabitation. In fact, living together is more common after a divorce than before a first marriage (Xu et al., 2006). Cohabitation, rather than dating, is especially appealing to older adults:

Their social scripts for dating may be outdated, and they may feel foolish, nervous, or uncertain about what to do. . . . Especially those who had been married for many years may be more comfortable setting up housekeeping with a partner than dating (Ganong and Coleman, 2004: 72).

In many societies, remarriages are based on practical considerations rather than romantic love. For example, after the deadly 2004 tsunami in Indonesia, young women came from their home villages to marry thousands of hardworking fishermen whose wives and children had perished.

Especially if there are children, combining two households may be more familiar and simpler than contending with the ups and downs of dating.

Cohabitation can hasten matrimony because most adults court for only brief periods before plunging into a remarriage. Some people may rush through the courtship process because they believe that they are running out of time or are desperate for financial or child-rearing help. Others believe that they don't need as much time to get to know each other because they have learned from past mistakes. As you'll see later in this chapter, high redivorce rates show that such convictions are often wrong.

Living together can also delay remarriage. If cohabitors move from one relationship to another over a number of years, it may take a long time to select a marriage partner. Or if one or both people are reluctant to marry, cohabitation may lead to a long-term relationship that includes children from a past marriage and those born to the cohabiting couple (Ganong et al., 2006; Xu et al., 2006).

Not all courtship ends in a remarriage. Many stepfamilies are formed through remarriage, but others are cohabiting stepfamily households, some lasting longer than others.

FORMING A STEPFAMILY

Stepfamily formation can follow a divorce of biological parents, nonmarital childbearing, or widowhood. Because same-sex marriage is still illegal in 45 states, most lesbians and gay men may form stepfamilies through long-term committed relationships in which

one or both partners raise children from previous unions. Before we look at remarriage, what, exactly, is a stepfamily?

What Is a Stepfamily?

In the past, sociologists defined a *stepfamily* as a household in which at least one of the *spouses* had a biological child from a previous marriage. Many sociologists are defining the term more broadly to include a greater diversity of families (see, for example, Pasley and Moorefield, 2004, and Stewart, 2007).

Since you asked . . .
- Are the terms *stepfamily* and *blended family* interchangeable?

A **stepfamily** is a household in which two adults who are biological or adoptive parents (heterosexual, gay, or lesbian) with a child from a previous relationship elect to marry or to cohabit. As in the case of defining *family* (see Chapter 1), not everyone would agree with this definition because it includes cohabitors. Nevertheless, this definition is more inclusive. It encompasses nontraditional stepfamilies because "concepts of and research about stepfamilies too often reflect the experiences of white, middle-class, heterosexual couples" (Stewart, 2007: 209).

Sometimes journalists and social scientists use terms such as *reconstituted family* and *binuclear family* interchangeably with *stepfamily*. However, *reconstituted* and *binuclear* are awkward and confusing terms, and family sociologists rarely use them (Kelley, 1996; Ganong and Coleman, 2004).

Some researchers use *blended family* interchangeably with *stepfamily,* but the leaders of some stepfamily organizations disagree. For example, according to Margorie Engel (2000), a past president of the Stepfamily Association of America, stepfamilies don't "blend." Instead, there are more parents, children have divided loyalties, and stepfamilies must develop new and unfamiliar roles for all their members, both adults and children.

How Common Are Remarriage and Stepfamilies?

Remarriage is so common that it has spawned a huge industry of services, magazines, and books. The readership of *Bride Again* magazine, for example, aimed at "encore brides" who marry more than once, is expanding widely.

The U.S. remarriage rate is the highest in the world, which suggests that many Americans haven't given up on marriage. For example, nearly 85 percent of Americans who divorce remarry, the median time between a divorce and a second marriage is short, and millions of Americans have married three or more times (see Data Digest).

The high divorce and remarriage rates have important implications for family structure and family roles in the future. For example, whereas 70- to 85-year-olds today have 2.4 biological children on average, by 2030 that group will average only 1.6 biological children but will have twice as many stepchildren as they do now (Wachter, 1997).

This means that the baby boom generation will have to rely more on stepchildren and stepgrandchildren rather than biological children and biological grandchildren for caregiving when they reach age 75 and older. If adult children perceive current and former stepparents to be family, it is more likely that they will provide them with help and financial support in later life (Schmeeckle et al., 2006). Because stepfamilies are common, close stepparent-stepchild ties are important for both current and future relationships. (We'll examine aging and caregiving in Chapter 17.)

Cohabitation, divorce, remarriage, and stepfamilies have created a variety of family structures, but remarried couples and stepfamilies have some common characteristics. We'll look at remarriages first and then examine stepfamilies.

CHARACTERISTICS OF REMARRIED COUPLES

Many factors affect people's decision to remarry. Among the most common are age, gender, race/ethnicity, social class, and the presence of children. These variables usually interact in explaining remarriage rates.

Age and Gender

For both sexes, being single after a divorce doesn't last long. The average age of a first remarriage is 33 for women and 35 for men. Across the life course, younger women (age 39 and younger) are more likely than their male counterparts to have been married twice, but men age 50 and older are more likely than women their age to marry a second time. The pattern is similar for those who have married three or more times. For example, of those ages 50 and older, 16 percent of women and 20 percent of men have been married three or more times (see *Figure 16.1*).

The women who are most likely to remarry are those who married at a young age the first time, have few marketable skills, and want children (Wu, 1994). These women are especially attractive to older divorced or widowed men who want a traditional wife to "spark" their lives. For example, Antonio, a 40-year-old divorced man who married

Marisa, 22, says that he loves his new life despite the family complexity and having a child from his second marriage:

"She was like a Barbie to me," recalls Antonio, a department manager at a Target store.... Marisa's attentions made him "feel young again," he said.... One of his daughters from his first marriage is two years younger than his second wife. Another daughter has married his wife's brother—making her both his daughter and sister-in-law. "We're all one happy family," he says, bouncing his toddler son on his lap (Herrmann, 2003: 6).

Remarriage rates are high for both sexes ages 50 and older, but higher for men (see *Figure 16.1*). Some older women, especially those who seek to remarry, may be attractive to older men because neither partner has children in the home who may create conflict. Also, the woman may be willing to devote her time to taking care of her husband instead of pursuing a career or higher education. If older women have few economic resources, and as their pool of eligible mates grows smaller, they might welcome a remarriage because they don't want to be alone in their aging years (see Chapter 17).

Generally, however, the older a woman is, the harder it is for her to attract a man for marriage or

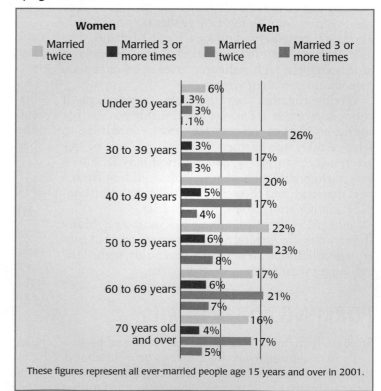

FIGURE 16.1 Percentage of Americans Who Have Remarried, by Age and Sex

These figures represent all ever-married people age 15 years and over in 2001.

Source: Based on Kreider, 2005: Table 3.

remarriage. In each age group, because men tend to choose women who are younger and women tend to choose men who are older, the pool of eligible (and acceptable) marriage partners expands for men but shrinks for women (see Chapters 7 and 8).

Gender and Race/Ethnicity

Overall, whites, particularly white women, have the highest remarriage rates. In 2004, and according to the most recent data, 19 percent of white women had been married two or more times

compared with 11 percent of African American women, 9 percent of Latinas, and about 6 percent of Asian American women (see *Figure 16.2*).

There are several interconnected reasons for the variations in remarriage rates across and within racial-ethnic groups. First, and as *Figure 16.2* shows, African Americans have the lowest marriage rates, which means that remarriage is less likely. Second, African Americans have the highest cohabitation rates (see *Figure 9.6* on p. 248 and the related discussion). Those with the highest cohabitation rates are the most likely to delay marriage or not marry at all, which affects remarriage rates (Wu and Schimmele, 2005). Third, Latinos and Asian Americans, especially recent immigrants, encourage marriage and

FIGURE 16.2 How Often We Marry and Remarry, by Gender and Race/Ethnicity, 2004
Percentage of Americans age 15 and older

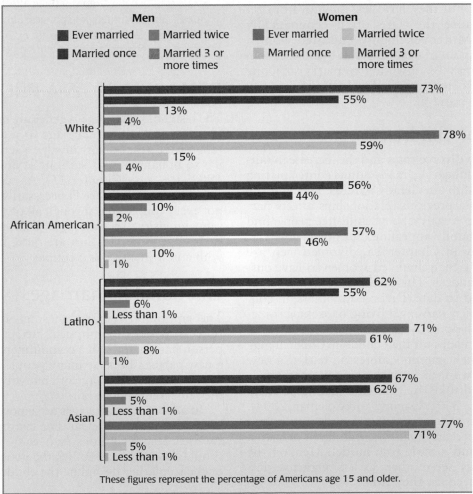

These figures represent the percentage of Americans age 15 and older.

Source: Based on data in U.S. Census Bureau, Survey of Income and Program Participation (SIPP), 2004 Panel, Wave 2 Topical Module, Table 3, 2007, http://www.census.gov/population/www/socdemo/marr-div/2004detailed_tables.html (accessed September 10, 2009).

discourage cohabitation and divorce (see Chapter 4). Thus, cultural values decrease the likelihood of remarrying, especially more than two times.

Social Class

In general, the wealthier a divorced man is, the more likely he is to remarry. In the marriage market, men tend to be worth more than women of the same age because they are usually financially better off. Divorced women, on the other hand, often have severe financial problems. For many women, then, the surest way to avoid or escape poverty is to remarry. Thus, young, less-educated, low-income divorcees are more likely to remarry than are divorced women who are older, highly educated, and financially independent (Folk et al., 1992; Ganong and Coleman, 1994; see, also, Chapter 15).

Men with higher educational attainment are more likely to remarry than are women with a similar education. Women with higher socioeconomic standing are more eligible remarriage candidates and are likely to attract a larger number of desirable marriage partners, but they have less to gain from remarriage because they are often economically independent. Moreover, highly educated women have a smaller pool of eligible mates to choose from because they may be unwilling to marry someone from a lower socioeconomic level (Wu, 1994; see, also, Chapters 8 and 9).

Presence of Children

Because of high divorce rates and the increase in out-of-wedlock childbearing, many adults contemplating a new relationship are already parents. The presence of children from previous relationships affects parents' decision to remarry. Some child-free people find a ready-made family appealing, but others don't.

As you saw in Chapter 15, divorced men are much less likely than divorced women to have custody of their children. This means that men are freer to socialize and to date. Divorced mothers, in contrast, may be busy earning a living or seeking someone who can help provide financial stability and economic advantages for their children. Children may also dampen their parents' interest in finding a new partner: They want to keep their single mothers to themselves or dislike their parents' dating partners (Schmiege et al., 2001; Ganong and Coleman, 2004).

Custodial mothers sometimes rush into a new marriage because they want their children to have a father figure and a male role model. Men, on the other hand, may see mothers as less attractive dating partners because they don't want to take on parental responsibilities.

The presence of children generally lowers the likelihood of remarriage, but this isn't always the case. Young children might encourage dating and

remarriage to replace an absent parent, especially a divorced father who never sees them. Older children who are living on their own may want a divorced or widowed parent to find a new companion, but may oppose a parent's remarriage for fear of losing their inheritance. In addition, custodial fathers are likely to remarry or to marry custodial mothers because they want to have a traditional family structure that includes both spouses and children (Goldscheider and Sassler, 2006).

Like divorce, remarriage is a process rather than a one-time act. And, like divorce, remarriage involves a series of stages.

⠿ **MAKING CONNECTIONS**

- Do you agree or disagree that the definition of stepfamilies should include cohabitors and people who have never married? Why?

- Besides variables such as age, gender, race/ethnicity, and social class, what else do you think affects remarriage rates? Think about religion, physical attractiveness, and the influence of family and friends, for example.

REMARRIAGE AS A PROCESS

The result of remarriage is generally much more complicated than a first marriage or a divorce, but the remarriage process may involve a series of steps similar to Bohannon's six stations of divorce (Goetting, 1982; see, also, Chapter 15). As with divorce, the stages of remarriage aren't necessarily sequential, and not every couple goes through all of them or with the same intensity. If partners can deal successfully with each stage, however, they are more likely to emerge with a new identity as a couple.

Emotional Remarriage

The emotional remarriage stage is often a slow process. Besides the physical attraction, a divorced person has to establish a commitment to and trust in a new partner. Because many people feel inadequate after a divorce, this stage often involves concern that the remarriage might fail.

In addition, remarriages are emotionally intricate because roles aren't clear. For example, what are a spouse's responsibilities to new steprelatives? And should the custodial mother, the noncustodial father, or the stepfather discipline the children?

Psychic Remarriage

People's identity changes from that of a single individual to that of part of a couple after they remarry.

Because social status and personal identity are independent of marital status for many men, a shift in marital status does not require an extreme change in personal identity.

The identify shift may be more difficult for women, however. For a traditional woman, the psychic remarriage represents recovery of a valued identity as a wife. A nontraditional woman, on the other hand, may worry about the loss of her highly valued independence.

Community Remarriage

People often change their community of friends when they remarry. During this stage of remarriage, they may sever close personal ties that they established after a divorce and lose valuable friendships.

In addition, people may move to another community after a remarriage. Such moves may entail meeting new neighbors, going to a different place of worship, and changing the children's schools. These transitions often loosen ties with previous friends and social networks.

Parental Remarriage

The parental remarriage involves developing relationships between a partner and the children of the new spouse. If the children's other biological parent still plays an active role in their lives, the stepparent may have to overcome many hurdles. He or she cannot assume the role of father or mother but must behave as a nonparent, deferring to the biological parent's rights.

In some families, the biological nonresidential father may step aside as the stepfather moves in. If divorced fathers live close to their biological children, however, they maintain ties through telephone calls or visits. Because there are no guidelines for this situation, the parental remarriage stage can lead to confusion and frustration for biological parents, stepparents, and children.

Especially when one or both partners have children from previous marriages, there may be little time to develop workable and comfortable marital relationships and to cement a husband-wife bond. Instead, both marital and parental roles must be

assumed simultaneously, and this may lead to conflict between the partners and between one or both partners and the children.

Economic Remarriage

Remarriage reestablishes a marital household as an economic unit. The main problems during this stage often stem from the presence of children from a former marriage. For example, a biological father's child-support payments may become unpredictable after a custodial mother remarries because he often feels less financial responsibility for the children regardless of the stepfather's income level.

There may also be friction about the distribution of resources. If, for example, the noncustodial parent is ignoring child-support payments, should the stepparent provide the money for recreational, educational, and other expenses for the stepchildren? Or should the custodial parent and stepparent take the nonpayer to court, even if doing so depletes their financial resources? In the case of parents who divorce and remarry when their children are younger than age 5 or so, who's responsible for the children's expenses, especially college costs—only the biological parents? Or the stepparents who played an important role in raising the children and encouraged them to go to college?

Legal Remarriage

Because the legal system does not specify remarriage responsibilities, people are left to struggle with many problems on their own (Hans, 2002; Skinner and Kohler, 2002). For example, a remarriage raises questions such as which wife deserves a man's life and accident insurance, medical coverage, retirement benefits, pension payments, and property—the former wife, who played a major role in building up the estate, or the current wife? And which children should a stepparent support, especially if an adult child is unemployed—his, hers, or theirs?

Most schools and other public institutions typically don't recognize a stepparent as a legal parent. Usually, school registration forms, field trip permission slips, and health emergency information are requested of biological parents, not stepparents. The message, whether intended or not, is that only biological parents count.

Even when stepchildren are mentioned in a will, many state inheritance laws do not recognize stepchildren as legitimate heirs. Stepchildren may have to go to court and battle biological children even when a stepparent has left the estate or other assets to a stepchild.

Some couples cope with the remarriage stages and move on. Others don't. Whether remarried couples succeed or fail, they must deal with new issues that people in first marriages rarely confront.

HOW FIRST MARRIAGES AND REMARRIAGES DIFFER

First marriages and remarriages differ in several important ways. Family composition tends to vary more in remarriages, role expectations are less defined, family members in remarriages may be at different points in their life cycles, and stress factors pile up as the stepfamily tries to readjust to its additional family relationships. People who remarry may also look for spouses who offer more than their first partners did in terms of communication, income, or companionship.

Since you asked . . .

• Why are remarriages often more complicated than first marriages?

Family Composition

Remarriages often result in myriad new relationships and a dramatic change in family composition. Children may suddenly find themselves with **stepsiblings**—brothers or sisters who share a biological or adoptive parent and a stepparent. Others have **half siblings**—brothers or sisters who share only one biological or adoptive parent. Children may also gain stepgrandparents, stepaunts, and a host of other steprelatives. As a result, the children's experiences may change dramatically. For example, they may have to share their biological parent's time, as well as their physical space, with stepsiblings. Listen to one 8-year-old:

We feel like guests in Jim's house. We are careful of what we do. It is like we are the intruders. And I feel very bad that we took Tommy's room. They fixed up a room for him in the basement, with posters and all, but he's still mad at us for taking his room (Fishman and Hamel, 1981: 185).

Remarriage creates a unique set of issues because it combines people from at least two families. Imagine the transition involved when a custodial mother marries a custodial father and the couple then has its own children. Each partner's children from the former marriage may fear that the new children will be loved more or receive more attention because they belong to both parents rather than to just one or the other.

A child who travels between two homes may feel left out of some everyday activities and treats. According to one 12-year-old, "I get jealous when I come back to my mom's and see candy wrappers laying around and I didn't get any" (Hamilton, 2002: J2).

For their part, the parents may worry about dividing their attention among three sets of children so that none feels left out. To complicate matters further, ex-spouses and ex-grandparents may want to

Jim Hensley, a multimillionaire, founded one of the largest beer distributorships in the nation. When he died in 2000, he left his fortune to his younger daughter, Cindy McCain (pictured here with her husband John McCain), from a second marriage and almost nothing to his older daughter, Kathleen, from a first marriage. During Senator John McCain's 2008 presidential campaign, Kathleen complained that Cindy referred to herself as an "only child," ignoring her half sister and making her feel like a "non-person" (Argetsinger and Roberts, 2008: C1). How does this example illustrate some of the complexity of stepfamily composition and role expectations?

have input into the new family that may not be welcomed by the remarried spouses.

Role Expectations

In first marriages, couples usually follow commonly accepted norms about enacting roles such as husband, wife, daughter-in-law, and so on. The absence of norms regarding role expectations for stepfamilies creates perplexing questions. For example, should stepparents have as much authority over children as the children's biological parents do? Should a noncustodial parent who has visitation rights have the same decision-making authority as a custodial parent does? And should a child born to a remarriage have more financial support than the stepchildren?

Role expectations are especially fuzzy when it comes to the extended family. Past and current in-laws and grandparents may be unsure how to treat their "instant" new family members. For example, step-grandparents may feel awkward around their new stepgrandchildren and avoid them or overindulge them to show that they're not playing favorites (LeBey, 2004).

Establishing trust in the new relationship is especially important for remarried couples as they grapple

Hagar © 2004. King Features Syndicate.

with their new roles. Violations of trust, particularly infidelity, are usually a major reason for a marital breakup (see Chapter 15). Because of past violations, remarried couples are especially firm about being honest, open, and trustworthy and are usually less willing to tolerate a betrayal of trust that they endured during the first marriage. For example, a woman who had been remarried for less than a year, said emphatically, "I wouldn't wait very long to be out of there or have him out because I've been there, done that, and did it too long" (Brimhall et al., 2008: 378). Thus, remarried relationships may be more fragile because some role expectations are stricter than in first marriages.

Changes across the Life Course

People who remarry sometimes find that they and their children are at different stages of the family life course. As a result, their goals may conflict. For example, a man with young adult children from his first marriage who is planning for his retirement may marry a younger woman who is looking forward to starting a family. Or his new wife may be an older woman who has already raised her family and now looks forward to a career:

Claire and Sydney had been married for 4 years. Sydney had two adult children, ages 25 and 27, who had never lived with the couple, and Claire had a daughter who was 18 and in college. Sydney had risen from working as a technician . . . to heading the marketing department for a large and successful electronics firm. He now had a month's vacation each year and looked forward to retirement in 10 years. Sydney wished to purchase a vacation home on a lake, as he had spent a number of years "dreaming about retiring there and fishing to his heart's content."

Claire, on the other hand, had gone to work at the telephone company to support herself and her daughter after her divorce. Now that she and

Sydney were married, she had been able to return to school and study to be a nurse. She was employed at a local hospital, loved her work, and hoped to become a supervisor before long. . . . Claire and Sydney worked out many of the stresses of their relationship arising from the joining of their two family groups, but they began to argue over weekend plans and future arrangements (Visher and Visher, 1988: 161–62).

On the other hand, an older man may look forward to remarriage and a new set of biological children. If he's at the top of his career ladder and economically secure, for example, he has time to enjoy watching his new children grow up and to participate in their upbringing. Also, his much younger second (or third) wife might encourage him to pursue recreational activities (such as skiing or socializing with friends) that he missed during his first marriage because of long work hours to pay the bills.

Recently, for example, actor/director Michael Douglas described raising his young children from a second marriage with actress Catherine Zeta-Jones (who's 25 years younger) as "the role of a lifetime." After becoming very successful, Douglas changed his priorities: "My life is centered around my family's schedule," he writes and says that he relishes watching the youngsters grow up. He admits, however, that "My oldest son from my first marriage, who is 28, did not benefit from my new priorities. He was short-changed" (Douglas, 2007: 82).

Stress and Resources

People who remarry usually seek someone who is more successful, more supportive, or more attractive than the ex-spouse. The most appealing mates for women are often older men who don't have custody of their children and have resources for their stepchildren, but such partners aren't always easy to find.

In most remarriages, partners must also cope with the stress of handling shifting resources. In the case of child support, for example, about two-thirds of the states calculate payments based on the income of both biological parents. Much of the general public believes that if a noncustodial parent, who is usually the father, remarries and has children, he should continue the same child-support payments (Hans, 2009). Noncustodial fathers, however, often believe that not decreasing their support payments is unfair because they have new expenses. And, if a stepfather has considerably more assets than the noncustodial father, shouldn't he provide more resources for his stepchildren?

There is also a question about the remarried couple's financial responsibilities toward aging parents. A nationally representative study of adults found that most Americans believe that adult children have a greater responsibility to provide financial assistance to their own parents rather than to stepparents. Remarried partners may experience conflict, however, if they disagree about whether parents or stepparents deserve more support depending on factors such as a feeling of closeness and making previous commitments for financial assistance (Hans et al., 2009).

Remarriage also increases resources. Children have more adults who care about them, may experience less conflict between biological parents, and have stepgrandparents who may be delighted to add more grandkids to the fold. According to some adolescents, the bright side of stepfamilies was having two Christmases, two vacations, and two birthday celebrations every year (Crosbie-Burnett and McClintic, 2000; Hamilton, 2002).

∷• MAKING CONNECTIONS

- If you, your parents, or friends have remarried, which of the remarriage stages described on pp. 450–451 were the most problematic? Why?

- Many financial planners and lawyers advise remarried couples to set up three separate savings and checking accounts—his, hers, and theirs. Doing so, they maintain, will avoid arguments over different spending styles and will help partners take care of themselves in case of a second divorce. Many marriage counselors, on the other hand, contend that separate funds show a lack of trust and can spark marital problems (Palmer, 2007). With which side do you agree? Why?

COUPLE DYNAMICS IN STEPFAMILIES

A well-known song tells us that "love is better the second time around." Often, however, people have fantasies about the second marriage resembling a

Since you asked . . .

∷• Why do many remarried couples divorce?

nuclear family that consists of the biological parents and their children living in one household. As you saw in Chapter 1, all family forms have been changing, but nuclear families are often idealized as the family structure that people should form and maintain.

Myths about Remarriage

Some couples are more realistic than others in how they think about a remarriage. Here are the most common myths that "can promote dangerous stepfamily expectations" (Hetherington and Kelly, 2002: 174):

- *The Nuclear Family Myth:* Believers of this fantasy expect family members to love and feel close to one another, children to show deference to parents, and "discomforting appendages" (such as a nonresidential parent) to disappear. Even in long-lasting stepfamilies, tight-knit relationships are usually uncommon.

- *The Compensation Myth:* The new mate is expected to be everything the problematic old mate wasn't—kind, sensitive, responsible, and true. Such expectations can create conflict because no one is perfect, and new partners want to be accepted for who they are rather than trying to make up for the qualities that the ex-spouse reportedly lacked.

- *The Instant Love Myth:* Believing marriage to be a form of parental entitlement, new stepparents presume an intimacy and authority that they have yet to earn. The instant love myth often produces disillusionment even faster than the nuclear family myth.

- *The Rescue Fantasy:* Stepparents think that they will "shape those kids up" and rescue them from a negative or lenient custodial parent. Custodial fathers expect the stepmother to take over responsibility for the care and nurturing of a stepchild, something a stepmother may be unable or unwilling to do because of employment, personality, or other factors.

Some couples continue to nurture these myths and fantasies, and eventually they break up. Others become more realistic and work on building satisfying relationships between themselves and the stepchildren.

Marital Roles and Power

Remarried couples report sharing decision making more equally than they did during their first marriage. They have a more egalitarian relationship because they believe that unequal power was a major problem in their first marriage and don't want to repeat the mistake (Ganong et al., 2006).

Another reason for more equitable power in remarriages may be that women feel obligated to earn income to help support their children from a previous relationship. Mothers are especially likely to work outside the home when they recognize that men may be reluctant to bear the full financial responsibility for the stepchildren. If women provide more economic resources, they are likely to have greater decision-making authority in the remarriage (Ganong and Coleman, 2004).

Shared power doesn't always mean that partners share household tasks equally. Remarried husbands often do more housework than husbands in first marriages, but much of the domestic work is based on traditional gender roles, and remarried women do most of the housework and child rearing (Deal et al., 1992; Pyke and Coltrane, 1996).

After a divorce, women who were employed in low-skilled jobs may seek partners who appreciate stay-at-home wives and have the money to support their doing so. In other cases, women enjoy their child care and domestic responsibilities, consider themselves to be good mothers, and neither need nor want parenting help from their partners. In such situations, the partners follow traditional gender roles: She does the housework and child care while he makes the major financial decisions (Pyke, 1994; Bray and Kelly, 1998).

Remarriage Satisfaction

The data on remarital satisfaction are mixed. People in first marriages report greater satisfaction than do remarried spouses, but the differences are small. Especially if the remarried parents have a stable relationship and the mother feels that the children's lives are going well, remarried mothers benefit psychologically from remarriage and are happier than divorced mothers (Vemer et al., 1989; Demo and Acock, 1996).

Other researchers report that remarried spouses are more likely to express criticism, anger, and irritation. The disagreements generally center on issues related to stepchildren, such as discipline and the distribution of resources (Coleman et al., 2002).

Negative interactions between remarried partners probably result from the strain and change associated with the new marriage and stepfamily formation. In the first few years of remarriage, stress could reflect the same poor communication and problem-solving skills that led to a previous divorce. Remarriages may also suffer from increased stress caused by the behavior problems of young adolescent children (Bray, 1999).

Remarriage Stability

About 60 percent of remarriages, compared with 45 percent of first marriages, end in divorce. The aver-

During a recent episode of *The Ellen DeGeneres Show*, DeGeneres noted that actor/director Will Smith's second marriage to actress Jada Pinkett Smith had lasted 10 years so far, which is rare in Hollywood. When DeGeneres asked Smith for the secret to their success, he said that he and his wife had decided that divorce just wasn't an option: "We're like listen, we're going to be together one way or the other, so we might as well try to be happy" (Dyball, 2008). Should other remarried couples adopt the Smiths' philosophy? Or is their stance unrealistic?

age duration of first marriages is approximately eight years. The average duration of second marriages is about the same, whereas third marriages that end in divorce typically last about five years (Kreider, 2005; see, also, Chapter 15).

Why are divorce rates higher for remarriages than for first marriages? There are many reasons. First, those who marry as teenagers and remarry at a young age are more likely to divorce after a second marriage (Wilson and Clarke, 1992). This may reflect a lack of problem-solving skills or immaturity in dealing with marital conflict.

Second, people most likely to redivorce see divorce as a quick solution for marital dissatisfaction. Having survived one divorce, people may feel that another divorce is a ready remedy for an unhappy marriage. Thus, they may exert less effort to make the remarriage work or they may be unwilling to invest the time and energy to try to resolve problems (Booth and Edwards, 1992; Pyke, 1994).

Third, women who have a child between marriages are more likely to divorce. Such *intermarital birth* may force a newly married couple to cope with an infant rather than devote time to their relationship (Wineberg, 1991).

Finally, remarried couples must deal with more boundary maintenance issues than people in first marriages. For example, those in remarriages often have to insulate themselves against interference from ex-spouses and ex–in-laws. Remarried couples must also devote more effort to establishing boundaries with new family members and new relatives, especially if one of the partners is a custodial parent (Browning, 1994).

THE DIVERSITY AND COMPLEXITY OF STEPFAMILIES

Since you asked . . .

❧• What are the some of the biggest problems facing stepfamilies?

Stepfamilies come in many shapes and sizes. We'll look at various types of stepfamilies first, consider the unique challenges of gay and lesbian families, and then examine some of ways in which stepfamilies differ from nuclear families.

Types of Stepfamilies

When a couple forms a stepfamily, new family networks emerge. These new networks are often traced through a **genogram,** a diagram showing the biological relationships among family members. The genogram in *Figure 16.3* shows some of the complexity of family systems that are created when two previously married parents marry each other.

Although they vary in parent–child relationships, there are three basic types of stepfamilies:

- In the **mother–stepfather family,** all the children are biological children of the mother and stepchildren of the father.

- In the **father–stepmother family,** all the children are biological children of the father and stepchildren of the mother.

- In the **joint stepfamily,** at least one child is the biological child of both parents, at least one child is the biological child of only one parent and the stepchild of the other parent, and no other type of child is present.

Stepfamilies can be even more complicated. In a *complex stepfamily,* both adults have children from previous marriages. And in *joint step–adoptive families*

FIGURE 16.3 **Stepfamily Networks**
Each set of parents of our target couple, Bill and Maria, are grandparents to at least two sets of children. For example, Maria's parents are the grandparents of her children with her former husband Bob (Billy, Mario, and Linda) and of her child with Bill (Joy). Depending on the closeness of the relationship Bill maintains with his former wife, Althea, however, Maria's parents might play a grandparental role to Peter and Julian, Bill and Althea's boys, as well.

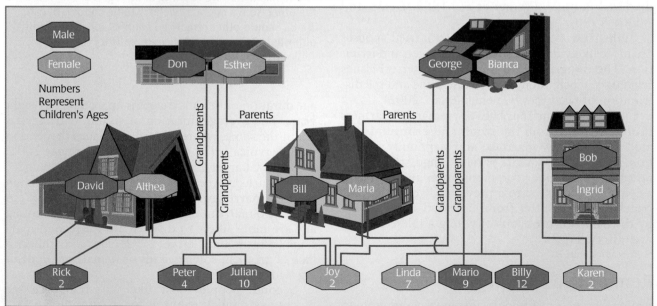

Source: Based on Everett and Everett, 1994: p. 132.

and *joint biological–step–adoptive families,* at least one child is a biological child of one parent and a stepchild of the other parent, and one or both parents have adopted at least one child. Nor does the term *complex stepfamily* take account of the relationships between cohabitors, one or both of whom may have been married and have children from previous unions.

Thus, stepfamilies can be fairly simple, composed of only a biological parent and his or her children and a stepparent. They can also be intricate because they include stepparents; stepsiblings; half siblings; and a combination of stepparents, stepsiblings, and half-siblings. The latter combination accounts for more than 2 percent of all stepfamilies (Kreider, 2008).

Gay and Lesbian Stepfamilies

Stepfamilies with gay and lesbian parents are similar to traditional stepfamilies and encounter many of the same problems, such as disciplining children and providing them with the necessary resources to be happy and healthy (Stewart, 2007). The usual difficulties often are aggravated, however, by the parent's and stepparent's sexual orientation because parents in lesbian and gay stepfamilies may encounter *triple stigmatization.* First, they are stigmatized for their homosexuality, which many people view as immoral. Second, gay and lesbian stepfamilies are still seen as deficient compared with nuclear families because they don't have adult role models of both sexes. Last, some gay men, especially, criticize parenthood in the homosexual community because they believe that the gay culture should emphasize the primacy of the couple relationship rather than parenting (Berger, 2000).

Despite such obstacles, there is evidence that lesbian stepfamilies are resilient and as diverse as heterosexual stepfamilies. For example, lesbian stepfamilies reflect three distinct stepparent roles (Wright, 1998):

- In the *co-parent family,* the nonbiological mother is a supporter of and helper and consultant to the biological mother, an active parent of the children, and a dedicated and committed family member.

- The *stepmother family* parallels heterosexual stepmother families. That is, the lesbian stepmother performs most of the traditional mothering tasks, but the biological mother (like the biological father in heterosexual families) retains most of the decision-making power.

- In the *co-mother family,* both mothers have equal rights and responsibilities in everyday decisions and child-rearing tasks.

Some Characteristics of Stepfamilies

Most children (87 percent) younger than age 18 live with their biological parents, and an additional 10 percent live with a biological parent and a stepparent. Among stepfamilies, the most common form is mother-stepfather. Across racial-ethnic groups, white children are most likely to live in a mother-stepfather family (Kreider, 2008).

Stepfamilies may look like nuclear families because they are composed of married adults and children living in the same household. However, stepparenting is more difficult for a number of reasons that range from the structure of stepfamilies to the ambiguous roles of stepfamily members.

1. *The structure of stepfamilies is complex.* It bears repeating that stepfamilies create new roles: stepparents, stepsiblings, half siblings, and stepgrandparents. Note that this structure does not make stepfamilies better or worse than nuclear families; they are simply different.

2. *A stepfamily must cope with unique tasks.* The stepparent may struggle to overcome rejection because the children may still be grieving over the breakup of the biological family, or the stepparent may disagree with the biological parent about discipline and rules (Hetherington and Kelly, 2002).

   One of the most common tasks is redefining and renegotiating family boundaries. This may include making "visiting" children feel welcome and working out "turf" problems:

   Consider the stepfamily in which the husband's three children rejoined the household every 3–4 days for a few days' time. The house was small, and the mother's three children who lived in the household had to shift where they slept, where they put their clothes, and where they could go to relax or to be alone to accommodate the extra family members. Bedrooms became dormitories, and the continual chaos created tension and instability for everyone (Visher and Visher, 1993: 241).

   In such situations, it's difficult to develop clear and consistent rules about property rights and private spaces for each family member.

3. *Stepfamilies often experience more stress and conflict than nuclear families.* As the previous example illustrates, much of the stress in stepfamilies is due to the vagueness and the lack of fit with cultural norms that, however unrealistic, endorse the nuclear family as the ideal family structure. Ambiguity may decrease as family members adjust to new roles and lifestyles. The sense that the family doesn't fit the ideal model may decrease as family functioning improves.

   A major source of tension is the adjustment that family members must make to one another all at once rather than gradually, as in a nuclear family. Stress may come from several sources:

It's important for stepfamilies to make sure that all the children receive love and attention. If signs of jealousy appear, both parents should listen to the children's concerns and try to resolve them.

More people make more demands, parents may differ on how to discipline children, one partner may feel excluded from the relationship between her or his spouse and the spouse's biological children, or there may not be enough resources to meet the larger family's needs (Whitsett and Land, 1992).

4. *Stepfamily integration typically takes years rather than months.* The age and sex of the children and the type of stepfamily (whether there is a stepmother or stepfather and whether there are children from one or both previous marriages) can affect adjustment. As "The Stepfamily Cycle" box shows, it may take as long as eight years for a couple to consolidate their family and to work as a team. And if the remarried couple has a baby or there are unexpected problems such as unemployment or a death in the family, the process may take even longer.

5. *Important relationships may be cut off or end abruptly, and others spring up overnight.* As you saw in Chapter 15, many noncustodial fathers have no contact with their children after a divorce. Moreover, siblings who are sometimes split between parents in split custody agreements may rarely see one another. Children are especially distressed if a parent's wedding announcement comes as a surprise:

One divorced father awakened his children one morning, asked them to get dressed, and drove them to the courthouse where he married a woman they had only recently met. The children were shocked and felt betrayed that they were not allowed to know that their father was serious about this woman and wanted to marry her. The woman also had a child, so that by 10 P.M.

these children went to bed in a house that now included a new stepmother and a new stepsister. The children were not happy about it (Knox and Leggett, 1998: 184).

According to both researchers and family clinicians, children should be given plenty of notice about an impending remarriage. The new partner and the children should get to know one another over the course of a year or two, go on vacations and have meals together, and just hang around the house, getting to know one another (Bray and Kelly, 1998; Knox and Leggett, 1998).

6. *There are continuous transitions and adjustments rather than stability.* In a stepfamily, the people living in a household can change continuously. The boundaries between who is a member of a stepfamily are sometimes blurry. For example, is the new spouse of a child's noncustodial parent a part of the child's family? And who decides the answer to this question?

Many families agree to have flexible boundaries so that at any age, including during adulthood, children have access to both of their biological parents and can move easily between households. If each child has parents who are divorced or remarried, there may be some difficulty in juggling individual needs, family traditions, and emotional ties between as many as four families.

7. *Stepfamilies are less cohesive than nuclear or single-parent households.* Stepchildren often feel closer to biological parents than to stepparents. As children grow up, they may also feel alienated because of differential economic support, as when only certain children in a stepfamily are supported during college. Or they may resent unequal favors and inheritances bestowed by stepgrandparents.

8. *Stepfamilies need great flexibility in their everyday behavior.* Varying custody and residential arrangements require different daily or weekly routines. Moreover, within the household, the expected ways in which a family operates may not apply. For example, is the clarinet at Mom's house or Dad's? It's Amy's day to stay at Mom's house, but over at Dad's they're going to play miniature golf.

The need for flexibility may decrease over time, but situations often arise (such as weddings, births, deaths, and holidays) that may demand unusual solutions and arrangements. For example, should a noncustodial father who rarely visits his children pay for his daughter's wedding, or should her stepfather do so? And if both the biological father and the stepfather are important in a young woman's life, who should walk down the aisle at her wedding? One or both of them?

The Stepfamily Cycle

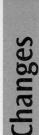

In a well-know study, family clinician Patricia Papernow (1993: 70–231) divides the process of becoming a stepfamily into three major stages. The early stage is characterized by fantasies, confusion, and slowly getting to know the other family members; in the middle stage, the family begins to restructure; and in the late stage the family achieves its own identity.

The Early Stages: Getting Started without Getting Stuck

Stage 1: Fantasy

Most remarrying couples start out with the fantasy that they will love the children of the person they love and be loved by them, and that they will be welcomed into a ready-made family. They see themselves as filling voids for the children, their spouses, and themselves.

Children in new stepfamilies also have fantasies that may encompass a mixture of hope and fear. Some children still hope that their biological parents will be reunited. Or they may fear losing or hurting one of their own parents if they come to love a stepparent.

Stage 2: Immersion

Chaos and confusion often characterize this stage. Biological parents, children, and stepparents may see problems differently. Stepparents may feel left out of the biological parent-child unit and may experience jealousy and resentment.

Biological parents are often caught in the middle. Some exhaust themselves trying to meet everyone's needs and make the stepfamily work; others ignore the difficulties. Particularly in the latter case, the children may feel lost or rejected. Some respond with angry outbursts; others withdraw.

Stage 3: Awareness

Members of the stepfamily get to know each other. Stepparents can learn about the children's likes and dislikes, their friends, and their memories without trying to influence the children.

Biological parents can try to find the right balance between overprotecting children and asking too much of them. Children should be encouraged to look at the positive aspects of the stepfamily, such as the parents' love.

The Middle Stages: Restructuring the Family

Stage 4: Mobilization

Many stepfamilies fall apart at this critical stage. The stepparent's task is to identify a few essential strategies for change (such as holding family meetings to deal with difficult issues) and make a sustained effort to communicate them to other family members while respecting the biological unit.

The biological parent's task is to voice the needs of her or his children and ex-spouse while supporting and addressing the stepparent's concerns. Children should voice their own needs to ease the pressures created by their conflicting loyalties.

Stage 5: Action

In this stage, the stepfamily can begin to make some joint decisions about how the family will operate. The stepparent begins to play a more active role in the family, and the biological parent doesn't feel the need to be all things to all people.

The Later Stages: Solidifying the Stepfamily

Stage 6: Contact

In this stage, family members begin to interact more easily. There is less withdrawal and more recognition of one another's efforts. The stepparent has a firm relationship with the spouse and has begun to forge a more intimate, authentic relationship with at least some of the stepchildren.

Stage 7: Resolution

Relationships begin to feel comfortable. The stepparent role is well defined and solid. Stepparents become mentors to some of their stepchildren. Other stepparent-stepchild relationships have achieved a mutually suitable distance.

In this stage, the adult couple has become a sanctuary, a place to turn for empathy, support, and cooperative problem solving, and the stepfamily finally has a sense of its own identity.

⁞• Stop and Think . . .

- Do you think that the stepfamily cycle differs for women and men, both as adults and children? Why or why not?

- The average duration of second marriages is about eight years. Why, then, do you think that many remarriages split up before then?

9. ***Stepfamily members often have unrealistic expectations.*** Stepfamilies often compare themselves with nuclear families and have idealized or naive expectations. There is no reason why members of the stepfamily—aside from newly remarried adults—should automatically feel any sort of familial relationship or affection. It's physically and emotionally impossible for a stepfamily to mirror a nuclear family; there are simply too many players and too many new relationships. As you saw in the box on "The Stepfamily Cycle" above, stepfamilies must forge their own rules and identities.

10. ***There is no shared family history.*** The stepfamily is a group of individuals who must develop meaningful, shared experiences. To do

Children in stepfamilies often feel divided loyalties between their noncustodial biological father, with whom they spend time periodically, their biological mother, and their stepfather.

this, they must learn one another's verbal and nonverbal communication patterns and to interact differently. New stepfamily members often speak of culture shock: When their own behavioral patterns and those of other members of the household differ, they sometimes feel as if they're in an alien environment. For example, mealtimes and the meals themselves may be different from those they were used to in the past.

One way to ease some of the strangeness is to mesh rituals. In one remarried family, when a major holiday was approaching, family members were asked to suggest favorite foods. By preparing and serving these dishes, the new family honors some of the traditions of the previous families (Imber-Black and Roberts, 1993).

11. *There may be many loyalty conflicts.* Accusations of liking one parent more than another often arise in all families, but loyalty conflicts are intensified in stepfamilies. For example, suppose that a child in the stepfamily feels closer to the noncustodial parent or to that parent's new spouse than to the biological

and custodial parent or that parent's new spouse. Should these relationships be nurtured despite the resentment of the custodial parent or stepparent?

Moreover, a newly remarried adult must make a sustained effort to be loyal to a new spouse despite her or his closeness with biological children. For example, when Gwen, who had lived with her mother and stepfather for nine years and then lived on her own while attending college, came back home for a time, her mother felt conflicted:

Hugh [Gwen's stepfather] wants her to pay rent. I don't want her to. I feel that at this point in her life I would be a little more lenient than Hugh is. A lot of the difficulty is that she's been away for five years and now she's back in the fold. Hugh's a very rigid person—everything is preplanned and set up that way and that's the way you do it. I'm a little more loose (Beer, 1992: 133).

Gwen's mother's task was to find ways to help her daughter that did not diminish her loyalty to her husband. Had her husband been as "loose" as she was, the adjustment might have been easier for this stepfamily.

12. *Stepfamily roles are often ambiguous.* A positive aspect of role ambiguity is that it provides freedom of choice because an adult may be able to play a variety of roles with children and other adults. For example, a stepparent who is willing to be a friend to the children, rather than a strict parent, can serve as a mediator when there is conflict between the children and the biological custodial parent.

However, ambiguity creates problems because people don't always know what's expected of them or what to expect from others. For instance, a partner may want a spouse who offers support, not mediation, when he or she disagrees with the children.

When adults have problems, so do children. If adults are resilient and adjust, so do children. What, more specifically, are the ways that stepfamilies affect children?

⋮• MAKING CONNECTIONS

- Did you or someone you know grow up in a stepfamily? Look at the list of 12 characteristics of stepfamilies on pp. 457–460. Which ones were the most difficult for you or someone you know?

- What are some advantages and disadvantages of growing up in a stepfamily compared with a nuclear family?

LIVING IN A STEPFAMILY

Stepparents don't have complete control over the relationships that develop in their new family. Often they must overcome stereotypes and work hard to merge members of several households into one.

Stereotypes about Stepfamilies

The *myth of the evil stepmother,* perpetuated in Western culture by classic tales such as "Cinderella," "Snow White," and "Hansel and Gretel," still exists. This myth, which depicts stepmothers as cruel, unloving, and abusive, has had a ripple effect over time. The harmful image persists even though many stepmothers neither wish nor expect to replace the stepchild's mother (Kheshgi-Genovese and Genovese, 1997; Orchard and Solberg, 1999).

Ex-wives who are still angry about a divorce sometimes refer to the stepmother as a witch in front of their children, deepening the rift between the stepmother and the stepchildren. Here's how one new stepmother, Melinda, describes her experiences when picking up her husband's sons at the custodial mother's house for weekend visits:

When I first started picking up the boys, I could sense how much his ex-wife resented me as the "other woman" who broke up her marriage, even though they had started divorce proceedings before I met Clark. I would often see her peeking out of an upstairs window, looking at me with pure venom. . . . As I sat there, I could hear the screaming accusations that his ex-wife was hurling at me in front of the boys (LeBey, 2004: 94–95).

Melinda and her husband Clark were raising her young daughter and their biological child and were experiencing financial difficulties. The boys from his previous marriage "ran wild" during weekends because Clark didn't impose any rules on their behavior. When the boys visited, Melinda, exhausted, was often "shrill, short-tempered, and angry. I was living up to the myth of the wicked stepmother." To make matters worse, Clark's parents often complained that their son had made a terrible mistake by marrying "that woman," an intruder and home wrecker (LeBey, 2004: 95).

To meet their husband's expectations, stepmothers often try to impose some kind of order on the household. Many stepchildren become angry, resenting and resisting the rules:

In our most contentious stepfamilies, a real demonizing of the stepmother often occurred. We heard stepmothers described by some stepchildren as "evil," "malevolent," "wicked," or as "monsters," and nicknamed "Dog Face" or "The Dragon." Stepfathers rarely encountered this level of vitriol. Many wellintentioned but angry, discouraged, and defeated stepmothers gradually gave up and pulled out of the marriage (Hetherington and Kelly, 2002: 193).

In contrast, the *myth of instant love,* as you saw earlier, maintains not only that remarriage creates an instant family but that stepmothers will automatically love their stepchildren. In *The Sound of Music,* for example, Julie Andrews wins the affections of the seven von Trapp children within a few months. Remarried parents, especially women, expect such instant love because, according to the *myth of motherhood,* mothering comes easily and naturally to all women (Braverman, 1989; Quick et al., 1994; see, also, Chapter 12 on motherhood myths).

Members of a newly constituted family who believe all these myths may experience a high degree of stress as they try to adapt to new personalities, lifestyles, schedules, and routines. And considering the unrealistic views that people hold of the nuclear family, it's not surprising that the stepfamily suffers by comparison (Gamache, 1997; see, also, Chapter 1 on the myths about the perfect family).

A woman who grew up believing that stepmothers are bad may try to become a super stepmom. She may be especially frustrated if her stepchildren rebel despite all her sincere and self-sacrificing efforts. By the same token, a child who grew up with the same ideas about stepmothers may have negative expectations and may resist her attempts to develop a positive relationship. Thus, a self-perpetuating cycle is set in motion. The children expect the stepmother to be nasty, and as a result they will be aloof. Their unpleasant behavior may cause the stepmother to become more demanding and critical (Berger, 2000).

Parenting in Stepfamilies

About 17 percent of American children live in a stepfamily (Kreider, 2008). Asian American children are the least likely to do so (see *Figure 16.4*). This is probably due to many Asian Americans' emphasizing the importance of families over individual self-fulfillment, which results in lower divorce rates and, consequently, lower remarriage rates (see Chapters 5 and 15).

FIGURE 16.4 Percentage of Children Living in Stepfamilies, 2004

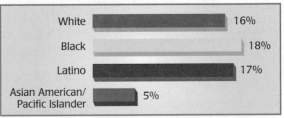

White	16%
Black	18%
Latino	17%
Asian American/ Pacific Islander	5%

Note: According to the most recent available data, in 1996, 21 percent of American Indian/Alaska Native children lived in stepfamilies.
Source: Based on Kreider, 2008: Table 6.

Most stepfamilies face a number of issues when they attempt to merge two households after a remarriage. These include naming, sexual boundaries, legal issues, distributing economic and emotional resources, developing the stepparent-stepchild relationship, establishing discipline and closeness, helping children adjust to the new family form, and developing intergenerational relationships.

NAMING The English language has fairly clear terms for relationships in biological families, such as "father," "mother," "brother," and "daughter." Suppose, however, that stepchildren want to call their stepfather "Dad." The biological children may feel threatened and annoyed if they don't accept their stepsiblings as "really" family. One of my friends admits that she feels pangs of anger and envy when her son calls his stepmother "Mom." Thus, bad feelings may result.

One stepmother was uncomfortable with her three young stepchildren's calling her by her first name (as her husband does) because it seemed impersonal and disrespectful. This was her solution:

I did not want to confuse the children by asking them to call me "Mom," since they already have a mother. So, I came up with a name that worked— "Smom." It's now a year later, and the kids are completely comfortable calling me Smom. Even my husband's ex-wife calls me that. Sometimes, the kids have variations, like "Smommy" or "Smama." I'm happy, they're happy (Ann Landers, 2000: C11).

The name children call a stepfather—whether he is married to or cohabiting with their mother—has special meaning for men. Actually hearing oneself called "Dad," as opposed to one's first name or "stepdad," is a sign of acceptance and belonging. Many stepfathers still remember first hearing "Daddy" or "Dad" as a thrilling and momentous occasion because the use of kinship terms goes hand in hand with a feeling of genuine fatherhood (Marsiglio and Hinojosa, 2006).

SEXUAL BOUNDARIES Our laws forbid sexual relations between siblings and between parents and children in biological families. However, there are rarely any legal restrictions on sexual relations between

Applying What You've Learned

⁑ Dealing with Sexual Boundaries in the Stepfamily

Only some states forbid romantic relationships between nonbiological members of a stepfamily. The weakened incest taboo in the stepfamily makes rules less clear, and sexual liaisons can create confusion, anger, and a sense of betrayal. Family practitioners Emily and John Visher (1982: 162–66) offer remarried partners these guidelines for dealing with sexuality in the stepfamily:

- Be affectionate and tender, but not passionate, with each other when the children are with you. Teenagers are particularly sensitive to open displays of affection because of their own emerging sexuality. Be aware of this sensitivity and forgo the kisses and embraces in the kitchen.

- Don't be sexually provocative. Walking around in a bra and underpants will counteract efforts to keep sexu-

ality under control in your household, even when only younger children are around. Set a limit on teenagers' sexual behavior. The first time a teenager parades around the house scantily clad, for example, he or she should be told to go back to his or her room and to dress properly. Be firm in setting limits for appropriate dress and behavior.

- Stop some forms of intimate behavior with children after they turn 10 or 11. For example, sitting on a stepfather's lap and showering him with kisses is inappropriate behavior for a teenage stepdaughter.

- If a teenager develops a crush on a stepparent, talk to him or her openly. Point out that the teen's affections are misplaced. Also, make it clear that there is a big difference

between feelings and behavior. Just because people are attracted to others does not mean that they should act on their impulses.

- Rearrange the living space between stepsiblings. For example, avoid adjoining bedrooms and change the bathroom-sharing arrangements so that older children have more privacy and less temptation.

- Do not tolerate sexual involvement in your home. In one family, the adults asked the college-aged son to move out of the house because they were unwilling to accept his sexual relationship with his stepsister. Stepparents can't control sexual attraction between stepsiblings, but they can control what happens in their home.

stepfamily members, either between stepchildren or between a stepparent and a stepchild.

Estimates of the extent of child abuse in stepfamilies vary, but researchers agree that children are at greater risk for both physical and sexual abuse if they live in a household with an adult who is not their biological parent than if they live with both biological parents. When sexual abuse occurs, the perpetrator is typically a male, and often a stepfather (Ganong and Coleman, 2004; Reading, 2006; see, also, Chapter 14).

Stepsiblings may also drift into romantic relationships that can damage family relationships. As the "Dealing with Sexual Boundaries in the Stepfamily" box shows, one way to handle sexual problems is to prevent them in the first place.

LEGAL ISSUES Financial matters are more complicated in stepfamilies than in first marriages. Financial planners and marriage educators are nearly unanimous in urging people who are planning a second marriage to spell out their financial obligations to each other in a legally binding prenuptial agreement. The issues include whether to share financial responsibility for children from previous marriages, how to divide estates, whether to merge assets and liabilities, and how to divide property acquired before and after the marriage in case of divorce (Ebeling, 2007; see, also, *Appendix F* on premarital and nonmarital agreements).

Unless there is a prenuptial agreement that allows a new spouse to waive his or her rights to a share of an estate, children from a previous marriage may be practically disinherited even though this was not the parent's intention. Some biological children may resent their inheritance being divided with stepsiblings. In other cases, adult children feel devastated when an aging dad has a new wife and changes his will, leaving most of the deceased mother's jewelry and other personal belongings to his stepchildren (Cohn, 2005).

Legal experts advise setting up a trust fund to safeguard the biological children's or grandchildren's inheritance. Trusts allow parents to transmit gifts and inheritances to whomever they choose while they are alive or after their death. In addition, to minimize family friction, attorneys advise people to discuss their estate plans with those who will be affected by them (Ebeling, 2007).

DISTRIBUTING ECONOMIC RESOURCES The children of remarried fathers typically are at a financial disadvantage if the children live with their custodial mother. The stepchildren living with their remarried father may receive more support, such as loans, gifts, and health coverage. Loss of economic support can impoverish biological children and create hostility.

In a stepfamily, the partners must decide whether to pool their resources and how to do so. They may

Involving both custodial and visiting (nonresidential) children in stepfamily activities can make the visiting children feel more welcome and a part of the family.

experience stress and resentment if there are financial obligations to a former family (such as child-support awards, mortgage payments, or outstanding debts). Disagreements may range from seemingly petty issues, such as how much should be spent on birthday presents for relatives, to drastically different attitudes about whether money should be saved or spent.

Because men typically have more economic resources than do women, stepfathers may have more decision-making power in the new family. Sometimes men use money to control their wives' and stepchildren's behavior ("If you don't shape up, you can pay for your own car insurance next time"). This kind of manipulation creates hostility.

DISTRIBUTING EMOTIONAL RESOURCES Resources such as time, space, and affection must also be distributed equitably so that all the family's members feel content with the new living arrangements. Mothers sometimes are angry about spending much of their time and energy on live-in stepchildren but receiving few rewards:

My husband's kids don't see me as their mother. They shouldn't because I'm not. But I've gone out of my way to hold my tongue and do special things for them. It's as if whatever I do can be sloughed off, because I really don't count.
I can do things for the kids and my husband gets the credit, not me. I resent them at those moments, and I resent him. It's really hard (Vissing, 2002: 193–94).

Custodial mothers can strengthen ties between their children and stepfathers by encouraging them to spend time together. As one mother said, "I'd send them off to the movies or to a park. They had to form a relationship without me intervening" (Wolcott, 2000: 16).

DEVELOPING THE STEPPARENT-STEPCHILD RELATIONSHIPS Relationships with stepchildren are often more difficult for stepmothers than for stepfathers. Stepfathers who don't monitor their stepchildren may have a long-term negative effect on the children's behavior, but stepmothers may be less likely to have good relationships with their stepchildren because they are more often the disciplinarian (Kurdek and Fine, 1993; MacDonald and DeMaris, 1996).

If the stepmother is at home more than her husband, she may be expected to be more actively involved in domestic duties, including raising the stepchildren. Regardless of the parent's gender, relations between children and parents both in biological and remarried homes are more positive when the parents include the children in decision making and are supportive rather than critical (Barber and Lyons, 1994; Crosbie-Burnett and Giles-Sims, 1994).

Noncustodial mothers and stepmothers seem to play a more important role than noncustodial fathers and stepfathers in shaping family dynamics. The women, not the men, are usually the *kinkeepers* who arrange visits between family members, remember birthday and holiday greetings and gifts, and give children affection and emotional support. They are also influential *gatekeepers* when they discourage relationships between noncustodial parents and biological children or cut off contact (Schmeeckle, 2007).

ESTABLISHING DISCIPLINE AND CLOSENESS Two of the biggest problems in stepfamilies are discipline and authority, especially in relationships between a stepfather and adolescent stepchildren. Teenagers complain, "He's not my father! I don't have to listen to him!" Stepfathers often resent not being obeyed, both because they consider themselves authority figures and because they may be working hard to support the family.

Mothers often feel caught in the middle. They love their husbands, but may feel guilty for having married someone the children don't like, or they may disagree with the stepfather's disciplinary methods (Hetherington and Stanley-Hagan, 2002).

Whether they intend it or not, when parents find themselves forming strong relationships with the children of a new partner, they may feel that they are betraying their biological children. Similarly, children may feel guilty if they find themselves liking a stepparent better than a biological parent because the stepparent is more fun, more understanding, or easier to get along with (Papernow, 1993).

Friendship may be the best way to enhance steprelationships. If stepparents go slowly in approaching stepchildren, especially adolescents, they have a better chance of establishing discipline or setting rules. Some stepparents act as *quasikin,* a role midway between that of parent and friend. That is, they assume some of the functions of parents but let the biological parents make final decisions about their children. Maintaining a quasikin relationship can be tricky, however:

Stepparents must balance daily parenting activities such as getting children ready for school, giving allowances, and supervising household chores while taking a more distant stance when the stepchildren's parents are making major decisions about the children (Coleman et al., 2001: 263).

Taking a quasikin role is easier with nonresidential (visiting) children than with custodial children and with older children than with younger children. This role is also more common among stepfathers than among stepmothers, who are often responsible for everyday monitoring and discipline.

Remarried partners sometimes have a child, hoping that the new addition will cement stepfamily bonds. A half sibling rarely affects adolescents, however. As in other types of families, teens typically become more involved with friends and school activities than with siblings. If, however, stepparents shift all of their focus to the baby, they may become less involved with preadolescent children who also need their attention (Stewart, 2005).

GENDER DIFFERENCES IN CHILDREN'S ADJUSTMENT Stepdaughter-stepfather relationships are usually more negative than those between stepsons and stepparents of either sex. Even when stepfathers make friendly overtures, stepdaughters may withdraw (Vuchinich et al., 1991).

One explanation for this distancing behavior is that daughters, who once had a privileged status in the family because they shared much of the authority in helping to raise younger children, may resent being replaced by someone with more power in the family. The stepdaughter-stepfather relationship may also be more distant because the stepfather has made sexual overtures or behaved in other inappropriate ways toward the stepdaughter (see Chapters 14 and 15).

Stepfathers, especially, must be patient in establishing new relationships. In describing the gradual process of developing a relationship with the stepchild, one stepfather commented, "Brian is different now. At first he was reclusive and jealous and he saw me as infringing. It was a slow progression" (Santrock et al., 1988: 159). The box on "The Ten Commandments of Stepparenting" offers some guidelines for stepparents.

INTERGENERATIONAL RELATIONSHIPS Ties across generations, especially with grandparents and stepgrandparents, can be close and loving or disruptive and intrusive. After a divorce or during a remarriage, grandparents can provide an important sense of continuity for children at a time when many other things are changing. Many children are not as attached to their new stepgrandparents as they are to their biological

The Ten Commandments of Stepparenting

Choices

All families, including stepfamilies, have to work at achieving a peaceful coexistence. Family practitioners (Turnbull and Turnbull, 1983; Visher and Visher, 1996) offer the following advice to stepparents who want to maintain harmony within the family:

1. **Provide neutral territory.** Most people have a strong sense of territoriality. Stepchildren may have an especially strong sense of ownership because some of their privacy has been invaded. If it is impossible to move to a new house in which each child has a bedroom, provide a special place that belongs to each child.

2. **Do not try to fit into a preconceived role.** Be honest right from the start. Each parent has faults and peculiarities and the children will have to get used to these weaknesses. Children detect phoniness and will lose respect for any adult who is insincere or too willing to please.

3. **Set limits and enforce them.** One of the most difficult issues in stepfamilies is discipline. Parents should work out the rules in advance and support each other in enforcing them. Rules can change as the children grow older, but there should be agreement from the beginning on issues such as mealtimes, bedtimes, resolving disagreements, and household responsibilities.

4. **Allow an outlet for the children's feelings for the biological parent.** The stepparent should not feel rejected if a child wants to maintain a relationship with a noncustodial biological parent. Children's affection for their biological parents should be supported so that the children do not feel disloyal.

5. **Expect ambivalence.** Children's feelings can fluctuate between love and hate, sometimes within a few hours. Ambivalence is normal in all relationships.

6. **Avoid mealtime misery.** Many families still idealize the dinner hour as a time when family members have intelligent discussions and solve family problems. Both parents should reinforce table manners but avoid an unpleasant experience. Some suggested strategies include letting the children prepare their own meals and having the stepfather do some of the cooking.

7. **Do not expect instant love.** It takes time to forge emotional bonds; sometimes this never occurs. Most children younger than age 3 adapt easily. Children older than age 5 may have more difficulty. Some children are initially excited at having a new mother or father but later find that the words "I hate you" are potent weapons. A thick skin helps during such hurtful times.

8. **Do not accept all the responsibility; the child has some, too.** Children, like adults, come in all types. Some are simply more lovable than others. Like it or not, the stepparent has to take what he or she gets. This does not mean assuming all the guilt for a troubled parent-child relationship, however.

9. **Be patient.** Good relationships take time. The first few months, and even six to seven years, are difficult. The support and encouragement of other parents who have had similar experiences can be invaluable.

10. **Maintain the primacy of the marital relationship.** The couple must remember that the marital relationship is primary in the family. The children need to see that the parents get along together, can settle disputes, and, most of all, will not be divided by the children.

⁑ Stop and Think . . .

- Some of my students, especially those who are stepparents, say that there should be a parallel list of ten commandments for stepchildren. Do you agree? Or do you think that peaceful coexistence is the adults' responsibility?

- If you were seeking a partner, would you use this list to screen a potential stepparent?

grandparents, but they may resent new stepgrandparents who seem to neglect or reject them:

One twelve-year-old girl in our practice became angry and aggressive toward her two new and younger stepsiblings following their first Christmas holiday together, even though she had been very loving with them before that. Several weeks later she revealed to her father that she was hurt and disappointed because the stepsiblings received twice as many gifts from their grandparents as she did in total from everyone in the family (Everett and Everett, 1994: 140).

Such distanced behavior can decrease contact and closeness between biological grandparents and

Children may feel anger and hostility when a parent or stepparent must go to court over issues such as child-support payments owed by the child's biological parent.

grandchildren. Even maternal grandparents may visit less often, call less often, and offer less baby-sitting time to remarried daughters than to married or divorced daughters. Generally, intergenerational relationships depend on how much effort the remarried partners and steprelatives put into maintaining or forging close family ties (Spitze et al., 1994; see, also, Chapter 17).

Some Effects of Stepfamilies on Children

Are stepfamilies beneficial or harmful to children? Among other factors, the results vary according to the family's socioeconomic status and degree of parental conflict.

HOW CHILDREN FARE Some studies report that there are few, if any, emotional or behavioral differences between stepchildren and other children. Other studies show that about 20 percent of stepchildren are at risk for negative outcomes, a somewhat higher percentage than for children living with both biological parents (see Pasley and Moorefield, 2004, for a summary of this research).

The results are mixed, but, overall, studies show that children in stepfamilies don't fare as well as children in biological families. They tend to have more problems academically, such as lower grades, scores on achievement tests, school attendance, and high school graduation rates. Even if the family's economic resources increase after a remarriage, alternating residences during the school year raises a child's risk of dropping out of school or having problems with school authorities (Bogenscheider, 1997; Pong, 1997; Tillman, 2007).

A recent national study found that the greater the involvement of cohabiting and married stepfathers

with adolescent males in grades 7 to 12, the less likely the boys were to have sex at an early age. Especially when the boys rarely saw their noncustodial fathers, the stepfathers were important role models who affected their stepsons' attitudes about sex and sexual behavior. For girls, however, the most important deterrents to early sexual activity were religiosity (e.g., attending religious services and teenage religious activities frequently), and the biological mothers' strong disapproval of early sexual activity and warning their daughters about doing so (Menning et al., 2007). Thus, both stepparents and biological mothers had a strong influence on their children's early sexual behavior.

Compared with children in first-marriage families, stepchildren often have more internalizing problems (not expressing their feelings), such as depression, and are at higher risk for emotional problems. Adolescent stepchildren also display more externalizing (acting out) behavioral problems, such as using drugs and alcohol, engaging in sexual intercourse, and having out-of-wedlock children (see Coleman et al., 2002, for a summary of some of these studies).

The most consistent findings on stepfamilies, however, show that how children fare depends greatly on the relationships among children, their custodial and noncustodial parents, and stepparents. Close relationships with stepfathers, noncustodial fathers, and noncustodial mothers are associated with better adolescent outcomes, such as decreasing the likelihood of externalizing behavior (e.g., delinquency, violence, and substance use) and internalizing behavior (e.g., depression, a negative outlook on life, and low self-esteem). Noncustodial fathers who remain involved with their children when they are young have a stronger relationship with their children in adulthood than those who lose contact. Also, stepfathers and noncustodial fathers who are cooperative rather than competitive in their relationships with children increase the children's well-being (Aquilino, 2006; Ganong et al., 2006; King, 2006, 2007; Marsiglio and Hinojosa, 2007). Thus, as in married and divorced families, children benefit when adults get along (see, also, Chapters 12 and 15).

SOME EXPLANATIONS FOR THE EFFECTS OF STEPFAMILIES ON CHILDREN There are about a dozen theoretical explanations for the effects of stepfamilies on children, but four of the most common are family stress theories, risk and resilience theories, social capital models, and the cumulative effects hypothesis.

Family stress theories say that living in a stepfamily creates numerous difficulties for children and other family members. The stressful events include possibly moving to another home or neighborhood, adapting to a variety of steprelatives after a parent's remarriage, following different rules and schedules, and experiencing ongoing hostility between divorced parents (Stewart, 2007). These and other factors contribute to the children's greater likelihood of externalizing and internalizing problem behaviors.

Risk and resilience theories suggest that the effects of remarriage on children reflect both costs (risks) and benefits (resources that increase resilience). Remarriage can lift many single mothers out of poverty. If children have a good relationship with a stepfather and a noncustodial father, they experience about the same number of problems as children from nuclear families. In addition, supportive schools and peers decrease the likelihood of adjustment problems. Children are less resilient, however, if the ex-spouses' "anger and acrimony undermine the happiness, health, and adjustment of family members" (Hetherington and Stanley-Hagan, 2000: 177; see, also, White and Gilbreth, 2001; Rodgers and Rose, 2002).

Social capital models maintain that children in stepfamily households have more problems than children in nuclear families because the stepparents often invest less time and energy in raising their children. Children thrive when their social capital includes parents who are involved in school activities and homework and value learning, and there is minimal tension between the adults (Pong, 1997; Kim et al., 1999). In many stepfamilies, however, children's social capital decreases because of poor parenting, a custodial parent's or stepparent's gatekeeping, and conflict between adults.

In the *cumulative effects hypothesis*, children whose parents have had several partners over time display more internalizing and externalizing problems than children who lived with a parent who had remarried only once. Thus, children who undergo multiple transitions experience more emotional and behavioral difficulties because the problems snowball (Kurdek and Fine, 1993; Cherlin, 2009a).

❖ MAKING CONNECTIONS

- Should stepparents be parents, friends, quasikin, or some combination of these roles?

- What kinds of traditions, rituals, and celebrations might stepfamilies implement to build a new identity for both stepchildren and stepparents?

SUCCESSFUL REMARRIAGES AND STEPFAMILIES

Since you asked . . .

❖ What can stepparents do to have happier families?

Many stepfamilies, as you've seen, encounter difficulties such as boundary problems, cohesiveness, and conflicting loyalties that biological families don't face, but we rarely hear about well-adjusted and happy stepfamilies. Forging a civil relationship with an ex-spouse or new spouse and raising stepchildren are daunting tasks, but they can be achieved.

Some Characteristics of Successful Stepfamilies

Seven characteristics are common to remarried families in which children and adults experience warm interpersonal relations and satisfaction with their lives (Visher and Visher, 1993). Some of these characteristics, as you might expect, are the opposite of the problems we examined earlier.

First, successful stepfamilies *develop realistic expectations*. They have rejected the myth of instant love because they realize that trying to force friendship or love simply doesn't work. In addition, they don't try to replicate the biological family because they accept the fact that the stepfamily is "under construction." Teenagers who are beginning to rebel against authority are particularly sensitive to adult supervision. As one teenager in a stepfamily put it, "Two parents are more than enough. I don't need another one telling me what to do" (Visher and Visher, 1993: 245).

Second, adults in successful stepfamilies *let children mourn their losses* because they are sensitive to children's feelings of sadness and depression after their parents' divorce. The stepparents also accept the children's expressions of fear, confusion, and anger, neither punishing them nor interpreting their reactions as rejection.

Third, the adults in well-functioning stepfamilies *forge a strong couple relationship*. This provides an atmosphere of stability because it reduces the children's anxiety about another parental breakup. It also gives children a model of a couple who can work together effectively as a team and solve problems rationally (Kheshgi-Genovese and Genovese, 1997).

Fourth, the *stepparenting role proceeds slowly*. A stepparent is catapulted into a parenting role, whereas a biological parent's relationship with a child develops over many years. One of the biggest mistakes that stepfathers make, usually with their wife's encouragement, is assuming an active parenting role too early in the marriage and presuming an intimacy and authority that they have not yet earned. Children might still be feeling the effects of emotional divorce even if their biological parents have recovered (see Chapter 15 on the stages of divorce).

Fifth, except when young children are present, the *stepparent should take on a disciplinary role gradually*. As one of my students stated, "My stepfather wasn't ever in my face, which was good, because I would have been mad if he had tried to discipline me." The biological parent should be the disciplinarian while the stepparent supports his or her rules. In

Stepfamilies often send photos of themselves to family members and friends during the holidays that show a happy and perfect family. Do you think that such photos reflect reality?

successful stepfamilies, adults realize that relations between a stepparent and stepchildren can be quite varied: The stepparent may be a parent to some of the children, a companion to others, or just a good friend to all. And even if there are no warm interpersonal ties, it is enough that family members are tolerant and respectful of one another.

Sixth, successful *stepfamilies develop their own rituals*. They recognize that there is more than one way to do the laundry, bake a turkey, or celebrate a birthday. Successful stepfamilies may combine previous ways of sharing household tasks or develop new schedules for the things they do together on the weekends. The most important criteria are flexibility and cooperation.

Finally, well-functioning stepfamilies *work out satisfactory arrangements between the children's households*. Adults don't have to like one another to get along during family events such as holidays, graduations, and weddings. Many black families, for example, have flexible familial boundaries so that children feel welcome in several households regardless of biological ownership. In addition, many African American families, including fictive kin, share material and emotional resources in raising children (Crosbie-Burnett and Lewis, 1993; see, also, Chapter 2 on fictive kin).

The most successful stepfamilies have two sets of parents but one set of rules. They collaborate at school functions, parent-teacher meetings, and after-school activities. For example, if each child has a list in his or her backpack, both sets of parents can check off items (such as homework, musical instruments, and gym shorts) when the children move back and forth from house to house.

Communication is critical in successful stepfamilies. If adult relationships are strained, relying on e-mail (or texting) can "take the 'feelings' out of communication. You can simply put the facts down, and you don't have to talk to the person" (Cohn, 2003: 13; see, also, Braithwaithe et al., 2006). Face-to-face interaction is usually more effective in stepchild-stepparent communication. Most important, adults should never criticize the children's biological parents or stepparents.

The Rewards of Remarriage and Stepparenting

Couples often say that their stepfamilies offer more benefits than their first marriage. Many believe that they learned valuable lessons in their first marriage and, as a result, have matured. They say that they know each other better than they knew their former spouse, talk more openly and more freely about issues that concern them, and are less likely to suppress their feelings (Brimhall et al., 2008).

Successful remarried couples say that they try harder, are more tolerant of minor irritations, and tend to be more considerate of each other's feelings than they were in their first marriages. They also report enjoying the new interests and new friends that a remarriage brings (Westoff, 1977).

When remarried partners are happy, the children benefit from living in a satisfying household. A well-functioning stepfamily increases the self-esteem and well-being of divorced parents and provides children who have minimal contact with their noncustodial parents with a caring and supportive adult. In addition, the children's economic situation often improves after a parent, especially a mother, remarries (Pill, 1990; see, also, Chapter 15 on the economic benefits and costs of divorce).

In many stepfamilies, the children benefit by having a more objective adult with whom to discuss problems, and they may be introduced to new ideas, different perspectives, and a new appreciation for art, music, literature, sports, or other leisure activities. Finally, if stepsiblings live together, they gain more experience in interacting, cooperating, and learning to negotiate with peers.

In many cases, children don't recognize the contributions of stepparents until they themselves are adults. One of my students, who admitted to being very rebellious and "a real pain" after her mother remarried, is now grateful that her stepfather didn't give up:

The best solution to my and my stepfather's problems was age. As I am getting older and supporting myself more and more, I realize just how much my stepfather has done for me. Even though he is not my "real" dad, he is the only father I have known. He has provided me with food, clothes, an education, and a home. Growing up, I thought I had it so rough. I now realize that he's my friend, and enjoy seeing him (Author's files).

CONCLUSION

As this chapter shows, there is life after separation or divorce. Of all the different marriage and family forms discussed in this textbook, stepfamilies are the most varied and complex. Thus, both children and adults must make many *changes* as family members adapt and work together.

Despite high redivorce rates, remarriage and stepparenting provide people more *choices* in establishing a satisfying family life. Stepfamilies must deal with many *constraints* after a remarriage, but there are also numerous rewards in establishing a new household. The new households can be especially beneficial to families as parents and siblings age, the topic of the next chapter.

SUMMARY

1. After a divorce, dating and courtship patterns vary by age and gender. Most divorced people marry within four years after a divorce.

2. Changes in family structure and makeup result from remarriage and the formation of stepfamilies. More than 40 percent of marriages are remarriages for one or both partners.

3. Remarriage rates vary by gender, race and ethnicity, age, social class, and marital status. Men tend to remarry more quickly than women do, but remarriage rates are higher for whites than for other racial-ethnic groups.

4. Remarriage is a process with emotional, economic, psychic, community, parental, and legal aspects. Some of these stages involve children, whereas others do not.

5. There are several important differences between first marriages and remarriages. Among these differences are the composition of the family, the children's experiences, the roles of stepfamily members, family goals and objectives, and family structure.

6. Stepfamilies are diverse in parent–child relationships and their ties to biological family members.

Stepfamilies can have three sets of children under the same roof, which may result in strained living arrangements.

7. Stepfamilies are similar to nuclear families in fulfilling basic functions and trying to raise happy and healthy children.

8. Stepfamilies must perform a number of unique tasks in merging two households. The most common difficulties include legal issues, integration of children into the family, and intergenerational relationships.

9. Two major tasks for stepfamilies are establishing discipline and developing closeness between family members. The data are mixed, but stepfather-stepdaughter relations are often more strained than those between stepsons and stepparents.

10. Many couples who have remarried say that they know each other better, communicate more openly, and are more considerate of each other's feelings than they were in their first marriages. Thus, although there are problems in remarriages, there are also many rewards.

KEY TERMS

stepfamily 447
stepsibling 452
half sibling 452

genogram 456
mother–stepfather family 456

father–stepmother family 456
joint stepfamily 456

PEARSON **myfamilylab** MyFamilyLab provides a wealth of resources. Go to www.myfamilylab.com<http://www.myfamilylab .com/>, to enhance your comprehension of the content in this chapter. You can take practice exams, view videos relevant to the subject matter, listen to audio files, explore topics further by using Social Explorer, and use the tools contained in MySearch-Lab to help you write research papers.

17 Families in Later Life

In 2007, 95-year-old Nola Ochs received a college diploma and was considering pursuing a master's degree. The mother of 4 and great-grandmother of 15 began taking classes after her husband died in 1972. Instead of viewing aging and her husband's death as setbacks, Ochs forged ahead: She had always yearned for a college education but was too busy raising the children on the family's farm (Lagorio, 2007). Her determination shows that throughout the life course, we have choices and need not be overwhelmed by constraints.

Are older people like Nola Ochs typical of most Americans? Probably not, but as we continue into the twenty-first century, more older people are vigorous and productive. Before you read any further, take the quiz in the "Ask Yourself" box on the next page to see how much you already know about our aging population.

As this chapter shows, aging changes older people, their families, and friends. Let's begin with a brief look at some demographic characteristics of our aging society.

DATA DIGEST

- The **percentage of the U.S. population older than age 65 has been increasing steadily:** 4 percent in 1900, 5 percent in 1920, 7 percent in 1940, 9 percent in 1960, and 13 percent in 2010. It is expected to grow to 16 percent by 2020.

- The **oldest-old** (people age 85 and older) are a small but growing group. In 2010, they made up 2 percent of the U.S. population, compared with 0.6 percent in 1900.

- The **average U.S. life expectancy** was 47 in 1900, 68 in 1950, and 78 in 2008 (80.4 years for women and 75.4 years for men).

- The **percentage of racial and ethnic minorities age 65 and older** in the U.S. population will increase from 19 percent in 2009 to 25 percent in 2030 and to 32 percent by 2050.

- American **grandparents are raising or helping raise more than 7.5 million children,** a 30 percent increase in the past 15 years.

- Over a lifetime, **medical costs are highest in the last 25 or so years of life:** 8 percent from birth to age 19; 12 percent from ages 20 to 39; 31 percent from ages 40 to 64; 37 percent from ages 65 to 84; and 12 percent for ages 85 and older.

- By 2015, worldwide and for the first time in history, **people ages 65 and older will outnumber children younger than age 5.**

Sources: Clarke, 2008; Federal Interagency Forum on Aging-Related Statistics, 2008; U.S. Census Bureau, 2008; "Grandparents Day," 2009; Kinsella and He, 2009.

Nola Ochs, 95, and her 21-year-old granddaughter, Alexandra, were in the same graduating class at Fort Hays State University in Kansas. Ochs plugged along over 35 years by taking correspondence courses and finally finishing at the university. When she was handed her degree, the crowd gave her a standing ovation, breaking a rule against applauding until the names of all 2,176 graduates had been read.

OUR AGING SOCIETY

In 1800, your chance of living to 100 was roughly 1 in 20 million; today it's 1 in 500 (Jeune and Vaupel, 1995, and author's calculations). Despite the high incidence of illnesses such as cancer and heart disease, more people are reaching age 65 than ever before. For example, American children born in 2007 have a **life expectancy**, the average length of time people of the same age will live, of almost 78 years compared with 47 years in 1900 and 71 years in 1970 (U.S. Census Bureau, 2007). As a result, the number of people age 65 and older is booming. (Many

researchers use the terms *older, aged, older people,* and sometimes *elderly* interchangeably.)

Despite our record high life expectancy in the United States, it falls short of 30 other countries' longevity rates. In 2008, for example, Japan and Singapore had a life expectancy of 82 years, and developing countries such as Costa Rica and Chile had a life expectancy of 77 years, just slightly lower than that of the United States. The life expectancy gaps between the United States and other countries have been attributed to factors such as high obesity rates, high infant mortality rates, and the lack of health coverage for all people (Stobbe, 2008; Kinsella and He, 2009; see, also, Chapter 11 on U.S. infant mortality rates).

> **Since you asked . . .**
> ❖ How does a longer life expectancy affect U.S. society?

The Growth of the Older Population

The older population has been increasing steadily since 1900 (see Data Digest). A graying America has several important implications for our society, especially a shrinking younger population, and, consequently, an expanding old-age dependency ratio.

THE SHRINKING YOUNGER POPULATION While the number of older Americans has increased, the proportion of younger people has decreased. By 2030, there will be only slightly more younger people than older people in the United States (see *Figure 17.1*). As a result, the years of parent-child relationships will be prolonged. Many adult children will care for frail older parents, and many young children will

---

ASK YOURSELF

How Much Do You Know about Aging?

The items in this quiz refer to people age 65 and older.

True   False
- ☐   ☐   **1.** Older adults are generally more depressed than younger people.
- ☐   ☐   **2.** Social contacts increase as people get older.
- ☐   ☐   **3.** Most older people become preoccupied with memories of their youth and childhood.
- ☐   ☐   **4.** The five senses (sight, hearing, taste, touch, smell) all tend to weaken in old age.
- ☐   ☐   **5.** A majority of older people have no interest in, nor capacity for, sexual relations.

True   False
- ☐   ☐   **6.** Retirement is usually more difficult for women than for men.
- ☐   ☐   **7.** The older I get, the sicker I'll get.
- ☐   ☐   **8.** Older people are usually more patient than younger people.
- ☐   ☐   **9.** People age 85 and older are more likely to die of Alzheimer's than of any other disease.
- ☐   ☐   **10.** Older people are more likely than teenagers or young adults to commit suicide.

The answers to this quiz are on page 477.

FIGURE 17.1 The Young and the Old, 1900 to 2030

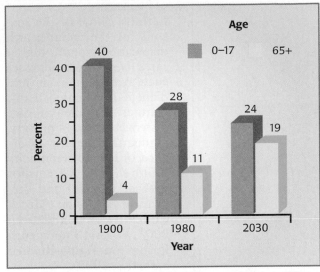

Source: Based on U.S. Senate Special Committee on Aging et al., 1991: 9, and U.S. Census Bureau, 2008.

TABLE 17.1	Old-Age Dependency Ratios: 1980 to 2030
Year	Older Support Ratio
1980	19.9
1990	21.4
2000	21.1
2010	21.7
2020	28.4
2030	36.2

Source: Based on He et al., 2005, Table 2-4.

have not only great-grandparents but also great-great-grandparents.

Gerontologists—scientists who study the biological, psychological, and social aspects of aging—emphasize that the aging population should not be lumped into one group. Instead, there are significant differences between the **young-old** (ages 65 to 74), the **old-old** (ages 75 to 84), and the **oldest-old** (age 85 and older) in living independently, working, and requiring health care.

One of the fastest-growing groups is the oldest-old, a population that increased from 100,000 in 1900 to 5.4 million in 2008. By 2030, this group will constitute almost 6 percent of the country's population. By 2020, about 135,000 Americans will be **centenarians**, people who are 100 years old or older (He et al., 2005; Federal Interagency Forum on Aging-Related Statistics, 2008; U.S. Census Bureau, 2008).

The percentage of older people is important in every society because older people are more likely than those who are younger to depend on the family, the government, or both, for financial, physical, and emotional support. As the number of older people increases, so does the old-age dependency ratio.

THE GROWING OLD-AGE DEPENDENCY RATIO The **old-age dependency ratio** (sometimes called a *dependency ratio*, an *age dependency ratio*, or a *support ratio*) is the number of people age 65 and older who are not in the labor force per 100 people ages 20 to 64 who are employed. In 2000, the old-age dependency ratio was 21, about one older person for every five working-age people. By 2030, this ratio is expected to be 36, which means that, unless older people continue working, fewer than three

working-age people will be supporting each older person (see *Table 17.1*).

As you saw in Chapter 13, unemployment rates have risen, and millions of Americans must accept part-time work or lower earnings. Even if the economy improves in the future, there will be a gender gap among older Americans.

The Gender Gap

As in most industrialized countries around the world, in the United States women live longer than men, and the proportion of older women increases with age. Women begin to outnumber men at about age 35, but the gender gap widens at age 70 and older (see *Figure 17.2*).

Women tend to live longer than men for a variety of reasons, especially gender roles and lifestyles. Compared with men, for example, women are more likely to seek medical attention, especially during their childbearing and postmenaupausal years, and to work fewer years in stressful jobs (see Chapter 13).

Men's more risky unhealthy behaviors are a major reason they die younger. Their higher rates of cigarette smoking, heavy drinking, gun use, employment in hazardous occupations, and risk taking in recreation and driving are responsible for many males' higher death rates due to lung cancer, accidents, suicide, and homicide. Men have historically had higher mortality rates, but the gender gap has narrowed during the last few decades. This change reflects women's increased smoking, use of alcohol and other drugs, and stresses related to multiple roles such as employment and caring for children and older family members (Yin, 2007).

Growing Racial and Ethnic Diversity

America's older population is more racially and ethnically diverse than ever before, reflecting changes in U.S. society over the past several decades. Our immigration rates are the highest in the world. Also,

FIGURE 17.2 Sex Ratio of Americans, by Age

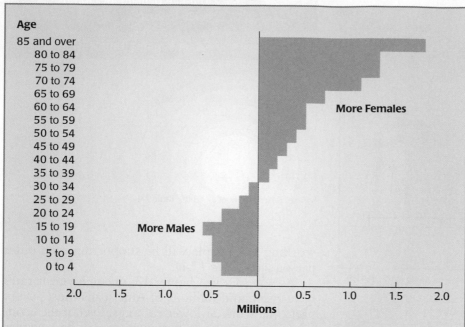

Note: The sex ratio is the number of men per 100 women (see Chapter 9).
Source: He et al., 2005, Figure 2–20.

because many racial and ethnic groups tend to have higher birth rates than whites, the ethnic population age 65 and older is expected to grow from 16 percent in 2000 to 36 percent in 2050 (see *Figure 17.3*).

Life expectancy has increased for all groups over the years, but the health status of racial and ethnic minorities lags far behind that of whites. In 2006, for example, 39 percent of white adults age 65 and older reported being in very good or excellent health, compared with 24 percent of blacks and 29 percent of Latinos. Some of the reasons for the racial health disparities include higher rates of chronic illnesses such as hypertension and diabetes and limited, if any, contact with health care systems because of poverty, inadequate health insurance, or limited community health services (Centers for Disease Control and Prevention and the Merck Company Foundation, 2007; Federal Interagency Forum on Aging-Related Statistics, 2008).

High rates of young immigrants have stabilized the old-age dependency ratio, but they, too, age. Low-skilled workers with low-paying jobs are the least likely to seek early treatment for chronic illnesses, but they will require medical care as they age (Population Reference Bureau, 2008).

Across all racial-ethnic groups, living longer has created millions of **later-life families,** families that are beyond the child-rearing years who have launched their children, or child-free families that are beginning to plan for retirement. As later-life families age, they experience a variety of physical and social changes.

FIGURE 17.3 Population Age 65 and Older, by Race and Ethnicity, 2000 and 2050

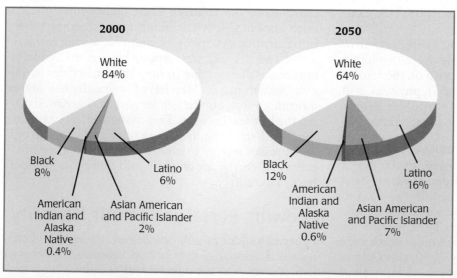

Source: "Older Americans 2000 . . .," 2000: 4.

HEALTH AND AGEISM

Every other summer, the National Senior Games Association, founded in 1985, sponsors the National Senior Games, the largest multisport event in the world for people age 50 and older. In 2009, almost 10,000 athletes from many countries competed in more than 800 events, including cycling, swimming, pole vaulting, tennis, and track and field (Chase, 2009). Why, however, does the association define senior athletes as those age 50 and older rather than 65 and older? Recently, for example, one of our friends, 53, was shocked and insulted when he ordered a meal at a fast food restaurant, and the worker called out "one senior meal!"

When Is "Old"?

What images come to mind when you hear words such as "old," "older," "aged," or "senior"? About a year before my mother died, she remarked, "It's very strange. When I look in the mirror, I see an old woman, but I don't recognize her. I know I'm 85, but I feel at least 30 years younger." She knew her health was failing; yet my mother's identity, like that of many older people, came from within, despite her chronological age.

For sociologists, age is largely a social construction. In societies where people rarely live past 50 (because of HIV/AIDS in many African nations, for example), 40 is old. In industrialized societies, where the average person lives to at least 75, 40 is considered young. Our perception and definition of old also depends on our age. A recent study of Americans age 18 and older found, perhaps not surprisingly, that the older people were, the more likely they were to define old at a later age (see *Figure 17.4*).

Whether people feel middle-aged or old depends on a number of factors, including personality, social status, and, perhaps most important, health. Still, and regardless of how we feel, society usually defines old in chronological age. In the United States, people are typically deemed old at age 65, 66, or 67 because they can retire and become eligible for Medicare and full Social Security benefits. Let's look first at physical and mental health and then at societal stereotypes about older people.

Physical Health

Almost every year, journalists discover a small town, village, or island where a large proportion of the people are age 90 or older and have few debilitating illnesses. A recent example is Ikaria, a small Greek island, where one of three of the 8,000 inhabitants reaches age 90 (compared with about one in 10 in the United States). Ikarians, like their long-living counterparts in other parts of the world, credit their long life to very similar reasons: unpolluted air; pure groundwater; a lean diet, especially homegrown vegetables; daily naps; good genes; working all day;

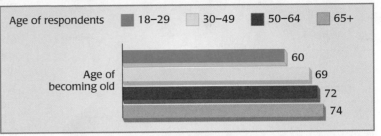

FIGURE 17.4 Perceptions of Who is Old, by Age, 2009

Percentage of responses to the question "At what age does the average person become old?"

Note: The number at the end of each bar shows the age at which respondents said that people were old.

Source: Taylor et al., 2009b, p. 21.

little intermarriage with outsiders; strong family networks that provide financial, emotional, and social help throughout life; and a daily glass or two of red wine (Buettner, 2005, 2009).

More than 43 percent of Americans ages 65 to 74 and 35 percent of those age 75 and older report being in very good or excellent health (Pleis and Lethbridge-Çejku, 2007). Far from becoming frail and losing their independence, nearly half of Americans ages 80 and older appear to enjoy generally good physical as well as mental health, and most live in their own homes. There is a decline in physical mobility once a person gets into his or her 90s, but the majority in this group also enjoys good mental health and continues to live independently (Saad, 2006).

According to conventional wisdom, most baby boomers (people born between 1946 and 1964) will retire in robust health. Such assumptions are fanned by journalists' (many of whom are themselves baby boomers) constant portrayal of boomers engaging in physical activity such as cycling, jogging, or exercising at gyms. However, a recent national study that compared Americans ages 51 to 56 (the boomers) with those who were in their mid and late sixties found that the boomers reported more difficulty with a range of everyday tasks as well as more pain, chronic ailments (such as diabetes and heart disease), more drinking, more mental health problems, and were more likely to be overweight or obese. The researchers noted that perhaps boomers report more health problems because they have unrealistic views of their aging bodies, but they concluded that the trend "portends poorly for the future health of Boomers as they age and incur increasing costs

Answers to "How Much Do You Know about Aging?"

Odd-numbered statements are **false**; even-numbered statements are **true**. The answers are based on the material in this chapter.

The people of Sardinia, Italy, and Okinawa, Japan, have the largest percentage of centenarians in the world. The centenarians credit their long life to a lean diet and staying active, such as the older Okinawan women practicing their local dance pictured here.

associated with health care and medications" (Soldo et al., 2006: 17).

PHYSICAL DECLINE IS NORMAL For a 90-year-old retired diplomatic correspondent, a long life comes down to "keeping your heart pumping, your noodle active, and your mood cheery" (Roberts, 2001: 16). Researchers agree, but physical decline is normal and inevitable among people in all age groups. A gradual process of physical deterioration begins during one's late 30s, affecting all of the body's systems: Reflexes slow, hearing and eyesight dim, and stamina and muscle strength decrease. No matter how well tuned we keep our bodies, the parts eventually wear down.

Some older people are healthier than others, of course. According to some gerontologists, living a long life (including becoming a centenarian) depends on a number of variables: About 50 percent is based on lifestyle, 30 percent on genes, and 20 percent on other factors, especially social class (Schneider, 2002). We can't change our genes or often our social class, but we can live longer and better by changing our lifestyles.

HOW TO LIVE LONGER AND BETTER A number of medical researchers have followed people's health from their 70s to their 90s and later and have drawn similar conclusions. Their findings can be condensed to a few rules about living to old age and staying relatively healthy:

- *Exercise physically.* Exercise increases blood and oxygen flow to the brain, which, in turn, cleanses the body of impurities and decreases the risk of disease and death.
- *Exercise mentally.* The brain is like a muscle that grows stronger with use. You can keep

your brain fit by engaging in behaviors that increase thinking, such as playing board games, playing musical instruments, doing crossword puzzles, and reading.

- *Lose weight and don't smoke.* Smoking and obesity are linked to diabetes, heart disease, some cancers, and arthritis, among other diseases.
- *Watch what you eat.* Eating a diet that includes fruit, vegetables, whole grains, and nuts while avoiding food that contains saturated fats is healthy at any age. Well before we reach 65, fat concentrates around vital organs and increases the risk of disease.
- *Control your blood pressure and avoid diabetes.* High blood pressure increases the likelihood of stroke, heart attack, and kidney failure. Diabetes, which affects every organ in the body, can cause blindness and kidney and heart failure.
- *Establish strong social networks.* Social relationships lower blood pressure (which decreases the risk of stroke) and reduces stress, anxiety, and depression (Tucker et al., 2005; Manini et al., 2006; Hall, 2008; Yates et al., 2008).

Following these rules won't ensure living to 100 because medical treatment also increases the chances of living longer and well. For example, a nationwide study of 739 women and men age 97 and older found that medications helped people even with chronic illnesses such as heart disease and diabetes delay serious disabilities. Many of these people were in fairly good physical health for their age already, but quitting smoking, exercising regularly, and taking the prescribed medications correctly enhanced their quality of life (Terry et al., 2008).

Mental Health

Americans are living longer, but are they happy? The mass media routinely feature articles on aging-related mental health problems such as depression and dementia. However, several recent national studies have challenged the stereotype that youth and young adulthood are the best times of life.

AGING AND HAPPINESS When researchers examine how happy people are at various ages, older people generally come out ahead. For example, those born earlier in the twentieth century are more likely than those born later, including baby boomers, to say that they are very happy (see *Figure 17.5*). It appears, then, that happiness often increases with age, but why?

One reason may be that happiness is affected by the social and economic pressures that a generation of people faces. For example, those who survived the

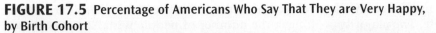

FIGURE 17.5 Percentage of Americans Who Say That They are Very Happy, by Birth Cohort

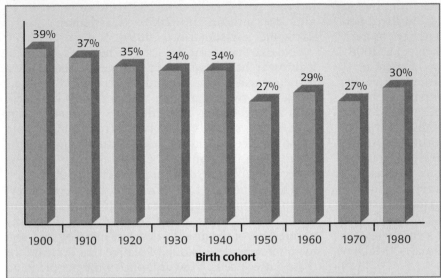

Birth cohort

Note: A *birth cohort* is a group of people born during a particular period or year, such as those born in 1980.
Source: Based on Yang, 2008b, Table 1.

hardships of the Great Depression and World War II (see Chapter 3) now live more comfortably than they had expected because of pensions, Social Security, and Medicare. A second and related reason is that people from earlier birth cohorts had lower expectations about the future than those born in later cohorts, especially the 1960s to 1980s, when the economy was strong and educational and job opportunities expanded. Third, as people age, they experience more health problems, but especially in their 70s, they feel more socially connected because they have stronger religious, family, and friend networks that improve their sense of well-being (Yang, 2008a; Yang, 2008b; Cagley, 2009).

One researcher describes baby boomers as "the gloomiest generation" because they are more pessimistic about their lives than are adults who are younger or older. Many baby boomers grew up in comfortable homes and were raised to believe that they could achieve anything. In addition, baby boomers, compared with younger and older age groups, have enjoyed higher median household incomes, have been less likely to be laid off, have had less trouble paying for medical care or housing, and are more likely to own stocks or bonds and to have retirement accounts. They are gloomier than other age groups, however, because they had very high expectations. Among other realities, many haven't attained the highest rung in their occupation, have had to compete all their lives with other baby boomers, feel financially stretched because of the sandwich phase of life during which they are supporting both children and aging parents, worry about

living comfortably in retirement, and, most of all, fear growing old (Cohn, 2008).

Two of the most common mental health problems among older people are depression and dementia. Depression is easier to spot and more treatable than dementia, but both have a negative impact on individuals and their families.

DEPRESSION *Depression* is a mental disorder characterized by pervasive sadness and other negative emotions that interfere with the ability to work, study, sleep, eat, and enjoy formerly pleasurable activities (see Chapter 14). Depression affects 14 percent of Americans age 65 and older compared with 9 percent of young adults ages 20 to 29. As people age, depression increases—from 13 percent for people ages 65 to 74 to 19 percent for those age 85 and older (Federal Interagency Forum on Aging-Related Statistics, 2008; National Center for Health Statistics, 2009).

Scientists believe that depression is due to a combination of genetic, personal history, and environmental factors. Older people who weather multiple stressful life experiences or crises (such as divorce, losing a job, or ongoing health and financial problems) are more likely to develop depression. Medical illnesses such as a stroke, a heart attack, cancer, Parkinson's disease, and hormonal disorders can lead to depression because of physical changes in the body. Depression can also be a side effect of some medications (Strock, 2002; Caspi et al., 2003).

Many baby boomers, believing that they can slow down the aging process, join health spas and gyms to exercise regularly.

DEMENTIA Dementia is the loss of mental abilities that most commonly occurs late in life. The majority of older adults don't experience dementia, but its prevalence increases with age, rising from 1 to 2 percent among those ages 65 to 74 to 30 percent or more among those age 85 or older (Chapman et al., 2006).

The most common form of dementia is **Alzheimer's disease,** a progressive, degenerative disorder that attacks the brain and impairs memory, thinking, and behavior. People age 65 and older are nine times more likely to die of heart disease than of Alzheimer's (Federal Interagency Forum on Aging-Related Statistics, 2008). Nevertheless, Alzheimer's has generated an enormous literature because the patients live an average of 10 years after the illness is diagnosed, and the emotional and financial costs for family members can be devastating. According to some estimates, by 2050 Alzheimer's care will cost Medicare more than $1 trillion annually (McDermott, 2007).

In 2007, about 5.1 million older Americans had Alzheimer's, but the disease afflicts only a small proportion of this population: 1 percent of people ages 65 to 69, 2 percent of those 70 to 74, 5 percent of those 75 to 79, 9 percent of those 80 to 84, and 18 percent of those age 85 or older. According to some estimates, because Americans are living longer, the number of people with Alzheimer's will increase to 7.7 million in 2030 and to between 11 and 16 million in 2050 (Castleman, 2007; Alzheimer's Association, 2009).

No one knows the cause of Alzheimer's, but medical researchers have linked it to genes that cause a dense deposit of protein and debris called "plaque," along with twisted protein "tangles" that kill nerve cells in the brain. According to neuroscientists, Alzheimer's spreads quickly, destroying more and more brain cells as it progresses. After two years, the disease engulfs almost the entire brain in some patients (Reilly, 2000; Thompson et al., 2003).

There is no cure for Alzheimer's, but there are several promising experimental drugs (among dozens that are being tested) that seem to slow down the progression of the disease, decrease memory loss, and might prevent the buildup of plaque that destroys the brain's nerve cells. Howard, one of the people in an experimental clinical trial, was a 77-year-old successful entrepreneur who was diagnosed with Alzheimer's four years earlier. After he took the drug MPC-7869 for 18 months, his wife reported that "He's living a normal life. Howard makes his breakfast, reads newspapers, goes out to dinner with friends, and plays

Applying What You've Learned

‡• Ten Warning Signs of Alzheimer's Disease

The Alzheimer's Association (www.alz.org) provides a list of symptoms that warrant medical evaluation. Have you seen any of these symptoms in family members or friends?

1. **Memory loss:** Although it's normal to forget names or telephone numbers, people with dementia forget such things more often and do not remember them later (for example, "I never made that doctor's appointment").

2. **Difficulty performing familiar tasks:** Not knowing the steps involved in preparing a meal, using a household appliance, or participating in a lifelong hobby.

3. **Problems with language:** Forgetting simple words. If someone with Alzheimer's can't find his or her toothbrush, for example, the person may ask for "that thing for my mouth."

4. **Disorientation to time and place:** Becoming lost on your own street, forgetting where you are and how you got there, and not knowing how to get back home.

5. **Poor or decreased judgment:** Dressing regardless of the weather, such as wearing several sweaters on a hot day or very little clothing in cold weather. Showing poor judgment about money, such as giving away large amounts of money to telemarketers or paying for home repairs or products one doesn't need.

6. **Problems with abstract thinking:** In balancing a checkbook, for example, someone with Alzheimer's could forget completely what the numbers are and what should be done with them.

7. **Misplacing things:** Putting things in unusual places, such as an iron in the freezer or a wristwatch in the sugar bowl.

8. **Changes in mood or behavior:** Showing rapid mood swings—from calm to tears or anger—for no apparent reason.

9. **Changes in personality:** Becoming extremely confused, suspicious, fearful, or suddenly very dependent on a family member.

10. **Loss of initiative:** Becoming very passive, such as sitting in front of the television for hours, sleeping much of the time, or not wanting to engage in usual activities.

with his grandchildren." When the researchers took him off the drug for five weeks, Howard said that he immediately regressed, becoming confused and depressed (Basler, 2007: 11). There's no way of knowing, however, how Howard fared compared with other people in the study because the results haven't been published in a peer-reviewed journal.

MEMORY LAPSE OR ALZHEIMER'S? During a recent interview, director Spike Lee commented that he must be getting old. When he watched one of his most recent movies, Lee said, "There was stuff I forgot we shot." When a reporter suggested that this might be a symptom of the early onset of Alzheimer's, Lee replied, "I've got Sometimers. Sometimes I remember and sometimes I forget" (Gostin, 2006: 70).

Like Lee, all of us experience memory slips such as misplacing car keys or cell phones, forgetting someone's name, or being unable to recall the name of a movie we saw a few weeks ago. The symptoms of Alzheimer's are much more severe (see the box "Ten Warning Signs of Alzheimer's Disease").

Some scientists are finding that depression and dementia (including Alzheimer's), which usually go hand in hand, may be due to the shrinkage of a certain area of the brain in old age. However, a number of studies report that regular exercise throughout life and avoiding obesity, especially during middle age, may prevent or at least delay the onset of dementia and even the forgetfulness often associated with normal aging (Whitmer et al., 2005; Simon et al., 2006; Wang et al., 2006). It appears, then, that our behavior affects how we age.

Ageism and Stereotypes

The late writer and feminist Betty Friedan, who died at the age of 85, admitted that her reaction to turning 60 was anything but jubilant:

"When my friends threw a surprise [birthday] party . . . I could have killed them all. Their toasts seemed [to be] . . . pushing me out of life . . . out of the race. Professionally, politically, personally, sexually . . . I was depressed for weeks" (Friedan, 1993: 13).

In our youth-oriented society, many people dread growing old because it results in exclusionary behavior. Americans often equate old age with disease and physical appearance with health and believe that we can control our appearance and health through exercise, pills, and beauty products. A major consequence of such beliefs is that "we stigmatize and exclude those who show signs of advancing age" and treat them unequally (Calasanti, 2007: 338).

FEAR OF AGING Aging is normal and inevitable, but it is often viewed as a disease. One of the best examples of negative attitudes about growing old is the deluge of antiaging beauty products and services that flood stores and Internet sites. Antiaging websites routinely tell visitors that "anyone who desires a more youthful appearance can have one" or that "aging is a treatable condition that can be slowed or reversed" (Calasanti, 2007: 342).

According to one physician, cosmetic surgery is a multi-million-dollar industry because many people don't want to look their age. In reality, cosmetic surgery doesn't restore your looks but is "repair work" for those who look old prematurely because of lifestyle decisions such as sunbathing, smoking, alcohol and drug abuse, or lack of exercise (McDaniel, 2006).

Do antiaging products work? No. In one five-month period, for example, 40,000 people sent complaints to the Federal Trade Commission (FTC) after one solicitor promised that his "human growth hormone" pills—at $80 a month—would regrow hair, remove wrinkles, increase muscle mass, reduce weight, and otherwise stop or reverse the aging process. An FTC attorney who settled some of the lawsuits remarked that "People would have gotten more growth hormones eating a steak" (Kirchheimer, 2005: 36).

According to scientists, there is no known way to stop, slow, or reverse human aging. Why, then, are antiaging products and services so popular? A major reason is that many Americans fear aging in a society that celebrates youth. As a result, we spend billions of dollars every year on "anti-aging quackery, hucksterism, and snake oil" that promises a fountain of youth (Perls, 2004: B682; see, also, Olshansky et al., 2004a, 2004b).

AGEISM In his classic book *Why Survive? Being Old in America,* physician Robert Butler (1975) coined

The Zimmers may be the world's oldest rock band. In 2009, the British group, composed of about 40 people, had a 92-year-old lead singer and a combined age of more than 3,000 years.

Don't "Sweetie," "Dear," and "Young Lady" Me!

Here's how a woman in her late 70s describes, angrily, a recent incident at one of the huge do-it-yourself home improvement stores when she was looking for a replacement part for her toilet tank:

I stopped at the front desk to inquire where I could find the particular item. The thirtysomething clerk looked at me and then made an announcement over the loudspeaker, "Will someone from plumbing please escort this young lady to aisle 14?"

I looked around to see who else was looking for the same thing that I was. Then I realized that the clerk meant me when he referred to "this young lady." In that brief moment, I suddenly became aware that it was I who was the object of his condescending description (Immel, 2006: 18).

She is not alone in experiencing such condescension. Many older people, especially women, say that it rankles them when store clerks, waiters, and others address them as "dear," "sweetie," or "young lady." "People think they're being nice," says an 83-year-old woman, "but when I hear 'dear,' it raises my hackles" (Leland, 2008: A1).

A 68-year-old police psychologist fumed when people called her "young lady," which she described as "mocking and disingenuous." To discourage such belittlement, she says that she often sprinkles her conversation with profanities when she is among people who don't know her: "That makes them think this is someone to be reckoned with. A little sharpness seems to help" (Leland, 2008: A1).

According to a columnist at the *Christian Science Monitor,* journalists who write about retirement and aging are in a quandary about how to refer to those in their midlife and later years because they realize that the words they use help define and shape attitudes in both positive and negative ways. The top choice seems to be "older," followed by "seniors." "Boomers" is fine, but not "baby boomers" because this generation is no longer babies. "Older" seems to grate the most, "the older" implies frailty and decline, but "elders" conveys respect (Gardner, 2007: 15).

⁞⁞• Stop and Think. . . .

■ Do you agree or disagree with older people who are offended by being addressed or referred to as "dear," "young lady," or "older"? Or do you think that people are being too sensitive?

■ Do you think that there is anything older people can do to counteract the words and phrases that they find demeaning?

■ How do you think we should refer to old people? And what do *you* mean by old?

---

the term **ageism** to refer to discrimination against people on the basis of age, particularly against older people. Among other things, Butler pointed out the persistence of the "myth of senility," the notion that if old people show forgetfulness, confusion, and inattention, they are senile.

If a 16-year-old boy can't remember why he went to the refrigerator, we say he's "off in the clouds" or in love; if his 79-year-old grandfather forgets why he went to the refrigerator, we're likely to call him senile. Our language is full of ageist words and phrases that stereotype and generally disparage older people: "biddy," "old bat," "old bag," "old fart," "old fogey," "old goat," "dirty old man," "geezer," and "over the hill" (see Palmore, 1999, for examples of historical and current ageist terms and humor). Older people are especially annoyed by ageist language that they believe devalues and demeans them. The box "Don't 'Sweetie,' 'Dear,' and 'Young Lady' Me!" examines some of this belittling language.

STEREOTYPES When you turn on the TV, what kinds of images of older people do you see? Probably those complaining about their health, such as bladder problems, dentures, diabetes, and other diseases. The media create and perpetuate negative images of aging. For example, less than 2 percent of prime-time television characters are age 65 or older, even though this group accounts for almost 13 percent of the population. Even then, only one-third of the older characters are women (International Longevity Center, 2006; see, also, Cruiksbank, 2003).

Children as young as 5 years old often have negative stereotypes of older people and see them as incompetent (Kwong See and Rasmussen, 2003). Young adults also have many stereotypes about getting old. For example, a recent national survey found that 63 percent of those ages 18 to 29 said that most older people experience memory loss, but only 25 percent of people age 65 and older sometimes do so (Taylor et al., 2009b).

A common stereotype is that older people are stuck in the past and have outdated interests and skills. In 2008, in fact, regular Internet users included large numbers of seniors: 56 percent of those 65 to 69, 45 percent of those 70 to 75, and 27 percent of people age 76 and older. A major reason for older people's not being online is the cost of computers and monthly fees for high-speed Internet connections rather than disinterest or fear of new technologies (Jones and Fox, 2009; Morales, 2009).

AGING AND PERSONALITY One of the most common stereotypes is that people become nasty as they age. In reality, most people's personalities are fairly stable throughout life (Belsky, 1988). If you're grumpy or unpleasant at 75, you were probably grumpy and unpleasant at 15, 35, and 55. Work, marriage, and other life experiences affect people, but generally those who are hostile, anxious, or self-centered in their 20s are likely to be hostile, anxious, or self-centered in old age.

Since you asked . . .

:::• Do most people become nastier as they age?

Our personalities aren't set in cement, however. As people mature, they often become more conscientious (organized and disciplined), more agreeable (warm and helpful), and less neurotic (prone to constant worry and emotional instability). As people become more aware of the limited time they have left to live, they tend to focus more on positive thoughts, activities, and memories than do people ages 18 to 53 (Charles et al., 2003; Srivastava et al., 2003).

Even if personalities are fairly stable over the life course, behavior can change. For example, and contrary to the popular notion that people become more stubborn as they age, seniors are usually more flexible than younger people. Older people are more likely to avoid confrontation and to be patient and less critical when there are interpersonal problems. In many stressful situations, older adults are more likely than young and midlife adults to do nothing rather than to argue or yell (Birditt et al., 2005; Birditt and Fingerman, 2005).

If some people seem harder to deal with as they age, it may be because they become less docile and submissive. When older people "suddenly" seem stubborn and defiant, they may simply be shedding some long-term inhibitions:

One of the greatest thrills of being a woman of 70 is having the luxury to be open about what I really think. When I was younger, I was so afraid of hurting people or worried about what they would think of me that I . . . kept my mouth shut. Now when I don't like something, I speak up. . . . Age has made me more truthful. And that's one of the reasons that I feel better about myself now than I have at any other time in life (Belsky, 1988: 65–66).

:::• MAKING CONNECTIONS

■ Do you use any antiaging products? Or plan to do so in the future? Why or why not?

■ Do you sometimes get impatient or mutter under your breath when older people fumble to pay for purchases in checkout lines or drive more slowly than you do?

As people age, their family roles change. Retirement is a major transition for most older adults, but whether or not older people reenter the labor force (out of either choice or necessity) depends on many factors, such as social class and health.

WORK AND RETIREMENT

In the United States, **retirement,** the exit from the paid labor force, is becoming more elusive. At age 66, Jerry Wood retired from his job as a field engineer, but he had to reenter the workforce two years later. He and his wife have diabetes, his wife suffers from related eye complications that require expensive treatments, and they could no longer cover their high health care costs. They had to move from Alabama to Kansas, where Wood now works at a construction job five days a week (Fleck, 2008).

Wood is one of millions of older Americans who have had to return to work or work much longer than they had expected because they can't afford to retire. According to economists and financial analysts, people who planned to retire at age 66 in 2012 will probably have to keep working for another nine years: They haven't saved enough for retirement to live as comfortably as they'd like to, the recent economic downturns have ravaged the value of their stocks and 401(k) investments, and health care costs keep rising (Gandel, 2009; Morin, 2009).

Since you asked . . .

:::• Why are many Americans rethinking their retirement plans?

Older People Are Working Longer

Anthropologist Margaret Mead once said, "Sooner or later I'm going to die, but I'm not going to retire." True to her word, Mead authored and co-authored several books before she died at age 77. Like Mead, many people work until they die.

Between 1998 and 2008, the share of men age 65 to 69 in the labor force jumped from 28 percent to 36 percent, and women's rates rose just as dramatically—from 18 percent to 26 percent (Lei, 2009). However, the poverty rate for Americans age 65 and older has dropped steadily—from 35 percent in 1959 to less than 10 percent in 2008, and this proportion is now lower than that for any other age group, including children (DeNavas-Walt et al., 2009).

Why, then, are so many older Americans working well past age 65, either full time or part time? Some of the reasons include the following:

■ **Social Security,** a public retirement pension system administered by the federal government, provides income to more than 90 percent of older Americans, but the benefits depend on how long people have been in the labor force and how much they have earned. Because Social Security replaces only about 42 percent of the average older person's preretirement income, many must continue to work (Munnell and Soto, 2005).

- Social Security changes have increased work incentives at older ages. The retirement age for full Social Security benefits increased from 65 to 66 for people born between 1943 and 1954, and gradually will rise to age 67 for those born after 1959. As a result, Americans must work longer to receive full retirement benefits (Mermin et al., 2008b).

- Between mid-2007 and mid-2009, retirement savings decreased, on average, by 31 percent because of the economic downturn that began in mid-2008 (Soto, 2009). Thus, a person age 65 who had $500,000 in a stock portfolio in early 2008 saw the amount plunge to about $333,000 in early 2009, a considerable decrease for someone on the verge of retirement.

- **Medicare,** created in 1965, is a federal health insurance program for people age 65 and older that provides almost universal health coverage. However, the higher one's retirement income, the higher are the monthly premiums. Also, Medicare doesn't cover dental and eye care and long-term care, and coverage of prescription drugs is minimal. This means that low- and middle-income retirees must pay these costs themselves or postpone retirement (Lei, 2009).

- Since the early 1990s, many companies (especially in the steel, airline, and auto industries) have reduced or eliminated their employee pension plans. As a result, many older people, including baby boomers, plan to continue working indefinitely (Mermin et al., 2008b).

Many older Americans work past retirement age because they need the money, but that's not always the case. As *Figure 17.6* shows, a majority of Americans age 65 and older work because they want to do so. Younger and middle-aged workers work because of the usual reasons, such as supporting themselves or their families or receiving health care benefits. In contrast, many older workers emphasize psychological and social factors, such as feeling useful and being with other people (Taylor et al., 2009a).

Many Older Americans Can't Find Work

There are also millions of older Americans who want and need work solely for economic reasons but are unemployed. In mid-2009, for example, almost 7 percent of people age 65 and older were unemployed and actively looking for work, more than twice as many as in late 2007, before the 2008 recession began. In mid-2009, the unemployment rates for those age 65 and older were 8 percent for men and 3 percent for women. These were the highest rates for this age group for men since 1948 and for women since 1992 (Johnson and Mommaerts, 2009).

As the recession deepened, unemployment rates for adults age 55 and older increased across nearly all industries, but more than tripled in construction, mining, agriculture, finance, and information (which includes telecommunications, publishing, and the media). Jobless rates increased for both college-educated older workers and those with limited schooling, but they were twice as high for men who did not complete college as they were for those with a college education. Unemployment rates have been lower for older women than older men but increased considerably for African Americans and Latinos (see *Figure 17.7*). Most of the job losses occurred in industries that don't require a college education, such as construction, manufacturing, and leisure and hospitality (Johnson and Mommaerts, 2009).

Many seniors claim that age discrimination in employment is pervasive, but the data are mixed. About 36 percent of workers age 65 or older are employed as managers and professionals, but 46 percent work in lower-paying occupations such as service, sales, and office/administrative support that are not intellectually stimulating but also not physically demanding. Most employer surveys indicate that firms generally value older workers' knowledge and experience, reliability, and work ethic. The surveys also show, however, that employers often question older workers' creativity, flexibility, and willingness to learn new things. Older workers are also more expensive than their younger counterparts. They usually have higher salaries and wages because they've been working longer. And, on average, in 2005 an employer paid only $2,500 a year for health benefits for a worker ages 30 to 39 compared with about $6,700 a year for those ages 60 to 69 (Mermin et al., 2008b).

FIGURE 17.6 Why Do Many Older Americans Work?

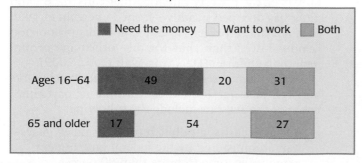

Source: Taylor et al., 2009a, p. 1.

FIGURE 17.7 Unemployment Rates for Americans Age 55 and Older, by Sex and Race, 2007 and 2009

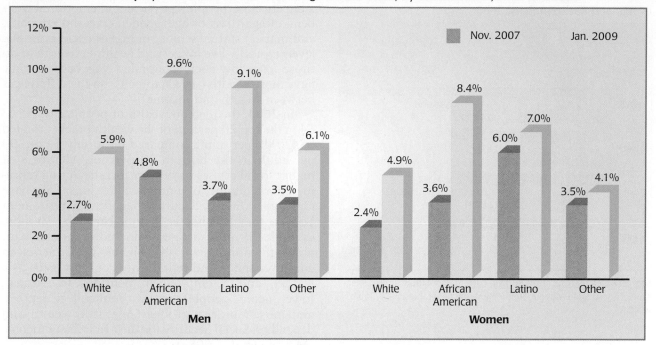

Source: Johnson and Mommaerts, 2009, Figure 4.

Variations in Retirement Income

Older Americans are economically and racially/ethnically diverse. In 2008, the annual median household income for people age 65 and older was almost $29,800, but there were large variations by gender, race and ethnicity, marital status, and social class. (Unless noted otherwise, the data in this section are based on U.S. Census Bureau, Current Population Survey, 2009).

GENDER In every age group, older women have a lower median income than men. For women age 65 and older, the median income in 2008 was about $24,130 a year compared with $33,680 for men in the same age group. Among those age 75 and older, almost twice as many women (13 percent) as men (8 percent) live below the poverty level.

There are many interrelated reasons for women's lower income during the retirement years (Fleck, 2007; "Women live longer but . . .," 2008). Compared with men, for example, women

- Earned less, even in comparable jobs (see Chapters 5 and 13)
- Spent less time in the labor force or never entered because of child-rearing responsibilities
- Didn't contribute at a high enough level to take advantage of the company match, which is typically 50 cents for every dollar up to 6 percent
- Invested more conservatively and started saving later

- Didn't make enough investments because 90 percent were unsure about how to manage their finances
- Withdrew funds before retirement
- Cashed out retirement savings rather than rolling them into other investments when changing jobs

On average, women are likely to live from 6 to 14 years longer than men. As a result, they are more likely than men to run out of financial resources in late life (Yin, 2008).

RACE AND ETHNICITY Older whites and Asian Americans have much higher median incomes than do African Americans and Latinos (see *Figure 17.8*). In 2008, 8.5 percent of whites age 65 and older lived in poverty, compared with 12 percent of Asian Americans and 19 percent of Latinos and 20 percent of African Americans. In this age group, the poorest were black women—16 percent compared with 14 percent of Latinas, 9 percent of Asian American women, and 6 percent of white women.

Among racial-ethnic groups, later life income varies considerably across subgroups. For example, a study of six Asian American groups in the United States age 65 and older found that the income of Japanese Americans was the highest, and very similar to that of older whites, whereas the poorest were older Korean and Vietnamese Americans. The researcher attributed the differences to factors such as educational attainment, household size, and recent immigration. Thus, older

FIGURE 17.8 Median Income of Older Households by Age and Race/Ethnicity, 2008

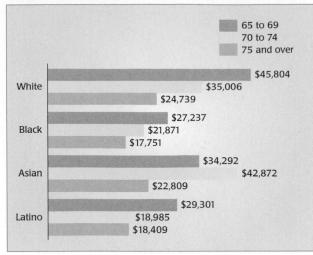

Legend:
- 65 to 69
- 70 to 74
- 75 and over

White
- $45,804
- $35,006
- $24,739

Black
- $27,237
- $21,871
- $17,751

Asian
- $34,292
- $42,872
- $22,809

Latino
- $29,301
- $18,985
- $18,409

Source: Based on U.S. Census Bureau, Current Population Survey, 2009 Annual Social and Economic Supplement, detailed tables, 2008, Table HINC-02.

Japanese Americans had the highest income because they had high education levels, small households (which result in fewer expenses and more savings), and had lived in the United States for at least six generations (Sharpe, 2008).

MARITAL STATUS Married couples have twice the median income of single men and more than twice that of single women. This difference characterizes every age group. Even at age 75 and older, when many people have depleted most of their savings, married couples have an annual income of almost $37,000, compared with $21,300 for single men and $16,000 for single women (Yin, 2008).

Divorced or separated older women are the most vulnerable because they have lower incomes and fewer economic resources. In 2008, the share of women age 65 and older living in poverty was highest among divorced or separated women (37 percent), followed by widows (28 percent), never-married women (22 percent), and married women (10 percent) (Yin, 2008).

Widows age 65 and older fare better than divorced or married women primarily because they usually receive spousal and survivor benefits, can cash in one or more of a late husband's life insurance policies, and inherit other holdings such as a home—the biggest middle-class asset—as well as cars, jewelry, and other property. In contrast, divorced women, especially if they don't get the house or a favorable legal settlement, are generally cut off from their ex-husband's assets (Favreault, 2005; Yin, 2008).

SOCIAL CLASS Social class—which includes education, occupation, and income—is probably the most

important factor in retirement income because it has a big effect on people's physical and emotional well-being. Regardless of age, gender, race and ethnicity, and marital status, seniors in higher socioeconomic levels typically live longer and healthier lives than do those from low socioeconomic levels because they have more wealth (see Chapter 13 on the differences between wealth and income).

In 2004, the median wealth of people ages 55 to 64 in the top 20 percent of the wealth bracket totaled $842,000 per adult compared with only $124,300 per adult in the bottom 20 percent. Members of higher social classes have more income during retirement for a number of interrelated reasons: They have (1) higher Social Security benefits at retirement because they had higher lifetime earnings, (2) more savings, (3) more property (including homes with paid-off mortgages), (4) higher investments in employer-sponsored retirement programs (such as a 401[k]), and (5) employment pensions. In contrast, lower-income people, those without college degrees, and most minority groups have little wealth and depend on Social Security for their retirement income (Mermin et al., 2008a).

Retirement and Marital Happiness

Retirement can affect marital happiness. Health and financial security are major factors in retirees' satisfaction with life, but among married couples, spouses are happier when they make joint decisions about the timing of retirement. For example, wives report less marital satisfaction if their already retired husbands insist that they retire or are always underfoot (Szinovacz and Davey, 2005). "The Retired Husband Syndrome in Japan" box examines a particularly unhappy outcome of many husbands' retirement.

People in higher social classes can enjoy their retirement years rather than having to go back to work or worrying about paying bills and ever-increasing health care costs.

Cross-Cultural and Multicultural Families

The Retired Husband Syndrome in Japan

In Tokyo, Sakura Terakawa, 63, describes her four decades of married life as a gradual transition from wife to mother to servant. Like most men of his generation, Terakawa's husband demanded strict obedience even though he spent his life almost entirely apart from her and their three children. He left home for the office just after dawn and stayed out late socializing after work. He even took most of his vacations with colleagues and clients.

Over the years, Terakawa developed her own life and her own way of doing things. She had many friends and enjoyed her life with the children.

Retirement cut the husband off from his long-time office social network, leaving him practically friendless. Within a few weeks of retirement, he forbade his wife to go out with her friends and criticized her meals and housework. She said she couldn't stand to look at her husband across the table and sat at an angle so she could stare out a window instead.

Within a few months, Terakawa developed stomach ulcers and polyps

in her throat, her speech began to slur, and rashes broke out around her eyes. When doctors couldn't find a medical reason for the symptoms, they referred her to a well-known Japanese psychiatrist, who diagnosed the problems as stress-related "retired husband syndrome" (RHS).

The psychiatrist estimates that as many as 60 percent of the wives of retired men in Japan suffer from some degree of RHS. Whereas 85 percent of soon-to-retire husbands are delighted by the idea of retirement, 40 percent of their wives describe themselves as depressed by the prospect. RHS may be one of the reasons that divorce rates among older Japanese couples have doubled since 1985.

Older wives are especially likely to experience RHS because the nature of Japanese family life has changed significantly over the past two decades. Members of younger generations are remaining single well into their 40s, and newly married couples, at least in urban areas, refuse to live with retired parents because they want more privacy. As a result, many older wives

must deal with the "curse" of their husband's retirement alone (Faiola, 2005).

Recently, a retired entrepreneur and a few of his colleagues founded a Friendship Network that encourages other older men to take on new roles, especially helping their wives care for aging relatives and persuading older people to stay active. The network had only 2,000 members in 2008, but the group has received monetary support from the government and hopes to thrive (Newcomb, 2008).

⠿ Stop and Think . . .

- Do you think that RHS is unique to Japan, or might it also be common in the United States?

- In 2008, Japan had the largest population (22 percent) of people age 65 and older (Kinsella and He, 2009). Are RHS problems in Japan exaggerated because of cultural gender roles and widespread retirements? Or can we expect similar results in the United States as millions of baby boomers retire?

Retirement is a significant role transition. Well before retirement, however, many adults take on another important role—that of grandparent.

⠿ MAKING CONNECTIONS

- Many women drop out of the labor force to raise children or to care for ill or aging relatives. In doing so, they forgo Social Security benefits later in life. Should the government compensate these women when they reach age 65?

- As you saw, many Americans haven't saved enough or even calculated how much they need for a comfortable retirement. When do *you* plan to retire? How much retirement planning have you done? Do you have enough wealth to retire at age 65, 66, 67, or earlier? If you've already retired, is your income adequate?

GRANDPARENTING

Grandparents are often the glue that keeps a family close. They typically represent stability in family relationships and a continuity of family rituals and values. Grandparents often help their adult children with parenting (such as babysitting) and provide support during emergencies or crises, including illness and divorce (see Szinovacz, 1998, and Smith and Drew, 2002, for good summaries of grandparenting across racial-ethnic groups).

No matter how strict they were with their own children, many grandparents are often family mediators, advocates for their grandchildren's point of view, and shoulders to cry on. Because today's grandparents are generally healthier and wealthier than those of previous generations, they engage in a wide range of activities and spend a fair amount of money on their grandchildren.

Grandparenting Styles

Grandparents usually take great pleasure in their grandchildren. The new role of grandparent often invigorates their lives and provides them with new experiences. There are a number of different grandparenting styles, however. Some of the most common are remote or detached, companionate and supportive, involved and influential, advisory and authoritative, and cultural transmitter.

Since you asked . . .

⠿• How does grandparenting affect grandchildren?

REMOTE OR DETACHED In the *remote or detached* relationship, the grandparents and grandchildren live far apart and see each other infrequently, maintaining a largely ritualistic, symbolic relationship. For example, some grandparents see their grandchildren only on holidays or special occasions. Such relationships may be cordial but are also uninvolved and fleeting (Thompson and Walker, 1991).

Only about 3 percent of grandparents never see their grandchildren and never write to them. The biggest barrier to face-to-face contacts is living too far away. In other cases, grandparents are remote or detached because they're experiencing health problems or their grandchildren's busy schedule makes it difficult to get together (Davies and Williams, 2002).

Grandparents may be close to one grandchild but detached from others. Sometimes grandparents see a particular grandchild as "special" because of the child's personality, accomplishments, or respect for his or her grandparents. Not surprisingly, then, grandparents sometimes spend more time with some grandchildren than with others (Smith and Drew, 2002; Mueller and Elder, 2003).

COMPANIONATE AND SUPPORTIVE The *companionate and supportive* style of grandparenting is the most common pattern. Supportive grandparents see their grandchildren often, frequently do things with them, and offer them emotional and instrumental support (such as giving them money), but they don't seek authority in the grandchild's life. These grandparents are typically on the maternal side of the family, are younger, and have more income than other grandparents, but they avoid getting involved in parental child-rearing decisions (Mueller and Elder, 2003).

Companionate grandparents generally don't want to share parenting and tend to emphasize loving, playing, and having fun. When visiting, grandparents and grandchildren usually spend their time eating together, watching TV shows, shopping for clothes or toys, playing sports, or attending church (Davies and Williams, 2002).

Grandparent–grandchild bonds are especially close, even when a grandchild becomes an adult, if a parent has a good relationship with his or her own

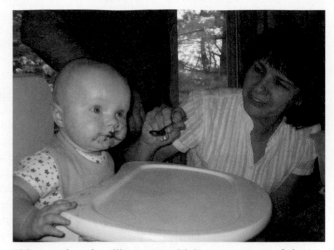

This grandmother illustrates which one or more of the grandparenting styles described in the text?

parents. Also, mothers are more likely than fathers to influence grandparent–grandchild relations with either side of the family. Thus, mothers play a key kin-keeping role in encouraging or discouraging grandparent-grandchild ties (Monserud, 2008).

INVOLVED AND INFLUENTIAL In the *involved and influential* grandparenting style, grandparents play an active role in their grandchildren's lives. They may be spontaneous and playful, but they also exert substantial authority over their grandchildren, imposing definite—and sometimes tough—rules. African American grandmothers, especially, say that they are concerned with teaching their grandchildren the value of education, providing emotional support, and involving them in the extended family and community activities (Gibson, 2005).

In a national survey, 42 percent of the respondents who plan to move after retirement will do so to be closer to their families, especially their grandchildren (Pulte Homes, 2005). Because many retirees may have another 15 healthy years ahead of them, the advantages of seeing their grandchildren grow up outweigh the disadvantages of moving to a new location.

Compared with past generations, many of today's grandfathers are more involved in their grandchildren's daily activities. According to a director of a child care center, for example, "We used to see grandfathers only at special events or in emergencies. Now, every day, grandfathers drive carpools, carry backpacks, and chat with teachers." Grandfathers are particularly influential in single-mother households. When grandfathers are involved, children (especially boys) have fewer social problems, are more self-confident, and do better academically (Zaslow, 2006: D1).

ADVISORY AND AUTHORITATIVE In the fourth type of grandparenting, *advisory and authoritative,* the grandparent serves as an advisor, or what Neugarten and Weinstein (1964) call a "reservoir of family wisdom." The grandfather, who may be the family patriarch, may also act as a financial provider, and the grandmother often plays a crucial advisory role in the grandchildren's lives.

Especially when the mother is very young, the maternal grandmother may help the "apprentice mother" make the transition to parenthood by supporting and mentoring—but not replacing—her in the parenting role. The grandmother provides emotional, financial, and child care support until the apprentice shows that she is responsive to and responsible for the baby (Apfel and Seitz, 1991).

School-age children whose parents suffer from depression or other physical or mental illnesses are at relatively high risk for a number of problems, including depression, misbehavior, substance abuse, and learning difficulties. Grandparents who have strong emotional ties with their grandchildren and are their confidantes reduce the likelihood of such problems, especially depression, when parents suffer from mental health problems, poverty, or stress (Silverstein and Ruiz, 2006).

Even when parents have healthy parenting skills, many adolescents turn to their grandparents for advice or understanding. According to a 17-year-old boy, "With my grandpa we discuss usually technical problems. But sometimes some other problems, too. He told me how to refuse to drink alcohol with other boys." A 16-year-old girl said that she and her grandmother go for walks and added, "I can tell her about everything" (Tyszkowa, 1993: 136). Sometimes the roles reverse, with teenage grandchildren helping their grandparents with errands or chores.

CULTURAL TRANSMITTERS Advisory grandparenting often overlaps with a fifth role, in which grandparents are *cultural transmitters* of values and norms. In American Indian families, for example, grandmothers often teach their grandchildren domestic chores, responsibility, and discipline that reflect tribal tradition. Grandfathers may transmit knowledge of tribal history and cultural practices through storytelling (Woods, 1996; see, also, Chapter 4).

Many recently arrived Asian immigrants live in extended families and are more likely to do so than any other group, including Latinos. In such co-residence, grandparents are often "historians" who transmit values and cultural traditions to their grandchildren even if there are language barriers. Chinese American grandparents, for example, help develop their grandchildren's ethnic identity by teaching them Chinese, passing on traditional practices and customs during holidays, and reinforcing cultural values such as respecting parents and other adults (Tam and Detzner, 1998; Tan, 2004).

Grandparents as Surrogate Parents

A grandparenting role is sometimes that of a *surrogate,* in which a grandparent provides regular care or replaces the parents in raising the grandchildren. Of the 1.5 million children being raised entirely by grandparents, many are white (see *Figure 17.9*).

The increase of grandchildren living with grandparents results from many factors: higher drug abuse by parents, teen pregnancy, divorce, unemployment, a parent's mental illness, child maltreatment or abandonment, and the death or incarceration of parents. Three of the most common groups of surrogate grandparents are custodial, living-with, and day-care grandparents (Jendrek, 1994).

CUSTODIAL GRANDPARENTS *Custodial* grandparents have a legal relationship with their grandchildren through adoption, guardianship, or custody. Most take custody of a grandchild only when a parental situation becomes intolerable. For example, at age 75, actor George Kennedy and his wife, 68, adopted their 5-year-old granddaughter because the little girl's mother could not kick her drug habit. In other cases, grandparents adopt a grandchild after the death of one or both parents.

For custodial grandparents, parenting a second time around is both enjoyable and challenging. It is enjoyable because they are wiser, more experienced, more relaxed, and can spend more time with their grandchildren than they did with their children. On

FIGURE 17.9 Grandparents Raising Grandchildren, 2008

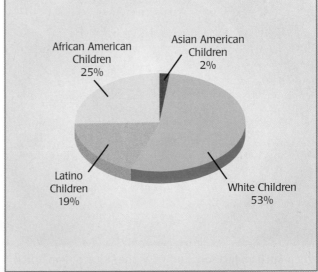

Note: "Other" includes grandchildren whose grandparents are from two or more racial groups.
Source: Based on data in U.S. Census Bureau, 2010 Census ACS U.S. Census ACS Table C4 Children/1 with Grandparents by Presence of Parents, Sex, Race, and Hispanic Origin/2 for Selected Characteristics: 2010 http://www.census.gov/population/www/socdemo/hh-fam/cps2010.html.

the other hand, they have less energy, more health problems, and worry more about their inability to protect their grandchildren from negative peer pressure, drugs and alcohol, and more liberal societal attitudes toward adolescent sex (Bachman and Chase-Landale, 2005; Dolbin-MacNab, 2006).

Grandchildren who were raised solely by grandparents also have mixed feelings about their upbringing. They love and respect their grandparents and are very grateful that they didn't grow up in a foster home. On the other hand, they worry about their grandparents' health and say that their grandparents' age and health problems limited their contacts with friends and participation in many extracurricular activities. They also report much conflict because of a generation gap regarding strict rules about clothes, dating, household chores, and leisure activities (Dolbin-MacNab and Keiley, 2009).

Older custodial grandparents also worry about the long-term care of a child. According to an African American grandfather, "I won't live long enough to see

When Michael Jackson, known as the "King of Pop," died in 2009, a judge named his mother, Katherine Jackson, 79 (pictured here with two of her grandchildren), as the permanent guardian of his three children, ages 7 to 12. Do you think that old-old grandparents (those between ages 75 and 84) should be given custody of their grandchildren?

her grow up because she [the grandchild] is still a baby. My wife might be around, but I probably won't be living to help her out. It worries me" (Bullock, 2005: 50).

LIVING-WITH GRANDPARENTS *Living-with* grandparents typically have the grandchild in their own home or, less commonly, live in the home of a grandchild's parents. Living-with grandparents take on child-rearing responsibilities either because their children have not yet moved out of the house or because teenage or adult parents can't afford to live on their own with their young children. These living arrangements have increased the number of **multigenerational households,** homes in which three or more generations live together. Such households represent almost 4 percent of all American households, up from about 2 percent in 2000 (U.S. Census Bureau, 2008).

In 2010, 7.5 million children lived with a grandparent, and the majority of these children lived in the grandparent's home (see Data Digest). Grandparent-run households are more common among African Americans than among other groups. In these families, children of single mothers have better outcomes than those who live in single-parent homes. Grandparents help young teen mothers, especially, by providing economic and emotional support in school, child care, and work, all of which are beneficial to their daughters' and grandchildren's well-being (DeLeire and Kalil, 2002).

However, grandchildren's outcomes vary depending on other factors. For example, mothers of unmarried adolescent daughters are more sensitive to their young grandchild's needs and interact with an infant more frequently than does the child's teenage mother. Grandparenting can be negative, on the other hand, if the multigenerational household is struggling with finances, the grandmother is also raising her own children, and the grandmother resents her daughter's becoming pregnant at a young age and not being able to raise the child herself (Barnett, 2008).

Children of single mothers who live in a multigenerational household often receive more cognitive stimulation from a grandparent, which increases the grandchildren's language skills and achievement in school. However, such positive outcomes characterize only households in which a grandparent provides an enriching home environment, such as engaging a grandchild in stimulating activities, including reading. If this isn't the case, grandchildren experience few benefits by living in a multigenerational household (Dunifon and Kowaleski-Jones, 2007).

Since the deployment of thousands of young parents to the wars in Iraq and Afghanistan, more grandparents have been taking care of grandchildren full or part time. The grandparents experience a double dose of stress—looking after their grandchildren and worrying about their children's safety overseas (Greider, 2003).

DAY-CARE GRANDPARENTS Because of the high cost of day care, in some families *day-care grandparents* assume responsibility for the physical care of their grandchildren, usually a daughter's, until the parents come home from work. Grandparents care for 30 percent of the children age 5 and younger while the parents are at work ("Grandparents Day," 2009).

African American grandmothers are more likely than their Latina and white counterparts to provide full-time care from the child's birth to age 3. In all ethnic groups, grandparents are most likely to care for these young grandchildren if the mothers are age 28 and younger, have full-time jobs, and work non-standard hours such as evenings and weekends (Vandell et al., 2003).

A national study of children ages 2 to 3 found that those cared for by a grandparent while the parent was working had half the injuries that required medical attention than children in other settings. Even when compared with organized day care or care by the mother or relatives, having a grandmother watch the child was associated with decreased injury for the child (Bishai et al., 2008).

Many grandmothers enjoy caring for their grandchildren, but they often combine caregiving with careers and express emotions ranging from joy and satisfaction to fatigue and resentment. As one grandmother said, "It's very sad that after a lifetime of working full time, grandparents should have a second full-time job of caring for their grandchildren unpaid. . . . Something's wrong here" (Gardner, 2002: 16).

Grandparents and Divorce

Traditionally, divorce meant that a grandparent would have to establish new relationships with the ex-spouse or stepparent. More recently, family ties have shifted because grandparents themselves are getting a divorce.

GRANDPARENTS AND THEIR CHILDREN'S DIVORCE Divorce creates both opportunities and dilemmas for grandparents. Grandparents on the custodial side often deepen their relationships with children and grandchildren, especially when they provide financial assistance, a place to live, and help in child rearing. In contrast, grandparents on the noncustodial side typically have less access to their grandchildren.

Many custodial parents move after the breakup, increasing the visiting distance. Troubled postdivorce relationships often result in a loss of contact between grandchildren and some of their grandparents because the mother feels a closer relationship to her biological kin than to her in-laws (Ganong and Coleman, 1999).

In other cases, because of estrangement or a poor relationship with their child's ex-spouse, grandparents aren't allowed to see their grandchildren. Grandchildren sometimes become pawns, used to punish grandparents for real or imagined misunderstandings and slights.

A divorce can also create unexpected financial burdens for grandparents. If grandparents anticipate being cut off from their grandchildren after the divorce, they may have to petition for visitation rights, thereby incurring legal expenses. In other cases, parents may provide financial help to children, especially daughters, to get a divorce. Such assistance often depletes the parents' savings. As one father noted, "I'm at the age where a lot of my friends are retiring, and I'm spending all my retirement savings on attorneys" (Chion-Kenney, 1991: B5).

GRANDCHILDREN AND THEIR GRANDPARENTS' DIVORCE Among those age 65 and older, in 1960, fewer than 2 percent of older men and women were divorced. In 2009, in contrast, 8 percent of men and 11 percent of women in this age group were divorced. Because divorce rates among older people are increasing, many grandchildren will experience their grandparents' breakup (He et al., 2005; U.S. Census Bureau, 2008).

When grandparents split up, both they and their grandchildren may suffer. Grandparents who divorce don't have as much contact with their grandkids, feel less close to them, and consider the role of grandparent less important in their lives. Grandfathers, especially, have less contact, fewer shared activities, and higher levels of conflict with their grandchildren than do grandmothers who have divorced. However, grandparents who can maintain a good relationship with adult children despite a divorce will be able to establish strong ties to their grandchildren (King, 2003).

Grandparents' Visitation Rights

Whether or not an adult child is divorced, do grandparents have the right to visit a grandchild if the child's parents object? As rates of divorce, out-of-wedlock births, and drug use increased, some states passed laws bolstering the rights of grandparents when parents died, divorced, separated, or were jobless or disabled.

Now the pendulum is swinging back. Because of a perception that parents' rights have eroded, more than a third of the states have narrowed their visitation laws. In some states, grandparents must prove that their visits are beneficial to the emotional, mental, or physical health of a grandchild.

Many parents welcome the changes because they have more control over grandparents' visitation and believe that they can decide what's best for their children. However, many groups argue that grandparents are part of an extended family and should have a right to visitation despite parents' objections, especially when high divorce rates fragment a family (Gearon, 2003).

⁝⁘ MAKING CONNECTIONS

- What are the grandparenting styles in your family? Do they differ depending on the grandparent's age and gender, for example?

- Should grandparents sue for visitation rights with their grandchildren? Or respect a parent's decision even if they disagree?

AGING PARENTS, ADULT CHILDREN, AND SIBLINGS

Most of us are living longer, but are our families happier? Let's examine this question in two areas—aging parents and adult child relationships and sibling ties in later life.

Relationships Between Parents and Adult Children

Parenting becomes less important in most people's daily lives as they age. Parent–child relationships typically last a lifetime, but they vary depending on a number of factors, such as geographic distance, amount of contact, emotional closeness, similar attitudes, and mutual assistance. For example, adult children who live nearby tend to have closer relationships with their aging parents than do those who live many miles away. These adult children often receive financial help and babysitting from their parents and reciprocate by assisting in household chores, especially yard work and home maintenance (Lin and Rogerson, 1995; Silverstein and Bengston, 2001).

Geographic closeness isn't the most critical factor that shapes intergenerational relationships, however. Parents tend to help children whom they see to be in need, especially those who are single, divorced, or widowed at a young age and if grandchildren are involved. For example, divorced daughters with child custody have more contact with their aging parents than married daughters do, and they often receive more help from their parents. Sons, on the other hand, receive more babysitting help from their parents when they are married because the grandparents are involved with their grandchildren. If sons are divorced or cohabiting, grandparents may see their grandchildren less often if the mother gets custody of the children or if the father remarries and starts a new family. In the latter case, the grandparents often split their time between their son's "old" and "new" families (Spitze et al., 1994; see, also, Chapters 15 and 16).

Parent–child relations are usually complex rather than positive, negative, or something in between. They often involve **intergenerational ambivalence**, contradictions that arise both from structured kinship roles

This out-of-town sister participated in a surprise 65th birthday party for her "little brother." She and her daughter compiled a photo album of his childhood and presented him with a traditional Lithuanian sash (saying "Congratulations!") that celebrates important events during the life course.

and from personal emotions. For example, our society's gendered division of domestic work obligates women to care for aging parents and in-laws, as you'll see shortly. In such caregiving situations, a daughter or daughter-in-law may feel close to her aging parents or in-laws but may also resent their critical or demanding behavior (Willson et al., 2003; see, also, Chapter 5).

Sibling Relationships in Later Life

About 80 percent of older people have siblings. Because brother–sister relationships usually last longer than any other family ties, siblings can be important sources of companionship and emotional support.

Since you asked . . .

⁝⁘ Do siblings become closer or more distant as they age?

According to medical sociologist Deborah Gold (1989, 1990), sibling relationships in later life generally fall into five groups, the last two of which are negative:

- *Intimate siblings* are close and consider each other to be best friends and close confidants. They help each other no matter what and are in frequent contact.

- *Congenial siblings* feel close and see each other as good friends, but they feel closer to a spouse or an adult child. They contact each other weekly or monthly but give help only when it doesn't conflict with their obligations to their spouse or children.

- *Loyal siblings* are available because of family bonds rather than affection or closeness. Disagreements don't erode the siblings' ties because they believe that family ties are important whether or not family members like each other.

- *Apathetic siblings* are indifferent, rarely think about each other, and have little contact with each other.
- *Hostile siblings* are angry and resentful and have had negative ties for a long time. They spend considerable time demeaning each other and arguing about the past, inheritances, and so on.

Adult sibling relationships vary by race, gender, and other factors. For example, black siblings tend to have more positive relationships than white siblings, sisters tend to be closer than brothers, and married siblings have more in common than those who are divorced or child free (Quadagno, 2002; Atchley and Barusch, 2004).

Sibling relationships can change over time, especially during family crises. Over the years, for instance, a number of my students in their 40s and 50s have said that their sibling relationships changed from apathetic to warm when a parent, grandparent, or great-grandparent became ill and needed ongoing care. In other cases, divorce and widowhood often bring indifferent siblings closer together.

Whether or not they have children and grandchildren, aging couples can enjoy many years together because of our greater life expectancy. Sooner or later, however, family members must cope with another important life course event: the death of a loved one.

DYING, DEATH, AND BEREAVEMENT

In 1900, the average U.S. life expectancy was 49 years (National Center for Health Statistics, 1997). Death was a normal part of everyday life at all life stages—from infancy to adulthood—because of infectious diseases; poor sanitation; unsafe work environments; and few medical interventions, such as antibiotics, that we now take for granted. Today, most deaths occur among the old-old and the oldest-old, and dying usually occurs in institutional settings (such as hospitals and nursing homes) rather than at home. Given these circumstances, death is an ever-present possibility primarily for the oldest Americans. Even then, however, many family members often avoid the topic.

Experiencing Death and Dying

American actor and director Woody Allen once said, "It's not that I'm afraid to die. I just don't want to be there when it happens." How we experience death depends on whether we are medical personnel treating the ill patient, relatives or friends of the patient, or the patient himself or herself. Each may have a different perspective on death and dying.

HEALTH CARE PROFESSIONALS Physicians and other health care professionals often use the term **dying trajectory**, which refers to the speed with which a person dies because of declining physical functions. In a *lingering trajectory*—for example, death from a terminal illness such as cancer—medical personnel do everything possible to treat the patient, but ultimately custodial care predominates. In contrast, the *quick trajectory* is an acute crisis caused by cardiac arrest or a serious accident. Staff members typically work feverishly to preserve the patient's life and well-being, sometimes successfully.

When an older person suffers from a terminal illness such as advanced cancer, health care professionals expect the patient to have a lingering death. Overworked hospital staff, especially, may respond to the patient's requests more slowly, place the patient in more remote wards, or even bathe and feed him or her less frequently. Family members, in contrast, typically expect their older relatives to be treated as painstakingly as any other patient (Atchley and Barusch, 2004).

PATIENTS, FAMILIES, FRIENDS Among the several perspectives on the dying process, probably the best

The Wizard of Id by Brant Parker and Johnny Hart. By permission of John L. Hart FLP and Creators Syndicate, Inc.

known is that of psychiatrist Elisabeth Kübler-Ross (1969). Based on work with 200 primarily middle-aged cancer patients, Kübler-Ross proposed five stages of dying: (1) *denial* ("The doctors must be wrong"), (2) *anger* ("Why me?"), (3) *bargaining* ("If you let me live longer, God, I promise to be a better person"), (4) *depression* ("There's no point in seeing family members or friends"), and (5) *acceptance* ("I might as well get my financial records in order").

Many have criticized this stage-based theory for several reasons. Some contend that the stages are not experienced by everyone, even middle-aged people, or in the same order. Others point out that the stages do not apply to older people. Because they are more accustomed to being sick, many older people have had to confront the possibility of death for many years.

Rather than deny death, some older people, especially the oldest-old, may welcome it. Many have seen their spouses and friends die over the years, and they often view death as a natural part of life. They may even await death as an end to pain, sorrow, social isolation, dependency, and loneliness. Thus, the oldest-old may not experience Kübler-Ross's stages because they have been undergoing a "social death" over the course of many years (Retsinas, 1988).

Moreover, the Kübler-Ross stages of dying ignore the feeling of relief that many family members experience after a loved one dies. For example, "there are those who suffered from chronic physical illness, the cancer that kept recurring, and the Alzheimer's victims who had died inside years earlier when they stopped recognizing family members." Thus, the death of a loved one can end the prolonged agony that family members endure: "Pain control during terminal illnesses is still inexact at best, causing the dying and their families untold suffering" (Elison, 2007: 18).

Hospice Care for the Dying

Derived from the medieval term for a place of shelter and rest for weary or sick travelers, a **hospice** is a place for the care of terminally ill patients. When death is imminent (generally a prognosis of six months or less to live), a hospice provides pain control, gives patients a sense of security and companionship, and tries to make them as comfortable as possible. Hospice care is available in a variety of settings: patients' homes, hospitals, nursing homes, or other inpatient facilities.

Ideally, physicians, nurses, social workers, and clergy associated with a hospice work as a team to meet the physical, emotional, and spiritual needs of the patient and his or her family to give dying people full and accurate information about their condition, and to help family members and friends deal with their feelings and sorrow.

In reality, hospice care—which Medicare and Medicaid (a federal government program for the poor) cover—is often unused, in part because of cultural and language barriers. For example, a comprehensive study of California—the most ethnically diverse state in America—found that 4 percent of Asian Americans, 6 percent of blacks, and 15 percent of Latinos, compared with 74 percent of whites, died at hospices. Some of the reasons for the differences were due to racial-ethnic groups' beliefs that people should die at home rather than an institutional setting, such as a hospice. There were also structural

Many people are personalizing their funerals. Here, mourners are treated to ice cream at the graveside of a man who had driven an ice cream truck for many years.

obstacles. Especially among many Latinos and Asian Americans, older immigrants weren't eligible for federal and state health care benefits, the terminally ill patients and their family members had problems communicating with hospice staff because of language barriers, or they found that staff members provided a low quality of care (Crawley and Singer, 2007).

The Right to Die with Dignity

Older men, especially those age 75 and older, have the highest suicide rates in the nation (see *Table 17.2*). This is especially true for white males age 65 and older, who commit suicide at almost triple the national rate (National Institutes of Health, 2009). It's not clear why suicide rates for older white men are so high and increase steadily after age 65. There are probably multiple reasons, including social isolation and loneliness, a feeling of uselessness, financial hardship, multiple losses of loved ones, or chronic illness and pain. White men, especially those from higher socioeconomic levels, may also fear becoming a burden to others and losing their control and dignity as their mental and physical capabilities diminish (DeSpelder and Strickland, 2005).

TABLE 17.2	American Suicide Rates, by Age and Sex, 2006

Suicide deaths per 100,000 population

Age group	Male	Female
15–19	11	3
20–29	20	4
30–44	21	6
45–54	26	9
55–64	21	7
65–74	22	3
75–84	27	4
85 and older	39	2
Total	17	5

Source: Based on Karch et al., 2009, Table 4.

Some maintain that older men's suicide rates would decrease if people had the legal right to die with dignity

Should Physician-Assisted Suicide Be Legal in Every State?

Originally, the Obama administration's health care bill included an end-of-life provision that was designed to allow Medicare to pay doctors who counsel patients about end-of-life decisions. The consultations would be voluntary and would provide information about **living wills**, health care proxies, paid medications, and hospice.

Widespread opposition to the bill emerged, especially from seniors, after former Alaska Governor Sarah Palin claimed that the administration was setting up "death panels" and implied that the panels would euthanize millions of older Americans against their will (Parsons and Zajac, 2009). It's not clear, as this book goes to press, whether the final health care bill will include or eliminate all end-of-life provisions.

How do Americans feel about PAS? According to several Gallup polls, 71 percent said that they support PAS if the patient and family request it, up from 54 percent in 1947 (Carroll, 2007). On a related but slightly different question, a larger proportion of Americans (84 percent) approves of laws that allow stopping medical treatment that is keeping a terminally ill patient alive if that is what the patient desires (Parker, 2009).

But who knows the dying person's wishes? At least 67 percent of cardiac arrests occur at home or in a public place. Family members may know that the afflicted person has signed a do-not-resuscitate (DNR) order, but the patient is usually resuscitated because family members can't produce the paperwork (Grudzen et al., 2009). Some patients recover, but others may be connected to a hospital's or nursing home's feeding tubes the rest of her or his life.

A living will is a legal document in which a person can specify which, if any, life-support measures he or she wants in the event of serious illness and whether and when such measures should be discontinued. Preparing such a document does not guarantee compliance, however. Physicians or hospitals may refuse to honor living wills if their policies support prolonging life at any cost, if family members contest the living will, or if there is any question about the patient's mental competence when the will was drawn up. For these reasons and because state laws and policies vary widely, people who want living wills to be enforced should consult an attorney to minimize legal problems and to make sure that their wishes will be carried out.

Stop and Think . . .

- What is your position on PAS? Why?
- Among those age 65 and older, 35 percent have never talked to their children about end-of-life medical decisions if they are unable to do so themselves (Parker, 2009). Have you discussed such issues with your parents, grandparents, or aging relatives? Why or why not?

Choices

on their own terms. Both historically and currently, one of the most controversial issues has involved end-of-life decisions. Oregon legalized physician-assisted suicide (PAS) in 1998 but strictly prohibits lethal injections or euthanasia (sometimes called mercy killing). Using Oregon's legal assisted suicide model, the state of Washington followed suit in late 2008.

The Oregon law allows mentally competent adults who declare their intentions in writing and have been diagnosed as terminally ill independently by two physicians to take a doctor-prescribed lethal drug themselves, orally, after a waiting period of 15 days. Opponents of the Death with Dignity law predicted massive PAS. Since the law went into effect, however, about 40 people a year have taken their own lives this way (Knickerbocker, 2009). The box "Should Physician-Assisted Suicide Be Legal in Every State?" on p. 495 examines this issue further.

Coping with Death

Bereavement is the process of recovery after the death of someone we felt close to. People who have experienced such a loss are known as the *bereaved*. Grief and mourning are two common emotional reactions during bereavement.

GRIEF AND MOURNING Grief is the emotional response to loss. It usually involves a variety and combination of feelings such as sadness, longing, bewilderment, anguish, self-pity, anger, guilt, and loneliness, as well as relief.

The grieving process may last a few months or continue throughout one's lifetime. However long it lasts, grieving usually encompasses physical, behavioral, and emotional responses. In terms of behavior, bereaved people may talk incessantly about the deceased and the circumstances of the death. Others may talk about everything except their loss because it's too painful to do so (DeSpelder and Strickland, 2005).

Mourning is the customary outward expression of grief. Mourning ranges from normal grief to pathological melancholy that may lead to physical illness or depression. Whether it's the death of a child, a parent, or a grandparent, most people don't "recover" and finish mourning. Instead, they adapt and change, such as donating the dead person's clothes to a charity and establishing new relationships (Silverman, 2000).

Coping with death varies in different social and cultural groups. Many U.S. ethnic groups are acculturating to the values of mainstream society, but traditional ceremonies reinforce family ties and religious practices (see the box "Death and Funeral Traditions among Racial-Ethnic Families").

PHASES OF GRIEF There are clusters or phases of grief (Hooyman and Kiyak, 2002). People generally respond *initially* with shock, numbness, and disbelief.

After one of my uncles died, for example, my aging aunt refused to get rid of any of his clothes because "he might need them when he comes back." The grieving person may be unable to sleep, lose interest in food, and not answer phone calls or even read sympathy cards because of an all-encompassing feeling of sorrow.

Since you asked . . .

How does grieving differ among people?

In the *intermediate stage* of grief, people often idealize loved ones who have died and may even actively search for them. A widow may see her husband's face in a crowd. Recent widows or widowers may also feel guilty, regretting every lapse: "Why wasn't I more understanding?" "Why did we argue that morning?" Survivors may also become angry, blowing up at children and friends over little things in a seemingly irrational way.

The *final stage* of grief, recovery and reorganization, may not occur for several years, although many people begin to adjust after about six months. In later life, grieving is often more complex than it is for younger people because an older person may experience, over a few years, the deaths of many people who were important to him or her.

DURATION AND INTENSITY OF GRIEF Death affects older people differently than it does younger people. A national study of couples age 65 and older found that up to 22 percent of spouses died within a year of being widowed. These "widower effects" (when a spouse dies shortly after being widowed) may reflect changes in the survivor's behavior, such as sleeping less, using sleep medications more often, consuming more alcohol, and losing weight. Even daily routines such as getting around, meal preparation, and household tasks may become more difficult both physically and emotionally (Christakis and Allison, 2006; Pienta and Franks, 2006; Utz, 2006).

For the most part, however, older bereaved people are very resilient. For example, almost half of those who have had satisfying marriages cope with the loss of their spouse with minimal grief: They accept the death as part of life and take great comfort in their memories. About 10 percent are relieved at the death of a partner because they had been trapped in a bad marriage or had provided stressful caregiving for a number of years. About 16 percent experience chronic grief lasting more than 18 months, but 24 percent show an improvement in psychological well-being within a year or so after a partner's death (Mancini et al., 2006).

The duration and intensity of a person's grief depend on a number of factors, including the quality of the lost relationship, the age of the deceased person, whether the death was sudden or anticipated, and the quality of care the dying person received at the end of his or her life (Carr et al., 2006). Most

Cross-Cultural and Multicultural Families

Death and Funeral Rituals among Racial-Ethnic Families

Despite acculturation, there are cultural, religious, and ethnic differences in how families cope with death. The variations include rituals, a display of emotion, the appropriate length of mourning, celebrating anniversary events, and beliefs about the afterlife. For example, many African American families give the deceased a "good sendoff" that includes buying the best casket the family can afford and a funeral in the home church with stirring songs and eulogies.

In many Middle Eastern families, traditional Muslim women display extreme emotions—crying, screaming, and pulling their hair—to express grief. Wearing black, Muslims usually mourn the death of a loved one for at least one year. They organize big gatherings of relatives and friends on the third day, the fortieth day, and one year after the death of a loved one.

Among many Mexican Americans, death brings family members and friends together even across geographic or psychological distances. Despite their heterogeneity, for Mexican American and other Latino families, funeral rites often strengthen family values and ties in several ways:

- There is a common belief that it is more important to attend a funeral than almost any other family event. During the funeral, the family and the community offer emotional and spiritual support.

- The funeral reflects traditional family values of respect for elders, tradition, and the importance of the family. Even if family members are not religious, they attend religious funerals.

- Socialization to death begins at a young age. Children attend wakes and funerals regularly and participate in memorial masses and family gatherings after the funeral.

- Many Mexican Americans cope with death through ritualistic acts such as a rosary, a mass, a graveside service, and the annual observance of All Souls' Day on November 2, which is more commonly known as the Day of the Dead (Día de los Difunios).

Recently, many cemeteries and mortuaries—whose directors are usually white—have adapted services to immigrant customs. Some funeral homes have removable pews so that Hindu and Buddhist mourners can sit on the floor. Funeral homes may also provide incense sticks and have common rooms where mourners can gather to snack and chat when funerals span several days.

Deceased Muslims are often propped on one shoulder inside their coffins so they face Mecca. Some funeral homes supply white shrouds, Egyptian spray perfume, and a particular soap that Muslims use to wash and dress the dead. Managers of funeral homes also make sure that women employees are working on days when female Muslims are washed in case an employee has to enter the preparation room.

Sources: Sharifzadeh, 1997; Willis, 1997; Murray, 2000; Martinez, 2001; Brulliard, 2006.

Stop and Think . . .

- How do some of these rituals differ from your family's? How are they similar?

- Talk to some of the international students on your campus or in class. How do their families cope with death? What kinds of rituals do the students practice? And why?

---

recently, many families have turned to the Internet to express their grief. Their Websites feature video montages of the deceased, Webcasts of funeral or memorial services, audio messages prepared by the terminally ill for distribution after death, and a space to leave condolences or to share funny anecdotes and memories of the deceased (Harris, 2007).

BEING WIDOWED AND SINGLE IN LATER LIFE

The death of a spouse often means not just the loss of a life companion but the end of a whole way of life. Friendships may change or even end because

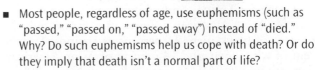

MAKING CONNECTIONS

- Most people, regardless of age, use euphemisms (such as "passed," "passed on," "passed away") instead of "died." Why? Do such euphemisms help us cope with death? Or do they imply that death isn't a normal part of life?

- Do you think that Internet sites about a dead family member are a good idea? Or do you think that grieving should be a private rather than a public affair? Why?

many close relationships during marriage were based on being a couple. Some ties, such as relationships with in-laws, may weaken or erode. Widowed persons

FIGURE 17.10 Marital Status of Americans Age 65 and Older, by Age Group and Sex, 2007

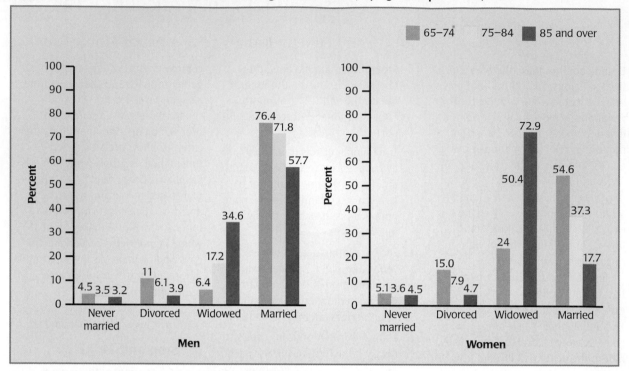

Source: Federal Interagency Forum on Aging-Related Statistics, 2008, p. 5.

may also forge new relationships through dating, cohabitation, and remarriage.

In 2007, a small proportion of the older population had never married (see *Figure 17.10*). A relatively small number of men age 65 and older (8 percent) and women (10 percent) were divorced. Older men were much more likely than older women to be married. Even among the oldest-old, the majority of men were married (60 percent) compared with only 15 percent of women.

Who Are the Widowed?

Across all older age groups, women are much more likely than men to be widowed, and these differences increase as people age (see *Figure 17.10*). Among racial-ethnic groups, African American widows age 70 and older comprise the largest proportion of African American women—58 percent compared with 51 percent each for Latinas and white women, and 47 percent for Asian American women. In contrast, only 23 percent of black men, 21 percent of Latinos, 19 percent of white men, and 14 percent of Asian American men are widowed (U.S. Census Bureau News, 2007).

There are three major reasons for the gender differences in widowhood. First, women tend to live longer than men (see Data Digest). Second, a wife typically is three or four years younger than her husband, which increases the likelihood that she will survive him. Third, widowers age 65 and older are eight times more likely than women to remarry. Especially

if they have the resources to attract a new mate, and given the large pool of eligible women (those who are younger, widowed, divorced, or never married) and the shortage of men, it's easier for older men than older women to remarry (see Chapters 8 and 16).

Facing Widowhood

Some recently widowed older people exhibit depressive symptoms such as insomnia, loss of appetite, and dissatisfaction with themselves. As you saw earlier, however, many usually recover within a year or so, especially if they no longer experience the stress of caring for a dying husband or wife.

Insurance benefits, when they exist, tend to be exhausted within a few years after a husband's death. Financial hardships may be especially great for a woman who cared for her spouse during a long illness or depleted their resources during the spouse's institutionalization. Moreover, many older widows have few opportunities to increase their income through paid employment because they were full-time homemakers and lack marketable skills.

If they are healthy and financially self-sufficient, most older Americans, including the widowed, value their independence and prefer to live alone rather than move in with their children. Others may feel isolated, especially when children or relatives live at a distance or rarely visit. Some of these seniors relocate and move in with adult children to help care for grandchildren, forming a multigenerational household.

How does widowhood affect a person's relationships? A national study examined the social networks of people age 65 and older at 6 and 18 months after a spouse's death. Initially, the widowed person had considerable support from adult children and relatives, who provided instrumental help (such as making funeral arrangements and help with relocating) and emotional support (such as listening and making the widowed person feel loved and cared for). Eighteen months later, however, friends played a more important role as confidants, people with whom the widowed person shared private feelings and concerns (Ha, 2008). Thus, social networks and support change over time as a person adjusts to being widowed.

Forging New Relationships

Some widows and many widowers begin to date within a few years of losing a mate. As a "Dear Ann Landers" letter shows, however, family members may disapprove:

My brother died a year ago. He left behind his wife of 30 years and two grown children. Two months after his death, my sister-in-law removed all his clothes from the closet, as well as the wall photos of him and the trophies he had won. Eight months later, she began to date. This has been quite painful for the rest of his family. We don't understand why she is dating so soon ("Ann Landers," 2001: 3E).

Ann Landers told the writer to stop being "petty and mean-spirited" because the sister-in-law had grieved for nearly a year (and this was enough) and should be allowed to enjoy male companionship and to go on with her life.

> **Since you asked . . .**
>
> :•• How soon should widowed people begin dating after a spouse's death?

Companionship is the most important reason for dating. Like younger people, older people enjoy having friends to share interests and whom they can call on in emergencies. After being widowed, older people who receive much emotional support from family and friends may be less likely to want to date or to remarry than are those who are more isolated (Carr, 2004).

If older widowed people form a romantic relationship, they often think seriously about whether to just date, move in together, or remarry. As you saw earlier and in Chapter 16, many older widowed people may increase their income taxes and reduce or lose an ex-spouse's Social Security benefits or pension if they remarry. Also, many widows aren't eager to provide caregiving to an older second or third husband because they've already done so. All of these issues can discourage remarriage, especially for older women. Nevertheless, caregivers become more vital in providing emotional and physical help as we age.

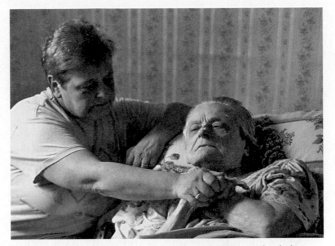

As life expectancy increases, many middle-aged adults find themselves caring for their aging parents. Most of the care is provided in the children's or the older person's home rather than in institutions such as nursing homes.

FAMILY CAREGIVING IN LATER LIFE

The *sandwich generation* is composed of midlife men and women who care for dependent children and their aging parents (see Chapters 1 and 13). Increasingly, the sandwich generation is morphing into a "club sandwich family" with four generations—children, parents, grandparents, and great-grandparents—requiring caregivers to help more people and over a longer period of time (Trafford, 2005).

A **caregiver** is a person, paid or unpaid, who attends to the needs of someone who is old, sick, or disabled. Nationally, about 1.4 million children between the ages of 8 and 18 (representing more than 3 percent of all households) are caregivers for a parent, grandparent, or sibling. About 20 percent of these caregivers, most of whom are girls, say that their responsibilities have made them miss school and after-school activities and have kept them from doing their homework (Hunt et al., 2005). For the most part, however, caregivers are usually spouses and adult children who provide more (and more extensive) care over much longer periods than their parents did in the so-called good old days.

Who Are the Caregivers and Recipients?

> **Since you asked . . .**
>
> :•• Why are women usually the caregivers for older family members?

The older we get, the more likely we are to give and receive help. Most people age 65 and older continue to develop disabilities as they grow older and eventually require assistance with the basic tasks of everyday life. And, as you might expect, the older people are, the more assistance they need. In 2005, for example, 7 percent of those ages 65 to 74 needed assistance compared with almost 20 percent of those age 75 or older (Gist et al., 2007).

RECIPIENTS Among people age 65 and older, 29 percent (about 10 million Americans) need help because they have one or more physical, mental, emotional, or memory problems that interfere with the activities of daily living (ADLs) or with instrumental activities of daily living (IADLs) (Interagency Forum on Aging-Related Statistics, 2008).

ADLs include dressing, walking across a room, bathing or showering, eating (such as cutting up food), getting in or out of bed, and using the toilet (including getting up or down). IADLs include preparing hot meals, shopping for groceries, making phone calls, taking medications, and managing money (such as paying bills and keeping track of expenses). The larger the number of ADL and IADL disabilities, the greater the reliance on caregivers (Johnson et al., 2007).

Many seniors need occasional help with transportation, house maintenance, and other tasks, but the nation's most vulnerable population is the *frail elderly*, older persons (usually 76 and older) who have physical or mental disabilities that interfere with their ability to perform everyday activities. The frail older population not in nursing homes or other institutions is disproportionately female (64 percent), age 75 or older (60 percent), white (79 percent), and widowed (41 percent) (Johnson et al., 2007).

CAREGIVERS There are almost 34 million Americans (16 percent of the adult population) who provide unpaid care to someone age 50 or older. A typical caregiver is female (61 percent), approximately 46 years old, has at least some college education (66 percent), and spends an average of 20 or more hours a week providing care (79 percent). A majority of caregivers are married, and most have to juggle work with caregiving responsibilities (Houser, 2007).

As in the case of providers for people age 50 and older, daughters and daughters-in-law are usually the caregivers of the frail elderly (see *Figure 17.11*). Even among the frail elderly themselves, most of the caregivers are wives because they live longer than men. On average, a caregiver provides about 25 hours of assistance per week to frail older people who are living at home. If an older person suffers from three or more ADL limitations, spouses typically provide 56 hours of care per week, and daughters and daughters-in-law provide 33 hours per week, even though at least half of the latter are employed full time (Johnson and Wiener, 2006).

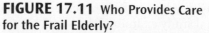

FIGURE 17.11 Who Provides Care for the Frail Elderly?

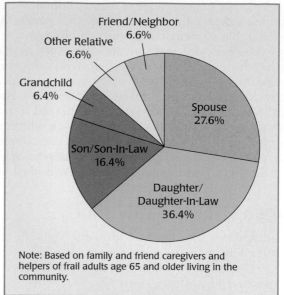

Note: Based on family and friend caregivers and helpers of frail adults age 65 and older living in the community.

Source: Johnson and Wiener, 2006, Figure 5.1.

Regardless of the older person's physical and emotional health, most frequently the caregiver is the female adult child who lives closest to the parent or relative or has the fewest career or family responsibilities. Even when they are employed full time, women are more likely than men to provide care, especially to parents and parents-in-law. According to some scholars, these gender differences reflect broader cultural norms that assign caretaking tasks to women, who are believed to be naturally more nurturing than men and who are expected to provide more care for children and aging parents (see Chapter 5).

Others maintain that the gender gap reflects structural factors such as employment. That is, women provide more caregiving to older adults because they are less likely than men to have lucrative, time-consuming, or satisfying jobs that they are unwilling to jeopardize. As a result, men in well-paying jobs are more likely to purchase help rather than take advantage of the Family and Medical Leave Act, which doesn't provide paid leave (Sarkisian and Gerstel, 2004; Neal and Hammer, 2007; see, also, the discussion of whom the Family and Medical Leave Act covers in Chapter 13).

Across all racial and ethnic groups, caregivers are more likely to be women, people who are married or cohabiting rather than single or divorced, and those who are employed. Overall, however, caregivers provide similar types of care and experience similar stresses regardless of their ethnic background, marital status, or other factors (National Alliance for Caregiving and AARP, 2004; Johnson and Wiener, 2006).

Caregiving Styles of Adult Children

Families help their older members in different ways—financially, physically, and emotionally—but adult children still provide most of the assistance (see *Figure 17.11* on p. 500). Because most of us grow up with brothers and sisters, how do siblings share the care? In one study, Matthews and Rosner (1988) found five primary types of caregiving for aging parents, some more cooperative than others.

ROUTINE HELP *Routine help* is the backbone of caring for older parents. The adult child incorporates assistance to the older parent into his or her ongoing activities and is regularly available. Routine involvement may include a wide range of activities: household chores, checking in with the person, providing outings, running errands, managing finances, and visiting.

BACKUPS In a second style, siblings serve as *backups*. One person gives routine care to an aging parent, but a brother or sister may step in when needed. For example, one sister explained, "I do what my sisters instruct me to do." She responded to her sisters' requests but did not initiate involvement. In other cases, a sibling may contact a "favorite child" when a parent refuses to do something that the routine caregiver thinks is necessary (such as taking medicine every day, regardless of its cost).

CIRCUMSCRIBED The *circumscribed* style of participation is limited but predictable and agreed upon. For example, one respondent said of her brother, "He gives a routine, once-a-week call," that a parent eagerly awaited. The brother was not expected to increase his participation in the care of his parent, however.

Siblings who adopt this style can be counted on to help but make clear the limits on their availability. For example, in one family, a son who was a physician gave medical advice but was not expected to assume any other responsibility.

SPORADIC In contrast to the first three types of caregiving, the *sporadic* style describes adult children who provide services to parents at their own convenience. As one daughter said, "My brother comes when he feels like it to take Mother out on Sunday, but it's not a scheduled thing." Some siblings don't mind this behavior, but others resent brothers and sisters who avoid the most demanding tasks:

[My sister and I] *were always very close, and we're not now. I don't think she comes down often enough. . . . She calls, big deal: that's very different from spending three to four hours a day. . . . She does not wheel my mother to the doctor, she does not carry her to the car, she does not oversee the help* (Abel, 1991: 154).

DISASSOCIATED The last style is *disassociation* from responsibility altogether; this occurs when sisters and brothers know that they can't count on a sibling at all. Siblings use geographic distance, employment, and other family responsibilities as excuses for not assuming caregiving responsibilities. Such justifications, however, may increase resentment among those who provide care (Ingersoll-Dayton et al., 2003).

Unequal caregiving burdens can create distance between siblings ("He never helps" or "I want to help but she rejects all my offers"). On the other hand, sisters and brothers sometimes overcome ancient grudges as they band together for their parents' sake. They might make mutual decisions about an aging parent's living in a retirement community, share information about a parent's health, and work out visiting schedules for siblings who are geographically scattered (Russo, 2005).

The Satisfactions and Strains of Caregiving

Exchange theory suggests that caregivers experience both costs and benefits. Even though the costs of caring for older family members sometimes outweigh the benefits, especially for women in a sandwich generation with full-time jobs, caregiving can also be satisfying (Raschick and Ingersoll-Dayton, 2004).

CAREGIVING SATISFACTION Some people enjoy caregiving, believing that family relationships can be renewed or strengthened by helping older family members. They see caregiving as a labor of love because of strong affection that has always existed in the family. For others, caregiving provides a feeling of being useful and needed. As one daughter said,

Some caregivers are monitoring older family members from afar. The technology includes video conferencing systems and webcams positioned throughout the house that track movement and notify caregivers if there are any deviations from a routine that might indicate an accident or illness.

"For me, that's what life's all about!" (Guberman et al., 1992: 611; see, also, Saldana and Dassori, 1999).

CAREGIVING STRAINS Caregiving also creates stress and strain. Older people usually need support at a time when their children's lives are complicated and demanding. Families are often unprepared for the problems involved in caring for an older person. Sandwiched caregivers frequently experience a lower quality of life because daily routines are disrupted and parent–child conflict may increase. Parents who are mentally impaired, can't perform basic daily self-care tasks, or engage in disruptive behavior are the ones who are most difficult to care for (Dilworth-Anderson et al., 1999; Rubin and White-Means, 2009).

Financial burdens include not only the direct costs of medical care but also indirect costs such as lost income or missed promotions. A national study of female caregivers ages 55 to 67 found that the women who spent time helping their parents cut back their work hours by 367 hours per year. These work-hour reductions translated into average compensation losses of about $8,600 ($6,300 in lost wages and $2,300 in lost benefits)—a considerable amount when it reduces the caregiver's income by up to 15 percent a year (Johnson, 2007).

Another national study found that long-distance caregivers spent almost twice as much every year (almost $9,000) as those living nearby (almost $4,600). The financial costs of those who live with the care recipient (whether it's a spouse, partner, or parent) are the highest—almost $15,000 a year—because they pitch in for groceries, over-the-counter drugs, medical and home maintenance expenses; have more transportation costs for doctor's and dentist's visits; and sometimes hire care attendants for temporary rest and relief (Evercare and National Alliance for Caregiving, 2007).

Other Support Systems

Only 5 percent of frail older Americans are institutionalized—typically in nursing homes—because family members are the primary source of assistance. This creates problems in the workplace.

Many employers complain about the costs of caregiving. In 2004, for example, the costs businesses bore because adult caregivers were absent, late, quit, or took unpaid leave totaled almost $34 billion (MetLife Mature Market Institute, 2006). Elder care issues have gained prominence in the workplace, but most companies, particularly those with fewer than 100 employees, "have yet to develop and implement policies that fully support their employees caring for older relatives" (Roberto and Jarrott, 2008: 107).

What are the options for care recipients? Most formal support systems are expensive or limited to people who can walk, can take care of their physical needs, or don't suffer from dementia. For example, day care centers for the aged can cost more than $1,000 a month, more than an average Social Security check. In 2007, the average monthly Social Security income for retired women was $905 and $1,178 for men (Social Security Administration, 2008). Also, most older people don't have long-term care insurance that might pay for higher-quality nursing care.

Retirement communities are attractive options because they include health care, housekeeping, meals, and many other services. But how many older people can afford to pay at least $300,000 for a house or apartment and another $4,000 or so per month for annual maintenance and other fees?

Similarly, assisted-living centers meet their residents' needs, but range from about $2,500 to $3,500 a month. The cost may be closer to $5,000 a month depending on the number of ADLs with which a person needs assistance, the geographic area, transportation services, and how often a family member has a meal with the resident (Absher, 2009).

Unless an older person is financially destitute and qualifies for Medicaid, nursing homes are expensive. The average cost can be more than $5,000 a month, depending on the level of care. Moreover, high-quality nursing homes don't accept Medicaid recipients because government programs don't cover the costs (Kalb and Juarez, 2005).

From 1975 to 2004, Medicaid spent about $600 billion on long-term care of older people, with nearly 90 percent going to institutions. According to some analysts, Medicaid can save an average of $15,000 a year for each person who receives care at home instead of in a nursing home. Thus, there is increased pressure for families to provide more care for the aged. About a dozen states have implemented programs that provide caregivers with respite care or allow families to purchase more of the goods and services they need for eldercare, including hospital-type beds and transportation (Feinberg et al., 2006; Lagnado, 2006).

You've seen that most caregivers experience emotional and financial burdens in caring for older family members and relatives, especially if they are dual earners in a sandwiched generation. On a macro level, assets are limited, which means that increasing numbers of Americans are competing for scarce resources.

COMPETITION FOR RESOURCES

When the Social Security Act was passed in 1935, life expectancy in the United States was just below 62 years, compared with about 78 today. In the years ahead, the increasing numbers of older Americans will put a significant strain on the nation's health care services and retirement income programs. What are some of the financial costs of our aging society? And are there any solutions?

Some Financial Costs of an Aging Society

Medical expenditures in the United States make up almost 20 percent of our gross domestic product (GDP), higher than any other country in the world. (A GDP is the market value of all goods and services produced within a country in a given period of time, such as a year.) In 2008, health care spending by American consumers, government agencies, businesses, and charities reached a record high of $2.6 trillion, and almost half of the medical costs were for people age 65 and older (Clarke, 2008; Trumbull, 2009).

These costs will increase in the future because boomers may live longer but have more chronic conditions, as you saw earlier, that will utilize more health care services. By 2030, half of the boomers will have arthritis, four times more hip replacements, and eight times more knee replacements; 33 percent will be obese (which results in numerous health problems); and 20 percent will have diabetes, which, like obesity, generates considerable health costs. However, because boomers have higher educational levels than previous generations, they are likely to demand more and more expensive health care services (American Hospital Association, 2007).

People who have worked all their lives should be able to live out their retirement years without enduring sickness and pain and without struggling with a pile of medical bills. According to some policy analysts, however, older people have benefited at the expense of others, especially children. From 1960 to 2007, federal spending on children rose from less than 1.9 percent to 2.6 percent of the GDP. Spending on the non-child portions of the big three entitlement programs for older people—Social Security, Medicare, and Medicaid—nearly quadrupled from 2 percent to almost 8 percent of the GDP. If current spending and revenue policies continue, in 2018 children's share of federal spending will decline to 2 percent while spending on older people will rise to almost 10 percent of the GDP (Carasso et al., 2008).

A major reason why older people have relatively generous health care coverage is that they complain the loudest. In 2009, for example, seniors showed up in large numbers in meetings with congressional representatives to protest the Obama administration's health care program that might have decreased some of their benefits (Schaller, 2009).

Also, older people are one of the largest and politically best organized groups in the nation. They vote in large numbers, follow issues carefully, and usually come to congressional hearings well prepared to defend their positions. An especially influential group is the AARP, which can "throw its weight around"

because the organization has at least a half million volunteers and one of the country's most influential lobbying groups in Congress that support politicians from both parties (Donnelly, 2007).

Older Americans have considerable political clout. In 2008, people age 65 and older made up less than 13 percent of the population, but accounted for 20 percent of the vote in the presidential election. In contrast, nearly 25 percent of all Americans who were under age 18 got no vote at all (Porter, 2009). Thus, the young have little say in their share of resources.

According to some analysts, younger generations won't enjoy similar retirement benefits in the future. Especially since the 2008 recession but also because the old-age dependency ratio has increased, the financial condition of the Social Security and Medicare systems is much more fragile than in the past. Medicare is now expected to run out of money in 2017, two years earlier than forecasted in 2008, and Social Security will be exhausted in 2037, four years earlier than predicted (The Board of Trustees . . ., 2009).

Are There Any Solutions?

One question is whether the oldest-old get too much treatment. A midlife son in Maryland, for example, whose mother was 88, initially authorized her biopsy for a mass on her lung that was possibly malignant. She had numerous other medical problems, including a series of ministrokes, blindness, emphysema that required oxygen around the clock, and severe heart disease and circulation problems. The mother became very upset when her son explained that the biopsy could puncture her lung and she might die or that she might have to undergo numerous chemotherapy treatments. She had already spent several years in hospitals for her ailments and didn't want to do so again. In the end, the son decided to forgo the biopsy even though all of the costs would've been covered by Medicare (Manger, 2009).

Some medical researchers also contend that we waste precious resources by providing care for dying elderly people to prolong their lives by a few weeks or months, especially since many of these patients spend most of their time in intensive-care units, connected to feeding tubes and oxygen tanks. The top U.S. medical centers spend anywhere from $30,000 to almost $94,000 a year per patient in his or her last two years of life, and all of the costs are covered by Medicare or Medicaid (Wennberg et al., 2008). Because physicians and family members know that such end-of-life treatments are fruitless, should the funds be redirected to children's health care and other programs that improve schools and decrease domestic violence?

There's no easy fix for our increasing health care costs for older Americans, but one solution might be to redefine old age. If, for example, the definition of old age and the time of mandatory retirement were pushed up to age 70 or later, many productive older Americans could continue to work and contribute to Social Security. As a result, the burden of supporting an aging population would not fall wholly on younger workers.

Another way to hold down the costs of health care is to make the health care industry more competitive because "health care markets are dominated by just a couple of large insurance firms." Greater competition would make it easier for new and less-profitable firms to enter the market and to offer consumers more options. Providing people, especially boomers, with incentives for healthier behaviors—including reducing smoking and obesity—would also lower health care costs in the future (Trumbull, 2009: 23).

CONCLUSION

As this chapter shows, because of increased life expectancy, many of us will have more *choices* in later life on how we will spend our later years. On the other hand, we will also face *constraints*, the most serious of which is how we will care for aging family members as longevity increases and health-related costs rise.

Another critical issue is how we will respond to the *changes* brought about by an aging population that has diverse social, health, and financial needs. One important question, for example, is whether boomers will adopt healthier lifestyles that can decrease health care costs in the future. Also, are older Americans willing to give up some other benefits to improve the lives of many children?

SUMMARY

1. Our society is aging at an exceedingly rapid pace for several reasons, especially an increase in life expectancy.

2. There is great diversity in the aged population, but people age 65 and older must confront similar issues, such as accepting a decline in health, dealing with stereotypes, and adjusting to retirement.

3. Many older Americans are working longer than ever, whereas others are involuntarily unemployed. How long people age 65 and older work depends on factors such as gender, race and ethnicity, marital status, and social class.

4. There are five common grandparenting styles: remote, companionate, involved, advisory, and cultural transmitter. These styles often reflect factors such as the grandparents' age, geographic distance, and relationships with their adult children. In some cases, grandparents act as surrogate parents.

5. Divorce by their adult children creates both opportunities and dilemmas for grandparents. In some cases, relationships with grandchildren grow stronger; in others, especially for in-laws, ties become weaker.

6. All families must deal with the death of older parents. Physicians and other health care professionals and families often view death differently.

7. Many families turn to hospice care, which makes the dying person more comfortable and provides companionship and pain control.

8. On average, women live at least five years longer than men. Most women outlive their husbands, but both widows' and widowers' coping strategies typically involve adapting to a change in income and dealing with loneliness and the emotional pain of losing a spouse.

9. Today adult children provide more care (and more extensive types of care) to older parents over much longer periods than ever before. As our population ages, more disabled and frail Americans will need long-term care.

10. A divisive issue is whether our society provides too much treatment to older people, especially the oldest-old who are terminally ill and, consequently, shortchanges children. There is also the question of who will pay for aging baby boomers who are generally less healthy than some earlier birth cohorts but who will demand more health care services.

KEY TERMS

life expectancy 474
gerontologist 475
young-old 475
old-old 475
oldest-old 475
centenarian 475
old-age dependency ratio 475
later-life family 476
dementia 480

Alzheimer's disease 480
ageism 482
retirement 483
Social Security 483
Medicare 484
multigenerational household 490
intergenerational ambivalence 492
dying trajectory 493
hospice 494

living will 495
bereavement 496
grief 496
mourning 496
caregiver 499

PEARSON
myfamilylab MyFamilyLab provides a
wealth of resources. Go to
www.myfamilylab.com <http://www.myfamily-
lab.com/>, to enhance your comprehension of the
content in this chapter. You can take practice

exams, view videos relevant to the subject matter,
listen to audio files, explore topics further by
using Social Explorer, and use the tools contained
in MySearchLab to help you write research
papers.

Glossary

A

abortion The expulsion of an embryo or fetus from the uterus.

absolute poverty Not having enough money to afford the most basic necessities of life such as food, clothing, or shelter.

acculturation The process of adapting to the language, values, beliefs, roles, and other characteristics of the host culture.

acquaintance rape The unwanted and forced sexual intercourse of a person who knows or is familiar with the rapist.

acquired immunodeficiency syndrome (AIDS) A degenerative disease caused by a virus that attacks the body's immune system and makes it susceptible to a number of diseases such as pneumonia and cancer.

adoption Taking a child into one's family through legal means and raising her or him as one's own.

agape Love that is altruistic and self-sacrificing and is directed toward all humankind.

ageism Discrimination against people on the basis of age, particularly against those who are old.

alimony Monetary payments made by one ex-spouse to the other after a divorce (sometimes called *spousal maintenance*).

Alzheimer's disease A progressive, degenerative disorder that attacks the brain and impairs memory, thinking, and behavior.

amniocentesis A procedure performed in the twentieth week of pregnancy, in which a sample of the amniotic fluid is withdrawn by a needle inserted into the abdomen; the fluid is analyzed for possible genetic disorders and biochemical abnormalities in the fetus.

androgyny A blend of culturally defined male and female characteristics.

annulment A ruling, usually by the Catholic Church, that a marriage is invalid for a variety of reasons, including adultery, pressure to marry, failure to consummate a marriage through vaginal intercourse, or a refusal to have children.

anorexia nervosa A dangerous eating disorder characterized by fear of obesity, together with a distorted body image and the conviction that one is fat, significant weight loss, and an absolute refusal to maintain weight within the normal limits for one's age and height.

arranged marriage A marriage in which parents or relatives choose the children's partners.

artificial insemination Sometimes called *donor insemination* (DI), a medical procedure in which semen is introduced artificially into the vagina or uterus at about the time of ovulation.

asexual Lacking any interest or desire for sex.

assimilation The conformity of ethnic group members to the culture of the dominant group, including intermarriage.

assisted reproductive technology (ART) A general term that includes all treatments and procedures that involve the handling of human eggs and sperm to establish a pregnancy.

attachment theory A theoretical perspective that proposes that our primary motivation in life is to be connected with other people because this is the only true security we will ever have.

authoritarian style An approach to parenting that is demanding, controlling, and punitive; emphasizes respect for authority, work, and order.

authoritative style An approach to parenting that is demanding but supportive and responsive; encourages autonomy and self-reliance; generally uses positive reinforcement instead of punitive, harsh discipline.

autoeroticism Arousal of sexual feeling without an external stimulus.

B

baby boomers People born in the post–World War II generation between 1946 and 1964.

battered woman syndrome A condition that describes a woman who has experienced many years of physical abuse and feels incapable of leaving her partner; used as a defense in cases in which such women have murdered their abusive husbands.

bereavement The period of recovery after the death of someone to whom we feel close.

bigamy Marrying a second person while a first marriage is still legal.

binge eating Consuming an unusually large amount of food and feeling that the eating is out of control.

birth rate The number of live births per 1,000 population.

bisexual A person who is sexually attracted to members of both sexes.

boomerang generation Young adults who move back into their parents' homes after living independently for a while.

bride price The required payment of money or property by the groom's family to the bride's family.

bulimia An eating disorder characterized by a cyclical pattern of eating binges followed by self-induced vomiting, fasting, excessive exercise, or the use of diuretics or laxatives.

bundling A courting custom in American colonial times in which a young man and woman, both fully dressed, spent the night in bed together, separated by a wooden board.

C

caregiver A person, paid or unpaid, who attends to the needs of someone who is sick or disabled.

centenarian A person who is 100 years old or older.

child abuse The physical or mental injury, sexual abuse, negligent treatment, or maltreatment of a child younger than age 18 by a person responsible for the child's welfare (often used interchangeably with *child maltreatment*).

child maltreatment A wide range of behaviors that place a child at serious risk, including physical abuse, sexual abuse, neglect, and emotional mistreatment.

child support Monetary payments by the noncustodial parent to the parent who has custody of children to help pay the expenses of raising the children.

chlamydia A sexually transmitted bacterial infection that can contribute to infertility.

chorionic villi sampling (CVS) A procedure in which some of the villi, or protrusions, of the membrane that surrounds the embryo are removed by a catheter through the vagina and analyzed for abnormalities in the fetus.

clinical research The study of individuals or small groups of people who seek help for physical and/or social problems from mental health professionals or other social scientists.

closed adoption The records of the adoption are kept sealed, the birth parent is not involved in the adoptee's life, and the child has no contact with the biological parents or little, if any, information about them.

co-custody Parents share physical and legal custody of their children equally.

cognitive development theory A theory positing that children learn on their own by thinking, reasoning, and interpreting information in their environment.

cohabitation A living arrangement in which two unrelated people are unmarried but live together and are in a sexual relationship.

collaborative divorce A method of trying to resolve disputes before finalizing a divorce in court.

common-law marriage A nonceremonial relationship that people establish by cohabitation.

commuter marriage A marriage in which partners live and work in separate geographic areas and get together intermittently.

compadrazgo A Mexican American family system in which close family friends are formally designated as godparents of a newborn, participate in the child's important rites of passage, and maintain continuing strong ties with their godchild.

companionate family A type of family that is built on mutual affection, sexual attraction, compatibility, and personal happiness between husband and wife.

companionate love Love that is characterized by feelings of togetherness, tenderness, and deep affection and sharing and supporting each other over time.

comparable worth A concept that calls for equal pay for men and women who are doing work that involves similar skill, effort, responsibility, and work conditions.

conflict-habituated marriage A marriage in which the partners fight both verbally and physically but do not believe that fighting is a good reason for divorce.

conflict theory A macro-level sociological theory that examines the ways in which groups disagree and struggle over power and compete for scarce resources; views conflict and its consequences as natural, inevitable, and often desirable.

contraception The prevention of pregnancy by behavioral, mechanical, or chemical means.

co-parenting A process in which divorced parents are involved in making decisions about the child's education, health care, religious training, and social activities.

corporate welfare An array of direct subsidies, tax breaks, and indirect assistance that the government has created for the special benefit of businesses.

cult of domesticity An ideology, which emerged during the 1880s, that glorified women's domestic roles.

cultural pluralism Maintaining aspects of immigrants' original cultures while living peacefully with the host culture.

cunnilingus Oral stimulation of a woman's genitals.

custody A court-mandated ruling as to which parent will have the primary responsibility for the welfare and upbringing of a child. *See also* joint custody.

D

date rape Unwanted, forced sexual intercourse in the context of a dating situation.

dating The process of meeting people socially for possible mate selection.

dating cohabitation A living arrangement that occurs when a couple who spends a great deal of time together eventually decides to move in together.

deindustrialization A process of social and economic change resulting from the reduction of industrial activity, especially manufacturing.

dementia The loss of mental abilities that most commonly occurs late in life.

depression A mental disorder characterized by pervasive sadness and other negative emotions that interfere with the ability to work, study, sleep, eat, and enjoy once-pleasurable activities.

developmental tasks Specific role expectations and responsibilities that must be fulfilled as people move through the family life cycle.

devitalized marriage A marriage in which the partners are initially in love, spend time together, and have a satisfying sex life but in time find they are staying together out of duty; because they see no alternatives, they do not consider divorce.

DEWK (dual-employed with kids) A family in which both parents are employed full time outside the home.

discouraged worker An unemployed person who wants to work and has looked for a job during the preceding year but has not searched in the past four weeks because she or he believes that job hunting is futile.

discretionary income Money remaining after the costs of basic necessities such as rent or mortgage, food, utilities, and transportation costs have been paid.

discrimination An *act* that treats people unequally or unfairly.

divorce The legal and formal dissolution of a marriage.

divorce mediation The technique and practice in which a trained arbitrator helps a divorcing couple come to an agreement and resolve issues such as support, child custody, and the division of property.

dominant group Any physically or culturally distinctive group that has the most economic and political power, the greatest privileges, and the highest social status.

dowry The money, goods, or property a woman brings to a marriage.

dual-career couple Both partners work in professional or managerial positions that require extensive training, a long-term commitment, and ongoing professional growth.

dual-earner couple Both partners work outside the home (also called *dual-income, two-income, two-earner,* or *dual-worker* couples).

dying trajectory The speed with which a person dies because of declining physical functions.

E

ecological theory A theoretical perspective that examines how a family influences and is influenced by its environment.

economy The social institution that determines how a society produces, distributes, and consumes goods and services.

egalitarian family A family structure in which both partners share power and authority about equally.

elder abuse Physical abuse, negligence, financial exploitation, psychological abuse, deprivation of necessities such as food and heat, isolation from friends and relatives, and failure to administer needed medications to people age 65 or older (sometimes called *elder mistreatment*).

emotional abuse A form of intimate partner violence that occurs when a partner threatens her or his loved one or her or his possessions or harms a partner's sense of self-worth.

endogamy The requirement that people marry or have sexual relations within a particular group (sometimes called *homogamy*).

endometriosis A condition in which tissue spreads outside the womb and attaches itself to other pelvic organs, such as the ovaries or the fallopian tubes.

engagement The formalization of a couple's decision to marry.

equity theory A theoretical perspective that proposes that an intimate relationship is satisfying and stable if both people see it as equitable and mutually beneficial.

eros Love based on beauty and physical attractiveness.

ethnic group A set of people who identify with a common national origin or cultural heritage.

evaluation research Research that assesses the effectiveness of social programs in both the public and private sectors.

exogamy The requirement that people marry outside the group, and not marry their relatives or members of the same clan or tribe (sometimes called *heterogamy*).

experiment A data collection method in a controlled situation in which the researcher manipulates variables and measures their cause and effect.

expressive role In structural-functional theory, the supportive and nurturing role of the wife/mother who sustains the family unit and supports the husband/father emotionally.

extended family A family that consists of parents and children as well as other kin, such as uncles and aunts, nieces and nephews, cousins, and grandparents.

F

familism The notion that within a given family, family relationships take precedence over the concerns of individual family members.

family An intimate group of two or more people who (1) live together in a committed relationship, (2) care for one another and any children, and (3) share activities and close emotional ties.

familycide Murdering one's spouse, ex-spouse, children, and/or other relatives before attempting or committing suicide.

family development theory A micro-level theory that examines the changes that families experience over the lifespan.

family life cycle The transitions that a family makes as it moves through a series of stages or events.

family of orientation The family into which a person is born or adopted.

family of procreation The family a person forms by marrying and having or adopting children.

family policy The measures that governments take to improve the well-being of families.

family systems theory A theoretical perspective that views the family as a functioning unit that solves problems, makes decisions, and achieves collective goals.

father–stepmother family A family in which all the children are biological children of the father and stepchildren of the mother.

fellatio Oral stimulation of a man's penis.

female infanticide The intentional killing of baby girls because of a preference for sons.

feminist theories Theoretical perspectives that analyze socially constructed expectations based on variables such as gender roles, social class, race, ethnicity, and sexual orientation.

feminization of poverty The likelihood that female heads of households will be poor.

fertility The number of live births in a population.

fertility drugs Medications that stimulate the ovaries to produce eggs.

fertility rate The number of live children born per year per 1,000 women ages 15 to 44.

fetal alcohol syndrome (FAS) Physical deformities and/or mental retardation in an infant caused by the mother's excessive use of alcohol during pregnancy.

fictive kin A family in which nonrelatives are accepted as part of a family.

field research A data collection method whereby researchers collect information by systematically observing people in their natural surroundings.

filter theory The theory that people in search of potential mates go through a process whereby they screen out eligible partners according to certain criteria and thus reduce the pool of eligibles to a relatively small number of candidates.

flextime A practice that allows workers to change their daily arrival and departure times.

foster home A home in which a family raises a child or children who are not their own for a period of time but does not formally adopt them.

G

gender The socially learned attitudes and behaviors that characterize a person of one sex or the other, based on differing social and cultural expectations of the sexes.

gender identity An individual's perception of him- or herself as either masculine or feminine.

gender pay gap The income difference between women and men (sometimes called the *wage gap*, *pay gap*, or the *gender wage gap*).

gender roles Distinctive patterns of attitudes, behaviors, and activities that society prescribes for females and males.

gender stereotype Expectations about how people will look, act, think, and feel based on their sex.

gender stratification Having unequal access to wealth, power, status, prestige, opportunity, and other valued resources because of one's gender.

generalized other People who do not have close ties to a child but who influence the child's internalization of society's norms and values.

genogram A diagram of the biological relationships among family members.

gerontologist A scientist who studies the biological, psychological, and social aspects of aging.

glass ceiling A collection of attitudinal and organizational biases in the workplace that prevents women from advancing to leadership positions.

globalization The growth and spread of investment, trade, production, communication, and new technology around the world.

grief The emotional response to loss.

H

half sibling A brother or sister who shares only one biological or adoptive parent.

heterogamy Dating or marrying someone from a social, racial, ethnic, religious, or age group different from one's own (sometimes called *exogamy*).

heterosexism The belief that heterosexuality is superior to and more "natural" than homosexuality.

heterosexual A person who is sexually attracted to members of the opposite sex.

homogamy Dating or marrying someone with similar social characteristics such as ethnicity, race, religion, age, and social class (sometimes called *endogamy*).

homophobia Fear and hatred of homosexuality.

homosexual A person who is sexually attracted to persons of the same sex.

hormones Chemical substances secreted into the bloodstream by glands of the endocrine system.

hospice A place for the care of terminally ill patients.

human immunodeficiency virus (HIV) The virus that causes AIDS.

hypergamy Dating or marrying someone in a higher social class to improve one's social standing.

hypogamy Dating or marrying someone who is in a lower social class than one's own.

I

identity bargaining A process in marriage in which newly married partners must modify their idealized expectations and deal with the realities of living together as husband and wife.

incest Sexual intercourse between family members who are closely related. *See also* incest taboo.

incest taboo Cultural norms and laws that forbid sexual intercourse between close blood relatives, such as brother and sister, father and daughter, or mother and son.

income The amount of money a person receives, usually through wages or salaries, but can also include rents, interest on savings accounts, dividends on stock, or the proceeds from a business.

infant mortality rate The number of babies under age 1 who die per 1,000 live births in a given year.

infertility The inability to conceive a baby.

instrumental role In structural-functional theory, the breadwinner role of the father or husband who provides food and shelter for the family and, at least theoretically, is hardworking, tough, and competitive.

intergenerational ambivalence Contradictions in relationships between parents and adult children that arise from both structured kinship roles and personal emotions.

intergenerational transmission of divorce The likelihood of divorce in later generations because an earlier generation passed down many of its problems.

intersexuals People whose medical classification at birth is not clearly male or female (this term has replaced *hermaphrodites*).

intimate partner violence (IPV) Abuse that occurs between two people in a close relationship.

in vitro fertilization (IVF) The surgical removal of eggs from a woman's ovaries, their fertilization in a petri dish (a specially shaped glass container) with sperm from her husband or another donor, and then the implantation of the embryos into the woman's uterus.

J

joint custody A custody arrangement in which the children divide their time between both parents; in *joint legal custody*, parents share decision making about the children's upbringing; in *joint physical custody*, the children live alternately and for specified periods in each parent's home.

joint stepfamily A family in which at least one child is a biological child of both parents, at least one child is the biological child of one parent and the stepchild of the other parent, and no other type of child is present.

K

kinship system A network of people who are related by marriage, blood, or adoption.

L

latchkey kids Children who return after school to an empty home and are alone and unsupervised until their parents or another adult arrives.

latent functions Functions that are not recognized or intended; present but not immediately visible.

later-life family A family that is beyond the years of child rearing and has launched the children or a childless family beginning to plan for retirement.

life expectancy The average length of time people of the same age will live.

living will A legal document in which a person can specify which, if any, life-support measures he or she wants in the event of serious illness and whether and when such measures should be discontinued.

ludus Love that is carefree and casual, "fun and games."

M

machismo A concept of masculinity that stresses attributes such as dominance, assertiveness, pride, and sexual prowess.

macro-level perspective A social science perspective that focuses on large-scale patterns that characterize society as a whole.

mania Love that is obsessive, jealous, and possessive.

manifest functions Functions that are recognized or intended and present in a clearly evident way.

marital burnout The gradual deterioration of love and, ultimately, the loss of an emotional attachment between marital partners.

marital rape An abusive act in which a husband forces his wife to engage in unwanted sexual intercourse (sometimes called *spousal rape* or *wife rape*).

marital roles The specific ways that married people define their behavior and structure their time.

marriage A socially approved mating relationship.

marriage market A courtship process in which prospective spouses compare the assets and liabilities of eligible partners and choose the best available mate.

marriage squeeze A sex imbalance in the ratio of available unmarried women and men.

masturbation Sexual self-pleasuring that involves some form of direct physical stimulation.

matriarchy A system in which the oldest females (usually grandmothers and mothers) control cultural, political, and economic resources and, consequently, have power over males.

matrilineal A kinship system in which children trace their family descent through their mother's line, and property is passed on to female heirs.

matrilocal A residential pattern in which newly married couples live with the wife's family.

Medicare A federal health insurance program for people age 65 and older that provides almost universal health coverage.

menopause The cessation of the menstrual cycle and the loss of reproductive capacity.

micro-level perspective A social science perspective that focuses on small-scale patterns of social interaction in specific settings.

minority group A group of people who may be treated differently or unequally because of their physical or cultural characteristics, such as gender, sexual orientation, religion, or skin color.

miscegenation Marriage or sexual relations between a man and a woman of different races.

monogamy The practice of having only one husband or wife.

motherhood penalty A gender pay gap attributed to being a mother, rather than just a woman (also called a *motherhood wage penalty* and *mommy penalty*).

mother-stepfather family A family in which all the children are biological children of the mother and stepchildren of the father.

mourning The customary outward expression of grief over the loss of a loved one.

multigenerational household A home in which three or more generations live together.

N

neolocal A residential pattern in which newly married couples set up their own residence, rather than live with either set of parents.

no-fault divorce A divorce process in which neither partner need establish the guilt or wrongdoing of the other.

norm A culturally defined rule for behavior.

nuclear family A family made up of a wife, a husband, and their biological or adopted children.

O

offshoring The sending of work or jobs to another country to cut a company's costs at home (sometimes called *international outsourcing* or *offshore outsourcing*).

old-age dependency ratio The number of people age 65 and older who are not in the labor force per 100 people ages 20 to 64 who are employed (sometimes called a *dependency ratio*, an *age dependency ratio*, or a *support ratio*).

old-old People between ages 75 and 84.

oldest-old People age 85 and older.

open adoption The practice of sharing information and maintaining contact between biological and adoptive parents throughout the child's life.

P

parenting style A general approach to interacting with and disciplining children.

passive-congenial marriage A marriage in which partners with minimal emotional investment and expectations maintain independent spheres of interests and activities and derive satisfaction from relationships with others rather than from each other.

patriarchy A system in which the oldest males (grandfathers, fathers, and uncles) control cultural, political, and economic resources and, consequently, have power over females.

patrilineal A kinship system in which children trace their family descent through their father's line, and property is passed on to male heirs.

patrilocal A residential pattern in which newly married couples live with the husband's family.

peer group A group of people who are similar in age, social status, and interests.

pelvic inflammatory disease (PID) An infection of the uterus that spreads to the fallopian tubes, ovaries, and surrounding tissues and produces scarring that blocks the fallopian tubes.

permissive style An approach to parenting that is highly responsive, warm, and indulgent; this approach places few requirements on children for orderly behavior or household tasks.

physical abuse A form of intimate partner violence that occurs when a person hurts or tries to hurt a partner using physical force.

polygamy A form of marriage in which a woman or man has two or more spouses.

population Any well-defined group of people (or things) that researchers want to know something about.

POSSLQs "Persons of the opposite sex sharing living quarters"; a U.S. Census Bureau household category.

postpartum depression (PPD) A serious illness that can occur up to a year after childbirth.

poverty line The minimum income level determined by the federal government to be necessary for individuals' and families' basic subsistence.

power The ability to impose one's will on others.

pragma Love that is rational and based on practical considerations, such as compatibility and perceived benefits.

preimplantation genetic diagnosis (PGD) A new assisted reproductive technology that enables physicians to identify genetic diseases in the embryo prior to implantation, before the pregnancy is established.

prejudice An *attitude* that prejudges people, usually in a negative way.

premarital cohabitation A living arrangement in which a couple tests its relationship before making a final commitment to get married.

primary group Important people, such as family members and close friends, characterized by close, long-lasting, intimate, and face-to-face interaction.

propinquity Geographic closeness.

Q

qualitative research A data collection process whereby social scientists examine nonnumerical material that they then interpret.

quantitative research A data collection process whereby researchers focus on a numerical analysis of people's responses or specific characteristics.

R

racial-ethnic group A group of people with distinctive racial and cultural characteristics.

racial group A category of people who share physical characteristics, such as skin color, that members of a society consider socially important.

racial socialization A process whereby parents teach their children to negotiate race-related barriers and experiences in a racially stratified society and to take pride in their ancestry.

racism A set of beliefs that one's own racial group is inherently superior to others.

relative poverty Not having enough money to maintain an average standard of living.

retirement Exit from the paid labor force.

role The obligations and expectations attached to a particular status or position in society.

role conflict The frustrations and uncertainties a person experiences when the expectations of two or more roles are incompatible.

role overload A feeling of being overwhelmed by multiple commitments.

role strain Conflicts that someone feels *within* a role.

S

sample A group of people (or things) that are representative of the population that researchers want to study.

sandwich generation Midlife men and women who feel caught between the need to care for both their own children and their aging parents.

secondary analysis An examination of data that have been collected by other researchers.

secondary group Groups characterized by relatively impersonal and short-term relationships and in which people work together on common tasks or activities.

self-disclosure Open communication in which one person offers his or her honest thoughts and feelings to another person in the hope that truly open communication will follow.

semi-open adoption Sometimes called *mediated adoption*, there is communication between the adoptive parents, birth parents, and adopted children, but through a third party (e.g., an agency caseworker or attorney) rather than directly.

separation A temporary period of living apart required by most states before a divorce is granted.

serial cohabitation Living with different sexual partners over time.

serial monogamy Marrying several people, one at a time; that is, marrying, divorcing, remarrying, divorcing again, and so on.

sex The biological—chromosomal, anatomical, hormonal, and other physical and physiological—characteristics with which we are born and that determine whether we are male or female.

sexism An attitude or behavior that discriminates against one sex, usually females, based on the assumed superiority of the other sex.

sex ratio The proportion of men to women in a country or group.

sexual abuse A form of intimate partner violence that occurs when a person forces a partner to take part in a sex act when she or he doesn't consent.

sexual harassment Any unwelcome sexual advance, request for sexual favors, or other conduct of a sexual nature that makes a person uncomfortable and interferes with her or his work.

sexual identity Our awareness of ourselves as male or female and the ways in which we express our sexual values, attitudes, feelings, and beliefs.

sexually transmitted diseases (STDs) Diseases that are spread by contact with body parts or fluids that harbor what are usually bacterial or viral microorganisms.

sexually transmitted infections (STIs) Diseases that are spread by contact, either sexual or nonsexual, with body parts or fluids that harbor specific microorganisms (generally bacterial or viral). (Corresponds to but has recently replaced another frequently used term, *sexually transmitted diseases,* or STDs.)

sexual orientation A preference for sexual partners of the same sex (homosexual), of the opposite sex (heterosexual), or of either sex (bisexual).

sexual response A person's physiological reaction to sexual stimulation.

sexual script Norms that specify what is acceptable and what is unacceptable sexual activity, identify eligible sexual partners, and define the boundaries of sexual behavior in time and place.

siblicide Killing a brother or sister.

significant others People in our primary groups—such as parents, friends, relatives, and teachers—who play an important role in our socialization.

social class A category of people who have a similar standing or rank based on wealth, education, power, prestige, and other valued resources.

social exchange theory A micro-level theory that proposes that the interaction between two or more people is based on the efforts of each to maximize rewards and minimize costs.

social integration The social bonds that people have with others and the community at large.

socialization The process of acquiring the language, accumulated knowledge, attitudes, beliefs, and values of one's society and culture and learning the social and interpersonal skills needed to function effectively in society.

social learning theory A theory that posits that people learn attitudes, beliefs, and behaviors through social interaction; learning is the result of reinforcement, imitation, and modeling.

Social Security A public retirement pension system administered by the federal government.

sociobiology The study of how biology affects social behavior.

socioeconomic status (SES) An overall rank of an individual's position in society based on income, education, and occupation.

sole custody A type of custody in which one parent has exclusive responsibility for raising a child and the other parent has specified visitation rights.

split custody A custody arrangement in which children are divided between the parents, usually female children going to the mother, male children to the father.

stepfamily A household in which two adults who are biological or adoptive parents (heterosexual, gay, or lesbian), with a child from a prior relationship, elect to marry or to cohabit.

stepsibling A brother or sister who shares a biological or adoptive parent and a stepparent.

storge Love that is slow burning, peaceful, and affectionate.

structural-functional theory A macro-level theoretical perspective that examines the relationship between the family and the larger society as well as the internal relationships among family members.

substance abuse An overindulgence in and dependence on a drug or other chemical that is detrimental to an individual's physical and mental health or the welfare of others.

substitute marriage A long-term commitment between two people who don't plan to marry.

surrogacy A woman who is capable of carrying a pregnancy to term serves as a substitute for a woman who cannot bear children.

surveys Data collection methods that systematically collect information from respondents either by a mailed or self-administered questionnaire or by a face-to-face or telephone interview.

symbolic interaction theory A micro-level theory that examines the everyday behavior of individuals.

T

telecommuting A flexible work style that allows working from home through electronic linkups to the central office.

theory A set of statements that explains why a particular phenomenon occurs.

total fertility rate (TFR) The average number of children born to a woman during her lifetime.

total marriage A marriage in which the spouses participate in each other's lives at all levels and have little tension or unresolved hostility.

trailing spouse A wife or husband who resigns from a position to search for another job in the location where her or his spouse has accepted a job.

transgendered A term that encompasses transsexuals, intersexuals, and transvestites.

transsexuals People who are born with one biologial sex but choose to live their life as another sex—either by consistently cross-dressing or by surgically altering their sex.

transvestites People who cross-dress at times but don't necessarily consider themselves a member of the opposite sex.

trial marriage An arrangement in which people live together to find out what marriage might be like.

two-person single career An arrangement in which one spouse partici-

pates in the other's career behind the scenes without pay or direct recognition.

U

underemployed worker A person who holds part-time jobs but would rather work full time or who accepts jobs below his or her experience, skill, and educational levels.

uninvolved style A parenting approach in which parents are neither supportive nor demanding because they are indifferent.

V

vital marriage A marriage in which spouses maintain a close relationship, resolve conflicts quickly through compromise, and often make sacrifices for each other.

W

wealth The money and economic assets that a person or family owns, including property and income.

welfare Government aid to those who can't support themselves, generally because they are poor or unemployed.

work Physical or mental activity that accomplishes or produces something, either goods or services.

working poor People who spend at least 27 weeks in the labor force (working or looking for work) but whose family or personal income falls below the official poverty level.

Y

young-old People between ages 65 and 74.

References

The references that are new to this edition are printed in blue.

A

ABAWI, A. 2009. Afghanistan "rape" law puts women's rights front and center. *New York Times*, April 7, www.nytimes.com (accessed April 9, 2009).

ABDULRAHIM, R. 2008. A match-making tradition with an up-to-date twist. *Los Angeles Times*, December 26, www.latimes.com (accessed December 27, 2008).

ABMA, J. C., AND G. M. MARTINEZ. 2006. Childlessness among older women in the United States: Trends and profiles. *Journal of Marriage and Family* 68 (November): 1045–56.

ABMA, J. C., G. M. MARTINEZ, W. D. MOSHER, AND B. S. DAWSON. 2004. Teenagers in the United States: Sexual activity, contraceptive use, and childbearing, 2002. *Vital and Health Statistics* (Series 23, No. 24). Hyattsville, MD: National Center for Health Statistics.

Abortion views by religious affiliation. 2009. January 15, www.pewforum.org (accessed June 30, 2009).

ABRAHAMS, G., AND S. AHLBRAND. 2002. *Boy v. girl? How gender shapes who we are, what we want, and how we get along.* Minneapolis: Free Spirit.

ABSHER, C. 2009. What does assisted living really cost? Care Pathways, www.carepathways.com (accessed September 27, 2009).

ACEVEDO, B. P., AND A. ARON. 2009. Does a long-term relationship kill romantic love? *Review of General Psychology* 13 (March): 59–65.

A child's day, 2006. 2009. Selected indicators of child well-being. Detailed table package. Survey of Income and Program Participation, 2004 Panel, Wave 8. U.S. Census Bureau, www.census.gov (accessed July 11, 2009).

ACKERMAN, D. 1994. *A natural history of love.* New York: Random House.

ACOCK, A. C., AND D. H. DEMO. 1994. *Family diversity and well-being.* Thousand Oaks, CA: Sage.

ACOSTA-BELÉN, E., AND C. E. SANTIAGO. 2006. *Puerto Ricans in the United States: A contemporary portrait.* Boulder, CO: Lynne Rienner.

ACS, G., AND P. LOPREST. 2008. Job differences by race and ethnicity in the low-skill job market. Urban Institute, February, www.urban.org (accessed June 1, 2009).

ACUNA, R. 1988. *Occupied America: A history of Chicanos*, 3rd ed. New York: Harper & Row.

ADAMS, B. 1980. *The family.* Chicago: Rand McNally.

ADAMS, B. N. 2004. Families and family study in international perspective. *Journal of Marriage and Family* 66 (December): 1076–88.

ADAMS, J. A., K. HARPER, S. KNUDSON, AND J. REVILLA. 1994. Examination findings in legally confirmed child sexual abuse: It's normal to be normal. *Pediatrics* 94 (September): 310–17.

ADIMORA, A., AND V. SCHOENBACH. 2005. Social context, sexual networks, and racial disparities in rates of sexually transmitted infections. *Journal of Infectious Diseases* 191, S115–S122.

ADLER-BAEDER, F., J. L. KERPELMAN, D. G. SCHRAMM, B. HIGGINBOTHAM, AND A. PAULK. 2007. The impact of relationship education on adolescents of diverse backgrounds. *Family Relations* 56 (July): 291–303.

AHITUV, A., AND R. LERMAN. 2004. Job turnover, wage rates, and marital stability: How are they related? The Urban Institute, November www.urban.org (accessed July 5, 2006).

AHRONS, C. 1994. *The good divorce: Keeping your family together when your marriage comes apart.* New York: HarperCollins.

AHRONS, C. 2004. *We're still family.* New York: HarperCollins.

AHRONS, C. R. 2006. Family ties after divorce: Long-term implications for children. *Family Process* 46 (March): 53–65.

AHRONS, C. R., AND R. H. RODGERS. 1987. *Divorced families: A multidisciplinary developmental view.* New York: Norton.

AINSWORTH, M., ET AL. 1978. *Patterns of attachment: A psychological study of the strange situation.* Hillsdale, NJ: Erlbaum.

AIZENMAN, N. C. 2005. In Afghanistan, new misgivings about an old but risky practice. *Washington Post*, April 17, A16.

AIZER, A., AND S. MC LANAHAN. 2005. The impact of child support enforcement on fertility, parental investment and child well-being. National Bureau of Economic Research, www.nber.org (accessed July 10, 2006).

ALBAS, D., AND C. ALBAS. 1987. The pulley alternative for the wheel theory of the development of love. *International Journal of Comparative Sociology* 28 (3–4): 223–27.

ALBERT, B., S. BROWN, AND C. M. FLANNIGAN, EDS. 2003. 14 and younger: The sexual behavior of young adolescents. The National Campaign to Prevent Teen Pregnancy. www.teenpregnancy.org (accessed June 10, 2003).

ALI, L. 2008. Having kids makes you happy. *Newsweek*, July 7/July 14, 62–63.

ALI, L., AND R. KELLEY. 2008. The curious lives of surrogates. *Newsweek*, April 7, 45–51.

ALI, L., AND L. MILLER. 2004. The secret lives of wives. *Newsweek,* July 12, 47–54.

ALIBHAI -BROWN, Y. 1993. Marriage of minds not hearts. *New Statesman & Society*, February 12, 28–29.

ALINI, E. 2007. In Italy, hard to get the kids to move out. *Christian Science Monitor*, November 15, 7.

AL-JADDA, S. 2006. Seeking love, American Muslim style. *Christian Science Monitor*, February 14, 9.

ALLAN, J. 2002. *Because I love you: The silent shadow of child sexual abuse.* Charlottesville, VA: Virginia Foundation for the Humanities Press.

ALLEN, E. B., D. C. ATKINS, D. H. BAUCOM, D. K. SNYDER, K. C. GORDON, AND S. GLASS. 2005. Intrapersonal, interpersonal, and contextual factors in engaging in and responding to infidelity. *Clinical Psychology: Science and Practice* 12 (June): 101–30.

ALLEN, K. R., AND B. K. BEITIN. 2007. Gender and class in culturally diverse families. In *Cultural diversity and families: Expanding perspectives*, eds. B. S. Trask and R. R. Hamon, 63–79. Thousand Oaks, CA: Sage.

ALLEN, K. R., E. H. HUSSER, D. J. STONE, AND C. E. JORDAL. 2008. Agency and error in young adults' stories of sexual decision making. *Family Relations* 57 (October): 517–29.

ALLGOR, C. 2002. *Parlor politics: In which the ladies of Washington help build a city and a government.* Charlottesville: University of Virginia Press.

ALMEIDA, R. V., ED. 1994. *Expansions of feminist family theory through diversity.* New York: Haworth.

ALSEVER, J. 2007. In the computer dating game, room for a coach. *New York Times*, March 11, 5.

ALTON, B. G. 2001. You think being a dad is a good deal? *Business Week*, April 2, 20.

ALTSTEIN, H. 2006. For adoption, leave race out of the discussion. *Baltimore Sun*, January 25, 15A.

ALVAREZ, L. 2006. (Name her) is a liar and a cheat. *New York Times* (February 16): E1–E2.

ALVEAR, M. 2003. The annual rite: Dumbing down love. *Christian Science Monitor*, February14, 11.

Alzheimer's Association. 2009. 2009 Alzheimer's disease: Facts and figures, www.alzheimers.org (accessed September 20, 2009).

AMATO, P. 2004. The future of marriage. In Vision 2004: What is the future of marriage? eds., Paul Amato and N. Gonzalez, 99–101. Minneapolis, MN: National Council on Family Relations.

AMATO, P. R. 2003. Reconciling divergent perspectives: Judith Wallerstein, quantitative family research, and children of divorce. *Family Relations* 52 (October): 332–339.

AMATO, P. R. 2007. Divorce and the well-being of adults and children. *Family Focus* 52 (December): F3–F4, F18.

AMATO, P. R., AND T. D. AFIFI. 2006. Feeling caught between parents: Adult children's relations with parents and subjective well-being. *Journal of Marriage and Family* 68 (February): 222–35.

AMATO, P. R., A. BOOTH, D. R. JOHNSON, AND S. J. ROGERS. 2007. *Alone together: How marriage in America is changing.* Cambridge, MA: Harvard University Press.

AMATO, P. R., AND J. CHEADLE. 2005. The long reach of divorce: Divorce and child well-being across three generations. *Journal of Marriage and Family* 67 (February): 191–206.

AMATO, P. R., AND J. G. GILBRETH. 1999. Nonresident fathers and children's well-being: A meta-analysis. *Journal of Marriage and the Family* 61 (August): 557–73.

AMATO, P. R., AND B. HOHMANN-MARRIOTT. 2007. A comparison of high- and low-distress marriages that end in divorce. *Journal of Marriage and Family* 69 (August): 621–38.

AMATO, P. R., D. R. JOHNSON, A. BOOTH, AND S. J. ROGERS. 2003. Continuity and change in marital quality between 1980 and 2000. *Journal of Marriage and Family* 65 (February): 1–22.

AMATO, P. R., C. E. MYERS, AND R. E. EMERY. 2009. Changes in nonresident father-child contact from 1976 to 2002. *Family Relations* 58 (February): 41–53.

AMBERT, A.-M. 1997. *Parents, children, and adolescents: Interactive relationships and development in context.* New York: Haworth.

AMBERT, A.-M. 2001. *The effect of children on parents,* 2nd ed. New York: Haworth.

American Academy of Pediatrics. 1998. Guidance for effective discipline. *Pediatrics* 101 (April): 723–728.

American Academy of Pediatrics. 2001. Children, adolescents, and television. *Pediatrics* 107 (February): 423–26.

American Hospital Association. 2007. When I'm 64: How boomers will change health care. www.aha.org (accessed September 27, 2009).

AMERICAN HUMANE ASSOCIATION. 2001. Answers to common questions about child abuse and neglect. www.americanhumane.org (accessed October 3, 2003).

American Indian and Alaska Native heritage month: November 2008. 2008. U.S. Census Bureau News, Facts for Features, CB08-FF.18, October 16, www.census.gov (accessed March 10, 2009).

American Indian– and Alaska Native–Owned Firms: 2002. 2006. U.S. Census Bureau, SB02-00CS-AIAN (RV), www.census.gov (accessed May 1, 2007).

American Kennel Club. 2006. AKC survey finds dog owners looking for canine qualities in human partners. January 30, www.akc.org (accessed May 29, 2009).

AMERICAN LAW INSTITUTE. 2002. *Principles of the law of family dissolution: Analysis and recommendations.* New York: Matthew Bender & Company.

American Rhetoric Online Speech Bank. 2004. Bill Cosby—address at the NAACP on the 50th anniversary of *Brown v. Board of Education.* May 17, www.americanrhetoric.com (accessed March 20, 2009).

American Society for Aesthetic Plastic Surgery. 2009. Cosmetic procedures in 2007. February 25, 2008, www.cosmeticplasticsurgery statistics.com (accessed April 20, 2009).

ANANAT, E. O., AND G. MICHAELS. 2008. The effect of marital breakup on the income distribution of women and children. *Journal of Human Resources* 43 (3), 611–29.

ANCHETA, A. N. 1998. *Race, rights, and the Asian American experience.* New Brunswick, NJ: Rutgers University Press.

ANDELIN, H. 1974. *Fascinating womanhood: A guide to a happy marriage.* Santa Barbara, CA: Pacific.

ANDERSON, E. 1999. *Code of the street: Decency, violence, and the moral life of the inner city.* New York: Norton.

ANDERSON, K. L. 1997. Gender, status, and domestic violence: An integration of feminist and family violence approaches. *Journal of Marriage and the Family* 59 (August): 655–69.

ANDERSON, K. L. 2002. Perpetrator or victim? Relationships between intimate partner violence and well-being. *Journal of Marriage and Family* 64 (November): 851–63.

ANDERSON, K. L. 2008. Is partner violence worse in the context of control? *Journal of Marriage and Family* 70 (December): 1157–68.

ANDERSSON, G., T. NOACK, A. SEIERSTAD, AND H. WEEDON-FEKJAER. 2006. The demographics of same-sex marriages in Norway and Sweden. *Demography* 43 (February): 79–98.

ANGIER, N. 1985. Finding trouble in paradise. *Time,* January 28, www.time.com (accessed March 3, 2009).

ANN LANDERS. 2000. *Washington Post,* May 9, C11.

ANN LANDERS. 2001. *Baltimore Sun,* August 10, 3E.

Anorexia Nervosa and Related Eating Disorders, Inc. 2006. Statistics: How many people have eating disorders? January 16, www.anred.com (accessed August 7, 2006).

ANTONUCCI, T. C., H. AKIYAMA, AND A. MERLINE. 2001. Dynamics of social relationships in midlife. In *Handbook of midlife development,* ed. M. E. Lachman, 571–98. New York: Wiley.

APPEL, N. H., AND V. SEITZ. 1991. Four models of adolescent mother-grandmother relationships in black inner-city families. *Family Relations* 40 (October): 421–29.

A profile of the working poor, 2007. 2009. U.S. Department of Labor, U.S. Bureau of Labor Statistics, March, Report 1012, www.dol .gov (accessed August 5, 2009).

APTER, T. 2009. *What do you want from me?: Learning to get along with in-laws.* New York: W. W. Norton.

AQUILINO, W. S. 2006. The non-custodial father-child relationship from adolescence into young adulthood. *Journal of Marriage and Family* 68 (November): 929–46.

AREND, L., AND S. SACHS. 2008. In Europe, a battle against ultrathin ideals for women. *Christian Science Monitor,* April 17, 1, 4.

ARDITTI, J. A. 1999. Rethinking relationships between divorced mothers and their children: Capitalizing on family strengths. *Family Relations* 48 (April): 109–19.

ARENDELL, T. 1997. A social constructionist approach to parenting. In *Contemporary parenting: Challenges and issues,* ed. T. Arendell, 1–44. Thousand Oaks, CA: Sage.

ARGETSINGER, A., AND R. ROBERTS. 2008. Sibling revelation: An overlooked branch of Cindy McCain's family tree. *Washington Post,* August 20, C1

ARIÈS, P. 1962. *Centuries of childhood.* New York: Vintage.

ARMARIO, C. 2005. More Muslims find online dating a good match. *Christian Science Monitor,* January 19, 16.

ARMOUR, S. 2008. Day care's new frontier: Your baby at your desk. *USA Today,* March 30, www.usatoday.com (accessed July 16, 2009).

ARMOUR, S. 2009. Foreclosure up: 1 in 84 homes affected in first half of year. *USA Today,* July 15, www.usatoday.com (accessed July 16, 2009).

ARMSTRONG, E. 2004. Gay marriages unite, and divide, families. *Christian Science Monitor,* May 20, 4–5.

ARMSTRONG, E. 2004. Should she pop the question? *Christian Science Monitor* (February 13): 1, 11.

ARONSON, E. 1995. *The social animal,* 7th ed. New York: W. H. Freeman.

ASHBURN, E. 2007. A race to rescue native tongues. *Chronicle of Higher Education,* September 28, B15.

Asian American Justice Center. 2006. Asian Pacific Americans in prime time: Setting the stage. www.advancingequality.org (accessed April 3, 2009).

Asian/Pacific American heritage month: May 2009. 2009. U.S. Census Bureau News, Facts for Features, CB09-FF.06, March 3, www .census.gov (accessed March 10, 2009).

Ask Amy. 2008. Ring on finger isn't the kind she wants. *Baltimore Sun,* January 18, 6C.

ASWAD, B. C. 1994. Attitudes of immigrant women and men in the Dearborn area toward women's employment and welfare. In *Muslim communities in North America,* eds. Y. Haddad and J. Smith, 501–20. Albany: State University of New York Press.

ASWAD, B. C. 1997. Arab American families. In *Families in cultural context: Strengths and challenges in diversity,* ed. M. K. DeGenova, 213–47. Mountain View, CA: Mayfield.

ASWAD, B. C. 1999. Attitudes of Arab immigrants toward welfare. In *Arabs in America: Building a new future,* ed. M. W. Suleiman, 177–91. Philadelphia: Temple University Press.

ATCHLEY, R. C., AND A. S. BARUSCH. 2004. *Social forces and aging: An introduction to social gerontology,* 10th ed. Belmont, CA: Wadsworth.

ATKIN, R. 2002. Keeping kids "clean." *Christian Science Monitor,* December 4, 11–13.

ATKINS, D. C., AND D. E. KESSEL. 2008. Religiousness and infidelity: Attendance, but not faith and prayer, predict marital fidelity. *Journal of Marriage and Family* 70 (May): 407–18.

ATKINSON, M. P., T. N. GREENSTEIN, AND M. M. LANG. 2005. For women, breadwinning can be dangerous: Gendered resource theory and wife abuse. *Journal of Marriage and Family* 67 (December): 1137–48.

Attitudes and characteristics of freshmen at 4-year colleges, Fall 2005. *Chronicle of Higher Education,* Almanac Issue 2006–7, 53 (August 25): 18.

AUNOLA, K., AND J.-E. NURMI. 2005. The role of parenting styles in children's problem behavior. *Child Development* 76 (November/December): 1144–59.

AUSTIN, A. 2009. Unequal unemployment: Racial disparities by state will worsen in 2010. Economic Policy Institute, July 21, www.epi.org (accessed August 9, 2009).

AUTOR, D. H., AND D. DORN. 2009. Inequality and specialization: The growth of low-skill service jobs in the United States. National Bureau of Economic Research, Working Paper 15150, July, www.nber.org (accessed July 30, 2009).

AVELLAR, S., AND P. SMOCK. 2005. The economic consequences of the dissolution of cohabiting unions. *Journal of Marriage and Family* 67 (May): 315–27.

AVNI, N. 1991. Battered wives: The home as a total institution. *Violence and Victims* 6 (2): 137–49.

B

BABBIE, E. R. 2007. *The basics of social research,* 7th ed. Belmont, CA: Wadsworth Press.

BABCOCK, J. C., J. WALTZ, N. S. JACOBSON, AND J. M. GOTTMAN. 1993. Power and violence: The relation between communication patterns, power discrepancies, and domestic violence. *Journal of Consulting and Clinical Psychology* 61 (1): 40–50.

BACA ZINN, M. 2000. Feminism and family studies for a new century. *Annals of the American Academy of Political and Social Science* 571 (September): 42–56.

BACA ZINN, M., AND A. Y. H. POK. 2002. Tradition and transition in Mexican-origin families. In *Minority families in the United States: A multicultural perspective,* 3rd ed., ed. R. L. Taylor, 79–100. Upper Saddle River, NJ: Prentice Hall.

BACA ZINN, M., AND B. WELLS. 2000. Diversity within Latino families: New lessons for family social science. In *Handbook of family diversity,* eds. D. H. Demo, K. R. Allen, and M. A. Fine, 252–73. New York: Oxford University Press.

BACHMAN, H. J., AND P. L. CHASE -LANSDALE. 2005. Custodial grandmothers' physical, mental, and economic well-being: Comparisons of primary caregivers from low-income neighborhoods. *Family Relations* 54 (October): 475–87.

BACHMAN, J. G., K. N. WADSWORTH, P. M. O'MALLEY, L. D. JOHNSTON, AND J. E. SCHULENBERG. 1997. *Smoking, drinking, and drug use in young adulthood: The impacts of new freedoms and new responsibilities.* Hillsdale, NJ: Erlbaum.

BACHRACH, C. A., P. F. ADAMS, S. SAMBRANO, AND K. A. LONDON. 1990. Adoption in the 1980s. *Vital Health Statistics,* no. 181, January 5, advance data. Hyattsville, MD: National Center for Health Statistics.

BADEN, A. 2001. Psychological adjustment of transracial adoptees: Applying the cultural–racial identity model. Paper presented at the American Psychological Association, San Francisco, August 2001.

BAER, J. S., P. D. SAMPSON, H. M. BARR, P. D. CONNOR, AND A. P. STREISSGUTH. 2003. A 21-year longitudinal analysis of the effects of prenatal alcohol exposure on young adult drinking. *Archives of General Psychiatry* 60 (April): 377–86.

BAHR, K. S., AND H. M. BAHR. 1995. Autonomy, community, and the mediation of value: Comments on Apachean grandmothering, cultural change, and the media. In *American families: Issues in race and ethnicity,* ed. C. K. Jacobson, 229–60. New York: Garland.

BAHRAMPOUR, T. 2009. Market for romance goes from bullish to sheepish. *Washington Post,* February 25, A1.

BAILEY, B. 1988. *From front porch to back seat: Courtship in twentieth-century America.* Baltimore: Johns Hopkins University Press.

BAILEY, J. M., R. C. PILLARD, M. C. NEALE, AND Y. AGYEI. 1993. Heritable factors influence sexual orientation in women. *Archives of General Psychiatry* 50 (March): 217–23.

BAILEY, W., M. YOUNG, C. KNICKERBOCKER, AND T. DOAN. 2002. A cautionary tale about conducting research on abstinence education: How do state abstinence coordinators define "sexual activity"? *American Journal of Health Education* 33 (September/October): 290–96.

BAIRD, J. 2008. Girls will be girls. Or not. *Newsweek*, March 31, 39.

BAKER, A. 2008. The girl gap. *Time*, January 28, 42–43.

BAKER, C. R., AND S. M. STITH. 2008. Factors predicting dating violence perpetration among male and female college students. *Journal of Aggression, Maltreatment & Trauma* 17 (September): 227–44.

BALDAUF, S. 2006. Indians crack down on gender abortions. *Christian Science Monitor.* March 31, 7.

BALDAUF, S. 2008. A refuge from painful rite for Kenyan girls. *Christian Science Monitor*, March 13, 7.

BALSAM, K. F., AND D. M. SZYMANSKI. 2005. Relationship quality and domestic violence in women's same-sex relationships: The role of minority stress. *Psychology of Women Quarterly* 29 (September): 258–69.

BANCROFT, L. 2002. *Why does he do that? Inside the minds of angry and controlling men.* New York: Berkley Trade.

BANDURA, A., AND R. H. WALTERS. 1963. *Social learning and personality development.* New York: Holt, Rinehart & Winston.

BANERJEE, A., E. DUFLO, M. GHATAK, AND J. LAFORTUNE. 2009. Marry for what: Caste and mate selection in modern India. National Bureau of Economic Research, Working Paper 14958, www.nber.org (accessed June 4, 2009).

BANFIELD, EDWARD C. 1974. *The unheavenly city revisited.* Boston: Little, Brown.

BANKS, S. 2006. Firehouse culture an ordeal for women. *Los Angeles Times*, December 3, www.latimes.com (accessed December 4, 2006).

BANNER, L. W. 1984. *Women in modern America: A brief history*, 2nd ed. New York: Harcourt Brace Jovanovich.

BANTA, C. 2005. Trading for a high. *Time*, August 1, 35.

Baptist missionaries must affirm doctrine. 2003. *The Guardian*, April 16. www.guardian.co.uk (accessed April 17, 2003).

BARABAK, M. Z. 2006. Guest-worker proposal has wide support. *Los Angeles Times*, April 30, www.latimes.com (accessed May 2, 2006).

BARASH, D. P. 2002. Evolution, males, and violence. *Chronicle of Higher Education*, May 24, B7–B9.

BARBER, B. K. 1994. Cultural, family, and personal contexts of parent-adolescent conflict. *Journal of Marriage and the Family* 56 (May): 375–86.

BARBER, B. L., AND D. H. DEMO. 2006. The kids are alright (at least, most of them): Links between divorce and dissolution and child well-being. In *Handbook of divorce and relationship dissolution*, eds. M. A. Fine and J. H. Harvey, 289–311. Mahwah, NJ: Lawrence Erlbaum.

BARBER, B. L., AND J. M. LYONS. 1994. Family processes and adolescent adjustment in intact and remarried families. *Journal of Youth and Adolescence* 23 (August): 421–36.

BARKIN, S., B. SCHEINDLIN, E. H. IP, I. RICHARDSON, AND S. FINCH. 2007. Determinants of parental discipline practices: A national sample from primary care practices. *Clinical Pediatrics* 46 (January): 64–69.

BARNES, C. 2006. China's "kingdom of women." *Slate*, November 17, www.slate.com (accessed June 12, 2007).

BARNES, G. M., A. S. REIFMAN, M. P. FARRELL, AND B. A. DINTCHEFF. 2000. The effects of parenting on the development of adolescent alcohol misuse: A six-wave latent growth model. *Journal of Marriage and the Family* 62 (February): 175–86.

BARNETT, M. A. 2008. Mother and grandmother parenting in low-income three-generation rural households. *Journal of Marriage and Family* 70 (December): 1241–57.

BARNETT, R. C., AND C. RIVERS. 1996. *She works, he works: How two-income families are happy, healthy, and thriving.* Cambridge, MA: Harvard University Press.

BARNETT, R. C., A. STEPTOE, AND K. C. GAREIS. 2005. Marital-role quality and stress-related psychobiological indicators. *Annals of Behavioral Medicine* 30: 1 (36–43).

BARNHARDT, L., AND J. SCHARPER. 2007. Dead tot bruised, underfed, police say. *Baltimore Sun*, December 29, 1A, 9A.

BAROVICK, H. 2002. Domestic dads. *Time*, August 15, B4–B10.

BARRET, R. L., AND B. E. ROBINSON. 1990. *Gay fathers.* Lexington, MA: Lexington Books.

BARRET-DUCROCQ, F. 1991. *Love in the time of Victoria: Sexuality, class and gender in nineteenth-century London.* New York: Verso.

BARRINGER, H. R., R. W. GARDNER, AND M. J. LEVIN. 1993. *Asians and Pacific Islanders in the United States.* New York: Russell Sage Foundation.

BARRY, E. 2005. It must be love, but let's be sure. *Los Angeles Times*, May 21, A1.

BARTKOWSKI, J. P. 2001. *Remaking the godly marriage: Gender negotiation in Evangelical families.* New Brunswick, NJ: Rutgers University Press.

BASLER, B. 2007. Closing in on Alzheimer's. *AARP Bulletin*, June, 10–11.

BATES, M. 2005. Tenured and battered. *Chronicle of Higher Education*, September 9, C1–C4.

BATTAN, M. 1992. *Sexual strategies.* New York: Putnam.

BAUER, G. 2007. Do Americans love pets too much? *Christian Science Monitor*, May 31, 9.

BAUER, M. 2007. Close to slavery: Guestworker programs in the United States. Southern Poverty Law Center, www.splcenter.org (accessed April 2, 2007).

BAUM, K., S. CATALANO, AND M. RAND. 2009. Stalking victimization in the United States. U.S. Department of Justice, Bureau of Justice Statistics, January, NCJ 224527, www.ojp.usdoj.gov (accessed May 2, 2009).

BAUMEISTER, R. F., AND S. R. WOTMAN. 1992. *Breaking hearts: The two sides of unrequited love.* New York: Guilford.

BAUMRIND, D. 1968. Authoritarian versus authoritative parental control. *Adolescence* 3, 255–72.

BAUMRIND, D. 1989. Rearing competent children. In *Child development today and tomorrow*, ed. W. Damon, 349–78. San Francisco: Jossey-Bass.

BAUMRIND, D. 1991. The influence of parenting styles on adolescent competence and substance use. *Journal of Early Adolescence* 11 (February): 56–95.

BAUMRIND, D., R. E. LARZELERE, AND P. A. COWAN. 2002. Ordinary physical punishment: Is it harmful? Comment on Gershoff (2002). *Psychological Bulletin* 128 (July): 580–89.

BAZAR, E. 2009. Economic casualties pile into tent cities. *USA Today*, May 5, www.usatoday.com (accessed May 16, 2009).

BAZAR, E., AND S. ARMOUR. 2005. Cities tackle day labor dilemma. *USA Today*, Oct 23, A3.

BAZELON, E. 2009. 2 kids + 0 husbands = family. *New York Times Magazine*, February 1, 30.

BEAN, F. D., AND G. STEVENS. 2003. *America's newcomers and the dynamics of diversity.* New York: Russell Sage Foundation.

BEARAK, B. 2006. The bride price. *New York Times Magazine*, July 9, 45–49.

BEARMAN, P. S., J. MOODY, AND K. STOVEL. 2004. Chains of affection: The structure of adolescent romantic and sexual networks. *American Journal of Sociology* 10 (July): 44–91.

BEATON, J. M., J. E. NORRIS, AND M. W. PRATT. 2003. Unresolved issues in adult children's marital relationships involving intergenerational problems. *Family Relations* 52 (April): 143–53.

BECK, A. T. 1988. *Love is never enough: How couples can overcome misunderstandings, resolve conflicts, and solve relationship problems through cognitive therapy.* New York: Harper & Row.

BEECH, H. 2005. Sex, please—we're young and Chinese. *Time*, December 12, 61.

BEER, W. R. 1992. *American stepfamilies.* New Brunswick, NJ: Transaction.

BEGLEY, S. 2008. Math is hard, Barbie said. *Newsweek*, October 27, 57.

BEHNKE, A. O., S. M. MACDERMID, S. L. COLTRANE, R. D. PARKE, AND K. F. WIDAMAN. 2008. Family cohesion in the lives of Mexican American and European American parents. *Journal of Marriage and Family* 70 (November): 1045–59.

BEIL, L. 2008. Just saying no to abstinence ed. *Newsweek*, October 27, 58–59.

BELCASTRO, P. A. 1985. Sexual behavior differences between black and white students. *Journal of Sex Research* 21, 56–57.

BELKIN, L. 2003. The opt-out revolution. *New York Times Magazine*, October 16, 42–47, 58, 85–86.

BELKIN, L. 2008. Smoother transitions. *New York Times*, September 4, 2.

BELLAH, R. N., R. MADSEN, W. M. SULLIVAN, A. SWIDLER, AND S. M. TIPTON. 1985. *Habits of the heart: Individualism and commitment in American life.* Berkeley: University of California Press.

BELLE, D. 1999. *The after-school lives of children: Alone and with others while parents work.* Mahwah, NJ: Erlbaum.

BELLUCK, PAM. 2008. Gay couples find marriage is a mixed bag. *New York Times*, June 15, 1.

BELSIE, L. 2001. An Iowa debate over newcomers. *Christian Science Monitor*, July 27, 1, 4.

BELSIE, L. 2003. Where do women out-earn men? Hint: not a city. *Christian Science Monitor*, August 1, 12.

BELSKY, J. K. 1988. *Here tomorrow: Making the most of life after fifty.* Baltimore: Johns Hopkins University Press.

BEM, S. L. 1975. Androgyny vs. the tight little lives of fluffy women and chesty men. *Psychology Today*, September, 58–62.

BENASSI, M. A. 1985. Effects of romantic love on perception of strangers' physical attractiveness. *Psychological Reports* 56 (April): 355–58.

BENNETT, J. 2009. Tales of a modern diva. *Newsweek*, April 6, 42–43.

BENNETT, R. L., ET AL. 2002. Genetic counseling and screening of consanguineous couples and their offspring: Recommendations of the National Society of Genetic Counselors. *Journal of Genetic Counseling* 11 (April): 97–119.

BENNETTS, L. 2008. The truth about American marriage. *Parade Magazine*, September 21, 4–5.

BENOKRAITIS, N. V., AND J. R. FEAGIN. 1995. *Modern sexism: Blatant, subtle, and covert discrimination*, 2nd ed. Upper Saddle River, NJ: Prentice Hall.

BENOKRAITIS, N. V., ED. 2000. *Feuds about families: Conservative, centrist, liberal, and feminist perspectives.* Upper Saddle River, NJ: Prentice Hall.

BERGER, E. M. 2008. Postnups. *Forbes Life Executive Woman*, Spring, 54–55.

BERGER, R. 2000. Gay stepfamilies: A triple-stigmatized group. *Families in Society* 81 (5): 504–16.

BERGMAN, P. M. 1969. *The chronological history of the Negro in America*. New York: Harper & Row.

BERK, B. R. 1993. The dating game. *Good House-keeping* (September.): 192, 220–21.

BERKMAN, N. D., ET AL. 2006. Management of eating disorders. Evidence Report/Technology Assessment No. 135. Rockville, MD: Agency for Healthcare Research and Quality.

BERLIN, I. 1998. *Many thousands gone: The first two centuries of slavery in North America*. Cambridge, MA: Belknap Press of Harvard University.

BERMUDEZ, E. 2008. Central American immigrants adopt Mexican ways in U.S. *Los Angeles Times*, November 3, www.latimes.com (accessed November 4, 2008).

BERNARD, J. 1973. *The future of marriage*. New York: Bantam.

BERNHARD, L. A. 1995. Sexuality in women's lives. In *Women's health care: A comprehensive handbook*, eds. C. I. Fogel and N. F. Woods, 475–95. Thousand Oaks, CA: Sage.

BERNARD, T. S. 2008. The key to wedded bliss? Money matters. *New York Times*, September 10, SPG-5.

BERNIER, J. C., AND D. H. SIEGEL. 1994. Attention-deficit hyperactivity disorder: A family and ecological systems perspective. *Families in Society: The Journal of Contemporary Human Services* (March): 142–50.

BERNSTEIN, J., E. GOULD, AND L. MISHEL. 2007. Poverty, income, and health insurance trends in 2006. Economic Policy Institute, August 28, www.epi.org (accessed August 29, 2008).

BERNSTEIN, N. 2007. Polygamy, practiced in secrecy, follows Africans to New York City. *New York Times*, March 23, A1, A20.

BERSAMIN, M. M., D. A. FISHER, S. WALKER, D. L. HILL, AND J. W. GRUBE. 2007. Defining virginity and abstinence: Adolescents interpretations of sexual behaviors. *Journal of Adolescent Health* 41 (August): 182–88.

BERSAMIN, M., M. TODD, D. A. FISHER, D. L. HILL, J. W. GRUBE, AND S. WALKER. 2008. Parenting practices and adolescent sexual behavior: A longitudinal study. *Journal of Marriage and Family* 70 (February): 97–12.

BERSCHEID, E., K. DION, E. WALSTER, AND G. W. WALSTER. 1982. Physical attractiveness and dating choice: A test of the matching hypothesis. *Journal of Experimental Social Psychology* 1, 173–89.

BEST, A. L. 2000. *Prom night: Youth, schools, and popular culture*. New York: Routledge.

BETCHER, W., AND W. POLLACK. 1993. *In a time of fallen heroes: The re-creation of masculinity*. New York: Atheneum.

BHATTACHARYA, S. 2003. Obesity breaks up sperm DNA. www.newscientist.com, October 17 (accessed April 27, 2006).

BIANCHI, S. M., L. SUBAIYA, AND J. R. KAHN. 1999. The gender gap in the economic well-being of nonresident fathers and custodial mothers. *Demography* 36 (May): 195–203.

BIANCHI, S. M., M. A. MILKIE, L. C. SAYER, AND J. P. ROBINSON. 2000. Is anyone doing the housework? Trends in the gender division of household labor. *Social Forces* 79 (September): 191–227.

BIANCHI, S. M., J. P. ROBINSON, AND M. A. MILKIE. 2006. *Changing rhythms of American family life*. New York: Russell Sage Foundation.

BIBBINS-DOMINGO, K., ET AL. 2009. Racial differences in incident heart failure among young adults. *New England Journal of Medicine* 360 (March 19): 1179–90.

BIBLARZ, T. J., AND G. GOTTAINER. 2000. Family structure and children's success: A comparison of widowed and divorced single-mother families. *Journal of Marriage and Family* 62 (May): 533–48.

BILLIONAIRES. 2008. *Forbes*, March 24, 80–86.

Binge eating disorder. 2008. National Institute of Diabetes and Digestive and Kidney Diseases. June, www.niddk.nih.gov (accessed August 23, 2009).

BIRD, G. W., AND A. SCHNURMAN-CROOK. 2005. Professional identity and coping behaviors in dual-career couples. *Family Relations* 54 (January): 145–60.

BIRDITT, K. S., AND K. L. FINGERMAN. 2005. Do we get better at picking our battles? Age group differences in descriptions of behavioral reactions to interpersonal tensions. *Journals of Gerontology: Psychological Sciences and Social Sciences* 60 (May): P121–P128.

BIRDITT, K. S., K. L. FINGERMAN, AND D. M. ALMEIDA. 2005. Age differences in exposure and reactions to interpersonal tensions: A daily diary study. *Psychology and Aging* 20 (June): 330–40.

BIRDITT, K. S., L. M. MILLER, K. L. FINGERMAN, AND E. S. LEFKOWITZ. 2009. Tensions in the parent and adult child relationship: Links to solidarity and ambivalence. *Psychology and Aging* 24 (June): 287–95.

BIRNS, B. 1999. Attachment theory revisited: Challenging conceptual and methodological sacred cows. *Feminism & Psychology* 9 (February): 10–21.

BIRNS, B., M. CASCARDI, AND S.-L. MEYER. 1994. Sex-role socialization: Developmental influences on wife abuse. *American Journal of Orthopsychiatry* 64 (January): 50–59.

BISHAI, D., ET AL. 2008. Risk factors for unintentional injuries in children: Are grandparents protective? *Pediatrics* 122 (November): e980–e987.

BISHAW, A., AND J. SEMEGA. 2008. *Income, earnings, and poverty data from the 2007 American Community Survey*. U.S. Census Bureau, ACS-09. Washington, DC: Government Printing Office.

BISSON, M. A., AND T. R. LEVINE. 2009. Negotiating a friends with benefits relationship. *Archives of Sexual Behavior* 38 (February): 66–73.

BIVENS, L. J. 2006. Offshoring. Economic Policy Institute. May, www.epinet.org (accessed June 1, 2007).

BLACK, M. C., AND M. J. BREIDING. 2008. Adverse health conditions and health risk behaviors associated with intimate partner violence—United States, 2005. *MMWR Weekly*, 57 (February 8): 113–17.

BLACKMAN, L., O. CLAYTON, N. GLENN, L. MALONE-COLON, AND A. ROBERTS. 2005. The consequences of marriage for African Americans: A comprehensive literature review. Institute for American Values, www.americanvalues.org (accessed April 12, 2006).

BLANK, R. M. 2008. How we measure poverty. *Los Angeles Times*, September 15, www.latimes.com (accessed September 16, 2008).

BLANKENHORN, D. 1995. *Fatherless America: Confronting our most urgent social problem*. New York: HarperPerennial.

BLAU, F. B., AND L. M. KAHN. 2006. The gender pay gap: Going, going . . . but not gone. In *The declining significance of gender?* eds. F. D. Blau, M. C. Brinton, and D. B. Grutsky, 37–66. New York: Russell Sage Foundation.

BLOCK, S., AND L. PETRECCA. 2009. For many minorities, saving isn't so easy. *USA Today*, July 6, www.usatoday.com (accessed July 7, 2009).

BLOMFIELD, J. 2009. Branded with the "Scarlet U." *Newsweek*, March 23, 22.

BLUESTEIN, G. 2005. 78-year-old accused of killing ex-flame. *Washington Post*, June 25, A2.

BLUESTONE, C., AND C. S. TAMIS-LE MONDA. 1999. Correlates of parenting styles in predominantly working- and middle-class African American mothers. *Journal of Marriage and the Family* 61 (November): 881–93.

BODMAN, D. A., AND G. W. PETERSON. 1995. Parenting processes. In *Research and theory in family science*, eds. R. D. Day, K. R. Gilbert, B. H. Settles, and W. R. Burr, 205–25. Pacific Grove, CA: Brooks/Cole.

BODNAR, J. 1985. *The transplanted: A history of immigrants in urban America*. Bloomington: Indiana University Press.

BOGENSCHNEIDER, K. 1996. An ecological risk/protective theory for building prevention programs, policies, and community capacity to support youth. *Family Relations* 45 (April): 127–38.

BOGENSCHNEIDER, K. 1997. Parental involvement in adolescent schooling: A proximal process with transcontextual validity. *Journal of Marriage and the Family* 59 (August): 718–33.

BOGLE, K. A. 2008. *Hooking up: Sex, dating, and relationships on campus*. New York: New York University Press.

BOHANNON, P. 1971. *Divorce and after*. New York: Doubleday.

BOLLAG, B. 2002a. Incident raises issue of harassment of women in Swedish universities. *Chronicle of Higher Education*, September 20, A41.

BOLLAG, B. 2002b. Wanted in Sweden: Female professors. *Chronicle of Higher Education*, September 20, A40–A42.

BOND, J. T., ELLEN G., STACY S. KIM, AND E. BROWNFIELD. 2005. 2005 National study of employers. Families and Work Institute, http://familiesandwork.org (accessed May 12, 2006).

BONNER, R. 2007. Male elementary teachers: Myths and realities. Men Teach, www.menteach.org (accessed June 12, 2008).

BONNIE, R. J., AND R. B. WALLACE, EDS. 2003. *Elder mistreatment: Abuse, neglect, and exploitation in an aging America*. Washington, DC: The National Academies Press.

BOODMAN, S. G. 1992. Questions about a popular prenatal test. *Washington Post Health Supplement*, November 3, 10–13.

BOONSTRA, H. D. 2009. Advocates call for a new approach after the era of "abstinence-only" sex education. *Guttmacher Policy Review* 12 (Winter): 6–11.

BOONSTRA, H. D., R. B. GOLD, C. L. RICHARDS, AND L. B. FINER. 2006. Abortion in women's lives. Guttmacher Institute, www.guttmacher.org (accessed September 21, 2006).

BOOTH, A., AND D. R. JOHNSON. 1994. Declining health and marital quality. *Journal of Marriage and the Family* 56 (February): 218–23.

BOOTH, A., AND J. N. EDWARDS. 1992. Starting over: Why remarriages are more unstable. *Journal of Family Issues* 13 (June): 179–94.

BOOTH, S. 2005. Very personal personals: Dating with an STD. *Washington Post*, May 10, C9.

BORAAS, S., AND W. M. RODGERS III. 2003. How does gender play a role in the earnings gap? An update." *Monthly Labor Review* 126 (March): 9–15.

BORDERS, L. D., L. K. BLACK, AND B. K. PASLEY. 1998. Are adopted children and their parents at greater risk for negative outcomes? *Family Relations* 47 (July): 237–41.

BORLAND, D. M. 1975. An alternative model of the wheel theory. *Family Coordinator* 24 (July): 289–92.

BORNSTEIN, M. H. 2002. Parenting infants. In *Handbook of parenting*, 2nd ed., Vol. 1: Children and parenting, ed. M. H. Bornstein, 3–43. Mahwah, NJ: Erlbaum.

BORST, J. 1996. Relatively speaking. *Newsweek*, July 29, 16.

BORZEKOWSKI, D. L. G., AND T. N. ROBINSON. 2005. The remote, the mouse, and the no. 2 pencil. *Archives of Pediatrics & Adolescent Medicine* 159 (July): 607–13.

BOSMAN, J. 2005. WPP executive resigns over remarks on women. *New York Times*, October 21, C1, C5.

BOSTIC, J. Q., AND M. C. MILLER. 2005. When should you worry? *Newsweek*, April 25, 60.

BOWLBY, J. 1969. *Attachment and loss*, Vol. 1: Attachment. New York: Basic Books.

BOWLBY, J. 1984. *Attachment and loss*, Vol. 1, 2nd ed. Harmondsworth, UK: Penguin.

BRADBURY, T. N., AND B. R. KARNEY. 2004. Understanding and altering the longitudinal course of marriage. *Journal of Marriage and Family* 66 (November): 862–79.

BRADBURY, T., R. ROGGE, AND E. LAWRENCE. 2001. Reconsidering the role of conflict in marriage. In *Couples in conflict*, eds. A. Booth, A. C. Crouter, and M. Clements, 59–81. Mahwah, NJ: Erlbaum.

BRADY, D., AND C. PALMERI. 2007. The pet economy. *Business Week*, August 6, 45–54.

BRADY, J. 1990. Why I still want a wife. *Ms.* (July/August): 17.

BRAIKER, B. 2007. Just don't call me Mr. Mom. *Newsweek*, October 8, 53–55.

BRAITHWAITE, D. O., P. SCHRODT, AND L. A. BAXTER. 2006. Understudied and misunderstood: Communication in stepfamily relationships. In *Widening the family circle: New research on family communication*, eds. K. Floyd and M. T. Moorman, 153–170. Thousand Oaks, CA: Sage.

BRAMLETT, M. D., AND W. D. MOSHER. 2002. Cohabitation, marriage, divorce, and remarriage in the United States. Centers for Disease Control and Prevention, Vital and Health Statistics. www.cdc.gov (accessed July 3, 2003).

BRANDER, B. 2004. *Love that works: The art and science of giving*. West Conshohocken, PA: Templeton Foundation Press.

BRANDON, J. 2005. Britain grapples with "honor killing" practice. *Christian Science Monitor*, October 19, 4.

BRASSARD, M. R., AND D. B. HARDY. 1997. Psychological maltreatment. In *The battered child*, 5th ed., eds. M. E. Helfer, R. S. Kempe, and R. D. Krugman, 392–412. Chicago: University of Chicago Press.

BRATTER, J. L., AND R. B. KING. 2008. "But will it last?": Marital instability among interracial and same-race couples. *Family Relations* 57 (April): 160–71.

BRAUN, M., N. LEWIN-EPSTEIN, H. STIER, AND M. K. BAUMGÄRTNER. 2008. Perceived equity in the gendered division of household labor. *Journal of Marriage and Family* 70 (December): 1145–56.

BRAUND, K. E. H. 1990. Guardians of tradition and handmaidens to change: Women's roles in Creek economic and social life during the eighteenth century. *American Indian Quarterly* 14 (Summer): 239–58.

BRAUNSTEIN, J. B., N. S. SHERBER, S. P. SCHULMAN, E. L. DING, AND N. R. POWE. 2008. Race, medical researcher distrust, perceived harm, and willingness to participate in cardiovascular prevention trials. *Medicine* 87 (January): 1–9.

BRAVERMAN, L. 1989. Beyond the myth of motherhood. In *Women in families: A framework for family therapy*, eds. M. McGoldrick and C. Anderson, 227–243. New York: W. W. Norton.

BRAY, J. H., AND J. KELLY. 1998. *Stepfamilies: Love, marriage, and parenting in the first decade*. New York: Broadway.

BREHM, S. S. 1992. *Intimate relationships*, 2nd ed. New York: McGraw-Hill.

BREHM, S. S., R. S. MILLER, D. PERLMAN, AND S. M. CAMPBELL. 2002. *Intimate relationships*, 3rd ed. Boston, MA: McGraw-Hill.

BREINES, W. 1992. *Young, white, and miserable: Growing up female in the fifties*. Boston: Beacon.

BREMER, J. 2005. The Internet and children: Advantages and disadvantages. *Child and Adolescent Psychiatric Clinics of North America* 14 (3): 405–28.

BRENDGEN, M., ET AL. 2005. Examining genetic and environmental effect on social aggression: A study of 6-year-old twins. *Child Development* 76 (July/August): 930–46.

BRENNAN, R. T., R. C. BARNETT, AND K. C. GAREIS. 2001. When she earns more than he does: A longitudinal study of dual-earner couples. *Journal of Marriage and Family* 63 (February): 168–82.

BRESCOLL, V. L., AND E. L. UHLMANN. 2008. Can an angry woman get ahead? Status conferral, gender, and expression of emotion in the workplace. *Psychological Science* 19 (March): 268–75.

BRETT, K., W. BARFIELD, AND C. WILLIAMS. 2008. Prevalence of self-reported postpartum depressive symptoms—17 states, 2004–2005. *MMWR Weekly* 57 (April 11): 361–66.

BRIERE, J. N. 1992. *Child abuse trauma: Theory and treatment of the lasting effects*. Thousand Oaks, CA: Sage.

BRIMHALL, A., K. WAMPLER, AND T. KIMBALL. 2008. Learning from the past, altering the future: A tentative theory of the effect of past relationships on couples who remarry. *Family Process* 47 (September): 373-387.

Bringing up baby. 1999. *Public Perspective* 10 (October/November): 19.

BRINK, S. 2007. This is your brain on love. *Los Angeles Times*, July 30, www.latimes.com (accessed August 1, 2007).

BRITNER, P. A., D. MOSSLER, AND I-M. EIGSTI. 2008. International adoption: Risk and resilience. *National Council on Family Relations Report* 53 (November): F8–F9.

BRITTINGHAM, A., AND G. P. DE LA CRUZ. 2005. We the people of Arab ancestry in the United States. Census 2000 Special Reports, CENSR-21, March, www.census.gov (accessed March 26, 2007).

BRIZENDINE, L. 2006. *The female brain*. New York: Morgan Road Books.

BRODERICK, C. B. 1988. To arrive where we started: The field of family studies in the 1930s. *Journal of Marriage and the Family* 50 (August): 569–84.

BRODERICK, C. B. 1993. *Understanding family process: Basics of family systems theory*. Thousand Oaks, CA: Sage.

BRODEY, D. 2005. Blacks join the eating-disorder mainstream. *New York Times*, September 20, 1, 8.

BRODY, G. H., S. DORSEY, R. FOREHAND, AND L. ARMISTEAD. 2002. Unique and protective contributions of parenting and classroom processes to the adjustment of African American children living in single-parent families. *Child Development* 63 (January–February): 274–86.

BRONFENBRENNER, U. 1979. *The ecology of human development: Experiments by nature and design*. Cambridge, MA: Harvard University Press.

BRONFENBRENNER, U. 1986. Ecology of the family as a context for human development: Research perspectives. *Developmental Psychology* 22: 723–42.

BRONSTAD, A. 2008. Is it creative style or harassment? *National Law Journal*, January 28, http://server.finklawfirm.crom (accessed March 15, 2008).

BROOK, J. S., C. M. CONNELL, C. M. MITCHELL, AND S. M. MASON. 2002. Drug use and neurobehavioral, respiratory, and cognitive problems: Precursors and mediators. *Journal of Adolescent Health* 30 (June): 433–41.

BROOKEY, R. A. 2002. *Reinventing the male homosexual: The rhetoric and power of the gay gene*. Bloomington: Indiana University Press.

BROOKS, D. 2003. Love, Internet style. *New York Times*, November 8, A15.

BROOKS, D. 2008. The culture of debt. *New York Times*, July 22, 19.

BROOKS-GUNN, J., P. K. KLEBANOV, AND G. J. DUNCAN. 1996. Ethnic differences in children's intelligence test scores: Role of economic deprivation, home environment, and material characteristics. *Child Development* 67 (April): 396–408.

BROTHERSON, S. E., AND W. C. DUNCAN. 2004. Rebinding the ties that bind: Government efforts to preserve and promote marriage. *Family Relations* 53 (October): 459–68.

BROWN, E., T. L. ORBUCH, AND J. A. BAUERMEISTER. 2008. Religiosity and marital stability among black American and white American couples. *Family Relations* 57 (April): 172–85.

BROWN, J. D., J. R. STEELE, AND K. WALSH-CHILDERS, eds. 2002. *Sexual teens, sexual media: Investigating media's influence on adolescent sexuality*. Mahwah, NJ: Lawrence Erlbaum.

BROWN, N. M., AND E. S. AMATEA. 2000. *Love and intimate relationships: Journeys of the heart*. Philadelphia: Brunner/Mazel.

BROWN, P. M. 1995. *The death of intimacy: Barriers to meaningful interpersonal relationships*. New York: Haworth.

BROWN, S. I. 2005. How cohabitation is reshaping American families. *Contexts* 4 (Summer): 33–37.

BROWN, S. L. 2004. Family structure and child well-being: The significance of parental cohabitation. *Journal of Marriage and Family* 66 (May): 351–67.

BROWN, T. N., E. E. TANNER-SMITH, C. L. LESANE-BROWN, AND M. E. EZELL. 2007. Child, parent, and situational correlates of familial ethnic/race socialization. *Journal of Marriage and Family* 69 (February): 14–25.

BROWNE, A. 1993. Family violence and homelessness: The relevance of trauma histories in the lives of homeless women. *American Journal of Orthopsychiatry* 63 (July): 370–84.

BROWNING, S. W. 1994. Treating stepfamilies: Alternatives of traditional family therapy. In *Stepparenting: Issues in theory, research, and practice*, eds. K. Pasley and M. Ihinger-Tallman, 175–98. Westport, CT: Greenwood.

BROWNSTEIN, C. A., AND J. S. BROWNSTEIN. 2008. Estimating excess mortality in post-invasion Iraq. *New England Journal of Medicine* 358 (January 31): 445–47.

BRÜCKNER, H., AND P. BEARMAN. 2005. After the promise: The STD consequences of adolescent virginity pledges. *Journal of Adolescent Health* 36 (April): 271–78.

BRULLIARD, K. 2006. Last rites, tailored to immigrant customs. *Washington Post*, April 24, A1.

BRYANT, C. M., R. D. CONGER, AND J. M. MEEHAN. 2001. The influence of in-laws on change in marital success. *Journal of Marriage and Family* 63 (August): 614–26.

BUCHANAN, C. M., E. E. MACCOBY, AND S. M. DORNBUSCH. 1996. *Adolescents after divorce.* Cambridge, MA: Harvard University Press.

BUCKS, B. K., A. B. KENNICKELL, T. L. MACH, AND K. B. MOORE. 2009. Changes in U.S. family finances from 2004 to 2007: Evidence from the Survey of Consumer Finances. *Federal Reserve Bulletin* 95 (February): A1–A56.

BUETTNER, D. 2005. The secrets of long life. *National Geographic*, November, 2–26.

BUETTNER, D. 2009. More good years. *AARP*, September/October, 22, 24.

BUHLE, M., T. MURPHY, AND J. GERHARD. 2008. *Women and the making of America*, vol. 2. Upper Saddle River, NJ: Prentice Hall.

BULCROFT, K., L. SMEINS, AND R. BULCROFT. 1999. *Romancing the honeymoon: Consummating marriage in modern society.* Thousand Oaks, CA: Sage.

BULCROFT, R. A., AND K. A. BULCROFT. 1993. Race differences in attitudinal and motivational factors in the decision to marry. *Journal of Marriage and the Family* 55 (May): 338–55.

BULCROFT, R., AND J. TEACHMAN. 2004. Ambiguous constructions: Development of a childless or child-free life course. In *Handbook of contemporary families: Considering the past, contemplating the future*, eds. M. Coleman and L. H. Ganong, 116–35. Thousand Oaks, CA: Sage.

BULIK, C. M., ET AL. 2006. Prevalence, heritability, and prospective risk factors for anorexia nervosa. *Archive of General Psychiatry* 63 (March): 305–12.

BULLERS, F. 2001. Suffrage doesn't please female Kansas state senator. September 27, christianparty.net (accessed April 17, 2009).

BULLOCK, K. 2005. Grandfathers and the impact of raising grandchildren. *Journal of Sociology and Social Welfare* 32 (March): 43–59.

BUMPASS, L., AND H.-H. LU. 2000. Trends in cohabitation and implications for children's family contexts in the United States. *Population Studies* 54 (March): 29–41.

Bureau of Labor Statistics. 2009. Employment situation summary, USDL 09-0742, July 2, www.bls.gov (accessed July 4, 2009).

Bureau of Labor Statistics News. 2009. Mass layoffs in June 2009. U.S. Department of Labor, USDL 09-0842, July 23, www.bls .gov (accessed June 28, 2009).

Bureau of Labor Statistics. 2009. Occupational employment and wages, May 2008. United States Department of Labor, www.bls.gov (accessed July 14, 2009).

Bureau of Labor Statistics News. 2009. Usual weekly earning of wage and salary workers: Second quarter 2009. Bureau of Labor Statistics, USDL 09-0814, July 16, www.bls .gov (accessed July 20, 2009).

BURGESS, E. W., AND H. J. LOCKE. 1945. *The family: From institution to companionship.* New York: American Book Company.

BURGESS, E. W., H. J. LOCKE, AND M. M. THOMES. 1963. *The family from institution to companionship.* New York: American Book Co.

BURLESON, B. R., AND W. H. DENTON. 1997. The relationships between communication skill and marital satisfaction: Some moderating effects. *Journal of Marriage and the Family* 59 (November): 884–902.

BURR, C. 1996. *A separate creation: The search for the biological origins of sexual orientation.* New York: Hyperion.

BURR, W. R. 1995. Using theories in family science. In *Research and theory in family science*, eds. R. D. Day, K. R. Gilbert, B. H. Settles, and W. R. Burr, 73–90. Pacific Grove, CA: Brooks/Cole.

BURRIS, J. 2009. First comes marriage, then . . . *Baltimore Sun*, June 19, 3.

BURTON, L. 2007. Childhood adultification in economically disadvantaged families:

A conceptual model. *Family Relations* 56 (October): 329–45.

BURTON, L. M., AND C. B. STACK. 1993. Conscripting kin: Reflections on family, generation, and culture. In *Family, self, and society: Toward a new agenda for family research*, eds. P. A. Cowan, D. Field, D. A. Hansen, A. Skolnick, and G. E. Swanson, 115–42. Hillsdale, NJ: Erlbaum.

BUSBY, D., M. BRANDT, C. GARDNER, AND N. TANIGUCHI. 2005. The family of origin parachute model: Landing safely in adult romantic relationships. *Family Relations* 54 (April): 254–64.

BUSBY, D. M., D. C. IVEY, S. M. HARRIS, AND C. ATES. 2007. Self-directed, therapist-directed, and assessment-based interventions for premarital couples. *Family Relations* 56 (July): 279–90.

BUSBY, D. M., T. B. HOLMAN, AND E. WALKER. 2008. Pathways to relationship aggression between adult partners. *Family Relations* 57 (January): 72–83.

BUSHMAN, B. J., A. M. BONACCI, M. VAN DIJK, AND R. F. BAUMEISTER. 2003. Narcissism, sexual refusal, and aggression: Testing a narcissistic reactance model of sexual coercion. *Journal of Personality and Social Psychology* 84 (May): 1027–40.

BUSS, D. M. 2000. *The dangerous passion: Why jealousy is as necessary as love and sex.* New York: Free Press.

BUSS, D. M., AND D. P. SCHMITT. 1993. Sexual strategies theory: An evolutionary perspective on human mating. *Psychological Review* 100 (April): 204–32.

BUSS, D. M., R. J. LARSEN, AND D. WESTEN. 1996. Commentary: Sex differences in jealousy: Not gone, not forgotten, and not explained by alternative hypotheses. *Psychological Science* 7 (November): 373–75.

BUSS, D. M., T. K. SHACKELFORD, L. A. KIRKPATRICK, AND R. J. LARSEN. 2001. A half century of mate preferences: The cultural evolution of values. *Journal of Marriage and Family* 63 (May): 491–503.

BUSSEY, K., AND A. BANDURA. 1992. Self-regulatory mechanisms governing gender development. *Child Development* 63 (October): 1236–50.

BUTLER, J. 2003. XXY marks the spot "X." FTM Australia, January 21. www.ftmaustralia .org (accessed June 11, 2003).

BUTLER, K., AND D. GILSON. 2008. 8 lbs, 21 inches, 3,800 diapers, and 1,525 tons of carbon. *Mother Jones*, May/June, 24–25.

BYERS, E. S., H. A. SEARS, AND A. D. WEAVER. 2008. Parents' reports of sexual communication with children in kindergarten to grade 8. *Journal of Marriage and Family* 70 (February): 86–96.

C

CACIOPPO, J. T., ET AL. 2002. Loneliness and health: Potential mechanisms. *Psychosomatic Medicine* 64 (May/June): 407–17.

CAFFARO, J. V., AND A. CONN-CAFFARO. 1998. *Sibling abuse trauma: Assessment and intervention strategies for children, families, and adults.* New York: Haworth.

CAGLEY, M. 2009. Social support, networks, and happiness. Population Reference Bureau, June, www.prb.org <http://www.prb.org/> (accessed September 12, 2009).

CALASANTI, T. 2007. Bodacious Berry, potency wood and the aging monster: Gender and age relations in anti-aging ads. *Social Forces* 86 (September): 335–55.

CALDWELL, M. A., AND L. A. PEPLAU. 1990. The balance of power in lesbian relationships. In *Perspectives on the family: History, class, and feminism*, ed., C. Carlton, 204–15. Belmont, CA: Wadsworth.

CALLAHAN, M. 2009. The rise of "familycide:" What's behind the shocking trend. *Washington Post*, April 26, 23.

CALLIS, R. R., AND L. B. CAVANAUGH. 2009. Census Bureau reports on residential vacancies and homeownership. U.S. Census Bureau News, CB09-57, April 27, www.census.gov (accessed May 15, 2009).

CALVERT, S. 2006. South Africans defend the price of tying the knot. *Baltimore Sun*, July 24, 1A, 10A.

CAMARILLO, A. 1979. *Chicanos in a changing society: From Mexican pueblos to American barrios in Santa Barbara and southern California, 1848–1930.* Cambridge, MA: Harvard University Press.

CAMPBELL, K. 2002. Today's courtship: White teeth, root beer, and e-mail? *Christian Science Monitor*, February 14, 1, 4.

CAMPBELL, W. K., C. A. FOSTER, AND E. J. FINKEL. 2002. Does self-love lead to love for others? A study of narcissistic game playing. *Journal of Personality and Social Psychology* 83 (August): 340–54.

CANARY, D. J., W. R. CUPACH, AND S. J. MESSMAN. 1995. *Relationship conflict: Conflict in parent–child, friendship, and romantic relationships.* Thousand Oaks, CA: Sage.

CANCIAN, F. M. 1990. The feminization of love. In *Perspectives on the family: History, class, and feminism*, ed. C. Carlson, 171–85. Belmont, CA: Wadsworth.

CANTWELL, H. B. 1997. The neglect of child neglect. In *The battered child*, 5th ed., eds. M. E. Helfer, R. S. Kempe, and R. D. Krugman, 347–73. Chicago: University of Chicago Press.

CAPIZZANO, J., G. ADAMS, AND J. OST. 2006. The child care patterns of white, black and Hispanic children. The Urban Institute, www .urban.org (accessed May 10, 2006).

CAPLAN, J. 2005. Metrosexual matrimony. *Time*, October 3, 67.

CAPPS, R., M. E. FIX, J. OST, J. REARDON-ANDERSON, AND J. S. PASSEL. 2005. The health and well-being of young children of immigrants. The Urban Institute, www .urban.org (accessed May 10, 2006).

CARASSO, A., C. E. STEUERLE, G. REYNOLDS, T. VERICKER, AND J. MACOMBER. 2008. Kids' share 2008: How children fare in the federal budget. The Urban Institute, www .urban.org (accessed September 27, 2009).

CARD, N. A., B. D. STUCKY, G. M. SAWALANI, AND T. D. LITTLE. 2008. Direct and indirect aggression during childhood and adolescence: A meta-analytic review of gender differences, intercorrelations, and relations to maladjustment. *Child Development* 79 (September/October): 1185–1229.

CAREY, B. 2005. Experts dispute Bush on gay-adoption issue. *New York Times*, January 29, A16.

CAREY, B. 2008. Psychiatrists revise the book of human troubles. *New York Times*, December 18, 1.

CAREY, K. 2005. One step from the finish line: Higher college graduation rates are within our reach. Education Trust, http://www2. edtrust.org (accessed January 18, 2005).

CARLSON, D. K. 2001. Over half of Americans believe in love at first sight. Gallup News Service, February 14. www.gallup.com (accessed May 19, 2003).

CARLSON, L. H., AND G. A. COLBURN, EDS. 1972. *In their place: White America defines her minorities, 1850–1950.* New York: Wiley.

CARLSON, M. J. 2006. Family structure, father involvement, and adolescent behavioral outcomes. *Journal of Marriage and Family* 68 (February): 137–54.

CARLSON, M., S. MCLANAHAN, AND P. ENGLAND. 2004. Union formation in fragile families. *Demography* 41 (May): 237–61.

CARMALT, J. H., J. CAWLEY, K. JOYNER, AND J. SOBAL. 2008. Body weight and matching with a physically attractive romantic partner. *Journal of Marriage and Family* 70 (December): 1287–96.

CARNOY, M., AND D. CARNOY. 1997. *Fathers of a certain age: The joys and problems of middle-aged fatherhood.* Minneapolis, MN: Fairview Press.

CARPENTER, C. 2008. "Tough love" pervades self-help books. *Christian Science Monitor*, February 7, 17.

CARPENTER, S. 2008. No recession for online dating sites. *Los Angeles Times*, December 28, www.latimes.com (accessed December 29, 2008).

CARR, D. 2004. The desire to date and remarry among older widows and widowers. *Journal of Marriage and Family* 66 (November): 1051–68.

CARR, D., C. B. WORTMAN, AND K. WOLFF. 2006. How older Americans die today: Implications for surviving spouses. In *Spousal bereavement in late life*, eds. D. Carr, R. M. Nesse, and C. B. Wortman, 49–78. New York: Springer.

CARRASQUILLO, H. 2002. The Puerto Rican family. In *Minority families in the United States: A multicultural perspective*, 3rd ed., ed. R. L. Taylor, 101–13. Upper Saddle River, NJ: Prentice Hall.

CARRELL, S. E., AND M. L. HOEKSTRA. 2009. Domino effect. *Education Next*, Summer, 59–63, www.educationnext.org (accessed August 16, 2009).

CARRIER, J. M., AND S. O. MURRAY. 1998. Woman-woman marriage in Africa. In *Boy-wives and female husbands: Studies of African homosexualities*, eds. S. O. Murray and W. Roscoe, 255–66. New York: St. Martin's.

CARROLL, B. T. 2003. Salvaging a career. *Chronicle of Higher Education*, May 16, C4.

CARROLL, J. 2006. Drugs, smoking, alcohol most important problem facing teens. Gallup Organization, February 17, www.gallup.com (accessed May 27, 2006).

CARROLL, J. 2006. Whites, minorities differ in views of economic opportunities in U.S. Gallup Organization, July 10, www.gallup.com (accessed July 18, 2006).

CARROLL, J. 2006. Women more likely than men to say they've been divorced. Gallup News Service, April 5, www.gallup.com (accessed April 8, 2006).

CARROLL, J. 2007. Americans: 2.5 children is "ideal" family size. Gallup News Service, June 26, www.gallup.com (accessed June 27, 2009).

CARROLL, J. 2007. Most Americans approve of interracial marriages. Gallup News Service, July 6, www.galluppoll.com (accessed October 10, 2007).

CARROLL, J. 2007. Public divided over moral acceptability of doctor-assisted suicide. Gallup News Service, May 31, www.gallup.com (accessed September 25, 2009).

CARROLL, J. S., AND W. J. DOHERTY. 2003. Evaluating the effectiveness of premarital prevention programs: A Meta-analytic review of outcome research. *Family Relations* 52 (April): 105–18.

CARSON, L. 2008. A shift in the workweek. *Baltimore Sun*, July 14, 1A, 8A

CARTER, S., AND J. SOKOL. 1993. *He's scared, she's scared: Understanding the hidden fears that sabotage your relationships.* New York: Delacorte.

CASHIN, S. 2004. *The failure of integration: How race and class are undermining the American dream.* New York: Public Affairs.

CASLER, L. 1974. *Is marriage necessary?* New York: Human Sciences Press.

CASPI, A., ET AL. 2003. Influence of life stress on depression: Moderation by a polymorphism in the 5-HTT gene. *Science* 301 (July 18): 386–89.

CASSIDY, M. L., AND G. R. LEE. 1989. The study of polyandry: A critique and synthesis. *Journal of Comparative Family Studies* 20 (Spring): 1–11.

CASSIDY, S. 1993. A single woman: The fabric of my life. In *Single women: Affirming our spiritual journeys*, eds. M. O'Brien and C. Christie, 35–48. Westport, CT: Bergin & Garvey.

CASTLEMAN, M. 2007. Myths about your body. *AARP Bulletin*, February, 43.

CATALANO, S. 2007. Intimate partner violence in the United States. Bureau of Justice Statistics, www.ojp.usdoj.gov/bjs (accessed July 30, 2009).

CATE, R. M., AND S. A. LLOYD. 1992. *Courtship.* Thousand Oaks, CA: Sage.

Causes and consequences. 2009. Centers for Disease Control and Prevention, August, www.cdc.gov (accessed August 23, 2009).

CAULFIELD, T., ET AL. 2009. Race and ancestry in biomedical research: Exploring the challenges. *Genome Medicine* 1 (January): 1–8.

CAVAN, R. S., AND K. H. RANCK. 1938. *The family and the Depression: A study of one hundred Chicago families.* Chicago: University of Chicago Press.

CAVANAGH, S. E., AND A. C. HUSTON. 2008. The timing of family instability and children's social development. *Journal of Marriage and Family* 70 (December): 1258–69.

CAVANAGH, S. E., S. R. CRISSEY, AND R. K. RALEY. 2008. Family structure history and adolescent romance. *Journal of Marriage and Family* 70 (August): 698–714.

CAWTHORNE, A. 2009. Weathering the storm: Black men in the recession. Center for American Progress, April, www.american progress.org (accessed August 9, 2009).

Celtics broadcaster apologizes on-air. 2007. February 28, www.boston.com (accessed April 17, 2009).

CENTERS FOR DISEASE CONTROL AND PREVENTION. 2003. First reports evaluating the effectiveness of strategies for preventing violence: Early childhood home visitation and firearms laws. Findings from the Task Force on Community Preventive Services. *Morbidity and Mortality Weekly Report* 52 (No. RR-14): 1–23.

CDC. 2006. Understanding intimate partner violence: Fact sheet. Centers for Disease Control and Prevention, www.cdc.gov (accessed July 29, 2009).

CDC. 2008a. Genital HPV infection—CDC fact sheet. April, www.cdc.gov (accessed May 26, 2009).

CDC. 2008b. HIV/AIDS in the United States. Revised August, www.cdc.gov (accessed May 22, 2009).

Centers for Disease Control and Prevention. 2008. *Sexually transmitted disease surveillance, 2007.* Atlanta, GA: U.S. Department of Health and Human Services.

CDC Press Release. 2008. Prevalence of sexually transmitted infections and bacterial vaginosis among female adolescents in the United States: Data from the national health and nutritional examination survey (NHANES) 2003–2004. Paper presented at the 2008 national STD prevention conference, March 11, Washington, DC. www.cdc.gov (accessed May 22, 2009).

Centers for Disease Control and Prevention, American Society for Reproductive Medicine, Society for Assisted Reproductive Technology. 2008. *2006 Assisted reproductive technology success rates: National summary and fertility clinic reports.* Atlanta, GA: U.S. Department of Health and Human Services.

Centers for Disease Control and Prevention and the Merck Company Foundation. 2007. *The state of aging and health in America 2007.* Whitehouse Station, NJ: Merck Company Foundation.

Center for American Women and Politics. 2009. Women in elective office 2009. New Brunswick, NJ: Rutgers University, www.cawp.rutgers.edu (accessed April 2, 2009).

Central Intelligence Agency. 2009. *The 2008 world factbook*, www.cia.gov (accessed April 19, 2009).

CHA, Y. 2009. Reinforcing the "separate spheres" arrangement: The effect of spousal overwork on the employment of men and women in dual-earner households. *American Sociological Review*, forthcoming.

CHADDOCK, G. R. 2003. For Hispanics, cultural shift and new tensions. *Christian Science Monitor*, January 23, 1, 3.

CHAFE, W. H. 1972. *The American woman: Her changing social, economic, and political roles, 1920–1970.* New York: Oxford University Press.

CHAMBERS, V. 2003. *Having it all? Black women and success.* New York: Doubleday.

CHAN, S. 1997. Families with Asian roots. In *Developing cross-cultural competence: A guide for working with children and families*, 2nd ed., eds. E. W. Lynch and M. J. Hanson, 251–353. Baltimore: Paul H. Brookes.

CHAN, S. 1999. Families with Asian roots. In *Developing cross-cultural competence: A guide for working with children and their families*, 2nd ed., eds. E. W. Lynch and M. J. Hanson, 251–344. Baltimore: Paul H. Brookes.

CHANCE, P. 1988. The trouble with love. *Psychology Today* (February): 22–23.

CHANDLER, M. A., AND M. GLOD. 2008. More schools trying separation of the sexes. *Washington Post*, June 15, A1.

CHANDRA, A., G. A. MARTINEZ, W. D. MOSHER, J.C. ABMA, AND J. JONES. 2005. Fertility, family planning, and reproductive health of U.S. women: Data from the 2002 national survey of family growth. *Vital and Health Statistics* (Series 23, No. 25). Hyattsville, MD: National Center for Health Statistics.

CHANDRA, A., ET AL. 2008. Does watching sex on television predict teen pregnancy? Findings from a national longitudinal survey of youth. *Pediatrics* 122 (November): 1047–54.

CHANG, A. 2008. Couples are finding ways to cut wedding costs. *Los Angeles Times*, August 27, www.latimes.com (accessed August 28, 2008).

CHANG, J., C. J. BERG, L. E. SALTZMAN, AND J. HERNDON. 2005. Homicide: A leading cause of injury deaths among pregnant and postpartum women in the United States, 1991–1999. *American Journal of Public Health* 95 (March): 471–77.

CHAO, R., AND V. TSENG. 2002. Parenting of Asians. In *Handbook of parenting*, 2nd ed., Vol. 4: Social conditions and applied parenting, ed. M. H. Bornstein, 59–93. Mahwah, NJ: Erlbaum.

CHAPMAN, D. P., S. M. WILLIAMS, T. W. STRINE, R. F. ANDA, AND M. J. MOORE. 2006. Dementia and its implications for public health. *Preventing Chronic Disease: Public Health Research, Practice, and Policy* 3 (April): A 34–A47.

CHARLES, S. T., AND L. L. CARSTENSEN. 2002. Marriage in old age. In *Inside the American couple: New thinking/new challenges*, eds. M. Yalom and L. L. Carstensen, 236–54. Berkeley: University of California Press.

CHARLES, S. T., M. MATHER, AND L. L. CARSTENSEN. 2003. Aging and emotional memory: The forget-table nature of negative images for older adults. *Journal of Experimental Psychology* 132 (June): 310–24.

CHASE, K. N. 2009. A showcase for senior athletes. *Christian Science Monitor*, August 16, 23

CHASE-LANSDALE, P. L., A. J. CHERLIN, AND K. E. KIERNAN. 1995. The long-term effects of parental divorce on the mental health of young adults: A developmental perspective. *Child Development* 66 (December): 1614–34.

CHATTERJI, P., AND S. MARKOWITZ. 2008. Family leave after childbirth and the health of new mothers. National Bureau of Economic Research, Working Paper 14156, July, www.nber.org (accessed August 12, 2009).

CHATTERS, L. M., AND R. J. TAYLOR. 2005. Religion and families. In *Sourcebook of family theory & research*, eds. V. L. Bengston, A. C. Acock, K. R. Allen, P. Dilworth-Anderson, and D. M. Klein, 517–30. Thousand Oaks, CA: Sage.

CHAUVIN, 2002. Catholic U. in Peru angers students by handing out pamphlets calling homosexuality an illness. *Chronicle of Higher Education*, September 19. http://chronicle.com (accessed September 20, 2002.)

CHEAH, C. S. L., C. Y. Y. LEUNG, M. TAHSEEN, AND D. SCHULTZ. 2009. Authoritative parenting among immigrant Chinese mothers of preschoolers. *Journal of Family Psychology* 23 (June): 311–20.

CHELALA, C. 2002. World violence against women a great unspoken pandemic. *Philadelphia Inquirer,* November 4. www.commondreams.org (accessed November 7, 2002).

CHEN, Z.-Y., AND H. B. KAPLAN. 2001. Intergenerational transmission of constructive parenting. *Journal of Marriage and Family* 63 (February): 17–31.

CHERLIN, A. J. 2009a. *The marriage-go-round: The state of marriage and the family in America today.* New York: Alfred A. Knopf.

CHERLIN, A. J. 2009b. Married with bankruptcy. *New York Times*, May 29, www.nytimes.com (accessed June 9, 2009).

CHERLIN, A. J., AND F. F. FURSTENBERG, JR. 1994. Stepfamilies in the United States: A reconsideration. *Annual Review of Sociology* 20: 359–81.

CHESHIRE. T. 2006. American Indian families: Strength and answers from our past. In *Families in global and multicultural perspective*, 2nd ed., eds. B. B. Ingoldsby and S. D. Smith, 315–27. Thousand Oaks, CA: Sage.

CHESHIRE, T. C. 2001. Cultural transmission in urban American Indian families. *American Behavioral Scientist* 44 (May): 1528–35.

CHESNEY-LIND, M., AND L. PASKO. 2004. *The female offender: Girls, women, and crime*, 2nd ed. Thousand Oaks, CA: Sage.

CHEVAN, A. 1996. As cheaply as one: Cohabitation in the older population. *Journal of Marriage and the Family* 58 (August): 656–67.

CHILDREN'S DEFENSE FUND. 2005. *State of America's children 2005*. Washington, DC: Children's Defense Fund.

Children's Defense Fund. 2008. *The state of America's children 2008.* www.unicef.org (accessed July 12, 2009).

CHILDTRENDS DATA BANK. Dating. 2005. www.childtrendsdatabank.org/pdf/73_PDF.pdf (accessed February 24, 2006).

Child Welfare Information Gateway. 2008. Child abuse neglect fatalities: Statistics and interventions. March, www.childwelfare.gov (accessed August 20, 2009).

Child Welfare Information Gateway. 2009. Foster care statistics. U.S. Department of

Health and Human Services, Administration for Children and Families. February, www.childwelfare.gov (accessed June 29, 2009).

CHIN, E. 2001. *Purchasing power: Black kids and American consumer culture*. Minneapolis: University of Minnesota Press.

CHION-KENNEY, L. 1991. Parents of divorce. *Washington Post*, May 6, B5.

CHLEBOWSKI, R. T., ET AL. 2008. Calcium plus vitamin D supplementation and the risk of breast cancer. *Journal of the National Cancer Institute* 100 (November): 1581–91.

CHO, H. 2008. Women wary of career breaks. *Baltimore Sun*, November 7, 18.

CHO, W., AND S. E. CROSS. 1995. Taiwanese love styles and their association with self-esteem and relationship quality. *Genetic, Social, and General Psychology Monographs* 121: 283–309.

CHOICE, P., AND L. K. LAMKE. 1997. A conceptual approach to understanding abused women's stay/leave decisions. *Journal of Family Issues* 18 (May): 290–314.

CHOMSKY, A. 2007. *"They take our jobs!" and 20 other myths about immigration*. Boston: Beacon Press.

CHOU, R. S., AND J. R. FEAGIN. 2008. *The myth of the model minority: Asian Americans facing racism*. Boulder, CO: Paradigm Publishers.

CHRISTAKIS, N. A., AND P. D. ALLISON. 2006. Mortality after the hospitalization of a spouse. *New England Journal of Medicine* 354 (February 16): 719–30.

CHRISTAKIS, N. A., AND J. H. FOWLER. 2007. The spread of obesity in a large social network over 32 years. *New England Journal of Medicine* 357 (July 26): 370–79.

CHRISTENSON, E. 2003. What women want. *Newsweek*, February 17, 11.

CHRISTIANSEN, S. 2009. The changing culture of Japanese fatherhood. *Family Focus* 54 (Spring): F12, F14.

CHRISTIE-MIZELL, C. A., E. M. PRYOR, AND E. R. B. GROSSMAN. 2008. Child depressive symptoms, spanking, and emotional support: Differences between African American and European American youth. *Family Relations* 57 (July): 335–50.

CHRISTOPHER, F. S. 2001. *To dance the dance: A symbolic interactional exploration of premarital sexuality*. Mahwah, NJ: Erlbaum.

CHRISTOPHER, F. S., AND T. S. KISLER. 2004. Sexual aggression in romantic relationships. In *The handbook of sexuality in close relationships*, eds. J. Harvey, A. Wenzel, and S. Sprecher, 287–409. Mahwah, NJ: Lawrence Erlbaum.

Chronicle of Higher Education. 2006. Attitudes and characteristics of freshmen at 4-year colleges, Fall 2005. Almanac Issue 2006–7, 53 (August): 19.

Chronicle of Higher Education. 2008. Students. *Almanac Issue 2008–9*. 55 (August 29): 18.

Chronicle of Higher Education. 2008. Faculty tenure. *Almanac Issue 2008–9, 55* (August 29): 25.

CHU, H. 2001. Chinese psychiatrists decide homosexuality isn't abnormal: New guidelines are hailed as a "leap forward" bringing nation more in line with the West. *Los Angeles Times*, March 6, A1.

CHU, H. 2006. Wombs for rent, cheap. *Los Angeles Times*, April 19, A1.

CHU, H. 2007. A gift for India's inter-caste couples. *Los Angeles Times*, November 4, www.latimes.com (accessed November 6, 2007).

CHUNG, G. H., M. B. TUCKER, AND D. TAKEUCHI. 2008. Wives' relative income production and household male dominance: Examining violence among Asian American enduring couples. *Family Relations* 57 (April): 227–38.

CIABATTARI, T. 2004. Cohabitation and housework: The effects of marital intentions. *Journal of Marriage and Family* 66 (February): 118–25.

CLARK, A. 2008. Tribes strive to save native tongues. *Christian Science Monitor*, May 23, 2.

CLARK, C. L., P. R. SHAVER, AND M. F. ABRAHAMS. 1999. Strategic behaviors in romantic relationship initiation. *Personality and Social Psychology Bulletin* 25: 707–20.

CLARK, J. M. 1999. *Doing the work of love: Men & commitment in same-sex couples*. Harriman, TN: Men's Studies Press.

CLARKE, G. Forever young. *Mother Jones*, July/August, 24–25.

CLARKE, S. C. 1995. Advance report of final divorce statistics, 1989 and 1990. *Monthly Vital Statistics Report* 43 (9[S]), March 22. Centers for Disease Control and Prevention.

CLARK-IBÁÑEZ, M., AND D. FELMLEE. 2004. Interethnic relationships: The role of social network diversity. *Journal of Marriage and Family* 66 (May): 292–305.

CLARKWEST, A. 2007. Spousal dissimilarity, race, and marital dissolution. *Journal of Marriage and Family* 69 (August): 639–53.

CLEARFIELD, M. W., AND N. M. NELSON. 2006. Sex differences in mothers' speech and play behavior with 6-, 9-, and 14-month-old infants. *Sex Roles* 54 (January): 127–37.

CLEMENTS, M. L., S. M. STANLEY, AND H. J. MARKMAN. 2004. Before they said "I do": Discriminating among marital outcomes over 13 years. *Journal of Marriage and Family* 66 (August): 613–26.

CLOUD, J. 2008. Are gay relationships different? *Time*, January 28, 78–80.

CLUNIS, D. M., AND G. D. GREEN. 2000. *Lesbian couples: A guide to creating healthy relationships*. Seattle: Seal.

COATES, T-N. 2008. This is how we lost to the white man. *Atlantic Monthly*, May, www.theatlantic.com (accessed March 20, 2009).

CODISPOTI, L., B. COURTOT, AND J. SWEDISH. 2008. Nowhere to turn: How the individual health insurance market fails women. National Women's Law Center, action.nwlc.org (accessed March 15, 2009).

COHAN, C. I., AND S. KLEINBAUM. 2002. Toward a greater understanding of the cohabitation effect: Premarital cohabitation and marital communication. *Journal of Marriage and Family* 64 (February): 180–92.

COHAN, W. D. 2009. *House of cards: A tale of hubris and wretched excess on Wall Street*. Garden City, NY: Doubleday.

COHANY, S. 2009. Ranks of discouraged workers and others marginally attached to the labor force rise during recession. Issues in Labor Statistics, U.S. Bureau of Labor Statistics, April, www.bls.gov (accessed August 9, 2009).

COHEN, C. E. 1994. The trailing-spouse dilemma. *Working Woman* (March): 69–70.

COHEN, S. A. 2008. Abortion and women of color: The bigger picture. *Guttmacher Policy Review* 11 (Summer): 2–5, 12.

COHN, C. 2008. Baby boomers: The gloomiest generation. Pew Research Center, June 25, http://pewresearch.org (accessed September 20, 2009).

COHN, D. 2000. Census complaints [in] home. *Washington Post*, May 4, A9.

COHN, L. 2003. One child, four parents. *Christian Science Monitor*, February 19, 11–13.

COHN, L. 2005. Remarriage after retirement. *Christian Science Monitor*, June 8, 11–12.

COLAPINTO, J. 1997. The true story of John/Joan. *Rolling Stone*, December 11, 54–73, 92–97.

COLAPINTO, J. 2001. *As nature made him: The boy who was raised as a girl.* New York: Harper Perennial.

COLAPINTO, J. 2004. What were the real reasons behind David Reimer's suicide? *Slate*, June 3, www.slate.com (accessed April 24, 2008).

COLE, A. 1996. Yours, mine and ours. *Modern Maturity* (September/October): 12, 14–15.

COLE, M. G., AND N. DENDUKURI. 2003. Risk factors for depression among elderly community subjects: A systematic review and meta-analysis. *American Journal of Psychiatry* 160 (June): 1147–56.

COLEMAN, M., L. H. GANONG, AND S. WEAVER. 2001. Relationship maintenance and enhancement in remarried families. In *Close romantic relationships: Maintenance and enhancement*, eds. J. H. Harvey and A. Wenzel, 255–76. Mahwah, NJ: Erlbaum.

COLEMAN, M., L. H. GANONG, AND M. FINE. 2002. Reinvestigating remarriage: Another decade of progress. In *Understanding families into the new millennium: A decade in review*, ed. R. M. Milardo, 507–26. Minneapolis: National Council on Family Relations.

COLEMAN, M., L. H. GANONG, AND T. C. ROTHRAUFF. 2006. Racial and ethnic similarities and differences in beliefs about intergenerational assistance to older adults after divorce and remarriage. *Family Relations* 55 (December): 576–87.

COLEMAN, T. F. 2007. Single women take large share of homebuyer market. Unmarried America, April 30, www.unmarried.org (accessed June 11, 2009).

COLEY, R. L. 2002. What mothers teach, what daughters learn: Gender mistrust and self-sufficiency among low-income women. In *Just living together: Implications of cohabitation on families, children, and social policy*, eds. A. Booth and A. C. Crouter, 97–106. Mahwah, NJ: Erlbaum.

COLL, STEVE. 2008. *The Bin Ladens: An Arabian family in the American century.* New York: Penguin.

COLLIER, J. 1947. *The Indians of the Americas.* New York: Norton.

COLLINS, C. 2005. N.H. adoptees gain access to records. *Christian Science Monitor*, Januaary 13, 11–12.

COLLINS, L. 2008. Pixel perfect—Pascal Dangin's virtual reality. *The New Yorker*, May 12, www.newyorker.com (accessed April 20, 2009).

COLLINS, R. L. 2005. Sex on television and its impact on American youth: Background and results from the RAND television and adolescent sexuality study. *Child and Adolescent Psychiatric Clinics of North America* 14 (July): 371–85.

COLLISON, M. N.-K. 1993. A sure-fire winner is to tell her you love her; women fall for it all the time. In *Women's studies: Thinking women*, eds. J. Wetzel, M. L. Espenlaub, M. A. Hagen, A. B. McElhiney, and C. B. Williams, 228–30. Dubuque, IA: Kendall/Hunt.

COLTRANE, S. 2000. Research on household labor: Modeling and measuring the social embeddedness of routine family work. *Journal of Marriage and the Family* 62 (November): 1208–33.

COLTRANE, S., R. D. PARKE, AND M. ADAMS. 2004. Complexity of father involvement in low-income Mexican American families. *Family Relations* 53 (March): 179–89.

COMERFORD, L. 2005. Co-custody may have unintended results. *National Council on Family Relations Report* 50 (June): F28–F29.

COMIJS, H. C., A. M. POT, H. H. SMIT, AND C. JONKER. 1998. Elder abuse in the community: Prevalence and consequences. *Journal of the American Geriatrics Society* 46 (7): 885–88.

CONDE-AGUDELO, A., A., ROSAS-BERMÚDEZ, AND A. C. KAFURY-GOETA. 2006. Birth spacing and risk of adverse perinatal outcomes: A meta-analysis. *JAMA* 295 (April 19): 1809–23.

CONGER, R. D., AND K. J. CONGER. 2002. Resilience in Midwestern families: Selected findings from the first decade of a prospective, longitudinal study. *Journal of Marriage and the Family* 64 (May): 361–73.

Congressional hearing explores high suicide rates among American Indian youth. 2009. Kaiser Family Foundation, March 3, www.kaisernetwork.org (accessed March 31, 2009).

CONLIN, J. 2009. Living apart for the paycheck. *New York Times,* January 2, 1.

CONLIN, M. 2007. The kids are all right. *Business Week*, October 8, 18.

CONLIN, M., J. MERRITT, AND L. HIMELSTEIN. 2002. Mommy is really home from work. *Business Week*, November 25, 101–3.

CONNOLLY, C. 2003. Texas teaches abstinence, with mixed grades. *Washington Post*, January 21, A1.

ConsumerReports.org. 2009. 6 top reasons for not having sex, February, www.consumerreports.org (accessed July 19, 2009).

CONWAY, T., AND R. Q. HUTSON. 2008. Healthy marriage and the legacy of child maltreatment: A child welfare perspective. CLASP Policy Brief, May, 1–13, www.clasp.org (accessed August 12, 2009).

COONTZ, S. 2005. *Marriage, a history: How love conquered marriage.* New York: Penguin.

COONTZ, S. 2006. A pop quiz on marriage. *New York Times*, February 19, 12.

COONTZ, S. 2007. The family revolution. *Greater Good Magazine* 4 (Fall), http://greatergood.berkeley.edu (accessed February 17, 2009).

COOPER, H. 2009. President delivers exhortation to fathers. *New York Times*, June 20, 10.

COPLAN, J. H. 2008. Reconcilable differences. *Working Wealth*, Winter, 16–21.

CORBETT, C., C. HILL, AND A. ST. ROSE. 2008. *Where the girls are: The facts about gender equity in education.* Washington, DC: American Association of University Women.

CORBETT, S. 2009. A prom divided. *New York Times*, May 24, 9.

CORDES, H. 2003. Doping kids. *Mother Jones*, Sep./October, 17–18.

CORNELIUS, M. D., AND N. L. DAY. 2000. The effects of tobacco use during and after pregnancy on exposed children: Relevance of findings for alcohol research. *Alcohol Research & Health* 24 (4): 242–49.

CORNELIUS, T. L., AND G. ALESSI. 2007. Behavioral and physiological components of communication training: Does the topic affect outcome? *Journal of Marriage and Family* 69 (August): 608–20.

CORRELL, S. H., S. BERNARD, AND I. PAIK. 2007. Getting a job: Is there a motherhood penalty? *American Journal of Sociology* 112 (March): 1297–338.

COSBY, B., AND A. F. POUSSAINT. 2007. *Come on people: On the path from victims to victors.* Nashville, TN: Thomas Nelson.

COSE, E. 1999. Deciphering the code of the street. *Newsweek*, August 30, 33.

COSE, E. 2003. The black gender gap. *Newsweek*, March 3, 46–51.

COSE, E. 2005. Does Cosby help? *Newsweek*, January 3, 66–69.

COSTIGAN, C. L., D. P. DORIS, AND T. F. SU. 2004. Marital relationships among immigrant Chinese couples. In *Vision 2004: What is the future of marriage?* eds. P. Amato and N. Gonzalez, 41–44. Minneapolis, MN: National Council on Family Relations.

COTT, N. F. 1976. Eighteenth century family and social life revealed in Massachusetts divorce records. *Journal of Social History* 10 (Fall): 20–43.

COTT, N. F. 1977. *The bonds of womanhood.* New Haven, CT: Yale University Press.

COTT, N. F., AND E. H. PLECK, EDS. 1979. *A heritage of her own: Toward a new social history of American women.* New York: Simon & Schuster.

COTTEN, S. R. 1999. Marital status and mental health revisited: Examining the importance of risk factors and resources. *Family Relations* 48 (July): 225–33.

COTTER, D., P. ENGLAND, AND J. HERMSEN. 2007. Trends in mothers' employment and which mothers stay home. Council on Contemporary Families, May 10, www.contemporaryfamilies.org (accessed June 3, 2009).

COVEL, S. 2003. Cheating hearts. *American Demographics* 25 (June): 16.

COVEL, S. 2003. The heart never forgets. *American Demographics* 25 (July/August): 15.

COWAN, C. P., AND P. A. COWAN. 2000. *When partners become parents: The big life change for couples.* Mahwah, NJ: Erlbaum.

COWAN, P. A., C. P. COWAN, M. K. PRUETT, AND K. PRUETT. 2009. Six barriers to father involvement and suggestions for overcoming them. *Family Focus* 54 (Spring): F1, F2, F4.

COWDERY, R. S., AND C. KNUDSON-MARTIN. 2005. The construction of motherhood: Tasks, relational connection, and gender equality. *Family Relations* 54 (July): 335–45.

COX, W. 2009. Executive summary: Improving quality of life through telecommuting. Information Technology & Innovation Foundation, January, www.itif.org (accessed August 9, 2009).

CRAIG, T. 2009. Uproar in D.C. as same-sex marriage gains. *Washington Post*, May 6, A1.

CRAIG-HENDERSON, K. M. 2006. *Black men in interracial relationships: What's love got to do with it?* New Brunswick, NJ: Transaction.

CRANDELL, S. 2005. Oh, baby. *AARP Magazine*, September/October, 108–18.

CRAWFORD, D. W., R. M. HOUTS, T. L. HUSTON, AND L. J. GEORGE. 2002. Compatibility, leisure, and satisfaction in marital relationships. *Journal of Marriage and Family* 64 (May): 433–49.

CRAWLEY, L., AND M. K. SINGER. 2007. Racial, cultural, and ethnic factors affecting the quality of end-of-life care in California: Findings and recommendations. California HealthCare Foundation, March, www.chcf.org (accessed September 20, 2009).

CRISPELL, D. 1992. Myths of the 1950s. *American Demographics* (August): 38–43.

CRISPELL, D. 1993. Planning no family, now or ever. *American Demographics*, 6 (October): 23–24.

CRITTENDEN, A. 2001. *The price of motherhood: Why the most important job in the world is still the least valued.* New York: Metropolitan.

CRITTENDEN, D. 1999. *What our mothers didn't tell us: Why happiness eludes the modern woman.* New York: Simon & Schuster.

CRNIC, K., AND C. LOW. 2002. Everyday stresses and parenting. In *Handbook of parenting*, 2nd ed., Vol. 5: ed. M. H. Bornstein, 243–68. Mahwah, NJ: Erlbaum.

CROCKETT, R. O. 2006. The rising stock of black directors. *Business Week*, February 27, 34.

CROSBIE-BURNETT, M., AND E. A. LEWIS. 1993. Use of African-American family structures and functioning to address the challenges of European-American postdivorce families. *Family Relations* 42 (July): 243–48.

CROSBIE-BURNETT, M., AND J. GILES-SIMS. 1994. Adolescent adjustment and stepparenting styles. *Family Relations* 43 (October): 394–99.

CROSBIE-BURNETT, M., AND K. M. MC CLINTIC. 2000. Remarriage and recoupling: A stress perspective. In *Families & change: Coping with stressful events and transitions,* 2nd ed., eds. P. C. McKenry and S. J. Price, 303–32. Thousand Oaks, CA: Sage.

CROSBY, F. J. 1991a. *Illusion and disillusion: The self in love and marriage,* 5th ed. Belmont, CA: Wadsworth.

CROSBY, F. J. 1991b. *Juggling: The unexpected advantages of balancing career and home for women and their families.* New York: Free Press.

CROSNOE, R., AND G. H. ELDER. 2002. Adolescent twins and emotional distress: The interrelated influence of nonshared environment and social structure. *Child Development* 73 (November/December): 1761–74.

CROSS, T. L. 1998. Understanding family resiliency from a relational world view. In *Resiliency in Native American and immigrant families,* eds. H. I. McCubbin, E. A. Thompson, A. I. Thompson, and J. E. Fromer, 143–57. Thousand Oaks, CA: Sage.

CROSSE, M. 2008. Abstinence education: Assessing the accuracy and effectiveness of federally funded programs. U.S. Government Accountability Office, GAO-08-664T, April 23, www.gao.gov (accessed May 2, 2009).

CROUSE, K. 2007. Fatherhood puts game in perspective. *New York Times,* November 2, 1.

CROWELL, J. A., AND E. WATERS. 1994. Bowlby's theory grown up: The role of attachment in adult love relationships. *Psychological Inquiry* 5 (1): 31–34.

CROWLEY, K., M. A. CALLANAN, H. R. TENENBAUM, AND E. ALLEN. 2001. Parents explain more often to boys than to girls during shared scientific thinking. *Psychological Science* 49 (May): 258–61.

CRUIKSBANK, M. 2003. *Learning to be old: Gender, culture, and aging.* Lanham, MD: Rowman & Littlefield.

CUBER, J., AND P. HAROFF. 1965. *Sex and the significant Americans.* Baltimore: Penguin.

CULLEN, L. T. 2007. Till work do us part. *Time,* October 8, 63–64.

CULLEN, L. T., AND C. MASTERS. 2008. We just clicked. *Time,* January 28, 86–89.

CUNNINGHAM, J. D., AND J. K. ANTILL. 1995. Current trends in nonmarital cohabitation: In search of the POSSLQ. In *Under-studied relationships: Off the beaten track,* eds. J. T. Wood and S. Duck, 148–72. Thousand Oaks, CA: Sage.

CUNNINGHAM, M., AND A. THORNTON. 2005. The influence of union transitions on white adults' attitudes toward cohabitation. *Journal of Marriage and Family* 67 (August): 710–20.

CUNRADI, C. B. 2009. Intimate partner violence among Hispanic men and women: The role of drinking, neighborhood disorder, and acculturation-related disorders. *Violence and Victims* 24 (January): 83–97.

CURRIE, J., AND E. TEKIN. 2006. Does child abuse cause crime? Cambridge, MA: National Bureau of Economic Research, Working Paper 12171, http://papers.nber.org/ (accessed June 12, 2006).

CUTRONA, C. E. 1996. *Social support in couples: Marriage as a resource in times of stress.* Thousand Oaks. CA: Sage.

D

DALLA, R. L., AND W. C. GAMBLE. 1997. Exploring factors related to parenting competence among Navajo teenage mothers: Dual techniques of inquiry. *Family Relations* 46 (April): 113–21.

DALY, K. J. 1999. Crisis of genealogy: Facing the challenges of infertility. In *The dynamics of resilient families,* eds. H. I. McCubbin, E. A. Thompson, A. I. Thompson, and J. A. Futrell, 1–40. Thousand Oaks, CA: Sage.

DANESI, M. 2003. *My son is an alien: A cultural portrait of today's youth.* Lanham, MD: Rowman & Littlefield.

DANG, D. T. 2008. Be wary in doing online survey. *Baltimore Sun,* June 10, 1D, 5D.

DANZIGER, S. 2008. The price of independence: The economics of early adulthood. *Family Focus* 53 (March): F7–F8.

DAUER, S. 2002. Pakistan: Violence against women continues. *Interact* (Summer): 1, 5.

DAUM, M. 2009. The age of friendaholism. *Los Angeles Times,* March 7, www.latimes.com (accessed March 8, 2009).

DAUM, M. 2009. Moms in their 60s—oh, baby! *Los Angeles Times,* July 23, www.latimes.com (accessed July 24, 2009).

Dave Thomas Foundation for Adoption. 2007. National foster care adoption attitudes survey. November, www.davethomasfoundation.org (accessed June 28, 2009).

DAVEY, M., AND D. LEONHARDT. 2003. Jobless and hopeless, many quit the labor force. *New York Times,* April 27.

DAVIES, C., AND D. WILLIAMS. 2002. *The grandparent study 2002 report.* AARP. http://research.aarp.org/general/gp_2002.pdf (accessed October 10, 2003).

DAVIS, E. C., AND L. V. FRIEL. 2001. Adolescent sexuality: Disentangling the effects of family structure and family context. *Journal of Marriage and Family* 63 (August): 669–81.

DAVIS, G. 2007. Muslims voice protests over school calendar. *Baltimore Sun,* May 9, 4B.

DAVIS, J. A., T. W. SMITH, AND P. V. MARSDEN. 2002. General Social Survey 2002 [United States] [computer file]. Chicago, IL: National Opinion Research Center [produce]; Storrs, CT: The Roper Center for Public Opinion Research, University of Connecticut [distributer].

DAVIS, J. B. 2009. For better or worse. *Texas Lawyer,* February 9, www.law.com (accessed August 26, 2009).

DAVIS, K. D., A. C. CROUTER, AND S. M. MCHALE. 2006. Implications of shift work for parent-adolescent relationships in dual-earner families. *Family Relations* 55 (October): 450–60.

DAVIS, K. D., W. B. GOODMAN, A. E. PIRRETTI, AND D. M. ALMEIDA. 2008. Nonstandard work schedules, perceived family well-being, and daily stressors. *Journal of Marriage and Family* 70 (November): 991–1003.

DAVIS, K. E. 1985. Near and dear: Friendship and love compared. *Psychology Today* 19: 22–30.

DAVIS, L. E., J. H. WILLIAMS, S. EMERSON, AND M. HOURD-BRYANT. 2000. Factors contributing to partner commitment among unmarried African Americans. *Social Work Research* 24 (March): 4–15.

DAVIS, M. 2002. Champion lovers share 83 years of marriage. *Lexington Herald-Leader,* April 9. www.kri.com/ (accessed July 23, 2003).

DAVIS, P. W. 1996. Threats of corporal punishment as verbal aggression: A naturalistic study. *Child Abuse & Neglect* 20 (4): 289–304.

DAVIS, S., M., AND T. N. GREENSTEIN. 2004. Cross-national variations in the division of household labor. *Journal of Marriage and Family* 66 (December): 1260–71.

DAWSON, J. M., AND P. A. LANGAN. 1994. *Murder in families.* Washington, DC: Bureau of Justice Statistics.

DAWSON, D. A., R. B. GOLDSTEIN, S. P. CHOU, W. J. RUAN, AND B. F. GRANT. 2008. Age at first drink and the first incidence of adult-onset DSM-IV alcohol use disorders. *Alcoholism: Clinical and Experimental Research* 32 (December): 2149–60.

DAY, R. D. 1995. Family-systems theory. In *Research and theory in family science,* eds. R. D. Day, K. R. Gilbert, B. H. Settles, and W. R. Burr, 91–101. Pacific Grove, CA: Brooks/Cole.

DEAL, J. E., M. STANLEY-HAGAN, AND J. C. ANDERSON. 1992. The marital relationships in remarried families. *Monographs of the Society for Research in Child Development* 57: 2–3, serial no. 227.

Dear Ann. 2001. *Washington Post,* April 13, C7.

DEBIAGGI, S. D. 2002. *Changing gender roles: Brazilian immigrant families in the U.S.* New York: LFB Scholarly Publishing.

DEE, T. S. 2006. The why chromosome. *Education Next* No 4. (Fall): 69–75.

Defining overweight and obesity. 2009. Centers for Disease Control and Prevention, August 12, www.cdc.gov (accessed August 23, 2009).

DEGLER, C. 1981. *At odds: Women and the family in America from the Revolution to the present.* New York: Oxford University Press.

DEGLER, C. N. 1983. The emergence of the modern American family. In *The American family in social-historical perspective,* 3rd ed., ed. M. Gordon, 61–79. New York: St. Martin's.

DEGARMO, D. S., AND C. R. MARTINEZ JR. 2006. A culturally informed model of academic well-being for Latino youth: The importance of discriminatory experiences and social support. *Family Relations* 55 (July): 267–78.

DE LA CANCELA, V. 1994. "Coolin": The psychosocial communication of African and Latino men. In *African American males: A critical link in the African American family,* ed. D. J. Jones, 33–44. New Brunswick, NJ: Transaction.

DELCASTILLO, R. G. 1984. *La familia: Chicano families in the urban Southwest, 1848 to the present.* Notre Dame, IN: University of Notre Dame Press.

DELEIRE, T., AND A. KALIL. 2002. Good things come in threes: Single-parent multigenerational family structure and adolescent adjustment. *Demography* 39 (May): 393–413.

DELEIRE, T., AND A. KALIL. 2005. How do cohabiting couples with children spend their money? *Journal of Marriage and Family* 67 (May): 286–95.

DELISLE, S. 1997. Preserving reproductive choice: Preventing STD-related infertility in women. *Siecus Report* 25 (March): 18–21.

DEMARIS, A. 2001. The influence of intimate violence on transitions out of cohabitation. *Journal of Marriage and Family* 63 (February): 235–46.

DEMARIS, A., AND W. MACDONALD. 1993. Premarital cohabitation and marital instability: A test of the unconventionality hypothesis. *Journal of Marriage and the Family* 55 (May): 399–407.

DEMO, D. H., AND A. C. ACOCK. 1996. Singlehood, marriage, and remarriage. *Journal of Family Issues* 17 (May): 388–407.

DEMOS, J. 1970. *A little commonwealth: Family life in Plymouth colony.* New York: Oxford University Press.

DEMOS, J. 1986. *Past, present, and personal: The family and the life course in American history.* New York: Oxford University Press.

DeMunck, V. C. 1998. Lust, love, and arranged marriages in Sri Lanka. In *Romantic love and sexual behavior: Perspectives from the social sciences,* ed. V. C. de Munck, 295–300. Westport, CT: Praeger.

DeNavas-Walt, C., B. D. Proctor, and C. H. Lee. 2006. *Income, poverty, and health insurance coverage in the United States: 2005.* Washington, DC: U.S. Government Printing Office.

DeNavas-Walt, C., B. D. Proctor, and J. C. Smith. 2008. Income, poverty, and health insurance coverage in the United States: 2007. *Current Population Reports,* P60-23. Washington, DC: U.S. Government Printing Office.

DeNavas-Walt, C., B. D. Proctor, and J. C. Smith. 2009. Income, poverty, and health insurance coverage in the United States: 2008. *Current Population Reports,* P60-236(RV). Washington, DC: U.S. Government Printing Office.

Denizet-Lewis, B. 2004. Friends, friends with benefits and the benefits of the local mall. *New York Times,* May 30, F30.

Denny, C. H., J. Tsai, R. L. Floyd, and P. P. Green. 2009. Alcohol use among pregnant and nonpregnant women of childbearing age—United States, 1991–2005. *MMWR Weekly* 58 (May 22): 529–32.

Dents in the dream. 2008. *Time,* July 28, 40–41.

DePaulo, B. 2006. *Single out: How singles are stereotyped, stigmatized, and ignored, and still live happily ever after.* New York: St. Martin's Griffin.

DeSpelder, L. A., and A. L. Strickland. 2005. *The last dance: Encountering death and dying,* 7th ed. New York: Mc-Graw Hill.

DeSteno, D., M. Y. Bartlett, J. Braverman, and P. Salovey. 2002. Sex differences in jealousy: Evolutionary mechanism or artifact of measurement? *Journal of Personality and Social Psychology* 83 (November): 1103–16.

Derlega, V. J., S. Metts, S. Petronio, and S. T. Margulis. 1993. *Self-disclosure.* Thousand Oaks, CA: Sage.

Deveny, K. 2003. We're not in the mood. *Newsweek,* June 30, 41–46.

De Vries, R., M. A. Anderson, and B. C. Martinson. 2006. Normal misbehavior: Scientists talk about the ethics of research. *Journal of Empirical Research on Human Research Ethics* 1 (March): 43–50.

Dew, J. 2008. Debt change and marital satisfaction change in recently married couples. *Family Relations* 57 (January): 60–71.

Dew, J. 2009. The gendered meaning of assets for divorce. *Journal of Family and Economic Issues* 30 (March): 20–31.

Dey, J. G., and C. Hill. 2007. Behind the pay gap. American Association of University Women Educational Foundation, www .aauw.org (accessed August 1, 2007).

Diamond, M., and K. Sigmundson. 1997. Sex reassignment at birth: Long-term review and clinical implications. *Archives of Pediatrics & Adolescent Medicine* 15 (March): 298–304.

Diener, M. L., S. C. Mangelsdorf, J. L. McHale, and C. A. Frosch. 2002. Infants' behavioral strategies for emotion regulation with fathers and mothers: Associations with emotional expressions and attachment quality. *Infancy* 3 (May): 153–74.

Diller, L. H. 1998. *Running on Ritalin: A physician reflects on children, society, and performance in a pill.* New York: Bantam.

Dilman, I. 1998. *Love: Its forms, dimensions, and paradoxes.* New York: St. Martin's.

Dilworth-Anderson, P., L. M. Burton, and W. L. Turner. 1993. The importance of values in the study of culturally diverse families. *Family Relations* 42 (July): 238–42.

Dilworth-Anderson, P., S. W. Williams, and T. Cooper. 1999. The contexts of experiencing emotional distress among family caregivers to elderly African Americans. *Family Relations* 48 (October): 391–96.

Dion, M. R., S. L. Braver, S. A. Wolchik, and I. N. Sandler. 1997. Alcohol abuse and psychopathic deviance in noncustodial parents as predictors of child-support payment and visitation. *American Journal of Orthopsychiatry* 67 (January): 70–79.

Dittmar, H., E. Halliwell, and S. Ive. 2006. Does Barbie make girls want to be thin? The effect of experimental exposure to images of dolls on the body image of 5-to 8-year old girls. *Developmental Psychology* 42 (March): 282–92.

Divoky, D. 2002. Utah women to highlight hazards of polygamy. Women's E-News. www .womensenews.org (accessed January 8, 2002).

Dixit, J. 2009. You're driving me crazy! *Psychology Today,* March/April, www .psychologytoday.com (accessed April 27, 2009).

Do, D. D. 1999. *The Vietnamese Americans.* Westport, CT: Greenwood.

Dodson, L., and L. Schmalzbauer. 2005. Poor mothers and habits of hiding: Participatory methods in poverty research. *Journal of Marriage and Family* 67 (November): 949–59.

Dogra, C. S. 2006. Death becomes her. *Outlook India,* February 27, www.outlookindia.com (accessed February 28, 2006).

Doherty, R. W., E. Hatfield, K. Thompson, and P. Choo. 1994. Cultural and ethnic influences on love and attachment. *Personal Relationships* 1: 391–98.

Doherty, W. J. 1999. How therapy can be hazardous to your marital health. Paper presented at the annual conference of the Coalition for Marriage, Family, and Couples Education, July 3, www.smartmarriages.org (accessed July 14, 2006).

Doherty, W. J. 2001. *Take back your marriage: Sticking together in a world that pulls us apart.* New York: Guilford.

Doherty, W. J. 2002. How therapists harm marriages and what we can do about it. *Journal of Couple and Relationship Therapy* 1 (February): 1–17.

Dohm, A., and L. Shniper. 2007. Occupational employment projections to 2016. *Monthly Labor Review* 130 (November): 86–125.

Dokoupil, T. 2009. Men will be men. *Newsweek,* March 12, 50.

Dolan, M. 2005. Affairs at work subject to suits. *Los Angeles Times,* July 19, A1.

Dolbin-MacNab, M. L. 2006. Just like raising your own? Grandmothers' perception of parenting a second time around. *Family Relations* 55 (December): 564–75.

Dolbin-MacNab, M. L., and M. K. Keiley. 2009. Navigating interdependence: How adolescents raised solely by grandparents experience their family relationships. *Family Relations* 58 (April): 162–75.

Donahue, E. H., R. Haskins, and M. Nightingale. 2008. Using the media to promote adolescent well-being. The Future of Children, Spring, Princeton-Brookings, www .futureofchildren.org (accessed June 1, 2009).

Donnelly, D. A., and E. O. Burgess. 2008. The decision to remain in an involuntarily celibate relationship. *Journal of Marriage and Family* 70 (May): 519–35.

Donnelly, S. B. 2007. Growing younger. *Time,* January, A13–A14.

Doss, B. D., G. K. Rhoades, S. M. Stanley, and H. J. Markman. 2009. The effect of the transition to parenthood on relationship quality: An 8-year prospective study. *Journal of Personality and Social Psychology* 96 (March): 601–19.

Dotinga, R. 2005. Online dating sites aren't holding people's hearts. *Christian Science Monitor,* January 27, 11.

Douglas, J. D., and F. C. Atwell. 1988. *Love, intimacy, and sex.* Beverly Hills, CA: Sage.

Douglas, M. 2007. The role of a lifetime. *Newsweek,* September 17, 82.

Douglas, S. J., and M. W. Michaels. 2004. *The mommy myth: The idealization of motherhood and how it has undermined women.* New York: Free Press.

Downey, D. B., J. W. Ainsworth-Darnell, and M. J. Dufur. 1998. Sex of parent and children's well-being in single-parent households. *Journal of Marriage and the Family* 60 (November): 878–93.

Doyle, A. B., and D. Markiewicz. 2005. Parenting, marital conflict, and adjustment from early- to mid-adolescence: Mediated by adolescent attachment style? *Journal of Youth and Adolescence* 34 (April): 97–110.

Dubberley, E. 2007. *I'd rather be single than settle: Satisfied solitude and how to achieve it.* London: Vision Press.

Duck, S. 1998. *Human relationships,* 3rd ed. Thousand Oaks, CA: Sage.

Dugas, C. 2009. Bankruptcy filings rise to 6,000 a day as job losses take toll. *USA Today,* June 3, www.usatoday.com (accessed July 16, 2009).

Dunbar, R. 1995. Are you lonesome tonight? *New Scientist* 145, February 11, 26–31.

Duncan, S. F., T. B. Holman, and C. Yang. 2007. Factors associated with involvement in marriage preparation programs. *Family Relations* 56 (July): 270–78.

Dunifon, R., and L. Kowaleski-Jones. 2007. The influence of grandparents in single-mother families. *Journal of Marriage and Family* 69 (May): 465–81.

Durose, M. R., C. W. Harlow, P. A. Langan, M. Motivans, R. R. Rantala, E. L. Smith, and E. Constantin. 2005. Family violence statistics: Including statistics on strangers and acquaintances. U.S. Department of Justice, Office of Justice Programs, June, www.ojp .usdoj.gov (accessed August 20, 2009).

Dush, C., M. Kamp, and P. R. Amato. 2005. Consequences of relationship status and quality for subjective well-being. *Journal of Social and Personal Relationships* 22 (October): 607–27.

Dush, K., C. Cohan, and P. Amato. 2003. The relationship between cohabitation and marital quality and stability: Change across cohorts? *Journal of Marriage and Family* (August): 539–49.

Duvall, E. M. 1957. *Family development.* Philadelphia: Lippincott.

Dyball, R. 2008. Will Smith: "Divorce is not an option." May 27, www.people.com (accessed September 10, 2009).

Dye, J. L. 2005. Fertility of American women: June 2004. U.S. Census Bureau, Current Population Reports, P20-555, www.census .gov (accessed April 16, 2006)

Dye, J. L. 2008. *Fertility of American women: 2006.* Current Population Reports, P20-558. Washington, DC: U.S. Census Bureau.

Dye, J. L., and T. D. Johnson. 2007. A child's day: 2003 (selected indicators of child well-being). Current Population Reports, P70-109. Washington, DC: U.S. Census Bureau.

Dyl, J., J. Kittler, K. A. Phillips, and J. I. Hunt. 2006. Body dysmorphic disorder and other clinically significant body image concerns in adolescent psychiatric inpatients: Prevalence and clinical characteristics. *Child Psychiatry & Human Development,* June, Online First, www.springerlink.com (accessed June 25, 2006).

Dyson, M. E. 2005. *Is Bill Cosby right? Or has the middle class lost its mind?* New York: Basic Civitas Books.

E

EARLE, A. M. 1899. *Child life in colonial days.* New York: Macmillan.

EASTMAN, K. L., R. CORONOA, G. W. RYAN, A. L. WARSOFSKY, AND M. A. SCHUSTER. 2005. Worksite-based parenting programs to promote healthy adolescent sexual development: A qualitative study of feasibility and potential content. *Perspectives on Sexual and Reproductive Health* 37 (June): 62–69.

EATON, D. K., R. LOWRY, N. D. BRENER, D. A. GALUSKA, AND A. E. CROSBY. 2005. Associations of body mass index and perceived weight with suicide ideation and suicide attempts among U.S. high school students. *Archives of Pediatrics & Adolescent Medicine* 159 (June): 513–19.

EATON, D. K., ET AL. 2008. Youth risk behavior surveillance—United States, 2007. *MMWR* 57, June 5, No. SS-4.

EBELING, A. 2007. The second match. *Forbes,* November 12, 86–89.

EBERSTADT, M. 2004. *Home-alone America: The hidden toll of day care, behavioral drugs, and other parent substitutes.* New York: Penguin.

EBERSTADT, N. 2009. Poor statistics. *Forbes,* March 2, 26.

EBLING, R., AND R. W. LEVENSON. 2003. Who are the marital experts? *Journal of Marriage and Family* 65 (February): 130–42.

ECCLES, J. S., C. FREEDMAN-DOAN, P. FROME, J. JACOBS, AND K. S. YOON. 2000. Gender-role socialization in the family: A longitudinal approach. In *The developmental social psychology of gender,* eds. T. Eckes and H. M. Trautner, 333–60. Mahwah, NJ: Erlbaum.

ECKHOLM, E. 2007. Mothers scrimp as states take child support. *New York Times,* December 1, www.nytimes.com (accessed December 5, 2007).

ECKHOLM, E. 2008. Blue-collar jobs disappear, taking families' way of life along. *New York Times,* January 16, 14.

ECKLAND, B. K. 1968. Theories of mate selection. *Eugenics Quarterly* 15 (1): 71–84.

EDIN, K., AND L. LEIN. 1997. *Making ends meet: How single mothers survive welfare and low-wage work.* New York: Russell Sage Foundation.

EDIN, K., AND M. KEFALAS. 2005. Unmarried with children. *Contexts* 4 (Spring): 16–22.

EDMONSTON, B. 1999. The 2000 census challenge. *Population Reference Bureau* 1 (February): 1.

EDMONSTON, B., S. M. LEE, AND J. S. PASSEL. 2002. Recent trends in intermarriage and immigration and their effects on the future racial composition of the U.S. population. In *The new race question: How the census counts multiracial individuals,* eds. J. Perlmann and M. Waters, 227–55. New York: Russell Sage Foundation.

EDWARDS, M. 2007. Protecting the vulnerable. *AARP Bulletin* 45 (July/August): 18–19.

EDWARDS, T. M. 2000. Flying solo. *Time,* August 28, 47–51.

EDWARDS, V. J., M. C. BLACK, S. DHINGRA, L. MCKNIGHT-ELLY, AND G. S. PERRY. 2009. Physical and sexual intimate partner violence and reported serious psychological distress in the 2007 BRFSS. *International Journal of Public Health* 54 (June): 37–42.

EGAN, T. 2005. Polygamous settlement defies state crackdown. *New York Times,* October 25, A16.

EGGEBEEN, D. J. 2005. Cohabitation and exchanges of support. *Social Forces* 83 (May): 1097–1110.

Egyptian activists strive to halt female circumcision. 2008. *Baltimore Sun,* August 4, 4A.

EHRENSAFT, M. K., ET AL. 2003. Intergenerational transmission of partner violence: A 20-year prospective study. *Journal of*

Consulting and Clinical Psychology 71 (August): 741–53.

EISENBERG, M. E., L. H. BEARINGER, R. E. SIEVING, C. SWAIN, AND M. D. RESNICK. 2004. Parents' beliefs about condoms and oral contraceptives: Are they medically accurate? *Perspectives on Sexual and Reproductive Health* 36 (March/April): 50–57.

EISENBERG, N., ET AL., 2005. Relations among positive parenting, children's effortful control, and externalizing problems: A three-wave longitudinal study. *Child Development* 76 (September/October): 1055–71.

EISENBERG, M. E., D. H. BERNAT, L. H. BEARINGER, AND M. D. RESNICK. 2008. Support for comprehensive sexuality education: Perspectives from parents of school-age youth. *Journal of Adolescent Health* 42 (April): 352–59.

EISENBREY, R. 2009. Downtime: Workers forced to settle for fewer hours. Economic Policy Institute, January 14, www.epi.org (accessed July 26, 2009).

EISENBREY, R., M. LEVINSON, AND L. MISHEL. 2007. The agenda for shared prosperity. *EPI Journal* 17 (Winter): 1–8.

ELISON, J. 2007. The stage of grief no one admits to: Relief. *Newsweek,* January 29, 18.

ELKIND, D. 2002. Empty parenthood: The loss of parental authority in the postmodern family. In *Taking parenting public: The case for a new social movement,* eds. S. A. Hewlett, N. Rankin, and C. West, 29–44. Lanham, MD: Rowman & Littlefield.

ELKIND, D. 2007. *The power of play: Learning what comes naturally.* New York: De Capo Press.

ELLINGWOOD, K. 2009. Kissing ban sparks a Mexican revolution. *Baltimore Sun,* February 15, 16.

ELLIS, A. 1963. *The origins and the development of the incest taboo.* New York: Lyle Stuart.

ELLIS, L., P. E. GAY, AND E. PAIGE. 2001. Daily hassles and pleasures across the lifespan. Paper presented at the Annual American Psychological Association meetings, San Francisco.

ELLISON, C., AND J. P. BARTKOWSKI. 2002. Conservative Protestantism and the division of household labor among married couples. *Journal of Family Issues* 23 (November): 950–985.

ELMORE, C. 2005. Child-support collection cutbacks are shameful. Women's e-news, November 27, www.womensenews.org (accessed November 28, 2005).

ELSHTAIN, J. B. 1988. What's the matter with sex today? Tikkun: A Bimonthly Jewish Critique of Politics, *Culture and Society* 3 (3): 42–43.

ELSHTAIN, J. B., E. AIRD, A. ETZIONI, W. GALSTON, M. GLENDON, M. MINOW, AND A. ROSSI. 1993. *A communitarian position paper on the family.* Washington, DC: Communitarian Network.

Employee compensation. 2006. U.S. Government Accountability Office, February, GAO-06-285, www.gao.gov (accessed May 15, 2006).

ENGEL, M. 2000. Stepfamilies are not blended. Stepfamily Association of America. www .saafamilies.org/faqs/faqs.htm (accessed September 29, 2003).

ENGELS, M. 2008. With HIV, growing older faster. *Los Angeles Times,* February 5, www.latimes.com (accessed February 6, 2008).

ENGLAND, P., E. F. SHAFER, AND A. C. K. FOGARTY. 2007. Hooking up and forming romantic relationships on today's college campuses. Unpublished paper.

ENGLAND, P., AND R. J. THOMAS. 2009. The decline of the date and the rise of the college hook up. In *Family in transition,* 15th

ed., eds. A. S. Skolnick and J. H. Skolnick, 141–52. Boston: Pearson Higher Education.

EPSTEIN, G. A. 2005. Matchmaking is just a walk in park. *Baltimore Sun* (August 3): 1A, 11A.

EPSTEIN, R. 2008. Same-sex marriage is too limiting. *Los Angeles Times,* December 4, 2008, www.latimes.com (accessed December 6, 2008).

ERICKSON, R. J. 1993. Reconceptualizing family work: The effect of emotion work on perceptions of marital quality. *Journal of Marriage and the Family* 55 (November): 888–900.

ERICKSON, R. J. 2005. Why emotion work matters: Sex, gender, and the division of household labor. *Journal of Marriage and Family* 67 (May): 337–51.

ERIKSON, E. 1963. *Childhood and society.* New York: Norton.

ESLER, A. 1994. *The Western world: Prehistory to the present,* 3rd ed. Upper Saddle River, NJ: Prentice Hall.

ESPELAGE, D. L., M. K. HOLT, AND R. R. HENKEL. 2003. Examination of peer-group contextual effects on aggression during early adolescence. *Child Development* 74 (February): 205–20.

ESPIRITU, Y. L. 1995. *Filipino American lives.* Philadelphia: Temple University Press.

ESPOSITO, J. L., AND D. MOGAHED. 2007. *Who speaks for Islam? What a billion Muslims really think.* New York: Gallup Press.

ESSED, P., AND D. T. GOLDBERG, EDS. 2002. *Race critical theories: Text and context.* Malden, MA: Blackwell Publishers.

ESTES, R. J., AND N. A. WEINER. 2002. The commercial sexual exploitation of children in the U.S., Canada, and Mexico. University of Pennsylvania, School of Social Work. http://caster.ssw.upenn.edu (accessed September 17, 2003).

Evan B. Donaldson Adoption Institute. 2008. Finding families for African American children: The role of race & law in adoption from foster care. May, www.adoption institute.org (accessed June 29, 2009).

EVANS, M. I. 2009. The truth about multiple births. *Newsweek,* March 2, 14.

EVANS, S. 2000. The children of divorce. *Washington Post,* May 9, C4.

Evercare and National Alliance for Caregiving. 2007. Family caregivers—what they spend, what they sacrifice: The personal financial toll of caring for a loved one. November, www.caregiving.org (accessed September 27, 2009).

EVERETT, C., AND S. V. EVERETT. 1994. *Healthy divorce.* San Francisco: Jossey-Bass.

EVERTSSON, M., AND M. NERMO. 2004. Dependence within families and the division of labor: Comparing Sweden and the United States. *Journal of Marriage and Family* 66 (December): 1272–86.

Expanding resources for children: Is adoption by gays and lesbians part of the answer for boys and girls who need homes? 2005. Evan B. Donaldson Adoption Institute, March, www.adoptioninstitute.org (accessed April 20, 2006).

F

FABRICIUS, W. V. 2003. Listening to children of divorce: New findings that diverge from Wallerstein, Lewis, and Blakeslee. *Family Relations* 52 (October): 385–96.

FAGAN, J., M. F. SCHMITZ, AND J. J. LLOYD. 2007. The relationship between adolescent and young fathers' capital and marital plans of couples expecting a baby. *Family Relations* 56 (July): 231–43.

FAIOLA, A. 2005. Sick of their husbands in graying Japan. *Washington Post,* October 17, A1.

FALLER, K. C. 1990. *Understanding child sexual maltreatment*. Beverly Hills, CA: Sage.

False reports of hate crimes lead to arrest. 2009. *New York Times*, March 21, www .nytimes.com (accessed April 2, 2009).

FAMILY VIOLENCE PREVENTION FUND. 2006. The facts on immigrant women and domestic violence. www.endabuse.org (accessed June 29, 2006).

Family Violence Prevention Fund. 2009. The facts on teens and dating violence. www .endabuse.org (accessed June 5, 2009).

FARAGHER, J. M. 1986. *Sugar Creek: Life on the Illinois prairie*. New Haven, CT: Yale University Press.

FARBER, B. 1972. *Guardians of virtue: Salem families in 1800*. New York: Basic Books.

FARLEY, J. 2002. Just a Hollywood ending. *Time*, April 8, 90.

FARLEY, N. 1996. A survey of factors contributing to gay and lesbian domestic violence. In *Violence in gay and lesbian domestic partnerships*, eds. C. M. Renzetti and C. H. Miley, 35–42. New York: Harrington Park Press.

FARNSWORTH, A. 2008. Some cubicles make room for baby. *Christian Science Monitor*, September 15, 15.

FARRELL, D. M. 1997. Jealousy and desire. In *Love analyzed*, ed. Roger E. Lamb, 165–88. Boulder, CO: Westview.

FARRIS, C., T. A. TREAT, R. J. VIKEN, AND R. M. McFALL. 2008. Perceptual mechanisms that characterize gender differences in decoding women's sexual intent. *Psychological Science* 19 (April): 348–54.

FASS, A. 2004. The dating game. *Forbes* (July 5): 137, 139

FAVREAULT, M. M. 2005. Women and Social Security. The Urban Institute, December, www.urban.org (accessed August 12, 2006).

Federal Bureau of Investigation. 2007. *Crime in the United States 2006*. Washington, DC: Government Printing Office.

Federal Bureau of Investigation. 2008. Hate crime statistics 2007. October, www.fbi.gov (accessed May 21, 2009).

Federal Interagency Forum on Aging-Related Statistics. 2008. *Older Americans 2008: Key indicators of well-being*. Washington, DC: U.S. Government Printing Office.

Federal Interagency Forum on Child and Family Statistics. 2008. *America's children in brief: Key national indicators of well-being 2008*. Washington, DC: U.S. Government Printing Office.

Federal Interagency Forum on Child and Family Statistics. 2009. *America's children: Key national indicators of well-being, 2009*. Washington, DC: U.S. Government Printing Office.

FEDERMAN, D. D., AND G. A. WALFORD. 2007. Is male menopause real? *Newsweek*, January 15, 58–60.

FEENEY, J. A., AND P. NOLLER. 2002. Allocation and performance of household tasks: A comparison of new parents and childless couples. In *Understanding marriage: Development in the study of couple interaction*, eds. P. Noller and J. A. Feeney, 411–36. New York: Cambridge University Press.

FEENEY, J., AND P. NOLLER. 1996. *Adult attachment*. Thousand Oaks, CA: Sage.

FEHR, B. 1993. How do I love thee? Let me consult my prototype. In *Individuals in relationships*, ed. S. Duck, 87–120. Thousand Oaks, CA: Sage.

FEHR, B. 1999. Laypeople's conceptions of commitment. *Journal of Personality and Social Psychology* 76 (January): 90–103.

FEINBERG, L. F., K. Wolkwitz, AND C. GOLDSTEIN. 2006. Ahead of the curve: Emerging trends and practices in family caregiver support. AARP Public Policy Institute, March, http:/ /assets.aarp.org (accessed August 5, 2006).

FEINBERG, M. E., M. L. KAN, AND E. M. HETHERINGTON. 2007. The longitudinal influence of coparenting conflict on parental negativity and adolescent maladjustment. *Journal of Marriage and Family* 69 (August): 687–702.

FEINGOLD, A. 1988. Matching for attractiveness in romantic partners and same-sex friends: A meta-analysis and theoretical critique. *Psychological Bulletin* 104 (September): 226–35.

FELDMAN, H. 1931. *Racial factors in American industry*. New York: Harper & Row.

FELDMANN, L. 2008. Women make modest gains in election 2008. *Christian Science Monitor*, November 17, 2.

FELDMAN, S. S., E. CAUFFMAN, AND J. J. ARNETT. 2000. The (un)acceptability of betrayal: A study of college students' evaluations of sexual betrayal by a romantic partner and betrayal of a friend's confidence. *Journal of Youth and Adolescence* 29 (August): 499–523.

FELSON, R. B., AND A. C. CARES. 2005. Gender and the seriousness of assaults on intimate partners and other victims. *Journal of Marriage and Family* 67 (December): 1182–95.

FELSON, R. B., AND P.-P. PARÉ. 2005. The reporting of domestic violence and sexual assault by nonstrangers to the police. *Journal of Marriage and Family* 67 (August): 597–610.

FENTON, K., AND J. M. DOUGLAS JR. 2009. Sexually transmitted diseases awareness month, April 2009. CDC Press Release, April 1, www.cdc.gov (accessed May 20, 2009).

FERNANDEZ, S. 2005. Getting to know you. *Washington Post* (May 30): C1.

FESTINOER, T. 2002. After adoption: Dissolution or permanence. *Child Welfare* 81: 515–33.

FETSCH, R. J., R. K. YANG, AND M. J. PETTIT. 2008. The RETHINK parenting and anger management program: A follow-up validation study. *Family Relations* 57 (December): 543–52.

FETTO, J. 2001. Gather 'round. *American Demographics* 23 (June): 11–12.

FETTO, J. 2003. Love stinks. *American Demographics* 25 (February): 10–11.

FEW, A. L., AND K. H. ROSEN. 2005. Victims of chronic dating violence: How women's vulnerabilities link to their decisions to stay. *Family Relations* 54 (April): 265–79.

FICHTER, M. M., N. QUADFLIEG, AND S. HEDLUND. 2006. Twelve-year course and outcome predictors of anorexia nervosa. *International Journal of Eating Disorders* 39 (March): 87–100.

FIELDS, J. 2001. Living arrangements of children: 1996. U.S. Census Bureau, Current Population Reports, 70–74. www.census .gov (accessed February 15, 2003).

FIELDS, J. 2004. America's families and living arrangements: 2003. Current Population Reports, P20–553. Washington, DC: U.S. Census Bureau.

FIELDS, J., AND L. M. CASPER. 2001. America's families and living arrangements: 2000. U.S. Census Bureau, Current Population Reports, P20–537. www.census.gov (accessed February 25, 2003).

FILION, K. 2009. Minimum wage issue guide. Economic Policy Institute, July 21, www .epi.org (accessed July 26, 2009).

FILKINS, D. 2009. Afghan schoolgirls undeterred by attack. *New York Times*, January 14, www.nytimes.com (accessed January 15, 2009).

FINE, G. A. 1993. Ten lies of ethnography: Moral dilemmas of field research. *Journal of Contemporary Ethnography* 22 (October): 267–94.

FINER, L. B., AND S. K. HENSHAW. 2003. Abortion incidence and services in the United States in 2000. *Perspectives on Sexual and Reproductive Health* 35 (January/February): 6–15.

FINER, L. B., L. F. FROHWIRTH, L. A. DAUPHINEE, S. SINGH, AND A. M. MOORE. 2005. Reasons U.S. women have abortions: Quantitative and qualitative perspectives. *Perspectives on Sexual and Reproductive Health* 37 (September): 110–18.

FINER, L. B. 2007. Trends in premarital sex in the United States, 1954–2003. *Public Health Reports* 122 (January–February): 73–78.

FINGERMAN, K. L., E. L. HAY, C. M. CAMP DUSH, D. E. CICHY, AND S. HOSTERMAN. 2007. Parents' and offspring's perception of change in continuity when parents transition to old age. *Advances in Life Course Research* 12 (June): 275–306.

FINK, D. 1992. *Agrarian women: Wives and mothers in rural Nebraska, 1880–1940*. Chapel Hill: University of North Carolina Press.

FINKELHOR, D., AND R. ORMROD. 2000. *Characteristics of crimes against juveniles*. Washington, DC: U.S. Department of Justice, Office of Juvenile Justice and Delinquency Prevention.

FINKELHOR, D., R. ORMROD, H. TURNER, AND S. L. HAMBY. 2005. The victimization of children and youth: A comprehensive, national survey. *Child Maltreatment* 10 (February): 5–25.

FINKELHOR, D., H. HAMMER, AND A. J. SEDLAK. 2008. Sexually assaulted children: National estimates and characteristics. U.S. Department of Justice, Office of Justice Programs, August, www.ojp.usdoj.gov (accessed August 20, 2009).

FISCELLA, K., AND K. HOLT. 2008. Racial disparity in hypertension control: Tallying the death toll. *Annals of Family Medicine* 6, No. 6 (November/December): 497–502.

FISCHER, K. 2008. Top colleges admit fewer low-income students. *Chronicle of Higher Education*, May 2, A1, A19–A20.

FISHER, H. 1999. *The first sex: The natural talents of women and how they are changing the world*. New York: Ballantine.

FISHER, H. 2004. *Why we love: The nature and chemistry of romantic love*. New York: Henry Holt.

FISHER, H. 2008. Of lost love and old bones. *Chronicle of Higher Education*, June 6, B5.

FISHER, L. 2005. New gloss on motherhood, but few changes. Women's e-news, February 18, www.womensenews.org (accessed February 20, 2005).

FISHMAN, B., AND B. HAMEL. 1981. From nuclear to stepfamily ideology: A stressful change. *Alternative Lifestyles* 4: 181–204.

FITZPATRICK, J., E. A. SHARP, AND A. REIFMAN. 2009. Midlife singles' willingness to date partners with heterogeneous characteristics. *Family Relations* 58 (February): 121–33.

FITZPATRICK, M. A., AND A. MULAC. 1995. Relating to spouse and stranger: Gender-preferential language use. In *Gender, power, and communication in human relationships*, eds. P. J. Kalbfleisch and M. J. Cody, 213–31. Hillsdale, NJ: Erlbaum.

FLECK, C. 2007. Two steps forward, one step back. *AARP Bulletin*, October, 24.

FLECK, C. 2008. Retirement on hold. *AARP Bulletin*, July–August, 10–11.

FLEISHMAN, J. 2007. Saudi rape victim's sentence sparks anger. *Los Angeles Times*, December 16, www.latimes.com (accessed December 18, 2007).

FLETCHER, C. 2009. Bollywood-style weddings face first recession test. Women's e-News, February 13, www.womensenews.org (accessed February 14, 2009).

FLETCHER, G. 2002. *The new science of intimate relationships.* Malden, MA: Blackwell.

FLORES, G., AND J. BROTANEK. 2005. The healthy immigrant effect: A greater understanding might help us improve the health of all children. *Archives of Pediatrics & Adolescent Medicine* 159 (3): 295–97.

FOGEL, C. I., AND N. F. WOODS. 1995. Midlife women's health. In *Women's health care: A comprehensive handbook,* eds. C. I. Fogel and N. F. Woods, 79–100. Thousand Oaks, CA: Sage.

FOLK, K. F., J. W. GRAHAM, AND A. H. BELLER. 1992. Child support and remarriage: Implications for the economic well-being of children. *Journal of Family Issues* 13, 142–57.

FONG, M. 2009. It's cold cash, not cold feet, motivating runaway brides in China. *Wall Street Journal,* June 5, A1.

FONG, T. P. 2002. *The contemporary Asian American experience: Beyond the model minority,* 2nd ed. Upper Saddle River, NJ: Prentice Hall.

FOO, L. J. 2002. *Asian American women: Issues, concerns, and responsive human and civil rights advocacy.* New York: Ford Foundation.

FORD, P. 2009. Foreign men lose appeal. *Christian Science Monitor,* April 19, 5.

FORD, C., AND E. BEACH. 1972. *Patterns of sexual behavior.* New York: Harper & Row. (Originally published 1951.)

FORMOSO, D., N. A. GONZALES, M. BARRERA JR., AND L. E. DUMKA. 2007. Interparental relations, maternal employment, and fathering in Mexican American families. *Journal of Marriage and Family* 69 (February): 26–39.

"For richer or poorer." 2005. *Mother Jones* 30 (January/February): 24–25.

FORRY, N. D., AND S. K. WALKER. 2006. *Public policy, child care, and families in the United States.* National Council on Family Relations, Family Focus on Families and Public Policy, March, F5–F6.

FORSLOFF, C. 2009. Health workers facilitate wife beating. *Digital Journal,* February 1, www.digitaljournal.com (accessed April 12, 2009).

FORTENBERRY, D. J. 2005. The limits of abstinence-only in preventing sexually transmitted infections. *Journal of Adolescent Health* 36 (April): 269–70.

FORWARD, S. 2002. *Obsessive love: When it hurts too much to let go.* New York: Bantam.

FOST, D. 1996. Child-free with an attitude. *American Demographics* 18 (April): 15–16.

FOUST-CUMMINGS, H., L. SABATTINI, AND N. CARTER. 2008. Women in technology: Maximizing talent, minimizing barriers. *Catalyst,* www.catalyst.org (accessed April 28, 2008).

FOX, G. L., AND V. M. MURRY. 2001. Gender and families: Feminist perspectives and family research. In *Understanding families into the new millennium: A decade of review,* ed. R. M. Milardo, 379–91. Lawrence, KS: National Council on Family Relations.

FOX, G. L., M. L. BENSON, A. A. DE MARIS, AND J. VAN WYK. 2002. Economic distress and intimate violence: Testing family stress and resources theories. *Journal of Marriage and Family* 64 (August): 793–807.

FOX, J. A., AND M. W. ZAWITZ. 2007. Homicide trends in the United States. Bureau of Justice Statistics, www.ojp.usdoj.gov/bjs (accessed July 30, 2009).

FOX, S. 2006. Online health search 2006. Pew Internet & American Life Project, October 29, www.pewinternetorg.org (accessed November 4, 2006).

FRANCE, D. 2006. "And then he hit me." *AARP Magazine,* January/February 81–85, 112–13, 118.

FRANK, G. K., ET AL. 2005. Increased dopamine D2/D3 receptor binding after recovery from anorexia nervosa measured by positron emission tomography and [^{11}C]raclopride. *Biological Psychiatry* 58 (December): 908–12.

FRAZIER, E. F. 1937. The impact of urban civilization upon Negro family life. *American Sociological Review* 2 (October): 609–18.

FRAZIER, E. F. 1939. *The Negro family in the United States.* Chicago: University of Chicago Press.

FRECH, A., AND K. WILLIAMS. 2007. Depression and the psychological benefits of entering marriage. *Journal of Health and Social Behavior* 48 (June): 149–63.

FREEMAN, D. 1983. *Margaret Mead and Samoa: The making and unmaking of an anthropological myth.* Cambridge, MA: Harvard University Press.

FREITAS, D. 2008. *Sex and the soul: Juggling sexuality, spirituality, romance, and religion on America's college campuses.* New York: Oxford University Press.

FRENCH, H. W. 2006. In a richer China, billionaires put money on marriage. *New York Times,* January 26, A4.

FRIAS, S. M., AND R. J. ANGEL. 2005. The risk of partner violence among low-income Hispanic subgroups. *Journal of Marriage and Family* 67 (August): 552–64.

FRIEDAN, B. 1963. *The feminine mystique.* New York: Norton.

FRIEDAN, B. 1993. *The fountain of age.* New York: Simon & Schuster.

FRISCO, M. L. 2005. Parental involvement and young women's contraceptive use. *Journal of Marriage and Family* 67 (February): 110–21.

FROMM, E. 1956. *The art of loving.* New York: Bantam.

FRYAR, C. D., R. HIRSCH, K. S. PORTER, B. KOTTIRI, D. J. BRODY, AND T. LOUIS. 2007. Drug use and sexual behaviors reported by adults: United States, 1999–2002. Advance Data from Vital and Health Statistics, no. 384. Hyattsville, MD: National Center for Health Statistics.

FU, V. K. 2001. Racial intermarriage pairings. *Demography* 38 (May): 147–59.

FUCHS, D. 2003. In Spain's lonely country side, a Cupid crusade. *Christian Science Monitor,* June 10, 1, 14.

FULIGNI, A. J., AND H. YOSHIKAWA. 2003. Socioeconomic resources, parenting, and child development among immigrant families. In *Socioeconomic status, parenting, and child development,* eds. M. H. Bornstein and R. H. Bradley, 107–24. Mahwah, NJ: Lawrence Erlbaum.

FULLER, N., AND A. GENCER. 2008. Father admits he drowned kids. *Baltimore Sun,* April 1, 1A, 4A.

FURGATCH, V. 1995. It's time to remove all barriers to adoption across racial lines. *Christian Science Monitor,* September 12, 19.

FURSTENBERG, F. F., AND K. E. KIERNAN. 2001. Delayed parental divorce: How much do children benefit? *Journal of Marriage and Family* 63 (May): 446–57.

FURSTENBERG, F. F., JR., AND J. O. TEITLER. 1994. Reconsidering the effects of marital disruption: What happens to children of divorce in early adulthood? *Journal of Family Issues* 15 (June): 173–90.

FUTRIS, T. G., AND S. J. SCHOPPE-SULLIVAN. 2007. Mothers' perceptions of barriers, parenting alliance, and adolescent fathers' engagement with children. *Family Relations* 56 (July): 258–69.

G

GABLE, S., R. C. ROTHRAUFF, K. R. THORNBURG, AND D. MAUZY. 2007. Cash incentives and turnover in center-based child care staff. *Early Childhood Research Quarterly* 22 (July): 363–78.

GAERTNER, B. M., T. L. SPINRAD, N. EISENBERG, AND K. A. GREVING. 2007. Parental childrearing attitudes as correlates of father involvement during infancy. *Journal of Marriage and Family* 69 (November): 962–76.

GAGER, C. T., AND L. SANCHEZ. 2003. Two as one?: Couples' perceptions of time spent together, marital quality, and the risk of divorce. *Journal of Family Issues* 24 (January): 21–50.

GALAMBOS, N. L., E. T. BARKER, AND H. J. KRAHN. 2006. Depression, self-esteem, and anger in emerging adulthood: Seven-year trajectories. *Developmental Psychology* 42 (March): 350–65.

GALINSKY, E., K. AUMANN, AND J. T. BOND. 2009. Times are changing: Gender and generation at work and at home. Families and Work Institute, www.familiesandwork.org (accessed April 12, 2009).

GALLAGHER, M. 1996. *The abolition of marriage: How we destroy lasting love.* Washington, DC: Regnery.

GALLAGHER, S. K. 2003. *Evangelical identity and gendered family life.* New Brunswick, NJ: Rutgers University Press.

GALLUP, G., JR., AND T. NEWPORT. 1990. Virtually all adults want children, but many of the reasons are intangible. *Gallup Poll Monthly* (June): 8–22.

GALVIN, K. M., AND B. J. BROMMEL. 2000. *Family communication: Cohesion and change,* 5th ed. New York: Addison-Wesley-Longman.

GAMACHE, D. 1990. Domination and control: The social context of dating violence. In *Dating violence: Young women in danger,* ed. B. Levy, 69–118. Seattle: Seal.

GAMACHE, S. J. 1997. Confronting nuclear family bias in stepfamily research. *Marriage & Family Review* 26 (1/2): 41–69.

GAMERMAN, E. 2006. Dating Web sites now trying to prevent divorce. *Wall Street Journal,* April 3, (accessed April 5, 2006).

GANDEL, S. 2009. Why boomers can't quit. *Time,* May 25, 46.

GANONG, L. H., AND M. COLEMAN. 1994. *Remarried family relationships.* Thousand Oaks, CA: Sage.

GANONG, L. H., AND M. COLEMAN. 1999. *Changing families, changing responsibilities: Family obligations following divorce and remarriage.* Mahwah, NJ: Erlbaum.

GANONG, L. H., AND M. COLEMAN. 2004. *Stepfamily relationships: Development, dynamics, and interventions.* New York: Kluwer Academic/Plenum Publishers.

GANONG, L., M. COLEMAN, AND J. HANS. 2006. Divorce as prelude to stepfamily living and the consequences of redivorce. In *Handbook of divorce and relationship dissolution,* eds. M. A. Fine and J. H. Harvey, 409–34. Mahwah, NJ: Lawrence Erlbaum.

GANS, H. J. 1971. The uses of poverty: The poor pay all. *Social Policy* (July/August): 78–81.

GANS, H. J. 1979. *Deciding what's news: A study of CBS Evening News, NBC Nightly News, Newsweek and Time.* New York: Pantheon.

GANTZ, W., N. SCHWARTZ, J. R. ANGELINI, AND V. RIDEOUT. 2007. *Food for thought: Television food advertising to children in the United States.* Kaiser Family Foundation, March, www.kff.org (accessed July 13, 2009).

GARBARINO, J. 2006. *See Jane hit: Why girls are growing more violent and what can be done about it.* New York: Penguin.

GARCÍA, A. M. 2002. *The Mexican Americans*. Westport, CT: Greenwood Press.

GARCÍA, C. Y. 1998. Temporal course of the basic components of love throughout relationships. *Psychology in Spain* 2(1): 76–86. www.psychologyinspain.com (accessed March 30, 2003).

GARCIA, M. T. 1980. La familia: The Mexican immigrant family, 1900–1930. In *Work, family, sex roles, language,* eds. M. Barrera, A. Camarillo, and F. Hernandez, 117–40. Berkeley, CA: Tonatiua-Quinto Sol International.

GARDNER, A., AND S. S. HSU. 2009. Airline apologizes for booting 9 Muslims. *Washington Post,* January 3, A1.

GARDNER, M. 2002. Grandmothers weigh in on providing child care. *Christian Science Monitor,* August 14, 16.

GARDNER, M. 2004. Is it cyber-flirting or cyber-betrayal? *Christian Science Monitor,* August 19, 12, 14.

GARDNER, M. 2007. Whatever you do, don't say "elderly." *Christian Science Monitor,* August 8, 15.

GARDNER, R., JR. 2002. Mom vs. mom. *New York Times Magazine,* October 21, 20ff.

GARDYN, R. 2002. The mating game. *American Demographics* 24 (July/August): 33–37.

GARFINKEL, I., S. S. MC LANAHAN, AND P. K. ROBINS, EDS. 1994. *Child support and child well-being.* Washington, DC: Urban Institute.

GARIETY, B. S., AND S. SHAFFER. 2007. Wage differentials associated with working at home. *Monthly Labor Review* 130 (March): 61-67.

GARRISON, J. 2007. Do-it-yourself doesn't always sever ties. *Los Angeles Times,* January 1, www.latimes.com (accessed January 5, 2007).

GARRISON, M. M., AND D. A. CHRISTAKIS. 2005. A teacher in the living room? Educational media for babies, toddlers and preschoolers. Kaiser Family Foundation, December. www.kff.org (accessed May 20, 2006).

GARROD, A., AND C. LARIMORE, EDS. 1997. *First person, first peoples: Native American college graduates tell their life stories.* Ithaca, NY: Cornell University Press.

GATES, G. J., AND J. OST. 2004. *The gay & lesbian atlas.* Washington, DC: The Urban Institute Press.

GATES, G., J. M. V. BADGETT, J. E. MACOMBER, AND K. CHAMBERS. 2007. Adoption and foster care by gay and lesbian parents in the United States. Urban Institute, March, www.urban.org (accessed June 27, 2009).

GATES, G., H. LAU, AND R. B. SEARS. 2006. Asians and Pacific Islanders in same-sex couples in the United States: Data from Census 2000. *Amerasia Journal* 32 (1): 15–32.

GATTAI, F. B., AND T. MUSATTI. 1999. Grandmothers' involvement in grandchildren's care: Attitudes, feelings, and emotions. *Family Relations* 48 (January): 35–42.

GAUNT, R. 2006. Couple similarity and marital dissatisfaction: Are similar spouses happier? *Journal of Personality* 74 (October): 1401–20.

GAYLIN, W. 1992. *The male ego.* New York: Viking.

GEARON, C. J. 2003. Visiting the "kids" gets harder. *AARP Bulletin,* February, 6–7.

GECAS, V., AND M. A. SEFF. 1991. Families and adolescents: A review of the 1980s. In *Contemporary families: Looking forward, looking back,* ed. A. Booth, 208–25. Minneapolis: National Council on Family Relations.

GEER, J. H., AND G. M. MANGUNO-MIRE. 1996. Gender differences in cognitive processes in sexuality. *Annual Review of Sex Research* 7: 90–124.

GELLES, R. J. 1997. *Intimate violence in families,* 3rd ed. Thousand Oaks, CA: Sage.

GELLES, R. J., AND C. P. CORNELL. 1990. *Intimate violence in families,* 2nd ed. Thousand Oaks, CA: Sage.

GELLES, R. J., AND M. A. STRAUS. 1988. *Intimate violence.* New York: Simon & Schuster.

GENOVESE, E. D. 1981. Husbands and fathers, wives and mothers, during slavery. In *Family life in America: 1620–2000,* eds. M. Albin and D. Cavallo, 237–51. St. James, NY: Revisionary Press.

GENTLEMAN, A. 2006. Doctor in India jailed for telling sex of a fetus. *New York Times,* March 30, A13.

GENTLEMAN, A. 2008. India nurtures business of surrogate motherhood. *New York Times,* March 10, 9.

GERBER, R. 2002. Girls need not apply. *Christian Science Monitor,* June 24, 11.

GERSHOFF, E. T. 2002. Corporal punishment by parents and associated child behaviors and experiences: A meta-analytic and theoretical review. *Psychological Bulletin* 128 (July): 539–79.

GERSON, K. 1997. The social construction of fatherhood. In *Contemporary parenting: Challenges and issues,* ed. T. Arendell, 119–53. Thousand Oaks, CA: Sage.

GERSON, K. 2003. Work without worry. *New York Times,* May 11 D13.

GERSTEL, N., AND N. SARKISIAN. 2006. Marriage: The good, the bad, and the greedy. *Contexts* 5 (Fall): 16–21.

GIBBS, A. 2009. After layoffs, couples wrestle with role reversal. Women's eNews, January 11, www.womensenews.org (accessed January 3, 2009).

GIBBS, N. 2002. Making time for a baby. *Time,* April 15, 48–53.

GIBBS, N. 2008. The pursuit of purity. *Time,* July 28, 46–49.

GIBBS, N. 2007. Abortion in America: 1 woman at a time. *Time,* February 26, 23–31.

GIBSON, P. A. 2005. Intergenerational parenting from the perspective of African American grandmothers. *Family Relations* 54 (April): 280–97.

GIBSON-DAVIS, C. M., K. MAGNUSON, L. A. GENNETIAN, AND G. J. DUNCAN. 2005. Employment and the risk of domestic abuse among low-income women. *Journal of Marriage and Family* 67 (December): 1149–68.

GILBERT, N. 2008. *A mother's work: How feminism, the market, and policy shape family life.* New Haven, CT: Yale University Press.

GILBERT, S. 2005. Married with problems? Therapy may not help. *New York Times,* April 19, F1.

GILES, L. C., G. F. V. GLONEK, M. A. LUSZCZ, AND G. R. ANDREWS. 2005. Effect of social networks on 10-year survival in very old Australians: The Australian longitudinal study of aging. *Journal of Epidemiology and Community Health* 59 (May): 574–79.

GILGOFF, D. 2004. The rise of the gay family. *U.S. News & World Report,* May 24, 40–45.

GILGUN, J. F. 2008. Child sexual abuse: One of the most neglected social problems of our time. *Family Focus* 53 (December): F5–F7.

GILLIS, J. R. 1996. *A world of their own making: Myth, ritual, and the quest for family values.* New York: Basic Books.

GILLIS, J. R. 2004. Marriages of the mind. *Journal of Marriage and Family* 66 (November): 988–91.

GILLMORE, M. R. ET AL. 2002. Teen sexual behavior: Applicability of the theory of reasoned action. *Journal of Marriage and Family* 64 (November): 885–97.

GIORDANO, P. C., M. A. LONGMORE, AND W. D. MANNING. 2006. Gender and the meanings of adolescent romantic relationships: A focus on boys. *American Sociological Review* 71 (April): 260–87.

Girl is stoned to death in Somalia after reporting rape. 2008. *Washington Post,* November 2, A15.

GIST, J., L. BEEDON, AND L. SOUTHWORTH. 2007. The state of 50+ America. AARP, www.aarp.org (accessed September 27, 2009).

GLASS, S. 2002. *Not "just friends": Protect your relationship from infidelity and heal the trauma of betrayal.* New York: Free Press.

GLAUBER, R. 2007. Marriage and the motherhood wage penalty among African Americans, Hispanics, and whites. *Journal of Marriage and Family* 69 (November): 951–61.

GLAUBKE, R., AND K. E. HEINTZ-SWENSON. 2004. Fall colors: 2003–04 prime time diversity report. Children Now, http://publications.childrennow.org (accessed December 4, 2005).

GLENN, E. N., AND S. G. H. YAP. 2002. Chinese American families. In *Minority families in the United States: A multicultural perspective,* 3rd ed., ed. R. L. Taylor, 134–63. Upper Saddle River, NJ: Prentice Hall.

GLENN, N. 2005. With this ring . . . : A national survey on marriage in America. National Fatherhood Initiative, www.fatherhood.org/doclibrary/nms.pdf (accessed April 2, 2006).

GLENN, N. D. 1991. Quantitative research on marital quality in the 1980s. In *Contemporary families: Looking forward, looking back,* ed. A. Booth, 28–41. Minneapolis: National Council on Family Relations.

GLENN, N. D. 1996. Values, attitudes, and the state of American marriage. In *Promises to keep: Decline and renewal of marriage in America,* eds. D. Popenoe, J. B. Elshtain, and D. Blankenhorn, 15–33. Lanham, MD: Rowman & Littlefield.

GLENN, N. D. 1997. A reconsideration of the effect of no-fault divorce on divorce rates. *Journal of Marriage and Family* 39 (November): 1023–30.

GLENN, N. D. 2002. A plea for greater concern about the quality of marital matching. In *Revitalizing the institution of marriage in the twenty-first century,* eds. L. D. Wardle and D. O. Coolidge, 45–58. Westport, CT: Praeger.

GLENN, N., AND T. SYLVESTER. 2006. The denial: Downplaying the consequences of family structure for children. Institute for American Values, www.familyscholarslibrary.org (accessed July 11, 2006).

GLYNN, L. M., N. CHRISTENFELD, AND W. GERIN 2002. The role of rumination in recovery from reactivity: Cardiovascular consequences of emotional states. *Psychosomatic Medicine* 64 (September/October): 714–26.

GODDARD, J. 2008. Supermom. *Christian Science Monitor,* December 23, 20.

GODDARD, H. W. 1994. *Principles of parenting.* Auburn, AL: Auburn University, Department of Family and Child Development.

GODFREY, S., C. L. RICHMAN, AND T. N. WITHERS. 2000. Reliability and validity of a new scale to measure prejudice: The GRISMS. *Current Psychology* 19 (March): 1046–1310.

GOETTING, A. 1982. The six stations of remarriage: Developmental tasks of remarriage after divorce. *Family Relations* 31 (April): 231–22.

GOFFMAN, E. 1959. *The presentation of self in everyday life.* New York: Doubleday Anchor Books.

GOFFMAN, E. 1963. *Stigma: Notes on the management of spoiled identity*. Upper Saddle River, NJ: Prentice Hall.

GOFFMAN, E. 1969. *Strategic interaction*. Philadelphia: University of Pennsylvania Press.

GOLD, D. T. 1989. Sibling relationships in old age: A typology. *International Journal on Aging and Human Development* 28 (1): 37–51.

GOLD, D. T. 1990. Late-life sibling relationships: Does race affect typological distribution? *The Gerontologist* 30 (December): 741–48.

GOLDBERG, A. E., AND A. SAYER. 2006. Lesbian couples' relationship quality across the transition to parenthood. *Journal of Marriage and Family* 68 (February): 87–100.

GOLDBERG, A. E., AND J. Z. SMITH. 2008. Social support and psychological well-being in lesbian and heterosexual preadoptive couples. *Family Relations* 57 (July): 281–94.

GOLDBERG, A. E., AND K. R. ALLEN. 2007. Imagining men: Lesbian mothers' perceptions of male involvement during the transition to parenthood. *Journal of Marriage and Family* 69 (May): 352–65.

GOLDEN, O., P. LOPREST, AND S. ZEDLEWSKI. 2006. Parents and children facing a world of risk: "Next steps toward a working families' agenda" roundtable report. The Urban Institute, March 10, www.urban.org (accessed May 4, 2006).

GOLDMAN, J., AND M. K. SALUS. 2003. *A coordinated response to child abuse and neglect: The foundation for practice*. U.S. Department of Health and Human Services, Administration for Children and Families, Administration on Children, Youth and Families, Children's Bureau, Office on Child Abuse and Neglect.

GOLDSCHEIDER, F., AND S. SASSLER. 2006. Creating stepfamilies: Integrating children into the study of union formation. *Journal of Marriage and Family* 68 (May): 275–91.

GOLDSTEIN, M. 2009. It's hard to find a date when you're looking for a job. *Boston Globe*, January 24, www.boston.com (accessed May 15, 2009).

GOLOMBOK, S., AND F. TASKER. 1996. Do parents influence the sexual orientation of their children? Findings from a longitudinal study of lesbian families. *Developmental Psychology* 32 (1): 3–11.

GONNERMAN, J. 2005. The unforgiven. *Mother Jones*, July/August, 38–43.

GONZAGA, G. C., B. CAMPOS, AND T. BRADBURY. 2007. Similarity, convergence, and relationship satisfaction in dating and married couples. *Journal of Personality and Social Psychology* 93 (July): 24–48.

GONZÁLEZ, R. 1996. *Muy macho: Latino men confront their manhood*. New York: Anchor.

GOODALE, G. 2008. First the marriage, *then* the courtship. *Christian Science Monitor*, September 9, 17.

GOODE, E. 1990. *Deviant behavior*, 3rd ed. Upper Saddle River, NJ: Prentice Hall.

GOODE, E., ET AL. 1994. Till death do them part? *U.S. News & World Report*, July 4, 24–28.

GOODE, W. J. 1963. *World revolution and family patterns*. New York: Free Press.

GOODMAN, E. 2008. What we demand of a political wife. *Baltimore Sun*, March 14, 21A.

GOODMAN, W. B., A. C. CROUTER, S. T. LANZA, AND M. J. COX. 2008. Paternal work characteristics and father-infant interactions in low-income, rural families. *Journal of Marriage and Family* 70 (August): 640–53.

GOODMARK, L. 2007. Where's outrage for athletes who abuse partners? *Baltimore Sun*, August 8, 11A.

GOODWIN, R., AND C. FINDLAY. 1997. "We were just fated together." Chinese love and the concept of yuan in England and Hong Kong. *Personal Relationships* 4: 85–92.

GORCHOFF, S. M., O. P. JOHN, AND R. HELSON. 2008. Contextualizing change in marital satisfaction during middle age: An 18-year longitudinal study. *Psychological Science* 19 (November): 1194–1200.

GORDON, L. H. 1993. Intimacy: The art of working out your relationships. *Psychology Today* 26 (September/October): 40–43, 79–82.

GORDON, R. J., AND I. DEW-BECKER. 2008. Controversies about the rise of American inequality: A survey. National Bureau of Economic Research, Working Paper 13982, April, www.nber.org (accessed July 30, 2009).

GORMAN, C. 1995. Trapped in the body of a man? *Time*, November 13, 94–95.

GORMAN, E. H. 2000. Marriage and money. *Work & Occupations* 27 (February): 64–88.

GOSE, B. 1994. Spending time on the reservation. *Chronicle of Higher Education*, August 10, A30–A31.

GOSTIN, N. 2006. Spike Lee. *Newsweek*, April 3, 70.

GOTTMAN, J. M. 1982. Emotional responsiveness in marital conversations. *Journal of Communication* 32, 108–20.

GOTTMAN, J. M. 1994. *What predicts divorce? The relationships between marital processes and marital outcome*. Hillsdale, NJ: Erlbaum.

GOTTMAN, J. M., AND J. DE CLAIRE. 2001. *The relationship cure: A five-step guide for building better connections with family, friends, and lovers*. New York: Crown.

GOTTMAN, J. M., AND N. SILVER. 1999. *The seven principles for making marriage work*. New York: Crown.

GOULD, D. C., R. PETTY, AND H. S. JACOBS. 2000. For and against: The male menopause—does it exist? *British Medical Journal* 320 (March): 858–60.

GRABE, S., L. M. WARD, AND J. S. HYDE. 2008. The role of the media in body image concerns among women: A meta-analysis of experimental and correlational studies. *Psychological Bulletin* 134 (May): 460–76.

GRACIA, E., AND J. HERRERO. 2006. Public attitudes toward reporting partner violence against women and reporting behavior. *Journal of Marriage and Family* 68 (August): 759–68.

GRACIA, E., AND J. HERRERO. 2008. Is it considered violence? The acceptability of physical punishment of children in Europe. *Journal of Marriage and Family* 70 (February): 210–17.

GRAHAM, L. O. 1996. *Member of the club: Reflections on life in a racially polarized world*. New York: HarperCollins.

GRALL, T. S. 2005. Support providers: 2002. U.S. Census Bureau, Current Population Reports, P70–99, www.census.gov (accessed July 9, 2006).

GRALL, T. S. 2007. Custodial mothers and fathers and their child support: 2005. U.S. Census Bureau, Current Population Reports, August, P60–234, www.census.gov (accessed July 1, 2009).

"Grandparents Day 2006: September 10." 2006, U.S. Census Bureau, Facts for Features, BB06-FF.13 (accessed July 28, 2006).

Grandparents Day. 2009. U.S. Census Bureau News, Facts for Features, July 13, www.census.gov (accessed September 27, 2009).

GRAVES, J. L., JR. 2001. *The emperor's new clothes: Biological theories of race at the millennium*. New Brunswick, NJ: Rutgers University Press.

GRAY, M. R., AND L. STEINBERG. 1999. Unpacking authoritative parenting: Reassessing a multidimensional construct. *Journal of Marriage and the Family* 61 (August): 574–87.

GRAY, P. S., J. B. WILLIAMSON, D. R. KARP, AND J. R. DALPHIN. 2007. *The research imagination: An introduction to qualitative and quantitative methods*. New York: Cambridge University Press.

GREEN, M. T. 2007. Florida shelter offers hope to women of means. Jewish Women International, June, www.jwi.org (accessed August 22, 2009).

GREEN, P. 2007. Whose bed is it anyway? *Baltimore Sun*, March 11, D1, D6.

GREENBERG, I. 2006. After a century, public polygamy is re-emerging in Tajikistan. *New York Times*, November 13, A10.

GREENBERG, J., AND M. RUHLEN. 1992. Linguistic origins of Native Americans. *Scientific American* 267: 94.

GREENBLATT, C. S. 1983. The salience of sexuality in the early years of marriage. *Journal of Marriage and the Family* 45 (May): 289–99.

GREENFIELD, D. 1999. *Virtual addiction*. Oakland, CA: New Harbinger Publications.

GREENHOUSE, S., AND M. BARBARO. 2005. Wal-Mart suggests ways to cut employee benefit costs. *New York Times*, October 26, C1–C2.

GREENSTEIN, T. N. 2000. Economic dependence, gender, and the division of labor in the home: A replication and extension. *Journal of Marriage and the Family* 62 (May): 322–35.

GREENSTEIN, T. N. 2006. *Methods of family research*, 2nd ed. Thousand Oaks, CA: Sage.

GREIDER, L. 2000. How not to be a monster-in-law. *Modern Maturity* (March/April): 57–59.

GREIDER, L. 2003. The old skills kick in. *AARP Bulletin*, May, 12.

GRISWOLD, R. L. 1993. *Fatherhood in America: A history*. New York: Basic Books.

GROSE, T. K. 2008. When "I do" is an order, not a choice. *U.S. News & World Report*, May 26/June 2, 13.

GROSS, J. 2008. AIDS patients face downside of living longer. *New York Times*, January 6, 1.

GROTEVANT, H. D. 2001. Adoptive families: Longitudinal outcomes for adolescents. Report to the William T. Grant Foundation. http://fsos.che.umn.edu (accessed August 17, 2003).

GROVES, E. R. 1928. *The marriage crisis*. New York: Longmans, Green.

GRUDZEN, C. R., W. J. KOENIG, J. R. HOFFMAN, J. BOSCARDIN, K. A. LORENZ, AND S. M. ASCH. 2009. Potential impact of a verbal prehospital DNR policy. *Prehospital Emergency Care* 13 (2): 166–72.

GRYCH, J. H. 2002. Marital relationships and parenting. In *Handbook of parenting*, 2nd ed., Vol. 4: Social conditions and applied parenting, ed. M. H. Bornstein, 203–25. Mahwah, NJ: Erlbaum.

GUBERMAN, N., P. MAHEU, AND C. MAILLE. 1992. Women as family caregivers: Why do they care? *The Gerontologist* 32 (5): 607–17.

GUESS, M. K., ET AL. 2006. Genital sensation and sexual function in women bicyclists and runners: are your feet safer than your seat? *Journal of Sexual Medicine* 3 (December): 1018–27.

GUEST, J. 1988. *The mythic family*. Minneapolis: Milkweed.

GUILMOTO, C. Z. 2007. Sex-ratio imbalance in Asia: Trends, consequences and policy responses. In *Sex-ratio imbalance in Asia: Trends, consequences and policy responses*.

Executive Summary, Regional Analysis, 1–12. United Nations Population Fund, www.unfpa.org (accessed June 12, 2009).

GUPTA, G. R. 1979. Love, arranged marriage and the Indian social structure. In *Cross-cultural perspectives of mate-selection and marriage*, ed. G. Kurian, 169–79. Westport, CT: Greenwood.

GURIAN, M. 2002. *The wonder girls: Understanding the hidden nature of our daughters.* New York: Pocket Books.

GURIAN, M., AND P. HENLY. 2000. *Boys and girls learn differently!: A guide for teachers and parents.* San Francisco, CA: Jossey-Bass.

GUTERMAN, L. 2005. Lost count. *Chronicle of Higher Education*, February 4, A10–A13.

GUTMAN, H. G. 1983. Persistent myths about the Afro-American family. In *The American family in socio-historical perspective*, 3rd ed., ed. M. Gordon, 459–81. New York: St. Martin's.

GUTNER, T. 2000. Getting your fair share in a divorce. *Business Week*, May 29, 250.

GUTNER, T. 2001. Househusbands unite! *Business Week*, January 22, 106.

GUTTMACHER INSTITUTE. 2005. An overview of abortion in the United States. 2005. Physicians for Reproductive Choice and Health and the Guttmacher Institute, June, www .guttmacher.org (accessed April 28, 2006).

Guttmacher Institute. 2008. Facts on induced abortion in the United States. July, www .guttmacher.org (accessed June 20, 2009).

Guttmacher Institute. 2009a. "Choose life" license plates. June 9, www.guttmacher.org (accessed June 25, 2009).

Guttmacher Institute. 2009b. An overview of abortion laws. June 1, www.guttmacher.org (accessed June 25, 2009).

GUZZO, K. B., AND H. LEE. 2008. Couple relationship status and patterns in early parenting practices. *Journal of Marriage and Family* 70 (February): 44–61.

H

HA, J-H. 2008. Changes in support from confidants, children, and friends following widowhood. *Journal of Marriage and Family* 70 (April): 306–18.

HACKER, A. 2003. *Mismatch: The growing gulf between women and men.* New York: Scribner.

HAFFNER, D. W. 1999. Facing facts: Sexual health for American adolescents. *Human Development & Family Life Bulletin* 4 (Winter): 1–3.

HAGAN, F. E. 2008. *Introduction to criminology: Theories, methods, and criminal behavior*, 6th ed. Los Angeles, CA: Sage.

HAGENBAUGH, B. 2009. Many of the jobless get no unemployment benefits. *USA Today*, March 4, www.usatoday.com (accessed March 5, 2009).

HAHN, R. A., AND D. M. KLEIST. 2000. Divorce mediation: Research and implications for family and couples counseling. *Family Journal* 8 (April): 165–71.

HALE, A. O. 2007. Practices and attitudes toward contraception in the black community. In *Black families*, 4th ed., ed. H. P. McAdoo, 297–315. Thousand Oaks, CA: Sage.

Half of older Americans report they are sexually active; 4 in 10 want more sex, says new survey. 1998. National Council on Aging. www.ncoa.org (accessed August 30, 2000).

HALFORD, W. K., K. L. WILSON, A. LIZZIO, AND E. MOORE. 2002. Does working at a relationship work? Relationship self-regulation and relationship outcomes. In *Understanding marriage: Development in the study of couple interaction*, eds. P. Noller and J. A. Feeney, 493–517. New York: Cambridge University Press.

HALL, S. S., AND S. M. MacDERMID. 2009. A typology of dual earner marriages based on work and family arrangements. *Journal of Family and Economic Issues* 30 (September): 215–25.

HALL, W. J. 2008. Centenarians: Metaphor becomes reality. *Archives of Internal Medicine* 168 (February 11): 262–63.

HALLORAN, L. 2008. An uncertain legacy. *U.S. News & World Report*, September, 34–37.

HALPERN, C. T., K. JOYNER, AND C. SUCHINDRAN. 2000. Smart teens don't have sex (or kiss much either). *Journal of Adolescent Health* 26 (March): 213–25.

HAMBY, S., AND A. BIBLE. 2009. Battered women's protective strategies. Applied Research Forum: National Online Resource Center on Violence Against Women, July, www.vawnet.org (accessed August 12, 2009).

HAMER, D. H., S. HU, V. MAGNUSON, N. HU, AND A. M. L. PATTATUCCI. 1993. A linkage between DNA markers on the X chromosome and male sexual orientation. *Science*, July 16, 321–27.

HAMER, J., AND K. MARCHIORO. 2002. Becoming custodial dads: Exploring parenting among low-income and working-class African American fathers. *Journal of Marriage and Family* 64 (February): 115–29.

HAMILTON, B. E., P. D. SUTTON, AND S. J. VENTURA. 2003. Revised birth and fertility rates for the 1990s and new rates for Hispanic populations, 2000 and 2001: United States. *National Vital Statistics Reports*, 51, August 4. www.cdc.gov (accessed August 25, 2003).

HAMILTON, B. E., J. A MARTIN, AND S. J. VENTURA. 2009. Births: Preliminary data for 2007. *National Vital Statistics Reports*, vol. 57, no 12. Hyattsville, MD: National Center for Health Statistics.

HAMILTON, T. F. 2002. Caitlin's families: Two families overcome their differences for the sake of a 12-year-old girl. *Grand Rapids Press*, September 15, J1.

HAMMOND, R. J., AND B. Bearnson. 2003. *The marriages and families activities workbook.* Belmont, CA: Wadsworth.

HAMPSON, R. 2006. Fear "as bad as after 9/11." *USA Today*, December 12, 1A.

HAN, B., J. GFROERER, AND J. COLLIVER. 2009. An examination of trends in illicit drug use among adults aged 50 to 59 in the United States. SAMSA, Office of Applied Studies, *OAS Data Review*, August, http://oas. samsa.gov (accessed August 13, 2009).

HANCOX, R. J., B. J. MINE, AND R. POULTON. 2005. Association of television viewing during childhood with poor educational achievement. *Archives of Pediatrics & Adolescent Medicine* 159 (July): 614–18.

HANDELSMAN, J. ET AL. 2005. Careers in science. *Science* 309 (August 19): 1190–91.

HANDLER, J. 2009. I won't roll the biological dice. *Newsweek*, April 27, 16.

HANES, S. 2004. Mail-order bride wins damage award. *Baltimore Sun* (November 19): 1A, 4a.

HANNA, S. L. 2003. *Person to person: Positive relationships don't just happen*, 4th ed. Upper Saddle River, NJ: Prentice Hall.

HANS, J. D. 2002. Stepparenting after divorce: Stepparents' legal position regarding custody, access, and support. *Family Relations* 51 (October): 301–7.

HANS, J. D. 2009. Beliefs about child support modification following remarriage and subsequent childbirth. *Family Relations* 58 (February): 65–78.

HANS, J. D., L. H. GANONG, AND M. COLEMAN. 2009. Financial responsibilities toward older parents and stepparents following

divorce and remarriage. *Journal of Family and Economic Issues* 30 (March): 55–66.

HANSEN, M. E., AND D. POLLACK. 2007. Transracial adoption of black children: An economic analysis. *Bepress Legal Series*, Working Paper 1942, January 17, http:// law.bepress.com (accessed June 28, 2009).

HARARI, S. E., AND M. A. VINOVSKIS. 1993. Adolescent sexuality, pregnancy, and childbearing in the past. In *The politics of pregnancy: Adolescent sexuality and public policy*, eds. A. Lawson and D. I. Rhode, 23–45. New Haven, CT: Yale University Press.

HARDY, S. A., AND M. RAFFAELLI. 2003. Adolescent religiosity and sexuality: An investigation of reciprocal influences. *Journal of Adolescence* 26 (December): 731–39.

HAREVEN, T. K. 1984. Themes in the historical development of the family. In *Review of child development research,* Vol. 7: The family, ed. R. D. Parke, 137–78. Chicago: University of Chicago Press.

HARLEY, W. F., JR. 2002. *Buyers, renters & freeloaders: Turning revolving-door romance into lasting love.* Grand Rapids, MI: Fleming H. Revell.

HARMON, A. 2003. Lost? Hiding? Your cellphone is keeping tabs. *New York Times*, December 21, A1.

HARRELL, W. A. 2005. *Are prettier kids protected better? A field observational study of child safety in grocery carts.* Population Research Laboratory, University of Alberta. Unpublished manuscript.

HARRELL, W. A. 2006. *Are ugly children at risk in grocery stores? The impact of imputed marital status and adult attractiveness.* Paper presented at the 17th annual Warren E. Kalbach Conference in Demography, University of Alberta, Canada, March 31.

HARRIS, L. 1996. The hidden world of dating violence. *Parade Magazine*, September 22, 4–6.

HARRIS, M. 1994. *Down from the pedestal: Moving beyond idealized images of womanhood.* New York: Doubleday.

HARRIS, M. 2007. Families turn to Internet to grieve. *Baltimore Sun*, February 23, 1A, 6A.

HARRIS, M. 2007. Same split with a lot less spat. *Baltimore Sun*, May 10, 1A, 10A.

HARRIS, T. 2003. Mind work: How a Ph.D. affects black women. *Chronicle of Higher Education*, April 11, B14–B15.

HARRYKISSOON, S. D., V. I. RICKERT, AND C. M. WIEMAN. 2002. Prevalence and patterns of intimate partner violence during the postpartum period. *Archives of Pediatrics & Adolescent Medicine* 156 (April): 325–30.

HART, S. N., M. R. BRASSARD, N. J. BINGGELI, AND H. A. DAVIDSON. 2003. Psychological maltreatment. In *International encyclopedia of marriage and family*, 2nd ed., ed. J. J. Ponzetti, Jr., 221–27. New York: Macmillan.

HARTILI, L. 2001. Vow or never. *Christian Science Monitor*, July 18, 15–17.

HARVEY, J. H., AND A. L. WEBER. 2002. *Odyssey of the heart: Close relationships in the 21st century*, 2nd ed. Mahwah, NJ: Erlbaum.

HARVEY, J. H., AND M. A. FINE. 2004. *Children of divorce: Stories of loss and growth.* Mahwah, NJ: Lawrence Erlbaum.

HARWOOD, R., B. LEYENDECKER, V. CARLSON, M. ASENCIO, AND A. MILLER. 2002. Parenting among Latino Families in the U.S. In *Handbook of parenting*, 2nd ed., Vol. 4: Social conditions and applied parenting, ed. M. H. Bornstein, 21–46. Mahwah, NJ: Erlbaum.

HASELTON, M. G. 2003. The sexual overperception bias: Evidence of a systematic bias in men from survey of naturally occurring events. *Journal of Personality and Social Psychology* 37 (January): 34–47.

HASLETT, A. 2004. *George Washington's rules of civility*. New York: Akashic Books.

HASS, A. 1979. *Teenage sexuality: A survey of teenage sexual behavior*. New York: Macmillan.

HATFIELD, E. 1983. What do women and men want from love and sex? In *Changing boundaries: Gender roles and sexual behavior*, eds. E. R. Allgeier and N. B. McCormick, 106–34. Mountain View, CA: Mayfield.

HAUB, C., AND M. M. KENT. 2008. 2008 world population data sheet. Washington, DC: Population Reference Bureau, wall chart.

HAUGEN, S. E. 2009. Measures of labor under-utilization from the Current Population Survey. U.S. Bureau of Labor Statistics, BLS Working Paper 424, March, www.bls.gov (accessed August 9, 2009).

HAUSMANN, R., L. D. TYSON, AND S. ZAHIDI. 2008. *The global gender gap report 2008*. Geneva, Switzerland: World Economic Forum.

HAUTALA, L. J., ET AL. 2008. Adolescents with fluctuating symptoms of eating disorders: A 1-year prospective study. *Journal of Advanced Nursing* 62 (June): 674–80.

HAWKE, D. F. 1988. *Everyday life in early America*. New York: Harper & Row.

HAYANI, I. 1999. Arabs in Canada: Assimilation or integration? In *Arabs in America: Building a new future*, ed. M. W. Suleiman, 284–303. Philadelphia: Temple University Press.

HAYASHI, G. M., AND B. R. STRICKLAND. 1998. Longterm effects of parental divorce on love relationships: Divorce as attachment disruption. *Journal of Social & Personal Relationships* 15 (February): 23–38.

HAYS, S. 1998. The fallacious assumptions and unrealistic prescriptions of attachment theory: A comment on parents' socioemotional investment in children. *Journal of Marriage and the Family* 60 (August): 782–95.

HAZAN, C., AND P. R. SHAVER. 1987. Conceptualizing romantic love as an attachment process. *Journal of Personality and Social Psychology* 52: 511–24.

HE, W., M. SENGUPIA, V. A. VELKOFF, AND K. A. DE BARROS. 2005. 65+ in the United States: 2005. U.S. Census Bureau, Current Population Reports, P23–209. Washington, DC: U.S. Government Printing Office.

HEALY, M. 2003. Fertility's new frontier. *Los Angeles Times*, July 21, F1.

HEALY, M. 2007. Are we too quick to medicate children? *Los Angeles Times*, November 5, www.latimes.com (accessed November 6, 2007).

HEALY, M. 2008. Sexy Halloween costumes . . . for little girls? *Los Angeles Times*, October 27, www.latimes.com (accessed October 28, 2008).

HEALY, M. 2009. Greater Internet threat to teens may be teens themselves. *Los Angeles Times*, January 26, www.latimes.com (accessed January 27, 2009).

HECHT, M. L., P. J. MARSTON, AND L. K. LARKEY. 1994. Love ways and relationship quality in heterosexual relationships. *Journal of Social and Personal Relationships* 11 (1): 25–43.

HEKKER, T. M. 2009. *Disregard first book*. Bloomington, IN: iUniverse.

HELM, B. 2008. Online polls: How good are they? *Business Week*, June 16, 86.

HELPER, S. 2008. Renewing U.S. manufacturing: Promoting a high-road strategy. Economic Policy Institute, February 13, www.epi.org (accessed July 4, 2008).

HENDRICK, C., AND S. HENDRICK. 1992a. *Liking, loving, and relating*, 2nd ed. Monterey, CA: Brooks/Cole.

HENDRICK, S., AND C. HENDRICK. 1992b. *Romantic love*. Thousand Oaks, CA: Sage.

HENDRICK, C., AND S. S. HENDRICK. 2003. Love. In *International encyclopedia of marriage and family*, 2nd ed., Vol. 3, ed. J. J. Ponzetti, Jr., 1059–65. New York: Macmillan.

HENDRICK, S. S., AND C. HENDRICK. 2002. Linking romantic love with sex: Development of the perceptions of love and sex scale. *Journal of Social and Personal Relationships* 19 (June): 361–78.

HENDRIX, H. 1988. *Getting the love you want: A guide for couples*. New York: Henry Holt.

HENNESSY-FISKE, M. 2009. Some jobless aren't down and out enough to qualify for aid. *Los Angeles Times*, March 26, www.latimes.com (accessed March 27, 2009).

HERRENKOHL, T. I., R. KOSTERMAN, W. A. MASON, AND J. DAVID. 2007. Youth violence trajectories and proximal characteristics of intimate partner violence. *Violence and Victims* 22 (July): 259–74.

HERRING, D. J. 2007. The Multiethnic Placement Act: Threat to foster child safely and wellbeing. University of Pittsburgh School of Law Working Paper Series, Paper 51, http://:law.bepress.com (accessed June 28, 2009).

HERRMANN, A. 2003. Children of divorce in no rush to repeat error. Chicago Sun Times, June 10. www.suntimes.com (accessed June 12, 2003).

HERTZ, R. 2006. *Single by chance, mothers by choice: How women are choosing parenthood without marriage and creating the new American family*. New York: Oxford University Press.

HETHERINGTON, E. M. 2003. Intimate pathways: Changing patterns in close personal relationships across time. *Family Relations* 52 (October): 318–31.

HETHERINGTON, E. M., AND J. KELLY. 2002. For better or for worse: Divorce reconsidered. New York: W. W. Norton.

HETHERINGTON, E. M., AND M. M. STANLEY-HAGAN. 2000. Diversity among stepfamilies. In *Handbook of family diversity*, eds. D. H. Demo, K. R. Allen, and M. A. Fine, 173–96. New York: Oxford University Press.

HETHERINGTON, E. M., AND M. M. STANLEY-HAGAN. 2002. Parenting in divorced and remarried families. In *Handbook of parenting*, 2nd ed., Vol. 3: Being and becoming a parent, ed. M. H. Bornstein, 287–315. Mahwah, NJ: Erlbaum.

HETHERINGTON, E. M., R. D. PARKE, AND V. O. LOCKE. 2006. *Child psychology: A contemporary viewpoint*, 6th ed. Boston: McGraw-Hill.

HEUBECK, E. 2005. Pressure grows to telecommute. *Baltimore Sun*, October 26, K1–K2.

HEWITT, B. 2009. Which spouse initiates marital separation when there are children involved? *Journal of Marriage and Family* 71 (May): 362–72.

HEYMANN, J., A. EARLE, AND J. HAYES. 2007. Implications for U.S. policy of the work, family, and equity index. Global Working Families, www.mcgill.ca (accessed June 3, 2009).

HEYMANN, J., H. J. RHO, J. SCHMITT, AND A. EARLE. 2009. Contagion nation: A comparison of paid sick day policies in 22 countries. Center for Economic and Policy Research, May, www.cepr.net (accessed August 9, 2009).

HEYN, D. 1997. Marriage shock: The transformation of women into wives. New York: Villard.

"High-tech gadgets help parents keep track of what their kids are doing," 2005. *Baltimore Sun*, September 5, B2.

HILL, G. 2008. Yemen confronts plight of child brides. *Christian Science Monitor*, August 22, 7.

HILL, R. B. 2003. *The strengths of black families*, 2nd ed. Lanham, MD: University Press of America.

HILL, S. A. 2005. *Black intimacies: A gender perspective on families and relationships*. Walnut Creek, CA: AltaMira Press.

HILLAKER, B. D., H. E. BROPHY-HERB, F. A. VILLARRUEL, AND B. E. HASS. 2008. The contributions of parenting to social competencies and positive values in middle school youth: Positive family communication, maintaining standards, and supportive family relationships. *Family Relations* 57 (December): 591–601.

HINES, D. A., AND K. MALLEY-MORRISON. 2005. *Family violence in the United States: Defining, understanding, and combating abuse*. Thousand Oaks, CA: Sage.

HINSCH, B. 1990. *Passions of the cut sleeve: The male homosexual tradition in China*. Berkeley: University of California Press.

HIRA, R. 2008. An overview of the offshoring of U.S. jobs. *Population Bulletin* 63 (June): 14–15.

HOBBS, F. 2005. Examining American household composition: 1990 and 2000. U.S. Census Bureau, Special Reports, CENSR-24. Washington, DC: U.S. Government Printing Office.

HOBBS, F., AND N. STOOPS 2002. Demographic trends in the 20th century. U.S. Census Bureau, 2000 Special Reports, Series CENSR-4. www.census.gov (accessed May 25, 2003).

HOBSON, K. 2004. The biological clock on ice. *U.S. News & World Report*, September 27, 62-63.

HOCHSCHILD, A., WITH A. MACHUNG. 1989. *The second shift: Working parents and the revolution at home*. New York: Penguin.

HOCK, R. R. 2007. *Human sexuality*. Upper Saddle River, NJ: Prentice Hall.

HOFKSTRA, M. J. 2006. "Just kidding, dear": Using dismissed divorce cases to identify the effect of parental divorce on student performance. University of Pittsburgh, Department of Economics. Unpublished paper.

HOFFERTH, S. L. 2005. Secondary data analysis in family research. *Journal of Marriage and Family* 67 (November): 891–907.

HOFFMAN, B. A. 2003. Gay rights as source of strength. *Baltimore Sun*, July 5, 11A.

HOFFMAN, J. 2009. Teenage girls stand by their man. *New York Times*, March 19, 1.

HOJAT, M., R. SHAPURIAN, D. FOROUGHI, H. NAYERAHMADI, M. FARZANEH, M. SHAFIEYAN, AND M. PARSI. 2000. Gender differences in traditional attitudes toward marriage and the family: An empirical study of Iranian immigrants in the United States. *Journal of Family Issues* 21 (May): 419–34.

HOLLINGSWORTH, L. D. 2003. When an adoption disrupts: A study of public attitudes. *Family Relations* 52 (April): 161–66.

HOLLIST, C. S., AND R. B. MILLER. 2005. Perceptions of attachment style and marital quality in midlife marriage. *Family Relations* 54 (January): 46–57.

HOLM-DENOMA, J. M., ET AL. 2005. Parents' reports of the body shape and feeding habits of 36-month-old children: An investigation of gender differences. *International Journal of Eating Disorders* 38 (November): 228–35.

HOLMAN, T. B., AND W. R. BURR. 1980. Beyond the beyond: The growth of family theories in the 1970s. *Journal of Marriage and the Family* 42 (November): 729–41.

HOLMAN, T. B., J. H. LARSON, AND S. L. HARMER. 1994. The development and predictive validity of a new premarital assessment instrument: The preparation for marriage questionnaire. *Family Relations* 43 (January): 46–52.

HOLT, T., L. GREENE, AND J. DAVIS. 2003. National survey of adolescents and young adults: Sexual health knowledge, attitudes and experiences. The Henry Kaiser Family Foundation. www.kff.org (accessed June 12, 2003).

HOLZER, H. J. 2001. Racial differences in labor market outcomes among men. In *America becoming: Racial trends and their consequences*, vol. 2, eds. N. J. Smelser, W. J. Wilson, and F. Mitchell, 98–123. Washington, DC: National Academy Press.

Homosexual relations. 2008. Gallup, www.gallup.com (accessed May 21, 2009).

HONEY, M. 1984. *Creating Rosie the Riveter: Class, gender, and propaganda.* Amherst: University of Massachusetts Press.

HOOYMAN, N. R., AND H. A. KIYAK. 2002. *Social gerontology: A multidisciplinary perspective,* 6th ed. Boston, MA: Allyn & Bacon.

HOPPER, J. 2001. The symbolic origins of conflict in divorce. *Journal of Marriage and Family* 63 (May): 430–45.

HORN, B., Ed. 2006. Progressive agenda for the states 2006: State policy leading America. Center for Policy Alternatives, www.stateaction.org (accessed May 2, 2006).

HORTON, S. 2008. What's tougher to get than a same-sex marriage? A same-sex divorce. *Los Angeles Times*, July 25, www.latimes.com (accessed July 27, 2008).

HORWITZ, A. V., H. R. WHITE, AND S. HOWELL-WHITE. 1996. Becoming married and mental health: A longitudinal study of a cohort of young adults. *Journal of Marriage and the Family* 58 (November): 895–907.

HORWITZ, A. V., AND J. C. WAKEFIELD. 2006. The epidemic in mental illness: Clinical fact or survey artifact? *Contexts* 5 (Winter): 19–23.

HOSSAIN, Z. 2001. Division of household labor and family functioning in off-reservation Navajo Indian families. *Family Relations* 50 (July), 255–61.

HOUSEKNECHT, S. K., AND S. K. LEWIS. 2005. Explaining teen childbearing and cohabitation: Community embeddedness and primary ties. *Family Relations* 54 (December): 607–20.

HOUSER, A. 2007. Women & long-term care. AARP Public Policy Institute, FS no. 77R, www.aarp.org (accessed September 27, 2009).

HOWARD, J. A., AND J. A. HOLLANDER. 1997. *Gendered situations, gendered selves: A gender lens on social psychology.* Thousand Oaks, CA: Sage.

How late is too late? 2001. Letter to the editor. *Newsweek*, September 3, 14.

HOWE, N., W. STRAUSS, and R. J. MATSON. 2000. *Millennials rising: The next great generation.* New York: Vintage.

HUANG, C-C. 2009. Mothers' reports of nonresident fathers' involvement with their children: Revisiting the relationship between child support payment and visitation. *Family Relations* 58 (February): 54–64.

HÜBNER, K., ET AL. 2003. Derivation of oocytes from mouse embryonic stem cells. *Science* 300 (May): 1251–56.

HUDAK, M. A. 1993. Gender schema theory revisited: Men's stereotypes of American women. *Sex Roles* 28 (5/6): 279–92.

HUDSON, J. I., E. HIRIPI, H. G. POPE JR., AND R. C. KESSLER. 2007. The prevalence and correlates of eating disorders in the national comorbidity survey replication. *Biological Psychiatry* 61 (February): 348–58.

HUDSON, J. W., AND L. F. HENZE. 1969. Campus values in mate selection: A replication. *Journal of Marriage and the Family* 31 (November): 772–75.

HUDSON, V. M., AND A. M. DEN BOER. 2004. *Bare branches: Security implications of Asia's surplus male population.* Cambridge, MA: MIT Press.

HUGHES, M. E., AND L. J. WAITE. 2009. Marital biography and health at mid-life. *Journal of Health and Social Behavior* 50 (September): 344–58.

HUNT, G., CAROL L., AND L. NAIDITCH. 2005. Young caregivers in the U.S.: Findings from a national survey. National Alliance for Caregiving and United Hospital Fund, September, www.caregiving.org (accessed August 2, 2006).

HUNT, J. 1991. Ten reasons not to hit your kids. In *Breaking down the wall of silence: The liberating experience of facing painful trust*, ed. A. Miller, 168–71. Meridian, NY: Dutton.

HUNT, J., AND M. GAUTHIER-LOISELLE. 2008. How much does immigration boost innovation? National Bureau of Economic Research, September, www.nber.org (accessed March 27, 2009).

HUPKA, R. B. 1991. The motive for the arousal of romantic jealousy: Its cultural origin. In *The psychology of jealousy and envy*, ed. P. Salovey, 252–70. New York: Guilford.

HURH, W. M. 1998. *The Korean Americans.* Westport, CT: Greenwood.

HUSTON, T. L., AND E. K. HOLMES. 2004. Becoming parents. In *Handbook of family communication*, ed. Anita L. Vangelisti, 105–33. Mahwah, NJ: Lawrence Erlbaum.

HUTCHINSON, E. O. 1994. *Black fatherhood. II: Black women talk about their men.* Los Angeles: Middle Passage.

HUTCHINSON, M. K. 2002. The influence of sexual risk communication between parents and daughters on sexual risk behaviors. *Family Relations* 51 (July): 238–47.

HUTTENLOCHER, J., M. VASILYEVA, E. CYMERMAN, AND S. LEVINE. 2002. Language input and child syntax. *Cognitive Psychology* 45 (November): 337–74.

HUTTER, M. 1998. *The changing family*, 3rd ed. Boston: Allyn & Bacon.

HWANG, A. C., A. KOYAMA, D. TAYLOR, J. T. HENDERSON, AND S. MILLER. 2005. Advanced practice clinicians' interest in providing medical abortion: Results of a California survey. *Perspectives on Sexual and Reproductive Health* 37 (June): 92–97.

HWANG, S.-S., R. SAENZ, AND B. F. AGUIRRE. 1994. Structural and individual determinants of outmarriage among Chinese-, Filipino-, and Japanese-Americans in California. *Sociological Inquiry* 64 (November): 396–414.

HYDE, J. S. 2005. The gender similarities hypothesis. *American Psychologist* 60 (September): 581–92.

HYDE, J. S. 2006. Gender similarities still rule. *American Psychologist* 61 (September): 641–42.

I

IHINGER-TALLMAN, M., AND K. PASLEY. 1987. *Remarriage.* Beverly Hills, CA: Sage.

IKONOMIDOU, C. P., ET AL., 2000. Ethanol-induced apoptotic neurodegeneration and fetal alcohol syndrome. *Science* 287, February 11, 1056–60.

ILKKARACAN, P., AND S. JOLLY. 2007. Gender and sexuality: Overview report. BRIDGE, January, www.bridge.ids.ac.uk (accessed February 20, 2007).

IMBER-BLACK, E., AND J. ROBERTS. 1993. Family change: Don't cancel holidays! *Psychology Today* 26 (March/April): 62, 64, 92–93.

IMMEL, M. B. 2008. I'm old—and I'm just fine with that. *Newsweek*, July 31, 18.

Indian Health Service. 2006. Facts on Indian health disparities. January, info.ihs.gov (accessed March 29, 2009).

Infant homicide. 2007. Child Trends Data Bank, www.childrendsdatabank.org (accessed August 15, 2009).

INGERSOLL-DAYTON, B., M. B. NEAL, J.-H. HA, AND L. B. HAMMER. 2003. Redressing inequity in parent care among siblings. *Journal of Marriage and Family* 65 (February): 201–12.

INGOLDSBY, B. B., S. R. SMITH, AND J. E. MILLER. 2004. *Exploring family theories.* Los Angeles, CA: Roxbury Publishing.

INTERNATIONAL LONGEVITY CENTER. 2006. Ageism in America. Open Society Institute, www.ilcusa.org (accessed July 28, 2006).

Inter-Parliamentary Union. 2009. Women in national parliaments. February 28, www.ipu.org (accessed April 10, 2009).

Iranian arbitrating body approves marriage age increase. 2002. Yahoo News, June 23. http://story.news.yahoo.com (accessed June 24, 2002).

Iranian gays present, hidden. *Baltimore Sun*, September 30, 16A.

ISHII-KUNTZ, M. 1993. Japanese fathers: Work demands and family roles. In *Men, work and family*, ed. J. C. Hood, 45–67. Thousand Oaks, CA: Sage.

ISHII-KUNTZ, M., 2004. Asian American families: Diverse history, contemporary trends, and the future. In *Handbook of contemporary families: Considering the past, contemplating the future*, eds. M. Coleman and L. H. Ganong, 369–84. Thousand Oaks, CA: Sage.

It's just lunch. 2006. January 5, www.consumeraffairs.com (accessed January 10, 2006).

J

JACKSON, S. A. 1998. "Something about the word": African American women and feminism. In *No middle ground: Women and radical protest*, ed. K. M. Blee, 38–50. New York: New York University Press.

JACKSON, S., L. FEDER, D. R. FORDE, R. C. DAVIS, C. D. MAXWELL, AND B. G. TAYLOR. 2003. *Batterer intervention programs: Where do we go from here?* Washington, DC: U.S. Department of Justice.

JACOBY, S. 2005. Sex in America. *AARP* (July/August): 57–62, 114.

JAGGER, A. M., AND P. S. ROTHENBERG, EDS. 1984. *Feminist frameworks*, 2nd ed. New York: McGraw-Hill.

JAIMES, M. A., WITH T. HALSEY. 1992. American Indian women: At the center of indigenous resistance in contemporary North America. In *The state of Native America: Genocide, colonization, and resistance*, ed. M. A. Jaimes, 311–44. Boston: South End.

JALALI, B. 1996. Iranian families. In *Ethnicity and family therapy*, 2nd ed., eds. M. McGoldrick, J. Giordano, and J. K. Pearce, 347–63. New York: Guilford.

JAMBUNATHAN, S., D. C. BURTS, AND S. PIERCE. 2000. Comparisons of parenting attitudes among five ethnic groups in the United States. *Journal of Comparative Family Studies* 31 (Autumn): 395–406.

JANKOWIAK, W. R., AND E. P. FISCHER. 1992. A cross-cultural perspective on romantic love. *Ethnology* 31 (April): 149–55.

JANSON, L. 2005. The many faces of Victoria's Secret. *Proteus* 52 (December): 27–30.

JARRETT, R. L. 1994. Living poor: Family life among single parent, African-American women. *Social Problems* 41 (February): 30–49.

JAYAKODY, R., AND A. KALIL. 2002. Social fathering in low-income, African American families with preschool children. *Journal of Marriage and Family* 64 (May): 504–16.

JAYAKODY, R., AND N. CABRERA. 2002. What are the choices for low-income families? Cohabitation, marriage, and remaining single. In *Just living together: Implications of cohabitation on families, children, and social policy,* eds. A. Booth and A. C. Crouter, 85–96. Mahwah, NJ: Erlbaum.

JAYSON, S. 2005. Hearts divide over marital therapy. *USA Today,* July 22, D1.

JAYSON, S. 2009. I want you to get married. *Chicago Sun-Times,* February 24, www.suntimes.com (accessed February 24, 2009).

JEFFREYS, S. 2005. Beauty and misogyny: Harmful cultural practices in the West. New York: Routledge.

JENDREK, M. P. 1994. Grandparents who parent their grandchildren: Circumstances and decisions. *The Gerontologist* 34 (2): 206–16.

JENKINS, C. 2008. Voices too often missing in op-ed land: Women's. *Christian Science Monitor,* July 16, 9.

JERVEY, G. 2005. She makes more than he does. *Money,* May, 41–44.

JEUNE, B., AND J. W. VAUPEL, EDS. 1995. *Exceptional longevity: From prehistory to the present.* Odense, Denmark: Odense University Press.

JIANG, J. 2009. Postcard: Beijing. *Time,* March 2, 7.

JO, M. H. 1999. *Korean immigrants and the challenge of adjustment.* Westport, CT: Greenwood.

JOHN, D., AND B. A. SHELTON. 1997. The production of gender among black and white women and men: The case of household labor. *Sex Roles* 36 (February): 171–93.

JOHN, R. 1988. The Native American family. In *Ethnic families in America: Patterns and variations,* 3rd ed., eds. C. H. Mindel, R. W. Habenstein, and R. Wright, Jr., 325–66. New York: Elsevier.

JOHNSON, D. R., AND J. WU. 2002. An empirical test of crisis, social selection, and role explanations of the relationship between marital disruption and psychological distress: A pooled time-series analysis of four-wave panel data. *Journal of Marriage and Family* 64 (February): 211–224.

JOHNSON, E. M., AND T. L. HUSTON. 1998. The perils of love, or why wives adapt to husbands during the transition to parenthood. *Journal of Marriage and the Family* 60 (February): 195–204.

JOHNSON, M. P. 2005. Domestic violence: It's not about gender—or is it? *Journal of Marriage and Family* 67 (December): 1126–30.

JOHNSON, M. P. 2008. *A typology of domestic violence: Intimate terrorism, violent resistance, and situational couple violence.* Boston, MA: Northeastern University Press.

JOHNSON, R. 1985. Stirring the oatmeal. In *Challenge of the heart: Love, sex, and intimacy in changing times,* ed. J. Welwood. Boston: Shambhala.

JOHNSON, R. W. 2007. The burden of caring for frail parents. The Urban Institute, May 16, www.urban.org (accessed September 27, 2009).

JOHNSON, R. W. AND J. M. WIENER. 2006. A profile of frail older Americans and their caregivers. The Urban Institute, February, www.urban.org (accessed August 3, 2006).

JOHNSON, R. W., AND C. MOMMAERTS. 2009. Unemployment rate hits all-time high for adults age 65 and older: March 2009. Urban Institute, Retirement Policy Program, www.retirementpolicy.org (accessed September 12, 2009).

JOHNSON, R. W., D. TOOHEY, AND J. W. WIENER. 2007. Meeting the long-term care need of baby boomers: How changing families will affect paid helpers and institutions. The Urban Institute, May, www.urban.org (accessed September 18, 2009).

JOHNSON, T. D. 2008. *Maternity leave employment patterns of first-time mothers: 1961–2003.* Current Population Report, P70-113. Washington, DC: U.S. Census Bureau.

JOHNSTON, J. 2005. Online dating finds some gray. *USA Today* August 30, www.usatoday.com (accessed September 3, 2005).

JOHNSTON, L. D., P. M. O'MALLEY, J. G. BACHMAN, AND J. E. SCHULENBERG. 2006. *Monitoring the Future: National results on adolescent drug use: overview of key findings, 2005.* Bethesda, MD: National Institute on Drug Abuse.

JONES, A. 1994. *Next time, she'll be dead: Battering and how to stop it.* Boston: Beacon.

JONES, A. 2009. Texas compound revives memory of her own escape. Women's eNews, January 5, www.womensenews.org (accessed January 5, 2009).

JONES, A., AND S. SCHECHTER. 1992. *When love goes wrong: What to do when you can't do anything right.* New York: HarperCollins.

JONES, H. W., Jr. 2007. Iatrogenic multiple births: A 2003 checkup. *Fertility and Sterility* 87 (March): 453–55.

JONES, J. 1985. *Labor of love, labor of sorrow: Black women, work and the family from slavery to the present.* New York: Basic Books.

JONES, J. M. 2006. Ideal age for marriage: 25 for women and 27 for men. Gallup News Service, June 22, www.gallup.com (accessed June 9, 2009).

JONES, J. M. 2008. Fewer Americans favor cutting back immigration. Gallup poll, July 10, www.gallup.com (accessed Sept. 9, 2008).

JONES, J. M. 2008. Most Americans not willing to forgive unfaithful spouse. Gallup, March 25, www.gallup.com (accessed June 2, 2008).

JONES, M. 2003. The mystery of my eggs. *New York Times,* March 16, 44.

JONES, M. 2004. The New Yankees. *Mother Jones* 29 (March/April): 65–69.

JONES, N. A. 2005. We the people of more than one race in the United States. U.S. Census Bureau, Census 2000 Special Reports, CENSR-22, April, www.census.gov (accessed March 1, 2009).

JONES, N. A., AND A. S. SMITH. 2001. The two or more races population: 2000. U.S. Census. www.census.gov (accessed April 16, 2003).

JONES, R. K. 1993. Female victim perceptions of the causes of male spouse abuse. *Sociological Inquiry* 63 (August): 351–61.

JONES, R. K., J. E. DARROCH, AND S. SINGH. 2005. Religious differentials in the sexual and reproductive behaviors of young women in the United States. *Journal of Adolescence* 36 (April): 279-2–88.

JONES, R. K., L. F. FROHWIRTH, AND A. M. MOORE. 2008a. "I would want to give my child, like, everything in the world." *Journal of Family Issues* 29 (January): 79–99.

JONES, R. K., M. R. S. ZOLNA, S. K. HENSHAW, AND L. B. FINER. 2008b. Abortion in the United States: Incidence and access to services, 2005. *Perspectives on Sexual and Reproductive Health* 40 (March): 6–16.

JONES, R. K., S. SINGH, AND A. PURCESS. 2005. Parent-child relations among minor females attending U.S. family planning clinics. *Perspectives on Sexual and Reproductive Health* 37 (December): 192–201.

JONES, S., AND S. FOX. 2003. Let the games begin: Gaming technology and entertainment among college students. Pew Internet & American Life Project, www.pewinternet.org (accessed December 12, 2004).

JONES, S. 2009. Generations online in 2009. Pew Internet & American Life Project, January 28, www.pewinternet.org (accessed February 12, 2009).

JONES, W. H., AND M. P. BURDETTE. 1994. Betrayal in relationships. In *Perspectives on close relationships,* eds. A. L. Weber and J. H. Harvey, 243–62. Boston: Allyn & Bacon.

JONSSON, P. 2006. Debate grows on out-of-wedlock laws. *Christian Science Monitor,* August 23, 3.

JOSEPH, S. ED. 1999. *Intimate selving in Arab families: Gender, self, and identity.* New York: Syracuse University Press.

JOSHI, P., AND K. BOGEN. 2007. Nonstandard schedules and young children's behavioral outcomes among working low-income families. *Journal of Marriage and Family* 69 (February): 139–56.

JOSSELSON, R. 1992. *The space between us: Exploring the dimensions of human relationships.* San Francisco: Jossey-Bass.

JOYCE, A. 2004. Lawsuits shed new light on sexual harassment of teens. *Washington Post,* December 2, A1.

JOYCE, A. 2006. Now it's time for women to get even. *Washington Post,* April 23, F1.

JOYCE, K. 2009. Extreme motherhood—understanding Quiverfull, the antifeminist, conservative Christian movement that motivates popular reality-TV families like the Duggars. *Newsweek* Web Exclusive, March 17, www.newsweek.com (accessed March 20, 2009).

JOYCE, T. J., S. K. HENSHAW, A. DENNIS, L. B. FINER, AND K. BLANCHARD. 2009. The impact of state mandatory counseling and waiting period laws on abortion: A literature review. Guttmacher Institute, April, www.guttmacher.org (accessed June 25, 2009).

JUSTICE, G. 1999. We're happily married and living apart. *Newsweek,* October 18, 12.

K

KACAPYR, E. 1998. How hard are hard times? *American Demographics* 20 (February): 30–32.

Kaiser Family Foundation. 2004. Birth control and protection: A series of national surveys of teens about sex. July, www.kff.org (accessed August 20, 2009).

Kaiser Family Foundation. 2008. Sexual health of adolescents and young adults in the United States. September, www.kff.org (accessed May 6, 2009).

KALATA, J. 2006. *Looking at act II of women's lives: Thriving & striving from 45 on.* AARP Foundation, April, www.aarp.org (accessed June 12, 2009).

KALB, C., AND V. JUAREZ. 2005. Small is beautiful. *Newsweek,* August 1, 46–47.

KALICK, S. M., AND T. E. HAMILTON. 1986. The matching hypothesis reexamined. *Journal of Personality and Social Psychology* 51 (October): 673–82.

KALIL, A. 2002. Cohabitation and child development. In *Just living together: Implications of cohabitation on families, children, and social policy,* eds. A. Booth and A. C. Crouter, 153–60. Mahwah, NJ: Erlbaum.

KALMIJN, M. 1998. Intermarriage and homogamy: Causes, patterns, trends. *Annual Review of Sociology* 24: 395–421.

KALMIJN, M., AND C. W. S. MONDEN. 2006. Are the negative effects of divorce on well-being dependent on marital quality? *Journal of Marriage and Family* 68 (December): 1197–213.

KAMBAYASHI, T. 2008. Japanese men shout the oft-unsaid: "I love you." *Christian Science Monitor,* February 13, 1, 11.

KAMEN, P. 2002. Her way: Women remake the sexual revolution. New York: Broadway.

KAMINSKI, J. W., AND X. FANG. 2009. Victimization by peers and adolescent suicide in three US samples. *Journal of Pediatrics* 155 (November): 683–88.

KAMP DUSH, C. M., M. G. TAYLOR, AND R. A. KROEGER. 2008. Marital happiness and psychological well-being across the life course. *Family Relations* 57 (April): 211–26.

KANTOR, R. M. 1970. Communes. *Psychology Today* (July): 53–57, 78.

KANTROWITZ, B. 2006. Sex & love: The new world. *Newsweek* (February 20): 51–59.

KANTROWITZ, B., AND P. WINGERT. 1999. The science of a good marriage. *Newsweek,* April 19, 52–57.

KANTROWITZ, B., AND P. WINGERT. 2001. Unmarried with children. *Newsweek,* May 28, 46–54.

KAO, L. C., ET AL. 2003. Expression profiling of endometrium from women with endometriosis reveals candidate genes for disease-based implantation failure and infertility. *Endocrinology* 144 (April 10): 2870–81.

KARCH, D. L., ET AL. 2009. Surveillance for violent deaths—National Violent Reporting System, 16 states, 2006. *MMWR* 58 (March 20): 1–44.

KARJANE, H. M., BONNIE S. F., AND F. T. CULLEN. 2005. Sexual assault on campus: What colleges and universities are doing about it. National Institute of Justice, December, www.ncjrs.gov (accessed March 10, 2006).

KARRAKER, M. W. 2008. *Global families.* Boston: Pearson Education.

KASHEF, Z. 2003. The fetal position. *Mother Jones* (January/February): 18–19.

KASS, L. R. 1997. The end of courtship. *The Public Interest* 126 (Winter): 39–63.

KAUFMANN, J-C. 2008. *The single woman and the fairytale prince.* Malden, MA: Polity Press.

KAUFMAN, M. 2006. Pregnancy centers found to give false information on abortion. *Washington Post,* July 18, A8.

KAUKINEN, C. 2004. Status compatibility, physical violence, and emotional abuse in intimate relationships. *Journal of Marriage and Family* 66 (May): 452–71.

KAWAMOTO, W. T., AND T. C. CHESHIRE. 1997. American Indian families. In *Families in cultural context: Strengths and challenges in diversity,* ed. M. K. DeGenova, 15–34. Mountain View, CA: Mayfield.

KAWAMOTO, W. T., AND T. C. CHESHIRE. 2004. A "seven-generation" approach to American Indian families. In *Handbook of contemporary families: Considering the past, contemplating the future,* eds. M. Coleman and L. H. Ganong, 385–93. Thousand Oaks, CA: Sage.

KAWAMOTO, W. T., AND R. P. VIRAMONTEZ ANGUINO. 2006. Asian and Latino immigrant families. In *Families in global and multicultural perspective,* 2nd ed., eds. B. B. Ingoldsby and S. D. Smith, 209–30. Thousand Oaks, CA: Sage.

KELLEY, P. 1992. Healthy stepfamily functioning. Families in Society: *The Journal of Contemporary Human Services* 73 (December): 579–87.

KELLY, D. 2005. Lost to the only life they knew. *Los Angeles Times,* June 13, A1.

KELLY, D. 2009. Polygamist who tortured his family is sentenced to 7 life terms. *Los Angeles Times,* February 14, www.latimes .com (accessed February 15, 2009).

KELLY, D., AND G. COHN. 2006. Blind eye to culture of abuse. *Los Angeles Times,* May 12, www.latimes.com (accessed May 13, 2006)

KELLY, G. F. 1994. *Sexuality today: The human perspective,* 4th ed. Guilford, CT: Dushkin.

KELLY, J. B., AND R. E. EMERY. 2003. Children's adjustment following divorce: Risk and resilience perspectives. *Family Relations* 52 (October): 352–62.

KELLY, J., AND S. L. SMITH. 2006. G movies give boys a D: Portraying males as dominant, disconnected and dangerous. Dads & Daughters Organization, www.seejane.org (accessed August 8, 2006).

KENDALL, D. 2002. *The power of good deeds: Privileged women and the social reproduction of the upper class.* Lanham, MD. Rowman & Littlefield.

KENEN, R. H. 1993. *Reproductive hazards in the workplace: Mending jobs, managing pregnancies.* New York: Haworth.

KENNEDY, D. E., AND L. KRAMER. 2008. Improving emotion regulation and sibling relationship quality: The More Fun with Sisters and Brothers program. *Family Relations* 57 (December): 567–78.

KENNEDY, R. 2002. *Nigger: The strange career of a troublesome word.* New York: Pantheon.

KENNEDY, T. L. M., A. SMITH, A. T. WELLS, AND B. WELLMAN. 2008. Networked families. Pew Internet & American Life Project, October 19, www.pewinternet.org (accessed February 25, 2009).

KENRICK, D. T., G. E. GROTH, M. R. TROST, AND E. K. SADALLA. 1993. Integrating evolutionary and social exchange perspectives on relationships: Effects of gender, self-appraisal, and involvement level on mate selection criteria. *Journal of Personality and Social Psychology* 64 (6): 951–69.

KENT, M. M., AND M. MATHER. 2002. What drives U.S. population growth? *Population Bulletin* 57 (December): 1–40. Washington, DC: Population Reference Bureau.

KERCKHOFF, A. C., AND K. E. DAVIS. 1962. Value consensus and need complementarity in mate selection. *American Sociological Review* 27 (June): 295–303.

KERN, S. 1992. *The culture of love: Victorians to moderns.* Cambridge, MA: Harvard University Press.

KERNIC, M. A., D. J. MONARY-ERNSDORFF, J. K. KOEPSELL, AND V. L. HOLT. 2005. Children in the crossfire: Child custody determinations among couples with a history of intimate partner violence. *Violence Against Women* 11 (August): 991–1021.

KERSHAW, S. 2003. Saudi Arabia awakes to the perils of inbreeding. *New York Times,* May 1, A3.

KERSTEN, K. K. 1990. The process of marital disaffection: Interventions at various stages. *Family Relations* 39 (July): 257–65.

KESTIN, S., AND P. FRANCESCHINA. 2007. Federal watchdog examines Seminoles' gambling profits. *South Florida Sun-Sentinel,* December 8, www.sun-sentinel.com (accessed December 10, 2007).

KETTNER, P. M., R. M. MORONEY, AND L. L. MARTIN. 1999. *Designing and managing programs: An effectiveness-based approach,* 2nd ed. Thousand Oaks, CA: Sage.

KHAW, L. B. L., AND J. L. HARDESTY. 2009. Leaving an abusive partner: Exploring boundary ambiguity using the stages of change model. *Journal of Family Theory & Review* 1(March): 38–53.

KHESHGI-GENOVESE, Z., AND T. A. GENOVESE. 1997. Developing the spousal relationship within stepfamilies. Families in Society: *The Journal of Contemporary Human Services* 78 (May/June): 255–64.

KIBRIA, N. 1997. The construction of "Asian American": Reflections on intermarriage and ethnic identity among second-generation Chinese and Korean Americans. *Ethnic and Racial Studies* 20 (July): 523–44.

KIECOLT-GLASER, J. K., AND T. L. NEWTON. 2001. Marriage and health: His and hers. *Psychological Bulletin* 127 (July): 472–503.

KIEFER, H. M. 2005. U.S. weddings: "Something borrowed" usually money. Gallup Organization, June 28, http://poll.gallup.com (accessed June 29, 2006).

KIEHL, S. 2007. It's not me; it's you. *Baltimore Sun,* September 30, 1E, 5E.

KILBOURNE, J. 1994. Still killing us softly: Advertising and the obsession with thinness. In *Feminist perspectives on eating disorders,* eds. P. Fallon, M. A. Katzman, and S. C. Wooley, 395–418. New York: Guilford.

KILBURN, J. C., JR. 1996. Network effects in care-giver to care-recipient violence: A study of care-givers to those diagnosed with Alzheimer's disease. *Journal of Elder Abuse & Neglect* 8 (1): 69–80.

KILPATRICK, D. G., B. E. SAUNDERS, AND D. W. SMITH. 2003. *Youth victimization: Prevalence and implications.* Washington, DC: U.S. Department of Justice.

KIM, H. K., H. K. LAURENT, D. M. CAPALDI, AND A. FEINGOLD. 2008. Men's aggression toward women: A 10-year panel study. *Journal of Marriage and Family* 70 (December): 1169–87.

KIM, J. E., E. M. HETHERINGTON, AND D. ROSS. 1999. Associations among family relationships, antisocial peers, and adolescents' externalizing behaviors. *Child Development* 70 (September/October): 1209–30.

KING, B. 2002. *Human sexuality today,* 4th ed. Upper Saddle River, NJ: Prentice Hall.

KING, J., AND G. GOMEZ. 2007. *The American college president: 2007 edition.* Washington, DC: American Council on Education.

KING, J. L. 2004. *On the down low: A journey into the lives of "straight" black men who sleep with men.* New York: Broadway Books.

KING, M., AND A. BARTLETT. 2006. What same sex civil partnerships may mean for health. *Journal of Epidemiology and Community Health* 60 (March): 188–91.

KING, M. L. 2007. Immigrants in the U.S. health care system: Five myths that misinform the American public. June 7, Center for American Progress, www.americanprogress.org (accessed March 13, 2009).

KING, M., AND A. BARTLETT. 2006. What same sex civil partnerships may mean for health. *Journal of Epidemiology and Community Health* 60 (March): 188–91.

KING, V. 2003. The legacy of a grandparent's divorce: Consequences for ties between grandparents and grandchildren. *Journal of Marriage and Family* 65 (February): 170–83.

KING, V. 2006. The antecedents and consequences of adolescents' relationships with stepfathers and nonresident fathers. *Journal of Marriage and Family* 68 (November): 910–28.

KING, V. 2007. When children have two mothers: Relationships with nonresident mothers, stepmothers, and fathers. *Journal of Marriage and Family* 69 (December): 1178–93.

KING, V., AND M. E. SCOTT. 2005. A comparison of cohabiting relationships among older and younger adults. *Journal of Marriage and Family* 67 (May): 271–85.

KING, W. 1996. "Suffer with them till death": Slave women and their children in nineteenth-century America. In *More than chattel: Black women and slavery in the Americas,* eds. D. B. Caspar and D. C. Hine, 147–68. Bloomington: Indiana University Press.

KINSELLA, K., AND W. HE. 2009. *An aging world: 2008.* Washington, DC: U.S. Government Printing Office.

KINSEY, A. C., W. B. POMEROY, AND C. E. MARTIN. 1948. *Sexual behavior in the human male.* Philadelphia: Saunders.

KINSEY, A. C., W. B. POMEROY, C. E. MARTIN, AND P. H. GEBHARD. 1953. *Sexual behavior in the human female*. Philadelphia: Saunders.

KIRBY, D. B. 2008. The impact of abstinence and comprehensive sex and STD/HIV education programs on adolescent sexual behavior. *Sexuality Research & Social Policy* 5 (September): 18–27.

KIRCHHEIMER, S. 2005. Anti-aging snake oil. *AARP Bulletin*, November, 36.

KISSLING, F., AND K. MICHELMAN. 2008. Abortion's battle of messages. *Los Angeles Times*, January 22, www.latimes.com (accessed January 23, 2008).

KISSMAN, K., AND J. A. ALLEN. 1993. *Single-parent families*. Beverly Hills, CA: Sage.

KITZINGER, S. 1989. *The crying baby*. New York: Penguin.

KIVISTO, P., AND W. NG. 2004. *Americans all: Race and ethnic relations in historical, structural, and comparative perspectives*, 2nd ed. Los Angeles, CA: Roxbury.

KLADKO, B. 2002. At computer camp, the gender gap is obvious. www.bergen.com (accessed July 29, 2002).

KLEIN, A. R. 2009. Practical implications of current domestic violence research: For law enforcement, prosecutors, and judges. NIJ Special Report, June, www.ojp.usdoj.gov/nij (accessed August 23, 2009).

KLEIN, K. 2006. Parents, wake up! Your kid is annoying. *Los Angeles Times*, January 3, B11.

KLINGAMAN, M. 2008. His brother's keeper. *Baltimore Sun*, March 9, 1, 8.

KLINKENBERG, D., AND S. ROSE. 1994. Dating scripts of gay men and lesbians. *Journal of Homosexuality* 26(4): 23–35.

KNAPP, M. L., AND J. A. HALL. 1992. *Nonverbal communication in human interaction*, 3rd ed. New York: Holt, Rinchard & Winston.

KNICKERBOCKER, B. 2006. Crackdown on polygamy group. *Christian Science Monitor*, May 9, 2, 4.

KNICKERBOCKER, B. 2009. Oregon's "death with dignity" law enters healthcare debate. *Christian Science Monitor*, August 22, www.csmonitor.com (accessed September 27, 2009).

KNICKMEYER, E. 2007. For young Libyans, old-style marriage is a dream too far. *Washington Post*, November 14, A13.

KNOESTER, C., D. L. HAYNIE, AND C. M. STEPHENS. 2006. Parenting practices and adolescents' friendship networks. *Journal of Marriage and Family* 68 (December): 1247–60.

KNOX, D., WITH K. LEGGETT. 1998. *The divorced dad's survival book: How to stay connected with your kids*. New York: Insight.

KNOX, N. 2006. Dream house, sans spouse: More women buy homes. *USA Today*, February 14, www.usatoday.com (accessed June 9, 2009).

KOCH, W. 2007. Russia curtails American adoptions. *USA Today*, April 11, 1A.

KOCH, W. 2009. Black leaders set records in state legislatures. *USA Today*, March 5, www.usatoday.com (accessed March 6, 2009).

KOCHANSKA, G., N. AKSAN, T. R. PRISCO, AND E. E. ADAMS. 2008. Mother-child and father-child mutually responsive orientation in the first 2 years and children's outcomes at preschool age: Mechanisms of influence. *Child Development* 79 (February): 30–44.

KOCHHAR, R. 2005. Survey of Mexican migrants: The economic transition to America. Pew Hispanic Center, December 6, www.pewhispanic.org (accessed March 15, 2009).

KOCHHAR, R. 2007. 1995–2005: Foreign-born Latinos make progress on wages. Pew Hispanic Center, August 21, www.pewhispanic.org (accessed March 16, 2009).

KOCHHAR, R. 2009. Unemployment rises sharply among Latino immigrants in 2008. Pew Hispanic Center, February 12, www.pewhispanic.org (accessed March 15, 2009).

KOHLBERG, L. 1969. Stage and sequence: The cognitive-developmental approach to socialization. In *Handbook of socialization theory and research*, ed. D. A. Goslin, 347–480. Chicago: Rand McNally.

KOHLER, P. K., L. E. MANHART, AND W. E. LAFFERTY. 2008. Abstinence-only and comprehensive sex education and the initiation of sexual activity and teen pregnancy. *Journal of Adolescent Health* 42 (April): 344–51.

KOHUT, A., C. DOHERTY, M. DIMOCK, AND S. KEETER. 2007. Trends in political values and core attitudes: 1987–2007; political landscape more favorable to Democrats. Pew Research Center for the People & the Press, March 22, www.people-press.org (accessed May 15, 2009).

KOHUT, A., AND K. PARKER. 2007. Motherhood today: Tougher challenges, less success. Pew Research Center for the People & the Press, May 2, http://people-press.org (accessed July 6, 2009).

KOHUT, A., ET AL. 2007. Blacks see growing values gap between poor and middle class. Pew Research Center, November 13, www.pewsocialtrends.org (accessed December 10, 2007).

KOROPECKYJ-COX, T., AND G. PENDELL. 2007. The gender gap in attitudes about childlessness in the United States. *Journal of Marriage and Family* 69 (November): 899–915.

KOSS-FEDER, L. 2009. Bunking in with mom and dad. *Time*, March 2, 45–46.

KOTZ, D. 2007. Sex ed for seniors: You still need those condoms. *U.S. News & World Report*, August 13, 45.

KOWAL, A. K., AND L. BLINN-PIKE. 2004. Sibling influences on adolescents' attitudes toward safe sex practices. *Family Relations* 53 (July): 377–84.

KREEGER, K. Y. 2002a. Sex-based differences continue to mount. *The Scientist* 16 (February 18). www.the-scientist.com (accessed July 14, 2002).

KREEGER, K. Y. 2002b. X and Y chromosomes concern more than reproduction. *The Scientist* 16 (February 4). www.the-scientist.com (accessed July 14, 2002).

KRACHE, D. 2008. How to ground a "helicopter parent." CNN, August 19, www.cnn.com (accessed July 10, 2009).

KREIDER, R. M. 2005. Number, timing, and duration of marriages and divorces: 2001. U.S. Census Bureau, Current Population Reports, P70–97, www.census.gov (accessed July 4, 2006).

KREIDER, R. M. 2008. *Living arrangements of children: 2004*. Current Population Reports, P70-114. Washington, DC: U.S. Census Bureau.

KREIDER, R. M., AND J. M. FIELDS. 2002. Number, timing, and duration of marriages and divorces: 1996. U.S. Census Bureau, Current Population Reports, 70–80. www.census.gov (accessed March 1, 2003).

KRIDEL, K. 2009. Going the distance for love. *Los Angeles Times*, March 9, www.latimes.com (accessed March 16, 2009).

KRISTOF, K. M. 2006. Will dating sites offer credit reports? *Los Angeles Times* (February 14): C1.

KROKOFF, L. J. 1987. The correlates of negative affect in marriage: An exploratory study of gender differences. *Journal of Family Issues* 8 (March): 111–35.

KRUK, E. 2008. Child custody, access and parental responsibility: The search for a just and equitable standard. Father Involvement Research Alliance (FIRA), December, www.fira.ca (accessed August 20, 2009).

KRUEGER, R. A. 1994. *Focus groups: A practical guide for applied research*, 2nd ed. Thousand Oaks, CA: Sage.

KÜBLER-ROSS, E. 1969. *On death and dying*. New York: Macmillan.

KUCZYNSKI, A. 2001. Men's magazines: How much substance behind the covers? *New York Times*, June 24, C1.

KULCZYCKI, A., AND A. P. LOBO. 2001. Deepening the melting pot: Arab-Americans at the turn of the century. *Middle East Journal* 3 (Summer): 459–73.

KULCZYCKI, A., AND A. P. LOBO. 2002. Patterns, determinants, and implications of intermarriage among Arab Americans. *Journal of Marriage and Family* 64 (February): 202–10.

KUNKEL, D., E. BIELY, K. EYAL, K. COPE-FERRAR, E. DONNERSTEIN, AND R. FANDRICH. 2003. Sex on TV3. Kaiser Family Foundation. www.kff.org (accessed June 15, 2003).

KUNKEL, D., K. EYAL, K. FINNERTY, E. BIELY, AND E. DONNERSTEIN. 2005. Sex on TV. Kaiser Family Foundation, www.kff.org (accessed January 6, 2006).

KURDEK, L. A. 1993. Predicting marital dissolution: A 5-year prospective longitudinal study of newlywed couples. *Journal of Personality and Social Psychology* 64 (2): 221–42.

KURDEK, L. A. 1994. Areas of conflict for gay, lesbian, and heterosexual couples: What couples argue about influences relationship satisfaction. *Journal of Marriage and the Family* 56 (November): 923–24.

KURDEK, L. A. 1998. Relationship outcomes and their predictors: Longitudinal evidence from heterosexual married, gay cohabiting, and lesbian cohabiting couples. *Journal of Marriage and the Family* 60 (August): 553–68.

KURDEK, L. A. 2006. Differences between partners from heterosexual, gay, and lesbian cohabiting couples. *Journal of Marriage and Family* 68 (May): 509–28.

KURDEK, L. A. 2007. The allocation of household labor by partners in gay and lesbian couples. *Journal of Family Issues* 28 (January): 132–48.

KURDEK, L. A., AND M. A. FINE. 1993. The relation between family structure and young adolescents' appraisals of family climate and parenting behavior. *Journal of Family Issues* 14: 279–90.

KURLAND, S. P. 2004. *Everlasting love*. Baltimore, MD: Noble House.

KURTH, B-M., AND U. ELLERT. 2008. Perceived or true obesity: Which causes more suffering in adolescents? *Deutsches Ärzteblatt International* 105 (23): 406–12.

KURZ, D. 1993. Physical assaults by husbands: A major social problem. In *Current controversies on family violence*, eds. R. J. Gelles and D. R. Loseke, 88–103. Thousand Oaks, CA: Sage.

KUTZ, G. D., AND J. T. MEYER. 2009. Wage and Hour Division's complaint intake and investigative processes leave low-wage workers vulnerable to wage theft. GAO, March 25, GAO-09-458T, www.gao.gov (accessed June 5, 2009).

KWONG SEE, S. T., AND C. RASMUSSEN. 2003. An early start to age stereotyping: Children's beliefs about an older experimenter. Cited in *University of Alberta News*. www.expressnews.ualberta.ca (accessed December 3, 2003).

L

LaFrance, M., M. A. Hecht, and E. L. Paluck. 2003. The contingent smile: A meta analysis of sex differences in smiling. *Psychological Bulletin* 129 (March): 305–35.

LaFraniere, S. 2005. Forced to marry before puberty, African girls pay lasting price. *New York Times*, Nov 27, 1A.

LaFraniere, S., and L. Goodstein. 2007. Anglicans rebuke U.S. branch on blessing same-sex unions. *New York Times*, February 20, A1, A11.

Lagnado, L. 2006. Staying put at 96. *Wall Street Journal*, May 6–7, A1, A5.

Lagorio, C. 2007. Meet a true college senior. CBS News, May 11, www.cbsnews.com (accessed May 15, 2007).

Laird, J. 1993. Lesbian and gay families. In *Normal family processes*, 2nd ed., ed. F. Walsh, 282–330. New York: Guilford.

Lakoff, R. T. 1990. *Talking power: The politics of language*. New York: Basic Books.

Lakshmanan, I. A. R. 1997. Marriage? Think logic, not love. *Baltimore Sun*, September 22, 2A.

Lampman, J. 2008. Global slave trade at a high, but reasons for hope. *Christian Science Monitor*, September 15, 1, 12.

Landale, N. S., and S. E. Tolnay. 1991. Group differences in economic opportunity and the timing of marriage. *American Sociological Review* 56 (February): 33–45.

Landers, A. 2001. Husband shows his love in small ways every day. *Baltimore Sun*, June 16, 3D.

Langer, G., C. Arnedt, and D. Sussman. 2004. Primetime Live poll: American sex survey. ABC News,: http://abcnews.go.com (accessed January 16, 2006).

Lantz, H. R. 1976. *Marital incompatibility and social change in early America*. Beverly Hills, CA: Sage.

LaPlante, M. D. 2007. Military divorce rates on the rise. Scripps News, December 24, www.scrippsnews.com (accessed August 29, 2009).

Lareau, A. 2003. *Unequal childhoods: Class, race, and family life*. Berkeley: University of California Press.

Large, E. 2002. Homeward bound. *Baltimore Sun*, June 9, 1N, 4N.

Larimer, M. E., A. R. Lydum, and A. P. Turner. 1999. Male and female recipients of unwanted sexual contact in a college student sample: Prevalence rates, alcohol use, and depression symptoms. *Sex Roles* 40 (February): 295–308.

LaRossa, R. 1986. *Becoming a parent*. Thousand Oaks, CA: Sage.

LaRossa, R. ed. 1984. *Family case studies: A sociological perspective*. New York: Free Press.

LaRossa, R., and D. C. Retizes. 1993. Symbolic interactionism and family studies. In *Sourcebook of family theories and methods: A contextual approach*, eds. P. G. Boss, W. J. Doherty, R. LaRossa, W. R. Schumm, and S. K. Steinmetz, 135–63. New York: Plenum.

Larzelere, R. E. 2000. Child outcomes of nonabusive and customary physical punishment by parents: An updated literature review. Unpublished manuscript, University of Nebraska Medical Center, Omaha, and Father Flanagan's Boys' Home, Boys' Town, NE.

Lasch, C. 1977. *Haven in a heartless world: The family besieged*. New York: Basic Books.

Laslett, P. 1971. *The world we have lost*, 2nd ed. Reading, MA: Addison-Wesley.

Lasswell, T. E., and M. E. Lasswell. 1976. I love you but I'm not in love with you.

Journal of Marriage and Family Counseling 2 (July): 211–24.

Latessa, D. 2005. From financial aid to fatherhood. *Chronicle of Higher Education*, October 21, C3.

Lau, A. S., D. T. Takeuchi, and M. Alegría. 2006. Parent-to-child aggression among Asian American parents: Culture, context, and vulnerability. *Journal of Marriage and Family* 68 (December): 1261–75.

Laumann, E. O., A. Paik, and R. C. Rosen. 2001. Sexual dysfunction in the United States: Prevalence and predictions. In *Sex, love, and health in America*, eds. E. O. Laumann and R. T. Michael, 352–76. Chicago: University of Chicago Press.

Laumann, E. O., J. H. Gagnon, R. T. Michael, and S. Michaels. 1994. *The social organization of sexuality: Sexual practices in the United States*. Chicago: University of Chicago Press.

Lawless, J. L., and R. L. Fox. 2005. *It takes a candidate: Why women don't run for office*. New York: Cambridge University Press.

Lawrance, K., and E. S. Byers. 1995. Sexual satisfaction in long-term heterosexual relationships: The interpersonal exchange model of social satisfaction. *Personal Relationships* 2: 267–85.

Lawson, E. J., and A. Thompson. 1999. *Black men and divorce*. Thousand Oaks, CA: Sage.

Leaper, C. 2002. Parenting girls and boys. In *Handbook of parenting*, 2nd ed., Vol. 1, ed. M. H. Bornstein, 189–215. Mahwah, NJ: Erlbaum.

Leaper, C., and M. M. Ayres. 2007. A meta-analytic review of gender variations in adults' language use: Talkativeness, affiliative speech, and assertive speech. *Personality and Social Psychology Review* 11 (November): 328–63.

Lebey, B. 2004. *Remarried with children: Ten secrets for successfully blending and extending your family*. New York: Bantam Books.

Lederer, W. J., and D. D. Jackson. 1968. *The mirages of marriage*. New York: Norton.

Lee, J. A. 1973. *The colors of love*. Upper Saddle River, NJ: Prentice Hall.

Lee, J. A. 1974. The styles of loving. *Psychology Today* (October): 46–51.

Lee, M. A., and M. Mather. 2008. U.S. labor force trends. *Population Bulletin* 63 (June): 1–17.

Lee, S. M., and B. Edmonston. 2005. New marriages, new families: U.S. racial and Hispanic intermarriage. *Population Bulletin* 60 (June): 1–40.

Lee, Y.-S., and L. J. Waite. 2005. Husbands' and wives' time spent on housework: A comparison of measures. *Journal of Marriage and Family* 67 (May): 328–36.

Lehmiller, J. J., and C. R. Agnew. 2007. Perceived marginalization and the prediction of romantic relationship stability. *Journal of Marriage and Family* 69 (November): 1036–49.

Lei, S. 2009. It's not easy being gray: The new rules of retirement. Urban Institute, February, no. 25, www.urban.org (accessed September 10, 2009).

Leinwand, D. 2006. Prescription drugs find place in teen culture. *USA Today*, June 13, www.usatoday.com (accessed June 14, 2006).

Leite, R., and P. C. Mc Kenry. 1996. Putting nonresidential fathers back into the family portrait. *Human Development and Family Life Bulletin* 2 (Autumn). www.hec .ohio-state.edu (accessed February 3, 1998).

Leitenberg, H., M. J. Detzer, and D. Srebnik. 1993. Gender differences in masturbation

and the relation of masturbation experience in preadolescence and/or early adolescence to sexual behavior and sexual adjustment in young adulthood. *Journal of Social Behavior* 22 (April): 87–98.

Leland, J. 2008. In "sweetie" and "dear," a hurt for the elderly. *New York Times*, October 7, A1.

Lemieux, R., and J. L. Hale. 2002. Cross-sectional analysis of intimacy, passion, and commitment: Testing the assumptions of the triangular theory of love. *Psychological Reports* 90 (June): 1009–14.

Leon, K. 2003. Risk and protective factors in young children's adjustment to parental divorce: A review of the research. *Family Relations* 52 (July): 258–70.

Leonard, K. I. 1997. *The South Asian Americans*. Westport, CT: Greenwood.

Leslie, L. A., and G. Morton. 2004. Family therapy's response to family diversity: Looking back, looking forward. In *Handbook of contemporary families: Considering the past, contemplating the future*, eds. M. Coleman and L. H. Ganong, 523–37. Thousand Oaks, CA: Sage.

Levaro, L. G. 2009. Living together or living apart together: New choices for old lovers. National Council on Family Relations newsletter, *Family Focus* (Summer): F9.

LeVay, S. 1993. *The sexual brain*. La Jolla, CA: MIP.

Levesque, R. J. R. 1993. The romantic experience of adolescents in satisfying love relationships. *Journal of Youth and Adolescence* 11 (3): 219–50.

Levey, N. L. 2009. Morning-after pill to be available to 17-year-olds over counter. *Los Angeles Times*, April 23, www.latimes.com (accessed April 24, 2009).

Levine, M. V. 1994. A nation of hamburger flippers? *Baltimore Sun*, July 31, 1E, 4E.

Leving, J. M., and G. Sacks. 2007. Ohio pizza box: "Deadbeat dad" campaign unfairly stigmatizes fathers. April 2, Fathers & Families, www.glennsacks.com (accessed September 1, 2009).

Levy, J. A. 1994. Sex and sexuality in later life stages. In *Sexuality across the life course*, ed. A. S. Rossi, 287–309. Chicago: University of Chicago Press.

Lewis, M. 1997. *Altering fate: Why the past does not predict the future*. New York: Guilford.

Lewis, O. 1966. The culture of poverty. *Scientific American* 115 (October): 19–25.

Li, Y.-F., B. Langholz, M. T. Salam, and F. D. Gilliland. 2005. Maternal and grandmaternal smoking patterns are associated with early childhood asthma. *Chest* 127 (April): 1232–41.

Libbon, R. P. 2000. MediaChannels. *American Demographics* 21 (February): 29.

Licht, J. 1995. Marriages that endure. Washington Post Health Supplement, October 31, 18–20.

Lichter, D. T., and M. L. Crowley. 2002. Poverty in America: Beyond welfare reform. *Population Bulletin* 57 (June). Washington, DC: Population Reference Bureau.

Lichter, D. T., D. R. Graefe, and J. B. Brown. 2003. Is marriage a panacea? Union formation among economically disadvantaged unwed mothers. *Social Problems* 50 (February): 60–86.

Lichter, D. T., Z. Qian, and L. M. Mellott. 2006. Marriage or dissolution? Union transitions among poor cohabiting women. *Demography* 43 (May): 223–40.

Lichter, D. T., and Z. Qian. 2008. Serial cohabitation and the marital life course. *Journal of Marriage and Family* 70 (November): 861–78.

LIEBOWITZ, S. W., D. C. CASTELLANO, AND I. CUELLAR. 1999. Factors that predict sexual behavior among young Mexican American adolescents: An exploratory study. *Hispanic Journal of Behavioral Sciences* 21 (November): 470–79.

Like a virgin? 2006. *Today Online*, January 11, www.todayonline.com/articles (accessed January 15, 2006).

LILLESTON, R. 2004. Survey: Gap between safe-sex claims, practices. *USA Today*, April 6, www.usatoday.com (accessed April 7, 2004).

LIN, G., AND P. A. ROGERSON. 1995. Elderly parents and the geographic availability of their adult children. *Research on Aging* 17 (September): 303–9.

LIN, M. H., V. S. Y. KWAN, A. CHEUNG, AND S. T. FISKE. 2005. Stereotype content model explains prejudice for an envied outgroup: Scale of anti-Asian American stereotypes. *Personality and Social Psychology Bulletin* 31 (January): 34–47.

LINCOLN, K. D., L. M. CHATTERS, AND R. J. TAYLOR. 2005. Social support, traumatic events, and depressive symptoms among African Americans. *Journal of Marriage and Family* 67 (August): 754–66.

LINDAU, S. T., L. P. SCHUMM, E. O. LAUMANN, W. LEVINSON, C. A. O'MUIRCHEARTAIGH, AND L. J. WAITE. 2007. A study of sexuality and health among older adults in the United States. *New England Journal of Medicine* 357 (August 23): 762–74.

LINDBERG, L. D., R. JONES, AND J. S. SANTELLI. 2008. Non-coital sexual activities among adolescents. *Journal of Adolescent Health* 42 (February): 44–45.

LINDBERG, L. D., AND S. SINGH. 2008. Sexual behavior of single adult American women. *Perspectives on Sexual and Reproductive Health* 40 (March): 27–33.

LINDSEY, L. L. 2005. *Gender roles: A sociological perspective*, 4th ed. Upper Saddle River, NJ: Prentice Hall.

LINO, M. 2008. *Expenditures on children by families, 2007*. U.S. Department of Agriculture, Center for Nutrition Policy and Promotion. Miscellaneous Publication No. 1528-2007, www.cnpp.usda.gov (accessed June 25, 2009).

LIPKA, S. 2008. The case for Mr. Not-Quite-Right. *The Atlantic Journal*, February 19, www.theatlantic.com (accessed June 9, 2009).

LIPS, H. M. 2008. *Sex & gender: An introduction*, 6th ed. New York: McGraw-Hill..

LIPTON, E. 2005. Report finds U.S. failing on overstays of visas. *New York Times*, October 22, A13.

LIU, H., AND D. J. UMBERSON. 2008. The times they are a changin': Marital status and health differentials from 1972 to 2003. *Journal of Health and Social Behavior* 49 (September): 239–53.

LIU, M. 2008. Sex, lies, and family planning. *Newsweek*, January 28, 9.

LIU, P., AND C. S. CHAN. 1996. Lesbian, gay, and bisexual Asian Americans and their families. In *Lesbians and gays in couples and families: A handbook for therapists*, eds. J. Laird and R.-J. Green, 137–54. San Francisco: Jossey-Bass.

LIU, R., AND D. TREFLER. 2008. Much ado about nothing: American jobs and the rise of service outsourcing to China and India. National Bureau of Economic Research, Working Paper 14061, June, www.nber.org (accessed June 1, 2009).

LIVINGSTON, J. N., AND J. L. McADOO. 2007. The roles of African American fathers in the socialization of their children. In *Black families*, 4th ed., ed. H. P. McAdoo, 219–37. Thousand Oaks, CA: Sage.

Liz Claiborne Inc. 2008. Tween and teen dating violence and abuse study. February, www .loveisnotabuse.com (accessed June 6, 2009).

LLANA, S. M. 2005. These Shakers won't be movers. *Christian Science Monitor*, December 20, 20.

LLANA, S. M. 2007. Why Guatemala is roiling over its adoption boom. *Christian Science Monitor*, September 12, 1, 4.

LLOYD, E. A. 2005. *The case of the female orgasm: Bias in the science of evolution*. Cambridge, MA: Harvard University Press.

LLOYD, S. A. 1991. The dark side of courtship: Violence and sexual exploitation. *Family Relations* 40 (January): 14–20.

LLOYD, S. A., AND B. C. EMERY. 2000. *The dark side of courtship: Physical and sexual aggression*. Thousand Oaks, CA: Sage.

LOEB, S., M. BRIDGE, D. BASSOK, B. FULLER, AND R. RUMBERGER. 2005. How much is too much? The influence of preschool centers on children's social and cognitive development. December, NBER Working paper No. W11812, www.nber.org (accessed May 20, 2006).

LONG, L. 2008. Painful lessons. *Baltimore Sun*, May 18, 11A.

LÓPEZ, R. A. 1999. Las comadres as a social support system. *Affilia* 14 (Spring): 24–41.

LOPEZ, S. 2009. Laid-off lawyer in predicament she never imagined. *Los Angeles Times*, February 15, www.latimes.com (accessed March 1, 2009).

LORBER, J. 2005. *Gender inequality: Feminist theories and politics*, 3rd ed. Los Angeles, CA: Roxbury.

LORENZ, F. O., K. A. S. WICKRAMA, R. D. CONGER, AND G. H. ELDER JR. 2006. The short-term and decade-long effects of divorce on women's midlife health. *Journal of Health and Social Behavior* 47 (June): 111–25.

LOWRY, S. M., AND O. TRUJILLO. 2008. Cross-system dialogue: An effective strategy to promote communication between the domestic violence community, child welfare system, and the courts. National Council of Juvenile and Family Court Judges, www .thegreenbook.info/documents/ crosssystemdialogue.pdf (accessed August 22, 2009).

LUCAS, R. E. 2005. Time does not heal all wounds: A longitudinal study of reaction and adaptation to divorce. *Psychological Science* 16 (December): 945–950.

LUCAS, S. R. 2008. *Theorizing discrimination in an era of contested prejudice*. Philadelphia, PA: Temple University Press.

LUGAILA, T. A. 1998. Marital status and living arrangements: March 1998 (update). Current Population Reports, P20–514, U.S. Census Bureau. www.census.gov (accessed August 8, 2000).

LUKEMEYER, A., M. K. MEYERS, AND T. SMEEDING. 2000. Expensive children in poor families: Out-of-pocket expenditures for the care of disabled and chronically ill children in welfare families. *Journal of Marriage and the Family* 62 (May): 399–415.

LUNDQUIST, J. 2006. The black-white gap in marital dissolution among young adults: What can a counterfactual scenario tell us? *Social Problems* 3 (August): 421–41.

LUO, M. 2009. Forced from executive pay to hourly wage. *New York Times*, March 1, 1.

LUO, S., AND E. C. KLOHNEN. 2005. Assortative mating and marital quality in newlyweds: A couple-centered approach. *Journal of Personality and Social Psychology* 88 (February): 304–26.

LUPTON, D., AND L. BARCLAY. 1997. *Constructing fatherhood: Discourses and experiences*. Thousand Oaks, CA: Sage.

LYNCH, F. R. 2007. Saving my cat: Why no price was too high. *Newsweek*, July 30, 14.

LYNN, D. B. 1969. *Parental and sex role identification: A theoretical formulation*. Berkeley, CA: McCutchen.

LYNN, M., AND M. TODOROFF. 1995. Women's work and family lives. In *Feminist issues: Race, class, and sexuality*, ed. N. Mandell, 244–71. Scarborough, Ont.: Prentice Hall Canada.

LYNSKEY, M. T., ET AL., 2003. Escalation of drug use in early-onset cannabis users vs. co-twin controls. *Journal of the American Medical Association* 289 (January 22): 427–33.

LYON, L. 2009. Helping teens steer clear of trouble. *U.S. News & World Report*, February, 40–43.

LYONS, L. 2004. How many teens are cool with cohabitation? The Gallup Organization, April 13, http://poll.gallup.com (accessed April 20, 2004).

LYTTON, H., AND L. GALLAGHER. 2002. Parenting twins and the genetics of parenting. In *Handbook of parenting*, 2nd ed., Vol. 1: Children and parenting, ed. M. H. Bornstein, 227–53. Mahwah, NJ: Erlbaum.

M

MACDONALD, G. J. 2003. Smarter toys, smarter tots? *Christian Science Monitor*, August 20, 12–13.

MACDONALD, W. L., AND A. DEMARIS. 1996. The effects of stepparents' gender and new biological children. *Journal of Family Issues* 17 (1): 5–25.

MACDORMAN, M. F., D. L. HOYERT, J. A. MARIN, M. L. MUNSON, AND B. E. HAMILTON. 2007. Fetal and perinatal mortality, United States, 2003. *National Vital Statistics Reports* 55 (February 21): 1–9.

MACDORMAN, M. F., AND T. J. MATHEWS. 2008. Recent trends in infant mortality in the United States. NCHS Data Brief, October, Centers for Disease Control and Prevention, National Center for Health Statistics, www.cdc.gov (accessed March 10, 2009).

MACMILLAN, R., AND R. GARTNER. 1999. When she brings home the bacon: Labor-force participation and the risk of spousal violence against women. *Journal of Marriage and the Family* 61 (November): 947–58.

MACPHEE, D., J. FRITZ, AND J. MILLER -HEYL. 1996. Ethnic variations in personal social networks and parenting. *Child Development* 67 (6): 3278–95.

MACCOBY, E. E. 1990. Gender and relationships: A developmental account. *American Psychologist* 45 (4): 513–20.

MACHAMER, A. M., AND E. GRUBER. 1998. Secondary school, family, and educational risk: Comparing American Indian adolescents and their peers. *Journal of Educational Research* 91 (July/August): 357–69.

MACOMBER, J. 2006. An overview of selected data on children in vulnerable families. Urban Institute and Child Trends, August 10, www.urban.org (accessed October 1, 2006).

MACUNOVICH, D. J. 2002. Using economics to explain U.S. fertility trends. *Population Bulletin* 57 (December): 8–9. Washington, DC: Population Reference Bureau.

MADDEN, M., AND A. LENHART. 2006. Online dating. Pew Internet & American Life Project, March 5, www.pewinternet.org (accessed June 4, 2009).

MADIGAN, N. 2003. Suspect's wife is said to cite polygamy plan. *New York Times*. www .nytimes.com (accessed March 16, 2003).

MADIGAN, N. 2009. Couple guilty in tot's death. *Baltimore Sun*, February 22, 1, 8.

MAGNIER, M. 2006. Sri Lanka still wed to system. *Los Angeles Times* (January 23): A1.

MAGNIER, M., AND P. RAMASWAMY. 2009. Indian extremist group targets Valentine's Day. *Los Angeles Times*, February 14, www.latimes .com (accessed February 15, 2009).

MAHAY, J., E. O. LAUMANN, AND S. MICHAELS. 2001. Race, gender, and class in sexual scripts. In *Sex, love, and health in America*, eds. E. O. Laumann and R. T. Michael, 197–238. Chicago: University of Chicago Press.

MAHONEY, J. L., A. L. HARRIS, AND J. S. ECCLES. 2006. Organized activity participation, positive youth development, and the over-scheduling hypothesis. *Social Policy Report* 20 (4): 3–32.

MAHONEY, M. 2002. The economic rights and responsibilities of unmarried cohabitants. In *Just living together: Implications of cohabitation on families, children, and social policy*, eds. A. Booth and A. C. Crouter, 247–54. Mahwah, NJ: Erlbaum.

MAHONEY, S. 2003. Seeking love. *AARP Magazine*, November/December. www .aarpmagazine.org (accessed September 28, 2003).

MAHONEY, S. 2004. Hello, old love. *AARP Magazine* (September-October): 62–68, 122.

MAIER, T. 1998. *Dr. Spock: An American life.* New York: Harcourt Brace.

MAJOR, B., M. APPELBAUM, L. BECKMAN, M. A. DUTTON, N. F. RUSSO, AND C. WEST. 2008. Report of the APA task force on mental health and abortion. August 13, American Psychological Association, www.apa.org (accessed September 5, 2008).

MALLEY-MORRISON, K., AND D. A. HINES. 2004. *Family violence in a cultural perspective: Defining, understanding, and combating abuse.* Thousand Oaks, CA: Sage.

MALM, K., J. MURRAY, AND R. GREEN. 2006. *What about the dads? Child welfare agencies' efforts to identify, locate, and involve nonresident fathers.* Washington, DC: U.S. Department of Health and Human Services.

MALM, K., E. ZIELEWSKI, AND H. CHER. 2008. More about the dads: Exploring associations between nonresident father involvement and child welfare case outcomes. U.S. Department of Health and Human Services, Children's Bureau, http://aspe.hhs.gov/hsp (accessed July 12, 2009).

MANCINI, A. D., D. L. PRESSMAN, AND G. A. BONANNO. 2006. Clinical interventions with the bereaved: What clinicians and counselors can learn from the changing lives of older couples study. In *Spousal bereavement in late life*, eds. D. Carr, R. M. Nesse, and C. B. Wortman, 255–78. New York: Springer.

MANDARA, J., AND C. L. PIKES. 2008. Guilt trips and love withdrawal: Does mothers' use of psychological control predict depressive symptoms among African American adolescents? *Family Relations* 57 (December): 602–12.

MANGAN, K. 2009. Industry ties rile Harvard U.S. medical school. *Chronicle of Higher Education* 55 (March 13): A11.

MANGER, P. 2009. What if the problem is too much care? *Baltimore Sun*, August 19, 15.

MANINI, T. M., ET AL. 2006. Daily activity energy expenditure and mortality among older adults. *Journal of the American Medical Association* 296 (July 12): 171–79.

MANLOVE, J., C. LOGAN, K. A. MOORE, AND E. IKRAMULLAH. 2008. Pathways from family religiosity to adolescent sexual activity and contraceptive use. *Perspectives on Sexual and Reproductive Health* 40 (June): 105–17.

MANNING, C. 1970. *The immigrant woman and her job.* New York: Ayer.

MANNING, W. D., AND K. A. LAMB. 2003. Adolescent well-being in cohabiting, married, and single-parent families. *Journal of Marriage and Family* 65 (December): 876–93.

MANNING, W. D., AND P. J. SMOCK. 2005. Measuring and modeling cohabitation: New perspectives from qualitative data. *Journal of Marriage and Family* 67 (November): 989–1002.

MANNING, W. D., S. D. STEWART, AND P. J. SMOCK. 2003. The complexity of fathers' parenting responsibilities and involvement with non-resident children. *Journal of Family Issues* 24 (July): 645–67.

MANNING, W. D., M. A. LONGMORE, AND P. C. GIORDANO. 2007. The changing institution of marriage: Adolescents' expectations to cohabit and to marry. *Journal of Marriage and Family* 69 (August): 559–75.

MANSFIELD, H. C. 2004. On the consensual campus. *Doublethink* (Winter): 24.

MARCUS, A. D. 2003. Guys, your clock is ticking, too: Doctors now say male fertility falls as early as age 35; the case for banking your sperm. *Wall Street Journal*, April 1, D1.

MARDER, D. 2002. For $9,600, women taught how to find a mate. *Knight Ridder News Service*, January 13. archives.his.com/smart-marriages (accessed January 15, 2002).

MARGOLIS, J., AND A. FISHER. 2002. *Unlocking the clubhouse: Women in computing.* Cambridge, MA: MIT Press.

MARIMOW, A. E. 2008. Ruling inspires new hope for transgender people. *Washington Post*, September 15, B1.

MARKHAM, M. S., L. H. GANONG, AND M. COLEMAN. 2007. Coparental identity and mothers' cooperation in coparental relationships. *Family Relations* 56 (October): 369–77.

MARKOWITZ, S., R. KAESTNER, AND M. GROSSMAN. 2005. An investigation of the effects of alcohol consumption and alcohol policies on youth risky sexual behaviors. *American Economic Review* 95 (May): 263–66.

MARKS, L. D., K. HOPKINS, C. CHANEY, P. A. MONROE, O. NESTERUK, AND D. D. SASSER. 2008. "Together, we are strong": A qualitative study of happy, enduring African American marriages. *Family Relations* 57 (April): 172–85.

MARQUARDT, E. 2005. *Between two worlds: The inner lives of children of divorce.* New York: Crown.

MARSHALL, M. J. 2002. *Why spanking doesn't work: Stopping this bad habit and getting the upper hand on effective discipline.* Springville, Utah: Bonneville Books.

MARSIGLIO, W., AND R. HINOJOSA. 2006. Stepfathers and the family dance. In *Couples, kids, and family life*, eds. J. F. Gubrium and J. A. Holstein, 178–96. New York: Oxford University Press.

MARSIGLIO, W., AND R. HINOJOSA. 2007. Managing the multifather family: Stepfathers as father allies. *Journal of Marriage and Family* 69 (August): 845–62.

MARTIN, A. 1993. *The lesbian and gay parenting handbook: Creating and raising our families.* New York: HarperPerennial.

MARTIN, C. L. 1990. Attitudes and expectations about children with nontraditional and traditional gender roles. *Sex Roles* 22 (February): 151–65.

MARTIN, C. L., AND R. A. FABES. 2001. The stability and consequences of young children's same-sex peer interactions. *Developmental Psychology* 37 (May): 431–66.

MARTIN, J. A., et al. 2005. Births: Final data for 2003. *National Vital Statistics Reports* 54 (September). Hyattsville, MD: National Center for Health Statistics.

MARTIN, K. A. 1998. Becoming a gendered body: Practices of preschools. *American Sociological Review* 63 (August): 494–511.

MARTIN, L. R., H. S. FRIEDMAN, K. M. CLARK, AND J. S. TUCKER. 2005. Longevity following the experience of parental divorce. *Social Science & Medicine* 61 (November): 2177–89.

MARTIN, P., AND G. ZÜRCHER. 2008. Managing migration: The global challenge. *Population Bulletin* 63 (March): 1–20.

MARTIN, S., AND K. OPPENHEIM. 2007. Video gaming: General and pathological use. *Trends & Tudes* 6 (March): 1–6.

MARTIN, T. C., AND L. L. BUMPASS. 1989. Recent trends in marital disruption. *Demography* 26 (February): 37–51.

MARTINEZ, E. A. 2001. Death: A family event for Mexican Americans. *Family Focus*, National Council on Family Relations, December, F4.

MARTINO, S. C., M. N. ELLIOTT, R. CORONA, D. E. KANOUSE, AND M. A. SCHUSTER. 2008. Beyond the "big talk": The roles of breadth and repetition in parent-adolescent communication about sexual topics. *Pediatrics* 21 (March): e612–e618.

MARTINSON, K., AND D. NIGHTINGALE. 2008. Ten key findings from responsible fatherhood initiatives. Urban Institute, February, www .urban.org (accessed September 2, 2009).

MARTIRE, L. M., M. P. STEPHENS, AND M. M. FRANKS. 1997. Multiple roles of women caregivers: Feelings of mastery and self-esteem as predictors of psychosocial well-being. *Journal of Women & Aging* 9 (1/2): 117–31.

MARVASTI, A., AND K. D. MC KINNEY. 2004. *Middle Eastern lives in America.* New York: Rowman & Littlefield.

MARZOLLO, J. 1993. *Fathers & babies: How babies grow and what they need from you from birth to 18 months.* New York: HarperCollins.

MARVASTI, A., AND K. D. MCKINNEY. 2004. *Middle Eastern lives in America.* Lanham, MD: Rowman & Littlefield.

MASCI, D. 2008a. Two perspectives on gay marriage. The Pew Forum on Religion & Public Life, April 24, http://pewforum.org (accessed June 13, 2009).

MASCI, D. 2008b. A stable majority: Most Americans still oppose same-sex marriage. Pew Forum on Religion and Public Life, April 1, http://pewforum.org (accessed June 13, 2009).

MASTERS, N. T., B. A. BEADNELL, D. M. MORRISON, M. J. HOPPE, AND M. R. GILLMORE. 2008. The opposite of sex? Adolescents' thoughts about abstinence and sex, and their sexual behavior. *Perspectives on Sexual and Reproductive Health* 40 (June): 87–93.

MASTERS, W. H., V. E. JOHNSON, AND R. C. KOLODNY. 1992. *Human sexuality*, 4th ed. New York: HarperCollins.

MATHER, M. 2007. Education and occupation separates two kinds of immigrants in the United States. Population Reference Bureau, September 12, www.prb.org (accessed October 10, 2007).

MATHER, M. 2008. High poverty rates in "mid-size" America. Population Reference Bureau, December, www.prb.org (accessed July 31, 2009).

MATHES, V. S. 1981. A new look at the role of women in Indian society. In *The American Indian: Past and present*, 2nd ed., ed. R. L. Nichols, 27–33. New York: Wiley.

MATHIAS, B. 1992. Yes, Va. (Md. & D.C.), there are happy marriages. *Washington Post*, September 22, B5.

MATTA, D. S., AND C. KNUDSON -MARTIN. 2006. Father responsivity: Couple processes and the coconstruction of fatherhood. *Family Process* 45 (March): 19–37.

MATTES, J. 1994. *Single mothers by choice*. New York: Times Books.

MATTHAEI, J. A. 1982. *An economic history of women in America: Women's work, the sexual division of labor, and the development of capitalism*. New York: Schocken.

MATTHEWS, S. H., AND T. T. ROSNER. 1988. Shared filial responsibility: The family as the primary caregiver. *Journal of Marriage and the Family* 50 (February): 185–95.

MATTHEWS, T. J., AND M. F. MACDORMAN. 2007. Infant mortality statistics from the 2004 period linked birth/infant death data set. *National Vital Statistics Reports* 55 (May 2): 1–32.

MATTHEWS, T. J., AND M. F. MACDORMAN. 2008. Infant mortality statistics from the 2005 period linked birth/infant death data set. *National Vital Statistics Reports* 55 (July 30): 109–11.

MAUME, DAVID J. 2006. Gender differences in restricting work efforts because of family responsibilities. *Journal of Marriage and Family* 68 (November): 859–69.

MAUSHART, S. 2002. *Wifework: What marriage really means for women*. New York: Bloomsbury.

MAY, E. T. 1995. *Barren in the promised land: Childless Americans and the pursuit of happiness*. New York: Basic Books.

MAY, P. A. 1999. The epidemiology of alcohol abuse among American Indians: The mythical and real properties. In *Contemporary Native American cultural issues*, ed. D. Champagne, 227–44. Walnut Creek, CA: AltaMira.

MAYNARD, R. A., ED. 1997. *Kids having kids: Economic costs and social consequences of teen pregnancy*. Washington, DC: Urban Institute.

MAYO, Y. 1997. Machismo, fatherhood, and the Latino family: Understanding the concept. *Journal of Multicultural Social Work* 5 (1/2): 49–61.

Mayo Clinic Staff. 2007. Male menopause: Myth or reality? May 26, www.mayoclinic.com (accessed May 19, 2009).

MAYS, V. M., L. M. CHATTERS, AND S. D. COCHRAN. 1998. African American families in diversity: Gay men and lesbians in family networks. *Journal of Comparative Family Studies* 29 (Spring): 73–88.

MAZARIO, S., AND D. SMITH. 2008. Inspectors find dirt on books at Southern Calif. Carwashes. *Los Angeles Times*, March 23, www.latimes.com (accessed March 24, 2008).

MCADOO, H. P. 2002. African American parenting. In *Handbook of parenting*, 2nd ed., Vol. 4: Social conditions and applied parenting, ed. M. H. Bornstein, 47–58. Mahwah, NJ: Erlbaum.

MCADOO, H. P. 2007. African American demographic images. In *Black families*, 4th ed., ed. H. P. McAdoo, 157–71. Thousand Oaks, CA: Sage.

MCADOO, J. L. 1986. Black fathers' relationships with their preschool children and the children's development of ethnic identity. In *Men in families*, eds. R. A. Lewis and R. E. Salt, 159–68. Thousand Oaks, CA: Sage.

MCBRIDE, B. A., G. L. BROWN, K. K. BOST, N. SHIN, B. VAUGHN, AND B. KORTH. 2005. Paternal identity, maternal gatekeeping, and father involvement. *Family Relations* 54 (July): 360–72.

MCCARROLL, C. 2002. Coed sleepovers: Platonic or premature? *Christian Science Monitor*, December 4, 1, 4.

MCCARTHY, B., AND T. CASEY. 2008. Love, sex, and crime: Adolescent romantic relationships and offending. *American Sociological Review* 73 (December): 944–69.

MCCURLEY, C., AND H. N. SNYDER. 2008. Co-occurrence of substance use behaviors in youth. U.S. Department of Justice, Office of Justice programs, November, www.ojp.usdoj.gov/ojjdp (accessed July 30, 2009).

MCDANIEL, D. H. 2006. Anti-aging: dreams fulfilled . . . or empty promises? *Cosmetic Surgery Times* 9 (July): 4.

MCDERMOTT, T. 2007. Scientists can't get their minds around Alzheimer's. *Los Angeles Times*, December 27, www.latimes.com (accessed December 28, 2007).

MCDONALD, R., E. N. JOURILES, S. RAMISETTY-MIKLER, R. CAETANO, and C. E. GREEN. 2006. Estimating the number of American children living in partner-violent families. *Journal of Family Psychology* 20 (March): 137–42.

MCELHANEY, K. B., J. ANTONISHAK, AND J. P. ALLEN. 2008. "They like me, they like me not": Popularity and adolescents' perceptions of acceptance predicting social functioning over time. *Child Development* 79 (May/June): 720–31.

MCELVAINE, R. S. 1993. *The great depression: America, 1929–1941*. New York: Times Books.

MCFADYEN, J. M., J. L. KERPELMAN, AND F. ADLER-BAEDER. 2005. Examining the impact of workplace supports: Work-family fit and satisfaction in the U.S. military. *Family Relations* 54 (January): 131–44.

MCFARLANE, J., AND A. MALECHA. 2005. Sexual assault among intimates: Frequency, consequences, and trauma. Unpublished report, U.S. Department of Justice, Document No. 211678.

MCFARLANE, M., S. S. BULL, AND C. A. RIETMEIJER. 2000. The Internet as a newly emerging risk environment for sexually transmitted diseases. *Journal of the American Medical Association* 284 (July 26): 443–46.

MCGINNIS, T. 1981. *More than just a friend: The joys and disappointments of extramarital affairs*. Upper Saddle River, NJ: Prentice Hall.

MCGOLDRICK, M., M. HEIMAN, AND B. CARTER. 1993. The changing family life cycle: A perspective on normalcy. In *Normal family processes*, 2nd ed., ed. F. Walsh, 405–43. New York: Guilford.

MCGONAGLE, K. A., R. C. KESSLER, AND I. H. GOTLIB. 1993. The effects of marital disagreement style, frequency, and outcome on marital disruption. *Journal of Social and Personal Relationships*, 10 (August): 385–404.

MCGRATH, E. 2002. The power of love. *Psychology Today*, December 1, www.psychologytoday.com (accessed April 27, 2009).

MCGUINESS, T., AND L. PALLANSCH. 2000. Competence of children adopted from the former Soviet Union. *Family Relations* 49 (October): 457–64.

MCGUIRE, M. 1996. Growing up with two moms. *Newsweek*, November 4, 53.

MCINTOSH, P. 1995. White privilege and male privilege: A personal account of coming to see correspondences through work in women's studies. In *Race, class, and gender: An anthology*, 2nd ed., eds. M. L. Andersen and P. H. Collins, 76–87. Belmont, CA: Wadsworth.

MCKINLEY, J. 2007. Lawmaker ends effort to make spanking a crime. *Baltimore Sun*, February 23, A15.

MCLOYD, V. C. 1990. The impact of economic hardship on black families and children: Psychological distress, parenting, and socioemotional development. *Child Development* 61 (April): 311–46.

MCLOYD, V. C., A. M. CAUCE, D. TAKEUCHI, AND L. WILSON. 2001. Marital processes and parental socialization in families of color: A decade review of research. In *Understanding families into the new millennium: A decade in review*, ed. R. M. Milardo, 289–312. Minneapolis: National Council on Family Relations.

MCMANUS, M. J. 2008. *How to cut America's divorce rate in half*. Potomac, MD: Marriage Savers, Inc.

MCMENAMIN, T. M. 2007. A time to work: Recent trends in shift work and flexible schedules. *Monthly Labor Review* 130 (December): 3–14.

MCNEELEY, C., AND R. CROSNOE. 2008. Social status, peer influence, and weight gain in adolescence. *Archives of Pediatrics & Adolescent Medicine* 162 (January): 91–92.

MCNEELY, C., ET AL. 2002. Mothers' influence on the timing of first sex among 14- and 15-year olds. *Journal of Adolescent Health* 31 (September): 256–65.

MCNEILL, D. 2008. Tolerance in Thailand. *Chronicle of Higher Education*, November 28, A6.

MCPHARLIN, P. 1946. *Love and courtship in America*. New York: Hastings House.

MCPHERSON, M., L. SMITH-LOVIN, AND M. BRASHEARS. 2008. The ties that bind are fraying. *Contexts* 7 (Summer): 32–36.

MCQUILLAN, J. A. L. GREI L, L. WHITE, and M. CASEY JACOB. 2003. Frustrated fertility: Infertility and psychological distress among women. *Journal of Marriage and Family* 65 (November): 1007–18.

MCRAE, S. 1999. Cohabitation or marriage? Cohabitation. In *The sociology of the family*, ed. G. Allan, 172–90. Malden, MA: Blackwell.

MEAD, G. H. 1934. *Mind, self, and society*. Chicago: University of Chicago Press.

MEAD, G. H. 1938. *The philosophy of the act*. Chicago: University of Chicago Press.

MEAD, G. H. 1964. *On social psychology*. Chicago: University of Chicago Press.

MEAD, L. M. 2008. Comment on "Helping poor working parents get ahead." Urban Institute, July 17, www.urban.org (accessed August 25, 2008).

MEAD, M. 1935. *Sex and temperament in three primitive societies*. New York: Morrow.

MEAD, S. 2006. The truth about boys and girls: The evidence suggests otherwise. Education Sector, June, www.educationsector.org (accessed August 8, 2006).

Medical memo: Marital stress and the heart. 2004. *Harvard Men's Health Watch* (May): 7.

MEHL, M. R., S. VAZIRE, N. RAMÍREZ-ESPARZA, R. B. SLATCHER, AND J. W. PENNEBAKER. 2007. Are women really more talkative than men? *Science* 317 (July): 82.

MELLO, M. M., B. R. CLARRIDGE, AND D. M. STUDDERT. 2005. Academic medical centers' standards for clinical-trial agreements with industry. *New England Journal of Medicine* 352 (May 26): 2202–10.

MELLOTT, L. M., Z. QIAN, AND D. T. LICHTER. 2005. Like mother, like daughter? The international transmission of union formation patterns. Paper presented at the annual meeting of the American Sociological Association, Philadelphia, August.

MELOSH, B. 2002. *Strangers and kin: The American way of adoption*. Cambridge, MA: Harvard University Press.

MELZER, S. A. 2002. Gender, work, and intimate violence: Men's occupational violence spillover and compensatory violence. *Journal of Marriage and Family* 64 (November): 820–32.

MENARD, S. 2002. *Short- and long-term consequences of adolescent victimization*. Washington, DC: U.S. Department of Justice.

MENCIMER, S. 2008. 10 ways to satisfy your president. *Mother Jones*, September-October, 62–65, 106.

MENDES, E., AND B. PELHAM. 2009. In U.S., worry about making monthly payments adding up. Gallup News Service, February 4, www.gallup.com (accessed July 27, 2009).

MENNING, C., M. HOLTZMAN, AND C. KAPINUS. 2007. Stepfather involvement and adolescents' disposition toward having sex. *Perspectives on Sexual and Reproductive Health* 39 (June): 82–89.

MERGENBAGEN, P. 1996. The reunion market. *American Demographics* 18 (April): 30–34, 52.

MERIDA, K. 2008. Racist incidents give some Obama campaigners pause. *Washington Post*, May 13, A1.

MERMIN, G. B. T., R. W. JOHNSON, AND E. J. TODER. 2008b. Will employers want aging boomers? The Urban Institute, July, www.urban.org (accessed September 25, 2009).

MERMIN, G. B. T., S. R. ZEDLEWSKI, AND D. J. TOOHEY. 2008a. Diversity in retirement wealth accumulation. The Urban Institute, December, www.urban.org (accessed September 25, 2009).

MERTEN, D. E. 1996. Going-with: The role of a social form in early romance. *Journal of Contemporary Ethnography* 24 (January): 462–84.

MESTON, C. M., AND D. M. BUSS. 2007. Why humans have sex. *Archives of Sexual Behavior* 36 (August): 477–507.

METEYER, K. B., AND M. PERRY-JENKINS. 2009. Dyadic parenting and children's externalizing symptoms. *Family Relations* 58 (July): 289–302.

MetLife Mature Market Institute. 2006. The MetLife caregiving cost study: Productivity losses to U.S. business. July, www.caregiving.org (accessed August 4, 2006).

METTS, S. 1994. Relational transgressions. In *The dark side of interpersonal communication*, eds. W. R. Cupach and B. H. Spitzberg, 217–39 Hillsdale, NJ: Erlbaum.

MEYER, C. L., AND M. OBERMAN. 2001. *Mothers who kill their children: Understanding the acts of moms from Susan Smith to the "prom mom."* New York: New York University Press.

MIALL, C. 1986. The stigma of involuntary childlessness. *Social Problems* 33 (April): 268–82.

MICHAEL, R. T., AND C. BICKERT. 2001. Exploring determinants of adolescents' early sexual behavior. In *Social awakening: Adolescent behavior as adulthood approaches*, ed. R. T. Michael, 137–73. New York: Russell Sage Foundation.

MICHELS, S. 2008. All in the family: Where does incest begin? ABC News, May 7, abcnews.go.com (accessed May 8, 2008).

MIDDLEMISS, W., AND W. MC GUIGAN. 2001. Ethnicity and adolescent mothers' benefit from participation in home-visitation services. *Family Relations* 54 (April): 212–24.

MIELL, D., AND R. CROGHAN. 1996. Examining the wider context of social relationships. In *Social interaction and personal relationships*, eds. D. Miell and R. Dallos, 267–318. Thousand Oaks, CA: Sage.

MILBOURN, T. 2006. Taking refuge. January 2, www.sacbee.com (accessed January 4, 2006).

MILKIE, M. A., M. J. MATTINGLY, K. M. NOMAGUCHI, S. M. BIANCHI, AND J. P. ROBINSON. 2004. The time squeeze: Parental statuses and feelings about time with children. *Journal of Marriage and Family* 66 (August): 739–61.

MILKMAN, R. 1976. Women's work and the economic crisis: Some lessons from the Great Depression. *Review of Radical Political Economics* 8 (Spring): 73–97.

MILLER, B. 1995. Household futures. *American Demographics* 17 (March): 4, 6.

MILLER, B. C. 1986. *Family research methods.* Beverly Hills, CA: Sage.

MILLER, M., S. J. LIPPMANN, D. AZRAEL, AND D. HEMENWAY. 2007. Household firearm ownership and rates of suicide across the 50 United States. *Journal of Trauma: Injury, Infection, and Critical Care* 62 (April): 1029–35.

MILLER, W. L., AND B. F. CRABTREE. 1994. Clinical research. In *Handbook of qualitative research*, eds. N. K. Denzin and Y. S. Lincoln, 340–52. Thousand Oaks, CA: Sage.

MILLNER, D., AND N. CHILES. 1999. *What brothers think, what sistahs know: The real deal on love and relationships.* New York: Morrow.

MIN, P. G. 2002. Korean American families. In *Minority families in the United States: A multicultural perspective*, 3rd ed., ed. R. L. Taylor, 193–211. Upper Saddle River, NJ: Prentice Hall.

MINTZ, S., AND S. KELLOGG. 1988. *Domestic revolution: A social history of American family life.* New York: Free Press.

MIRANDA, C. A. 2004. Fifteen candles. *Time*, July 19, 6.

MIRANDE, A. 1985. *The Chicano experience: An alternative perspective.* Notre Dame, IN: University of Notre Dame Press.

MIROWSKY, J. 2005. Age at first birth, health, and mortality. *Journal of Health and Social Behavior* 46 (March): 32–50.

MIROWSKY, J., AND C. E. ROSS. 2007. Creative work and health. *Journal of Health and Social Behavior* 48 (December): 385–403.

MISHEL, L., J. BERNSTEIN, AND H. SHIERHOLZ. 2009. *The state of working America 2008/2009.* Ithaca, NY: Cornell University Press.

MISRA, D., ED. 2001. *Women's health data book: A profile of women's health in the United States*, 3rd ed. Washington, DC: Jacobs Institute of Women's Health and The Henry J. Kaiser Family Foundation.

MITCHELL, B. A., AND E. M. GEE. 1996. "Boomerang kids" and midlife parental marital satisfaction. *Family Relations* 45 (October): 442–48.

MITCHELL, A. A. 2002. Infertility treatment: More risks and challenges. *New England Journal of Medicine* 346 (March 7): 769–70.

MOCK, M. S. 2005. Confined by the stained-glass window. *Chronicle of Higher Education*, November 4, B24.

MODO, I. V. OGO. 2005. Nigerian families. In *Handbook of world families*, eds. B. N. Adams and J. Trost, 25–46. Thousand Oaks, CA: Sage.

MODO, V. O. 2005. Nigerian families. In *Handbook of world families*, eds. B. N. Adams and J. Trost, 25–46. Thousand Oaks, CA: Sage.

MOEN, P. 1992. *Women's two roles: A contemporary dilemma.* Westport, CT: Auburn House.

MOHR, J. 1981. The great upsurge of abortion, 1840–1880. In *Family life in America: 1620–2000*, eds. M. Albin and D. Cavallo, 119–30. St. James, NY: Revisionary Press.

MONASTERSKY, R. 2007. Who's minding the teenage brain? *Chronicle of Higher Education*, January 12, A14–A17.

MONEY, J., AND A. A. EHRHARDT. 1972. *Man & woman, boy & girl.* Baltimore: Johns Hopkins University Press.

MONSERUD, M. A. 2008. Intergenerational relationships and affectual solidarity between grandparents and young adults. *Journal of Marriage and Family* 70 (February): 182–95.

MONTENEGRO, X. P. 2004. *Divorce experience: A study of divorce at midlife and beyond.* Washington, DC: AARP.

MONTGOMERY, M. J., AND G. T. SORELL. 1997. Differences in love attitudes across family life stages. *Family Relations* 46 (January): 55–61.

MONTLAKE, S. 2006. A town of foreign marriages. *Christian Science Monitor*, July 20: 20.

MOORE, D. M. 2005. Lobster and love? Think again. Gallup poll, February 1, http://poll.gallup.com (accessed March 1, 2005).

MOORE, F. R., C. CASSIDY, M. HANE L. SMITH, AND D. I. PERRETT. 2006. The effects of female control of resources on sex-differentiated mate preferences. *Evolution and Human Behavior* 27 (May): 193–205.

MOORE, J., AND H. PACHON. 1985. *Hispanics in the United States.* Upper Saddle River, NJ: Prentice Hall.

MOORE, K. A., Z. REDD, M. BURKHAUSER, K. MBWANA, AND A. COLLINS. 2009. Children in poverty: Trends, consequences, and policy options. Child Trends Research Brief, April, www.childrends.org (accessed August 9, 2009).

MOORE, K. A., ET AL. 2006. Depression among moms: Prevalence, predictors, and acting out among third grade children. Child Trends Research Brief, March, www.childtrends.org (accessed September 22, 2006).

MOORE, M. R., AND P. L. CHASE-LANSDALE. 2001. Sexual intercourse and pregnancy among African American girls in high-poverty neighborhoods: The role of family and perceived community environment. *Journal of Marriage and Family* 63 (November): 1146–57.

MOORE, R. L. 1998. Love and limerence with Chinese characteristics: Student romance in the PRC. In *Romantic love and sexual behavior: Perspectives from the social sciences*, ed. V. C. deMunck. 251–88. Westport, CT: Praeger.

MORALES, E. 1996. Gender roles among Latino gay and bisexual men: Implications for family and couple relationships. In *Lesbians and gays in couples and families: A handbook for therapists*, eds. J. Laird and R.-J. Green, 272–97. San Francisco: Jossey-Bass.

MORALES, L. 2009. Nearly half of Americans are frequent Internet users. Gallup News Service, January 2, www.gallup.com (accessed February 24, 2009).

MORENO, M. A., A. VANDERSTOEP, M. R. PARKS, F. J. ZIMMERMAN, A. KURTH, AND D. A. CHRISTAKIS. 2009. Reducing at-risk adolescents' display of risk behavior on a social networking Web site. *Archives of Pediatrics & Adolescent Medicine* 163 (January): 35–41.

MORGAN, D. I., ED. 1993. *Successful focus groups: Advancing the state of the art.* Thousand Oaks, CA: Sage.

MORGAN, P. D. 1998. *Slave counterpoint: Black culture in the eighteenth-century Chesapeake & lowcountry.* Chapel Hill: University of North Carolina Press.

MORGAN, W. L. 1939. *The family meets the depression: A study of a group of highly selected families.* Westport, CT: Greenwood.

MORIN, R. 1994. How to lie with statistics: Adultery. *Washington Post*, March 6, C5.

MORIN, R. 2009. Most middle-aged adults are rethinking retirement plans. Pew Research Center, May 28, http://pewsocialtrends.org (accessed September 16, 2009).

MORIN, R., AND D. COHN. 2008. Women call the shots at home; public mixed on gender roles in jobs. Pew Research Center, September 28, www.pewresearch.org (accessed November 20, 2008).

MORRIS, M. 2003. Love in a hurry. *Baltimore Sun*, January 12, 1N, 4N.

MORR SEREWICZ, M. C. 2008. Toward a triangular theory of the communication and relationships of in-laws: Theoretical proposal and social relations analysis of relational satisfaction and private disclosure in in-law triads. *Journal of Family Communication* 8 (October): 264–92.

MOSHER, W. D., and W. F. PRATT. 1991. Fecundity and infertility in the United States: Incidence and trends. *Fertility and Sterility* 56 (August): 192–93.

MOSHER, W. D., A. CHANDRA, AND J. JONES. 2005. Sexual behavior and selected health measures: Men and women 15–44 years of age, United States, 2002. National Center for Health Statistics, *Vital and Health Statistics,* September 15, www.cdc.gov (accessed January 10, 2006).

MOSS, P., AND K. WALL, EDS. 2007. International review of leave policies and related research 2007. Department for Business Enterprise & Regulatory Reform, Employment Relations Research Series No. 80, July, www.berr.gov.uk (accessed August 9, 2009).

Mother, 4 kids fatally beaten, autopsy finds. 2008. *Baltimore Sun,* March 27, 4A.

MOWRER, E. R. 1972. War and family solidarity and stability. In *The American family in World War II,* ed. R. A. Abrams, 100–106. New York: Arno and New York Times.

MOYNIHAN, D. P., ED. 1970. *Toward a national urban policy.* New York: Basic Books.

MUELLER, M. M., AND G. H. ELDER, JR. 2003. Family contingencies across the generations: Grandparent–grandchild relationships in holistic perspective. *Journal of Marriage and Family* 65 (May): 404–17.

MUELLER, T. E., L. E. GAVIN, AND A. KULKARNI. 2008. The association between sex education and youth's engagement in sexual intercourse, age at first intercourse, and birth control use at first sex. *Journal of Adolescent Health* 42 (January): 89–96.

MULAC, A. 1998. The gender-linked language effect: Do language differences really make a difference? In *Sex differences and similarities in communication: Critical essays and empirical investigations of sex and gender in interaction,* eds. D. J. Canary and K. Dindia, 127–53. Mahwah, NJ: Lawrence Erlbaum Associates.

MULLEN, N. 2009. Problem of female genital mutilation growing in the EU. *Irish Medical Times,* April 3, www.imt.ie (accessed May 7, 2009).

MULSOW, M., Y. M. CALDERA, M. PURSLEY, A. REIFMAN, AND A. C. HUSTON. 2002. Multilevel factors influencing maternal stress during the first three years. *Journal of Marriage and Family* 64 (November): 944–56.

MUMME, D. L., AND A. FERNAND. 2003. The infant as onlooker: Learning from emotional reactions observed in a television scenario. *Child Development* 74 (January/February): 221–37.

MUNCY, R. L. 1988. Sex and marriage in utopia. *Society* 25 (January/February): 46–48.

MUNDELL, E. J. 2002. Bye, bye love: How men, women dish out rejection. ABC News, February 5. http://abcnews.go.com (accessed February 6, 2002).

MUNDELL, E. J. 2003. No sex until marriage? Don't bet on it, study finds. Reuters Health, June 23. www.reutershealth.com (accessed August 3, 2003).

MUNK-OLSEN, T., T. M. LAURSEN, C. B. PEDERSON, O. MORS, AND P. B. MORTENSEN. 2006. New parents and mental disorders: A population-based register study. *JAMA* 296 (December 6): 2582–89.

MUNNELL, A. H., AND M. SOTO. 2005. How much pre-retirement income does Social Security replace? Center for Retirement Research,

Boston College, November, no. 36, www.bc.edu/images/stories (accessed September 21, 2009).

MUNSON, L. 2009. Colleges still have money enough to share. *Chronicle of Higher Education* 55 (March 13): A36.

MUNTER, C. 1984. Fat and the fantasy of perfection. In *Pleasure and danger: Exploring female sexuality,* ed. C. Vance, 225–31. Boston: Routledge & Kegan Paul.

MURPHY, E., AND E. J. GRAFF. 2005. *Getting even: Why women don't get paid like men—and what to do about it.* New York: Simon & Schuster.

MURRAY, C. I. 2000. Coping with death, dying, and grief in families. In *Families & change: Coping with stressful events and transitions,* 2nd ed., eds. P. C. McKenry and S. J. Price, 120–53. Thousand Oaks, CA: Sage.

MURRAY, J. E. 2000. Marital protection and marital selection: Evidence from a historical-prospective sample of American men. *Demography* 37 (November): 511–21.

MURSTEIN, B. I. 1974. *Love, sex, and marriage through the ages.* New York: Springer.

MUSGROVE, M. 2009. Challenging assumptions about online predators. *New York Times,* January 25, www.nytimes.com (accessed January 26, 2009).

MYERS, J. P. 2007. *Dominant-minority relations in America: Convergence in the new world,* 2nd ed. Boston, MA: Allyn and Bacon.

MYERS, S. M., AND A. BOOTH. 1999. Marital strains and marital quality: The role of high and low locus of control. *Journal of Marriage and the Family* 61 (May): 423–36.

N

NAGOURNEY, E. 2005. Nicotine changes sperm, and not for the better. *New York Times,* October 25, D6.

NAIMI, T. S., ET AL. 2008. Alcohol-attributable deaths and years of potential life lost among American Indians and Alaska Natives—United States, 2001–2005. *MMWR Weekly* 57 (August 29): 938–41.

NAJIB, A., J. P. LORBERBAUM, S. KOSE, D. E. BOHNING, AND M. S. GEORGE. 2004. Regional brain activity in women grieving a romantic relationship breakup. *American Journal of Psychiatry* 161 (December): 2245–56.

NAKONEZNY, P. A., R. D. SHULL, AND J. L. RODGERS. 1995. The effect of no-fault divorce law on the divorce rate across the 50 states and its relation to income, education, and religiosity. *Journal of Marriage and the Family,* 57 (May): 477–88.

NANCE-NASH, S. 2005. African American women gaining in biz starts. Women's e-news, February 18, www.womensenews.org (accessed February 20, 2005).

NASS, G. D., R. W. LIBBY, AND M. P. FISHER. 1981. *Sexual choices: An introduction to human sexuality.* Belmont, CA: Wadsworth.

NATHAN, R. 2005. *My freshman year: What a professor learned by becoming a student.* Ithaca, NY: Cornell University Press.

NATIONAL ABORTION FEDERATION. 2006. Crisis pregnancy centers: An affront to choice. Washington, DC, www.prochoice.org (accessed September 19, 2006).

NATIONAL ADOPTION INFORMATION CLEARINGHOUSE. 2002. Pros and cons of each type of adoption for the involved parties. U.S. Department of Health & Human Services. www.calib.com (accessed August 17, 2003).

NATIONAL ADOPTION INFORMATION CLEARINGHOUSE. 2006. Openness in adoption: A bulletin for professionals. U.S. Department of Health and Human Services, http://naic.acf.hhs.gov (accessed April 27, 2006).

NATIONAL ALLIANCE FOR CAREGIVING AND AARP. 2004. Caregiving in the U.S. April, www.caregiving.org (accessed August 4, 2006).

National Cancer Institute. 2004. NCI cancer bulletin 1 (November 16): 1–8.

National Center for Health Statistics. 1997. Vital statistics of the United States, 1993. www.cdc.gov (accessed September 21, 2009).

National Center for Health Statistics. 2009. *Health, United States, 2008, with special feature on the health of young adults.* Washington, DC: U.S. Government Printing Office.

National Center for Health Statistics. 2009. National marriage and divorce rate trends. June 2, www.cdc.gov (accessed August 28, 2009).

National Center on Addiction and Substance Abuse. 2008. National survey of American attitudes on substance abuse XIII: Teens and parents. August, www.casacolumbia.org (accessed July 13, 2009).

NATIONAL CENTER ON ELDER ABUSE. 2005. *Fact sheet: Elder abuse prevalence and incidence.* Washington, DC: National Center on Elder Abuse.

National Coalition for the Homeless. 2008a. How many people experience homelessness? NCH Fact Sheet #2, June, www.nationalhomeless.org (accessed August 9, 2009).

National Coalition for the Homeless. 2008b. Why are people homeless? NCH Fact Sheet #1, June, www.nationalhomeless.org (accessed August 9, 2009).

National Conference of State Legislatures. 2009. Common law marriage. www.ncsl.org (accessed February 18, 2009).

National Healthy Marriage Resource Center. 2009. Young people want "happily ever after," but lack skills to make marriage work. February 19, www.twoofus.org (accessed March 5, 2009).

National Institutes of Health. 2009. Suicide in the U.S.: Statistics and prevention. National Institute of Mental Health, www.nimh.nih.org (accessed September 25, 2009).

NATIONAL MENTAL HEALTH ASSOCIATION. 2006. Eating disorders. www.nmha.org (accessed June 26, 2006).

NATIONAL RESEARCH COUNCIL. 1998. *Violence in families: Assessing prevention and treatment programs.* Washington, DC: National Academy Press.

NAUCK, B., AND D. KLAUS. 2005. Families in Turkey. In *Handbook of world families,* eds. B. N. Adams AND J. TROST, 364–388. Thousand Oaks, CA: Sage.

NAURATH, N. 2007. Perceived acceptance of homosexuals differs around the globe. Gallup, November 1, www.gallup.com (accessed May 21, 2009).

NEAL, M. B., AND L. B. HAMMER. 2007. *Working couples caring for children and aging parents.* Mahwah, NJ: Lawrence Erlbaum.

NELSON, G. 1994. Emotional well-being of separated and married women: Long-term follow-up study. *American Journal of Orthopsychiatry* 64 (January): 150–60.

NEUGARTEN, B. L., AND K. K. WEINSTEIN. 1964. The changing American grandparents. *Journal of Marriage and the Family* 26 (May): 199–204.

NEUMAN, R. J., E. LOBOS, W. REICH, C. A. HENDERSON, L-W. SUN, AND R. D. TODD. 2007. Prenatal smoking exposure and dopaminergic genotypes interact to cause a severe ADHD subtype. *Biological Psychiatry* 61 (June): 1320–28.

NEWCOMB, A. 2008. In Japan, retired men find new role as caregivers. *Christian Science Monitor,* October 21, 1, 12.

NEWPORT, F. 2001. Americans see women as emotional and affectionate, men as more aggressive. *Gallup Poll Monthly* 425 (February 2001): 34–38.

NEWPORT, F. 2007. Americans continue to express slight preference for boys. Gallup News Service, July 5, www.gallup.com (accessed April 12, 2009).

NEWPORT, F. 2008. Gauging the public's reaction to Edwards' extramarital affair. Gallup Poll, August 12, www.gallup.com (accessed August 18, 2008).

NEWPORT, F. 2008. Wives still do laundry, men do yard work. Gallup News Service, April 4, www.gallup.com (accessed June 2, 2008).

NEWPORT, F. 2009. Views on government aid depend on the program. Gallup News Service, February 24, www.gallup.com (accessed August 9, 2009).

Newspaper content: What makes readers more satisfied. 2001. Readership Institute: Media Management Center at Northwestern University. www.readership.org (accessed May 23, 2003).

NG, F. 1998. *The Taiwanese Americans.* Westport, CT: Greenwood.

NICHD EARLY CHILD CARE RESEARCH NETWORK. 2003. Does amount of time in child care predict socioemotional adjustment? *Child Development* 74 (July/August): 976–1005.

NICHD. 2006. The NICHD study of early child care and youth development: Findings for children up to age 4 1/2 years. National Institute of Child Health and Human Development, January, www.nichd.nih.gov (accessed June 20, 2009).

NICHOLS, A. 2006. Understanding recent changes in child poverty. Urban Institute, August 25, www.urban.org (accessed February 15, 2007).

NICOLOSI, A., ET AL. 1994. The efficiency of male-to-female and female-to-male sexual transmission of the human immunodeficiency virus: A study of 730 stable couples. *Epidemiology* 5 (November): 570–75.

NIE, N. H., AND L. ERBRING. 2000. Internet and society: A preliminary report. www .stanford.edu.

NISSINEN, S. 2000. *The conscious bride: Women unveil their true feelings about getting hitched.* Oakland, CA: New Harbinger.

NOCK, S. L. 1998. *Marriage in men's lives.* New York: Oxford University Press.

NOGUCHI, Y. 2005. Life and romance in 160 characters or less. *Washington Post* (December 29): A1.

NOLAND, V. J., K. D. LILLER, R. J. MC DERMOTT, M. L. COULTER, AND A. E. SERAPHINE. 2004. Is adolescent sibling violence a precursor to college dating violence? *American Journal of Health Behavior* 28 (April): S13–S23.

NOMAGUCHI, K. M. 2006. Maternal employment, nonparental care, mother-child interactions, and child outcomes during preschool years. *Journal of Marriage and Family* 68 (December): 1341–69.

NOLLER, P. 1984. *Nonverbal communication and marital interaction.* New York: Pergamon.

NOLLER, P., AND M. A. FITZPATRICK. 1993. *Communication in family relationships.* Upper Saddle River, NJ: Prentice Hall.

No passports for scofflaws. 2007. *Baltimore Sun*, August 15, 2A.

NORTHRUP, C. 2001. *The wisdom of menopause: Creating physical and emotional health and healing during the change.* New York: Bantam.

NOWINSKI, J. 1993. *Hungry hearts: On men, intimacy, self-esteem, and addiction.* New York: Lexington.

NURIUS, P. S., J. NORRIS, L. A. DIMEFF, AND T. L. GRAHAM. 1996. Expectations regarding acquaintance sexual aggression among sorority and fraternity members. *Sex Roles* 35 (7/8): 427–44.

NUTA, V. R. 1986. Emotional aspects of child support enforcement. *Family Relations* 35 (January): 177–82.

NYE, F. I., AND F. M. BERARDO, EDS. 1981. *Emerging conceptual frameworks in family analysis.* New York: Praeger.

O

OATES, R. K., AND R. S. KEMPE. 1997. Growth failure in infants. In *The battered child*, 5th ed., eds. M. E. Helfer, R. S. Kempe, and R. D. Krugman, 374–91. Chicago: University of Chicago Press.

OBERMAN, M., AND C. L. MEYER. 2008. *When mothers kill: Interviews from prison.* New York: New York University Press.

OCAMPO, V. W., G. A. SHELLEY, AND L. H. JAYCOX. 2007. Latino teens talk about help seeking and help giving in relation to dating violence. *Violence Against Women* 13 (February): 172–89.

ODEN, T. J. 2008. The first gentleman. *Chronicle of Higher Education*, March 21, C2–C3.

O'DONNELL, L., G. AGRONICK, R. DURAN, A. MYINT-U, AND A. STUEVE. 2009. Intimate partner violence among economically disadvantaged young adult women: Associations with adolescent risk-taking and pregnancy experiences. *Perspectives on Sexual and Reproductive Health* 41 (June): 84–91.

O'DONNELL, P., S. STEVENSON, V. S. STEFANAKOS, AND K. PERAINO. 1999. Click and split. *Newsweek*, November 22, 8.

OFFICE OF NATIONAL DRUG CONTROL POLICY. 2006. Girls and Drugs. February 9, www .mediacampaign.org (accessed June 10, 2006).

Office of National Drug Control Policy. 2009. Club drugs facts & figures. www .whitehousedrugpolicy.gov (accessed June 7, 2009).

Office of the Deputy Chief of Staff for Intelligence. 2006. Arab cultural awareness: 58 factsheets. January, www.fas.org (accessed March 4, 2009).

OGUNWOLE, S. U. 2006. We the people: American Indians and Alaska Natives in the United States. U.S. Census Bureau, Census 2000 Special Reports, CENSR-28, www .census.gov (accessed March 26, 2007).

O'HANLON, M. E., AND J. H. CAMPBELL. 2008. Iraq index: Tracking variables of reconstruction & security in post-Saddam Iraq. Brookings Institute, November 20, www .brookings.edu (accessed December 5, 2008).

OJEDA, L., R. ROSALES, AND G. E. GOOD. 2008. Socioeconomic status and cultural predictors of male role attitudes among Mexican American men: ¿Son más machos? *Psychology of Men & Masculinity* 9 (no. 3): 133–38.

OLDENBURG, DON. 2006. Experts rip "Sesame" TV aimed at tiniest tots. *Washington Post*, March 21, C1.

Older Americans 2000: Key indicators of well-being. 2000. Federal Interagency Forum on Aging-Related Statistics. www.agingstats .gov (accessed October 28, 2000).

OLECK, J. 2000. The kids are all right. *Business Week*, February 14, 74, 78.

OLEN, H., AND K. BLAKELEY. 2009. My turn, your turn. *Forbes Woman*, April 22, 55–57.

OLFSON, M., C. BLANCO, L. LIU, C. MORENO, AND G. LAJE. 2006. *Archives of General Psychiatry* 63 (June): 679–85.

OLIVER, M. L., AND T. M. SHAPIRO. 2001. Wealth and racial stratification. In *America becoming: Racial trends and their consequences*, Vol. 2, eds. N. J. Smelser, W. J. Wilson, and F. Mitchell, 222–51. Washington, DC: National Academy Press.

OLSHANSKY, S. J., L. HAYFLICK, AND T. T. PERLS. 2004a. Anti-aging medicine: the hype and the reality—part I. *Journal of Gerontology: Biological Sciences* 59A (6): 513–14.

OLSHANSKY, S. J., L. HAYFLICK, AND T. T. PERLS. 2004b. Anti-aging medicine: the hype and the reality—part II. *Journal of Gerontology: Biological Sciences* 59A (7): 649–51.

OLSHEN, E., K. H. MCVEIGH, R. A. WUNSCH-HITZIG, AND V. I. RICKERT. 2007. Dating violence, sexual assault, and suicide attempts among urban teenagers. *Archives of Pediatrics & Adolescent Medicine* 161 (June): 539–45.

OLSON, D. H., AND A. K. OLSON. 2000. *Empowering couples: Building on your strengths.* Minneapolis: Life Innovations.

OLSON, D. H., AND A. OLSON -SIGG. 2002. Overview of cohabitation research: For use with PREPARECC. Life Innovations. www .lifeinnovation.com (accessed July 15, 2003).

OLSON, I. R., AND C. MARSHUETZ. 2005. Facial attractiveness is appraised in a glance. *Emotion* 5 (December): 498–502.

O'MARA, R. 1997. Who am I? *Baltimore Sun*, June 29, 1J, 4J.

ONISHI, N. 2007. Betrothed at first sight: A Korean-Vietnamese courtship. *New York Times*, February 22, A1, A12.

ONISHI, N. 2008. Korea aims to end stigma of adoption and stop "exporting" babies. *New York Times*, October 9, 6.

OOMS, T. 2002. Strengthening couples and marriage in low-income communities. In *Revitalizing the institution of marriage for the twenty-first century*, eds. A. J. Hawkins, L. D. Wardle, and D. O. Coolidge, 79–100. Westport, CT: Praeger.

OOMS, T. 2005. The new kid on the block: What is marriage education and does it work? Center for Law and Social Policy, July, www.clasp.org (accessed April 14, 2006).

OOMS, T., S. BOUCHET, AND M. PARKE. 2004. Beyond marriage licenses: Efforts in states to strengthen marriage and two-parent families. Center for Law and Social Policy, www.clasp.org/publications/beyond_marr. pdf (accessed November 2, 2005).

ORCHARD, A. L., AND K. B. SOLBERG. 1999. Expectations of the stepmother's role. *Journal of Divorce & Remarriage* 31 (1/2): 107–23.

ONISHI, N. 2007. Betrothed at first sight: A Korean-Vietnamese courtship. *New York Times*, February 22, A1, A12.

ONISHI, N. 2008. Korea aims to end stigma of adoption and stop "exporting" babies. *New York Times*, October 9, 6.

ORDONEZ, J. 2007. Tying the financial knot. *Newsweek*, April 9, 46–48.

ORENSTEIN, P. 2000. *Flux: Women on sex, work, kids, love, and life in a half-changed world.* New York: Doubleday.

ORMAN, S. 2008. *Suze Orman's 2009 action plan.* New York: Spiegel & Grau.

ORNISH, D. 2005. Love is real medicine. *Newsweek*, October 3, 56.

OROPESA, R. S., AND N. S. LANDALE. 2004. The future of marriage and Hispanics. *Journal of Marriage and Family* 66 (November): 901–20.

ORR, A. 2009. Minimum wage still low by historic measures. Economic Policy Institute, www.epi.org (accessed August 26, 2009).

ORR, K., AND M. STOUT. 2007. Harlequin romance report 2007: The romance revolution. http://www.harlequinromancereport. com (accessed May 1, 2009).

OSBORNE, C., AND S. MCLANAHAN. 2007. Partnership instability and child well-being. *Journal of Marriage and Family* 69 (November): 1065–83.

OSBORNE, C., W. D. MANNING, AND P. J. SMOCK. 2007. Married and cohabiting parents' relationship stability: A focus on race and ethnicity. *Journal of Marriage and Family* 69 (December): 1345–66.

OSHERSON, S. 1992. *Wrestling with love: How men struggle with intimacy with women, children, parents and each other.* New York: Fawcett Columbine.

O'SULLIVAN, L. F., AND E. S. BYERS. 1993. Eroding stereotypes: College women's attempts to influence reluctant male sexual partners. *Journal of Sex Research* 30 (August): 270–82.

O'SULLIVAN, L. F., M. M. CHENG, K. M. HARRIS, AND J. BROOKS-GUNN. 2007. I wanna hold your hand: The progression of social, romantic and sexual events in adolescent relationships. *Perspectives on Sexual and Reproductive Health* 39 (November/December): 100–107.

OSWALD, R. F. 2002. Resilience within the family networks of lesbians and gay men: Intentionality and redefinition. *Journal of Marriage and Family* 64 (May): 374–83.

OUTCALT, T. 1998. *Before you say "I do:" Important questions for couples to ask before marriage.* New York: Perigee.

OVERTURF JOHNSON, J. 2005. Who's minding the kids? Child care arrangements: Winter 2002. *Current Population Reports,* P70–101. Washington, DC: U.S. Census Bureau.

OVERTURF JOHNSON, J., AND B. DOWNS. 2005. Maternity leave and employment patterns: 1961–2000. *Current Population Reports,* P70 103. Washington, DC: U.S. Census Bureau.

P

PAASCH, K. M., AND J. D. TEACHMAN. 1991. Gender of children and receipt of assistance from absent fathers. *Journal of Family Issues* 12 (December): 450–66.

PAGE, C. 2008. Another alpha male caught behaving badly: Why do they do it? *Baltimore Sun,* March 18, 15A.

PAGE, M. E., AND A. H. STEVENS. 2005. Understanding racial differences in the economic costs of growing up in a single-parent family. *Demography* 42 (February): 75–90.

Pakistani girl describes punitive gang-rape. 2002. *Baltimore Sun,* July 4, 13A.

PALEY, A. R. 2008. For Kurdish girls, a painful ancient ritual. *Washington Post,* December 29, A9.

PALFREY, J. 2008. Enhancing child safety and online technologies. Berkman Center for Internet & Society, Harvard University, December 31, http://cyber.law.harvard.edu (accessed March 8, 2009).

PALMER, K. 2007. Accountability: His and hers. *U.S. News & World Report,* October 8, 51–53.

PALMER, K. 2007. The new mommy track. *U.S. News & World Report.* September 3, 40–45.

PALMER, K. 2008. Not making it like mom and dad. *U.S. News & World Report,* July 7/July 14, 16.

PALMER, K. 2008. Keeping money unmarried. *U.S. News & World Report,* April 16, 58–59.

PALMORE, E. B. 1999. *Ageism: Negative and positive.* New York: Springer.

PAN, L., ET AL. 2009. Differences in prevalence of obesity among black, white, and Hispanic adults—United States, 2006–2008. *MMWR Weekly,* 58 (July 17): 740–44.

PAPERNOW, P. L. 1993. *Becoming a step family: Patterns of development in remarried families.* San Francisco: Jossey-Bass.

PAPP, L. M., E. M. CUMMINGS, AND M. C. GOEKE-MOREY. 2009. For richer, for poorer: Money as a topic of marital conflict in the home. *Family Relations* 58 (February): 91–103.

PARAMESWARAN, L. 2003. Battered wives often recant or assume blame. Women's E-News, August 2. www.womensenews.org (accessed August 4, 2003).

Parenting in the Workplace Institute. 2009. Babies in the workplace. www.babiesat work.org (accessed August 8, 2009).

Parents Television Council. 2008. What are your children watching? November, www .parents.org (accessed April 18, 2009).

PARIS, R., AND N. DUBUS. 2005. Staying connected while nurturing an infant: A challenge of new motherhood. *Family Relations* 54 (January): 72–83.

PARK, R. L. 2003. The seven warning signs of bogus science. *Chronicle of Higher Education,* January 31, B20.

PARKE, R. D. 1996. *Fatherhood.* Cambridge, MA: Harvard University Press.

PARKER, K. 2009. Coping with end-of-life decisions. Pew Research Center, August 20, www.pewresearch.org (accessed September 25, 2009).

PARKER, R., AND C. CÁCERES. 1999. Alternative sexualities and changing sexual cultures among Latin American men. *Culture, Health, & Sexuality* 1: 201–6.

PARKER, S. 1996. Full brother-sister marriage in Roman Egypt: Another look. *Cultural Anthropology* 11 (August): 362–76.

PARKER-POPE, T. 2009. What are friends for? A longer life. *New York Times,* April 21, 1.

PARKS, K. A., AND D. M. SCHEIDT. 2000. Male bar drinkers' perspective on female bar drinkers. *Sex Roles* 43 (December): 927–941.

PARMELEE, L. F. 2002. Among us always. *Public Perspective* 13 (March/April): 17–18.

PARSONS, T., AND R. F. BALES. 1955. *Family, socialization and interaction process.* Glencoe, IL: Free Press.

PARTINGTON, S. N., D. L. STEBER, K. A. BLAIR, AND R. A. CISLER. 2009. Second births to teenage mothers: Risk factors for low birth weight and preterm birth. *Perspectives on Sexual and Reproductive Health* 41 (June): 101–9.

Partnership for a Drug-Free America. 2008. Teen culture: The lingo. www.drugfree.org (accessed August 16, 2009).

Partnership for a Drug-Free America. 2009. The partnership attitude tracking study (PATS): Teens 2008 report. February 26, www.drugfree.org (accessed July 13, 2009).

PASCOE, C. J. 2007. *Dude, you're a fag: Masculinity and sexuality in high school.* Berkeley: University of California Press.

PASLEY, K., AND B. S. MOOREFIELD. 2004. Stepfamilies: Changes and challenges. In *Handbook of contemporary families: Considering the past, contemplating the future,* eds. M. Coleman and L. H. Ganong, 317–330. Thousand Oaks, CA: Sage.

PASSEL, J. S. 2008. U.S. immigration trends: A focus on agriculture & California. Paper presented at Labor Market in a Global Economy International Agricultural Trade Research Consortium, Washington, DC, January 7.

PASSEL, J. S., AND D. COHN. 2008. *Trends in unauthorized immigration: Undocumented inflow now trails legal inflow.* Washington, DC: Pew Hispanic Center.

PASSEL, J. S., AND D. COHN. 2009. A portrait of unauthorized immigrants in the United States. Pew Research Center, April 14 (accessed May 16, 2009).

PATNER, M. M. 1990. Between mothers and daughters: Pain and difficulty go with the territory. *Washington Post,* November 8, C5.

PATTERSON, C. J. 2001. Family relationships of lesbians and gay men. In *Understanding families into the new millennium: A decade in review,* ed. R. M. Milardo, 271–88. Minneapolis: National Council on Family Relations.

PATTERSON, C. J. 2002. Lesbian and gay parenthood. In *Handbook of parenting,* 2nd ed., Vol. 3: Being and becoming a parent, ed. M. H. Bornstein, 317–38. Mahwah, NJ: Erlbaum.

PATTERSON, J. M. 2002. Integrating family resilience and family stress theory. *Journal of Marriage and Family* 64 (May): 349–60.

PATTERSON, J., AND P. KIM. 1991. *The day America told the truth: What people really believe about everything that really matters.* Upper Saddle River, NJ: Prentice Hall.

PATZ, A. 2000. Will your marriage last? *Psychology Today* 33 (January/February): 58–63.

PAUL, P. 2001. Childless by choice. *American Demographics* 23 (November): 45–50.

PAUL, P. 2002. Make room for granddaddy. *American Demographics* 24 (April): 41–45.

PAUL, P. 2003. The permaparent trap. *Psychology Today* 36 (September/October): 40–53.

PAULOZZI, L., A. CROSBY, AND G. RYAN. 2007. Increases in age-group—specific injury mortality—United States, 1999–2004. *MMWR Weekly,* 56 (December 14): 1281–84.

PAYNE, B. K. 2000. *Crime and elder abuse: An integrated perspective.* Springfield, IL: Charles C. Thomas.

PAYNE, J. W. 2008. The black woman's burden: An epidemic of HIV. *U.S. News & World Report,* October 13, 64.

PEAR, R. 2008. Women buying health policies pay a penalty. *New York Times,* October 30, 23.

PEARCE, D. 1978. The feminization of poverty: Women, work, and welfare. *Urban and Social Change Review* 11: 28–36.

PEARSON, J. C. 1985. *Gender and communication.* Dubuque, IA: Wm. C. Brown.

PEAVY, L., AND U. SMITH. 1994. *Women in waiting in the westward movement: Life on the home frontier.* Norman: University of Oklahoma Press.

PEELE, S., WITH A. BRODSKY. 1976. *Love and addiction.* New York: New American Library.

PELCZARSKI, Y., AND S. P. KEMP. 2006. Patterns of child maltreatment referrals among Asian and Pacific Islander families. *Child Welfare* 85 (January/February): 5–31.

PELLERIN, L. A. 2005. Applying Baumrind's parenting typology to high schools: Toward a middle-range theory of authoritative socialization. *Social Science Research* 34 (June): 282–303.

PENHA-LOPES, V. 1995. "Make room for daddy": Patterns of family involvement among contemporary African American men. In *American families: Issues in race and ethnicity,* ed. C. K. Jacobson, 179–99. New York: Garland.

PEPLAU, L. A., R. C. VENIEGAS, AND S. M. CAMPBELL. 1996. Gay and lesbian relationships. In *The lives of lesbians, gays, and bisexuals: Children to adults,* eds. R. C. Savin-Williams and K. M. Cohen, 250–73. New York: Harcourt Brace.

PERCHESKI, C. 2008. Opting out? Cohort differences in professional women's employment rates from 1960 to 2005. *American Sociological Review* 73 (November): 497–517.

PÉREZ, L. 1992. Cuban Miami. In *Miami now! Immigration, ethnicity, and social change*, eds. G. J. Grenier and A. Stepick III, 83–108. Gainesville: University Press of Florida.

PÉREZ, L. 2002. Cuban American families. *In Minority families in the United States: A multicultural perspective*, 3rd ed., ed. R. L. Taylor, 114–30. Upper Saddle River, NJ: Prentice Hall.

PERITZ, I. 2003. Miracle birth signals male moms? *Toronto Globe and Mail*, August 15, A14.

PERLS, T. T. 2004. Anti-aging quackery: Human growth hormone and tricks of the trade—more dangerous than ever. *Journals of Gerontology: Biological and Medical Sciences* 59 (July): B682–B691.

PERLSTEIN, L. 2005. A user's guide to middle school romance. *Washington Post Magazine*, February 13, 20–23, 33.

PERRIN, E. C. 2002. Technical report: Coparent or second-parent adoption by same-sex parents. *Pediatrics* 109 (February): 341–44.

PERRY, S. W. 2004. American Indians and crime. U.S. Department of Justice, Bureau of Justice Statistics, December, www.ojp.usdoj.gov (accessed March 25, 2009).

PERRY, T., C. STEELE, AND A. HILLIARD III. 2003. *Young, gifted and black: Promoting high achievement among African-American students*. New York: Beacon.

PERRY-JENKINS, M., AND K. FOLK. 1994. Class, couples, and conflict: Effects of the division of labor on assessments of marriage in dual-earner families. *Journal of Marriage and the Family* 56 (February): 165–80.

PERRY-JENKINS, M., C. P. PIERCE, AND A. E. GOLDBERG. 2004. Discourses on diapers and dirty laundry: Family communication about child care and housework. In *Handbook of family communication*, ed. Anita L. Vangelisti, 541–61. Mahwah, NJ: Lawrence Erlbaum.

PERRY-JENKINS, M., A. E. GOLDBERG, C. P. PIERCE, AND A. G. SAYER. 2007. Shift work, role overload, and the transition to parenthood. *Journal of Marriage and Family* 69 (February): 123–38.

PESSAR, P. R. 1995. *A visa for a dream: Dominicans in the United States*. Boston: Allyn & Bacon.

PETERS, M. F. 2007. Parenting of young children in black families: A historical note. In *Black families*, 4th ed., ed. H. P. McAdoo, 203–18. Thousand Oaks, CA: Sage.

PETERSEN, W. 1966. Success story, Japanese American style. *New York Times Magazine*, January 6, 20ff.

PETERSON, B. D., C. R. NEWTON, K. H. ROSEN, AND R. S. SCHULMAN. 2006. Coping processes of couples experiencing infertility. *Family Relations* 55 (April): 227–39.

PETERSON, J. 2006. Many forced to retire early. *Los Angeles Times*, May 15, A8.

PETERSON, J. L., J. J. CARD, M. B. EISEN, AND B. SHERMAN-WILLIAMS. 1994. Evaluating teenage pregnancy prevention and other social programs: Ten stages of program assessment. *Family Planning Perspectives* 26 (May): 116–20, 131.

Pew Center on the States. 2009. One in 31: The long reach of American corrections. March, www.pewcenteronthestates.org (accessed May 30, 2009).

Pew Forum on Religion & Public Life. 2008. An overview of the same-sex marriage debate. April 1, http://pewforum.org (accessed June 13, 2009).

Pew Forum on Religion & Public Life. 2008. *U.S. religious landscape survey*. February, www.pewforum.org (accessed March 1, 2008).

Pew Hispanic Center. 2004. Assimilation and language. March, www.pewhispanic.org (accessed March 15, 2009).

Pew Hispanic Center. 2006. Cubans in the United States. August 25, www.pewhispanic.org (accessed May 1, 2007).

Pew Internet & American Life Project. 2008. Demographics of Internet users. February 15, www.pewinternet.org (accessed April 23, 2008).

PEWEWARDY, C. 1998. Fluff and feathers: Treatment of American Indians in the literature and the classroom. *Equity & Excellence in Education* 31 (April): 69–76.

PHILLIPS, J. A., AND M. M. SWEENEY. 2005. Premarital cohabitation and marital disruption among white, black, and Mexican American women. *Journal of Marriage and Family* 67 (May): 296–314.

PHILLIPS, K. A., AND W. MENARD. 2006. Suicidality in body dysmorphic disorder: A prospective study. *American Journal of Psychiatry* 163 (July): 1280–82.

PHILLIPS, K. R. 2004. Getting time off: Access to leave among working parents. The Urban Institute, April 22, www.urban.org (accessed May 3, 2006).

PHINNEY, J. S. 1996. Understanding ethnic diversity. *American Behavioral Scientist* 40 (November/December) 143–52.

PHINNEY, J. S., B. HORENCZYK, K. LIEBKIND, AND P. VEDDER. 2001. Ethnic identity, immigration, and well-being: An interactional perspective. *Journal of Social Issues* 57: 493–510.

PIAGET, J. 1932. *The moral judgment of the child*. New York: Harcourt, Brace.

PIAGET, J. 1954. *The construction of reality in the child*. New York: Basic Books.

PIAGET, J. 1960. *The child's conception of the world*. London: Routledge.

PIENTA, A. M., AND M. M. FRANKS. 2006. A closer look at health and widowhood: Do health behaviors change after loss of a spouse? In *Spousal bereavement in late life*, eds. D. Carr, R. M. Nesse, and C. B. Wortman, 117–142. New York: Springer.

PILL, C. J. 1990. Stepfamilies: Redefining the family. *Family Relations* 39 (April): 186–92.

PILLEMER, K., AND J. J. SUTTOR. 1991. Will I ever escape my child's problems? Effects of adult children's problems on elderly parents. *Journal of Marriage and the Family* 53 (August): 585–94.

PIÑA, D. L., AND V. L. BENGSTON. 1993. The division of household labor and wives' happiness: Ideology, employment, and perceptions of support. *Journal of Marriage and the Family* 55 (November): 901–12.

PIORE, A. 2007. The dog wears Prada. *Christian Science Monitor*, February 21, 20.

PIORKOWSKI, G. K. 1994. *Too close for comfort: Exploring the risks of intimacy*. New York: Plenum.

PITTMAN, F. 1990. *Private lies: Infidelity and the betrayal of intimacy*. New York: W.W. Norton.

PITTMAN, F. 1999. *Grow up! How taking responsibility can make you a happy adult*. New York: Golden Books.

PLANTY, M., W. HUSSAR, T. SNYDER, S. PROVASNIK, G. KENA, R. DINKES, A. KEWAL RAMANI, AND J. KEMP. 2008. *The condition of education 2008* (NCES 2008-031). Washington, DC: National Center for Education Statistics, Institute of Education Sciences, U.S. Department of Education.

PLANTY, M., ET AL. 2007. *The condition of education 2007* (NCES 2007-064). Washington, DC: U.S. Government Printing Office.

PLATERIS, A. A. 1973. *100 years of marriage and divorce statistics: 1867–1967*. Rockville, MD: National Center for Health Statistics.

PLATT, S. F. 2006. *Letters from the front lines: Iraq and Afghanistan*. Point Roberts, WA: Granville Island Publishing.

PLEIS, J. R., AND M. LETHBRIDGE-ÇEJKU. 2007. Summary health statistics for U.S. adults: National Health Interview Survey, 2006. *Vital and Health Statistics* 10 (December): 1–163.

Police in Iran crack down on vice: Valentine's Day. 2003. *Baltimore Sun*, February 13, 12A.

POLISI, C. J. 2009. Spousal rape laws continue to evolve. Women's eNews, July 1, www.womensenews.org (accessed August 23, 2009).

POMFRET, J. 2001. In China's countryside, "it's a boy!" too often. *Washington Post*, May 29, A1.

PONG, S.-L. 1997. Family structure, school context, and eighth grade math and reading achievement. *Journal of Marriage and the Family* 59 (August): 734–46.

PONG, S.-L. HAO, AND E. GARDNER. 2005. The roles of parenting styles and social capital in the school performance of immigrant Asian and Hispanic adolescents. *Social Science Quarterly* 86 (December): 928–50.

PONIEWOZIK, J. 2002. The cost of starting families. *Time*, April 15, 56–57.

POOL, B., AND C. BOUSADA. 2007. Fooling nature, and the fertility doctor. *Los Angeles Times*, January 30, www.latimes.com (accessed February 2, 2007).

POORTMAN, A-R., AND J. A. SELTZER. 2007. Parents' expectations about childrearing after divorce: Does anticipating difficulty deter divorce? *Journal of Marriage and Family* 69 (February): 254–69.

POPE, J. R., H. G. R. OLIVARDIA, AND J. BOROWIECKI. 1999. Evolving ideals of male body image as seen through action toys. *International Journal of Eating Disorders* 26 (July): 65–72.

POPENOE, D. 1996. *Life without father: Compelling new evidence that fatherhood and marriage are indispensable for the good of children and society*. New York: Free Press.

POPENOE, D. 2002. The top ten myths of marriage. The National Marriage Project, March, http://marriage.rutgers.edu (accessed April 6, 2006).

POPENOE, D. 2007. The future of marriage in America. The state of our unions 2007. The National Marriage Project, http://marriage.rutgers.edu (accessed March 2, 2009).

POPENOE, D. 2008. Cohabitation, marriage and child wellbeing: A cross-national perspective. The National Marriage Project, http://marriage.rutgers.edu (accessed December 30, 2008).

POPENOE, D., AND B. D. WHITEHEAD. 2002. *Should we live together? What young adults need to know about cohabitation before marriage: A comprehensive review of recent research*, 2nd ed. New Brunswick, NJ: The National Marriage Project, Rutgers University. http://marriage.rutgers.edu (accessed July 12, 2003).

POPENOE, D., AND B. D. WHITEHEAD. 2003. The state of our unions, 2003: The social health of marriage in America. The National Marriage Project, Rutgers University. http://marriage.rutgers.edu (accessed July 4, 2003).

POPENOE, D., AND B. D. WHITEHEAD. 2006. The state of our unions 2006: The social health of marriage in America. The National Marriage Project, http://marriage.rutgers.edu (accessed September 7, 2006).

POPENOE, D., AND B. D. WHITEHEAD. 2009. The state of our unions 2008: The social health of marriage in America. The National

Marriage Project, Rutgers University, http://marriage.rutgers.edu (accessed June 1, 2009).

Population Division, U.S. Census Bureau. 2008. Projections of the population by race and Hispanic origin for the United States: 2008 to 2050. August 14, www.census.gov (accessed September 8, 2008).

Population Reference Bureau. 2008. Interview with Ron Lee on what are the financial implications of aging in the United States. November 6, www.prb.org (accessed September 16, 2009).

POTTS, L. 2003. PBS looks at how oral contraceptives changed women's lives. www.abqjournal.com (accessed February 23, 2003).

POWELL, E. 1991. *Talking back to sexual pressure.* Minneapolis: CompCare.

PORTER, N., AND Y. SANO. 2009. Father involvement in Japanese families. *Family Focus* 54 (Spring): F13, F15.

POWERS, C. H. 2004. *Making sense of social theory: A practical introduction.* Lanham, MD: Rowman & Littlefield.

PREUSS, U. W., ET AL. 2003. Predictors and correlates of suicide attempts over 5 years in 1,237 alcohol-dependent men and women. *American Journal of Psychiatry* 160 (January): 56–63.

PREVITI, D., AND P. R. AMATO. 2003. Why stay married? Rewards, barriers, and marital stability. *Journal of Marriage and Family* 65 (August): 561–73.

PRICE, J. A. 1981. North American Indian families. In *Ethnic families in America: Patterns and variations,* 2nd ed., eds. C. H. Mindel and R. W. Habenstein, 245–68. New York: Elsevier.

PRICE, R. H., J. N. CHOI, AND A. D. VINOKUR. 2002. Links in the chain of adversity following job loss: How financial strain and loss of personal control lead to depression, impaired functioning, and poor health. *Journal of Occupational Health Psychology* 7 (4): 302–12.

PR Newswire. 2007. 65 percent of Americans spend more time with their computer than their spouse. January 27, http://sev.prnewswire.com (accessed February 24, 2009).

PRESSER, H. B., J. C. GORNICK, AND S. PARASHAR. 2008. Gender and nonstandard work hours in 12 European countries. *Monthly Labor Review* 131 (February): 83–103.

PROCTOR, B. D., AND J. DALAKER. 2003. Poverty in the United States: 2002. U.S. Census Bureau, *Current Population Reports,* P60–222. www.census.gov (accessed October 5, 2003).

PROTHROW-STITH, D., AND H. R. SPIVAK. 2005. *Sugar and spice and no longer nice: How can we stop girls' violence?* San Francisco, CA: Jossey-Bass.

PROVASNIK, S., AND S. DORFMAN. 2005. Mobility in the teacher workforce (NCES 2005-114). U.S. Department of Education, National Center for Education Statistics. Washington, DC: U.S. Government Printing Office.

PRUSHER, I. R. 2001. South Korea: Gay confession ignites debate. *Christian Science Monitor,* January 17, 7.

PRUSHER, I. R. 2007. As order slides, Palestinian women face honor killings. *Christian Science Monitor,* November 20, 1, 4.

PRYOR, J. H., S. HURTADO, V. B. SAENZ, J. L. SANTOS, AND W. S. KORN. 2007. *The American freshman: Forty year trends.* Los Angeles: Higher Education Research Institute, UCLA.

PULTE HOMES. 2005. Baby boomer study: Full report. Harris Interactive Market Research, May, www.harrisinteractive.com (accessed August 1, 2006).

PURCELL, P., AND D. B. WHITMAN. 2006. Topics in aging: Income of Americans age 65 and older, 1969 to 2004. CRS Report for Congress, www.policyarchive.org (accessed February 25, 2009).

PYKE, K. D. 1994. Women's employment as a gift or burden? Marital power across marriage, divorce, and remarriage. *Gender and Society* 8 (March): 73–91.

PYKE, K., AND S. COLTRANE. 1996. Entitlement, obligation, and gratitude in family work. *Journal of Family Issues* 17 (January): 60–82.

Q

QIAN, Z. 2005. Breaking the last taboo: Interracial marriage in America. *Contexts* 4 (Fall): 33–37.

QIAN, Z., D. T. LICHTER, L. M. MELLOTT. 2005. Out-of-wedlock childbearing, marital prospects and mate selection. *Social Forces* 84 (September): 473–91.

QIAN, Z., AND D. T. LICHTER. 2007. Social boundaries and marital assimilation: Interpreting trends in racial and ethnic intermarriage. *American Sociological Review* 72 (February): 68–94.

QUADAGNO, J. 2002. *Aging and the life course: An introduction to social gerontology,* 2nd ed. New York: McGraw-Hill.

QUEEN, S. A., R. W. HABENSTEIN, AND J. S. QUADAGNO. 1985. *The family in various cultures,* 5th ed. New York: Harper & Row.

QUENQUA, D. 2007. Little love among matchmakers. *New York Times,* December 24, 6.

QUICK, B. 1992. Tales from the self-help mill. *Newsweek,* August 31, 14.

QUICK, D. S., P. C. MC KENRY, AND B. M. NEWMAN. 1994. Stepmothers and their adolescent children: Adjustment to new family roles. In *Stepparenting: Issues in theory, research, and practice,* eds. K. Pasley and M. Ihinger-Tallman, 119–25. Westport, CT: Greenwood.

QUINTANA, S. M., AND V. M. VERA. 1999. Mexican American children's ethnic identity, understanding of ethnic prejudice, and parental ethnic socialization. *Hispanic Journal of Behavioral Sciences* 21 (November): 387–404.

R

RAGHAVAN, A. 2009. Wall Street's disappearing women. *Forbes,* March 16, 72–78.

RAINE, A., C. REYNOLDS, P. H. VENABLES, AND S. A. MEDNICK. 2002. Stimulation seeking and intelligence: A prospective longitudinal study. *Journal of Personality and Social Psychology* 82 (April): 663–74.

RAINIE, L., AND M. MADDEN. 2006. Not looking for love: Romance in America. Pew Research Center, February 13, http://pewresearch.org (accessed March 12, 2006).

RAJ, A., AND J. G. SILVERMAN. 2002. Intimate partner violence against South Asian women in greater Boston. *Journal of the American Medical Women's Association* 57 (April): 111–14.

RALEY, R. K., AND E. WILDSMITH. 2004. Cohabitation and children's family instability. *Journal of Marriage and Family* 66 (February): 210–19.

RAMACHANDRAN, N. 2005. The parent trap: Boomerang kids. *U.S. News & World Report,* December 12, 64.

RANK, M. R. 1987. The formation and dissolution of marriages in the welfare population. *Journal of Marriage and the Family* 49 (February): 15–20.

RASCHICK, M., AND B. INGERSOLL-DAYTON. 2004. The costs and rewards of caregiving among aging spouses and adult children. *Family Relations* 53 (April): 317–25.

RATHUS, J. H., AND K. D. O'LEARY. 1997. Spouse-specific dependency scale: Scale development. *Journal of Family Violence* 12 (June): 159–68.

RAY, R., AND J. SCHMITT. 2007. No-vacation nation. Center for Economic and Policy Research, May, www.cepr.net (accessed July 4, 2008).

RAYBECK, D., S. DORENBOSCH, M. SARAPATA, AND D. HERRMAN. 2000. The quest for love and meaning in the personals. Unpublished paper.

READ, J. G. 2004. Family, religion, and work among Arab American women. *Journal of Marriage and Family* 66 (November): 1042–50.

READING, R. 2006. Child deaths resulting from inflicted injuries: Household risk factors and perpetrator characteristics. *Child: Care, Health & Development* 32 (March): 253.

REARDON-ANDERSON, J., M. STAGNER, J. E. MACOMBER, and J. MURRAY. 2005. Systematic review of the impact of marriage and relationship programs. Urban Institute, February 11, www.urban.org (accessed November 1, 2005).

REAY, A. M., AND K. D. BROWNE. 2001. Risk factors for caregivers who physically abuse or neglect their elderly dependents. *Aging and Mental Health* 5 (1): 56–62.

REEFHUIS, J., M. A. HONEIN, L. A. SCHIEVE, A. CORREA, C. A. HOBBS, AND S. A. RASMUSSEN. 2009. Assisted reproductive technology and major structural birth defects in the United States. *Human Reproduction* 24 (February): 360–66.

REGAN, P. 2003. *The mating game: A primer on love, sex, and marriage.* Thousand Oaks, CA: Sage.

REGAN, P. C., AND E. BERSCHEID. 1999. *Lust: What we know about human sexual desire.* Thousand Oaks, CA: Sage.

REGNERUS, M. D. 2007. *Forbidden fruit: Sex & religion in the lives of American teenagers.* New York: Oxford University Press.

REGNIER, P., AND A. GENGLER. 2006. Men, women, and money. *Money,* March 14, http://magazines.ivillage.com (accessed April 14, 2006).

REID, J. 1993. Those fabulous '50s. *Utne Reader* 55 (January): 18–19.

REILLY, P. R. 2000. *Abraham Lincoln's DNA and other adventures in genetics.* New York: Cold Spring Harbor Laboratory.

REIMER, S. 1999. Sex questions show how little our kids know. *Baltimore Sun,* September 9, 1e, 4e.

REINER, W. G., AND J. P. GEARHART. 2004. Discordant sexual identity in some genetic males with cloacal exstrophy assigned to female sex at birth. *New England Journal of Medicine* 350 (January 22): 333–41.

REINISCH, J. M., WITH R. BEASLEY. 1990. *The Kinsey Institute new report on sex: What you must know to be sexually literate.* New York: St. Martin's.

REISS, I. 1960. Toward a sociology of the heterosexual love relationship. *Marriage and Family Living* 22 (May): 139–45.

REISS, I. L. 1971. *The family system in America.* New York: Holt, Rinehart & Winston.

REISS, I. L., AND G. R. LEE. 1988. *Family systems in America,* 4th ed. New York: Holt, Rinehart & Winston.

REITMAN, V. 2002. Self-immolations on rise in Afghanistan. *Los Angeles Times,* November 17, A5.

RENN, J. A., AND S. L. CALVERT. 1993. The relation between gender schemas and adults' recall of stereotyped and counterstereotyped televised information. *Sex Roles* 28 (7/8): 449–59.

Rennison, C. M. 2001. *Intimate partner violence and age of victim, 1993–99.* Washington, DC: U.S. Department of Justice.

Rennison, C. M. 2003. *Intimate partner violence, 1993–2001.* Washington, DC: U.S. Department of Justice.

Rennison, C. M., and S. Welchans. 2000. *Intimate partner violence.* Washington, DC: U.S. Department of Justice.

Rentz, E. D., S. W. Marshall, D. Loomis, C. Casteel, S. L. Martin, and D. A. Gibbs. 2007. Effect of deployment on the occurrence of child maltreatment in military and nonmilitary families. *American Journal of Epidemiology* 165 (May): 1199–206.

Renout, F. 2005. Immigrants' second wives find few rights. *Christian Science Monitor,* May 25, 17.

Retherford, D., and N. Ogawa. 2006. Japan's baby bust: Causes, implications, and policy responses. In *The baby bust: Who will do the work? Who will pay the taxes?* ed. F. R. Harris, 5–47. Lanham, MD: Rowman & Littlefield.

Retsinas, J. 1988. A theoretical reassessment of the applicability of Kübler-Ross's stages of dying. *Death Studies* 12 (3): 207–16.

Reuters highlights a Chinese periodical targeting gay men that discusses "taboo" subjects of homosexuality and HIV/AIDS. 2002. The Henry Kaiser Family Foundation, October 1. www.kaisernetwork.org (accessed June 12, 2003).

Reynolds, A. J., and D. Robertson. 2003. School-based early intervention and later child maltreatment in the Chicago longitudinal study. *Child Development* 74 (January/February): 3–26.

Reynolds, S. S. 2007. Book review: *Leap! What will we do with the rest of our lives? Los Angeles Times,* April 6, www.latimes.com (accessed April 7, 2007).

Rhee, K. E., J. C. Lumeng, D. P. Appugliese, N. Kaciroti, and R. H. Bradley. 2006. Parenting styles and overweight status in first grade. *Pediatrics* 117 (June): 2047–54.

Rheingold, H. L. 1969. The social and socializing infant. In *Handbook of socialization theory and research,* ed. D. A. Goslin, 779–90. Chicago: Rand McNally.

Rice, G., C. Anderson, N. Risch, and G. Ebers. 1999. Male homosexuality: Absence of linkage to microsatellite markers at Xq28. *Science* 284 (April 23): 665–67.

Rich, M. 2005. Living in a retirement village, back home with mom and dad. *New York Times,* May 22, A1.

Richardson, B. 2004. What Japanese women want: A western husband. *Christian Science Monitor* (December 6): 1, 10.

Richardson, C. R., P. J. Resnick, D. L. Hansen, H. A. Derry, and V. J. Rideout. 2002. Does pornography-blocking software block access to health information in the Internet? *Journal of the American Medical Association* 288 (December 11): 2887–94.

Richardson-Bouie, D. 2003. Ethnic variation/ethnicity. In *International encyclopedia of marriage and family,* 2nd ed., Vol. 2, ed. J. J. Ponzetti, Jr., 525–30. New York: Macmillan.

Rideout, V. 2007. Parents, children & media: A Kaiser Family Foundation survey. Kaiser Family Foundation, June, www.kff.org (accessed May 5, 2009).

Rideout, V. 2008. Television as a health educator: A case study of *Grey's Anatomy.* Kaiser Family Foundation, September, www.kff .org (accessed October 15, 2008).

Rideout, V., and E. Hamel. 2006. The media family: Electronic media in the lives of infants, toddlers, preschoolers and their parents. Kaiser Family Foundation, May, www .kff.org (accessed September 22, 2006).

Rideout, V., C. Richardson, and P. Resnik. 2002. See no evil: How Internet filters affect the search for online health information. The Henry Kaiser Family Foundation. www.kff.org (accessed June 10, 2003).

Rideout, V., D. F. Roberts, and U. G. Foehr. 2005. *Generation M: Media in the lives of 8–18 year-olds.* Menlo Park, CA: Kaiser Family Foundation.

Rieger, G., M. Chivers, and M. J. Bailey. 2005. Sexual arousal patterns of bisexual men. *Psychological Science* 16 (August): 579–84.

Ringle, K. 1999. Unamicable partners. *Washington Post,* March 15, C1, C7.

Rivers, C. 2001. Study: Young people seeking soul mates to marry. Women's E-News, June 20. www.womensenews.org (accessed July 15, 2003).

Rivers, C. 2002. Pop science book claims girls hard-wired for love. Women's E-News, June 28. www.womensenews.org (accessed June 29, 2002).

Rivers, C., and R. C. Barnett. 2005. Holiday toys sell girls on primping and passivity. Women's e-news, November 27, http://womensenews .org (accessed November 28, 2005).

Roan, S. 2005. Breasts, redefined. *Los Angeles Times,* June 13, F1.

Roberto, K. A., and S. E. Jarrott. 2008. Family caregivers of older adults: A life span perspective. *Family Relations* 57 (January): 100–111.

Roberts, B., and D. Povich. 2008. Working hard, still falling short: New findings on the challenges confronting America's working families. Working Poor Families Project, www.workingpoorfamilies.org (accessed August 9, 2009).

Roberts, C. M. 2001. The view from 90. *Washington Post Health Supplement,* January 23, 15–16.

Roberts, L. J. 2000. Fire and ice in marital communication: Hostile and distancing behaviors as predictors of marital distress. *Journal of Marriage and the Family* 62 (August): 693–707.

Robey, E. B., D. J. Canary, and C. S. Burggraf. 1998. Conversational maintenance behaviors of husbands and wives: An observational analysis. In *Sex differences and similarities in communication: Critical essays and empirical investigations of sex and gender in interaction,* eds. D. J. Canary and K. Dindia, 373–92. Mahwah, NJ: Lawrence Erlbaum Associates.

Robinson, B. 2008. The disruption of marital e-harmony: Distinguishing mail-order brides from online dating in evaluating "good faith marriage." *Loyola Public Interest Law Reporter* 13 (Summer): 252–70.

Roche, T. 2002. The Yates odyssey. *Time,* January 28, 40–50.

Rochman, B. 2009. The ethics of octuplets. *Time,* February 16, 43–44.

Rock, E. M., M. Ireland, M. D. Resnick, and C. A. Mc Neely. 2005. A rose by any other name? Objective knowledge, perceived knowledge, and adolescent male condom use. *Pediatrics* 115 (March): 667–72.

Rodberg, G. 1999. Woman and man at Yale. www.culturefront.org (accessed August 29, 2000).

Rodgers, J. L., P. A. Nakonezny, and R. D. Shull. 1997. The effect of no-fault divorce legislation on divorce rates: A response to a reconsideration. *Journal of Marriage and the Family* 59 (November): 1026–30.

Rodgers, K. B., and H. A. Rose. 2002. Risk and resiliency factors among adolescents who experience marital transitions. *Journal of Marriage and Family* 64 (November): 1024–37.

Rogers, S. J., and D. D. De Boer. 2001. Changes in wives' income: Effects on marital happiness, psychological well-being, and the risk of divorce. *Journal of Marriage and Family* 63 (May): 458–72.

Rohner, R. P., and R. A. Veneziano. 2001. The importance of father love: History and contemporary evidence. *Review of General Psychology* 5 (4): 382–405.

Rohypnol. 2003. Office of National Drug Control Policy, www.whitehousedrugpolicy.gov (accessed March 10, 2006).

Roisman, G. I., E. Clausell, A. Holland, K. Fortuna, and C. Elieff. 2008. Adult romantic relationships as contexts of human development: A multimethod comparison of same-sex couples with opposite-sex dating, engaged, and married dyads. *Developmental Psychology* 44 (January): 91–101.

Romano, L. 2006. Multiple single moms, one nameless donor. *Washington Post,* February 27, A2.

Roschelle, A. R., M. I. Toro -Morn, and E. Facio. 2005. Families in Cuba: From colonialism to revolution. In *Handbook of world families,* eds. B. N. Adams and J. Trost, 414–39. Thousand Oaks, CA: Sage.

Rose, S., and I. H. Frieze. 1993. Young singles' contemporary dating scripts. *Sex Roles* 28 (May): 499–509.

Rosemond, J. 2000. *Raising a nonviolent child.* Kansas City, MI: Andrews McMeel Publishing.

Rosen, B. C. 1982. *The industrial connection: Achievement and the family in developing societies.* New York: Aldine.

Rosen, K. H., and S. M. Stith. 1993. Intervention strategies for treating women in violent dating relationships. *Family Relations* 42 (October): 427–33.

Rosenbaum, J. E. 2006. Reborn a virgin: Adolescents' retracting of virginity pledges and sexual histories. *American Journal of Public Health* 96 (June): 1098–103.

Rosenbaum, J. E. 2009. Patient teenagers? A comparison of the sexual behavior of virginity pledgers and matched nonpledgers. *Pediatrics* 123 (May): e110–e120.

Rosenberg, D. 2007. (Rethinking) gender. *Newsweek,* May 21, 50–57.

Rosenberg, J. 1993. Just the two of us. *In Reinventing love: Six women talk about lust, sex, and romance,* eds. L. Abraham, L. Green, M. Krance, J. Rosenberg, J. Somerville, and C. Stoner, 301–7. New York: Plume.

Rosenblatt, P. C. 1994. *Metaphors of family systems theory: Toward new constructions.* New York: Guilford.

Rosenblatt, P. C., and R. A. Phillips, Jr. 1975. Family articles in popular magazines: Advice to writers, editors, and teachers of consumers. *Family Coordinator* 24 (July): 267–71.

Rosenfeld, M. J. 2002. Measures of assimilation in the marriage market: Mexican Americans 1970–1990. *Journal of Marriage and Family* 64 (February): 152–62.

Rosenthal, C. J. 1985. Kinkeeping in the familial division of labor. *Journal of Marriage and the Family* 47 (November): 965–74.

Rosenzweig, P. M. 1992. *Married and alone: The way back.* New York: Plenum.

Ross, C. E., and J. Mirowsky. 1999. Parental divorce, life-course disruption, and adult depression. *Journal of Marriage and the Family* 61 (November): 1034–45.

Rothenberg, P. S. 2008. *White privilege: Essential readings on the other side of racism.* New York: Worth.

ROTHMAN, B. K. 1984. *Hands and hearts: A history of courtship in America.* New York: Basic Books.

ROTHMAN, E. K. 1983. Sex and self-control: Middle-class courtship in America, 1770–1870. In *The American family in social-historical perspective,* 3rd ed., ed. M. Gordon, 393–410. New York: St. Martin's.

ROTHMAN, S. M. 1978. *Women's proper place: A history of changing ideals and practices, 1870 to the present.* New York: Basic Books.

ROUG, L. 2005. The time seems ripe to tie the knot in Iraq. *Los Angeles Times,* June 12, A1.

RUBIN, B. M. 2008. Adoption ban targets gay couples, critics say. *Los Angeles Times,* December 4, www.latimes.com (accessed December 5, 2008).

RUBIN, L. B. 1985. *Just friends: The role of friendship in our lives.* New York: Harper & Row.

RUBIN, R. M., AND S. I. WHITE-MEANS. 2009. Informal caregiving: Dilemmas of sandwiched caregivers. *Journal of Family and Economic Issues* 30 (September): 252–67.

RUSSO, F. 2002. That old feeling. *Time,* February 13, G1–G3.

RUSSO, F. 2005. Who cares more for mom? *Time,* June 20, F7–F10.

RYAN, M. P. 1983. *Womanhood in America: From colonial times to the present,* 3rd ed. New York: Franklin Watts.

S

SAAD, L. 2004. Romance to break out nationwide this weekend. Gallup Organization, February 13, http://poll.gallup.com (accessed February 17, 2004).

SAAD, L. 2006. Americans have complex relationship with marriage. Gallup Organization, May 30, www.gallup.com (accessed May 31, 2006).

SAAD, L. 2006. Americans still oppose gay marriage. Gallup Organization, May 22, www.gallup.com (accessed September 16, 2006).

SAAD, L. 2006. Growing old doesn't necessarily mean growing infirm. Gallup News Service, November 30, www.gallup.com (accessed December 1, 2006).

SAAD, L. 2007. A downturn in black perceptions of racial harmony. Gallup News Service, July 6, www.gallup.com (accessed April 6, 2009).

SAAD, L. 2007. Women slightly more likely to prefer working to homemaking. Gallup News Service, August 31, www.gallup.poll (accessed April 17, 2009).

SAAD, L. 2008. Americans evenly divided on morality of homosexuality. Gallup, June 18, www.gallup.com (accessed May 21, 2009).

SAAD, L. 2008. By age 24, marriage wins out. Gallup News Service, August 11, www.gallup.com (accessed June 9, 2009).

SAAD, L. 2008. Cultural tolerance for divorce grows to 70%, May 19, Gallup News Service, www.gallup.com (accessed July 8, 2008).

SAAD, L. 2008. Telecommuting still a rare perk. Gallup News Service, August 15, www.gallup.com (accessed August 14, 2008).

SAAD, L. 2009. Americans tell Obama what they want to hear in speech. Gallup News Service, February 24, www.gallup.com (accessed February 24, 2009).

SAAD, L. 2009. More Americans "pro-life" than "pro-choice" for first time. Gallup News Service, May 15, www.gallup.com (accessed June 30, 2009).

SA'AH, R. J. 2006. Cameroon girls battle "breast ironing." BBC News (June 23), http://news.bbc.co.uk (accessed June 25, 2006).

SABAH, A. 2006. Parents disapprove, but Internet romance a big hit. *USA Today,* October 12, www.usatoday.com (accessed October 14, 2006).

SABATELLI, R. M., AND S. BARTLE -HARING. 2003. Family-of-origin experiences and adjustment in married couples. *Journal of Marriage and Family* 65 (February): 159–69.

SABATTINI, L., N. M. CARTER, J. PRIME, AND D. MEGATHLIN. 2007. The double-bind dilemma for women in leadership: Damned if you do, doomed if you don't. *Catalyst,* www.catalyst.org (accessed April 28, 2008).

SADKER, M., AND D. SADKER. 1994. *Failing at fairness: How America's schools cheat girls.* New York: Scribner's.

SAENZ, R. 2007. The growing color divide in U.S. infant mortality. Population Reference Bureau, October, www.prb.org (accessed March 28, 2009).

SAENZ, R. 2008. A demographic profile of U.S. workers around the clock. Population Reference Bureau, September, www.prb.org (accessed July 31, 2009).

SAFILIOS -ROTHSCHILD, C. 1977. *Love, sex, and sex roles.* Upper Saddle River, NJ: Prentice Hall.

SAGIRI, Y. 2001. *United National Indian Tribal Youth, Inc.* Washington, DC: U.S. Department of Justice.

ST. GEORGE, D. 2008. Women are gaining ground in family decision making. *Washington Post,* September 26, B1.

ST. GEORGE, D., AND P. DVORAK. 2008. Child neglect cases multiply as economic woes spread. *Washington Post,* December 29, B1.

SAITO, L. T. 2002. *Ethnic identity and motivation: Socio-cultural factors in the educational achievement of Vietnamese American students.* New York: LFB Scholarly Publishing.

SALDANA, D. H., AND A. M. DASSORI. 1999. When is caregiving a burden? Listening to Mexican American women. *Hispanic Journal of Behavioral Sciences* 21 (August): 283–301.

SALTZMAN, A. 1999. From diapers to high heels. *U.S. News & World Report,* July 26, 57–58.

SALUTER, A. F. 1994. Marital status and living arrangements: March 1993. U.S. Census Bureau, *Current Population Reports,* Series P20–478. Washington, DC: U.S. Government Printing Office.

SALUTER, A. F. 1996. Marital status and living arrangements: March 1995 (Update). U.S. Census Bureau, Department of Commerce, Economics and Statistics Administration.

SAMPSON, O., ET AL. 2009. Barriers to adolescents' getting emergency contraception though pharmacy access in California: Differences by language and religion. *Perspectives on Sexual and Reproductive Health* 41 (June), www.guttmacher.org (accessed June 30, 2009).

SAMPSON, R. 2002. Acquaintance rape of college students. U.S. Department of Justice, Office of Community Oriented Policing Services, Guide No. 17, www.cops.usdoj.gov (accessed March 5, 2006).

SAMPSON, R. 2009. Bullying in schools. U.S. Department of Justice, Office of Community Oriented Policing Services, www.cops.usdoj.gov (accessed July 25, 2009).

SAMUELS, G. M. 2009. "Being raised by white people": Navigating racial difference among adopted multiracial adults. *Journal of Marriage and Family* 71 (February): 80–94.

SAMUELS, L. 2008. Stay in the closet, or else. *Newsweek,* September 8, 8.

SANCHEZ-WAY, R., AND S. JOHNSON. 2000. Cultural practices in American Indian prevention programs. *Juvenile Justice* 7 (December): 20–30.

SANDBERG, J. G., R. B. MILLER, AND J. M. HARPER. 2002. A qualitative study of marital process and depression in older couples. *Family Relations* 51 (July): 256–64.

SANG-HUN, C. 2007. Where boys were kings, a shift toward baby girls. *New York Times,* December 23, 1.

SANG-HUN, C. 2007. Traditional Korean marriage meets match on the Internet. *New York Times,* June 6, 13.

SANTANA, W. 2008. Vietnam women marry foreigners to escape poverty. *Los Angeles Times,* August 23, www.latimes.com (accessed August 24, 2008).

SANTOS, F. 2008. After the war, a new battle to become citizens. *New York Times,* February 24, 1.

SANTROCK, J. W., K. A. SITTERLE, AND R. A. WARSHAK. 1988. Parent–child relationships in stepfather families. In *Fatherhood today: Men's changing role in the family,* eds. S. P. Bronstein and C. P. Cowan, 144–65. New York: Wiley.

SAPPENFIELD, M. 2007. In India, a public kiss is *not* just a kiss. *Christian Science Monitor,* April 30, 1, 10.

SARCH, A. 1993. Making the connection: Single women's use of the telephone in dating relationships with men. *Journal of Communications* 43 (Spring): 128–44.

SARKISIAN, N., AND N. GERSTEL. 2004. Explaining the gender gap in help to parents: The importance of employment. *Journal of Marriage and Family* 66 (May): 431–51.

SARKISIAN, N., M. GERENA, AND N. GERSTEL. 2007. Extended family integration among Euro and Mexican Americans: Ethnicity, gender, and class. *Journal of Marriage and Family* 68 (February): 40–54.

SARMIENTO, S. T. 2002. *Making ends meet: Income-generating strategies among Mexican immigrants.* New York: LFB Scholarly Publishing.

SASSLER, S. 2004. The process of entering into cohabiting unions. *Journal of Marriage and Family* 66 (May): 491–505.

SAUL, S. 2008. In sour economy, some scale back on medications. *New York Times,* October 22, 1.

SAUL, S. 2009. Birth of octuplets puts focus on fertility clinics. *New York Times,* February 11, 1.

SAVIN -WILLIAMS, R. C., AND E. M. DUBÉ. 1998. Parental reactions to their child's disclosure of a gay/lesbian identity. *Family Relations* 47 (January): 7–13.

SAYER, L. C. 2006. Economic aspects of divorce and relationship dissolution. In *Handbook of divorce and relationship dissolution,* eds. M. A. Fine and J. H. Harvey, 385–406. Mahwah, NJ: Lawrence Erlbaum.

SCHECTER, S., AND A. GANELY. 1995. *Domestic violence: A national curriculum for family preservation practitioners.* San Francisco: Family Violence Prevention Fund.

SCELFO, J. 2007. Come back, Mr. Chips. *Newsweek,* September 17, 44.

SCELFO, J. 2007. Facing darkness. *Newsweek,* February 26, 43–49.

SCHALLER, T. F. 2009. Seniors complain loudest, benefit most from public health care. *Baltimore Sun,* September 15, 13.

SCHEFFT, J. 2007. *Better single than sorry: A no-regrets guide to loving yourself and never settling.* New York: HarperCollins.

SCHIEBINGER, L., A. D. HENDERSON, AND S. K. GILMARTIN. 2008. Dual-career academic couples: What universities need to know. Michelle R. Clayman Institute for Gender Research, www.stanford.edu (accessed April 1, 2009).

SCHINDLER, M. 2009. Failed relationships attributed to 60 percent of Army-wide suicides. The Military Wire, March 6, blog.seattlepi.com/militarywire (accessed April 26, 2009).

SCHMEECKLE, M. 2007. Gender dynamics in stepfamilies: Adult stepchildren's views. *Journal of Marriage and Family* 69 (February): 174–89.

SCHMEECKLE, M., R. GIARRUSSO, D. FENG, AND V. L. BENGSTON. 2006. What makes someone family? Adult children's perceptions of current and former stepparents. *Journal of Marriage and Family* 68 (August): 595–610.

SCHMIEGE, C., L. RICHARDS, AND A. ZVONKOVIC. 2001. Remarriage: For love or money? *Journal of Divorce and Remarriage* 36 (January/February): 123–140.

SCHMITT, D. P., AND D. M. BUSS. 2001. Interpersonal relations and group processes: Human mate poaching—tactics and temptations for infiltrating existing mateships. *Journal of Personality and Social Psychology* 80 (June): 894–917.

SCHNEIDER, J. 2002. 100 and counting. *U.S. News & World Report*, June 3, 86.

SCHOEN, R., AND V. CANUDAS-ROMO. 2006. Timing effects on divorce: 20th century experience in the United States. *Journal of Marriage and Family* 68 (August): 749–58.

SCHOEN, R., AND Y.-H. A. CHENG. 2006. Partner choice and the differential retreat from marriage. *Journal of Marriage and Family* 68 (February): 1–10.

SCHOENBORN, C. A. 2004. *Marital status and health: United States, 1999–2002. Advance data from vital and health statistics.* Hyatsville, MD: National Center for Health Statistics.

SCHOPPE-SULLIVAN, S. J., S. C. MANGELSDORF, C. A. FROSCH, AND J. L. MC HALE. 2004. Association between coparenting and marital behavior from infancy to the preschool years. *Journal of Family Psychology* 18 (March): 194–207.

SCHOPPE-SULLIVAN, S. J., G. L. BROWN, E. A. CANNON, S. C. MANGELSDORF, AND M. S. SOKOLOWSKI. 2008. Maternal gatekeeping, coparenting quality, and fathering behavior in families with infants. *Journal of Family Psychology* 22 (June): 389–98.

SCHOR, J. B. 2002. Time crunch among American parents. In *Taking parenting public: The case for a new social movement*, eds. S. A. Hewlett, N. Rankin, and C. West, 83–102. Lanham, MD: Rowman & Littlefield.

SCHVANEVELDT, P. L., B. C. MILLER, E. H. BERRY, AND T. R. LEE. 2001. Academic goals, achievement, and age at first sexual intercourse: Longitudinal, bidirectional influences. *Adolescence* 36 (Winter): 767–87.

SCHWARTZ, D. J., V. PHARES, S. TANTLEFF-DUNN, AND J. K. THOMPSON. 1999. Devin body image, psychological functioning, and parental feedback regarding physical appearance. *International Journal of Eating Disorders* 25: 339–43.

SCHWARTZ, E. 2007. A host of trouble. *U.S. News & World Report*, October 8, 47-49.

SCHWARTZ, M. J. 2000. *Born in bondage: Growing up enslaved in the antebellum South.* Cambridge, MA: Harvard University Press.

SCHWARTZ, P. 2006. *Finding your perfect match.* New York: Penguin.

SCHWARTZBERG, J. 2009. Slouching toward fatherhood. *Newsweek*, April 15, 17.

SCHWEIGER, W. K., AND M. O'BRIEN. 2005. Special needs adoption: An ecological systems approach. *Family Relations* 54 (October): 512–22.

SCHWETZER, M. M., ED. 1999. *American Indian grandmothers: Traditions and transitions.* Albuquerque: University of New Mexico Press.

SCOMMEGNA, P. 2002. Increased cohabitation changing children's family settings. *Population Today* 30 (October): 3, 6.

SCOTT, D., AND B. WISHY, EDS. 1982. *America's families: A documentary history.* New York: Harper & Row.

SCOTT, M. E., A. BOOTH, V. KING, AND D. R. JOHNSON. 2007. Postdivorce father-adolescent closeness. *Journal of Marriage and Family* 69 (August): 1194–209.

SCOTT, W. 2009. Personality. *Parade Magazine*, July 12, 2.

SCOTT, M. E., A. BOOTH, V. KING, AND D. R. JOHNSON. 2007. Postdivorce father-adolescent closeness. *Journal of Marriage and Family* 69 (August): 1194–209.

SCOTT, W. 2009. Personality. *Parade Magazine*, July 12, 2.

SEAGER, J. 2009. *The Penguin atlas of women in the world*, 4th ed. New York: Penguin Books.

SECCOMBE, K. 2002. "Beating the odds" versus "changing the odds": Poverty, resilience, and family policy. *Journal of Marriage and Family* 64 (May): 384–94.

SECCOMBE, K. 2007. *"So you think I drive a Cadillac?": Welfare recipients' perspectives on the system and its reform*, 2nd ed. Boston, MA: Allyn and Bacon.

Secret to wedded bliss. 2005. www.msnbc.com, June 1 (accessed June 3, 2006).

SEEMAN, T. E., B. H. SINGER, C. D. RYFF, G. D. LOVE, AND L. LEVY-STORMS. 2002. Social relationships, gender, and allostatic load across two age cohorts. *Psychosomatic Medicine* 64 (May/June) 395–406.

SEGAL, J. 1989. 10 myths about child development. *Parents* (July): 81–84, 87.

SEGAL, J., G. KEMP, J. JAFFE, AND D. RUSSELL. 2009. Raising kids with your ex: Co-parenting after a separation or divorce. Helpguide.org, www.helpguide.org (accessed August 31, 2009).

SEGAL, M. W., AND J. J. HARRIS. 1993. *What we know about army families* (Special Report 21). Alexandria, VA: U.S. Army Research Institute for the Behavioral and Social Sciences.

SEGRÉ, F. 2007. This is to inform you of our new life apart. *New York Times*, October 28, 18.

SÉGUIN, V., H. B. SINGER, AND A. S. DAAR. 2008. Bidil: Recontextualizing the race debate. *Pharmacogenomics Journal* 8 (January): 169–73.

SEGURA, D. A. 1994. Working at motherhood: Chicana and Mexican immigrant mothers and employment. In *Mothering: Ideology, experience, and agency*, eds. E. N. Glenn, G. Chang, and L. R. Forcey, 211–33. New York: Routledge.

SELTZER, J. A. 2004a. Cohabitation and family change. In *Handbook of contemporary families: Considering the past contemplating the future*, eds. M. Coleman and L. H. Ganong, 57–78. Thousand Oaks, CA: Sage.

SELTZER, J. A. 2004b. Cohabitation in the United States and Britain: Demography, kinship, and the future. *Journal of Marriage and Family* 66 (November): 921–28.

SELVIN, M. 2007. Taking better care of caregivers. *Los Angeles Times*, May 12, www.latimes.com (accessed May 13, 2007).

SEMPLE, K. 2008. With economy, day laborer jobs dwindle. *New York Times*, October 20, A25.

SEMUELS, A. 2006. You can date now, meet later. *Los Angeles Times*, October 12, www.latimes.com (accessed October 13, 2006).

SEMUELS, A. 2008. Gay marriage may be a gift to California's economy. *Los Angeles Times*, June 2, www.latimes.com (accessed June 9, 2008).

SEMUELS, A. 2008. R U ready to txt for D8s? Don't LOL. *Los Angeles Times*, October 31, www.latimes.com (accessed November 1, 2008).

SESSO, H. D., ET AL. 2008. Vitamins E and C in the prevention of cardiovascular disease in men. *JAMA* 300 (November 12): 212-33.

SETOODEH, R. 2007. Need a lift? *Newsweek*, February 26, 12.

SHACKELFORD, T. K., A. T. GOETZ, D. M. BUSS, H. A. EULER, AND S. HOIER. 2005. When we hurt the ones we love: Predicting violence against women from men's mate retention. *Personal Relationships* 12 (December): 447–63.

SHADISH, W. R., AND S. A. BALDWIN. 2005. Effects of behavioral marital therapy: A meta-analysis of randomized controlled trials. *Journal of Consulting and Clinical Psychology* 73 (February): 6–14.

SHAH, A. 2009. Dell settles discrimination suit for $9.1 million. *PC World*, July 24, www.pcworld.com (accessed July 28, 2009).

SHAKIR, E. 1997. *Bint Arab: Arab and Arab American women in the United States.* Westport, CT: Praeger.

SHANKMAN, P. 1996. The history of Samoan sexual conduct and the Mead-Freeman controversy. *American Anthropologist* 98 (3): 555–67.

SHAPIRO, C. H. 2005. The infertile couple as an evolving family. *National Council on Family Relations Report* 50 (June): F15–16.

SHAPIRO, L. 1990. Guns and dolls. *Newsweek*, May 28, 57–65.

SHAPIRO-MENDOZA, C. K., M. KIMBALL, K. M. TOMASHEK, R. N. ANDERSON, AND S. BLANDING. 2009. US infant mortality trends attributable to accidental suffocation and strangulation in bed from 1984 through 2004: Are rates increasing? *Pediatrics* 123 (February): 533–39.

SHARIFZADEH, V.-S. 1997. Families with Middle Eastern roots. In *Developing cross-cultural competence: A guide for working with children and families*, eds. E. W. Lynch and M. J. Hanson, 441–82. Baltimore: Paul H. Brookes.

SHARP, E. A., D. SORELLE-MINER, J. M. BERMUDEZ, AND M. WALKER. 2008. "The glass ceiling is kind of a bummer": Women's reflections on a gender development course. *Family Relations* 57 (October): 530–41.

SHARPE, D. L. 2008. Economic status of older Asians in the United States. *Journal of Family and Economic Issues* 29 (December): 570–83.

SHATZKIN, K. 1996. Battered wife wants husband to keep job. *Baltimore Sun*, December 7, A1, A4.

SHATZKIN, K. 2004. Meeting of the minds. *Baltimore Sun*, June 6, 1N, 4N.

SHATZKIN, K. 2005. A twist in healthful benefits of marriage. Baltimore Sun, November 4, 1D-2D.

SHAVER, P., C. HAZAN, AND D. BRADSHAW. 1988. Love as attachment. In *The psychology of love*, eds. R. J. Sternberg and M. L. Barnes, 68–99. New Haven, CT: Yale University Press.

SHEA, J. A., AND G. R. ADAMS. 1984. Correlates of romantic attachment: A path analysis study. *Journal of Youth and Adolescence* 13 (1): 27–44.

SHELLENBARGER, S. 2008. When 20-somethings move back home, it isn't all bad. *Wall Street Journal*, May 21, D1.

SHENG, X. 2005. Chinese families. In *Handbook of world families*, eds. B. N. Adams and Jan Trost, 99–128. Thousand Oaks, CA: Sage.

SHERMAN, L. 1992. *Policing domestic violence: Experiment and dilemmas.* New York: Free Press.

SHEVELL, T., ET AL., 2005. Assisted reproductive technology and pregnancy outcome. *Obstetrics & Gynecology* 106 (November): 1039–45.

SHIERHOLZ, H. 2009. Nine years of job growth wiped out. Economic Policy Institute, July 2, www.epi.org (accessed August 9, 2009).

SHIERHOLZ, H., AND E. GARR. 2008. Paid maternity leave still on the wishlist for many U.S. mothers. Economic Policy Institute, May 7, www.epi.org (accessed August 8, 2009).

SHIN, A. 2009. As cuts loom, will working from home lead to a layoff? *Washington Post*, March 23, A1.

SHIN, A. 2009. Fewer new households formed in recession. *Washington Post*, July 10, A16.

SHIN, H. B., AND R. BRUNO. 2003. Language use and English-speaking ability: 2000. U.S. Census Bureau, C2KBR, October, www.census.gov (accessed July 18, 2006).

SHINAGAWA, L. H., AND G. Y. PANG. 1996. Asian American panethnicity and intermarriage. *Amerasia Journal* 22 (Spring): 127–52.

SHTARKSHALL, R. A., J. S. SANTELLI, AND J. S. HIRSCH. 2007. Sex education and sexual socialization: Roles for educators and parents. *Perspectives on Sexual and Reproductive Health* 39 (June): 116–19.

SIFAKIS, F., ET AL. 2005. HIV prevalence, unrecognized infection, and HIV testing among men who have sex with men—five U.S. cities, June 2004–April 2005. *JAMA* 294 (August 10): 674–76.

SILLIMAN, B., AND W. R. SCHUMM. 2000. Marriage preparation programs: A literature review. *The Family Journal: Counseling and Therapy for Couples and Families* 8 (April): 133–42.

SILVERMAN, I. 2006. *I married my mother-in-law*. New York: Riverland.

SILVERMAN, J. G., A. RAJ, L. A. MUCCI, AND J. E. HATHAWAY. 2001. Dating violence against adolescent girls and associated substance use, unhealthy weight control, sexual risk behavior, pregnancy, and suicidality. *JAMA* 286 (August 1): 572–79.

SILVERMAN, P. R. 2000. *Never too young to know: Death in children's lives*. New York: Oxford University Press.

SILVERMAN, R. E. 2003. Provisions boost rights of couples living together. *Wall Street Journal*, March 5, D1.

SILVERSTEIN, M., AND V. L. BENGSTON. 2001. Intergenerational solidarity and the structure of adult child-parent relationships in American families. In *Families in later life: Connections and transitions*, eds. A. J. Walker, M. Manoogian-O'Dell, L. A. McGraw, and D. L. G. White, 53–61. Thousand Oaks, CA: Pine Forge.

SILVERSTEIN, M., AND S. RUIZ. 2006. Breaking the chain: How grandparents moderate the transmission of maternal depression to their grandchildren. *Family Relations* 55 (December): 601–12.

SIMMONS, T. AND M. O'CONNELL. 2003. Married-couple and unmarried-partner households: 2000. *Census 2000 Special Reports*, CENSR-5. Washington, DC: U.S. Census Bureau.

SIMON, G. E., ET AL. 2006. Association between obesity and psychiatric disorders in the U.S. adult population. *Archives of General Psychiatry* 63 (July): 824–30.

SIMON, J. P. 1996. Lebanese families. In *Ethnicity and family therapy*, 2nd ed., eds. M. McGoldrick, J. Giordano, and J. K. Pearce, 364–75. New York: Guilford.

SIMON, R. J. 1993. *The case for transracial adoption*. Washington, DC: American University Press.

SIMON, R. J., AND H. ALTSTEIN. 2000. *Adoption across borders: Serving the children in transracial and intercountry adoptions*. Lanham, MD: Rowman & Littlefield.

SIMON, R. W. 2002. Revisiting the relationships among gender, marital status, and mental health. *American Journal of Sociology* 107 (January): 1065–96.

SIMON, R. W. 2008. The joys of parenthood, reconsidered. *Contexts* 7 (Spring): 40–45.

SIMON, R. W., AND L. E. NATH. 2004. Gender and emotion in the United States: Do men and women differ in self-reports of feelings and expressive behavior? *American Journal of Sociology* 109 (March): 1137–76.

SIMON, S. 2007. States fund antiabortion advice. *Los Angeles Times*, February 11, www.latimes.com (accessed February 12, 2007).

SIMONELLI, C. J., T. MULLIS, A. N. ELLIOTT, AND T. W. PIERCE. 2002. Abuse by siblings and subsequent experiences of violence within the dating relationship. *Journal of Interpersonal Violence* 17 (February): 103–21.

SIMPSON, J. A., W. A. COLLINS, S. TRAN, AND K. C. HAYDON. 2007. Attachment and the experience and expression of emotions in romantic relationships: A developmental perspective. *Journal of Personality and Social Psychology* 92 (February): 355–67.

SIMPSON, S. 2006. Divorce can mean loss of job at university. *The Oklahoman*, January 11, www.newsok.com (accessed January 20, 2006).

SINGH, G. K., AND M. D. KOGAN. 2007. Persistent socioeconomic disparities in infant, neonatal, and postneonatal mortality rates in the United States, 1969–2001. *Pediatrics* 119 (April): e938–e939.

SINGH, J. P. 2005. The contemporary Indian family. In *Handbook of world families*, eds. B. N. Adams and J. Trost, 129–66. Thousand Oaks, CA: Sage.

SINGLETARY, M. 2005. Financial infidelity? *Washington Post*, October 23, F1.

SINHA, G. 2004. The identity dance. *Psychology Today* 37 (March/April): 52–95.

SISSON, C. K. 2007. In college, a focus on homemaking. *Christian Science Monitor*, December 3, 20.

SIWOLOP, S. 2002. In Web's divorce industry, bad (and good) advice. *New York Times*.

SKINNER, D. A., AND J. K. KOHLER. 2002. Parental rights in diverse family contexts: Current legal developments. *Family Relations* 51 (October): 293–300.

SKOLNICK, A. 1991. *Embattled paradise: The American family in an age of uncertainty*. New York: Basic Books.

SLACKMAN, M. 2008. Generation faithful. *New York Times*, May 12, A1.

SLACKMAN, M. 2008. Stifled, Egypt's young turn to Islamic fervor. *New York Times*, Feb. 17, 1.

SLEVIN, P. 2009. Antiabortion efforts move to the state level. *Washington Post*, June 8, A1.

SLIVINSKI, S. 2007. The corporate welfare state: How the federal government subsidizes U.S. businesses. *Policy Analysis*, no. 592, May 14, Cato Institute, www.cato.org (accessed August 12, 2009).

SMALL, S. A., AND D. KERNS. 1993. Unwanted sexual activity among peers during early and middle adolescence: Incidence and risk factors. *Journal of Marriage and the Family* 55 (November): 941–52.

SMITH, C. A. 2005. Abduction, often violent, a Kyrgyz wedding rite. *New York Times* (April 30): A1.

SMITH, C. S. 2002. Kandahar journal. Shh, it's an open secret: Warlords and pedophilia. *New York Times*, February 21, A4.

SMITH, G. F. 2007. Visa denied: How anti-Arab visa policies destroy US exports, jobs and higher education. Institute for Research: Middle Eastern Policy, www.irmep.org (accessed May 7, 2007).

SMITH, J., AND H. ROSS. 2007. Training parents to mediate sibling disputes affects children's negotiation and conflict understanding. *Child Development* 78 (May): 790–805.

SMITH, K. 2009. Nohabitation: A less than ideal situation. National Council on Family Relations newsletter, *Family Focus* (Summer): F15–F16.

SMITH, K., B. DOWNS, AND M. O'CONNELL. 2001. Maternity leave and employment patterns: 1961–1995. U.S. Census Bureau, Current Population Reports, 70–79. www.census.gov (accessed September 10, 2003).

SMITH, P. K., AND L. M. DREW. 2002. Grandparenthood. In *Handbook of parenting*, 2nd ed., Vol. 3: Being and becoming a parent, ed. M. H. Bornstein, 141–72. Mahwah, NJ: Erlbaum.

SMITH, T. W. 1994. Can money buy you love? *Public Perspective* 5 (January/February): 33–34.

SMITH, T. W. 2006. American sexual behavior: Trends, socio-demographic differences, and risk behavior. National Opinion Research Center, University of Chicago, March, www.norc.org (accessed May 22, 2009).

SMITH, W. L. 1999. *Families and communes: An examination of nontraditional lifestyles*. Thousand Oaks, CA: Sage.

SMOCK, P. J. 2004. The wax and wane of marriage: Prospects for marriage in the 21st century. *Journal of Marriage and Family* 66 (November): 966–73.

SMOCK, P. J., W. D. MANNING, AND M. PORTER. 2005. "Everything's there except money": How money shapes decisions to marry among cohabitors. *Journal of Marriage and Family* 67 (August): 680–96.

SMOLAK, L., M. P. LEVINE, AND F SCHERMER. 1999. Parental input and weight concerns among elementary school children. *International Journal of Eating Disorders* 25: 263–71.

SNIPP, C. M. 2002. American Indians: Clues to the future of other racial groups. In *The new race question: How the census counts multiracial individuals*, eds. J. Perlmann and M. C. Waters, 189–214. New York: Russell Sage Foundation.

SNYDER, H. N., AND C. MCCURLEY. 2008. Domestic assaults by juvenile offenders. U.S. Department of Justice, Office of Justice Programs, November, www.ojp.usdoj.gov/ojjdp (accessed July 30, 2009).

SNYDER, K. A. 2007. A vocabulary of motives: Understanding how parents define quality time. *Journal of Marriage and Family* 69 (May): 320–40.

SOARES, C. 2006. Women rethink a big size that is beautiful but brutal. *Christian Science Monitor*, July 11, 4.

Social Security Administration. 2008. Annual statistical supplement to the Social Security bulletin, 2007. SSA Publication No. 13-11700, April, www.ssa.gov (accessed September 27, 2009).

SOCIETY FOR ADOLESCENT MEDICINE. 2004. College students engage in "risky business," exposing themselves to the dangers of sexually transmitted diseases. Unpublished material provided by April Starling, Cohn & Wolfe, February 1, 2006.

SOGUEL, D. 2009. Wage gap study arrives in time for Equal Pay Day. Women's eNews, April 28, www.womensenews.org (accessed April 28, 2009).

SOLDO, B. J., O. S. MITCHELL, R. TFAILY, AND J. F. MCCABE. 2006. Cross-cohort differences in health on the verge of retirement. National Bureau of Economic Research, December, NBER Working Paper No. 12762, www.nber.org (accessed September 20, 2009).

SOLOMON, R. C. 2002. Reasons for love. *Journal for the Theory of Social Behaviour* 32 (March): 1–28.

SOLOT, D., and M. MILLER. 2002. *Unmarried to each other: The essential guide to living together as an unmarried couple.* New York: Marlowe & Company.

SOMMERS, M., AND K. BIRCH. 2009. Combat the terror of rape in Congo. *Christian Science Monitor,* January 27, 9.

SONTAG, D. 2002. Fierce entanglements. *New York Times Magazine,* November 17, 52.

SORENSEN, E., AND C. ZIBMAN. 2000. Child support offers some protection against poverty. Washington, DC: Urban Institute. newfederalism.urban.org (accessed October 21, 2000).

SORENSON, S. B., AND K. A. THOMAS. 2009. Views of intimate partner violence in same- and opposite-sex relationships. *Journal of Marriage and Family* 71 (May): 337–52.

SORIANO, C. G. 2006. "Bored" by her kids, she's getting it full-bore. *USA Today,* July 31, www.usatoday.com (accessed August 3, 2006).

SOTO, M. 2009. How is the financial crisis affecting retirement savings? May 2009, update. Urban Institute, Retirement Policy Program, www.retirementpolicy.org (accessed September 5, 2009).

SOUKUP, E. 2005. Happy-V-Day! (Just not in Pittsburgh.) *Newsweek,* February 14, 11.

SOUTH, S. J., K. D. CROWDER, AND K. TRENT. 1998. Children's residential mobility and neighborhood environment following parental divorce and remarriage. *Social Forces* 77: 667–93.

SPAKE, A. 1998. Adoption gridlock. *U.S. News & World Report,* June 22, 30–37.

SPENCER, R. F., and J. D. JENNINGS. 1977. *The Native Americans: Ethnology and backgrounds of the North American Indians.* New York: Harper & Row.

SPIEKER, S. J., N. C. LARSON, AND L. GILCHRIST. 1999. Developmental trajectories of disruptive behavior problems in preschool children of adolescent mothers. *Child Development* 70 (March): 443–58.

SPITZE, G., J. R. LOGAN, G. DEANE, AND S. ZERGER. 1994. Adult children's divorce and intergenerational relationships. *Journal of Marriage and the Family* 56 (May): 279–93.

SPRECHER, S. 1999. "I love you more today than yesterday": Romantic partners' perceptions of changes in love and related affect over time. *Journal of Personality and Social Psychology* 76 (January): 46–53.

SPRECHER, S. 2001. Equity and social exchange in dating couples: Associations with satisfaction, commitment, and stability. *Journal of Marriage and Family* 63 (August): 509–613.

SPRECHER, S., AND K. MC KINNEY. 1993. *Sexuality.* Thousand Oaks, CA: Sage.

SQUIER, D. A., AND J. S. QUADAGNO. 1988. The Italian American family. In *Ethnic families in America: Patterns and variations,* 3rd ed., eds. C. J. Mindel, R. W. Habenstein, and R. Wright, Jr., 109–37. New York: Elsevier.

SRABSTEIN, J., B. L. LEVENTHAL, AND J. MERRICK. 2008. Bullying: A global public health risk. *International Journal of Adolescent Medicine and Health* 20 (2): 99–100.

SRINIVASAN, P., AND G. R. LEE. 2004. The dowry system in northern India: Women's attitudes and social change. *Journal of Marriage and Family* 66 (December): 1108–17.

SRIVASTAVA, S., O. P. JOHN, S. D. GOSLING, AND J. POTTER. 2003. Development of personality in early and middle adulthood: Set like plaster or persistent change? *Journal of Personality and Social Psychology* 84 (May): 1041–53.

STACEY, J. 2003. Gay and lesbian families: Queer like us. In *All our families: New policies for a new century,* 2nd ed., eds. M. A. Mason, A. Skolnick, and S. D. Sugarman, 144–69. New York: Oxford University Press.

STACEY, J., AND T. J. BIBLARZ. 2001. (How) does the sexual orientation of parents matter? *American Sociological Review* 66 (April): 159–83.

STAFFORD, F. 2008. Exactly how much housework does a husband create? University of Michigan News Service, April 3, www.ns .umich.edu (accessed June 2, 2008).

STANCZYK, A. 2009. Low-income working families: Updated facts and figures. Urban Institute, June 1, www.urban.org (accessed August 9, 2009).

STANLEY, A. 2008. Mars and Venus dissect the Spitzer scandal on the TV talk shows. *New York Times,* March 12, 1.

STANLEY, S. M., AND G. SMALLEY. 2005. *The power of commitment: A guide to active, lifelong love.* San Francisco, CA: Jossey-Bass.

STANLEY, S. M., H. J. MARKMAN, AND S. W. WHITTON. 2002. Communication, conflict, and commitment: Insights on the foundations of relationship success from a national survey. *Family Process* 41 (Winter): 659–75.

STANLEY, S. M. 2007. Assessing couple and marital relationships: Beyond form and toward a deeper knowledge of function. In *Handbook of measurement issues in family research,* eds. L. M. Casper and S. L. Hofereth, 85–100. Mahwah, NJ: Lawrence Erlbaum & Associates.

STANLEY, S. M., AND G. K. RHOADES. 2009. "Sliding vs. deciding": Understanding a mystery. National Council on Family Relations newsletter, *Family Focus* (Summer): F1–F4.

STANLEY, S. M., S. W. WHITTON, AND H. J. MARKMAN. 2004. Maybe I do: Interpersonal commitment and premarital or nonmarital cohabitation. *Journal of Family Issues* 25 (May): 496–519.

STANNARD, D. E. 1979. Changes in the American family: Fiction and reality. In *Changing images of the family,* eds. V. Tufte and B. Myerhoff, 83–98. New Haven, CT: Yale University Press.

STAPLES, R. 1988. The black American family. In *Ethnic families in America: Patterns and variations,* 3rd ed., eds. C. H. Mindel, R. W. Habenstein, and R. Wright, Jr., 303–24. New York: Elsevier.

STARK, E. 2007. *Coercive control: How men entrap women in personal life.* New York: Oxford University Press.

STARK, M. 1998. *What no one tells the bride.* New York: Hyperion.

STARR, A. 2001. Shotgun weddings by Uncle Sam? *Business Week,* June 4, 68.

State of the world's mothers 2003: Protecting women and children in war and conflict. 2003. Save the Children. www.savethe children.org (accessed May 25, 2003).

Stats & facts: Love and money. 2005. *Redbook,* November, http://lawyers.com/lawyers/ (accessed April 14, 2006).

STAUSS, J. H. 1995. Reframing and refocusing American Indian family strengths. In *American families: Issues in race and ethnicity,* ed. C. K. Jacobson, 105–18. New York: Garland.

STEAD, D. 2008. What mom and dad are buying. *Business Week,* December 15, 19

STEIL, J. M. 1997. *Marital equality: Its relationship to the well-being of husbands and wives.* Thousand Oaks, CA: Sage.

STEIN, P. J., ED. 1981. *Single life: Unmarried adults in social context.* New York: St. Martin's.

STEIN, R. 2008. "Pro-life" drugstores market beliefs. *Washington Post,* June 16, A1.

STEINBERG, L., AND R. M. LERNER. 2004. The scientific study of adolescence: A brief history. *Journal of Early Adolescence* 24 (February): 45–54.

STERNBERG, R. J. 1986. A triangular theory of love. *Psychological Review* 93 (2): 119–35.

STERNBERG, R. J. 1988. *The triangle of love.* New York: Basic Books.

STEWART, S. D. 2003. Nonresident parenting and adolescent adjustment. *Journal of Family Issues* 24 (March): 217–44.

STEWART, S. D. 2005. How the birth of a child affects involvement with stepchildren. *Journal of Marriage and Family* 67 (May): 461–73.

STEWART, S. D. 2007. *Brave new stepfamilies: Diverse paths toward stepfamily living.* Thousand Oaks, CA: Sage.

STILLARS, A. L. 1991. Behavioral observation. In *Studying interpersonal interaction,* eds. B. M. Montgomery and S. Duck, 197–218. New York: Guilford.

STINNETT, N., AND J. DE FRAIN. 1985. *Secrets of strong families.* Boston: Little, Brown.

STIRLING, K., AND T. ALDRICH. 2008. Child support: Who bears the burden? *Family Relations* 57 (July): 376–89.

STOBBE, M. 2008. Life expectancy tops 78. *Baltimore Sun,* June 12, 3C.

STOCKEL, H. H. 1991. *Women of the Apache nation.* Reno: University of Nevada Press.

STOLBERG, S. G., AND M. CONNELLY. 2009. Obama is nudging views on race, a survey finds. *New York Times,* April 28.

STOLZENBERG, R. M. 2001. It's about time and gender: Spousal employment and health. *American Journal of Sociology* 107 (July): 61–100.

STOMBLER, M. 2009. In the hot seat. *Chronicle of Higher Education,* May 1, A31, A33.

STONE, L., AND N. P. MC KEE. 2002. *Gender and culture in America,* 2nd ed. Upper Saddle River, NJ: Prentice Hall.

STONE, P. 2007. *Opting out? Why women really quit careers and head home.* Berkeley: University of California Press.

STOUT, H. 2005. Family matters: Singles therapy. *Wall Street Journal* (April 28): D1.

STRASBURGER, V. C. AND B. J. WILSON. 2002. *Children, adolescents, & the media.* Thousand Oaks, CA: Sage.

STRASBURGER, V. C., ET AL. 2006. Children, adolescents, and advertising. *Pediatrics* 118 (December): 2563–69.

STRASSER, J. 2004. *Black eye: Escaping a marriage, writing a life.* Madison: University of Wisconsin Press.

STRATTON, J. L. 1981. *Pioneer women: Voices from the Kansas frontier.* New York: Simon & Schuster.

STRAUCH, B. 2003. *The primal teen: What the new discoveries about the teenage brain tell us about our kids.* New York: Doubleday.

STRAUS, M. 2007. Do we need a law to prohibit spanking? *Family Focus* 52 (June): F7, F19.

STRAUS, M. 2008. Ending spanking can make a major contribution to preventing physical abuse. *Family Focus* 53 (December): F14–F16.

STRAUS, M. A. 2006. Dominance and symmetry in partner violence by male and female university students in 32 nations. Paper presented at conference on Trends in Intimate Violence Intervention, New York University, May 23.

STRAUS, M. A., AND C. J. FIELD. 2003. Psychological aggression by American parents: National data on prevalence, chronicity, and severity. *Journal of Marriage and Family* 65 (November): 795–808.

STRAUS, M. A., AND C. L. YODANIS. 1996. Corporal punishment in adolescence and physical assaults on spouses in later life: What accounts for the link? *Journal of Marriage and the Family* 58 (November): 825–41.

STRAUS, M. A., AND J. H. STEWART. 1999. Corporal punishment by American parents: National data on prevalence, chronicity, severity, and duration, in relation to child and family characteristics. *Clinical Child and Family Psychology Review* 2 (June): 55–70.

STRAUS, M. A., ED. 2001. *Beating the devil out of them: Corporal punishment in American families and its effects on children*, 2nd ed. Somerset, NJ: Transaction Publishers.

STREISAND, B. 2006. Who's your daddy? *U.S. News & World Report*, February 13, 53–56.

STRIEGEL-MOORE, R. H., ET AL. 2003. Eating disorders in white and black women. *American Journal of Psychiatry* 160 (July): 1326–31.

STROCK, M. 2002. Depression. National Institutes of Mental Health. www.nimh.nih.gov (accessed October 9, 2003).

STROEBE, M., M. VAN SON, W. STROEBE, R. KLEBER, H. SCHUT, AND J. VAN DEN BOUT. 2000. On the classification and diagnosis of pathological grief. *Clinical Psychology Review* 20 (January): 57–75.

STROH, M. 2006. Biological clock ticks for men, too, studies say. *Baltimore Sun*, September 10, 1A, 10A.

STROHSCHEIN, L. 2005. Parental divorce and child mental health trajectories. *Journal of Marriage and Family* 67 (December): 1286–1300.

Substance Abuse and Mental Health Services Administration. 2005. *Results from the 2004 National Survey on Drug Use and Health: National Findings*. Rockville, MD: Office of Applied Studies.

Substance Abuse and Mental Health Services Administration. 2006. *Results from the 2005 national survey on drug use and health: National findings*. Rockville, MD: Office of Applied Studies, NSDUH Series H-30, DHHS Publication No. SMA 06-4194.

Substance Abuse and Mental Health Services Administration. 2008. *Results from the 2007 national survey on drug use and health: National findings*. Office of Applied Studies, www.samsa.gov (accessed August 9, 2009).

SUDARKASA, N. 2007. African American female-headed households: Some neglected dimensions. In *Black families*, 4th ed., ed. H. P. McAdoo, 172–83. Thousand Oaks, CA: Sage.

SUGG, D. K. 2000. Subtle signs of heart disease in women are often missed. *Baltimore Sun*, January 25, 1A, 13A.

Suicide. 2008. Centers for Disease Control and Prevention, Summer, www.cdc.gov/injury (accessed March 31, 2009).

Suicide. 2009. Centers for Disease Control and Prevention, Summer, www.cdc.gov (accessed August 23, 2009).

SULLIVAN, A. 2003. The conservative case for gay marriages. *Time*, June 30, 76.

SULLIVAN, A., ED. 1997. *Same-sex marriage, pro and con: A reader*. New York: Vintage.

SULLIVAN, J. 2006. The Cupid index. *Christian Science Monitor* (February 14): 20.

SULLIVAN, M. 2009. How to end the war over sex ed. *Time*, March 30, 40–43.

SULLIVAN, O., AND S. COLTRANE. 2008. Men's changing contribution to housework and child care. Council on Contemporary Families, www.contemporaryfamilies.org (accessed April 17, 2009).

SUN, Y. 2001. Family environment and adolescents' well-being before and after parents' marital disruption: A longitudinal analysis.

Journal of Marriage and Family 63 (August): 697–713.

SUN, Y., AND Y. LI. 2002. Children's well-being during parents' marital disruption process: A pooled time-series analysis. *Journal of Marriage and Family* 64 (May): 472–88.

SUN, Y., AND Y. LI. 2007. Racial and ethnic differences in experiencing parents' marital disruption during late adolescence. *Journal of Marriage and Family* 69 (August): 742–62.

SUN, Y., AND Y. LI. 2008. Stable postdivorce family structures during late adolescence and socioeconomic consequences in adulthood. *Journal of Marriage and Family* 70 (February): 129–43.

SUNDERAM, S., ET AL. 2009. Assisted reproductive technology surveillance—United States, 2006. *MMWR* 58 (June 12): 1–25.

SURDIN, A. 2009. In several states, a push to stem cyber-bullying. *Washington Post*, January 1, A3.

SURO, R. 1998. *Strangers among us: How Latino immigration is transforming America*. New York: Knopf.

SWANBERG, J. E., AND T. K. LOGAN. 2003. Intimate partner violence and employment: A qualitative study of rural and urban women. *Family Focus* (March): F8–F9.

SWANBROW, D. 2007. Time, money, and who does the laundry. University of Michigan, Institute for Social Research, January, www .isr.umich.edu (accessed April 20, 2009).

SWANBROW, D. 2008. Exactly how much housework does a husband create? University of Michigan News Service, April 3, http:// michigantoday.umich.edu (accessed June 21, 2009).

SWARNS, R. L. 2008. Bipartisan calls for new federal poverty measure. *New York Times*, September 2, 14.

SWEENEY, M. M., AND J. A. PHILLIPS. 2004. Understanding racial differences in marital disruption: Recent trends and explanations. *Journal of Marriage and Family* 66 (August): 639–650.

SWINFORD, S. P., A. DE MARIS, S. A. CERNKOVICH, AND P. G. GIORDANO. 2000. Harsh physical discipline in childhood and violence in later romantic involvements: The mediating role of problem behaviors. *Journal of Marriage and the Family* 62 (May): 508–19.

SZABO, L., AND J. APPLEBY. 2009. 21% of Americans scramble to pay medical, drug bills. *USA Today*, March 10, www.usatoday.com (accessed July 7, 2009).

SZINOVACZ, M. E., AND A. DAVEY. 2005. Retirement and marital decision making effects on retirement satisfaction. *Journal of Marriage and Family* 67 (May): 387–98.

SZINOVACZ, M. E., ED. 1998. *Handbook on grandparenthood*. Westport, CT: Greenwood.

SZYMANSKI, L. A., A. S. DEVLIN, J. C. CHRISLER, AND S. A. VYSE. 1993. Gender roles and attitudes toward rape in male and female college students. *Sex Roles* 29 (1/2): 37–57.

T

TACH, L., AND S. HALPERN-MEEKIN. 2009. How does premarital cohabitation affect trajectories of marital quality? *Journal of Marriage and Family* 71 (May): 298–317.

TAKAGI, D. Y. 2002. Japanese American families. In *Minority families in the United States: A multicultural perspective*, 3rd ed., ed. R. L. Taylor, 164–80. Upper Saddle River, NJ: Prentice Hall.

TALBOT, L. 2007. *Singular existence: Because it's better to be alone than wish you were!* New York: Citadel Press.

TAM, V. C.-W., AND D. F. DETZNER. 1998. Grandparents as a family resource in Chi-

nese-American families: Perceptions of the middle generation. In *Resiliency in Native American and immigrant families*, eds. H. I. McCubbin, E. A. Thompson, A. I. Thompson, and J. E. Fromer, 243–64. Thousand Oaks, CA: Sage.

TAN, A. L. 2004. *Chinese American children & families: A guide for educators & service providers*. Olney, MD: Association for Childhood Education International.

TANNEN, D. 1990. *You just don't understand: Women and men in conversation*. New York: Ballantine.

TANNEN, D. 1994. *Talking 9 to 5: Women and men at work*. New York: Quill.

TANUR, J. M. 1994. The trustworthiness of survey research. *Chronicle of Higher Education*, May 25, B1–B3.

TAVRIS, C. 1992. *The mismeasure of woman*. New York: Simon & Schuster.

TAVRIS, C. 2003. Mind games: Psychological warfare between therapists and scientists. *Chronicle of Higher Education*, February 28, B7–B9.

TAYLOR, J. B., AND J. P. KALT. 2005. *American Indians on reservations: A databook of socioeconomic change between the 1990 and 2000 censuses*. Harvard Project on American Indian Economic Development, January, www.ksg.harvard.edu (accessed April 20, 2007).

TAYLOR, L. R., AND N. GASKIN-LANIYAN. 2007. Sexual assault in abusive relationships. *NIJ Journal*, no. 256, January, www.ojp.usdoj .gov (accessed July 9, 2009).

TAYLOR, P., C. FUNK, AND P. CRAIGHILL. 2006a. Are we happy yet? Pew Research Center, February 13, http://pewresearch.org (accessed June 14, 2006).

TAYLOR, P., C. FUNK, AND P. CRAIGHILL. 2006b. Once again, the future ain't what it used to be. Pew Research Center May 2, http:pewresearch.org (accessed May 10, 2006).

TAYLOR, P., R. KOCHHAR, R. MORIN, W. WANG, AND D. DOCKTERMAN. 2009a. Recession turns a graying office grayer. Pew Research Center, September 3, http://pewsocialtrends. org (accessed September 16, 2009).

TAYLOR, P., C. FUNK, AND A. CLARK. 2007. As marriage and parenthood drift apart, public is concerned about social impact. Pew Research Center, July 1, www.pewresearch .org (accessed June 15, 2009).

TAYLOR, P., C. FUNK, AND P. CRAIGHILL. 2006. A barometer of modern morals: Sex, drugs, and the 1040. Pew Research Center, March 28, http://pewresearch.org (accessed May 20, 2009).

TAYLOR, P., R. MORIN, D. COHN, R. FRY, R. KOCHHAR, AND A. CLARK. 2008. Inside the middle class: Bad times hit the good life. Pew Research Center, April 9, http:// pewresearch.org (accessed May 20, 2008).

TAYLOR, P., R. MORIN, K. PARKER, D. COHN, AND W. WANG. 2009b. Growing old in America: Expectations vs. reality. Pew Research Center, June 29, http://pewsocialtrends.org (accessed September 5, 2009).

TAYLOR, S. C. 2003. *Brown skin: Dr. Susan Taylor's prescription for flawless skin, hair, and nails*. New York: HarperCollins.

TAZ, V. 2005. Not dead yet. *Chronicle of Higher Education*, October 28, C1, C4.

TEACHMAN, J. D. 2002. Childhood living arrangements and the intergenerational transmission of divorce. *Journal of Marriage and Family* 64 (August): 717–29.

TEACHMAN, J. D. 2003. Premarital sex, premarital cohabitation, and the risk of subsequent marital dissolution among women. *Journal of Marriage and Family* 65 (May): 444–55.

TEACHMAN, J. D., AND L. TEDROW. 2008. Divorce, race, and military service: More than equal pay and equal opportunity. *Journal of Marriage and Family* 70 (November): 1030–44.

TEASTER, P. B. ET AL. 2006. The 2004 survey of state adult protective services: Abuse of adults 60 years of age and older. National Center on Elder Abuse, February, www .elderabusecenter.org (accessed June 6, 2006).

Teens, video games, and civics. 2008. Pew Research Center, September 16, http:// pewresearch.org (accessed September 18, 2008).

TEJADA-VERA, B., AND P. D. SUTTON. 2009. Births, marriages, divorces, and deaths: Provisional data for 2008. *National Vital Statistics Reports* 57 (July 29): 1–6.

TELLEEN, S., S. MAHER, AND R. C. PESCE. 2003. Building community connections for youth to reduce violence. *Psychology in the Schools* 40 (September): 549–63.

TERESI, D. 1994. How to get a man pregnant. *New York Times Magazine*, November 27, 54–55.

TERGESEN, A. 2001. Cutting the knot—but not the benefits. *Business Week*, July 16, 87–88.

TERRY, D. F., P. SEBASTIANI, S. L. ANDERSEN, AND T. T. PERLS. 2008. Disentangling the roles of disability and morbidity in survival to exceptional old age. *Archives of Internal Medicine* 168 (February 11): 277–83.

TERZIEFF, J. 2006. New law puts brakes on international bride brokers. Women's e-news, March 8, www.womensenews.com (accessed March 12, 2006).

TESSIER, M. 2007. Custody disputes often bypass abuse assessments. Women's eNews, July 6, www.womensenews.org (accessed July 20, 2007).

TESSIER, M. 2008. Intimate violence remains a big killer of women. Women's eNews, August, www.womensenews.org (accessed August 9, 2009).

The best interests of the child. 2009. Editorial. *New York Times*, January 6, A24.

The Board of Trustees, Federal Old-Age and Survivors Insurance and Federal Disability Insurance Trust Funds. 2009. *The 2009 annual report of the board of trustees of the federal old-age and survivors insurance and disability insurance trust funds.* Washington, DC: U.S. Government Printing Office.

THEE, M. 2007. Cellphones challenge poll sampling. *New York Times*, December 7, 29.

The FASD Center. 2009. Alcohol and pregnancy. www.fasdcenter.samhsa.gov (accessed June 26, 2009).

The merits of gay marriage. 2003. Editorial, *Washington Post*, November 20, A40.

The National Campaign to Prevent Teen and Unplanned Pregnancy and *CosmoGirl.com.* 2008. Sex and tech: Results from a survey of teens and young adults. www.thenational campaign.org (accessed May 15, 2009).

THERNSTROM, M. 2005. The new arranged marriage. *New York Times Magazine,* February 13, 35–41, 72–78.

The State of Our Unions 2007. 2007. Social indicators of marital health and wellbeing: Trends of the past four decades. The National Marriage Project, http://marriage. rutgers.edu (accessed March 2, 2009).

THOMAS, A. J., AND S. L. SPEIGHT, 1999. Racial identity and racial socialization attitudes of African American parents. *Journal of Black Psychology* 25 (May): 152–70.

THOMAS, J. 2009. Virginity pledgers are just as likely as matched nonpledgers to report premarital intercourse. *Perspectives on Sexual and Reproductive Health* 41 (March): 63.

THOMAS, W. I., AND F. ZNANIECKI. 1927. *The Polish peasant in Europe and America*, vol. 2. New York: Knopf. (Originally published 1918 by the University of Chicago Press.)

THOMPSON, K. M., AND F. YOKOTA. 2004. Violence, sex, and profanity in films: Correlation of movie ratings with content. *Medscape General Medicine* 6 (3): 1–19.

THOMPSON, L., AND A. J. WALKER. 1991. Gender in families. In *Contemporary families: Looking forward, looking back*, ed. A. Booth, 76–102. Minneapolis: National Council on Family Relations.

THOMPSON, P. M., ET AL. 2003. Dynamics of gray matter loss in Alzheimer's disease. *Journal of Neuroscience* 23 (February 1): 994–1005.

THOMPSON, R. S., ET AL. 2006. Intimate partner violence: Prevalence, types, and chronicity in adult women. *American Journal of Preventive Medicine* 30 (June): 447–57.

THOMSON, E. 1997. Couple childbearing desires, intentions, and births. *Demography* 34 (August): 343–54.

THORNBERRY, T. P., C. A. SMITH, C. RIVERA, D. HUIZINGA, AND M. STOUTHAMER -LOEBER. 1999. *Family disruption and delinquency.* Washington, DC: U.S. Department of Justice, Office of Justice Programs, Office of Juvenile Justice and Delinquency Prevention.

THORNTON, A. 2001. The developmental paradigm, reading history sideways, and family change. *Demography* 38 (November): 449–65.

THORNTON, A., AND L. YOUNG-DE MARCO. 2001. Four decades in attitudes toward family issues in the United States: The 1960s through the 1990s. *Journal of Marriage and the Family* 63 (November): 1009–37.

THORNTON, E. 1994. Video dating in Japan. *Fortune*, January 24, 12.

TICHENOR, V. J. 2005. *Earning more and getting less: Why successful wives can't buy equality.* New Brunswick, NJ: Rutgers University Press.

TILLMAN, K. H. 2007. Family structure pathways and academic disadvantage among adolescents in stepfamilies. *Sociological Inquiry* 77 (August): 383–424.

TIMBERLAKE, C. A., AND W. D. CARPENTER. 1990. Sexuality attitudes of black adults. *Family Relations* 39 (January): 87–91.

TIMMER, S. G., AND T. L. ORBUCH. 2001. The links between premarital parenthood, meanings of marriage, and marital outcomes. *Family Relations* 50 (April): 178–85.

TITUS, S. L., J. A. WELLS, AND L. J. RHOADES. 2008. Repairing research integrity. *Nature* 453 (June 19): 980–82.

TJADEN, P., AND N. THOENNES. 2000. *Extent, nature, and consequences of intimate partner violence: Findings from the National Violence against Women Survey.* Washington, DC: U.S. Department of Justice, Office of Justice Programs.

TJADEN, P., AND N. THOENNES. 2006. *Extent, nature, and consequences of rape victimization: Findings from the National Violence against Women Survey.* Washington, DC: U.S. Department of Justice, Office of Justice Programs.

TOHID, O. 2003. Pakistanis abroad trick daughters into marriage. *Christian Science Monitor,* May 15, 1, 7.

TOPPO, G. 2008. In-laws in White House may add new meaning to domestic policy. *USA Today,* December 4, www.usatoday.com (accessed December 5, 2008).

TORO-MORN, M. I. 1998. The family and work experiences of Puerto Rican women migrants in Chicago. In *Resiliency in Native American and immigrant families,* eds. H. I. McCubbin, E. A. Thompson, A. I. Thompson, and J. E. Fromer, 277–94. Thousand Oaks, CA: Sage.

TOTH, J. F., AND X. XU. 1999. Ethnic and cultural diversity in fathers' involvement: A racial/ethnic comparison of African American, Hispanic, and white fathers. *Youth & Society* 31 (September): 76–99.

TOTH, J. F., AND X. XU. 2002. Fathers' child-rearing involvement in African American, Latino, and white families. In *Contemporary ethnic families in the United States: Characteristics, variations, and dynamics,* ed. N. V. Benokraitis, 130–40. Upper Saddle River, NJ: Prentice Hall.

TOWER, R. B., S. V. KASL, AND A. S. DAREFSKY. 2002. Types of marital closeness and mortality risk in older couples. *Psychosomatic Medicine* 64: 644–59.

TOWNER, B. 2009. 50 and still a doll. *AARP Bulletin* (March): 35.

TRAFFORD, A. 2005. Grandparents help define family values. *Washington Post,* March 1, HE6.

TREAS, J., AND D. GIESEN. 2000. Sexual infidelity among married and cohabiting Americans. *Journal of Marriage and the Family* 62 (February): 48–60.

TRENHOLM, C., B. DEVANEY, K. FORTSON, M. CLARK, L. QUAY, AND J. WHEELER. 2008. Impacts of abstinence education on teen sexual activity, risk of pregnancy, and risk of sexually transmitted diseases. *Journal of Policy Analysis and Management* 27 (March): 255–76.

TRIMBLE, J. E., AND B. MEDICINE. 1993. Diversification of American Indians: Forming an indigenous perspective. In *Indigenous psychologies,* eds. U. Kim and J. W. Berry, 133–51. Newbury Park, CA: Sage.

TROST, J., AND I. LEVIN. 2005. Scandinavian families. In *Handbook of world families,* eds. Bert N. Adams and Jan Trost, 347–63. Thousand Oaks, CA: Sage.

TROTTER, R. J. 1986. Failing to find the father-infant bond. *Psychology Today* (February): 18.

TRU. 2009. Teens worldwide rate mom the most influential person in their lives. Press release, May 6, www.tru-insight.com (accessed June 6, 2009).

TRUMBULL, D. A., AND D. RAVENEL. 1999. Spare the rod? New research challenges spanking critic. Family Policy, Family Research Council, January 22.

TRUMBULL, M. 2009. A shift in home economics. *Christian Science Monitor,* June 7, 21.

TRUMBULL, M. 2009. Americans are working fewest hours on record. *Christian Science Monitor,* July 2, www.csmonitor.com (accessed July 5, 2009).

TRUMBULL, M. 2009. Healthcare hurdles. *Christian Science Monitor,* September 13, 23.

Trust for America's Health. 2009. F as in fat: How obesity policies are failing in America. Robert Wood Johnson Foundation, July, www.healthyamericans.org (accessed July 18, 2009).

TSAI, G., AND J. GRAY. 2000. The eating disorders inventory among Asian American college women. *Journal of Social Psychology* 140 (August): 527–29.

TSAI, J. L., D. E. PRZYMUS, AND J. L. BEST. 2002. Toward an understanding of Asian American interracial marriage and dating. In *Inside the American couple: New thinking/new challenges,* eds. M. Yalom and L. L. Carstensen, 189–210. Berkeley: University of California Press.

TUCKER, C. 2007. Lingering sexism impedes women's path to highest level of power. *Baltimore Sun,* January 8, A9.

TUCKER, K. L., J. HALLFRISCH, N. QIAO, D. MULLER, R. ANDRES, AND J. L. FLEG. 2005. The combination of high fruit and vegetable and low saturated fat intakes is more protective against mortality in aging men than is either alone: The Baltimore longitudinal study of aging. *Journal of Nutrition* 135 (March): 556–61.

TUCKER, R. K. 1992. Men's and women's ranking of thirteen acts of romance. *Psychological Reports* 71: 640–42.

TURETSKY, V. 2006. Families will lose at least $8.4 billion in uncollected child support if Congress cuts funds—and could lose billions more. Center for Law and Social Policy, January 18, www.clasp.org/ (accessed July 10, 2006).

TURNBULL, S. K., AND J. M. TURNBULL. 1983. To dream the impossible dream: An agenda for discussion with stepparents. *Family Relations* 32: 227–30.

TURNER, M. A., AND K. FORTUNY. 2009. Residential segregation and low-income working families. The Urban Institute, February, www.urban.org (accessed March 15, 2009).

TURNER, M. J., C. R. YOUNG, AND K. I. BLACK. 2006. Daughters-in-law and mothers-in-law seeking their place within the family: A qualitative study of differing viewpoints. *Family Relations* 55 (December): 588–600.

TUTTLE, W. M., JR. 1993. *Daddy's gone to war: The Second World War in the lives of America's children*. New York: Oxford University Press.

TWENGE, J. M., W. K. CAMPBELL, AND C. A. FOSTER. 2003. Parenthood and marital satisfaction: A meta-analytic review. *Journal of Marriage and Family* 65 (August): 574–83.

TWENGE, J., AND W. CAMPBELL. 2003. "Isn't it fun to get the respect that we're going to deserve?" Narcissism, social rejection, and aggression. *Personality and Social Psychology Bulletin* 29 (2): 261–72.

TWENGE, J. M., AND W. K. CAMPBELL. 2009. *The narcissism epidemic: Living in an age of entitlement*. New York: Free Press.

TYSZKOWA, M. 1993. Adolescents' relationships with grandparents: Characteristics and developmental transformations. In *Adolescence and its social worlds*, eds. S. Jackson and H. Rodriguez-Tomé, 121–43. East Sussex, UK: Erlbaum.

U

UNAIDS. 2008. Report on the global AIDS epidemic 2008: Global facts and figures. August, www.unaids.org (accessed May 25, 2009).

Understanding suicide. 2009. Centers for Disease Control and Prevention, www.cdc.gov (accessed August 23, 2009).

UNICEF. 2005. Child poverty in rich countries, 2005: Innocent Report Card No. 6. Florence: UNICEF Innocenti Research Centre, www.unicef-icdc.org (accessed May 28, 2006).

UNICEF. 2006. The state of the world's children 2006: Excluded and invisible. www.unicef.org (accessed March 12, 2009).

UNICEF. 2007. Child poverty in perspective: An overview of child well-being in rich countries. *Innocenti Report Card 7*, www.unicef.org/irc (accessed July 13, 2009).

UNITED NATIONS CHILDREN'S FUND. 2005. Changing a harmful social convention: Female genital mutilation/cutting. New York, www.unicef-icdc.org (accessed January 5, 2006).

United Nations Population Fund. 2007. Sex-ratio imbalance in Asia: Trends, consequences and policy responses. *Executive Summary, Regional Analysis*. www.unfpa.org (accessed June 12, 2009).

U.S. Bureau of Labor Statistics. 2008. Table 39: Median weekly earning of full-time wage and salary workers by detailed occupation and sex. www.bls.gov (accessed July 2, 2008).

U.S. CENSUS BUREAU. 2002. *Statistical abstract of the United States: 2002*. Washington, DC: U.S. Government Printing Office.

U.S. Census Bureau. 2005. Interim projections of the population by selected age groups for the United States and states: April 1, 2000 to July 1, 2030. Population Division, Interim State Population Projections, 2005, www.census.org (accessed September 18, 2009).

U.S. Census Bureau News. 2007. Most people make only one trip down the aisle, but first marriages shorter. Census Bureau reports, September 19, CB07-131, www.census.gov (accessed August 28, 2009).

U.S. Census Bureau. 2008. *Statistical abstract of the United States 2009* (128th edition). Washington, DC: U.S. Government Printing Office.

U.S. Census Bureau. 2008. Table MS-1. Marital status of the population 15 years old and over, by sex and race: 1950 to present. July, Current Population Survey, March and Annual Social and Economic Supplements, 2007 and earlier, www.census.gov (accessed February 23, 2009).

U.S. Census Bureau, Current Population Survey, 2008 Annual Social and Economic Supplement. 2009. Detailed table package, www.census.gov (accessed July 13, 2009).

U.S. Census Bureau, Current Population Survey. 2008. Table MS-2: Estimated median age at first marriage, by sex: 1890 to the present. July, March and Annual Social and Economic Supplements, 2007 and earlier, www.census.gov (accessed February 23, 2009).

U.S. Census Bureau, Current Population Survey, 2009. 2008 Annual Social and Economic Supplement, January, Tables A1 and AVG1, www.census.gov (accessed June 6, 2009).

U.S. Census Bureau, Current Population Survey, 2009. March and Annual Social and Economic Supplements, 2008 and earlier, January, Table MS-2, www.census.gov (accessed June 6, 2009).

U.S. Census Bureau, Current Population Survey. 2009. Poverty data. 2009 Annual Social and Economic Supplement, www.census.gov (accessed September 22, 2009).

U.S. Census Bureau News. 2008. Unmarried and single Americans week Sept. 21–27, 2008. U.S. Census Bureau, www.census.gov (accessed February 24, 2009).

U.S. Census Bureau News. 2009. Facts for features: Older Americans month, May 2009. CB09-FF.07, March 3, www.census.gov (accessed June 13, 2009).

U.S. Census Bureau News. 2009. Mother's Day: May 10, 2009. Facts for Features, CB09-FF.09, March 10, www.census.gov (accessed April 3, 2009).

U.S. Census Bureau News. 2009. Unmarried and single Americans week Sept. 20–26, 2009. U.S. Census Bureau, www.census.gov (accessed February 24, 2009).

U.S. Census Bureau Newsroom. 2008. Facts for features: Valentine's Day 2009: Feb. 14, CB09-FF.02, December 16, www.census.gov (accessed June 22, 2009).

U.S. DEPARTMENT OF COMMERCE. 1993. We the American foreign born. U.S. Bureau of the Census. Washington, DC: U.S. Government Printing Office.

U.S. Department of Education. 2006. *Digest of education statistics 2005*, National Center for Education Statistics, Table 246.

nces.ed.gov/programs (accessed August 8, 2006).

U.S. DEPARTMENT OF HEALTH AND HUMAN SERVICES. 2006. Teen chat: A guide to discussing healthy relationships. http://4Parents.gov (accessed September 22, 2006).

U.S. Department of Health and Human Services. 2009a. *Child maltreatment 2007*. Washington, DC: U.S. Government Printing Office.

U.S. Department of Health and Human Services. 2009b. *Protecting children in families affected by substance use disorders*. Washington, DC: U.S. Government Printing Office.

U.S. Department of Housing and Urban Development. 2008. The third annual homeless assessment report to Congress. July, www.hud.gov (accessed July 29, 2009).

U.S. Department of Labor. 2008. *Women in the labor force: A databook*. Washington, DC: U.S. Government Printing Office.

U.S. Department of State. 2008. Total adoptions to the United States. http://adoption.state.gov (accessed June 28, 2009).

U.S. Department of State. 2008. Trafficking in persons report. June, www.state.gov (accessed February 3, 2009).

U.S. Equal Employment Opportunity Commission. 2009a. Sexual harassment charges: EEOC & FEPAs combined: FY 1997–FY 2008. www.eeoc.gov (accessed August 8, 2009).

U.S. Equal Employment Opportunity Commission. 2009b. Pregnancy discrimination charges: EEOC & FEPAs combined: FY 1997–FY 2008. www.eeoc.gov (accessed August 8, 2009).

U.S. General Accounting Office. 2004. Defense of Marriage Act: Update to prior report. January 23, GAO-04-353R, www.gao.gov (accessed June 11, 2009).

U.S. Hispanic population surpasses 45 million, now 15 percent of total. 2008. U.S. Census Bureau News, CB08-67, May 1, www.census.gov (accessed March 10, 2009).

UNITED STATES HOUSE OF REPRESENTATIVES. 2006. False and misleading health information provided by federally funded pregnancy resource centers. Committee on Government Reform—Minority Staff, Special Investigations Division, July, http://reform.democrats.house.gov (accessed September 19, 2006).

United States of Mayors. 2008. Hunger and homelessness survey. December, http://usmayors.org (accessed July 29, 2009).

U.S. Senate Special Committee on Aging, American Association of Retired Persons, Federal Council on the Aging, and U.S. Administration on Aging. 1991. Aging America: Trends and projections, 1991. Washington, DC: Department of Health and Human Services.

UMAÑA-TAYLOR, A. J., AND M. A. FINE. 2003. Predicting commitment to wed among Hispanic and Anglo partners. *Journal of Marriage and Family* 65 (February): 117–39.

UMAÑA-TAYLOR, A. J., AND M. Y. BÁMACA. 2004. Conducting focus groups with Latino populations: Lessons from the field. *Family Relations* 53 (April): 261–72.

UMBERSON, D., K. WILLIAMS, D. A. POWERS, H. LIU, AND B. NEEDHAM. 2005. Stress in childhood and adulthood: Effects on marital quality over time. *Journal of Marriage and Family* 67 (December): 1332–47.

Underage drinkers at higher risk of brain damage than adults, American Medical Association report reveals. 2002. American Medical Association. www.alcoholpolicysolutions.net (accessed September 17, 2003).

University of Connecticut, Center for Survey Research & Analysis. 2007. Two Americas but one American dream. July 6, www.csra .uconn.edu (accessed May 25, 2008).

UPCHURCH, D. M., L. A. LILLARD, AND C. W. A. PANIS. 2001. The impact of nonmarital child-bearing on subsequent marital formation and dissolution. In *Out of wedlock: Causes and consequences of nonmarital fertility,* eds. L. L. Wu and B. Wolfe, 344–80. New York: Russell Sage Foundation.

UPDEGRAFF, K. A., S. M. THAYER, S. D. WHITEMAN, D. J. DENNING, AND S. M. MC HALE. 2005. Relational aggression in adolescents' sibling relationships: Links to sibling and parent–adolescent relationship quality. *Family Relations* 54 (July): 373–85.

Urban Institute. 2008. Child care. June 4, www.urban.org (accessed July 15, 2009).

UTZ, R. L. 2006. Economic and practical adjustments to late life spousal loss. In *Spousal bereavement in late life,* eds. D. Carr, R. M. Nesse, and C. B. Wortman, 167–92. New York: Springer.

V

VACCARINO, V., ET AL. 2002. Sex differences in hospital mortality after coronary artery bypass surgery: Evidence for a higher mortality in younger women. *Circulation* 105 (February 18): 1176–81.

VAKILI, B., ET AL. 2002. Sex-based differences in early mortality of patients undergoing angioplasty for first acute myocardial infarction. *Circulation* 104 (December 18): 3034–38.

Valentine's a "worthless" day? 2002. Reuters News, February 14, http://story.news. yahoo.com (accessed February 15, 2002).

VALENZUELA, A., JR., N. THEODORE, E. MELÉNDEZ, AND A. LUZ GONZALEZ. 2006. On the corner: Day labor in the United States. Center for the Study of Urban Poverty, January, www .sscnet.ucla.edu (accessed April 3, 2009).

VANAUSDALE, D., AND J. R. FEAGIN. 2001. *The first R: How children learn race and racism.* Lanham, MD: Rowman & Littlefield.

VAN DYK, D. 2005. Parlez-vous twixter? *Time,* January 24, 49.

VAN HOOF, H. B., AND M. J. VERBEETEN. 2005. Wine is for drinking, water is for washing: Student opinions about international exchange programs. *Journal of Studies in International Education* 9 (Spring): 42–61.

VANDELL, D. L., K. MC CARTNEY, M. T. OWEN, C. BOOTH, AND A. CLARKE-STEWART. 2003. Variations in child care by grandparents during the first three years. *Journal of Marriage and Family* 65 (May): 375–81.

VANDELLO, J. A., AND D. COHEN. 2003. Male honor and female fidelity: Implicit cultural scripts that perpetuate domestic violence. *Journal of Personality and Social Psychology* 84 (May): 997–1010.

VANDEWATER, E. A., D. S. BICKHAM, J. H. LEE, H. M. CUMMINGS, E. A. WARTELLA, AND V. J. RIDEOUT. 2005. When the television is always on: Heavy television exposure and young children's development. *American Behavioral Scientist* 48 (January): 562–77.

VANDIVERE, S., K. TOUT, J. CAPIZZANO, AND M. ZASLOW. 2003. Left unsupervised: A look at the most vulnerable children. Washington, DC: Child Trends. www.childtrends.org (accessed August 23, 2003).

VARGAS, J. A. 2004. Married men with another life to live. *Washington Post* (August 14): C1.

VEEVERS, J. 1980. *Childless by choice.* Toronto: Butterworth.

VEMER, E., M. COLEMAN, L. H. GANONG, AND H. COOPER. 1989. Marital satisfaction in remarriage: A meta-analysis. *Journal of Marriage and the Family* 51 (August): 713–25.

VENKATESH, S. 2008. *Gang leader for a day: A rogue sociologist takes to the streets.* New York: Penguin Press.

VENTURA, S. J., J. A. MARTIN, S. C. CURTIN, T. J. MATHEWS, AND M. M. PARK. 2000. Births: final data for 1998. *National Vital Statistics Reports* 48, March 28, Centers for Disease Control and Prevention. www.cdc.gov (accessed September 22, 2000).

VESELY, R. 2005. Hospital program identifies more domestic violence. Women's e-news, June 13, www.womensenews.org (accessed June 15, 2005).

VESTAL, C. 2009. Gay marriage legal in six states. June 4, Stateline.org, www.stateline .org (accessed June 13, 2009).

VIDEON, T.M. 2002. The effects of parent-adolescent relationships and parental separation on adolescent well-being. *Journal of Marriage and Family* 64 (May): 489–503.

VINICK, B. H. 2000. Sexuality among older couples: Perceptions of spouse and self. In *With this ring: Divorce, intimacy, and cohabitation from a multicultural perspective,* eds. R. R. Miller and S. L. Browning, 111–26. Stamford, CT: JAI.

Violence Policy Center. 2008. When men murder women: An analysis of 2006 homicide data. September, www.vpc.org (accessed August 22, 2009).

VIORST, J. 2003. *Grown-up marriage.* New York: Free Press.

VISHER, E. B., AND J. S. VISHER. 1988. *Old loyalties, new ties: Therapeutic strategies with stepfamilies.* New York: Brunner/Mazel.

VISHER, E. B., AND J. S. VISHER. 1993. Remarriage families and stepparenting. In *Normal family processes,* 2nd ed., ed. F. Walsh, 235–53. New York: Guilford.

VISHER, E. B., AND J. VISHER. 1982. *How to win as a stepfamily.* New York: Dembner.

VISHER, E. B., AND J. S. VISHER. 1996. *Therapy with stepfamilies.* New York: Brunner/Mazel.

VISSING, Y. 2002. *Women without children: Nurturing lives.* New Brunswick, NJ: Rutgers University Press.

VITELLO, P. 2006. The trouble when Jane becomes Jack. *New York Times* (August 20): H1, H6.

VOGEL, N. 2007. A spanking ban: Are we gonna get it? *Los Angeles Times,* January 20, www .latimes.com (accessed January 25, 2007).

VOSS, K. W. 2003. New anti-violence campaigns aim at boys, young men. Women's E-News, February 28. www.womensenews.org (accessed March 3, 2003).

VOTRUBA-DRZAL, E. 2003. Income changes and cognitive stimulation in young children's home learning environments. *Journal of Marriage and Family* 65 (May): 341–55.

VREEMAN, R. C., AND A. E. CARROLL. 2008. Seasonal medical myths that lack evidence. *British Medical Journal* 337 (Dec. 17): 1442–43.

VUCHINICH, S. 1987. Starting and stopping spontaneous family conflicts. *Journal of Marriage and the Family* 49 (August): 591–601.

VUCHINICH, S., E. M. HETHERINGTON, R. A. VUCHINICH, AND W. G. CLINGEMPEEL. 1991. Parent-child interaction and gender differences in early adolescents' adaptation to stepfamilies. *Developmental Psychology* 27 (4): 618–26.

W

WACHTER, K. W. 1997. Kinship resources for the elderly. *Philosophical Transactions: Biological Sciences* 352 (December 29): 1811–17.

WADE, C., AND S. CIRESE. 1991. *Human sexuality,* 2nd ed. New York: Harcourt Brace Jovanovich.

WAGNER, J. S. 2008. When play turn to trouble. *U.S. News & World Report,* May 19, 51–53.

WAHLBERG, D. 2005. Secret sex, drug use fuel rise in AIDS. *The Atlanta Journal-Constitution,* June 16, 4E.

WAINRIGHT, J. L., S. T. RUSSELL, AND C. J. PATTERSON. 2004. Psychosocial adjustment, school outcomes, and romantic relationships of adolescents with same-sex partners. *Child Development* 75 (November/December): 1886–98.

WAITE, L. J., AND K. JOYNER. 2001. Emotional satisfaction and physical pleasure in sexual unions: Time horizon, sexual behavior, and sexual exclusivity. *Journal of Marriage and Family* 63 (February): 247–64.

WAITE, L. J., AND L. A. LILLARD. 1991. Children and marital disruption. *American Journal of Sociology* 96 (January): 930–53.

WAITE, L. J., ED. 2000. *The ties that bind: Perspectives on marriage and cohabitation.* New York: Aldine de Gruyter.

WAITE, L. J., D. BROWNING, W. J. DOHERTY, M. GALLAGHER, Y. LUO, AND S. M. STANLEY. 2002. Does divorce make people happy? Findings from a study of unhappy marriages. Institute for American Values. www .americanvalues.org (accessed September 24, 2003).

WAKEMAN, J. 2008. Misogyny's greatest hits. *Extra!* Fairness & Accuracy and Reporting, May/June, 6–7.

WAKSCHLAG, L. S., B. L. LEVENTHAL, D. S. PINE, K. E. PICKETT, AND A. S. CARTER. 2006. Elucidating early mechanisms of developmental psychopathology: The case of prenatal smoking and disruptive behavior. *Child Development* 77 (July/August): 893–906.

WALDREF, J. 2008. Women at work find reinforced glass ceilings. Women's eNews, August, www.womensenews.org (accessed September 2, 2008).

WALKER, L. 1978. Treatment alternatives for battered women. In *The victimization of women,* eds. J. R. Chapman and M. Gates, 143–74. Beverly Hills, CA: Sage.

WALKER, L. E. A. 2000. *The battered woman syndrome,* 2nd ed. New York: Springer.

WALLER, W. 1937. The rating and dating complex. *American Sociological Review* 2 (October): 727–34.

WALLERSTEIN, J. S. 2003. Children of divorce: A society in search of policy. In *All our families: New policies for a new century,* 2nd ed., eds. M. A. Mason, A. Skolnick, and S. D. Sugarman, 66–95. New York: Oxford University Press.

WALLERSTEIN, J. S., J. M. LEWIS, AND S. BLAKESLEE. 2000. *The unexpected legacy of divorce: A 25 year landmark study.* New York: Hyperion.

WALSH, A. 1991. *The science of love: Understanding love and its effects on mind and body.* Buffalo, NY: Prometheus.

WALSH, F., ED. 1993. *Normal family processes,* 2nd ed. New York: Guilford.

WALSH, W. 2002. Spankers and nonspankers: Where they get information on spanking. *Family Relations* 51 (January): 81–88.

WALSTER, E., E. BERSCHEID, AND G. W. WALSTER. 1973. New directions in equity research. *Journal of Personality and Social Psychology* 25 (2): 151–76.

WALTHER, A. N. 1991. *Divorce hangover.* New York: Pocket Books.

WALZER, S. 1998. *Thinking about the baby: Gender and transitions into parenthood.* Philadelphia: Temple University Press.

WANG, C-T., AND J. HOLTON. 2007. Total estimated cost of child abuse and neglect in the United States. Prevent Child Abuse America, September, www.preventchildabuse.org (accessed August 21, 2009).

WANG, L., E. B. LARSON, J. D. BOWEN, AND G. VAN BELLE. 2006. Performance-based physical function and future dementia in older people. *Archives of Internal Medicine* 166 (May 22): 1115–20.

Want ad proves a woman's work is never done. 1997. Ann Landers column. *Baltimore Sun*, September 20, 3D.

WARDRIP, K. E., D. PELLETIERE, AND S. CROWLEY. 2009. Out of reach 2009. National Low Income Housing Coalition, April, www.nlihc.org (accessed August 9, 2009).

WARNER, J. 2005. *Perfect madness: Motherhood in the age of anxiety.* New York: Riverhead Books.

WARNER, J. 2008. The other home equity crisis. *New York Times*, July 24, A4.

WARNER, W. L., AND P. S. LUNT. 1941. *The social life of a modern community.* New Haven, CT: Yale University Press.

WARREN, E., AND A. W. TYAGI. 2003. *The two income trap: Why middle-class mothers & fathers are going broke.* New York: Basic Books.

WARSHAK, R. A. 2003. Payoffs and pitfalls of listening to children. *Family Relations* 52 (October): 373–84.

WARTIK, N. 2005. The perils of playing house. *Psychology Today* (July/August): 42–52.

WASSERMAN, G. A., ET AL. 2003. *Risk and protective factors of child delinquency.* Washington, DC: U.S. Department of Justice.

WATKINS, G. 2002. Inuit ingenuity finds a warm reception. *Christian Science Monitor*, October 2, 14.

WATKINS, M. L., S. A. RASMUSSEN, M. A. HONEIN, L. D. BOTTO, AND C. A. MOORE. 2003. Maternal obesity and risk for birth defects. *Pediatrics* 111 (May): 1152–58.

WATKINS, T. H. 1993. *The great depression: America in the 1930s.* New York: Little, Brown.

WATSON, M., M. SARAIYA, F. AHMED, C. J. CARDINEZ, M. E. REICHMAN, H. K. WEIR, AND T. B. RICHARDS. 2008. Using population-based cancer registry data to assess the burden of human papillomavirus-associated cancers in the United States: Overview of methods. *Cancer* 113, S10 (November): 2841–54.

WATTERS, E. 2003. *Urban tribes: A generation redefines friendship, family and commitment.* New York: Bloomsbury.

WAX, E. 2005. Namibia chips away at African taboos on homosexuality. *Washington Post*, October 24, A1.

WAX, E. 2008. Can love conquer caste? *Washington Post*, November 22, A1.

WAX, E. 2008. For gays in India, fear rules. *Washington Post*, November 15, A13.

WAX, E. 2008. In thriving India, wedding sleuths find their niche. *Washington Post*, Feb. 23, A1.

WEATHERFORD, D. 1986. *Foreign and female: Immigrant women in America, 1840–1930.* New York: Schocken.

WEAVER, J. 2007. Lust, love & loyalty. msnbc.com, April 16, www.msnbc.msn.com (accessed May 4, 2009).

WEBLEY, K. 2009. Behind the drop in Chinese adoptions. *Time*, June 15, 55.

WEINER-DAVIS, M. 2003. *The sex-starved marriage: A couple's guide to boosting their marriage libido.* New York: Simon & Schuster.

WEIR, F. 2002. East meets West on love's risky cyberhighway. *Christian Science Monitor*, June 11, 1, 7.

WEIR, F. 2007. Orphanages brim, but Russia thwarts foreign adoption. *Christian Science Monitor*, April 19, 1, 4.

WEISS, C. H. 1998. *Evaluation research: Methods for assessing program effectiveness*, 2nd ed. Upper Saddle River, NJ: Prentice Hall.

WELLNER, A. S. 2002. The female persuasion. *American Demographics* 24 (February): 24–29.

WELLNER, A. S. 2003. The wealth effect. *American Demographics* 24 (January): 35-47

WELTER, B. 1966. The cult of true womanhood: 1820–1860. *American Quarterly* 18 (2): 151–74.

WENNBERG, J. E., E. S. FISHER, D. C. GOODMAN, AND J. S. SKINNER. 2008. *Tracing the care of patients with severe chronic illness/The Dartmouth Institute for Health Policy and Clinical Practice*, www.dartmouthatlas.org (accessed September 27, 2009).

WEST, C. M. 2008. "A thin line between love and hate?" Black men as victims and perpetrators of dating violence. *Journal of Aggression, Maltreatment & Trauma* 16 (June): 238–57.

WEST, C., AND D. H. ZIMMERMAN. 1987. Doing gender. *Gender and Society* 1 (June): 125–51.

WEST, M. S., AND J. W. CURTIS. 2006. *AAUP faculty gender equity indicators 2006.* Washington, DC: American Association of University Professors.

WESTHOFF, C., L. PICARDO, AND E. MORROW. 2003. Quality of life following early medical or surgical abortion. *Contraception* 67 (1): 41–47.

WESTOFF, L. A. 1977. *The second time around: Remarriage in America.* New York: Viking.

WHEELER, L. 1998. Excavation reveals slaves as entrepreneurs. *Washington Post*, October 13, B3.

Where the jobs are. 2009. Editorial, *New York Times*, July 10, A24.

WHIPPLE, E. E., AND C. A. RICHEY. 1997. Crossing the line from physical discipline to child abuse: How much is too much? *Child Abuse & Neglect* 21 (May): 431–44.

WHISMAN, M. A., K. C. GORDON, AND Y. CHATAV. 2007. Predicting sexual infidelity in a population-based sample of married individuals. *Journal of Family Psychology* 21 (June): 320–24.

WHISMAN, M. A., AND D. K. SNYDER. 2007. Sexual infidelity in a national survey of American women: Differences in prevalence and correlates as a function of method of assessment. *Journal of Family Psychology* 21 (June): 147–54.

WHITE, J. 2005. Four-star general relieved of duty. *Washington Post* (August 10), A1.

WHITE, J. W., AND D. M. KLEIN. 2002. *Family theories*, 2nd ed. Thousand Oaks, CA: Sage.

WHITE, L. K. 1991. Determinants of divorce. In *Contemporary families: Looking forward, looking back*, ed. A. Booth, 150–61. Minneapolis: National Council on Family Relations.

WHITE, L., AND J. G. GILBRETH. 2001. When children have two fathers: Effects of relationships with stepfathers and noncustodial fathers on adolescent outcomes. *Journal of Marriage and Family* 63 (February): 155–67.

WHITE, M. 2003. What's your favorite way to say "be mine": Card, candy, flowers? *Christian Science Monitor*, February 12, 20.

WHITE, R. D., AND M. LIFSHER. 2009. Blacks lose ground in job slump. *Los Angeles Times*, March 21, B1.

WHITE, T. 2008. Seniors reach digital age. *Baltimore Sun*, March 14, 1B, 10B.

WHITEFORD, L. M., AND L. GONZALEZ. 1995. Stigma: The hidden burden of infertility. *Social Science and Medicine* 40 (January): 27–36.

WHITEHEAD, B. D. 1996. The decline of marriage as the social basis of childrearing. In *Promises to keep: Decline and renewal of marriage in America*, eds. D. Popenoe, J. B. Elshtain, and D. Blankenhorn, 3–14. Lanham, MD: Rowman & Littlefield.

WHITEHEAD, B. D. 2002. *Why there are no good men left: The romantic plight of the new single woman.* New York: Broadway.

WHITEHEAD, B. D., AND D. POPENOE. 2001. The state of our unions 2001: The social health of marriage in America. The National Marriage Project, Rutgers University. http://marriage.rutgers.edu (accessed July 12, 2003).

WHITEHEAD, B. D., AND D. POPENOE. 2008. Life without children: The social retreat from children and how it is changing America. The National Marriage Project, Rutgers University, http://marriage.rutgers.edu (accessed June 10, 2009).

WHITEMAN, S. D., S. M. MCHALE, AND A. C. CROUTER. 2007. Longitudinal changes in marital relationships: The role of offspring's pubertal development. *Journal of Marriage and Family* 69 (November): 1005–20.

WHITING, J. B., AND R. E. LEE III. 2003. Voices from the system: A qualitative study of foster children's stories. *Family Relations* 52 (July): 288–95.

WHITMER, R. A., ERICA P. GUNDERSON, E. BARRETT-CONNOR, C. P. QUESENBERRY, JR., AND K. YAFFE. 2005. Obesity in middle age and future risk of dementia: A 27 year longitudinal population based study. *British Medical Journal* 330 (June 11): 1360–65.

WHITSETT, D., AND H. LAND, 1992. The development of a role strain index for stepparents. *Families in Society: The Journal of Contemporary Human Services* 73 (January): 14–22.

WHORISKEY, P. 2008. Skilled-worker visa demand expected to far exceed supply. *Washington Post*, April 1, D3.

WHORISKEY, P. 2009. Out of work and challenged on benefits, too. *Washington Post*, February 12, A1.

WHYTE, M. K. 1990. *Dating, mating, and marriage.* New York: Aldine de Gruyter.

WICKRAMA, K. A. S., F. O. LORENZ, R. D. CONGER, AND G. H. ELDER, JR. 1997. Marital quality and physical illness: A latent growth curve analysis. *Journal of Marriage and the Family* 59 (February): 143–55.

WIDOM, C. S., AND M. G. MAXFIELD. 2001. *An update on the "cycle of violence."* Washington, DC: U.S. Department of Justice.

WIEHE, V. R., WITH T. HERRING. 1991. *Perilous rivalry: When siblings become abusive.* Lexington, MA: Lexington.

WIGHT, D., A. PARKES, V. STRANGE, E. ALLEN, C. BONELL, AND M. HENDERSON. 2008. The quality of young people's heterosexual relationships: A longitudinal analysis of characteristics shaping subjective experience. *Perspectives on Sexual and Reproductive Health* 40 (December): 226–37.

WILCOX, W. B. 2002. Religion, convention, and paternal involvement. *Journal of Marriage and Family* 64 (August): 780–92.

WILCOX, W. B. 2002. Sacred vows, public purposes: Religion, the marriage movement and marriage policy. The Pew Forum on Religion and Public Life. http://pewforum.org (accessed March 3, 2003).

WILCOX, W. B., AND S. L. NOCK. 2006. What's love got to do with it? Equality, equity, commitment and women's marital quality. *Social Forces* 84 (March): 1321–45.

WILKINSON, D. 2005. True love: Finding a second act on the Internet. *New York Times*, April 12, www.nytimes.com (accessed April 13, 2005).

WILKINSON, T. 2008. Italy grapples with polygamy. *Los Angeles Times*, July 15, www.latimes.com (accessed July 16, 2008).

WILLIAMS, A. 2004. E-dating bubble springs leak. *New York Times*, December 12, I1.

WILLIAMS, C. J. 2009. Another sign of tough times: Legal aid for the middle class. *Los Angeles Times*, March 10, www.latimes.com (accessed March 16, 2009).

WILLIAMS, K. 2005. Tenacity drives immigrant's dream. *Washington Post*, August 7, A1.

WILLIAMS, K., AND A. DUNNE-BRYANT. 2006. Divorce and adult psychological well-being: Clarifying the role of gender and child age. *Journal of Marriage and Family* 68 (December): 1178–96.

WILLIAMS, L. 2002. Hispanic female athletes few and far between. *New York Times*, November 6, D1.

WILLIAMS, N. 1990. *The Mexican American family: Tradition and change*. New York: General Hall.

WILLIAMS, W. M. 2001. Women in academe, and the men who derail them. *Chronicle of Higher Education*, July 20, B20.

WILLIAMS, R. A. ED. 2007. *Eliminating health-care disparities in America: Beyond the IOM report*. Totowa, NJ: Humana.

WILLIAMS, T., AND T. MAHER. 2009. Iraq's newly open gays face scorn and murder. *New York Times*, April 8, www.nytimes.com (accessed April 9, 2009).

WILLIE, C. V., AND R. J. REDDICK. 2003. *A new look at black families*, 5th ed. Walnut Creek, CA: AltaMira.

WILLINGER, M., C. W. KO, H. J. HOFFMAN, R. C. KESSLER, AND M. J. CORWIN. 2003. Trends in infant bed sharing in the United States, 1993–2000. *Archives of Pediatrics & Adolescent Medicine* 157 (January): 43–49.

WILLIS, S. L., AND J. D. REID, EDS. 1999. *Life in the middle: Psychological and social development in middle age*. San Diego, CA: Academic Press.

WILLIS, W. 1997. Families with African American roots. In *Developing cross-cultural competence: A guide for working with children and families*, eds. E. W. Lynch and M. J. Hanson, 165–202. Baltimore: Paul H. Brookes.

WILLSON, A. E., K. M. SHUEY, AND G. H. ELDER, JR. 2003. Ambivalence in the relationship of adult children to aging parents and in-laws. *Journal of Marriage and Family* 65 (November): 1055–1072.

WILMOT, W. W., AND J. L. HOCKER. 2007. *Interpersonal conflict*, 7th ed. Boston: McGraw-Hill.

WILSON, B. F., AND S. C. CLARKE. 1992. Remarriages: A demographic profile. *Journal of Family Issues* 13 (June): 123–41.

WILSON, C. 2001. Living single grows in USA. *USA Today*, October 23, D1.

WILSON, E. K., AND H. P. KOO. 2008. Association between low-income women's relationship characteristics and their contraceptive use. *Perspectives on Sexual and Reproductive Health* 40 (September): 171–79.

WILSON, J. Q. 2002. *The marriage problem: How our culture has weakened families*. New York: HarperCollins.

WILSON, R. 2005. Second sex. *Chronicle of Higher Education*, October 7, A10–A12.

WILSON, R. 2008. 2 colleges, 2 presidents, one marriage. *Chronicle of Higher Education*, February 22, A1, A8.

WILSON, R. F. 2006. Sexually predatory parents and the children in their care: Remove the threat, not the child. In *Handbook on children, culture, and violence*, eds. N. E. Dowd, D. G. Singer, and R. F. Wilson, 39–58. Thousand Oaks, CA: Sage.

WILSON, S. 2002. The health capital of families: An investigation of the inter-spousal correlation in health status. *Social Science & Medicine* 55 (October): 1157–72.

WILSON, S. M., L. W. NGIGE, AND L. J. TROLLINGER. 2003. Connecting generations: Kamba and Maasai paths to marriage in Kenya. In *Mate selection across cultures*, eds. R. R. Hamon and B. B. Ingoldsby, 95–118. Thousand Oaks, CA: Sage.

WILTENBURG, M. 2002. Minority. *Christian Science Monitor*, January 31, 14.

WINCH, R. F. 1958. *Mate selection: A study of complementary needs*. New York: Harper & Row.

WINEBERG, H. 1991. Intermarital fertility and dissolution of the second marriage. *Social Science Quarterly* 75 (January): 62–65.

WINEBERG, H. 1996. The prevalence and characteristics of blacks having a successful marital reconciliation. *Journal of Divorce & Remarriage* 25 (1/2): 75–86.

WINEBERG, H., AND J. MC CARTHY. 1993. Separation and reconciliation in American marriages. *Journal of Divorce & Remarriage* 20: 21–42.

WINGERT, P. 2008. Wanted: A bundle of joy. *Newsweek*, October 13, 12.

WINSLOW-BOWE, S. 2006. The persistence of wives' income advantage. *Journal of Marriage and Family* 68 (November): 824–42.

WINTON, C. A. 1995. *Frameworks for studying families*. Guilford, CT: Dushkin.

WISEMAN, R. 2002. *Queen bees and wannabes: A parent's guide to helping your daughter survive cliques, gossip, boyfriends, and other realities of adolescence*. New York: Crown.

WITT, G. E. 1998. Vote early and often. *American Demographics* 20 (December): 23.

WITTSTEIN, I. S. ET AL. 2005. Neurohumoral features of myocardial stunning due to sudden emotional stress. *New England Journal of Medicine* 352 (February 10): 539–48.

WIZEMANN, T. M., AND M. L. PARDUE, EDS. 2001. *Exploring the biological contributions to human health: Does sex matter?* Washington, DC: National Academy Press.

WOLANIN, T. R. 2005. Higher education opportunities for foster youth: A primer for policymakers. The Institute for Higher Education Policy, www.ihep.org (accessed May 10, 2006).

WOLCOTT, J. 2000. Finding Mrs. Right (and all the little Rights). *Christian Science Monitor*, February 23, 15–17.

WOLCOTT, J. 2003. Single moms find roommates. *Christian Science Monitor*, March 12, 11, 14.

WOLCOTT, J. 2004. Is dating dated on college campuses? *Christian Science Monitor* (March 2): 11, 14.

WOLF, D. L. 1997. Family secrets: Transnational struggles among children of Filipino immigrants. *Sociological Perspectives* 40 (3): 457–82.

WOLFE, L. 1981. *The Cosmo report*. New York: Arbor House.

WOLFF, EDWARD N. 2007. Recent trends in household wealth in the United States: Rising debt and the middle-class squeeze. The Levy Economics Institute, June, www.levy.org (accessed May 20, 2008).

WOLFINGER, N. H. 2005. *Understanding the divorce cycle: The children of divorce in their own marriages*. New York: Cambridge University Press.

WOLFRADT, J. J., S. HEMPEL, AND J. N. V. MILES. 2003. Perceived parenting styles, depersonalization, anxiety and coping behavior in adolescents. *Personality and Individual Differences* 34 (February): 521–32.

Women live longer but aren't saving enough for it. *Baltimore Sun*, July 10, 6C.

WOOD, D. B. 2009. In hard times, illegal immigrants lose healthcare. *Christian Science Monitor*, March 24, 1, 3.

WOOD, H. M., B. J. TROCK, AND J. P. GEARHART. 2003. In vitro fertilization and the cloacal–bladder exstrophy–epispadias complex: Is there an association? *Journal of Urology* 169 (April): 1512–15.

WOOD, R. G., S. AVELLAR, AND B. GOESLING. 2008. Pathways to adulthood and marriage: Teenagers' attitudes, expectations, and relationship patterns. ASPE Research Brief, October, U.S. Department of Health and Human Services, Office of Human Services Policy, October, www.aspe.hhs.gov (accessed June 11, 2009).

WOODS, R. D. 1996. Grandmother roles: A cross cultural view. *Journal of Instructional Psychology* 23 (December): 286–92.

Working to Halt Online Abuse. 2008. Online harassment/Cyberstalking statistics. www.haltabuse.org (accessed May 1, 2009).

World Bank. 2007. World development indicators. April 23, siteresources.worldbank.org (accessed June 2, 2007).

WORLD HEALTH ORGANIZATION. 2005. WHO multi-country study on women's health and domestic violence against women: Summary report of initial results on prevalence, health outcomes and women's responses. Geneva: World Health Organization.

WORTH, K. A., J. G. CHAMBERS, D. H. NASSAU, B. K. RAKHRA, AND J. D. SARGENT. 2008. Exposure of US adolescents to extremely violent movies. *Pediatrics* 122 (August): 306–12.

WORTH, R. E. 2008. Tiny voices defy child marriage in Yemen. *New York Times*, June 29, A8.

WRIGHT, C. L., AND L. S. FISH. 1997. Feminist family therapy: The battle against subtle sexism. In *Subtle sexism: Current practices and prospects for change*, ed. N. V. Benokraitis, 201–15. Thousand Oaks, CA: Sage.

WRIGHT, C. N., A. HOLLOWAY, AND M. E. ROLOFF. 2007. The dark side of self-monitoring: How high self-monitors view their romantic relationships. *Communication Reports* 20 (October): 101–14.

WRIGHT, J. 1997. Motherhood's gray area. *Washington Post*, July 29, E5.

WRIGHT, J. C., A. C. HUSTON, AND K. C. MURPHY. 2001. The relations of early television viewing to school readiness and vocabulary of children from low-income families: the Early Window Project. *Child Development* 72 (September/October): 1347–66.

WRIGHT, J. M. 1998. *Lesbian step families: An ethnography of love*. New York: Haworth.

WRIGLEY, J., AND J. DREBY. 2005. Fatalities and the organization of child care in the United States, 1985–2003. *American Sociological Review* 70 (October): 729–57.

WRIGLEY, J., AND J. DREBY. 2006. Violent fatalities in child care. *Contexts* 5 (Fall): 35–40.

WU, L. L. 1996. Effects of family instability, income, and income instability on the risk of a premarital birth. *American Sociological Review* 61 (June): 386–406.

WU, L. L., AND E. THOMSON. 2001. Race difference in family experience and early sexual initiation: Dynamic models of family structure and family change. *Journal of Marriage and Family* 63 (August): 682–96.

WU, Z. 1994. Remarriage in Canada: A social exchange perspective. *Journal of Divorce & Remarriage* 21 (3/4): 191–224.

WU, Z., AND C. M. SCHIMMELE. 2005. Repartnering after first union disruption. *Journal of Marriage and Family* 67 (February): 27–36.

WU, Z., AND M. S. POLLARD. 2000. Economic circumstances and the stability of nonmarital cohabitation. *Journal of Family Issues* 21 (April): 303–28.

WULFHORST, E. 2006. U.S. mothers deserve $134,121 in salary. May 3, http://today .reuters.com (accessed May 10, 2006).

WULFHORST, E. 2007. Stay-at-home mother's work worth $138,095 a year. Yahoo! News, May 2, news.yahoo.com (accessed May 15, 2007).

X

XIE, Y., J. RAYMO, K. GOYETTE, AND A. THORNTON. 2003. Economic potential and entry into marriage and cohabitation. *Demography* 40 (May): 351–67.

XU, X., CLARK, D. HUDSPETH., AND J. P. BARTKOWSKI. 2006. The role of cohabitation in remarriage. *Journal of Marriage and Family* 68 (May): 261–74.

XU, X., C. D. HUDSPETH, AND S. ESTES. 1997. The effects of husbands' involvement in child rearing activities and participation in household labor on marital quality: A racial comparison. *Journal of Gender, Culture, and Health* 2(3): 171–93.

Y

YANCEY, A. K., J. M. SIEGEL, AND K. L. MCDANIEL. 2002. Role models, ethnic identity, and health-risk behaviors in urban adolescents. *Archives of Pediatrics & Adolescent Medicine* 156 (January): 55–61.

YANG, Y. 2008a. Long and happy living: Trends and patterns of happy life expectancy in the U.S., 1970–2000. *Social Science Research*, 37 (December): 1235–52.

YANG, Y. 2008b. Social inequalities in happiness in the United States, 1972 to 2004: An age-period-cohort analysis. *American Sociological Review* 73 (April): 204–26.

YARNALL, K. S. H., ET AL. 2003. Factors associated with condom use among at-risk women students and nonstudents seen in managed care. *Preventive Medicine* 37 (August): 163–70.

YATES, L. B., L. DJOUSSÉ, T. KURTH, J. E. BURING, AND M. GAZIANO. 2008. Exceptional longevity in men. *Archives of Internal Medicine* 168 (February 11): 284–90.

YELLOWBIRD, M., AND C. M. SNIPP. 2002. American Indian families. In *Minority families in the United States: A multicultural perspective*, 3rd ed., ed. R. L. Taylor, 227–49. Upper Saddle River, NJ: Prentice Hall.

YEOMAN, B. 2008. When wounded vets come home. *AARP Magazine*, July/August, 60–64, 82–83.

YIN, S. 2002. Off the map: Looking for love. *American Demographics* 24 (February): 48.

YIN, S. 2007. Gender disparities in health and mortality. Population Reference Bureau, November, www.prb.org (accessed March 10, 2007).

YIN, S. 2007. PopWire: Younger U.S. baby boomers less likely to divorce by 40 than older boomers. Population Reference Bureau, October, www.prb.org (accessed August 28, 2009).

YIN, S. 2008. How older women can shield themselves from poverty. Population Reference Bureau, March, www.prb.org (accessed September 22, 2009).

YOON, I.-J. 1997. *On my own: Korean businesses and race relations in America.* Chicago: University of Chicago Press.

YOSHIHAMA, M., A. L. PAREKH, AND D. BOYINGTON. 1991. Dating violence in Asian/Pacific communities. In *Dating violence: Young women in danger*, ed. B. Levy, 184–95. Seattle: Seal.

YOUNG, K. 2001. *Tangled in the Web: Understanding cybersex from fantasy to addiction.* Bloomington, IN: 1st Books Library.

YOUNG, L. 2009. Love: Neuroscience reveals all. *Nature* 457 (January 8): 148.

YOUSAFZAI, S., AND R. MOREAU. 2008. The opium brides of Afghanistan. *Newsweek*, April 7, 38–40.

YU, E., AND J. LIU. 2007. Environmental impacts of divorce. *Proceedings of the National Academies of Sciences* 104 (December 18): 20629–34.

Z

ZAFF, J. F., J. CALKINS, L. J. BRIDGES, AND N. G. MARGIE. 2002. Promoting positive mental and emotional health in teens: Some lessons from research. Washington, DC: Child Trends. www.childtrends.org (accessed August 23, 2003).

ZAGORSKY, J. L. 2003. Husbands' and wives' view of the family finances. *Journal of Socio-Economics* 32 (May): 127–46.

ZAGORSKY, J. L. 2005. Marriage and divorce's impact on wealth. *Journal of Sociology* 41 (December): 406–24.

ZAIDI, A. U., AND M. SHURAYDI. 2002. Perceptions of arranged marriages by young Pakistani Muslim women living in a Western society. *Journal of Comparative Family Studies* 33 (Autumn): 495–514.

ZAREMBO, A. 2009. DNA can reveal ancestors' lies and secrets. *Los Angeles Times*, January 18, www.latimes.com (accessed January 19, 2009).

ZAREMBO, A., AND K. YOSHINO. 2009. Surrogacy makes for a perilous path to parenthood.

Los Angeles Times, March 29, www .latimes.com (accessed March 30, 2009).

ZASLOW, J. 2006. Mr. moms grow up: A new generation of granddads is helping raise the kids. *Wall Street Journal*, June 8, D1.

ZHANG, Y., AND J. VAN HOOK. 2009. Marital dissolution among interracial couples. *Journal of Marriage and Family* 71 (February): 95–107.

ZHANG, Z., AND M. D. HAYWARD. 2001. Childlessness and the psychological well-being of older persons. *Journal of Gerontology: Social Sciences* 56B: S311–20.

ZHANG, Z., AND M. HAYWARD. 2006. Gender, the marital life course, and cardiovascular diseases in late midlife. *Journal of Marriage and Family* 68 (August): 639–57.

ZHU, W. X., AND T. HESKETH. 2009. China's excess males, sex selective abortion, and one child polity: Analysis of data from 2005 national intercensus survey. *British Medical Journal* online, April 9, www.bmj .com (accessed June 15, 2009).

ZIELINSKI, D. S. 2005. Long-term socioeconomic impact of child abuse and neglect: Implications for public policy. Center for Child and Family Policy, www.pubpol.duke.edu (accessed June 25, 2006).

ZIMMERMAN, F. J., AND D. A. CHRISTAKIS. 2005. Children's television viewing and cognitive outcomes: A longitudinal analysis of national data. *Archives of Pediatrics & Adolescent Medicine* 159 (July): 619–25.

ZIMMERMAN, F. J., D. A. CHRISTAKIS, AND A. N. MELTZOFF. 2007. Associations between media viewing and language development in children under age 2 years. *Journal of Pediatrics* 151 (October): 364–68.

ZITO, J. M. ET AL. 2003. Psychotropic practice patterns for youth. *Archives of Pediatrics & Adolescent Medicine* 157 (January): 17–25.

ZOROYA, G. 2005. Letters home from Iraq. *USA Today,* October 25, (www.usatoday.com accessed online October 26, 2006).

ZOROYA, G. 2009. Online dating sites: Cupid's arrow lands in war zone. *USA Today*, May 18, www.usatoday.com (accessed May 19, 2009).

ZURBRIGGEN, E. L., ET AL. 2007. *Report of the APA task force on the sexualization of girls.* Washington, DC: American Psychological Association.

Photo Credits

Name Index

Subject Index